D0466640

TREASURY OF PHILOSOPHY

TREASURY

of

PHILOSOPHY

edited by
DAGOBERT D. RUNES

PHILOSOPHICAL LIBRARY
New York

COPYRIGHT, 1955, BY

THE PHILOSOPHICAL LIBRARY, Inc.
15 East 40th Street, New York, N. Y.

PRINTED IN THE UNITED STATES OF AMERICA

CONTENTS

vii

ix

xi

xiii

xvi

xix

xx

A Few Words to the Reader

Man is a meditative creature, and wherever we come across his traces we find indications of his perennially philosophical mind.

What philosophy be has been defined a great many times. None of the definitions, however, seems to be entirely satisfactory, and even now, standing at the end of this book —like all prefaces, this is being written, not at the beginning, but at the completion of a work—I can say only that "philosophy is the search for the indefinable."

Of the almost four hundred searchers represented in this collection, none has really set out to solve an issue or a problem once and for all, as do mathematicians, physicists, chemists, or engineers. Rather, all these men whom I have brought together under the roof of this volume have, at certain times in their lives, sat down to meditate upon the wondrous themata that came to their minds in uncharted realms: the essence of being, the nature of man, the principles of ethics, the "where from" of existence, the "where to" of human purpose, the "where in" of beauty, the undercurrents of emotional life, the structure of reason, the limitations of knowledge, and the quest for God.

There are about ten thousand men and a score of women who have some claim to be classed as philosophers. If there was any notable difficulty in my task, I would point only to the process of selecting the few hundred from the many thousands. Many, even of the well-known, were not thinkers but rather teachers, others were not pundits but rather preachers—and some were just clever.

I have taken care to include in this anthology a considerable number of Hebrew, Chinese, and other Oriental minds who have generally been ignored by our Western-focussed historians. I have also listed American philosophers who still seem to be step-children in the house of European lexicographers. In going through European reference books, I sometimes felt that their authors had not heard of the discovery of America!

In my efforts to keep this book within the prescribed limits of space, and perhaps also through the unavoidable coloring of choice by personal taste, I may have done injustice by omitting one philosopher or another, and I shall, in this sense, welcome suggestions from serious readers.

I should like to thank, for their advice and valuable assistance, the Doctors Vergilius Ferm, John White, and Kurt F. Leidecker, without whose cooperation my task could not have been accomplished.

And now, may I wish the readers of this Treasury the same benign pleasure in perusing the following pages that I experienced in assembling them.

D. D. R.

Treasury of Philosophy

$\mathcal{A}$

ABAILARD, PETER

ABAILARD, PETER (1079-1142). Abailard's life is a portrait of the triumphs and vicissitudes of philosophy, faith, and love. He was born in a little town in Brittany, and having been ordained as priest, returned there to tutor Héloïse, the niece of Canon Fulbert. His secret love affair with her, and Astrolabius, the son she bore him, caused him considerable misfortune, for when the canon discovered the secret relationship he had the priest physically mutilated. Abailard persuaded Héloïse to take the veil: he himself retired to a quiet place near Troyes.

His disciples, however, sought him out, and once again the handsome, eloquent schoolman attracted students from all over Europe. He established an oratory called the Paraclete. His subtle argumentation persuaded his listeners to found their beliefs on reason. He tabulated the contradictions of the Bible and the Church Fathers for easy reference; he made freedom of the will the basis of all ethics; he opposed the teachings of the famous schoolmen, and expounded those concepts which hold that the Aristotelian precepts, called universals in scholastic philosophy (such as genus and species), have only intellectual significance.

The story of his "calamities" (he wrote a book by that title) was never-ending. His interpretation of the Trinity was twice condemned as heretical. Finally, weary of the fight, he burned his book on the Trinity and lived out his life, a subdued follower of the faith. Upon his death Héloïse, twenty-one years younger than he, claimed his body and buried him. The ashes of both lovers now rest at the Père-Lachaise in Paris.

ON SIN

WHEN the Scripture says: 'Go not after your own desires' (Eccles. xviii, 30), and: 'Turn from your own will' (ibid.), it instructs us not to fulfil our desires. Yet it does not say

1

that we are to be wholly without them. It is vicious to give in to our desires; but not to have any desires at all is impossible for our weak nature.

The sin, then, consists not in desiring a woman, but in consent to the desire, and not the wish for whoredom, but the consent to the wish is damnation.

Let us see how our conclusions about sexual intemperance apply to theft. A man crosses another's garden. At the sight of the delectable fruit his desire is aroused. He does not, however, give way to desire so as to take anything by theft or rapine, although his mind was moved to strong inclination by the thought of the delight of eating. Where there is desire, there, without doubt, will exists. The man desires the eating of that fruit wherein he doubts not that there will be delight. The weakness of nature in this man is compelled to desire the fruit which, without the master's permission, he has no right to take. He conquers the desire, but does not extinguish it. Since, however, he is not enticed into consent, he does not descend to sin.

What, then, of your objection? It should be clear from such instances, that the wish or desire itself of doing what is not seemly is never to be called sin, but rather, as we said, the consent is sin. We consent to what is not seemly when we do not draw ourselves back from such a deed, and are prepared, should opportunity offer, to perform it completely. Whoever is discovered in this intention, though his guilt has yet to be completed in deed, is already guilty before God in so far as he strives with all his might to sin, and accomplishes within himself, as the blessed Augustine reminds us, as much as if he were actually taken in the act.

God considers not the action, but the spirit of the action. It is the intention, not the deed wherein the merit or praise of the doer consists. Often, indeed, the same action is done from different motives: for justice sake by one man, for an evil reason by another. Two men, for instance, hang a guilty person. The one does it out of zeal for justice; the other in resentment for an earlier enmity. The action of

2

hanging is the same. Both men do what is good and what justice demands. Yet the diversity of their intentions causes the same deed to be done from different motives, in the one case good, in the other bad. [1]

ABRAVANEL, ISAAC

ABRAVANEL, ISAAC (1437-1508). A Spanish Sephardic Jew who was in the court of Alfonso V, King of Portugal, but had to flee, at great loss of personal fortune, when a new ruler ascended the throne. From Lisbon he went to the House of Castile, and when the Jews were banished from Spain, he went to Naples, once again in the service of a king, until he was banished by the French rulers. He then fled to Venice where he remained until his death. He was buried in Padua.

Abravanel is generally considered the last great Aristotelian. Sometimes a philosophic eclectic, he was principally concerned with the teachings of the Bible and the modifications of doctrine expounded by the Jews. He was a believer in the Torah and considered the history of the Jews a revelation of God. His studies of the Bible are frequently used as reference by Christian scholars.

THE INTERRUPTED WORK

THUS spake Isaac, the son of my Lord, of the prince and great man in Israel, Judah Abravanel, of the root of Jesse the Bethlehemite, of the seed of David, a leader and commander to my people, of a people scattered abroad and dispersed, one of those exiled from Jerusalem to Spain:

Behold, in expounding the books, that is to say, Joshua, Judges, Samuel, and Kings, I encountered in reverse order what Hiel the Bethelite encountered when he built up Jericho, he who laid the foundation thereof with the loss of his first-born, and with the loss of his youngest son he set up the gates of it. But I opened my mouth to God in former days that were better than these, settling on my leas in the kingdom of Portugal, the land of my birth, to expound those four books, since I saw that those who had expounded them had done so inadequately. But with the burden of the king and

3

princes it came up upon my neck, and I could not complete it until the hand of the Lord touched me, and the king of Portugal held me for his enemy, not for any injustice in my hands. He stood with his right hand as an adversary to destroy me utterly; he took all that was mine, durable and lawful possessions, and I saved myself, I alone, fleeing to the kingdom of Castile from the oppressing sword. And when I arrived there, a stranger in the land, a wayfaring man that turneth aside to tarry for a night, I sought to repay that which God had lent me by expounding the three first books, Joshua, Judges, and Samuel.

All this happened at the beginning of the two hundred and forty-fourth year, in the sixth millennium of the creation. And when I was about to begin expounding the Books of the Kings, I was called to come in unto the king, to the king of Spain, the greatest of all the kings on earth, who ruled over the kingdoms of Castile, Aragon, Catalunia, and Sicilia, and the other islands of the sea. I came to the court of the king and the queen, was with them many days, and the Lord gave me favor in their eyes, in the eyes of the princes that sat first in the kingdom, and I wrought in their service for eight years.

And both riches and honor, which if a man do, he lives by them, I gained in their towns and in their castles. Therefore the Torah was slacked and the work hindered. Because I served the kings of peoples who are not of the children of Israel, I left mine heritage, the kingdom of Judah and of Israel, and the expounding of their books.

In the year two hundred and fifty-two, [1492] the king of Spain conquered the entire kingdom of Granada and the great city of Granada, great among nations and princess among the provinces, and in his might and pride he turned from his former ways. He imputed his might unto his God. "And Esau said in his heart": For wherewith could I reconcile myself unto my master, who has girded me with strength to battle, wherewith shall I come before the Lord, who has put this city into my hands, if not that I bring under his wings the people that walks in darkness, the scattered sheep of Israel, and either lead back to his law and his faith the backsliding daughter, or banish them from my countenance and cast them into another land, so that they may no longer dwell in my land nor tarry in my sight.

And because of this the king's commandment and his decree went forth, and a herald loudly proclaimed: "To you it is commanded, to all the families of the house of Israel, that if you 'go through the water,' if you fall down and worship the gods of those peoples, you shall eat the good of the land, as we are doing this very day, and you shall dwell and trade therein. But if you refuse and rebel, if you do not mention the name of my God, and if you do not worship my God, rise up, and get you forth from among my people, out of the lands of Spain, Sicily, Mallorca, and Sardinia, which are under my rule, and three months after, there shall not a hoof be left behind of all who call themselves by the name of Jacob, or by the name of Israel, in any of the provinces of my kingdom."

Now since I was in the court of the king's house, I wore myself out with crying and my throat dried. Oftentimes I spoke to the king, I entreated him with my mouth, and said: "Help, O king, wherefore dealest thou thus with thy servants? Ask me never so much dowry and gift, gold and silver and all that a man of the house of Israel has, will he give for his land."

I called for my lovers that see the king's face, to plead for my people. The nobles took counsel together, with all their might to implore the king to reverse the letters of his anger and fury, and to destroy the scheme he had devised against the Jews. But like the dead adder he stopped his ear and answered nothing at all to anyone. And the queen stood at his right hand to accuse. With her much fair speech she caused him to yield, and bring to pass his act, to begin and also make an end. We labored but our fears were not mitigated. I was not at ease, neither was I quiet, neither had I rest; but trouble came.

5

And they went without strength, three hundred thousand on foot, the people among whom I am, young and old, little children and women, in one day, from all the provinces of the king. "Whither the spirit was to go, they went."

I too chose out their way, the way of a ship in the midst of the sea. I, among the captives, came with all my house— "the children are my children, and the flocks are my flocks" —came here to Naples, to that exalted city, whose kings are merciful kings, and I spoke with my own heart: I will pay that which I have vowed, I will expound the Books of the Kings, which I have not done until now; and I shall do this also because "it it time to work for the Lord," to commemorate the destruction of our holy and glorious house, and the exile that has come upon our people, as they are written in this book, and as I will expound with the help of God.

Now, after this: Hiel the Bethelite, in the building of Jericho, had laid "the foundation thereof with his first-born, and with his youngest son set up the gates thereof," but I, a man that hath seen affliction, began my explanation of these four books, and founded it upon the least of the banishments and exiles that came upon me, that is, the particular exile from the kingdom of Portugal, and with the greatest of the exiles, the bitter and hasty exile, the great and dreadful destruction, devoured and swallowed, driven from abiding in Spain—with this I "set up the gates" of this commentary and completed it.   [2]

ABRAVANEL, JUDAH

ABRAVANEL, JUDAH (c. 1460-1530). Abravanel was one of the outstanding figures of the period of transition between the Middle Ages and the Renaissance. He lived not only at the conjunction of two eras, but also in contact with three cultures—Jewish, Spanish, and Italian. He and his father, Don Isaac Abravanel fled in 1483 from their native Portugal to Spain, and thence to Italy in 1492. Judah practised medicine, but he was mainly interested in philosophy, mathematics, and astronomy. For a time he lectured at the

Universities in Naples and Rome. The intellectuals of both cities requested his friendship; his was a close association with Pico della Mirandola. During his sojourn in Italy, Judah assumed the name of Leone, the translation of Judah, the Lion.

His most famous work, *Dialoghi di Amore* (Dialogues about Love), was published in Italian, and soon after translated into Hebrew, Latin, French, Spanish, and English. A portion of the book was incorporated in a rabbinical commentary on the Song of Songs. The Dialogues are landmarks in the history of aesthetics and of great consequence to the history of metaphysics and ethics. The book promulgates love as a cosmic principle inseparable from being; its spirit, the mirror of reality. The Dialogues stressed the spiritual character of physical beauty and helped develop the field of aesthetic idealism. He maintained that true happiness is the "union of the human intellect with the Divine intelligence," and that it is directly connected to aesthetic enjoyment. There is a pantheistic strain in Abravanel's philosophy, but he always emphasized his orthodox Judaism, and tried to reconcile his pantheistic feelings with the Biblical concept of God.

KNOWLEDGE, LOVE AND DESIRE

KNOWLEDGE must precede all love; for we could not love anything we had not first known to be good. Nor can we love anything before we conceive of it as an actuality. Our mind is a mirror and model, or to be more specific, an image of real things. Therefore we can love nothing, until we can perceive its existence as reality.

It cannot be denied that knowledge precedes desire. Knowledge is not only concerned with what *is*, but also that which *is not*. For our mind judges things as it perceives them to be; it judges things which are not, in the same fashion. Thus I would say that love presupposes a knowledge of things which are, and a desire of those things which are not or which we lack.

Knowledge without love is of those things which are not beautiful, and therefore not desirable; or of bad and ugly things that are hated; or of things which are neither desired nor hated. All other knowledge of good and beautiful things either has love or desire as its end.

7

Every degree of being in the universe is subordinate to another, and graded from the lowest to the highest. In man himself, the lesser faculties are subordinate to the greater; to wit: those of the vegetable soul to those of the sensitive; those of the sensitive to those of the intellectual. The intellectual is the finest and highest faculty, not only in Man, but in all of the lower world. Even in the intellectual, activities are graded from the lowest to the highest in order of intelligible objects. The highest and final intelligible object is the highest being, and the ultimate end to which all things are ordered. The acme and objective of intellectual activity is that celestial, angelic intellect, to which all others are subordinate. In the same way . . . the various loves in the created universe are subordinate, from the lowest to the highest, up to that final and supreme love, that of the universe for its creator.

[2A]

ACOSTA, URIEL

ACOSTA, URIEL (1590-1647). Born in Portugal, the descendant of a Marrano family, religiously observant of Catholicism, the young Acosta prepared himself for the priesthood. But, tortured by doubts about the Christian religion, he decided to flee to Holland. Here he embraced Judaism, not because he was convinced of the truth of his new faith, but he was resolved to deny his former beliefs. He defied Jewish orthodoxy, the very basis of Judaism, because he was incapable of integrating himself into the Jewish community or of understanding its precarious situation and vital needs. His attacks upon the fundamental doctrines of Christianity, which he wrote as a member of the Jewish congregation of Amsterdam angered the congregation because they felt the Christian authorities who had given the Jews refuge would be offended. Banished, he recanted, revolted anew, was banished anew, and ostracized for seven years. No longer able to endure solitude, he was willing to withstand the most severe penance in order to be allowed to re-enter the Jewish community. But the rigors of the ceremony destroyed his will to survive. Soon thereafter, he committed suicide, unrepenting and irreconcilable. To some extent, he was the victim of his temper, but more so of an era in which it was impossible for an independent thinker to live unharmed outside a religious community.

Many novelists and dramatists, Jew and non-Jew, have idealized his life and thoughts, for the poetic transfiguration of his fate is the tragedy of an uprooted man in revolt against tradition and any community based on tradition—the tragedy of a humiliated man, unable to live in isolation, whose only alternative was death. He entitled his autobiography *Exemplar Humanae Vitae* (Example of a Human Life), but his life was certainly anything but typical.

THE HUMAN SOUL

SINCE we have to deal with the mortality or immortality of the human soul, it is appropriate to ask what that soul is. Many ignorant fools speak of it as though it were a virgin personified; others describe it as something emergent from purgatory. We say that the human soul is man's vital spirit, by means of which he lives. This spirit is in the blood, and with it man acts and moves in the world. Man lives as long as the vital spirit works in his body. He dies when the spirit is either naturally or accidentally extinguished. The only difference between the animal soul and the human soul is that the human soul is endowed with reason, while the animal soul lacks reason.

We know that we have something called the soul, and we must ask what it is that creates this soul in the human body. Man creates, by a natural process, the soul of another man, just as an animal creates the soul of another animal similar to itself. That can be the only indubitable answer . . . . Those who assert that the soul is different from the body; that it was created by a God who deposed it, are not worth being heeded. . . . Man would not die if his vital spirit, his soul, could not die.   [3]

ADAMS, JOHN

ADAMS, JOHN (1735-1826). The second president of the United States regarded himself as "one of those Protestants who do not believe in anything." He repudiated Platonism, the doctrines of the Christian churches, deism, materialism, and scoffed at the belief in the perfectibility of human nature and the progressive development of the human intellect. An austere, cynical, selfless, and stubborn man, he opposed democracy because he distrusted the people, yet he devoted himself to the welfare of the entire nation. He maintained that an aristocratic class could provide for the interests of the poor more adequately than the masses of plain people whose very interests might be at stake.

Adams was a political philosopher despite his contemptuous attitude toward philosophy. His concepts of government were based upon the arguments of Aristotle and Montesquieu. He admired the ideas of these men, even though they were philosophers, and in the same way, he revered Bolingbroke, Hume and Voltaire as "comets" of thought. He staunchly defended the governmental system of checks and balances against the demands for centralized power or an extension of democracy.

Adams played a leading part in the opposition to the Stamp Act of 1765 and in the organization of the War of Independence; but he remained a Tory in his persistent sympathy for the British form of government. Thus the constitution for the State of Massachusetts, written by him, was very conservative. As President, Adams resisted Alexander Hamilton's requests for a declaration of war against France and the negation of the lower-class demands. Adams' domestic policy of taking the middle course was a failure; his Presidential experiences reinforced his feelings of detached cynicism. After he left the Capitol, he declared that "a fine load of manure was a fair exchange for the honors and virtues of the world."

ON SELF-DELUSION

NOTHING in the science of human nature is more curious or deserving of critical attention than the principle, referred to by moralists, as self-deceit. This principle is the spurious offspring of self-love. It is, perhaps, the greatest source and the worst part of the vices and calamities of mankind. The most distorted minds are ingenious in contriving excuses for their crimes. They will explain that compulsion, necessity, the strength or suddenness of temptation, or the violence of passion caused them to commit the crime. These excuses also serve to assuage their consciences and to make them, by degrees, even more insensible.

Indeed it must be confessed . . . that those eyes, which

have been given us to see, are willingly suffered, to be obscured, and those consciences, which by the commission of the Almighty God have a rightful authority over us, are often deposed by prejudices, appetites, and passions; disagreeable qualities that ought to have an inferior position in our intellectual and moral systems. . . .

Let not writers and statesmen deceive themselves. The springs of conduct and opinion are not always clear and pure, nor are those of our political antagonists so polluted and corrupt, as they would have the world believe.

[4]

ADLER, ALFRED

ADLER, ALFRED (1870-1937). Adler is important for his formulation of the theory of "individual psychology," the most widely accepted technique (next to psychoanalysis, founded by Sigmund Freud) in the treatment of neuroses. This concept is largely based upon the general theory of psychology and human character. Because "individual psychology" is based on medical practice as well as philosophy, it is easily distinguishable from the various social psychologies.

Adler, a disciple and collaborator of Freud, is said to have influenced his teacher in some ways. Like Freud, Adler attributed primary importance to infantile experiences. But, whereas Freud considered sexuality or its repression as the formative force of character and the cause of certain types of neuroses, Adler stated that the formative force is the desire of the individual to secure authority in the social milieu. Neurosis, according to Adler, is the effect of inferior feelings that result from the individual's failure to gain superiority or dominance. Inferior feelings may be caused either by physical or mental shortcomings. Consequently, the individual tends to compensate or even over-compensate. He assumes superior attitudes which cause abnormal behavior patterns.

Freud endeavored to discover the sexual components of the healthy or neurotic personality, while Adler deviated from this overemphasis of sexuality. He maintained that no component could be evaluated accurately without regard for the unity of character which manifests itself in the individual's "style of life." The weak individual, unable to overcome his shortcomings or to discipline himself, adopts a "style of life" which enables him to enjoy illu-

11

sions of superiority. He expects social prestige because of his imagined superiority instead of actual efficiency. Consequently he becomes a stranger to reality, pursuing "fictive goals." The function of the psychologist, according to Adler, is to induce the patient (whose fundamental "style of life" cannot be changed after early childhood) to avoid conflicts with society by recognizing its dangers, to act in accordance with reality and abstain from a reversion to delusions. Because of the emphasis on early childhood, Adler and his disciples were interested in educational reform.

His principal works are *The Neurotic Constitution* (1912) and *Individual Psychology* (1924).

THE STYLE OF LIFE

IF we look at a pine tree growing in the valley we will notice that it grows differently from one on top of a mountain. It is the same kind of a tree, but there are two distinct styles of life. Its style on top of the mountain is different from its style when growing in the valley. The style of life of a tree is the individuality of a tree expressing itself and moulding itself in an environment. We recognize a style when we see it against a background of an environment different from what we expect, for then we realize that every tree has a life pattern and is not merely mechanical reaction to the environment.

It is much the same with human beings. We see the style of life under certain conditions of environment, and it is our task to analyze its exact relation to the existing circumstances, since our mind changes with alteration of the environment. As long as a person is in a favorable situation we cannot see his style of life clearly. In new situations, however, where he is confronted with difficulties, the style of life appears clearly and distinctly. . . . The style of life is a unity because it has grown out of the difficulties of early life and out of the striving for a goal. [5]

ADLER, FELIX

ADLER, FELIX (1851-1933). Brought to the United States at the age of six by his father, a rabbi, Felix Adler was also educated for the rabbinical office. He received his doctorate from Heidelberg University and returned to preach at the Temple Emanu-El in New York City. It was here that he failed to refer to God in his sermons. Although he was not disloyal to Judaism, as a rationalist he could not accept the rituals in any literal sense.

He left the rabbinate and his friends established a professorship of Hebrew and Oriental literature for him at Cornell University.

It was his belief that the principle of the good life can be achieved independently of religious ritual and dogma that led him to found the American Ethical Union and the Society for Ethical Culture in New York. (From there it spread to many groups throughout America and the Continent.) He maintained that the idea of a personal God is unnecessary; that the social and ethical behavior of man, if it makes for harmonious relationships among men, constitutes the Godhead; that man's personality because of its unique and inviolable nature is the central force of the religion. He advocated more than mere religious tolerance: men should reverently respect the religious differences among themselves.

In his books *Creed and Deed* (1878) and *Moral Instruction of Children* (1892) he was able to fuse his heterogeneous influences: Judaism, Christianity, Kant, Emerson, and the cogent socialistic ideas of his lifetime. He is noted for his social efforts in such areas as kindergarten and manual training schools, and the abolition of child labor.

IMMORTALITY

TRUE disinterestedness is the distinguishing mark of every high endeavor. The pursuit of the artist is unselfish, the beauty he creates is his reward. The toil of the scientist in the pursuit of abstract truth is unselfish, the truth he sees is his reward. Why should we hesitate to acknowledge in the domain of ethics what we concede in the realm of art and science? To say that unselfishness itself is only the more refined expression of a selfish instinct, is to use the term selfish with a double meaning, is a mere empty play on words. We have the innate need of harmony in the moral relations; this is our glory, and the stamp of the Divine upon our nature. We cannot demonstrate the existence of disinterested motives any more than we can demonstrate that there is joy in the sunlight and freedom in the mountain breeze. The fact that

13

we *demand unselfishness* in action alone assures us that the standard of enlightened self-interest is false.

And indeed, if we consult the opinions of men where they are least likely to be warped by sophistry, we shall find that disinterestedness is the universal criterion by which moral worth is measured. If we suspect the motive we condemn the act. If a person gives largely for some object of public usefulness, or charity, we do not permit the munificence of the gift to deceive our judgment. Perhaps he is merely desirous of vaunting his wealth, perhaps it is social standing he aims at, perhaps he is covetous of fame. If these suspicions prove well founded, the very men who accept his bounty will, in their secret hearts, despise him, and by a certain revulsion of feeling we shall resent his action all the more, because, not only is he destitute of honorable purpose, but he has filched the fair front of virtue, and defiled the laurel even in the wearing of it.

We do not even accord the name of goodness to that easy, amiable sympathy which leads us to alleviate the sufferings of others, unless it be guided by wise regard for their permanent welfare. The tattered clothes, the haggard looks, the piteous pleading voice of the pauper on the public highway may awaken our pity, but the system of indiscriminate alms-giving is justly condemned as a weakness rather than a virtue.

On the other hand, obedience to duty, when it involves pain and self-abnegation, seems to rise in the general estimation. Clearly because in this instance even the suspicion of interested motives is removed, since hardship, injury in estate and happiness, and even the possible loss of life, are among the foreseen consequences of the act. It is for this reason that the Book of Martyrs has become the golden book of mankind, and that the story of their lives never fails to fill us with mingled sorrow and admiration and pride. They are monuments on the field of history, and milestones on the path of human progress. We regard them and gain new courage and confidence in our better selves. The blazing pyre on the

Campo Fiore, whereon Giordano Bruno breathes his last, be· comes a beacon-light for the truth-seeker; the dying Socrates still pours benignant peace over many a sufferer's couch; the Man of Sorrows, on Calvary, comforts the hearts of the Chris· tian millions. In the presence of these high examples the in· adequacy of the selfish standard becomes clearly apparent. We recognize what a sublime quality that is in man which enables him, not only to triumph over torment and suffering, but to devote his very self to destruction for the sake of honor and truth. Freely must Virtue be wooed, not for the dowry she may bring; by loyal devotion to her for her own sake only, can she be won!

If thus it appears that not only is there nothing in the nature of Virtue to warrant a claim to reward, but that it is her very nature to disclaim any reward, it will become plain that the problem, as stated in the beginning, rests upon an entirely false foundation. That the unrighteous and unprin· cipled should enjoy temporal happiness, does not offend the law of justice. That you, my good sir, honest in all your deal· ings, truthful in all your acts, should be unhappy, is greatly to be deplored. Why evil and happiness should have been allowed at all to enter a world created by an all good and all powerful Being may fairly be asked. Why those who pos· sess the treasure of a clear conscience should not also possess the lesser goods of earth is a question with which moral· ity is in nowise concerned.

Virtue can have no recompense, save as it is its own recompense, and vice can receive no real punishment, save as it is its own avenger. The hope of immortality, in so far as it is based upon the supposed necessity of righting in a future state what is here wrong, is therefore untenable, for it is based upon the assumption of a wrong which exists in the imagination merely. *And he who claims a reward because of his virtue, has thereby forfeited his right to maintain the claim, since that is not virtue which looks for reward.*

[6]

AHAD HAAM. See Ginzberg, Asher.

ALBERTUS MAGNUS

ALBERTUS MAGNUS (1193-1280). Considered the first representative of humanism during the Middle Ages, Albertus Magnus was
born in Germany, a descendant of the Counts of Bollstadt in Bavaria.
He was educated in Padua and Bologna. Endowed with an encyclopedic mind, he was rightly called "Doctor Universalis."

His reputation as a professor of theology at the University of
Paris was known throughout Europe, and he was highly esteemed as
a scholar of Arab and Jewish philosophy (studies which had been
encouraged under the influence of Emperor Frederick II). In fact,
no other Christian scholar of the Middle Ages quoted as many
Jewish philosophers as did Albertus. He learned much from Solomon ibn Gabirol's *Fons Vitae* (Source of Life), although he recognized that this book was not in accordance with the accepted precepts
of philosophy.

In physics and cosmology, he was a disciple of Maimonides.
As a trained scientist he stressed the importance of observation and
experiment. Interested in the study of metals and inorganic elements,
Albertus is perhaps best remembered as a scientist for his observation of the comet in 1240 and for his contributions to experimental
science.

In 1223, Albertus entered the Dominican Order, despite the
protestations of his former teachers. He believed in the defense of
knowledge for its intrinsic value, and that philosophy was an integral part of that knowledge, rather than an accessory study. He
maintained that his essential ideas were best expressed in his theological works. He was more the compiler than the systematic thinker,
the commentator rather than the creator of constructive and consistent philosophies. Although he always presented a speculative
philosophy with great clarity, he never succeeded in integrating contemporary philosophies into Christian thought.

He taught at Cologne from 1248 to 1254 and after served as
Bishop of Ratisbon for two years. His most famous pupil was
Thomas Aquinas, and they were devoted friends until Aquinas'
death in 1274. One of Albertus' last works was written in defense of
his former pupil.

ANALOGY BETWEEN GOD AND MAN

THERE is no excellence among the creatures which is not
to be found in a much higher style, and as an archetype, in

16

the Creator; among created beings it exists only in footmarks and images. This is true also of the Trinity. No artistic spirit can accomplish his work without first forming to himself an outline of it. In the spirit, therefore, first of all, the idea of its work is conceived, which is, as it were the offspring of the spirit in every feature resembling the spirit, representing it in its acting. Thus, therefore, the spirit reveals himself in the idea of the spirit. Now, from the acting spirit this idea passes into reality, and for this purpose the spirit must find a medium in outward action. This medium must be simple, and of the same substance with him who first acted, if indeed the latter is so simple that being, nature, and activity are one in him. From this results the idea in reference to God, of the formative spirit, of the planned image, and of the spirit by which the image is realized. The creation in time is a revelation of the eternal acting of God, the eternal generation of his Son. The revelation of God in time for the sanctification of nature, is an image of the eternal procession of the spirit from the Father and the Son. Our love is only a reflection of the divine love; the archetype of all love is the Holy Spirit, who, like all love, proceeds from God. The one love spread abroad through all holy souls proceeds from the Holy Spirit. Love in God neither diminishes nor increases, but we diminish or increase it in ourselves according as we receive this love into our souls, or withdraw from it.

[7]

ALBO, JOSEPH

ALBO, JOSEPH (c. 1380-1445). Very little is known about the life of Albo, but the few facts that are available present interesting aspects of medieval Jewish life midst Gentile surroundings. Albo was the representative of the Jewish community of Daroca, where the impact and resultant clash of Jewish, Christian, and Islamic thought gave rise to a number of intellectual disputes. He participated in the great religious controversy at Tortosa (1413-14), where he vigorously defended the Jewish viewpoint of the Talmud.

He attained popularity among medieval Jews because of his book

Sefer-Ha-Ikkarim (Book of Principles), a defense of Judaism against philosophical criticism and Christianity. Although no new ideas are introduced, the book is important to the general philosophy of religion because it established the criterion whereby the primary fundamental doctrines of Judaism may be distinguished from those of secondary importance. Albo stated that three principles are basic to every revelational religion: a belief in God, the concept of divine revelation, and divine retributive justice.

LAUGHTER

"LAUGHTER" (Heb. *sehok*) is a homonymous term. It applies to joy, as in the expression, "Then Abraham fell upon his face and laughed." Here "laughed" means "was glad," as is also the interpretation of Onkelos.

Laughter may also denote scorn, as in the expression, "I am as one that is a laughing-stock to his neighbour." And sometimes laughter and scorn are combined, and the words are used synonymously, as in the expression, "He that sitteth in heaven laugheth, the Lord hath them in derision," for laughter is often due to the feeling of contempt for that which deserves it, as when a person observes a defect in the words or deeds of another, while being conscious of superiority in himself, as not likely to err in word or deed as his neighbor has done. Thus laughter arises from the feeling of contempt when he observes his neighbor doing or saying something that is unbecoming to human nature or the person's dignity.

In the same way, laughter and derision are ascribed to God in the expression, "He that sitteth in heaven laugheth, the Lord hath them in derision." The reason is because He hears them saying, "Let us break their bands asunder," words a human being should not use; as our Rabbis say: The reason that the Psalm of Absalom stands next to that dealing with Gog and Magog, is that if any one should say, Is it possible that a servant should rebel against his master? you say to him, Is it possible that a son should rebel against his father? And yet the latter actually happened, so the former will happen. It is clear from this that it is an unusual thing for a man to say, and that he who says it deserves derision and contempt. In such cases, then, laughter is attributed to God or man.

Sometimes a person laughs when he deceives another in a matter about which the latter should have taken caution and did not. Accordingly the cause of laughter in all cases is a feeling of superiority in the person laughing, when he sees another commit a folly or exhibit ignorance or foolishness. When the scientists say that laughter is a human property, i.e. the cause of laughter is not known, they mean to say that we do not know why laughter is accompanied by certain bodily motions or why laughter is caused by touching the armpits or feeling other sensitive places in the body. But derision as a cause of laughter is well known, as we have shown in explaining the verse, "He that sitteth in heaven laugheth."

[8]

ALCOTT, AMOS BRONSON

ALCOTT, AMOS BRONSON (1799-1888). Alcott is frequently referred to as a dreamer because of his unsystematic, deeply veiled philosophy. Yet, like his friend, Emerson, he is truly representative of the New England transcendentalist movement. He was best received at small gatherings, where people listened patiently to his rambling ideas, eager to catch the secret meaning of his orthodoxy. His critics like to dwell upon his personal oddities with the result that his virtues and thoughts are little known. However, many of his lectures throughout the East and Middle West were published in *The Dial*. He is also the author of *Orphic Sayings*, *Tablets*, and *Concord Days*. Principally a distributor of ideas, a reiterator of previously formulated concepts, he was a teacher by conversation rather than indoctrination. He established several schools based upon these ideas, and was a member of the short-lived Utopian experiment at Fruitlands. Through his solid friendships with Ralph Waldo Emerson and William T. Harris, he was able to realize his dream of a school of philosophy at Concord, Massachusetts.

It is frequently said, despite his contributions to American letters and philosophy, that his life was a failure—largely because his household larder was empty most of the time. This in no way detracted from his family's allegiance to him. His daughter, Louisa May Alcott, portrayed him as the grandfather in *Little Women*. In

19

spite of his critics, this peripatetic lover of wisdom remains one of New England's most lovable sons.

TABLE TALK

LIKE its suburban neighbor beside the Charles, our village, seated along the banks of its Indian stream, spreads a rural cradle for the fresher literature; and aside from these advantages it well deserves its name for its quiet scenery and plain population. Moreover, few spots in New England have won a like literary repute. The rural muse has traversed these fields, meadows, woodlands, the brook-sides, the river; caught the harmony of its changing skies, and portrayed their spirit in books that are fit to live while Letters delight, and Nature charms her lovers. Had Homer, had Virgil, fairer prospects than our landscape affords? Had Shakespeare or Goethe a more luxuriant simplicity than ours? Only the wit to say or sing these the poet needs; and of this our neighborhood has not less than many sounding cities. Plain as our landscape is, it has special attractions for the scholar who courts quiet surroundings, scenery not too exciting, yet stimulating to genial and uninterrupted studies. If the hills command no very broad horizon, the prospect is sufficiently sylvan to give an agreeable variety without confusing the mind, while the river in good part compensates for the sameness, as it winds sluggishly along the confines of the village, flowing by the monument into the distance through the meadows. Thoreau, writing of it jocosely says: "It is remarkable for the gentleness of its current, which is hardly perceptible, and some have ascribed to its influence the proverbial moderation of the inhabitants of Concord, as celebrated in the Revolution and on other occasions. It has been suggested that the town should adopt for its coat-of-arms a *field verdant* with the Concord River circling nine times round it."

* * *

Not in stirring times like ours, when the world's affairs come posted with the succesive sun rising or setting, can we ignore magazines, libraries, and ephemera of the press. Newspapers intrude into every house, almost supersede the primers and text-books of the schools, proffering alike to hand and eye intelligence formerly won only by laborious studies and much expense of time and money. Cheap literature is now in vogue; the age, if not profound, has chances for attaining some superficial knowledge, at least, of the world's doings and designings; the experiments of the few being hereby popularized for the benefit of the many everywhere, the humblest even partaking largely of the common benefit.

* * *

Life and literature need the inspiration which idealism quickens and promotes. The history of thought shows that a people given to sensationalism and the lower forms of materialism have run to ruin. Only that which inspires life and nobility of thought can maintain and preserve itself from speedy and ignoble decay. And we have too palpable evidences of corruption, public and private, to leave us in doubt as to the tendency of not a little of the cultivation and teachings in our times. . . The idealists have given deeper insight into life and nature than other schools of thought. If inclined to visionariness, and seemingly sometimes on the verge of lunacy even, they have revealed depths of being, a devotion to the spirit of universality, that render their works most edifying. They, more than any other, hold the balance between mind and matter, and illuminate literature, while they furthered the science, art, and religion of all times. An age deficient in idealism has ever been one of immorality and superficial attainment, since without the sense of ideas, nobility of character becomes of rare attainment, if possible.

* * *

If the speaker cannot illuminate the parlor, shall he adorn the pulpit? Who takes most of private life into the desk comes nearest heaven and the children who have not lapsed out of it. Is it not time in the world's history to have less familiarity with sin and the woes of the pit? Commend me to him who holds me fast by every sense, persuades me—against every bias of temperament, habit, training, culture—to espouse the just and lovely, and he shall be in my eyes thereafter the Priest of the Spirit and the Sent of Heaven. It is undeniable that, with all our teaching and preaching—admirable as these often are— the current divinity falls behind our attainments in most things else; the commanding practical sense and adventurous thoughts of our time being unawakened to the concerns wherein faith and duty have their seats, and from whose fountains life and thought are spiritualized and made lovely to men. Though allegory is superseded in good part by the novel, the field for this form of writing is as rich and inviting as when Bunyan wrote. A sacred allegory, treating of the current characteristics of the religious world, would be a powerful instrumentality for awakening and stimulating the piety of our times.

* * *

Every dogma embodies some shade of truth to give it seeming currency. Take the theological trinity as an instance which has vexed the literal Church from its foundation, and still perplexes its learned doctors. An intelligible psychology would interpret the mystery even to the unlearned and unprofessional. Analyse the attributes of your personality—that which you name yourself—and you will find herein the threefold attributes of instinct, intelligence, will, incarnate in your own person:—the root plainly of the trinitarian dogma.—Not till we have fathomed the full significance of what we mean when we pronounce *"I myself,"* is the idea of person clearly discriminated, philosophy and religion established upon immutable foundations.

* * *

Ever present and operant is *That* which never becomes a party in one's guilt, conceives never an evil thought, consents never to an unrighteous deed, never sins; but holds itself impeccable, immutable, personally holy — the Conscience — counsellor, comforter, judge, and executor of the spirit's decrees. None can flee from the spirit's presence, nor hide himself. The reserved powers are the mighty ones. Side by side sleep the Whispering Sisters and the Eumenides. Nor is Conscience appeased till the sentence is pronounced. There is an oracle in the beast, an unsleeping police; and ever the court sits, dealing doom or deliverance. Our sole inheritance is our deeds. While remorse stirs the sinner, there remains hope of his redemption. "Only he to whom all is one, who draweth all things to one, and seeth all things in one, may enjoy true peace and rest of spirit." None can escape the *Presence*. The *Ought* is everywhere and imperative. Alike guilt in the soul and anguish in the flesh affirm His ubiquity. Matter—in particle and planet, mind and macrocosm—is quick with spirit.

* * *

Born daily out of a world of wonders into a world of wonders, that faith is most ennobling which, answering to one's highest aspirations, touches all things meanwhile with the hues of an invisible world. And how vastly is life's aspect, the sphere of one's present activity, widened and ennobled the moment there step spiritual agents upon the stage, and he holds conscious communication with unseen powers! "He to whom the law which he is to follow," says Jacobi, "doth not stand forth as a God, has only a dead letter which cannot possibly quicken him." The religious life transcends the scientific understanding, its light shining through the clouds to those alone whose eyes are anointed to look behind the veils by lives of purity and devotion.

* * *

Personal Identity is the sole Identity. "That which knows and that which is known," says Aristotle, "are really the same thing." The knowing that *I am* affirms also the personality

23

immanent in all persons; and hence of the Supreme Person, since distinct from personality neither mind nor God were thinkable. And it were impossible to have like conceptions in our minds, if we did not partake of one and the same intellect.

> Were God not *God*, I were not *I*;
> Myself in Him myself descry.

An impersonal God were an absurdity. Personality is essential to the idea of spirit, and man, as man, were unthinkable without the presupposition of personality. It is the *I* that gives subsistence to nature and reality to mind. Where the *I* is not, nothing is. Religion and science alike presuppose its presence as their postulate and ground. It is the essence of which substance is the manifestation. Qualities are inherent in substance, and substance is one and spiritual. Personal Identity is spiritual, not numerical, souls being one, bodies not one. Any number of bodies can never attain to unity, since it is the one in each that defines and denotes it. The personality is inclusive of the one in each and in all.

*   *   *

Our sleep is a significant symbol of the soul's antecedence. Shall I question that I now am, because I am unconscious of being myself while I slept; or because I am conscious of being then unconscious? I am sure of being one and the same person I then was, and thread my identity through my successive yesterdays into the memory out of which my consciousness was born; nor can I lose myself in the search of myself. At best, our mortality is but a suspended animation, the soul meanwhile awaiting its summons to awaken from its slumbers. Every act of sleep is a metamorphosis of bodies and a metempsychosis of souls. We lapse out of the senses into the pre-existent life of memory through the gate of dreams, memory and fancy opening their folding-doors into our past and future periods of existence:—the soul freed for the moment from its dormitory in space and time. The more of sleep the more of retrospect; the more of wakefulness, the more of prospect. Memory marks the nadir of our consciousness, imagination its zenith. Before the heavens thou art, and shall survive their decay. Were man personally finite, he could not conceive of infinity; were he mortal he could not conceive of immortality. Whatever had a beginning comes of necessity to its end, since it has not the principle of perpetuity inherent in itself. And there is that in man which cannot think annihilation, but thinks continuance. All life is eternal; there is no other. Despair snuffs the sun from the firmament.

> For souls that of His own good life partake
> He loves as His own self; dear as His eye
> They are to Him. He'll never them forsake.
> When they shall die, then God Himself shall die.
> They live, they live in blest eternity.   [9]

ALCUIN, FLACCUS ALBINUS

ALCUIN, FLACCUS ALBINUS (c. 735-804). Well-known as a teacher, poet, and monastic, Alcuin achieved his greatest fame as the educator of Charlemagne. The emperor probably met him on his journeys through Italy. Alcuin had returned to Parma from England because of a declining interest in education there, and when Charlemagne invited him to take charge of his court school, the Schola Palatina, he gladly accepted. There, and later at Tours, where he had been given the monastery of St. Martin, Alcuin lived the life of a teacher, always abreast of the literary developments of the period. According to him, he "dispensed the honey of the Holy Scripture, intoxicated his students with the wine of ancient learning, fed them the apples of grammatical refinement, and adorned them with the knowledge of astronomy."

The erudition of Charlemagne is directly traceable to the influence of his versatile teacher. Alcuin was a lover of poetry, and wrote quite acceptable hexameters. But posterity remembers him best as a great letter writer; more than three hundred of his letters have been preserved. Each was written to a distinguished friend, addressed either by some name which characterized the recipient,

25

or a Latin paraphrase of the real name. They are still interesting for their philosophical content as well as for their references to historic events.

DIALOGUE ON THE VIRTUES

Charlemagne—I wonder that we Christians should so often depart from virtue, though we have eternal glory promised as its recompense by Jesus Christ, who is Truth itself whilst the heathen philosophers steadily pursued it merely on account of its intrinsic worth, and for the sake of fame.

Alcuin—We must rather deplore than wonder, that most of us will not be induced to embrace virtue, either by the fear of punishment or the hope of promised reward.

Charlemagne—I see it, and must, alas! acknowledge that there are many such. I beg you, however, to inform me as briefly as possible, how we, as Christians, are to understand and regard these chief virtues.

Alcuin—Does not that appear to you to be wisdom, whereby God, after the manner of human understanding, is known and feared, and his future judgment believed?

Charlemagne—I understand you; and grant that nothing is more excellent than this wisdom. I also remember that it is written in Job, *Behold, the wisdom of man is the fear of God!* And what is the fear of God but the worship of God.

Alcuin—It is so: and further, what is righteousness but the love of God, and the observance of his commandments?

Charlemagne—I perceive this also, and that nothing is more perfect than this righteousness, or rather that there is no other than this.

Alcuin—Do you not consider that to be valor whereby a man overcomes the "Evil One," and is enabled to bear with firmness the trials of the world?

Charlemagne—Nothing appears to me more glorious than such a victory.

26

Alcuin—And is not that temperance which checks desire, restrains avarice, and tranquillizes and governs all the passions of the soul?

[10]

ALDEN, JOSEPH

ALDEN, JOSEPH (1807-1885). Principally known as a pedagogue, Alden began his career at the age of fourteen when he became a teacher in a district school. His skill and ability were soon recognized. He became a professor at Williams College in 1835 and remained there until 1852. He was appointed president of Jefferson College in 1857, and was principal of the State Normal School at Albany, New York from 1867 to 1882.

He excelled in directing and developing logical thought in young people and was equally successful as an administrator and author. He published more than seventy books, most of which dealt with philosophy, religion, and government in such a manner that they were popularly acceptable for classroom use. Aware that his talents were chiefly of a didactic nature, Alden refrained from pretentious expression and adopted his aims to his methods. Of his many books, *Christian Ethics or the Science of Duty* (1866), *The Science of Government* (1867), and *Thoughts on the Religious Life* (1879) were the most widely read.

CONCEPTIONS OF THE INFINITE

THERE has been a great deal written about the absolute and the infinite which conveys no meaning to such as have not the faculty of understanding the unintelligible. For example, Mansel says: "That which is conceived of as absolute and infinite must be conceived of as combining within itself the sum not only of all actual but of all possible modes of being."—There is no such thing as a general infinite. There are infinite things or attributes, just as there are true propositions. But the infinite and the true are not independent entities. We cognize infinite objects, and can thus form an abstract idea of infinity. The idea is not definable. As we say, "Truth is that in which all true proportions agree," so we may say, that the infinite is that in which all infinite objects agree.

27

That is infinite which has no limit. That which we cognize as limitless is to us infinite. We must distinguish between the infinite and the indefinite. God's wisdom is infinite; it transcends all our powers of expression. So of his mercy and his benevolence. Infinite existence is everlasting existence. When we speak of God as the Infinite Existence, we mean that all his attributes are infinite. The human mind can form no adequate apprehension of infinite things; and yet it is not, properly speaking, a negative apprehension which we have of it. The fact that we cannot know everything about a subject or object does not prove that we cannot know anything about it. The fact that we cannot by searching find out God to perfection, does not prove that we cannot know many things respecting him. God is infinite: that is, His existence and attributes are without limit—transcend all our power of apprehension. We know nothing than can be added to them.

[11]

ALEXANDER, SAMUEL

ALEXANDER, SAMUEL (1859-1938). A teacher at Oxford, Glasgow and Victoria Universities, Alexander's fame rests principally on his book *Space, Time and Deity*, which evolved out of his Gifford Lectures at Glasgow given in 1915. This book has been referred to as the most significant British metaphysical contribution since that of Hobbes. Classed as both idealist and realist, he tended more toward realism as he grew older. In 1889, his prize essay *Moral Order and Progress* (which he disowned some twenty years later) fanned the Anglo-Aristotelian-Hegelian movement in British ethics toward the direction of a sophisticated evolutionary theory.

PHILOSOPHY AND THEOLOGY

PHILOSOPHY approaches theology, in the character of the philosophy of religion, in the same spirit as it approaches the other sciences, the spirit of criticism and comprehension. Necessarily, in Bacon's fine phrase, philosophy takes all knowledge for its province; not in the sense of arrogating an impossible erudition, but in the sense that it asks whether the ideas used in any science are compatible with those used in other sciences or in the ordinary unscientific possessions of the mind. No topic raised in the sciences, so far as it does not fall strictly within that art which is the special province of the science—and is therefore subject to the rules of the scientific artist (what philosopher in his senses would question the demonstration of the binomial theorem? He leaves such doubts to the skilled craftsman, the mathematician)—is exempt from his enquiry. His dearest privilege indeed is to organize knowledge, to find a comprehensive view of the whole. But comprehension means scrutiny. Of theology it asks, granted that the object of religion is such and such, what place is there in the rest of the universe for such a being? Is the being so described consistent with other well-attested facts? Hence, as in regard to the ordinary things of sense, it asks whether these are indeed real, apart from our awareness of them, or exist only in so far as there is a knower of them; so it asks of theology, may not the object of religion be a fancy projected into reality by the wishes of man?

Philosophy is critical of theology in another fashion, which is more to my immediate purpose. Theology is exposed to a peculiar danger. The more it penetrates by reflection into the notions of religion the more it tends to employ conceptions on the borderland of philosophy. Some theologies do more or less without philosophy; it is always said that the Jews are not a philosophical people on the whole, and are content with moral notions. But Christian theology has been, in its more abstract parts, very philosophical, and has attracted to itself some of the greatest speculative intellects. Now the danger arises thus: the demands of the religious consciousness—I mean, of course, the clarified religious consciousness— are insistent and must be met, and they lead to ideas which are mysterious indeed, but whose mystery passes more or less unnoticed by the ordinary mind; which are indeed pictorial embodiments of these insistent claims. Thus the intimate harmonising of God and man, their communion in the relation of child to father, is embodied in the idea of a God-made man, which is found in other religions, but in none with such grace and winningness as in Christianity. But the purely religious data of the Incarnation, the Atonement, the Resurrection, data which are the starting points of Christian theology, lead on to the subtlest metaphysical conceptions, such as that of the Trinity, which are introduced to satisfy rationally the data contained in the religious consciousness, which is not of itself rational at all in its inception. It is in the employment of philosophical conceptions that theology has to tread most warily and to beware of taking them over except after scrutiny. Much of the theology which I have read of to-day (and it is very little) seems to me not to avoid this danger; one instance is the indiscriminate appeal made to the idea of value or the valuable, as something which must be accepted as admitting no further analysis, although psychologists and writers on morals have offered such analyses more than once.   [12]

AL-FARABI

AL-FARABI (c. 870-950). Born of a Turkish family, educated by a Christian physician at Baghdad, Al-Farabi has been ranked with Aristotle as one of the greatest of all teachers.

A versatile man, his chief occupation was that of philosopher, either by way of comment or original contribution. He is best known for his analyses of the Greek philosophers. Whatever he wrote was syncretistic in nature, for he sought for the compatible concepts of God, soul, time, and space among the diverse philosophies. Thus he found Plato and Aristotle in perfect accord, and historians of philosophy have ever since despaired over his treatise *On the Agreement of the Philosophy of Plato and Aristotle.*

He wrote many works on various aspects of the soul: its intellect, the unity of the soul, its substance, and many of its problems. All his thinking was characterized by an idealism bordering on mysticism.

Al-Farabi was principally influenced by Plotinus whose belief that the materially comprehensive world emanated from God still exerts influence over Moslem scholastic thought, and by Aristotle who assumed there was a Prime Mover of the universe and therefore the world had no beginning in time, that time is relative to motion and could not have preceded God, who himself was the first mover.

Al-Farabi was not only a great philosopher but also a noted musicologist. Dervishes in the East can still be heard singing the chants he composed. He was also a Utopian whose *Model City* envisioned his desires for the heavenly city on this earth.

ON CONCEPTS

I. KNOWLEDGE is divided into (a) generally accepted concepts (concepts of the sun, moon, intellect, and the soul), and (b) those concepts that require verification (such as making certain that the heaven consists of spheres, one in the other; or that the world has been created in time).

It is necessary for every concept to have a prior concept. The concluding concept may be established without connecting it to a concept preceding it. This is true of being: the necessary and the possible. These concepts do not require one to previously perceive that something comprises them. These three are rather distinct, correct concepts, innate to understanding. If someone desires to verbally clarify these concepts, then this is only a stimulus to understanding; but they cannot be clarified beyond the clarity of the concepts themselves.

II. It is impossible for us to understand the verifications of concepts without previously having understood other things. For instance, if we wish to know that the world has been created in time, then we must have the prior certainty that the world is composite. However, all that is composite has also been originated in time; consequently we know also that the world has been originated in time. Without doubt, this verification ultimately ends in another which then does not require another to precede it for confirmation.

These, then, are the basic principles that are clearly present in the intellect: of two sides of an opposite, one must always be true, the other false; the whole is greater than any part of it. Logic is the science by which we get acquainted

31

with these methods so that they assist us in our concepts of things and guide us to their verification. The two methods mentioned here aid us in distinguishing between complete and deficient concepts, between the certain and those only approximately certain; as well as the preponderant opinion and the doubtful one. By doing this we become aware of all the aspects of the complete concept as well as the certain verification of those that do not contain any doubt.

III. Thus we maintain: All that there is is divided into two categories. In the first category it is unnecessary to cogitate the nature of the things, since they are of a possible existence. If we reflect on the nature of the second category of things, we find that their being is a necessary one and we say accordingly, it is of necessary existence. It is not absurd to postulate that some things of possible existence are not present; for in order for a thing to exist, it must have a cause; however, if it becomes a necessary being, then it attains necessary existence through something other than that which it itself is. From this it follows that it is necessary for it to belong to that which naturally always has a possible existence and became a necessary being only by virtue of something else. This possibility either never ceases or it takes place at a particular time. The possibility cannot move forever as cause and effect, as it were, in a circle; instead it must end in something necessary to itself. The latter would be that which would be present at first.

IV. However, if we postulate that which is necessary as not present, then we state an absurdity. For its being has no cause, and furthermore, it cannot have its being by virtue of something else. It is the first cause of the being of things, and its being must of necessity be the prime being. We are compelled to imagine the same in every way free of want. Its being is thus complete. Moreover, its being must of necessity be the most perfect one, free from causes, i.e., matter, form, creation, and the final goal. [13]

ALGHAZZALI, ABU HAMID MOHAMMED IBN GHAZZALI

ALGHAZZALI, ABU HAMID MOHAMMED IBN GHAZZALI (1059-1111). Alghazzali was a Persian philosopher born in the northeastern part of the empire. The greatest teachers of Islam have bestowed upon him innumerable encomiums, among them, "the guide to the True Faith," "the embodiment of religious thought," "the living reaffirmation of Islam." To this day his writings are considered classic throughout the Moslem world.

Alghazzali, never a bigoted orthodox, both advocated and practiced tolerance. He often advised his co-religionists to take the pious Jew as their model in religious reverence. In fact, Jewish philosophers of the Middle Ages soon became aware that Alghazzali's principles and teachings were closely akin to those of Judaism, a fact that has often been confirmed by modern Christian scholars.

Alghazzali was deeply influenced by Sufism despite his faithful study of the Koran. His doctrine of emanation was derived from neo-Platonic writings. He classified those who denied this doctrine as children, for both confuse marionettes or wooden idols with reality. His criticisms of causality pre-dated David Hume's parallel theories by several centuries, and he exerted great influence over William of Ockham and other Christian philosophers. He compared the pursuit of knowledge to the process involved in digging a well: both involved probing; the desired object in both cases was necessary to life.

THE NATURE OF MAN

THOUGH man shares with the other animals external and internal senses, he is at the same time also endowed with two qualities peculiar to himself, knowledge and will. By knowledge is meant the power of generalization, the conception of abstract ideas, and the possession of intellectual truths. By will is meant that strong desire to acquire an object which after due consideration of its consequences has been pronounced by reason to be good. It is quite different from animal desire, nay, it is often the very opposite of it.

In the beginning children also lack these two qualities. They have passion, anger, and all the external and internal

33

senses, but will finds its expression only later. Knowledge differs according to the capacity for it, according to the latent powers in a man. Hence there is a variety of stages amongst Prophets, the Ulamas, the Sufis and the Philosophers. Further progress is possible even beyond these stages, for divine knowledge knows no bounds. The highest stage is reached by one to whom all truths and realities are revealed intuitively, who by virtue of his exalted position enjoys direct communion and close relation with the Most Holy. The real nature of this position is known only to him who enjoys it. We verify it by faith. A child has no knowledge of the attainments of an adult; an adult is not aware of the acquisitions of a learned man. Similarly a learned man is not cognizant of the holy communion of the saints and the prophets, and of the favors bestowed on them. Although the divine blessings descend freely, those are fit recipients of them, whose hearts are pure and wholly devoted to Him. "Verily," says the Hadis, "the desire of the virtuous is to hold communion with me, and I long to look at them." "He who approaches me a span, I approach him an arm." The divine favors are not withheld, but hearts bedimmed by impurity fail to receive them. "Had it not been that the devils hover round the hearts of men, they would have seen the glories of the Kingdom of the Heaven."

The superiority of man consists thus in his being cognizant of divine attributes and actions. Therein lies his perfection; thus he may be worthy of admission to God's presence.

The body serves as a vehicle for the soul, and the soul is the abode for knowledge which is its fundamental character as well as its ultimate object. The horse and the ass are both beasts of burden, but a superiority of the former is found in its being gracefully adapted for use in battle. If the horse fails in this it is degraded to the rank of mere burden bearing animals. Similarly with man. In certain qualities man resembles a horse and an ass, but his distinguishing trait is his participation in the nature of the angels, for he holds a middle position between the beast and the angel. Considering the mode of his nourishment and growth he is found to belong to the vegetable world. Considering his power of movement and impulses he is a denizen of the animal kingdom. The distinguishing quality of knowledge lifts him up to the celestial world. If he fails to develop this quality and to translate it into action he is no better than a grunting pig, a snarling dog, a prowling wolf, or a crafty fox.

If he wishes for true happiness, let him look upon reason as a monarch sitting on the throne of his heart, imagination as its ambassador, memory as treasurer, speech as interpreter, the limbs as clerks, and the senses as spies in the realms of color, sound, smell, etc. If all these properly discharge the duties allotted to them, if every faculty does that for which it was created—and such service is the real meaning of thanksgiving to God—the ultimate object of his sojourn in this transitory world is realized.

Man's nature is made up of four elements, which produce in him four attributes, namely, the beastly; the brutal, the satanic, and the divine. In man there is something of the pig, the dog, the devil, and the saint. The pig is the appetite which is repulsive not for its form but for its lust and its gluttony. The dog is passion which barks and bites, causing injury to others. The devil is the attribute which instigates these former two, embellishing them and bedimming the sight of reason which is the divine attribute. Divine reason, if properly attended to, would repel the evil by exposing its character. It would properly control appetite and the passions. But when a man fails to obey the dictates of reason, these three other attributes prevail over him and cause his ruin. Such types of men are many. What a pity it is that these who would find fault with those who worship stones do not see that on their part they worship the pig and the dog in themselves: Let them be ashamed of their deplorable condition and leave no stone unturned for the suppression of these evil attributes. The pig of appetite begets shamelessness, lust, slander, and such like: the dog of passion begets pride, vanity, ridicule, wrath and tyranny. These two, controlled by the satanic power produce deceit, treachery, perfidy, meanness etc. but if divinity in man is uppermost the qualities of knowledge, wisdom, faith, and truth, etc. will be acquired.

Know then that mind is like a mirror which reflects images. But just as the mirror, the image, and the mode of reflection are three different things so mind, objects, and the way of knowing are also distinct. There are five reasons which may prevent the object from being reflected in the mirror. 1. There may be something wrong with the mirror. 2. Something other than the mirror may prevent the reflection. 3. The object may not be in front of it. 4. Something may come between the object and the mirror. 5. The position of the object may not be known, so that the mirror may be properly placed. Similarly, for five reasons, the mind fails to receive knowledge. 1. The mind may be imperfect, like the child's. 2. Sin and guilt may bedim the mind and throw a veil over it. 3. The mind may be diverted from the real object. For example, a man may be obedient and good, but instead of rising higher to the acquisition of truth and contemplation of God is contented with bodily devotions and aquirement of means of living. Such a mind, though pure, will not reflect the divine image for his objects of thought are other than this. If this is the condition of such mind, think what will be the state of those minds which are absorbed in the gratification of their inordinate passions. 4. An external screen, may as it were, come before the objects. Sometimes a man who has subjugated his passions still through blind imitation or prejudice fails to know the truth. Such types are found amongst the votaries of the Kalam. Even many virtuous men also fall a prey to it and blindly stick to their dogmas. 5. There may be ignorance of the means for the acquisition of truth. Thus for illustration, a man wants to see his back in a mirror: if he places the mirror before his eyes he fails to see his back; if he keeps it facing his back it will still be out of sight. Let him then take another mirror and place one before his eyes and the other facing his back in such a position that the image of the latter is reflected in the former. Thus he will be able to see his back. Similarly the knowledge of the unknown from the known.

The divine dispensation is liberal in the distribution of its bounties, but for reasons mentioned above, minds fail to profit by them. For human minds partake of the nature of the divine and the capacity to apprehend truth is innate. The Koran says: "Surely we offered the trust to the heavens and the earth and the mountains, but they declined to bear it up and were afraid of it and man took it up. Surely he is not just (to himself) and is ignorant." In this passage the innate capacity of man is hinted at and refers to the secret power of knowing God, latent in human minds by virtue of which they have preference over other objects and the universe. The Prophet says: "Every child is born in the right state (Fitrat) but his parents make him a Jew, a Christian, or a Magian." And again: "Had it not been that evil spirits hover round the hearts of the sons of Adam they would have seen the kingdom of heaven." Ibn Umar reports that the Prophet was once asked as to where God is found either on earth or in heaven. "He is in the hearts of his faithful servants," replied the Prophet.

It will not be out of place to throw some light here on the following terms which are often vaguely applied while dealing with the question of human nature.

1. Qalb (heart) has two meanings. (a) A conical shaped piece of flesh on the left side of the chest, circulating blood, the source of animal spirits. It is found in all animals. The heart thus belongs to the external world and can be seen with the material eyes. (b) A mysterious divine substance which is related to the material heart like the relation between the dweller and the house or the artisan and his implements. It alone is sentient and responsible.

2. Ruh (spirit) means (a) a vapory substance which issues from the material heart, and quickens every part of the body. It is like a lamp which is placed in a house and sheds its light on all sides. (b) The soul which is expressed

in the Koran as "divine commanament" and is used in the same sense as the second meaning of Qalb, mentioned above.

3. Nafs (self) which means (*a*) the substratum for appetite and passion. The Sufis call it the embodiment of vices. (*b*) The ego which receives different names in accordance with the qualities acquired from changes in its conditions. When in subjugating passions it acquires mastery over them and feels undisturbed, it is called *the peaceful self* (Nafsi mutmainna). The Koran says: "Nafs that art at rest. Return to thy Lord well pleased with Him, well pleasing." When it upbraids man for his actions it is called *conscience* (Nafsi lauwama). When it freely indulges in the gratification of his passions, it is called *the inordinate self* (Nafsi ammara).

[14]

AL·KINDI

AL-KINDI (died 873 A.D.). The son of a South Arabian governor, Al-Kindi was given the best possible education at Basra and Baghdad. His life was spent in the service of the court as tutor, astrologer, translator and editor of many Greek philosophical works. We possess few of his writings in the original Arabic, probably because, at one time, his extensive library was temporarily confiscated. His optical and astronomical calculations were valued for centuries. He was the first to apply mathematics not only to the physical world but also to Materia Medica where he calculated the effect of medicines from the proportions and qualities represented in the various mixtures.

From Latin translations of his works and literary activities, we learn that his eclecticism was equally characteristic of many Arab philosophers throughout the Middle Ages. He respected Plato, Aristotle and Pythagoras, but remained blind to their essential doctrinal differences. He, thus, shared the tendencies of most Neo-Platonists and Neo-Pythagoreans. In philosophy, he regarded God as the intelligent cause of the universe, the Greek *nous*, that has communicated itself from above through successive emanations of the soul to the sphere in which we live. Through this process, man became free and immortal, though his body remained subject to the influence of the stars.

I HAVE taken note that you ask that a brief discussion of the intellect [and the object of comprehension], according to the theory of Plato and Aristotle, be communicated to you. Their theory is that intellect falls into four types. The first is the intellect which is always active; the second is the intellect potentially in the mind; the third is the intellect when it becomes an efficient agent by virtue of [its] power in the mind; the fourth is the intellect which we call demonstrative, and it is this intellect which Aristotle approximates to sensation, because of the propinquity of sensation to truth and because it is in complete communion with it.

For Aristotle has said that there are two kinds of form. One of them has matter and it is that which underlies sensation; but the other is that which is devoid of matter and is that which forms the substratum of intellect. Indeed, the former has to do with things, while the latter is above that.

Now, the form that resides in matter, is actually perceived; for if it were not actually perceived it would not lie within the range of sensation. Now, if the mind apprehends it, then it is as such in the mind. But it does not apprehend it unless it was first potentially in the mind. Therefore, when the mind apprehends it, it becomes actual in the mind. However, it is not in the mind as something is in a vase, nor does it chase through the body; for the mind is not the body, nor is it limited. Therefore, it is in the mind, and the mind is one, identical with itself, and not anything other than itself; nor is it again different by virtue of a twisting of terms.

Similarly, the faculty of feeling does not exist except in the soul. But it is not part of the soul as a member is part of the body; rather, it is the soul itself, and as such is feeling. Likewise, the form of the sense datum is not in the mind as something distinct or different. Therefore, as Aristotle has declared, the sense datum in the mind is the perceiving agent in conformity to what is in the mind. But, the sense datum as a material thing is outside the perceiving mind. Now, therefore, that which is in matter is the sense datum, not the perceiving agent.

Similarly, Aristotle has explained intelligence as the mind when it apprehends the object of comprehension, or THE form which has neither matter nor sensuous representation and is one with mind, and is then in actuality in the mind; for it was not previously in actuality, but [only] potentially in the mind. This form, therefore, which hasn't any matter or sensuous representation as yet, is the intellect which the mind has attained through primal intelligence, the concept of all, ever active. However, this does not become contributive, unless the mind has attained the power to receive it, since the mind is [only] potentially an agent of intelligence, whereas primal intelligence is always active. For nothing assimilates anything through its own receptivity except that which belonged to it potentially and not in actuality. Nothing, to be sure, that a thing possesses potentially works as an efficient cause by itself; for if it were self-existent, it would always be in activity; since its essence would always be its own and spontaneous. Therefore, nothing that exists potentially becomes an efficient cause unless by virtue of something that is an efficient cause. Hence, the mind is potentially an agent of intelligence, yet it becomes an efficient cause at the instigation of primal intelligence, looking to which it becomes an agent of intelligence in actuality. And, when an intelligible form is conjoined with it, it is not one thing, and the intelligible form another, because it is not divisible, allowing it to be changed. But when a union is brought about with the intelligible form, then it and the intellect are one, if you will allow the agent of intelligence and that which is comprehended. Thus, the intellect and the object of comprehension are one when they exist in the mind. In truth, the intellect as such, which is always active and draws forth the mind so it may become an agent of intelligence in fact, after it was potentially intelligent, and the object of comprehension as such are not one and the same thing. Therefore, the object of comprehension in the mind and the first type of intellect derived from primal intelligence are not the same; however, the intellect derived from the mind and the object of comprehension are one and the same.

But the intellect, which in simplicity is more like the soul, is much higher in comparison with the thing comprehended than sensation, as compared with the sense datum. The first type of intellect, therefore, is the cause of all that is comprehended. But the second type of intellect is potentially in the mind.

Intellect is, thus, either of the first type in that it is for all that is comprehended, or it is of the second type and then it is potentially in the mind; at all events, the mind is not an actual agent of intelligence. The third type of intellect, however, is the one that is working efficiently in the mind which has already acquired it. And, it is kept there in such a manner that, when it wills, it may use it and cause it to be in one other than itself. In the same way, writing is ready and easy for a scribe because he has already become proficient in it and it has become second nature to him. Consequently, he communicates and practices it whenever he is so inclined. The fourth type of intellect is that which goes forth from the mind which, when you desire to communicate it, will work an effect in someone other than yourself.

The second type of intellect derives, therefore, from the the third and fourth, for the reason that the third is an acquisition of the mind and causes it to appear whenever it wishes, either at the first instance of its acquisition in us, or in the second instance of its appearance outside us. Then the mind uses it. Therefore, the third is the one that is an acquisition of the mind, which is prior to it, and, if it so wills, becomes spontaneous in it. But the fourth is that which appears to work as an efficient cause from the mind.

These are, therefore, the parts into which the foremost

philosophers have divided the intellect. May this explanation suffice for what you had in mind.

[15]

ALLEN, ETHAN

ALLEN, ETHAN (1738-1789). Ten years prior to the publication of
Thomas Paine's *Age of Reason*, Ethan Allen's book, *Reason The
Only Oracle of Man*, (1784), enunciated the principles of deism op-
erative in American life. Condemned by the clergy and New England
universities, it was admiringly referred to by freethinkers as
"Ethan's Bible." When a fire at the publishing house destroyed the
stock of copies, the orthodox welcomed the incident as "an act of
God."

Though Allen was a contemplative man, he led an active life,
engaging in farming, mining, manufacturing, and real-estate transactions. He was a soldier during the French and Indian War, and,
during the War for Independence, he commanded the Green Mountain Boys of Vermont and captured from the British Fort Ticon-
deroga, the main approach to Canada. He was a pioneer in the development of American economic life and built a blast furnace in
the Litchfield Hills of Connecticut, his native state. Vermont was
his adopted state, and he vociferously defended its boundary and
land claims against those of New York and New Hampshire.

Allen was reared in Arminianism. This religious belief, though
tolerant of Calvinist orthodoxy, emphasized human duties more than
theological speculation. Allen rebelled against any accepted dogma,
publicly protesting that he was not a Christian but a deist. He opposed authority of all kinds and declared that tradition was fallible,
reason the highest gift of God, and faith less reliable and unimportant. He viewed human beings as "the most selfish, oddest, and most
cunning medley of beings of that size in the universe." And though
his opinions of contemporary human conditions were equally pessimistic, he was confident that the ultimate victory of virtue would
make for human progress. He was convinced that the existence of
Man was necessary for the maintenance of the world created by
God and, therefore, there "can be no ultimate failure." He held that
the future was beyond human comprehension and that goodness and
happiness would prevail in the last stage of human development, for
so had God ordained.

THE period of life is very uncertain, and at the longest is but short: a few years bring us from infancy to manhood, a few more to a dissolution; pain, sickness and death are the necessary consequences of animal life. Through life we struggle with physical evils, which eventually are certain to destroy our earthly composition; and well would it be for us did evils end here; but alas! moral evil has been more or less predominant in our agency, and though natural evil is unavoidable, yet moral evil may be prevented or remedied by the exercise of virtue.

Morality is of more importance to us than any or all other attainments; as is a habit of mind, which, from a retrospective consciousness of our agency in this life, we should carry with us into our succeeding state of existence, as an acquired appendage of our rational nature, and as the necessary means of our mental happiness. Virtue and vice are the only things in this world, which, with our souls, are capable of surviving death; the former is the rational and only procuring cause of all intellectual happiness, and the latter of conscious guilt and misery; and therefore, our indispensable duty and ultimate interest is, to love, cultivate and improve the one, as the means of our greatest good, and to hate and abstain from the other, as productive of our greatest evil. And in order thereto, we should so far divest ourselves of the incumbrances of this world, (which are too apt to engross our attention) as to acquire a consistent system of the knowledge of religious duty, and make it our constant endeavour in life to act conformably to it.

The knowledge of the being, perfections, creation and providence of GOD, and of the immortality of our souls, is the foundation of religion. And as the Pagan, Jewish, Christian and Mahometan countries have been overwhelmed with a multiplicity of revelations diverse from each other, and which, by their respective promulgators, are said to have been immediately inspired into their souls, by the spirit of God, or immediately communicated to them by the intervening agency of angels (as in the instance of the invisible Gabriel to Mahomet) and as those revelations have been received and credited, by far the greater part of the inhabitants of the several countries of the world (on whom they have been obtruded) as supernaturally revealed by God or Angels, and which, in doctrine and discipline, are in most respects repugnant to each other, it fully evinces their imposture, and authorizes us, without a lengthy course of arguing, to determine with certainty, that not more than one if any one of them, had their original from God; as they clash with each other; which is ground of high probability against the authenticity of each of them.

A revelation, that may be supposed to be really of the institution of God, must also be supposed to be perfectly consistent or uniform, and to be able to stand the test of truth; therefore such pretended revelations, as are tendered to us as the contrivance of heaven, which do not bear that test, we may be morally certain, were either originally a deception, or has since, by adulteration become spurious. Furthermore, should we admit, that among the numerous revelations on which the respective priests have given the stamp of divinity, some one of them was in reality of divine authority, yet we could not otherwise, as rational beings, distinguish it from others, but by reason.

Reason therefore must be the standard by which we determine the respective claims of revelation; for otherwise we may as well subscribe to the divinity of the one as of the other, or to the whole of them, or to none at all. So likewise on this thesis, if reason rejects the whole of those revelations, we ought to return to the religion of nature and reason.

Undoubtedly it is our duty, and for our best good, that we occupy and improve the faculties, with which our Creator has endowed us, but so far as prejudice, or prepossession of opinion prevails over our minds, in the same proportion, reason is excluded from our theory or practice. Therefore if we would acquire useful knowledge, we must first divest ourselves of those impediments; and sincerely endeavour to search out the truth; and draw our conclusions from reason and just argument, which will never conform to our inclination, interest or fancy; but we must conform to that if we would judge rightly. As certain as we determine contrary to reason, we make a wrong conclusion; therefore, our wisdom is, to conform to the nature and reason of things, as well in religious matters, as in other sciences. Preposterously absurd would it be, to negative the exercise of reason in religious concerns, and yet, be actuated by it in all other and less occurrences of life. All our knowledge of things is derived from God, in and by the order of nature, out of which we cannot perceive, reflect or understand any thing whatsoever; our external senses are natural and so are our souls; by the instrumentality of the former we perceive the objects of sense, and with the latter we reflect on them. And those objects are also natural; so that ourselves, and all things about us, and our knowledge collected therefrom, is natural, and not supernatural.

We may and often do, connect or arrange our ideas together, in a wrong or improper manner, for the want of skill or judgment, or through mistake or the want of application, or through the influence of prejudice; but in all such cases, the error does not originate from the ideas themselves, but from the composer; for a system, or an arrangement of ideas justly composed always contain the truth; but an unjust composition never fails to contain error and falsehood. Therefore an unjust connection of ideas is not derived from nature, but from the imperfect composition of man. Misconnection of ideas is the same as misjudging, and has no positive existence, being merely a creature of the imagination; but nature and truth are real and uniform; and the rational mind by reasoning, discerns the uniformity, and is thereby enabled to make a just composition of ideas, which will stand the test of truth. But the fantastical illuminations of the credulous and superstitious part of mankind, proceed from weakness, and as far

45

as they take place in the world, subvert the religion of REASON
and TRUTH. [16]

AL-MUKAMMAS, DAVID IBN MERWAN

AL-MUKAMMAS, DAVID IBN MERWAN (died c. 937). Born in
Babylonia, author of the earliest known Jewish philosophical work of
the Middle Ages—a commentary to the Sefer Yetzirah (the Book
of Formation)—chiefly responsible for the development of the Cabala, Al-Mukammas' manuscripts lay forgotten for centuries. The
aforementioned was discovered in 1898 in the Tsarist Library;
fragments of another work on the unity of God were found in the
basement of a Cairo synagogue. Al-Mukammas established three ascending categories of science: practical philosophy, theoretical philosophy, and knowledge of the Torah.

THE THREE GRADES OF SCIENCE

THE science of ethics and the mind clarifies the opinions of
men and guides them in the path of understanding.

The study of applied mathematics is an aid to the thorough understanding of the practical arts; the study of rational mathematics is a guide to the understanding of the
speculative arts. For the science of mathematics is one of the
gates which lead to a knowledge of the substance of the soul.
This knowledge is the beginning of science, the constituent
element of wisdom, and the root of the practical and theoretical arts.

Philosophy is the knowledge of all things according to
the measure of their form, the secret of their nature, and the
impartation of truth. . . . The "impartation of truth" includes that science, superior to all other sciences, namely
the science of the Torah. These three are essential gradations of philosophy.

No one who acknowledges the existence of God, prophet,
or law, can deny the authority of the Torah. To deny it is
an important omission. Some deniers add or invent mysterious things for the purpose of self-aggrandizement. For it

46

was God's own goodness that prompted Him to benefit man by giving him laws for his guidance; not the innate merits of man that gave him prior claim to God's protection, since God neither benefits from man's obedience, nor receives injury from his disobedience.

[17]

ANAXAGORAS

ANAXAGORAS (c. 500-428 B.C.). Renowned as the last of the great Ionian philosophers, Anaxagoras was born at Klazomene on the Lydian coast of Asia Minor. A friend of Pericles and a teacher of Thucydides, Euripides, and other noted Greeks, he was the first philosopher to choose Athens as his home. He was held in great reverence until, at the instigation of a bigot, he was accused of blasphemy in speculating that the sun was a red, hot mass of stone and the moon an earthy substance. Although he was condemned to death, his influential friends helped him escape.

FRAGMENTS

ALL things were together infinite both in number and in smallness,—for the small, too, was infinite. And when all things were together, none of them could be distinguished because of their smallness. For air and æther prevailed over all things, being both of them infinite; for amongst all things these are the greatest both in quantity and size.

For air and æther are separated off from the mass that surrounds the world, and the surrounding mass is infinite in quantity.

And since these things are so, we must suppose that there are contained many things and of all sorts in all (the worlds) that are brought together, germs of all things, with all sorts of shapes, and colours and savours, and that men have been formed in them, and the other animals that have life, and that these men have inhabited cities and cultivated fields, as with us; and that they have a sun and moon and the rest, as with us; and that their earth brings forth for them many things of all kinds, of which they gather together the

47

best and use them for their dwellings. Thus much have I said with regard to separating off, but elsewhere too.

. . . As these thus revolve and are separated off by the force and speed. And the speed makes the force. And their speed is like nothing in speed of the things that are now among men, but in every way many times as quick.

. . . .

But before they were separated off, when all things were together, not even was any colour distinguishable; for the mixture of all things prevented it,—of the moist and of the dry, and the warm and the cold, and the light and dark [and much earth being in it], and of a multitude of innumerable germs in no way like each other. For none of the other things either is like any other.

In everything there is a portion of everything except Nous, and there are some things in which there is Nous (mind) also.

All other things partake in a portion of everything, while Nous is infinite and self-ruled, and is mixed with nothing, but is alone, itself by itself. For if it were not by itself, but were mixed with anything else, it would partake in all things if it were mixed with any; for in everything there is a portion of everything, as has been said by me in what goes before, and the things mixed with it would hinder it, so that it would have power over nothing in the same way that it has now being alone by itself. For it is the thinnest of all things and the purest, and it has all knowledge about everything and the greatest strength; and Nous has power over all things, both greater and smaller, that have life. And Nous had power over the whole revolution, so that it began to revolve in the beginning. And it began to revolve first from a small beginning; but the revolution now extends over a large space, and will extend over a larger still. And all the things that are mingled together and separated off and distinguished are all known by Nous. And Nous set in order all things that were to be and that were, and all things that are now and that are, and this revolution in which now revolve the stars and the sun and the moon, and the air and the æther that are separated off. And this revolution caused the separating off, and the rare is separated from the dense, the warm from the cold, the light from the dark; and the dry from the moist. And there are many portions in many things. But no thing is altogether separated off nor distinguished from anything else except Nous. And all Nous is alike, both the greater and the smaller; while nothing else is like anything else, but each single thing is and was most manifestly those things of which it has most in it.

. . . .

And when Nous began to move things, separating off took place from all that was moved, and so far as Nous set in motion all was separated. And as things were set in motion and separated, the revolution caused them to be separated much more.

The dense and the moist and the cold and the dark came together where the earth is now, while the rare and the warm and the dry (and the bright) went out towards the further part of the æther.

From these as they are separated off earth is solidified: for from mists water is separated off, and from water earth. From the earth stones are solidified by the cold, and these rush outwards more than water.

But Nous has power over all things that are, and it is now where all the other things are, in the mass that surrounds the world, and in the things that have separated off and that are being separated off.

Nor are the things that are in one world divided nor cut off from one another with a hatchet, neither the warm from the cold nor the cold from the warm.

And when those things are being thus distinguished, we must know that all of them are neither more nor less; for it is not possible for them to be more than all, and all are always equal.

Nor is there a least of what is small, but there is always a smaller; for it is impossible that what is should cease to be by being divided. But there is always something greater than what is great, and it is equal to the small in amount, and, compared with itself, each thing is both great and small.

And since the portions of the great and of the small are equal in amount, for this reason, too, all things will be in everything; nor is it possible for them to be apart, but all things have a portion of everything. Since it is impossible for there to be a least thing, they cannot be separated, nor come to be by themselves; but they must be now, just as they were in the beginning, all together. And in all things many things are contained, and an equal number both in the greater and in the smaller of the things that are separated off.

The Hellenes are wrong in using the expressions coming into being and passing away; for nothing comes into being or passes away, but mingling and separation takes place of things that are. So they would be right to call coming into being mixture, and passing away separation.

The earth is flat in shape, and remains suspended because of its size and because there is no vacuum. For this reason the air is very strong, and supports the earth which is borne up by it.

Of the moisture on the surface of the earth, the sea arose from the waters in the earth, . . . and from the rivers which flow into it.

Rivers take their being both from the rains and from the waters in the earth; for the earth is hollow, and has waters in its cavities. And the Nile rises in summer owing to the water that comes down from the snows in Ethiopia.

The sun and the moon and all the stars are fiery stones ignited by the rotation of the æther. Under the stars are the sun and moon, and also certain bodies which revolve with them, but are invisible to us.

We do not feel the heat of the stars because of the greatness of their distance from the earth; and, further, they are not so warm as the sun, because they occupy a colder region. The moon is below the sun, and nearer to us.

The sun surpasses the Peloponnesos in size. The moon has not a light of her own, but gets it from the sun. The course of the stars goes under the earth.

The moon is eclipsed by the earth screening the sun's light from it. The sun is eclipsed at the new moon, when the moon screens it from us. Both the sun and the moon turn in their courses owing to the repulsion of the air. The moon turns frequently, because it cannot prevail over the cold.

Anaxagoras was the first to determine what concerns the eclipses and the illumination of the sun and moon. And he said the moon was of earth, and had plains and ravines in it. The Milky Way was the reflection of the light of the stars that were not illuminated by the sun. Shooting stars were sparks, as it were, which leapt out owing to the motion of the heavenly vault.

Winds arose when the air was rarefied by the sun, and when things were burned and made their way to the vault of heaven and were carried off. Thunder and lightning were produced by heat striking upon clouds.

Earthquakes were caused by the air above striking on that beneath the earth; for the movement of the latter caused the earth which floats on it to rock.

But Anaxagoras says that perception is produced by opposites; for like things cannot be affected by like. He attempts to give a detailed enumeration of the particular senses. We see by means of the image in the pupil; but no image is cast upon what is of the same colour, but only on what is different. With most living creatures things are of a different colour to the pupil by day, though with some this is so by night, and these are accordingly keen-sighted at that time. Speaking generally, however, night is more of the same colour with the eyes than day. And an image is cast on the pupil by day, because light is a concomitant cause of the image, and because the prevailing colour casts an image more readily upon its opposite.

It is in the same way that touch and taste discern their objects. That which is just as warm or just as cold as we are neither warms us nor cools us by its contact; and, in the same way, we do not apprehend the sweet and the sour by means of themselves. We know cold by warm, fresh by salt, and sweet by sour, in virtue of our deficiency in each; for all these are in us to begin with. And we smell and hear in the same manner; the former by means of the accompanying respiration, the latter by the sound penetrating to the brain, for the bone which surrounds this is hollow, and it is upon it that the sound falls.

And all sensation implies pain, a view which would seem to be the consequence of the first assumption, for all unlike things produce pain by their contact. And this pain is made perceptible by the long continuance or by the excess of a sensation. Brilliant colours and excessive noises produce pain, and we cannot dwell long on the same things. The larger animals are the more sensitive, and, generally, sensation is proportionate to the size of the organs of sense. Those animals which have large, pure and bright eyes see large objects and from a great distance, and contrariwise.

And it is the same with hearing. Large animals can hear great and distant sounds, while less sounds pass unperceived; small animals perceive small sounds and those near at hand. It is the same too with smell. Rarefied air has more smell; for, when air is heated and rarefied, it smells. A large animal when it breathes draws in the condensed air along with the rarefied, while a small one draws in the rarefied by itself; so the large one perceives more. For smell is better perceived when it is near than when it is far by reason of its being more condensed, while when dispersed it is weak. But, roughly speaking, large animals do not perceive a rarefied smell, nor small animals a condensed one.

[18]

52

ANAXIMANDER

ANAXIMANDER (610-c. 547 B.C.). Known as Anaximander of Miletus, he was the earliest Greek philosophical essayist. A pupil of Thales, he was also the first Greek cartographer, and has been credited with the invention of a number of astronomical instruments.

His treatise *On Nature* dealt with the development of matter. In the search of the basic principles from which all things in existence were derived, Anaximander ignored those elements experienced by perception. He upheld the concept of *apeiron,* wherein the universe developed from the infinite by means of rotation.

Neither Anaximander nor his contemporaries analyzed the concept of the infinite. However, he did advance theories concerning infinite space, the infinite possibilities of combinations of qualities, and the infinite power of production.

FRAGMENTS

ANAXIMANDER of Miletus, son of Praxiades, a fellow-citizen and associate of Thales, said that the material cause and first element of things was the Infinite, he being the first to introduce this name for the material cause. He says it is neither water nor any other of what are now called the elements, but a substance different from them which is infinite, from which arise all the heavens and the worlds within them.

And into that from which things take their rise they pass away once more, "as is ordained; for they make reparation and satisfaction to one another for their injustice according to the appointed time."

And besides this, there was an external motion, in the course of which was brought about the origin of the worlds.

He did not ascribe the origin of things to any alteration in matter, but said that the oppositions in the substratum, which was a boundless Body, were separated out.

He says that something capable of begetting hot and cold was separated off from the eternal at the origin of this world. From this arose a sphere of flame which grew round the air encircling the earth, as the bark grows round a tree.

When this was broken up and enclosed in certain rings, the sun, moon, and stars came into existence.

Rain was produced by the moisture drawn up from the earth by the sun.

The sea is what is left of the original moisture. The fire has dried up most of it and turned the rest salt by scorching it.

The earth swings free, held in its place by nothing. It stays where it is because of its equal distance from anything.

Living creatures arose from the moist element as it was evaporated by the sun. Man was like another animal, namely, a fish, in the beginning.

Further, he says that in the beginning man was born from animals of a different species. His reason is, that, while other animals quickly find food for themselves, man alone requires a prolonged period of sucking. Hence, had he been originally such as he is now, he could never have survived.

The first living creatures were produced in the moist element, and were covered with prickly integuments. As time went on they came out upon the drier part, and, the integument soon breaking off, they changed their manner of life.

[19]

ANAXIMENES

ANAXIMENES (c. 585-525 B.C.). Along with Thales and Anaximander, Anaximenes was one of the triumvirate of important Milesian philosophers. His importance is due to his formulation of the method whereby change is represented as the result of the processes of condensation and rarefication. This theory anticipated the development of physical laws and mechanics and physics.

He also attempted to define the fundamental substance that constitutes the universe. Anaximenes endeavored to synthesize the doctrines of his two Milesian predecessors by stating that the qualities of air were sufficient to explain whatever exists perceptually and intellectually. He maintained that air was as infinite as Anaximander's *apeiron* and as real as the water which Thales considered the fundamental cosmic matter.

ANAXIMENES of Miletus, son of Eurystratos, who had been an associate of Anaximander, said, like him, that the underlying substance was one and infinite. He did not, however, say it was indeterminate, like Anaximander, but determinate; for he said it was Air.

From it, he said, the things that are, and have been, and shall be, the gods and things divine, took their rise, while other things come from its offspring.

"Just as," he said, "our soul, being air, holds us together, so do breath and air encompass the whole world."

And the form of the air is as follows. Where it is most even, it is invisible to our sight; but cold and heat, moisture and motion, make it visible. It is always in motion; for, if it were not, it would not change so much as it does.

It differs in different substances in virtue of its rarefaction and condensation.

When it is dilated so as to be rarer, it becomes fire; while winds, on the other hand, are condensed Air. Cloud is formed from Air by "felting;" and this, still further condensed, becomes water. Water, condensed still more, turns to earth; and when condensed as much as it can be, to stones.

He says that, as the air was "felted," the earth first came into being. It is very broad, and is accordingly supported by the air.

In the same way, the sun and the moon and the other heavenly bodies, which are of a fiery nature, are supported by the air because of their breadth. The heavenly bodies were produced from the earth by moisture rising from it. When this is rarefied, fire comes into being, and the stars are composed of the fire thus raised aloft. There were also bodies of earthy substance in the region of the stars, revolving along with them. And he says that the heavenly bodies do not move under the earth, as others suppose, but round it, as a cap turns round our head. The sun is hidden from sight, not because it goes under the earth, but because it is concealed by the higher parts of the earth, and because its distance from us becomes greater. The stars give no heat because of the greatness of their distance.

Winds are produced when condensed air rushes into rarefied; but when it is concentrated and thickened still more, clouds are generated; and, lastly, it turns to water.

[20]

ANSELM OF CANTERBURY, SAINT

ANSELM OF CANTERBURY, SAINT (1033-1109). A prominent figure in the struggle for power (in this period) between the secularists and ecclesiastics, Anselm was of even greater importance as a Christian philosopher. Although he was not a Scholastic, this school of church philosophy embodied many of his concepts.

Anselm, first as abbot and later as archbishop, defended the authority of the Pope to William Rufus and Henry I, kings of England. This resulted in his exile. But regardless of whether he was living in poverty or splendor, he always maintained an ascetic existence. His monastic life of contemplation and meditation was frequently interrupted by political activity.

His philosophy, largely a justification of Church practices and dogma, was publicized because he felt its position needed strengthening. He was convinced that the comprehension of divine truth was the result of faith, not reason. He stated that believing is a necessary condition of knowledge, and that in order to believe, one need not probe. In his most famous book, *Cur Deus Homo* (Why God Made Man), he tried to answer questions concerning the doctrine of man's redemption. He stated that man is created for an immortal life but is frustrated by sin, and that the Messiah has the power of redemption because His virginal birth excludes Him from the inheritance of sin. His theory of atonement and satisfaction has determined Christian thought and piety throughout the centuries. Anselm is held responsible for the ontological argument for the existence of God. This thesis, elaborated in his *Monologium*, was accepted by theologians and such eminent philosophers as Descartes and Leibniz.

NO GREATER BEING

AND so, Lord, do thou, who dost give understanding to faith, give me, so far as thou knowest it to be profitable, to under-

56

stand that thou art as we believe; and that thou art that which we believe. And, indeed, we believe that thou art a being than which nothing greater can be conceived. Or is there no such nature, since the fool hath said in his heart, there is no God? (Psalms xiv. 1). But, at any rate, this very fool, when he hears of this being of which I speak—a being than which nothing greater can be conceived—understands what he hears, and what he understands is in his understanding; although he does not understand it to exist.

For, it is one thing for an object to be in the understanding, and another to understand that the object exists. When a painter first conceives of what he will afterwards perform, he has it in his understanding, but he does not yet understand it to be, because he has not yet performed it. But after he has made the painting, he both has it in his understanding, and he understands that it exists, because he has made it.

Hence, even the fool is convinced that something exists in the understanding, at least, than which nothing greater can be conceived. For, when he hears of this, he understands it. And whatever is understood, exists in the understanding. And assuredly that, than which nothing greater can be conceived, cannot exist in the understanding alone. For, suppose it exists in the understanding alone: then it can be conceived to exist in reality; which is greater.

Therefore, if that, than which nothing greater can be conceived, exists in the understanding alone, the very being, than which nothing greater can be conceived, is one, than which a greater can be conceived. But obviously this is impossible. Hence, there is no doubt that there exists a being, than which nothing greater can be conceived, and it exists both in the understanding and in reality.

[21]

ANTISTHENES

ANTISTHENES (c. 445-365 B.C.). Son of a lower-class Athenian father and either a Thracian or Phrygian-slave mother, Antisthenes was the founder of the Cynic school of Greek philosophy. The name of his school was derived from the building in which he taught, the *Cynosarges* (dog's tomb), for Cynic philosophy bears no relation to the modern meaning of cynicism in which human values or moral scruples are held in contempt. He was originally a disciple of Gorgias, the sophist, who came to Athens in 427 B.C. Later he became one of the most faithful pupils of Socrates, tramping five miles each day to the city in order to listen to his master's words. He was present when Socrates drank the cup of hemlock.

Antisthenes was opposed to Plato's doctrine of ideas and to Aristippus' philosophy of pleasure. He interpreted the teachings of Socrates as the doctrine of virtue which can be taught with disregard of feelings, independence of judgment, contempt for conventional opinions, and discrimination between social status, birth and wealth. Later Cynics, exaggerating Antisthenes' statements, were strongly opposed to Stoics and Epicureans.

APOPHTHEGMS

O Plato, I can see a horse but I do not see horseness.

I would rather be mad than feel pleasure.

Virtue is a matter of action.

Virtue is sufficient in itself to secure happiness.

The wise man is self-sufficient.

The wise man does not follow established laws but only the law of virtue.

It is better to side a handful of good men in their struggle against an army of bad men than to side an army of bad men in their battle against a handful of good men.

[22]

AQUINAS, THOMAS

AQUINAS, THOMAS (1225-1274). Recognized as the leading philosopher of the Roman Catholic Church, Aquinas' authority was officially established by Pope Leo XIII in the encyclical *Aeterni Patris* (1879).

All non-Catholic philosophers and historians regard the doctrines promulgated by Aquinas as the quintessence of the Scholastic spirit of the Middle Ages. He surpassed all Christian predecessors in his ability to deal with the crucial problems of reason and faith by mediating variant tendencies within the Church and systematizing its theology so that it was consistent and precise.

Aquinas subordinated philosophy to theology; natural law to the revelations of Christ; human society to the dogma of the Church. He endeavored to demonstrate that these subordinations benefit philosophy, natural law, and human society, and that the dignity of each of these is reinforced in its subordination to theology. Aquinas tried to show that reality has value because it is created by God. For this reason he opposed Averroism because it rejected the theological control of philosophy; and Platonism because it depreciated the real world. He accepted Aristotelian philosophy because it was compatible with the doctrines of Christianity and met the desires and needs of human society. Many of his pronouncements were directly influenced by Jewish thinkers. His proof for the existence of God was adapted from Maimonides, and one of his proofs for the unity of God was taken from Bahya ibn Pakuda.

He was the son of the Count of Aquino, and a relative of the emperor, Frederick II. He was glorified as the "Doctor Angelicus," and, after his death, canonized as a saint.

WHETHER THE INTELLIGIBLE SPECIES ARE DERIVED BY THE SOUL FROM CERTAIN SEPARATE FORMS?

Objection 1. It seems that the intelligible species are derived by the soul from some separate forms. For whatever is such by participation is caused by what is such essentially; for instance, that which is on fire is reduced to fire as the cause thereof. But the intellectual soul forasmuch as it is actually understanding, participates in the thing understood: for, in a way, the intellect in act is the thing understood in act. Therefore what in itself and in its essence is understood in act, is the cause that the intellectual soul actually understands. Now that which in its essence is actually understood is a form existing without matter. Therefore the intelligible species, by which the soul understands, are caused by some separate forms.

Objection 2. Further, the intelligible is to the intellect, as the sensible is to the sense. But the sensible species which are in the senses, and by which we feel, are caused by the sensible object which exists actually outside the soul. Therefore the intelligible species by which our intellect understands, are caused by some things actually intelligible, existing outside the soul. But these can be nothing else than forms separate from matter. Therefore the intelligible forms of our intellect are derived from some separate substances.

Objection 3. Further, whatever is in potentiality is reduced to act by something actual. If, therefore, our intellect, previously in potentiality, actually understands, this must needs be caused by some intellect which is always in act. But this is a separate intellect. Therefore the intelligible species, by which we actually understand, are caused by some separate substances.

On the contrary, If this were true we should not need the senses in order to understand. And this is proved to be false especially from the fact that if a man be wanting in a sense, he cannot have any knowledge of the sensibles corresponding to that sense.

I answer that, Some have held that the intelligible species of our intellect are derived from certain separate forms or substances. And this in two ways. For Plato, as we have said, held that the forms of sensible things subsist by themselves without matter; for instance, the form of a man which he called *per se* man, and the form or idea of a horse which he called *per se* horse, and so forth. He said therefore that these forms are participated both by our soul and by corporeal matter; by our soul, to the effect of knowledge thereof, and by corporeal matter to the effect of existence: so that, just as corporeal matter by participating the idea of a stone, becomes an individual stone, so our intellect, by participating the idea of a stone, is made to understand a stone. Now participation of an idea takes place by some image of the idea in the participator, just as a model is participated by a copy. So just as he held that the sensible forms, which are in corporeal matter, are derived from the ideas as certain images thereof: so he held that the intelligible species of our intellect are images of the ideas, derived therefrom. And for this reason, as we have said above, he referred sciences and definitions to those ideas.

But since it is contrary to the nature of sensible things that their forms should subsist without matter, as Aristotle proves in many ways, Avicenna setting this opinion aside, held that the intelligible species of all sensible things, instead of subsisting in themselves without matter, pre-exist immaterially in the separate intellects: from the first of which, said he, such species are derived by a second, and so on to the last separate intellect which he called the *active intelligence,* from which, according to him, intelligible species flow into our souls, and sensible species into corporeal matter. And so Avicenna agrees with Plato in this, that the intelligible species of our intellect are derived from certain separate forms; but these Plato held to subsist of themselves, while Avicenna placed them in the *active intelligence.* They differ, too, in this respect, that Avicenna held that the intelligible species do not remain in our intellect after it has ceased actually to understand, and that it needs to turn (to the active intellect) in order to receive them anew. Consequently he does not hold that the soul has innate knowledge, as Plato, who held that the participated ideas remain immovably in the soul.

But in this opinion no sufficient reason can be assigned for the soul being united to the body. For it cannot be said that the intellectual soul is united to the body for the sake of the body: for neither is form for the sake of matter, nor is the mover for the sake of the moved, but rather the reverse. Especially does the body seem necessary to the intellectual soul, for the latter's proper operation which is to understand: since as to its being the soul does not depend on the body. But if the soul by its very nature had an inborn aptitude for receiving intelligible species through the influence of only certain separate principles, and were not to receive them from the senses, it would not need the body in order to understand: wherefore to no purpose would it be united to the body.

61

But if it be said that our soul needs the senses in order to understand, through being in some way excited by them to the consideration of those things the intelligible species of which it receives from the separate principles: even this seems an insufficient explanation. For this excitation does not seem necessary to the soul, except in as far as it is overcome by sluggishness, as the Platonists expressed it, and by forgetfulness, through its union with the body. Consequently the reason of the union of the soul with the body still remains to be sought.

And if it be said with Avicenna, that the senses are necessary to the soul, because by them it is roused to turn to the *active intelligence* from which it receives the species: neither is this sufficient explanation. Because if it is natural for the soul to understand through species derived from the *active intelligence*, it follows that at times the soul of an individual wanting in one of the senses can turn to the active intelligence either from the inclination of its very nature, or through being aroused by another sense, to the effect of receiving the intelligible species of which the corresponding sensible species are wanting. And thus a man born blind could have knowledge of colors; which is clearly untrue. We must therefore conclude that the intelligible species, by which our soul understands, are not derived from separate forms.

Reply Objection 1.   The intelligible species which fall to the share of our intellect are reduced, as to their first cause, to a first principle which is by its essence intelligible—namely, God. But they proceed from that principle by means of the forms of sensible and material things, from which we gather knowledge, as Dionysius says.

Reply Objection 2.   Material things, as to the being which they have outside the soul, may be actually sensible, but not actually intelligible. Wherefore there is no comparison between sense and intellect.

Reply Objection 3.   Our passive intellect is reduced from potentiality to act by some being in act, that is, by the active intellect, which is a power of the soul as we have said; and not by a separate intelligence, as a proximate cause, although perchance as remote cause.

[23]

ARCESILAUS

ARCESILAUS (c. 315-240 B.C.). From 270 to 240 B.C., Arcesilaus directed the Platonic Academy at Athens and helped it to regain its former splendor. During his administration, the doctrine of the Academy turned to a scepticism similar to that of Pyrrho and Timon, although it had developed independently of them and was somewhat milder in form.

Arcesilaus studied mathematics with Autolycus, a predecessor of Euclid at Sardes, Asia Minor. He was also an experienced musician, and a brilliant speaker and teacher. He regarded himself as the true disciple of Plato, haranguing against Speusippus and Xenocrates whom he accused of distorting Plato's doctrines. According to Arcesilaus, the correct understanding of Plato results in doubt, suspension of judgment, and a complete spiritual freedom equivalent to the supreme good. With a vehemence equal to that of other Platonists, Arcesilaus attacked the Stoics, who, in turn, severely criticized him. Epicurus was the only contemporary philosopher he acknowledged. Only a few sayings of Arcesilaus are extant.

ASSENT AND SUSPENSION

SUSPENDED judgment of particular objects is good, but assent of particulars is bad.

Whereas these statements are not made dogmatically, but in accordance with the appearance of things, they are made as statements of real facts. Therefore suspension is really good and assent bad.

Suspension is accompanied by quietude.

What the Stoics call apprehension, assent, and apprehensive presentation occurs neither in a wise man nor in a fool.

He who suspends judgment about everything, will regulate his inclinations, aversions, and his general actions with application of the rule of Reason, and by proceeding in accordance with this criteria he will act rightly. For happiness is attained through wisdom; wisdom consists in right actions, and right actions, when performed, possess reasonable justification. [24]

ARDIGO, ROBERTO

ARDIGO, ROBERTO (1828-1920). A former Catholic priest and influential leader of Italian positivism, Ardigo abandoned theology in 1869 and resigned from the Church in 1871. He was appointed a professor of theology at the University of Padua in 1881, and from that time until 1900, when an idealistic reaction had taken place, exerted considerable influence in philosophic circles. His positivism, inspired by Auguste Comte, differed from that of his master. Ardigo considered thought more important than matter and insisted on psychological disquisitions. He stated that thought is dominant in every action, the result of every action, and that it vanishes only in a state of general corruption; according to him, thought is a natural formation, unrelated to an alleged absolute; facts are the contents of consciousness, in which the subjective and objective elements are developed from an originally indistinct state. His principal works are *Psychology As A Positive Science* (1870) and *The Moral of the Positivists* (1879).

TRUTH AND REASON

TRUTH is essentially the conscious datum because consciousness incontestably attests to reality. Conscious datum is the only reality. Simple or complex sensations and the rhythm of concurring groups of sensations are facts. Truth is essentially the result of sensation because in consciousness the only datum that can be met is that of sensation.

Reason is the rhythm of experiences of the species or the individual remembered by the organism. When it functions it makes itself partly known in consciousness, but a part remains concealed. The individual does not make this rhythm, and therefore often succumbs to the delusion that the rhythm is dictated by an eternal truth which always illuminated his mind and the mind of every man in the same way.
[25]

ARISTIPPUS

ARISTIPPUS (c. 435-366 B.C.). All the writings of Aristippus are lost, but if the ancient sources about him are not entirely misleading, he seems, of all the disciples of Socrates, to have been the least congenial with his teacher. The only Socratic point in Aristippus' doctrine was the praise of inner freedom and true independence. Unlike Socrates, he denied social responsibility, was indifferent to reason, and conceived of wisdom as that which is concerned with the enjoyment of pleasure and the avoidance of pain. He is said to have been the first disciple of Socrates to request fees for his lessons. When this action aroused Socrates' indignation, he offered his master part of his gain as a royalty.

Aristippus was born in Cyrene, North Africa. Early in life, he settled in Athens to study first with Protagoras and then with Socrates. The little that is known about him through anecdotes reveal him to have been wily, greedy, and ever eager to ridicule Plato. He also seems to have been optimistic, of a serene disposition, and kindly disposed to his fellow-men, except those whom he regarded as his competitors.

PLEASURE AND PAIN

THERE are only two states of the soul, namely pleasure and pain. Pleasure is a soft and easy motion. Pain is a rough and violent one. There is no other pleasure than that of the body. No pleasure is more pleasant than another one. But a pleasure may be composed of a multitude of elementary pleasures. Pleasure is agreeable, and pain is repellent to all living creatures.

[26]

ARISTOTLE

ARISTOTLE (384-322 B.C.). Still accepted by thousands as the world's leading philosopher, Aristotle possessed one of the few really encyclopedic minds ever produced by the West. His was an unique combination of philosophic insight and keen powers of observation. He was a great thinker, systematic historian, and natural scientist. Although his contributions to the subject matter of physics are important and still used, his subsequent reflections on the causes and principles of physical matter established the field of metaphysics, literally those things beyond or after physics.

The substance of his philosophy, influenced by the highly developed state of Greek art, is that there are two dichotomies: matter and form. Everything is either matter or form. For example, in a brass statue, brass is matter with a variety of potentialities and possibilities; the statue is form, the actuality. It is the form or shape of one of the possibilities of brass. Development is the process by which matter becomes form, and every form the matter for the next highest form. God, the prime mover, is pure form or thought. In man, reason represents the highest form. Entelechy is the formative principle in which purpose and cause unite for a final end.

To Aristotle, man's happiness consisted in virtue—the mean between two extremes. "Even if happiness is not sent by the Gods, but is the result of virtue and of learning of discipline of some kind, it is apparently one of the most divine things in the world; for it would appear that that which is the prize and end of virtue is the supreme good, and in its nature divine and blessed."

He conceived the perfect state to be a democracy in which the masses are restricted and where education is aimed at the development of bodily vigor and the virtues.

Aristotle was born at Stagira, and went to Athens to become a pupil (and later a critic) of Plato. He spent some years in the company of the tyrant, Hermias, whose niece he married. Shortly afterwards, he accepted the task of educating the son of Philip of Macedonia, who became known to posterity as Alexander the Great. After the death of Plato, he returned to Athens to found a school. He taught art, politics, physics, systems of natural science, logic, and philosophy at the Lyceum. In his last years, he was condemned as godless and banished from Athens. He died shortly thereafter.

THE PROCESS OF CHANGE

EVERYTHING which comes into being is brought about by something, that is, by a source from which its generation comes. And it is composed of something. Now this latter is best described not as the absence of the thing but as the matter from which it comes. And it becomes a particular thing, as a sphere or a circle or some other thing. Now one does not "make" the material—as the bronze—of which a thing is composed; so one does not make the sphere, except in

66

a secondary sense, in so far as the bronze circle is a circle and one makes it. For the act of making a particular thing is a process of making it out of some material in general. I mean that to make the bronze round is not to make the "round" or the "sphere," but quite a different thing—that of putting this form into what did not have it previously. If one made the "form," one would make it out of something else, for this would underlie it, as when one makes a sphere out of bronze. This is done by making of a particular kind of substance, namely bronze, a special sort of thing, namely a sphere. And if one makes this "sphere" also in the same way, it is evident that he will make it in the same manner, and the process of origination will go on to infinity. It is evident therefore that the form, or whatever one ought to call the shape of the perceived object is not "made." It does not "become," nor does it have an origin. Nor is there any for the essential conception of a thing. For this is what is implanted in another entity, either by training or by nature or by force. But one does cause the "bronze sphere" to *be*. For one makes it out of bronze and the form of "sphere." One puts the form into this matter, and it is then a bronze sphere. But if there is an origin for "the idea of sphere in general" it will be something generated from something else. That which is generated will have to be analyzed again in turn, and each reduced to something further, then that to something else; I mean in one aspect into matter, in another into form. A sphere is a figure whose surface is everywhere equally distant from a center. One aspect of it is the material into which the form is to be put; the other the form which is to be put into it. The whole is what results, namely, the bronze sphere.

It is evident from what we have said that the part which is spoken of as the form or the essence does not originate; but the combination which derives its name from this does; and in everything which originates there is matter, and it is now this thing, now that. Is there then a "sphere" beside the particular spheres? Or is there a "house" beside the houses of brick? Or would there never be any particular things if this were so? The genus gives the general character, but is not a definite particular thing. But one makes and produces such and such a thing out of "this" particular substance. And when it has been produced it is "this thing of such and such a kind." This concrete existing thing is "Kallias" or "Socrates," just as the other was "this bronze sphere," but it is man and animal in general just as the other was a bronze sphere in general. It is evident then that the formal principle, as some are accustomed to speak of forms, if they are something aside from the particulars and beside the acts of generation and the essences, is of no use. For not by virtue of them would there be particular instances of them. In some cases indeed it is evident that that which causes is the same sort of thing as that which is caused, yet not identically the same, nor one numerically, but in form—as in the case of the products of nature. Man begets man, (and so it is), except where something arises of different nature, as when a horse begets a mule. Yet these cases also are really similar to the others; but what is common to a horse and an ass has not been given a name as a "proximate genus"; perhaps it would be "mule."

So it is evident that it is not at all necessary to supply forms as patterns, (for they would have to be found in these cases especially, since these are certainly substances). The begetter is adequate to the production of the effect and to the embodiment of the form in the matter. And the compound— such and such a form in this flesh and these bones—is Kallias or Socrates. They differ because of their matter, for it is different, but they are the same in form. For the form is indivisible.

Of things which come into existence some are generated by nature, some by art, some by chance. And all things which are generated are generated by something and from something and as some particular thing. Some particular thing, I mean with respect to each category, such as substance, quantity, quality or place. Origination by nature occurs in the case of those things whose origin is through the processes of nature. The substance of which they are formed we call matter; the source from which they arise is some thing in nature; the kind of thing which they become is "man" or "plant" or some other thing of the kind which we are especially accustomed to call "substances." All things which have an origin, whether by nature or by art, have a material. Each of them might exist or not exist; and the seat of this double possibility is the material part of them. In general that out of which and in accordance with which they arise is some natural thing. For that which comes into being has some natural character as that of a plant or an animal. And that under the influence of which it arises is a natural object which with reference to its form may be said to be homogeneous. And this form is found in another individual; as one man begets another man. In this way arise the things which come about by nature; but other originations are called artificial creations.

Artificial creations result from acquired skill, or external power, or deliberate planning. Some of these also come about spontaneously and by chance, in nearly the same manner as some things are generated by nature. For there some kind of things arise in some instances from seed, in other instances without seed. Into these things we shall have to look later; but those things arise by art, the forms of which are in some one's mind. And by form I mean the essential conception of the thing and its fundamental essence. And indeed in a certain sense opposites have the same form. The opposed essence is that of the absence of the given thing, as health is the absence of disease. For by the absence of the former disease becomes manifest. But health is the determining principle, in the soul and in knowledge. The healthy condition of one who has been ill comes about as follows: since such and such a condition is health it is necessary, if there is to be health, that some other condition exist, as uniform temperature, and if there is to be uniform temperature then warmth. And in this manner one continues one's analysis until one arrives at a certain thing which one can do as the first step. The activity which comes from this is an artificial productivity, in this case the production of health. So in this sense it is true that health comes from health, and a house from a house, that which has material content from that which does not. The essence of the physician's art and of the builder's art is the form of health and the form of the house. And the essence without matter I call the essential conception.

One aspect of the process of production and of action is called the intellectual contemplation, the other the practical effecting of them. The one which has to do with the principle and the form is intellectual contemplation. That which refers to the aim of the intellectual contemplation is the practical application. And each of the intermediate steps has the like phases. For instance, if one will be healthy it is necessary to have an even temperature. What does the maintenance of an even temperature involve? This: it will result if one is kept warm. And what will do this? The following; but this exists only as a possibility. Yet it is in one's power. So then the action and the source from which the development of the healthy state springs, if it is from an artificial source, is the "form" in one's mind; but if from chance, still it results from something which at sometime or other is the source of activity used by him who acts with conscious skill. In the case of medical treatment perhaps the source is in causing warmth, and one produces this by rubbing. So the warmth in the body is either a part of health or there follows it something of a kind which is a part of health, or is so after some intermediate stages. And this last step is what causes the essential part and what is thus a part is to health as the stones are to a house; and likewise with other things.

As we have said, nothing can arise unless something pre-exists. Therefore that some part necessarily exists is evident. For the material part is a part. And it enters into a thing and pervades its changes. And so it is also with the things mentioned in our statement. We tell what bronze circles are by distinguishing two phases; saying of the material that it is

70

bronze; and of the form that it is such and such a shape. And this is the genus under which it is placed first. The brazen circle includes matter in its notion. Some things receive names from the matter out of which they come when they arise, being said, of course, to be not " that substance" but "of that substance," as the image of a man is said to be not "stone" but "of stone." But a healthy man is not designated from that out of which he has come. The reason for this is that he has come from a condition opposite to his present one, as well as out of a substance which we call his material being. Thus it is both a man and a sick man who becomes well. But the statement is made rather with reference to the negative state; one becomes healthy from being ill rather than from being a man. Consequently the well person is not said to be ill, but a man and a healthy man. But in those things to which there is no evident opposite, or none with a name, as of any kind of form in bronze, or the bricks or boards of a building, generation is said to be out of these, as in the other case it was out of the condition of illness. Wherefore, as in that case that from which this comes is not used in the name, so here the image of the man is not called "wood" but is styled "wooden," or "brazen" not "bronze," or "stony" not "stone"; and a house is said to be "of brick" not "bricks." Nor does the image come from wood, nor the house from bricks, if one looks at the matter exactly; and one could not say this without qualification, for it is necessary that generation come through the changing of a source—through its not remaining permanent. For these reasons then we use such modes of expression.

[27]

AURELIUS AUGUSTINUS
(Saint Augustine)

AURELIUS AUGUSTINUS (SAINT AUGUSTINE) (354-430). Born in Tagaste, near Carthage, North Africa, Augustine was the son of a pagan father and a pious Christian mother, Monica (who was later canonized). By the time he was thirty-three, he had embraced Christianity, although much earlier he had been an adherent of Manicheanism and scepticism. Shortly after his conversion, he was ordained, and from 395 until his death he served as bishop of Hippo, North Africa. He died when the Vandals besieged his episcopal town.

Living in the period of the disintegration of the Roman Empire, Augustine, through his writings, contributed much to strengthening the position of the Christian church. He defended its established doctrines against heretical attacks, and gave it a philosophy of ethics, metaphysics, and a lasting philosophy of history. His writings show him to have been trained in rhetoric, a sincere confessor, a man of both passion and serenity, and humble, though in an authoritative position.

His works deal with the problems of divine omnipotence, predestination, God, the Trinity, and creation. They consistently affirm that the Catholic Church is the only reliable guide of human reason; that founded by Christ, it practices His teachings. In addition to hundreds of sermons and pamphlets, most of which are devoted to the refutation of heresy, he made world-wide lasting contributions to the history of philosophy and literature. His major works are: *Expositio Fideis Christianae* (397); *De Trinitate* (c. 416); a commentary on *Genesis* the first parts of which were published in 414; *De Civitate Dei;* and *Confessiones.* He spent the years from 410 to 427 in writing *The City of God* (De Civitate Dei). In this work, he enunciated the famous doctrine of the four epochs of human history, a doctrine that was impressed upon the consciousness of Western civilization until the time of Hegel and Comte. However, it is not the originality of his ideas but the profundity of psychological analysis that makes Augustine a great figure in the history of philosophy. His autobiographical *Confessions* has been regarded for many centuries as a manual of self-analysis. His influence, though immeasurable, is especially notable in the teachings of Luther, Pascal, Descartes, and Leibniz.

WHAT WE ARE TO BELIEVE

WHEN, then, the question is asked what we are to believe in regard to religion, it is not necessary to probe into the nature of things, as was done by those whom the Greeks call *physici;* nor need we be in alarm lest the Christian should be ignorant of the force and number of the elements,—the motion, and order, and eclipses of the heavenly bodies; the form of the heavens; the species and the natures of animals, plants, stones, fountains, rivers, mountains; about chronology and distances; the signs of coming storms; and a thousand other things which those philosophers either have found out, or think they have found out. For even these men themselves, endowed though they are with so much genius, burning with zeal, abounding in leisure, tracking some things by the aid of human conjecture, searching into others with the aids of history and experience, have not found out all things; and even their boasted discoveries are oftener mere guesses than certain knowledge. It is enough for the Christian to believe that the only cause of all created things, whether heavenly or earthy, whether visible or invisible, is the goodness of the Creator, the one true God; and that nothing exists but Himself that does not derive its existence from Him; and that He is the Trinity—to wit, the Father, and the Son begotten of the Father, and the Holy Spirit proceeding from the same Father, but one and the same Spirit of Father and Son.

[28]

AURELIUS, MARCUS ANTONINUS

AURELIUS, MARCUS ANTONINUS (121-180). While thousands cheered hysterically when the victorious gladiator plunged his sword into his vanquished opponent, a boy in the imperial box buried himself even deeper in a book on moral philosophy. The boy, an adopted son of Antoninus Pius, became Roman emperor in 161 A.D. Ascetic in his ways, his stoical outlook had been carefully nursed by excellent teachers, and he tried to apply it during his reign, turbulent though the times proved to be.

Like his foster father, he believed that no price was too great which might buy peace and good will. Never before in the Western world had a philosopher sat on the throne, none, surely, that had tried so consistently to extol the virtues of the intellect, none that dismissed pleasure and fought with righteous zeal the ignorance which is at the base of the fear, desire and sorrow that constitute the evil in this world. Even the Christians, whom he never understood and who suffered in consequence, acknowledged the saintliness of his character and could not help but admire his half agnostic, half faith-inspired belief in God or gods as the font of wisdom and power.

While the political situation worsened throughout the empire which was no longer protected by Roman armies but by foreign armed bands, while his adoptive brother, Lucius Verus, wasted himself and the empire's opportunities in debauchery in the East, while Rome was gripped in the Oriental plague and the Italian peninsula threatened by the Marcomanni, throughout all this Antoninus remained true to himself. He honored his faithless, scheming wife, Faustina, by consecrating a temple to her at Halala where she died and one at Rome, and by establishing a foundation for poor girls. Her damning letters he nobly burned unread.

His best-known work, the *Meditations,* this emperor-saint wrote on the battlefield. His life and writings show Stoicism at its best although he was judged wanting in ability to cope wih empire problems where force was deemed necessary for their successful solution.

VANITAS

MEN seek retreats for themselves, houses in the country, seashores, and mountains; and thou too art wont to desire such things very much. But this is altogether a mark of the most common sort of men, for it is in thy power whenever thou shalt choose to retire into thyself. For nowhere either with more quiet or more freedom from trouble does a man retire than into his own soul, particularly when he has within him such thoughts that by looking into them he is immediately in perfect tranquillity; and I affirm that tranquillity is nothing else than the good ordering of the mind. Constantly then give to thyself this retreat, and renew thyself; and let thy principles be brief and fundamental, which, as soon as thou shalt recur to them, will be sufficient to cleanse the soul completely, and to send thee back from all discontent with the things to which thou returnest. For with what art thou discontented? With the badness of men? Recall to thy mind this conclusion, that rational animals exist for one another, and that to endure is a part of justice, and that men do wrong involuntarily; and consider how many already, after mutual enmity, suspicion, hatred, and fighting have been stretched dead, reduced to ashes; and be quiet at last.—But perhaps thou art dissatisfied with that which is assigned to thee out of the universe.—Recall to thy recollection this alternative; either there is providence or atoms [fortuitous concurrence of things]; or remember the arguments by which it has been proved that the world is a kind of political community [and be quiet at last].—But perhaps corporeal things will still fasten upon thee.—Consider then further that the mind mingles not with the breath, whether moving gently or violently, when it has once drawn itself apart and discovered its own power, and think also of all that thou hast heard and assented to about pain and pleasure [and be quiet at last].—But perhaps the desire of the thing called fame will torment thee.—See how soon everything is forgotten, and look at the chaos of infinite time on each side of [the present], and the emptiness of applause, and the changeableness and want of judgment in those who pretend to give praise, and the narrowness of the space within which it is circumscribed [and be quiet at last]. For the whole earth is a point, and how small a nook in it is this thy dwelling, and how few are there in it, and what kind of people are they who will praise thee.

This then remains: Remember to retire into this little territory of thy own, and above all do not distract or strain thyself, but be free, and look at things as a man, as a human being, as a citizen, as a mortal. But among the things readiest to thy hand to which thou shalt turn, let there be these, which are two. One is that things do not touch the soul, for they are external and remain immovable; but our perturbations come only from the opinion which is within. The other is that all these things, which thou seest, change immediately and will no longer be; and constantly bear in mind how many of these changes thou hast already witnessed. The universe is transformation: life is opinion.

Take away thy opinion, and then there is taken away the complaint, 'I have been harmed.' Take away the complaint, 'I have been harmed,' and the harm is taken away.

*   *   *

Do not act as if thou wert going to live ten thousand years. Death hangs over thee. While thou livest, while it is in thy power, be good.

How much trouble he avoids who does not look to see what his neighbor says or does or thinks, but only to what he does himself, that it may be just and pure; or as Agathon says, look not round at the depraved morals of others, but run straight along the line without deviating from it.

He who has a vehement desire for posthumous fame does not consider that every one of those who remember him will himself also die very soon; then again also they who have succeeded them, until the whole remembrance shall have been extinguished as it is transmitted through men who foolishly admire and perish. But suppose that those who will remember are even immortal and that the remembrance will be immortal, what then is this to thee? And I say not what is it to the dead, but what is it to the living. What is praise, except indeed so far as it has a certain utility? For thou now rejectest unseasonably the gift of nature, clinging to something else.

Everything harmonizes with me, which is harmonious to thee, O Universe. Nothing for me is too early nor too late, which is in due time for thee. Everything is fruit to me which thy seasons bring, O Nature: from thee are all things, in thee are all things, to thee all things return.

Occupy thyself with few things, says the philosopher, if thou wouldst be tranquil.—But consider if it would not be better to say, Do what is necessary, and whatever the reason of the animal which is naturally social requires, and as it requires. For this brings not only the tranquillity which comes from doing well, but also that which comes from doing few things. For the greatest part of what we say and do being unnecessary, if a man takes this away, he will have more leisure and less uneasiness. Accordingly on every occasion a man should ask himself, Is this one of the unnecessary things? Now a man should take away not only unnecessary acts, but also unnecessary thoughts, for thus superfluous acts will not follow after.

Try how the life of a good man suits thee, the life of him who is satisfied with his portion out of the whole, and satisfied with his own just acts and benevolent disposition.

Hast thou seen those things? Look also at these. Do not disturb thyself. Make thyself all simplicity. Does any one do wrong? It is to himself that he does the wrong. Has anything happened to thee? Well; out of the universe from the beginning everything which happens has been apportioned and spun out to thee. In a word, thy life is short. Thou must turn to profit the present by the aid of reason and justice. Be sober in thy relaxation.

Either it is a well arranged universe or a chaos huddled together, but still a universe. But can a certain order subsist in thee, and disorder in the All? And this too when all things are so separated and diffused and sympathetic.

*   *   *

The words which were formerly familiar are now antiquated: so also the names who were famed of old, are now in a manner antiquated, Camillus, Caeso, Volesus, Leonnatus, and a little after also Scipio and Cato, then Augustus, then also Hadrianus and Antoninus. For all things soon pass away and become a mere tale, and complete oblivion soon buries them. And I say this of those who have shone in a wondrous way. For the rest, as soon as they have breathed out their breath they are gone, and no man speaks of them. And, to conclude the matter, what is even an eternal remembrance? A mere nothing. What then is that about which we ought to employ our serious pains? This one thing, thoughts just, and acts social, and words which never lie, and a disposition which gladly accepts all that happens, as necessary, as usual, as flowing from a principle and source of the same kind.

[28 A.]

AUROBINDO, SRI

AUROBINDO, SRI (1872-1950). The son of a prominent Bengalese physician, Sri Aurobindo was educated in England, where he was sent at the age of seven. Returning to India at the age of twenty-one, he served the State of Baroda for the next three years in various administrative and teaching capacities; in 1906 he resigned from the Baroda State Service. He anticipated Gandhi in organizing the national action of passive resistance during his next few years of political activity in Bengal. Imprisoned by the government for one year on a false political charge, he left Bengal upon his release in 1910, went to live in French Pondicherry, and from then on devoted his interests exclusively to philosophical writing and teaching.

Two books synthesize his teachings: "The Life Divine", his philosophy, and "The Synthesis of Yoga", his system of Yoga. He also completed three volumes of poetry, and from 1914 to 1921, he was the editor of ARYA, a philosophical journal. In 1926, he retired to the *Ashrama*, where he lived in isolation except for a few public appearances during the course of each year.

THE INDIAN CONCEPTION OF LIFE

THE VALUE of the Indian conception for life must depend on the relations and gradations by which this perfection is connected with our normal living. Put over against the latter without any connection, without any gradations leading up to it, it would either be a high unattainable ideal or the detached remote passion of a few exceptional spirits, or discourage the springs of our natural life by the too great contrast between this spiritual being and natural being. Something of the kind has happened in later times and given some room for the current Western impression about the exaggerated asceticism and other-worldliness of Indian religion and philosophy. But we must not be misled by the extreme over-emphasis of certain tendencies. To get to the real meaning of the Indian idea of life we must go back to its best times and look not at this or that school of philosophy or at some side of it, but at the totality of the ancient philosophical thinking, religion, literature, art, society. The Indian conception in its soundness made no such mistake; it did not imagine that this great thing can or even ought to be done by some violent, intolerant, immediate leap. Even the most extreme philosophies do not go so far. Whether the workings of the Spirit in the universe are a reality or only a half reality, self-descriptive *Lila* or illusory *Maya*, whether it be an action of the Infinite Energy, *Sakti*, or a figment of some secondary paradoxical consciousness in the Eternal, *Maya*, life as an intermediate reality is nowhere denied by any school of Indian thinking. Indian thought recognized that the normal life of man has to be passed through conscientiously, developed with knowledge, its forms perused, interpreted, fathomed, its values worked out, possessed and lived, its enjoyments taken on their own level, before we can go on to self-existence or a supra-existence. The spiritual perfection which opens before man is the crown of a long, patient, millennial outflowering of the spirit in life and nature. This belief in a gradual spiritual progress and evolution is the secret of the almost universal Indian acceptance of the truth of reincarnation. By millions of lives in inferior forms the secret soul in the universe, conscious even in the inconscient, *cetano acetanesu,* has arrived at humanity: by hundreds, thousands, perhaps millions of lives man grows into his divine self-existence. Every life is a step which he can take backward or forward; by his action, his will in life, by the thought and knowledge that governs it, he determines what he is yet to be, *yatha karma yatha srutam.*

This conception of a spiritual evolution with a final spiritual perfection or transcendence of which human life is the means and an often repeated opportunity, is the pivot of the Indian conception of existence. It gives to our life a figure of ascent, in spirals or circles, which has to be filled in with knowledge and action and experience. There is room within it for all human aims, activities and aspirations; there is place in the ascent for all types of human character and nature. The spirit in the world assumes hundreds of forms, follows many tendencies, gives many shapes to his play or *lila*, and all are part of the mass of necessary experience; each has its justification, its law, its reason of being, its utility. The claim of sense satisfaction is not ignored, nor the soul's need of labour and heroic action, nor the hundred forms of the pursuit of knowledge, nor the play of the emotions or the demand of the aesthetic faculties. Indian culture did not deface nor impoverish the richness of the grand game of human life or depress or mutilate the activities of our nature. On the contrary it gave them, subject to a certain principle of harmony and government, their full, often their extreme value; it bade man fathom on his way all experience, fill in life opulently with colour and beauty and enjoyment and give to his character and action a large rein and heroic proportions. This side of the Indian idea is stamped in strong relief over the epic and the classical literature, and to have read the *Ramayana*, the *Mahabharata*, the dramas, the literary epics, the romances, the lyric and the great abundance of gnomic poetry, to say nothing of the massive remains of other cultural work and social and political system and speculation without perceiving this breadth, wealth and greatness, one must have read without eyes to see or without a mind to understand. But while the generous office of culture is to enrich, enlarge and encourage human life, it must also find in it a clue, give it a guiding law and subject it to some spiritual, moral and rational government. The greatness of the ancient Indian civilization consists in the power with which it did this work and the high and profound wisdom and skill with which, while basing society, ordering the individual life, encouraging and guiding human nature and propensity, it turned them all towards the realization of its master idea and never allowed the mind it was training to lose sight of the use of life as a passage of the Infinite and a discipline for spiritual perfection.

Two main truths are always kept in sight by the Indian mind whether in the government of life or in the discipline of spirituality. First, our being in its growth has stages through which it must pass. Then again, life is complex, the nature of man is complex, and in each life man has to figure a certain sum of its complexity. The initial movement of life is that form of it which develops the powers of the ego in man; *kama, artha,* self interest and desire are the original human motives. Indian culture gave a large recognition to this primary turn of our nature. These powers have to be accepted; the ego-life must be lived and the forces it evolves in the human being brought to fullness. But to get its full results and inspire it eventually to go beyond itself, it must be kept from making any too unbridled claim or heading furiously towards its satisfaction. There must be no internal or external anarchy. A life governed in any absolute or excessive degree by self-will, by passion, sense-attraction, self-interest, desire cannot be the whole natural rule of a human or a humane existence. The tempting imagination that it can, with which the Western mind has played in leanings or outbursts of what has been called Paganism, not at all justly, for the Greek or Pagan intelligence had a noble thought for self-rule, law and harmony,—is alien to the Indian mentality. It perceived very well the possibility of a materialistic life and its attraction worked on certain minds and gave birth to the Carvaka philosophy; but this could not take hold or stay. Even it allowed to it when lived on a grand scale a certain perverse greatness, but a colossal egoism was regarded as the nature of the Asura and Raksasa, the Titanic, gigantic or demoniac type of spirit, not the proper life for man. Another power claims man, overtopping desire and self-interest and self-will, the power of the Dharma.

The Dharma, religious law of action, is not as in the Western idea, only a religious creed and cult inspiring an ethical and social rule, but the complete rule of our life, the harmony of the whole tendency of man to find a right and just law of his living. Every thing has its dharma, its law of life imposed on it by its nature, but the dharma for a man is a conscious imposition of a rule of ideal living on all his members. This Dharma develops, evolves, has stages, grada-

81

tions of spiritual and ethical ascension. All men cannot follow in all things one common and invariable rule of action. Nature, the position, the work, aim and bent, the call of life, the call of the spirit within, the degree and turn of development, the *adhikara* or capacity differ too much in different men; life is too complex to admit of such an ideal simplicity. Man lives in society and by society, and every society has its own general dharma, its law of right stability and right functioning, and into this law the individual life must be fitted; but the individual's part in society, his own nature, the needs of his capacity and temperament all vary, and the social law on its side must make room for this variety. The man of knowledge, the man of power, the productive and acquisitive man, the priest, scholar, poet, artist, ruler, fighter, trader, tiller of the soil, craftsman, labourer, servant cannot all have the same training, be shaped in the same pattern, follow the same way of living or be all put under the same tables of the law. Each has his type of nature and there must be a rule for the perfection of that type, or each his function and there must be a canon and ideal of the function. The main necessity is that, that there must be in all things some wise and understanding canon and ideal; a lawless impulse of desire and interest and propensity cannot be allowed; even in the frankest following of desire and interest and propensity there must be a rule, a guidance, an ethic and science arising from and answering to some truth of the thing sought, a restraint, an order, a standard of perfection. The rule and training and result differ with the type of the man and the type of the function. The idea of the Indian social system was a harmony of this complexity of *artha, kama* and *dharma*.

[28B]

ANONYMOUS

AUTHOR OF THE IMITATION OF CHRIST, AN UNKNOWN CARTHUSIAN MONK. Carlyle said about this work, "None, except the Bible, is so universally read and loved by Christians of all tongues and sects," a statement confirmed by all lovers of devotional literature. Whoever wrote the book described the trials and temptations, the joys of mystical intercourse with Christ, and the readiness to suffer with him. The debates about the author of this work began around 1430 and have continued up to the present day. For a long time, it was attributed to Thomas á Kempis (1380-1471), who signed a copy of his writing in 1441. But none of his other numerous books is comparable to the *Imitatio*, and the oldest extant manuscript was written in 1383 when Thomas á Kempis was three years old. However, he may be considered as the editor who improved the Latin phraseology. The assumption that the *Imitatio* is based upon the diaries of Gerard Root is also untenable. In all probability, the author was a Carthusian monk who, after many wordly experiences, composed this work, which has been described by Matthew Arnold as "the most exquisite document of Christian spirit after the New Testament."

THE THOUGHTS OF DEATH

1. VERY quickly will it be over with thee here; see then how matters stand with thee. A man is here to-day, and to-morrow he is no longer seen.

And when he is taken away from the sight, he is also quickly out of mind.

Oh! the dullness and hardness of the human heart, which thinks only of what is present and does not look rather forward to things to come.

Thou oughtest in every action and thought so to order thyself, as if thou wert immediately to die.

If thou hadst a good conscience, thou wouldst not much fear death.

It were better for thee to avoid sin, than to escape death.

If thou are not prepared to-day, how wilt thou be to-morrow?

To-morrow is an uncertain day; and how dost thou know that thou shalt be alive to-morrow?

2. What good is it to live long, when we advance so little?

Ah! long life does not always make us better, but often rather adds to our guilt.

Would that we had behaved ourselves well in this world, even for one day!

Many reckon up the years of their conversion; but oftentimes the fruit of amendment is but small.

If it be frightful to die, perhaps it will be more dangerous to live longer.

Blessed is he that has always the hour of his death before his eyes, and every day prepares himself to die.

If thou hast at any time seen a man die, think that thou also must traverse the same path.

3. In the morning, think that thou mayest not live till night; and when evening comes, presume not to promise thyself the next morning.

Be therefore always prepared, and live in such a manner, that death may never find thee unprepared.

Many die suddenly, and when they little think of it: For in such an hour as ye think not the Son of Man will come.

When that last hour shall come, thou wilt begin to have quite other thoughts of thy whole past life, and be exceeding sorry that thou hast been so negligent and remiss.

4. How happy and prudent is he who strives now to be such in this life, as he desires to be found at his death.

A perfect contempt of the world, a fervent desire to advance in virtue, a love of discipline, labor in penitence, readiness in obedience, self-denial, and patience in affliction for the love of Christ, will give us great assurance of dying happily.

Thou mayest do many good things whilst thou art well; but when thou art sick, I know not what thou wilt be able to do.

Few are improved by sickness; so they also that rove about much, seldom become holy.

5. Trust not in thy friends and kinsfolk, nor put off the welfare of thy soul to hereafter; for men will forget thee sooner than thou thinkest.

It is better now to provide in time, and send some good before thee, than to depend upon the help of others.

If thou art not now careful for thyself, who will be careful for thee hereafter?

The present time is very precious. Now is the acceptable time; now is the day of salvation.

But oh, the sorrow that thou dost not spend this time more profitably, wherein thou mayest earn life for ever! The time will come, when thou wilt wish for one day or hour to amend; and I know not whether thou wilt obtain it.

6. O dearly beloved, from how great a danger mayest thou deliver thyself, from how great a fear mayest thou rescue thyself, if thou wilt but now be always fearful, and looking for death!

Strive now so to live, that in the hour of thy death thou mayest be able to rejoice rather than fear.

Learn now to die to the world, that thou mayest then begin to live with Christ.

Learn now to despise all things, that thou mayest then freely go to Christ.

Chasten thy body now by penitence, that thou mayest then have a sure confidence.

7. Ah, fool! why dost thou think to live long, when thou art not sure of one day?

How many thinking to live long have been deceived, and snatched unexpectedly away?

How often hast thou heard related, that such a one was slain by the sword; another drowned; another, from a height, broke his neck; one died eating, another playing?

Some have perished by fire; some by the sword; some by pestilence; and some by robbers.

And so death is the end of all; and man's life suddenly passeth away like a shadow.

8. Who will remember thee when thou art dead? and who will pray for thee?

Do now, beloved, do now all thou canst, because thou knowest not when thou shalt die, nor does thou know what shall befall thee after death.

Whilst thou hast time, gather up for thyself everlasting riches; think of nothing but thy salvation; care for nothing but the things of God.

Make now to thyself friends, by honoring the saints of God, and imitating their actions; that when thou failest, they may receive thee into everlasting habitations.

9. Keep thyself as a pilgrim and a stranger upon earth, whom none of the affairs of this world concern.

Keep thy heart free, and raised upwards to God; for here thou hast no continuing city.

Send thither thy daily prayers with sighs and with tears; that after death thy spirit may be worthy happily to pass to our Lord. Amen.

[29]

AVENARIUS, RICHARD

AVENARIUS, RICHARD (1843-1896). Empirio-criticism was a radical positivist doctrine formulated by Avenarius. He maintained that scientific philosophy must be confined to the descriptive, generalized definitions of experience; that pure experience must be kept free of metaphysics or materialism. This doctrine assumes that there is a constancy in the mutual relationship between the ego and its environment; that only parts of our environment constitute pure experience; that those occasions where experience is said to transcend the environment must be regarded and repudiated as an extraneous element or invention of the mind. Substance and causality are such inventions. Avenarius accepted a parallelism between brain changes and states of consciousness, but emphasized that neither thoughts nor sensations are to be explained as functions of the brain. He stated that since men are equal, the experience of each ego has equal validity, provided that individual variations are recognized; that the experience of each ego can be used to construct a natural concept of the world. His opposition to the materialist as-

sertions of Karl Vogt resulted in a violent attack upon empirio-criticism by Lenin. Avenarius, whose principal works are *Critique of
Pure Experience* (1888-90) and *The Human Concept of the World*
(1891) influenced Ernst Mach and, to some extent, William James.

THE TWO AXIOMS OF EMPIRIO-CRITICISM

IT is perhaps not unsuitable to advance two assumptions
which I should like to call empirio-critical axioms: The first
is the axiom of the contents of knowledge, the second the
axiom of the forms of knowledge.

One could formulate these two axioms in the following
manner.

(1) Each human individual originally supposes an environment with multiple elements; other human individuals
with multiple assertions as well as a certain dependence of
that which is asserted in the environment. All the contents
of knowledge of the philosophical concept of the world
(whether it be critical or uncritical) are alterations of this
original supposition.

That means whatever the conclusions of a Plato, Spinoza or Kant might be . . . these philosophers came to their
results by positive or negative additions to the particular supposition which they too made at the beginning of their development.

(2) The scientific cognition has essentially no other
forms or means than the nonscientific cognition. All the special forms or means of knowledge are transformations of pre-
scientific ones. That means that whatever methods mathematics or mechanics may have developed they must be reducible
to simple and general human functions.

One who accepts the first proposition will most likely
admit that it is also advisable in our research, to proceed
from this original assumption and not from later transformations. . . .

To proceed from "consciousness" or "reasoning" in
order to develop one's own opinion on cognition or even to

judge other people's opinion on it would mean, in order not to use a more drastic comparison, to start with the end.

If one admits, however, that one has to proceed from the original supposition as we have mentioned . . . one should also admit that it would be inadvisable to proceed from the environment and the asserting individual, in his relationship to the environment. When the influences of irritation on the nervous center are noticed, one cannot immediately proceed from the changes of this organ to "consciousness," "reasoning," and the "images" of the individual. The changes, and their various ramifications, which the irritation has produced in the organ must be followed up. After that, one may go on to the phenomena dependent upon these changes.

Whoever admits the second proposition will be inclined to admit that it is advisable not to reflect immediately or exclusively on complicated and special forms and means of a highly developed scientific knowledge. One must keep in mind the ordinary life, the natural, unprejudiced cognition which draws upon its own resources; scientific cognition is developed from this. Thus is shown the relationship of the scientific form of knowledge to its prescientific form.

[30]

AVENPACE (Ibn Badjdja)

AVENPACE (IBN BADJDJA) (End of 11th Century—1138). Avenpace was a high dignitary in Islamic Spain, for twenty years when he was poisoned by his enemies who decried him as an atheist and scorner of the Koran. He was a reputed musician and well acquainted with the natural sciences, mathematics and astronomy. Avenpace wrote commentaries on several works of Aristotle, whom he interpreted in accordance with Neo-Platonism, and treatises among which *The Hermit's Guide* was most famous. It was used by Averroës and the Jewish author Moses of Narbonne, as well as by Albertus Magnus and Aquinas. He distinguished between "animal" and "human" activities, regarded the human intellect as the emanation of the Agens Intellect, the supreme Being, and described their mystical union.

88

ON HUMAN PERFECTION

THE word "regime," in its most popular sense, signifies a concurrence of actions which are directed toward a certain end. The word regime cannot, therefore, be applied to a single action, since it is used for a complex of actions, as military regime or political regime. Thus, we say that God governs and rules over the world. For this regime, according to vulgar opinion, is similar to that of the governments of states, though, from the philosophical point of view, these words are a simple homonym. This regulated concurrence of actions which demands reflection, cannot be formed but by a solitary man. The regime of the solitary man must be the image of the perfect government of a state, where judges and physicians are absent because they are useless. . . . In a perfect state, every individual will have the highest degree of perfection of which man is capable. There, everyone thinks in accordance with the highest justice, and does not neglect, when he is acting, any law and custom. There will be no fault, no joke, no ruse.

In an imperfect state the solitary man shall become the element of the future perfect state.

He who acts under the influence of reflection and justice only, without regard to the animal soul, must be called divine rather than human. Such a man must excel in moral virtues so that when the rational soul decides in favor of a thing, the animal soul, far from objecting, decides in favor of the same thing. It is the nature of the animal soul to obey the rational soul. This is, however, not the case with men who are not in the natural state but who allow themselves to give way to rage. He who allows himself to give way to passions acts in accordance not with human but with animal nature. He is even worse than the animal which obeys its own nature.

[31]

89

AVERROÖS (Ibn Roshd)

AVERROÖS (IBN ROSHD) (1126-1198). Due to a mistake made in translating the works of Mohammed ibn Ahmed ibn Mohammed ibn Roshd from the Arabic into Latin, this great Islamic philosopher for about two centuries deeply influenced Christian thinkers, by whom he was known under the name Averroës. In reality, Averroës taught that there is one eternal truth which, according to the various levels of education, can be formulated and comprehended in two ways, namely, the way of revelation, by the Koran, or the way of natural knowledge, with the aid of Aristotle and other philosophers. He maintained on occasion that there is a double truth, and that a proposition may be theologically true and philosophically untrue, and vice versa. Christian Averroism flourished in the thirteenth century, especially at the University of Paris where Siger of Brabant was the leader of that school. In 1277, Averroism was condemned by the Church. Averroës also influenced Jewish philosophers of the Middle Ages.

Apart from his ascendancy over Christian and Jewish philosophy, Averroës has become important as the last great philosopher of Islamic Spain, and as the last and greatest of all Arabian Aristotelians. He studied medicine and jurisprudence, and was a judge in Sevilla and Cordova. Although he was fully acquainted with natural sciences, his approach to philosophy was determined to a great extent by his legal training. As a jurist, Averroës insisted on the literal meaning of religious and secular documents, and was eager to refute misinterpretations, particularly those which were advanced by theologians. In this way, Averroës studied, explained and annotated Aristotle whom he glorified as a "man chosen by God." Violently attacked by the Mohammedan clergy, Averroës' doctrines were condemned and his books burned.

His theories of the evolution of pre-existent forms and of the intellect anticipated modern concepts.

ON METAPHISICS

IT has already been demonstrated in natural science that everything that is moved presupposes a moving principle; that, furthermore, the moved is moved only in so far as it exists potentially and that the mover carries out a movement in so far as he is *in actu;* and that the mover, if one time he

90

carries out a movement but the next time does not produce such, must, in a certain manner, be passively moved, since active motion exists only potentially in him if he does not actually move. If we thus assume in this case that the first mover of the world one time carries out a movement, but not the next time, then we have to conclude inevitably that a further mover, prior to this one, must exist in the world. This one is, therefore, not the prime mover. Now, if we thus assume in the case of the second one that he moves one time and does not move the next time, we necessarily get the same result with respect to it as we got in the first case. Therefore, it is an irrefutable consequence that either this succession yields an infinite chain or that we admit that in the "here" [i.e., the world] there exists a mover who is in no manner moved nor may yet be moved, neither as concerns his essence, nor yet *per accidens*. Since matters lie thus, this mover is consequently of necessity eternal; the object that is put in motion by him is likewise eternally in motion; for if something existed that, at a given time, were potentially in a position to be moved by the eternal mover, then a mover who would precede the eternal mover, would inevitably have to exist "beyond." For this reason, the mover whose existence has been demonstrated in the 16th Book of Zoology, would not possess the qualification sufficient for carrying out a special movement without the aid of the mover of the whole world.

If it is thus clear that an eternal motion exists in the "here," and if it is impossible that there is an eternal motion, leaving out of account the circular and spatial one—this has been discussed in natural science—then it is evident that this demonstration yields the necessity of an eternal, spatial motion existing in the "here." However, this is in no manner ascertainable by sensual perception, if you except the motion of the heavenly body. The motion of this body must, therefore, be the eternal motion of which we are in search. The mover of this body is at the same time the eternal mover whose existence has become intelligible through former dis-

91

cussions. The existence of an eternal, continuous motion with respect to time has likewise been proved; for, time, as has been demonstrated, is one of the accidents of motion. Time cannot be slowly composed, not even by him who is raised above time. The reason for this lies in what follows: Let us admit that time arises by degrees; then it would exist after it was nonexistent previously, indeed already prior to its existence. The earlier and the later are, however, two designations for parts of time. Therefore, time would have to exist before there was any. Furthermore, if time were something that originates, then it would happen that time which might be a present time did not precede a particular thing. However, it is quite impossible to imagine that no past preceded a particular thing which is in actuality and exists in a "present" moment, let alone that we could imagine such a state of affairs were we to reflect on the real nature of time. An error in these ideas can occur only when we think of time in terms of a line; for, in so far as the line possesses spatial motion—this exists in actuality—it is by necessity finite, not to mention the fact that one cannot even imagine infinity in connection with it. Now, if you should imagine time in this sense as a straight line, it is impossible for it to be infinite. This type of error belongs to those that fall under the topic of spatial motion and substitution. Farabi has composed long dissertations concerning this problem with respect to things that exist and change.

This being so, and it being evident that time forms an eternal continuum, it follows inevitably upon an eternal motion which is continuous and uniform; for a motion which in the proper sense of the word is uniform, is the continuous motion. If, now, there exists in the "here" an eternal motion, it follows that there must also be present an eternal mover who is ever the same; for, if there were many moving principles existing, the motion would not be one and the same, nor would it be continuous. Now, that this first mover cannot be of a material nature, has become intelligible by virtue of the fact that his motion, which takes place in time, proceeds without end. However, every mover that exists in some matter must have quantity adhering to him, that is, must possess a body. Every potentiality, however, which has its seat in something quantitative, is divisible, corresponding to the divisibility of quantity. It follows likewise in the determination of finiteness and infinity, as has been demonstrated in natural science, be it that one presupposes this potentiality as blended with the body or only as "engraved" upon it. Of such nature are heat in fire and cold in water. This potentiality is in some sort of necessary internal dependence on the *hyle*, that is to say, a dependence absolutely necessary for its existence. Thus with respect to the psychic principle. Since, now, in essence, form is material, no material force can exist which, as moving principle, is infinite. All this was demonstrated in natural science. . . .

[32]

AVICENNA

AVICENNA (979-1037). Nearly a thousand years have passed and the name of Avicenna is still revered in the East. One of the wisest of physicians, he is referred to in the West as the Galen of the Moslem world. The name Avicenna is the Latinized form of the Hebrew, Aven Sina; or the Arabic, Abu Ali al-Husain ibn Abdullah ibn Sina. While still a youth in his teens, Avicenna was called upon to cure the Sultan of Bokhara. The potentate, in gratitude, opened his library to the young man. This good fortune enabled Avicenna, (who had memorized the Koran by the age of ten) to write the *Canon*, the basis of his medical fame, before he had attained his legal majority.

In addition to his medical accomplishments, he studied logic, metaphysics, mathematics, and physics. He studied Aristotelian and neo-Platonic philosophy with Al-Farabi. As a result of this, Avicenna wrote voluminously on Aristotle. He said that cause and effect are simultaneous and therefore God and the world are co-eternal; that God created intelligence or the soul, and these emanate from the heavens and reach the earth in huge chains; that intelligence is sustained by God, and though that is innately eternal, its multiple extensions are not dependent on Him, for He is not concerned with matter.

Avicenna was probably a pantheist. His work, *Philosophia Orientalis*, in which his position was apparently clarified, is lost. His mysticism is said to have been derived from Mazdaism. For a time he occupied the office of Vizier at Hamadan.

MENTAL ESSENCE

As to the mental essence, we find it in infants devoid of every mental form. Then, later on in life, we find in it self-evident axiomatic mentally-grasped notions, without effort of learning and without reflections. So that the arising of them within it will not fail of being either through sense and experience, or else through divine outpouring reaching to it. But it is not licit to hold that the arising of such primary mental form will be through experience, seeing that experience does not afford and supply a necessary and inevitable judgment, since experience does not go so far as to believe or disbelieve definitely the existence of something different to the judgment drawn from what it has perceived. Indeed experience, although it shows us that every animal we perceive moves on chewing the lower jaw, yet it does not supply us with a convincing judgment that such is the case with every animal; for were this true, it would not be licit for the crocodile to exist which moves his upper jaw on chewing. Therefore not every judgment we have arrived at, as to things, through our sensuous perception, is applicable to and holds good of all that we have perceived or have not perceived of such things, but it may so be that what we have not perceived differ from what we have perceived. Whereas our conception that a whole is greater than a part is not [formed] because we have sensuously felt every part and every whole that are so related, seeing that even such an experience will not guaranty to us that there will be no whole and no part differently related.

Likewise the dictum concerning the impossibility of two opposites (contrasts) coming together in one and the same thing, and that things which are equal to one and the same thing are equal to one another. And likewise the dictum concerning our holding proofs to be true if they be valid, for the belief in and conviction of their validity does not become valid by and through learning and effort of study; else this would draw out ad infinitum [inasmuch as each proof rests upon given presuppositions, whose validity would in its turn have to be proved]. Nor is this gained from sense, for the reason that we have mentioned. Consequently both the latter as well as the former [certainty] are gained from a godly outflow reaching unto the rational soul, and the rational soul reaching unto it; so that this mental form arises therein. Also, as to this outflow, unless it have in its own self such a generic (universal) mental form, it would not be able to engrave it within the rational soul. Hence such form is in the outflow's own self. And whatsoever Self has in it a mental form is an essence, other than a body, and not within a body, and standing of itself. Therefore this outflow unto which the soul reaches is a mental essence, not a body, not in a body, standing of itself, and one which stands towards the rational soul in the stead of light to sight; yet however with this difference, namely that light supplies unto sight the power of perceiving only, and not the perceived form, whereas this essence supplies, exclusively by and through its sole and single self, unto the rational power, the power of perceiving, and brings about therein the perceived forms also, as we have set forth above.

Now, if the rational soul's conceiving rational forms be a source of completion and perfection for it, and be effected and brought about on reaching unto this essence, and if worldly earthy labors, such as its thought, its sorrows and joy, its longings, hamper the power and withhold it from reaching thereunto, so that it will not reach thereunto save only through abandoning these powers and getting rid of them, there being nothing to stop it from continued Reaching save the living body,—then consequently if it quit the body it will not cease to be reaching unto its Perfector and attached to Him.

Again, what reaches unto its Perfector and attaches itself to Him is safe against corruption, all the more so if even during disconnection from Him it has not undergone corruption. Wherefore the soul after death shall ever remain and continue unwavering [and undying] and attached to this noble essence, which is called generic universal mind, and in the language of the lawgivers the Divine Knowledge.

As to the other powers, such as the animal and the vegetable: Whereas every one of them performs its proper peculiar action only by and through the live body, and in no other way, consequently they will never quit live bodies, but will die with their death, seeing that every thing which is, and yet has no action, is idle and useless. Yet nevertheless the rational soul does gain, by its connection with them, from them their choicest and purest lye and wash, and leaves for death the husks. And were it not so, the rational soul would not use them in consciousness. Wherefore the rational soul shall surely depart (migrate, travel) taking along the kernels of the other powers after death ensues.

We have thus made a clear statement concerning souls, and got at which souls are [ever-] lasting, and which of them will not be fitted out and armed with [ever]lastingness. It still remains for us, in connection with this research, to show how a soul exists within live bodies, and the aim and end for which it is found within the same, and what measure will be bestowed upon it, in the hereafter, of eternal delight and perpetual punishment, and of [temporary] punishment that ceases after a duration of time that shall ensue upon the decease of the live body; and to treat of the notion that is designated by the lawgivers as intercession (mediation), and of the quality (attribute) of the four angels and the throne-bearers. Were it not however that the custom prevails to isolate such research from the research whose path we have been treading, out of high esteem and reverence for it, and to make the latter research precede in order of treatment the former, to the end of levelling the road and paving it solidly, I should (would) have followed up these [ten] sections with a full and complete treatment of the subject dealt with in them. Notwithstanding all this, were it not for fear of wearying by prolixity, I would have disregarded the demands of custom herein. Thus, then whatever it may please the Prince—God prolong his highness—to command as to treating singly of such notions, I shall put forth, in humble compliance and obedience, my utmost effort, God Almighty willing; and may wisdom never cease to revive through him after fainting, to flourish after withering, so that its sway may be renewed through his sway, and through his days its days may come back again, and that through his prestige the prestige of its devotees be exalted, and the seekers after its favor abound, so God almighty will.   [33]

AXELROD, PAVEL BORISSOVICH

AXELROD, PAVEL BORISSOVICH (1850-1928). Brought up in a small provincial town in Russia, the son of a poor Jewish innkeeper, Axelrod realized that his quest for knowledge was inseparable from the struggle for human progress; that his desire for self-education was only an aspect of his desire to educate the masses of the people.

In his youth he was a disciple of Bakunin, and he remained an idealist even after adopting the Marxist concept of historical materialism. With his lifelong friend, Plekhanov, he became one of the founders of the Russian Social Democratic Party. Plekhanov was the leading theorist of the movement, and Axelrod directed its propaganda and applied the theories to practical politics. It was largely due to his efforts that the labor movement of Russia participated in the political struggle against Tsarist absolutism instead of concentrating their activities upon economic improvement. He took a leading part in directing and formulating the policies of the Menshevist Party, and was elected a member of the executive committee of the Second Internationale. One of the principal aims of his activities was to organize the Russian worker and make him as politically active as his Western European counterpart. He was often referred to as the great Westerner among the Russian Socialists. From 1903 until his death, he and Plekhanov combatted Lenin and the Bolshevists.

A MARXIST'S IDEALISM

THE motivation of my idealism, of all my public activities is that the relative progress of human nature is infinite. It may appear curious, but the more clearly I recognize the fallibility of human nature in the present time, the more passionately do I long for its future perfection, even though it may take millennia. It doesn't matter to me that the distance is nebulous and seemingly endless. For it is just that aspect, coupled with the "supermen" of the future that serve as a strong incentive and source of enthusiasm. I think this strange phenomenon is rooted in a kind of religious feeling, which I'm unable to characterize, except to say that my devoted respect for thought, conscientiousness, and spirit may be paralleled with fanaticism.

If there is no God, no creator of the universe, then may God be praised for His nonexistence. For we can behead kings, but we would be powerless against a despotic Jehovah. If there is no God, then we must prepare for the arrival of earthly gods; of beings, omnipotent because of their reason and energy of will, capable of comprehending the knowledge of the world and of their own selves, and of embracing and dominating the world by virtue of their spirit.

[34]

B

BAADER, FRANCIS XAVIER VON

BAADER, FRANCIS XAVIER VON (1765-1841). An expert on mints and mining, and consultant in both these fields, Baader was also a writer, a Catholic layman whose works were read by both Protestant and Catholic philosophers. The latter found him stimulating if unorthodox, particularly in view of the fact that he once stated that should the devil appear on earth, it would be in the garb of a professor of moral philosophy. During a five-year sojourn in England, Baader acquainted himself with the opposing ideologies of David Hartley, the sensualist, David Hume, the sceptic, and Jacob Boehme, the mystic. His writings, as a result of these influences, contained many unpredictable flashes of insight and startling affirmations. Mysticism influenced him more than did philosophies. Baader never strove for a system, but aimed at the deep and profound; he frequently appeared paradoxical. Rationalism was abhorrent to him; human knowledge required the greater wisdom of God, which he viewed as the real spontaneity in all forms of knowledge. The phrase, *con-scientia* symbolized to him man's participation in God's knowledge. He disapproved of some aspects of the papacy, but, nonetheless, elected to stay within the fold, striving, in his lectures, for a philosophic rationale of Catholicism, and making the love of God and neighbor the mainstay of his sociology, which also incorporated his ideas of liberty and equality. In 1826 he was called to assume the chair of professor of speculative dogmatics at the University of Munich, his native city. However, he was compelled in 1838 to exchange this for a chair in anthropology because he was barred from lecturing on the philosophy of religion for the reason that he was a layman.

GOD AND THE WORLD

THE only criterion of truth is the intimate consciousness of what we feel. The seed of all knowledge, of all Good and

Evil, lies in myself; all external things can only ripen it. All books can only render the service of a midwife.

The so-called sensual, material nature is a symbol, a copy of inner, spiritual nature. Every action and deed of God in both animated and inanimated nature, in nature and the Bible, are the semantic symbolic, fulfillment and revelation of the past, the germ and seal of the future.

God is universal. He is called God only in the sphere of light. The non-manifest God is only one; the divine Himself in Revelation. The ground is not undivided; it always remains the same. It is only manifestation that divides itself; unity must be laid in the ground, not in manifestations. God is the spirit of all spirits; the essence of all essences.

Theologians are correct in distinguishing the immanent revelation of God from His eminence, and asserting that the form is mediated by a generation begetting. Only begetting is true action, creation. The word is born, not made. The word is not the creature but co-substantial with it.

[35]

BAAL SHEM-TOV

BAAL SHEM-TOV (1700-1760). After seven years of solitary meditation, Israel ben Eliezer began to teach, in 1740, a mysticism which later became known as Hasidism. This earned him the title of Baal Shem-Tov (Master of the Good Name), even though in his early years he had been despised by his people as an ignorant and inefficient man.

He taught that the divine spirit is omnipresent in each man and in everything that exists. Therefore, it is possible to serve God in even the most trifling of actions. In contradistinction to other schools of mysticism and to various Jewish mystical doctrines, he declared that the pleasures of the senses are not sinful, because man must serve God with his body as well as with his soul. In his teachings, all things, including the lowest acts, had dignity. Although he did not reject learning, he put prayer above scholarship, insisting that his followers pray "with gladness" and forget, through religious concentration, all the sufferings imposed by life.

The teachings of Baal Shem-Tov gained a large number of adherents among the Jews of Eastern Europe who, at that time, were subject to frequent persecutions and whose economic situation was constantly growing worse. These people were impressed by his kind and humble personality and revered him as a saint. He received gifts of immense value, but ended each day by distributing all his wealth among the poor. He saved many co-religionists from despair, enabled them to endure extreme hardship, and imbued them with the spirit of confident piety.

THE END-ALL OF KNOWLEDGE

"Had they but abandoned Me," says God, "and kept faith with My Torah!"

This must be interpreted as follows: The end-all of knowledge is to know that we cannot know anything. But there are two sorts of not-knowing. The one is the immediate not-knowing, when a man does not even begin to examine and try to know, because it is impossible to know. Another, however, examines and seeks, until he comes to know that one cannot know. And the difference between these two—to whom may we compare them? To two men who wish to see the king. The one enters all the chambers belonging to the king. He rejoices in the king's treasure rooms and splendid halls, and then he discovers that he cannot get to know the king. The other tells himself; "Since it is not possible to get to know the king, we will not bother to enter, but put up with not knowing."

This leads us to understand what those words of God mean. They have abandoned Me, that is, they have abandoned the search to know me, because it is not possible. But oh, had they but abandoned me with searching and understanding, so keeping faith with my Torah!

Why do we say: "Our God and the God of our fathers?" There are two sorts of persons who believe in God. The one believes because his faith has been handed down to him by his fathers; and his faith is strong. The other has arrived at faith by dint of searching thought. And this is the difference between the two: The first has the advantage that his faith cannot be shaken, no matter how many objections are raised to it, for his faith is firm because he has taken it over from his fathers. But there is a flaw in it: it is a commandment given by man, and it has been learned without thought or reasoning. The advantage of the second man is that he has reached faith through his own power, through much searching and thinking. But his faith too has a flaw: it is easy to shake it by offering contrary evidence. But he who combines both kinds of faith is invulnerable. That is why we say: "Our God," because of our searching, and "the God of our fathers," because of our tradition.

And a like interpretation holds when we say, "The God of Abraham, the God of Isaac, and the God of Jacob," for this means: Isaac and Jacob did not merely take over the tradition of Abraham, but sought out the divine for themselves.

[36]

BACON, FRANCIS

BACON, FRANCIS (1561-1626). The first philosophical work written originally in English was Francis Bacon's *The Advancement of Learning* (1605). Its author was a native of London, son of Nicholas Bacon, Lord Keeper of the Great Seal. Versed, from early age, in political and legal affairs, he advanced to the position of Lord Chancellor. In 1621 he was accused and convicted of accepting bribes from litigants. He subsequently retired from public life and spent his remaining years in scientific research.

Bacon's personal character has been severely condemned by both his contemporaries and posterity. Like many of the men of his time, he placed his career ahead of the public welfare and his personal integrity. But despite his moral shortcomings, Bacon must be credited with his devotion to science, with his sincere efforts to use his power and authority for scientific promotion, and as one of the greatest propagandists for scientific research. He earnestly endeavored to protect scientists against possible Church condemnation, a danger inherent in the very nature of scientific conclusions. He tried to do this by declaring his reverence for orthodox religion, by proclaiming and defending the secularization of science and philosophy, and by resorting to reason and revelation wherein "double truth" was an acceptable medieval doctrine. Bacon regarded and trusted secularized thought as the instrument for the future improvement of human conditions.

He categorized himself as the "trumpeter of the new age." Actually, he represents an age in transition. Although he emphatically stressed the importance of experiment and the inductive method, he ignored most of the real progress science had made during his lifetime. He was more interested in the effects of knowledge on human behavior than he was in knowledge for its own sake. He asserted that "human knowledge and human power meet in one"; therefore, "knowledge is power." He cautioned against the possible abuse of power. Yielding to prejudice or "idols" might result in this. His claim to have permanently established "a true and lawful marriage between the empirical and rational faculty" is a disputable one. However, it is to his incontestable merit that he saw that true philosophy is concerned with "the real business and fortunes of the human race."

IDOLS WHICH BESET MAN'S MIND

MAN, being the servant and interpreter of nature, can do and understand so much and so much only as he has observed in fact or in thought of the course of nature: beyond this he neither knows anything nor can do anything.

*　　*　　*

Human knowledge and human power meet in one; for where the cause is not known the effect cannot be produced. Nature to be commanded must be obeyed; and that which in contemplation is as the cause is in operation as the rule.

*　　*　　*

There are and can be only two ways of searching into and discovering truth. The one flies from the senses and particulars to the most general axioms, and from these principles, the truth of which it takes for settled and immovable, proceeds to judgment and to the discovery of middle axioms. And this way is now in fashion. The other derives axioms from the senses and particulars, rising by a gradual and unbroken ascent, so that it arrives at the most general axioms last of all. This is the true way, but as yet untried.

The understanding left to itself takes the same course (namely, the former) which it takes in accordance with logi-

103

cal order. For the mind longs to spring up to positions of higher generality, that it may find rest there; and so after a little while wearies of experiment. But this evil is increased by logic, because of the order and solemnity of its disputations.

The understanding left to itself, in a sober, patient, and grave mind, especially if it be not hindered by received doctrines, tries a little that other way, which is the right one, but with little progress; since the understanding, unless directed and assisted, is a thing unequal, and quite unfit to contend with the obscurity of things.

Both ways set out from the senses and particulars, and rest in the highest generalities; but the difference between them is infinite. For the one just glances at experiment and particulars in passing, the other dwells duly and orderly among them. The one, again, begins at once by establishing certain abstract and useless generalities, the other rises by gradual steps to that which is prior and better known in the order of nature.

*   *   *

The axioms now in use, having been suggested by a scanty and manipular experience and a few particulars of most general occurrence, are made for the most part just large enough to fit and take these in: and therefore it is no wonder if they do not lead to new particulars. And if some opposite instance, not observed or not known before, chance to come in the way, the axiom is rescued and preserved by some frivolous distinction; whereas the truer course would be to correct the axiom itself.

The conclusions of human reason as ordinarily applied in matter of nature, I call for the sake of distinction *Anticipations of Nature* (as a thing rash or premature). That reason which is elicited from facts by a just and methodical process, I call *Interpretation of Nature*.

Anticipations are a ground sufficiently firm for consent;

for even if men went mad all after the same fashion, they might agree one with another well enough.

For the winning of assent, indeed, anticipations are far more powerful than interpretations; because being collected from a few instances, and those for the most part of familiar occurrence, they straightway touch the understanding and fill the imagination; whereas interpretations on the other hand, being gathered here and there from very various and widely dispersed facts, cannot suddenly strike the understanding; and therefore they must needs, in respect of the opinions of the time, seem harsh and out of tune; much as the mysteries of faith do.

In sciences founded on opinions and dogmas, the use of anticipations and logic is good; for in them the object is to command assent to the proposition, not to master the thing.

Though all the wits of all the ages should meet together and combine and transmit their labours, yet will no great progress ever be made in science by means of anticipations; because radical errors in the first concoction of the mind are not to be cured by the excellence of functions and remedies subsequent.

It is idle to expect any great advancement in science from the superinducing and engrafting of new things upon old. We must begin anew from the very foundations, unless we would revolve forever in a circle with mean and contemptible progress.

The honour of the ancient authors, and indeed of all, remains untouched; since the comparison I challenge is not of wits or faculties, but of ways and methods, and the part I take upon myself is not that of a judge, but of a guide.

This must be plainly avowed: no judgment can be rightly formed either of my method or of the discoveries to which it leads, by means of anticipations (that is to say, of the reasoning which is now in use); since I cannot be called on to abide by the sentence of a tribunal which is itself on its trial.

Even to deliver and explain what I bring forward is no

easy matter; for things in themselves new will yet be apprehended with reference to what is old.

It was said by Borgia of the expedition of the French into Italy, that they came with chalk in their hands to mark out their lodgings, not with arms to force their way in. I in like manner would have my doctrine enter quietly into the minds that are fit and capable of receiving it; for confutations cannot be employed, when the difference is upon first principles and very notions and even upon forms of demonstration.

One method of delivery alone remains to us; which is simply this: we must lead men to the particulars themselves, and their series and order; while men on their side must force themselves for awhile to lay their notions by and begin to familiarise themselves with facts.

The doctrine of those who have denied that certainty could be attained at all, has some agreement with my way of proceeding at the first setting out; but they end in being infinitely separated and opposed. For the holders of that doctrine assert simply that nothing can be known; I also assert that not much can be known in nature by the way which is now in use. But then they go on to destroy the authority of the senses and understanding; whereas I proceed to devise and supply helps for the same.

The idols and false notions which are now in possession of the human understanding, and have taken deep root therein, not only so beset men's minds that truth can hardly find entrance, but even after entrance obtained, they will again in the very instauration of the sciences meet and trouble us, unless men being forewarned of the danger fortify themselves as far as may be against their assaults.

There are four classes of Idols which beset men's minds. To these for distinction's sake I have assigned names,—calling the first class *Idols of the Tribe;* the second, *Idols of the Cave;* the third, *Idols of the Market-place;* the fourth, *Idols of the Theatre.*

The formation of ideas and axioms by true induction is

no doubt the proper remedy to be applied for the keeping off and clearing away of idols. To point them out, however, is of great use; for the doctrine of Idols is to the Interpretation of Nature what the doctrine of the refutation of Sophisms is to common Logic.

The Idols of the Tribe have their foundation in human nature itself, and in the tribe or race of men. For it is a false assertion that the sense of man is the measure of things. On the contrary, all perceptions as well of the sense as of the mind are according to the measure of the individual and not according to the measure of the universe. And the human understanding is like a false mirror, which, receiving rays irregularly, distorts and discolours the nature of things by mingling its own nature with it.

The Idols of the Cave are the idols of the individual man. For every one (besides the errors common to human nature in general) has a cave or den of his own, which refracts and discolours the light of nature; owing either to his own proper and peculiar nature; or to his education and conversation with others; or to the reading of books, and the authority of those whom he esteems and admires; or to the differences of impressions, accordingly as they take place in a mind preoccupied and predisposed or in a mind indifferent and settled; or the like. So that the spirit of man (according as it is meted out to different individuals) is in fact a thing variable and full of perturbation, and governed as it were by chance. Whence it was well observed by Heraclitus that men look for sciences in their own lesser worlds, and not in the greater or common world.

There are also Idols formed by the intercourse and association of men with each other, which I call Idols of the Market-place, on account of the commerce and consort of men there. For it is by discourse that men associate; and words are imposed according to the apprehension of the vulgar. And therefore the ill and unfit choice of words wonderfully obstructs the understanding. Nor do the definitions or explanations wherewith in some things learned men are wont to guard and defend themselves, by any means set the matter right. But words plainly force and overrule the understanding, and throw all into confusion, and lead men away into numberless empty controversies and idle fancies.

Lastly, there are Idols which have immigrated into men's minds from the various dogmas of philosophies, and also from wrong laws of demonstration. These I call Idols of the Theatre; because in my judgment all the received systems are but so many stage-plays, representing worlds of their own creation after an unreal and scenic fashion. Nor is it only of the systems now in vogue, or only of the ancient sects and philosophies, that I speak; for many more plays of the same kind may yet be composed and in like artificial manner set forth; seeing that errors the most widely different have nevertheless causes for the most part alike. Neither again do I mean this only of entire systems, but also of many principles and axioms in science, which by tradition, credulity, and negligence have come to be received.

[37]

BACON, ROGER

BACON, ROGER (c. 1214-1294). A member of the Order of the Franciscans, Roger Bacon was educated at Oxford and Paris. He was known to some as *Doctor mirabilis,* the wonderful doctor; to others as Friar Bacon; and to still others, as a necromancer, feared and respected for the powers he presumably possessed. His ambitions to pry into the secrets of nature, to make physical calculations and experiment with chemicals roused the suspicion and envy of his Brothers who forthwith complained to the Pope. He was denounced as a "sorcerer" for any number of reasons—because he cited the Greeks and Arabs as authorities, made magnifying glasses, investigated the properties of light, discovered a powder similar to gunpowder, enumerated the errors in the Julian calendar, criticized the Schoolmen (he called St. Thomas Aquinas "a teacher yet unschooled"), and attempted to establish ethics as a basis for monastic life. Finally his opponents prevailed upon the Pope to prevent him from teaching. He was confined for ten years with neither books nor instruments. His *Opus Majus* is a defense of himself, but neither this work nor a condensed version, the *Opus Minus,* called forth any notice from Rome. He made a third revision, *Opus Tertium,* with little success. In many ways the struggles of Roger Bacon parallel those of his fellow countryman, Francis Bacon.

ON THE IMPORTANCE OF EXPERIENCE

THERE are two modes of acquiring knowledge, namely, by reasoning and experience. Reasoning draws a conclusion and makes us grant the conclusion, but does not make the conclusion certain, nor does it remove doubt so that the mind may rest on the intuition of truth, unless the mind discovers it by the path of experience; since many have the arguments relating to what can be known, but because they lack experience they neglect the arguments, and neither avoid what is harmful nor follow what is good. For if a man who has never seen fire should prove by adequate reasoning that fire burns and injures things and destroys them, his mind would not be satisfied thereby, nor would he avoid fire, until he placed his hand or some combustible substance in the fire, so that he might prove by experience that which reasoning taught. But when he has had actual experience of combustion his mind is made certain and rests in the full light of truth. Therefore reasoning does not suffice, but experience does.

This is also evident in mathematics, where proof is most convincing. But the mind of one who has the most convincing proof in regard to the equilateral triangle will never cleave to the conclusion without experience, nor will he heed it, but will disregard it until experience is offered him by the intersection of two circles, from either intersection of which two lines may be drawn to the extremities of the given line; but then the man accepts the conclusion without any question. Aristotle's statement, then, that proof is reasoning that causes us to know is to be understood with the proviso that the proof is accompanied by its appropriate experience, and is not to be understood of the bare proof. His statement also in the first book of the Metaphysics that those who understand the reason and the cause are wiser than those who have empiric knowledge of a fact, is spoken of such as know only the bare truth without the cause. But I am here speaking of the man who knows the reason and the cause through experience. These men are perfect in their wisdom, as Aristotle maintains in the sixth book of the Ethics, whose simple statements must be accepted as if they offered proof, as he states in the same place.

He therefore who wishes to rejoice without doubt in regard to the truths underlying phenomena must know how to devote himself to experiment. For authors write many statements, and people believe them through reasoning which they formulate without experience. Their reasoning is wholly false. For it is generally believed that the diamond cannot be broken except by goat's blood, and philosophers and theologians misuse this idea. But fracture by means of blood of this kind has never been verified, although the effort has been made; and without that blood it can be broken easily. For I have seen this with my own eyes, and this is necessary, because gems cannot be carved except by fragments of this stone. Similarly it is generally believed that the castors employed by physicians are the testicles of the male animal. But this is not true, because the beaver has these under its breast, and both the male and female produce testicles of this kind. Besides these castors the male beaver has its testicles in their natural place; and therefore what is subjoined is a dreadful lie, namely, that when the hunters pursue the beaver, he himself knowing what they are seeking cuts out with his teeth these glands. Moreover, it is generally believed that hot water freezes more quickly than cold water in vessels, and the argument in support of this is advanced that contrary is excited by contrary, just like enemies meeting each other. But it is certain that cold water freezes more quickly for any one who makes the experiment. People attribute this to Aristotle in the second book of the Meteorologics; but he certainly does not make this statement, but he does make one like it, by which they have been deceived, namely, that if cold water and hot water are poured on a cold place, as upon ice, the hot water freezes more quickly, and this is true. But if hot water and cold are placed in two vessels, the cold will freeze more quickly. Therefore all things must be verified by experience.

But experience is of two kinds; one is gained through our external senses, and in this way we gain our experience of those things that are in the heavens by instruments made for this purpose, and of those things here below by means attested by our vision. Things that do not belong in our part of the world we know through other scientists who have had experience of them. As, for example, Aristotle on the authority of Alexander sent two thousand men through different parts of the world to gain experimental knowledge of all things that are on the surface of the earth, as Pliny bears witness in his Natural History. This experience is both human and philosophical, as far as man can act in accordance with the grace given him; but this experience does not suffice him, because it does not give full attestation in regard to things corporeal owing to its difficulty, and does not touch at all on things spiritual. It is necessary, therefore, that the intellect of man should be otherwise aided, and for this reason the holy patriarchs and prophets, who first gave sciences to the world, received illumination within and were not dependent on sense alone. The same is true of many believers since the time of Christ. For the grace of faith illuminates greatly, as also do divine inspirations, not only in things spiritual, but in things corporeal and in the sciences of philosophy; as Ptolemy states in the Centilogium, namely, that there are two roads by which we arrive at the knowledge of facts, one through the experience of philosophy, the other through divine inspiration, which is far the better way, as he says.

[38]

BAHYA IBN PAKUDA

BAHYA IBN PAKUDA (c. 1050). Little is known of the personal life of Bahya, except that he was a *dayyan* (judge at the rabbinical court) in Saragossa toward the end of the eleventh century. His book, *Hobot ha-Lebatot* (The Duties of the Heart), expressed his

111

personal feelings more elaborately than was usual for the Middle Ages. It depicted the noble, humble soul and pure, imperturbable mind of a man ever-grateful to God, motivated by his love of God. Bahya regarded the soul elevated toward God and liberated from the shackles of earthly existence as evidence of purification, communion with God as the ultimate goal. However, his teachings neither imply nor result in neo-Platonic ecstasy. He remained faithful to the Bible and the Talmud. Unlike many other schools of mysticism, he differentiated between man and God. Although a religious moralist, he resolutely subordinated moral righteousness and lawful action to the pious contemplation of God, for the latter served as the most effective control of egoistic instincts and passions.

ADMONITIONS OF THE SOUL

BLESS the Lord, O my soul; and all that is within me, bless His holy name.

O my soul, march on with strength, and bless thy Creator. Prepare a supplication for Him, and pour out thy meditation before Him. Awake from thy sleep, and consider thy place, whence thou camest, and whither thou goest.

O my soul, awake from thy slumber, and utter a song to thy Creator; sing praises unto His name, declare his wonders, and fear Him wherever thou dwellest.

O my soul, be not as the horse, or as the mule, which have no understanding; nor shouldst thou be as a drunkard that is fast asleep, or as a man that is stupefied; for out of the fountain of understanding wast thou formed, and from the spring of wisdom wast thou taken; from a holy place wast thou brought forth, and from the city of the mighty, from heaven, wast thou taken out by God.

O my soul, put on garments of prudence, and gird on a girdle of understanding, and free thyself from the vanities of thy body, in which thou dwellest. Let not thy heart beguile thee with the sweetness of its desires, and let it not allure thee with the visions of its pleasures which melt away like water that runs apace. Remember that the beginning of these pleasures is without help or profit, and their end is shame and also reproach.

O my soul, run to and fro through the streets of thy

understanding, and go about in the chambers of thy wisdom, and come unto the structure of the building of thy imagery, whose foundation is in dust; is it not a despised body and a carcass trodden under foot? It is formed out of a troubled fountain and corrupted spring, built of a fetid drop; it is burned with fire, it is cut down. It is an unformed substance resembling a worm, it is nought but terror. It is kept in a foul womb, closed up in an impure belly; it is born with pangs and sorrows to see trouble and vanities. All day long it covets pleasures, and departs from instruction and from commandments; it comes in the dark, and goes away in the dark; it is a poor, needy, and destitute wayfarer. It has no knowledge without thee, and no understanding beside thee. While alive, it is dust; and when it dies, it is ashes. As long as it lives, worms surround it, and when its end comes, vermin and clods of dust cover it. It cannot discern between its right hand and its left hand; its lot is hidden in the ground. Go thou, therefore, and reign over it, for sovereignty is meet unto the children of wisdom, and the foolish is a servant to the wise of heart. Walk not in the stubbornness of thy wicked heart, be not ensnared by its counsels, and despise the gain of its frauds; trust not in oppression, and become not vain in robbery; for oppression makes a wise man foolish, and a bribe destroys the heart.

O my soul, set thy heart toward the highway, even the way by which thou didst go; for all was made of dust, and indeed unto dust shall all return. Every thing that was created and fashioned has an end and a goal to return unto the ground, whence it was taken. Life and death are brothers that dwell together; they are joined to one another; they cling together, so that they cannot be sundered. They are joined together by the two extremes of a frail bridge over which all created beings travel: life is the entrance, and death is the exit thereof. Life builds, and death demolishes; life sows, and death reaps; life plants, and death uproots; life joins together, and death separates; life links together, and death scatters. Know, I pray thee, and see that also unto thee shall the cup pass over, and thou shalt soon go out from the lodging-place which is on the way, when time and chance befall thee, and thou returnest to thine everlasting home. On that day shalt thou delight in thy work, and take thy reward in return for thy labor wherein thou hast toiled in this world, whether it be good or bad. Therefore hearken, I pray thee, and consider, and incline thine ear; forget thy people and thy father's house. Arise, and sing unto thy King all thy day and all thy night; lift up thy hands toward Him, and bow down unto Him with thy face to the ground; let thine eyelids gush out with waters, and kneel thou upon thy knees; the King may perchance desire thy beauty, and lift up His countenance unto thee, and give thee peace. He will be gracious unto thee in the days of the affliction in this world, and also after thou hast returned to thy rest. For as long as thou didst live He dealt bountifully with thee.

O my soul, prepare provision in abundance, prepare not little, while thou art yet alive, and while thy hand has yet strength, because the journey is too great for thee. And say not: 'I shall prepare provision to-morrow'; for the day has declined, and thou knowest not what the next day may bring forth. Know likewise that yesterday shall never come back, and that whatever thou hast done therein is weighed, numbered, and counted. Nor shouldst thou say: 'I shall do it to-morrow'; for the day of death is hidden from all the living. Hasten to do thy task every day, for death may at any time send forth its arrow and lightning. Delay not to do thy daily task, for as a bird wanders from its nest, so does a man wander from his place. Think not with thyself that after thou hast gone forth from the prison of thy body thou wilt turn to correction from thy perpetual backsliding; for it will not be possible for thee then to turn away from backsliding or to repent of wickedness, guilt, and transgression. For that world has been established to render accounts—the book of the hidden and concealed deeds which every man commits is sealed—and it has been prepared to grant a good reward to them that fear the Lord and think upon His name, and to

execute the vengeance of the covenant upon them that forget
God, who say unto God: 'Depart from us, for we desire not
the knowledge of Thy ways. What is the Almighty, that we
should serve Him? and what profit should we have, if we
pray unto Him?'

O my soul, if thou art wise, thou art wise for thyself;
and if thou scoffest, thy error remains with thee. Hear instruction, and be wise, and refuse it not. Lay continually to
thy heart the words of Koheleth the son of David: 'The end
of the matter, all having been heard: fear God, and keep His
commandments; for this is the whole man. For God will
bring every work into judgment concerning every hidden
thing, whether it be good or whether it be evil.' Forget not
that He seals up the hand of every man, that all men whom
He has made may know it. Remember likewise that there is
no darkness and no thick darkness wherein the workers of
iniquity may hide themselves. Seek the Lord thy Maker with
all thy might and strength. Seek righteousness, seek meekness; it may be that thou wilt be hidden in the day of God's
anger, and in the day of His fierce wrath, and that thou wilt
shine as the brightness of the firmament and as the sun when
it goes forth in its might. The sun of righteousness with healing in its wings shall shine upon thee. Now arise, go and
make supplication unto thy Lord, and take up a melody unto
thy God. Praise thou God, for it is good to sing praises to
our God; for it is pleasant, and praise is comely.

[39]

BAKUNIN, MICHAEL

BAKUNIN, MICHAEL (1814-1876). For nearly thirty years, he was
an active participant in all European revolutions. Neither failure
nor defeat could discourage his anarchistic spirit. To him, revolution meant the destruction of a corrupt and doomed society, and the
desire for destruction served as a creative outlet for him. He detested
the quiet life and often reiterated: "We need a tempestuous lawlessness to secure a free world."

A lawless world seemed both possible and good to Bakunin It

would produce "the free initiative of free individuals within free groups." It would destroy the uniformity of the social order (which to him meant death) and create the variety which he considered identical with the life spirit. He was a grim adversary of all contemporary governments and of the socialism advocated by Karl Marx.

Bakunin, the prophet of destruction, who exalted radicals as the most honorable enemies of decadent institutions, was a nobleman and former officer of the Tsar's imperial guard.

SCIENCE AND LIFE

HISTORICALLY speaking, there are three fundamental principles that constitute the essential conditions for all human development. These principles apply to the individual as well as to collective humanity. They are: human animality, thought, and rebellion. The first corresponds with individual and socialized relationships; the second with science; the third with liberty.

The gradual development of the material world is one of a natural movement from the simple to the complex. Organic and animal life, the historically progressive intelligence of man, individually and socially, has been from the lowest species to the highest; from the inferior to the superior. This movement conforms with all our daily experiences, and consequently it also conforms with our natural logic; with the distinctive laws of our mind, which are formed and developed only by the aid of these same experiences; that is, the mental and cerebral reproduction or reflected summary.

Real and living individuality is perceptible only to another living individuality, not to a thinking individuality; not to the man who, by a series of abstractions, puts himself outside of and above immediate contact with life; to such a man, it can exist only as a more or less perfect example of the species—as a definite abstraction. . . .

Science is like a rabbit. Both are incapable of grasping the individuality of a man. Science is not ignorant of the principle of individuality; it conceives of it perfectly as a principle, but not as a fact.

What I preach, then, is to a certain extent, the revolt of life against science, or rather against the government of science; not to destroy science—that would be treason to humanity—but to remand it to its place so that it can never leave it again.

[40]

BARTH, KARL

BARTH, KARL (1886-   ). Barth is the first religious man since Kierkegaard violently to attack the churches. He tried to restore the theology of early Lutheran and Calvinist reform. Although a member of the Calvinist church, his "dialectical theology" and his concept of the active effect of the divine word in man is more akin to the personal spirit of Luther. He agrees and extends Calvin's belief in man's inability to know God, by emphasizing the "wholly otherness" of God. Like Luther and Calvin, he endeavors to isolate piety and salvation from knowledge. Like them, he insists that man, without the intervention of divine Grace, is helpless and forlorn. Barth consistently refutes all attempts to vindicate even the slightest autonomous values of humanity. He repudiates all idealism as an exaltation of the human mind and declines the idealist concept of the absolute as "a man-made abstraction." He does not favor optimism because its confidence is generally based upon purely human qualities. To him, the only truths are those known through revelation.

The deep earnestness and stern resoluteness of Barth's theology has attracted many adherents in almost all countries. His doctrine is one of conversion and struggle rather than one of knowledge. His ethical demands, religious convictions, and theological doctrines are manifest in his *The Word of God and the Word of Man* (1928), *Credo* (1936), *The Holy Ghost and the Christian Life* (1938), and *Dogmatics in Outline* (1949).

FAITH AS KNOWLEDGE

POSSIBLY you may be struck by the emergence of the concept of *reason*. I use it deliberately. The saying, 'Despise only reason and science, man's supremest power of all', was ut-

117

tered not by a prophet, but by Goethe's Mephisto. Christendom and the theological world were always ill-advised in thinking it their duty for some reason or other, either of enthusiasm or of theological conception, to betake themselves to the camp of an opposition to reason. Over the Christian Church, as the essence of revelation and of the work of God which constitutes its basis, stands the Word: 'The Word was made flesh.' The Logos became man. Church proclamation is language, and language not of an accidental, arbitrary, chaotic and incomprehensible kind, but language which comes forward with the claim to be true and to uphold itself as the truth against the lie. Do not let us be forced from the clarity of this position. In the Word which the Church has to proclaim the truth is involved, not in a provisional secondary sense, but in the primary sense of the Word itself—the Logos is involved, and is demonstrated and revealed in the human reason, the human *nous*, as the Logos, that is, as meaning, as truth to be learned. In the word of Christian proclamation we are concerned with *ratio* reason, in which human *ratio* may also be reflected and reproduced. Church proclamation, theology, is no talk or babbling; it is not propaganda unable to withstand the claim, Is it then true as well, that this is said? Is it really so? You have probably also suffered from a certain kind of preaching and edifying talk, from which it becomes only too clear that there is talking going on, emphatic talk with a plenteous display of rhetoric, which does not however stand up to this simple question as to the truth of what is said. The Creed of Christian faith rests upon knowledge. And where the Creed is uttered and confessed knowledge should be, is meant to be, created. Christian faith is not irrational, not anti-rational, not supra-rational, but rational in the proper sense. The Church which utters the Creed, which comes forward with the tremendous claim to preach and to proclaim the glad tidings, derives from the fact that it has apprehended something—*Vernunft* comes from *vernehmen*— and it wishes to let what it has apprehended be apprehended again. These were always unpropitious periods in the Christian Church, when Christian histories of dogmatics and theology separated *gnosis* and *pistis*. *Pistis* rightly understood is *gnosis*; rightly understood the act of faith is also an act of knowledge. Faith means knowledge.

But once this is established, it must also be said that Christian faith is concerned with an illumination of the reason. Christian faith has to do with the object, with God the Father, the Son, and the Holy Spirit, of which the Creed speaks. Of course it is of the nature and being of this object, of God, the Father, the Son, and the Holy Spirit that He cannot be known by the powers of human knowledge, but is apprehensible and apprehended solely because of His own freedom, decision and action. What man can know by his own power according to the measure of his natural powers, his understanding, his feeling, will be at most something like a supreme being, an absolute nature, the idea of an utterly free power, of a being towering over everything. This absolute and supreme being, the ultimate and most profound, this 'thing in itself,' has nothing to do with God. It is part of the intuitions and marginal possibilities of man's thinking, man's contrivance. Man is able to think this being; but he has not thereby thought God. God is thought and known when in His own freedom God makes Himself apprehensible. We shall have to speak later about God, His being and His nature, but we must now say that God is always the One who has made Himself known to man in His own revelation, and not the one man thinks out for himself and describes as God. There is a perfectly clear division there already, epistemologically, between the true God and the false gods. Knowledge of God is not a possibility which is open for discussion. God is the essence of all reality, of that reality which reveals itself to us. Knowledge of God takes place where there is actual experience that God speaks, that He so represents Himself to man that he cannot fail to see and hear Him, where, in a situation which he has not brought about, in which he becomes incomprehensible to himself, man sees himself faced with the fact that he lives with God and God with him, be-

119

cause so it has pleased God. Knowledge of God takes place where divine revelation takes place, illumination of man by God, transmission of human knowledge, instruction of man by this incomparable Teacher.

We started from the point that Christian faith is a meeting. Christian faith and knowledge of Christian faith takes place at the point where the divine reason, the divine Logos, sets up His law in the region of man's understanding, to which law human, creaturely reason must accommodate itself. When that happens, man comes to knowledge; for when God sets up His law in man's thought, in his seeing and hearing and feeling, the revelation of the truth is also reached about man and his reason, the revelation of man is reached, who cannot bring about of himself what is brought about simply by God Himself.

Can God be known? Yes, God can be known, since it is actually true and real that He is knowable through Himself. When that happens, man becomes free, he becomes empowered, he becomes capable—a mystery to himself—of knowing God. Knowledge of God is a knowledge completely effected and determined from the side of its object, from the side of God. But for that very reason it is genuine knowledge; for that very reason it is in the deepest sense free knowledge. Of course it remains a relative knowledge, a knowledge imprisoned within the limits of the creaturely. Of course it is especially true here that we are carrying heavenly treasures in earthen vessels. Our concepts are not adequate to grasp this treasure. Precisely where this genuine knowledge of God takes place it will also be clear that there is no occasion for any pride. There always remains powerless man, creaturely reason within its limitations. But in this area of the creaturely, of the inadequate, it has pleased God to reveal Himself. And since man is foolish in this respect too, He will be wise; since man is petty, He will be great; since man is inadequate, God is adequate. 'Let my grace suffice for thee. For my strength is mighty in the weak' holds good also for the question of knowledge.

In the opening statement we said that Christian faith has to do with the illumination of the reason, in which men become free to live in the truth of Jesus Christ. For the understanding of Christian knowledge of faith it is essential to understand that the truth of Jesus Christ is living truth and the knowledge of it living knowledge. This does not mean that we are to revert once more to the idea that here knowledge is not basically involved at all. It is not that Christian faith is a dim sensation, an a-logical feeling, experiencing and learning. Faith is knowledge; it is related to God's Logos, and is therefore a thoroughly logical matter. The truth of Jesus Christ is also in the simplest sense a truth of facts. Its starting-point, the Resurrection of Jesus Christ from the dead, is a fact which occurred in space and time, as the New Testament describes it. The apostles were not satisfied to hold on to an inward fact; they spoke of what they saw and heard and what they touched with their hands. And the truth of Jesus Christ is also a matter of thoroughly clear and, in itself, ordered human thinking; free, precisely in its being bound. But—and the things must not be separated—what is involved is living truth. The concept of knowledge, or *scientia*, is insufficient to describe what Christian knowledge is. We must rather go back to what in the Old Testament is called wisdom, what the Greeks called *sophia* and the Latins *sapientia*, in order to grasp the knowledge of theology in its fullness. *Sapientia* is distinguished from the narrower concept of *scientia*, wisdom is distinguished from knowing, in that it not only contains knowledge in itself, but also that this concept speaks of a knowledge which is practical knowledge, embracing the entire existence of man. Wisdom is the knowledge by which we may actually and practically live; it is empiricism and it is the theory which is powerful in being directly practical, in being the knowledge which dominates our life, which is really a light upon our path. Not a light to wonder at and to observe, not a light to kindle all manner of fireworks at—not even the profoundest philosophical speculations—but the light on our road which may stand above our action and above our talk, the light on our healthy and on our sick days, in our poverty and our wealth, the light which does not only lighten when we suppose ourselves to have moments of insight, but which accompanies us even into our folly, which is not quenched when all is quenched, when the goal of our life becomes visible in death. To live by this light, by this truth, is the meaning of Christian knowledge. Christian knowledge means living in the truth of Jesus Christ. In this light we live and move and have our being (Acts 17. 28) in order that we may be of Him, and through Him and unto Him, as it says in Romans 11. 36. So Christian knowledge, at its deepest, is one with what we termed man's trust in God's Word. Never yield when they try to teach you divisions and separations in this matter. There is no genuine trust, no really tenable, victorious trust in God's Word which is not founded in His truth; and on the other hand no knowledge, no theology, no confessing and no Scripture truth which does not at once possess the stamp of this living truth. The one must always be measured and tested and confirmed by the other.

And just because as Christians we may live in the truth of Jesus Christ and therefore in the light of the knowledge of God and therefore with an illumined reason, we shall also become sure of the meaning of our own existence and of the ground and goal of all that happens. Once more a quite tremendous extension of the field of vision is indicated by this; to know this object in its truth means in truth to know no more and no less than all things, even man, oneself, the cosmos, and the world. The truth of Jesus Christ is not one truth among others; it is *the* truth, the universal truth that creates all truth as surely as it is the truth of God, the *prima veritas* which is also the *ultima veritas*. For in Jesus Christ God has created all things, He has created all of us. We exist not apart from Him, but in Him, whether we are aware of it or not; and the whole cosmos exists not apart from Him, but in Him, borne by Him, the Almighty Word. To know Him is to know all. To be touched and gripped by the Spirit in this realm means being led into all truth. If a man believes and knows God, he can no longer ask, What is the meaning of my life? But by believing he actually lives the meaning of his life, the meaning of his creatureliness, of his individuality, in the limits of his creatureliness and individuality and in the fallibility of his existence, in the sin in which he is involved and of which daily and hourly he is guilty; yet he also lives it with the aid which is daily and hourly imparted to him through God's interceding for him, in spite of him and without his deserving it. He recognises the task assigned to him in this whole, and the hope vouchsafed to him in and with this task, because of the grace by which he may live and the praise of the glory promised him, by which he is even here and now secretly surrounded in all lowliness. The believer confesses this meaning of his existence. The Christian Creed speaks of God as the ground and goal of all that exists. The ground and goal of the entire cosmos means Jesus Christ. And the unheard-of thing may and must be said, that where Christian faith exists, there also exists, through God's being trusted, inmost familiarity with the ground and goal of all that happens, of all things; there man lives, in spite of all that is said to the contrary, in the peace that passeth all understanding, and which for that very reason is the light that lightens our understanding.

[41]

BEECHER, HENRY WARD

BEECHER, HENRY WARD (1813-1887). One of the outstanding public figures of American life and a brilliantly persuasive preacher, Henry Ward Beecher was regarded, in his youth, as unusually stupid by his parents, teachers, and playmates. He decided to study navigation and become a sailor, for he felt unsuited for other occupations. A great change took place in him during his sojourn at Mount Pleasant Classical Institute, Amherst, Massachusetts; his extraordinary vitality broke through. He became active in sports, read omnivorously, and resolved to become a preacher. He subsequently continued his studies at Lane Theological Seminary in Cincinnati. Here, he revolted against Calvinism and professed independent Presbyterianism in the name of life and the beauty of nature.

Beecher was not a man of original thought; he started no new movement, but he succeeded in attracting and educating Church people, and helped them to develop the power to withstand life's tests and conflicts. He used his sermons to advocate social reforms; he was strongly opposed to slavery despite his dislike for radical abolitionists. He taught a disbelief of hell; defended evolution, and advocated that of which he was so terribly fond, the outdoor life. Despite their great success, his sermons did not satisfy him. He carefully scrutinized and adhered to the methods of Jonathan Edwards, the leader of the "Great Awakening" in New England, and those of the Apostles as they are described in the book of *Acts*. His last years were troubled by a highly publicized trial in which charges of adultery were brought against him. The jury could not agree and an ecclesiastical council acquitted him. Beecher was minister, from 1847 until his death, at Plymouth Church, Brooklyn, New York. Though often ranged on the side of unpopular causes, Beecher's powers of persuasion were such that his sermons gained nation-wide hearing and swayed popular opinion.

SOME OBSERVATIONS

IT is a shiftless trick to lie about stories and groceries, arguing with men that you have *no time,* in a new country, for nice farming, for making good fences for smooth meadows without a stump, for draining wet patches which disfigure fine fields; to raise your own frogs in your own yard; to permit, year after year, a dirty, stinking, mantled puddle to stand before your fence in the street; to plant orchards, and allow your cattle to eat the trees up, and when gnawed down, to save your money by trying to nurse the stubs into good trees, instead of getting fresh ones from the nursery; to allow an orchard to have blank spaces, where trees have died; and when the living trees begin to bear, to wake up, and put young whips in the vacant spots. It is a filthy trick to use tobacco at all; and it puts an end to all our affected squeamishness at the Chinese taste in eating rats, cats, and bird's nests. It is vile economy to lay up for remastication a half-chewed cud; to pocket a half-smoked cigar; and finally to bedrench one's self with tobacco juice; to so besmoke one's clothes that a man can be scented as far off as a whaleship can be smelt at sea. It is a vile trick to borrow a choice book; to read it with unwashed hands, that have been used in the charcoal-bin; and finally to return it daubed on every leaf with nose-blood spots, tobacco-spatter, and dirty finger-marks. It is an unthrifty trick to bring in eggs from the barn in one's coat pocket, and then to sit down upon them. It is a filthy trick to borrow of or lend for others' use a tooth-brush or a toothpick; to pick one's teeth at table with a fork or a jackknife; to put your hat upon the dinner-table among the dishes; to spit generously into the fire, or at it, while the hearth is covered with food set to warm—for sometimes a man hits what he don't aim at. It is an unmannerly trick to neglect the scraper outside the door, but to be scrupulous in cleaning your feet, after you get inside, on the carpet, rug, or andiron; to bring your drenched umbrella into the entry, where a black puddle may leave to the housewife melancholy evidence that you have been there. It is a soul-trying trick for a neat dairy-woman to see her "man" watering the horse out of her milk-bucket; or filtering horse medicine through her milk-strainer; or feeding his hogs with her water-pail; or, after barn-work, to set the well-bucket outside the curb, and wash his hands out of it.

*   *   *

There is something peculiarly impressive to me in the old New England custom of announcing a death. In a village of a few hundred inhabitants all are known each to each. There are no *strangers*. The village church, the Sabbath-school, and the district-school have been channels of inter-communication; so that one is acquainted not only with the persons, but, too often, with the affairs—domestic, social, and secular—of every dweller in the town.

A thousand die in the city every month, and there is no void apparent. The vast population speedily closes over the emptied space. The hearts that were grouped about the deceased doubtless suffer alike in the country and in the city. But, outside of the special grief, there is a moment's sadness, a dash of sympathy, and then life closes over the grief, as waters fill the void made when a bucketful is drawn out of the ocean. There goes a city funeral! Well, I wonder who it is that is journeying so quietly to his last home. He was not of my house, nor of my circle; his life was not a thread woven with mine; I did not see him before, I shall not miss him now. We did not greet at the church; we did not vote at the town meeting; we had not gone together upon sleigh-rides, skatings, huskings, fishings, trainings, or elections. Therefore it is that men of might die daily about us, and we have no sense of it, any more than we perceive it when a neighbor extinguishes his lamp.

It was upon the very day that we arrived in Woodstock, upon this broad and high hill-top, in the afternoon, as we were sitting in ransomed bliss rejoicing in the boundless hemisphere above, and in the beautiful sweep of hills feathered with woods, and cultivated fields ruffled with fences; and full, here and there, of pictures of trees, single or in rounded groups; it was as we sat thus—the children, three families of them, scattered out, racing and shouting upon the village-green before us—that the church-bell swung round merrily, as if preluding, or clearing its throat for some message. It is five o'clock: What can that bell be ringing for? Is there a meeting? Perhaps a "preparatory lecture." It stops. Then one deep stroke is given, and all is still. Every one stops. Some one is dead. Another solemn stroke goes vibrating through the crystal air, and calls scores more to the doors. Who can be dead? Another solitary peal wafts its message tremulously along the air; and that long gradually dying vibration of a country bell—never heard amid the noises of the air in a city—swelling and falling, swelling and falling; aerial waves, voices of invisible spirits communing with each other as they bear aloft the ransomed one!

But now its warning voice is given. All are listening. Ten sharp, distinct strokes, and a pause. Some one is ten years old of earth's age. No; ten more follow; twenty years is it? Ten more tell us that it is an adult. Ten more, and ten more, and twice ten again, and one final stroke, count the age of *seventy-one*. Seventy-one years! Were they long, weary, sorrowful years? Was it a venerable sire, weary of waiting for the silver cord to be loosed? Seventy-one years! Shall I see as many? And if I do, the hill-top is already turned, and I am going down upon the farther side. How long to look forward to! How short to look back upon! Age and youth look upon life from opposite ends of the telescope: It is exceedingly long; it is exceedingly short! To one who muses this, the very strokes of the bell seem to emblem life. Each is like a year, and all of them roll away as in a moment, and are gone.

*   *   *

It is plain that Mary was imbued with the spirit of the Hebrew Scriptures. Not only was the history of her people familiar to her, but her language at the annunciation shows that the poetry of the Old Testament had filled her soul. She was fitted to receive her people's history in its most romantic and spiritual aspects. They were God's peculiar people. Their history unrolled before her as a series of wonderful providences. The path glowed with divine manifestations. Miracles blossomed out of every natural law. But to her there were no "laws of nature." Such ideas had not yet been born. "The earth was the Lord's." All its phenomena were direct manifestations of his will. Clouds and storms came on errands from God. Light and darkness were the shining or the hiding of his face. Calamities were punishments; harvests were divine gifts; famines were immediate divine penalties. To us, God acts through instruments; to the Hebrew, he acted immediately by his will. "He spake, and it was done; he commanded, and it stood fast."

To such a one as Mary there would be no incredulity as to the reality of this angelic manifestation. Her only surprise would be that *she* should be chosen for a renewal of those divine interpositions in behalf of her people of which their history was so full. The very reason which would lead us to suspect a miracle in our day, gave it credibility in other days. It is simply a question of adaptation. A miracle, as a blind appeal to the moral sense, without use of the reason, was adapted to the earlier periods of human life. Its usefulness ceases when the moral sense is so developed that it can find its own way through the ministration of the reason. A miracle is a substitute for moral demonstration, and is peculiarly adapted to the early conditions of mankind.

Of all miracles, there was none more sacred, more congruous, and grateful to a Hebrew than an angelic visitation. A devout Jew, in looking back, saw angels flying thick between the heavenly throne and the throne of his fathers. The greatest events of national history had been made illustrious by their presence. Their work began with the primitive pair. They had come at evening to Abraham's tent. They had waited upon Jacob's footsteps. They had communed with Moses, with the judges, with priests and magistrates, with prophets and holy men. All the way down from the beginning of history the pious Jew saw the shining foot-steps of these heavenly messengers. Nor had the faith died out in the long interval through which their visits had been withheld. Mary could not, therefore, be surprised at the coming of angels, but only that they should come to her.

It may seem strange that Zacharias should be struck dumb for doubting the heavenly messenger, while Mary went unrebuked. But it is plain that there was a wide difference in the nature of the relative experiences. To Zacharias was promised an event external to himself, not involving his own sensibility. But to a woman's heart there can be no other announcement possible that shall so stir every feeling and sensibility of the soul as the promise and prospect of her first child. Motherhood is the very center of womanhood. The first awakening in her soul of the reality that she bears a double life—herself within herself—brings a sweet bewilderment of wonder and joy. The more sure her faith of the fact, the more tremulous must her soul become. Such an announcement can never mean to a father's what it does to a mother's heart. And it is one of the exquisite shades of subtle truth,

and of beauty as well, that the angel who rebuked Zacharias for doubt, saw nothing in the trembling hesitancy of Mary, inconsistent with a childish faith. If the heart swells with the hope of a new life in the common lot of mortals, with what profound feeling must Mary have pondered the angel's promise to her son:
He shall be great, and shall be called the son of the Highest,
And the Lord God shall give him the throne of his father
    David;
And he shall reign over the house of Jacob forever.
And of his kingdom there shall be no end.

[42]

BENDA, JULIEN

BENDA, JULIEN (1867-   ). Although Benda had retired to a solitary existence prior to the collapse of France, his life was particularly endangered during the German occupation of France because he was a Jew, a defender of democracy, and an adversary of German nationalism.

Throughout his lifetime, he has consistently opposed the main currents of French spiritual life and has fought untiringly against the cult of vagueness, subjectivism, romanticism, mystic nationalism, and the blending of other arts with music. He is a successful novelist, sensitive to poetry. He maintains the superiority of science to literature; Descartes, Kant, and Darwin to Dante and Victor Hugo; and intelligence to sensibility. He has been an ardent opponent of Henri Bergson, and, although he rejected the aesthetics of Paul Valery, he has adopted his phrase, "Thought by its very nature is without style."

Benda's works proclaim his hatred of injustice, his contempt of scepticism, and his "ideal of disinterested values," those universal ideas which are independent of historical conditions. *La Trahison des Clercs* (The Treason of the Intellectuals.) (1927) accused the intellectuals of disloyalty to those concepts which, according to Benda, are the basis of individual rights and mandatory for everyone who actively participates in a spiritual life. *Uriel's Report*, written in 1926 with cruel objectivity, is a satirical picture of humanity. *Exercises of a Man Buried Alive* (1947) violently attacks almost all French celebrities, except Paul Claudel.

129

HUMANITARIANISM

I SHOULD like to draw a distinction between humanitarianism as I mean it here—a sensitiveness to the abstract quality of what is human, to Montaigne's "whole form of human condition"—and the feeling which is usually called humanitarianism, by which is meant the love for human beings existing in the concrete. The former impulse (which would more accurately be called humanism) is the attachment to a concept. It is a pure passion of the intelligence, implying no terrestrial love. It is quite easy to conceive of a person plunging into the concept of what is human without having the least desire even to see a man. This is the form assumed by love of humanity in the great patricians of the mind like Erasmus, Malebranche, Spinoza, Goethe, who all were men, it appears, not very anxious to throw themselves into the arms of their neighbors. The second humanitarianism is a state of the heart and therefore the portion of plebeian souls. It occurs among moralists in periods when lofty intellectual discipline disappears among them and gives way to sentimental exaltation, I mean in the eighteenth century (chiefly with Diderot) and above all in the nineteenth century, with Michelet, Quinet, Proudhon, Romain Rolland, Georges Duhamel. This sentimental form of humanitarianism and forgetfulness of its conceptual form explain the unpopularity of this doctrine with so many distinguished minds, who discover two equally repulsive commonplaces in the arsenal of political ideology. One of them is "the patriotic bore" and the other "the universal embrace."

The humanitarianism which holds in honor the abstract quality of what is human, is the only one which allows us to love *all* men. Obviously, as soon as we look at men in the concrete, we inevitably find that this quality is distributed in different quantities, and we have to say with Renan: "In reality one is *more or less* a man, *more or less* the son of God . . . I see no reason why a Papuan should be immortal."

130

Modern equalitarians, by failing to understand that there can be no equality except in the abstract and that inequality is the essence of the concrete, have merely displayed the extraordinary vulgarity of their minds as well as their amazing political clumsiness.

Humanism, as I have defined it, has nothing to do with internationalism. Internationalism is a protest against national egotism, not on behalf of a spiritual passion, but on behalf of another egotism, another earthly passion. It is the impulse of a certain category of men—laborers, bankers, industrialists—who unite across frontiers in the name of private and practical interests, and who only oppose the national spirit because it thwarts them in satisfying those interests.

In comparison with such impulses, national passion appears an idealistic and disinterested impulse. In short, humanism is also something entirely different from cosmopolitanism, which is the simple desire to enjoy the advantages of all nations and all their cultures, and is generally exempt from all moral dogmatism.

[43]

BENTHAM, JEREMY

BENTHAM, JEREMY (1748-1832). Noted as an English social philosopher and sympathizer of the American and French revolutions, Bentham's ideas paralleled those of the American founding fathers more closely than those of the French Jacobins. His treatise, *Fragment on Government*, was revised and republished in 1789, the year of the French Revolution, as *An Introduction to the Principles of Morals and Legislation.*

Bentham defined the function of good government as the effort to promote the greatest happiness of the greatest number of citizens and to effect harmony between public and private interests. He declared that the American government was the only good government because it upheld these principles. According to Bentham, happiness is identical with pleasure, and serves as the underlying motivation of human behavior; thus happiness can be the only criterion of morals and legislation. Originally, Bentham called this criterion Utility, but by 1822 he felt that the word did not adequately crystallize his ideas. However, James Mill, a disciple of Bentham, revived the term, Utilitarianism, shortly afterward and henceforth Bentham has been known as the "father of the Utilitarian school."

Bentham had been nicknamed "philosopher" at the age of five.

THE FOUR SOURCES OF PLEASURE AND PAIN

THE happiness of the individuals, of whom a community is composed, that is their pleasures and their security, is the end and the sole end which the legislator ought to have in view: the sole standard, in conformity to which each individual ought, as far as depends upon the legislator, to be *made* to fashion his behaviour. But whether it be this or any thing else that is to be *done,* there is nothing by which a man can ultimately be *made* to do it, but either pain or pleasure. Having taken a general view of these two grand objects (*viz.* pleasure, and what comes to the same thing, immunity from pain) in the character of *final* causes; it will be necessary to take a view of pleasure and pain itself, in the character of efficient causes or means.

There are four distinguishable sources from which pleasure and pain are in use to flow: considered separately, they may be termed the *physical,* the *political,* the *moral,* and the *religious*: and inasmuch as the pleasures and pains belonging to each of them are capable of giving a binding force to any law or rule of conduct, they may all of them be termed *sanctions.*

If it be in the present life, and from the ordinary course of nature, not purposely modified by the interposition of the will of any human being, nor by any extraordinary interposition of any superior invisible being, that the pleasure or the pain takes place or is expected, it may be said to issue from or to belong to the *physical sanction.*

If at the hands of a *particular* person or set of persons in the community, who under names correspondent to that of *judge,* are chosen for the particular purpose of dispensing it, according to the will of the sovereign or supreme ruling power in the state, it may be said to issue from the *political sanction*.

If at the hands of such *chance* persons in the community, as the party in question may happen in the course of his life to have concerns with, according to each man's spontaneous disposition, and not according to any settled or concerted rule, it may be said to issue from the *moral* or *popular sanction*.

If from the immediate hand of a superior invisible being, either in the present life, or in a future, it may be said to issue from the *religious sanction*.

Pleasures or pains which may be expected to issue from the *physical, political,* or *moral* sanctions, must all of them be experienced, if ever, in the *present* life: those which may be expected to issue from the *religious* sanction, may be expected to be experienced either in the *present* life or in a *future*.

·   ·   ·   ·   ·   ·   ·   ·   ·   ·

Of these four sanctions the physical is altogether, we may observe, the ground-work of the political and the moral: so is it also of the religious, in as far as the latter bears relation to the present life. It is included in each of those other three. This may operate in any case, (that is, any of the pains or pleasures belonging to it may operate) independently of *them*: none of *them* can operate but by means of this. In a word, the powers of nature may operate of themselves; but neither the magistrate, nor men at large, *can* operate, nor is God in the case in question *supposed* to operate, but through the powers of nature.

[44]

BERACHYAH

BERACHYAH (c. 12th or 13th century). The literary fame of Berachyah is chiefly founded upon his *Mishle Shualim* (Fox Fables). Some of these were of his own invention; others were derived from the fables of Aesop, the Talmud, and the Hindus, but even in the adaptation of plots to his own Hebrew style, he displayed poetic originality and narrative talents. The best-known of his philosophical works, encyclopedic in quality, is *Sefer Hahibbur* (The Book of Compilation). Here, he developed the ideas of Saadia, Bahya Ibn Pakuda, and Solomon Ibn Gabirol. He was versed in the eastern and western branches of Jewish philosophy, and was well acquainted with medieval French and English literature.

The personal life of Berachyah is solely conjecture. He was called Berachyah Ben Natronai Hanakdan. His father's name indicates descent from the Jewish scholars of Babylonia, which may help to explain Berachyah's knowledge of Hindu stories. His surname means "punctuator," probably an allusion to his profession of scribe or grammarian. There is no agreement as to the time, place, or country in which he lived. Some of his biographers assume that he wrote during the twelfth century; others during the thirteenth century. Some maintain that he lived in Provence; others in Northern France, and still others in England. It is not improbable that he was an itinerant teacher, scholar, and writer.

THE COMPENDIUM

ON THE SOURCES OF KNOWLEDGE

THERE are three distinct forms of knowledge. First, the knowledge resulting from observation, *i.e.*, knowledge gained through the senses, which are the primary sources of feeling known as the five senses, viz: sight, hearing, smell, taste, and touch. Secondly the knowledge of the intellect that is, the instrument of sense, and without the association of the emotions; for instance, determining in our mind the beauty of truth and the abhorring of falsehood, without having before us any presentative images. Thirdly, intuitive knowledge, which a man is bound to believe, and the perception of which is forced upon him, his consciousness being compelled to accept it as true; for if he did not accept it as true, he would, as a natural consequence, have to deny the existence of mind altogether, and to make out knowledge to be a liar.

ON THE CLASSIFICATION OF KNOWLEDGE

All knowledge may be divided into three parts: First, the science of created matter, *i.e.*, the science of the nature of all bodies, and their accidental properties. This is required for the purposes of this world, and it is the lowest form of knowledge. Midway stands the science, which we might term the "auxiliary science," such as the science of numbers and their computations, the science of astronomy, and the science of music. These two departments of knowledge form the basis of all the secrets of the world and of the several advantages to be derived from them; inasmuch as they enlighten us with regard to the various handicrafts, and all forms of tactics, which are necessary for the development of the human body, and for worldly acquisitions. The third science is that of theology, viz: the science of the knowledge of God, and the knowledge of His Law and Commandments, such as may be grasped by the soul and the intellect. Now, every subdivision of this science, however diverse in various interests, becomes so many introductions, afforded us by God, to become acquainted with the Torah. It is the highest form of knowledge; we are bound to cultivate it for the purpose of attaining a proper understanding of our Law, and not for the purpose of attaining worldly advantages thereby.

[45]

BERDYAEV, NICHOLAS

BERDYAEV, NICHOLAS (1874-1948). Berdyaev was educated in the military school of the Tsarist cadet corps. Later he became a Marxist, was arrested in 1898 for his socialist activities, and banished to the north of Russia for three years. Around 1905 he reverted to the Christian faith, but was accused, in 1914, of insulting the Holy Synod. His trial in 1917 was ended by the Russian Revolution. The Bolshevist government had him arrested in 1920 and then again in 1922. He was expelled from the Soviet Union because of his persistent support of faithful Christians. His remaining years were spent in France.

He regarded himself as the prophet of a new world about to be born; the eventide of history whose means of research, adequate as they might appear for the sun-lit day of rationalism, would be completely inadequate for the new era. He predicted a "New Middle Ages" which would spell the end of humanism, individualism, for-

135

mal liberalism, nationalism, socialism, and communism. It would be the beginning of a new religious collectivity, which would not be ruled by an ecclesiastic hierarchy, but would imbue knowledge, morality, art, and economic and political institutions with a religious spirit free from external constraint. Berdyaev's philosophy conceives of man as the conjunction of the natural and divine world. Man, created by a creator, must necessarily continue the creative process in order to prove the creative character of his cognitive faculties and use them for the perfection of true civilization. Berdyaev arrived at this point of view after considerable changes in his personal philosophy.

ON SOCIALISM

Socialism cannot be fought with "bourgeois ideas"; it is useless to set over against it the middle-class, democratic, capitalist society of the nineteenth and twentieth centuries. It is precisely this bourgeois society that has bred Socialism and involved us in it. Socialism is flesh of the flesh and blood of the blood of Capitalism. They both belong to the same world; they are animated by a common spirit—or rather, by a common negation of spirit. Socialism has inherited the middle-class atheism of the capitalist nineteenth-century, which was, indeed, the most atheistical society known to history. It falsified the relation between man and man, and between man and physical nature. Its political economy corrupted the hierarchical organization of society and gave birth to economic materialism, which is an exact reflection of the actual state of that nineteenth-century civilization. The life of the spirit became almost less than an accident, a speculative adaptation to less high things. The worship of Mammon instead of God is a characteristic of Socialism as well as of Capitalism. Socialism is no longer an utopia or a dream: it is an objective threat, and a warning to Christians to show them unmistakably that they have not fulfilled the word of Christ, that they have in effect apostatized. A basis is sometimes assigned to Capitalism by the statement that human nature is sinful and that sin cannot be got rid of by force, while the essence of Socialism is in the supposition that this nature is entirely good. But it is forgotten that the moment of history can come when the evil in human nature, namely, the sin in which it is involved, will have taken on a new shape. It is the sinful part of our nature that begets Socialism. Capitalism, considered spiritually and morally, arose because human nature is prone to evil. But Socialism has arisen for exactly the same reason. Apostasy from the Christian faith, abandonment of spiritual principles and disregard of the spiritual ends of life, must of necessity lead first to the stage called Capitalism and then to the stage called Socialism. It follows clearly enough that we must begin to make our Christianity effectively real by a return to the life of the spirit, that a normal hierarchical harmony of life must be recovered, that that which is economic must be subordinated to that which is spiritual, that politics must be again confined within their proper limits.

[46]

BERGSON, HENRI

BERGSON, HENRI (1859-1941). When Bergson was asked how a philosopher should state his ideas, his reply was, "There are general problems which interest everybody and must be dealt with in language comprehensible to everybody. The solutions to these problems are frequently subordinated to those questions which interest only scholars. These may be dealt with in technical terms." While he admitted the occasional use of professional terminology, Bergson always wrote with a vocabulary easily comprehensible, inspiring, and exciting to philosophical laymen. When he used or coined technical terms, he was capable of making them popular. His mastery of language and subject matter extended his influence far beyond the realm of philosophy into such areas as the history of poetry, the social sciences, and religion. He also influenced the opinions of many contemporary philosophers.

According to Bergson, philosophy is the conscientious and reflective return to the immediate data of intuition. He classified reason as an impersonal faculty, emphasizing that every philosopher consciously proceeds from a chosen point of view. He regarded the philosopher as a man who faced the essentials of thought in order to discover the conditions for the totality of knowledge. He advocated the concept of duration as contrasted with the mechanistic concept of time. From duration, immediately felt in mental life, he

137

proceeded to the ideas of the vital impetus and creative evolution which manifest themselves in organic nature as well as in spiritual life, social processes, and individual actions. He was one of the few modern thinkers convinced of the unlimited progress of humanity.

His international fame was so great that after the collapse of France in 1940, the Vichy government offered him exemption from the Jewish laws, patterned after the Nuremberg Laws. Bergson declined the offer and resigned his professorship at the Collège de France.

ANIMAL AND HUMAN CONSCIOUSNESS

RADICAL is the difference between animal consciousness, even the most intelligent, and human consciousness. For consciousness corresponds exactly to the living being's power of choice; it is coextensive with the fringe of possible action that surrounds the real action: consciousness is synonymous with invention and with freedom. Now, in the animal, invention is never anything but a variation on the theme of routine. Shut up in the habits of the species, it succeeds, no doubt, in enlarging them by its individual initiative; but it escapes automatism only for an instant, for just the time to create a new automatism. The gates of its prison close as soon as they are opened; by pulling at its chain it succeeds only in stretching it. With man, consciousness breaks the chain. In man, and in man alone, it sets itself free. The whole history of life until man has been that of the effort of consciousness to raise matter, and of the more or less complete overwhelming of consciousness by the matter which has fallen back on it. The enterprise was paradoxical, if, indeed, we may speak here otherwise than by metaphor of enterprise and of effort. It was to create with matter, which is necessity itself, an instrument of freedom, to make a machine which should triumph over mechanism, and to use the determinism of nature to pass through the meshes of the net which this very determinism had spread. But, everywhere except in man, consciousness has let itself be caught in the net whose meshes it tried to pass through: it has remained the captive of the mechanisms it has set up. Automatism, which it tries to draw in the direction of freedom, winds about it and drags it down.

138

It has not the power to escape, because the energy it has provided for acts is almost all employed in maintaining the infinitely subtle and essentially unstable equilibrium into which it has brought matter. But man not only maintains his machine, he succeeds in using it as he pleases. Doubtless he owes this to the superiority of his brain, which enables him to build an unlimited number of motor mechanisms, to oppose new habits to the old ones unceasingly, and by dividing automatism against itself, to rule it. He owes it to his language, which furnishes consciousness with an immaterial body in which to incarnate itself and thus exempts itself from dwelling exclusively on material bodies, whose flux would soon drag it along and finally swallow it up. He owes it to social life, which stores and preserves efforts as language stores thought, fixes thereby a mean level to which individuals must raise themselves at the outset, and by this initial stimulation prevents the average man from slumbering and drives the superior man to mount still higher. But our brain, our society, and our language are only the external and various signs of one and the same internal superiority. They tell, each after its manner, the unique exceptional success which life has won at a given moment of its evolution. They express the difference of kind, and not only of degree, which separates man from the rest of the animal world. They let us guess that, while at the end of the vast spring-board from which life has taken its leap, all the others have stepped down, finding the cord stretched too high, man alone has cleared the obstacle.

It is in this quiet special sense that man is the "term" and the "end" of evolution. Life, we have said, transcends finality as it transcends the other categories. It is essentially a current sent through matter, drawing from it what it can. There has not, therefore, properly speaking, been any project or plan. On the other hand, it is abundantly evident that the rest of nature is not for the sake of man: we struggle like other species, we have struggled against other species. Moreover, if the evolution of life had encountered other accidents in its course, if thereby, the current of life had been otherwise divided, we should have been, physically and morally, far different from what we are. For these various reasons it would be wrong to regard humanity, such as we have it before our eyes, as prefigured in the evolutionary movement. It cannot even be said to be the outcome of the world of evolution, for evolution has been accomplished on several divergent lines, and while the human species is at the end of one of them, other lines have been followed with other species at their end. It is in quite a different sense that we hold humanity to be the ground of evolution.

From our point of view, life appears in its entirety as an immense wave which, starting from a centre, spreads outwards, and which on almost the whole of its circumference is stopped and converted into oscillation: at one single point the obstacle has been forced, the impulsion has passed freely. It is this freedom that the human form registers. Everywhere but in man, consciousness has had to come to a stand; in man alone it has kept on its way. Man, then, continues the vital movement indefinitely, although he does not draw along with him all that life carries in itself. On other lines of evolution there have travelled other tendencies which life implied, and of which, since everything interpenetrates, man has, doubtless, kept something, but of which he has kept only very little. *It is as if a vague and formless being, whom we may call, as we will,* man *or* superman, *had sought to realize himself, and had succeeded only by abandoning a part of himself on the way*. The losses are represented by the rest of the animal world, and even by the vegetable world, at least in what these have that is positive and above the accidents of evolution.

From this point of view, the discordances of which nature offers us the spectacle are singularly weakened. The organized world as a whole becomes as the soil on which was to grow either man himself or a being who morally must resemble him. The animals, however distant they may be from our species, however hostile to it, have none the less been useful traveling companions, on whom consciousness has unloaded whatever encumbrances it was dragging along, and who have enabled it to rise, in man, to heights from which it sees an unlimited horizon open again before it.

It is true that it has not only abandoned cumbersome baggage on the way; it has also had to give up valuable goods. Consciousness, in man is pre-eminently intellect. It might have been, it ought, so it seems, to have been also intuition. Intuition and intellect represent two opposite directions of the work of consciousness: intuition goes in the very direction of life, intellect goes in the inverse direction, and thus finds itself naturally in accordance with the movement of matter. A complete and perfect humanity would be that in which these two forms of conscious activity should attain their full development. And, between this humanity and ours, we may conceive any number of possible stages, corresponding to all the degrees imaginable of intelligence and of intuition. In this lies the part of contingency in the mental structure of our species. A different evolution might have led to a humanity either more intellectual still or more intuitive. In the humanity of which we are a part, intuition is, in fact, almost completely sacrificed to intellect. It seems that to conquer matter, and to reconquer its own self, consciousness has had to exhaust the best part of its power. This conquest, in the particular conditions in which it has been accomplished, has required that consciousness should adapt itself to the habits of matter and concentrate all its attention on them, in fact determine itself more especially as intellect. Intuition is there, however, but vague and above all discontinuous. It is a lamp almost extinguished, which only glimmers now and then, for a few moments at most. But it glimmers wherever a vital interest is at stake. On our personality, on our liberty, on the place we occupy in the whole of nature, on our origin and perhaps also on our destiny, it throws a light feeble and vacillating, but which none the less pierces the darkness of the night in which the intellect leaves us.

These fleeting intuitions, which light up their object

141

only at distant intervals, philosophy ought to seize, first to sustain them, then to expand them and so unite them together. The more it advances in this work, the more will it perceive that intuition is mind itself, and, in a certain sense, life itself: the intellect has been cut out of it by a process resembling that which has generated matter. Thus is revealed the unity of the spiritual life. We recognize it only when we place ourselves in intuition in order to go from intuition to the intellect, for from the intellect we shall never pass to intuition.

Philosophy introduces us thus into the spiritual life. And it shows us at the same time the relation of the life of the spirit to that of the body. The great error of the doctrines on the spirit has been the idea that by isolating the spiritual life from all the rest, by suspending it in space as high as possible above the earth, they were placing it beyond attack, as if they were not thereby simply exposing it to be taken as an effect of mirage! Certainly they are right to listen to conscience when conscience affirms human freedom; but the intellect is there, which says that the cause determines its effect, that like conditions like, that all is repeated and that all is given. They are right to believe in the absolute reality of the person and in his independence toward matter; but science is there, which shows the interdependence of conscious life and cerebral activity. They are right to attribute to man a privileged place in nature, to hold that the distance is infinite between the animal and the man; but the history of life is there, which makes us witness the genesis of species by gradual transformation, and seems thus to reintegrate man in animality. When a strong instinct assures the probability of personal survival, they are right not to close their ears to its voice; but if there exist "souls" capable of an independent life, whence do they come? When, how and why do they enter into this body which we see arise, quite naturally, from a mixed cell derived from the bodies of its two parents? All these questions will remain unanswered, a philosophy of intuition will be a negation of science, will be sooner or later swept away by science, if it does not resolve to see the life of the body just where it really is, on the road that leads to the life of the spirit. But it will then no longer have to do with definite living beings. Life as a whole, from the initial impulsion that thrust it into the world, will appear as a wave which rises, and which is opposed by the descending movement of matter. On the greater part of its surface, at different heights, the current is converted by matter into a vortex. At one point alone it passes freely, dragging with it the obstacle which will weigh on its progress but will not stop it. At this point is humanity; it is our privileged situation. On the other hand, this rising wave is consciousness, and, like all consciousness, it includes potentialities without number which interpenetrate and to which consequently neither the category of unity nor that of multiplicity is appropriate, made as they both are for inert matter. The matter that it bears along with it, and in the interstices of which it inserts itself, alone can divide it into distinct individualities. On flows the current, running through human generations, subdividing itself into individuals. This subdivision was vaguely indicated in it, but could not have been made clear without matter. Thus souls are continually being created, which, nevertheless in a certain sense pre-existed. They are nothing else than the little rills into which the great river of life divides itself, flowing through the body of humanity. The movement of the stream is distinct from the river bed, although it must adopt its winding course. Consciousness is distinct from the organism it animates, although it must undergo its vicissitudes. As the possible actions which a state of consciousness indicates are at every instant beginning to be carried out in the nervous centres, the brain underlies at every instant the motor indications of the state of consciousness; but the interdependency of consciousness and brain is limited to this; the destiny of consciousness is not bound up on that account with the destiny of cerebral matter. Finally, consciousness is essentially free; it is freedom itself; but it cannot pass through matter without settling on it, without adapting itself to it: this adaptation is what we call intellectuality; and the intellect, turning itself back toward active, that is to say free, consciousness, naturally makes it enter into the conceptual forms into which it is accustomed to see matter fit. It will therefore always perceive freedom in the form of necessity; it will always neglect the part of novelty or of creation inherent in the free act; it will always substitute for action itself an imitation artificial, approximative, obtained by compounding the old with the old and the same with the same. Thus, to the eyes of a philosophy that attempts to reabsorb intellect in intuition many difficulties vanish or become light. But such a doctrine does not only facilitate speculation; it gives us also more power to act and to live. For, with it, we feel ourselves no longer isolated in humanity, humanity no longer seems isolated in the nature that it dominates. As the smallest grain of dust is bound up with our entire solar system, drawn along with it in that undivided movement of descent which is materiality itself, so all organized beings, from the humblest to the highest, from the first origins of life to the time in which we are, and in all places as in all times, do but evidence a single impulsion, the inverse of the movement of matter, and in itself indivisible. All the living hold together, and all yield to the same tremendous push. The animal takes its stand on the plant, man bestrides animality, and the whole of humanity, in space and in time, is one immense army galloping beside and before and behind each of us in an overwhelming charge able to beat down every resistance and clear the most formidable obstacles, perhaps even death.

[47]

BERKELEY, GEORGE

BERKELEY, GEORGE (1685-1753). A keen thinker and an excellent writer, unafraid of attacking the commonplace, Berkeley's literary style persuaded many antagonistic readers. He was a champion of idealism, or rather of theistic immaterialism. His main purpose was to make evident the existence of God, and to prove that God is the true cause of all things. Proceeding from Locke's examination of the nature and range of human knowledge, Berkeley stressed the distinction between ideas and the mind itself. He conceived of the latter as an active being, distinct from the passivity of its content, and concluded that matter does not exist, that all reality is mental, and that nature is a manifestation of God. The development of his thinking shows the constant influence of Malebranche rather than Plato. In Berkeley's last philosophical works, he stated that the universe assumes a symbolic character and function. This thesis attracted the interest of Thomas de Quincey, William Blake, and Samuel Taylor Coleridge. His most important philosophical works were *A New Theory of Vision* (1709), *The Principles of Human Knowledge* (1710), and *The Dialogues of Hylas and Philonous* (1713).

Berkeley was born in Ireland. He was a militant apologist for the Anglican Church and subsequently became the Bishop of Cloyne. In 1728, he came to America and resided in Rhode Island for three years. During this period, he helped found the University of Pennsylvania, contributed land and a collection of books to Yale University, and wrote verse in praise of America. His poem, "Verses on . . . America" is chiefly remembered for the line: "westward the course of empire takes its way."

OBJECTS OF HUMAN KNOWLEDGE

1. IT is evident to any one who takes a survey of the *objects of human knowledge,* that they are either *ideas* actually imprinted on the senses; or else such as are perceived by attending to the passions and operations of the mind; or lastly, *ideas* formed by help of memory and imagination—either compounding, dividing, or barely representing those originally perceived in the aforesaid ways. By sight I have the ideas of light and colors, with their several degrees and variations. By touch I perceive hard and soft, heat and cold, motion and resistance, and of all these more and less either as to quantity or degree. Smelling furnishes me with odors; the palate with tastes; and hearing conveys sounds to the mind in all their variety of tone and composition. And as several of these are observed to accompany each other, they come to be marked by one name, and so to be reputed as one thing. Thus, for example, a certain color, taste, smell, figure and consistence having being observed to go together, are accounted one distinct thing, signified by the name *apple;* other collections of

ideas constitute a stone, a tree, a book, and the like sensible things; which as they are pleasing or disagreeable excite the passions of love, hatred, joy, grief, and so forth.

2. But, besides all that endless variety of ideas or objects of knowledge, there is likewise something which knows or perceives them, and exercises divers operations, as willing, imagining, remembering, about them. This perceiving, active being is what I call *mind, spirit, soul,* or *myself.* By which words I do not denote any one of my ideas, but a thing entirely distinct from them, wherein they exist, or, which is the same thing, whereby they are perceived—for the existence of an idea consists in being perceived.

3. That neither our thoughts, nor passions, nor ideas formed by the imagination, exist without the mind, is what everybody will allow. And to me it is no less evident that the various sensations, or ideas imprinted on the sense, however blended or combined together (that is, whatever objects they compose), cannot exist otherwise than in a mind perceiving them.—I think an intuitive knowledge may be obtained of this by any one that shall attend to what is meant by the term *exist,* when applied to sensible things. The table I write on I say exists, that is, I see and feel it; and if I were out of my study I should say it existed—meaning thereby that if I was in my study I might perceive it, or that some other spirit actually does perceive it. There was an odor, that is, it was smelt; there was a sound, that is, it was heard; a color or figure, and it was perceived by sight or touch. This is all that I can understand by these and the like expressions. For as to what is said of the absolute existence of unthinking things without any relation to their being perceived, that is to me perfectly unintelligible. Their *esse* is *percipi,* nor is it possible they should have any existence out of the minds or thinking things which perceive them.

4. It is indeed an opinion strangely prevailing amongst men, that houses, mountains, rivers, and in a word all sensible objects, have an existence, natural or real, distinct from their being perceived by the understanding. But, with how

146

great an assurance and acquiescence soever this principle may be entertained in the world, yet whoever shall find in his heart to call it in question may, if I mistake not, perceive it to involve a manifest contradiction. For, what are the forementioned objects but the things we perceive by sense? and what do we perceive besides our own ideas of sensations? and is it not plainly repugnant that any one of these, or any combination of them, should exist unperceived?

5. If we thoroughly examine this tenet, it will, perhaps, be found at bottom to depend on the doctrine of *abstract ideas*. For can there be a nicer strain of abstraction than to distinguish the existence of sensible objects from their being perceived, so as to conceive them existing unperceived? Light and colors, heat and cold, extension and figures—in a word the things we see and feel—what are they but so many sensations, notions, ideas, or impressions on the sense? and is it possible to separate, even in thought, any of these from perception? For my part, I might as easily divide a thing from itself. I may, indeed, divide in my thoughts, or conceive apart from each other, those things which, perhaps, I never perceived by sense so divided. Thus, I imagine the trunk of a human body without the limbs, or conceive the smell of a rose without thinking on the rose itself. So far, I will not deny, I can abstract—if that may properly be called *abstraction* which extends only to the conceiving separately such objects as it is possible may really exist or be actually perceived asunder. But my conceiving or imagining power does not extend beyond the possibility of real existence or perception. Hence, as it is impossible for me to see or feel anything without an actual sensation of that thing, so it is impossible for me to conceive in my thoughts any sensible thing or object distinct from the sensation or perception of it.

6. Some truths there are so near and obvious to the mind that a man need only open his eyes to see them. Such I take this important one to be, viz., that all the choir of heaven and furniture of the earth, in a word all those bodies which compose the mighty frame of the world, have not any sub-

sistence without a mind, that their *being* is to be perceived or known; that consequently so long as they are not actually perceived by me, or do not exist in my mind or that of any other created spirit, they must either have no existence at all, or else subsist in the mind of some Eternal Spirit—is being perfectly unintelligible, and involving all the absurdity of abstraction, to attribute to any single part of them an existence independent of a spirit. To be convinced of which, the reader need only reflect, and try to separate in his own thoughts the *being* of a sensible thing from its *being perceived*.

7. From what has been said it is evident there is not any other Substance than *Spirit*, or that which perceives. But, for the fuller demonstration of this point, let it be considered the sensible qualities are color, figure, motion, smell, taste, &c., i.e. the ideas perceived by sense. Now, for an idea to exist in an unperceiving thing is a manifest contradiction, for to have an idea is all one as to perceive; that therefore wherein color, figure, &c. exist must perceive them; hence it is clear there can be no unthinking substance or *substratum* of those ideas.

8. But, say you, though the ideas themselves do not exist without the mind, yet there may be things like them, whereof they are copies or resemblances, which things exist without the mind in an unthinking substance. I answer, an idea can be like nothing but an idea; a color or figure can be like nothing but another color or figure. If we look but never so little into our own thoughts, we shall find it impossible for us to conceive likeness except only between our ideas. Again, I ask whether those supposed *originals* or external things, of which our ideas are the pictures or representations, be themselves perceivable or no? If they are, then *they* are ideas and we have gained our point; but if you say they are not, I appeal to any one whether it be sense to assert a color is like something which is invisible; hard or soft, like something which is intangible; and so of the rest.

9. Some there are who make a distinction betwixt *pri-*

mary and *secondary* qualities. By the former they mean extension, figure, motion, rest, solidity or impenetrability, and number; by the latter they denote all other sensible qualities, as colors, sounds, tastes, and so forth. The ideas we have of these they acknowledge not to be the resemblances of anything existing without the mind, or unperceived, but they will have our ideas of the primary qualities to be patterns or images of things which exist without the mind, in an unthinking substance which they call *Matter*. By Matter, therefore, we are to understand an inert, senseless substance, in which extension, figure, and motion do actually subsist. But it is evident, from what we have already shewn, that extension, figure, and motion are only ideas existing in the mind, and that an idea can be like nothing but another idea, and that consequently neither they nor their archetypes can exist in an unperceiving substance. Hence, it is plain that the very notion of what is called *Matter* or *corporeal substance,* involves a contradiction in it.

10. They who assert that figure, motion, and the rest of the primary or original qualities do exist without the mind in unthinking substances, do at the same time acknowledge that colors, sounds, heat, cold, and such like secondary qualities, do not—which they tell us are sensations existing in the mind alone, that depend on and are occasioned by the different size, texture, and motion of the minute particles of matter. This they take for an undoubted truth, which they can demonstrate beyond all exception. Now, if it be certain that those original qualities are inseparably united with the other sensible qualities, and not, even in thought, capable of being abstracted from them, it plainly follows that they exist only in the mind. But I desire any one to reflect and try whether he can, by any abstraction of thought, conceive the extension and motion of a body without all other sensible qualities. For my own part, I see evidently that it is not in my power to frame an idea of a body extended and moving, but I must withal give it some color or other sensible quality which is acknowledged to exist only in the mind. In short, extension,

149

figure, and motion, abstracted from all other qualities, are inconceivable. Where therefore the other sensible qualities are, there must these be also, to wit, in the mind and nowhere else.

11. Again, *great* and *small, swift* and *slow,* are allowed to exist nowhere without the mind, being entirely relative, and changing as the frame or position of the organs of sense varies. The extension therefore which exists without the mind is neither great nor small, the motion neither swift nor slow, that is, they are nothing at all. But, say you, they are extension in general, and motion in general: thus we see how much the tenet of extended movable substances existing without the mind depends on the strange doctrines of *abstract ideas.* And here I cannot but remark how neatly the vague and indeterminate description of Matter or corporeal substance, which the modern philosophers are run into by their own principles, resembles that antiquated and so much ridiculed notion of *material prima,* to be met with in Aristotle and his followers. Without extension solidity cannot be conceived; since therefore it has been shewn that extension exists not in an unthinking substance, the same must also be true of solidity.

12. That *number* is entirely the creature of the mind, even though the other qualities be allowed to exist without, will be evident to whoever considers that the same thing bears a different denomination of number as the mind views it with different respects. Thus, the same extension is one, or three, or thirty-six, according as the mind considers it with reference to a yard, a foot, or an inch. Number is so visibly relative, and dependent on men's understanding, that it is strange to think how any one should give it an absolute existence without the mind. We say one book, one page, one line, &c.; all these are equally units, though some contain several of the others. And in each instance, it is plain, the unit relates to some particular combination of ideas arbitrarily put together by the mind.

13. Unity I know some will have to be a simple or uncompounded idea, accompanying all other ideas into the

mind. That I have any such idea answering the word *unity* I do not find; and if I had, methinks I could not miss finding it: on the contrary, it should be the most familiar to my understanding, since it is said to accompany all other ideas, and to be perceived by all the ways of sensation and reflexion. To say no more, it is an *abstract idea.*

14. I shall farther add, that, after the same manner as modern philosophers prove certain sensible qualities to have no existence in Matter, or without the mind, the same thing may be likewise proved of all other sensible qualities whatsoever. Thus, for instance, it is said that heat and cold are affections only of the mind, and not at all patterns of real beings, existing in the corporeal substances which excite them, for that the same body which appears cold to one hand seems warm to another. Now, why may we not well argue that figure and extension are not patterns or resemblances of qualities existing in Matter, because to the same eye at different stations, or eyes of a different texture at the same station, they appear various, and cannot therefore be the images of anything settled and determinate without the mind? Again, it is proved that sweetness is not really in the sapid thing, because the thing remaining unaltered the sweetness is changed into bitter, as in case of a fever or otherwise vitiated palate. Is it not as reasonable to say that motion is not without the mind, since if the succession of ideas in the mind become swifter, the motion, it is acknowledged, shall appear slower without any alternation in any external object?

15. In short, let any one consider those arguments which are thought manifestly to prove that colors and taste exist only in the mind, and he shall find they may with equal force be brought to prove the same thing of extension, figure, and motion. Though it must be confessed this method of arguing does not so much prove that there is no extension or color in an outward object, as that we do not know by sense which is the true extension or color of the object. But the arguments foregoing plainly shew it to be impossible that any color or extension at all, or other sensible quality whatsoever, should

exist in an unthinking subject without the mind, or in truth, that there should be any such thing as an outward object.
[48]

BERNARD OF CLAIRVAUX, SAINT

BERNARD OF CLAIRVAUX, SAINT (1091-1153). "The visionary of the century" was the way Bernard characterized himself, for he felt that he had been selected by God to guide Christianity along the right paths. He sincerely tried to lead the life of a saint, although he was cognizant of those temptations that led men astray. An objective observer, John of Salisbury, noticed that he often lost his temper and behaved unjustly, and Bishop Otto of Freising, a pious church member, accused him of jealousy and habitual weaknesses. Bernard asserted that his inner life was based on the stages of the ascent of his soul toward God, and upon supernatural grace. His book *De Gradibus Humilitatis et Superbiae* (published c. 1121) established him as the founder of Christian mysticism of the Middle Ages. Here, he condemned the acquisition of knowledge for merely the sake of knowledge. To him, knowledge is only justified when it promotes the purification of the soul and leads it toward union with God. Humility is the basic condition for this union, and it, in turn, engenders love. He stated that there are twelve degrees of humility— the highest constitutes the cognition of truth, and this is identical with union with God. This stage is psychologically characterized as the extinction of all sensitive life, but it does not remove the essential difference between man, a finite being, and God. With this reservation, Bernard's philosophy separates him from the monism of later mystics.

Bernard excelled as an ecclesiastical ruler, as the organizer of a monastic order, as an irresistibly persuasive orator and an experienced administrator. As abbot of the monastery at Clairvaux, he was incapable of imposing his will on popes, kings, and emperors, but his ascendency over the masses was unfailing. However, shortly before his death, the terrible disasters of the Second Crusade took place. Because he had agitated for this crusade with all his power, its failure aroused doubt and opposition. His abhorrence of knowledge for the sake of knowledge made him a grim adversary of Abailard and Gilbert de la Porrée. He succeeded in persecuting the former, but was defeated in his controversy with the latter. Bernard wrote many sermons, epistles, and hymns.

152

SOME EXCLAMATIONS

BERNARD'S APPEAL

I AM no longer able to veil my grief, to suppress my anxiety, to dissemble my sorrow. Therefore, contrary to the order of justice, I who have been wounded am constrained to recall him who hath wounded me; I, the despised, must seek after him who hath despised me; after suffering injury, I must offer satisfaction to him from whom the injury has come; I must, in a word, entreat him who ought rather to entreat me. But grief does not deliberate, it knows no shame, it does not consult reason, it does not fear any lowering of dignity, does not conform itself to rule, does not submit itself to sound judgment; it ignores method and rule; the mind is wholly and only occupied with this: to seek to be rid of what it pains it to have, or to gain what it grieves it to want. I am wretched because I miss thee, because I do not see thee, because I live without thee, for whom to die would be to me life, to live without whom is to die! Only come back, and all will be peace. Return, and I shall be at rest. Return, I say: return! and I shall joyfully sing, "He that was dead is alive again; he was lost, and is found." No doubt it may have been my fault that you departed. I must have appeared severe to so delicate a youth, and in my own hardness have treated thy tenderness too harshly. What I say, my son, I do not say to confound thee, but to admonish my most dear boy; for though thou mayest have many teachers in Christ, thou hast not many fathers. If thou wilt permit me to say so, I myself have brought thee forth into the life of religion, by instruction and example. How can it please thee that another should glory in thee who has in no way labored for thee?

Lectures on Bernard, R. S. Storr.

ST. BERNARD'S HYMN

Jesu, the very thought of thee
  With sweetness fills the breast;

But sweeter far Thy face to see
    And in Thy presence rest.
No voice can sing, no heart can frame,
    Nor can the memory find,
A sweeter sound than Jesus' name,
    The Saviour of mankind.
O hope of every contrite heart,
    O joy of all the meek,
To those who fall how kind Thou art!
    How good to those who seek!
But what to those who find? Ah this
    Nor tongue nor pen can show;
The love of Jesus, what it is
    None but His lov'd ones know.
Jesu our only joy be Thou,
    As Thou our prize wilt be
In Thee be all our glory now,
    And through eternity.

MY ENEMIES

The world lays close siege, and my five senses are the avenues by which it enters and attacks me. They give free passage to the fatal darts, and here death makes its approaches to my heart. My eye gazes about, and by admitting variety of engaging subjects, draws off my attention from the one thing necessary. The ear is open to pleasing sounds, and these disturb the mind in its meditations. The smell amuses, and obstructs serious thinking. The tongue is lavish in speech, and lets itself loose in flattery and falsehood. The touch kindles impure fires, takes every slight occasion to defile itself with lust, and unless the first motions be carefully guarded, and resolutely rejected, it seizes, vanquishes, and inflames the whole body: the steps by which it advances in this conquest are, first to tickle the imagination with unclean thoughts, then to pollute the mind with unlawful delight, and

at last to subdue the reason by consenting to wicked inclinations. Lastly, the devil bends his bow, and makes ready his
arrows within the quiver.

[49]

BOEHME, JACOB

BOEHME, JACOB (1575-1624). One day, Jacob Boehme, a shoemaker, turned from his work and stared at the cupboard, gazing at
the reflection of a sunbeam on pewter. He interpreted this as the
manifestation of divine truth, revealing the universe as the theater
of an eternal conflict between spirit and matter. Boehme regarded
matter as an embodiment of evil, but a necessary condition for the
existence of all beings. Without its existence, even the divine spirit
would evaporate. He thought that contemporary events reiterated
and confirmed neo-Platonic and Gnostic ideas. Untiringly he contrasted his vision of the divine order with the reality he saw dominated by evil. His intrepid criticism of church and state, of economic
exploitation and political oppression caused the authorities to charge
him with heresy in 1612. His *Aurora* and other writings were interdicted. When Boehme tried to penetrate the mysteries of creation
and salvation, his unschooled mind often appeared more confused
than enlightened. He displayed a powerful originality, but became
entangled in fallacies. His descriptions of the anxieties and temptations of the soul have interested many modern readers who dislike
his metaphysical speculations. He exerted considerable influence
among German romantics and mystics in France, Russia, England,
and the United States.

GOD IS ALL

Now therefore we say (as the Scripture informs us) that God
dwells in Heaven, and it is the Truth. Now mark, *Moses*
writes, that God created the Heaven out of the Midst of the
Waters, and the Scripture says, God dwells in Heaven; therefore we may now observe, that the water has its Original
from the Longing of the eternal Nature after the eternal
Light of God; but the eternal Nature is made manifest by
the Longing after the Light of God, as is mentioned before;

155

and the Light of God is present every where, and yet remains hidden to Nature; for Nature receives only the Virtue of the Light, and the Virtue is the Heaven wherein the Light of God dwells and is hid, and so shines in the Darkness. The Water is the *Materia,* or Matter that is generated from the Heaven, and therein stands the third, which again generates a Life, and comprehensible Essence, or Substance, out of itself, *viz.* the Elements and other Creatures.

Therefore, O noble Man, let not Antichrist and the Devil befool you, who tell you that the Deity is far off from you, and direct you to a Heaven that is situated far above you; whereas there is nothing nearer to you than the Heaven is. You only stand before the Door of Heaven, and you are gone forth with *Adam* out of the paradisaical Heaven into the third Principle; yet you stand in the Gate, do but as the eternal Mother does, which by great desiring and longing after the Kingdom of God, attains the Kingdom of Heaven, wherein God dwells, wherein Paradise springs up; do you but so, set all your Desire upon the Heart of God, and so you will pass in by Force, as the eternal Mother does; and then it shall be with thee as Christ said, *The Kingdom of Heaven Suffereth Violence, and the Violent take it by Force*: So you shall make to yourself Friends in Heaven with your unrighteous *Mammon,* and so you come to be the true Similitude and Image of God, and his proper own; for all the three Principles, with the Eternity, are in you, and the holy Paradise is again generated in you, wherein God dwells. Then where will you seek for God? Seek him in your Soul only that is proceeded out of the eternal Nature, wherein the divine Birth stands.

O that I had but the Pen of Man, and were able therewith to write down the Spirit of Knowledge. I can but stammer of the great Mysteries like a Child that is beginning to speak; so very little can the earthly Tongue express what the Spirit comprehends and understands; yet I will venture to try, whether I may procure some to go about to seek the Pearl, whereby also I might labour in the Works of God in my paradisaical Garden of Roses; for the Longing of the eternal Matrix drives me on to write and exercise myself in this my Knowledge.

Now if we will lift up our minds, and seek after the Heaven wherein God dwells, we cannot say that God dwells only above the Stars, and has inclosed himself with the Firmament which is made out of the Waters; in which none can enter except it be opened (like a Window) for him; with which Thoughts Men are altogether befooled [and bewildered]. Neither can we say (as some suppose) that God the Father and the Son are only with Angels in the uppermost inclosed Heaven, and rule only here in this World by the Holy Ghost, who proceeds from the Father and the Son. All these Thoughts are void of the very Knowledge of God. For then God should be divided and circumscriptive, like the Sun that moves aloft above us, and sends its Light and Virtue to us, whereby the whole Deep becomes light and active all over.

Reason is much befooled with these Thoughts; and the Kingdom of Antichrist is begotten in these Thoughts, and Antichrist has by these Opinions set himself in the Place of God, and means to be God upon Earth, and ascribes divine Power to himself, and stops the Mouth of the Spirit of God, and will not hear him speak; and so strong Delusions come upon them, that they believe the Spirit of Lies, which in Hypocrisy speaks strong Delusions, and seduces the Children of Hope, as *St. Paul* witnesses.

The true Heaven wherein God dwells, is all over, in all Places [or Corners,] even in the Midst [or Center] of the Earth. He comprehends the Hell where the Devils dwell, and there is nothing without God. For wheresoever he was before Creation of the World, there he is still, *viz.* in himself; and is himself the Essence of all Essences: All is generated from him, and is originally from him. And he is therefore called God, because he alone is the Good, the Heart, or [that which is] best; understand, he is the Light and Virtue, [or Power,] from whence Nature has its Original.

If you will meditate on God, take before you the eternal

157

Darkness, which is without God; for God dwells in himself, and the Darkness cannot in its own Power comprehend him; which Darkness has a great [Desire of] longing after the Light, caused by the Light's beholding itself in the Darkness, and shining in it. And in this Longing or Desiring, you find the Source, and the Source takes hold of the Power or Virtue of the Light, and the Longing makes the Virtue material, and the material Virtue is the Inclosure to God, or the Heaven; for in the Virtue stands the Paradise, wherein the Spirit which proceeds from the Father and the Son works. All this is incomprehensible to the Creation, but not impossible to be found in the Mind; for Paradise stands open in the Mind of a holy Soul.

Thus you [may] see how God created all Things out of Nothing, but only out of Himself; and yet the Out-Birth is not from his Essence, [or Substance,] but it has its Original from the Darkness. The Source of the Darkness is the first Principle, and the Virtue [or Power] of the Light is the second Principle, and the Out-Birth, [generated] out of the Darkness by the Virtue of the Light, is the third Principle; and that is not called God: God is only the Light, and the Virtue of the Light, and that which goes forth out of the Light is the Holy Ghost. [50]

BOETHIUS

BOETHIUS (475-524). It was while Boethius was rigorously confined to prison, awaiting execution, that he expressed in writing his meditations of his own fate and the destiny of mankind. For years he had served as minister to King Theodoric, the Goth. He fought corruption and, as a result, aroused the hostility of many depraved dignitaries who finally succeeded in making Theodoric believe that Boethius was a traitor in the service of the Byzantine emperor. The false accusations caused Boethius to be sentenced without trial.

The vicissitudes of his life led Boethius to consider the general problem of whether fortune or divine providence governed the world. His *De Consolatione Philosophiae*, which contains his thoughts while imprisoned, has been translated into almost every European language. It asserts that man is superior to the blind forces of nature; that the power of fortune, affecting the practical

158

affairs of mankind, is irrelevant; and that Providence is infinite. Many persons of considerable achievement, such as Dante, Chaucer, and Queen Elizabeth, have found that the writings of Boethius enabled them to face life with courage and renewed confidence whenever they were beset by doubts or alarmed by the mystery of the future.

EVERY MAN HAS HIS CROSS

VERY narrow and very paltry is human happiness, for either it cometh not to any man, or abideth not steadily with him such as it was when it came; this I will show more clearly later on.

We know that many have worldly riches enough, but they are ashamed of their wealth if they are not as well born as they would desire. Some again are noble and famous from their high birth, but they are oppressed and saddened by their base estate and their poverty, so that they would rather be of mean birth than so poor, were it but in their power. Many are both well born and well endowed, yet are joyless, being wedded to an ill-matched or unpleasing wife. Many are happy enough in their marriage, but being childless must leave all the wealth they amass to strangers to enjoy, and therefore they are sad. Some have children enough, but these are perhaps weakly, or wicked and ignoble, or they die young, so that their parents sorrow for them all their days. Therefore no man may in this present life altogether withstand Fate; for even if he have nothing now to grieve about, yet he may grieve not to know what his future will be, whether good or evil, even as thou also didst not know; and moreover, that which he enjoys so happily while he hath it, he dreads to lose. Show me, I pray thee, the man who to thy mind is most happy, and who is most given over to self-indulgence; I will soon cause thee to see that he is often exceedingly put out by the veriest trifles if anything, however slight, thwart his will or his habits, unless he can beckon every one to run at his bidding. A very little thing may make the happiest of men in this world believe his happiness to be impaired or altogether lost. Thou art thinking now, for instance, that thou art very unhappy, and yet I know that many a man would fancy himself raised up to heaven if he had any part of the happiness which is still remaining to thee. Why, the place where thou art now imprisoned, and which thou callest exile, is a home to them that were born there, and also to them that live in it by choice. Nothing is bad, unless a man think it bad; and though it be hard to bear and adverse, yet is it happiness if a man does it cheerfully and bears it with patience. Few are so wise as not to wish in their impatience that their fortune may be changed. With the sweets of this world much bitterness is mingled; though they seem desirable, yet a man cannot keep them, once they begin to flee from him. Is it not then plain that worldly happiness is a poor thing? It is unable to satisfy poor man, who ever desireth what he hath not at the time, and even with men of patience and of sober life it will never long abide.

[51]

BOLZANO, BERNARD

BOLZANO, BERNARD (1781-1848). The personal fate of Bolzano affords a dramatic insight into the dangers to which really independent thinkers are exposed when the internal revolutions of a reactionary period are manifest. Bolzano was born shortly prior to the outbreak of the French Revolution and died during the year of multiple European revolutions. Although he was not burned at the stake, he was compelled to live in complete retirement for the last thirty years of his life. Bolzano, whose writings were forbidden publication, was a Catholic priest and professor of philosophy at the University of Prague. However, he continued to work ceaselessly, and some of his friends arranged to have his books published anonymously outside his own country. Half a century after his death, his works were discovered and read eagerly by leading modern philosophers. His consistent distinction between logic and psychology was of great importance to Husserl and his disciples. In a sense, Bolzano anticipated the modern theory of transfinite numbers. He was firmly convinced that human knowledge can be enlarged infinitely and insisted on methodical research, cautioning against wishful thinking.

160

ON CORRECT THINKING

It is quite possible to know many rules of logic without previous purposeful meditation, or without having studied logic. Without knowing these rules, one can follow some of them, either through intuition, or by observing the methods of his fellow-men who are more acquainted with them. In this way, it is possible to obtain considerable skill in correct thinking, even on scientific matters. But one is more successful in avoiding mistakes, finding previously hidden new truths, and in coordinating and utilizing them, if one has completely learned the rules which must take place with all this.

The same principles that apply to careful speech also apply to careful thought, or many of the other activities where man can exercise them perfectly without having previously been taught their rules of procedure. Everyone admits that the study of the rules of language is useful; if one speaks correctly, he can follow these rules with more certainty. For the same reason, similar advantages arise from a proper study of the rules of logic and science.

The knowledge of these rules becomes particularly necessary, if one is not to be led astray by artificially invented paralogisms. One should be capable of refuting sophisms in an intelligible manner. A knowledge of the rules of logic, obtained without a proper study of logic, is insufficient if one is to disprove clearly to others the fallacious premise of a paralogism. If one is incapable of logical analysis, then he cannot guard himself or others against the dangers of manifold deceptions, especially when the senses welcome error. For it becomes difficult for rationality to disclose fallacy when one's emotions rejoice in accepting erroneous conclusions. Unfortunately there are too many ubiquitous paralogisms. Their nature is such, that they lead us astray in both our moral and religious convictions. It is therefore desirable, that each man study logic, if only to guard himself and his fellow man against seduction by paralogism.

It is impossible to treat successfully some of the more

difficult sciences, such as metaphysics, without being conscious of all the rules which must be adhered to in sequential order for a scientific demonstration. Probably the reason for the unlimited confusion in metaphysics and some of the other philosophical sciences, is the lack of a highly developed science of logic. Every useful, elaborated manual of logic is written, more or less strictly, in a scientific form; containing explanations, proofs, objections, refutations, etc. The study of such books makes for correct thinking; a training not inferior to that which may be gained through the study of many other sciences.

[52]

BONAVENTURA, SAINT

BONAVENTURA, SAINT (1221-1274). John Fidanza was born in Tuscany in 1221, and, in 1240, he entered the Order of Franciscans, where he was renamed Fra Bonaventura. He studied with Alexander of Hales in Paris, and later became a teacher of theology. In 1255 he was excluded from the University of Paris because he supported Aquinas in a dispute, but was readmitted in 1257 and elected general of the Franciscan Order. He became a cardinal in 1273, and died in 1274 at the Council of Lyons. Bonaventura, called "Doctor Seraphicus," was canonized in 1482.

A complex personality, Bonaventura was a philosopher, mystic, and dogmatic theologian. He was never a radical thinker, for he was too fond of tradition, too cautious and adverse to controversy, even though he was involved in several. He definitely formulated Franciscan doctrine, but he has been accused of having been greatly influenced by Aquinas and the Dominicans.

Bonaventura's mystical writings were of considerable influence. His central theme concerned the study of God. He stated that man possesses an imperfect but very certain knowledge of the supreme being. His path of thought proceeds from stable faith, to reason, and then to contemplation. Knowledge, derived from human science, is differentiated from mystical knowledge, which is the work of divine grace. His *Itinerarium Mentis* (Journey of the Mind) describes seven stages of ascent, three of which are the result of imagination, reason, and memory; at the fourth stage supernatural grace intervenes. The seventh stage provides knowledge of the Trinity, and is described as a psychological experience of speechless ecstasy. His

162

doctrine of human knowledge is voluntaristic. Knowledge is a spontaneous activity which stems from God and is directed toward God. It beholds the world as a symbol which mirrors divine beauty. Knowledge for its own sake is branded as error. World opinion may consider philosophy great, but in the light of the Christian faith, it is of little value. Bonaventura established the concrete image of the world in accordance with Platonism, corrected by the idea of Biblical omnipotence. He did not consider Plato as the representative of wisdom, nor Aristotle as the representative of science. But he viewed Augustine as the manifestation of holy inspiration, and his teachings as the correct guide to human knowledge. The imagery of Bonaventura's prose creates a more lasting impression than does the originality of his thoughts.

ON FRANCIS OF ASSISI

THE grace of God our Saviour hath appeared in these our latter days in His faithful and devout servant Francis, and hath been manifested through him to all those who are truly humble and lovers of holy poverty; who honouring and devoutly adoring the superabundance of the divine mercy, which was so bountifully poured forth upon him, have been taught by his example to forsake all impiety and worldly desires, to conform their lives to the life of Christ, and with intense and burning desire to thirst after the hope of heavenly beatitude. For so graciously did God look upon this truly poor and contrite man, that He not only raised the poor and needy from the vile dust of worldly conversation, but also set him to be a light to the faithful, making him to become a true professor, leader, and herald of evangelical perfection, that, bearing witness to the light, he might prepare before the Lord a way of light and peace in the hearts of the faithful. For, shining like a morning star in the midst of a dark cloud, he enlightened by the bright rays of his pure doctrine and holy life those who lay in darkness and in the shadow of death, and thus guided them onwards by his bright shining to the perfect day. And like the glorious rainbow set in the darkness of the clouds, he came forth as the angel of true peace and the sign of the covenant between God and man, bringing glad tidings of peace and salvation: being sent by God, like the Precursor of Christ, to prepare in the desert of this world the highway of holy poverty, and by word and example to preach penance to men. Thus prevented by the gifts of heavenly grace, enriched with the merits of invincible virtue, filled with the spirit of prophecy, and ordained to the angelic office of declaring good tidings, burning with seraphic fire, and raised above all human things in the fiery chariot of divine love, it may be reasonably affirmed from the clear testimony of His whole life that he came in the spirit and power of Elias.

We may also say that he was truly shadowed forth by that other friend of Christ, the Apostle and Evangelist St. John, under the similitude of the angel whom he saw ascending from the east with the sign of the living God. Under this figure we may assuredly discern Francis, the servant, herald, and messenger of God, the beloved of Christ, the pattern for our imitation, the wonder of the world, if we carefully observe and mark the excellency of his marvellous sanctity, by which, during his life, he imitated the purity of the Angels, so that he may be set forth as an example to all the perfect followers of Christ.

[53]

BOOLE, GEORGE

BOOLE, GEORGE (1815-1864). Compared with other philosophers, it was relatively late in his lifetime that George Boole began to specialize in the field that ultimately made him famous. At the age of sixteen, he taught school in an English provincial town; by the time he was twenty, he had opened his own school; at thirty, he began to concentrate upon mathematics. In 1847 he published a pamphlet, *The Mathematical Analysis of Logic*, which contained the principal ideas he later developed in his book, *Laws of Thought* (1854). This book marks the beginning of symbolic logic, a new and efficient method of formal logic, designed to avoid the ambiguities of ordinary language. Boole recognized that the canonical forms of Aristotelian syllogism are really symbolical, but less perfect than the symbolism of mathematics. Furthermore, he realized that ordinary language is an inadequate medium for the expression of ideas. He tried to devise a symbolic language, the terms of which would express exactly what he thought. He was less interested in reducing logic to mathematics than in employing symbolic language and notation in a wide generalization of purely logical processes. He organized deductive logic as an algebra, interpretable spatially and proportionally. With this, he paved the way for Frege, Peano, Bertrand Russell, Whitehead, Hilbert, and others.

THE PLACE OF MATHEMATICS IN THE SYSTEM OF HUMAN KNOWLEDGE

THOSE who have maintained that the position of Mathematics is . . . a fundamental one, have drawn one of their strongest arguments from the actual constitution of things. The material frame is subject in all its parts to the relations of number. All dynamical, chemical, electrical, thermal actions seem not only to be measurable in themselves, but to be connected with each other, even to the extent of mutual convertibility, by numerical relations of a perfectly definite kind. But the opinion in question seems to me to rest upon a deeper basis than this. The laws of thought, in all its processes of conception and of reasoning, in all those operations of which language is the expression or the instrument, are of the same kind as are the laws of the acknowledged processes of Mathematics. It is not contended that it is necessary for us to acquaint ourselves with those laws in order to think coherently, or, in the ordinary sense of the terms, to reason well. Men draw inferences without any consciousness of those elements upon which the entire procedure depends. Still less is it desired to exalt the reasoning faculty over the faculties of observation, of reflection, and of judgment. But upon the very ground that human thought, traced to its ultimate elements, reveals itself in mathematical forms, we have a presumption that the mathematical sciences occupy, by the constitution of our nature, a fundamental place in human knowledge, and that no system of mental culture can be complete or fundamental, which altogether neglects them.

But the very same class of considerations shows with equal force the error of those who regard the study of Mathe-

matics, and of their applications, as a sufficient basis either
of knowledge or of discipline. If the constitution of the material frame is mathematical, it is not merely so. If the mind,
in its capacity of formal reasoning, obeys, whether consciously or unconsciously, mathematical laws, it claims through
its other capacities of sentiment and action, through its perceptions of beauty and of moral fitness, through its deep
springs of emotion and affection, to hold relation to a different order of things. There is, moreover, a breadth of
intellectual vision, a power of sympathy with truth in all its
forms and manifestations, which is not measured by the
force and subtlety of the dialectic faculty. Even the revelation
of the material universe in its boundless magnitude, and
pervading order, and constancy of law, is not necessarily
the most fully apprehended by him who has traced with
minutest accuracy the steps of the great demonstration. And
if we embrace in our survey the interests and duties of life,
how little do any processes of mere ratiocination enable us
to comprehend the weightier questions which they present!
As truly, therefore, as the cultivation of the mathematical
or deductive faculty is a part of intellectual discipline, so
truly is it only a part. The prejudice which would either
banish or make supreme any one department of knowledge
or faculty of mind, betrays not only error of judgment, but
a defect of that intellectual modesty which is inseparable
from a pure devotion to truth.

[54]

BOSANQUET, BERNARD

BOSANQUET, BERNARD (1848-1923). The best known (next to
Bradley) of the British idealist philosophers, Bosanquet descended
from an old Huguenot family. For eleven years he lectured on
Greek history and philosophy at University College, Oxford. Then
he left this to devote himself to charity and the study of ethics,
logic, and aesthetics.

His interests, later shared by his wife, included the London
Ethical Society (later known as the London School of Ethics and

Social Philosophy) and the Charity Organization Society. This work was not the hobby of a leisure-class gentleman, but the practical application of Bosanquet's philosophy.

His emphasis was on the importance of the individual, the fruition of a cosmoramic view which could only be realized in the individual. Accordingly, he defined the Absolute (and in this he was profoundly influenced by Hegel) not as a personality lacking coherence and unity, but as a whole being. Similarly in his logic, he defined truth as a cohering, comprehensive whole. He perceived ethics as the endeavor towards a unity of pleasure and responsibility, all the while emphasizing the importance of the individual in his relationships with others. His philosophy may be said to bear the stamp of conciliation.

His personal charm, his sympathetic attitudes, and his "critically appreciative powers" were hallmarks of his warm personality. His writings include *Knowledge and Reality, A History of Aesthetic, The Essentials of Logic, The Psychology of the Moral Self,* and *The Philosophic Theory of the State.*

ON THE STATE

THE State . . . is to the general life of the individual much as . . . the family . . . with regard to certain of his impulses. The idea is that in it, or by its help, we find at once discipline and expansion, the transfiguration of partial impulses, and something to do and to care for, such as the nature of a human self demands. If, that is to say, you start with a human being as he is in fact, and try to devise what will furnish him with an outlet and a stable purpose capable of doing justice to his capacities—a satisfying object of life— you will be driven on by the necessity of the facts at least as far as the State, and perhaps further. Two points may be insisted on to make this conception less paradoxical to the English mind.

(*a*) The State, as thus conceived, is not merely the political fabric. The term State accents indeed the political aspect of the whole, and is opposed to the notion of an anarchical society. But it includes the entire hierarchy of institutions by which life is determined, from the family to the trade, and from the trade to the Church and the University.

It includes all of them, not as the mere collection of the growths of the country, but as the structure which gives life and meaning to the political whole, while receiving from it mutual adjustment, and therefore expansion and a more liberal air. The State, it might be said, is thus conceived as the operative criticism of all institutions—the modification and adjustment by which they are capable of playing a rational part in the object of human will. And criticism, in this sense, is the life of institutions. As exclusive objects, they are a prey to stagnation and disease—think of the temper which lives solely for the family or solely for the Church; it is only as taken up into the movement and circulation of the State that they are living spiritual beings. It follows that the State, in this sense, is, above all things, not a number of persons, but a working conception of life. It is the conception by the guidance of which every living member of the commonwealth is enabled to perform his function, as Plato has taught us. If we ask whether this means that a complete conception of the aims and possibilities of the common life exists even in the minds of statesmen, not to speak of ordinary citizens, the question answers itself in the negative. And yet the State can only live and work in as far as such a conception, in however fragmentary, one-sided shapes, pervades the general mind. It is not there mostly in reflective shape; and in so far as it is in reflective shape it is according to ultimate standards contradictory and incomplete. But everyone who has a fair judgment of what his own place demands from him, has, at his own angle, so to speak, a working insight into the end of the State; and, of course, practical contradictions would be fewer if such conceptions were completer and more covered by each other. But a complete reflective conception of the end of the State, comprehensive and free from contradiction, would mean a complete idea of the realization of all human capacity, without waste or failure. Such a conception is impossible owing to the gradual character of the process by which the end of life, the nature of the good, is determined for man. The Real Will, as represented by the State, is only a partial embodiment of it.

(*b*) The State, as the operative criticism of all institutions, is necessarily force; and in the last resort, it is the only recognised and justified force. It seems important to observe that force is inherent in the State, and no true ideal points in the direction of destroying it. For the force of the State proceeds essentially from its character of being our own mind extended so to speak, beyond our immediate consciousness. Not only is the conduct of life as a whole beyond the powers of the average individual at his average level, but it is beyond the powers of all the average individuals in a society taken together at their average level. We made a great mistake in thinking of the force exercised by the State as limited to the restraint of disorderly persons by the police and the punishment of intentional lawbreakers. The State is the fly-wheel of our life. Its system is constantly reminding us of our duties, from sanitation to the incidents of trusteeship, which we have not the least desire to neglect, but which we are either too ignorant of or too indolent to carry apart from instruction and authoritative suggestion. We profit at every turn by institutions, rules, traditions, researches, made by minds at their best, which, through State action are now in a form to operate as extensions of our own minds. It is not merely the contrast between the limited activity of one individual and the greater achievement of millions put together. It is the contrast between individuals working in the order and armed with the laws, customs, writings, and institutions devised by ages, and the same individuals considered as their daily average selves, with a varying but always limited range of immediate consciousness. For at any given moment no judge knows all the law; no author knows all his own books, not to mention those of others; no official of an institution has the whole logic and meaning of the institution before his mind. All individuals are continually reinforced and carried on, beyond their average immediate consciousness, by the knowledge, resources, and energy which surround them in the social order, with its inheritance, of which the order itself

is the greatest part. And the return of this greater self, forming a system adjusted to unity, upon their isolated minds, as
an expansion and stimulus to them, necessarily takes the
shape of force, in as far as their minds are inert. And this
must always be the case, not merely so long as wills are
straightforwardly rebellious against the common good, but
so long as the knowledge and energy of the average mind are
unequal to dealing, on its own initiative and out of its own
resources, with all possible conjunctions in which necessary
conditions of the common good are to be maintained. In
other words, there must be inertia to overcome, as long as
the limitations of our animal nature exist at all. The State
is, as Plato told us, the individual mind writ large, or, as we
have said, our mind reinforced by capacities which are of its
own nature, but which supplement its defects. And this being
so, the less complete must clearly submit to find itself in the
more complete, and be carried along with it so far as the
latter is able to advance.

[55]

BOUTROUX, EMILE

BOUTROUX, EMILE (1845-1921). It is a rare occurrence for
European scholars to hail a doctoral thesis in philosophy as a turning point in the history of thought. However, this was the case with
Boutroux's thesis published in 1874, *De la Contingence des Lois de
la Nature* (On the Contingency of the Laws of Nature). Subsequently he became one of the most influential teachers of philosophy
at the Sorbonne in Paris; Henri Bergson was one of his many
famous pupils.

He demonstrated that the concept of natural law in all branches
of science (from mathematics to biology) is a result rather than a
principle, for it does not prove the universal reign of necessity.
According to Boutroux, generally the relatively invariable relationship between causes and effects comes about because of an inadequate grasp of such true and profound realities as life and liberty.
He encountered the objection that contingency connotes hazard and
disorder by stating that necessity implies immutability and death.
Many of Boutroux's arguments on the problem of liberty and the
extent to which necessity can be admitted have become classic. He

always endeavored to strengthen the conviction that man is able to act upon nature. His adherence to the ideas advanced in his first book helped to pave the way for new progress in science. When asked what the good life involved, he replied "a thought conceived in early years and developed in maturity." His opinion was internationally revered as the expression of "Europe's conscience."

ALL BEINGS TEND TOWARD GOD

GOD is the creator of the essence and existence of beings. Moreover, it is His activity, His incessant providence, that gives the higher forms the faculty of employing the lower ones as instruments. Nor is there any reason to regard a special providence as more unworthy of Him than the creation of a manifold and changing universe.

The contingency shown in the hierarchy of the general laws and forms of the world finds its explanation in this doctrine of divine freedom. . . .

The progress of the events of life may be likened unto a sea voyage. While the main concern of the sailors is to avoid hidden reefs and come safe out of storms, their efforts do not stop there. They have a goal to reach, and, however circuitous the routes they may have to traverse, they constantly aim for this goal. To advance is not to avoid, more or less completely, the dangers along the track, it is to draw nearer the goal. But though the sailors have a mission, they also have the freedom of action necessary for its accomplishment; and those whose duty it is more especially to steer the vessel are entrusted with greater authority. Of course the power of these men is nothing compared with the might of the ocean; but then, it is an intelligent and organized power; it is put into action at the right moment. By means of a series of manoeuvres and contrivances which do not appreciably change the outer conditions, but are all calculated to make use of them in view of the goal to be attained, man succeeds in making the winds and waves obey his will.

Similarly, it is not the sole end of the beings of nature to continue in existence, amid the obstacles surrounding them, and to yield to outer conditions: they have an ideal to realize;

and this ideal consists in drawing nearer to God, in re-sembling Him, each after its kind. The ideal varies with the different beings, since each has a special nature and is cap-able of imitating God only and through its own distinctive nature.

The perfection for which creatures were born entitles them to a certain degree of spontaneity, necessary in order to transcend themselves. The higher the mission of a being, *i.e.* the more its nature admits of perfection, the wider is its liberty, the means of attaining its end.

[56]

BOWNE, BORDEN PARKER

BOWNE, BORDEN PARKER (1847-1910). For more than thirty years, Bowne was professor of philosophy at Boston University where, although the spiritual atmosphere of religious traditionalism was agreeable to him, he endeavored to and succeeded in liberalizing religious thought.

An acute critic of positivism and naturalism, he untiringly maintained the cause of theism, defending it from the viewpoints of epistemology, logic, psychology, metaphysics, and religious and so-cial thought. He categorized his views as Kantianized Berkeleyanism, transcendental empiricism and, finally, Personalism—a term used by other philosophers, who differ from Bowne in all fundamental theses, to characterize their systems. Bowne's was chiefly influenced by Lotze.

Bowne's religious and philosophical problems conjoin in their attitude toward change and identity. Epistemologically and psy-chologically, Bowne regarded identity as the foundation of person-ality. He argued that without identity, recognition is impossible; without recognition, memory cannot be formed; that memory, the essence of the self, is the primary condition of mental life. He in-sisted that the mind, not the sense, gives evidence of reality; that reality is comprehended by more than the cognitive faculties; that life and aspiration are more deeply rooted in the person than logical thought; therefore, it becomes necessary to justify aesthetics, ethics, and metaphysics. Bowne stated that no fundamental antagonism exists between thought and feeling. The question of freedom inti-mately enters into the structure of reason. All knowledge is the result of considerable searching effort. Science is the consequence

172

of human freedom, not of automatically functioning truth. Bowne applied his philosophy of change and identity to the experiences of daily social life, and tried to establish a balance between the claims of progress and conservatism.

THE MORAL LIFE

THAT was not first which was spiritual, but that which was natural, and afterward that which was spiritual. But the spiritual is not something apart from the natural, as a kind of detached movement; it is rather the natural itself, rising toward its ideal form through the free activity of the moral person. The natural can be understood only through the spiritual, to which it points; and the spiritual gets contents only through the natural, in which it roots.

As a consequence, the field of ethics is life itself, and, immediately, the life that now is. And our moral task is to make this life, so far as possible, an expression of rational good-will. In this work we have a double guide. Internally, we have a growing moral ideal; externally, we have a growing insight into the tendencies of conduct. Neither of these can be deduced from the other, and both are alike necessary.

For life has two poles. It demands for its perfection both outward fortune and happiness and inward worth and peace. A conditioned life like ours cannot reach an ideal form, unless it be in harmony both with its objective environment and with its subjective ideals. Either of these elements, when viewed apart from the other, is an abstraction of theory, and a source of confusion, if not a mischief. If we consider only the inner worth and peace, ethics runs to leaves. If we consider only the outer fortune and happiness, ethics runs to weeds. There is no need to ask which factor is first, as both should be first, last and always.

The moral life finds its chief field in the service of the common good. Neither virtue nor happiness is attainable as a direct abstract aim. It is a commonplace that happiness eludes direct pursuit; and it is equally true, though less generally recognized, that virtue is alike elusive. Our nature acts spontaneously and normally only when we are taken out of ourselves and our attention is directed to our normal objects. The man who is seeking to do as he would be done by, and to love his neighbor as himself, is in a much better way than the man who is engaged in self-culture and the pursuit of virtue.

The greatest need in ethics is the impartial and unselfish will to do right. With this will, most questions would settle themselves; and, without it, all theory is worthless. The selfish will is the great source not only of wars and fightings, but also of dishonest casuistry and tampering with truth and righteousness. One bent on doing wrong never lacks an excuse; and one seeking to do right can commonly find the way.

Presupposing this will to do right, the great need in ethical theory is to renounce abstractions, as virtue, pleasure, happiness, and come into contact with reality. Most of the theoretical contentions of the world would vanish if brought out of their abstraction. Mr. Mill did once suggest that two and two might make five, but he prudently located the possibility in another planet. That is, it was a purely verbal doubt, which neither he nor any one else ever dreamed of tolerating in concrete experience. Ethics, in particular, has suffered from this verbalism; and all the more because it is a practical science, which has to do with life rather than speculation. Concrete relations and duties have been overlooked in the name of various abstractions—all of them thin and bloodless, and admitting of endless verbal manipulation. It is in this region of abstractions that most ethical debate has been carried on. Hence its sterility of anything but mischief. As Mr. Mill's doubt did not touch practical arithmetic, so the doubts of the ethical schools vanish before concrete matter. The men of good will who are desirous of leading a helpful and worthy human life will generally agree in the great outlines, and also in the details, of duty, whatever their ethical philosophy. And even the tedious vaporers about the indifference of vice and virtue succeed in believing their own whims only so long as they keep clear of the concrete. A blindness more than judicial can easily be induced concerning the facts of human life by bringing in a few such terms as sin and plunging into the labyrinths of theological controversy. So great is the deceit of words! Hence the importance of rescuing ethics from its abstractions and bringing it into contact with life.

The great need of ethical practice, next to the good will, is the serious and thoughtful application of intellect to the problems of life and conduct. As error arises less from wilful lying than from indifference to truth, so misconduct and social evils in general arise less from a will to do wrong than from an indifference to doing right. As of old, the "people do not consider;" and in the ignorance thus engendered terrible things are done or ignored. There is really moral life enough to make vast and beneficent reforms, if the people would only consider. And until they do consider we must worry along in the old way, with an embryonic conscience, drugged by custom and warped into artificiality, while life is directed not by wise and serious reflection, but by conflicting passion and selfishness. We shall escape from this condition only as we control the mechanical drifting of thoughtlessness, and advance beyond the narrowness of the conventional conscience, and devote all our good will and all our intellect to the rationalization and moralization of life.

We shall also do well to remember that righteousness is nothing which can be achieved once for all, whether for the individual or for the community. The living will to do right must be ever present in both, forever reaffirming itself and adjusting itself to new conditions. The tacit dream of the half-way righteous in both fields is that some stage may be reached where the will may be relaxed, and given a vacation. But this dream also must be dismissed. Both individual and social righteousness are likely long to remain militant. As we are now constituted, righteousness cannot be so stored away in habits as to dispense with the continuous devotion of the living will. Especially is this devotion demanded in social righteousness. Here the error is perennial of thinking

175

that justice and wisdom may be so stored up in laws and constitutions as to run of themselves, while the citizens are left free to go to their farms and merchandise. This is one of the most pernicious practical errors of our time. Social righteousness may be expressed in laws, but it lives only in the moral vigilance of the people.

In a very important sense the respectable class is the dangerous class in the community. By its example it degrades the social conception of the meaning of life, and thus materializes, vulgarizes, and brutalizes the public thought. Also, by its indifference to public duties, it constitutes itself the guilty accomplice of all the enemies of society. By this same indifference, too, it becomes the great breeder of social enemies; for only where the carcass is are the vultures gathered together. The ease with which self-styled good people ignore public duties and become criminal accomplices in the worst crimes against humanity is one of the humorous features of our ethical life.

In the application of principles to life there will long be a neutral frontier on the borders of the moral life, where consequences and tendencies have not so clearly declared themselves as to exclude differences of opinion among men of good will. Here men will differ in judgment rather than in morals. It is very common to exaggerate this difference into a moral one; and then the humorous spectacle is presented of friends who ignore the common enemy and waste their strength in mutual belaborings. This is one of the great obstacles to any valuable reform.

Finally, in reducing principles to practice we must be on our guard against an abstract and impracticable idealism. Even in the personal life conscience may be a measureless calamity, unless restrained by a certain indefinable good sense. Many principles look fair and even ideal when considered in abstraction from life, which cannot, however, be applied to life without the most hideous or disastrous results. Here is the perennial oversight of off-hand reformers and socialistic quacks. Ethics when divorced from practical wis-

dom prevents the attainment of its own ends. The abstract
ethics of the closet must be replaced by the ethics of life, if
we would not see ethics lose itself in barren contentions and
tedious verbal disputes.

[57]

BRADLEY, FRANCIS HERBERT

BRADLEY, FRANCIS HERBERT (1846-1924). Noted for his contribution to English philosophy, Bradley was, at first, a disciple of
Hegel. He lost sympathy with Hegelian philosophy, and left it to
revitalize the musty logic of Mills. Subsequently he opposed utilitarianism and supported the ethics of Kant, by insisting that good
will was a universal principle, as well as a human quality. He found,
by testing the relation of each claim to fundamental reality, that
experience, as such, is nonrelational and contains within itself the
essential features of thought which make for explicit logic. He
stated that truth can only reside in judgment; that not all judgments
are true; that when a subject is circumspect and sufficiently inclusive, then its judgment is true; and that truth really requires the
absolute. Bradley lucidly restated the fundamental idealism and
spiritual monism that form the bases for the analysis of individual
experience. This analysis gradually develops into the realization of a
universal coherent unity, infinite in character.

In his youth, Bradley accepted a fellowship at Merton College,
Oxford, tenable for life, but terminable at marriage. He enjoyed
its benefits for more than half a century. As an athlete at University College, he contracted typhoid fever and subsequently suffered
from an inflammation of the kidneys. These illnesses probably resulted in his being a crochety recluse. Yet his literary efforts have
polish, style, and even humor. His *Appearance and Reality* (1893)
and *Essays on Truth and Reality* (1914) are philosophical classics.

THE ABSOLUTE

WE can find no province of the world so low but the Absolute
inhabits it. Nowhere is there even a single fact so fragmentary and so poor that to the universe it does not matter. There
is truth in every idea however false, there is reality in every
existence however slight; and, where we can point to reality
or truth, there is the one undivided life of the Absolute.

177

Appearance without reality would be impossible, for what then could appear? And reality without appearance would be nothing, for there certainly is nothing outside appearances. But on the other hand Reality . . . is not the sum of things. It is the unity in which all things, coming together, are transmuted, in which they are changed all alike, though not changed equally. And, as we have perceived, in this unity relations of isolation and hostility are affirmed and absorbed. These also are harmonious in the Whole, though not of course harmonious as such, and while severally confined to their natures as separate. Hence it would show blindness to urge, as an objection against our view, the opposition found in ugliness and in conscious evil. The extreme of hostility implies an intenser relation, and this relation falls within the Whole and enriches its unity. The apparent discordance and distraction is overruled into harmony, and it is but the condition of fuller and more individual development. But we can hardly speak of the Absolute itself as either ugly or evil. The Absolute is indeed evil in a sense and it is ugly and false, but the sense, in which these predicates can be applied, is too forced and unnatural. Used of the Whole each predicate would be the result of an indefensible division, and each would be a fragment isolated and by itself without consistent meaning. Ugliness, evil, and error, in their several spheres, are subordinate aspects. They imply distinctions falling, in each case, within one subject province of the Absolute's kingdom; and they involve a relation, in each case, of some struggling element to its superior, though limited, whole. Within these minor wholes the opposition draws its life from, and is overpowered by the system which supports it. The predicates evil, ugly, and false must therefore stamp, whatever they qualify, as a mere subordinate aspect, an aspect belonging to the province of beauty or goodness or truth. And to assign such a position to the sovereign Absolute would be plainly absurd. You may affirm that the Absolute *has* ugliness and error and evil, since it owns the provinces in which these features are partial elements. But to assert that it *is* one of its own fragmentary and dependent details would be inadmissible.

It is only by a license that the subject-systems, even when we regard them as wholes, can be made qualities of Reality. It is always under correction and on sufferance that we term the universe either beautiful or moral or true. And to venture further would be both useless and dangerous at once.

If you view the Absolute morally at all, then the Absolute is good. It cannot be one factor contained within and overpowered by goodness. In the same way, viewed logically or aesthetically, the Absolute can only be true or beautiful. It is merely when you have so termed it, and while you still continue to insist on these preponderant characters, that you can introduce at all the ideas of falsehood and ugliness. And, so introduced, their direct application to the Absolute is impossible. Thus to identify the supreme universe with a partial system may, for some end, be admissible. But to take it as a single character within this system, and as a feature which is already overruled, and which as such is suppressed there, would, we have seen, be quite unwarranted. Ugliness, error, and evil, all are owned by, and all essentially contribute to the wealth of the Absolute. The Absolute, we may say in general, has no assets beyond appearances; and again, with appearances alone to its credit, the Absolute would be bankrupt. All of these are worthless alike apart from transmutation. But, on the other hand once more, since the amount of change is different in each case, appearances differ widely in their degrees of truth and reality. There are predicates which, in comparison with others, are false and unreal.

To survey the field of appearances, to measure each by the idea of perfect individuality, and to arrange them in an order and in a system of reality and merit—would be the task of metaphysics.

[58]

179

BRANDEIS, LOUIS DEMBITZ

BRANDEIS, LOUIS DEMBITZ (1856-1941). Notable as a Justice of the United States Supreme Court Brandeis was a juridical heretic, who had the satisfaction of seeing his views acknowledged by orthodox jurists. Many of his dissenting opinions have since become the law of the land. He was greatly inspired by Oliver Wendell Holmes, Jr., a colleague of his on the Supreme Court bench, and he subsequently had great influence over his former teacher. Both of them stressed the historical development of law, the necessity of adapting legislation to the dynamic economic and social changes, and the social and broad cultural responsibilities of jurists and legislators. Both frequently dissented from the majority Court opinion.

Brandeis was opposed to socialism and claimed it did not increase industrial efficiency. He was favorably inclined toward labor, small businessmen, and cooperative enterprises. Although he protested that he had no general philosophy and thought only within the context of the facts that came before him, he was not only a philosopher of law, but also a social and political philosopher. His views never lost their vital contact with the facts of daily life. He distrusted those whose reasoning bounded far ahead of the facts, and considered those thinkers inadequate whose lack of imagination did not enable their ideas to withstand the test of experience and subsequent events. He always treated opponents fairly when they indicated a willingness to compromise. He firmly believed in the ultimate possibility of reconciling the varied interests of individuals, in overcoming the antagonism between the individual and society and in espousing a basic loyalty to one's fellow man and to the community. He hoped that a humanistic education would culminate in the realization of his ideas.

LAW AND DEMOCRACY

WHAT are American ideals? They are the development of the individual for his own and the common good; the development through liberty, and the attainment of the common good through democracy and social justice.

Our form of government, as well as humanity, compels us to strive for individual man. Under universal suffrage every voter is a part ruler of the state. Unless the rulers have, in the main, education and character, and are free men, our great experiment in democracy must fail. It devolves upon the state, therefore, to fit its rulers for their tasks.

Democracy must be on its toes. You cannot get democracy by doing nothing, or even by passing laws. It has to come from the people. Law is no substitute for the efforts of the citizen. We make laws for the community. We cannot make the community fit the laws. If we desire respect for the law we must first make the law respectable.

We are particularly at fault in America in making private things public and keeping public things private. There used to be a certain glamour about big things; anything big, simply because it was big, seemed to be good and great. We are now coming to see that big things may be very bad and mean.

Big business is not more efficient than small business. Within certain limits you may get through size a relatively smaller cost unit, but the size of greatest efficiency is reached at a comparatively early stage. With the growth in size comes an increasing cost of organization and administration, which is so much greater than the increase in the volume of business that the law of diminishing returns applies.

The real test of efficiency comes when success has to be struggled for; when natural or legal conditions limit the charges which may be made for the goods sold or the services rendered. Real efficiency in any business in which conditions are ever changing must ultimately depend, in large measure, upon the correctness of the judgment exercised, from day to day, on important problems as they arise.

I believe that the possibilities of human advancement are unlimited. I believe that the resources of productive enterprise are almost untouched, and that the world will see a vastly increased supply of comforts, a tremendous social surplus out of which the great masses will be apportioned a degree of well-being that is now hardly dreamed of.

[59]

BRENTANO, FRANZ

BRENTANO, FRANZ (1838-1917). The intellectual milieu of his early background is not manifest in Franz Brentano's writings. He was uninterested in literature and politics, and declined to exploit the influence of his relatives. He was educated by his father, Christian, a devout Catholic and religious author. Franz became a Catholic priest, but after nine years, he abandoned the Catholic Church in 1873. He then became a professor at Wuerzburg and Vienna, and spent the remaining twenty years of his life in Italy and Switzerland. He maintained friendly relations only with his brother, Lujo Brentano, who was noted as a political economist and champion of free trade.

Brentano's chief contributions were in the fields of epistemology, logic, axiology, and psychology. He declared that psychology was the basis of philosophy and the path to metaphysics. He did not believe in metaphysical systems, but believed that reliable metaphysical knowledge was possible. He thought that constant change might lead to increasing perfection. Resolutely opposed to German idealism, he stated that the natural sciences were the true method of philosophic thought. He was disdainful of the "physiological psychology" of Wilhelm Wundt and others who tried to found a psychology based upon experimental methods. Brentano revived those concepts of Scholasticism that deal with the intentional relation of the consciousness to the object. He considered this to be the essential character of psychological experience. He also made great efforts to demonstrate that psychological analysis was not the way to achieve knowledge of an object. He stressed the fundamental differences between judgment and presentation—two completely different means by which the consciousness of an object is perceived. His energetic rejection of the attempts to reduce logic to psychology were of great importance to his disciples: Husserl, Stumpf, Marty, Meinong, Kraus, and Ehrenfels.

Brentano's exemplary character and sincerity of thought enabled him to proceed courageously and independently in his defiance of religious and and secular authority. He never yielded to a need for popular approval, or paid much attention to ideas merely because they were the current vogue.

THE THREE CLASSES OF PSYCHIC PHENOMENA

IN order to adequately express the concepts concerning the

different manner of relationships to content, we have to distinguish three main classes of psychic phenomena. These
three species are not the same as those generally accepted,
and since more appropriate names are not at hand, the first
may be called "image"; the second, "judgment"; and the
third, "emotion," "interest," or "love."

We speak of image whenever something appears to us.
If we see something, we imagine its color; if we hear something, we imagine its sound; if we indulge in fancies, we
imagine fanciful creations.

By virtue of the general sense in which the word is used,
it can be said that it is impossible for the activity of the soul
to bear on some thing that cannot be imagined. Whenever I
hear and understand a name, I imagine what it stands for,
and generally speaking, it is the purpose of a name to provoke "images."

The meaning of "judgment" is in accordance with customary philosophical usage. That is, anything we accept is
true; anything we reject is false.

Unfortunately, there is no unifying expression for the
third major class: the phenomena called emotions; or the
phenomena of interests; or the phenomena of love. This class
comprises all psychic phenomena, not included in the first
two classes. Emotions are only affective phenomena which
are combined with noticeable physical excitement. Everyone
comprehends anger, fear, violence, and desire as emotions.
In the general sense in which the term "emotion" is used it
also comprises any wish, decision, or intention.

The term interest is preferably used only for certain
acts that belong to a particular sphere; those cases there is a
desire for knowledge, or where curiosity is aroused. A wish,
hope, or decision of the will is also an act of interest; similarly delight or aversion may also be categorized as interest.

Instead of calling this class by the simple name of love,
it should, strictly speaking, have been called love or hatred,
only because they are opposites. Just as when one speaks of
"judging" as an act of accepting, or when one speaks of the

phenomenon of true desire. For the sake of brevity, I have applied a simple term for the pair of names, even though the term does not embrace the meaning in every sense or sphere. One means something quite different, to be sure, when one says that one loves one's friend, as when one says that he loves wine. The former is loved by wishing him well; the latter is loved by desiring it as something good and enjoying it with pleasure. Using the sense of the word in the latter instance, each act that belongs to this third class is something that is loved, or more precisely speaking, something that is loved or hated.

In an analogous manner, each judgment takes an object as true or false; each phenomenon that belongs to the third class takes an object as good or bad.

[60]

BRIDGMAN, P. W.

BRIDGMAN, P. W. (1882-   ). A professor of mathematics and natural philosophy at Harvard University, an authority on thermodynamics, electricity, and various other physical sciences, Percy Bridgman is noted for his promulgation of the "operational" theory of meaning in his books *The Logic of Modern Physics* (1927) and *The Nature of Physical Theory* (1936). He asserts that the classical concepts of physics are inadequate. He defines concept as a set of operations comprised of mental and physical activity. Truth is identical with verifiability, and the criterion of scientific truth is the experimental method. Although Bridgman has been influenced by neither Dewey nor James, his operationalism parallels John Dewey's instrumentalism.

Bridgman enlarged his scope of observation and thought in *The Intelligent Individual and Society* (1938). His starting point is the irrationality of Man in contemporary society; Man's awareness of this makes him long for an intelligent, orderly life, even though such longing may not be directed at the perfectibility of human desires. If a perfect life is unattainable, a satisfactory life can be secured by apprehending the relations, consequences, implications of the drive, or by intelligently satisfying these drives. These drives are not subject to argument, but only to examination and modification through education. Rationality does not have all the qualities requisite for this task. Emotional adjustment can complete it.

Ideally, education should provide the technique for criticism and modification of the specific drives by the individual. Thus, Bridgman seeks to secure individual freedom in society. His human ideal is a synthesis of intellectual and emotional honesty.

SCIENTIST AND SOCIAL RESPONSIBILITY

WHAT is the relation of the scientist to ideal society? It seems to me that he occupies a position of high strategic importance, a position impossible of attainment for the man who has not directly experienced the significant factors basic to this type of society. The conception of what constitutes the good life does not present itself as a primitive datum in consciousness, but is a product of cultivation and education. Furthermore, various ideals of the good life are possible, competitive with one another and to a certain extent mutually exclusive. The ideals that come to prevail will to a large extent depend on the self-conscious activities of those most concerned. It may even be that the ideals will have to be fought for. What constitutes the good life for the scientist does not at once appeal to the majority as constituting the good life. Nay, more than this, without education the majority cannot be trusted to see that it is to the advantage of the community as a whole that the scientist be allowed to lead his good life. With education, however, I believe that this can be accomplished, and that the scientist is strategically situated to impart this education. It is, of course, easy for anyone to see that the material benefits we now enjoy would not have been possible without scientific activity and to see that for this reason science should be supported. What I have in mind, however, is something less material. I think the scientist, in endeavoring to impart the vision of what this is, would do well not to take a too narrow view. The scientific life, which for him is a good life, is a special kind of a more general life which is also a good life, namely, the life of the intellect.

I think the scientist's most important educative task is to get the average man to feel that the life of the intellect not only is a good life for those who actively lead it, but that it is also good for society as a whole that the intellectual life should be made possible for those capable of it, and that it should be prized and rewarded by the entire community. It is perhaps a gamble that society as a whole can be made to feel this. But I believe it is a gamble to which the scientific man is committed. If the human race is such a sort of creature that it cannot be made to feel that intellectual activity and satisfaction of the craving for understanding are goods in themselves, then we might as well shut up shop here and now, and those of us who are made that way henceforth get the intellectual satisfactions necessary to us as best we can, surreptitiously and in spite of our fellows. Example itself can be educative. Appreciation of the element of high adventure in achieving understanding of the ways of nature should not be difficult to impart. In other fields human beings do this. There must be widespread sympathy with, and understanding of the mountain climber who, when asked why he had to climb mountains, replied, "Because the mountain is there." I believe that most men similarly can be made to feel the challenge of an external world not understood and can be made to see that the scientist has to understand nature "because nature is there." The challenge to the understanding of nature is a challenge to the utmost capacity in us. In accepting the challenge, man can dare to accept no handicaps. That is the reason that scientific freedom is essential and that artificial limitations of tools or subject matter are unthinkable. The average man, I believe, can be made to see that scientific freedom is merely freedom to be intelligent, and that the need for this freedom is born with us, and that we will practice it in the inmost recesses of our thoughts no matter what the external constraints. And I believe also that the average man can be made to see that the imposition of restraints on the freedom to be intelligent betrays fear of the unknown and of himself, and that he can be made to feel

186

that this fear is an ignoble thing. My gamble is that the human race, once it has caught the vision, will not be willing to yield to fear of the consequences of its own intelligence.

It may appear that we have been straying rather far from our ostensible topic. I think, however, that from the broad point of view we have not. What we have been saying amounts to saying that the most intelligent way of dealing with the problems arising from scientific discoveries is to create an appropriate society. This society will be a society that recognizes that the only rational basis for its functions is to be sought in its relations to the individuals of which it is composed; a society in which the individual in his capacity as a member of society will have the integrity not to stoop to actions he would not permit himself as an individual; a society broadly tolerant and one which recognizes intellectual achievement as one of the chief glories of man; a society imaginative enough to see the high adventure in winning an understanding of the natural world about us, and a society which esteems the fear of its own intellect an ignoble thing. In a society so constituted I venture to think the problems created by scientific discoveries will pretty much solve themselves.

[61]

BRUNO, GIORDANO

BRUNO, GIORDANO (1548-1600). Poet, playwright, philosopher, Bruno is less representative of the development of the modern scientific spirit than he is of the fermentation produced by the contact of Scholastic philosophy with the natural sciences. His enthusiasm for Copernicus' astronomical discovery enabled him to enlarge his cosmic concepts. But instead of thinking empirically, he continued to think in terms of Aristotelian ideas, all the while attacking Aristotle. Bruno was convinced that true philosophy was no different than poetry, music, or painting, since the arts are bound to express divine wisdom. He believed in the infinite perfectibility of knowledge, and conceived of the universe as an imperfect mirror of God's essence in which God's infinity and unity are inadequately depicted.

Throughout his life, Bruno was beset by a restless spirit. He

187

quarreled with the Catholic Church, Calvinists, Lutherans, mathematicians, and physicists. During a fifteen-year period, he lived in Genoa, Venice, Toulouse, Lyons, Paris, Oxford, Wittenberg, and Prague. Wherever he lived he was first admired and then detested for his intolerant attitudes. Like Gabirol, he was both litterateur and philosopher. He wrote many lyrical poems, imbued with an heroic spirit, and ribald comedies—both equally characteristic of the Baroque age. After seven years of imprisonment due to his renunciation of the Dominican Order, he was burned (February 17, 1600) at the stake during the Inquisition in Rome because of his staunch refusal to recant.

A PHILOSOPHY OF THE INFINITE UNIVERSE

THESE are the doubts, difficulties and motives, about the solution whereof I have said enough in our dialogues to expose the intimate and radicated errors of the common philosophy, and to show the weight and worth of our own. Here you will meet with the reasons why we should not fear that any part of this Universe should fall or fly off, that the least particle should be lost in empty space, or be truly annihilated. Here you will perceive the reason of that vicissitude which may be observed in the constant change of all things, whereby it happens, that there is nothing so ill but may befall us or be prevented, nor anything so good but may be lost or obtained by us; since in this infinite field the parts and modes do perpetually vary, though the substance and the whole do eternally persevere the same.

From this contemplation (if we do but rightly consider), it will follow that we ought never to be dispirited by any strange accidents through excess of fear or pain, nor ever be elated by any prosperous event through excess of hope or pleasure; whence we have the way to true morality, and, following it, we would become the magnanimous despisers of what men of childish thoughts do fondly esteem, and the wise judges of the history of nature which is written in our minds, and the strict executioners of those divine laws which are engraven in the centre of our hearts. We would know that it is no harder thing to fly from hence up into heaven, than to fly from heaven back again to the earth, that ascending thither and ascending hither are all one; that we are no more circumferential to the other globes than they are to us, nor they more central to us than we are to them, and that none of them is more above the stars than we, as they are no less than we covered over or comprehended by the sky. Behold us therefore free from envying them! behold us delivered from the vain anxiety and foolish care of desiring to enjoy that good afar off, which in as great a degree we may possess so near at hand, and even at home! Behold us freed from the terror that they should fall upon us, any more than we should hope that we might fall upon them; since every one as well as all of these globes are sustained by infinite ether, in which this our animal freely runs, and keeps to his prescribed course, as the rest of the planets do to theirs. . . .

We fear not, therefore, that what is accumulated in this world, should, by the malice of some wandering spirit, or by the wrath of some evil genius, be shook and scattered, as it were, into smoke or dust, out of this cupola of the sky, and beyond the starry mantle of the firmament; nor that the nature of things can otherwise come to be annihilated in substance, than, as it seems to our eyes, that the air contained in the concavity of a bubble is become nothing when that bubble is burst; because we know that in the world one thing ever succeeds another, *there being no utmost bottom*, whence, as by the hand of some artificer, things are irreparably struck into nothing. There are no ends, limits, margins, or walls, that keep back or subtract any parcel of the infinite abundance of things. Thence it is that the earth and sea are ever equally fertile, and thence the perpetual brightness of the sun, eternal fuel circulating to those devouring fires, and a supply of waters being eternally furnished to the evaporated seas, from the infinite and ever renewing magazine of matter: so that Democritus and Epicurus, who asserted the infinity of things with their perpetual variableness and restoration were so far more in the right than he who endeavored to account for the

189

eternally same appearance of the Universe, by making homogeneous particles of matter ever and numerically to succeed one another.

Thus the excellency of God is magnified, and the grandeur of his Empire made manifest; he is not glorified in one, but in numberless suns, not in one earth nor in one world, but in ten hundred thousand, of infinite globes: so that this faculty of the intellect is not vain or arbitrary, that ever will or can add space to space, quantity to quantity, unity to unity, member to member. By this science we are loosened from the chains of a most narrow dungeon, and set at liberty to rove in a most august empire; we are removed from conceited boundaries and poverty, to the innumerable riches of an infinite space, of so worthy a field, and of such beautiful worlds: this science does not, in a word, make a horizontal circle feigned by the eye on earth, and imagined by the fancy in the spacious sky.

[62]

BRUNSCHWICG, LÉON

BRUNSCHWICG, LÉON (1869-1944). When the Germans occupied Paris in 1940, they compelled Léon Brunschwicg to leave his position as professor of philosophy at the Sorbonne, robbed him of his collection of precious books, and destroyed his manuscripts. Even though the Germans knew hardly any of his works, the fact that he was a Jew and that his wife had been an under-secretary in the Popular Front cabinet of Léon Blum was sufficient cause for his removal. Despite all the possible dangers, Brunschwicg refused to leave France and spent the remaining years of his life in complete isolation. During this period, he wrote valuable studies of Montaigne, Descartes, and Pascal which were printed in Switzerland and the United States. For his granddaughter, who was then in her teens, he composed a manual of philosophy, entitled *Héritage de Mots, Héritage d'Idées* (Legacy of Words, Legacy of Ideas) which was published posthumously in 1945 after the liberation of France.

To Brunschwicg, philosophy meant not a system of doctrines, but the expression of an attitude toward the totality of material and spiritual beings. It was essentially a reflection on the activities of the human mind in the fields of mathematics, physics, morality, the arts,

190

and the history of civilization. Brunschwicg energetically emphasized the creative power of the human mind and demonstrated its
function in the network of relationships that make up the framework
of the universe.

Brunschwicg made highly important contributions to the history of science and philosophy, and at the same time contributed to
the understanding and solution of practical problems. His reinter-
pretation of Descartes has become the foundation for a new idealism. He was a man of universal interests as evidenced by his lectures which criticized newspaper editorials as well as Plato or Kant.
He was a friend of Marcel Proust, the novelist, and of Marcel Denis,
the painter; a patron of the theater and modern art exhibits; an
ardent French patriot, and a fighter for human rights.

ON GOD

Modern science, from the time of Galileo and Copernicus
to Einstein and the theorists of quantum mathematics, has
progressively revealed the true reality of the world. This
revelation reaffirms our concepts and ideas of truth. It is
characteristic for the philosopher to view this as a unified
and indivisible idea. He cannot tolerate the mind in a changing situation, to add epithet or substantive, or in any way
slacken the rigorous method of verification. Inflexibility is the
exigency of the method. Religious truth must, therefore, be
absolute truth; one need not look for the foundation or content of the religion. From the viewpoint of speculation or
rationalism, it must not be said that the basic idea of religion
is yet to be discovered. It is the *Word* which Greece received
from Egypt; which formed the center of Judaic-Christian
theology; the inner light that shines for all mankind and
whose comforting universality and unlimited productivity is
felt by all those who are able to extend and coordinate ideas.
Therefore, religion is the *Word* of God; it confirms the innermost, unparalleled certainty that there is a presence in
each of us, which makes our intelligence different from the
mere passive accumulation of images; makes our love different from the egoistic urge of instinct; keeps us from sev-
ering us from ourselves, and unites us with the community
of minds.

The very manner of attaining this proposition involves the immediate consideration of its negative. For the philosopher, there should not be any other God than the *Word*, comprehended in the immanence which secures His perfect spirituality, with no relation to external forms which would make Him dependent upon the conditions of space and time, and would, in this way, cause the relapse of the religious idea from the sphere of spirit to the inferior regions of matter or life. This new proposition broaches the problem from a negative or somewhat more restrictive aspect. Compared with the essential instincts that determine the origin of religions, the ascetic rationalism of the *Word* seems somewhat deficient and incomplete. In reality, from the viewpoint of pure philosophy, it represents the progress attained by the gradual development from the spontaneous, primitive type of religion to that of a higher type. For the sake of precision, we may call it progress from the religion of *sublimated nature* to the religion of *surmounted* nature.

The first type is derived from constant experience: the inability of the will to realize its aims with certainty; those impervious obstacles which often frustrate the most carefully prepared enterprises: sudden catastrophes, inevitable death. This leads man to form active dreams of superior striving which are at times contradictory to and at other times in accordance with his personal desires. This earthly diffuse striving becomes embodied in the psychology of a transcendent almighty being; a god who inspires fear; who for the same reason becomes the source of hope. We do anything to soften his ire and receive his grace. The supernatural powers at his disposal, secure success for us, or at least we are confident that he will compensate us for our failures and sufferings in immortal time, which according to the common creed succeeds the duration of life.

The renunciation involved in Pascal's mortification and Kant's rigorism is only an ephemeral attitude, accepted and transformed by the expectation of posthumous eternity, where the fruits of peace, denied to us on earth, will be enjoyed.

With this concept, God is defined according to his relations with mankind. He is the providential agent, prepared to guard the fate of our planet and the interests of its inhabitants. He is the vital source of precious comfort. Such a God is perfectly adapted to the vicissitudes and ends of human conditions.

It is needless to emphasize the difficulties secular reason, aided by logic, encounters in the analysis of those spontaneous creeds, whose echoes are transmitted to us from remote epochs, and which ethnographers again discover in contemporary primitive societies. The proof of causality *in* the world does not prove that there is a causality *of* the world. Quite the contrary. The conditions of thought which establish the relationships that shape the texture of the universe, as it is known to us, exclude extrapolation, which by pronouncing an abstract principle makes the Absolute emerge as a being that transcends the knowable reality. The more the mind becomes conscious of the proper order of its constituents, whether they belong to the realm of matter or life, the more difficult does it become to regard God as the reason that explains the animate and inanimate universe. The optimism of metaphysics was not only unsuccessful, in divining and justifying the design of creation, but in order to conceive the very idea of such a design, one had to assume first that the earth and mankind were the central interest of the Almighty. Science has considerably enlarged our speculative horizon in terms of space and time. Therefore, the former supposition must be considered a poor one, it contradicts the concept of divinity. Theology, founded upon physics or biology, projecting a supernatural vision of the world, cannot, through conjecture or speculation, solve the problem of religion.

It seems, therefore, reasonable and noble, if not easy, to understand that this speculative inability is the counterpart of moral weakness. If both are to be overcome, we must resolutely convert ourselves to the spirit of truth and change our concept of God, and remove the responsibility of our personal care from Him. God recovers all of His dignity

193

when our concept of him is not charged with the intermediate, involuntary arrogance of terrestrial and human privilege. He does not assimilate Himself with our particular experiences or concepts that result from abstract reasoning. He is not an object of truth, detachable from itself in an unknown region of reality. He is not an object of love which enters into competition with other objects. Rather, he is the cause of our capabilities to comprehend and love without exhausting the resources of our intelligence, or limiting our affection, or reverting it solely to our personal interests. He is the reason we are able to live the life of the spirit.

[63]

BUBER, MARTIN

BUBER, MARTIN (b. 1878-). Martin Buber is one of the leading exponents of Hasidic philosophy. His grandfather, Solomon Buber, was the Hasidic scholar who provided impetus to the mystical movement, and the revival of some of the early tenets and practices of Judaism that resulted in a cultural renaissance among the 18th-century Jews of Eastern Europe.

Martin Buber, a student of the mystical religions of China and India, as well as that of medieval Christianity, maintains that the Judaic experience of divine immanence, as it is expressed in the Talmud and realized in prayer, has a unique importance for all peoples. He accepts the mystical concept of man's communion with God. Religious redemption is the central theme of his spirituality. He believes that the philosophies of religion and sociology have made for greater human cohesiveness.

GOD AND THE SOUL

A definition of mysticism is always open to question, if, with any other religious teaching, it is made on the basis of subject matter or chief principle; for then we only have an idea or sentence that is at the same time abstract and somewhat vague, and that fails to comprehend what makes mysticism in its historical manifestations such a singular and remarkable type of religious life. We do better if we take as our starting point that experience of the soul, which is clearly

194

common to all mystics, for they all speak of it in one way or another and, if only in a veiled reference or even in so objective an expression that the personal foundation, that very experience, does not come within our range of vision; here too are moments when a powerful recollection suddenly pulsates through the firm notes of the objective statement. Of course that experience may be called an experience of Unity; but once again we shall only have something abstract and indefinite, if we think merely of a contemplation of Unity, in which to be sure the one contemplating recedes, his essential position however, which he still feels to some extent in the midst of his experience, is no other than the essential position of all our human contemplation, the division of Being into the contemplating and the contemplated. One of the greatest among the mystics, Plotinus, leaves much room for such a misunderstanding when, as a true Greek still in the late period of the fusion of all spiritual elements, he interprets that experience in visual language as the image of the eye contemplating the light. In Plotinus also we perceive on closer observation that this is only one, if also the thinnest, of the garments in which mystical experience cloaks itself so as to be able to reveal itself, or rather to enable the wearer to fit his experience into the framework of his inner life and then into the framework of his cognition. Indeed the crucial factor in that experience is not that the multiplicity of manifestations collapses into the one, that the interplay of colours gives place to the absoluteness of the white light, but that in the one contemplating the act of contemplation is obliterated; it is not the dissolution of phenomenal diversity but of constructive dualism, the dualism of the I experiencing and the object experienced, which is the crucial factor, the peculiarity of mysticism in the true sense. And indeed we can only speak of mysticism in the true sense where we are concerned, not with men in an early state of semi-consciousness preceding a clear distinction between subject and object, but with those to whom the fundamental position has become a matter of course: an I complete in itself and a world complete in itself facing one another.

This fundamental dualism, itself perceived only slowly by the human spirit, is at certain moments in an individual life swept aside in favor of an overwhelming experience of union; this it is which excites that deep and ever-recurring awe which, though in varying degrees of expression, we find in all mystics.

In all mysticism, however, which springs from the soil of the so-called theistic religions, there is an additional factor to which a specifically religious significance is to be attributed. Here the mystic is conscious of a close personal contact with God, and this contact has, it is true, as its goal a union with God, a union which is often felt and presented in images of the earthly Eros, but in this as in every contact between Being and Being it is the very dualism of these beings which is the primary condition of what is occurring between them. It is not the dualism of subject and object, i.e., neither is to the other merely an object of contemplation, itself having no part in the relationship, but it is the dualism of I and Thou, both entering into reciprocal relationship. However God be comprehended as an absolute Being, He is here not the whole, but the Facing, the One facing this man; He is what this man is not, and is not what this man is; it is precisely upon this that the longing for union can be based. In other words, in this close association experienced by the mystic, God, even if the mystic wants to be merged in Him, is and remains a Person. The I of the mystic seeks to lose itself in the Thou of God, but this Thou of God, or, after the I of the mystic has been merged therein, this absolute I of God cannot pass away. That man's "I am" shall perish, so that the "I am" of God remains alone. "Between me and thee," says al-Hallaj, the great martyr of Moslem mysticism, "there is an 'I am' that grieves me. Ah! through thy 'I am' take away my 'I am' from betwixt us both." The mystic never thinks of calling into question the personality of this divine "I am." "I call thee," says al-Hallaj, ". . . no, it is thou who callest me to thee! How could I have said to thee 'It is thou,' if thou hadst not whis-

196

pered to me 'It is I.' " The I of the revealing God, the I of the God Who accords to the mystic the intercourse with Him, and the I of God, in Whom the human I merges itself, are identical. The mystic remains in the sphere of intercourse, as he was in the sphere of revelation, a theist.

It is otherwise when mysticism, penetrating beyond the sphere of experienced intercourse, dares to deal with God as He is in Himself, that is beyond the relation to man, and indeed beyond the relation to the created world generally. Of course it knows well that, as the greatest thinker of western mysticism, Meister Eckhart, put it, no one can really say what God is. But its conception of absolute unity, a unity therefore that nothing can face any more, is so strong that even the highest idea of the person must yield place to it. Unity which is in relationship to something other than itself is not perfect unity; and perfect unity can no more be personal. By that mysticism, sprung from the soil of a theistic religion, in no way means to deny the personal nature of the God; but it strives to raise that perfect unity, which is faced by nothing, above the God of revelation, and to differentiate between the Godhead abiding in pure being and the active God. Perfect unity merely *is*, it does not work. "Never," says Eckhart, "has the Godhead worked this or that, it is God Who creates all things." To that primal existence before the creation, to that unity transcending all dualism, the mystic strives finally to return; he wishes to become as he was before the creation.

Theistic mysticism does not always strain its conception of unity to the extreme of setting up thereby a dualism in the very being of God. Islamic mysticism avoids it by seeking to raise the attribute of work to an abstract height, where it is compatible with perfect unity. Certainly its success here is only apparent, for it transfigures as it were mystically the monotheistic tradition of the active God, without allowing any of the work of the worker to penetrate the mystical sphere itself;—the one is directed towards the world, the other is essentially acosmic; the one displays

197

God's doings in the community of mankind, the other is only acquainted with Him in His contacts with the soul; so Islamic mysticism, at the price of dividing religious life into two, achieves a questionable unity of God. Christian mysticism, in the best of its theology, proceeds here more boldly and more consistently. With unsurpassable precision it locates the tension in the divine itself. "God and Godhead," says Eckhart, "are as different as heaven and earth. . . . God becomes (wird) and vanishes (entwird)." So here "God" is the name of the Divine, in so far as from perfect unity, faced by nothing, It made Itself in creation and revelation the One facing the world, and thereby the partaker in Its becoming and vanishing. For "God" only exists for a world, by the Divine becoming its, the world's, God; when "world" becomes, God becomes; and if there is no world, God ceases to be, and again there is only Godhead.

Already here it can be seen that it would be a grave error to attribute to mysticism the view that the distinction between Godhead and God is only one of perspective, that is, one consisting not in itself but in the viewpoint of the world. Apart from all else such a view would nullify the historical revelation. Such is far from genuine theistic mysticism, which sees the distinction instead as founded in God's very being and consummated by Him.

Thus far has Christian mysticism proceeded with Eckhart, as Indian mysticism earlier in Sankara; further it has not attempted to penetrate. But by that an enigma that confronts us on the borderline of human being, at the point where it touches the Divine, has been only shifted into the Divine itself, and so for the time being withdrawn from further investigation. Not for ever; for there is in the history of later mysticism yet one more endeavour, even if only fragmentary and if apparently coming to a standstill in its very start, to penetrate still further and here again to ask "Why?" The question may be formulated provisionally thus: Why did God become Person? That Hasidism (and, so far as I can see, Hasidism alone) has ventured to attempt to answer this question—or rather, as will be shown, a related question—is indicated by the words of its greatest thinker, the Maggid of Mesritch, which we are able to extract from the notes of disciples and to some extent to put together. Here is one of the few points, in which Hasidic theology surpasses that of the later Kabbala, whose paths it follows here too, even if only gropingly.

[64]

BUDDHA, GAUTAMA

BUDDHA, GAUTAMA (c. 563-483 B.C.). The term "Buddha" means the "enlightened one who enlightens" or "the awakened who awakens the sense of truth in his fellow men." Buddhism is conceived of as the possession of perfect wisdom and supernatural powers. According to Buddhist doctrine, there is a line of Buddhas who appear in the course of human history from the time of remote antiquity to the distant future. The man who, in world history, is known as Buddha, was originally named Siddhartha (he who has accomplished his aim) or Sakyamuni (sage of the Sakya tribe). He belonged to the Gautama family, a warrior caste that ruled over the Sakya tribe. According to some scholars, the earliest reports of his life were written some two hundred to four hundred years after his death. But all these reports undoubtedly are rephrasings of verbal traditions based upon his life which appear in the detailed summaries of his original doctrines. With the exception of a few radical sceptics, most scholars agree that he married his cousin, Yasodhara, at the age of nineteen, and that a son, Rahula, was born of this union. There is no agreement as to the character of his activities.

In all probability, Buddha began to meditate upon the meaning of life in his early years, and became so disturbed by his awareness of human misfortunes and sufferings that he resolved to find the ways by which mankind could be comforted and redeemed. In India, and throughout the East, the path to knowledge that would enable him to rescue humanity, meant a nomadic life in order to obtain the advice of wise men, who themselves were wanderers, and to meditate in isolation. After six years of studying mankind, life, and doctrines, he was convinced that he had discovered Truth, and thereupon devoted the remainder of his lifetime to converting others to his ideas. He renounced his fortune and family and traveled through the valley of the Ganges as a mendicant, surrounded by an ever-increasing host of disciples, who also lived as mendicants, and finally formed an order.

Buddhism teaches four "Noble Truths," namely; Suffering; Knowledge of its cause, explained by the twelvefold Chain of Causation; Getting rid of passions as the means of deliverance from suffering; Truth, the way of removing suffering by a system of moral discipline. Buddha called his truths "noble," because he regarded nobility as moral. Whether rationalist or mystic, Buddha was a teacher of moral behavior. He avoided metaphysics and religion.

Buddhism has spread throughout Eastern Asia, and is the living faith in Ceylon, Japan, China, Indo-China, Siam, Burma, and Tibet, although it has undergone many modifications in these countries. In India the country where Buddha and Buddhism were born, Buddhism has been all but extinct since 1200 A.D. Modern Hindus are so estranged from Buddhism that Gandhi had to defend himself against the "accusation" of spreading Buddhistic teachings under the guise of Sanatana Hinduism. Gandhi did state, however, that in his "deliberate opinion, the essence of Buddha's teachings now form an integral part of Hinduism."

SOME TEACHINGS

INSIGHT into the causes of error results in the cessation of the consciousness of the self.

Phenomena, those sensuous objects that are striven for, are the cause of error.

However, the cause of error is the incorrect concept of wholeness.

Doubt arises because knowledge and ignorance are two different things.

There can be no doubt concerning the fact that the whole exists, for it has been previously demonstrated.

At the same time that we are not in doubt, other philosophers may state that it does *not* exist; that the whole or a part of the relationship is an impossible one; that there is no whole, nor are there any parts that comprise the whole; for actually there are no parts, and therefore there is no whole because there are no parts.

Moreover, continue these philosophers, there is no whole because it is not independent of its parts; nor do the parts constitute the whole.

200

These assertions create an unreal problem; for it does not make sense to talk of differences in the One, because it does not countenance differences.

The reason advanced by our opponents is only apparent because of the fact that the whole would not be in the parts, even if it had these parts.

To this they may object and say, that perception of the whole is like a wad of hair that dims vision.

A sense organ, like perception, whether it be keen or dull, does no more than sense its proper object. It fails to function in respect to an object that does not belong to its field.

Thus, our opponents will claim that the part-whole relationship could be continued until the dissolution of the world.

However, there is no dissolution of the world, because there are atoms.

Indeed it is said that the atom is finer than the mote in the sunbeam.

Some thinkers maintain that this is not the case, for the atom is pervaded by *akasa* (ether), and that *akasa* does not possess the quality of universal penetration.

However we say that the inner and outer parts exist only in a thing that is produced, just as one speaks of cause as something other than the thing that is produced. In anything that is not produced, there is no inner and outer.

Moreover, *akasa* has the quality of all-pervasiveness; its conjunction with sound is universally present.

Akasa has the qualities of nondispersion and nonresistance, and is omnipresent.

Some, however, do maintain that there are parts to the atom, because things possessed of form have a structure and because atoms are conjoined.

There is no valid objection to such reasoning, for that would lead to a *regressus ad infinitum*, and a *regressus ad infinitum* is not permissible.

At this point, our adversaries will say that on the basis

of intellectual analysis, one does not arrive at the nature of things, just as one does not perceive the existence of a piece of cloth except by its threads, so one does not perceive the whole except by its parts.

To this we retort, that this is not a valid reason, it confuses the issue.

The whole is not perceived as a separate entity, its parts are inherent in it.

In addition, objects are dependent upon the source of knowledge whether that source of knowledge is correct or incorrect.

Some opponents among the Buddhists tell us that this is an erroneous concept of the source and object of knowledge; just as they maintain that cognition of the image in dreams is erroneous; or that cognition is similar to the magic of the Fata Morgana of the city of Gandharvas or to the desert mirage called "thirst of the antelopes."

This is without foundation, for there is no ground for such comparison. Incorrect cognition of images in dreams is similar to the cognition involved in memory and desire. These, in turn, involve a cognition similar to our conscious existence.

Wrong perceptions disappear by virtue of knowing what is true, just as the wrong cognition of images in dreams vanishes upon waking.

Similarly, we arrive at truth by the recognition of the reality of that which is the basis of thought, as well as by the fact that there is dual knowledge: one is true, the other is false, and by the virtue of distinguishing that which is real from that which is perceived to be wrong.

Truth becomes known through special exercises for collecting one's thoughts.

Some will aver from this, because certain objects are over-powering and because one is driven by hunger and the like, thus making the collection of one's thoughts an impossibility.

Collection, by means of Yoga, should be practiced in the forest, in caves, and along river banks.

One might conclude that in the final liberation there is a disturbing influence of externals.

This is not so, because there must be a body, capable of receiving such disturbing impressions. Yet, such does not exist, nor is any longer countenanced in the liberated condition.

With this in mind, we must prepare ourselves, with physical and mental restraint, and avail ourselves of the prescriptions regarding the self in Yoga discipline.

One should practice the acquisition of insight and discuss it with those who have such wisdom.

The truth-seeker should invite discussions with students, teachers, associates, distinguished people, those who strive for the *summum bonum*, and those who have a serene disposition.

If he desires, he may seek such discussion, without antithesis, merely for the occasion to solidify his own views.

Contests and disputes should be sought out in order to establish and guard the truth; just as one surrounds the seed corn with thorns and branches to protect it as it grows.

In these two kinds of argumentation, debates engaged in accordance with the rules for winning the argument are in order.

[65]

BURCKHARDT, JAKOB

BURCKHARDT, JAKOB (1818-1897). Burckhardt taught history and lived quietly, frugally, undisturbed, and independent of the good and evil of modern civilization in his native town of Basle. His *Kultur der Renaissance* (1860) made him famous in all civilized countries, but his dislike for publicity was so great, that even though he continued to study and collect ample material to fill many more volumes, he refrained from publishing any further works during his lifetime. His skill as a teacher, his gift for narrating facts and events and integrating them with all branches of knowledge and cultural activity as part of a continuous evolutionary pattern attracted students from many countries. After his death, his lectures were edited, and those entitled *Reflections on History* have been acknowledged as a major contribution to modern historiography.

Burckhardt, the historian, was an austere judge of morality. He often condemned morally that which he admired aesthetically. He regarded history as the best means for ridding the world of its illusion, for though he saw beyond the superficial veil, nevertheless he loved and admired its fallacious charm. His sympathy was always with defeated minorities; their defeat confirmed his conviction that success had little to do with merit insofar as active life was concerned. However, he did admit that in poetry and art, greatness and success were often identical. His disapproval of results never prevented him from studying their causes.

ON WAR

IT is part of the wretchedness of life on earth that even the individual believes that he can only attain a full consciousness of his own value if he compares himself with others and, in certain circumstances, actually makes others feel it. The State, law, religion and morality are hard put to it to keep this bent within bounds, that is, to prevent its finding public expression. In the individual the open indulgence of it is regarded as ridiculous, intolerable, ill-mannered, dangerous, criminal.

On a big scale, however, nations from time to time assume that it is allowable and inevitable for them to fall upon each other on some pretext or other. The main pretext is that in international relations there is no other way of arriving at a decision, and: "If we don't, others will." We shall leave aside for the moment the highly diverse internal histories of the outbreaks of wars, which are often extremely complex.

A people actually feels its full strength as a people only in war, in the comparative contest with other peoples, because it only exists at that time. It must then endeavor to sustain its power at that level. Its whole standard has been enlarged.

In philosophic form, the dictum of Heraclitus, "war is the father of all things," is quoted in proof of the benefits of war. Lasaulx accordingly explains that antagonism is the cause of all growth, that harmony is born only of the conflict of forces, the "discordant harmony" or the "harmonious conflict" of things. This means, however, that both sides are still in possession of some vital energy, and not that one triumphs while the other lies prostrate. Indeed, according to him, war is divine in character, a world law and present in all nature. Not without cause do the Indians worship Shiva, the god of destruction. The warrior, he says, is filled with the joy of destruction, wars clear the air like thunderstorms, they steel the nerves and restore the heroic virtues, upon which States were originally founded, in place of indolence, double-dealing and cowardice. We might here also recall H. Leo's reference to "fresh and cheerful war, which shall sweep away the scrofulous mob."

Our conclusion is—men are men in peace as in war, and the wretchedness of earthly things lies equally upon them both. In any case, we generally suffer from an optical illusion in favour of those parties and their members with whose interests our own are in any way connected.

Lasting peace not only leads to enervation; it permits the rise of a mass of precarious, fear-ridden, distressful lives which would not have survived without it and which nevertheless clamour for their "rights," cling somehow to existence, bar the way to genuine ability, thicken the air and as a whole degrade the nation's blood. War restores real ability to honour. As for these wretched lives, war may at least reduce them to silence.

Further, war, which is simply the subjection of all life and property to *one* momentary aim, is morally vastly superior to the mere violent egoism of the individual; it develops power in the service of a supreme general idea and under a discipline which nevertheless permits supreme heroic virtue to unfold. Indeed, war alone grants to mankind the magnificent spectacle of a general submission to a general aim.

And since, further, only real power can guarantee a

peace and security of any duration, while war reveals where real power lies, the peace of the future lies in such a war.

Yet it should, if possible, be a just and honourable war —perhaps a war of defense such as the Persian War, which developed the powers of the Hellenes gloriously in all ways, or such as the war of the Netherlands against Spain.

Further, it must be a genuine war, with existence at stake. A permanent smouldering of small feuds, for instance, may replace war but is without value as a crisis. The German feudal heroes of the fifteenth century were highly astonished when they were confronted with an elemental power like the Hussites.

Nor did the disciplined "sport of kings" of the eighteenth century lead to much more than misery.

In quite a special sense, however, the wars of today are certainly aspects of a great general crisis, but individually they lack the significance and effect of genuine crises. Civilian life remains in its rut in spite of them, and it is precisely the pitiable existences referred to above which survive. But these wars leave behind them vast debts, i.e. they bequeath the main crisis to the future. Their brevity too deprives them of their value as crises. The full forces of despair do not come into play, and hence do not remain victorious on the field of battle, and yet it is they, and they alone, which could bring about a real regeneration of life, i.e. reconciliation in the abolition of an old order by a really vital new one.

Finally, it is quite unnecessary—as unnecessary as in the case of the barbarian invasion—to prophesy of all destruction that regeneration will come of it. It may be that this globe is already aged (nor does it matter how old it is in the absolute sense, i.e. how many times it has revolved round the sun—it may be very young for all that). We cannot imagine, in great tracts of denuded country, that new forests will ever arise to replace those which have been destroyed. And so peoples may be destroyed, and not even survive as component elements of other races.

And often it is the most righteous defense that has

proved most futile, and we must be thankful that Rome went so far as to proclaim the glory of Numantia, that conquerors have a sense of the greatness of the conquered.

The thought of a higher world plan, etc., is cold comfort. Every successful act of violence is a scandal, i.e. a bad example. The only lesson to be drawn from an evil deed successfully perpetrated by the stronger party is not to set a higher value on earthly life than it deserves.

[66]

BURKE, EDMUND

BURKE, EDMUND (1729-1797). The political pamphlets, parliamentary speeches, and essays of Burke proved him to be a genuine philosopher. His contemporaries, regardless of whether they shared his opinions, admired his talent for discerning the basic principles and elucidating the philosophical issues inherent in the disputes and interests of practical matters. Some of his essays, like *The Sublime and the Beautiful,* manifest the influence of Kant, Hegel, and many aestheticians of the eighteenth century. Despite his philosophical attitude toward the events of contemporary politics, Burke was always an ardent partisan, for his theoretical insights blended with his factious spirit and his realism with his romanticism. His morality demanded a rigorous honesty and cautious regard for actual circumstances, traditions, and expediences. He was always prepared to combat imminent dangers and great evil.

For more than three decades, Burke participated in political struggles. An Irishman by birth, and master of the English language, he was one of the greatest orators in the history of the British Parliament. Basically, he was convinced that the human individual is incapable of creating newness; that all useful and legitimate innovations must result from the slow growth of the collective mind in accordance with tradition. He strongly opposed changes in the British Constitution, whose excellent form was dogma to him. He fought for the removal of administrative abuses; opposed corruption, particularly the attempts of King George III to enslave both houses of Parliament. He denounced the French Revolution as a crime because it manifested a break with the past, served as a challenge to true wisdom and experience, and was a threat to liberty and prosperity. With his derision of the theory of the "Rights of Man," Burke became the vanguard of the European counter-revolution.

IT is an undertaking of some degree of delicacy to examine into the cause of public disorders. If a man happens not to succeed in such an inquiry, he will be thought weak and visionary; if he touches the true grievance, there is a danger that he may come near to persons of weight and consequence, who will rather be exasperated at the discovery of their errors, than thankful for the occasion of correcting them. If he should be obliged to blame favorites of the people, he will be considered as the tool of power; if he censures those in power, he will be looked on as an instrument of faction. But in all exertions of duty something is to be hazarded. In cases of tumult and disorder, our law has invested every man, in some sort, with the authority of a magistrate. When the affairs of the nation are distracted, private people are by the spirit of that law, justified in stepping a little out of their ordinary sphere. They enjoy a privilege, of somewhat more dignity and effect, than that of idle lamentation over the calamities of their country. They may look into them narrowly; they may reason upon them liberally; and if they should be so fortunate as to discover the true source of the mischief, and to suggest any probable method of removing it, though they may displease the rulers for the day, they are certainly of service to the cause of Government. Government is deeply interested in everything which, even through the medium of some temporary uneasiness, may tend finally to compose the minds of the subjects, and to conciliate their affections. I have nothing to do here with the abstract value of the voice of the people. But as long as reputation, the most precious possession of every individual, and as long as opinion, the great support of the State, depend entirely upon that voice, it can never be considered as a thing of little consequence either to individuals or to Government. Nations are not primarily ruled by laws; less by violence. Whatever original energy may be supposed either in force or regulation;

the operation of both is, in truth, merely instrumental. Nations are governed by the same methods, and on the same principles, by which an individual without authority is often able to govern those who are his equals or his superiors; by a knowledge of their temper, and by a judicious management of it; I mean—when public affairs are steadily and quietly conducted: not when the Government is nothing but a continued scuffle between the magistrate and the multitude; in which sometimes the one and sometimes the other is uppermost; in which they alternately yield and prevail, in a series of contemptible victories and scandalous submissions. The temper of the people amongst whom he presides ought therefore to be the first study of a Statesman. And the knowledge, of this temper it is by no means impossible for him to attain, if he has not an interest in being ignorant of what it is his duty to learn.

To complain of the age we live in, to murmur at the present possessors of power, to lament the past, to conceive extravagant hopes of the future, are the common dispositions of the greatest part of mankind; indeed the necessary effects of the ignorance and levity of the vulgar. Such complaints and humors have existed in all times; yet as all times have not been alike, true political sagacity manifests itself, in distinguishing that complaint which only characterizes the general infirmity of human nature, from those which are symptoms of the particular distemperature of our own air and season.

[67]

BURROUGHS, JOHN

BURROUGHS, JOHN (1837-1921). Characterized as a nature lover, friend of birds and squirrels, scientist and poet in his descriptions of animal and plant life, John Burroughs stated that his two greatest sources of inspiration were Emerson, in his youth, and Bergson, in later life. In 1882 he wrote, "With Emerson dead it seems folly to be alive." When Bergson lectured at Columbia University, Burroughs assiduously attended each lecture (although

209

he did not understand French), and hailed the French philosopher as "the prophet of the soul" who had opened new vistas to him.

Throughout his lifetime, Burroughs longed for the solitude which would allow him to enjoy the "company of one's self." He liked to live in his cabin in the woods and devote himself to "prophets of the soul" and sensory perception. He strove to attain large perspectives, but he also thought that "little things explain great things." This principle directed his observations of nature, which to him epitomized the spirit. He regarded natural objects as spiritual symbols and relished their variety, but maintained that chance does not exist in nature, but that laws dominate even the oddest singularity. He rejected materialism, but declared that "the greatest materialists I know are the spiritualists." He believed in the unity of matter and spirit. A man of action as well as of contemplation, Burroughs was an efficient bank examiner and receiver. Among his steadfast friends, he numbered Walt Whitman and Theodore Roosevelt. Whether he was leading an isolated life or a socialized existence, his spirit and actions were always forcefully compelling. His books, *Wake-Robin* (1871), *Birds and Poets* (1877), *Fresh Fields* (1884), *Ways of Nature* (1905), and *Accepting the Universe* (1920), have become favorite reading.

CONTRADICTIONS IN LIFE

LIFE and nature and philosophy are full of contradictions. The globe upon which we live presents the first great contradiction. It has no under or upper side; it is all outside. Go around it from east to west, or from north to south, and you find no bottom or top such as you see on the globe in your study, or as you apparently see on the moon and the sun in the heavens. A fly at the South Pole of the schoolroom globe is in a reversed position, but the discoverers of the South Pole on our earth did not find themselves in a reversed position on their arrival there, or in danger of falling off. The sphere is a perpetual contradiction. It is the harmonization of opposites. Our minds are adjusted to planes and to right lines, to up and down, to over and under. Our action upon things is linear. Curves and circles baffle us. My mind cannot adjust itself to the condition of free empty space.

Transport yourself in imagination away from the earth to the vacancy of the interstellar regions. Can you convince yourself that there would be no over and no under, no east and no west, no north and no south? Would one not look down to one's feet, and lift one's hand to one's head? What could one do?—No horizontal, no vertical—just the negation of all motion and direction. If one rode upon a meteorite rushing toward the earth, would one have the sensation of falling? Could one have any sensation of motion at all in absolutely vacant space—no matter at what speed with reference to the stars one might be moving? To have a sense of motion must we not have also a sense of something not in motion? In your boat on the river, carried by the tide or the current, you have no sense of motion till you look shoreward. With your eye upon the water all is at rest. The balloonist floats in an absolute calm. The wind does not buffet him because he goes with it. But he looks down and sees objects beneath him, and he looks up and sees clouds or stars above him. Fancy him continuing his journey on into space till he leaves the earth behind him—on and on till the earth appears like another moon. Would he look up or down to see it? Would he have a sense of rising or of falling? If he threw out ballast, would it drop or soar, or would it refuse to leave him?

Such speculations show how relative our sense standards are, how the law of the sphere upon which we live dominates and stamps our mental concepts. Away from the earth, in free space, and we are lost; we cannot find ourselves; we are stripped of everything but ourselves; we are stripped of night and day, of up and down, of east and west, of north and south, of time and space, of motion and rest, of weight and direction. Just what our predicament would be, who can fancy?

[68]

BUTLER, SAMUEL

BUTLER, SAMUEL (1835-1902). Butler's novel *Erewhon*, published in 1872, has been compared with Swift's *Gulliver's Travels* and Voltaire's *Candide*. Together with *The Way of All Flesh*, written

211

1872-1885 and published posthumously in 1903, Butler's position as a master of the English novel was firmly established. It has been a matter of considerable speculation among biographers as to what caused Butler to delay publication of his second novel and forego success as a novelist. He was a man of wide interests and abilities: he painted; composed; critically examined the evidence for the Resurrection of Christ; criticized Darwin by maintaining that the principle of natural selection deprived life of its purposiveness and "banished mind from the universe"; outlined his own theory of evolution in *Life and Habit* (1877) and *Evolution Old and New* (1879); developed his ideas in *Unconscious Memory* (1880); and advanced a new hypothesis concerning the authorship of the *Odyssey*.

Butler liked to call himself the "enfant terrible" of literature and science. He was fond of destroying the idols of his contemporaries and treating ironically those convictions generally classed as fundamentally important to the substance of civilization. He was often disturbed by his own destructive tendencies and suffered because his dissent differed from the common creed. Butler, though a diffident personality and daring humorist was incapable of liberating his emotions from the fear and hatred of his father, even after the latter's death. In his human relationships, he was alternately an attractive and repugnant personality. He disliked the past, despised the present, feared the future, and most of all, was terrified by the technological developments in engineering and machinery that he considered fatal to humanity. His acute penetration of the shortcomings of his time made him a great satirist, but he owed his deepest insights to his constant dismay at the independence of his own thoughts.

NOTES

A DEFINITION is the enclosing a wilderness of ideas within a wall of words.

To live is to love; all reason is against it, and all healthy instinct for it.

NATURE. As the word is now commonly used, it excludes nature's most interesting productions: the works of man. Nature is usually taken to mean mountains, rivers, clouds, undomesticated animals, and plants. I am not indifferent to this half of nature, but it interests me much less than the other half.

Imagination depends mainly upon memory, but there is a small percentage of creation of something out of nothing with it. We can invent a trifle more than can be got by mere combination of remembered things.

All men can do great things, if they know what great things are. So hard is this last that even where it exists the knowledge is as much unknown as known to them that have it, and is more a leaning upon the Lord than a willing of one who willeth. And yet all this leaning on the Lord in Christendom fails if there be not a will of him that willeth to back it up. God and man are powerless without one another.

GENIUS and PROVIDENCE. Among all the evidences for the existence of an overruling Providence that I can discover, I see none more convincing than the elaborate and, for the most part, effectual provision that has been made for the suppression of genius. The more I see of the world, the more necessary I see it to be, that by far the greater part of what is written or done should be of so fleeting a character as to take itself away quickly. That is the advantage in the fact that so much of our literature is journalism.

Schools and colleges are not intended to foster genius and to bring it out. Genius is a nuisance, and it is the duty of schools and colleges to abate it by setting genius-traps in its way. They are as the artificial obstructions in a hurdle race, tests of skill and endurance, but in themselves useless. Still, so necessary is it that genius and originality should be abated that, did not academies exist, we should have had to invent them.

[69]

213

C

CALKINS, MARCY WHITON

CALKINS, MARCY WHITON (1863-1930). The creed of Calkins is expressed in four principal statements which are developed in her books: *The Persistent Problems of Philosophy* (1907) and *The Good Man and The Good* (1918). She proceeded from the conviction that the universe contained distinct mental realities; that although the mind had emerged from a lower level of existence, it no longer belonged to that level, but rather to a new order of existence which had special laws of behavior. These mental realities were ultimately personal; consciousness never occurred impersonally. She defined psychology as a "science of the self as conscious." She also asserted that the universe was throughout, mental; that whatever was real was ultimately mental and therefore personal. She concluded that the universe was an all-inclusive Self; an absolute Person; a conscious being. She maintained that philosophy meant metaphysics, which she defined as "the attempt by reasoning to know what is ultimately real." To her, metaphysics did not imply a return to animism, and she stated that it was compatible with the concepts of scientific laws and that reasoning separated metaphysics from mysticism. She was considerably influenced by Royce; opposed logical atomism and instrumentalism. On several problems, she agreed with Samuel Alexander, but claimed a greater consistency.

EGOISM AND ALTRUISM

PERHAPS the most fundamental contrast between conceptions of the good is that between individualistic or (as they used to be named) egoistic theories on the one hand, and social, or altruistic, conceptions on the other. It must, however, carefully be borne in mind that there is a sense in which a

214

elf is always egoistic, for, whatever else a man is conscious of, he is always (though often very vaguely) conscious of himself. Similarly, there is a sense in which a self is always altruistically, or socially, conscious, for there is no really isolated self and even such predominantly "impersonal" experiences as thinking and perceiving have a social reference. That is to say, we are aware that other people, similarly placed, see what we see and hear what we hear; and we regard the laws of thought as universal, held by everybody. The clear understanding that every man is, in this fundamental sense, both egoist and altruist and that the two attitudes are not incompatible is an important introduction to the study of ethical egoism and altruism. For when a moral system is designated as egoistic (individualistic) or altruistic (social) either term is used, in a sense far narrower than that which has just been formulated, to indicate a basal form of willing.

It will be convenient first to present in a relatively uncritical fashion both the egoistic and the altruistic theory. Egoistic willing is, as we know, self-assertion, the subordination of my environment, personal or impersonal, to myself. And, from the standpoint of ethical egoism, the good which I ought to seek is precisely my own good, not that of anybody else. The argument for ethical individualism (or egoism), is variously stated. It is sometimes urged that the supreme object of will is a man's own good since only so can his will be directed toward that part of the universe, himself, which is under his own control. A man can not, it is argued, by his willing, alter the course of the sun or the conduct of a tradesman but he can affect his own conduct and he may gain his own pleasure, advantage, enlargement. Or again, it may be argued empirically that men actually reach their highest levels of achievement, develop their utmost strength and capacity, only under the spur of ambition, only in conditions of widest freedom, only through stressing their own individual purposes. The culmination of such a view is Nietzsche's teaching (as it is usually interpreted)—the doc-

215

trine that human progress is forever impossible except as each man relentlessly seeks his own advantage in total disregard of the needs of other men so that, out of the welter of failing, defeated beings there may emerge the superman —the man strong enough to trample down all rivalry and opposition and to win against all odds. Most often, however, egoism is argued negatively by the destructive criticism (presently to be summarized) of altruistic conceptions coupled with the implication that egoism is the only alternative to altruism.

Altruistic (or social) will—sharply contrasted with egoistic self-assertion—is loyalty, or devotion, the subordination of myself to a cause, a person, an ideal—in a word, to some object other than my narrow and individual self. The altruist conceives the moral self as furthering the happiness or the perfection no longer of himself but of another self or selves. To the altruist (in the strict meaning of the term) the good man is one who lavishes and sacrifices his own possessions, health, opportunities, his very life, for others. To be good consists in turning from one's own end, in crucifying, in torturing, in annihilating one's self so that one may thereby rescue, help, or enrich others. The mother who completely subordinates herself to her children is thus the never failing embodiment of the altruist's ideal. But there are as many forms of altruism as there are types of personal and social relationship. The cavalier who gives himself, body and soul, to the king's cause, the Jesuit who yields himself to his order, the union workman who goes on a sympathetic strike—these all are (or may well be) altruists. For the altruist abjures his own good and seeks that of other self or selves. And he appeals alike to the casual observer and to the close student of biography to confirm his view that the good men are altruists and that conversely, in Spencer's words, "an unchecked satisfaction of personal desires—in absolute disregard of all other beings would cause . . . social dissolution." Clearly, the altruist repeats, men who are ever seeking others' gains—devoted physicians, tireless teachers, lavish givers—

216

re willing a good to which the merely individual egoistic
ood must be subordinate. But the egoist is never silenced
y this appeal to experience. He first notes as incidental to
is argument, the patent fact that many alleged altruists are
eally egoists in disguise, seeking, under the cloak of avowed
ltruism, their individual ends: reputation or material gain.
And next, admitting the sincerity of genuinely altruistic
deals, the egoist emphasizes the divergence among them
nd the difficulty of harmonizing the objects of the personal,
he domestic, and the patriotic altruist. It is, on the face
f it, equally altruistic to sacrifice oneself for one's parents,
ne's children, one's state; but altruism contains no prin-
iple by which to decide between these conflicting objects.
With greatest effect, however, the critic attacks the fundamental position of altruism strictly defined, namely, dis-
egard of oneself. Herein, he insists, the altruistic concep-
ion is essentially irrational. The mother who wears her-
elf out in the passionate pursuit of what she deems best
or her children is purposing to defeat her own end (for
he is actually choosing a course which makes her useless
o the very beings whose good she is willing); and the object of her will, involving as it does disregard of an individual life, her own, can not possibly be viewed as the in-
controvertibly ultimate good. With Herbert Spencer, the
critic of altruism, one may go further and argue that a completely altruistic world is inherently impossible since if literally every self wills another's good, thereby giving up his
own, nobody experiences good and so the end sought by each
altruistically willing self is nonexistent.

[70]

CAMPANELLA, TOMMASO

CAMPANELLA, TOMMASO (1568-1639). A resident of Naples,
Campanella was sentenced to lifetime imprisonment during the
Spanish rule, for political plotting and heresy. During this time,
he wrote a valiant and courageous vindication of Galileo, who

217

had been tried by the Inquisition. After twenty-seven years of incarceration, Campanella succeeded in escaping to France, where he remained for the remainder of his life under the aegis of Cardinal Richelieu. His work was a source of inspiration for Mersenne and other French philosophers; as well as Leibniz. His philosophy was a blend of medieval thought combined with the methods of modern science. A Dominican and partisan of the secular power of the Pope, his communistic utopia, outlined in *City of the Sun*, was ruled by an ideal Pope. He regarded the world as the "living statue of God." Eternal truth is perceptible through the study of nature and the Bible. Many of his ideas are similar to those of modern day existentialists; for to him, neither the reports of the senses nor the speculations of reason, but only the feelings of one's own existence offer a reliable basis for the knowledge of God, man and nature. Preservation of existence is the aim of all human activities, and the laws that make for this preservation not only compel man to love God, but also to make him desire to return to Him.

ON STATE CONTROLLED MARRIAGE

THE race is managed for the good of the commonwealth, and not of private individuals, and the magistrates must be obeyed. They deny what we hold—viz., that it is natural to man to recognize his offspring and to educate them, and to use his wife and house and children as his own. For they say that children are bred for the preservation of the species and not for individual pleasure, as St. Thomas also asserts. Therefore the breeding of children has reference to the commonwealth, and not to individuals, except in so far as they are constituents of the commonwealth. And since individuals for the most part bring forth children wrongly and educate them wrongly, they consider that they remove destruction from the State, and therefore for this reason, with most sacred fear, they commit the education of the children, who, as it were, are the element of the republic, to the care of magistrates; for the safety of the community is not that of a few. And thus they distribute male and female breeders of the best natures according to philosophical rules. Plato thinks that this distribution ought to be made by lot, lest some men seeing that they are kept away from the beautiful women, hould rise up with anger and hatred against the magistrates; nd he thinks further that those who do not deserve cohabitation with the more beautiful women, should be deceived vhile the lots are being led out of the city by the magistrates, so that at all times the women who are suitable should all to their lot, not those whom they desire.

This shrewdness, however, is not necessary among the nhabitants of the City of the Sun. For with them deformity s unknown. When the women are exercised they get a clear omplexion, and become strong of limb, tall and agile, and vith them beauty consists in tallness and strength. Therefore, f any woman dyes her face, so that it may become beautiful, or uses high-heeled boots so that she may appear tall, or garments with trains to cover her wooden shoes, she is condemned to capital punishment. But if the women should even desire them, they have no facility for doing these hings. For who indeed would give them this facility? Further, they assert that among us abuses of this kind arise from he leisure and sloth of women. By these means they lose heir color and have pale complexions, and become feeble and small. For this reason they are without proper complexions, use high sandals, and become beautiful not from strength, but from slothful tenderness. And thus they ruin heir own tempers and natures, and consequently those of heir offspring. Furthermore, if at any time a man is taken captive with ardent love for a certain woman, the two are allowed to converse and joke together, and to give one another garlands of flowers or leaves, and to make verses. But if the race is endangered, by no means is further union between them permitted. Moreover, the love born of eager desire is not known among them; only that born of friendship.

[71]

CARDOZO, BENJAMIN NATHAN

CARDOZO, BENJAMIN NATHAN (1870-1938). It has been said of Justice Cardozo, that "by the magic of his pen, he transmuted law

219

into justice." He was one of the greatest American philosophers o law; chief judge of the Supreme Court of the State of New York for more than ten years; Justice of the Supreme Court of the United States, and recipient of many honorary degrees.

Justice, to Cardozo, was "a concept far more subtle and indefinite than any that is yielded by mere obedience to a rule. It remains, to some extent, when all is said and done, the synonym of an aspiration, a mood of exaltation, a yearning for what is fine and high."

Despite all his sensitivity to the indefinite, Cardozo was also a thinker whose profundity never excluded clear and distinct concepts and definitions. He was aware of the paradoxes and tensions of his profession, yet remained capable of viewing things with plain and simple common sense. He always tried to synthesize law and life, by comprehending the stream of historical life and the chaotic drives of social and economic forces. He was conscious of the necessity for adapting existing forms to newly emergent trends. He was not a radical, but he was imbued with the spirit of democracy. Franklin D. Roosevelt, upon the death of Cardozo, called this scholar and wise man, a "great soul." Cardozo was devoted to the welfare of the nation, defended the rights of the individual, strove for harmony between contradictory interests, staunchly opposed selfish interests, and was a courageous fighter for liberty and truth.

LAW AND LIBERTY

WHEN we speak of law and liberty, and the need of compromise between them, what is uppermost in our minds is commonly the kind of problem that is involved in the definition of the constitutional immunity. In essence, however, the problem is not different whenever a rule of law is extended into fields unoccupied before. "Shall A answer to B for the consequences of an act?" means this and nothing more, "Shall the freedom of A to work damage to B be restrained so as to preserve to B the freedom to be exempt from damage?" In determining whether it shall, we must again evaluate the social interests concerned. We have regard to the social interest of certainty. The force of precedent and analogy may lead us to refuse an extension that we would otherwise concede. If these guides are silent or inconclusive, we give heed to the prompting of justice or of expediency, which may shade down from considerations of supreme importance to those of mere convenience. "Das Recht," as Binding puts it, "ist eine Ordnung menschlicher Freiheit." The opposites, liberty and restraint, the individual and the group, are phases of those wider opposites, the one and the many, rest and motion, at the heart of all being. Dichotomy is everywhere.

One of the marks by which we recognize a social interest as worthy of protection is the spontaneity and persistence with which groups are established to conserve it. The mark, of course, is not infallible. There are groups, spontaneous and persistent enough,—camorras, secret orders, revolutionary bands—whose aims are anti-social. Even so, spontaneity and persistence are tokens not to be ignored that the associative process is moving toward a social end. A striking instance of this truth is seen in the history of trade-unions. At first the law held them anathema. They were combinations in restraint of trade, pernicious, it was thought, in so far as they were effective, and, in the long run, as futile as they were pernicious, since economic "laws," then supposed to be inexorable, would nullify the gains of victory, and restore the pre-existing level. The result belied the prophecy. The urge to associate and unify was too spontaneous and persistent for any interdict to stifle it. The courts perceived and yielded. They were helped at times by legislation. In many jurisdictions, however, they reached the same result unaided. They gave up denouncing as lawless and unsocial a form of grouping that appeared and reappeared in response to a social pressure akin in steadiness and intensity to the pressure that makes law. Whether the unions were to be classified as jural persons was another question of quite subsidiary importance. What mattered most was that they were lawful. The state would hold them in check as it would hold in check the individual and even the agencies of government, it would not repudiate or destroy them. In the struggle between liberty and restraint, a new liberty, asserting itself persistently and clamorously in the minds and hearts of men, became a liberty secured by law. Out of the psychical urge there had been born the jural right. The peace of a new compromise had been declared between the warring opposites.

[72]

CARLYLE, THOMAS

CARLYLE, THOMAS (1795-1881). The writings of Carlyle differ considerably from those of Locke, Hume, Pope, Fielding, Macaulay, and John Stuart Mill. For Carlyle wrote emotionally; his language expressed passion, love, hate, enthusiasm, or scorn; nothing left him unmoved. He was a bitter enemy of the Age of Reason, and detested cold logic, intellectual abstraction, and scientific aloofness.

Although not an orthodox Protestant, he classed himself as a Christian for whom faith was the source of wisdom and the standard of criticism for life and art. Society, as he conceived it, was the brotherhood of men and the union of souls. He categorized political constitutions, class distinctions, political parties, and trade unions as the artificial products of human arrogance. He distrusted material progress, opposed the advances of modern civilization, and scoffed at the diseases and misfortunes of modern life. He maintained that the latter were curable, provided mankind was guided by great men. He derided universal suffrage, even though he sympathized with the Chartist movement. He preferred a kind of patriarchal feudalism to the governmental regulation of wages, or the bargaining process between management and labor.

Surely he was not a misanthrope, for he sincerely desired: the improvement of human conditions, a continuing spiritual development, and increased education for the masses. He asserted that great men would serve as the instruments by which those things would be accomplished, that they were the real trustees of the common interests of human happiness and could not be judged by the moral standards of the middle and lower classes. His theories led him to exalt Frederick William I of Prussia, the soldier king, whose principles became the tenets of fascism, and to praise the regime and wars of his son, Frederick II. A great admirer of German poetry and metaphysics, he considered both to be imbued with the true Christian spirit. Until his death he remained an optimist, always hoping for those events which would lead mankind back to a true Christian way of life.

WE have undertaken to discourse here for a little on Great Men, their manner of appearance in our world's business, how they have shaped themselves in the world's history, what ideas men formed of them, what work they did;—on Heroes, namely, and on their reception and performance; what I call Hero-worship and the Heroic in human affairs. Too evidently this is a large topic; deserving quite other treatment than we can expect to give it at present. A larger topic; indeed, an illimitable one; wide as Universal History itself. For, as I take it, Universal History, the history of what man has accomplished in this world, is at bottom the History of the Great Men who have worked here. They were the leaders of men, these great ones; the modellers, patterns, and in a wide sense creators, of whatsoever the general mass of men contrived to do or to attain; all things that we see standing accomplished in the world are properly the outer material result, the practical realization and embodiment, of Thoughts that dwelt in the Great Men sent into the world: the soul of the whole world's history, it may justly be considered, were the history of these. Too clearly it is a topic we shall do no justice to in this place!

One comfort is, that Great Men, taken up in any way, are profitable company. We cannot look, however imperfectly, upon a great man, without gaining something by him. He is the living light-fountain, which it is good and pleasant to be near. The light which enlightens, which has enlightened the darkness of the world; and this not as a kindled lamp only, but rather as a natural luminary shining by the gift of Heaven; a flowing light-fountain, as I say, of native original insight, of manhood and heroic nobleness;—in whose radiance all souls feel that it is well with them. On any terms whatsoever, you will not grudge to wander in such neighbourhood for a while. These Six classes of Heroes, chosen out of widely distant countries and epochs, and in mere external figure differing altogether, ought, if we look faithfully at them, to illustrate several things for us. Could we see *them* well, we should get some glimpses into the very marrow of the world's history.

[73]

CARNEADES

CARNEADES (c. 214-129 B.C.). Carneades was born in Cyrene, North Africa. A radical sceptic, he was the first of the philosophers to pronounce the failure of metaphysicians who endeavored to discover rational meanings in religious beliefs. By 159 B.C. he had begun to refute all dogmatic doctrines, particularly Stoicism; nor did he spare the Epicureans as previous sceptics had done. The original theory of probability that he developed was profound and of great consequence. While he attacked the efforts of the Stoics to reconcile popular religions with their philosophical convictions, he also denied the immortality of the gods, their super-human qualities, pantheism, fatalism, and providence. He refused to accept moral values as absolute, although he taught the necessity of learning how to conduct one's life in an artful manner by combining sagacity and reflective thought. In his practical ethics, he professed a moderate Platonism, devoid of all religious or metaphysical elements. He founded the third or New Academy. However, his philosophy had very little in common with Plato, the original founder of the Academy.

THE FALLACY OF THE CRITERION OF TRUTH

THERE is absolutely no criterion for truth. For reason, senses, ideas, or whatever else may exist are all deceptive.

Even if such criterion were at hand, it could not stand apart from the feelings which sense impressions produce. It is the faculty of feeling that distinguishes the living creature from inanimate things. By means of that feeling, the living creature becomes perceptive of both itself and the external world. There is no sensation or perception of anything unless the sense is irritated, agitated, or perturbed. When an object is indicated, then the senses become irritated and somewhat disturbed. It is impossible that there be an unperturbed presentation of external things.

The subject is more or less persuaded by the image it perceives. The strength of that persuasion depends on the disposition of the subject and on the degree of irritation produced by the image. It is not the distinctness of the image that constitutes its credibility.

The only way we can ever obtain certitude is by the difficult process of examination. We cannot be satisfied with evidence that is incomplete and only probable. Our certitude is always a precarious one. Science relies on probability, not on certitude.

[74]

CARTESIUS. See DESCARTES, RENÉ.

CARUS, PAUL

CARUS, PAUL (1852-1919). The memory of the eclectic Paul Carus is kept alive by the Carus Foundation, the Carus Lectures, and the American Philosophical Association. Carus preferred to consider himself a theologian rather than a philosopher. He referred to himself as "an atheist who loved God." The fact was that he was a pantheist who insisted that God, as a cosmic order, was a name comprising "all that which is the bread of our spiritual life." He held the concept of a personal God as untenable. Carus' monism was more frequently associated with a kind of pantheism, although it was occasionally identified with positivism. His pantheistic theology regarded every law of nature as a part of God's being. Although when he maintained that the laws of mechanics represented the action of spiritual existence, it was never quite clear whether he meant that mechanics were a part of God's being, or more simply, that the matter was identical with mind; thus he did not commit himself as to the character of divinity. He acknowledged Jesus Christ as a redeemer, but not as the only one, for he believed that Buddha and other religious founders were equally endowed with the same qualities.

Carus tried to steer a middle course between idealistic metaphysics and materialism. He disagreed with metaphysicians because they "reified" words and dealt with them as though they were realities. He objected to materialism because it ignored or overlooked the importance of form. Carus constantly emphasized form by conceiving of the divinity as a cosmic order. He also objected to any monism which sought the unity of the world not in the unity of truth but in the oneness of a logical assumption of ideas. He referred to such concepts as *henism*, not monism. He stated that truth was independent of time, human desire, and human action. Therefore, science was not a human invention, but a human revelation which needed to be apprehended; discovery meant apprehension; it was the result or manifestation of the cosmic order in which all truths were ultimately harmonious.

MONISM

THE Monism which I represent insists on the reality of form and of relations, and on the significance of ideas. The soul of man is . . . his mind. He is not a mere heap of atoms. He consists of ideas. His existence is not purely material. It is also and principally spiritual. We grant there is no ego soul. There is as little a metaphysical thing-in-itself in man as there is a thing-in-itself of a watch or a tree, or a natural law. But nevertheless, just as much as that combination called a watch is not a nonentity but a reality, in the same way man's soul, in spite of the non-existence of a metaphysical ego soul, is not a nonentity but a reality; and the mold into which we have been cast is that divinity of the world which was at the beginning and will remain forever and aye.

The term Monism is often used in the sense of one substance theory that either mind alone or matter alone exists. These views generally called materialism, idealism or spiritualism, are pseudomonisms and would better be called henism. For either view attempts to explain the world from one single concept, deriving therefrom all natural phenomena. Monism does not attempt to subsume all phenomena under one category but remains conscious of the truth that spirit and matter, soul and body, God and world are different, not entities but abstract ideas denoting certain features of reality.

Monism is a unitary conception of the world—one inseparable and indivisible entirety.

Monism stands upon the principles that all the dif-

erent truths are but so many different aspects of one and
1e same truth.

[75]

CASSIRER, ERNST

ASSIRER, ERNST (1874-1945). Cassirer's philosophy proceeds
·om the basic conviction that historical investigation and systematic
rder do not contradict each other, but rather are conditional and
1utually support one another. Their result is the demonstration of
1e "immanent logic of history," based upon the critical examina-
on of abundant empirical materials. Cassirer's works contributed
) historical development of epistemology. In *Philosophie der Sym-
lischen Formen* (1924), he dealt with the functions of linguistic
nd mythical thinking, coordinating the world of pure knowledge
ith religious, mythical, and artistic ideas. Cassirer was firmly
onvinced that the different approaches to reality cooperate in the
)rmation of a totality of meaning.

During the Kaiser's reign in Germany, he was denied appoint-
1ent as a professor and tolerated only as a lecturer. Under the
Iitler regime, he was compelled to emigrate—first, to Sweden,
here he was a professor at the University of Goetenborg, then to
1e United States.

MAN, AN ANIMAL SYMBOLISM

N the human world we find a new characteristic which ap-
·ears to be the distinctive mark of human life. The func-
ional circle of man is not only quantitatively enlarged; it
as also undergone a qualitative change. Man has, as it
/ere, discovered a new method of adapting himself to his
nvironment. Between the receptor system and the effector
ystem, which are to be found in all animal species, we find
n man a third link which we may describe as the *symbolic
ystem*. This new acquisition transforms the whole of human
ife. As compared with the other animals man lives not
nerely in a broader reality; he lives, so to speak, in a new
limension of reality. There is an unmistakable difference
·etween organic reactions and human responses. In the first
ase a direct and immediate answer is given to an outward

stimulus; in the second case the answer is delayed. It is interrupted and retarded by a slow and complicated process of thought. At first sight such a delay may appear to be a very questionable gain. Many philosophers have warned man against this pretended progress. "L'Homme qui médite," says Rousseau, "est un animal dépravé": it is not an improvement but a deterioration of human nature to exceed the boundaries of organic life.

Yet there is no remedy against this reversal of the natural order. Man cannot escape from his own achievement. He cannot but adopt the conditions of his own life. No longer in a merely physical universe, man lives in a symbolic universe. Language, myth, art, and religion are parts of this universe. They are the varied threads which weave the symbolic net, the tangled web of human experience. All human progress in thought and experience refines upon and strengthens this net. No longer can man confront reality immediately; he cannot see it, as it were, face to face. Physical reality seems to recede in proportion as man's symbolic activity advances. Instead of dealing with the things themselves man is in a sense constantly conversing with himself. He has so enveloped himself in linguistic forms, in artistic images, in mythical symbols or religious rites that he cannot see or know anything except by the interposition of this artificial medium. His situation is the same in the theoretical as in the practical sphere. Even here man does not live in a world of hard facts, or according to his immediate needs and desires. He lives rather in the midst of imaginary emotions, in hopes and fears, in illusions and disillusions, in his fantasies and dreams. "What disturbs and alarms man," said Epictetus, "are not the things, but his opinions and fancies about the things."

From the point of view at which we have just arrived we may correct and enlarge the classical definition of man. In spite of all the efforts of modern irrationalism this definition of man as an *animal rationale* has not lost its force. Rationality is indeed an inherent feature of all human activ ties. Mythology itself is not simply a crude mass of super-stitions or gross delusions. It is not merely chaotic, for it possesses a systematic or conceptual form. But, on the other hand, it would be impossible to characterize the structure of myth as rational. Language has often been identified with reason, or with the very source of reason. But it is easy to see that this definition fails to cover the whole field. It is a *pars pro toto;* it offers us a part for the whole. For side by side with logical or scientific language there is a language of poetic imagination. Primarily language does not express thoughts or ideas, but feelings and affections. And even a religion "within the limits of pure reason" as conceived and worked out by Kant is no more than a mere abstraction. It conveys only the ideal shape, only the shadow, of what a genuine and concrete religious life is. The great thinkers who have defined man as an *animal rationale* were not em-piricists, nor did they ever intend to give an empirical ac-count of human nature. By this definition they were express-ing rather a fundamental moral imperative. Reason is a very inadequate term with which to comprehend the forms of man's cultural life in all their richness and variety. But all these forms are symbolic forms. Hence, instead of de-fining man as an *animal rationale,* we should define him as an *animal symbolicum.* By so doing we can designate his specific difference, and we can understand the new way open to man—the way to civilization.

[76]

CHERNYSHEVSKY, NICOLAI GAVRILOVICH

CHERNYSHEVSKY, NICOLAI GAVRILOVICH (1828-1889). After the assassination of Czar Alexander II of Russia, the secret police, in order to avoid a similar recurrence on the occasion of the coronation of the new Czar, affected a compromise with the revolu-tionary groups. The latter demanded the liberation of Chernyshev-sky as the principal condition for their refraining from an attempt on the Czar's life.

Chernyshevsky did not belong to any revolutionary organiza-

tion or party. He had been sentenced, after two years of imprison
ment in a fortress, to seven years hard labor and lifelong banishmen
to Siberia.

The son of an orthodox priest, educated in the spirit of Russiar
orthodoxy, he adopted the views of Feuerbach, Fourier, Proudhon
and John Stuart Mill, whose *Principles of Political Economy* h
had translated into Russian. His interpretation and critical note
on Mill's work not only proved Chernyshevsky's independent mind
but also pointed up the social problems of Russia. As a member
of the staff of the influential periodical, *Sovremennik* (Contempor
ary), he introduced the spirit of Western civilization into Russi
and defended the interests of the peasants against the great land
owners before and after the emancipation of the serfs. He believe
that philosophical materialism was the basis for social progress
but that ethics of self-discipline and altruism were also needed
As prisoner in the Peter and Paul fortress, he wrote the novel
What Is To Be Done, (1863) which was a source of inspiratior
to Russian youth until the First World War.

Chernyshevsky returned to St. Petersburg in 1881, his health
undermined, forced to live in isolation, and dependent upon trans
lating as a means of livelihood. Until the 1905 Russian revolution
censorship did not permit any mention of his name. His works
were printed anonymously, but the Russian people recognized him
as the author, and revered him as the martyr of free thought.

THE EVOLUTION OF LANGUAGE

PHILOLOGY shows that all languages begin with that stage in
which there is no declension, no conjugation, and no change
of aspect or inflection in the word, and each case of everything assumes one and the same form. Modern Chinese serves
as an example of this.

As language becomes more developed, inflection appears with greater frequency. The composition of the word
reaches the kind of flexibility that is characteristic of the
Semitic dialects. Language acquires the extreme abundance
of grammatical suffixes that are observable in Tartarian
where the verb has seven or eight moods, a full dozen tenses,
and ten gerundial forms. In our own linguistic family, the
highest point of that evolution is marked by Sanskrit. But
evolution continues; in Latin and Old Slavic, there is less

inflection than there is in Sanskrit. The longer a language lives, and the more people develop it by speaking, the more it tends to get rid of the old richness of inflection. Modern Slavic dialects are poorer than Old Slavic. There is less inflection in Italian, French, Spanish, and other Romance languages than there is in Latin; less inflection in German, Danish, Swedish, and Dutch, than in Gothic. English is indicative of the goal towards which all European languages will march, as far as inflection is concerned.

At the onset of linguistic evolution, there are no cases; neither are there any at the end. In the grammatical evolution of language, the end corresponds to the beginning. The same fact is reproduced in all forms of intellectual and social life which have language as the common condition of their subsistence.

[77]

CHRYSIPPUS

CHRYSIPPUS (c. 280-207 B.C.). The Stoic school of philosophy, established by Zeno, would not have had as lasting an influence had not Chrysippus developed and solidified its concepts. He was born in Soli, Cilicia, Asia Minor, and went to Athens in 260 B.C. There he succeeded Cleanthes as director of the Stoic school. Chrysippus is said to have written some seven hundred books on a variety of topics. Although his literary style was far from masterful, he was a systematic thinker, logician, and psychologist. He anticipated several important propositions which were of considerable consequence in later eras. He particularly investigated sentiments and ideas, and tried to obtain through logical and dialectical disquisitions the irrefutable truths upon which his ethics and theology were based. He stated that the essential characteristic of man which distinguished him from the animals was that his judgment became active as soon as his sensations were irritated. In ethics, Chrysippus assumed that a natural impetus operated in all living creatures. This impetus was conscious in man. He did not see any dichotomy between the decision of human will and that of natural impetus. Nature, striving for virtue, made the natural impetus.

231

THE slightest thing that happens takes place in accordance with nature and its reason.

Common nature is spread throughout all things. Therefore whatever happens in the universe is in accordance with common nature and its reason, and therefore proceeds in an unhindered fashion. There is nothing outside the universe to oppose its working, nor can any of its parts be moved or conditioned in a fashion other than that which is agreeable to common nature.

Sometimes good men suffer misfortunes, not as punishment for wickedness, but in accordance with some other lines of administration.

Just as states which have a surplus population send great numbers of their people out to the colonies, and stir up wars against their neighbor, so God provides occasion for our destruction.

It is unreasonable to say that the deity is the cause of base deeds. Just as law cannot be the cause for misdemeanor, so God cannot be the cause of impiety.

Homer correctly stated: "The will of Zeus is done"; referring to the fate and nature of the universe by which all things are governed.

[78]

CHUANG CHOU

CHUANG CHOU (c. 340-280 B.C.). Modern experts on Chinese philosophy consider Chuang Chou as among the most brilliant of all the Chinese philosophers. He was a scholar, a poet, and a master of dialectic and logic. Aware of the unity of the universe, he longed for "the transcendental bliss" which brought peace of mind and enabled man to live harmoniously with nature. His ability at logic and dialectics made him appear to be a cynical debunker, fond of destroying renowned illusions, but his love of freedom was too great to allow him to deny the values of government and society; he often declined high office in order to retain his personal

232

independence. As a formidable adversary of Confucius, he was frequently and severely criticized by Mencius. If Chuang Chou was
not the founder of that which was subsequently called Taoism,
certainly he was its precursor, and the extent of his soaring imagination, the profundity of his thought, and the power of his style
were never matched by any of the Taoists.

EXCURSIONS INTO FREEDOM

IN THE Northern Ocean there is a fish, its name the Kun
[Leviathan], its size I know not how many *li*. By metamorphosis it becomes a bird called the P'eng ['Roc'], with
a back I know not how many *li* in extent. When it rouses
itself and flies, its wings darken the sky like clouds. With
the sea in motion this bird transports itself to the Southern
Ocean, the Lake of Heaven. In the words of Ch'i Hsieh, a
recorder of marvels, 'When the P'eng transports itself to the
Southern Ocean, it thrashes the water for three thousand *li*,
and mounts in a whirlwind to the height of ninety thousand
li, and flies continuously for six months before it comes to
rest.'

A mote in a sunbeam (that in one sense is all that this
vast Roc is): flying dust which living creatures breathe in
and out! And that blueness of the sky! Is it an actual color,
or is it the measureless depth of the heavens which we gaze
at from below and see as 'blue,' just like that and nothing
more? Again take water, without the dense accumulation of
which there is no power for the floating of a great ship. And
(think of) a cup of water upset in a corner of the hall. A
tiny mustard seed becomes a ship (afloat), but the cup which
held the water will remain aground because of the shallowness of the water and the size of the cup as a ship.

So with the accumulation of wind, without sufficient
density it has no power to float huge wings. Thus it is that
the P'eng has to rise ninety thousand *li* and cut off the wind
beneath it. Then and not before, the bird, borne up by the
down-pressed wind, floats in the azure heavens with secure
support. Then and not before, it can start on its journey
south.

A cicada and a young dove giggled together over the P'eng. The cicada said, 'When we exert ourselves to fly up on to the tall elms, we sometimes fail to get there and are pulled back to the ground; and that is that. Why then should any one mount up ninety thousand *li* in order to go south?' Well, the man who goes out to the grassy country near by takes only three meals with him and comes back with his stomach well filled. But the man who has to travel a hundred *li* grinds flour for one night on the way; and the man who has to travel a thousand *li* requires food for three months. These two little creatures (the cicada and the dove), what can they know?

Small knowledge is not equal to great knowledge, just as a short life is not equal to a long one. How do we know this to be so? The mushroom with one brief morning's existence has no knowledge of the duration of a month. The chrysalis knows nothing of the spring and the autumn.

Thus it is that the knowledge of some men qualifies them for a small office and for effecting unity in one district, whilst the moral power of another man fits him to be a ruler and proves itself throughout a whole country. These men have a view of themselves which is like the quail's view of himself.

On the other hand, Master Yung of Sung State just laughs at these men. If the whole world should admire or criticize him, he would neither be encouraged nor discouraged. Having determined the difference between what is intrinsic and what extrinsic, he disputed the accepted boundaries of honor and dishonor. In this he was himself, and there are very few such men in the world. Nevertheless he was not really rooted.

Take Master Lieh. He could drive the wind as a team and go, borne aloft, away for fifteen days before returning. Such a man attains a happiness which few possess. Yet in this although he had no need to walk, there was still something on which he was dependent [viz. the wind]. Supposing, however, that he were borne on the normality of the heavens and earth, driving a team of the six elements in their changes, and thus wandered freely in infinity-eternity, would there be anything then on which he was dependent?

Thus it is that I say, 'The perfect man has no self, the spirit-endowed man no achievements, the sage no reputation.'

[79]

CICERO, MARCUS TULLIUS

CICERO, MARCUS TULLIUS (106-43 B.C.). The tremendous historical influence of Cicero's philosophical writings cannot be underestimated. It is evident in the works of the Church fathers, Petrarch, Erasmus, and Copernicus. Even Voltaire, among whose many talents the quality of admiration was the least developed, praised two of Cicero's books as "of the noblest works that were ever written." The founding fathers of the United States were equally ardent in their admiration of Cicero. Thomas Jefferson read *De Senectute* (On Old Age) every year; John Adams, the second President of the United States, declared that "all the epochs of world history combined were unable to produce statesman or philosopher as great as Cicero. His authority should have considerable weight." His son, John Quincy Adams, while lecturing at Harvard University, supported Cicero's doctrine that eloquence was the mainstay of liberty. Theodor Mommsen, in his famous *Roman History*, used all his education, ability, and authority to debunk Cicero; for it had become fashionable to abuse and sneer at Cicero as a politician and philosopher. Thadaeus Zielinski, the great Russian philologist, asserted that of all Julius Caesar's achievements none was as important to the history of human civilization as the fact that Caesar, by compelling Cicero to retire to the country, forced the latter to state his philosophy in writing.

It is somewhat difficult to define either Cicero's originality or lack of it, since the works of those Greek philosophers from whom he allegedly borrowed his ideas are lost. One idea was certainly his own: the doctrine that "no war should be undertaken, except to maintain good faith or security."

ON FRIENDSHIP

THE right course is to choose for a friend one who is frank, sociable and sympathetic—that is, one who is likely to be influenced by the same motives as yourself—since all these

235

qualities induce to loyalty; for it is impossible for a man to be loyal whose nature is full of twists and twinings; and, indeed, one who is untouched by the same influences as yourself and is naturally unsympathetic cannot be loyal.

Since happiness is our best and highest aim we must, if we would attain it, give our attention to virtue, without which we can obtain neither friendship nor any other desirable thing; on the other hand, those who slight virtue and yet think that they have friends perceive their mistake at last when some grievous misfortune causes them to put their friends to the test. Virtue both creates the bond of friendship and preserves it. For in virtue is complete harmony, in her is permanence, in her is fidelity; and when she has raised her head and shown her own light, and recognized the same light in another, she moves towards it and in turn receives its beams; as a result love or friendship leaps into flame.

We must despair of the safety of the man whose ears are so closed to truth that he cannot hear what is true from a friend. For there is shrewdness in that well-known saying of Cato: "Some men are better served by their bitter-tongued enemies than by their sweet-smiling friends; because the former often tell the truth; the latter, never."

*   *   *

New friendships are not to be scorned if they offer hope of bearing fruit, like green shoots of corn that do not disappoint us at harvest time; yet the old friendships must preserve their own place, for the force of age and habit is very great.

In the intimacy existing between friends and relatives the superior should put himself on a level with his inferior, so the latter ought not to grieve that he is surpassed by the former in intellect, fortune or position. Even if you could bestow upon another any honor you chose, yet you must consider what he is able to bear.

Difference of character is attended by difference of

taste and it is this diversity of taste that severs friendships; nor is there any other cause why good men cannot be friends to wicked men, or wicked men to good men, except that there is the greatest possible difference between them in character.

We must be ever on the search for some persons whom we shall love and who will love us in return; for if good will and affection are taken away, every joy is taken from life.

[80]

ON JUSTICE

THE great foundation of justice is faithfulness, which consists in being constantly firm to your word, and a conscientious performance of all compacts and bargains. The vice that is opposite to justice is injustice, of which there are two sorts: the first consists in the actual doing an injury to another; the second, in tamely looking on while he is injured, and not helping and defending him though we are able. He that injuriously falls on another, whether prompted by rage or other violent passion, does, as it were, leap at the throat of his companion; and he that refuses to help him when injured, and to ward off the wrong if it lies in his power, is as guilty of injustice as though he had deserted his father, his friends or native country.

It is observable that the limits of justice are not fixed. Respect must be had to general rules as the ground and foundation of all justice—first, that no injury be done to another; and, secondly, that we make it our earnest endeavor to promote the good of all mankind: so that our duty is not always the same, but various, according to circumstances.

*   *   *

There are certain duties to be strictly observed, even towards those who have injured us; for we ought not to go beyond certain bounds in exacting revenge and punishment of another; in which particular it may, perhaps, be enough

237

to make him that has wronged us repent of the wrong done, so that both he himself may abstain from the like, and others may be discouraged from injuring us in the future.

There are certain peculiar laws of war, also, which are of all things most strictly to be observed in the commonwealth; for there being two sorts of disputing in the world, the one by reason, and the other by open force; and the former of these being that which is agreeable to the nature of man, and the latter to that of brutes. When we cannot obtain what is our right by the one, we must of necessity have recourse to the other. It is allowable, therefore, to undertake wars, but it must always be with the design of obtaining a secure peace; and when we have got the better of our enemies, we should rest content with the victory alone unless they are such as have been very cruel and committed inhuman barbarities in the war. In my opinion, it is always our duty to do what we can for a fair and safe peace.

Unless a man be governed by the rules of justice, and fight for the safety and good of the public, his is a sort of courage that is altogether blamable.

[80A]

CLAIRVAUX, SAINT BERNARD OF. See BERNARD OF CLAIRVAUX, SAINT.

CLEANTHES

CLEANTHES (310-232 B.C.). Noted as a director of the oldest Stoic school for thirty-one years, Cleanthes, an indigent scholar, worked mostly as a porter until finally, at the age of fifty, he was enabled to enter a philosopher's school. He became a devoted disciple of Zeno, the Stoic, studied under his master for nineteen years, and upon Zeno's death, assumed the directorship of the school. Cleanthes slightly modified Zeno's doctrine. He was also famous as a poet; of his forty works, all of them very short, many fragments are extant. A large portion of his most famous poem, *Hymn to Zeus*, has been preserved. Even as head of the school, and despite his advanced years, Cleanthes continually astonished his friends by hoisting heavy loads and earning his living by manual work.

HYMN TO ZEUS

Great Jove, most glorious of the immortal gods,
Wide known by many names, Almighty One,
King of all nature, ruling all by law,
We mortals thee adore, as duty calls;
For thou our Father art, and we thy sons,
On whom the gift of speech thou hast bestowed
Alone of all that live and move on earth.
Thee, therefore, will I praise; and ceaseless show
To all thy glory and thy mighty power.
This beauteous system circling round the earth
Obeys thy will, and, whereso'er thou leadest,
Freely submits itself to thy control.
Such is, in thine unconquerable hands,
The two-edged, fiery, deathless thunderbolt;
Thy minister of power, before whose stroke
All nature quails, and, trembling, stands aghast;
By which the common reason thou dost guide,
Pervading all things, filling radiant worlds,
The sun, the moon, and the host of stars.
So great art thou, the universal King.
Without thee naught is done on earth, O God!
Nor in the heavens above nor in the sea;
Naught save the deeds unwise of sinful men.
Which sinful men, blinded, forsake and shun,
Deceived and hapless, seeking fancied good.
Yet harmony from discord thou dost bring;
That which is hateful, thou dost render fair;
Evil and good dost so co-ordinate,
That everlasting reason shall bear sway;
The law of God they will not see nor hear;
Which if they would obey, would lead to life.
But thou, O Jove! the giver of all good,
Darting the lightning from thy home of clouds,
Permit not man to perish darkling thus;
From folly save them; bring them to the light;
Give them to know the everlasting law

By which in righteousness thou rulest all;
That we, thus honored, may return to thee
Meet honor, and with hymns declare thy deeds,
And, though we die, hand down thy deathless praise.
Since nor to men nor gods is higher meed,
Than ever to extol with righteous praise
The glorious, universal King Divine.

[81]

CLEMENCEAU, GEORGES

CLEMENCEAU, GEORGES (1841-1929). When Woodrow Wilson promulgated his famous Fourteen Points, Clemenceau remarked that "Our Father in Heaven would have been content with ten." This and others of his sayings caused Americans to regard his character as that of a cynical politician, narrow-minded French nationalist, advocate of power politics, and victim of French propaganda. The Germans did not like him. In 1871 he had protested against the peace dictated by Bismarck; he always expressed a hope for the return of Alsace to France; during World War I, he encouraged the French to resist and vanquish the German onslaught; and he was held responsible for the harsh conditions of the Treaty of Versailles. Clemenceau was feared and detested by a large group of the French people, by the majority of the deputies, and by those of the radical party, to which he himself belonged. French rightists hated him because as a defender of the Republic, he was also an opponent of clericalism; French leftists hated him because he crushed strikes and persecuted defeatists. Clemenceau was not only the most striking and vigorous of the French statesmen of his time, a formidable enemy, and genius of invective; he was also sincerely and fanatically devoted to the ideals of reason and freedom, which he regarded as compatible with his stern patriotism. He always remained a democrat. One of the last acts of his administration was the introduction of the eight-hour day for France. He had also been a resolute defender of Alfred Dreyfus. It was Clemenceau who formulated the title of Zola's famous letter, *J'Accuse*, who fully rehabilitated Dreyfus, and who appointed Colonel Picquart, (who had been persecuted because he was a witness to the innocence of Dreyfus), to the post of minister of war.

Clemenceau, a highly educated man, had lived in the United States, and intimately knew Latin America and many European countries. He was a trained art critic, a successful dramatist and novelist, and a profound thinker who meditated on the meaning of life, the charm of illusion, and the destiny of mankind. Almost all of his plays and novels are imbued with a philosophical spirit; so is his historical study, *Demosthenes* (1926). His great work, *In the Evening of My Thought* (1929), stands as proof that he overcame those temptations which make for lulled minds among many aged philosophers.

KNOWLEDGE AND EMOTION

IDEALISM is not the result of logical thinking. It grows from man's making the greatest effort of which he is capable. Since the directing principle of man cannot be the avoidance of suffering at any price, and if it is, in fact, a fine thing to accept suffering, yet scorn it, to seek it, yet despise it, as did the ancient martyrs in their generous ardor for noble achievement, then idealism can lift man to the highest pinnacle of his destiny, through supreme suffering in the service of an idea. The beauty of great causes, to which what is best in human life is attached, is revealed in the band of heroic men, known and unknown, who chose to sacrifice their lives without thought of reward for the keen joy of unselfishly doing their duty.

What then can we gain by refusing to admit scientific facts, in order to accept the hallucination of a future life beyond the confines of this world, charming only because of its unreality? Can we successfully substitute for the positive world the dream of an imaginary existence upon which to expend our energies? It is a great temptation to make promises which we have no intention of keeping. That is what is most obvious about the march to the imaginary star of eternal human felicity.

Evolution of knowledge must increase the instruments of our activity. Will it then make us happier, more powerful, longer-lived? To answer these questions with certainty would require nothing short of a precise definition of eternal happiness—than which nothing is less stable, less subject to definition, or more various for each and all of us. Experience proves that to our innermost sensibility, the fleeting

241

happiness of each of us is in himself and in the satisfaction that lies in his power to adapt himself to his surroundings. Thus decrees the subjective character of the sensation of happiness, sometimes common and sometimes refined, to which we aspire, usually without being able to realize it except through anticipations that are found baseless as soon as they are formed. Knowledge supplies the means for momentary or durable happiness. These means we must utilize. Each person can be at least temporarily happy within his own limitations, according to how high or how low is his conception of life, and according to how great is the personal will-power which acquired knowledge and strength of character have allowed him to devote to the task.

How many will be able to understand this fact, and amid the vicissitudes of human society, such as invasions, wars, epidemics, and every other form of catastrophe, how many will have the chance even partly to act on it? The pitiless struggle for existence in time of peace has on the whole caused as much misery and death as have pitched battles. The simple-minded ideologue suggests that a remedy will be found in new social conditions which will do away with these evils, and which will automatically bring peace to men. Just so their even more simple-minded predecessors thought to alleviate earthly woe by the promise of an indefinitely adjourned happiness in an unknown, but eternal paradise—an enchanting land of inaction which, since happiness is dependent on action, is a contradiction in terms. To see what effect it has had on matters earthly one need only examine human history.

The inevitable growth of knowledge, freed through the growth of character from being dominated by emotion, could then only facilitate our achievement of that happiness which we never cease to desire, but which seems only too often to vanish when we think we have grasped it. Our ancestors of 1789 were innocent enough to believe that a mild, indulgent code would bring about a state of perfect happiness. Apt pupils of the Church, those 'liberators,' trusting at first, like their masters, to the formulae of universal love, soon came to enforce them on the scaffold. To suppress the adversary in order to suppress his opinions is the dogmatic idea. The first benefit brought us by relative knowledge is the doctrine of universal tolerance. It is unfortunate that our empiricism has not progressed beyond the point of doing more than recommending its practice.

[82]

CLEMENT OF ALEXANDRIA

CLEMENT OF ALEXANDRIA (c. 150-215 A.D.). The pagan philosopher, Celsus, one of the most ardent opponents of Christianity, noticed (c. 150 A.D.) that the dispersed Christian communities were tending toward a closer organization, toward a unified doctrine and common acceptance of a canon of sacred scriptures, and toward a uniformity in their methods of interpretation. What Celsus apprehended was the early formation of a Church that claimed to be Catholic. The first spiritual representative of that Church was Clement. He was also the father of Christian apologetics based upon a faith in divine revelation, but adapted to philosophical concepts. These prevail unto modern days. He adapted the *Philo* (the general concepts of the Jews) to the aims and needs of the nascent Christian Church, although the details of his system of defense of Christianity more closely paralleled the theology of the Stoics. He is principally remembered as the creator of Christian apologetics, but the other doctrines he enunciated were not permanently accepted by the Church.

Prior to his conversion to Christianity, he traveled extensively through Egypt, Italy, Syria, and Palestine. He was initiated into the mysteries of Eleusis; imbued with the Gnostic spirit, and with the pre-Christian doctrines of salvation which were rooted in Oriental mysticism and integrated with Greek philosophy. He was well acquainted with the books of the Bible, including those which were not incorporated into the canon, and he was well versed in pagan philosophy. His books, *Protrepticus* (Exhortations), *Paidagogus*, and *Stromateis* (Carpet-Bags), were appeals to both educated Christians and pagans. He stated that the simple Christian faith was sufficient for the salvation of man and promised greater knowledge to those who were initiated with Christian philosophy. Logos, not God nor Christ, was the centrifugal point of his teachings. He defined

243

faith as obedience to the reason of Logos. He maintained that philosophy did not make faith a verity but opened the way to complete safety from error, and strengthened the elan toward the deity. He promised pagans deification if they adopted the Christian faith.

EXHORTATION TO THE GREEKS

BUT, you say, it is not reasonable to overthrow a way of life handed down to us from our forefathers. Why then do we not continue to use our first food, milk, to which, as you will admit, our nurses accustomed us from birth? Why do we increase or diminish our family property, and not keep it for ever at the same value as when we received it? Why do we no longer sputter into our parents' bosoms, nor still behave in other respects as we did when infants in our mothers' arms, making ourselves objects of laughter? Did we not rather correct ourselves, even if we did not happen to have good attendants for this purpose? Again, in voyages by sea, deviations from the usual course may bring loss and danger, but yet they are attended by a certain charm. So, in life itself, shall we not abandon the old way, which is wicked, full of passion, and without God? And shall we not, even at the risk of displeasing our fathers bend our course towards the truth and seek after Him who is our real Father, thrusting away custom as some deadly drug? This is assuredly the noblest of all the tasks we have in hand, namely, to prove to you that it was from madness and from this thrice miserable custom that hatred of godliness sprang. For such a boon, the greatest that God has ever bestowed upon the race of men, could never have been hated or rejected, had you not been clean carried away by custom, and so had stopped your ears against us. Like stubborn horses that refuse to obey the reins, and take the bit between their teeth, you fled from our arguments. You yearned to shake yourselves free from us, the charioteers of your life; yet all the while you were being carried along by your folly towards the precipices of destruction, and supposed the holy Word of God to be accursed. Accordingly the recompense of your choice attends upon you, in the words of Sophocles,

Lost senses, useless ears, and fruitless thoughts;

and you do not know that this is true above all else, that the good and god-fearing, since they have honored that which is good, shall meet with a reward that is good; while the wicked, on the other hand, shall meet with punishment corresponding to their deeds: and torment hangs over the head of the prince of evil. At least, the prophet Zechariah threatens him: "He that hath chosen Jerusalem take vengeance upon thee! Behold, is not this a brand plucked out of the fire?" What a strange longing, then, is this for a self-chosen death which still presses upon men? Why have they fled to this death-bearing brand, with which they shall be burnt up, when they might live a noble life according to God, not according to custom? For God grants life; but wicked custom inflicts unavailing repentance together with punishment after we depart from this world. And "by suffering even a fool will learn" that daemon-worship leads to destruction, and the fear of God to salvation.

Let any of you look at those who minister in the idol temples. He will find them ruffians with filthy hair, in squalid and tattered garments, complete strangers to baths, with claws for nails like wild beasts; many are also deprived of their virility. They are an actual proof that the precincts of the idols are so many tombs or prisons. These men seem to me to mourn for the gods, not to worship them, and their condition provokes pity rather than piety. When you see sights like this, do you still remain blind and refuse to look up to the Master of all and Lord of the universe? Will you not fly from the prisons on earth, and escape to the pity which comes from heaven? For God of His great love still keeps hold of man; just as, when a nestling falls from the nest, the mother bird flutters above, and if perchance a serpent gapes for it,

Flitting around with cries, the mother mourns
for her offspring.

245

Now God is a Father, and seeks His creature. He remedies the falling away, drives off the reptile, restores the nestling to strength again, and urges it to fly back to the nest. Once more, dogs who have lost their way discover their master's tracks by the senses of smell, and horses who have thrown their rider obey a single whistle from their own master; "the ox," it is written, "knoweth his owner, and the ass his master's crib, but Israel doth not know Me." What then does the Lord do? He bears no grudge; He still pities, still requires repentance of us. I would ask you, whether you do not think it absurd that you men who are God's last creation, who have received your soul from Him, and are entirely His, should serve another master; aye, and more than that, should pay homage to the tyrant instead of to the rightful king, to the wicked one instead of to the good? For, in the name of truth, what man in his senses forsakes that which is good to keep company with evil? Who is there that flees from God to live with daemons? Who is pleased with slavery, when he might be a son of God? Or who hastens to a region of darkness, when he might be a citizen of heaven; when it is in his power to till the fields of paradise, and traverse the spaces of heaven, when he can partake of the pure and life-giving spring, treading the air in the track of that bright cloud, like Elijah, with his eyes fixed on the rain that brings salvation? But there are some who, after the manner of worms, wallow in marshes and mud, which are the streams of pleasure, and feed on profitless and senseless delights. These are swinish men; for swine, says one, "take pleasure in mud" more than in pure water; and they "are greedy for offal," according to Democritus. Let us not then, let us not be made slaves, nor become swinish, but as true "children of the light," direct our gaze steadily upward towards the light, lest the Lord prove us bastards as the sun does the eagles.

Let us therefore repent, and pass from ignorance to knowledge, from senselessness to sense, from intemperance to temperance, from unrighteousness to righteousness, from godlessness to God.

[83]

COHEN, HERMANN

COHEN, HERMANN (1842-1918). The basis of Cohen's philosophy was that God made truth possible. His system of critical idealism dealt with the logic of pure knowledge, the ethics of pure will, and the aesthetics of pure feeling. He emphasized that basically his ethical philosophy was connected with the teachings of Judaism.

For many years, he was a professor at the University of Marburg. Upon his retirement at the age of seventy, he spent his last years as a teacher of Jewish philosophy at the Institute for the Science of Judaism in Berlin. In addition to educating rabbinical students, he directed discussions each Friday for the benefit of the general public. Many non-Jewish scholars attended these, eager to profit by Cohen's answers to questions concerning the whole range of science and philosophy. His method for teaching the rudiments of philosophy to beginners was greatly admired. He listened patiently to his students, helped them articulate their thoughts and express themselves methodically. He regarded this technique of discussion with beginners a test of his doctrine wherein thought was "pure creation," not the result but the condition of experience. His interpretations of the critiques of Kant, in his early years, gave new direction to the Neo-Kantian movement.

KANT AS THE FOUNDER OF THE
PHILOSOPHY OF SCIENCE

THE mere title, *Prolegomena to Every Future Metaphysic Which May Present Itself As Science*, by Kant is indicative of his historical influence. It was neither Kant's intention to end all philosophical endeavors, nor to confine the spirit of future thought to the terms of his literary language; but he did claim to have written the most methodical introduction (the prolegomena) of both past and future metaphysics. His claim was founded upon the limitations of metaphysics in presenting itself "as a science." The words "as a science" signify the peculiarity of Kant's system and method; for no inspirational frenzy shall supersede the genius of wisdom in the future, nor shall proud resignation (*scio me veram intellegere philosophiam*) make the feeling of truth the ultimate fundament of certainty; for metaphysics will become science and coordinate itself with the "steady pace of science." That is the historical meaning of Kant's eminent fundamental thought. From it we may also derive the direction and manner in which Kant's historical influence may be pursued.

The mathematical science of nature had been accepted as real science about one hundred and fifty years before Kant. That earlier period witnessed the publication of Newton's *Philosophiae Naturalis Principia* (1687) and Galileo's *Discorsi* (1638). Scientific abstraction was prevalent in both these works. Galileo formulated the fundamental idea of modern science, according to which all things consisted of motions determinable by laws, and explorable only as such. Newton's theories that all motions belonged to a coherent system whose center was the astronomical system was fundamentally related to Galileo's concepts. They form the historical basis for Kant's thesis that the system of the universe is the disposition of the system of reason.

The general attitude of philosophy toward science is similar to that of Kant's attitude toward science. It is similar to that of poetry toward myth; the myth creates its images in a naive fashion as a means of conceiving things; poetry utilizes such images as symbols and metaphors, and the poet reflects upon the material of the myths. Science, in parallel ways, unsophisticatedly uses the natural power of the mind "rightly conscious of an obscure impulse." Philosophy must clarify the obscure impulse in order that science may proceed, without necessarily being led, along the right path. The obscure impulse presents a problem; it is a natural phenomenon undeterminable by psychological laws, even if psychology were in perfect accordance with the standards of natural science. Humanity, in general, like each child, begins by thinking mythically. Civilization, through poetry and art, obtains its freedom of the soul. Human reason and science acquire their free self-consciousness, their certainty of spontaneous action, the awareness of their purposes, and the knowledge of their limits through philosophy. In this sense, science is to philosophy what nature is to art.

Thus, philosophy, itself, becomes a science when it verifies the mentioned metaphor. Its object cannot be nature as such, but the science of nature. Newton systematized nature and those who accept his theories must also accept that as his underlying purpose. One may well question: How is the science of nature possible? What epistemological conditions does it presuppose? Upon which principles is it founded? According to Kant, the answers to all these questions make philosophy a science. Philosophy becomes science by recognizing the realities of science, and by inquiring into the conditions that make science possible. The title, *Prolegomena to Every Future Metaphysics Which May Present Itself As Science*, means the aforementioned. In fact the theoretical aspects of Kant's philosophy are nothing but proof of their physical examples; the demonstration of their epistemological value within the bounds of the science of nature based upon mathematics. Such demonstration is the performance of philosophical genius. Throughout the history of philosophy, whether it be Plato, Descartes, Leibniz, or Kant, the philosophical genius becomes evident whenever the question: "What is science?" is raised.

[84]

COHEN, MORRIS RAPHAEL

COHEN, MORRIS RAPHAEL (1880-1947). When Cohen was a boy in Minsk, Russia, he was called Kallyeleh, the Yiddish equivalent of moron. At the age of twelve, he emigrated to the United States. People from Cohen's native town were considerably astonished to hear, in later years, that the so-called moron was generally acknowledged as one of the strongest intellectual forces in American education and philosophy. Many of the greatest contemporary minds—Einstein, Woodbridge, Dewey, Russell, Oliver Wendell Holmes, Jr., and Cardozo—considered Cohen their equal. His disciples admired his

249

wisdom and his teaching methods. His cardinal virtue was his
integrity of mind and conscience. He was outstanding as a logician
and mathematician, and was chiefly responsible for the renaissance
of philosophy in American law.

Cohen's interest in the philosophy of law and religion dated
back to his "moronic" boyhood, when he was educated in Biblical
and Talmudic law and read Maimonides and Judah Halevi's *Kuzari*.
As a young man, he was attracted to Marxian socialism, but his
strong belief in democracy helped him to discover other ways of
serving the common good and acting in accordance with his social
conscience. Felix Adler influenced his approach to ethics; but Cohen
was essentially a logician, devoted to mathematical logic and to the
investigation of the relationships between science and philosophy.
He characterized himself as a realistic rationalist who conceived of
reason as "the use of both deductive and inductive inferences working upon the material of experience." He regarded reality as a
category that belonged to science not religion.

PHILOSOPHY AND LITERATURE

UNLIKE SCIENCE, philosophy has never been able entirely to
dispense with pure speculation, nor has it been able entirely
to eliminate the bias of temperament, and in these respects
philosophy resembles a certain art, viz., the art of poetry and
of reflective literature generally. Actual scientific knowledge
is too fragmentary to enable us to so form a complete picture
of the world to which we must react, and so imagination
must be called in. Sometimes imagination and science work
together, but often imagination does all the work and science is a silent spectator, as in the case of Fechner's "Zend-
Avesta."

It has generally been assumed that of two opposing
systems of philosophy, *e. g.*, realism and idealism, one only
can be true and one *must* be false; and so philosophers have
been hopelessly divided on the question, which is the true
one. The assumption back of this attitude is that philosophy
is determinate knowledge which will not admit of variation.
But is this assumption necessary? Can not two pictures of
the same object both be true, in spite of radical differences?
The picture which the philosopher draws of the world is

surely not one in which every stroke is necessitated by pure logic. A creative element is surely present in all great systems, and it does not seem possible that all sympathy or fundamental attitudes of will can be entirely eliminated from any human philosophy. The method of exposition which philosophers have adopted leads many to suppose that they are simply inquiries, that they have no interest in the conclusions at which they arrive, and that their primary concern is to follow their premises to their logical conclusions. But it is not impossible to think that the minds of philosophers sometimes act like those of other mortals, and that, having once been determined by diverse circumstances to adopt certain views, they then look for and naturally find reasons to justify these views.

There are a number of points in which the method of philosophers is precisely that of literary essayists of the type of St. Benre, Matthew Arnold, Stevenson, or Lowell. Both use examples to suggest or illustrate rather than to demonstrate. In science this would be called the fallacy of one example. In both literature and philosophy the temper of the lesser Napoleon, *aut Caesar aut nullus*, is very prominent. In science this might be called the "all or nothing" fallacy. Constant reservations and numerous qualifications destroy literary sweep, and take away the air of profundity from philosophic discussion. Some philosophers, notably Aristotle and St. Thomas, might perhaps be excepted from the last statement, but in spite of all our hankering after the epithet science, I can not see that we have been making much progress in this habit of self-control against the extravagance of generalization. Again, both literature and philosophy work by appealing to certain reigning idols. These idols came into vogue in different ways. They are seldom refuted or directly overthrown. Generally they are simply outlived, or they do not survive the change of fashion. In the latter eighties or in the earlier nineties the term *relation* was a magic word to conjure with. It was brought into mode by Thomas Hill Green, and died a natural death with the eclipse of his influence. To-day if anything is characterized as *experimental, functional,* or *dynamic,* that is enough to allow it to pass all the watch-dogs of philosophic criticism, and to characterize anything as *static* is to consign it to the lowermost depths from which no power can rescue it. I am not anxious to bring down the wrath of the gods by questioning the all-sufficient potency of such terms as *experience, evolution,* etc.; but may I ask what progress would mathematical physics have made if every time one approached a problem of stresses, he were frightened off by the warning that he must not for a moment entertain that most heinous criminal, the static point of view? I humbly agree with those who claim that the static point of view is mechanical and lifeless and, therefore, inapplicable to the entire universe, but I am quite sure that the dynamic point of view itself may be mechanical and lifeless.

Lastly, literature and philosophy both allow past idols to be resurrected with a frequency which would be truly distressing to a sober scientist. If a philosophic theory is once ruled out of court, no one can tell when it will appear again.

In thus pointing out certain respects in which philosophy resembles literature more than science, I do not mean, of course, to imply that it would be well for philosophy if it ceased to aim at scientific rigor. Let philosophy resolutely aim to be as scientific as possible, but let her not forget her strong kinship with literature.

[85]

COLERIDGE, SAMUEL TAYLOR

COLERIDGE, SAMUEL TAYLOR (1772-1834). A gifted poet and leader of the English romantic movement, Coleridge found life a continuous struggle against passion and physical suffering. His unhappy marriage and his love for another married woman caused him grave psychological disturbance and his addiction to opium undermined his physical health. Coleridge did not do justice to his philosophical expositions and often said that he found no comfort "except in the driest speculations." His psychological observations of the activities of the mind under abnormal and morbid conditions are invaluable. The results of his keen self-examination anticipate many of the researches of modern psychopathology. From 1816 to 1834 Coleridge lived in the house of a physician who finally succeeded in curing him, and the last years of the poet were spent in relative psychological security.

Coleridge's philosophy was largely the result of his changing political sentiments. At first an ardent supporter of the French Revolution, he turned to fanatical conservatism and traditionalism. He staunchly opposed almost all of the eighteenth century British philosophers—particularly Locke, Hartley, Hume, and Bentham— and subsequently was converted to German idealism. His *Biographia Literaria*, which developed a theory of literary criticism, influenced British and American aesthetics and philosophy.

PRECISION IN THE USE OF TERMS

I ADVERTISE to the prevailing laxity in the use of terms: this is the principal complaint to which the moderns are exposed; but it is a grievous one in as much as it inevitably tends to the misapplication of words, and to the corruption of language. . . . The word 'taste' . . . applies not merely to substantives and adjectives, to things and their epithets, but to verbs: thus, how frequently is the verb 'indorsed' strained from its true signification, as given by Milton in the expression, 'And elephants endorsed with towers.' Again, 'virtue' has been equally perverted: originally it signified merely strength; then it became strength of mind and valor, and it has now been changed to the class term for moral excellence in all its various species. I only introduce these as instances by the way, and nothing could be easier than to multiply them.

At the same time, while I recommend precision both of thought and expression, I am far from advocating a pedantic niceness in the choice of language: such a course would only render conversation stiff and stilted. Dr. Johnson used to say that in the most unrestrained discourse he always sought for the properest word—that which best and most exactly conveyed his meaning: to a certain point he was right, but because he carried it too far, he was often laborious where he ought to have been light, and formal where he ought to have been familiar. Men ought to endeavor to distinguish subtly, that they may be able afterwards to assimilate truly.

[86]

INWARD BLINDNESS

TALK to a blind man—he knows he wants the sense of sight, and willingly makes the proper allowances. But there are certain internal senses which a man may want, and yet be wholly ignorant that he wants them. It is most unpleasant to converse with such persons on subjects of taste, philosophy, or religion. Of course, there is no *reasoning* with them, for they do not possess the facts, on which the reasoning must be grounded. Nothing is possible but a naked dissent, which implies a sort of unsocial contempt; or—what a man of kind disposition is very likely to fall into—a heartless tacit acquiescence, which borders too nearly on duplicity.

[86A]

TYPES OF READERS

READERS may be divided into four classes:

1. Sponges, who absorb all they read and return it nearly in the same state, only a little dirtied.

2. Sand-glasses, who retain nothing and are content to get through a book for the sake of getting through the time.

3. Strain-bags, who retain merely the dregs of what they read.

4. Mogul diamonds, equally rare and valuable, who profit by what they read, and enable others to profit by it also.

[86B]

THE LOVE OF NATURE

THE love of nature is ever returned double to us, not only (as) the delighter in our delight, but by linking our sweetest, but of themselves perishable feelings to distinct and vivid images, which we ourselves, at times, and which a thousand casual recollections recall to our memory. She is the preserver, the treasurer, of our joys. Even in sickness and nervous diseases she has peopled our imagination with lovely forms, which have sometimes overpowered the inward pain and brought with them their old sensations. And even when all men have seemed to desert us, and the friend of our heart has passed on with one glance from his "cold disliking eye—" yet even then the blue heaven spreads itself out and bends over us, and the little tree still shelters us under its plumage as a second cope, a domestic firmament, and the low creeping gale will sigh in the heath plant and soothe us by sound of sympathy, till the lulled grief lose itself in fixed gaze on the purple heath-blossom, till the present beauty becomes a vision of memory.

[86C]

THE WORTH AND PRICE OF KNOWLEDGE

IT IS not true that ignorant persons have no notion of the advantages of truth and knowledge. They see and confess those advantages in the conduct, the immunities, and the superior powers of the possessors. Were these attainable by pilgrimages the most toilsome, or penances the most painful, we should assuredly have as many pilgrims and self-tormentors in the service of true religion and virtue as now exist under the tyranny of Papal and Brahman superstition. This inefficacy of legitimate reason, from the want of fit objects— this its relative weakness, and how narrow at all times its immediate sphere of action must be—is proved to us by the impostors of all professions. What, I pray you, is their fortress, the rock which is both their quarry and their foundation, from which and on which they are built?—the desire of arriving at the end without the effort of thought and will which are the appointed means.

Let us look back three or four centuries. Then, as now, the great mass of mankind were governed by the three main wishes: the wish for vigor of body, including the absence of painful feelings; for wealth, or the power of procuring the external conditions of bodily enjoyment—these during life; and security from pain and continuance of happiness here-

after. Then, as now, men were desirous to attain them by
some easier means than those of temperance, industry, and
strict justice. They gladly therefore applied to the Priest,
who could ensure them happiness hereafter without the performance of their duties here; to the Lawyer, who could
make money a substitute for a right cause; to the Physician,
whose medicines promised to take the sting out of the tail
of their sensual indulgences, and let them fondle and play
with vice, as with a charmed serpent; to the Alchemist, whose
gold-tincture would enrich them without toil or economy;
and to the Astrologer, from whom they could purchase foresight without knowledge or reflection.

[86D]

INTRODUCTORY APHORISMS

In philosophy, equally as in poetry, it is the highest and
most useful prerogative of genius to produce the strongest
impressions of novelty, while it rescues admitted truths from
the neglect caused by the very circumstance of their universal
admission. Extremes meet. Truths of all others the most awful
and interesting are often considered as so true that they lose
all the power of truth, and lie bed-ridden in the dormitory
of the soul, side by side with the most despised and ex-
ploded errors.

*   *   *

As a fruit-tree is more valuable than any one of its
fruits singly, or even than all its fruits of a single season,
so the noblest object of reflection is the mind itself, by which
we reflect. And as the blossoms, the green and ripe fruit of
an orange-tree are more beautiful to behold when on the tree,
and seen as one with it, than the same growth detached and
seen successively, after their importation into another country and different climate; so it is with the manifold objects
of reflection, when they are considered principally in reference to the reflective power, and as part and parcel of the
same. No object, of whatsoever value our passions may represent it, but becomes foreign to us as soon as it is altogether

256

unconnected with our intellectual, moral, and spiritual life. To be ours, it must be referred to the mind, either as a motive, or consequence, or symptom.

* * *

Life is the one universal soul, which, by virtue of the enlivening Breath and the informing Word, all organized bodies have in common, each after its kind. This, therefore, all animals possess—and Man, as an animal. But, in addition to this, God transfused into man a higher gift, and specially imbreathed:—even a Living (that is, self-subsisting) Soul; a Soul having its life in itself:—"And Man became a Living Soul." He did not merely possess it—he *became* it. It was his proper being, his truest self—the Man in the man. None, then, not one of human kind, so poor and destitute but there is provided for him, even in his present state, "a house not built with hands;" aye, and in spite of the philosophy (falsely so-called) which mistakes the causes, the conditions, and the occasions of our becoming conscious of certain truths and realities for the truths and realities themselves—a house gloriously furnished. Nothing is wanted but the eye, which is the light of this house, the light which is the eye of the soul. This very light, this enlightening eye, is Reflection. It is more, indeed, than is ordinarily meant by that word; but it is what a Christian ought to mean by it, and to know, too, whence it first came, and still continues to come:—of what Light even this light is but a reflection. This, too, is Thought; and all thought is but unthinking that does not flow out of this or tend toward it.

* * *

It may be an additional aid to reflection to distinguish the three kinds severally, according to the faculty to which each corresponds—the part of our human nature which is more particularly its organ. Thus: the *prudential* corresponds to the sense and the understanding; the *moral* to the heart and conscience; the *spiritual* to the will and the reason; that is, to the finite will reduced to harmony with, and in subordi-

257

nation to the reason, as a ray from that true light which is both reason and will absolute.

[86E]

COMENIUS, JOHANN AMOS

COMENIUS, JOHANN AMOS (1592-1670). A bishop of the Bohemian Brethren and the first great democrat among Christian educational philosophers, Comenius fled from Czechoslovakia in 1628 when that country lost its liberty and its national culture was threatened with extinction by the Hapsburg emperor. He roamed throughout Europe working untiringly for the salvation of his nation and the realization of his educational, political, and scientific projects. Despite his misfortunes and precarious existence, Comenius never lost confidence in the rational mind or in human progress.

His ultimate aim was universal peace. He recognized that the necessary steps, preliminary to the attainment of this goal involved the unification of rival Christian denominations, fundamental reforms in education, and a new approach to natural science. It was largely the result of his initiative that scientific societies promoting research were founded throughout Europe during the seventeenth century. He insisted that education should be free, universally available, and compulsory for every child; that automatic memorization should be replaced by teaching words with perceptual objects; and that the sensual faculties of school children should be taken into consideration. Comenius stands as a transitional figure in the area of science—halfway between the medieval Aristotelianism and modern empiricism. He believed that independent study and observation offered greater intellectual rewards than did constant reliance upon Aristotle or Pliny. His textboks, translated into more than seventeen languages, were used in the early years of Harvard University, and throughout the seventeenth century schools of New England, Asia, and Europe. His principal works were: *The Gates of Unlocked Tongues* (1631); *The Way of Light* (1642); *Patterns of Universal Knowledge* (1651); and *The Great Didactic* (1657).

LAST DECLARATION

WHERE shall I now begin, after so many labyrinths and Sisyphian stones, with which I have been plagued all my life? Shall I say with Elias: "Now, O Lord, take away my life from me, since I am no better than my fathers;" or with

258

David: "Forsake me not, O Lord, in my age, until I have prophesied all that thine arm shall bring to pass." Neither; that I may not be unhappy with painful longing for the one or the other; but I will have my life and death, my rest and my labor, according to the will of God; and with closed eyes will follow wherever He leads me, full of confidence and humility, praying, with David: "Lead me in thy wisdom, and at last receive me into glory." And what I shall do hereafter, shall happen no otherwise than as if directed by Christ, so that the longer I live the more I may be contented with what is needful for me, and may burn up or cast away all that is unnecessary. Would that I were soon to depart to the heavenly country, and leave behind me all earthly things! Yea, I will cast away all the earthly cares which I yet have, and will rather burn them in the fire, than to encumber myself further with them.

To explain this, my last declaration, more clearly, I say that a little hut, wherever it be, shall serve me instead of a palace; or if I have no place whereto lay my head, I will be contented after the example of my Master, though none receive me under his roof. Or I will remain under the roof of the sky, as did He during that last night upon the Mount of Olives, until, like the beggar Lazarus, the angels shall receive me into their company. Instead of a costly robe, I will be contented, like John, with a coarse garment. Bread and water shall be to me instead of a costly table, and if I have therewith a few vegetables, I will thank God for them. My library shall consist of the threefold book of God; my philosophy shall be, with David, to consider the heavens and the works of God, and to wonder that He, the Lord of so great a kingdom, should condescend to look upon a poor worm like me. My medicine shall be, a little eating and frequent fasting. My jurisprudence, to do unto others as I would that they do unto me. If any ask after my theology, I will, like the dying Thomas Aquinas—for I, too, shall die soon—take my Bible, and say with tongue and heart, "I believe what is written in this book." If he ask further about my creed, I will repeat to him the apostolic one, for I know none shorter, simpler, or more expressive, or that cuts off all controversy. If he ask for my form of prayer, I will show him the Lord's Prayer; since no one can give a better key to open the heart of the father than the son, his own off-spring. If any ask after my rule of life, there are the ten commandments; for I believe no one can better tell what will please God than God Himself. If any seek to know my system of casuistry, I will answer, everything pertaining to myself is suspicious to me; therefore I fear even when I do well, and say humbly, "I am an unprofitable servant, have patience with me!"

[87]

COMTE, AUGUSTE

COMTE, AUGUSTE (1798-1857). The Utopian socialist, Saint-Simon influenced Comte in his youth. Comte had little use either for logic or psychology, but instead advocated the study of phrenology. His object was to show that philosophy was in the stage of being absorbed by science. Theology was the first stage of philosophy, wherein nature was explained by the supernatural; metaphysics constituted the second stage, and philosophy was concerned with such abstractions as purpose, life, and the *a priori*; the third and last stage was positivism, which Comte said implied experiment, observation, and the consequences derived from the laws of phenomena. His best known work, *Cours de Philosophie Positive* was published (1830-42) in six volumes. He maintained that science had always been experimental and observational, and therefore positivistic; that it never required metaphysics either to help determine its course or its limits. His ethics was based on the factor of egotism. This, he said, would lead to a consideration of others, or altruism, and thence to mankind as the guarantor of a social order that would be beneficial to the individual. In order to insure the effectiveness of this, he formalized this attitude into a religion with saints, holy days, sacraments and prayers, and made himself the high priest of the cult. Although he died in 1857, there still are remnants of sects that uphold the religion he founded.

The personal life of Comte had many unhappy aspects. He was twice committed to an insane asylum: the first time, as a result of his unhappy marriage to a woman of the streets; the second, after the death of Clotilde de Vaux, the wife of a man imprisoned for life. It was Clotilde, who served as liaison between the *grand être* (that is, mankind) and its high priest. John Stuart Mill was one of Comte's principal sponsors, helping him to remain solvent, write, and spread his cult. The positivist philosophy was a reaction to the speculative phase that developed in philosophy after Kant.

POSITIVE PHILOSOPHY

IN order to explain properly the true nature and peculiar character of the Positive Philosophy, it is indispensable that we should first take a brief survey of the progressive growth of the human mind, viewed as a whole; for no idea can be properly understood apart from its history.

In thus studying the total development of human intelligence in its different spheres of activity, from its first and simplest beginning up to our own time, I believe that I have discovered a great fundamental Law, to which the mind is subjected by an invariable necessity. The truth of this Law can, I think, be demonstrated both by reasoned proofs furnished by a knowledge of our mental organization, and by historical verification due to an attentive study of the past. This Law consists in the fact that each of our principal conceptions, each branch of our knowledge, passes in succession through three different theoretical states: the Theological or fictitious state, the Metaphysical or abstract state, and the Scientific or positive state. In other words, the human mind —by its very nature—makes use successively in each of its researches of three methods of philosophising, whose characters are essentially different, and even radically opposed to each other. We have first the Theological method, then the Metaphysical method, and finally the Positive method. Hence there are three kinds of philosophy or general systems of conceptions on the aggregate of phenomena, which are mutually exclusive of each other. The first is the necessary starting-point of human intelligence: the third represents its fixed and definite state: the second is only destined to serve as a transitional method.

In the Theological state, the human mind directs its researches mainly towards the inner nature of beings, and towards the first and final causes of all the phenomena which it observes—in a word, towards Absolute knowledge. It therefore represents these phenomena as being produced by the direct and continuous action of more or less numerous supernatural agents, whose arbitrary intervention explains all the apparent anomalies of the universe.

In the Metaphysical state, which is in reality only a simple general modification of the first state, the supernatural agents are replaced by abstract forces, real entities or personified abstractions, inherent in the different beings of the world. These entities are looked upon as capable of giving rise by themselves to all the phenomena observed, each phenomenon being explained by assigning it to its corresponding entity.

Finally, in the Positive state, the human mind, recognizing the impossibility of obtaining absolute truth, gives up the search after the origin and destination of the universe and a knowledge of the final causes of phenomena. It only endeavors now to discover, by a well-combined use of reasoning and observation, the actual *laws* of phenomena— that is to say, their invariable relations of succession and likeness. The explanation of facts, thus reduced to its real terms, consists henceforth only in the connection established between different particular phenomena and some general facts, the number of which the progress of science tends more and more to diminish.

The Theological system arrived at its highest form of perfection, when it substituted the providential action of a single being, for the varied play of the numerous independent gods which had been imagined by the primitive mind. In the same way, the last stage of the Metaphysical system consisted in replacing the different special entities by the idea of a single great general entity—Nature—looked upon as the sole source of all phenomena. Similarly, the ideal of the Positive system, towards which it constantly tends, although in all probability it will never attain such a stage, would be reached if we could look upon all the different phenomena observable as so many particular cases of a single general fact, such as that of Gravitation, for example.

This is not the place to give a special demonstration of this fundamental Law of Mental Development, and to deduce from it its most important consequences. We shall make a direct study of it, with all the necessary details, in the part of this work relating to social phenomena. I am only considering it now in order to determine precisely the true character of the Positive Philosophy, as opposed to the two other philosophies which have successively dominated our whole intellectual system up to these latter centuries. For the present, to avoid leaving entirely undemonstrated so important a law, the applications of which will frequently occur throughout this work, I must confine myself to a rapid enumeration of the most evident general reasons which prove its exactitude.

In the first place, it is, I think, sufficient merely to enumerate such a law for its accuracy to be immediately verified, by all those who are fairly well acquainted with the general history of the sciences. For there is not a single science which has to-day reached the Positive stage, which was not in the past—as each can easily see for himself—composed mainly of metaphysical abstractions, and, going back further still, it was altogether under the sway of theological conceptions. Unfortunately, we shall have to recognize on more than one occasion in the different parts of this course, that even the most perfect sciences still retain to-day some very evident traces of these two primitive states.

This general revolution of the human mind can, moreover, be easily verified to-day, in a very obvious, although indirect, manner, if we consider the development of the individual intelligence. The starting-point being necessarily the same in the education of the individual as in that of the race, the various principal phases of the former must reproduce the fundamental epochs of the latter. Now, does not each of us in contemplating his own history recollect that he has been successively—as regards the most important ideas—a *theo-*

logian in childhood, a *metaphysician* in youth, and a *natural philosopher* in manhood? This verification of the law can easily be made by all who are on a level with their age.

But, in addition to the proofs of the truth of this law furnished by direct observation of the race or the individual, I must, above all, mention in this brief summary the theoretical considerations which show its necessity.

The most important of these considerations arises from the very nature of the subject itself. It consists in the need at every epoch of having some theory to connect the facts, while, on the other hand, it was clearly impossible for the primitive human mind to form theories based on observation.

All competent thinkers agree with Bacon that there can be no real knowledge except that which rests upon observed facts. This fundamental maxim is evidently indisputable if it is applied, as it ought to be, to the mature state of our intelligence. But, if we consider the origin of our knowledge, it is no less certain that the primitive human mind could not, and indeed ought not to, have thought in that way. For if, on the one hand, every Positive theory must necessarily be founded upon observations, it is, on the other hand, no less true that, in order to observe, our mind has need of some theory or other. If in contemplating phenomena we did not immediately connect them with some principles, not only would it be impossible for us to combine these isolated observations, and therefore to derive any profit from them, but we should even be entirely incapable of remembering the facts, which would for the most part remain unnoted by us.

Thus there were two difficulties to be overcome: the human mind had to observe in order to form real theories, and yet had to form theories of some sort before it could apply itself to a connected series of observations. The primitive human mind, therefore, found itself involved in a vicious circle, from which it would never have had any means of escaping, if a natural way out of the difficulty had not fortunately been found by the spontaneous development of

264

Theological conceptions. These presented a rallying-point for the efforts of the mind, and furnished materials for its activity. This is the fundamental motive which demonstrated the logical necessity for the purely Theological character of Primitive Philosophy, apart from those important social considerations relating to the matter which I cannot even indicate now.

This necessity becomes still more evident, when we have regard to the perfect congruity of Theological Philosophy, with the peculiar nature of the researches on which the human mind, in its infancy, concentrated to so high a degree all its powers. It is, indeed, very noticeable how the most insoluble questions—such as the inner nature of objects, or the origin and purpose of all phenomena—are precisely those which the human mind proposes to itself, in preference to all others, in its primitive state; all really soluble problems being looked upon as hardly worthy of serious thought. The reason for this is very obvious, since it is experience alone which has enabled us to estimate our abilities rightly, and if man had not commenced by over-estimating his forces, these would never have been able to acquire all the development of which they are capable. This fact is a necessity of our organization. But, be that as it may, let us picture to ourselves as far as we can this early mental disposition, so universal and so prominent, and let us ask ourselves what kind of reception would have been accorded at such an epoch to the Positive Philosophy, supposing it to have been then formed. The highest ambition of this Philosophy is to discover the *laws* of phenomena, and its main characteristic is precisely that of regarding as necessarily interdicted to the human reason, all those sublime mysteries which Theological Philosophy, on the contrary, explains with such admirable facility, even to the smallest detail. Under such circumstances, it is easy to see what the choice of primitive man would be.

The same thing is true, when we consider from a practical standpoint the nature of the pursuits which the human mind first occupies itself with. Under that aspect, they offer to man the strong attraction of an unlimited control over the exterior world, which is regarded as being entirely destined for our use, while all its phenomena seem to have close and continuous relations with our existence. These chimerical hopes, these exaggerated ideas of man's importance in the universe, to which the Theological Philosophy gives rise, are destroyed irrevocably by the first-fruits of the Positive Philosophy. But, at the commencement, they afforded an indispensable stimulus without the aid of which we cannot, indeed, conceive how the primitive human mind would have been induced to undertake any arduous labours.

We are at the present time so far removed from that early state of mind—at least as regards the majority of phenomena—that it is difficult for us to appreciate properly the force and necessity of such considerations. Human reason is now so mature that we are able to undertake laborious scientific researches, without having in view any extraneous goal capable of strongly exciting the imagination, such as that which the astrologers or alchemists proposed to themselves. Our intellectual activity is sufficiently excited by the mere hope of discovering the laws of phenomena, by the simple desire of verifying or disproving a theory. This, however, could not be the case in the infancy of the human mind. Without the attractive chimeras of Astrology, or the example, where should we have found the perseverance and ardour necessary for collecting the long series of observations and experiments which, later on, served as a basis for the first Positive theories of these two classes of phenomena?

The need of such stimulus to our intellectual development was keenly felt long ago by Kepler in the case of astronomy, and has been justly appreciated in our own time by Berthollet in chemistry.

The above considerations show us that, although the Positive Philosophy represents the true final state of human intelligence—that to which it has always tended more and more—it was none the less necessary to employ the Theological Philosophy at first and during many centuries, both as a method and as furnishing provisional doctrines. Since the Theological Philosophy is spontaneous in its character, it is, for that reason, the only one possible in the beginning; it is also the only one which can offer a sufficient interest to our budding intelligence. It is now very easy to see that, in order to pass from this provisional form of philosophy to the final stage, the human mind was naturally obliged to adopt Metaphysical methods and doctrines as a transitional form of philosophy. This last consideration is indispensable, in order to complete the general sketch of the great law which I have pointed out.

It is easily seen that our understanding, which was compelled to progress by almost insensible steps, could not pass suddenly, and without any intermediate stages, from Theological to Positive philosophy. Theology and Physics are so profoundly incompatible, their conceptions are so radically opposed in character, that, before giving up the one in order to employ the other exclusively, the human intelligence had to make use of intermediate conceptions, which, being of a hybrid character, were eminently fitted to bring about a gradual transition. That is the part played by Metaphysical conceptions, and they have no other real use. By substituting, in the study of phenomena, a corresponding inseparable entity for a direct supernatural agency—although, at first, the former was only held to be an offshoot of the latter— Man gradually accustomed himself to consider only the facts themselves. In that way, the ideas of these metaphysical agents gradually became so dim that all right-minded persons only considered them to be the abstract names of the phenomena in question. It is impossible to imagine by what other method our understanding could have passed from frankly supernatural to purely natural considerations, or, in other words, from the Theological to the Positive *régime*.

[88]

267

CONDILLAC, ETIENNE BONNOT DE

CONDILLAC, ETIENNE BONNOT DE (1715-1780). Often referred to as the "philosophers' philosopher," historically, the influence of Condillac is still important, although his prestige has waned. He was an eighteenth century abbot, whose ecclesiastical garment neither hampered his enjoyment of life, nor interfered with his secular thinking.

Condillac professed spiritualism in the area of metaphysics; metaphysics was only loosely connected with his principal interests and occupied a very small part of his writings. In his chief works, *Essai Sur L'Origine des Connaissances Humaines* (An Essay on the Origin of Human Knowledge) (1746) and *Traité des Sensations* (1754) Condillac, like Locke and some of the Cartesians who in some respects deviated from Descartes, denied the usefulness of speculating about the metaphysical nature of the mind. He preferred to study the human mind as a psychologist in order to understand its operations. He thought that the analysis of sensation contained the elements of any judgment connected with the sensation. He regarded the human individual as composed of two egos, that of habit and that of reflection. The ego of habit acted unconsciously: it was capable of the senses of sight, hearing and smell. The ego of reflection was conscious of its acts while performing them. Instinct was derived from the ego of habit, and reason from the habit of reflection. Many of his solutions were considered rash; today, it is recognized that his critics, Kant and Helmholtz among others, were wrong. Condillac was also interested in the psychology of animals, logic and mathematics. His work in economics, *Le Commerce et Le Gouvernement*, deals with ideas and problems very similar to those treated by Adam Smith in his *Wealth of Nations*, both published simultaneously (1776).

TREATISE ON SENSATIONS

NOTIONS OF A MAN POSSESSING THE SENSE OF SMELL ONLY

THE notions of our statue being limited to the sense of smell, can include odors only. It cannot have any conception of extent, of form, of anything external to itself, or to its sensations, any more than it can have of color, sound or taste.

If we offer the statue a rose, it will be, in its relation to us, a statue which smells a rose; but in relation to itself, it will be merely the scent itself of the flower.

Therefore, according to the objects which act upon its organ, it will be scent of rose, of carnation, of jasmine, of violet. In a word, odors are, in this respect merely modifications of the statue itself or modes of being; and it is not capable of believing itself aught else, since these are the only sensations it can feel.

Let those philosophers to whom it is so evident that everything is material, put themselves for a moment in the place of the statue, and let them reflect how they could suspect that there exists anything resembling what we call *matter*.

We may then already be convinced that it is sufficient to increase or to diminish the number of the senses to cause us to come to conclusions wholly different from those which are at present so natural to us, and our statue, limited to the sense of smell, may thus enable us to comprehend somewhat the class of beings whose notions are the most restricted.

THE SLEEP AND DREAMS OF A MAN LIMITED TO THE SENSE OF SMELL

Our statue may be reduced to the condition of being merely the remembrance of an odor; then the sense of its existence appears to be lost to it. It feels less that it is existing than that it has existed, and in proportion as memory recalls ideas to it with less intensity, this remnant of feeling becomes weaker yet. Like a light which goes out gradually, the feeling ceases wholly when the faculty of memory becomes entirely inactive.

Now, our own experience compels us to believe that exercise must in the end fatigue the memory and the imagination of the statue. Let us therefore consider these faculties at rest, and refrain from exciting them by any sensation: the resultant condition will be that of sleep.

If the repose of these faculties be such that they are completely inactive, there is nothing to note, save that the sleep is the soundest possible. If, on the contrary, these faculties continue to act, they will act upon a part only of the notions acquired. A number of links in the chain will be cut out, and the succession of ideas, during sleep, will necessarily differ from the order in a waking state. Pleasure will no longer be the sole cause determining the action of the imagination. This faculty will awaken those ideas only over which it still exercises a measure of power, and it will tend just as frequently to make the statue unhappy as to make it happy.

This is the dreaming state: it differs from the waking state only in that the ideas do not preserve the same order and that pleasure is not always the law which governs the imagination. Every dream, therefore, involves the interception of a number of ideas, on which the faculties of the soul are unable to act.

Since the statue is unacquainted with any difference between imagining intensely and having sensations, it cannot distinguish any difference between dreaming and waking. Whatever, therefore, it experiences while asleep is as real, so far as it is concerned, as what it has experienced before falling asleep.

OF THE EGO, OR PERSONALITY OF A MAN — LIMITED TO THE SENSE OF SMELL

Our statue being capable of remembering, it is no sooner one odor than it remembers that it has been another. That is its personality, for if it could say *I*, it would say it at every instant of its own duration, and each time its *I* would comprise all the moments it remembered.

True, it would not say it at the first odor. What is meant by that term seems to me to suit only a being which notes in the present moment, that it is no longer what it has been. So long as it does not change, it exists without thought of itself; but as soon as it changes, it concludes that it is the selfsame which was formerly in such another state, and it says *I*.

This observation confirms the fact that in the first instant of its existence the statue cannot form desires, for before being able to say *I wish,* one must have said *I.*

The odors which the statue does not remember do not therefore enter into the notion it has of its own person. Being as foreign to its *Ego* as are colors and sounds, of which it has no knowledge, they are, in respect of the statue, as if the statue had never smelled them. Its *Ego* is but the sum of the sensations it experiences and of those which memory recalls to it. In a word, it is at once the consciousness of what it is and the remembrance of what it has been.

CONCLUSIONS

Having proved that the statue is capable of being attentive, of remembering, of comparing, of judging, of discerning, of imagining; that it possesses abstract notions, notions of number and duration; that it is acquainted with general and particular truths; that desires are formed by it, that it has the power of passions, loves, hates, wills; and finally that it contracts habits, we must conclude that the mind is endowed with as many faculties when it has but a single organ as when it has five. We shall see that the faculties which appear to be peculiar to us are nothing else than the same faculties which, applied to a greater number of objects, develop more fully.

If we consider that to remember, compare, judge, discern, imagine, be astonished, have abstract notions, have notions of duration and number, know general and particular truths, are but different modes of attention; that to have passions, to love, to hate, to hope, to fear and to will are but different modes of desire, and that, finally, attention and desire are in their essence but sensation, we shall conclude that sensation calls out all the faculties of the soul.

If we consider that there are no absolutely indifferent sensations, we shall further conclude that the different degrees of pleasure and of pain constitute the law according to which the germ of all that we are has developed in order to produce all our faculties.

This principle may be called want, astonishment, or otherwise, but it remains ever the same, for we are always moved by pleasure or by pain in whatever we are led to do by need or astonishment.

The fact is that our earliest notions are pain or pleasure only. Many others soon follow these, and give rise to comparisons, whence spring our earliest needs and our earliest desires. Our researches, undertaken for the purpose of satisfying these needs and desires, cause us to acquire additional notions which in their turn produce new desires. The surprise which makes us feel intensely any extraordinary thing happening to us, increases from time to time the activity of our faculties, and there is formed a chain the links of which are alternately notions and desires, and it is sufficient to follow up this chain to discover the progress of the enlightening of man.

Nearly all that I have said about the faculties of the soul, while treating of the sense of smell, I might have said if I had taken any other sense; it is easy to apply all to each of the senses.

[89]

CONFUCIUS

CONFUCIUS (556-479 B.C.). Kung Fu Tse, the Grand Master or Confucius, was officially worshipped from 195 B.C. to 1912, but the traditional cult still continues in almost every district of China. Kung lived during a period of cultural decadence, but his teachings and exemplary personal conduct effected a moral and spiritual recovery and cultural renaissance among the people of China. Despite the many foreign influences and internal political conflicts, the stamp of Confucius on Chinese civilization has been more or less permanent.

Kung, a contemporary of Pythagoras and some of the later Hebrew prophets, roamed for some fourteen years throughout China, observing, teaching, and acquiring a steadily increasing number of disciples about him. He taught poetry, history, music, and adherence to tradition. He promulgated an ideal conduct of life, the basis of

272

which was learning, wisdom, moral perfection, and decency in behavior. His doctrine of reciprocity in man's relations with his fellow
man paralleled, with almost the same words, the concept of the
Golden Rule. He demanded that his followers practice the virtues
of sincerity, justice, benevolence, courtesy, respect for older people,
and ancestor reverence. He urged them to live in harmony with
themselves because that was a requisite condition for harmony
between the individual and the universe. He sometimes referred to
"Heaven," without, however, expressing belief in a supreme deity.
He constantly exhorted that all intellectual and moral energies be
channeled for self-perfection, the common good, and social and
universal peace.

For a short time he held high office, using his power for reforms, and for the punishment of evil-doers, even when they were
mandarins. His services, however, were not adequately appreciated
by the ruler.

THE GREAT LEARNING

1. WHAT the Great Learning teaches, is—To illustrate illustrious virtue; to renovate the people; and to rest in the highest
excellence.—2. The point where to rest being known, the
object of pursuit is then determined; and, that being determined, a calm unperturbedness may be attained. To that
calmness there will succeed a tranquil repose. In that repose
there may be careful deliberation, and that deliberation will
be followed by the attainment [of the desired end].—3.
Things have their root and their completion. Affairs have
their end and their beginning. To know what is first and what
is last will lead near to what is taught [in the Great Learn-
ing].—4. The ancients who wished to illustrate illustrious
virtue throughout the empire, first ordered well their own
States. Wishing to order well their States, they first regulated
their families. Wishing to regulate their families, they first
cultivated their persons. Wishing to cultivate their persons,
they first rectified their hearts. Wishing to rectify their hearts,
they first sought to be sincere in their thoughts. Wishing to
be sincere in their thoughts, they first extended to the utmost
their knowledge. Such extension of knowledge lay in the investigation of things.—5. Things being investigated, knowl-

273

edge became complete. Their knowledge being complete, their thoughts were sincere. Their thoughts being sincere, their hearts were then rectified. Their hearts being rectified, their persons were cultivated. Their persons being cultivated, their families were regulated. Their families being regulated, their States were rightly governed. Their States being rightly governed, the whole empire was made tranquil and happy. —6. From the emperor down to the mass of the people, all must consider the cultivation of the person the root [of everything besides].—7. It cannot be, when the root is neglected, that what should spring from it will be well ordered. It never has been the case that what was of great importance has been slightly cared for, and, at the same time, that what was of slight importance has been greatly cared for.

[90]

THE DOCTRINE OF THE MEAN

1. WHAT heaven has conferred is called *The Nature;* an accordance with this nature is called *The Path* of duty; the regulation of this path is called *Instruction.*—2. The path may not be left for an instant. If it could be left, it would not be the path. On this account, the superior man does not wait till he sees things, to be cautious, nor till he hears things, to be apprehensive—3. There is nothing more visible than what is secret, and nothing more manifest than what is minute. Therefore the superior man is watchful over himself, when he is alone.—4. While there are no stirrings of pleasure, anger, sorrow, or joy, the mind may be said to be in the state of *Equilibrium.* When those feelings have been stirred, and they act in their due degree, there ensues what may be called the state of *Harmony.* This *Equilibrium* is the great root from which grow all the human actings in the world, and this Harmony is the universal path which they all should pursue.—5. Let the states of Equilibrium and Harmony exist in perfection, and a happy order will prevail throughout heaven and earth, and all things will be nourished and flourish.

[90A]

274

COOK, JOSEPHUS FLAVIUS

COOK, JOSEPHUS FLAVIUS (1838-1901). A descendant of the Pilgrim fathers, Josephus Cook achieved his fame as a lecturer. His direction of the Monday noon prayer meeting in Tremont Temple, Boston, received considerable public attention, and for more than twenty years the meetings were among Boston's greatest attractions. So popular were they that he was invited to repeat them throughout the United States, England, and many other countries, and their printed editions were translated into several languages.

He was extremely popular as a lecturer because he awakened and confirmed in his audience the conviction that modern science could not disrupt faith in Christianity. Though he was orthodox in his sympathies, he advised his listeners to follow him in a friendly understanding of the sciences. He attempted to prove that where science was not harmonious with Christian religion, it was easily refutable. He frequently used colorful descriptions and quotations to illustrate his points and drew upon his fund of diverse reading and his travels in Germany, Southern Europe, Palestine, Egypt, India, Japan, and Australia. Many of his friends admitted, however, that he often pretended to know that which he had not understood and lacked real erudition.

THE UNITY OF CONSCIOUSNESS

THERE is a great fact known to us more certainly than the existence of matter: it is the unity of consciousness. I know that I exist, and that I am One. Hermann Lotze's supreme argument against materialism is the unity of consciousness. I know that I am *I*, and not *you*; and I know *this* to my very finger-tips. That finger is part of my organism, not of yours. To the last extremity of every nerve, I know that I am One. The unity of consciousness is a fact known to us by much better evidence than the existence of matter. I am a natural realist in philosophy, if I may use a technical term: I believe in the existence of both matter and mind. There are two things in the universe; but I know the existence of mind better than I know the existence of matter. Sometimes in dreams we fall down precipices and awake, and find that the gnarled savage rocks had no existence. But we touched them; we felt them; we were bruised by them. Who knows but that some day we may awake, and find that all matter is merely a dream? Even if we do that, it will yet remain true that I am *I*. There is more support for idealism than for materialism; but there is no sufficient support for either. If we are to reverence all, and not merely a fraction, of the list of axiomatic or self-evident truths, if we are not to play fast and loose with the intuitions which are the eternal tests of verity, we shall believe in the existence of both tests of verity, we shall believe in the existence of both matter and mind. Hermann Lotze holds that the unity of consciousness is a fact absolutely incontrovertible and absolutely inexplicable on the theory that our bodies are woven by a complex of physical arrangements and physical forces, having no co-ordinating presiding power over them all. I know that there is a coordinating presiding power somewhere in me. I am *I*. I am One. Whence the sense of a unity of consciousness, if we are made up according to Spencer's idea, or Huxley's, of infinitely multiplex molecular mechanisms? We have the idea of a presiding power that makes each man one individuality from top to toe. How do we get it? It must have a sufficient cause. To this hour, no man has explained the unity of consciousness in consistency with the mechanical theory of life.

[91]

COURNOT, ANTOINE AUGUSTINE

COURNOT, ANTOINE AUGUSTINE (1801-1877). Modesty and resignation are the repetitious themes of Cournot's philosophy. His concept of truth was founded upon probability rather than certainty. He renounced those inquiries into what other philosophers termed the essence of truth. He was satisfied with investigating the role of truth in the development of the sciences and determined to find the most adequate expression for that kind of truth instrumental in the promotion of scientific research. His efforts to determine the foundation of human knowledge were not directed to an analysis of general human faculties, but to a study of those principles which make for progress in the positive sciences. The major conclusions of Cournot's reflections were that chance is a positive factor in the sum total of reality; that contingency maintained its position beside order; and that the total continuity of evolution could not be proved. He believed that man could approach truth even though he might not be able to attain it and elaborated this point of view in his books: *Considérations sur la Marche des Idées* (1872) and *Traité de L'Enchanement des Idées Fondamentales dans les Sciences et dans L'Histoire* (A Treatise on the Relationships of the Fundamental Concepts in the Sciences and History, 1881). In his early years, Cournot was a tutor in the house of Marshalie Gouvion St. Cyr; later, he became an important dignitary, but regardless of his position, he always led a modest and unpretentious existence. He declined to head a school, and for that reason, his philosophy was neglected for a long time.

EXAMPLES OF THE CREATION AND DESTRUCTION OF WEALTH

THE abstract idea of *wealth* or of *value in exchange,* a definite idea, and consequently susceptible of rigorous treatment in combinations, must be carefully distinguished from the accessory ideas of utility, scarcity, and suitability to the needs and enjoyments of mankind, which the word *wealth* still suggests in common speech. These ideas are variable, and by nature indeterminate, and consequently ill suited for the foundation of a scientific theory. The division of economists into schools, and the war waged between practical men and theorists, have arisen in large measure from the ambiguity of the word *wealth* in ordinary speech, and the confusion which has continued to obtain between the fixed, definite idea of *value in exchange,* and the ideas of utility which every one estimates in his own way, because there is no fixed standard for the utility of things.

It has sometimes happened that a publisher, having in store an unsalable stock of some work, useful and sought after by connoisseurs, but of which too many copies were originally printed in view of the class of readers for whom it was intended, has sacrificed and destroyed two-thirds of the number, expecting to derive more profit from the remainder than from the entire edition.

There is no doubt that there might be a book of which it would be easier to sell a thousand copies at sixty francs, than three thousand at twenty francs. Calculating in this way, the Dutch Company is said to have caused the destruction in the islands of the Sound of a part of the precious spices of which it had a monopoly. Here is a complete destruction of objects to which the word *wealth* is applied because they are both sought after, and not easily obtainable. Here is a miserly, selfish act, evidently opposed to the interests of society; and yet it is nevertheless evident that this sordid act, this actual destruction, is a real creaion of *wealth* in the commercial sense of the word. The publisher's inventory will rightly show a greater value for his assets; and after the copies have left his hands, either wholly or in part, if each individual should draw up his inventory in commercial fashion, and if all these partial inventories could be collated to form a general inventory or balance sheet of the wealth in circulation, an increase would be found in the sum of these items of wealth.

On the contrary, suppose that only fifty copies exist of a curious book, and that this scarcity carries up the price at auction to three hundred francs a copy. A publisher reprints this book in an edition of a thousand copies, of which each will be worth five francs, and which will bring down the other copies to the same price from the exaggerated value which their extreme scarcity had caused. The 1050 copies will therefore only enter for 5250 francs into the sum of wealth which can be inventoried, and this sum will thus have suffered a loss of 9750 francs. The decrease will be even more considerable if (as should be the case) the value of the raw materials is considered, from which the reprints were made, and which existed prior to the reprinting. Here is an industrial operation, a material production, useful to the publisher who undertook it, useful to those whose products and labor it employed, useful even to the public if the book contains valuable information, and which is nevertheless a real destruction of wealth, in the abstract and commercial meaning of the term.

[92]

COUSIN, VICTOR

COUSIN, VICTOR (1792-1867). The disrespect largely prevalent for the philosophy of Victor Cousin is based upon his emphasis of *eclecticism*, a term he used to characterize his method, disregarding the pejorative meaning of the word which implied shallowness and dependence. Although Cousin does not belong to that small nucleus of great philosophers, many of his ideas influenced American transcendentalism while others parallel modern American views, and continue to inspire European philosophers.

Cousin was attracted by that which is common to humanity. He was convinced that mankind could not be sceptical; that it needed a common faith, (not necessarily a religious faith, but certainty). He maintained that the mission of philosophy was to explain faith, not destroy it. His philosophical studies were principally aimed at the elevation of the soul, not at insight into the mystery of things. His cardinal principle asserted that truth was contained in each of the philosophical systems known throughout historical time; that every major philosopher had made a contribution to the knowledge of truth, and that their composite contributions comprised the whole truth, even though they contained some errors. Modifications of Cousin's concepts are manifest in Wilhelm Dilthey's "doctrine of philosophical types," and Benedetto Croce's identification of philosophy with its history. Cousin believed that he had discovered a method of intellectual distillation whereby the method of essential truth could be extrapolated from the various historical systems. He called this method of critical choice *eclecticism*. It was based upon his belief that spontaneous reason, freed from the control of the will, became pure in its contemplation, and thereby was able to behold essential truth.

As a young man, Cousin adhered to the Scottish school of Thomas Reid; in the period from 1815 to 1833 he was seized by a "metaphysical fever," and studied Hegel and Schelling, both of whom he later came to know personally. In 1840 he returned to the Scottish school of philosophy, and severely criticized his earlier writings. However, it was the writings of his "metaphysical fever"

279

that had the greatest influence on American thought. Cousin was the intermediary whereby the transcendentalists acquainted themselves with German idealism, for his was a more lucid, if not altogether correct, presentation. For a time, James Marsh (the founder of Transcendentalism), Theodore Parker, Charles Sumner, and George Bancroft were his devoted adherents; James Walker and Caleb Henry maintained his views somewhat later. Emerson, too, was indebted to Cousin, although he rightly declared that Cousin's method of "distillation" was the result of optical delusion. Cousin became a peer of France, royal councillor, and minister of public education during the régime of Louis Philippe. He was attacked by the clergy for his defense of the liberty of science, and later by the radical leftists. He became politically obscure after the coup d'état of Napoleon III.

WHAT IS ECLECTICISM

PHILOSOPHY, at the present day, can do only one of these three things:

Either abdicate, renounce its independence, submit again to the ancient authority, return to the Middle Ages;

Or continue its troubled motion in the circle of worn-out systems which mutually destroy each other;

Or finally disengage what is true in each of these systems, and thus construct a philosophy superior to all systems, which shall be no longer this or that philosophy, but philosophy itself in its essence and in its unity.

*   *   *

The third course remains. In the absence of fanaticism for this or that specific system, which a tendency to enthusiasm and an incomplete view of things would perhaps produce, and of which we must almost despair with our present characteristics, both good and bad, I see no resource left to philosophy, if it is unwilling to pass under the yoke of theocracy, but equity, moderation, impartiality, wisdom. It is, I confess, somewhat of a desperate resource but for myself, I see no other. It would be strange if there were no longer any thing but common sense which could produce an effect on the imagination of men. But it is certain that every other charm appears to be worn out. All the parts of fanaticism in philosophy, all the parts which have been performed at once by injustice and by folly, that is to say again, all the inferior parts have been taken from the nineteenth century by the preceding centuries; it is condemned to a new part, the most humble in appearance, but the most elevated and important in reality—that of being just towards all systems, and the dupe of none of them; of making them all the object of study, and instead of following in the train of any one, whatever it may be, of enrolling them all under its own banner, and thus marching at their head to the discovery and the conquest of truth. This procedure—to reject no system and to accept none entirely, to neglect this element and to take that, to select in all what appears to be true and good, and consequently everlasting—this, in a single word, is ECLECTICISM.

[93]

ANALYSIS OF FREE ACTION

FREE action is a phenomenon which contains several different elements combined together. To act freely, is to perform an action with the consciousness of being able not to perform it; now, to perform an action with the consciousness of being able not to perform it, supposes that we have preferred performing it to not performing it; to commence an action when we are able not to commence it, is to have preferred commencing it; to continue it when we are able to suspend it, is to have preferred continuing it; to carry it through when we are able to abandon it, is to have preferred accomplishing it. Now, to prefer supposes that we had motives for preferring, motives for performing this action, and motives for not performing it; that we were acquainted with these motives, and that we have preferred a part of them to the rest; in a word, preference supposes the knowledge of motives for and against. Whether these motives are passions or ideas, errors or truths, this or that, is of no consequence; it is important only to ascertain what faculty is here in operation; that is to say, what it is that recognizes these motives, which prefers one to the other, which judges that one is preferable to the other; for this is precisely what we mean by preferring. Now what is it that knows, that judges, but intelligence? Intelligence therefore is the faculty which prefers. But in order to prefer certain motives to others, to judge that some are preferable to others, it is not sufficient to know these different motives, we must moreover have weighed and compared them; we must have deliberated on these motives in order to form a conclusion; in fact, to prefer, is to judge definitively, to conclude. What, then, is it to deliberate? It is nothing else than to examine with doubt, to estimate the relative value of different motives without yet perceiving it with the clear evidence that commands judgment, conviction, preference.

Now, what is it that examines, what is it that doubts, what is it that judges that we should not yet judge in order to judge better? Evidently it is intelligence—the same intelligence which, at a subsequent period, after having passed many provisional judgments, will abrogate them all, will judge that they are less true, less reasonable than a certain other; will pass this latter judgment, will conclude and prefer after having deliberated. It is in intelligence that the phenomenon of preference takes place, as well as the other phenomena which it supposes. Thus far, then, we are still in the sphere of intelligence, and not in that of action. Assuredly intelligence is subjected to conditions; no one examines who does not wish to examine; and the will intervenes in deliberation; but this is the simple condition, not the foundation, of the phenomena; for, if it be true, that without the faculty of willing, all examination and all deliberation would be impossible, it is also true that the faculty itself which examines and which deliberates—the faculty which is the peculiar subject of examination, of deliberation, and of all judgment, provisional or definitive, is intelligence. Deliberation and conclusion, or preference, are therefore facts purely intellectual. Let us continue our analysis.

We have conceived different motives for performing or

not performing an action; we have deliberated on these motives, and we have preferred some of them to others; we have concluded that we ought to perform it rather than not to perform it; but to conclude that we ought to perform, and to perform, are not the same thing. When intelligence has judged that we ought to do this or that, for such or such motives, it remains to proceed to action; in the first place to resolve to assume our part, to say to ourselves, not I *ought* to do, but I *will* to do. Now, the faculty which says I ought to do, is not and cannot be the faculty which says I will to do, I resolve to do. The office of intelligence here closes entirely. I ought to do is a judgment; I will to do is not a judgment, nor consequently an intellectual phenomenon. In fact, at the moment when we form the resolution of doing a particular action, we form it with the consciousness of being able to form the contrary resolution. Here then is a new element which should not be confounded with the preceding; this element is will; just before it was our business to judge and to know; now it is our business to will. To will, I say, and not to do; for precisely as to judge that we ought to do is not to will to do, so to will to do is not in itself to do. To will is an act, not a judgment; but an act altogether internal. It is evident that this act is not action properly so called; in order to arrive at action we must pass from the internal sphere of will to the sphere of the external world, in which is definitively accomplished the action which you had at first conceived, deliberated on, and preferred; which you then willed; and which it was necessary to execute. If there were no external world, there would be no consummated action; and there must not only be an external world; the power of will also, which we have recognized after the power of comprehending and of judging, must be connected with another power, a physical power, which serves it as an instrument with which to attain the external world. Suppose that the will were not connected with organization, there would be no bridge between the will and the external world; no external action would be possible. The physical power, necessary to action, is organization; and in this organization it is acknowledged that the muscular system is the special instrument of the will. Take away the muscular system, no effort would any longer be possible, consequently, no locomotion, no movement whatever would be possible; and if no movement were possible, no external action would be possible. Thus, to recapitulate, the whole action which we undertook to analyze is resolved into three elements perfectly distinct: (1) the intellectual element, which is composed of the knowledge of the motives for and against, of deliberation, of preference, of choice; (2) the voluntary element, which consists entirely in an internal act, namely the resolution to do; (3) the physical element, or the external action.

[93A]

CREIGHTON, JAMES EDWIN

CREIGHTON, JAMES EDWIN (1861-1924). To have his own philosophical system would have been contrary to Creighton's fundamental conviction that human thoughts are never completely the work of an isolated mind. He was an ardent advocate of social cooperation in philosophy, repeatedly pointing to the successes that resulted from cooperation in science. He regarded intellectual life as a form of experience which can be realized only in common with others through participation in a social community. With this point of view, Creighton concluded first, that the philosopher must participate intimately in the mental activities and interests of other people; and second, that he must define the task of philosophy as that of determining the real, stressing the importance of a precise concept of experience. He regarded "concept of experience" as an ambiguous term which was generally appealed to in a very uncritical and too confident fashion. Though he endeavored to define experience as strictly as possible, he was influenced in his earlier years by Kant, Bradley, and Bosanquet. Later, he accepted some views of Windelband and Rickert, without sharing all of their opinions. Creighton differentiated between that which is intelligible in philosophy and that which is intelligible in the natural sciences.

INDIVIDUAL AND SOCIETY

IN our theories as to the practical relations of men in society, we have at length come to see that it is necessary to

284

read the facts in a new way. If it is true that the individual, as a moral, political, or religious being, includes as an essential element within himself relations to his fellow-men that involve some form of organized society, then it is evidently a wrong scientific procedure to assume as the fundamental reality a self-centered individual whose activities are all concerned with the promotion of his own happiness. The older theories of politics and ethics accepted unquestioningly the notion of the individual as a self-contained given entity, endowed with certain properties and principles, *e.g.*, "self-love to move and reason to direct." Guided by a similar logic, the older physical theories assumed as their unquestioned datum of fact the self-enclosed atom with its properties of attraction and repulsion. From these isolated atoms, physical and social alike, the nature of the physical world and of human society had to be explained. But the same logic that overthrew the notion of the hard atom led in the social field to a truer view of the nature of the human individual. In both cases alike, a dynamic and relative view came to displace the older static and external set of conceptions. This new doctrine teaches that nothing is isolated and nothing fixed: that the parts live in and through their relation to the whole; and that change finds its way to the very heart of things.

I do not feel competent to speak of the results which the application of these new categories have brought about in the physical sciences. We know, however, that the older hypotheses have been revolutionized, and that much has happened and is happening in these departments of knowledge that was wholly undreamed of in the old philosophy. Similarly, the abandonment of atomistic conceptions of man and of society has brought about consequences that seem in many respects even more strikingly revolutionary. In order to give an account of these changes, it would be necessary to undertake to write the history of recent thought in these fields. We have only to consider the older political philosophy which was based on the conception of a social contract, the

285

hedonistic or intuitional theories of morality, or the classical forms of political economy, in order to realize how great is the gulf that separates our thought from the individualism of the eighteenth and early nineteenth centuries. Even those of us who still call ourselves individualists no longer base our arguments upon a conception of the rights, duties, or interests of the formal or nominal individual; we have been forced to abandon the notion of *exclusive* individuality, and to recognize that individuals have reality and significance, not in themselves and by natural or divine right; but in so far as they embody and express the life and purpose of a larger social whole of which they are members. It is as *members of society*, not as self-subsistent entities, that individuals must be interpreted. Individuality involves partnership with others, coöperation in a common cause, loyalty to interests that carry the individual out beyond the limits of his merely private life. This conception of concrete individuality, as deriving its positive content from social relationships, is leading at the present day to new methods of inquiry and to new problems in the fields of social and political life. Even in religion, which has never been entirely deprived of social significance, emphasis has in recent times been laid less upon the individual's so-called inner life, and more upon his relations to his fellows. It must, of course, be added that this whole process of reconstruction is still going on, and that many questions as to the lines of its detail are still under debate. For our present purpose, however, it is not necessary to give an account of the results so far achieved, or to attempt a criticism or justification of the doctrines of any particular writer. These references are intended only to introduce the question whether the adoption of a similar standpoint is not necessary in order to understand the significance of the individual's thinking, and the influences which go toward the development of the intellectual life.

It might seem that this view would require only to be stated in order to find assent. For it is impossible to separate the concrete life of the mind into separate departments. The mind is a whole, and if its social nature is demonstrated in certain forms of experience, we should hardly expect to find it, in any one of its aspects, remaining isolated and self-centered. Nevertheless, both in popular thinking and in psychological analysis there is a tendency to regard the thinking mind as a particular form of existence, somehow enclosed within a body, and expressing the functioning of a brain. Just as one body keeps another body out of the same space, so the thinking mind of the individual is regarded as isolated, repellent, exclusive. The thinker is taken to be a solitary being, wrestling with his own problems alone and unassisted. By the power of his mind he is supposed to create truth through his own analysis and meditations. And, again, as an independent thinker, *Athanasius contra mundum,* he is supposed to be capable of bearing witness to this truth, and of making it prevail. As opposed to this contention, I wish to suggest that the process of verification always involves, either directly or indirectly, the coöperation and interplay of a plurality of thoughts of other men so that the individual is able to free himself from subjective fancies and hasty generalizations, and so to attain to universal truth. The result is not original in the sense that it has sprung wholly from his brain, but it is the product of many minds working together. In short, I am expressing again the doctrine that I have already suggested: thinking is the outcome of the functioning of a society of minds, not of an abstract individual mind, just as morality, and political institutions, and religion spring from and belong to such an organic unity of individuals. "Without society no individual," is a statement that applies to man as a thinker no less than to man as a moral or political being.

[94]

CRESCAS, HASDAI

CRESCAS, HASDAI (1340-1410). Like almost all Jewish philosophers of the Middle Ages, Crescas developed his philosophy in the face of persecution and imminent personal danger. He was born in Barcelona and was denounced and victimized there, imprisoned and fined, despite the recognition of his innocence. He moved and settled in Saragossa, where he declined appointment as rabbi of the congregation. He then became an authority on Jewish law and ritual tradition, and often intervened diplomatically on behalf of his co-religionists in Aragon and neighboring kingdoms. In a letter from him to the Jews of Avignon, he described the personal pain he and other Jews endured during the persecution of Jews in Spain. It was during this Inquisition period (1391), that he lost his only son.

Crescas did not content himself with bemoaning the fate of the Jews. He endeavored to defend the spirit and doctrines of Judaism against its religious and philosophical opponents. His criticism of Christianity, written in Spanish, is lost, except for those fragments which were translated into Hebrew by Joseph ibn Shemtob in 1451. Crescas' principal work, *Or Adonai* (The Light of God), completed in 1410, the year of his death, was of great consequence. It refuted Neo-Platonism and Aristotle, and implied a sharp criticism of Gersonides and Maimonides because of their efforts to reconcile Judaism with Greek philosophy. Crescas rejected Aristotle's physics, metaphysics, and axiology. He defended the cause of Judaism with a spiritual originality, radicalism, and courage, uncommon in the history of the Middle Ages. The importance of his thinking was by no means confined to the history of Jewish philosophy. His rejection of Aristotle, by stating that "there are no other worlds" than the one system in which the earth is situated, inspired such Christian thinkers as Nicholas Cusanus, Giordano Bruno, Marsilio Ficino, and Pico della Mirandola. There is little doubt that Spinoza was indebted to Crescas for his concept of the universe.

ON TIME AND CHANGE

THE correct definition of time is that it is the measure of the duration of motion or of rest between two instants. It is, moreover, evident that the genus most essentially appropriate of time is magnitude, for time belongs to continuous quantity and number to discrete. If we describe time as number, we describe it by a genus which is not essential nor primary. It is indeed measured by both motion and rest because it is our supposition of the measure of duration that is time. It seems therefore that the existence of time is only in the soul. . . .

Time may exist without motion . . . what we may reasonably maintain is that, since rest is the privation of motion, when we measure time by rest, we inevitably conceive of motion; but to say that the idea of time cannot be conceived except if it be connected with motion, must be denied.

Every change has two aspects. First it may be regarded with respect to the substratum, in which case change means the transition of that which underlies the change from one accident to another. In this respect, change exists in the other categories, and is in no-time. Second, change may also be regarded with respect to the matter of the change, the matter being, e.g., quantity, quality and place. In this respect it exists in that category in which the matter of the change is to be found.

Aristotle's statement that every motion is a change is evident. The proposition, however, is not convertible, for not every change is motion, inasmuch as there is a kind of change that takes place in no-time, as, e.g., generation and corruption and the transition of the substratum from one accident to another, in which latter respect, change is to be included under the category of action and passion.

While indeed the division of numbers into odd and even is true and unavoidable, still infinite number, not being limited, is not to be described by either evenness or oddness. And so an infinite number is not impossible in the case of intellects and souls.

That the possibility of infinite increase is not incompatible with being actually limited, may appear from the case of infinite decrease, for the examination into contraries is by one and the same science. . . . It is possible for a distance infinitely to decrease and still never completely to disappear. It is possible to assume, for instance, two lines which, by how much farther they are extended, are brought by so much nearer to each other and still will never meet, even if they are produced to infinity. If, in the case of decrease, there is always a certain residual distance which does not disappear, a *fortiori* in the case of increase it should be possible for a distance, though infinitely increased, always to remain limited.

CROCE, BENEDETTO

CROCE, BENEDETTO (1866-1952). The changing relations between the various forms of the human mind interested Croce far more than the solution of metaphysical problems. According to him, there is nothing that does not represent a manifestation of spirit either in nature or in the realm of science. He is opposed to materialism, naturalism, and the dualism of Kant, and often resorts to a renewal of Scholastic concepts. He considers himself to be a disciple of Plato and De Sanctis in aesthetics; of Herbart in ethics. To read Hegel, is to Croce "a debate within my own consciousness." He never intended to construct a system of philosophy, but, rather, a series of systematizations. He regards all philosophical thoughts as transitional steps, "because philosophy is the history of philosophy."

Croce began with historical studies, became engrossed with records and deeds, and astonished his colleagues with his keen critical faculties. He turned to philosophy around 1893, because his method of examining documents and interpreting historical facts involved an inquiry into the relations between history and the sciences, and an examination of those general concepts from which historical ideas may be derived or with which they may be integrated. The first result of these studies was *Aesthetics* (1902), conceived as the science of expression. Together with three volumes dealing with logic, ethics, and the theory of history, it is a part of his *Philosophy of Spirit* which was completed in 1917.

Croce lost his parents and sister in the earthquake of 1883, and was severely injured himself. However, it was not this experience that made him broach philosophical questions. The news of such events had made Voltaire and Goethe think about metaphysics. Under the Fascist regime of Mussolini, Croce was neither arrested nor compelled to emigrate; he continued to defy the Duce's claims of infallibility within his own country. He was neither intimidated by threats nor lured by promises; continuing to profess idealistic liberalism before, during, and after the reign of terror.

THE HUMANITY OF HISTORY

ENFRANCHISING itself from servitude to extra-mundane ca-

290

price and to blind natural necessity, freeing itself from transcendency and from false immanence (which is in its turn transcendency), thought conceives history as the work of man, as the product of human will and intellect, and in this manner enters that form of history which we shall call *humanistic*.

This humanism first appears as in simple contrast to nature or to extra-mundane powers, and posits dualism. On the one side is man, with his strength, his intelligence, his reason, his prudence, his will for the good; on the other there is something that resists him, strives against him, upsets his wisest plans, breaks the web that he has been weaving and obliges him to weave it all over again. History, envisaged from the viewpoint of this conception, is developed entirely from the first of these two sides, because the other does not afford a dialectical element which can be continually met and superseded by the first, giving rise to a sort of interior collaboration, but represents the absolutely extraneous, the capricious, the accidental, the meddler, the ghost at the feast. Only in the former do we find rationality combined with human endeavor, and thus the possibility of a rational explication of history. What comes from the other side is announced, but not explained: it is not material for history, but at the most for chronicle.

This first form of humanistic history is known under the various names of *rationalistic, intellectualistic, abstractistic, individualistic, psychological* history, and especially under that of *pragmatic* history. It is a form generally condemned by the consciousness of our times, which has employed these designations, especially *rationalism* and *pragmatism*, to represent a particular sort of historiographical insufficiency and inferiority, and has made proverbial the most characteristic pragmatic explanations of institutions and events, as types of misrepresentation into which one must beware of falling if one wishes to think history seriously. But as happens in the progress of culture and science, even if the condemnation be of culture and science, even if the condemnation be cordially accepted and no hesitation entertained as to drawing practical consequences from it in the field of actuality, there is not an equally clear consciousness of the reasons for this, or of the thought process by means of which it has been attained. This process we may briefly describe as follows.

Pragmatic finds the reasons for historical facts in man, but in man *in so far as he is an individual made abstract,* and thus opposed as such not only to the universe, but to other men, who have also been made abstract. History thus appears to consist of the mechanical action and reaction of beings, each one of whom is shut up in himself. Now no historical process is intelligible under such an arrangement, for the sum of the addition is always superior to the numbers added. To such an extent is this true that, not knowing which way to turn in order to make the sum come out right, it became necessary to excogitate the doctrine of 'little causes,' which were supposed to produce 'great effects.' This doctrine is absurd, for it is clear that great effects can only have real causes (if the illegitimate conceptions of great and small, of cause and effect, be applicable here). Such a formula, then, far from expressing the law of historical facts, unconsciously expresses the defects of the doctrine, which is inadequate for its purpose. And since the rational explanation fails, there arise crowds of fancies to take its place, which are all conceived upon the fundamental motive of the abstract individual. The pragmatic explanation of religious is characteristic of this; these are supposed to have been produced and maintained in the world by the economic cunning of the priests, taking advantage of the ignorance and credulity of the masses. But historical pragmatic does not always present itself in the guise of this egoistic and pessimistic inspiration. It is not fair to accuse it of egoism and utilitarianism, when the true accusation should, as we have already said, be levelled at its abstract individualism. This abstract individualism could be and sometimes was conceived even as highly moral, for we certainly find among the pragmatics sage

legislators, good kings, and great men, who benefit humanity by means of science, inventions, and well-organized institutions. And if the greedy priest arranged the deceit of
religions, if the cruel despot oppressed weak and innocent
people, and if error was prolific and engendered the strangest
and most foolish customs, yet the goodness of the enlightened
monarch and legislator created the happy epochs, caused the
arts to flourish, encouraged poets, aided discoveries, encouraged industries. From these pragmatic conceptions is
derived the verbal usage whereby we speak of the age of
Pericles, of that of Augustus, of that of Leo X, or of that of
Louis XIV. And since fanciful explanations do not limit
themselves merely to individuals physically existing, but also
employ facts and small details, which are also made abstract
and shut up in themselves, being thus also turned into what
Vico describes as 'imaginative universals,' in like manner
all these modes of explanation known as 'catastrophic' and
making hinge the salvation or the ruin of a whole society
upon the virtue of some single fact are also derived from
pragmatic. Examples of this, which have also become proverbial, because they refer to concepts that have been persistently criticized by the historians of our time, are the fall
of the Roman Empire, explained as the result of barbarian
invasions, European civilization of the twelfth and thirteenth
centuries, as the result of the Crusades, the renascence of
classical literatures, as the result of the Turkish conquest of
Constantinople and of the immigration of the learned Byzan-
tines into Italy—and the like. And in just the same way as
when the conception of the single individual did not furnish a sufficient explanation recourse was for that reason
had to a multiplicity of individuals, to their co-operation and
conflicting action, so here, when the sole cause adduced soon
proved itself too narrow, an attempt was made to make up
for the insufficiency of the method by the search for and
enumeration of multiple historical causes. This enumeration threatened to proceed to the infinite, but, finite or infinite as it might be, it never explained the process to be

explained, for the obvious reason that the continuous is never made out of the discontinuous, however much the latter may be multiplied and solidified. The so-called theory of the causes or factors of history, which survives in modern consciousness, together with several other mental habits of pragmatic, although generally inclined to follow other paths, is rather a confession of powerlessness to dominate history by means of individual causes, or causes individually conceived, than a theory; far from being a solution, it is but a reopening of the problem.

[96]

CUDWORTH, RALPH

CUDWORTH, RALPH (1617-1688). A theologian, Cudworth constantly warned against the over-estimation of dogmatic differences. He was Regius professor of Hebrew at Cambridge University, England, from 1645 to 1688 and while there became known as the leader of the Cambridge Platonists. In his *True Intellectual System of the World* (1678), he concentrated upon the refutation of all the atheistic schools, particularly those of Democritus, Lucretius, and Hobbes. However, he did consider it incumbent upon him to present fairly the disputed doctrines. This caused many critics, among them Dryden, to express apprehension lest readers of these presentations become converts to atheism, and stop reading before perusing Cudworth's refutation. Cudworth maintained that a primitive monotheistic creed could be found even in ancient paganism. In his explanation of the universe, he tried to avoid both the assumption of chance and the hypothesis of a steady interference of God. Therefore, he introduced the concept of "plastic nature" which was to act in a creative manner in accordance with its own laws. This concept, very likely, influenced Spinoza, and the nineteenth century French philosopher, Paul Janet, whose work was based on the idea of "plastic nature."

When the Stuarts resumed their reign of England in 1660, Cudworth encountered some governmental difficulties. They hesitated to reappoint him because he had been an intimate friend of Thurloe, Cromwell's secretary, and Cromwell had consulted Cudworth in 1655 on the question of the readmission of the Jews to England.

For, first, *Sense* only Suffering and receiving from without, and having no *Active Principle* of its own, to take Acquaintance with what it receives, it must needs be a Stranger to that which is altogether adventitious to it, and therefore cannot know or understand it. For to *Know* or *Understand* a thing, is nothing else but by some Inward Anticipation of the Mind, that is Native and Domestic, and so familiar to it, to take Acquaintance with it; of which I shall speak more afterward.

Sense is but the Offering or Presenting of some Object to the Mind, to give it an Occasion to exercise its own Inward *Activity* upon. Which two things being many times nearly conjoined together in Time, though they be very different in Nature from one another, yet they are vulgarly mistaken for one and the same thing, as if it were all nothing but mere Sensation or Passion from the Body. Whereas *Sense* itself is but the *Passive Perception* of some Individual Material Forms, but to *Know* or *Understand,* is Actively to Comprehend a thing by some Abstract, Free and Universal *Reasonings, from whence the Mind as it were looking down (as Boetius expresseth it) upon the individuals below it, views and understands them.* But *Sense* which lies Flat and Grovelling in the Individuals, and is stupidly fixed in the Material Form, is not able to rise up or ascend to an Abstract Universal Notion; For which Cause it never *Affirms* or *Denies* any thing of its Object, because (as *Aristotle* observes) in all Affirmation, and Negation at least, the Predicate is always Universal. The Eye which is placed in a Level with the sea, and touches the Surface of it, cannot take any large Prospect upon the Sea, much less see the whole Amplitude of it. But an Eye Elevated to a higher Station, and from thence looking down, may comprehensively view the whole Sea at once, or at least so much of it as is within our Horizon. The Abstract Universal *Reasons* are that higher Station of the Mind, from whence looking down upon

Individual things, it hath a Commanding view of them, and as it were *a priori* comprehends or Knows them.

But Sense, which either lies in the same Level with that Particular Material Object which it perceives, or rather under it and beneath it, cannot emerge to any Knowledge or Truth concerning it.

[97]

CUSA, NICHOLAS OF

CUSA, NICHOLAS OF (1401-1464). Nicholas Krebs, the son of a poor boatman, was born in Cues à Moselle, France. He rose to become bishop and cardinal, and distinguished himself as a mystical theologian, jurist, and diplomat. He was educated by the Brethren of the Common Life at Deventer, Holland and studied law, mathematics, astronomy, and theology at the Universities of Heidelberg, Padua, Rome and Cologne. He achieved great repute as a scholar and bibliophile, and was especially famous for his large collection of the manuscripts of Augustine and other authors of that period.

Although he was highly respected by the early Italian humanists, he remained, essentially, a scholastic Platonist. To some extent he was also influenced by Arabic and Jewish philosophy. His attempts to integrate metaphysics and mathematics were the result of numerous influences: the theosophical arithmetic of the Jewish Cabala; the *Zohar* or *Book of Splendor;* and the writings of Bonaventura (from whom he borrowed the term *"docta ignorantia"*). Although he was interested in astronomy, he maintained that God, not the sun, was the center of the universe. He upheld the Ptolemaic system, even though he had adopted the views of Jewish and Arabic thinkers that the earth really did move.

Cusanus said that there were two directions which enabled the human spirit to arrive at the truth. The first was reason, whose realm was measureable; the second, intellect, whose objectives were infinite. Reason was solely a human activity wherein God could only be expressed by antinomies, that is by the coincidence of opposites, so that pure reason was compelled to conceive God, at one and the same time, as both a being and one who was not a being, or as an infinite circle. Intellect was understanding illuminated by faith. This activity had supernatural qualities which enabled God to be viewed as an absolute unity without finite proportions. Since God was infinite, he remained undefinable by the concepts of reason, and therefore generally remained ignored by reason; he was conceived without being comprehended. Cusanus conceived of God as the concentrated unity of all essences; the world as the multiple explications of Divine essences. He used the theory of emanation as the basis for this concept. The essence of God comprised not only all existing creation but all possible creation. Cusanus deviated from one of the principal tenets of Christianity by adopting a statement of William of Ockham that the earth was the peculiar place of death and corruption.

THE VISION OF GOD

APART from Thee, Lord, naught can exist. If, then, Thine essence pervade all things, so also doth Thy sight, which is Thine essence. For even as no created thing can escape from its own proper essence, so neither can it from Thine essence, which giveth essential being to all beings. Wherefore, neither can it from Thy sight. Accordingly, Thou, Lord, seest all things and each thing at one and the same time, and movest with all that move, and standest with them that stand. And because there be some that move while others stand, Thou, Lord, dost stand and move at the same time, at the same time Thou dost proceed and rest. For if both motion and rest be individuated at the same time in divers beings, and if naught can exist apart from Thee, and no motion be apart from Thee, nor any rest; then Thou, Lord, art wholly present to all these things, and to each, at one and the same time. And yet Thou dost not move nor rest, since Thou art exalted above all, and freed from all that can be conceived or named. Wherefore, Thou standest and proceedest, and yet at the same time dost not stand or proceed, and that this painted face showeth me. For, if I move, its glance seemeth to move because it quitteth me not; if, while I am moving, another look on the face while standing still, its glance in like manner quitteth not him, but standeth still as he doth. Howbeit, the condition of motion or standing cannot rightly suit with a face that is freed from such conditions, for it is above all standing or motion, in simplest and absolute infinity; and 'tis on the hither side of this infinity that are found motion, and rest, and their opposition, and whatever may be uttered or conceived.

Hence I observe how needful it is for me to enter into the darkness, and to admit the coincidence of opposites, beyond all the grasp of reason, and there to seek the truth where impossibility meeteth me. And beyond that, beyond even the highest ascent of intellect, where I shall have attained unto that which is unknown to every intellect, and which every intellect judgeth to be most far removed from truth, there, my God, art Thou, who art Absolute Necessity. And the more that dark impossibility is recognised as dark and impossible, the more truly doth His Necessity shine forth and is more unveiledly present, and draweth nigh.

Wherefore I give Thee thanks, my God, because Thou makest plain to me that there is none other way of approaching Thee than that which to all men, even the most learned philosophers, seemeth utterly inaccessible and impossible. For Thou hast shown me that Thou canst not be seen elsewhere than where impossibility meeteth and faceth me. Thou hast inspired me, Lord, who art the Food of the strong, to do violence to myself, because impossibility coincideth with necessity, and I have learnt that the place wherein Thou art found unveiled is girt round with the coincidence of contradictories, and this is the wall of Paradise wherein Thou dost abide. The door whereof is guarded by the most proud spirit of Reason, and, unless he be vanquished, the way in will not lie open. Thus 'tis beyond the coincidence of contradictories that Thou mayest be seen, and nowhere this side thereof. If, then, in Thy sight, Lord, impossibility be necessity, there is naught that Thy sight seeth not.

[98]

$\mathcal{D}$

D'ALEMBERT, JEAN BAPTISTE LE ROND

D'ALEMBERT, JEAN BAPTISTE LE ROND (1717-1783). Considered the father of positivism, and in many ways the progenitor of pragmatism, D'Alembert maintained that truth is hypothetical but useful. In his introduction to the famous encyclopedia that he and Diderot edited, D'Alembert outlined the psychological genesis of knowledge, and the logical order and historical sequence of the sciences. He classed mathematics with natural philosophy, stating that it could be developed into a science of general dimensions contrary to the mathematical theories of Plato and Descartes. One of the most eminent mathematicians of his century, his theory of mathematics was consistent with his perceptual empiricism. He also made valuable contributions to physics, meteorology, and astronomy. In his literary works, he violently opposed all religious organization.

Abandoned as an infant, he was found on November 16, 1717, near the entrance to the Church St. Jean-Le-Rond by a glazier's wife. Brilliant and talented as a child, he achieved membership in the Academy of Science at the age of twenty-four. When he had become famous, his real mother, Madame de Tencin, socially important in Paris, recognized him, but he remained attached to his foster mother. He declined the presidency of the Prussian Academy of Sciences, offered him by Frederick II of Prussia, and the offer of Catherine II of Russia who wanted him to become a tutor for her grandson, who later became Czar Paul I.

ANECDOTES OF BOSSUET

BOSSUET's talents for the pulpit disclosed themselves almost from his infancy. He was announced as a phenomenon of early oratory at the hotel de Rambouillet, where merit of all kinds was summoned to appear, and was judged of, well or ill. He there, before a numerous and chosen assembly, made a sermon on a given subject, almost without preparation, and with the highest applause. The preacher was only sixteen years old, and the hour was eleven at night; which gave occasion to Voiture, who abounded in plays on words, to say that he had never heard so early or so late a sermon.

One of those persons who make a parade of their unbelief, wished to hear, or rather to brave him. Too proud to confess himself conquered, but too just to refuse the homage due to a great man, he exclaimed, on leaving the place, "This man to me is the first of preachers; for I feel it is by him I should be converted, if I were ever to be so."

He one day presented to Louis XIV Father Mabillon, as "the most learned Religieux of his Kingdom."— "And the humblest too," said le Tellier, Archbishop of Rheims, who thereby thought to epigrammatise adroitly the modesty of the prelate. The famed Archbishop, however, humiliated as he felt himself by the elevated genius of Bossuet, was too just to suffer it to be slighted. Some young court chaplains, one of whom has since occupied high stations, talking one day in his presence, with French levity, of the works and abilities of the Bishop of Meaux, whom they ventured to ridicule; "Be silent," said le Tellier, "respect your master and ours."

[99]

DARWIN, CHARLES

DARWIN, CHARLES (1809-1882). The age-old dispute between Biblical cosmology and modern natural science was completely overshadowed by Darwin's *Origin of Species* (1859) which resulted in innumerable arguments on evolution. Darwin's earlier book and his *Descent of Man* (1871) revolutionized biology and deeply affected philosophy, historical perspectives, religious controversies, and political, social, and economic criteria.

Darwin, humble, of delicate health, and adverse to publicity, upheld Christian behavior, though he had abandoned theism. He had never intended to provoke religious or philosophical debates. The aim of his special studies, which occupied him for more than twenty-five years, was to show that higher species had come into existence as a result of the gradual transformation of lower species; that the process of transformation could be explained through the selective effects of the natural environment upon organisms. His theory was based upon the propositions that all organisms and instincts are variable, that the gradual perfection of any organism or instinct is the result of an adaptation to the environment, and that the general struggle for existence (which Darwin considered to be the powerful method of selection) allowed only those organisms which were fit for adaptation to survive. Heredity continued this survival and reproduction of parental and ancestral qualities for many epochs. Darwin stated that although natural selection was the essential factor, it was not the sole factor in transformation. He admitted the possibility of inheriting acquired characteristics; this was denied by later Darwinists. Darwin did not exclude man from his theory that the higher organisms are the result of long processes of transformation which began with the lowest on the scale.

His work was based upon painstaking observation. His principle of the struggle for existence was not based upon his primary studies of nature. For years, he had sought for a principle by means of which he could arrange the collected facts. Neither his thoughts as a natural scientist nor his observations of nature led him to this. Malthus' *Essay on Population* which Darwin read (1838) clarified for him the entire problem of variation in plants and animals. Malthus maintained that more individuals are born than are able to survive and that the capability of adaptation to the environment is the reason for the survival of the fittest. This principle, borrowed by Darwin from a political economist, has become one of the most disputed portions of his theory.

Since the appearance of the *Origin of Species,* Darwinism and evolutionism have become synonymous. It was Herbert Spencer, to whom Darwin fondly referred as "our philosopher," who characterized Darwin's theory as evolutionism, and to which Darwin agreed. Darwin's concept of evolution is entirely different from other evolutionary theories which assumed a metaphysical entity as the evolving or directing power. Natural selection, regardless of whether it is valid, was conceived and kept by Darwin, free from any metaphysics. Darwin's hypothesis that transformation or evolution proceeds by minute gradations, has been disputed by Thomas Huxley, who, despite this dissension, was an important champion of Darwinism. Most modern biologists share Huxley's views on this question.

"Everyone believing, as I do, that all the corporeal and mental organs (excepting those which are neither advantageous nor disadvantageous to the possessor) of all beings have been developed through natural selection, or the survival of the fittest, together with use or habit, will admit that these organs have been formed so that their possessors may compete successfully with other beings, and thus increase in number. Now an animal may be led to pursue that course of action which is most beneficial to the species by suffering, such as pain, hunger, thirst, and fear; or by pleasure, as in eating and drinking, and in the propagation of the species, &c.; or by both means combined, as in the search for food. But pain or suffering of any kind, if long continued, causes depression and lessens the power of action, yet is well adapted to make a creature guard itself against any great or sudden evil. Pleasurable sensations, on the other hand, may be long continued without any depressing effect; on the contrary, they stimulate the whole system to increased action. Hence it has come to pass that most or all sentient beings have been developed in such a manner, through natural selection, that pleasurable sensations serve as their habitual guides. We see this in the pleasure from exertion, even occasionally from great exertion of the body or mind,— in the pleasure of our daily meals, and especially in the pleasure derived from sociability, and from our loving families. The sum of such pleasures as these, which are habitual or frequently recurrent, give, as I can hardly doubt, to most sentient beings an excess of happiness over misery, although many occasionally suffer much. Such suffering is quite compatible with the belief in Natural Selection, which is not perfect in its action, but tends only to render each species as successful as possible in the battle for life with other species, in wonderfully complex and changing circumstances.

"That there is much suffering in the world no one disputes. Some have attempted to explain this with reference to man by imagining that it serves for his moral improvement. But the number of men in the world is as nothing compared with that of all other sentient beings, and they often suffer greatly without any moral improvement. This very old argument from the existence of suffering against the existence of an intelligent First Cause seems to me a strong one; whereas, as just remarked, the presence of much suffering agrees well with the view that all organic beings have been developed through variation and natural selection.

"At the present day the most unusual argument for the existence of an intelligent God is drawn from the deep inward conviction and feelings which are experienced by most persons.

"Formerly I was led by feelings such as those just referred to (although I do not think that the religious sentiment was ever strongly developed in me), to the firm conviction of the existence of God and of the immortality of the soul. In my Journal I wrote that whilst standing in the midst of the grandeur of a Brazilian forest, 'it is not possible to give an adequate idea of the higher feelings of wonder, admiration, and devotion which fill and elevate the mind.' I well remember my conviction that there is more in man than the mere breath of his body; but now the grandest scenes would not cause any such convictions and feelings to rise in my mind. It may be truly said that I am like a man who has become color-blind, and the universal belief by men of the existence of redness makes my present loss of perception of not the least value as evidence. This argument would be a valid one if all men of all races had the same inward conviction of the existence of one God; but we know that this is very far from being the case. Therefore I cannot see that such inward convictions and feelings are of any weight as evidence of what really exists. The state of mind which grand scenes formerly excited in me, and which was intimately connected with a belief in God, did not essentially differ from that which is often called the sense of sublimity; and however difficult it may be to explain the genesis of this

303

sense, it can hardly be advanced as an argument for the existence of God, any more than the powerful though vague and similar feelings excited by music.

"With respect to immortality, nothing shows me [so clearly] how strong and almost instinctive a belief it is as the consideration of the view now held by most physicists, namely, that the sun with all the planets will in time grow too cold for life, unless indeed some great body dashes into the sun and thus gives it fresh life. Believing as I do that man in the distant future will be a far more perfect creature than he now is, it is an intolerable thought that he and all other sentient beings are doomed to complete annihilation after such long-continued slow progress. To those who fully admit the immortality of the human soul, the destruction of our world will not appear so dreadful."

[100]

DE BROGLIE, LOUIS

DE BROGLIE, LOUIS (1892-   ). Albert Einstein evaluated De Broglie's genius and achievements as something which "happens only in large intervals of history." He also expressed great satisfaction with the decision of the Nobel Prize Committee to award the 1929 Nobel Prize to De Broglie.

De Broglie's principal achievement is his formulation of "undulatory mechanics" or "wave mechanics." He overcame the constant antagonism between the theories of emission and undulation by showing the interaction between radiation and matter. The almost-forgotten wave principle of optics was discussed during the seventeenth and eighteenth centuries, and applications of this principle to physics were considered to be completely out of the question. De Broglie's theory assimilates the photons as particulars of light, and the electrons as particulars of matter. These have been confirmed experimentally by noted British and American physicists. De Broglie has always acknowledged that Einstein's theory of relativity was his constant inspiration. He established a relativist mechanics of a more physical character; whereas Einstein's physics is of a more mathematical nature. De Broglie's theory has been stated to be of equal importance with those of Einstein and Planck. It allows for a more rigorous approximation of measurement and a more concrete objectivity of scientific symbolism. It makes for progress in the exactitude of theoretical physics and increasingly reconciles the principles of continuity and discontinuity.

THE MARCH OF SCIENCE

In the history of thought, particularly scientific thought, there are moments when great, earth-shaking evolutions are produced, and decisive distances that formerly existed, disappear. These mutations are slowly and secretly prepared during anterior periods and occur with the same abruptness, frequency, and similarity that contemporary biologists have demonstrated in the evolution of living organisms.

The progressive formation and coincidence of individual efforts converging toward the same end often takes place without knowledge of those engaged in the work. Powerful currents of thought emerge simultaneously. The exact form of whole branches of science whose great features had only been vaguely seen by precursors is suddenly illumined by the work of superior minds. It is as though the chisel of an inspired artist sculpts a statue that is admired for centuries. Sometimes the effect of pre-established harmony is the discovery of more than one exceptional mind; it becomes the simultaneous flowering of ingenious savants; an ensemble of imperishable discoveries whose production a privileged generation is witness to in its lifetime. It becomes a glorious epoch of scientific thought from which all progress issues forth in ensuing years.

[101]

DEDEKIND, RICHARD

DEDEKIND, RICHARD (1831-1916). When Dedekind was seventy-three years old, he read in a mathematical annual, an obituary that stated he had died on September 4, 1899. As a cautious mathematician, he wrote to the editor of the annual, pointing out that as far as he could see, September 4 might be proved to be correct in the future, but that the year, 1899, as the year of his death was certainly not correct. The incident was characteristic of Dedekind's modesty and aversion to publicity, which resulted in his remaining unknown even to mathematical experts, who daily utilized his findings and studies.

Dedekind's principal works: *Continuity and Irrational Numbers* (1871) and *The Nature and Meaning of Numbers* (1888) are highly important contributions to the theory of numbers. Dedekind's "cut," in the first book, is considered to be the foundation of irrational numbers. In the second, the concept and the fundamental qualities of natural numbers are developed by the pure theory of quantity, beginning with the idea of imaged systems. A system (totality or quantity) is called infinite if it cannot be imaged homologously.

THE NATURE AND MEANING OF NUMBERS

IN science nothing capable of proof ought to be accepted without proof. Though this demand seems so reasonable yet I cannot regard it as having been met even in the most recent methods of laying the foundations of the simplest science; viz., that part of logic which deals with the theory of numbers. In speaking of arithmetic (algebra, analysis) as a part of logic I mean to imply that I consider the number-concept entirely independent of the notions or intuitions of space and time, that I consider it an immediate result from the laws of thought. My answer to the problems propounded in the title of this paper is, then, briefly this: numbers are free creations of the human mind; they serve as a means of apprehending more easily and more sharply the difference of things. It is only through the purely logical process of building up the science of numbers and by thus acquiring the continuous number-domain that we are prepared accurately to investigate our notions of space and time by bringing them into relation with this number-domain created in our mind. If we scrutinise closely what is done in counting an aggregate or number of things, we are led to consider the ability of the mind to relate things to things, to let a thing correspond to a thing, or to represent a thing by a thing, an ability without which no thinking is possible.

I like to compare this action of thought, so difficult to trace on account of the rapidity of its performance, with the action which an accomplished reader performs in reading; this reading always remains a more or less complete repetition of the individual steps which the beginner has to take in his wearisome spelling-out; a very small part of the same, and therefore a very small effort or exertion of the mind, is sufficient for the practiced reader to recognize the correct, true word, only with very great probability, to be sure; for, as is well known, it occasionally happens that even the most practiced proof-reader allows a typographical error to escape him, i.e., reads falsely, a thing which would be impossible if the chain of thoughts associated with spelling were fully repeated. So from the time of birth, continually and in increasing measure we are led to relate things to things and thus to use that faculty of the mind on which the creation of numbers depends; by this practice continually occurring, though without definite purpose, in our earliest years and by the attending formation of judgments and chains of reasoning we acquire a store of real arithmetic truths to which our first teachers later refer as to something simple, self-evident, given in the inner consciousness; and so it happens that many very complicated notions (as for example that of the number [*Anzahl*] of things) are erroneously regarded as simple.

[102]

DELMEDIGO, JOSEPH SOLOMON

DELMEDIGO, JOSEPH SOLOMON (1591-1655). A restless spirit made Delmedigo the prototype of the wandering Jew. He peregrinated from Candia, Crete, his native town, to Padua, Italy; thence to Egypt, Turkey, Poland, Hamburg, Amsterdam, Frankfort, Worms, and then finally died in Prague. He earned his living either as physician or teacher but wherever he sojourned, he remembered to study the natural sciences. He was a disciple of Galileo and a keen critic of the medieval philosophy of nature; but he had to be careful, lest the ecclesiastical and secular authorities were offended by his ideas. He was shrewd enough to avoid such disturbances. His only known works are: *Elim* (Palms) dealing with mathematics, the natural sciences, and metaphysics, and some of letters and essays.

GOOD AND BAD BOOKS

PEOPLE say that the art of printing has brought us great advantages, whereas it has in fact been detrimental to us. For in former days authors were handsomely paid and people would buy from them only the good, pleasing, useful books, while the useless, vain books would of themselves disappear. Not so, however, in our days, when many ignorant people assume airs, and, though benighted and smaller than the least throughout their lives, seek to set themselves up as shining lights to another generation that has not learned to know them. And everyone who possibly can, and whose wealth is greater than his understanding, connives to publish books in which he is arbitrarily referred to as a great and worthy man, whereas he is no more an authority than is a carpenter's apprentice.

The only concern for the publishers is for new books. No one pays any attention to the writings of the early authors, or makes effort to preserve them and to shake the dust from them. Because of the art of printing you find a topsy-turvy world—the native below and the stranger on top.

It seems to me that books are subject to the same process as souls: they migrate from one body to another. Not by chance are son and book designated in Latin by the same term, *liber*. And so it is in the case of scholarly books that are translated from one language into another, in a different style, in other words, and in changed order. The language becomes different but the content is the same. And the book is given a new title—for example, a book originally entitled *Precious Vessel* will be called *Costly Vessel*. The matter remains exactly the same except that it has been poured from one receptacle into another. Ecclesiastes has taught us all this in these his words: "That which hath been is that which shall be, and that which hath been done is that which shall be done; and there is nothing new under the sun. Is there a thing whereof it is said: 'See, this is new'?—it hath been already, in the ages which were before us. There is no remembrance of them of former times; neither shall there be any remembrance of them of latter times that are to come, among those that shall come after." He also said: "Seeing that in the days to come all will long ago have been forgotten."

It is true indeed that there is no cause for concern about the good, useful, pleasing authors, for under any circumstances their names will live for many days, perhaps they will even shine forever, like stars. But not so in the case of those who pen spurious writings, who have consumed their time and their money to no advantage. When their ignorance is laid bare and their mischief gives offense, their shortcomings are recognized and their hope turns to despair. For their eye is dimmed. Even if they were to offer their books as gifts, no one would accept them. They become like thorns in their eyes, they are piled high in their houses, heaps upon heaps, and the rats feed upon and glut themselves with them. And the rain falls, drips down upon them drop upon drop, and the birds, pigeons, and chickens nest among them. The sun sets at noon for the authors of these books, before their very eyes, and their books die in their lifetime.

But if the authors were only wise enough to realize all this, they would recoil from "much study that is a weariness of the flesh." But their love for themselves is great, and they shut their minds to the fact that the ultimate end of their books is but a vain one, for no one would ever commit the folly of publishing them anew. Thus one who writes a number of inferior books will live unto all generations just as little as the name of one who begets many illegitimate children.

[103]

DEMOCRITUS OF ABDERA

DEMOCRITUS OF ABDERA (460-c. 360 B.C.). Although only scarce fragments of the numerous works of Democritus are extant, sufficient pieces have remained to prove that he was one of the greatest of the Greek thinkers; equally outstanding as a scientist and philosopher; a peer of Plato and Aristotle; and a man whose thoughts and feelings were close to the common people. Many legends have been formed about his life. He is said to have traveled from Ethiopia and Egypt to Persia and India. He certainly visited Athens, but no one there took notice of him. Plato, his contemporary, never mentioned Democritus, but Aristotle and Hippocrates quoted him frequently. The legends depicted Democritus as a man easily disposed to laughter; an incurable optimist; moderate, serene, and always prepared to understand the errors and failures of his fellow men.

Democritus conceived the universe to be composed of essential transitory combinations of an infinite number of atoms and their separations as the necessary condition for eternal change; that atomic theory was a working hypothesis which would help explain the experiences of mind and nature; his concepts were comparable to idealistic metaphysics. He was not only an important systematizer of Greek atomism, anticipating the underlying principle of modern physics, but also an acute psychologist; a sage moralist, inspired by humanitarian ideals, without illusions about human nature. He taught that equanimity and fortitude must prevail in all life situations, and that there must be resistance to evil and temptations. He contributed to epistemology, physics, mathematics, and technics. He dealt with logical and musical problems; avoided politics in his writings.

THE SYMMETRY OF LIFE

In truth we know nothing about anything, but every man shares the generally prevailing opinion.

In fact we do not know anything infallibly, but only that which changes according to the condition of our body and of the [influences] that reach and impinge upon it.

There are two forms of knowledge, one genuine, one obscure. To the obscure belong all of the following: sight, hearing, smell, taste, feeling. The other form is the genuine, and is quite distinct from this. (And then distinguishing the genuine from the obscure, he continues:) Whenever the obscure [way of knowing] has reached the *minimum sensible* of hearing, smell, taste, and touch, and when the investigation must be carried farther into that which is still finer, then arises the genuine way of knowing, which has a finer organ of thought.

310

By convention sweet is sweet, by convention bitter is bitter, by convention hot is hot, by convention cold is cold, by convention color is color. But in reality there are atoms and the void. That is, the objects of sense are supposed to be real and it is customary to regard them as such, but in truth they are not. Only the atoms and the void are real.

Of practical wisdom these are the three fruits: to deliberate well, to speak to the point, to do what is right.

If one choose the goods of the soul, he chooses the diviner [portion]; if the goods of the body, the merely mortal.

'Tis not in strength of body nor in gold that men find happiness, but in uprightness and in fullness of understanding.

Not from fear but from sense of duty refrain from your sins.

He who does wrong is more unhappy than he who suffers wrong.

Many who have not learned wisdom live wisely, and many who do the basest deeds can make most learned speeches.

Fools learn wisdom through misfortune.

One should emulate works and deeds of virtue, not arguments about it.

Strength of body is nobility in beasts of burden, strength of character is nobility in men.

The hopes of the right-minded may be realized, those of fools are impossible.

Neither art nor wisdom may be attained without learning.

It is better to correct your own faults than those of another.

Those who have a well-ordered character lead also a well-ordered life.

Good means not [merely] not to do wrong, but rather not to desire to do wrong.

There are many who know many things, yet are lacking in wisdom.

311

Fame and wealth without wisdom are unsafe possessions.

You can tell the man who rings true from the man who rings false, not by his deeds alone, but also by his desires.

False men and shams talk big and do nothing.

My enemy is not the man who wrongs me, but the man who means to wrong me.

The enmity of one's kindred is far more bitter than the enmity of strangers.

The friendship of one wise man is better than the friendship of a host of fools.

No one deserves to live who has not at least one good-man-and-true for a friend.

Seek after the good, and with much toil shall ye find it; the evil turns up of itself without your seeking it.

In the weightiest matters we must go to school to the animals, and learn spinning and weaving from the spider, building from the swallow, singing from the birds,—from the swan and the nightingale, imitating their art.

An evil and foolish and intemperate and irreligious life should not be called a bad life, but rather, dying long drawn out.

Fortune is lavish with her favors, but not to be depended on. Nature on the other hand is self-sufficing and therefore with her feebler but trustworthy [resources] she wins the greater [meed] of hope.

The right-minded man, ever inclined to righteous and lawful deeds, is joyous day and night, and strong, and free from care. But if a man take no heed of the right, and leave undone the things he ought to do, then will the recollection of no one of all his transgressions bring him any joy, but only anxiety and self-reproaching.

Now as of old the gods give men all good things, excepting only those that are baneful and injurious and useless. These, now as of old, are not gifts of the gods: men stumble into them themselves because of their own blindness and folly.

A sensible man takes pleasure in what he has instead of pining for what he has not.

The pleasures that give most joy are the ones that most rarely come.

Throw moderation to the winds, and the greatest pleasures bring the greatest pains.

Men achieve tranquility through moderation in pleasure and through the symmetry of life. Want and superfluity are apt to upset them and to cause great perturbations in the soul. The souls that are rent by violent conflicts are neither stable nor tranquil. One should therefore set his mind upon the things that are within his power, and be content with his opportunities, nor let his memory dwell very long on the envied and admired of men, nor idly sit and dream of them. Rather, he should contemplate the lives of those who suffer hardship, and vividly bring to mind their sufferings, so that your own present situation may appear to you important and to be envied, and so that it may no longer be your portion to suffer torture in your soul by your longing for more. For he who admires those who have, and whom other men deem blest of fortune, and who spends all his time idly dreaming of them, will be forced to be always contriving some new device because of his [insatiable] desire, until he ends by doing some desperate deed forbidden by the laws. And therefore one ought not to desire other men's blessings, and one ought not to envy those who have more, but rather, comparing his life with that of those who fare worse, and laying to heart their sufferings, deem himself blest of fortune in that he lives and fares so much better than they. Holding fast to this saying you will pass your life in greater tranquillity and will avert not a few of the plagues of life—envy and jealousy and bitterness of mind.

[104]

DE MORGAN, AUGUSTUS

DE MORGAN, AUGUSTUS (1806-1871). De Morgan made a number of important contributions to an algebra of logic, and his laws

313

of the propositional calculus have been widely discussed. He is also acknowledged as the founder of the logic of relations. However, the author of *Formal Logic* (1847) never renounced his claims of promoting metaphysics in no lesser degree than he did mathematics and logic. For more than thirty years, De Morgan, as professor at University College in London, acted and taught in accordance with his principle that positive theism must be made the basis of psychological explanation and that, in elucidating mathematical principles, it is necessary to refer to an intelligent and disposed Creator when mental organization is to be dealt with as effect of a cause.

Although a convinced theist, De Morgan never joined a religious congregation. He was a staunch adversary of religious discrimination and was fond of his nonconformism. He renounced his professorship in 1866, when James Martineau was denied a chair at University College because he was a Unitarian. De Morgan, who was admired for his "reading algebra like a novel," was an intimate friend of George Boole who shared his views on mathematics as well as those on religion and ethics.

I D E A S

The word *idea*, as here used, does not enter in that vague sense in which it is generally used, as if it were an opinion that might be right or wrong. It is that which the object gives to the mind, or the state of the mind produced by the object. Thus the idea of a horse is *the horse in the mind*: and we know no other horse. We admit that there is an external *object*, a horse, which may give a *horse in the mind* to twenty different persons: but no one of these twenty knows the object; each one only knows his *idea*. There is an object, because each of the twenty persons receives an idea without communicating with the others: so that there is something external to give it them. But when they talk about it, under the name of a horse, they talk about their ideas. They all refer to the object, as being the thing they are talking about, until the moment they begin to differ: and then they begin to speak, not of external horses, but of impressions on their minds; at least this is the case with those who know what knowledge is; the positive and the unthinking part of them still talk of the *horse*. And the

314

latter have a great advantage over the former with those who are like themselves.

Why then do we introduce the term *object* at all, since all our knowledge lies in ideas? For the same reason as we introduce the term *matter* into natural philosophy, when all we know is form, size, color, weight, &c., no one of which is matter, nor even all together. It is convenient to have a word for that external source from which *sensible* ideas are produced: and it is just as convenient to have a word for the external source, material or not, from which *any* idea is produced. Again, why do we speak of our power of considering things ideally or objectively, when as we can know nothing but ideas, we can have no right to speak of any thing else? The answer is that, just as in other things, when we speak of an object, we speak of the *idea of an object*. We learn to speak of the external world, because there are others like ourselves who evidently draw ideas from the same sources as ourselves: hence we come to have the idea of those sources, the idea of external objects, as we call them. But we do not know those sources; we know only our ideas of them.

We can even use the terms ideal and objective in what may appear a metaphorical sense. When we speak of ourselves in the manner of this chapter, we put ourselves, as it were, in the position of spectators of our own minds: we speak and think of our own minds objectively. And it must be remembered that by the word object, we do not mean *material* object only. The mind of another, any one of its thoughts or feelings, any relation of minds to one another, a treaty of peace, a battle, a discussion upon a controverted question, the right of conveying a freehold,—are all objects, independently of the persons or things engaged in them. They are things external to our minds, of which we have ideas.

An object communicates an idea: but it does not follow that every idea is communicated by an object. The mind can create ideas in various ways; or at least can derive, by combinations which are not found in external existence, new collections of ideas. We have a perfectly distinct idea of unicorn, or a flying dragon: when we say there are no such things, we speak objectively only: ideally, they have as much existence as a horse or a sheep; to a herald, more. Add to this, that the mind can separate ideas into parts, in such manner that the parts alone are not ideas of any existing separate material objects, any more than the letters of a word are constituent parts of the meaning of the whole. Hence we get what are called *qualities* and *relations*. A ball may be hard and round, or may have hardness and roundness: but we cannot say that hardness and roundness are separate external material objects, though they are objects the ideas of which necessarily accompany our perception of certain objects. These ideas are called *abstract* as being removed or abstracted from the complex idea which gives them: the abstraction is made by comparison or observation of resemblances. If a person had never seen any thing round except an apple, he would perhaps never think of roundness as a distinct object of thought. When he saw another round body, which was evidently not an apple, he would immediately, by perception of the resemblance, acquire a separate idea of the thing in which they resemble one another.

[105]

DE SANCTIS, FRANCESCO

DE SANCTIS, FRANCESCO (1817-1883). In the 1848 revolution in Naples, when the revolutionaries struggled against the king's troops, one barricade, in particular, attracted wide attention. It was led by De Sanctis, then the director of a boys' school, who commanded and organized his pupils as a company of trained soldiers. When the revolution was defeated, De Sanctis was imprisoned for more than four years. He utilized this period of enforced idleness to study the philosophy of Hegel and to translate several German works into Italian. Upon his release, he earned his living as a private tutor and free-lance writer; he later became a professor at Zurich, Switzerland, with the German Hegelian, Friederich Theodor Vischer, and the historian, Jacob Burckhardt, as his colleagues. When the unified kingdom of Italy was achieved, King Victor Emmanuel II appointed De Sanctis minister of public education (1861), and he was later made professor of comparative literature at the University of Naples (1871). There, De Sanctis had many faithful disciples, among whom Benedetto Croce was the most outstanding.

De Sanctis' chief contribution was to aesthetics. Although he remained a Hegelian, he did not found his aesthetic views upon ideas; instead he concentrated upon form. He stated that living form was the essence of art, rather than the ideal or beauty. He opposed all psychological approaches to the arts, especially poetry, and insisted upon formal analysis. His influence upon Italian literary criticism remained strong up to the present time.

THE INTELLECTUAL FUTURE

ITALY, compelled to struggle for a whole century to win independence and liberal institutions, kept by that struggle in a circle of ideas too general, too uniform, subordinated to political ends, is witnessing the falling to pieces of that whole theological-metaphysical-political system, which has nothing left to give her. The positive tendencies were vanquished by ontology with its brilliant synthesis; and now ontology is failing too, is stale and repetitive. It has sunk into the Arcadian and academic, as happens inevitably to systems that have ceased to progress. Ontology's heir is criticism, a criticism bearing on its face the stamp of the fantastic and dogmatic it received at its birth; but visibly inclined to investigate, rather than to postulate and demonstrate. Philosophical and literary synthesis are declining; their place is being taken by the humble and patient monograph. Systems are suspect, laws are received with diffidence, principles until now regarded as absolute are being tested in the crucible. Nothing is admitted that has not been proved by a series of ascertained facts—the verification of a fact is an event of greater importance than the establishment of a law. That whole collection of ideas, maxims, and formulae that once gave rise to such struggles and excitements, has sunk into a conventional repertory no longer representative of opinion as it really is: Giacomo Leopardi has left his touch on them. It would seem that at this very moment when Italy at last has formed herself, that the intellectual and political world which made her formation possible, was dissolving. That Italy herself is alive we know from the new horizon that has dawned—vague as yet and shadowy, but unmistakable. A never-flagging force is driving her onward; no sooner is one aspiration appeased than another appears.

Italy till now has been dazzled by her brilliant sphere —the sphere of nationality and liberty. Her philosophy has sprung from a thing outside of her, even if around her. Now she must look into her heart, must seek for her very self. The sphere must develop and become concrete as her inner life. The religious hypocrisies, the academic habits, the political necessities, the long periods of lying fallow, the foreign motives superimposed on her liberal development, the memories of a servitude that lasted for centuries—all these have led to an artificial and vacillating consciousness, preventing absorption and intimacy. Her life, even today, is external and artificial. Let her look into her heart with clear eyes, unhindered by veil or obstacle; let her look for the "effectual thing" with the spirit of Galileo and Machiavelli. In this search for the elements of the real in her life the Italian spirit will create its culture once more, will restore her moral world, will refresh her impressions, will find in her own inner life new sources of inspiration—woman, the family, love, nature, liberty, science, and virtue—and not as brilliant ideas revolving in space around and about her but as concrete, definite things, become her content.

[106]

DESCARTES, RENÉ

DESCARTES, RENÉ (1595-1650). Descartes represented the spirit of the age which rid itself of ancient authority and conventions. His personal life manifested a change from bon vivant to that of recluse. The life-loving, teeming existence of Paris did not deter him. He had been a soldier of fortune with different armies during the Thirty Years' War, a scholar, traveler, pilgrim, and firm adberent to the Catholic faith.

On November 10, 1619 a dream revealed to him the synthetic

and analytic method which he was to follow. He never published it in the form he had originally intended because news of the persecution of Galileo, with whom he had sympathized, reached him. Like everyone in that age, he doubted everything; even his own existence. The more he doubted, the more certain he became of himself as a thinking being. He tersely couched this insight with the phrase: "I think, therefore I am." His constant intellectual search led him to the idea of an infinite God, which fact he then took as proof that God exists. He argued thus: nothing so great as a divine being could be without a real basis in fact. He stated that the existence of a perfect being was comprised in the idea of it, just as the equality of the three angles to two right ones is comprised in the idea of a triangle. Since God was truthful, he could not be thought of as wishing to deceive man. Hence God guaranteed the truth of whatever is clear and distinct to man's reason and perception.

Thus Descartes, or Cartesius—the Latin form of his name—became the father of modern rationalism. He was also a mechanist, explaining matter by differently shaped corpuscles interacting mechanically. He and his disciples maintained that even animals are living automata; that man is also a machine, except for his spirit which represents thinking substance, as distinct from extended substance. Descartes died unhappily in the service of Queen Christina of Sweden who meant to make full use of his talents for philosophy, mathematics, and natural science.

THE NATURE OF THE HUMAN MIND

I SUPPOSE . . . that all the things which I see are fictitious; I believe that none of those objects which my fallacious memory represents ever existed; I suppose that I possess no senses; I believe that body, figure, extension, motion, and place are merely fictions of my mind. What is there, then, that can be esteemed true? Perhaps this only, that there is absolutely nothing certain.

But how do I know that there is not something different altogether from the objects I have now enumerated, of which it is impossible to entertain the slightest doubt? Is there not a God, or some being, by whatever name I may designate him, who causes these thoughts to arise in my mind? But why suppose such a being, for it may be I myself am capable of producing them? Am I, then, at least not something? But

319

I before denied that I possessed senses or a body; I hesitate, however, for what follows from that? Am I so dependent on the body and the senses that without these I cannot exist? But I had the persuasion that there was absolutely nothing in the world, that there was no sky and no earth, neither minds nor bodies; was I not, therefore, at the same time, persuaded that I did not exist? Far from it; I assuredly existed, since I was persuaded. But there is I know not what being, who is possessed at once of the highest power and the deepest cunning, who is constantly employing all his ingenuity in deceiving me. Doubtless, then, I exist, since I am deceived; and, let him deceive me as he may, he can never bring it about that I am nothing, so long as I shall be conscious that I am something. So that it must, in fine, be maintained, all things being maturely and carefully considered, that this proposition I am, I exist, is necessarily true each time it is expressed by me, or conceived in my mind.

But I do not yet know with sufficient clearness what I am, though assured that I am; and hence, in the next place, I must take care, lest perchance I inconsiderately substitute some other object in room of what is properly myself, and thus wander from the truth, even in that knowledge which I hold to be of all others the most certain and evident. For this reason, I will now consider anew what I formerly believed myself to be, before I entered on the present train of thought; and of my previous opinion I will retrench all that can in the least be invalidated by the grounds of doubt I have adduced, in order that there may at length remain nothing but what is certain and indubitable. What then did I formerly think I was? Undoubtedly I judged that I was a man. But what is a man? Shall I say a rational animal? Assuredly not; for it would be necessary forthwith to inquire into what is meant by animal, and what by rational, and thus, from a single question, I should insensibly glide into others, and these more difficult than the first; nor do I now possess enough of leisure to warrant me in wasting my time amid subtleties of this sort. I prefer here to attend to the thoughts that sprung up of themselves in my mind, and were inspired by my own nature alone, when I applied myself to the consideration of what I was. In the first place, then, I thought that I possessed a countenance, hands, arms, and all the fabric of members that appears in a corpse, and which I called by the name of body. It further occurred to me that I was nourished, that I walked, perceived, and thought, and all those actions I referred to the soul; but what the soul itself was I either did not stay to consider, or, if I did, I imagined that it was something extremely rare and subtile, like wind, or flame, or ether, spread through my grosser parts. As regarded the body, I did not even doubt of its nature, but thought I distinctly knew it, and if I had wished to describe it according to the notions I then entertained, I should have explained myself in this manner: By body I understand all that can be terminated by a certain figure; that can be comprised in a certain place, and so fill a certain space as therefrom to exclude every other body; that can be perceived either by touch, sight, hearing, taste, or smell; that can be moved in different ways, not indeed of itself, but by something foreign to it by which it is touched [and from which it receives the impression]; for the power of self-motion as likewise that of perceiving and thinking, I held as by no means pertaining to the nature of body; on the contrary, I was somewhat astonished to find such faculties existing in some bodies.

But [as to myself, what can I now say that I am], since I suppose there exists an extremely powerful, and, if I may so speak, malignant being, whose whole endeavors are directed towards deceiving me? Can I affirm that I possess any one of all those attributes of which I have lately spoken as belonging to the nature of body? After attentively considering them in my own mind, I find none of them that can properly be said to belong to myself. To recount them were idle and tedious. Let us pass, then, to the attributes of the soul. The first mentioned were the powers of nutrition and walking; but, if it be true that I have no body, it is true likewise that I am capable neither of walking nor of being nourished. Perception is another attribute of the soul; but perception too is impossible without the body: besides, I have frequently, during sleep, believed that I perceived objects which I afterwards observed I did not in reality perceive. Thinking is another attribute of the soul; and here I discover what properly belongs to myself. This alone is inseparable from me. I am—I exist: this is certain; but how often? As often as I think; for perhaps it would even happen, if I should wholly cease to think, that I should at the same time altogether cease to be. I now admit nothing that is not necessarily true: I am therefore, precisely speaking, only a thinking thing, that is, a mind, understanding, or reason,— terms whose signification was before unknown to me. I am, however, a real thing, and really existent; but what thing? The answer was, a thinking thing. The question now arises, am I aught besides? I will stimulate my imagination with a view to discover whether I am not still something more than a thinking being. Now it is plain I am not the assemblage of members called the human body; I am not a thin and penetrating air diffused through all these members, or wind, or flame, or vapour, or breath, or any of all the things I can imagine; for I supposed that all these were not, and, without changing the supposition, I find that I still feel assured of my existence.

But it is true, perhaps, that those very things which I suppose to be non-existent, because they are unknown to me, are not in truth different from myself whom I know. This is a point I cannot determine, and do not now enter into any dispute regarding it. I can only judge of things that are known to me: I am conscious that I exist, and I who know that I exist inquire into what I am. It is, however, perfectly certain that the knowledge of my existence, thus precisely taken, is not dependent on things, the existence of which is as yet unknown to me: and consequently it is not dependent on any of the things I can feign in imagination. Moreover, the phrase itself, I frame an image, reminds me of my error; for I should in truth frame one if I were to imagine myself to be anything, since to imagine is nothing more than to contemplate the figure or image or a corporeal thing; but I already know that I exist, and that it is possible at the same time that all those images, and in general all that relates to the nature of body, are merely dreams [or chimeras]. From this I discover that it is not more reasonable to say, I will excite my imagination that I may know more distinctly what I am, than to express myself as follows: I am now awake, and perceive something real; but because my perception is not sufficiently clear, I will of express purpose go to sleep that my dreams may represent to me the object of my perception with more truth and clearness. And, therefore, I know that nothing of all that I can embrace in imagination belongs to the knowledge which I have of myself, and that there is need to recall with the utmost care the mind from this mode of thinking, that it may be able to know its own nature with perfect distinctness.

But what, then, am I? A thinking thing, it has been said. But what is a thinking thing? It is a thing that doubts, understands, [conceives], affirms, denies, wills, refuses, that imagines also, and perceives. Assuredly it is not little, if all these properties belong to my nature. But why should they not belong to it? Am I not that very being who now doubts of almost everything; who, for all that, understands and conceives certain things; who affirms one alone as true, and denies the others; who desires to know more of them, and does not wish to be deceived; who imagines many things, sometimes even despite his will; and is likewise percipient of many, as if through the medium of the senses. Is there nothing of all this as true as that I am, even although I should be always dreaming, and although he who gave me being employed all his ingenuity to deceive me? Is there also any one of these attributes that can be properly distinguished from my thought, or that can be said to be separate from myself? For it is of itself so evident that it is I who doubt, I who understand, and I who desire, that it is here unnecessary to add anything by way of rendering it more clear. And I am as certainly the same being who imagines; for, although it may be (as I before supposed) that nothing I imagine is true, still the power of imagination does not cease really to exist in me and to form part of my thought. In fine, I am the same being who perceives, that is, who apprehends certain objects as by the organs of sense, since, in truth, I see light, hear a noise, and feel heat. But it will be said that these presentations are false, and that I am dreaming. Let it be so. At all events it is certain that I seem to see light, hear a noise, and feel heat; this cannot be false, and this is what in me is properly called perceiving, which is nothing else than thinking. From this I begin to know what I am with somewhat greater clearness and distinctness than heretofore.

But, nevertheless, it still seems to me, and I cannot help believing, that corporeal things, whose images are formed by thought, [which fall under the senses], and are examined by the same, are known with much greater distinctness than that I know not what part of myself which is not imaginable; although, in truth, it may seem strange to say that I know and comprehend with greater distinctness things whose existence appears to me doubtful, that are unknown, and do not belong to me, than others of whose reality I am persuaded, that are known to me, and appertain to my proper nature; in a word, than myself. But I see clearly what is the state of the case. My mind is apt to wander, and will not yet submit to be restrained within the limits of truth. Let us therefore leave the mind to itself once more, and, according to it every kind of liberty, [permit it to consider the objects that appear to it from without], in order that, having afterwards withdrawn it from these gently and opportunely, [and fixed it on the consideration of its being and the properties it finds in itself], it may then be the more easily controlled.

Let us now accordingly consider the objects that are commonly thought to be [the most easily, and likewise] the most distinctly known, viz., the bodies we touch and see; not, indeed, bodies in general, for these general notions are usually somewhat more confused, but one body in particular. Take, for example, this piece of wax; it is quite fresh, having been but recently taken from the bee-hive; it has not yet lost the sweetness of the honey contained; it still retains somewhat of the odor of the flowers from which it was gathered; its color, figure, size, are apparent (to the sight); it is hard, cold, easily handled; and sounds when struck upon with the finger. In fine, all that contributes to make a body as distinctly known as possible, is found in the one before us. But, while I am speaking, let it be placed near the fire—what remained of the taste exhales, the smell evaporates, the color changes, its figure is destroyed, its size increases, it becomes liquid, it grows hot, it can hardly be handled, and, although struck upon, it emits no sound. Does the same wax still remain after this change? It must be admitted that it does remain; no one doubts it, or judges otherwise. What, then, was it I knew with so much distinctness in the piece of wax? Assuredly, it could be nothing of all that I observed by means of the senses, since all the things that fell under taste, smell, sight, touch, and hearing are changed, and yet the same wax remains. It was perhaps what I now think, viz., that this wax was neither the sweetness of honey, the pleasant odor of flowers, the whiteness, the figure, nor the sound, but only a body that a little before appeared to me conspicuous under these forms, and which is now perceived under others. But, to speak precisely, what is it that I imagine when I think of it in this way? Let it be attentively considered, and, retrenching all that does not belong to the wax, let us see what remains. There certainly remains nothing, except something extended, flexible, and movable. But what is meant by flexible and movable? Is it not that I imagine that the piece of wax, being round, is capable of becoming square, or of passing from a square into a triangular figure? Assuredly such is not the case, because I conceive that it admits of an infinity of similar changes; and I am, moreover, unable to compass this infinity by imagination, and consequently this conception which I have of the wax is not the product of the faculty of imagination. But what now is this extension? Is it not also unknown? for it becomes greater when the wax is melted, greater when it is boiled, and greater still when the heat increases; and I should not conceive [clearly and] according to truth, the wax as it is, if I did not suppose that the piece we are considering admitted even of a wider variety of extension than I ever imagined. I must, therefore, admit that I cannot even comprehend by imagination what the piece of wax is, and that it is the mind alone which perceives it. I speak of one piece in particular; for, as to wax in general, this is still more evident. But what is the piece of wax that can be perceived only by the [understanding or] mind? It is certainly the same which I see, touch, imagine; and, in fine, it is the same which, from the beginning, I believed it to be. But (and this it is of moment to observe) the perception of it is neither an act of sight, of touch, nor of imagination, and never was either of these, though it might formerly seem so, but is simply an intuition of the mind, which may be imperfect and confused, as it formerly was, or very clear and distinct, as it is at present, according as the attention is more or less directed to the elements which it contains, and of which it is composed.

But, meanwhile, I feel greatly astonished when I observe [the weakness of my mind, and] its proneness to error. For although, without at all giving expression to what I think, I consider all this in my own mind, words yet occasionally impede my progress, and I am almost led into error by the terms of ordinary language. We say, for example, that we see the same wax when it is before us, and not that we judge it to be the same from its retaining the same color and figure: whence I should forthwith be disposed to conclude that the wax is known by the act of sight, and not by the intuition of the mind alone, were it not for the analogous instance of human beings passing on in the street below, as observed from a window. In this case I do not fail to say that I see the men themselves, just as I say that I see the wax; and yet what do I see from the window beyond hats and cloaks that might cover artificial machines, whose motions might be determined by springs? But I judge that there are human beings from these appearances, and thus I comprehend, by the faculty of judgment alone which is in the mind, what I believed I saw with my eyes.

The man who makes it his aim to rise to knowledge superior to the common, ought to be ashamed to seek occasions of doubting from the vulgar forms of speech: instead, therefore, of doing this, I shall proceed with the matter in hand, and inquire whether I had a clearer and more perfect perception of the piece of wax when I first saw it, and when I thought I knew it by means of the external sense itself, or, at all events, by the common sense, as it is called, that is, by the imaginative faculty; or whether I rather apprehend it more clearly at present, after having examined with greater care, both what it is, and in what way it can be known. It would certainly be ridiculous to entertain any doubt on this point. For what, in that first perception, was there distinct? What did I perceive which any animal might not have perceived? But when I distinguish the wax from its exterior forms, and when, as if I had stripped it of its vestments, I consider it quite naked, it is certain, although some error may still be found in my judgment, that I cannot, nevertheless, thus apprehend it without possessing a human mind.

But, finally, what shall I say of the mind itself, that is, of myself? for as yet I do not admit that I am anything but mind. What, then! I who seem to possess so distinct an apprehension of the piece of wax,—do I not know myself, both with greater truth and certitude, and also much more distinctly and clearly? For if I judge that the wax exists because I see it, it assuredly follows, much more evidently, that I myself am or exist, for the same reason: for it is possible that what I see may not in truth be wax, and that I do not even possess eyes with which to see anything; but it cannot be that when I see, or, which comes to the same thing,

327

when I think I see, I myself who think am nothing. So like-wise, if I judge that the wax exists because I touch it, it will also follow that I am; and if I determine that my imagination, or any other cause, whatever it be, persuades me of the existence of the wax, I will still draw the same conclusion. And what is here remarked of the piece of wax, is applicable to all the other things that are external to me. And further, if the [notion or] perception of wax appeared to me more precise and distinct, after that not only sight and touch, but many other causes besides, rendered it manifest to my apprehension, with how much greater distinctness must I now know myself, since all the reasons that contribute to the knowledge of the nature of wax, or of any body whatever, manifest still better the nature of my mind? And there are besides so many other things in the mind itself that contribute to the illustration of its nature, that those dependent on the body, to which I have here referred, scarcely merit to be taken into account.

But, in conclusion, I find I have insensibly reverted to the point I desired; for, since it is now manifest to me that bodies themselves are not properly perceived by the senses nor by the faculty of imagination, but by the intellect alone; and since they are not perceived because they are seen and touched, but only because they are understood [or rightly comprehended by thought], I readily discover that there is nothing more easily or clearly apprehended than my own mind. But because it is difficult to rid one's self so promptly of an opinion to which one has been long accustomed, it will be desirable to tarry for some time at this stage, that, by long continued meditation, I may more deeply impress upon my memory this new knowledge.

[107]

DEWEY, JOHN

DEWEY, JOHN (1859-1952). At the celebration of his ninetieth anniversary, John Dewey declared that losing faith in our fellow men means losing faith in ourselves, "and that is the unforgivable sin." Dewey is generally recognized as America's leading philosopher, and the foremost apostle of the faith in the essential union of the democratic and philosophical spirit. Since his revolt against German philosophy, he repudiated the separation of the individual and the social, both of which, according to him, are concrete traits and capacities of human beings. He always regarded reason, not as something existing timelessly in the nature of things, but simply as a fortunate and complex development of human behavior. His criticism of the traditional notions of truth is embodied in his theory of *instrumentalism*, which he defines as "an attempt to constitute a precise logical theory of concepts, judgments and inferences in their various forms, by primarily considering how thought functions in the experimental determinations of future consequences." Dewey made inquiry, rather than truth or knowledge, the essence of logic.

He regarded philosophy as the criticism of those socially important beliefs which are part and parcel of the social and cultural life of human communities. This criticism involves an examination of the way in which ideas, taken as solutions of specific problems, function within a wider context. It is in this way that a theory of knowledge—logic, ethics, psychology, aesthetics, and metaphysics becomes necessary and explainable. These are not to be derived from the assumption of an abstract truth, that is, a higher reality or a reality different from that within which we live and act, nor from everlasting values. Dewey objects to transcendental philosophers, because they ignore the kind of empirical situations to which their themes pertain; even the most transcendental philosophers use empirical subject matter, if they philosophize at all. But they become nonempirical because they fail to supply directions for experimentation. The supply of such directions is the core of Dewey's philosophy. His standard of belief and conduct claims to lie within, rather than outside of, a situation of life, that can be shared. Idealists, in contradistinction to Dewey's search for a guide to the beliefs of a shareable situation, deny to common life the faculty of forming its own regulative methods; they claim to have private access to truth. In Dewey's democratic philosophy, common life is the reality of a dignity equivalent to that of nature or the individual.

Dewey devoted his studies not only to the conditions but also to the consequences of knowledge. He never made philosophy subservient to the vested interests of any class or nation; nor was he afraid to hurt any sensibility. He insisted that philosophy, in contrast to all other human activities, must be allowed to remain outside and above the public domain in order to maintain sound relations with these other human activities and to whose progress it must contribute. Dewey was opposed to any isolation of cognitive experience and its subject matter from other modes of experience and their subject matter, because he attempted to integrate spiritual life into the precise framework of natural phenomena, and, for the sake of all-embracing experience, tried to do away with the distinction between the objective and the subjective, and the psychical and the physical. He denied that the characteristic object of knowledge has a privileged position of correspondence with an allegedly ultimate reality; he insisted that action is involved in knowledge and that knowledge is not subordinate to action or practice; that it is in experimental knowing that genuine intellectual integrity is found.

Dewey did not accept any alternative between knowledge or intelligence and action. To him it is "intelligent action" that matters. The failure of human intelligence in social areas has made Dewey strongly emphasize the social aspects of his philosophy. Throughout his long life he tried not only to apply his experimental methods to social philosophy, but he also actively participated in disputes and struggles of political, social, and cultural relevance. Political, social, cultural, and theoretical motives have enhanced Dewey's interest in education. He recognized the important role education plays in the survival of democracy, and the importance of democratic thought and action in the improvement of education. For more than forty years, Dewey maintained a leadership in American education, bringing increased human interest into school life and work, making for the increased encouragement of pupil initiative and responsibility. Dewey's instrumentalism was first expressed in his *Studies in Logical Theory* (1903) where he acknowledged his obligation to William James. His other principal works are: *Democracy and Education* (1916); *Essays in Experimental Logic* (1917); *Reconstruction in Philosophy* (1920); *Human Nature and Conduct* (1922); *The Quest for Certainty* (1929), and *Logic: The Theory of Inquiry* (1938).

ON THE USE OF THE WORD "OBJECT"

It is not a new discovery that the word "object" is highly ambiguous, being used for the sticks and the stones, the cats and the dogs, the chairs and tables of ordinary experiences, for the atoms and electrons of physics, and for any kind of "entity" that has logical subsistence—as in mathematics. In spite of the recognized ambiguity, one whole

330

branch of modern epistemology is derived from the assumption that in the case of at least the first two cases, the word "object" has the same general meaning. For otherwise the subject matter of physics and the things of everyday experience would not have presented themselves as rivals, and philosophy would not have felt an obligation to decide which is "real" and which is "appearance," or at least an obligation to set up a scheme in which they are "reconciled." The place occupied in modern philosophy by the problem of the relation of the so-called, "scientific objects" and "common-sense objects" is proof, in any case, of the dominating presence of a distinction between the "objective" and the "subjective" which was unknown in ancient philosophy. It indicates that at least in the sense of awareness of an ever-present problem, modern philosophy is "objective-subjective," not just subjective. I suggest that if we give up calling the distinctive material of the physical sciences by the name "objects" and employ instead the neutral term "scientific subject matter," the genuine nature of the problem would be greatly clarified. It would not of itself be solved. But at least we should be rid of the implication which now prevents reaching a solution. We should be prepared to consider on its merits the hypothesis here advanced: namely, that scientific subject matter represents the *conditions* for having and not-having things of direct experience.

Genuinely complete empirical philosophy requires that there be a determination *in terms of experience* of the relation that exists between physical subject-matter and the things of direct perception, use, and enjoyment. It would seem clear that historic empiricism, because of its commitment to sensationalism, failed to meet this need. The obvious way of meeting the requirement is through explicit acknowledgement that direct experience contains, as a highly important direct ingredient of itself, a wealth of *possible* objects. There is no inconsistency between the idea of direct experience and the idea of objects of that experience which are as yet unrealized. For these latter objects are directly experienced as

331

possibilities. Every plan, every protection, yes, every forecast and anticipation, is an experience in which some non-directly experienced object is directly experienced *as a possibility*. And, as previously suggested, modern experience is marked by the extent to which directly perceived, enjoyed, and suffered objects are treated as signs, indications, of what has *not* been experienced in and of itself, or/and are treated as means for the realization of these things of possible experience. Because historic empirical philosophy failed to take cognizance of this fact, it was not able to account for one of the most striking features of scientific method and scientific conclusions—preoccupation with generality as such.

For scientific methods and scientific subject matter combine highly abstract or "theoretical" considerations with directly present concrete sensible material, and the generality of conclusions reached is directly dependent upon the presence of the first-named type of considerations. Now in modern philosophy, just as scientific "objects" have been set over against objects in direct experience, thereby occasioning the *ontological* problem of modern philosophy (the problem of where "reality" is to be found) so identification of the experimental with but one of the two factors of the method of knowing has created the *epistemological* problem of modern philosophy; the relation of the "conceptual" and "perceptual"; of sense and understanding. In terms of our hypothesis, the distinction and the connection of the distinguished aspects rests upon the fact that what *is* (has been) experienced is of cognitive importance in connection with what *can* be experienced: that is, as evidence, sign, test, of forecast, anticipation, etc. while, on the other hand, there is no way of valid determination of objects of possible experiences save by employing what *has* been experienced, and hence is sensible. Anticipation, foresight, prediction, depend upon taking what is "given" (what has indubitably been experienced) as ominous, or of prospective reference. This is a speculative operation, a wager about the future. But

332

the wager is subject to certain techniques of control. Although every projection of a possible object of experience goes beyond what has been experienced and is in so far risky, this fact does not signify that every idea or projected possibility has an equal claim. Techniques of observation on one side and of calculation (in its broad sense) on the other side have been developed with a view to effective cooperation. Interactivity *of the two factors* constitutes the method of science. Were it not for the influence of the inertia of habit it would be fairly incredible that empiricists did not long ago perceive that material provided by direct sense perception is limited and remains substantially the same from person to person and from generation to generation. Even when we take into account the additional sense data furnished by artificial instruments, the addition bears no proportionate ratio to the expansion of the subject matter of the sciences that is constantly taking place. Were it not that "rationalist" theories are in no better case with respect to accounting for increase in scientific knowledge (which is its most striking trait in modern times), the marked impotency of sensationalist empiricism would long ago have effected its disappearance.

[108]

DIDEROT, DENIS

DIDEROT, DENIS (1713-1784). As a philosopher, Diderot has often been underestimated. His unique versatility of mind was amazing. The journalistic vein (characteristic of his mentality) enabled him to enlarge, rectify, and communicate his philosophical knowledge and his personal concepts of man, nature, life, and moral and cultural values. His arguments were founded upon those recent scientific discoveries whose philosophical consequences he grasped with extraordinary agility.

Diderot, in addition to being the editor of the most influential and famous encyclopedia, was himself a living encyclopedia; well versed in the natural and social sciences, in the history of literature and the arts; in philosophy and religion. He never confined his achievements to the mere summarization of the knowledge of his

333

time; he was an innovator in many fields. He was the first modern art critic. He rebelled against the authority of classicism in the literary and artistic life of continental Europe. He criticised the civil and religious institutions of his time and demonstrated the necessity for change. As a dramatist, he pioneered in dealing with social problems and in representing modern middle-class life on the stage.

All of these activities were compatible with his philosophical outlook which conceived of life and spirit as eternal and eternally changing. He stated that the formation of moral values could be traced back to the experiences of early childhood of both the individual and mankind. He made many studies of the blind, mute, and deaf, and proceeded to epistemological, psychological, aesthetic, and sociological points of view that have since had great consequence. His daring spirit caused Diderot to incur royal and papal interdictions and imprisonment.

ON REASON

DOUBTS in religious matters, far from being blamable—far from being acts of impiety, ought to be regarded as praiseworthy, when they proceed from a man who humbly acknowledges his ignorance, and arise from the fear of offending God by the abuse of reason.

To admit any conformity between the reason of man, and the eternal reason of God, and to pretend that God demands the sacrifice of human reason, is to maintain that God wills one thing, and intends another thing at the same time.

When God, of whom I hold my reason, demands of me to sacrifice it, he becomes a mere juggler that snatches from me what he pretended to give.

If I renounce my reason, I have no longer a guide—I must then blindly adopt a *secondary principle*, and the matter in question becomes a supposition.

If *reason* be a gift of Heaven, and we can say as much of *faith*, Heaven has certainly made us two presents not only incompatible, but in direct contradiction to each other. In order to solve the difficulty, we are compelled to say either that *faith* is a chimera, or that reason is useless.

334

Pascal, Nicole and others have said, that God will punish
with eternal torments the faults of a guilty father upon all
his innocent offspring; and that this is a proposition *superior*
to reason, and not in *contradiction* to it; but what shall we
propose as being contradictory to reason if such blasphemy
as this is not so?

Bewildered in an immense forest during the night, and
having only one small torch for my guide, a stranger approaches and thus addresses me:—*"Friend, blow out thy
light if thou wouldst make sure of the right path."* This
stranger was a priest.

If my reason be the gift of Heaven, it is the voice of
Heaven that speaks; shall I hearken to it?

Neither merit nor demerit is applicable to the judgment
of our rational faculties, for all the submission and good
will imaginable could not assist the blind man in the perception of colors.

I am compelled to perceive evidence where it is, or the
want of evidence where it is not, so long as I retain my
senses; and if my judgment fail me, it becomes a *misfortune,* not a *sin.*

The Author of Nature would not reward me for having
been a *wit,* surely, then, he will not *damn* me for having been
a *fool.* Nay, more; he will not *damn* me even for being
wicked. Is not my own conscience a sufficient punishment for
me?

[109]

DILTHEY, WILHELM

DILTHEY, WILHELM (1833-1911). Wilhelm Dilthey was born
two years after Hegel's death. He devoted much of his energy to
the task of investigating the structure of the human mind and in
writing its history. This had been Hegel's purpose, but Dilthey
was strongly opposed to the Hegelian system, as well as to any
metaphysical inquiry into the realm of the supernatural.

Hegel regarded the human mind as one of the manifestations
of the cosmic spirit, and when he wrote the history of the human

335

mind, he believed that he had recognized and defined the essence of mind. Dilthey, on the other hand, relied upon empiricism: historical facts, biographies, the extant works of great personalities, documents on the currents of cultural life, religious traditions, and social institutions supplied the answer to the question of what man really is. Dilthey, the historian of the human mind, stated that philosophical definitions were the historical documents which informed him about the mental situation of an epoch; poems, laws, and customs of that epoch did the same.

He saw history as a means of comprehending man as a thinking, feeling, willing, creating being who lived in the historical stream of life. His total activities were designed to elaborate "a critique of historical reason," as necessary for the completion of Kant's three critiques. It was to be founded upon an "understanding and analyzing psychology" whose starting point was the analysis of consciousness, and whose development was necessary for understanding the way of civilization and its functional relation to the totality of spontaneous impulses, which he considered to be the stream of life.

Dilthey left great and important fragments of his projected work. His academic career was extremely brilliant, but his real influence was felt only after he died.

STRUCTURAL COHERENCE OF THE PSYCHE

THE psychical sciences form a cognitive whole which strives to achieve a factual and objective knowledge of the chain of human experiences in the human-historical-social world. The history of the sciences of the mind reveals a constant struggle with the difficulties which confront us here. These are gradually overcome to a certain degree, and the inquiry approaches, though remotely, this goal which hovers incessantly before each and every true scholar. The inquiry into the possibility of factual and objective knowledge forms the foundation of the mental sciences. I submit the following contributions toward this end.

The mental sciences are confronted by the human-historical world; this world is often an inexact picture of the reality that exists outside these sciences. Such a thing cannot produce knowledge. It is and remains bound up with the means of intuition, understanding, and conceptual think-

336

ing. The mental sciences do not desire to produce the exact picture; rather they refer to that which has occurred and occurs: this unique, accidental, and momentary happening back to a sensible and value-giving coherence. Progressive cognition seeks to penetrate ever deeper into this. It becomes ever more objective in its understanding of it, without ever being able to reveal its fundamental nature; so that, in fact, it discovers that which is always a mere after-feeling, constructing, uniting, and separating in abstract connections of a conceptual nexus. Thus the historical description of what has once happened can approximate these events only upon the foundations of the analytic sciences whose only common purpose is to attain an objective grasp of their object within the bounds of the medium of understanding and conceptual comprehension.

A knowledge of those events in which the mental sciences specialize is a condition for an understanding of their history. It clarifies the relationship of the individual mental sciences to the coexistence and succession of experience on which they are based.

PLAN FOR A CRITIQUE OF HISTORICAL REASON

THE current of life is composed of parts and experiences which bear an inner relation to each other. Each single experience refers to a self, of which it is a part; it is united structurally with other parts in a coherence. Coherence is found in all mind, so that coherence is a category which springs from life. We comprehend coherence by virtue of the unity of consciousness. This is the condition under which all comprehension stands; but it is clear that the appearance of cohesion will not follow from this mere fact, or that a manifoldness of experiences is granted to the unity of consciousness. Only because life itself is a structural coherence to which experiences (i.e. relations of experience) inhere, is it possible for us to have a coherence of life. This coherence is included in a more comprehensive category which is a mode of predication regarding all reality; the relation of the whole to the parts.

[110]

DRIESCH, HANS

DRIESCH, HANS (1867-1941). A discovery made in 1895 by Hans Driesch attracted international attention and firmly placed him among the important figures in the history of biology. Driesch, by experiment, demonstrated that it was possible to remove large pieces from eggs; shuffle the blastomeres at will; take several blastomeres away; interfere in many ways, and yet not affect the resulting embryo. The fact that despite such operations, a normal, though small-sized embryo emerged was taken as proof that any single monad in the original egg cell was capable of forming any part of the completed embryo. This discovery made Driesch internationally famous as a zoologist. Until then he had been a disciple and adherent of Ernest Haeckel, but the success of the experiments led him to abandon the mechanistic point of view and to profess a renovated vitalism. At this time, he turned from biology to philosophy.

His system was comprised of three parts: the first dealt with causality and consciousness; the second with logic, which he called "a doctrine of order"; the third was a doctrine of reality. Driesch was converted to vitalism because he believed that physical laws were insufficient to explain his discovery, which he declared to be beyond the powers of any machine ever constructed by man. Thus far, he encountered no objections. When he tried to prove the autonomy of life by introducing a nonphysical cause: entelechy (using Aristotle), he met with violent opposition. This opposition held for all other arguments that he advanced. Until his death, Driesch energetically continued to defend his views. Though he was an unscholarly thinker, his style was animated and colorful.

CAUSALITY

CAUSALITY, in the proper sense of the word, is the determination of events within the natural stream of things expressly so that the effects of events are determined by earlier causes. Here we deal with fairly new matter as compared with mere functionality, namely the concept of "temporal," expressed by such words as "cause" and "effect" and concatenated with the meaning of "because." The effects of events do not only follow the cause, but it is because of the cause that the events have occurred.

Just as substance is the objectivated concept of identity, that is to say a concept "thrown out" into nature, so causality is consequence "thrown out." A judgment is valid *because* one or more judgments are valid. A concept subsists *because* it is a component of earlier concepts; its attributes make it a partial totality of other concepts. Thus in the pure sense of words, meanings deal with proper consequences; that is, they are "posited together." Events happen *because* under certain constant "conditions" the causes of the event happened. Thus we say: this is causality.

Events have a sequential relationship to time. The aspect of consequence is that means of partial identity which makes for a "positing together." This makes for the transmission of events.

Mathematical physics is essentially incapable of coming close to causality. It cannot even approach such temporal sequence as *post hoc*, let alone the *propter* in *post*.

Those who question the aforementioned statement should consider the well-known fact that mathematical physics uses equations. Equations can be read from left to right *and* from right to left. They are indifferent to direction. But causality, even temporal sequence is *not* indifferent to direction. If a cigar is thrown into a powder keg it causes an explosion; the explosion is not the cause of the throwing.

Mathematical physics can only extract from the totality a part of the true cause, the quantitative equivalences, or more precisely those *coupled* quantities which are expressed by the equal sign. It takes out something that accompanies causality or is in it. It never meets causality itself. This is typically illustrated by the principle of the conservation of energy: a given amount lost in one area is gained in another. The two areas may be infinitely close together; however, one can never state that the cause of the loss makes for the effect of the gain; or that gain takes place *because*, in the course of time, there is loss.

Although mathematical physics cannot come close to causality, the concept of causality is quite indispensable to the true science of nature. In fact that "I can push" might psychologically evoke the concept of causality in an individual; its proper basis is logical, the application of the meaning of *because* to temporal succession.

Suffice it to say, that I do not consider "causality" a true category which can be analyzed, a "pure principle of understanding," as Kant did. Rather, it is a concept composed of true original meanings. The meanings of "because" and "events" are here joined.

It goes without saying that causality is only a postulate; a logical desire. It is one that up to now has always been demonstrated empirically. Up to now, we have always found or invented successful causes when or where changes, referred to as effects, have taken place.

[111]

DÜHRING, EUGEN

DÜHRING, EUGEN (1833-1921). "Heroic materialism" characterized Dühring's philosophy. The only reality he acknowledged was the world of the natural sciences. He regarded thinking and feeling as "states of irritation of matter." He substituted ethical education for religion in the "direction of the mind." He asserted that the universe was spatially finite, and that the beginning of the formation of the world was fixable in time. He attacked capitalism, Marxism, organized Christianity and Judaism, and the faculties of the German universities. Had it not been for his blindness, he probably would have played a much more important role in German political life.

PESSIMISM

PESSIMISM is itself the peak of moral evil, in the sense that it adores nothing and condemns nature. Scepticism tries to do that with regard to reason. It is the theoretical supplement to practical corruption. It is incompatible with the trust of

340

healthy knowledge, and is opposed to real logical knowledge as a final possibility. When it remains faithful to its essence (or rather its nuisance), it implies that there can be deviation for personal contingencies; therefore it assists wickedness.

Since everything is basically bad, people consider it only right for them not to consider some of their own base acts. If they resign themselves to demoralization and thereby adjust themselves to the character of the world, they're merely following the pattern of all things. If they commit an evil act and extend it further; or even approve of it (in a particular case), they contribute their share to the moral evil. They try to protect themselves with the hypocritical excuse that they are redeeming the world with their demoralized behavior; that they help make for that saintly order which tends toward the adoration of *nil*.

Even with better people, there is some demoralization too; it takes the form of discouragement, or the reduction of confidence in the state of things, and makes for a sapping of strength. That kind of demoralization parallels the circumstances involved in the demoralization of troops. In the struggle for existence, the opinion that the good have no chance in the sphere of the knowledge of things, or the possibility of doing good, must certainly produce a demoralizing effect. A philosophy hostile to life, which professes the total evilness of nature and explains the world as a single and great evil is in itself the greatest thing that makes for demoralization, because of necessity it eradicates the courage for life and good will.

[112]

DUNS SCOTUS, JOHN

DUNS SCOTUS, JOHN (1270-1308). The popular identification of the words "dunce" and "blockhead," which were sanctioned by Alexander Pope's satiric poem, signifies the age-old contempt in which posterity has held the man who probably was born in the

341

Scottish village of Duns. Although he was so famous and successful as a professor at Oxford that the numerous foreign students
could not be accommodated in the town, and although he taught
at Paris with even greater success, his name was disparaged by his
opponents who, after his premature death, publicly burned his
books and distorted the meaning of his doctrine. For Duns Scotus
had dared to criticize Augustine and Aquinas, and had attempted
to destroy their notions of matter, form and potency, the indispensable resources of Peripatetic philosophers. Victorious Thomism
did not pardon this challenge, and imposed its prejudice against
Duns Scotus on its opponents, namely, enlightenment.

But, since Charles S. Peirce adopted Duns Scotus' realism, more
and more historians have become convinced that Duns Scotus is to
be ranked among the great constructive thinkers. In the Middle
Ages, Duns Scotus, the inveterate antagonist of Aquinas was called
"Doctor Subtilis." Now he is acknowledged to be not only subtle but
vigorous. His insistence on demonstrative proof led him to a demarcation between rationalism and empiricism that has followers
among recent philosophers. Instead of matter and form, he established the extremely modern concept of "haecceity," or principle
of individuation, which is explained as ontological independence,
singularity, or the undefinable quality of ultimate reality, anticipating ways of *Gestalt psychology, Gegenstands theory* and existentialism. Duns Scotus admitted that there is no science of the singular,
but he maintained that this indicates only a limit of the human
intellect, not of reality. His psychology is essentially voluntaristic.
In several of his views, Duns Scotus was inspired by Solomon ibn
Gabirol's *Fons Vitae* (Source of Life) which influenced many Franciscans, to whose order Duns Scotus belonged; however he shows
strong originality in their elaboration.

UNDERSTANDING AND EXPERIENCE

WHEN the evidence or the certitude of first principles has
been had, it is evident how certitude may be had of conclusions inferred from them, because of the evidence of the
perfect forms of the syllogism, since the certitude of the
conclusions depends only on the certitude of the principles
and inference.

But will not the understanding err in this knowledge of
principles and conclusions, if the senses are deceived concerning all the terms? I reply that, with respect to the
knowledge, the understanding does not have the senses for

cause, but only for occasion, for the understanding cannot have knowledge of simples unless it has received that knowledge from the senses: still, having received it, it can compound simples with each other by its own power; and if, from the relation of such simples, there is a combination which is evidently true, the understanding will assent to that combination by its own power and by the power of the terms, not by the power of the senses by which it receives the terms from without. . . .

Concerning things known by experience, I say that although experience is not had of all singulars, but of a large number, and that although it is not always had but in a great many cases, still one who knows by experience knows infallibly that it is thus, and that it is always thus, and that it is thus in all, and he knows that by the following proposition reposing in the soul: whatever occurs as in a great many things from some cause which is not free, is the natural effect of that cause, which proposition is known to the understanding, even though it has accepted the terms of it from erring senses; for a cause which is not free cannot produce as in a great many things an effect to the opposite of which it is ordered, or to which it is not ordered by its form; but a casual cause is ordered to the producing of the opposite of the casual effect or to not producing it: therefore nothing is the casual cause in respect to an effect produced frequently by it, and if it is not free, it is a natural cause.

That, however, this effect occurs by such a cause producing as in a great many cases, this must be learned by experience.

[113]

DURKHEIM, DAVID EMILE

DURKHEIM, DAVID EMILE (1858-1917). A founder of the science of sociology, Durkheim regarded sociology neither as a branch of philosophy, psychology, nor biology, though he always stressed the importance of psychological and biological knowledge. Similarly, he was well versed in ethnology and utilized many of its results; but he carefully defined the method and object of sociology as distinct from the former.

Even as a sociologist, Durkheim retained his belief in moral values. He stated that these could not be explained without taking into account the existence of society; that society formed and enlightened the individual; that it was impossible to separate the individual from society, or to regard society as the mere totality of individuals. He conceived of the group mind as a reality distinct from the minds of the individuals who comprised the group.

Durkheim's real starting point was his study of the division of labor. He regarded the division of labor not only as an important social and economic phenomenon but as a proof that the individual was incapable of controlling his life. From this he proceeded to demonstrate that the concepts of causality, space, and time had to be derived from collective sources. He was a man of wide perspectives. His inquiries embraced religion (particularly its elementary forms), law, criminology, ethics, moral data, economics, aesthetics, and the histories of language and the arts. He was particularly interested in education which he viewed as the birth of social man from the embryo of the individual.

All who met Durkheim were deeply impressed by his ascetic appearance. He seemed to be the embodiment of the scientific spirit. His disciples, among whom Lucien Lévy-Bruhl was the outstanding, never forgot the inspiration engendered by Durkheim for methodical investigation. Even his opponents respected the austerity of his devotion to the cause of truth.

THE HEALTHY AND MORBID

PAIN is commonly regarded by the layman as the index of morbidity; and in general it is true that there is a relation between these two conditions, but a relation which lacks uniformity and precision. There are serious but painless maladies; while less serious afflictions, such as those resulting from a speck of coal dust in the eye, may cause real torture. In certain cases the very absence of pain, or even actual pleasure, are symptoms of morbidity. There is an insensibility to pain which is pathological. Circumstances causing suffering to a healthy man may give to a neurasthenic a sensation of enjoyment of an incontestably morbid nature. Conversely, pain accompanies many states belonging to normal physiology, such as hunger, fatigue, and parturition.

Shall we say that health, consisting in successful development of the vital forces, is recognizable by the perfect adaptation of the organism to its environment; and shall we, on the contrary, term "morbidity" whatever disturbs this adaptation? But first . . . it has by no means been proved that every state of the organism corresponds to some external state of the environment. And, further, even if this criterion of adaptation were truly distinctive of the state of health, another criterion would be needed in order to recognize it. We must be able to distinguish varying degrees of completeness of adaptation.

Or shall we take as this criterion the effect health and morbidity may have on our probabilities of survival? Health would then be the state of an organism in which these probabilities are at a maximum; and morbidity, on the contrary, would include everything which reduces them. Unquestionably, morbidity weakens the organism. But it is not alone in producing this result. The functions of reproduction inevitably cause death in certain lower species, and they are accompanied by risks even in the higher orders. They are, however, normal. Senility and infancy have the same effects, for both the old and the very young are peculiarly susceptible to the causes of destruction. Are infancy and old age morbid types then? And can only the adult be healthy? How strangely would the domain of health and physiology then be restricted!

If, moreover, old age is already synonymous with morbidity, how distinguish the healthy from the diseased old person? From the same point of view, one is obliged to place menstruation among the morbid phenomena, for the disturbances it causes increase female susceptibility to disease. But would we then be justified in designating as "morbid" a state whose absence or premature disappearance constitutes an incontestably pathological phenomenon? People argue about this question as if, in a healthy organism, each element played a useful role, as if each internal state corresponded exactly to some external condition and, consequently, helped to maintain vital equilibrium and to diminish the chance of death. But it is, on the contrary, legitimate to suppose that some anatomical or functional arrangements are of no direct use, but are merely the products of the general conditions of life. We cannot, however, call them morbid, for morbidity is, above all, something escapable, something not essential to the constitution of the organism. It may even be true that, instead of strengthening the organism, these anatomical and functional arrangements diminish its resistance and, consequently, increase the risks of death.

[114]

E

ECKHART, JOHANNES

ECKHART, JOHANNES (c. 1260-1327). "Wouldst thou be perfect, do not yelp about God." This sentence, uttered by Johannes Eckhart, characterized him as a man of deepest spirituality whose sermons utilized the Bible as an opportunity to lead his listeners to the oneness of God, to make them realize that the approach to God was through the self and silence. A Dominican monk, he rose to high office in the service of the Church. He was prior at Erfurt; vicar-provincial of Thuringia; provincial of Saxony; and vicar-general of Bohemia. A Master of Sacred Theology and Doctor of Divinity, he preached his "sweet doctrine" at the College of St. James, Paris, and in the nunneries of Strassburg and Cologne. Always welcome, he was reverently referred to as the "Holy Master Eckhart."

A "Brother of the Free Spirit," he differed markedly from the schoolmen and their arid teachings. His message paralleled the best of Hindu teachings in *Sankara Acharya*: that God is in every human being; nothing is apart from God, and the complete dissolution of all opposites and self-abandonment to Him constitutes salvation. In the early stages of the Inquisition his mystic teachings and symbolic interpretations were not opposed, but charges were preferred against him in 1327. He was unwilling to recant all his teachings and appealed to Rome. Pope John XXII issued a bull condemning the majority of his propositions as heretical and the rest as "ill-sounding, rash, and probably heretic." It was during that year that Eckhart died; however, official condemnation did not prevent his followers from clinging to his teachings.

SECLUSION

I HAVE read many writings of both Pagan masters and the Prophets of the old and new Covenant, and have investigated seriously and with great zeal which would be the best and highest virtue by which Man could best become similar to God, and how he could resemble again the archetype such as he was in God when there was no difference between him and God until God made the creatures. If I go down to the bottom of all that is written as far as my reason with its testimony and its judgment can reach, I find nothing but mere seclusion of all that is created. In this sense our Lord says to Martha: "One thing is needed," this means: He who wants to be pure and untroubled has to have one thing, Seclusion.

Many teachers praise Love as the highest virtue, like Saint Paul when he says: "Whatever exercises I undergo, if I have no Love I have nothing." I however place seclusion higher than love. First: The best about love is that it forces me to love God. But it is much more important that I force God down to me than that I force myself up to God. For my eternal bliss rests upon my being united with God. For God is more able to penetrate into me and to become united with me, than I with Him. That seclusion forces God down to me, I can prove in the following way: Every creature likes to be in its natural abode, the abode that is appropriate for it is the most natural, the most appropriate abode of God, unity and purity. Both rest upon seclusion. That is why God cannot help abandoning himself to a secluded heart.

The second reason why I place seclusion above love is: If love induces me to suffer anything for God, seclusion induces me to be receptive only to God. This however is superior. For while suffering, Man is still aiming at the creature through which he is suffering, though seclusion is free from all other creatures so that seclusion is receptive only for God I can prove by the following: What shall be received has to be received somewhere. Seclusion is so near to sheer nothing that there is nothing that would be fine enough that it could find space in it, but God. He is so simple and so fine that he finds room in the secluded heart.

[115]

348

EDWARDS, JONATHAN

EDWARDS, JONATHAN (1703-1758). Until the very end of the nineteenth century, Jonathan Edwards was considered America's greatest philosopher. Only in later manuals of philosophy published in the United States were men like Charles Peirce and William James hesitantly acknowledged as his equals. Outside of the United States Edwards' philosophy remains virtually unknown; his name is mentioned only in the histories of American religious life.

Edwards, who, in his early years, admired Locke and adopted the ideas of Cudworth and other Cambridge Platonists, lost interest in theoretical philosophy after he was ordained minister (1726) in the church of Northampton. A persuasive preacher and devoted spiritual leader of his congregation, he was also very influential as the author of religious and theological treatises. His sermon *Justification by Faith* (1734) marked the beginning of "New England Theology" which dominated the congregationalism of New England until 1880. Edwards had revolted against Calvinism in his youth and initiated what has been called "Consistent Calvinism," "Strict Calvinism," or the "New Divinity." He defended its fundamental doctrines against Arminians and deists, and preached the doctrine of divine immanence and divine initiative. He denied the freedom of human will and affirmed election by predestination. His congregation was the starting point of the "Great Awakening" of New England. Edwards was not only the theologian of this movement, but also its historian and psychologist. His *Treatise Concerning Religious Affections* (1746) tried to distinguish between sincere religious emotion, genuine conversion, hysteria, false sentimentality, and enthusiastic exaggeration. William James praised Edwards' descriptions as "admirably rich and delicate."

Unfortunately, the life of piety and purity to which Edwards tried to convert his people was beyond their comprehension. He was dismissed in 1750 by his parishioners when he excluded from full communion those members of the congregation who did not correspond to his ideal. He turned to missionary work among the Indians and wrote voluminous works on topics he had previously dealt with in shorter form. In 1757 he was elected president of the College of New Jersey, later to become Princeton University.

GOD AND THE EVIL IN THE WORLD

THAT there is a great difference between God's being concerned thus, by his *permission,* in an event and act, which,

349

in the inherent subject and agent of it, is sin, (though the event will certainly follow on his permission) and his being concerned in it by *producing* it and exerting the act of sin; or between his being the *orderer* of its certain existence, by *not hindering* it, under certain circumstances, and his being the proper *actor* or *author* of it, by a *positive agency* or *efficiency*. And this, notwithstanding what Dr. Whitby offers about a saying of philosophers, that *causa deficiens, in rebus necessariis, ad causam per se efficientem reducenda est.* As there is a vast difference between the sun's being the cause of the lightsomeness and warmth of the atmosphere, and brightness of gold and diamonds, by its presence and positive influence; and its being the occasion of darkness and frost in the night, by its motion, whereby it descends below the horizon. The motion of the sun is the occasion of the latter kind of events; but it is not the proper cause, efficient, or producer of them; though they are necessarily consequent on that motion under such circumstances: no more is any action of the Divine Being the cause of the evil of men's wills. If the sun were the proper *cause* of cold and darkness, it would be the *fountain* of these things, as it is the fountain of light and heat; and then something might be argued from the nature of cold and darkness, to a likeness of nature in the sun; and it might be justly inferred, that the sun itself is dark and cold, and that his beams are black and frosty. But from its being the cause no otherwise than by its departure, no such thing can be inferred, but the contrary: it may justly be argued, that the sun is a bright and hot body, if cold and darkness are found to be the consequence of its withdrawment; and the more constantly and necessarily these effects are connected with and confined to its absence, the more strongly does it argue the sun to be the fountain of light and heat. So, inasmuch as sin is not the fruit of any positive agency or influence of the Most High, but, on the contrary, arises from the withholding of his action and energy, and, under certain circumstances, necessarily follows on the want of his influence; this is no argument that he is sinful, or his operation evil, or has anything of the nature of evil; but on the contrary, that he, and his agency, are altogether good and holy, and that he is the fountain of all holiness. It would be strange arguing, indeed, because men never commit sin, but only when God leaves them *to themselves,* and necessarily sin when he does so, that therefore their sin is not *from themselves,* but from God; and so that God must be a sinful being: as strange as it would be to argue, because it is always dark when the sun is gone, and never dark when the sun is present, that therefore all darkness is from the sun, and that his disc and beams must needs be black.

It properly belongs to the supreme and absolute Governor of the universe to order all important events within his dominion by his wisdom: but the events in the moral world are of the most important kind; such as the moral actions of intelligent creatures, and their consequences.

These events will be ordered by something. They will either be disposed by wisdom, or they will be disposed by chance; that is, they will be disposed by blind and undesigning causes, if that were possible, and could be called a disposal. Is it not better that the good and evil which happen in God's world, should be ordered, regulated, bounded, and determined, by the good pleasure of an infinitely wise Being, —who perfectly comprehends within his understanding and constant view the universality of things, in all their extent and duration, and sees all the influence of every event, with respect to every individual thing and circumstance throughout the grand system, and the whole of the eternal series of consequences,—than to leave these things to fall out by chance, and to be determined by those causes which have no understanding or aim? Doubtless, in these important events there is a better and a worse, as to the time, subject, place, manner, and circumstances of their coming to pass, with regard to their influence on the state and course of things.

And if there be, it is certainly best that they should be determined to that time, place, etc. which is best. And therefore it is in its own nature fit, that wisdom, and not chance, should order these things. So that it belongs to the Being who is the Possessor of infinite wisdom, and is the Creator and Owner of the whole system of created existences, and has the care of all; I say it belongs to him to take care of this matter; and he would not do what is proper for him if he should neglect it. And it is so far from being unholy in him to undertake this affair, that it would rather have been unholy to neglect it; as it would have been a neglecting what fitly appertains to him; and so it would have been a very unfit and unsuitable neglect.

Therefore the sovereignty of God doubtless extends to this matter; especially considering, that if it should be supposed to be otherwise, and God should leave men's volitions, and all moral events, to the determination and disposition of blind unmeaning causes, or they should be left to happen perfectly without a cause; this would be no more consistent with liberty, in any notion of it, and particularly not in the Arminian notion of it, than if these events were subject to the disposal of Divine Providence, and the will of man were disposed by Divine wisdom, as appears by what has been already observed. But it is evident, that such a providential disposing and determining men's moral actions, though it infers a moral necessity of those actions, yet it does not in the least infringe the real liberty of mankind; the only liberty that common sense teaches to be necessary to moral agency, which, as has been demonstrated, is not inconsistent with such necessity.

On the whole it is manifest, that God may be, in the manner which has been described, the orderer and disposer of that event, which, in the inherent subject and agent is moral evil; and yet his so doing may be no moral evil. He may will the disposal of such an event, and its coming to pass, for good ends, and his will not be an immoral or sinful will, but a perfectly holy will. And he may actually, in his providence, so dispose and permit things, that the event may be certainly and infallibly connected with such disposal and permission, and his act therein not be an immoral or unholy, ut a perfectly holy act. Sin may be an evil thing; and yet that there should be such a disposal and permission as that it should come to pass, may be a good thing. This is no contradiction or inconsistence. Joseph's brethren selling him into Egypt, consider it only as it was acted by them, and with respect to their views and aims, which were evil, was a very bad thing; but it was a good thing, as it was an event of God's ordering, and considered with respect to his views and aims, which were good. Gen. 1.20. "As for you, ye thought evil against me; but God meant it unto good." So the crucifixion of Christ, if we consider only those things which belong to the event as it proceeded from his murderers, and are comprehended within the compass of the affair considered as their act, their principles, dispositions, views, and aims; so it was one of the most heinous things that ever was done, in many respects the most horrid of all acts: but consider it as it was willed and ordered of God, in the extent of his designs and views, it was the most admirable and glorious of all events; and God's willing the event was the most holy volition of God that ever was made known to men; and God's act in ordering it was a divine act, which, above all others, manifests the moral excellency of the Divine Being.

*   *   *

There is no inconsistency in supposing, that God may hate a thing as it is in itself, and considered simply as evil, and yet that it may be his will it should come to pass, considering all consequences. I believe there is no person of good understanding, who will venture to say, he is certain that it is impossible it should be best, taking in the whole compass and extent of existence, and all consequences in the endless series of events, that there should be such a thing as moral evil in the world. And if so, it will certainly follow, that an infinitely wise Being who always chooses what is best, must choose that there should be such a thing. And if so, then such a choice is not an evil, but a wise and holy choice. And if so, then that providence which is agreeable to such a choice,

353

is a wise and holy providence. Men do *will* sin as sin, and so are the authors and actors of it: they love it as sin, and for evil ends and purposes. God does not will sin as sin, or for the sake of anything evil; though it be his pleasure so to order things, that, he permitting, sin will come to pass; for the sake of the great good that by his disposal shall be the consequence. His willing to order things so that evil should come to pass, for the sake of the contrary good, is no argument that he does not hate evil as evil: and if so, then it is no reason why he may not reasonably forbid evil as evil and punish it as such.

[116

EINSTEIN, ALBERT

EINSTEIN, ALBERT (1879-). The overwhelming majority of scientists continually testify that Einstein has accomplished "one of the greatest generalizations of all time" and "has revolutionized our nineteenth century concepts not only of astronomy, but also of the nature of time, space, and of the fundamental ideas of science." Modern humanity reveres Einstein as one of its profoundest thinkers, as well as a man of the highest intellectual integrity, free of personal ambition, an intrepid fighter for human rights, social justice, and social responsibility. In the few decades that have passed between the time that Einstein made his theory of relativity known to the public and his seventieth birthday, more than five thousand books and pamphlets in every language have been published about him and his work. Although Einstein himself did nothing to popularize his ideas, his fame spread internationally after he predicted that the deflection of light in a gravitational field would occur in 1916 and 1919. He had and still has opponents some of whom are prejudiced against him because he remains conscious of his Jewish origin. But humble people throughout the world are comforted by the knowledge that Einstein, whose thoughts pervade the universe, feels with all who suffer from oppression and persecution. Seldom has it happened that any man has become so popular, even though his theory is largely beyond popular imagination and common-sense thought. While the achievements of Copernicus, Galileo, Newton, and Darwin have been, at least in broad outline, explicable to the public, it has been impossible up to the present time to translate Einstein's theory of relativity adequately into the non-technical language of popular literature.

The most important consequence of Einstein's special theory of relativity for scientific and philosophical thought has been the change in the concepts of time and space. Einstein destroyed the assumption that there is a single all-embracing time in which all events in the universe have their place. He has shown that "it is impossible to determine absolute motion by any experiment whatever." As long as time and space are measured separately, there always remains a kind of subjectivity which affects not only human observers but all other things. Time and space, which for classical physics are absolute constituents of the world, are conceived by Einsteinian physics as dependent upon each other, forming a relationship which can be analyzed in many different ways into what is referred to as spatial distance or lapse of time. Time which previously had been regarded as a cosmic measure is presented by Einstein as "local time" connected with the motion of the earth. He conceives of time as so completely analogous to the three dimensions of space that physics can be transformed into a kind of four-dimensional geometry. On the other hand, the special theory of relativity confers an absolute meaning on a magnitude, namely the velocity of light, which had only a relative significance in classical physics.

After this special theory, Einstein formulated his general theory of relativity which offers new explanations of the size of the universe, of gravitation and inertia. Einstein's achievements are by no means limited to the special and general theories of relativity. He was awarded the Nobel Prize in 1922 for his studies in photochemical equivalents. Later, he took a leading part in the investigation of atomic energy. On many occasions, he has expressed his personal views on problems of daily life, contemporary history, war, peace, education, religion, science and the fate of the Jews.

RELIGION AND SCIENCE

EVERYTHING that the human race has done and thought is concerned with the satisfaction of felt needs and the assuagement of pain. One has to keep this constantly in mind if one wishes to understand spiritual movements and their development. Feeling and desire are the motive forces behind all human endeavor and human creation, in however exalted a guise the latter may present itself to us. Now what are the feelings and needs that have led men to religious thought and belief in the widest sense of the words? A little consideration will suffice to show us that the most varying emotion preside over the birth of religious thought and experienc With primitive man it is above all fear that evokes religiou notions—fear of hunger, wild beasts, sickness, death. Since this stage of existence understanding of causal connection is usually poorly developed, the human mind creates fo itself more or less analogous beings on whose wills and ac tions these fearful happenings depend. One's object now to secure the favor of these beings by carrying out action and offering sacrifices which, according to the traditio handed down from generation to generation, propitiate the or make them well disposed towards a mortal. I am speak ing now of the religion of fear. This, though not created, is i an important degree stabilized by the formation of a specia priestly caste which sets up as a mediator between the peopl and the beings they fear, and erects a hegemony on thi basis. In many cases the leader or ruler whose position de pends on other factors, or a privileged class, combine priestly functions with its secular authority in order to mak the latter more secure; or the political rulers and the priestl caste make common cause in their own interests.

The social feelings are another source of the crystall ization of religion. Fathers and mothers and the leaders o larger human communities are mortal and fallible. The de sire for guidance, love, and support prompts men to forn the social or moral conception of God. This is the God o Providence who protects, disposes, rewards, and punishes, th God who, according to the width of the believer's outlook loves and cherishes the life of the tribe or of the human race or even life as such, the comforter in sorrow and unsatisfie longing, who preserves the souls of the dead. This is the so cial or moral conception of God.

The Jewish scriptures admirably illustrate the develop ment from the religion of fear to moral religion, which continued in the New Testament. The religions of all civilize peoples, especially the peoples of the Orient, are primaril moral religions. The development from a religion of fea

356

to moral religion is a great step in a nation's life. That primitive religions are based entirely on fear and the religions of civilized peoples purely on morality is a prejudice against which we must be on our guard. The truth is that they are all intermediate types, with this reservation, that on the higher levels of social life the religion of morality predominates.

Common to all these types is the anthropomorphic character of their conception of God. Only individuals of exceptional endowments and exceptionally high-minded communities, as a general rule, get in any real sense beyond this level. But there is a third state of religious experience which belongs to all of them, even though it is rarely found in a pure form and which I will call cosmic religious feeling. It is very difficult to explain this religious feeling to anyone who is entirely without it, especially as there is no anthropomorphic conception of God corresponding to it.

The individual feels the nothingness of human desires and aims, and the sublimity and marvellous order which reveal themselves both in nature and in the world of thought. He looks upon individual existence as a prison of the spirit and wants to experience the universe as a single significant whole. The beginnings of cosmic religious feeling already appear in earlier stages of development—e.g., in many of the Psalms of David and in some of the Prophets. Buddhism, as we have learnt from the wonderful writings of Schopenhauer especially, contains a much stronger element of it.

The religious geniuses of all ages have been distinguished by this kind of religious feeling, which knows no dogma and no God conceived in man's image; so that there can be no Church whose central teachings are based on it. Hence, it is precisely among the heretics of every age that we find men who are filled with the highest kind of religious feeling and were in many cases regarded by their contemporaries as Atheists, sometimes also as saints. Looked at in this light, men like Democritus, Francis of Assisi, and Spinoza are closely akin to one another.

How can cosmic religious feeling be communicated

from one person to another, if it can give rise to no definite notion of a God and no theology? In my view, it is the most important function of art and science to awaken this feeling and keep it alive in those who are capable of it.

We thus arrive at a conception of the relation of science to religion very different from the usual one. When one views the matter historically one is inclined to look upon science and religion as irreconcilable antagonists, and for a very obvious reason. The man who is thoroughly convinced of the universal operation of the law of causation cannot for a moment entertain the idea of a being who interferes in the course of events—that is, if he takes the hypothesis of causality really seriously. He has not use for the religion of fear and equally little for social or moral religion. A God who rewards and punishes is inconceivable to him for the simple reason that a man's actions are determined by necessity, external and internal, so that in God's eyes he cannot be responsible, any more than an inanimate object is responsible for the motions it goes through. Hence science has been charged with undermining morality, but the charge is unjust. A man's ethical behavior should be based effectually on sympathy, education, and social ties; no religious basis is necessary. Man would indeed be in a poor way if he had to be restrained by fear and punishment and hope of reward after death.

It is therefore easy to see why the Churches have always fought science and persecuted its devotees. On the other hand, I maintain that cosmic religious feeling is the strongest and noblest incitement to scientific research. Only those who realize the immense efforts and, above all, the devotion which pioneer work in theoretical science demands, can grasp the strength of the emotion out of which alone such work, remote as it is from the immediate realities of life, can issue. What a deep conviction of the rationality of the universe and what a yearning to understand, were it but a feeble reflection of the mind revealed in this world, Kepler and Newton must have had to enable them to spend years

358

or solitary labor in disentangling the principles of celestial mechanics! Those whose acquaintance with scientific research is derived chiefly from its practical results easily develop a completely false notion of the mentality of the men, who, surrounded by a skeptical world, have shown the way to those like-minded with themselves, scattered through the earth and the centuries. Only one who has devoted his life to similar ends can have a vivid realization of what has inspired these men and given them the strength to remain true to their purpose in spite of countless failures. It is cosmic religious feeling that gives a man strength of this sort. A contemporary has said, not unjustly, that in this materialistic age of ours the serious scientific workers are the only profoundly religious people.

[117]

ELIEZER, ISRAEL BEN. See BAAL SHEM-TOV.

ELIOT, GEORGE

ELIOT, GEORGE (1819-1880). Mary Ann Evans is best known by her pseudonym of George Eliot. Her novels are regarded, today, as classics. She was educated by her father in a spirit of rigorous evangelism, but she broke with Christian orthodoxy after studying the writings of David Friederich Strauss and Ludwig Feuerbach. She translated some of their works into English. Her novels attempt to illustrate that character is a process of mental and moral unfolding, that each individual must face his own nemesis and that departure from orthodoxy does not corrupt moral standards. They also contain many comments on moral and philosophical questions. Many critics have thought that she placed too much emphasis on ethical problems. Inclined as she was to meditation, her observations of life were very keen. She excelled in painting rural life, in presenting the tragic and comic aspects of ordinary people, and in characterizing them with the utmost detail. She also depicted great historical figures sympathetically. In *Daniel Deronda* (1876), Eliot dealt with the question of Jewish national survival in such manner that, according to Nahum Sokolow (a Zionist leader), it significantly prepared the way for Theodor Herzl's work.

For many years, Eliot lived together with G. H. Lewes in a

common-law relationship. Though she was a conscientious non-conformist, she never scorned tradition light-heartedly. Her best known works are *Scenes of Clerical Life* (1858), *Middlemarch* (1872), *Silas Marner* (1861), *Adam Bede* (1859), and *The Mill on The Floss* (1860).

VALUE IN ORIGINALITY

THE supremacy given in European cultures to the literature of Greece and Rome has had an effect almost equal to that of a religion in binding the Western nations together. It is foolish to be forever complaining of the consequent uniformity, as if there were an endless power of originality in the human mind. Great and precious origination must always be comparatively rare, and can only exist on condition of a wide and massive uniformity. When a multitude of men have learned to use the same language in speech and writing, then, and then only can the greatest masters of language arise.

For in what does their mastery consist? They use words which are already a familiar medium of understanding and sympathy in such a way as greatly to enlarge understanding and sympathy. Origination of this order changes the wild grasses into world-feeding grain. Idiosyncrasies are pepper and spices of questionable aroma.

[118]

EMERSON, RALPH WALDO

EMERSON, RALPH WALDO (1803-1882). William James pointed out that there were two Emersons: one was the instinctive New Englander whose sharp eyes penetrated the defects of the American republic without despairing of it; the other was the Plotinizing Emerson who exalted the Over-Soul, and before whom revelations of time, space, and nature shrank away. Emerson was often aware of the fact that his readiness to perceive various phenomena and to expand his spiritual interests could lead his mind in disparate directions. The elder Henry James asserted that Emerson "had no conscience, in fact he lived by perception." Emerson looked upon consistency as the hob-goblin of little minds. In *Self-Reliance*, he stated: "With consistency a great soul has simply nothing to do."

360

In *History,* he declared: "It is the fault of our rhetoric that we cannot state one fact without seeming to belie some other."

When Emerson spoke of the realm of the soul which embraced the mind and the spirit, it was with certainty and strong conviction, not theoretical knowledge. He distinguished between philosophers like Spinoza, Kant, and Coleridge and others like Locke, Paley, Mackintosh, and Stewart. He held that the former spoke from within or from experience as parties to or possessors of the fact; while the others spoke from without, as spectators whose acquaintance with the fact came from the evidence of third persons. He treated the latter and their doctrines contemptuously, and characterized them as coarse translators of things into conscience, ignorant of the relationship of the soul to the divine spirit. The latter relationship was the only thing that mattered to Emerson, for him no facts as such were sacred; none unworthy but which became instantly important when they indicated or symbolized the history of the living soul, regardless of whether they voiced a mythical imagination, history, law, customs, proverbial wisdom, the creative spirit of artists and poets, the contemplation of a saint, the decision of a hero, or the conversation of ordinary persons. He believed that the worth of any individual man was derived from the universe which contained all human life and was therefore mysterious. He regarded every man as the entrance to the universal mind, capable of feeling and comprehending that which at any time befell any man

SELF-RELIANCE

I READ the other day some verses written by an eminent painter which were original and not conventional. The soul always hears an admonition in such lines, let the subject be what it may. The sentiment they instill is of more value than any thought they may contain. To believe your own thought, to believe that what is true for you in your private heart is true for all men,—that is genius. Speak your latent conviction, and it shall be the universal sense; for the inmost in due time becomes the outmost, and our first thought is rendered back to us by the trumpets of the Last Judgment. Familiar as the voice of the mind is to each, the highest merit we ascribe to Moses, Plato and Milton is that they set at naught books and traditions, and spoke not what men, but what *they* thought. A man should learn to detect and watch

361

that gleam of light which flashes across his mind from within, more than the luster of the firmament of bards and sages. Yet he dismisses without notice his thought, because it is his. In every work of genius we recognize our own rejected thoughts; they come back to us with a certain alienated majesty. Great works of art have no more affecting lesson for us than this. They teach us to abide by our spontaneous impression with good-humored inflexibility then most when the whole cry of voices is on the other side. Else tomorrow a stranger will say with masterly good sense precisely what we have thought and felt all the time, and we shall be forced to take with shame our own opinion from another.

There is a time in every man's education when he arrives at the conviction that envy is ignorance; that imitation is suicide; that he must take himself for better for worse as his portion; that though the wide universe is full of good, no kernel of nourishing corn can come to him through his toil bestowed on that plot of ground which is given to him to till. The power which resides in him is new in nature, and none but he knows what that is which he can do, nor does he know until he has tried. Not for nothing one face, one character, one fact, makes much impression on him, and another none. This sculpture in the memory is not without pre-established harmony. The eye was placed where one ray should fall, that it might testify of that particular ray. We but half express ourselves, and are ashamed of that divine idea which each of us represents. It may be safely trusted as proportionate and of good issues, so it be faithfully imparted, but God will not have his work made manifest by cowards. A man is relieved and gay when he has put his heart into his work and done his best; but what he has said or done otherwise shall give him no peace. It is a deliverance which does not deliver. In the attempt his genius deserts him; no muse befriends; no invention, no hope.

Trust thyself: every heart vibrates to that iron string. Accept the place the divine providence has found for you, the society of your contemporaries, the connection of events.

Great men have always done so, and confided themselves childlike to the genius of their age, betraying their perception that the absolutely trustworthy was seated at their heart, working through their hands, predominating in all their being. And we are now men, and must accept in the highest mind the same transcendent destiny; and not minors and invalids in a protected corner, not cowards fleeing before a revolution, but guides, redeemers and benefactors, obeying the Almighty effort and advancing on Chaos and the Dark.

What pretty oracles nature yields us on this text in the face and behavior of children, babes, and even brutes! That divided and rebel mind, that distrust of a sentiment because our arithmetic has computed the strength and means opposed to our purpose, these have not. Their mind being whole, their eye is as yet unconquered, and when we look in their faces we are disconcerted. Infancy conforms to nobody; all conform to it; so that one babe commonly makes four or five out of the adults who prattle and play to it. So God has armed youth and puberty and manhood no less with its own piquancy and charm, and made it enviable and gracious and its claims not to be put by, if it will stand by itself. Do not think the youth has no force, because he cannot speak to you and me. Hark! in the next room his voice is sufficiently clear and emphatic. It seems he knows how to speak to his contemporaries. Bashful or bold then, he will know how to make us seniors very unnecessary.

The nonchalance of boys who are sure of a dinner, and would disdain as much as a lord to do or say aught to conciliate one, is the healthy attitude of human nature. A boy is in the parlor what the pit is in the playhouse; independent, irresponsible, looking out from his corner on such people and facts as pass by, he tries and sentences them on their merits, in the swift, summary way of boys, as good, bad, interesting, silly, eloquent, troublesome. He cumbers himself never about consequences, about interests; he gives an independent, genuine verdict. You must court him; he does not court you. But the man is as it were clapped into jail by his consciousness. As soon as he has once acted or spoken with *éclat* he is a committed person, watched by the sympathy or the hatred of hundreds, whose affections must now enter into his account. There is no Lethe for this. Ah, that he could pass again into his neutrality! Who can thus avoid all pledges and, having observed, observe again from the same unaffected, unbiased, unbribable, unaffrighted innocence,—must always be formidable. He would utter opinions on all passing affairs, which being seen to be not private but necessary, would sink like darts into the ear of men and put them in fear.

These are the voices which we hear in solitude, but they grow faint and inaudible as we enter into the world. Society everywhere is in conspiracy against the manhood of every one of its members. Society is a joint-stock company, in which the members agree, for the better securing of his bread to each shareholder, to surrender the liberty and culture of the eater. The virtue in most request is conformity. Self-reliance is its aversion. It loves not realities and creators, but names and customs.

Whoso would be a man, must be a nonconformist. He who would gather immortal palms must not be hindered by the name of goodness, but must explore if it be goodness. Nothing is at last sacred but the integrity of your own mind. Absolve you to yourself, and you shall have the suffrage of the world. I remember an answer which when quite young I was prompted to make to a valued adviser who was wont to importune me with the dear old doctrines of the church. On my saying, "What have I to do with the sacredness of traditions, if I live wholly from within?" my friend suggested,—"But these impulses may be from below, not from above." I replied, "They do not seem to me to be such; but if I am the Devil's child, I will live then from the Devil." No law can be sacred to me but that of my nature. Good and bad are but names very readily transferable to that or this; the only right is what is after my constitution; the only wrong what is against it. A man is to carry himself in the presence of all opposition as if everything were titular and

ephemeral but he. I am ashamed to think how easily we capit-
ulate to badges and names, to large societies and dead institutions. Every decent and well-spoken individual affects and
sways me more than is right. I ought to go upright and vital,
and speak the rude truth in all ways.

*   *   *

The other terror that scares us from self-trust is our consistency; a reverence for our past act or word because the
eyes of others have no other data for computing our orbit
than our past acts, and we are loth to disappoint them.

But why should you keep your head over your shoulder?
Why drag about this corpse of your memory, lest you contradict somewhat you have stated in this or that public place?
Suppose you should contradict yourself; what then? It seems
to be a rule of wisdom never to rely on your memory alone,
scarcely even in acts of pure memory, but to bring the past
for judgment into the thousand-eyed present, and live ever
in a new day. In your metaphysics you have denied personality to the Deity, yet when the devout motions of the soul
come, yield to them heart and life, though they should clothe
God with shape and color. Leave your theory, as Joseph his
coat in the hand of the harlot, and flee.

A foolish consistency is the hobgoblin of little minds,
adored by little statesmen and philosophers and divines. With
consistency a great soul has simply nothing to do. He may as
well concern himself with his shadow on the wall. Speak
what you think now in hard words and tomorrow speak what
tomorrow thinks in hard words again, though it contradict
every thing you said today.—"Ah, so you shall be sure to be
misunderstood."—Is it so bad then to be misunderstood?
Pythagoras was misunderstood, and Socrates, and Jesus, and
Luther, and Copernicus, and Galileo, and Newton and every
pure and wise spirit that ever took flesh. To be great is to be
misunderstood.

[119]

EMPEDOCLES

EMPEDOCLES (c. 490-435 B.C.). Born in Acragas (Agrigentum) on the south coast of Sicily, Empedocles, like his teacher Parmenides, was bred in the Pythagorean tradition. He tried to combine this with the more naturalistic philosophy and science of the Milesians. He did not share Parmenides' distrust of the senses, and like him, composed his philosophy in verse. Fragments of two treatises, one entitled *On Nature* and the other *Purification*, are extant. The term *catharsis*, which became highly important in poetry and aesthetics, was first used in *Purification*. The doctrine of the four elements, water, fire, air, and earth, which dominated the popular thinking about nature for more than two thousand years, was probably originated by Empedocles. According to him, change was produced by the two fundamental forces, love and strife. The first was the cause of combination; the other of separation. He explained cosmic nature, the functions of the human body, and the activities of the soul as the result of conflicting forces. His philosophy was a blend of mythological imagination and scientific observation. He was an opponent of tyranny and a miracle-worker who claimed to be a God. Hundreds of stories abounded about him throughout ancient Greece and Italy. He was credited with founding the first great medical school. His legendary death is supposed to have taken place by jumping into the crater of Mount Etna; this has been a source of inspiration for many poets, among them: Matthew Arnold and Friedrich Hoelderlin.

FRAGMENTS

But, O ye Gods, turn aside from my tongue the madness of those men. Hallow my lips and make a pure stream flow from them! And thee, much-wooed, white-armed Virgin Muse, do I beseech, that I may hear what is lawful for the children of a day! Speed me on my way from the abode of Holiness and drive my willing car! Constrain me not to win garlands of honor and glory at the hands of mortals on condition of speaking in my pride beyond that which is lawful and right, and only so to gain a seat upon the heights of wisdom.

Go to now, consider with all thy powers in what way each thing is clear. Hold nothing that thou seest in greater credit than what thou hearest, nor value thy resounding ear above the clear instructions of thy tongue; and do not with-hold thy confidence in any of thy other bodily parts by which there is an opening for understanding, but consider every-thing in the way it is clear.

*   *   *

And thou shalt learn all the drugs that are a defense against ills and old age, since for thee alone shall I accomp-lish all this. Thou shalt arrest the violence of the weariless winds that arise and sweep the earth, laying waste the corn-fields with their breath; and again, when thou so desirest, thou shalt bring their blasts back again with a rush. Thou shalt cause for men a seasonable drought after the dark rains, and again after the summer drought thou shalt produce the streams that feed the trees as they pour down from the sky. Thou shalt bring back from Hades the life of a dead man.

*   *   *

And I shall tell thee another thing. There is no coming into being of aught that perishes, nor any end for it in bane-ful death; but only mingling and separation of what has been mingled. Coming into being is but a name given to these by men.

*   *   *

But, when the elements have been mingled in the fashion of a man and come to the light of day, or in the fashion of the race of wild beasts or plants or birds, then men say that these come into being; and when they are separated, they call that, as is the custom, woeful death. I too follow the custom, and call it so myself.

*   *   *

Fools!—for they have no far-reaching thoughts—who deem that what before was not comes into being, or that aught can perish and be utterly destroyed. For it cannot be that aught arise from what it no way is, and it is impossible and unheard of that what is should perish; for it will always be,

367

wherever one may keep putting it.

A man who is wise in such matters would never surmise in his heart that, so long as mortals live what men choose to call their life, they are, and suffer good and ill; while, before they were formed and after they have been dissolved they are, it seems, nothing at all.

I shall tell thee a twofold tale. At one time things grew to be one only out of many; at another, that divided up to be many instead of one. There is a double becoming of perishable things and a double passing away. The coming together of all things brings one generation into being and destroys it; the other grows up and is scattered as things become divided. And these things never cease, continually changing places, at one time all uniting in one through Love, at another each borne in different directions by the repulsion of Strife. Thus, as far as it is their nature to grow into one out of many, and to become many once more when the one is parted asunder, so far they come into being and their life abides not. But, inasmuch as they never cease changing their places continually, so far they are immovable as they go round the circle of existence.

*   *   *

Nor is any part of the whole empty. Whence, then, could aught come to increase it? Where, too, could these things perish, since no place is empty of them? They are what they are; but, running through one another, different things continually come into being from different sources, yet ever alike.

*   *   *

Come now, look at the things that bear virtues. Behold the sun, everywhere bright and warm, and all the immortal things that are bathed in its heat and bright radiance. Behold the rain, everywhere dark and cold; and from the earth issue forth things close-pressed and solid. When they are in strife all these things are different in form, and separated; but they come together in love, and are desired by one another.

For out of these have sprung all things that were and are and shall be,—trees and men and women, beasts and birds and the fishes that dwell in the waters, yea, and the gods that live long lives and are exalted in honor.

For these things are what they are; but, running through one another, they take different shapes—so much does mixture change them.

* * *

For, of a truth, they (i.e. Love and Strife) were aforementioned and shall be; nor ever, methinks, will boundless time be emptied of that pair. And they prevail in turn as the circle comes round, and pass away before one another, and increase in their appointed turn.

* * *

For all of them—sun, earth, sky, and sea,—fit in with all the parts of themselves, the friendly parts which are separated off in perishable things. In the same way, all those things that are more adapted for mixture, are united to one another in Love, made like by the power of Aphrodite. But they themselves (i.e. the elements) differ as far as possible in their origin and mixture and the forms imprinted on each, being altogether unaccustomed to come together, and very hostile, under the influence of Strife, since it has wrought their birth.

Thus all things have thought by the will of fortune. . . . And, inasmuch as the rarest things come together in their fall. . . .

Fire is increased by Fire, Earth increases its own mass, and Air swells the bulk of Air.

And the kindly earth in its well-wrought ovens received two parts of shining Nestis out of the eight, and four of Hephaistos; and they became white bones, divinely fitted together by the cements of Harmony.

And the earth meets with these in nearly equal proportions, with Hephaistos and Water and shining Air, anchoring

369

in the perfect haven of Kypris,—either a little more of it, or
less of it and more of them. From these did blood arise
and the various forms of flesh.

[120]

ENGELS, FRIEDRICH

ENGELS, FRIEDRICH (1820-1895). As long as Karl Marx lived,
Engels was his intimate friend, collaborator, and supporter. Though
he remained in the background, were it not for Engels' money,
moral encouragement, and innumerable other services, Marx would
have perished. Several of the writings were the collaboration of
both; Engels was always ready to recognize Marx as his superior.
After Marx died, Engels edited the second and third volumes of
Marx's *Capital;* when socialists disagreed about the meaning of the
work, or adversaries distorted it, Engels untiringly interpreted his
late friend's meaning.

Engels was the descendant of a dynasty of German industrialists
who adhered to religious orthodoxy and political conservatism. He
had planned, in his youth, to become a poet, for he was an enthusiast of German romanticism, the historical past and beauty and
nature in art. When a new Oriental crisis threatened to cause war
between France and Germany (1840), Engels, still an excited nationalist, dreamed of German military victories. A sojourn in
London and military service in the Prussian army made him revise
his beliefs. He abandoned German nationalism, and all prospects
of succeeding his father in his well-to-do business. Thereafter, he
devoted his life to the fight for the rights of the working class
and for the realization of Marx's plans. In 1845 Engels published
his pamphlet, *On The Situation of The Working Class*, in England.
He was greatly indebted for this to Constantin Pecqueur, who also
wrote a pamphlet dealing with the same subject. Engels' subsequent
collaboration with Marx was so close that it is impossible to define
his part in it with exactness. In his later years, Engels blended
dialectical materialism (as Marx had conceived of it) with philosophical materialism. He also tried to expand the meaning of
Marx's terminology. He developed a great interest in ethnology in
order to attack social conventions with arguments that demonstrated
the relativity of social values. Until his death, he remained the
executor of Marx's will.

MORALITY IS CLASS MORALITY

THE conceptions of good and bad have varied so much from
nation to nation and from age to age that they have often

been in direct contradiction to each other. But all the same, someone may object, good is not bad and bad is not good; if good is confused with bad there is an end to all morality, and everyone can do and leave undone whatever he cares. This is also, stripped of his oracular phrases, Herr Dühring's opinion. But the matter cannot be so simply disposed of. If it was such an easy business there would certainly be no dispute at all over good and bad; everyone would know what was good and what was bad. But how do things stand today? What morality is preached to us today? There is first Christian-feudal morality, inherited from past centuries of faith; and this again has two main sub-divisions, Catholic and Protestant moralities, each of which in turn has no lack of further subdivisions from the Jesuit-Catholic and Orthodox-Protestant to loose "advanced" moralities. Alongside of these we find the modern bourgeois morality and with it too the proletarian morality of the future, so that in the most advanced European countries alone the past, present and future provide three great groups of moral theories which are in force simultaneously and alongside of each other. Which is then the true one? Not one of them, in the sense of having absolute validity; but certainly that morality which contains the maximum of durable elements is the one which, in the present, represents the overthrow of the present, represents the future: that is, the proletarian.

But when we see that the three classes of modern society, the feudal aristocracy, the bourgeoisie and the proletariat, each have their special morality, we can only draw the one conclusion, that men, consciously or unconsciously, derive their moral ideas in the last resort from the practical relations on which they carry on production and exchange.

But nevertheless there is much that is common to the three moral theories mentioned above—is this not at least a portion of a morality which is externally fixed? These moral theories represent three different stages of the same historical development, and have therefore a common historical background, and for that reason alone they necessarily have much in common. Even more. In similar or approximately similar stages of economic development moral theories must of necessity be more or less in agreement. From the moment when private property in movable objects developed, in all societies in which this private property existed there must be this moral law in common: Thou shalt not steal. Does this law thereby become an eternal moral law? By no means. In a society in which the motive for stealing has been done away with, in which therefore at the very most only lunatics would ever steal, how the teacher of morals would be laughed at who tried solemnly to proclaim the eternal truth: Thou shalt not steal!

We therefore reject every attempt to impose on us any moral dogma whatsoever as an eternal, ultimate and forever immutable moral law on the pretext that the moral world has its permanent principles which transcend history and the differences between nations. We maintain on the contrary that all former moral theories are the product, in the last analysis, of the economic stage which society had reached at that particular epoch. And as society has hitherto moved in class antagonisms, morality was always a class morality; it has either justified the domination and the interests of the ruling class, or, as soon as the oppressed class has become powerful enough, it has represented the revolt against this domination and the future interests of the oppressed.

[121]

EPICTETUS

EPICTETUS (c. 60-110). The son of a slave, himself crippled by a brutal master, Epictetus was legally emancipated and became the example of an upright, independent, free man. Often, when men were afflicted by misfortune, they declined religious consolation and read the *Encheiridion* (Manual) to regain peace of mind. The manual was not written by the Stoic philosopher, Epictetus, but by his faithful disciple Arrian (a military commander and important dignitary of the Roman Empire) who had made notes on his teacher's psychological observations, moral meditations, lectures, and conversations. About half the original manual is extant.

Epictetus was born in Phrygia, Asia Minor. He was sold to one of the retinue of Emperor Nero. He was allowed to attend the lectures of the Stoic philosopher Caius Musonius Rufus whom he greatly admired. From Musonius he learned how to make theoretical discussions personal confessions. When Musonius died (81), Epictetus, who by this time had been freed from slavery, held philosophical lectures in Rome. Emperor Domitian, who disliked freedom of expression, banished Epictetus (90) and all other philosophers from the capital. Epictetus went to Nicopolis, in Epirus, Greece, where among the members of his large audience was the future Emperor Hadrian. He also exerted considerable influence over Emperor Marcus Aurelius; the latter's views almost consistently agreed with those of Epictetus. Epictetus taught that reason governed the world and was identical with God. Sometimes he paralleled Christian doctrines. He mentioned the "Galileans"; praised their courage, but maintained that they were devoid of reason. His work, expressed in simple and frank language, attracted many thinkers of later centuries, notably Montaigne and Kant.

TO THOSE WHO FEAR WANT

ARE you not ashamed of being more cowardly and more mean than fugitive slaves? How do they when they run away leave their masters? on what estates do they depend, and what domestics do they rely on? Do they not after stealing a little which is enough for the first days, then afterwards move on through land or through sea, contriving one method after another for maintaining their lives? And what fugitive slave ever died of hunger? But you are afraid lest necessary things should fail you, and are sleepless by night. Wretch, are you so blind, and don't you see the road to which the want of necessaries leads?—Well, where does it lead?—To the same place to which a fever leads, or a stone that falls on you, to death. Have you not often said this yourself to your companions? have you not read much of this kind, and written much? and how often have you boasted that you were easy as to death?

Yes: but my wife and children also suffer hunger.— Well then does their hunger lead to any other place? Is there not the same descent to some place for them also? Is not there not the same state below for them? Do you not choose then to look at that place full of boldness against every want and deficiency, to that place to which both the richest and those who have held the highest offices, and kings themselves and tyrants must descend? or to which you will descend hungry, if it should so happen, but they burst by indigestion and drunkenness. What beggar did you hardly ever see who was not an old man, and even of extreme age? But chilled with cold and night, and lying on the ground, and eating only what is absolutely necessary they approach near to the impossibility of dying. Cannot you write? Cannot you teach (take care of) children? Cannot you be a watchman of another person's door?—But it is shameful to come to such a necessity.—Learn then first what are the things which are shameful, and then tell us that you are a philosopher: but at present do not, even if any other man call you so, allow it. Is that shameful to you which is not your own act, that of which you are not the cause, that which has come to you by accident, as a headache, as a fever? If your parents were poor, and left their property to others, and if while they live they do not help you at all, is this shameful to you? Is this what you learned with the philosophers? Did you ever hear that the thing which is shameful ought to be blamed, and that which is blamable is worthy of blame? Whom do you blame for an act which is not his own, which he did not do himself? Did you then make your father such as he is, or is it in your power to improve him? Is this power given to you? Well then, ought you to wish the things which are not given to you, or to be ashamed if you do not obtain them? And have you also been accustomed while you were studying philosophy to look to others and to hope for nothing from yourself? Lament then and groan and eat with fear that you may not have food to-morrow. Tremble about your poor slaves lest they steal, lest they run away, lest they die. So live and continue to live, you who in name only have approached philosophy, and have disgraced its theorems as far as you can by showing them to be useless and unprofitable to those who take them up; you who have never sought

374

constancy, freedom from perturbation, and from passions: you who have not sought any person for the sake of this object, but many for the sake of syllogisms; you who have never thoroughly examined any of these appearances by yourself, Am I able to bear, or am I not able to bear? What remains for me to do? But as if all your affairs were well and secure, you have been resting on the third topic, that of things being unchanged, in order that you may possess unchanged —what? cowardice, mean spirit, the admiration of the rich, desire without attaining any end, and avoidance which fails in the attempt? About security in these things you have been anxious.

Ought you not to have gained something in addition from reason, and then to have protected this with security? And whom did you ever see building a battlement all round and not encircling it with a wall? And what door-keeper is placed with no door to watch? But you practice in order to be able to prove—what? You practice that you may not be tossed as on the sea through sophisms, and tossed about from what? Shew me first what you hold, what you measure, or what you weigh; and shew me the scales or the mediums (the measure); or how long will you go on measuring the dust? Ought you not to demonstrate those things which make men happy, which make things go on for them in the way as they wish, and why we ought to blame no man, accuse no man, and acquiesce in the administration of the universe? Shew me these. 'See, I shew them; I will resolve syllogisms for you.'—This is the measure, slave; but it is not the thing measured. Therefore you are now paying the penalty for what you neglected, philosophy: you tremble, you lie awake, you advise with all persons; and if your deliberations are not likely to please all, you think that you have deliberated ill. Then you fear hunger, as you suppose: but it is not hunger that you fear, but you are afraid that you will not have a cook, that you will not have another to purchase provisions for the table, a third to take off your shoes, a fourth to dress you, others to rub you, and to follow you, in order that in the bath, when you have taken off your clothes and stretched yourself out like those who are crucified you may be rubbed on this side and on that, and then the aliptes (rubber) may say (to the slave), Change his position, present the side, take hold of his head, shew the shoulder; and then when you have left the bath and gone home, you may call out, Does no one bring something to eat? And then, Take away the tables, sponge them: you are afraid of this, that you may not be able to lead the life of a sick man. But learn the life of those who are in health, how slaves live, how laborers, how those live who are genuine philosophers; how Socrates lived, who had a wife and children; how Diogenes lived, and how Cleanthes who attended to the school and drew water. If you choose to have these things, you will have them everywhere, and you will live in full confidence. Confiding in what? In that alone in which a man can confide, in that which is secure, in that which is not subject to hindrance, in that which cannot be taken away, that is in your own will. And why have you made yourself so useless and good for nothing that no man will choose to receive you into his house, no man to take care of you?: but if a utensil entire and useful were cast abroad, every man who found it, would take it up and think it a gain; but no man will take you up, and every man will consider you a loss. So cannot you discharge the office even of a dog, or of a cock? Why then do you choose to live any longer, when you are what you are?

Does any good man fear that he shall fail to have food? To the blind it does not fail, to the lame it does not; shall it fail to a good man? And to a good soldier there does not fail to be one who gives him pay, nor to a laborer, nor to a shoemaker: and to the good man shall there be wanting such a person? Does God thus neglect the things he has established, his ministers, his witnesses, whom alone he employs as examples to the uninstructed, both that he exists, and administers well the whole, and does not neglect human affairs, and that to a good man there is no evil either when

376

he is living or when he is dead? What then when he does not supply him with food? What else does he do than like a good general he has given me the signal to retreat? I obey, I follow, assenting to the words of the commander, praising his acts: for I came when it pleased him, and I will also go when it pleases him; and while I lived, it was my duty to praise God both by myself, and to each person severally and to many. He does not supply me with many things, nor with abundance, he does not will me to live luxuriously; for neither did he supply Hercules who was his own son; but another (Eurystheus) was king of Argos and Mycenae, and Hercules obeyed orders, and labored, and exercised. And Eurystheus was what he was, neither king of Argos nor of Mycenae, for he was not even king of himself; but Hercules was ruler and leader of the whole earth and sea, who purged away lawlessness, and introduced justice and holiness; and he did these things both naked and alone. And when Ulysses was cast out shipwrecked, did want humiliate him, did it break his spirit? but how did he go off to the virgins to ask for necessaries, to beg which is considered most shameful?

As a lion bred in the mountains trusting in his strength.

Relying on what? Not on reputation nor on wealth nor on the power of a magistrate, but on his own strength, that is, on his opinions about the things which are in our power and those which are not. For these are the only things which make men free, which make them escape from hindrance, which raise the head (neck) of those who are depressed, which make them look with steady eyes on the rich and on tyrants. And this was the gift given to the philosopher. But you will not come forth bold, but trembling about your trifling garments and silver vessels. Unhappy man, have you thus wasted your time till now?

What then, if I shall be sick? You will be sick in such

377

a way as you ought to be.—Who will take care of me?—
God; your friends—I shall lie down on a hard bed—But
you will lie down like a man—I shall not have a convenient
chamber—You will be sick in an inconvenient chamber—
Who will provide for me the necessary food?—Those who
provide for others also. You will be sick like Manes.—
And what also will be the end of the sickness? Any other
than death?—Do you then consider this the chief of all
evils to man and the chief mark of mean spirit and of
cowardice is not death, but rather the fear of death? Against
this fear then I advise you to exercise yourself: to this let
all your reasoning tend, your exercises, and reading; and
you will know that thus only are men made free.

[122]

EPICURUS

EPICURUS (341-270 B.C.). According to Epicurus, philosophy
must be a cure for the mind and soul; it must be a guide to happiness. He taught that pleasure was the beginning and end of the
blessed life; that wisdom and culture must be directed toward this
end. Contrary to other hedonists, Epicurus regarded the permanent
absence of pain as the only true pleasure, rather than joy or debauchery. The pleasure he conceived of demanded self-control; prudence was necessary for the pursuit of happiness. He recommended
an extremely frugal life; he himself was ordinarily satisfied with
bread and water. The essential part of his philosophy was devoted
to ethics and teaching a wise conduct of life. Logic, epistemology,
physics, and metaphysics were regarded as helpful toward securing
tranquility of soul or disturbing it. He thus concluded that fear
of death and religion were the main sources of psychic disorder.
He staunchly opposed superstition or any belief in supernatural
interference. His concept of nature mainly followed that of Democritus. Although he adopted atomism, he disaffirmed determinism,
and established the doctrine of cosmic chance. The latter doctrine
has been revived in contemporary times.

In 310 B.C. he founded the oldest sanatorium, in Mytilene,
for persons suffering from psychic or nervous disorders, depressions,
or the consequences of failure or disappointment. Four years later
the sanatorium was removed to Athens. Epicurus, himself, always
suffered from diseases of the stomach, bladder, or kidneys. His

378

philosophy enabled him to endure pain and he was able to cure many of the patients in his sanatorium by teaching them his philosophy. Many were indebted to his knowledge whereby psychic disorders could be avoided. Persons of all origins, professions, and social stature were admitted to his sanatorium or school. Neither slaves nor hetaerae were excluded. His teachings, though often distorted, were spread throughout the ancient world. They have had considerable influence through all of history, up to the present time.

ON PLEASURE

WE must consider that of desires some are natural, others vain, and of the natural some are necessary and others merely natural; and of the necessary some are necessary for happiness, others for the repose of the body, and others for very life. The right understanding of these facts enables us to refer all choice and avoidance to the health of the body and (the soul's) freedom from disturbance, since this is the aim of the life of blessedness. For it is to obtain this end that we always act, namely, to avoid pain and fear. And when this is once secured for us, all the tempest of the soul is dispersed, since the living creature has not to wander as though in search of something that is missing, and to look for some other thing by which he can fulfill the good of the soul and the good of the body. For it is then that we have need of pleasure, when we feel pain owing to the absence of pleasure; (but when we do not feel pain), we no longer need pleasure. And for this cause we call pleasure the beginning and end of the blessed life. For we recognize pleasure as the first good innate in us, and from pleasure we begin every act of choice and avoidance, and to pleasure we return again, using the feeling as the standard by which we judge every good.

And since pleasure is the first good and natural to us, for this very reason we do not choose every pleasure, but sometimes we pass over many pleasures, when greater discomfort accrues to us as the result of them: and similarly we think many pains better than pleasures, since a greater pleasure comes to us when we have endured pains for a long time. Every pleasure then because of its natural kinship to us is good, yet not every pleasure is to be chosen: even as every pain also is an evil, yet not all are always of a nature to be avoided. Yet by a scale of comparison and by the consideration of advantages and disadvantages we must form our judgment on all these matters. For the good on certain occasions we treat as bad, and conversely the bad as good.

And again independence of desire we think a great good—not that we may at all times enjoy but a few things, but that, if we do not possess many, we may enjoy the few in the genuine persuasion that those have the sweetest pleasure in luxury who least need it, and that all that is natural is easy to be obtained, but that which is superfluous is hard. And so plain savors bring us a pleasure equal to a luxurious diet, when all the pain due to want is removed; and bread and water produce the highest pleasure, when one who needs them puts them to his lips. To grow accustomed therefore to simple and not luxurious diet gives us health to the full, and makes a man alert for the needful employments of life, and when after long intervals we approach luxuries disposes us better towards them, and fits us to be fearless of fortune.

When, therefore, we maintain that pleasure is the end, we do not mean the pleasures of profligates and those that consist in sensuality, as is supposed by some who are either ignorant or disagree with us or do not understand, but freedom from pain in the body and from trouble in the mind. For it is not continuous drinkings and revellings, nor the satisfaction of lusts, nor the enjoyment of fish and other luxuries of the wealthy table, which produce a pleasant life, but sober reasoning, searching out the motives for all choice and avoidance, and banishing mere opinions, to which are due the greatest disturbance of the spirit.

Of all this the beginning and the greatest good is prudence. Wherefore prudence is a more precious thing even than philosophy: for from prudence are sprung all the other virtues, and it teaches us that it is not possible to live pleasantly without living prudently and honorably and justly, (nor again, to live a life of prudence, honor, and justice) without living pleasantly. For the virtues are by nature bound up with the pleasant life, and the pleasant life is inseparable from them.

[123]

ERASMUS, DESIDERIUS

ERASMUS, DESIDERIUS (1466-1536). Born in Rotterdam, Erasmus was brought up in the tradition of the Brethren of the Common Life. He believed in Christ and His mission and regarded Christianity not only as a religion and doctrine of salvation, but also as a guide to moral life. He held that philosophy and the arts could also show the right way. In his later years, he conceived of Christianity more as a religion of the spirit based upon confidence in human reason. He stated that all human evils were rooted in ignorance and infatuation and therefore education of humanity was the essential task of his life.

Although he suffered from living in "a century of fury," he endeavored to stem the tide of fanaticism, by complaining and despising religious exaltation and partisanship, thereby exposing himself to the fury of all religious parties. Sometimes referred to as the Voltaire of the Age of Reformation, he was essentially a man of deep religious feeling and conviction; an independent thinker; the greatest philologist of his time and one of the greatest of all times; a staunch defender of human reason, opposed Luther's teachings; a fearless critic of clerical abuses; and a religious reformer who tried to avoid schisms.

Though he disapproved of Luther's theology, of his doctrine of predestination, and his derogation of human reason, he defended Luther only for the sake of freedom of conscience and because he approved of Luther's criticisms of the existing Church, which he himself had severely criticized. In fact, it was Erasmus' courageous intervention that saved Luther's life at the very beginning of the latter's reforming activities. Luther essentially relied on St. Paul; Erasmus maintained that the *Sermon on the Mount* was the principal basis of the Christian religion. He refused to give dogma primary importance, placed piety above tenets, moral righteousness above orthodoxy, and nothing above "true and perfect friendship, dying and living with Christ." Erasmus exerted considerable influence in the spiritual life of England. He died in Basle in 1536.

LITERARY EDUCATION

IF the ancient teachers of children are commended for alluring them with wafers that they might be willing to learn their first rudiments, I think it ought not to be charged as a fault upon me that, by the like regard, I allure youth either to the elegance of Latin or to piety. Besides, it is a good part of prudence to know the foolish affections of the common people and their absurd opinions. I judge it to be much better to instruct those out of my little book than by experience, the mistress of fools. The rules of grammar are crabbed things to many persons. Aristotle's *Moral Philosophy* is not fit for children. Scotus' *Divinity* is less fit, nor is it, indeed, of great use to men to give them understanding. And it is a matter of great moment to disseminate a taste of the best things into the tender minds of children. I cannot tell that anything is learned with greater success than what is learned by playing, and this is in truth a very harmless fraud to trick a person into his own profit. . . .

There is nothing more base than to find fault with that which thou dost not understand. That view vilifies everything; it produces but bitterness and discord. Therefore, let us candidly interpret other men's work and not esteem our own as oracles, nor look upon the judgments of those men who do not understand what they read. Where there is hatred in judgment, judgment is blind.

[124]

ERIUGENA, JOHANNES SCOTUS

ERIUGENA, JOHANNES SCOTUS (c. 815-877). The translator of Pseudo-Dionysius from Greek to Latin adopted Neo-Platonism and tried to reconcile this with Christianity. He regarded Church doctrine as dynamic and therefore attempted an original approach to religion and philosophy. For this heresy, he narrowly escaped persecution.

He asserted that there was only one reality, namely God, who created all things by emanation and to whom all creatures return.

In his principal work, *On the Division of Nature,* he stated that God emanates nature in four forms: the highest is God himself, who creates but is not created; then there are those which are created and create; those which are created but do not create, and finally God again, who rests neither created nor creating. Eriugena declined to speculate on God's attributes. He declared: "God is not a what but a that." True religion and true philosophy are identical. Both of them rest upon the unity of God who is not subject to necessity but creates by his own free will. Man is a microcosmos with his own unique soul, but in the last analysis "all our souls are but one soul." His concept of the dogma of Trinity is more similar to Plotinus' triad than it is to the doctrine of the Church. Eriugena also wrote about predestination, reducing this concept to a vagueness which makes it little different from free will. Although he never claimed that he was an independent thinker, he actually was. At any rate, he succeeded in fitting what were apparently his personal thoughts within the framework of accepted doctrines. His influence was greater with the mystics than it was with the logicians of the later Middle Ages. An Irish monk, he had mastered Greek and Latin, and was responsible for the revival of philosophical thought which had remained dormant in Western Europe after the death of Boethius. He taught at the royal palace school of Charles the Bald of France and was often entrusted by him to settle theological disputes.

THE HUMAN MIND

It would suffice for me to answer you briefly when you ask why God should have created man, whom he proposed to make in his own image, in the genus of animals. He wished so to fashion him, that there would be a certain animal in which he manifested his own express image. But whoever asks why He wished that, asks the cause of the divine will; to ask that is too presumptuous and arrogant. . . .

I should not, therefore, say why He willed, because that is beyond all understanding, but I shall say, as He has permitted, what He has willed to do. He has made all creation, visible and invisible, in man since the whole spread of created nature is understood to be in him. For although it is still unknown how much the first creation of man, after the transgression, is in defect of the eternal light, nevertheless there is nothing naturally present in the celestial

383

essences which does not subsist essentially in man. For there is understanding and reason, and there is naturally implanted the sound reason of possessing a celestial and angelic body, which after the resurrection will appear more clearly than light both in the good and the evil. For it will be common to all human nature to rise again in eternal incorruptible spiritual bodies. . . .

Man is a certain intellectual idea, formed eternally in the divine mind. . . . The human mind, its idea by which it knows itself, and the discipline by which it learns itself that it knows itself, subsists as one and the same essence. . . . Reason teaches us . . . that the human mind assuredly knows itself and does not know itself. For it knows that it is, but it does not know what it is. . . . The divine likeness in the human mind . . . is recognized most clearly in that it is known only to be, but what it is, is not known.

[125]

EUCKEN, RUDOLF

EUCKEN, RUDOLF (1846-1926). The core of Eucken's philosophy was that the concept of life manifests its mere existence through sensual experience, activity, and in a world of relationships comprehensible to the spirit. He explained the history of the world as a blending of reason and blind necessity. Throughout the course of history, spiritual life was evolved as a new level of reality. It was not the human individual, nor the sum of individuals, who created the new order of things and relationships, but the motion of the universe. Eucken thought that his concept corresponded more to the nature of man than that of Fichte, Schelling, or Hegel who overestimated the range of the human mind. Eucken accused positivism, materialism, and naturalism of ignoring the faculties of the mind.

His colleagues, professors of philosophy at the German universities, were surprised when he was awarded the Nobel Prize (1908); they felt that the selection of candidates for the prize should be made more carefully. Eucken, however, maintained that German philosophers were indifferent to his writings; that he was popular in England, America, and China before he even began to attract attention in Germany. During World War I, Eucken pro-

amusement, for work, and getting his bodily and mental growth; he, too, is indeed there for himself; but his body and mind are also but a dwelling place into which new and higher impulses enter, mingle, and develop, and engage in all sorts of processes together, which both constitute the feeling and thinking of the man, and have their higher meaning for the third stage of life.

The mind of man is alike indistinguishably his own possession and that of the higher intelligences, and what proceeds from it belongs equally to both always, but in different ways. Just as in this figure, which is intended not for a representation but only a symbol, the central, colored, six-rayed star (looking black here) can be considered as independent and having unity in itself; its rays proceeding from the middle point are all thereby dependently and harmoniously bound together; on the other hand, it appears again mingled together from the concatenation of the six single colored circles, each one of which has its own individuality. And as each of its rays belongs as well to it as to the circles, through the overlapping of which it is formed, so is it with the human soul.

Man does not often know from whence his thoughts come to him: he is seized with a longing, a foreboding, or a joy, which he is quite unable to account for; he is urged to a force of activity, or a voice warns him away from it, without his being conscious of any special cause. These are the visitations of spirits, which think and act in him from another center than his own. Their influence is even more manifest in us, when, in abnormal conditions (clairvoyance or mental disorder) the really mutual relation of dependence between them and us is determined in their favor, so that we only passively receive what flows into us from them, without return on our part.

But so long as the human soul is awake and healthy, it is not the weak plaything or product of the spirits which grow into it or of which it appears to be made up, but precisely that which unites these spirits, the invisible center, possessing primitive living energy, full of spiritual power of attraction, in which all unite, intersect, and through mutual communication engender thoughts in each other. This is not brought into being by the mingling of the spirits, but is inborn in man at his birth; and free will, self-determination, consciousness, reason, and the foundation of all spiritual power are contained herein. But at birth all this lies still latent within, like an unopened seed, awaiting development into an organism full of vital individual activity.

So when man has entered into life other spirits perceive it and press forward from all sides and seek to add his strength to theirs in order to reinforce their own power, but while this is successful, their power becomes at the same time the possession of the human soul itself, is incorporated with it and assists its development.

The outside spirits established within a man are quite as much subjected to the influence of the human will, though in a different way, as man is dependent upon them; he can, from the center of his spiritual being, equally well produce new growth in the spirits united to him within, as these can definitely influence his deepest life; but in harmoniously developed spiritual life no will has the mastery over another. As every outside spirit has only a part of itself in common with a single human being, so can the will of the single man have a suggestive influence alone upon a spirit which with its whole remaining part lies outside the man; and since every human mind contains within itself something in common with widely differing outside spirits, so too can the will of a single one among them have only a quickening influence upon the whole man, and only when he, with free choice, wholly denies himself to single spirits is he deprived of the capacity to master them.

All spirits cannot be united indiscriminately in the same soul; therefore the good and bad, the true and false spirits contend together for possession of it, and the one who conquers in the struggle holds the ground.

The interior discord which so often finds place in men

is nothing but this conflict of outside spirits who wish to get possession of his will, his reason, in short, his whole innermost being. As the man feels the agreement of spirits within him as rest, clearness, harmony, and safety, he is also conscious of their discord as unrest, doubt, vacillation, confusion, enmity, in his heart. But not as a prize won without effort, or as a willing victim, does he fall to the stronger spirits in this contest, but, with a source of self-active strength in the center of his being, he stands between the contending forces within which wish to draw him to themselves and fights on whichever side he chooses; and so he can carry the day even for the weaker impulses, when he joins his strength to theirs against the stronger. The Self of the man remains unendangered so long as he preserves the inborn freedom of his power and does not become tired of using it. As often, however, as he becomes subject to evil spirits, is it because the development of his interior strength is hindered by discouragement, and so, to become bad, it is often only necessary to be careless and lazy.

The better the man already is, the easier it is for him to become still better; and the worse he is, so much the more easily is he quite ruined. For the good man has already harbored many good spirits, which are now associated with him against the evil ones remaining and those freshly pressing for entrance, and are saving for him his interior strength. The good man does good without weariness, his spirits do it for him; but the bad man must first overcome and subdue by his own will all the evil spirits which have striven against him. Moreover, kin seeks and unites itself to kin, and flees from its opposites when not forced. Good spirits in us attract good spirits outside us, and the evil spirits in us the evil spirits outside. Pure spirits turn gladly to enter a pure soul, and evil without fastens upon the evil within. If only the good spirits in our souls have gained the upper hand, so of itself the last devil still remaining behind in us flees away, he is not secure in good society; and so the soul of a good man becomes a pure and heavenly abiding place for happy indwelling spirits. But even good spirits, if they despair of winning a soul from the final mastery of evil, desert it, and so it becomes at last a hell, a place fit only for the torments of the damned. For the agony of conscience and the inner desolation and unrest in the soul of the wicked are sorrows which, not they alone, but the condemned spirits within them also, feel in still deeper woe.

[128]

FEUERBACH, LUDWIG

FEUERBACH, LUDWIG (1804-1872). Modern existentialists ought to recognize Feuerbach as well as Kierkegaard as their forerunners, instead of regarding the former as a mere materialist. It is true that Feuerbach, while opposing Hegel's idealism, professed materialistic views, but materialism, to him, meant only a part of the truth, not its entirety. He defined philosophy as "the science of reality in its truth and totality." To find the total truth, he resorted to a concept of anthropology which included theology. He did not deny the existence of God, but explained the formation of the idea of God as the result of the longing of sensual man to reconcile the apparent contradictions of life. He accused the idealist philosophers of having deprived man of his feelings of immediateness and existence. According to Feuerbach, man was nothing without the world of objects with which he was connected: existence was defined as the abundance of relations; sensuality was the criterion of existence, but not its only characteristic. He maintained that the cooperation of physical and psychic elements made for the unity of man. He denied the possibility of reducing mental phenomena to the physical level or deriving God from nature. The antinomy between mind and nature was described by Feuerbach with ironic humor. He enjoined his fellow men not to ignore the contradictions of life, and to concentrate upon the tasks of the present day.

ABOVE RELIGION

OUR relation to religion is not a merely negative, but a critical one; we only separate the true from the false;—though we grant that the truth thus separated from falsehood is a new truth, essentially different from the old. Religion is the first form of self-consciousness. Religions are sacred because

394

they are the traditions of the primitive self-consciousness. But that which in religion holds the first place,—namely, God,—is, as we have shown, in itself and according to truth, the second, for it is only the the nature of man regarded objectively; and that which to religion is the second,—namely, man,—must therefore be constituted and declared the first. Love to man must be no derivative love; it must be original. If human nature is the highest nature to man, then practically also the highest and first law must be the love of man to man. *Homo homini Deus est*:—this is the great practical principle: —this is the axis on which revolves the history of the world. The relations of child and parent, of husband and wife, of brother and friend,—in general of man to man,—in short, all the moral relations are *per se* religious. Life as a whole is, in its essential, substantial relations, throughout of a divine nature. Its religious consecration is not first conferred by the blessing of the priest. But the pretension of religion is that it can hallow an object by its essentially external co-operation; it thereby assumes to be itself the only holy power; besides itself it knows only earthly, ungodly relations; hence it comes forward in order to consecrate them and make them holy.

But marriage—we mean, of course, marriage as the free bond of love—is sacred in itself, by the very nature of the union which is therein effected. That alone is a religious marriage, which is a true marriage, which corresponds to the essence of marriage—of love. And so it is with all moral relations. Then only are they moral,—then only are they enjoyed in a moral spirit, when they are regarded as sacred in themselves. True friendship exists only when the boundaries of friendship are preserved with religious conscientiousness, with the same conscientiousness with which the believer watches over the dignity of his God. Let friendship be sacred to thee, property sacred, marriage sacred,— sacred the well-being of every man; but let them be sacred *in and by themselves*.

In Christianity the moral laws are regarded as the commandments of God; morality is even made the criterion of piety; but ethics have nevertheless a subordinate rank, they have not in themselves a religious significance. This belongs only to faith. Above morality hovers God, as a being distinct from man, a being to whom the best is due, while the remnants only fall to the share of man. All those dispositions which ought to be devoted to life, to man,—all the best powers of humanity, are lavished on the being who wants nothing. The real cause is converted into an impersonal means, a merely conceptional, imaginary cause usurps the place of the true one. Man thanks God for those benefits which have been rendered to him even at the cost of sacrifice by his fellow man. The gratitude which he expresses to his benefactor is only ostensible; it is paid, not to him, but to God. He is thankful, grateful to God, but unthankful to man. Thus is the moral sentiment subverted in religion! Thus does man sacrifice man to God! The bloody human sacrifice is in fact only a rude, material expression of the innermost secret of religion. Where bloody human sacrifices are offered to God, such sacrifices are regarded as the highest thing, physical existence as the chief good. For this reason life is sacrificed to God, and it is so on extraordinary occasions; the supposition being that this is the way to show him the greatest honor. If Christianity no longer, at least in our day, offers bloody sacrifices to its God, this arises, to say nothing of other reasons, from the fact that physical existence is no longer regarded as the highest good. Hence the soul, the emotions are now offered to God, because these are held to be something higher. But the common case is, that in religion man sacrifices some duty towards man—such as that of respecting the life of his fellow, of being grateful to him— to a religious obligation,—sacrifices his relation to man to his relation to God. The Christians, by the idea that God is without wants, and that he is only an object of pure adoration, have certainly done away with many pernicious conceptions. But this freedom from wants is only a metaphysical idea, which is by no means part of the peculiar nature of religion. When the need for worship is supposed to exist only on one side, the subjective side, this has the invariable effect of one-sidedness, and leaves the religious emotions cold; hence, if not in express words, yet in fact, there must be attributed to God a condition corresponding to the subjective need, the need of the worshipper, in order to establish reciprocity. All the positive definitions of religion are based on reciprocity. The religious man thinks of God, because God thinks of him; he loves God, because God has first loved him. God is jealous of man; religion is jealous of morality; it sucks away the best forces of morality; it renders to man only the things that are man's, but to God the things that are God's; and to Him is rendered true, living emotion,—the heart.

When in times in which peculiar sanctity was attached to religion, we find marriage, property, and civil law respected, this has not its foundation in religion, but in the original, natural sense of morality and right, to which the true social relations are sacred *as such*. He to whom the Right is not holy for its own sake, will never be made to feel it sacred by religion. Property did not become sacred because it was regarded as a divine institution; but it was regarded as a divine institution because it was felt to be in itself sacred. Love is not holy, because it is a predicate of God, but it is a predicate of God because it is in itself divine. The heathens do not worship the light or the fountain, because it is a gift of God, but because it has of itself a beneficial influence on man, because it refreshes the sufferer; on account of this excellent quality they pay it divine honors.

Wherever morality is based on theology, wherever the right is made dependent on divine authority, the most immoral, unjust, infamous things can be justified and established. I can found morality on theology only when I myself have already defined the divine being by means of morality. In the contrary case, I have no criterion of the moral and immoral, but merely an *un*moral, arbitrary basis, from which I may deduce anything I please. Thus, if I would found

397

morality on God, I must first of all place it in God: for Mo rality, Right, in short, all substantial relations, have their only basis in themselves, can only have a real foundation— such as truth demands—when they are thus based. To place anything in God, or to derive anything from God, is nothing more than to withdraw it from the test of reason, to institute it as indubitable, unassailable, sacred, without rendering an account *why*. Hence self-delusion, if not wicked, insidious design, is at the root of all efforts to establish morality, right, on theology. Where we are in earnest about the right we need no incitement or support from above. We need no Christian rule of political right; we need only one which is rational, just, human. The right, the true, the good, has always its ground of sacredness in itself, in its quality. Where man is in earnest about ethics, they have in themselves the validity of a divine power. If morality has no foundation in itself, there is no inherent necessity for morality; morality is then surrendered to the groundless arbitrariness of religion.

Thus the work of the self-conscious reason in relation to religion is simply to destroy an illusion:—an illusion, however, which is by no means indifferent, but which, on the contrary, is profoundly injurious in its effects on mankind; which deprives man as well of the power of real life, as of the genuine sense of truth and virtue; for even love, in itself the deepest, truest emotion, becomes by means of religiousness merely ostensible, illusory, since religious love gives itself to man only for God's sake, so that it is given only in appearance to man, but in reality to God.

And we need only, as we have shown, invert the religious relations—regard that as an end which religion supposes to be a means—exalt that into the primary which in religion is subordinate, the accessory, the condition,—at once we have destroyed the illusion, and the unclouded light of truth streams in upon us. The sacraments of Baptism and the Lord's Supper, which are the characteristic symbols of the Christian religion, may serve to confirm and exhibit this truth.

The water of Baptism is to religion only the means by which the Holy Spirit imparts itself to man. But by this conception it is placed in contradiction with reason, with the truth of things. On the one hand, there is virtue in the objective, natural quality of water; on the other, there is none, but it is a merely arbitrary medium of divine grace and omnipotence. We free ourselves from these and other irreconcilable contradictions, we give a true significance to Baptism, only by regarding it as a symbol of the value of water itself. Baptism should represent to us the wonderful but natural effect of water on man. Water has in fact not merely physical effects, but also, and as a result of these, moral and intellectual effects on man. Water not only cleanses man from bodily impurities, but in water the scales fall from his eyes: he sees, he thinks, more clearly; he feels himself freer; water extinguishes the fire of appetite. How many saints have had recourse to the natural qualities of water, in order to overcome the assaults of the devil! What was denied by Grace has been granted by Nature. Water plays a part not only in dietetics, but also in moral and mental discipline. To purify oneself, to bathe, is the first, though the lowest of virtues. In the stream of water the fever of selfishness is allayed. Water is the readiest means of making friends with Nature. The bath is a sort of chemical process, in which our individuality is resolved into the objective life of Nature. The man rising from the water is a new, a regenerate man. The doctrine that morality can do nothing without means of grace, has a valid meaning if, in place of imaginary, supernatural means of grace, we substitute natural means. Moral feeling can effect nothing without Nature; it must ally itself with the simplest natural means. The profoundest secrets lie in common every-day things, such as supranaturalistic religion and speculation ignore, thus sacrificing real mysteries to imaginary, illusory ones; as here, for example, the real power of water is sacrificed to an imaginary one. Water is the simplest means of grace or healing for the maladies of the soul as well as of the body. But water is effectual only where its use is constant and regular. Baptism, as a single act, is either an altogether useless and unmeaning institution, or, if real effects are attributed to it, a superstitious one. But it is a rational, a venerable institution, if it is understood to typify and celebrate the moral and physical curative virtues of water.

But the sacrament of water required a supplement. Water, as a universal element of life, reminds us of our origin from Nature, an origin which we have in common with plants and animals. In Baptism we bow to the power of a pure Nature-force; water is the element of natural equality and freedom, the mirror of the golden age. But we men are distinguished from the plants and animals, which together with the inorganic kingdom we comprehend under the common name of Nature;—we are distinguished from Nature. Hence we must celebrate our distinction, our specific difference. The symbols of this our difference are bread and wine. Bread and wine are, as to their materials, products of nature; as to their form, products of man. If in water we declare: man can do nothing without Nature; by bread and wine we declare: Nature needs man, as man needs Nature. In water, human, mental activity is nullified; in bread and wine it attains self-satisfaction. Bread and wine are supernatural products,—in the only valid and true sense, the sense which is not in contradiction with reason and Nature. If in water we adore the pure force of Nature, in bread and wine we adore the supernatural power of mind, of consciousness, of man. Hence this sacrament is only for man matured into consciousness; while baptism is imparted to infants. But we at the same time celebrate here the true relation of mind to Nature: Nature gives the material, mind gives the form. The sacrament of Baptism inspires us with thankfulness towards Nature, the sacrament of bread and wine with thankfulness towards man. Bread and wine typify to us the truth that Man is the true God and Saviour of man.

Eating and drinking is the mystery of the Lord's Supper;—eating and drinking is in fact in itself a religious act; at least, ought to be so. Think, therefore, with every morsel of bread which relieves thee from the pain of hunger, with every draught of wine which cheers thy cheer, of the God, who confers these beneficent gifts upon thee,—think of Man! But in thy gratitude towards man forget not gratitude towards holy Nature! Forget not that wine is the blood of plants, and flour the flesh of plants, which are sacrificed for thy well-being! Forget not that the plant typifies to thee the essence of nature, which lovingly surrenders itself for thy enjoyment! Therefore forget not the gratitude which thou owest to the natural qualities of bread and wine! And if thou art inclined to smile that I call eating and drinking religious acts, because they are common every day acts, and are therefore performed by multitudes without thought, without emotion; reflect, that the Lord's Supper is to multitudes a thoughtless, emotionless act, because it takes place often; and, for the sake of comprehending the religious significance of bread and wine, place thyself in a position where the daily act is unnaturally, violently interrupted. Hunger and thirst destroy not only the physical but also the mental and moral powers of man; they rob him of his humanity—of understanding, of consciousness. Oh! if thou shouldst ever experience such want, how wouldst thou bless and praise the natural qualities of bread and wine, which restore to thee thy humanity, thy intellect! It needs only that the ordinary course of things be interrupted in order to vindicate to common things an uncommon significance, *to life, as such, a religious import.* Therefore let bread be sacred for us, let wine be sacred, and also let water be sacred! Amen.

[129]

FICHTE, JOHANN GOTTLIEB

FICHTE, JOHANN GOTTLIEB (1762-1814). Fichte, a German philosopher, studied at Meissen, Pforta, Jena and Leipzig to be a theologian. Shortly thereafter, he accepted a tutoring position in

Switzerland, but dissatisfied with it, he intended to accept one in Poland. En route there he met Kant whose moral and religious doctrines attracted him and caused him to change all his plans. Forthwith he wrote *An Essay Towards A Critique of All Revelation*. For some unaccountable reason, the publisher neglected to place Fichte's name on the title page; everyone hailed the essay as a new work of Kant. When the real author became known, Fichte, overnight, was recognized as a first-rate philosopher and was called to Jena to lecture on the vocation of the scholar.

Fichte lost his position because he regarded God as the moral order of the universe; he went to Berlin, and lectured on occasion at the University of Erlangen. When the French occupied Berlin, (1806) Fichte left. He returned the following year and devoted himself wholeheartedly to freeing Prussia of foreign domination. As rector of the new Berlin university, he fired his listeners with enthusiasm. His addresses to the German nation are still famous. His view of the state was socialistic, and he had visions of a league of peoples united in a moral endeavor and in true culture.

As a philosopher, he was a transcendental subjective idealist; his system reversed the idea of I, the non-I or the world, and their synthesis in experience. In his *Science of Knowledge,* he sought a complete system of reason. His life was devoted to ideals and he exemplified his thesis that the world is but the occasion for man to exercise his moral duty. "The system of freedom satisfies my heart; the opposite system destroys and annihilates it. To stand cold and unmoved, amid the current of events, a passive mirror of fugitive and passing phenomena—this existence is impossible for me. I scorn and detest it. I will love; I will lose myself in sympathy; I will know the joy and grief of life."

THE EGO

WE have to search for the absolute, first, and unconditioned fundamental principle of human knowledge. It cannot be proven, nor determined if it is to be absolute first principle.

This principle is to express that *deed-act* which does not occur among the empirical determinations of our consciousness, nor can so occur, since it is rather the basis of all consciousness, and first and alone makes consciousness possible. In representing this deed-act it is not so much to be feared that my readers will *not* think what they ought to think, as that they will think what they ought not to think. This renders necessary a *reflection* on what may perhaps for the present be taken for that deed-act, and an *abstraction* from all that does not really belong to it.

Even by means of this abstracting reflection, that deed-act, which is not empirical *fact* of consciousness, cannot become fact of consciousness: but by means of this abstracting reflection we may recognize so much; that this deed-act must necessarily be *thought* as the basis of all consciousness.

The laws according to which this deed-act must necessarily be thought as basis of human knowledge, or, which is the same, the rules according to which that abstracting reflection proceeds, have not yet been proven as valid, but are for the present tacitly presupposed as well known and agreed upon. As we proceed we shall deduce them from that fundamental principle, the establishment whereof is correct only if they are correct. This is a circle, but an unavoidable circle. And since it is unavoidable and freely admitted, it is also allowable to appeal to all the laws of general logic in establishing this highest fundamental principle.

In undertaking this abstracting reflection, we must start from some proposition which every one will admit without dispute. Doubtless there are many such. We choose the one which seems to us to open the shortest road to our purpose. In admitting this proposition, the deed-act, which we intend to make the basis of our whole science of knowledge, must be admitted; and the reflection must show *that* this deed-act is admitted the moment that proposition is admitted.

Our course of proceeding in this reflection is as follows: Any fact of empirical consciousness, admitted as such valid proposition, is taken hold of, and from it we separate one of its empirical determinations after the other, until only that remains, which can no longer be separated and abstracted from.

As such admitted proposition we take this one: A is A.

Every one admits this proposition, and without the least hesitation. It is recognized by all as completely certain and evident.

If any one should ask a proof of its certainty, no one would enter upon such a proof, but would say: This proposition is *absolutely* (*that is, without any further ground*) *certain;* and by saying this would ascribe to himself the power of *absolutely positing something.*

In insisting on the in-itself certainty of the above proposition, you posit *not* that A *is.* The proposition A is A is by no means equivalent to A *is. Being* when posited without predicate is something quite different from being when posited with a predicate. Let us suppose A to signify a space enclosed within two straight lines, then the proposition A is A would still be correct; although the proposition A *is* would be false, since such a space is impossible.

But you posit by that proposition: *If* A is, *then* A is. The question *whether* A is at all or not, does not, therefore, occur in it. The *content* of the proposition is not regarded at all: merely its *form.* The question is not whereof you know, but *what* you know of any given subject. The only thing posited, therefore, by that proposition is the *absolutely* necessary connection between the two A's. This connection we shall call X.

In regard to A itself nothing has as yet been posited. The question, therefore, arises: Under what condition *is* A?

X at least is in the Ego, and posited *through* the Ego, for it is the Ego, which asserts the above proposition, and so asserts it by virtue of X as a law, which X or law must, therefore, be given to the Ego; and, since it is asserted absolutely, and without further ground, must be given to the Ego through itself.

Whether and *how* A is posited we do not know; but since X is to designate a connection between an unknown positing of A (of the first A in the proposition A is A) and a positing of the same A, which latter positing is absolute on condition of the first positing, it follows that A, *at least in so far as that connection is posited,* is posited *in* and *through* the Ego, like X. Proof: X is only possible in relation to an A; now X is really posited in the Ego; hence, also, A must be posited in the Ego, in so far as X is related to it.

X is related to that A, in the above proposition, which occupies the logical position of subject, and also to that A which is the predicate, for both are united by X. Both, therefore, are posited in the Ego, in so far as they are posited; and the A of the predicate is posited *absolutely* if the first one is posited. Hence the above proposition may be also expressed: If A is posited *in the Ego,* then *it is posited,* or then it *is.*

Hence, by means of X, the Ego posits; that A *is* absolutely for the asserting Ego, and *is* simply because it is posited in the Ego: or that there is something in the Ego which always remains the same, and is thus able to connect or posit: and hence the absolutely posited X may also be expressed, Ego=Ego, or I am I.

Thus we have already arrived at the proposition I *am;* not as expression of a deed-act, it is true, but, at least, as expression of a *fact.*

For X is absolutely posited; this is a fact of empirical consciousness, as shown by the admitted proposition. Now X signifies the same as I am I; hence, this proposition is also absolutely posited.

But Ego is Ego, or I am I, has quite another significance than A is A. For the latter proposition had content only on a certain condition, namely, *if* A is posited. But the proposition I am I is unconditionally and absolutely valid, since it is the same as X; it is valid not only in form but also in content. In it the Ego is posited not on condition, but absolutely, with the predicate of self-equality; hence, it is posited, and the proposition may also be expressed, I *am.*

This proposition, *I am,* is as yet only founded upon a fact, and has no other validity than that of a fact. If "A= A" (or X) is to be certain, then "I am" must also be certain. Now, it is fact of empirical consciousness that we are compelled to regard X as absolutely certain; hence, also "I am" is certain, since it is the ground of the X. It follows from this, that the *ground of explanation of all facts of em-*

pirical consciousness is this: before all positing, the Ego must oe posited through itself.

I say of *all* facts; and to prove this I must show that X is the highest fact of empirical consciousness, is the basis of all others, and contained in all other facts; which, perhaps, would be admitted by all men, without proof, although the whole science of knowledge busies itself to prove it.

The proposition A is A is *asserted.* But all asserting is an act of the human mind; for it has all the conditions of such an act in empirical consciousness, which must be pre-supposed as well known and admitted in order to advance our reflection. Now, this act is based on something which has no higher ground, namely X or I am.

Hence, that which is *absolutely posited and in itself grounded* is the ground of *a certain* (we shall see hereafter of *all*) acting of the human mind; hence its pure character; the pure character of activity in itself, altogether abstracting from its particular empirical conditions.

The positing of the Ego through itself is, therefore, the pure activity of the Ego. The Ego *posits* itself; and the Ego is by virtue of this mere self-positing. Again, *vice versa:* the Ego *is* and *posits* its being, by virtue of its mere being. It is both the acting and the product of the act; the active and the result of the activity; deed and act in one; and hence the *I am* is expressive of a deed-act; and of the *only possible* deed-act, as our science of knowledge must show.

Let us again consider the proposition *I am I.* The Ego is absolutely posited. Let us assume that the first Ego of this proposition (which has the position of formal subject) is the *absolutely posited* Ego, and that the second Ego (that of the predicate) is the *being* Ego; then the absolutely valid assertion that both are one signifies: the Ego is, *because* it has posited itself.

This is, indeed, the case according to the logical form of the proposition. In A=A the first A is that which is posited in the Ego, (either absolutely, like the Ego itself, or conditionally, like any non-Ego) and in this positing of A

406

the Ego is absolutely subject; and hence the first A is also called the subject. But the second A designates that which the Ego, in now making itself the object of its own reflection discovers thus *as* posited in itself, (since it has just before itself posited the A in itself). The Ego, in asserting that proposition A=A, predicates in truth not something of A, but of itself, namely, that it has found an A posited in itself; and hence the second A is called predicate.

The Ego in the former and the Ego in the latter significance are to be absolutely Equal. Hence, the above proposition may be turned around, and then it reads: The Ego posits itself simply *because* it is. It posits itself through its mere being, and *is* through its mere being posited.

This, then, will explain clearly in what significance we here use the word Ego (I), and will lead us to a definite explanation of the Ego as absolute subject. The Ego as absolute subject is *that, the being, essence, whereof consists merely in positing itself as being.* As soon as it posits itself, it is; and as soon as it is, it posits itself; and hence the Ego is for the Ego absolute and necessary. Whatsoever is not for itself is not an Ego.

The question has been asked, What *was* I before I became self-conscious? The answer is, *I* was not at all, for I was not I. The Ego is only, in so far as it is conscious of itself. The possibility of that question is grounded upon mixing up of the Ego as *subject,* and the Ego as *object* of the reflection of the absolute subject; and is in itself altogether improper. The Ego represents itself, and in so far takes itself up in the form of representation, and now first becomes a *somewhat,* that is, an object. Consciousness receives in this form of representation a substrate, which *is,* even without the real consciousness, and which, moreover, is thought bodily. Such a condition is thought, and the question asked, *What* was the Ego at that time? that is, what is the substrate of consciousness? But even in this thought you unconsciously *add in thinking* the *absolute subject* as looking at that substrate; and hence you unconsciously add in thought the very

407

thing whereof you wanted to abstract, and thus you contradict yourself. The truth is, you cannot think anything at all without adding in thought your Ego as self-conscious; you cannot abstract from your self-consciousness; and all questions of the above kind are not to be answered, since maturely considered, they cannot be asked.

If the Ego *is* only so far as it posits itself, then it also is only *for* the positing, and posits only for the being Ego. *The Ego is for the Ego;* but if it posits itself absolutely, as it is, then it posits itself necessarily, and is necessary for the Ego. *I am only for me; but for me I am necessarily.* (By saying *for me,* I already posit my being.) *To posit itself* and *to be* is, applied to the Ego, the same. Hence, the proposition I am because I have posited myself, can also be expressed; *I am absolutely because I am.*

Again, the Ego as positing itself and the Ego as being are one and the same. The Ego is as *what* it posits itself and posits itself as *what* it is. Hence, *I am absolutely what I am.*

The immediate expression of the thus developed deed-act may be given in the following formula: *I am absolutely because I am, and I am absolutely what I am for myself.*

If this narration of the original deed-act is to be placed at the head of a science of knowledge as its highest fundamental principle, it may perhaps be best expressed thus:

The Ego posits originally its own being.

(In other words, the Ego is necessarily identity of subject and object; is itself subject-object; and it is this without further meditation.)

We started from the proposition A=A, not as if the proposition, I am, could be proven by it, but because we had to start from some one certain proposition given in empirical consciousness. And our development, also, has shown that A=A does not contain the ground of "I am," but, on the contrary, that the latter proposition is the ground of the former.

By abstracting from the content of the proposition I am, and looking merely to its form, namely, the form of drawing a conclusion from the being posited of something to its being, as we must abstract for the sake of logic, we thus obtain as *fundamental principle of logic* the proposition A=A, which can only be proven and determined through the science of knowledge. *Proven*: for A is A because the Ego which has posited A is the same as the Ego in which A is posited. *Determined*: for whatever is, is only in so far as it is posited in the Ego, and there is nothing outside of the Ego. No possible A (no *thing*) can be any thing else but an A posited in the Ego.

By abstracting, moreover, from all asserting as a determined acting, and looking merely to the general *manner* of acting, of the human mind, which is given through that form, we obtain the *category of reality*. Every thing to which the proposition A=A is applicable has reality, *in so far as that proposition is applicable to it*. That which is posited through the mere positing of any thing (in the Ego)is its reality, its essence.

[130]

FRANKLIN, BENJAMIN

FRANKLIN, BENJAMIN (1706-1790). At the beginning of his *Autobiography*, Franklin states that if Providence allowed him the choice, "he should have no objection to go over the same life from beginning to the end, requesting only the advantage authors have of correcting, in a second edition, the faults of the first." Franklin was always fond of such harmless and shrewd remarks which prevented his earnestness from being pathetic. This inclination resulted in the legend that he was not entrusted with writing the *Declaration of Independence*, because the Founding Fathers feared he might include a joke in the writing of the solemn proclamation.

Franklin, throughout his lifetime, made strenuous efforts to perfect his mind and character. He regarded a lack of moderation as incompatible with human perfection, human dignity, efficiency, and success. The story of his love and courtship of his wife proved his talents for tempering his passion. He read poetry for amusement and for the improvement of his literary style, but he did not allow himself to become absorbed in its charms. He always reacted to life zestfully, and with humorous detachment. He re-

409

garded reason as the means by which life could be conducted intelligently. In his youth, he was greatly interested in metaphysics, but he later disavowed this branch of philosophy; the problem of absolute and consistent truth left him unmoved.

He was a famous inventor and philanthropist; a skillful politician and diplomat. He always accomplished his tasks and fulfilled his duties because his moral conscience directed him to take care of the common good. Though very busy, he was always ready to obey the demands of his community and country, for he was never that completely absorbed in his own affairs. It was only to science that he was deeply devoted. In science he sought for laws that govern nature and point toward the orderliness of cosmic and human relations, though he was aware that the moral sciences of his time lagged far behind the standards of the natural sciences.

Franklin summarized his experiences by eliminating the words "certainly" and "undoubtedly" from his vocabulary. In place of them, he adopted: "I conceive; I apprehend; I imagine a thing to be so; or so it appears to me at present." Other thinkers, before and after Franklin, have gone the same way. To him, it was not only the result of reasoning, but a means of success. He especially appreciated the "advantage of change," whether it concerned his own manners, or his relations to his fellow men. Truth that is not useful was not truth to him. He formulated his creed by the words: "truth; sincerity, and integrity" as "of the utmost importance for the felicity of life." Franklin was not absorbed in utilitarianism; he enjoyed truth and integrity, "a naïve lustre," independently and successfully.

WISE SAYINGS

THE eyes of Christendom are upon us, and our honor as a people is becoming a matter of the utmost consequence to be taken care of. If we give up our rights in this contest, a century to come will not restore us to the opinion of the world; we shall be stamped with the character of . . . poltroons and fools . . . Present inconveniences are, therefore, to be borne with fortitude, and better times expected.

We make daily great improvement in *natural* [philosophy], but there is one I wish to see in *moral* philosophy; the discovery of a plan, that would induce and oblige nations to settle their disputes without first cutting one another's throats. When will human reason be sufficiently improved to see the advantage of this! When will we be convinced that even successful wars at length become misfortunes to those who unjustly commenced them and who triumphed blindly in their success, not seeing all its consequences.

I think with you, that nothing is of more importance for the public weal, than to form and train up youth in wisdom and virtue. Wise and good men are, in my opinion, the strength of a state far more so than riches or arms, which, under the management of ignorance and wickedness, often draw on destruction, instead of providing for the safety of a people. Though the culture bestowed on *many* should be successful only with a *few*, yet the influence of those few and the service in their power may be very great. . . . General virtue is more probably to be expected and obtained from the *education* of youth, than from the *exhortation* of adult persons; bad habits, and vices of the mind being, like diseases of the body, more easily prevented than cured . . .

Commerce among nations, as well as between private persons, should be fair and equitable, by equivalent exchanges and mutual supplies. Taking unfair advantages of a neighbor's necessities tho' attended with temporary success, always breeds bad blood.

The rapid progress *true* science now makes occasions my regretting sometimes that I was born so soon. It is impossible to imagine the height to which may be carried, in a thousand years, the power of man over matter. We may perhaps learn to deprive large masses of their gravity, and give them absolute levity, for the sake of easy transport. Agriculture may diminish its labor and double its produce; all diseases may by sure means be prevented or cured, not excepting even that of old age, and our lives lengthened even beyond the antediluvian standard.

Righteousness, or *justice*, is, undoubtedly of all the virtues, the surest foundation on which to create and establish a new state. But there are two nobler virtues, *industry* and *frugality*, which tend more to increase the wealth, power and grandeur of the community, than all the others without them.

411

Lost time is never found again; and what we call time enough, always proves little enough.

Diligence overcomes difficulties, sloth makes them.

The busy man has few idle visitors; to the boiling pot, the flies come not.

Laziness travels so slowly that poverty soon overtakes him.

Beware of little expenses; a small leak will sink a great ship.

Industry pays debts, despair increases them.

Mad kings and mad bulls are not to be held by treaties and packthread.

But dost thou love life, then do not squander Time, for that's the stuff Life is made of.

Glass, china, and reputation, are easily cracked, and never well mended.

Three may keep a secret, if two of them are dead.

[131]

G

GANDHI, MOHANDAS KARAMCHAND

GANDHI, MOHANDAS KARAMCHAND (1869-1948). Not only the vast majority of Hindus but also many Westerners have accorded to Gandhi the title of "Mahatma," the "great soul," and have revered him as a master of wisdom and saintliness, while also recognizing his political skill and steadfastness. At least in modern times, Gandhi has had no equal in his ability to use spiritual weapons for political aims, in his power to make the resistance of the powerless irresistible. He has been adored as the father of the new State of India. But shortly after he had realized the ideal of a free India, for which he had struggled for nearly half a century, he was assassinated by a fanatical son of his own people.

Gandhi restored the self-reliance of Hinduism after he had been imbued with the spirit of Western civilization and had rejected it. In 1889 he was called to the bar in London. Then, for seventeen years, he was a lawyer in South Africa before becoming the champion of the cause of the Indian settlers in that country. In 1914 he returned to India and in 1919 started the Satyagraha (Truth-seeking movement). From 1920 on he campaigned for non-cooperation with the British government. Devoted to Hinduism as Gandhi was, he was also inspired by Tolstoy's doctrine of non-violence which became his principal battle-cry in the struggle against British domination and was considered by him the panacea for every evil. Non-violence was conceived by him as "conscious suffering," not as meek submission to the will of the evil-doer, but "the putting of one's whole soul against the will of the tyrant." It means the restitution of the ancient Indian law of self-sacrifice. He repeatedly protested against being regarded as a visionary. Instead, he described himself as a "practical idealist" and rightly claimed "to know my millions" and to "recognize no God except the God that is to be found in the hearts of the dumb millions." But he also claimed that he recognized God's presence while the millions could not see it.

LET me for a few moments consider what Hinduism consists of, and what it is that has fired so many saints about whom we have historical record. Why has it contributed so many philosophers to the world? What is it in Hinduism that has so enthused its devotees for centuries? Did they see untouchability in Hinduism and still enthuse over it? In the midst of my struggle against untouchability I have been asked by several workers as to the essence of Hinduism. We have no simple *Kalema*, they said, that we find in Islam, nor have we *John*, Chapters 3-16 of the *Bible*. Have we or have we not something that will answer the demands of the most philosophic among the Hindus or the most matter-of-fact among them? Some have said, and not without good reason, the *Gayatri* answers that purpose. I have perhaps recited the *Gayatri Mantra* a thousand times, having understood the meaning of it. But still it seems to me that it did not answer the whole of my inspirations. Then as you are aware I have, for years past, been swearing by the *Bhagavad Gita*, and have said that it answers all my difficulties and has been my *Kamadhenu*, my guide, my open sesame, on hundreds of moments of doubts and difficulty. I cannot recall a single occasion when it has failed me. But it is not a book that I can place before the whole of this audience. It requires a prayerful study before the *Kamadhenu* yields rich milk she holds in her udders.

But I have fixed upon one *Mantra* that I am going to recite to you as containing the whole essence of Hinduism. Many of you I think, know the *Ishopanishad*. I learnt it by heart in Yervada Jail. But it did not then captivate me, as it has done during the past few months, and I have now come to the final conclusion that if all the *Upanishads* and all the other scriptures happened all of a sudden to be reduced to ashes, and if only the first verse in the *Ishopanishad* were left intact in the memory of Hindus, Hinduism would live for ever.

Now this *Mantra* divides itself in four parts. The first part is:

All this that we see in this great Universe is pervaded by God. Then come the second and third parts which read together, as I read them:

I divide these into two and translate them thus: *Renounce it and enjoy it.* There is another rendering which means the same thing: *Enjoy what He gives you.* Even so you can divide it into two parts. Then follows the final and most important part, which means: *Do not covet anybody's wealth or possession.* All the other *Mantras* of that ancient *Upanishad* are a commentary or an attempt to give us the full meaning of the first *Mantra.* As I read the *Mantra* in the light of the *Gita* or the *Gita* in the light of the *Mantra* I find that the *Gita* is a commentary on the *Mantra.* It seems to me to satisfy the craving of the socialist and the communist. I venture to suggest to all who do not belong to the Hindu faith that it satisfies their cravings also. And if it is true—and I hold it to be true—you need not take anything in Hinduism which is inconsistent with or contrary to the meaning of this *Mantra.* What more can a man in the street want to learn than this that the one God and Creator and Master of all that lives pervades the Universe? The three other parts of the *Mantra* follow directly from the first. If you believe that God pervades everything that He has created you must believe that you cannot enjoy anything that is not given by Him. And seeing that He is the Creator of His numberless children, it follows that you cannot covet anybody's possession. If you think that you are one of His numerous creatures, it behooves you to renounce everything and lay it at His feet. That means the act of renunciation of everything is not a mere physical renunciation but represents a second or new birth. It is a deliberate act, not done in ignorance. It is therefore a regeneration. And then since he who holds the body must eat and drink and clothe himself, he must naturally seek all that he needs from Him. And he gets it as a natural reward of that renunciation. As if this

415

was not enough the *Mantra* closes with this magnificent thought: *Do not covet anybody's possession*. The moment you carry out these precepts, you become a wise citizen of the world, living at peace with all that lives. It satisfies one's highest aspirations on this earth and hereafter. No doubt it will not satisfy the aspirations of him who does not believe in God and His undisputed sovereignty. It is no idle thing that the Maharaja of Travancore is called *Padmabhadas*. It is a great thought we know that God himself has taken the title of *Dasanudas* Servant of servants. If all the princes would call themselves servants of God, they would be correctly describing themselves, but they cannot be servants of God unless they are servants of the people. And if *zamndars* and moneyed men and all who have possessions would treat themselves as trustees and perform the act of renunciation that I have described, this world would indeed be a blessed world to live in.

[133]

GASSENDI, PIERRE

GASSENDI, PIERRE (1592-1655). When, in 1633, Galileo was tormented by his condemnation and was watched narrowly by the Inquisition, many scholars were terrified, and not a few denied any connection with him. But Gassendi, a Catholic priest, known by his writings on astronomy, physics and mathematics, wrote a letter to Galileo that had to pass the censorship of the Inquisition, as Gassendi knew. He comforted Galileo by protesting that the ecclesiastical sentence had nothing to do with the conscience of a scientist, and Galileo had no reason to accuse himself of any moral failure. There were not many savants who acted as frankly as Gassendi did.

Gassendi himself was wise, or at least cautious enough to avoid persecution on the part of the Church, although he professed materialism and criticized Descartes' idealistic views. For Gassendi combined his atomistic materialism with the belief in the Biblical God, and asserted that the atoms, conceived in accordance with the doctrines of Democritus and Epicurus, were created by the Christian God. Gassendi therefore was called the "Christianized Epicurus." Also in his personal life, Gassendi knew how to be a dignified priest, a learned theologian, and how to enjoy the society of witty

416

and gay men, no matter whether they were faithful Christians or libertines.

ACTIVE HAPPINESS

SUPPOSING that there are two kinds of life and thus two sorts of happiness, the philosophers have always preferred the contemplative to the active life. Nevertheless, that does not prevent those whom birth or genius, hazard or necessity has pushed into any business from keeping a laudable and convenient tranquility. For he who undertakes it not at random but after mature consideration, looks at human things not from the midst of the crowd but from an elevated point. He knows that in the actual course of affairs a hundred things might happen which human sagacity might not foresee. He provides not specifically, but generally for all the difficulties that might happen. He is prepared to be ready often to make up his mind on the spot. He recognizes that he is the master of what is within him, but not of the things that are not depending on his free will. He performs as much as is possible for him, the duties of an honest man. He thinks that finally he shall be happy and satisfied whatever might occur. He is never too sure about the good outcome of his enterprises as not to think that they might turn out to be different from what he wished and he adjusts his mind in such a manner that although he might have to stand bad luck he would nevertheless bear it constantly and patiently. This one, I say, who is endowed and disposed in such a manner, will be engaged in any business, will be able to act in the outside world in such a way that in the middle of all agitation and troubles of his affairs he will keep inwardly and within himself a sweet and calm tranquillity.

[134]

GENTILE, GIOVANNI

GENTILE, GIOVANNI (1875-1944). Gentile was the official philosopher of Italian fascism. After having been a professor of philosophy at the University of Palermo from 1907 to 1914, and later at the University of Pisa, he was Mussolini's minister of Public Education from 1922 to 1924. Then he became senator of the kingdom, and was entrusted with what Mussolini called "reform of the educational system." In this position, he dismissed all teachers who were suspected of being liberals or democrats; but, since he was not a member of the Fascist Party, Gentile did not satisfy all demands concerning the curriculum. Benedetto Croce protested against Gentile's purge with vigor but without result.

According to Gentile, as he explained it in his principal works *General Theory of the Spirit as Pure Act* (1916) and *Logic as Theory of Knowledge* (1917), philosophy isolated from life and life isolated from philosophy are equally symptoms of cultural bankruptcy. Philosophy must penetrate into human life, govern and mould it. Thought is all-embracing. No one can go out of the sphere of thinking or exceed thought. Reality is not thinkable but in relation to an activity by means of which it becomes thinkable. Every experience occurs between a subject which is one, a center, and of spiritual nature, and a multitude of phenomena which lack such a center. The Real can be thought of only as posing itself, not as being. Reality therefore is spiritual. The spirit is both unity and multitude, and is recognized in the pure act. Gentile added that the "one-multiple" spirit is the same as the ineffable one of the mystics. By this remark, Gentile deviated from Hermann Cohen who characterized thinking as pure creation. Benedetto Croce objected that Gentile's "pure act" is nothing other than Schopenhauer's will. While Gentile followed Hegel, in general he tried to combine the Hegelian phenomenology of the spirit with Berkeley's ideas on perception.

SCIENCE AND PHILOSOPHY

WE not only distinguish philosophy from art and religion, we also distinguish it from science. Although science has the cognitive character of philosophy yet *stricto sensu* it is not philosophy. It has not the universality of its object which philosophy has, and therefore it has not the *critical and systematic* character of philosophy. Every science is one among others and is therefore particular. When a particular science transcends the limits of its own special subject matter it tends to be transformed into philosophy. As particular, that is, concerned with an object which itself is particular and can

418

have its own meaning apart from other objects which co-exist with it, science rests on the naturalistic presupposition. For it is only when we think of reality as nature that it presents itself to us as composed of many elements, any one of which can be made the object of a particular investigation. A naturalistic view is the basis, then, of the analytical character of every science. Thence the logically necessary tendency of science in every period towards mechanism and materialism.

Again, every science presupposes its object. The science arises from the presupposition that the object exists before it is thought, and independently altogether of being known. Had science to apprehend the object as a creation of the subject, it would have first to propound the problem of the position of the real in all its universality, and then it would no longer be science, but philosophy. In presupposing the object as a datum to be accepted not proved, a natural datum, a fact, every particular science is necessarily empirical, unable to conceive knowledge otherwise than as a relation of the object to the subject extrinsic to the nature of both. This relation is sensation or a knowing which is a pure fact on which the mind can then work by abstraction and generalization. Science, therefore, is *dogmatic*. It does not prove and it cannot prove its two fundamental presuppositions: (1) that its object exists; (2) that the sensation, the initial and substantial fact of knowledge, which is the immediate relation with the object, is valid.

Philosophy, on the other hand, proposes to prove the value of the object, and of every form of the object, in the system of the real, and its why and how. It gives, or seeks to give, an account not only of the existence of the objects which the particular sciences dogmatically presuppose, but even of the knowing (which itself also is at least a form of reality) whereby every science is constituted. And therefore philosophy, in being systematic, is critical.

[135]

419

GEORGE, HENRY

GEORGE, HENRY (1839-1897). John Dewey called Henry George "one of the world's great social philosophers, certainly the greatest which our country has produced." Dewey's appraisal of George has not been shared by many Americans. The great majority of American economists have severely criticized George's insistence on nationalization of land and on the "single tax," the two principal tenets of his system. In 1941, George R. Geiger stated that Henry George was neglected and even ignored in liberal and progressive circles and that he had been forgotten by his conservative critics. But the statement is true for America only. In England and Germany the doctrine of Henry George always had greater influence than in his homeland, and it still has many adherents there. His *Progress and Poverty* (1880) became of special consequence for British socialism, as well as for the *Socialist League,* led by William Morris, and the *Fabian Society,* the great training school for labor leaders.

George regarded political economy as justified only when directed by moral principles and social consciousness. He founded his movement for abolition of private landed property upon both religious and political grounds. Land, he said, is the creation of God; it therefore must be common property of all people. Land, he also argued, is the physical foundation of the entire economic process. Therefore, he concluded, no democracy is secure as long as it is in private hands.

George repudiated materialism and evolutionism. He vigorously attacked Herbert Spencer because he had, in 1850, declared that property in land was wrong and in 1882 recanted what George considered the fundamental truth.

DEMOCRACY'S DANGER

To turn a republican government into a despotism the basest and most brutal, it is not necessary formally to change its constitution or abandon popular elections. It was centuries after Caesar before the absolute master of the Roman world pretended to rule other than by authority of a Senate that trembled before him.

But forms are nothing when substance is gone, and the forms of popular government are those from which the substance of freedom may most easily go. Extremes meet, and a government of universal suffrage and theoretical equality may, under conditions which impel the change, most readily become a despotism. For there despotism advances in the name and with the might of the people. The single source of power once secured, everything is secured. There is no unfranchised class to whom appeal may be made, no privileged orders who in defending their rights may defend those of all. No bulwark remains to stay the flood, no eminence to rise above it. They were belted barons led by a mitered archbishop who curbed the Plantagenet with Magna Charta; it was the middle classes who broke the pride of the Stuarts; but a mere aristocracy of wealth will never struggle while it can hope to bribe a tyrant.

And when the disparity of condition increases, so does universal suffrage make it easy to seize the source of power. . . . Given a community with republican institutions, in which one class is too rich to be shorn of its luxuries, no matter how public affairs are administered, and another so poor that a few dollars on election day will seem more than any abstract consideration; in which the few roll in wealth and the many seethe with discontent as a condition of things they know not how to remedy, and power must pass into the hands of jobbers who will buy and sell it as the Praetorians sold the Roman purple, or into the hands of demagogues who will seize and wield it for a time, only to be displaced by worse demagogues.

[136]

GERSONIDES

GERSONIDES (1288-1344). Levi ben Gershom, called Gersonides, was the greatest astronomer of his time. His writings attracted the interest of Kepler and his inventions, the "Jacob's staff" to measure visual angles and the *camera obscura*, became of great use. He also wrote on physics, physiology, mathematics, logic, ethics, psychology, metaphysics, the Bible and Talmud. Whatever he dealt with, he did so in a new manner. In some regards he was a precursor of

421

Galileo, in others even of modern thinkers like Bertrand Russell, for Gersonides' principal problem in general philosophy was the relation between individual experience and the body of scientific knowledge, or the way science can be developed and subsist in the course of history. As a philosopher of religion, Gersonides, in his principal work *Milhamoth Adonai* (The Wars of the Lord), made a vigorous effort to integrate the historical experience of the Jewish people into a conception of the universe that rests upon the secular sciences of astronomy, physics and the other branches with which he was acquainted. He insisted that scientific research must be conducted independently of the Torah, which, he said, does not compel men to believe what is not true. But he was convinced that truth, in accordance with modern science, is contained in the Torah, though not explicitly, and that the history of the Jewish people reflects and confirms the universal truth, in whose discovery time plays an important part.

A large part of Gersonides' writings is either lost or still unpublished.

IS THE UNIVERSE CREATED OR EXTERNAL?

IT behooves us first of all to point out the great difficulty of this investigation, as this will lead us to some extent to make the investigation into this problem more complete. For by being aware of the difficulty of a problem, we are guided to the way which leads us to the attainment of the truth thereof.

The fact that the philosophers who have hitherto investigated it greatly differ from one another in their opinions concerning it points to its difficulty; for this proves that arguments may be derived from the nature of existing things, wherewith each of the conflicting views can be either established or refuted. And it is very difficult to investigate a problem with such a peculiarity.

What undoubtedly points to the great difficulty inherent in this enquiry is the fact that we have to investigate whether all existing things were created by God, who is blessed, after a period of non-existence, or were never created at all. Now it is manifest that if we desire to fathom one of the attributes of an object, by the way of speculative investigation, whether that object possesses that attribute or not, it is

422

first of all necessary that we should know the essence of the object and its attributes. For it is only through them that we may attain to that which we seek to know. It is thus evident that one who desires to investigate this problem thoroughly must first of all know the essence and attributes of the thing under examination as far as it is possible for man to perceive. This would necessitate that a man desirous of thoroughly investigating this subject should know the nature and the attributes of all existing things, so that he may be able to explain whether there is among them a thing or an attribute which would lead us to the conclusion that the universe was not created; or whether there is among them a thing or an attribute which would lead us to the conclusion that the universe was created; or whether there is not among them a thing or an attribute from which it could be concluded either that the universe was created, or that it was not created. The matter being so, a man, to whom the knowledge of one of the existing things or of the attributes thereof, so far as a human being can possibly know, is inaccessible, is unable to make as thorough an investigation of this problem as is humanly possible. Now it is evident that to obtain as thorough a knowledge of all existing things and of their attributes as is humanly possible is extremely difficult.

What makes this investigation more difficult is the fact that the investigator must necessarily have some knowledge of the First Cause as far as it is possible. For this enquiry leads him to investigate whether God, who is blessed, could possibly have existed at first without this world, which He afterwards brought into existence and created, or it is necessary that the world should have always existed with Him. It is, however, evident from the preceding argument itself that it is necessary for a man, desirous of making this investigation as perfect as possible, to know of the essence of God, who is blessed, all that can be attained, so that he may be able to decide accurately whether God, who is blessed, can possibly be active at one time, and cease to be active

423

at another time, or whether this is impossible. This greatly adds to the difficulty of this investigation, since our knowledge of the essence of the First Cause is necessarily slight, as has become manifest from the preceding.

Another point which makes this investigation still more difficult is the circumstance that it is hard to know from which essences or attributes of existing things it is possible for us to attain to the truth of this problem. For it is necessary that a man, desirous of making this investigation perfect, should know this at the very outset, otherwise he can only attain to the truth thereof by accident.

The statement of the philosopher, as recorded by the author of the *Guide*, points to the difficulty of this investigation. It is as follows: 'As for the things concerning which we have no argument, and which are too high for us, our statement about them is, according to this, as difficult as our statement whether the world is eternal or not.' This shows that this question was considered extremely difficult by the philosopher, so that he was perplexed and doubtful about it, despite the numerous arguments he mentioned to prove that the universe is eternal. The reason for that is undoubtedly because the philosopher assumed that there were numerous arguments likewise to prove that the universe was created, and that his own arguments did not in any way establish the truth in this matter; and this is the very truth, as will be explained further on. Now if this question was considered difficult by the philosopher, despite his high rank of wisdom, how much more difficult would it be to other men who are lower than he on the ladder of knowledge.

And indeed we find that the opinions of the ancients concerning this investigation are diametrically opposed to one another. Some maintain that the universe was created and destroyed an endless number of times. Others hold that it was created only once; these are divided into two opinions: some of them think that the universe was created out of something, as, for instance, Plato and the later philosophers who follow his doctrine; while others think that the universe was created out of absolute non-existence, as for instance the early Mutakallimites, like Yahya the grammarian, according to what Ibn Roshd recorded of him in his commentary on the *Metaphysics*. In this theory they were followed by the Mutakallimites. This view was also adopted by the great philosopher, the author of the *Guide*, and by many of the sages of our religion. But there are still others who maintain that the universe is eternal. This is the theory of the philosopher and his followers. It is evident that the cause of their disagreement concerning these doctrines is the variety of objects from which they derived their proofs with regards to the nature of existing things, or because they were compelled by the Torah, or because of these two causes combined.

[137]

GEULINCX, ARNOLD

GEULINCX, ARNOLD (1624-1669). For twelve years, Geulincx was professor at the University of Louvain, Belgium, a stronghold of Catholic orthodoxy. Then he was converted to Calvinism, and became professor at the University of Leyden, Holland, at that time the center of learning, and an asylum for scholars who had been persecuted in their native country. He wrote all of his works in Latin, and died before his principal books, namely *Ethica* and *Metaphysica* could be published.

Although Geulincx often and intensely dealt with metaphysical questions, he was even more interested in ethics, but did not separate one from another. On the contrary, his ethics is founded upon metaphysics, though he also used psychological experience for his argumentation. He summed up his doctrine in the words: *Ita est, ergo ita sit* (So it is, therefore be it so). His view on life is colored with optimistic resignation. His steady confidence in God does not shut his eyes to the shortcomings of the existing world; if he expressed the idea of what Leibniz, about twenty-five years after Geulincx' death, has called the "pre-established harmony," he did not intend to assert that the existing world was good or the best of all possible but rather that it were good enough for Man who is morally and intellectually far from perfection.

Geulincx was a man of moderation, opposite to any kind of extremism. Following Descartes, he regarded doubt as the force

425

that makes Man ask for truth. He appreciated the educational value of provisional scepticism, but demanded that mature men must believe in God whom he regarded as the first cause of all things, without denying second causes. Geulincx therefore, while adopting the Scholastic term of occasional cause, held that occasionalism was an indispensable hypothesis, apt to explain natural and mental facts, but was far from the radical standpoint of Malebranche who published his views only five years after Geulincx' death.

THE PHILOSOPHER'S VIEW ON PASSION

AFTER philosophers noticed that the activities of the mob are directed by passion, they resolved to insist on a contrary conduct of life and tried to act against their own passions. But, in doing so, they became not wiser than the mob, though, in a different, maybe more brilliant, manner, insane. Thus they came to the same state of mind as the mob, although sometimes by a sideways or roundabout route.

Some of these philosophers endeavored to extinguish all of their passions, as did the Cynics and Stoics. That is evidently madness, for we cannot extinguish passion without destroying our whole body.

If there really is something that is permanently certain, it is the certainty that passion cannot be eliminated because it is a constituent of what is good in human conditions. Passions are not bad. Some of them are morally neutral, others are good by nature, and we are obliged to tolerate them.

Just a little wiser are those philosophers who are not prepared to extinguish all passions—what would be insane, impossible, inadmissible—but to omit or to suspend all actions which they consider caused by passion. Plato belongs to this group.

In this regard we can discern four strata of philosophers —namely, first, Cynics and Stoics; second, Platonists; and finally two schools of mortification.

They all are acting against reason. They, therefore, are themselves directed by passion. For, whenever we act, we act

426

deliberately, and our impulse is either reason or any kind of passion.

[138]

GILSON, ETIENNE

GILSON, ETIENNE (1884-   ). While Jacques Maritain is the outstanding militant exponent of the philosophy of Aquinas in our time, Gilson is its outstanding historian. But, in analyzing Thomism historically, Gilson does not lack the fighting spirit. He defends his master by attacking what is called modern philosophy, and he does so both by special studies and by outlining large aspects, in order to prove that Thomism has not the ambition of achieving philosophy once and for all but rather of keeping philosophical thought alive, and that Thomism is able to offer a basis for relating reality as we know it to the permanent principles in whose light all the changing problems of science, of ethics or of the arts must be solved. To Gilson, Thomism is by no means identical with Scholasticism, but rather a revolt against it. Gilson does not believe in systems of philosophy. He believes firmly in the guidance of such principles which, in the course of the history of philosophy, have become evident as an impersonal necessity for philosophical inquiry and orientation. History of philosophy, therefore, is, for him, by far more a part of philosophy itself than history of science is a part of science. It is possible, he says, to become a competent scientist without knowing much about history of science, but no man can carry very far his own philosophical reflections, unless he first studies the history of philosophy. For Gilson, there have been only three really great metaphysicians, viz., Plato, Aristotle and Aquinas, and none of them had a philosophical system, which would have meant the abolition of philosophy. From the Middle Ages until the present time three great experiments for founding a system have been attempted, and all of them have failed. The medieval, the Cartesian and the modern experiment, represented by Immanuel Kant and Auguste Comte have broken down. The result, as Gilson sees it, is the reduction of philosophy to science. Its consequences would be the abdication of the right to judge and rule nature, the conception of Man as a mere part of nature, and the green light for the most reckless social adventures to play havoc with human lives and institutions. Gilson is convinced that the revival of the philosophy of Aquinas opens the way out of that zone of danger.

427

THE only way to ascertain what the free will can do is to define what it is. Knowing its nature, you will find in that knowledge a safe rule to define the power of the will as well as its limitations. If, on the contrary, you start on the assumption that it is safer to keep a little below the line, where are you going to stop? Why, indeed, should you stop at all? Since it is pious to lessen the efficacy of free will, it is more pious to lessen it a little more, and to make it utterly powerless should be the highest mark of piety. In fact, there will be mediaeval theologians who come very close to that conclusion, and even reach it a long time before the age of Luther and Calvin. Nothing, of course, would have been more repellent to St. Bonaventura than such a doctrine; the only question here is: was St. Bonaventura protected against it? If we allow pious feelings to decree what nature should be, we are bound to wrong nature, for how could we find in piety a principle of self-restriction? In theology, as in any other science, the main question is not to be pious, but to be right. For there is nothing pious in being wrong about God!

If piety is not theology, still less is it philosophy. Yet it cannot be denied that, as a philosopher, St. Bonaventura sometimes allowed himself to be carried away by his religious feelings. In dealing with the nature of causality, for instance, two different courses were open to him. First, he could favor the view that where there is efficient causality, something new, which we call effect, is brought into existence by the efficacy of its cause; in this case, every effect can be rightly considered as a positive addition to the already existing order of reality. Or St. Bonaventura could maintain, with St. Augustine, that God has created all things present and future at the very instant of creation. From this second point of view, any particular being, taken at any time of world history, should be considered, so to speak, as the seed of all those other beings, or events, that are to flow from it according to the laws of divine providence. It is typical of St. Bonaventura's theologism that he always clung to this second interpretation of causality. He never could bring himself to think that efficient causality is attended by the springing up of new existences. To him, such a view practically amounted to crediting creatures with a creative power that belongs only to God. An effect, says Bonaventura, is to its cause as the rose is to the rosebud. It is permissible to appreciate the poetic quality of his comparison and the religious purity of his intention, without overlooking its philosophical implications.

[139]

GINZBERG, ASHER

GINZBERG, ASHER (1856-1927). Best known under his pseudonym, Ahad Haam, (one of the people), Ginzberg became noted as a philosopher and contributor to the revival of the Hebrew language and Hebrew literature. He also played a significant role in the modern Jewish nationalist movement.

Although his writings deal principally with Jewish affairs, his fundamental ideas are of general interest. Dissatisfied with material evolution, he emphasized the importance of spiritual evolution. He concentrated upon the moral aspects of all problems, rejecting that relationship between ethics and religion where the role of ethics is limited only to the confines of a sociological frame of reference. He regarded ethics as the most important determinant in national character and, for that reason, insisted that the national development of ethical views precedes all political activity. His aim was to harmonize nationalistic sentiments with the necessary sense of responsibility for the future of human civilization. The success of that aim will depend on one's devotion to the ideals of justice enunciated by the prophets of the Old Testament.

His concept of Zionism established him as a genuine philosopher. It is founded upon an original explanation of reality and ideals. For many years he was opposed to political Zionism, advocating, instead, the establishment of a Jewish cultural center in Palestine. This, he hoped, would become a "center of emulation" for Jews dispersed all over the world, effectively raising their cultural standards, and inspiring them to produce a genuine Jewish culture.

EVEN when the world as a whole is at peace, there is no rest or peace for its inhabitants. Penetrate to the real life, be it of worms or of men, and beneath the veil of peace you will find an incessant struggle for existence, a constant round of aggression and spoliation, in which every victory involves a defeat and a death.

Yet we do distinguish between time of war and time of peace. We reserve the term "war" for a visible struggle between two camps, such as occurs but seldom—a struggle that we can observe, whose causes and effects we can trace, from beginning to end. But to all the continual petty wars between man and man, of which we know in a general way that they are in progress, but of which we cannot envisage all the details and particulars, we give the name of "peace," because such is the normal condition of things.

In the spiritual world also there is war and peace; and here also "peace" means nothing but a number of continual petty wars that we cannot see—wars of idea against idea, of demand against demand, of custom against custom. The very slightest change in any department of life—as, for instance, the substitution of one letter for another in the spelling of a word—can only be brought about by a battle and a victory; but these tiny events happen silently, and escape observation at the time. It is only afterwards, when the sum total of all the changes has become a considerable quantity, that men of intelligence look backwards, and find to their astonishment that everything—opinions, modes of life, speech, pronunciation—has undergone vast changes. These changes appear to have taken place automatically; we do not know in detail when they came about, or through whose agency.

Peace, then, is the name that we give to a continuous, gradual development. But in the spiritual world, as in the material, there is sometimes a state of war; that is, a visible struggle between two spiritual camps, two complete systems,

430

the one new, the other old. The preparations for such a war are made under cover, deep down in the process of continuous development. It is only when all is in readiness that the war breaks out openly, with all its drums and tramplings; and then a short space of time sees the most far-reaching changes.

The character of these changes, as well as the general course of the war, depends chiefly on the character of the new system of thought that raises the storm. They differ according as the system is wholly positive, wholly negative, or partly positive and partly negative.

A new *positive* system comes into existence when the process of continuous development produces in the minds of a select few some new positive concept. This may be either a belief in some new truth not hitherto accepted by society, or the consciousness of some new need not hitherto felt by society; generally the two go together. This new conception, in accordance with a well-known psychological law, gives rise to other conceptions of a like nature, all of which strengthen one another, and become knit together, till at last they form a complete system. The center point of the system is the new positive principle; and round this center are grouped a number of different beliefs, feelings, impulses, needs, and so forth, which depend on it and derive their unity from it.

A new system such as this, though essentially and originally it is wholly positive, cannot help including unconsciously some element of negation. That is to say, it cannot help coming into contact, on one side or another, with some existing system that covers the same ground. It may not damage the essential feature, the center, of the old system; but it will certainly damage one of the conceptions on its circumference, or, at the very least, it will lessen the strength of men's attachment to the old principles. When, therefore, the reformers begin to put their system into practice, to strive for the attainment of what they need by the methods in which they believe, their action necessarily arouses opposition on the part of the more devoted adherents of the old system,

with which the reformers have unwittingly come into conflict. The result of this opposition is that the new system
spreads, and attracts to its ranks all those who are adapted
to receive it. As their number increases, the animosity of
their opponents grows in intensity; and so the opposition
waxes stronger and stronger, until it becomes war to the
knife.

At first the disciples of the new teaching are astounded
at the accusations hurled at them. They find themselves
charged with attempting to overthrow established principles;
and they protest bitterly that no such thought ever entered
their minds. They protest with truth: for, indeed, their whole
aim is to add, not to take away. Intent on their task of addition, they overlook the negation that follows at its heels;
even when the negation has been made plain by their opponents, they strive to keep it hidden from others, and to ignore
its existence themselves, and they do not recognize the artificiality of the means by which they attain this end.

The older school, on the other hand, who derive all
their inspiration from the old doctrine, are quick to see or
feel the danger threatened by the new teaching; and they
strive, therefore, to uproot the young plant while it is still
tender. But as a rule they do not succeed. Despite their
efforts, the new system finds its proper place; gradually the
two systems, the new and the old, lose some of their more
sharply opposed characteristics, share the forces of society
between them in proportion to their relative strength, and
ultimately come to terms and live at peace. By this process
society has been enriched; its tree of life has gained a new
branch; its spiritual equipment has received a positive addition.

[140]

GIOBERTI, VINCENZO

GIOBERTI, VINCENZO (1801-1852). The part Gioberti acted in
the history of the Italian struggle for national unity is more im-

portant than the consequence of his philosophical thoughts. Gioberti was a faithful son of the Catholic Church and a convinced
liberal in the sense of early nineteenth-century liberalism. An ordained priest in 1825, he sympathized with the revolutionaries who
endeavored to liberate Italy from Austrian domination but differed
from them because he intended to entrust the Pope with the task
of organizing the country politically. Popes Leo XII, and Pius VIII
and Gregory XVI were opposed to any change of both the political
and the cultural order, and Gioberti was exiled to France in 1833.
When Pius IX was elected Pope in 1846, Gioberti built his hopes
upon him, and for a short time, the new Pope seemed to justify
Gioberti's expectations. After the outbreak of the revolution in
1848, Gioberti returned to Italy but he was soon disappointed, for
the revolution was crushed and Pius IX denied his early liberalism.
Gioberti continued in his efforts to reconcile the papacy and political liberalism and to defend the holy see against reproaches on
the part of the liberals. But his strength was broken by his painful
experiences, and he died soon after the end of the revolution.

In Gioberti's philosophy there is a conspicuous difference between his fundamental concepts and his method. While his method
relied upon immediate intuition of the Absolute, his system was concerned with the dialectical relations between essence and existence.
He stated that there is a permanent processus by virtue of which
essence creates existence, and existence returns to essence. The individual, whose source is divine, is subject to the same processus. The
universal spirit returns to universality after having passed the
stages from sensibility to intelligibility. Gioberti's last years were
all the more unhappy since, in addition to his political failure, he
became aware of the severe opposition of Italian philosophers to
his doctrine.

THE TWO HUMANITIES

ONE can distinguish two orders of humanities: One of nature and one of grace. Stemming both from one man they
grew successively. But the natural order, having lost any
moral unity, propagates by generation, while the predestined
order propagates by election and maintains the spiritual
unity which confers on it its privilege. The former is a
material society consisting more of bodies than of souls,
lacking as it does the integrity of the ideal principle. The
latter is a spiritual society, a council of intelligences that

originate in the Idea and that are strictly united within only one body. Both proceed from one Individual and pass successively through the threefold ring of the family, the nation and the assemblage of nations. Both are tending toward a great universality of the future from which both are still far off. Both are progressive and move from the individual unity in order to reach the universal unity. Unity is their beginning and their end. Divided in their march toward the future type, they are imperfect; for one is lacking the unity characteristic of the elected race, the other, embracing only one part of humanity, does not possess all the variety characteristic of the natural race. But when each of them will have completed its course, they will merge again and will complete each other naturally. The natural species will become, still in the order of time, the elected species and the restored primitive unity of our species will be led to its ultimate perfection. At the present moment, the Church through election and spiritual generation represents the human race set up in a superhuman fashion. It can be defined, in this respect, as the reorganization of the human generation divided and reunited by grace by means of the ideal unity.

[141]

GOBINEAU, JOSEPH ARTHUR, COMTE DE

GOBINEAU, JOSEPH ARTHUR, COMTE DE (1816-1882). Not only in his youth but in later years, Gobineau was enthralled by dreams of his miraculous greatness. He felt that he was the descendant of Vikings and condottieri, and in the midst of the plain 19th century he planned to astonish humanity by his leadership in war on sea and land. Reality forced him to acquiesce in a more modest conduct of life. But, after a short period of difficulty, he did not reject nepotism on his behalf, and, due to the protection of high-ranking relatives, he became a diplomat who could afford to visit, or stay in, many countries, from Germany to Persia, from Sweden to Brazil.

All these favors could not overcome Gobineau's feelings of tediousness, his disdain of modern civilization which he regarded as decadent and doomed. In his book *The Inequality of Human Races* (1855-57), which was ignored in his native country, France, but hailed in Germany, Gobineau expressed his longing for and admiration of the Teutons who had once conquered Europe, shaped its civilization, and surpassed all other peoples in beauty, physical strength and spiritual creativeness. The restitution of Teutonic supremacy was considered by Gobineau as the only way to salvation. Although he carefully declined to identify modern Germans with his ideal Teutons, Gobineau's doctrine became favorite reading in Pan-German circles, above all in Richard Wagner's Bayreuth and at the court of Emperor William II who was initiated into Gobineau's doctrine by Prince Philip Eulenburg, an intimate friend of Gobineau's. A "Gobineau-Society," founded in Germany, continued to propagate his ideas until Hitler's accession. Gobineau also wrote novels and dramatic scenes in which he displayed artistic skill.

THE MEANING OF DEGENERATION

THE word *degenerate,* when applied to a people, means (as it ought to mean) that the people has no longer the same intrinsic value as it had before, because it has no longer the same blood in its veins, continual adulterations having gradually affected the quality of that blood. In other words, though the nation bears the name given by its founders, the name no longer connotes the same race; it fact, the man of a decadent time, the *degenerate* man properly so called, is a different being, from the racial point of view, from the heroes of the great ages. I agree that he still keeps something of their essence; but the more he degenerates the more attenuated does this "something" become. The heterogeneous elements that henceforth prevail in him give him quite a different nationality—a very original one, no doubt, but such originality is not to be envied. He is only a very distant kinsman of those he still calls his ancestors. He, and his civilization with him, will certainly die on the day when the primordial race unit is so broken up and swamped by the influx of foreign elements, that its effective qualities have no longer a sufficient freedom of action. It will not, of course, absolutely disappear, but it will in practice be so beaten down and enfeebled, that its power will be felt less and less as time goes on. It is at this point that all the results of degeneration will appear, and the process may be considered complete.

If I manage to prove this proposition, I shall have given a meaning to the word "degeneration." By showing how the essential quality of a nation gradually alters, I shift the responsibility for its decadence, which thus becomes, in a way, less shameful, for it weighs no longer on the sons but on the nephews, then on the cousins, then on collaterals more or less removed. And when I have shown by examples that great peoples, at the moment of their death, have only a very small and insignificant share in the blood of the founders, into whose inheritance they come, I shall thereby have explained clearly enough how it is possible for civilizations to fall—the reason being that they are no longer in the same hands. At the same time I shall be touching on a problem which is much more dangerous than that which I have tried to solve in the preceding chapters. This problem is: "Are there serious and ultimate differences of value between human races; and can these differences be estimated?"

[142]

GOEDEL, KURT

GOEDEL, KURT (1906-   ). Goedel's important discovery of the existence of nondemonstrable mathematical theorems which can neither be proved nor refuted has been considered as proof of the essential incompleteness and incompletability of mathematics.

Examining the two most comprehensive formal systems of our time, namely the *Principia Mathematica* (by Alfred N. Whitehead and Bertrand Russell) and Fraenckel's and Zermelo's system of axioms of quantity, Goedel shows that in both of these systems there are even relatively simple problems of the theory of ordinary whole numbers which cannot be decided on the ground of the axiom, and that this is not the fault of the two systems but is valid for all formal systems. Goedel holds that if we submit mathematical demonstrations to certain limitations, there certainly are undecidable formulas. But he also shows that the truth or falsehood of these formulas can be found out by methods using the metalanguage. He has prepared the proof of his own theorems by his device of arithmetization of syntax, a way of attacking syntactical problems by means of a mathematical algorism. In his lecture on *The Consistency of the Continuum Hypothesis* (1941), Goedel proves that the axiom of choice and Cantor's continuum hypothesis are consistent with the other axioms of set theory, if these axioms are consistent. His purpose is to show how the proof for theorems of a certain kind can be accomplished by a general method.

APHORISMS

THE true reason for the incompleteness inherent to all formal systems of mathematics lies in the fact that the formation of more and more higher types can be continued to the transfinite.

THE general existence theorem is a *metatheorem,* that is a theorem about the system, not in the system, and merely indicates, once and for all, how the formal derivation would proceed in the system for any given proof.

[142 A]

GOETHE, JOHANN WOLFGANG VON

GOETHE, JOHANN WOLFGANG VON (1749-1832). Goethe often expressed his resentment when he was hailed and exalted as the author of *Faust, Werther* and so many other dramatic, epic and lyrical poems but ignored as a scientist. In his later years, he constantly declared that no adequate appraisal of his work was possible without taking into account the importance of his contributions to anatomy, mineralogy, meteorology, botany, zoology, optics, and most modern scientists agree with his biographers that Goethe was right. It is true, Goethe's theory of colors is disputed, but in all the other fields, his scientific activities, especially concerning comparative morphology, are acknowledged as of high value. Moreover, there is today an almost general agreement that Goethe's life and personality cannot be comprehensively understood and appreciated without due regard to his studies on natural sciences. It was science to which Goethe devoted most of his time during many years, even decades, and it was his scientific activities that formed a conspicuous strain in his character and mind.

437

To Goethe, science meant exact observation of the phenomena, inquiry into their conditions, effects, coherence and variety. His methods were both analytical and synthetical, study of the characteristics of the individual and of general laws of formation. But, as far as science is concerned with measuring and counting, with mathematical methods, Goethe did not like it. The instrument he regarded as the most sure and precious was the human eye, and he passionately protested confidence in sensory experience.

Goethe's science and poetry were founded upon general views of philosophical character, although he remained distrustful of any technical philosophy. The only philosopher he admired without reserve, was Spinoza. He adopted his pantheism but not his determinism. Or, more precisely, he adopted his determinism to a certain extent but did not believe that life and the universe are totally determined. He even did not believe in the general validity of causality. Goethe repeatedly declared that freedom is blended, in a mysterious manner, with necessity, and that law and arbitrary forces rule the universe, working side by side. It was for these reasons that Goethe regarded man as both subject to necessity and capable of free will. In his autobiography *Fiction and Truth*, in his studies on French literature and on oriental poetry, he tried to penetrate into the realm of necessity, by inquiring into historical factors that condition the existence of the individual, but he felt himself obliged to state that all knowable factors of historical development are not sufficient to explain the peculiarity of the human individual. On the other hand, he repeatedly warned against miscalculation or neglect of historical, social and natural conditions which limit the freedom of the individual.

Goethe's philosophy spells serene resignation. But it does not mean easy acquiescence in the fact that human knowledge is limited. He constantly admonished mankind to inquire as far as possible and not to give up too quickly. It is quite another thing, said Goethe, to resign near the boundaries of human thought, than to rest within one's narrow-minded ego. What he regarded as the greatest happiness of thinking man was "to have explored whatever is explorable, and to revere silently what is inexplorable."

ACTIONS AND WORDS

ART is long, life short, judgment difficult, opportunity transient. To act is easy, to think is hard; to act according to our thought is troublesome. Every beginning is cheerful; the threshold is the place of expectation. The boy stands astonished, his impressions guide him; he learns sportfully, seriousness comes on him by surprise. Imitation is born with us; what should be imitated is not easy to discover. The excellent is rarely found, more rarely valued. The height charms us, the steps to it do not; with the summit in our eye, we love to walk along the plain. It is but a part of art that can be taught; the artist needs it all. Who knows it half, speaks much and is always wrong; who knows it wholly, inclines to act and speaks seldom or late. The former have no secrets and no force; the instruction they can give is like baked bread, savoury and satisfying for a single day; but flour cannot be sown, and seed corn ought not to be ground. Words are good, but they are not the best. The best is not to be explained by words. The spirit in which we act is the highest matter. Action can be understood and again represented by the spirit alone. No one knows what he is doing while he acts aright; but of what is wrong we are always conscious. Whoever works with symbols only is a pedant, a hypocrite, or a bungler. There are many such, and they like to be together. Their babbling detains the scholar; their obstinate mediocrity vexes even the best. The instruction which the true artist gives us opens the mind; for where words fail him, deeds speak. The true scholar learns from the known to unfold the unknown, and approaches more and more to being a master.

[143]

GORGIAS

GORGIAS (About 483-375 B.C.). Next to Protagoras, the most important and respected sophist was Gorgias, born in Leontini in Sicily, who, as leader of an embassy which was sent by his native city to Athens in order to ask for help against Syracusan aggression, succeeded in persuading the Athenians who were deeply impressed by his powerful eloquence.

Gorgias has often been mentioned as an example of longevity, and this has been attributed to his great egoism. He did not marry, and was always indifferent to both the sufferings and the happiness of other people. He developed rhetoric as an art whose possibilities are not restricted by anything, least of all by philosophy. To prove this thesis, Gorgias proceeded from Empedocles' theory of perception. He wrote a treatise *On Nature*, a *Technic of Rhetorics*, and several eulogies. Only two small fragments, probably from the treatise *On Nature*, are extant.

FRAGMENTS

NOTHING exists.

If ever anything did exist, it would be unknowable. If anything existed and would be knowable, the knowledge of it could not be conveyed to other people. For he who knows it, would be incapable to describe it to his fellow-men.

Every sign is different from what it signifies. How can anyone communicate the idea of color by means of words, since the ear does not hear colors but only sounds? And how can two persons, different one from another, have the same idea?

[144]

GREEN, THOMAS HILL

GREEN, THOMAS HILL (1836-1882). "Shut up your Mill and Spencer," Green, professor of moral philosophy at Oxford, admonished his audience, "and open your Kant and Hegel." Green repudiated the whole tradition of British philosophy, especially Locke and Hume, and became the leader of the opposition against positivism and utilitarianism in England. His oratoric power enabled him to convert many British students of philosophy to German idealism. He praised Kant's categories as "the connective tissue of the known world," derived from Kant his conception of self-distinguishing consciousness as a combining agency, and, although he did not adopt Hegel's dialectical method, he did agree with him regarding history and organized society as embodiments of divine will. He flatly rejected Locke's and Hume's assumption that sensations are the raw material of knowledge. According to Green, every experience takes place by forming relations which, consequently, are the real elements of that which is regarded as sensation. Since relations are

440

the work of human mind, reality is characterized as essentially spiritual.

Bitterly opposed as Green was to Darwin, his mind was nevertheless influenced by biological as well as Hegelian evolutionism. He held that an animal organism which has its history in time, gradually becomes the vehicle of an eternally complete consciousness, which, in itself, can have a history of the process by which the animal organism becomes its vehicle. Green even described mystical union as an evolutionary process. He exposed the foundations of his metaphysics and ethics in *Prolegomena to Ethics* (1883).

UTILITARIANISM EVALUATED

ON the whole there is no doubt that the theory of an ideal good, consisting in the greatest happiness of the greatest number, as the end by reference to which the claim of all laws and powers and rules of action on our obedience is to be tested, has tended to improve human conduct and character. This admission may be made quite as readily by those who consider such conduct and character an end in itself, as by those who hold that its improvement can only be measured by reference to an extraneous end, consisting in the quantity of pleasure produced by it; perhaps, when due account has been taken of the difficulty of deciding whether quantity of pleasure is really increased by "social progress," *more* readily by the former than by the latter. It is not indeed to be supposed that the Utilitarian theory, any more than any other theory of morals, has brought about the recognition or practice of any virtues that were not recognized and practised independently of it; or that any one, for being a theoretic Utilitarian, has been a better man—i.e. one more habitually governed by desire for human perfection in some of its forms—than he otherwise would have been. But it has helped men, acting under the influence of ideals of conduct and rules of virtuous living, to fill up those ideals and apply those rules in a manner beneficial to a wider range of persons—beneficial to them in the sense of tending to remove certain obstacles to good living in their favor. It has not given men a more lively sense of their duty to others—no theory can do that—but it has led those in whom that sense has already been awakened to be less partial in judging who the "others" are, to consider all men as the "others," and, on the ground of the claim of all men to an equal chance of "happiness," to secure their political and promote their social equality. To do this is not indeed directly to advance the highest living among men, but it is to remove obstacles to such living, which in the name of principle and authority have often been maintained.

*   *   *

Those who are glad of a topic for denunciation may, if they like, treat the prevalence of such opinions among educated men as encouraging the tendency to vicious self-indulgence in practice. No such unfairness will here be committed. There is no good reason to apprehend that there is relatively more—we may even hope that there is less—of self-indulgence than in previous generations; though, for reasons just indicated, it has a wider scope for itself, talks more of itself and is more talked about, than at times when men were more tied down by the necessities of their position. We are no more justified in treating what we take to be untrue theories of morals as positive promoters of vice, than in treating what we deem truer theories as positive promoters of virtue. Only those in whom the tendencies to vicious self-indulgence have been so far overcome as to allow the aspirations after perfection of life to take effect, are in a state to be affected either for better or for worse by theories of the good. The worst that can truly be objected against the prevalence of Hedonistic theory, just noticed, is that it may retard and mislead those who are already good, according to the ordinary sense of goodness as equivalent to immunity to vice, in their effort to be better; and the most that can be claimed for the theory which we deem truer, is that it keeps the way clearer of speculative impediments to the operation of motives, which it seeks to interpret but does not pretend to supply.

*   *   *

We should accept the view, then, that to think of ulti-mate good is to think of an intrinsically desirable form of conscious life; but we should seek further to define it. We should take it in the sense that to think of such good is to think of a state of self-conscious life as intrinsically desir-able for oneself, and for that reason is to think of it as something else than pleasure—the thought of an object as pleasure for oneself, and the thought of it as intrinsically de-sirable for oneself, being thoughts which exclude each other. The pleasure anticipated in the life is not that which renders it desirable; but so far as desire is excited by the thought of it as desirable, and so far as that desire is re-flected on, pleasure comes to be anticipated in the satisfac-tion of that desire. The thought of the intrinsically desirable life, then, is the thought of something else than pleasure, but the thought of what? The thought, we answer, of the full realization of the capacities of the human soul, of the ful-filment of man's vocation, as of that in which alone he can satisfy himself—a thought of which the content is never final and complete, which is always by its creative energy further determining its own conduct, but which for practical purposes, as the mover and guide of our highest moral ef-fort, may be taken to be the thought of such a social life as that described. The thought of such a life, again, when applied as a criterion for the valuation of the probable ef-fects of action, may be taken to be represented by the ques-tion . . . "Does this or that law or usage, this or that course of action—directly or indirectly, positively or as pre-ventive of the opposite—contribute to the better being of society, as measured by the more general establishment of conditions favorable to the attainment of the recognized virtues and excellencies, by the more general attainment of those excellencies in some degree, or by their attainment on the part of some persons in higher degree without detraction from the opportunities of others?"

The reader, however, will be weary of hearing of this ideal, and he will be waiting to know in what particular way it can afford guidance in cases of the kind supposed, where conventional morality and Utilitarian theory alike fail to do so. We have argued that no man could tell whether, by denying himself according to the examples given, he would in the whole result increase the amount of pleasant living in the world, present and to come. Can he tell any better whether he will further that realization of the ideal just described, in regard to which we admit the impossibility of saying positively what in its completeness it would be?

We answer as follows. The whole question of sacrificing one's own pleasure assumes a different aspect, when the end for which it is to be sacrificed is not an addition to a general aggregate of pleasures, but the harmonious exercise of man's proper activities in some life resting on a self-sacrificing will. According to the latter view, the individual's sacrifice of pleasure does not—as so much loss of pleasure—come into the reckoning at all; nor has any balance to be attempted of unascertainable pains and pleasures spreading over an indefinite range of sentient life. The good to be sought is not made up of pleasures, nor the evil to be avoided made up of pains. The end for which the sacrifice is demanded is one which in the sacrifice itself is in some measure attained,— in some measure only, not fully, yet so that the sacrifice is related to the complete end, not as a means in itself valueless, but as a constituent to a whole which it helps to form. That realization of the powers of the human spirit, which we deem the true end, is not to be thought of merely as something in a remote distance, towards which we may take steps now, but in which there is no present participation. It is continuously going on, though in varying and progressive degrees of completeness; and the individual's sacrifice of an inclination, harmless or even in its way laudable, for the sake of a higher good, is itself already in some measure an attainment of the higher good.

[145]

GROTIUS, HUGO (Hugues De Groot)

GROTIUS, HUGO (HUGUES DE GROOT) (1583-1645). At the age of sixteen, Grotius was already a highly successful lawyer in Leyden. He excelled as a jurist, theologian, historian, philologist, poet and diplomat. In 1619, after the defeat of the Dutch republicans, he was tried by the victorious monarchists and sentenced to prison for life, but, in 1621, he escaped to France. Thereafter he lived as an exile, internationally respected as a scholar, and later was recognized by his own country as one of the greatest Dutchmen of all times. For about fifteen years, Grotius was Swedish minister to Paris and accomplished a number of difficult tasks while negotiating with Richelieu.

Grotius was not the first to expound natural law, but he was first to construct a system of international jurisprudence in which the distinction between natural and historical law was essential. According to Grotius, the principle of natural morality is written by God in the hearts and minds of mankind. It is to be ascertained by reason. On the other hand, the existing institutions and laws of the nations are products of human will. The ultimate end of legal development must be the establishment of the supreme command of natural law. For the time being, some minimum demands must be formulated in order to eliminate license in making and conducting war. Grotius' significant work *On the Law of Peace and War* (1625) was directed against arbitrary power policy and radical pacifists, although just wars were admitted. Previously, Grotius, in his *Mare Liberum* (Free Sea, 1609), had tried to secure the rights of neutral ships against ruthless force on the parts of Portugal, Spain and England.

Grotius also had a great effect on Old Testament exegesis by his cold lucidity which secured his independence of Christian traditions and enabled him to recognize the historical uniqueness of the Hebrew Bible.

THE RATIONAL BASIS OF INTERNATIONAL LAW

THE civil law, both that of Rome and that of each nation in particular, has been treated of by many, with a view either to elucidate it, through commentaries, or to present it in a compendious form. But that law which regards the relations between peoples, or between rulers of peoples, whether it proceed from nature or be instituted by divine commands or introduced by custom and tacit agreement, has been touched on by few, and has by no one been treated as a whole and in an orderly manner. And yet that this be done is of concern to the human race.

And such a work is the more necessary because of the fact that persons in our time, as well as in former ages, have held in contempt what has been done in this province of jurisprudence, as if no such thing existed, as a mere name. Every one is familiar with the saying of Euphemius in Thucydides, that for a king or city who has authority to maintain, nothing is unjust which is useful; and to the same effect is the saying that with good fortune equity is where strength is, and that the commonwealth cannot be administered without doing some wrong. To this we add that the controversies which arise between peoples and between kings commonly have war as their arbiter. But that war has nothing to do with laws is not only the opinion of the ignorant; even wise and learned men often let fall expressions which support such an opinion. For nothing is more common than to place laws and arms in opposition to each other. . . .

Since our discussion of law is undertaken in vain if there is no law, it will serve both to commend and fortify our work if we refute briefly this very grave error. And that we may not have to deal with a mob of opponents, let us appoint an advocate to speak for them. And whom can we select fitter than Carneades, who had arrived at the point— the supreme aim of his academic philosophy—where he could use the strength of his eloquence for falsehood as easily as for truth? When he undertook to argue against justice—especially, the justice of which we here treat, he found no argument stronger than this: that men had, as utility prompted, established laws, differing among different peoples as manners differed, and, among the same people, often changing with the change of times; but that there is no natural law, since all men, as well as other animals, are impelled by nature to seek their own advantage; and that either there is no justice, or if it exist, it is the highest folly since through it one harms oneself in consulting the interests of others.

But what this philosopher says, and, following him, the poet—"Nature cannot distinguish the just from the unjust," must by no means be admitted. For though man is indeed an animal, he is an uncommon animal, differing much more from all other animals than they differ from one another; this is evidenced in many actions peculiar to the human species. Among the attributes peculiar to man is the desire for society—that is for communion with his fellow-men, and not for communion simply, but for a tranquil association and one suited to the quality of his intellect; this the Stoics called *Oykeiosin*. Therefore, the statement that by nature every animal is impelled to seek only its own advantage cannot be conceded in this general form.

Even in other animals their desires for their own good are tempered by regard for their offspring and for others of their species; this we believe to proceed from some intelligence outside of themselves; for with regard to other acts not at all more difficult than these an equal degree of intelligence does not appear. The same is to be said of infants, in whom, previous to all teaching, there is manifested a certain disposition to do good to others, as is sagaciously remarked by Plutarch; for example, at that age compassion breaks forth spontaneously. A man of full age knows how to act similarly in similar cases, and he has exceptional craving for society, whose peculiar instrument, language, he alone among all animals possesses; accordingly, he has the faculty of knowing and acting according to general principles; the tendencies which agree with this faculty do not belong to all animals, but are the peculiar properties of human nature.

This concern for society, which we have now stated in a rude manner, and which is in agreement with the nature of the human intellect, is the source of law, properly so called, of which we are speaking. It is law that determines the abstention from another's property; the restitution of another's goods which we have in our possession and of any gain we have derived from such possession; the obligation to fulfill promises; the reparation for damage wrongfully done; and the retribution of punishments.

From this signification of law there has flowed another larger meaning. For man is superior to other animals not only in the social impulse, of which we have spoken, but also in his judgment in estimating what is pleasant and what is injurious—not only for the present but for the future also, and the things which may lead to good or to ill. We know, therefore, that, in accordance with the quality of the human intellect, it is congruous to human nature to follow, in such matters, a judgment rightly formed and not to be misled by fear or by the enticement of present pleasure, or to be carried away by heedless impulse; and that what is plainly repugnant to such judgment is likewise contrary to natural law, that is, to natural human law.

And here comes the question of a wise assignment in bestowing upon each individual and each body of men the things which peculiarly belong to them; this disposition will sometimes prefer the wiser man to the less wise, the neighbor to a stranger, the poor man to the rich man, according as the nature of each act and each matter requires. This question some have made a part of law, strictly and properly so called; though law, properly speaking, has a very different nature; for it consists in this—that each should leave to another what is his and give to him what is his due.

What we have said would still be in point even if we should grant, what we cannot without great wickedness, that there is no God, or that He bestows no regard upon human affairs. Since we are assured of the contrary, partly by our reason and partly by constant tradition, confirmed by many arguments and by miracles attested by all ages, it follows that God, as our creator to whom we owe our being and all that we have, is to be obeyed by us without exception, especially since He has in many ways shown himself to be supremely good and supremely powerful. Wherefore, He is able to bestow upon those who obey Him the highest rewards, even eternal rewards, since He himself is eternal; and He must be believed to be willing to do this, particularly if He has promised to do so in plain words; and this we as Christians believe, convinced by the indubitable faith of testimonies.

And here we find another origin of law, besides that natural source of which we have spoken; it is the free will of God, to which our reason indisputably tells us we must submit ourselves. But even natural law—whether it be the natural social law, or law in the looser meaning of which we have spoken—may yet be rightfully ascribed to God, though it proceed from the principles of man's inner nature; for it was in accordance with His will that such principles came to exist within us. In this sense Chrysippus and the Stoics said that the origin of law was not to be sought in any other source than Jove himself; and it may be conjectured that the Latins took the word *jus* from the name *Jove*.

It may be added that God has made these principles more manifest by the commandments which He has given in order that they might be understood by those whose minds have weaker powers of reasoning. And He has controlled the aberrations of our impulses, which drive us this way and that, to the injury of ourselves and of others; bridling our more vehement passions, and restraining them within due limits.

In the next place, since it is conformable to natural law to observe compacts (for some mode of obliging themselves was necessary among men, and no other natural mode can be imagined) civil rights were derived from that very source. For those who joined any community, or put themselves in subjection to any man or men, either expressly promised or from the nature of the case must have been understood to promise tacitly, that they would conform to

449

that which either the majority of the community, or those whom power was assigned, should determine.

And therefore what Carneades said, and what has been said by others—that utility is the mother of justice and right—is, if we are to speak accurately, not true. For the mother of natural law is human nature itself, which would lead us to desire mutual society even though we were driven thereto by other wants. The mother of civil law is obligation by compact; and since compacts derive their force from natural law, nature may be said to be the great-grandmother of civil law. But utility supplements (*accedit*) natural law. For the Author of nature ordained that we, as individuals, should be weak and in need of many things for living well, in order that we might be the more impelled to cherish society. But utility furnished the occasion for civil law; for that association or subjection of which we have spoken, was at the first instituted for the sake of some utility. Accordingly, those who prescribe for others ordinarily design, or should design, some utility in their laws.

But just as the laws of each state regard the utility of that state, so also between all states, or, at least, between most of them, certain laws could be established by consent—and it appears that laws have been established—which regard the utility, not of particular communities but of the great aggregate of communities. And this is what is called the law of nations (*jus gentium*), in so far as we distinguish it from natural law. This part of law is omitted by Carneades, who divides all law into natural law and the civil law of particular peoples; although as he was about to treat of that law which obtains between one people and another (for he subjoins a discussion upon war and acquisitions by war), he was especially called upon to make mention of law of this kind.

Moreover, Carneades improperly traduces justice when he calls it folly. For since, as he himself acknowledges, the citizen is not foolish who in a state obeys the civil law, although in consequence of such respect for the law he may lose some things which are useful to him, so too a people is not to be deemed foolish which does not estimate its interests so highly as to disregard the common laws between peoples for the sake of its own advantage. The reason is the same in both cases. For as a citizen who disobeys the civil law for the sake of present utility destroys that in which the perpetual utility of himself and his posterity is bound up, so too a people which violates the laws of nature and of nations breaks down the bulwark of its own tranquillity for future time. Even though no utility were to be looked on from the observation of law, such a course would be one not of folly but of wisdom, to which we feel ourselves drawn by nature.

Wherefore, that saying that we were compelled to establish laws from fear of wrong, is not universally true; this opinion is explained by a speaker in Plato's dialogues, who says that laws were introduced because of the fear of receiving wrong, and that men are driven to respect justice by a certain compulsion. But this applies only to those institutions and statutes which were devised for the more easy enforcement of law; as when many, individually weak, fearing oppression by those who were stronger, combined to establish judicial authorities and to protect them by their common strength, so that those whom they could not resist singly, they might, united, control. Only in this sense may we properly accept the statement that law is that which pleases the stronger party: namely, that we are to undersand that law does not attain its external end unless it has force as its servant. Thus Solon accomplished great things, as he himself said, *by linking together force and law.*

But even law that is unsupported by force is not destitute of all effect; for justice brings serenity to the conscience, while injustice brings torments and remorse such as Plato describes as afflicting the hearts of tyrants. The common feeling of upright men approves justice and condemns injustice. The important point is that justice has for its friend, God,

451

while injustice has Him as an enemy; He reserves his judgments for another life, yet in such manner that He often exhibits their power in this life; we have many examples of this in history.

The error which many commit who, while they require justice in citizens, hold it to be superfluous in a people or the ruler of a people, is caused primarily by this fact: they are regarding only the utility which arises from the law. This utility is evident in the case of citizens, who individually are too weak to secure their own protection. Great states, on the other hand, which seem to embrace within themselves all that is necessary to support life, do not appear to have need of that virtue which regards extraneous parties and is called justice.

But—not to repeat what I have already said, that law is not established for the sake of utility alone—there is no state so strong that it may not at some time need the aid of others external to itself, either in the way of commerce or in order to repel the force of many nations combined against it. Hence we see that alliances are sought even by the most powerful peoples and kings; the force of such alliances is entirely destroyed by those who confine law within the boundaries of a state. It is most true that everything becomes uncertain if we withdraw from law.

Since, for the reasons which I have stated, I hold it to be completely proved that there is between nations a common law which is of force with respect to war and in war, I have had many and grave reasons why I should write a work on that subject. For I saw prevailing throughout the Christian world a license in making war of which even barbarous nations would have been ashamed, recourse being had to arms for slight reasons or for no reason; and when arms were once taken up, all reverence for divine and human law was lost, just as men were henceforth authorized to commit all crimes without restraint.

It remains now that I briefly explain with what aids

and with what care I have undertaken this work. In the first place, it was my object to refer to the truth of the things which belong to natural law to certain notions so certain that no one can deny them without doing violence to his own nature. For the principles of that law, if you attend to them rightly, are of themselves patent and evident almost in the same way as things which we perceive by our external senses; for these do not deceive us, if the organs are rightly disposed and other necessary things are not wanting.

For the demonstration of natural law I have used the testimonies of philosophers, historians, poets, and finally orators. Not that these are to be trusted indiscriminately; for they are ordinarily writing to serve their sect, their argument, or their cause. But when many, writing in different times and places, affirm the same thing as true, their unanimity must be referred to some universal cause, which, in the questions with which we are here concerned, can be no other than either a right deduction proceeding from principles of nature, or some common agreement. The former cause points to the law of nature, the latter to the law of nations; the difference between these two is to be discerned not in the testimonies themselves (for writers everywhere confound the law of nature and the law of nations), but in the quality of the matter. For what can not be deduced from certain principles by unerring reasoning, and yet is seen to be observed everywhere, must have its origin in free consent.

Passages of history have a two-fold use in our argument: they supply both examples and judgments. In proportion as examples belong to better times and better nations, they have greater authority; we have therefore preferred the examples from ancient Greece and Rome. Nor are judgments to be despised, especially when many of them agree; for natural law is, as we have said, to be proved by such concord; and the law of nations can be proved in no other manner.

The opinions of poets and orators have not so much weight; and these we often use not so much to gain confirmation from them as to give to what we are trying to say some ornamentation from their modes of expression.

The books written by men inspired by God, or approved by them, I often use as authority, with a distinction between the Old and the New Testament.

[146]

H

HAEBERLIN, PAUL

HAEBERLIN, PAUL (1878-   ). The evolution of Haeberlin's thinking has proceeded from the religious belief of a Protestant minister
to idealism, returned to a prevalently religious attitude, then approached a purely theoretical standpoint, and returned again to the
view that religious experience, and not philosophical knowledge,
is able to master the problems of life and to comprehend the
meaning of existence. Haeberlin assigns a very important task
to philosophy but he does not give it the last word. Haeberlin
maintains that life, and existence are essentially problematical,
and concludes that knowledge also is necessarily problematical.
The human mind is characterized by him as the constant protest
against this inevitable fact which remains a mystery to man but
is not a mystery to God. Man is capable of becoming aware of his
real situation only by assuming a religious attitude. Philosophy,
provided it recognizes its true function, can help man to obtain
knowledge of his real situation.

Haeberlin has made valuable contributions to psychology,
characterology, pedagogics and psychotherapeutics. He was especially successful in treating psychopathic children and young people in their teens. Since 1922 he has been a full professor of philosophy, psychology and pedagogics at the University of Basel. His
principal works are: *The Object of Psychology* (1921), *Aesthetics*
(1929), *The Essence of Philosophy* (1934) and *Possibilities and
Limits of Education* (1936).

THE PRINCIPLES OF SCIENTIFIC KNOWLEDGE

KNOWLEDGE supposes correct thinking. Correct thinking lies
in correct judgment. The essence of knowledge is the absolute correctness of judgment. The task of knowledge is to
make correct judgment. Its object is the content of this judgment. Judgment does not mean any single judgment or the

judgment of a definite judging subject, e.g., a human subject, but judgment altogether, and therewith judgment independent of the kind of the subject. The absolute judging subject corresponds to the absolute judgment. This is, however, of lesser importance than the fact that knowledge is correct thinking and therefore can be found only in correct judgment. In this connection, "correctness" means absolute correctness or objective correctness. But when is judgment in this sense correct? There is only one possible answer to this question. It can only be found if one considers that all judging is acting, that every judgment is an action. An action is correct in this object sense if it corresponds to an absolutely valid objective demand, or, as we also can say, if it is the realization of a norm. The concept of correctness of acting supposes the concept of an objective norm. The norm of acting corresponds to absolutely correct acting. Furthermore, if judging is a modification of acting, the concept of correctness of judgment supposes the concept of norm of judgment as a definite modification of the norm of acting altogether. The absolute norm of judgment corresponds to the correct judgment, and is the modification of the norm altogether. Correct judgment is the realization of this norm of judgment. A judgment is correct if it fulfils its norm of judgment and therewith fulfils, on its part and in its way, the norm of judgment. Knowledge, as totality of correct judgment, consequently, means the realization of the absolute norm of judgment.

Every judgment has a content, or, as we also could say, a result. That means what is "made" by the judgment, in the sense of a position or statement. For every judgment does notify something, and this something is just its content. But such a statement is an action by means of which that something is formed; in as far the content is a formation. The content of a correct judgment is correctly formed. It is a correct formation. In general, we characterize the correctness of a formation made by judgment, in contradistinction to a formation by action altogether, as truth. Correct judgments have true contents. The content of correct judgment altogether is the very truth. Truth, therefore, is the content of knowledge. The correct judgment, consequently, can also be defined from the viewpoint of the content. A judgment is correct if its content is true. This definition is quite as valid as the inverse: the content of a judgment is true if the judgment is correct. Both of them mean realization of the norm of judgment.

[147]

HALEVI, JUDAH

HALEVI, JUDAH (About 1080-1140). As a "flaming pillar of song," Judah Halevi, the greatest Jewish poet of the Middle Ages, was exalted by Heinrich Heine, who, himself an undeniable expert, sensed through the medium of a translation Halevi's mastership of versification and his fervent soul. Halevi sang of love and friendship, of virtue and beauty, and most passionately of the fate of the Jewish people, of Zion and God. Several of his sacred poems form part of Jewish prayer-books in every country where Jewish congregations exist.

But Halevi was also an important philosopher of religion. His *Kitab Al Khazari,* written in Arabic and translated into Hebrew under the title *Sefer Ha-Kuzari* (Book of the Khazar), referring to the conversion to Judaism of the Khazar King Bulan II (about 740), is a defense of the Jewish faith against Christian and Islamic attacks and at the same time, a profound meditation on Jewish history and an acute demarcation between philosophy and religion. The close connection between the revealed religion and the history of the Jewish people is characteristic of Halevi's position. He maintained that Judaism does not center in the person of its founder as the religions of Christ and Mohammed do but in the people to whom the Torah has been given, and he goes so far as to declare: "If there were no Jews there would be no Torah." But he by no means idolizes his people in the way modern nationalists do. Jewish history is the work of Divine Providence which he regarded as the continuation of the Divine creative activity. Halevi was opposed to Aristotelianism which he reproached for subjecting the Deity to necessity and for being incompatible with the idea of a personal God. Platonic tradition seemed more fitting to him, for he was inclined to regard God as the principle of form that moulds the eternal material principle. Fundamentally, however, Halevi re-

457

mained reluctant to use philosophical categories in matters that concern religion, and he often expressed his dislike of philosophy and philosophers, although he proved to be one of them.

ON REVELATION

OUR intellect which, a priori, is only theoretical, being sunk in matter, cannot penetrate to the true knowledge of things, except by the grace of God, by special faculties which He has placed in the senses. There is no difference between my perception and thine that this circumscribed disc, giving forth light and heat is the sun. Should even these characteristics be denied by reason, this does no harm, because we can derive it from argument for our purposes. Thus also a sharp-eyed person, looking for a camel, can be assisted by a weak-eyed and squinting one who tells him that he has seen two cranes at a certain place. The sharp-eyed person then knows that the other has only seen a camel, and the weakness of his eyes made him believe that it was a crane, and his squint that there were two cranes. In this way the sharp-eyed person can make use of the evidence of the weak-eyed one, whilst he excuses his faulty description by his faulty sight. A similar relation prevails between senses and imagination on one side and reason on the other. The Creator was as wise in arranging this relation between the exterior senses and the things perceived, as He was in fixing the relation between the abstract sense and the uncorporeal substratum. To the chosen among His creatures He has given an inner eye which sees things as they really are, without any alteration. Reason is thus in a position to come to a conclusion regarding the true spirit of these things. He to whom this eye has been given is clear-sighted indeed. Other people, who appear to him as blind, he guides on their way. It is possible that this eye is the power of imagination as long as it is under the control of the intellect. It beholds, then, a grand and awful sight which reveals unmistakable truths among the whole of this species and those sights. By this I mean all the prophets. For they witnessed things which are described to the other in the same manner as we do with things we have seen. We testify to the sweetness of honey and the bitterness of the colocynth; and if any one contradicts us, we say that he has failed to grasp a fact of natural history. Those prophets without doubt saw the divine world with the inner eye; they beheld a sight which harmonized with their natural imagination. Whatever they wrote down, they endowed with attributes as if they had seen them in corporeal form. Those attributes are true as far as regards what is sought by inspiration, imagination, and feeling; they are untrue as regards the reality sought by reason.

[148]

HAMANN, JOHANN GEORG

HAMANN, JOHANN GEORG (1730-1788). During a stay in London, where he was bound to become acquainted with British business methods, Hamann, a native of Königsberg, Prussia, had a mystical experience which made him a grim adversary of rationalism and the spirit of enlightenment that fascinated most of his contemporaries. With the aid of allegorical interpretation, Hamann regarded the Bible as the fundamental book of all possible knowledge, including that of nature. Allegory and symbol gave Hamann truer knowledge than notions. Myths and poetry were to him of greater validity than scientific research and logical conclusions. Language was the key that opens the door to reality. Hamann was a past master in sensing the unconscious tendencies of speech. But in his style there are no consequences, no development of ideas. He tried to grasp the flux of life, but, according to his own avowal, often forgot the meaning of the similes he had used and to which he alluded in later pages of the same treatise. His fugitive associations, therefore, are of greater value than his efforts to express his intentions elaborately. Devout and coquettish, excessive in his piety and repentance of transgressions with which his imagination remained fascinated, Hamann tried to embrace spirit and sensuality, sometimes illuminating their relations, sometimes becoming hopelessly confused. His writings were inspired by sublime earnestness and brilliant irony. He accused the rationalistic spirit of his age of ignoring God and nature, human genius, creative action and the enjoyment of real life. His views deeply impressed Herder, Goethe, Friedrich Heinrich Jacobi, Hegel and Kierkegaard.

459

NATURE is a book, a letter, a fairy tale (in the philosophical sense) or whatever you want to call it. Suppose we know all the letters in this book as well as possible, suppose we know how to spell the words and how to pronounce them, suppose we know even the language in which it is written—is that enough to understand the book, to judge it, to give an account of it or to make an excerpt of it? You need more physics in order to interpret nature. Physics is nothing but the ABC's. Nature is an equation with an unknown, a Hebrew word which is written only with consonants to which reason has to add the dots. I stick to the letters, to the visible and to the natural, like the hands of the watch. But what is behind the dial plate? That is where you find the art of the master, wheels and springs which like the mosaic serpent need an Apocalypse. The entire visible nature is nothing but a dial and the hand; the wheels and the right weight are stones, winds and flames of fire. . . .

Reason discovers in us nothing more than what Hiob saw . . . the misfortune of our birth, the advantage of the grave and the uselessness and the shortcomings of the human life, since we have no insight and feel passion and urges in us whose purposes are unknown to us. All human wisdom works and has worries and grief as reward. The farther reason looks the greater is the haze in which it loses itself. Everything is vain and tortures the spirit instead of calming and satisfying it. It is with reason, as with eyes with lenses, whereby the most tender skin becomes nauseating, whereby the most delicate dish becomes a heap of worms and the most refined work of art becomes a bungling work. We see the impossibility of remedying all inequalities in human society and we see an overwhelming number of deficiencies and flaws in it. The weakness of ourselves and of our reason makes us see flaws in beauties by making us consider everything piece by piece.

[149]

460

HAMILTON, ALEXANDER

HAMILTON, ALEXANDER (1757-1804). "A great man, but not a great American," "a great Englishman bred in America"—so Hamilton was called by Woodrow Wilson. Other historians have equally assumed that Hamilton threw himself into the American Revolution as much out of ambition as through adherence to the principle of popular government. However, Hamilton's services to the cause of America's independence and to the formation of the republic cannot be questioned. He stormed the redoubt at York-town; his activities were instrumental in the ratification of the Constitution; as Washington's Secretary of the Treasury, he secured the credit of the national government, and some historians call him the greatest finance minister in American history. His efficiency, his talents for organization were of inestimable value to the establishment of public order in the young republic. In addition to his brilliancy and his personal charm, some defects of his character, however, must not be overlooked. He was quarrelsome and excitable, and, although he was undeniably a great statesman, there was also in his personality a quixotic strain, and he not only favored a strong, centralized government but also avowedly admired the British monarchy and the institution of the House of Lords.

Even as a youth of eighteen, Hamilton showed his great literary talents. He was well acquainted with Locke, Montesquieu and Hume, and was always eager to read and to learn. His most important contribution to American political philosophy was his articles in the *Federalist Papers*. It was their aim to explain the Constitution and to recommend its acceptance by the people of the thirteen colonies. "No constitution," said Chancellor Kent, "ever received a more masterly and successful vindication."

ON A JUST PARTITION OF POWER

It is of great importance in a republic not only to guard the society against the oppression of its rulers, but to guard one part of the society against the injustice of the other part. Different interests necessarily exist in different classes of citizens. If a majority be united by a common interest, the rights of the minority will be insecure. There are but two methods of providing against this evil: the one by creating a will in the community independent of the majority, that is, of the

461

society itself; the other by comprehending in the society so many separate descriptions of citizens as will render an unjust combination of a majority of the whole very improbable, if not impracticable. The first method prevails in all governments possessing a hereditary or self-appointed authority. This at best is but a precarious security; because a power independent of the society may as well espouse the unjust views of the major as the rightful interests of the minor party, and may possibly be turned against both parties. The second method will be exemplified in the federal republic of the United States. While all authority in it will be derived from and dependent on the society, the society itself will be broken into so many parts, interests, and classes of citizens that the rights of individuals or of the minority will be in little danger from interested combinations of the majority. In a free government the security for civil rights must be the same as that for religious rights. It consists in the one case in the multiplicity of interests, and in the other in the multiplicity of sects. The degree of security in both cases will depend on the number of interests and sects; and this may be presumed to depend on the extent of country and number of people comprehended under the same government. This view of the subject must particularly recommend a proper federal system to all the sincere and considerate friends of republican government; since it shows that in exact proportion as the territory of the Union may be formed into more circumscribed confederacies, or States, oppressive combinations of a majority will be facilitated; the best security under republican forms, for the rights of every class of citizens, will be diminished; and, consequently, the stability and independence of some member of the government, the only other security, must be proportionally increased. Justice is the end of government. It is the end of civil society. It ever has been and ever will be pursued until it be obtained or until liberty be lost in the pursuit. In a society, under the forms of which the stronger faction can readily unite and oppress the weaker, anarchy may as truly be said to reign, as in a

state of nature, where the weaker individual is not secured against the violence of the stronger; and as in the latter state even the stronger individuals are prompted by the uncertainty of their condition to submit to a government which may protect the weak as well as themselves, so in the former state will the more powerful factions or parties be gradually induced by a like motive to wish for a government which will protect all parties, the weaker as well as the more powerful. It can be little doubted that if the State of Rhode Island was separated from the confederacy, and left to itself, the insecurity of rights under the popular form of government within such narrow limits would be displayed by such reiterated oppressions of factious majorities that some power altogether independent of the people would soon be called for by the voice of the very factions whose misrule had proved the necessity of it. In the extended republic of the United States, and among the great variety of interests, parties, and sects which it embraces, a coalition of a majority of the whole society could seldom take place on any other principles than those of justice and the general good; while there being thus less danger to a minor from the will of a major party, there must be less pretext, also, to provide for the security of the former, by introducing into the government a will not dependent on the latter; or, in other words, a will independent of the society itself. It is no less certain than it is important, notwithstanding the contrary opinions which have been entertained, that the larger the society, provided it lie within a practical sphere, the more duly capable it will be of self-government. And happily for the republican cause, the practical sphere may be carried to a very great extent, by a judicious modification and mixture of the federal principle.
[150]

HAN FEI

HAN FEI (died 233 B.C.). Han Fei, a disciple of Hsun Ching and the greatest Chinese philosopher of law, committed suicide because he, as an unofficial adviser of a ruler, had aroused the jealousy of the latter's responsible minister.

Han Fei concentrated upon the problems of government, state-craft, authority and public welfare, and advanced views similar to those of Jeremy Bentham and other British utilitarians. But he also adopted Taoist ideas on essential truth.

ESSAYS

NOTHING is more valuable than the royal person, more honorable than the throne, more powerful than the authority of the sovereign, and more august than the position of the ruler. These four excellences are not obtained from outside, nor secured from anybody else, but are deliberated in the ruler's own mind and acquired thereby. . . . This the ruler of men must keep firmly in mind.

Master Shen [i.e. Shen Tao, fourth century] said, 'A flying dragon rides the winds, a floating serpent wanders through the mist on the water; but when the clouds disperse and the mist is gone, a dragon and a serpent are no different from a cricket or an ant. They have lost what they depended on. Thus the reason why a man of worth may be overpowered by a worthless one is that the able man's power is weak and his position humble. And the reason why a worthless man submits to a man of worth is that the able man's power is strong and his position high. Yao [the Sage-king] as a common man could not have governed three people, whilst Chieh [the villain-king] as Son of Heaven could bring the whole of society into confusion. Thus I know that authority and position are to be trusted, ability and wisdom are not particularly desirable. . . . It was when Yao ascended the throne and was king over the Great Society that what he commanded was done, what he banned was not done. From this angle I see that worth and wisdom are not enough to subdue a population whilst authority and position are enough to overpower men of worth.'

To this the reply is made, 'In the case of a dragon . . . riding the clouds, I do not regard the dragon as not depending on the clouds. . . . None the less, if worth is discarded and reliance put solely on authority, is it enough to produce good government? If it is, I have never seen it. There is something which goes along with the particular prestige of clouds and makes the dragon able to ride them . . .; and this something is the dragon's or the serpent's, special quality. . . . However thick the clouds and mist might be, the quality of the cricket or the ants is not up to the mark. In the case of a Chieh, seated on the throne and using the majesty of the son of Heaven as clouds and mist, society nevertheless cannot escape great confusion; and this because a Chieh's quality is inadequate. What is more, supposing a sovereign using the authority of a Yao to govern the Great Society, how different that authority is from the kind which makes confusion! . . . The sovereigns who use their authority to make confusion are many, those who use their authority to make order are few. . . .'

*　　*　　*

No country is permanently strong, nor is any country permanently weak. If conformers to law are strong, the country is strong; if conformers to law are weak, the country is weak. . . . Any ruler able to expel private crookedness and uphold public law finds the people become law-abiding and the state ordered; and any ruler able to eradicate individualistic action and act on public law finds his army become strong and his enemy weak. So, find out men who follow the discipline of laws and regulations, and place them above the body of officials. Then the sovereign cannot be deceived by anybody with fraud and falsehood. . . .

Now supposing promotions were made because of mere reputation, then ministers would be estranged from the sovereign and all officials would associate for treasonable purposes. Supposing officials were appointed on account of their partisanship, then the people would strive to cultivate friendships and never seek employment in accordance with the law. Thus, with the government lacking able men, the state will fall into confusion. If rewards are bestowed according to mere reputation, and punishments are inflicted according to mere defamation, then men who love rewards and hate punishments will discard public law and practice self-seeking tricks and associate for rebellious purposes. . . . Therefore, the intelligent sovereign makes the law select men, and makes no arbitrary regulation himself. In consequence able men cannot be obscured, bad characters cannot be disguised, falsely praised fellows cannot be advanced, wrongly defamed people cannot be degraded. In consequence the distinction between the ruler and minister becomes clear and order is attained. . . .

Hence to govern the state by law is to praise the right and blame the wrong. The law does not fawn on the noble, (just as) an inked string does not follow a crooked line. Whatever the law applies to, the wise cannot reject it nor the brave defy it. Punishment for fault never skips ministers, and reward for good never misses commoners. Therefore for correcting the faults of the high, for rebuking the vices of the low, for suppressing disorders, for deciding against mistakes, for subduing the arrogant, for straightening the crooked, and for unifying the folk-ways of the masses, nothing can match with the law: for warning officials and overaweing the people, for rebuking obscenity and danger and for forbidding falsehood and deceit, nothing can match with penalties. If they are strictly administered, no discrimination is made between noble and commoner. If the law is definite, superiors are esteemed and not flouted. If superiors are not flouted, the sovereign will become strong and able to maintain the proper course of government. This was the reason why the early kings esteemed legalism and handed it down to posterity.

[151]

HARRIS, WILLIAM TORREY

HARRIS, WILLIAM TORREY (1835-1909). When passions ran high at the beginning of the Civil War, a group met together in St. Louis and calmly interpreted the events as part of a universal plan, the working out of an eternal dialectic which Hegel had explained in all his works, particularly his *Philosophy of History*. One of the key men of that philosophical society was Harris who rose from teacher in the public schools to the superintendency and the United States Commissionership of Education, which post he held for 17 years, longer than any other incumbent. He might be termed the idealist in education in that he organized all phases of it on the principles of a philosophical pedagogy in which the German idealists Hegel, Kant, Fichte and Goethe were his principal teachers, apart from Froebel, Pestalozzi and the rest.

Harris founded and edited the first philosophical periodical in America, the *Journal of Speculative Philosophy*, in which men like William James, Josiah Royce and John Dewey first spread their wings. He initiated, with Brokmeyer, the St. Louis Movement in Philosophy which had far-reaching influence. Together with Amos Bronson Alcott and with the support of Emerson, he revived New England transcendentalism but gave it a more logical, metaphysical twist. Lecturing from coast to coast as one of America's most popular educators, he made his hearers realize the importance of philosophy, of having objectives in an education for democracy, and of viewing things in their whole.

Far from being a dreamer, he was practical in his activities. As editor-in-chief of Webster's, he originated the divided page. He expanded the functions of the Bureau of Education; presented the United States in graphic exhibits at many an international exposition; incorporated the first kindergarten into an American public school system, and was responsible for introducing the reindeer into Alaska as a condition for educating the natives who were thus supplied with an industry and a livelihood which the whalers and trappers had brought to the verge of extinction.

THE LAST JUDGMENT

MICHELANGELO passes by all subordinate scenes and seizes at once the supreme moment of all history—of the very world itself and all it contains. This is the vastest attempt that the artist can make, and is the same that Dante had ventured upon in the *Divina Commedia*. In religion we seize the absolute truth as a process going on in time: the deeds of humanity are judged "after the end of the world." After death Dives goes to torments, and Lazarus to the realm of the blest. In this supreme moment all worldly distinctions fall away, and the naked soul stands before eternity with naught save the pure essence of its deeds to rely upon. All souls are equal before God, so far as mere worldly eminence is concerned. Their inequality rests solely upon the degree that they have realized the eternal will by their own choice.

But this dogma, as it is held in the christian religion, is not merely a dogma; it is the deepest of speculative truths. As such it is seized by Dante and Michelangelo, and in this universal form every one must recognize it if he would free it from all narrowness and sectarianism. The point of view is this:—The whole world is seized at once under the form of eternity; all things are reduced to their lowest terms. Every deed is seen through the perspective of its own consequences. Hence every human being under the influence of any one of the deadly sins—anger, lust, avarice, intemperance, pride, envy, and indolence—is being dragged down into the inferno just as Michelangelo has depicted. On the other hand any one who practises the cardinal virtues—prudence, justice, temperance, and fortitude—is elevating himself toward celestial clearness.

If any one will study Dante carefully, he will find that the punishments of the inferno are emblematical of the very states of the mind one experiences when under the influence of the passion there punished. To find the punishment for any given sin, Dante looks at the state of mind which it causes in the sinner, and gives it its appropriate emblem. . . .

So Michelangelo in this picture has seized things in their essential nature; he has pierced through the shadows of time, and exhibited to us at one view the world of humanity as it is in the sight of God, or as it is in its ultimate analysis. Mortals are there, not as they seem to themselves or to their companions, but as they are when measured by the absolute standard—the final destiny of spirit. This must recommend the work to all men of all times, whether one holds to this or that theological creed; for it is the last judgment in the sense that it is the ultimate or absolute estimate to be pronounced upon each deed, and the question of the eternal punishment of any individual is not necessarily brought into account. Everlasting punishment is the true state of all who persist in the commission of those sins. The sins are indissolubly bound up in pain. Through all times anger shall bring with it the "putrid mud" condition of the soul; the indulgence of lustful passions, the stormy tempest and spiritual night; intemperance, the pitiless rain of hail and snow and foul water. The wicked sinner—shall be tormented forever; for we are now and always in eternity. . . . Just as we strive in our human laws to establish justice by turning back upon the criminal effects of his deeds, so *in fact* when placed "under the form of Eternity," all deeds do return to the doer; and this is the final adjustment, the "end of all things"—it is *the last judgment*. And this judgment is always the only actual fact in the world.

[152]

HARTMANN, EDUARD VON

HARTMANN, EDUARD VON (1842-1906). An officer in the Prussian army, Eduard von Hartmann became disabled, suffering from a nervous disease that forced him to lie on his back. After quitting military service, he studied philosophy, and soon became famous because of the great success of his *Philosophie des Unbewussten* (Philosophy of the Unconscious, 1869). Later, he published many other books, none of which attracted as much attention as his first work.

By no means was Hartmann a precursor of modern investigation of unconscious or subconscious activities. He is rather to be regarded as one of the last constructors of systems, each of whom was immediately inspired by Schelling. Avowedly Hartmann tried to form a synthesis of Leibniz, Schelling, Hegel, Schopenhauer and the results of modern natural sciences. What he called the Unconscious combines the qualities of Hegel's absolute spirit and Schopenhauer's blind will. It is proclaimed as the "thing in itself," the origin of the cosmic order and the mental life of the human individual. Hartmann called his system "transcendental realism" and claimed to have constructed the reliable bridge to metaphysics and, at the same time "the only possible bridge to natural science."

469

I SHOULD like to . . . call every original philosopher a mystic, so far as he is truly original; for in the history of philosophy no high thought has ever been brought to light by laborious conscious trial and induction, but has always been apprehended by the glance of genius, and then elaborated by the understanding. Add to that, that philosophy essentially deals with a theme which is most intimately connected with the one feeling *only* to be *mystically* apprehended, namely, the *relation of the individual to the Absolute.* All that has gone before only concerned such matter of consciousness as can or could arise in no other way, thus is here only called mystical, because the *form of its origin* is mystical; but now we come to an item of consciousness, which, in its inmost character, is *only* to be apprehended mystically, which thus also, *materially*, may be called mystical; and a human being who can produce this mystical content will have to be called pre-eminently a mystic.

To wit, *conscious thought* can comprehend the identity of the individual with the Absolute by a rational method, as we too have found ourselves on the way to this goal on our inquiry; but the Ego and the Absolute and their identity stand before it as three *abstractions,* whose *union* in the *judgment* is made probable, it is true, through the preceding proofs, yet an *immediate feeling of this identity* is not attained by it. The *authoritative belief* in an external revelation may credulously repeat the dogma of such a unity—the living feeling of the same cannot be engrafted or thrust on the mind from without, it can only spring up in the mind of the believer himself; in a word, it is to be attained neither by philosophy nor external revelation, but only mystically, by one with equal mystical proclivities, the more easily, indeed, the more perfect and pure are the philosophical notions or religious ideas already possessed. Therefore this feeling is the content of mysticism, *Kat exochen,* because it finds its existence *only* in it, and, at the same time, the *highest* and *ulti-mate,* if also, as we have seen before, by no means the only aim of all those who have devoted their lives to mysticism. Nay, we may even go so far as to assert that the production of a certain degree of this mystical feeling, and the enjoy-ment lurking in it, is the sole *inner* aim of all religion, and that it is, therefore, not incorrect, if less significative, to ap-ply the name *religious* feeling to it.

Further, if the highest blessedness lurks in this feeling for its possessor, as is confirmed by the experience of all mystics, the transition is manifestly easy to the endeavor to heighten this feeling in degree, by seeking to make the union between the Ego and the Absolute ever closer and more intimate. But it is also not difficult to see that we have here arrived at the point previously indicated, where mysticism spontaneously degenerates into the morbid, by overshooting its mark. Undoubtedly we must elevate ourselves for this purpose a little above the standpoint hitherto attained in our investigations. The unity, namely of the Absolute and the individual, whose individuality or egoity is given through consciousness, thus, in other words, the unity of the uncon-scious and conscious, is once for all given, inseparable and indestructible, except by destruction of the individual; where-fore, however, every attempt to make this unity more close than it is, is so absurd and useless. The way which, his-torically, has almost always been taken, is that of the an-nihilation of consciousness—the endeavor to let the individ-ual perish in the Absolute. This, however, contains a great error, as if, when the goal of annihilation of consciousness was reached, the individual still existed; the Ego at once desires to be annihilated, and to subsist in order to enjoy this annihilation. Consequently this goal has hitherto been always imperfectly attained on both sides, although the ac-counts of the mystics enable us to perceive that many on this path have attained an admirable height, or rather depth.

[153]

471

HARTMANN, NICOLAI

HARTMANN, NICOLAI (1882-1950). Born and educated in Tsarist Russia, Hartmann, shortly after 1900, emigrated to Germany where he became naturalized. During World War I, he fought in the German army. In his adopted country, Hartmann was at first a follower of Hermann Cohen, but later became an adversary of Neo-Kantianism. Since this change, Hartmann has developed his philosophical views with progressive consistency.

Hartmann emphasizes the necessity that the philosopher must take into account the fact that no one begins with his own thinking, but rather meets a historically conditioned situation in which ideas and problems, already developed by previous thinkers, or expressed in various spiritual creations of the time direct the way a beginner selects the questions which interest him, and formulate his problems and principles. From this standpoint, Hartmann proceeds to the establishment of the science of ontology, which, to him, is at least equally as important as epistemology. According to Hartmann, the realm of reason covers only a sector of reality. It is impossible to solve the metaphysical problem because irrational remainders always defy reason. But, if metaphysics is impossible in the form of any system, it remains the principal business of the philosopher to mark the boundary between the rational and the irrational and to recognize the metaphysical elements in all branches of philosophy. His inquiry results in the statement that epistemology, ethics, and aesthetics can offer partial solutions only, and that the notions of logic are subject to historical change, although their ideal structure remains unalterable. The history of the notions forms the center of the history of philosophy and science. As to ethics and axiology, Hartmann tries to harmonize the absolute character of the moral duty with the historical variety of evaluations.

VALUE AND VALIDITY

THE so-called "relativity of values" is nothing but the historical instability of their actuality which results in the instability of validity. That solves the puzzle why it is so often asserted that the values themselves are relative. For validity has always been considered the sort of being of the values themselves. But that has been recognized as an error, and therefore the relativity of the "being valuable" is untenable.

Notwithstanding all regarding the change of the real, there remains a definite kind of independence of the value-character itself, or of the "being valuable" (for instance the being valuable of a certain manner of acting in certain circumstances). This absoluteness is very evident in the fact of the super-temporariness of the being valuable, even if the valuable real is only ephemeral. It is an error to think that only the eternal could have eternal value. Just the transient has eternal value. Its value-character is the eternal in it. The value of a thing is as little dependent on its duration as the truth of a proposition is dependent on the flash or disappearance of the insight in human minds.

Upon this footing, a synthesis of the right value relativism and the right value-absolutism is possible. If both of them limit themselves strictly to the phenomena and refrain from constructing theories, they can complete one another harmoniously. Relativism may be satisfied with the historical conditionality of actuality and "validity," which is conceded by the adversary. Absolutism, on its part, may be satisfied with the continuance of the "being valuable," even when it is not actual and not "valid," and that does not affect the facts of historical relativity.

Both of these theories not only contain a truth but are indispensable to each other. For only the relativity of validity demonstrates the meaning of independent continuance, and only that meaning can make evident what relativity really is. Moreover, only these two theories together can clarify the mystery of the value-consciousness.

If the perception of values is dependent on historical circumstances, it seems to be unreliable for that reason. Since, however, we have no other knowledge about values, that would mean that any kind of comprehending values is uncertain. It therefore is important to recognize that it really does matter that certain values are at certain times non-valid while they are valid at other times. This phenom-

473

enon is clarified entirely by the historical conditionality of actuality. This explanation is completed by Scheler's notion of "value-blindness" and the notion of "narrowness of the value-consciousness" introduced by myself. To understand this phenomenon, we do not need the assumption of a deceivableness of the valuing feelings. It is sufficient to think that all valuing feelings are limited as far as their contents are concerned, incapable of comprehending all of the values, and may become seeing only in accordance with the degree of their maturing, though conditional upon the historical change of the shape of life. However, the valuing feeling can grasp values only in accordance with the laws of its own development.

The notion of "narrowness of the value-consciousness" needs as its complementary notion that of the "wandering of the valuing glance" whose horizon is inside the plane of the values. Seen from the realm of the values this wandering means just the same as the historical conditionality of "validity." For it is moving in the course of time, and is dependent on the changing conditions of life. For at any time the consciousness is in touch with only a sector of the realm of values. This sector is another one at any time. The values themselves, however, remain motionless.

[154]

HEGEL, GEORG WILHELM FRIEDRICH

HEGEL, GEORG WILHELM FRIEDRICH (1770-1831). Long after Hegel lost his once immense authority, many of his intellectual formulas continued to attract the philosophers of various schools in various countries. Hegel's philosophy is often regarded as typically German, and certainly some of its main features represent the very characteristics of the German way of reacting to reality. Numerous great philosophers in England and America, in Italy and France, and in other countries have testified that they owed to Hegel not only an increase of knowledge but the fundamental principles of their own thinking. Outstanding Hegelians in England were T. H. Green, Edward and John Caird, J. H. Bradley and Bernard Bosanquet, and in America, W. T. Harris, Royce, Creighton and alkins. John Dewey said that "acquaintance with Hegel has left a permanent deposit in my thinking."

Hegel's philosophy has often been despised as abstract speculation. Yet soon after his death it became evident that his thoughts could offer an ideological basis to political parties which were radically opposed to each other. Bismarck and the Prussian Junkers adopted Hegel's view on the state. So did Fascism and National Socialism, while Marx, and after him, Lenin, adapted Hegel's dialectical method to give reasons for the doctrine of the dictatorship of the proletariat. And even staunch defenders of liberalism and democracy have appealed to Hegel's philosophy of history.

In a similar way, the champions of religious orthodoxy and liberalism have used Hegel's ideas to justify their respective positions. King Frederick William III of Prussia and his minister of public education favored Hegelianism as the firmest bulwark of Christianity, while King Frederick William IV of Prussia and his minister of public education persecuted the Hegelians whom they accused of undermining the Christian faith.

Hegel has been glorified and vilified as the protector of reactionary conservatism and as the prophet of revolutionary change because his system tries to synthesize antagonistic tendencies. On the one hand, he put becoming above being, and conceived of the world as an eternally evolutionary process; on the other hand, he claimed to have laid the groundwork for definite knowledge and for the understanding of timeless perfection.

In a lecture on the history of philosophy, Hegel, from his chair at the University of Berlin, called to his audience: "Man cannot over-estimate the greatness and power of his mind." For he regarded human mind as one of the manifestations of the Absolute which he defined as spirit. The world, Hegel stated, is penetrable to thought which is, on its part, a description of the Absolute. Cosmic reason operates within the soul of man, whose consciousness is the area of the subjective spirit, while the objective spirit becomes manifest in cultural and social institutions like law and morality, and the absolute spirit can be grasped in the arts, in religion and philosophy. Human history and social life, culminating in the state, represent the highest level of a gradation that rises from inorganic nature to human genius, from "mere existence" to consciousness, knowledge of truth and action in accordance with recognized duties. The history of the world means the progressive realization of freedom which can be demonstrated by purely logical development. For Hegel does not acknowledge any other cause of historical change than the movement of thought by integrating a thesis and its antithesis into a synthesis which, on its part, pro-

475

vokes a new antithesis with which it becomes integrated into a new synthesis. These succeeding syntheses will bring the world to reason. Hegel thought that he had found the pattern for both human and cosmic reason in this conflict of thesis and antithesis which he called the dialectics. For becoming was regarded by Hegel as the modification of a being by factors which he defined as the negation of the being to be modified. In this way, evolution was conceived by Hegel as a purely logical procedure for which he claimed the acknowledgment of real necessity.

ON THE NATURE OF SPIRIT

THE nature of spirit may be understood by a glance at its direct opposite—*Matter.* As the essence of matter is gravity so, on the other hand, we may affirm that the substance, the essence, of spirit is freedom. All will readily assent to the doctrine that spirit, among other properties, is also endowed with freedom; but philosophy teaches that all the qualities of spirit exist only through freedom; that all are but means for attaining freedom; that all seek and produce this and this alone. It is a result of speculative philosophy, that freedom is the sole truth of spirit. Matter possesses gravity in virtue of its tendency towards a central point. It is essentially composite; consisting of parts that *exclude* each other. It seeks its unity; and therefore exhibits itself as self-destructive, as verging towards its opposite [an indivisible point]. If it could attain this, it would be matter no longer, it would have perished. It strives after the realization of its idea; for in unit it exists *ideally.* Spirit, on the contrary, may be defined as that which has its center in itself. It has not a unity outside itself, but has already found it; it exists *in* and *with* itself. Matter has its essence out of itself; spirit is *self-contained existence.* Now this is freedom, exactly. For if I am dependent, my being is referred to something else which I am not; I cannot exist independently of anything external. I am free, on the contrary, when my existence depends upon myself. This self-contained existence of spirit is none other than self-consciousness—consciousness of one's own being. Two things must be distinguished in consciousness; first, the fact

476

that I know; secondly *what I know.* In *self*-consciousness these are merged in one; for spirit knows itself. It involves an appreciation of its own nature, as also an energy enabling it to realize itself; to make itself *actually* that which it is *potentially.* According to this abstract definition it may be said of universal history, that it is the exhibition of spirit in the process of working out the knowledge of that which it is potentially. . . .

This vast congeries of volitions, interests, and activities, constitutes the instruments and means of the world-spirit for attaining its object; bringing it to consciousness, and realizing it. And this aim is none other than finding itself— coming to itself—and contemplating itself in concrete actuality. But that those manifestations of vitality on the part of individuals and peoples, in which they seek and satisfy their own purposes, are, at the same time, the means and instruments of a higher and broader purpose of which they know nothing,—which they realize unconsciously,—might be made a matter of question; rather has been questioned, and in every variety of form negatived, decried, and contemned as mere dreaming and "Philosophy." But on this point I announced my view at the very outset, and asserted our hypothesis,—which, however, will appear in the sequel, in the form of a legitimate inference, and our belief that reason governs the world, and has consequently governed its history. In relation to this independently universal and substantial existence—all else is subordinate, subservient to it, and the means for its development. The union of universal abstract existence generally with the individual, the subjective, that this alone is truth, belongs to the department of speculation, and is treated in this general form in logic. But in the process of the world's history itself—as still incomplete,—the abstract final aim of history is not yet made the distinct object of desire and interest. While these limited sentiments are still unconscious of the purpose they are fulfilling, the universal principle is implicit in them and is realizing itself through them. The question also assumes the form of the union of *freedom* and *necessity;* the latent abstract process of spirit being regarded as *necessity,* while that which exhibits itself in the conscious will of men, as their interest, belongs to the domain of *freedom.* As the metaphysical connection (*i.e.* the connection in the idea) of these forms of thought, belongs to logic, it would be out of place to analyze it here. The chief and cardinal points only shall be mentioned.

Philosophy shows that the idea advances to an infinite antithesis; that, viz. between the idea in its free, universal form—in which it exists for itself—and the contrasted form of abstract introversion, reflection on itself, which is formal existence-for-self, personality, formal freedom, such as belongs to spirit only. The universal idea exists thus as the substantial essence of free volition on the other side. This reflection of the mind on itself is individual self-consciousness—the polar opposite of the idea in its general form, and therefore existing in absolute limitation. This polar opposite is consequently limitation, particularization for the universal absolute thing; it is the side of its *definite existence;* the sphere of its formal reality, the sphere of the reverence paid to God. To comprehend the absolute connection of this antithesis, is the profound task of metaphysics. This limitation originates all forms of particularity of whatever kind. The formal volition (of which we have spoken) wills itself; desires to make its own personality valid in all that it purposes and does; even the pious individual wishes to be saved and happy. This pole of the antithesis, existing for itself, is— in contrast with the absolute universal being— a special separate existence, taking cognizance of specialty only, and willing that alone. In short it plays its part in the region of mere phenomena. This is the sphere of particular purposes, in effecting which individuals exert themselves on behalf of their individuality—give it full play and objective realization. This is also the sphere of happiness and its opposite. He is happy who finds his condition suited to his special character, will, and fancy, and so enjoys himself in that condition.

The history of the world is not the theater of happiness. Periods of happiness are blank pages in it, for they are periods of harmony,—periods when the antithesis is in abeyance. Reflection on self,—the freedom above described—is abstractly defined as the formal element of the activity of the absolute idea. The realizing *activity* of which we have spoken is the middle term of the syllogism, one of whose extremes is the universal essence, the *idea,* which reposes in the penetralia of spirit; and the other, the complex of external things,—objective matter. That activity is the medium by which the universal latent principle is translated into the domain of objectivity.

*   *   *

What is the material in which the ideal of reason is wrought out? The primary answer would be,—personality itself—human desires—subjectivity, generally. In human knowledge and volition, as its material element, reason attains positive existence. We have considered subjective volition where it has an object which is the truth and essence of a reality, viz. where it constitutes a great world-historical passion. As a subjective will, occupied with limited passions, it is dependent, and can gratify its desires only within the limits of this dependence. But the subjective will has also a substantial life—a reality,—in which it moves in the region of *essential* being, and has the essential itself as the object of its existence. This essential being is the union of the *subjective* with the *rational* will: it is the moral whole, the *state,* which is that form of reality in which the individual has and enjoys his freedom; but on the condition of his recognizing, believing in and willing that which is common to the whole. And this must not be understood as if the subjective will of the social unit attained its gratification and enjoyment through that common will; as if this were a means provided for its benefit; as if the individual, in his relations to other individuals, thus limited his freedom, in order that this universal limitation—the mutual constraint of all—

might secure a small space of liberty for each. Rather, we affirm, are law, morality, government, and they alone, the positive reality and completion of freedom. Freedom of a low and limited order, is mere caprice; which finds its exercise in the sphere of particular and limited desires.

Subjective volition—passion—is that which sets men in activity, that which effects "practical" realization. The idea is the inner spring of action; the state is the actually existing, realized moral life. For it is the unity of the universal, essential will, with that of the individual; and this is "morality." The individual living in this unity has a moral life; possesses a value that consists in this substantiality alone. Sophocles in his Antigone says, "The divine commands are not of yesterday, nor of to-day; no, they have an infinite existence, and no one could say whence they came." The laws of morality are not accidental, but are the essentially rational. It is the very object of the state, that what is essential in the practical activity of men, and in their dispositions, should be duly recognized; that it should have a manifest existence, and maintain its position. It is the absolute interest of reason that this moral whole should exist; and herein lies the justification and merit of heroes who have founded states, —however rude these may have been. In the history of the world, only those peoples can come under our notice which form a state. For it must be understood that this latter is the realization of freedom, *i.e.* of the absolute final aim, and that it exists for its own sake. It must further be understood that all the worth which the human being possesses—all spiritual reality, he possesses only through the state. For his spiritual reality consists in this, that his own essence— reason—is objectively present to him, that it possesses objective immediate existence for him. Thus only is he fully conscious; thus only is he a partaker of morality—of a just and moral social and political life. For truth is the unity of the universal and subjective will; and the universal is to be found in the state, in its laws, its universal and rational arrangements. The state is the divine idea as it exists on

arth. We have in it, therefore, the object of history in a
more definite shape than before; that in which freedom obtains objectivity, and lives in the enjoyment of this objectivity. For law is the objectivity of spirit; volition in its true
form. Only that will which obeys law is free; for it obeys
itself—it is independent and so free. When the state or our
country constitutes a community of existence; when the subjective will of man submits to laws,—the contradiction between liberty and necessity vanishes. The rational has necessary existence, as being the reality and substance of things,
and we are free in recognizing it as law, and following it as
the substance of our own being. The objective and the subjective will are then reconciled, and present one identical
homogeneous whole. For the morality of the state is not of
that ethical reflective kind, in which one's conviction bears
sway; this latter is rather the peculiarity of the modern time,
while the true antique morality is based on the principle of
abiding by one's duty (to the State at large). An Athenian
citizen did what was required of him, as it were from instinct:
but if I reflect on the object of my activity, I must have the
consciousness that my will has been called into exercise.
But morality is duly—substantial right—a "second nature"
as it has been justly called; for the *first* nature of man is his
primary merely animal existence.

*   *   *

Summing up what has been said of the state, we find
that we have been led to call its vital principle, as actuating
the individuals who compose it,—morality. The state, its
laws, its arrangements, constitute the rights of its members;
its natural features, its mountains, air, and waters are *their*
country, their fatherland, their outward material property;
the history of this state, *their* deeds; what their ancestors
have produced belongs to them and lives in their memory.
All is their possession, just as they are possessed by it; for
it constitutes their existence, their being.

Their imagination is occupied with the ideas thus pre-

481

sented, while the adoption of these laws, and of a fatherland so conditioned is the expression of their will. It is this matured totality which thus constitutes *one* being, the spirit of *one* people. To it the individual members belong; each unit is the son of his nation, and at the same time—in so far as the state to which he belongs is undergoing development—the son of his age. None remains behind it, still less advances beyond it. This spiritual being (the spirit of his time) is his; he is a representative of it; it is that in which he originated and in which he lives. Among the Athenians the word Athens had a double import; suggesting primarily, a complex of political institutions, but no less, in the second place, that goddess who represented the spirit of the people and its unity.

This spirit of a people is a *determinate* and particular spirit, and is, as just stated, further modified by the degree of its historical development. This spirit, then, constitutes the basis and substance of those other forms of a nation's consciousness, which have been noticed. For spirit in its self-consciousness must become an object of contemplation to itself, and objectivity involves, in the first instance, the rise of differences which make up a total of distinct spheres of objective spirit, in the same way as the soul exists only as the complex of its faculties, which in their form of concentration in a simple unity produce that soul. It is thus *one individuality* which, presented in its essence as God, is honored and enjoyed in *religion;* which is exhibited as an object of sensuous contemplation in *art;* and is apprehended as an intellectual conception in *philosophy*. In virtue of the original identity of their essence, purport, and object, these various forms are inseparably united with the spirit of the state. Only in connection with this particular religion, can this particular political constitution exist; just as in such or such a state, such or such a philosophy or order of art.

The remark next in order is, that each particular national genius is to be treated as only one individual in the process of universal history. For that history is the exhibition

f the divine, absolute development of spirit in its highest
forms,—that gradation by which it attains its truth and consciousness of itself. The forms which these grades of progress assume are the characteristic "national spirits" of history, the peculiar tenor of their moral life, of their Government, their art, religion, and science. To realize these grades
is the boundless impulse of the world-spirit—the goal of its
irresistible urging; for this division into organic members,
and the full development of each, is its idea. Universal history is exclusively occupied with showing how spirit comes
to a recognition and adoption of the truth: the dawn of knowledge appears; it begins to discover salient principles, and
at last it arrives at full consciousness.

Having, therefore, learned the abstract characteristics
of the nature of spirit, the means which it uses to realize its
idea, and the shape assumed by it in its complete realization
in phenomenal existence,— namely, the state, nothing further
remains for this introductory section to contemplate, but—
the course of the world's history.

[155]

HEHASID, JUDAH BEN SAMUEL
OF REGENSBURG

HEHASID, JUDAH BEN SAMUEL OF REGENSBURG (12th and
13th centuries). The Hebrew word *Hehasid* means "the Saint."
Judah's co-religionists revered him because he was an extremely
pious man, absorbed in mystical contemplation, a great teacher,
scholar and a careful leader of the Jewish community of Regensburg where he settled in 1195. He was the initiator of Jewish mysticism in Germany, a way of thinking and feeling that is different
from cabalistic mysticism because it insists more on prayer and
moral conduct. Judah denied all possibility of human understanding of God. Man must fulfill his religious duties, as they are prescribed in the Bible, without reasonable knowledge of the Almighty,
but, by purification, obedience to ceremonial life and asceticism, he
may obtain union with God that is beyond reasoning. In this way,
Judah tried to reconcile the demands of orthodox Judaism with enjoyment of mystical ecstasy.

483

Judah's biography is adorned with many legends which testify to the admiration of his contemporaries and succeeding generations. He wrote *Sefer Hasidim* (Book of the Pious), and *Sefer Hakahod* (Book of Glory). The second book has been lost. It is known only by quotations other authors have made from it.

CERTAIN FORMS OF VIRTUE LEAD TO SIN

THERE is a kind of humility which inherits Gehenna, and causes the heirs of the humble to inherit a burning fire in Gehenna. In what manner is it? If a man sees that his children, relatives, or pupils are of bad behavior, and it lies within his power to correct them, by reprimanding or by beating them, but he says to himself: 'I shall rather be agreeable to them and not reprimand or beat them,' he causes them to inherit Gehenna. For they will corrupt their way, and will even do mischief to their father and their mother, so that they will despise them, and curse the day wherein they were born. It is in connection with such a case that it is written: 'He that spareth the rod hateth his son.' It is also said that he who smites his grown-up son transgresses the injunction: 'Put not a stumbling-block before the blind.' But a son that is accustomed to reproofs of instruction, and is beaten while small, will not resent if his father beats him when he is grown up. It is also written: 'Unless I had believed to see the goodness of the Lord;' there are some dots on the word *Unless,* for David said: 'Peradventure I caused my sons to sin, and am not able to make amends by repenting'; for it is written: 'And his father had not grieved him all his life in saying: "Why hast thou done so?"'

There is another kind of humility which likewise brings a man down to Gehenna. For instance, a man sits in a court of justice, and knows that the judges are in error; or a private man knows that the court is in error, but says: 'How shall I go and put them to shame?' or a man knows that the judges are not well-versed in law, while he is well-versed, and when they say to him: 'Sit with us that we may not go astray', he replies: 'I shall not take a seat, for ye are well-versed.' It is obvious that if they go astray, the sin is to be attached to him. Another instance is, when a man hears that the congregation speak falsely, and he says: 'Who am I that I should speak before them?' Behold, it is written: 'And in thy majesty prosper, ride on, in behalf of truth and humility of righteousness'; from this we infer that there is a kind of humility which is not righteousness, as the above and similar cases show. It is also said: 'An untutored priest should not say the benedictions in the presence of scholars.'

There is a kind of charity which is pernicious. In what manner is it? One who gives alms to adulterers or to a glutton or a drunkard. For it is written: 'She shall not fall into harlotry,' and thou mayest read: 'She shall not cause to fall into harlotry;' 'Thou shall not commit adultery,' and thou mayest read: 'Thou shall not cause to commit adultery.' 'Thou shalt not murder,' and it may be read: 'Thou shalt not cause to murder.' He who supplies weapons of destruction to murderers is regarded as if he himself had committed murder. For it is written: 'He hath also prepared for him the weapons of death.' He who gives food to robbers is like their accomplice. Similarly, he who gives alms to adulterers is regarded as though he had aided them and brought them together, for they take the money that is given to them, and offer it as hire to harlots. It is also said that a man should give no alms at all rather than give it publicly. In a similar sense it is also said that if a man who cannot pay his debts gives alms, it is obvious that his charity is robbery.

There is a kind of piety which is bad. For instance, a man whose hands are unclean sees a holy book fall into the fire, and says: 'It is better that it should be burned,' and does not touch the book. Another instance has also been cited: a man sees a woman drown in the river, and says: 'It is better that she should drown than that I should touch her.'

There is also false piety. For instance: a man brings out a Scroll of the Law into the public thoroughfare on the Sabbath on account of a fire; or when a man says: 'How shall I save a man's life and profane the Sabbath?' Another instance is: a question about declaring a thing forbidden or unlawful is referred to a man who knows that he is well-versed in the Law, though there are others like him in the city, and he says: 'Address the question to others;' behold, his meekness may lead to sin: peradventure if he had given his decision, he would have forbidden that which others had declared lawful.

There is sometimes a righteous judge that perishes in his righteousness. For instance: he sees two litigants, one being a swindler, and the other a simpleton; the swindler knows how to plead, but the simpleton, who does not know how to plead, is right; concerning him it is written: 'Open thy mouth for the dumb.' Likewise, if he knows that the verdict is unjust, one of the litigants having hired false witnesses, he should say: 'Let the sin be attached to the witnesses.'

A favor sometimes turns out to be harmful, and is regarded as an evil for its author and his offspring. In what manner is it? For instance: a man causes that sinners and they that lead others astray should dwell in the city. Now since it is bad for the people of the city, it is evident that he and his offspring will stumble over them, and they will do mischief to his offspring. It is in connection with such a case that it is written: 'And he did that which is not good among his people.' (Another explanation: *And he did that which is not good among his people* refers to him who disgraces his family; he is punished, because he sinned by inflicting shame and injury upon his people). Another instance: he who does a good deed in order to be honored and to praise himself thereby.

[156]

HEIDEGGER, MARTIN

HEIDEGGER, MARTIN (1889-). Heidegger is a modern German philosopher who has a considerable French following despite the fact that he had leanings toward the socio-political views of the Third Reich. As a keen analyst of being, Being, existence being present and thus-being (even the French speak of *le Sosein* and *le*

Desein) he has no equal and the fine distinctions which he draws have earned him derision and the charge of mental acrobatics among those incapable of following him. Yet he is no more abstruse than his teacher Husserl, and in his philosophy he is continually reaching down into the very core of personality in which he discovers grave guilt, anxiety and fear which make our existence one for death. Man is lost in utter loneliness, he is totally isolated. Only against the background of historical fate does his present existence attain value.

Heidegger himself is conscious of the difficult style in which his main work *Sein und Zeit* and all the others are written, and he is now clarifying his position, controversial on that account, by occupying himself with the problem of language and communication. Spending his summers in a tiny cottage deep in the Black Forest (but not deep enough to exclude philosophical and journalistic pilgrims), his winters in Freiburg (where he accepted the rectorship at the University in 1933, but resigned it the following year to continue as professor of philosophy), he has a number of significant works on his desk ready for publication if history so decrees.

NOTHINGNESS

FROM ancient times, metaphysics has spoken about nothingness in an ambiguous sentence. *Ex nihilo nihil fit.* Nothing becomes out of nothing. Although "nothing" has never been a problem in the discussion of that sentence, the leading and fundamental concept of being is expressed in it.

Ancient metaphysics conceives nothingness in the sense of not being, of unshaped matter that is incapable of shaping itself into a formed being. Formed being offers an aspect, appearance (*eidos*). Being is form that represents something in an image. Origin, right and limit of that concept of being are as little discussed as nothingness itself.

But Christian dogmatics denies the truth of the sentence *Ex nihilo nihil fit* and gives nothingness a changed meaning, in the sense of absolute absence of non-godly being. *Ex nihilo ens creatum.* Being has been created out of nothing. Now nothingness has become the contradiction of the true being, of the *summum ens*, of God as the *ens increatum*, the uncreated being. Here, too, the interpretation of nothingness indicates a fundamental concept of the Being. The metaphysical discussion of the Being maintains itself on the same level as the question concerning nothingness. It, therefore, does not care about the difficulty that, if God creates out of nothing, He just must have an attitude toward nothingness. If, however, God is God, then He cannot know nothingness, provided that the "Absolute" excludes from itself all nothingness.

This sketchy historical survey shows nothingness as the counter-concept of the true Being, as its negation. But if nothingness becomes a problem anyhow, then this counter-relation is not only more distinctly determined, but then the very metaphysical question of the "being of being" is broached. Nothingness does not remain the indefinite contrary to Being, but is revealed as belonging to the "Being of Being."

"Pure Being and pure non-being are the same thing"—this sentence of Hegel is true. Being and nothing belong together, but not because, as from Hegel's point of view, both agree in their indefiniteness and immediateness, but because Being is essentially finite and becomes manifest only in the transcendence of Being taken into the realm of nothingness.

[157]

HELMHOLTZ, HERMANN VON

HELMHOLTZ, HERMANN VON (1821-1894). When Helmholtz, in 1847, delivered his lecture on the conservation of energy, he was prepared to be reproached by the authorities of his time for talking about old stuff. Instead he was hailed by some as a discoverer, and blamed by others as a fanciful speculative philosopher. Most of the physicists had ignored the principle of persistence of energy. Helmholtz knew better. He did not claim to have discovered it. His intention was rather to demonstrate what it means to physical phenomena and to what numerical consequences it leads everywhere.

The universality of Helmholtz' mind is proved by the mere fact that he was successively appointed full professor of physiology, anatomy and physics at the greatest universities of Germany. He promoted optics and acoustics, mechanics, the general theory of electricity, thermodynamics, hydrodynamics, electrodynamics, geometry and the theory of numbers. In 1850 he invented the ophthalmoscope, and received no other material profit from his invention than about fifteen dollars as honorarium for the treatise in which he communicated it.

Helmholtz was also interested in philosophy which, according to him, is concerned with the inquiry into the cognitive faculties and performances of man. He characterized sensation as a symbol, not an image of the external world, and the world of these symbols as the mirror of the real world. If man learns to read the symbols correctly, he becomes able to arrange his actions in a way that the effects correspond to the aims. Helmholtz conceded the theoretical possibility of interpreting the facts in terms of subjective idealism but held that the realist interpretation is the simpler one. Helmholtz, one of whose maternal ancestors was William Penn, was respected internationally not only because of his scientific performances but as the very incarnation of the dignity and probity of science.

THE INTERDEPENDENCE OF THE SCIENCES

MEN of science form, as it were, an organized army, laboring on behalf of the whole nation, and generally under its direction, and at its expense, to augment the stock of such knowledge as may serve to promote industrial enterprise, to increase wealth, to adorn life, to improve political and social relations, and to further the moral development of individual citizens. After the immediate practical results of their work we forbear to inquire; that we leave to the instructed. We are convinced that whatever contributes to the knowledge of the forces of nature or the powers of the human mind is worth cherishing, and may, in its own due time, bear practical fruit, very often where we should least have expected it. Who, when Galvani touched the muscles of a frog with different metals, and noticed their contraction, could have dreamt that eighty years afterward, in virtue of the self-same process, whose earliest manifestations attracted his attention in his anatomical researches, all Europe would be traversed with wires, flashing intelligence from Madrid to St. Petersburg with the speed of lightning? In the hands of Galvani, and at first even in Volta's, electrical currents were phenomena capable of exerting only the feeblest forces, and could not be detected except by the most delicate apparatus. Had they been neglected, on the ground that the investigation of them promised no immediate practical result, we should now be ignorant of the most important and most interesting of the links between the various sources of nature. When young Galileo, then a student at Pisa, noticed one day during divine service a chandelier swinging backward and forward, and convinced himself, by counting his pulse, that the duration of the oscillations was independent of the arc through which it moved, who could know that this discovery would eventually put it in our power, by means of the pendulum, to attain an accuracy in the measurement of time till then deemed impossible, and would enable the storm-tossed seaman in the most distant oceans to determine in what degree of longitude he was sailing?

Whoever, in the pursuit of science, seeks after immediate practical utility, may generally rest assured that he will seek in vain. All that science can achieve is a perfect knowledge and a perfect understanding of the action of natural and moral forces. Each individual student must be content to find his reward in rejoicing over new discoveries, enjoying the aesthetic beauty of a well-ordered field of knowledge, where the connection and the filiation of every detail is clear to the mind, and where all denotes the presence of a ruling intellect; he must rest satisfied with the consciousness that he too has contributed something to the increasing fund of knowledge on which the dominion of man over all the forces hostile to intelligence reposes. . . .

The sciences have, in this respect, all one common aim, to establish the supremacy of intelligence over the world: while the moral sciences aim directly at making the resources of intellectual life more abundant and more interesting, and seek to separate the pure gold of Truth from alloy, the physical sciences are striving indirectly toward the same goal, inasmuch as they labor to make mankind more and more independent of the material restraints that fetter their activity. Each student works in his own department, he chooses for himself those tasks for which he is best fitted by his abilities and his training. But each one must be convinced that it is only in connection with others that he can further the great work, and that therefore he is bound, not only to investigate, but to do his utmost to make the results of his investigation completely and easily accessible. If he does this, he will derive assistance from others, and will in his turn be able to render them his aid. The annals of science abound in evidence of how such mutual services have been exchanged, even between departments of science apparently most remote. Historical chronology is essentially based on astronomical calculations of eclipses, accounts of which are preserved in ancient histories. Conversely, many of the important data of astronomy—for instance, the invariability of the length of the day, and the periods of several comets, rest upon ancient historical notices. Of late years, physiologists, especially Brücke, have actually undertaken to draw up a complete system of all the vocables that can be produced by the organs of speech, and to base upon it propositions for a universal alphabet, adapted to all human languages. Thus physiology has entered the service of comparative philology, and has already succeeded in accounting for many apparently anomalous substitutions, on the ground that they are governed, not as hitherto supposed, by the laws of euphony, but by similarity between the movements of the mouth that produce them. Again, comparative philology gives us information about the relationships, the separations, and the migrations of tribes in prehistoric times, and of the degree of civilization which they had reached at the time when they parted. For the names of objects to which they had already learnt to give distinctive appellations reappear as words common to their later languages. So that the study of languages actually gives us historical data for periods respecting which no other historical evidence exists. Yet again I may notice the help which not only the sculptor, but the archaeologist, concerned with the investigation of ancient statues, derives from anatomy. And if I may be permitted to refer to my own most recent studies, I would mention that it is possible, by reference to physical acoustics and to the physiological theory of the sensation of hearing, to account for the elementary principles on which our musical system is constructed, a problem essentially within the sphere of aesthetics. In fact, it is a general principle that the physiology of the organs of sense is most intimately connected with psychology, inasmuch as physiology traces in our sensations the results of mental processes which do not fall within the sphere of consciousness, and must therefore have remained inaccessible to us.

I have been able to quote only some of the most striking instances of this interdependence of different sciences, and such as could be explained in a few words. Naturally, too, I have tried to choose them from the most widely separated sciences. But far wider is of course the influence which allied sciences exert upon each other.

[158]

HELVÉTIUS, CLAUDE ADRIEN

HELVÉTIUS, CLAUDE ADRIEN (1715-1771). Many moralists of many ages have complained that personal interest in the pursuit of happiness is the only efficient principle of human actions. The awareness of this fact has made some of them melancholy, others resigned to that fate, and still others fundamentally pessimistic, or indignant, or hypocritical. There has been no lack of efforts to deny such statements or to change the character of man if the statement were true. Helvétius, contrary to all of these critics of egoism, was the first to draw an optimistic conclusion from the conviction that personal interest was the real rule of human behavior. His book *De l'Esprit* (On the Mind, 1758), in which Helvétius explained his views and founded them upon Condillac's sensualism, was condemned by the Sorbonne and burned in Paris after the judges had declared it dangerous to state and society.

Helvétius was a clever financier by profession. He used his

492

large income for the promotion of literature, philosophy and social welfare. He was one of the first to insist on taking the social
environment and economic conditions into consideration before sen-
tencing a defendant. Not this demand but other suggestions advanced by Helvétius were later realized by the legislation of the
First French Republic and by Napoleon.

Helvétius' book *On the Mind* was studied by Bentham and,
through him, influenced British utilitarianism.

OF THE ERRORS OCCASIONED BY PASSION

THE passions lead us into error because they fix our attention to that particular part of the object they present to us,
not allowing us to view it on every side. A king passionately
affects the title of Conqueror. Victory, says he, calls me to
the remotest part of the earth: I shall fight; I shall gain the
victory; I shall load mine enemy with chains, and the terror
of my name, like an impenetrable rampart, will defend the
entrance of my empire. Inebriated with this hope, he forgets
that fortune is inconstant; and, that the victor shares the
load of misery almost equally with the vanquished. He does
not perceive, that the welfare of his subjects is only a pretence for his martial frenzy; and that pride alone forges
his arms, and displays his ensigns: his whole attention is
fixed on the pomp of the triumph.

Fear, equally powerful with pride, will produce the
same effect; it will raise ghosts and phantoms, and disperse
them among the tombs, and in the darkness of the woods,
present them to the eyes of the affrighted traveler, seize on
all the faculties of his soul, without leaving any one at liberty to reflect on the absurdity of the motives for such a
ridiculous terror.

The passions not only fix the attention on the particular
sides of the objects they present to us; but they also deceive
us, by exhibiting the same objects, when they do not really exist. The story of a country clergyman and an amorous lady is
well known. They had heard, and concluded, that the moon
was peopled, and were looking for the inhabitants through
their telescopes. If I am not mistaken, said the lady, I per-

ceive two shadows; they mutually incline towards each other: doubtless they are two happy lovers.—O fie! madam, replied the clergyman, these two shadows are the two steeples of a cathedral. This tale is our history, it being common for us to see in things what we are desirous of finding there: on the earth, as in the moon, different passions will cause us to see either lovers or steeples. Illusion is a necessary effect of the passions, the strength of force of which is generally measured by the degree of obscurity into which they lead us. This was well known to a certain lady, who being caught by her lover in the arms of his rival, obstinately denied the fact of which he had been a witness. How! said he, have you the assurance—Ah! perfidious creature, cried the lady, it is plain you no longer love me; for you believe your eyes, before all I can say. This is equally applicable to all the passions, as well as to love. All strike us with the most perfect blindness. When ambition has kindled a war between two nations, and the anxious citizens ask one another the news, what readiness appears, on one side, to give credit to the good; and, on the other, what incredulity with regard to the bad? How often have christians, from placing a ridiculous confidence in monks, denied the possibility of the antipodes. There is no century which has not, by some ridiculous affirmation or negation, afforded matter of laughter to the following age. A past folly is seldom sufficient to show mankind their present folly.

The same passions, however, which are the germ of an infinity of errors, are also the sources of our knowledge. If they mislead us, they, at the same time, impart to us the strength necessary for walking. It is they alone that can rouse us from that sluggishness and torpor always ready to seize on the faculties of our soul.

[159]

HERACLITUS

HERACLITUS (about 540-480 B.C.). One of the most vigorous thinkers of Greek antiquity, proud and independent, Heraclitus stated with utter candor his opinion of his fellow citizens of Ephe sus: They ought to go and hang themselves and hand over the city to juveniles, having expelled Hermodoros, the best among them. So disgusted was he with political intrigue and the wrangles of small minds, that he left the city and sought solace and inspiration in the beauty and grandeur of nature. But for the Ephesians he had a strange wish: Would that their wealth never decline so that their worthlessness might appear to even better advantage!

Himself of noble birth, he disdained the masses. His admirer, Nietzsche, would have concurred in this: "One man to me is worth as much as 10,000, provided he be the best." The masses, he believed, cannot comprehend the divine nature. Indeed, they could not follow Heraclitus in the flight of his spirit, and thus they called him the Dark Philosopher.

From his spiritual height he flayed their idolatry and base thinking, and aligned himself with fate and a divine being for whom all is beautiful, good and just. The world, not created in time but existing from all eternity, he considered as ever in flux, and war as the father of all things. There is a cycle, however, from the eternal fire through want to the manifold of things, and back again through satedness, harmony and peace. Everything is relative— the most beautiful ape is ugly compared to man; illness makes health sweet, evil the good . . . Contentment is achieved by submission to order, reason and wisdom. The soul, a spark of the substance of the stars, is immortal and returns upon death to the all-soul to which it is related.

FRAGMENTS

It is wise to hearken not to me but my argument, and to confess that all things are one.

Though this discourse is true evermore, yet men are as unable to understand it when they hear it for the first time as before they have heard it at all. For, although all things happen in accordance with the account I give, men seem as if they had no experience of them, when they make trial of words and works such as I set forth, dividing each thing according to its nature and explaining how it truly is. But other men know not what they are doing when you wake them up, just as they forget what they do when asleep.

Fools when they do hear are like the deaf; of them

does the proverb bear witness that they are absent when present.

Eyes and ears are bad witnesses to men, if they have souls that understand not their language.

The many have not as many thoughts as the things they meet with; nor, if they do remark them, do they understand them, though they believe they do.

Knowing not how to listen nor how to speak.

If you do not expect the unexpected, you will not find it; for it is hard to be sought out and difficult.

Those who seek for gold dig up much earth and find a little.

Nature loves to hide.

The lord whose is the oracle at Delphi neither utters nor hides his meaning, but shows it by a sign.

And the Sibyl, with raving lips uttering things solemn, unadorned, and unembellished, reaches over a thousand years with her voice because of the god in her.

Am I to prize these things above what can be seen, heard, and learned?

. . . bringing untrustworthy witnesses in support of disputed points.

The eyes are more exact witnesses than the ears.

The learning of many things teacheth not understanding, else would it have taught Hesiod and Pythagoras, and again Xenophanes and Hekataios.

Pythagoras, son of Mnesarchos, practised inquiry beyond all other men, and made himself a wisdom of his own, which was but a knowledge of many things and an art of mischief.

Of all whose discourses I have heard, there is not one who attains to understanding that wisdom is apart from other things.

Wisdom is one thing. It is to know the thought by which all things are steered through all things.

This order, which is the same in all things, no one of gods or men has made; but it was ever, is now, and ever shall be everliving Fire, fixed measures of it kindling and fixed measures going out.

The transformations of Fire are, first of all, sea (and half of the sea is earth, half fiery storm-cloud). . . .

All things are exchanged for Fire, and Fire for all things, as wares are exchanged for gold and gold for wares.

(The earth) is liquified, and the sea is measured by the same tale as before it became earth.

Fire is want and satiety.

Fire lives the death of earth, and air lives the death of fire; water lives the death of air, earth that of water.

Fire will come upon and lay hold of all things.

How can one hide from that which never sinks to rest?

It is the thunderbolt that steers the course of all things.

The sun will not exceed his measures; if he does, the Erinyes, the avenging handmaids of Justice, will find him out.

The limit of East and West is the Bear; and opposite the Bear is the boundary of bright Zeus.

If there were no sun, it would be night.

The sun is new every day.

The seasons that bring all things.

Hesiod is most men's teacher. Men think he knew very many things, a man who did not know day or night! They are one.

God is day and night, winter and summer, war and peace, satiety and hunger; but He takes various shapes, just as fire, when it is mingled with different incenses, is named according to the savour of each.

If all things were turned to smoke, the nostrils would distinguish them.

Souls smell in Hades.

It is cold things that become warm, and what is warm that cools; what is wet dries, and the parched is moistened.

It scatters things and brings them together; it approaches and departs.

You cannot step twice into the same rivers; for fresh waters are ever flowing in upon you.

Homer was wrong in saying: "Would that strife might perish from among gods and men!" He did not see that he was praying for the destruction of the universe; for, if his prayer were heard, all things would pass away.

War is the father of all and the king of all; and some he has made gods and some men, some bond and some free.

Men do not know how that which is drawn in different directions harmonises with itself. The harmonious structure of the world depends upon opposite tension, like that of the bow and the lyre.

It is opposition that brings things together.

The hidden harmony is better than the open.

Let us not conjecture at random about the greatest things.

Men who love wisdom must be acquainted with very many things indeed.

The straight and the crooked path of the fuller's comb is one and the same.

Asses would rather have straw than gold.

Oxen are happy when they find bitter vetches to eat.

The sea is the purest and the impurest water. Fish can drink it, and it is good for them; to men it is undrinkable and destructive.

Swine like to wash in the mire rather than in clean water, and barnyard fowls in dust.

Every beast is tended with blows.

Good and ill are the same.

Physicians who cut, burn, stab, and rack the sick, then complain that they do not get any adequate recompense for it.

You must couple together things whole and things not whole, what is drawn together and what is drawn asunder, the harmonious and the discordant. The one is made up of all things, and all things issue from the one.

Men would not have known the name of justice if there were no injustice.

Men themselves have made a law for themselves, not knowing what they made it about; but the gods have ordered the nature of all things. Now the arrangements which men have made are never constant, neither when they are right nor when they are wrong; but all the arrangements which the gods have made are always right, both when they are right and when they are wrong; so great is the difference.

We must know that war is the common and justice is strife, and that all things come into being and pass away(?) through strife.

... for they are undoubtedly allotted by destiny.

All the things we see when awake are death, even as the things we see in slumber are sleep.

Wisdom is one only. It is willing and unwilling to be called by the name of Zeus.

The bow (bios') is called life (bi'os), but its work is death.

Mortals are immortals and immortals are mortals, the one living the other's death and dying the other's life.

For it is death to souls to become water, and death to water to become earth. But water comes from earth; and from water, soul.

The way up and the way down is one and the same.

The beginning and the end are common (to both paths).

You will not find the boundaries of soul by travelling in any direction.

It is pleasure to souls to become moist.

A man, when he gets drunk, is led by a beardless lad, knowing not where he steps, having his soul moist.

The dry soul is the wisest and best.

Man is kindled and put out like a light in the night-time

The quick and the dead, the waking and the sleeping, the young and the old are the same; the former are changed and become the latter, and the latter in turn are changed into the former.

Time is a child playing draughts, the kingly power is a child's.

I have sought to know myself.

We step and do not step into the same rivers; we are and are not.

It is a weariness to labor at the same things and to be always beginning afresh.

It finds rest in change.

Even the ingredients of a posset separate if it is not stirred.

Corpses are more fit to be cast out than dung.

When they are born, they wish to live and to meet with their dooms—or rather to rest, and they leave children behind them to meet with dooms in turn.

A man may be a grandfather in thirty years.

Those who are asleep are fellow-workers. . . .

Wisdom is common to all things. Those who speak with intelligence must hold fast to the common as a city holds fast to its law, and even more strongly. For all human laws are fed by one thing, the divine. It prevails as much as it will, and suffices for all things with something to spare.

Though wisdom is common, yet the many live as if they had a wisdom of their own.

They are estranged from that with which they have most constant intercourse.

It is not meet to eat and speak like men asleep.

The waking have one and the same world, but the sleeping turn aside each into a world of his own.

The way of man has no wisdom, but that of the gods has.

Man is called a baby by God, even as a child by a man.

The wisest man is an ape compared to God, just as the most beautiful ape is ugly compared to man.

The people must fight for its law as for its walls.

Greater deaths win greater portions.

Gods and men honor those who are slain in battle.

Wantonness needs to be extinguished even more than a conflagration.

It is not good for men to get all they wish to get. It is disease that makes health pleasant and good; hunger, plenty; and weariness, rest.

It is hard to fight with desire. Whatever it wishes to get, it purchases at the cost of soul.

It is best to hide folly; but it is a hard task in times of relaxation, over our cups.

And it is the law, too, that we obey the counsel of one.

For what thought or wisdom have they? They follow the poets and take the crowd as their teacher, knowing not that there are many bad and few good. For even the best of them choose one thing above all others, immortal glory among mortals, while most of them fill their bellies like beasts.

In Priene lived Bias, son of Teutamas, who is of more account than the rest. (He said, "Most men are bad.")

One is as ten thousand to me, if he be the best.

The Ephesians would do well to hang themselves, every grown man of them, and leave the city to beardless youths; for they have cast out Hermodoros, the best man among them, saying: "We will have none who is best among us; if there be any such, let him be so elsewhere and among others."

Dogs bark at every one they do not know.

. . . (The wise man) is not known because of men's want of belief.

The fool is fluttered at every word.

The most esteemed of those in estimation knows how to feign; yet of a truth justice shall overtake the artificers of lies and the false witnesses.

Homer should be turned out of the lists and whipped, and Archilochos likewise.

One day is equal to another.

Man's character is his fate.

There await men when they die such things as they look not for nor dream of.

501

... that they rise up and become the guardians of the hosts of the quick and dead.

Night-walkers, Magians, priests of Bakchos and priestesses of the wine-vat, mystery-mongers. . . .

The mysteries into which men are initiated are unholy.

And they pray to these images, as if one were to talk with a man's house, knowing not what gods or heroes are.

For if it were not to Dionysos that they made a procession and sang the shameful phallic hymn, they would be acting most shamelessly. But Hades is the same as Dionysos in whose honor they go mad and keep the feast of the wine-vat.

They purify themselves by defiling themselves with blood, just as if one who had stepped into the mud were to go and wash his feet in mud.

[160]

HERBART, JOHANN FRIEDRICH

HERBART, JOHANN FRIEDRICH (1776-1841). American thinking was influenced by Herbart during the two decades which preceded the First World War. But even those who declined to follow him thereafter could not but acknowledge that Herbart was a pioneer in psychological research and pedagogics.

Herbart, who occupied Immanuel Kant's chair at the University of Königsberg for many years, was regarded by Fichte, Schelling and Hegel as their most formidable adversary. In some regards, Herbart maintained the Kantian tradition but more often he relied upon Leibniz, Hume and British associationism. He was an excellent musician, a master of the piano, the violin, the violoncello and the harp, and liked to explain psychological laws by examples taken from the theory of harmony.

Contrary to Fichte, Schelling and Hegel, Herbart always took great care to tally his thoughts with the results of the empirical sciences. To him, philosophy was the reflection upon the conceptions which are commonly used in experience, both daily and scientific. The philosopher must ask what is it that in reality corresponds to the empirical conceptions which are called substance and causality. While German idealists proceeded from the individual knower, the subject, to the metaphysics of nature and mind, Herbart re

502

garded the subject as the highest metaphysical problem. At the same time, the subject was known to him as the changing product of ideas, and, therefore, was explorable by means of psychological research. Psychology, to Herbart, was founded upon experience, metaphysics and mathematics. He followed Locke and Hume by trying to conceive complex psychic phenomena in terms of simple ideas, each of which was supposed to have a certain degree of strength. His great dream was a future psychodynamics determined by mathematical laws.

CHIEF CLASSES OF INTEREST

INSTRUCTION must be joined to the knowledge furnished by experience, and to the disposition which is nourished by intercourse. Experience corresponds immediately with empirical, intercourse with sympathetic, interest. Progressive thought about the objects of experience develops speculative interest,—thought about the more complex relationships of intercourse develops social interest. To these we add on the one side aesthetic, on the other religious, interest. Both have their origin not so much in progressive thought, as in a quiet contemplation of things and their destiny.

It must not be expected that all these various kinds of interest will develop equally in each individual, but on the other hand we may expect to find them all more or less amongst a number of pupils. The required many-sidedness will be more perfectly attained, the more closely each individual approaches the standard of mental culture in which all these interests are aroused with equal energy.

That these six classes of interest naturally fall into two groups, has been already indicated when pointing out the historical and scientific divisions. This tallies with what has been generally observed in the Gymnasia (classical schools), that the pupils generally show a leaning either to the one side or the other. But it would be a great mistake to put for this reason, the historic interest in opposition to the scientific, or even to substitute in the place of these two the philological and mathematical, as is often done. This confusion of ideas must not be continued, otherwise entirely wrong views on instruction will be the result. This erroneousness will be most easily demonstrated, by a consideration of the many varieties of one-sidedness already occurring even *within* the two classes mentioned. In this way, at least, the many varieties it is necessary to distinguish here, will become more clearly separated. For the possible one-sided varieties of interest are much more widely differentiated from each other, than could be indicated by the previous six-fold classification.

Empirical interest will be in its way one-sided, if a certain class of objects of experience are dwelt on to the exclusion of others. So it will be, for instance, if a man desires to be a botanist only, or a mineralogist, or zoologist; or if he only cares for languages, perhaps only dead or only modern languages, or even but for one; or again, if a traveller (like many so-called tourists) only wishes to see certain celebrated districts during his journey, in order to be able to say he has seen them; or again, if as a collector he has only this or that particular hobby; or if as an historian he only cares for the annals of one country and one parish, and so on.

Speculative interest will be in its way one-sided, if it deals only with logic or mathematics, possibly with merely a branch of the latter, such as the geometry of the ancients,— or with metaphysics only, which again may be limited to the views of one school,—or with physics only, perhaps limited to the establishment of one hypothesis,—or finally, with pragmatic history alone.

Aesthetic interest tends to confine itself exclusively to painting or sculpture or poetry—perhaps the latter only of a lyric or dramatic class; or to music, or even only to a variety thereof, etc., etc.

Sympathetic interest will become one-sided, if an individual only cares to live with people of his own class, or with his compatriots, or only with members of his own family, and has no feeling for any others.

Social interest becomes one-sided, when a man is entirely devoted to his own political party, and measures all weal and woe by its interests alone.

Religious interest becomes one-sided, when it leads a man to adhere to certain sects and dogmas, and to despise those who think otherwise.

Many of these species of one-sidedness are brought about in later life, by the individual's vocation, but it ought not to isolate the man. It would certainly do so if such narrowness ruled him in earlier years.

It would be possible to analyze one-sided tendencies still further, but this is not necessary in order to determine what place the studies in the Gymnasia referred to, occupy amongst the subjects that serve to animate interest. Languages are the first on the list, as we know from experience, but why is the preference among so many given to Latin and Greek? Clearly because of their literature and history. Literature with the poets and orators belongs to aesthetic interest, history awakens sympathy for excellent men and for social weal and woe; through both channels it has a direct influence in developing religious interest. No better centre of unity for so many various stimuli can be found. Even speculative interest is not neglected, when the grammatical construction of these languages is added. But history does not stand still with the ancients; literary knowledge also widens, and aids in animating still more completely the interests before mentioned. The pragmatic treatment of history assists speculative interest from another side. In this respect however, mathematics have the preference, only, in order to gain a firmer footing and permanent influence, they must be combined with the natural sciences which arouse both empiric and speculative interest.

Now if these studies *co-operate* thoroughly, they achieve, conjoined with religious instruction, a good deal towards guiding the young mind in the direction conducive to many-sided interest. But were philology and mathematics to be separated, the connecting links removed, and every individual be left the choice of one or the other according to his own preference, the result would then show specimens of

pure one-sidedness such as have been sufficiently characterized in the preceding remarks.

It is generally admitted now that the higher citizens'
schools ought to introduce just this same many-sided education,—that is to say, they should make use of the very same
main classes of interest as the Gymnasia, etc. The only difference is, that the pupils of the Gymnasia begin the exercise of their future calling later than do those of the citizens'
schools. Consequently modern literature and history receive
more consideration in the latter, and to those who are
capable of going beyond these subjects, the higher ones necessary to complex mental activity can be given, but not *quite
so fully* as in the Gymnasia. The same applies to all those
lower schools which give a general education. It is different
with technical schools and polytechnics, in short with such
as presuppose that education is already finished, at least in
so far as circumstances will allow.

Accordingly when a higher citizens' school has a correct
curriculum, it will be seen from it, just as from that of a
Gymnasium, that an attempt has been made, through that
curriculum, to avoid the *extreme* one-sidedness which results
if one only of the *six main classes of interest* be disregarded.

But no instruction whatever is able to avoid those special
one-sidednesses which occur within each main class. When
once observation, reflection, taste for the beautiful, sympathy,
social instincts, and religious feeling have been called into
activity, though but in a narrow circle of subjects, it is chiefly
left to the individual and opportunity to initiate further expansion, including a greater number and variety of subjects.
To talented individuals, still more to geniuses, sufficient
breadth of view may be given by instruction, to show them
what has been done before by others of talent and genius;
their idiosyncrasies however they must retain, and be responsible for themselves.

Nor are all these subordinate one-sided tendencies
equally disadvantageous, for not all assert themselves exclusively to the same extent. Although all of them may be-

506

come arrogant, yet they are not all equally liable to do so.

Under favorable conditions as regards time and opportunity, such as Gymnasia and higher citizens' schools have, the aim of instruction is not as is well known restricted to merely first efforts. The question then comes up, in what sequence should the interests which have been aroused be cultivated further? There is no lack of teaching matter; it is necessary to choose and systematize. For this purpose we must apply in general what has been said regarding the conditions of manysidedness and of interest. These conditions are, to proceed from the simple to the complex, and to provide suitable opportunities for the exercise of involuntary apperceptive attention. It is useless however to deceive ourselves about the difficulties and all that is required to carry this out.

Empirical subject-matter (in languages, history, geography, etc.) requires certain complications and series of presentations, together with their interconnections. To start with, the mere words consist of roots and those particles that pertain to modification and derivation, and these again of single articulate sounds. History has its periods in time, and geography its interconnections in space. The psychological laws of reproduction determine the acts of learning by memory, and of memory itself.

The mother-tongue serves as medium for the comprehension of foreign languages, but at the same time the child's mind struggles against foreign sounds and idioms. Besides this, a younger boy takes a long while to get accustomed to the idea, that at a remote time and place there were, and still are, human beings who speak and have spoken differently to himself—human beings who concern us here and now. The illusion also of many masters is very common and injurious, that because their expression (language) is clear, it must therefore be comprehended by the boy, whose child's language only grows slowly. These clogging influences can be overcome. Geography helps with respect to spatial distances, though the visible presentation of mountains is wanting to the inhabitants of a flat country, and that of plains to one who lives in a valley, and again of the sea to the majority of people. That the earth is a ball and turns on its axis, and revolves round the sun, sounds to children for a long time like a fairy-tale, and there are cultivated youths who doubt the theory of the planetary system, because they do not comprehend how it can be known. Such obstructions must be got rid of, and not multiplied unnecessarily. Old ruins might be made use of as a starting point for history, if they were not far too meagre and too near in time, when the young are to be introduced to Jewish, Greek and Roman antiquities. Recourse can only be had to stories to arouse a lively interest; these become the fulcrum of thought about a long vanished past, but the estimation of chronological distances leading up to our own time is still wanting, and can only be gradually realized by subsequent insertions.

Practice in thinking, and together with it, the animation of speculative interest, is stimulated by everything which reveals or even only suggests connection by general laws in nature, in human affairs, in the structure of languages, in religious teaching. But everywhere, even in the things most commonly used, in general arithmetic and grammar, the pupil is confronted by general concepts, judgments and conclusions. He remains however attached to the single, familiar, sensuous. The abstract is strange to him; even geometrical figures drawn for the eye are but individual concrete things to him, and he only recognizes their general import with difficulty. The general notion ought to drive the special example out of his thoughts, but *vice versa* the special instance comes to the front in the usual series of presentations, and of the generalization, little remains to the boy but the words with which it is designated. If he is to draw a conclusion, he loses sight of one premise in dealing with the other, and the teacher must continually begin again, and illustrate the concepts and connect them, and gradually bring the premises together. When the middle terms in the premises have at last been correctly united, the union is still at first incomplete; the very same syllogisms are often forgotten, and afterwards too frequently repetitions have to be avoided, lest interest be extinguished instead of animated.

It is advisable to allow much of what has already been arrived at through conclusions to be for a time forgotten, as this cannot be prevented, and to return to the principal points later *by different routes*. The first preliminary exercises attain their purpose, if they give a glimpse of the general as revealed in the particular, before the concepts become the subjects of formulae, and before the propositions are formed into series of conclusions. Association must be made between the first demonstrations of the generalization and the syste- matic teaching of its interconnection.

Manifold external interests and also excited emotions may be the causes of aesthetic contemplation. But it only takes place spontaneously, when the spirit is sufficiently tranquil, to enable it to perfectly comprehend the simultan- eously beautiful, and to follow the successively beautiful with answering rhythm. Comprehensible objects must be offered, contemplation must not be forced; but inappropriate re- marks and, still more, damage done to objects of aesthetic value to which respect is due must certainly be forbidden. Frequently imitation, even if at first but roughly done, in drawing, singing, and reading aloud, and later on in trans- lating, is a sign of attracted attention; such imitation may be encouraged, but certainly not praised. The true enthusiasm which grows spontaneously in aesthetic culture, is easily spoiled by being over-stimulated. To overburden is injurious; works of art that belong to a higher stage of culture must not be drawn down to a lower, and opinions and art criticisms should not be forced upon pupils.

The interests of sympathy are still more dependent on intercourse and home life than the former interests are on experience. If children are frequently moved from place to place, their attachment cannot take root anywhere. Even the change of masters and school is injurious. The pupils make comparisons of their own; an authority which is not perma-

nent counts for little; on the contrary, efforts to obtain freedom act against it. Instruction cannot do away with such
evils, the less because it is itself constantly obliged to change
its form, which causes the master to appear different. It is
consequently all the more necessary that in giving historical
instruction, such warmth and sympathy should be expressed
as is due to the personalities and events in question. For this
reason, which is so important for the whole of education, we
should carefully avoid making history a mere chronological
skeleton. Specially should this be observed in the earlier instruction in history, as on it mainly depends what impression
history as a whole will make later on.

It is needless to add, how much religious instruction
should make the children feel their dependence, and how just
are our expectations that it will not leave their souls untouched. In all this, historical must be combined with religious instruction, otherwise religious doctrine will occupy
an isolated position, and will run the danger of not duly
influencing the teaching and learning in all other subjects.

[161]

HERDER, JOHANN GOTTFRIED

HERDER, JOHANN GOTTFRIED (1744-1803). It would not be
incorrect to derive the growth, if not the origin, of modern German nationalism from Herder's writings. But it would not do
justice to him to ignore his humanitarian cosmopolitanism. In fact,
Slavic national feelings have been equally strengthened by Herder
who spoke and wrote German but was a descendant from German-
ized Lithuanians. More than once, Herder not only expressed his
fondness of Slavic literature but protested against German oppression of the Baltic Slavs. He attributed a high value to nationality
as a medium of human civilization. But he denied any claim to
superiority.

To Herder, love of the historical past was a cultural force, a
way to psychic renovation. He believed that acquaintance with the
poetry of the Bible, with Homer, Shakespeare and medieval folk
songs would refresh and enhance the sentiments of modern humanity. But he was an enthusiast of history because he was no less

510

an enthusiast of the future of civilization, and he was firmly convinced that humanitarian ideals were the manifestations of God's
will. In his *Ideen zur Philosophie der Geschichte der Menschheit*
(Ideas on the Philosophy of History of Humanity, 1784-91), Herder
combined biological, ethnological and literary studies with the ideas
of Spinoza, Leibniz, Shaftesbury, Montesquieu and Voltaire. His
work began with the stars, among which earth is one of many others,
and described the influence of climate, geography, customs and individual fates on the history of mankind. Change, growth, and
development were of basic importance to Herder's image of the
world.

Originally a disciple of Kant, Herder, in his later years, opposed his teacher, especially his ideas concerning the "depraved
nature" of man, as a consequence of original sin. He also tried to
refute Kant's Critiques.

MAN, A LINK BETWEEN TWO WORLDS

EVERY thing in nature is connected: one state pushes forward
and prepares another. If then man be the last and highest
link, closing the chain of terrestrial organization, he must
begin the chain of a higher order of creatures as its lowest
link, and is probably, therefore, the middle ring between
two adjoining systems of the creation. He cannot pass into
any other organization upon earth, without turning backwards, and wandering in a circle: for him to stand still is
impossible; since no living power in the dominions of the
most active goodness is at rest; thus there must be a step
before him, close to him, yet as exalted above him, as he is
preeminent over the brute, to whom he is at the same time
nearly allied. This view of things, which is supported by all
the laws of nature, alone gives us the key to the wonderful
phenomenon of man, and at the same time to the only *philosophy* of his *history*. For thus,

I. The singular *inconsistency* of man's condition becomes clear. As an animal he tends to the earth, and is attached to it as his habitation: as a man he has within him
the seeds of immortality, which require to be planted in
another soil. As an animal he can satisfy his wants; and men
that are contented with this feel themselves sufficiently happy

here below: but they who seek a nobler destination find every thing around them imperfect and incomplete; what is most noble is never accomplished upon earth, what is most pure is seldom firm and durable: this theatre is but a place of exercise and trial for the powers of our hearts and minds. The history of the human species, with what it has attempted, and what has befallen it, the exertions it has made, and the revolutions it has undergone sufficiently proves this. Now and then a philosopher, a good man, arose, and scattered opinions, precepts, and actions on the flood of time: a few waves played in circles around them, but these the stream soon carried away and obliterated: the jewel of their noble purposes sunk to the bottom. Fools overpowered the councils of the wise; and spendthrifts inherited the treasures of wisdom collected by their forefathers. Far as the life of man here below is from being calculated for eternity, equally far is this incessantly revolving sphere from being a repository of permanent works of art, a garden of never-fading plants, a seat to be eternally inhabited. We come and go: every moment brings thousands into the world, and takes thousands out of it. The earth is an inn for travellers; a planet, on which birds of passage rest themselves, and from which they hasten away. The brute lives out his life; and, if his years be too few to attain higher ends, his inmost purpose is accomplished: his capacities exist, and he is what he was intended to be. Man alone is in contradiction with himself, and with the earth: for, being the most perfect of all creatures, his capacities are the farthest from being perfected, even when he attains the longest term of life before he quits the world. But the reason is evident: his state, being the last upon this earth, is the first in another sphere of existence, with respect to which he appears here as a child making his first essays. Thus he is the representative of two worlds at once; and hence the apparent duplicity of his essence.

II. Thus it becomes clear, what part must predominate in most men here below. The greater part of man is of the animal kind: he has brought into the world only a capacity for humanity, which must be first formed in him by diligence and labor. In how few is it rightly formed! and how slender and delicate is the divine plant even in the best! Throughout life the brute prevails over the man, and most permit it to sway them at pleasure. This incessantly drags man down, while the spirit ascends, while the heart pants after a freer sphere: and as the present appears more lively to a sensual creature than the remote, as the visible operates upon him more powerfully than the invisible, it is not difficult to conjecture, which way the balance will incline. Of how little pure delight, of how little pure knowledge and virtue, is man capable! And were he capable of more, to how little is he accustomed! The noblest compositions here below are debased by inferior propensities, as the voyage of life is perplexed by contrary winds; and the creator, mercifully strict, has mixed the two causes of disorder together, that one might correct the other, and that the germ of immortality might be more effectually fostered by tempests, than by gentle gales. A man who has experienced much has learned much: the careless and indolent knows not what is within him; and still less does he feel with conscious satisfaction how far his powers extend. Thus life is a conflict, and the garland of pure immortal humanity is with difficulty obtained. The goal is before the runner: by him who fights for virtue, in death the palm will be obtained.

III. Thus, if superior creatures look down upon us, they may view us in the same light as we do the *middle species*, with which nature makes a transition from one element to another. The ostrich flaps his feeble wings to assist himself in running, but they cannot enable him to fly: his heavy body confines him to the ground. Yet the organizing parent has taken care of him, as well as of every middle creature; for they are all perfect in themselves, and only appear defective to our eyes. It is the same with man here below: his defects are perplexing to an earthly mind; but a superior spirit, that inspects the internal structure, and sees more links of the chain, may indeed pity, but cannot despise him. He perceives why man must quit the world in so many different states, young and old, wise and foolish, grown gray in second childhood, or an embryo yet unborn. Omnipotent goodness embraces madness and deformity, all the degrees of cultivation, and all the errors of man, and wants not balsams to heal the wounds that death alone could mitigate. Since probably the future state springs out of the present, as our organization from inferior ones, its business is no doubt more closely connected with our existence here than we imagine. The garden above blooms only with plants, of which the seeds have been sown here, and put forth their first germs from a coarser husk. If, then, as we have seen, sociality, friendship, or active participation in the pains and pleasures of others, be the principal end, to which humanity is directed; this finest flower of human life must necessarily there attain the vivifying form, the overshadowing height, for which our heart thirsts in vain in any earthly situation. Our brethren above, therefore, assuredly love us with more warmth and purity of affection, than we can bear to them: for they see our state more clearly, to them the moment of time is no more, all discrepancies are harmonized, and in us they are probably educating, unseen, partners of their happiness and companions of their labors. But one step farther, and the oppressed spirit can breathe more freely, the wounded heart recovers: they see the passenger approach and stay his sliding feet with a powerful hand.

[162]

HESS, MOSES

HESS, MOSES (1812-1875). Hess, who assumed the first name Moses instead of Moritz in order to show his adherence to Judaism, provoked the indignation of his relatives by marrying a prostitute in order to show his contempt of the existing moral standards. He lived with her in happiness until his death. He was, however, a man who willingly obeyed those ethical demands that his thinking recognized as right. He was an early apostle of socialism, and a precursor of Zionism. Because of his participation in the revolution of 1848, Hess was sentenced to death and on escaping had to wander through many countries of Europe before he found refuge in Paris.

In his youth, Hess abounded in ideas. His influence with Karl Marx was considerable. For a time they were closely associated. Later Marx felt himself superior to Hess, and made him smart for his previous ascendancy. Although Hess recognized the importance of economic and social forces, he conceived socialism as a prevalently humanitarian ideal, dissenting from Marx who regarded it as the inevitable result of economic evolution. It was also for the sake of humanity that Hess agitated for the establishment of a Jewish commonwealth in Palestine by publishing his book *Rome and Jerusalem* (1862) and numerous essays in which he expresses Messianic hopes. According to Hess, Judaism has no other dogma but "the teaching of the unity." As already shown by his *Holy Story of Humanity* (1837), he deviated from the Jewish conception of God and called the history of humanity holy because, in his opinion, it is really the history of God, then conceived by him partly in accordance with Spinoza, partly with the Christian doctrine of Trinity. In *European Triarchy* (1841) he outlined a new order of Europe which he claimed was in accordance with "human nature." His socialism is not strictly egalitarian but an effort to satisfy the wants of "human nature," which remained his principal standard of judging human institutions. In his later years he came closer to the views developed in Jewish traditions, but he built his hopes for the settlement of the Jews in the Holy Land upon France, which he regarded as the champion of liberty. After France's defeat in the war of 1870, he admonished the nations of Europe to ally with one another against German militarism.

ORGANIC LIFE

EVERY transformation of matter on behalf of the life of humanity means working, creating, producing, acting—in short, living. For, in reality, whatever is living is working. Concerning human life, not only head and hands but also all the other members and organs of the body work to transform the matter received from outside. The mouth works up the matter for the stomach, which, on its part, digests it for the blood, and so on. That means that every organ of the human body and every member of human society is producing, on behalf of the whole. Every man is working while apparently only consuming or enjoying, and he enjoys his

515

life, while apparently working or producing for the whole. But the harmony between work and enjoyment takes place only in organic or organized life, not in a life that lacks organization.

[163]

HIYYA, ABRAHAM BAR

HIYYA, ABRAHAM BAR (About 1065-1136). While Christianity and Islam met each other on the battlefield, Abraham bar Hiyya, called by his fellow Jews "the prince," and by non-Jews "Savasorda" (Latinization of his Arabic title Sahib al Shurta, governor of a city), took a leading part in promoting spiritual interchange between the representatives of the Christian and Arabic civilizations. without neglecting his principal task, namely the vindication of the Jewish faith and its harmonization with science and philosophy.

His treatise on areas and measurements which introduced new scientific terms and new methods for the measurement of surfaces, was translated into Latin under the title *Liber Embadorum,* and, for centuries, it remained a standard work. His contributions to mathematics, astronomy, music and optics were highly appreciated by Jewish, Christian and Moslem scholars. In his *Hegyon Hanefesh* (Reflection on the Soul), Abraham bar Hiyya, while exposing his ideas on creation and the destiny and conduct of Man, showed a strong inclination to an ascetic conception of life.

THE LIFE OF THE PIOUS

THOSE people of the law who do not uphold the faith are not helped much by their learning.

Those separated unto God eat food they have, not to satisfy a desire for its good taste but to silence the pain of hunger, and they wrap themselves with any garment to protect the body against the cold without being concerned as to whether it is of wool or flax.

Any potentiality the actualization of which wisdom affirms must have already changed to actuality.

[164]

516

HOBBES, THOMAS

HOBBES, THOMAS (1588-1679). Born prematurely due to his mother's anxiety over the approach of the Spanish Armada, Hobbes had a streak of timidity in him which did not jibe with the philosophy propounded in his *Leviathan* and *Behemoth*. Influenced by the greatest thinkers of the times—among them Descartes, Gassendi and Galileo, whom he met on the Continent as tutor to Charles II and during an 11-year self-imposed, needless exile—Hobbes professed materialism, seeking to explain everything on mechanical principles. All knowledge comes by way of the senses, he held, and the objects of knowledge are material bodies obeying physical forces. Man too, in his natural state is "brutish and nasty." Realizing, that if man were to continue as wolf to man, chaos and destruction would result, men have, therefore, entered into a social contract, delegating the control of their fellow men to the state, which is governed and thus insures them a measure of security. In essence, therefore, the state and the kingship is a thing bargained for.

Uninfluenced by Francis Bacon, whose secretary he was for a time, "gaping on mappes" while supposed to be studying at Oxford, reading few books, getting himself into trouble with every publication because either conceptions or Parliament had changed, absorbed in mathematics for which he did not have the talent to make original contributions, and translating Homer and other Greeks, he attained the age of 89 complaining of having trouble keeping the flies "from pitching on the baldness" of his head. With consistency he had resisted the gains of the Renaissance as well as the resuscitation of scholasticism. His books were condemned by Parliament. Although the clergy hated him as an atheist, he nevertheless played safe by affiliating himself with a church and showing devoutness in the face of death.

STATE AND SOVEREIGNTY

THE final cause, end, or design of men, who naturally love liberty, and dominion over others, in the introduction of that restraint upon themselves, in which we see them live in commonwealths, is the foresight of their own preservation, and of a more contented life thereby; that is to say, of getting themselves out from that miserable condition of war, which

517

is necessarily consequent . . . to the natural passions of men, when there is no visible power to keep them in awe, and tie them by fear of punishment to the performance of their covenants, and observation of those laws of nature set down in the fourteenth and fifteenth chapters.

For the laws of nature, as "justice," "equity," "modesty," "mercy," and, in sum, "doing to others as we would be done to," of themselves, without the terror of some power to cause them to be observed, are contrary to our natural passions, that carry us to partiality, pride, revenge, and the like. And covenants, without the sword, are but words and of no strength to secure a man at all. Therefore notwithstanding the laws of nature which every one hath then kept, when he has the will to keep them, when he can do it safely, if there be no power erected, or not great enough for our security, every man will and may lawfully rely on his own strength and art, for caution against all other men. And in all places where men have lived by small families, to rob and spoil one another has been a trade, and so far from being reputed against the law of nature, that the greater spoils they gained, the greater was their honor; and men observed no other laws, therein, but the laws of honor; that is, to abstain from cruelty, leaving to men their lives, and instruments of husbandry. And as small families did then, so now do cities and kingdoms, which are but greater families, for their own security, enlarge their dominions, upon all pretences of danger, and fear of invasion, or assistance that may be given to invaders, and endeavor as much as they can to subdue or weaken their neighbors, by open force and secret arts, for want of other caution, justly; and are remembered for it in after ages with honor.

Nor is it the joining together of a small number of men that gives them this security; because in small numbers, small additions on the one side or the other make the advantage of strength so great as is sufficient to carry the victory; and therefore gives encouragement to an invasion. The multitude sufficient to confide in for our security is not determined by any certain number, but by comparison with the enemy we fear; and is then sufficient, when the odds of the enemy is not of so visible and conspicuous moment to determine the event of war, as to move him to attempt.

And be there never so great a multitude; yet if their actions be directed according to their particular judgments and particular appetites, they can expect thereby no defence, nor protection, neither against a common enemy, nor against the injuries of one another. For being distracted in opinions concerning the best use and application of their strength, they do not help but hinder one another; and reduce their strength by mutual opposition to nothing: whereby they are easily, not only subdued by a very few that agree together; but also when there is no common enemy, they make war upon each other, for their particular interests. For if we could suppose a great multitude of men to consent in the observation of justice, and other laws of nature, without a common power to keep them all in awe, we might as well suppose all mankind to do the same; and then there neither would be nor need to be any civil government or commonwealth at all; because there would be peace without subjection.

Nor is it enough for the security, which men desire should last all the time of their life, that they be governed and directed by one judgment, for a limited time: as in one battle, or one war. For though they obtain a victory by their unanimous endeavor against a foreign enemy; yet afterwards, when either they have no common enemy, or he that by one part is held for an enemy is by another part held for a friend, they must needs by the difference of their interests dissolve, and fall again into a war amongst themselves.

It is true that certain living creatures, as bees and ants, live sociably one with another, which are therefore by Aristotle numbered amongst political creatures; and yet have no other direction than their particular judgments and appetites; nor speech, whereby one of them can signify to another what he thinks expedient for the common benefit: and therefore

519

some man may perhaps desire to know why mankind cannot do the same. To which I answer,

First, that men are continually in competition for honor and dignity, which these creatures are not; and consequently amongst men there ariseth on that ground, envy and hatred, and finally war; but amongst these not so.

Secondly, that amongst these creatures, the common good differeth not from the private; and being by nature inclined to their private, they procure thereby the common benefit. But man, whose joy consisteth in comparing himself with other men, can relish nothing but what is eminent.

Thirdly, that these creatures, having not, as man, the use of reason, do not see, nor think they see any fault in the administration of their common business; whereas amongst men there are very many that think themselves wiser and abler to govern the public better than the rest; and these strive to reform and innovate, one this way, another that way, and thereby bring it into distraction and civil war.

Fourthly, that these creatures, though they have some use of voice, in making known to one another their desires and other affections; yet they want that art of words by which some men can represent to others that which is good in the likeness of evil, and evil in the likeness of good, and augment or diminish the apparent greatness of good and evil; discontenting men, and troubling their peace at their pleasure.

Fifthly, irrational creatures cannot distinguish between injury and damage; and therefore as long as they be at ease, they are not offended with their fellows: whereas man is then most troublesome when he is most at ease; for then it is that he loves to show his wisdom, and control the actions of them that govern the commonwealth.

Lastly, the agreement of these creatures is natural; that of men is by covenant only, which is artificial: and therefore it is no wonder if there be somewhat else required, besides covenant, to make their agreement constant and lasting; which is a common power, to keep them in awe, and to direct their actions to the common benefit.

The only way to erect such a common power as may be able to defend them from the invasion of foreigners and the injuries of one another, and thereby to secure them in such sort as that by their own industry, and by the fruits of the earth, they may nourish themselves and live contentedly, is to confer all their power and strength upon one man, or upon one assembly of men, that may reduce all their wills, by plurality of voices, unto one will: which is as much as to say, to appoint one man, or assembly of men, to bear their person; and every one to own and acknowledge himself to be author of whatsoever he that so beareth their person shall act, or cause to be acted, in those things which concern the common peace and safety; and therein to submit their wills, every one to his will, and their judgments to his judgment. This is more than consent, or concord; it is a real unity of them all in one and the same person, made by covenant of every man with every man, in such manner as if every man should say to every man, "I authorize and give up my right of governing myself, to this man or to this assembly of men, on this condition, that thou give up thy right to him and authorize all his actions in like manner." This done, the multitude so united in one person is called a "commonwealth," in Latin *civitas*. This is the generation of that great leviathan, or rather, to speak more reverently, of that mortal god, to which we owe under the immortal God, our peace and defence. For by this authority, given him by every particular man in the commonwealth, he hath the use of so much power and strength conferred on him, that by terror thereof, he is enabled to perform the wills of them all, to peace at home, and mutual aid against their enemies abroad. And in him consisteth the essence of the commonwealth; which, to define it, is "one person, of whose acts a great multitude, by mutual covenants one with another, have made themselves every one the author, to the end he may use the strength and means of them all, as he shall think expedient, for their peace and common defence."

And he that carrieth this person is called sovereign, and

said to have sovereign power; and every one besides, his subject.

The attaining to this sovereign power is by two ways. One, by natural force; as when a man maketh his children to submit themselves, and their children, to his government, as being able to destroy them if they refuse; or by war subdueth his enemies to his will, giving them their lives on that condition. The other is when men agree amongst themselves to submit to some man, or assembly of men, voluntarily, on confidence to be protected by him against all others. This latter may be called a political commonwealth, or commonwealth by institution; and the former, a commonwealth by acquisition.

*   *   *

A commonwealth is said to be instituted when a multitude of men do agree and covenant, every one with every one, that to whatsoever man or assembly of men shall be given by the major part the right to present the person of them all, that is to say, to be their representative; every one, as well he that voted for it as he that voted against it, shall authorize all the actions and judgments of that man or assembly of men in the same manner as if they were his own, to the end to live peaceably amongst themselves and be protected against other men.

From this institution of a commonwealth are derived all the rights and faculties of him, or them, on whom sovereign power is conferred by the consent of the people assembled.

First, because they covenant, it is to be understood, they are not obliged by former covenant to anything repugnant hereunto. And consequently that they have already instituted a commonwealth, being thereby bound by covenant to own the actions and judgments of one, cannot lawfully make a new covenant amongst themselves, to be obedient to any other in any thing whatsoever, without his permission. And therefore, they that are subjects to a monarch, cannot without his leave cast off monarchy, and return to the confusion of a disunited multitude; nor transfer their person from him that beareth it, to another man, or other assembly of men: for they are bound, every man to every man, to own and be reputed author of all that he that already is their sovereign shall do, and judge fit to be done: so that any one man dissenting, all the rest should break their covenant made to that man, which is injustice: and they have also every man given the sovereignty to him that beareth their person; and therefore if they depose him, they take from him that which is his own, and so again it is injustice. Besides, if he that attempteth to depose his sovereign be killed, or punished by him for such attempt, he is author of his own punishment, as being by the institution author of all his sovereign shall do: and because it is injustice for a man to do anything for which he may be punished by his own authority, he is also upon that title unjust. And whereas some men have pretended for their disobedience to their sovereign, a new covenant, made not with men, but with God, this also is unjust: for there is no covenant with God but by meditation of somebody that representeth God's person; which none doth but God's lieutenant, who hath the sovereignty under God. But this pretence of covenant with God is so evident a lie, even in the pretenders' own consciences, that it is not only an act of an unjust, but also of a vile and unmanly disposition.

Secondly, because the right of bearing the person of them all is given to him they make sovereign, by covenant only of one to another, and not of him to any of them, there can happen no breach of covenant on the part of the sovereign: and consequently none of his subjects, by any pretence of forfeiture, can be freed from his subjection. That he which is made sovereign maketh no covenant with his subjects beforehand, is manifest; because either he must make it with the whole multitude, as one party to the covenant, or he must make a several covenant with every man. With the whole, as one party, it is impossible; because as yet they are not one person; and if he make so many several covenants as there be men, those covenants after he hath the sovereignty are void; because what act soever can be pretended by any one of them for breach thereof, is the act both of himself and of all the rest, because done in the person and by the right of every one of them in particular. Besides, if any one or more of them pretend a breach of the covenant made by the sovereign at his institution; and others, or one other of his subjects, or himself alone, pretend there was no such breach, there is in this case no judge to decide the controversy; it returns therefore to the sword again, and every man recovereth the right of protecting himself by his own strength, contrary to the design they had in the institution. It is therefore in vain to grant sovereignty by way of precedent covenant. The opinion that any monarch receiveth his power by covenant, that is to say, on condition, proceedeth from want of understanding this easy truth, that covenants being but words and breath, have no force to oblige, contain, constrain, or protect any man, but what they have from the public sword; that is, from the united hands of that man or assembly of men that hath the sovereignty, and whose actions are avouched by them all, and performed by the strength of them all, in him united. But when an assembly of men is made sovereign, then no man imagineth any such covenant to have passed in the institution; for no man is so dull as to say, for example, the people of Rome made a covenant with the Romans to hold the sovereignty on such or such conditions; which not performed, the Romans might lawfully depose the Roman people. That men see not the reason to be alike in a monarchy and in a popular government, proceedeth from the ambition of some that are kinder to the government of an assembly, whereof they may hope to participate, than of monarchy, which they despair to enjoy.

Thirdly, because the major part hath by consenting voices declared a sovereign, he that dissented must now consent with the rest, that is, be contented to avow all the actions he shall do, or else justly be destroyed by the rest.

For if he voluntarily entered into the congregation of them that were assembled, he sufficiently declared thereby his will, and therefore tacitly covenanted to stand to what the major part should ordain: and therefore if he refuse to stand thereto, or make protestation against any of their decrees, he does contrary to his covenant, and therefore unjustly. And whether he be of the congregation or not, and whether his consent be asked or not, he must either submit to their decrees, or be left in the condition of war he was in before; wherein he might without injustice be destroyed by any man whatsoever.

Fourthly, because every subject is by this institution author of all the actions and judgments of the sovereign instituted, it follows that whatsoever he doth it can be no injury to any of his subjects, nor ought he to be by any of them accused of injustice. For he that doth anything by authority from another doth therein no injury to him by whose authority he acteth: but by this institution of a commonwealth every particular man is author of all the sovereign doth; and consequently, he that complaineth of injury from his sovereign complaineth of that whereof he himself is author and therefore ought not to accuse any man but himself; no, nor himself of injury, because to do injury to one's self is impossible. It is true that they that have sovereign power may commit iniquity, but not injustice or injury in the proper signification.

Fifthly, and consequently to that which was said last, no man that hath sovereign power can justly be put to death, or otherwise in any manner by his subjects punished. For seeing every subject is author of the actions of his sovereign, he punisheth another for the actions committed by himself.

And because the end of this institution is the peace and defence of them all, and, whosoever has right to the end has right to the means, it belongeth of right to whatsoever man or assembly that hath the sovereignty to be judge both of the means of peace and defence, and also of the hindrances and disturbances of the same, and to do whatsoever he shall think necessary to be done, both beforehand, for the preserving of peace and security, by prevention of discord at home and hostility from abroad; and, when peace and security are lost, for the recovery of the same.

Sixthly, it is annexed to the sovereignty to be judge of what opinions and doctrines are averse and what conducting to peace; and consequently, on what occasions, how far, and what men are to be trusted withal, in speaking to.multitudes of people, and who shall examine the doctrines of all books before they be published. For the actions of men proceed from their opinions, and in the well governing of opinions consisteth the well governing of men's actions, in order to their peace and concord. And though in matter of doctrine nothing ought to be regarded but the truth; yet this is not repugnant to regulating the same by peace. For doctrine repugnant to peace can be no more true than peace and concord can be against the law of nature. It is true that in a commonwealth, where, by the negligence or unskilfulness of governors and teachers, false doctrines are by time generally received, the contrary truths may be generally offensive. Yet the most sudden and rough bursting in of a new truth that can be, does never break the peace, but only sometimes awake the war. For those men that are so remissly governed, that they dare take up arms to defend or introduce an opinion, are still in war; and their condition not peace, but only a cessation of arms for fear of one another; and they live, as it were, in the precincts of battle continually. It belongeth therefore to him that hath the sovereign power to be judge, or constitute all judges, of opinions and doctrines, as a thing necessary to peace, thereby to prevent discord and civil war.

Seventhly, is annexed to the sovereignty, the whole power of prescribing the rules whereby every man may know what goods he may enjoy and what actions he may do, without being molested by any of his fellow-subjects; and this is it men call "propriety." For before constitution of sovereign power, as hath already been shown, all men had right to all things, which necessarily causeth war: and therefore this propriety, being necessary to peace, and depending on sovereign power, is the act of that power, in order to the public peace. These rules of propriety, or *meum* and *tuum*, and of good, evil, lawful, and unlawful in the actions of subjects, are the civil laws; that is to say, the laws of each commonwealth in particular; though the name of civil law be now restrained to the ancient civil laws of the city of Rome, which being the head of a great part of the world, her laws at that time were in these parts the civil law.

Eighthly, is annexed to the sovereignty, the right of judicature, that is to say, of hearing and deciding all controversies which may arise concerning law, either civil or natural, or concerning fact. For without the decision of controversies, there is no protection of one subject against the injuries of another; the laws concerning *meum* and *tuum* are in vain, and to every man remaineth, from the natural and necessary appetite of his own conservation, the right of protecting himself by his private strength, which is the condition of war, and contrary to the end for which every commonwealth is instituted.

Ninthly, is annexed to the sovereignty, the right of making war and peace with other nations and commonwealths, that is to say, of judging when it is for the public good, and how great forces are to be assembled, armed, and paid for that end, and to levy money upon the subjects to defray the expenses thereof. For the power by which the people are to be defended consisteth in their armies, and the strength of an army, in the union of their strength under one command, which command the sovereign instituted, therefore hath; because the command of the "militia," without other institution, maketh him that hath it sovereign. And therefore whosoever is made general of an army, he that hath the sovereign power is always generalissimo.

Tenthly, is annexed to the sovereignty, the choosing of all counsellors, ministers, magistrates, and officers, both in peace and war. For seeing the sovereign is charged with the end, which is the common peace and defence, he is understood to have power to use such means as he shall think most fit for his discharge.

Eleventhly, to the sovereign is committed the power of rewarding with riches or honor, and of punishing with corporal or pecuniary punishment, or with ignominy, every subject according to the law he hath formerly made; or if there be no law made, according as he shall judge most to conduce to the encouraging of men to serve the commonwealth, or deterring of them from doing disservice to the same.

Lastly, considering what value men are naturally apt to set upon themselves, what respect they look for from others, and how little they value other men, from whence continually arise amongst them, emulation, quarrels, factions, and at last war, to the destroying of one another and diminution of their strength against a common enemy, it is necessary that there be laws of honor, and a public rate of the worth of such men as have deserved or are able to deserve well of the commonwealth; and that there be force in the hands of some or other, to put these laws in execution. But it hath already been shown that not only the whole "militia," or forces of the commonwealth, but also the judicature of all controversies, is annexed to the sovereignty. To the sovereign therefore it belongeth also to give titles of honor; and to appoint what order of place and dignity each man shall hold; and what signs of respect, in public or private meetings, they shall give to one another.

These are the rights which make the essence of sovereignty, and which are the marks whereby a man may discern in what man, or assembly of men, the sovereign power is placed and resideth. For these are incommunicable, and inseparable. The power to coin money, to dispose of the estate and persons of infant heirs, to have preemption in markets, and all other statute prerogatives, may be transferred by the sovereign, and yet the power to protect his subjects be retained. But if he transfer the "militia," he retains the judicature in vain, for want of execution of the laws: or if he grant away the power of raising money, the "militia" is in vain; or if he give away the government of doctrines, men will be frighted into rebellion with the fear of spirits. And so if we consider any one of the said rights, we shall presently see that the holding of all the rest will produce no effect in the conservation of peace and justice, the end for which all commonwealths are instituted. And this division is it whereof it is said, "a kingdom divided in itself cannot stand:" for unless this division precede, division into opposite armies can never happen. If there had not first been an opinion received of the greatest part of England that these powers were divided between the King, and the Lords, and the House of Commons, the people had never been divided and fallen into this civil war, first between those that disagreed in politics, and after between the dissenters about the liberty of religion; which have so instructed men in this point of sovereign right, that there be few now in England that do not see that these rights are inseparable, and will be so generally acknowledged at the next return of peace, and so continue, till their miseries are forgotten; and no longer, except the vulgar be better taught than they have hitherto been.

And because they are essential and inseparable rights, it follows necessarily that in whatsoever words any of them seem to be granted away, yet if the sovereign power itself be not in direct terms renounced, and the name of sovereign no more given by the grantees to him that grants them, the grant is void: for when he has granted all he can, if we grant back the sovereignty, all is restored, as inseparably annexed thereunto.

This great authority being indivisible and inseparably annexed to the sovereignty, there is little ground for the opinion of them that say of sovereign kings, though they be *singulis majores,* of greater power than every one of their subjects, yet they be *universis minores,* of less power than them all together. For if by "all together" they mean not the collective body as one person, then "all together" and "every one" signify the same; and the speech is absurd. But if by "all together," they understand them as one person, which person the sovereign bears, then the power of all together is the same with the sovereign's power; and so again the speech is absurd: which absurdity they see well enough, when the sovereignty is in an assembly of the people; but in a monarch they see it not; and yet the power of sovereignty is the same in whomsoever it be placed.

And as the power, so also the honor of the sovereign, ought to be greater than that of any or all the subjects. For in the sovereignty is the fountain of honor. The dignities of lord, earl, duke, and prince are his creatures. As in the presence of the master the servants are equal, and without any honor at all; so are the subjects in the presence of the sovereign. And though they shine some more, some less, when they are out of his sight; yet in his presence, they shine no more than the stars in the presence of the sun.

But a man may here object that the condition of subjects is very miserable; as being obnoxious to the lusts, and other irregular passions of him or them that have so unlimited a power in their hands. And commonly they that live under a monarch, think it the fault of monarchy; and they that live under the government of democracy, or other sovereign assembly, attribute all the inconvenience to that form of commonwealth; whereas the power in all forms, if they be perfect enough to protect them, is the same: not considering that the state of man can never be without some incommodity or other; and that the greatest, that in any form of government can possibly happen to the people in general, is scarce sensible, in respect of the miseries and horrible calamities that accompany a civil war, or that dissolute condition of masterless men, without subjection to laws and a coercive power to tie their hands from rapine and revenge: nor considering that the greatest pressure of sovereign governors proceedeth not from any delight or profit they can expect in the damage or weakening of their subjects, in whose vigor consisteth their own strength and glory; but in the restiveness of themselves, that unwillingly contributing to their own defence, make it necessary for their governors to draw from them what they can in time of peace, that they may have means on any emergent occasion, or sudden need, to resist, or take advantage on their enemies. For all men are by nature provided of notable multiplying glasses, that is their passions and self-love, through which every little payment appeareth a great grievance; but are destitute of those prospective glasses, namely, moral and civil science, to see afar off the miseries that hang over them, and cannot without such payments be avoided.

[165]

HOCKING, WILLIAM ERNEST

HOCKING, WILLIAM ERNEST (1873-). The strength of Hocking's religious and philosophical convictions is rooted not only in his actual belief but also in the memory of his childhood. He grew up in a home where, according to him, "religious life was concrete, vivid and regulatory." If he has not really been influenced by such recollections, he nevertheless has reason to be satisfied with the fact that the development of his thinking has not involved conflict with his family traditions.

At first, Hocking intended to become a civil engineer. It was not an incident of external nature that prevented him from choosing this profession definitely, but rather his spiritual interests which were attracted at first by Herbert Spencer, then by Royce, and, decisively, by the study of German idealism. Hocking went to Germany, and attended lectures of almost all important philosophers in that country at that time, particularly Dilthey, Natorp, Husserl, Windelband and Rickert.

Hocking must be considered the outstanding recent defender of idealism in America. His allegiance to this way of thinking is strong enough to allow him occasional concessions to pragmatism, although he declares that it cannot supply idealism whatever the latter's deficiencies may be. Furthermore, Hocking is very critical toward the actual performances of idealism, which he has accused of having been incapable of finding the way "to worship, to the particular and historical in religion, to the authoritative and super-

531

personal." In many regards, Hocking seems to agree with Wilhelm Luetgert, a German critic of idealism; however, he does not abandon its cause. To him, idealism means "in name and truth the unlimited right of Idea in a world where nothing is ultimately irrational." While declaring that there is no inaccessible truth, no "unknowable," contrary to Spencer, he agrees with Santayana, but his idea of the possibility of perceiving and experiencing God is more intensively colored by mysticism even though he far from ignores the dangers and aberrations of mysticism.

AN ART PECULIAR TO MAN

USING the word art in the widest sense, as including all conscious efforts to remake the world, we may say that all animal behavior includes some degree of outwardly directed art. While life permits its world to shape it, it promotes thereby the artisanship by which it shapes the world.

There is but one exception, presumably, to the rule that the arts of animals are directed to the environment. The human being does deliberately undertake, while reshaping his outer world, to reshape himself also. In meeting unsatisfactory conditions,—scarcity of food, danger, etc.,—the simpler animal does what it can to change those conditions. The human being does likewise; but there sometimes occurs to him the additional reflection, "perhaps there should be some change in myself also." Scarcity of food may become to him an argument for greater foresight or industry, danger for more caution. If a beast is threatened, it may either fight or retreat: if a man is threatened, he may (while dealing with the facts) become a critic also of his own fear or anger.

Man thus becomes for himself an object of artful reconstruction, and this is an art peculiar to man. Whatever is done in the world by way of producing better human individuals, whether for the benefit of the species or for the ends of individuals themselves, man is an agent in it: it is done not merely to him but by him. He has become judge of his own nature and its possibilities. "Evolution" leaves its work in his hands—so far as he is concerned.

I do not say that man is the only creature that has a part in its own making. Every organism may be said (with due interpretation of terms) to build itself, to regenerate itself when injured, to recreate itself and, in striving for its numerous ends, to develop itself—to grow. It may be, as we were saying, an agent in evolution. But in all likelihood, it is only the human being that does these things with conscious intention, that examines and revises his mental as well as his physical self, and that proceeds according to a preformed idea of what this self should be. To be human is to be self-conscious; and to be self-conscious is to bring one's self into the sphere of art, as an object to be judged, altered, improved.

Human beings as we find them are accordingly artificial products; and for better or for worse they must always be such. Nature has made us: social action and our own efforts must continually remake us. Any attempt to reject art for "nature" can only result in an artificial naturalness which is far less genuine and less pleasing than the natural work of art.

[166]

HODGSON, SHADWORTH HOLLWAY

HODGSON, SHADWORTH HOLLWAY (1832-1912). Hodgson neither held any post as a University teacher nor did he ever seek one. He lived a retired, happy life, devoted to philosophy. He regarded the poets Wordsworth and Coleridge as his principal teachers, especially the latter from whom he adopted the idea of intimate union of intellectual and emotional elements in human nature, although not his identification of religious experience with theological dogma.

In his principal work *The Metaphysic of Experience* (1898) Hodgson, by his criticism of Kant, prepared the way for New Realism. His method was to analyze the content of consciousness without any assumption concerning its origin or nature. Contrary to Kant, he did not take the existence of the ego for granted. While Kant proceeded from consciousness as a synthetic agency, Hodgson held that this agency is also part of experience and must be analyzed. He objected to empiricism in its postulating of things and persons. Against both Kant and empiricism, Hodgson insisted that neither subject nor object are warranted as initial assumptions of philosophy. From this depth of experience, Hodgson ascended to the metaphysical heights of speculation on God and the Universe, but maintained that thinking about invisible reality is not a matter of knowledge but rather the consequence of moral drives.

FAITH

THE faith of the man lies in his conscious and volitional reciprocation of the love of God, but the ultimate source of its efficacy, that which calls it into existence as a redeeming agency, lies not in the belief, but in the thing believed, the fact that it is *love* which is believed in, and that love the love of God, man's response to which is love and faith at once, a response whereby he places himself in conscious union and harmony with the Divine Object of his faith.

From the twofold fact, that this ultimate source both lies wholly beyond the man, and also, as the love of God, is unchanging and eternal, and therefore demands a response at every moment and in all circumstances, it follows, that the act of response, which is the initial act of faith, must be constantly sustained or perpetually repeated. Consequently it involves an immanent and permanent change in the dominant principle of life, a change from seeking the realization of the ideals of the Self to bringing the Self and its ideals into conformity with the will of God; a change of heart, *metanoia*, repentance, self-surrender. Love to God then becomes the *sine qua non* condition of the man's whole conduct.

From this the love of mankind also follows. For how can anyone, whose life is centered in the primal source of love and righteousness, indulge in enmity or even indifference to those who are objects of the divine love equally with himself? Love is the great subduing, transforming, and harmonizing emotion in human nature. And it is love alone by which responsive love is awakened, or on account of which love is felt in return. Ultimately, therefore, it is the love of

God for man, and that alone, which redeems the man; because that love alone calls forth in return that love of man for God, by which the man's whole nature is transformed. But to be efficacious in man, it must be appropriated by man, that is, believed in and reciprocated by conscious acts of will.

It would appear, that there is no human consciousness so depraved, that the thought of the love of God cannot occur to it, and consequently no kind of degree of abjectness from which the redeeming faith, founded on that thought, cannot uplift a man. Even at its first arising, and in moments at which (provided it be genuine) it is accompanied by the deepest sense of shame, humility, and unworthiness, it gives a certain sense of security, of dignity, and of hopefulness. It ennobles, even while it humbles. In repentance the man begins, or begins again so often as repentance is renewed, to feel himself in communion and fellowship with the sole almighty Power, and the sole righteous Judge. His state in this respect has nothing to do with the estimation in which he may be held by his fellow-men. This was no doubt the hidden reason of Christianity spreading so rapidly as it did throughout the mixed and struggling populations of the great cities of the ancient world. A new life was laid open before every soul of them. For though founded in the strictest individualism, it was for that very reason universal, the same kernel of human nature being the one thing common to all individuals alike.

This is the true source and meaning of the universality of Christianity. It is not confined to men of a particular race (Jews), or of a particular degree of intellectual enlightenment (philosophers), or of a particular standard of moral attainment (the "ninety and nine just persons who need no repentance" of the parable); but is capable of arising independently from the emotional and volitional endowment of all men as men by nature, apart from circumstances of every other kind, whether of the organism or of the environment.

[167]

HÖFFDING, HARALD

HÖFFDING, HARALD (1843-1931). After a long, difficult struggle, Höffding resolved to renounce theology and to devote his life to philosophy. It was his great esteem for Kierkegaard, the adversary of the established church and inquirer into the mystery of personal faith, that fortified Höffding in his decision. He became Denmark's most important modern philosopher, and his works have also been read and highly appreciated in France, England and Germany.

Höffding was more interested in philosophical problems than in systems. Asked which philosopher was his personal ideal, Höffding answered Spinoza. But he rejected Spinoza's system. He only loved and revered his personality. Höffding called himself a critical positivist. He held that experience is of decisive importance to all a philosopher might think, but declared that experience is a problem that defies the efforts of all philosophers. To Höffding, philosophy alone frees human mind from habits, prejudices and traditions. It enlarges the spiritual horizon in such a manner as no special science can.

PLURALISM AND MONISM

THE importance of pluralism, *i.e.*, of the tendency to accentuate the multiplicity and the difference of phenomena, depends on its power to raise problems. Both thought and sensations suppose difference, contrast, variation. Already Thomas Hobbes saw that, when he said that to have always one single sensation would be the same as to have no sensation at all. The psychology of our time has, generally speaking, confirmed this view. Fechner's law on the relation between physical impression and psychical sensation points in this direction. And our thought starts with greatest energy when two judgments contradict one another, *i.e.*, when a problem arises.

I believe there is reason for accentuating this point in the actual state of philosophy. There seems to be too much metaphysics in the air, and it is important not to forget what we have learnt from positivism and criticism. The old

English school had the mission to keep the attention of philosophers on experience, and it started the great movement against dogmatism in the last three centuries. It is no accident that the greatest setter of problems, David Hume, belonged to this school. In evolutionism this school has said its last word—the widening of the concept of experience to connote not only the experience of the single individual, but the organized experience of the whole species. We may hope that a new, refreshing start will be made.

Pluralism makes the world new for us and necessitates a revision of our categories, our principles and our methods. A dogmatic sleep is too tempting for the human mind. We are inclined to suppose that we can develop—or perhaps already have developed—thoughts in which all existence can be expressed. But, as a Danish thinker, Sören Kierkegaard, has said we live forward, but we understand backward. Understanding comes after experience. Only when life is closed can it be thoroughly understood. This is our tragicocomical situation. Even a divine thinker could only understand the world when the life of the world was finished.

But pluralism as such brings no understanding, no intelligence. To understand is to connect one fact with other facts, to find a uniting principle. Multiplicity as such would only make description and classification possible, and even this only under the condition that the manifold phenomena were not only different, but also similar. The only meaning of 'understanding' which a consistent pluralism can acknowledge is understanding as mere recognition, not as explanation.

. . . Now, it is a fact that we in many cases have found such connection of continuity in nature. It is the ideal of knowledge to find it in all domains of observation. Our mind can only understand by synthesis, and the principle of continuity is therefore the presupposition, the working hypothesis, of all science. But we must also acknowledge continuity as a characteristic of reality. We have no right to suppose that the fact that we can not understand phenomena, if we can find no connection or continuity, should be without ground in reality itself. If we will build our philosophy on experience, we ought to give full importance to connection, unity and continuity, as well as to difference and multiplicity. Experience shows us both, and pluralism can, therefore, not be the sole or the last word of the philosopher. And there is an inner connection between continuity and multiplicity. All qualities, powers and characters which we ascribe to the single elements or beings which pluralism acknowledges are only known through the connection of these elements or beings with a whole order of things. We can, for example, only ascribe energy to a being because we experience that it actually does a certain work, that alterations in it or out of it have their cause in it. If it were absolutely isolated, we could not ascribe any predicate to it, we could not know it at all.

Perhaps it is impossible to develop a metaphysical theory which shall give both facts their full right. But this ought not to lead us to forget the urgency of the problem.

I, for my part, call myself a monist, because connection and continuity seem to me to be more important facts than multiplicity; it is, as I have shown, only through their connection one with another and with us, that things can be understood.

[168]

HOLBACH, PAUL HENRI THIRY BARON D'

HOLBACH, PAUL HENRI THIRY BARON D' (1723-1789). Friends and foes of the French Revolution used to regard Holbach, who died some months before its outbreak, as one of its most important prophets. His writings were deemed responsible for the anti-clerical and anti-Christian excesses which took place. This may be true. But Holbach's atheism was detested by such influential leaders as Robespierre just as by the priests who had been attacked constantly in Holbach's pamphlets and books.

All who knew Holbach personally liked him. He was gentle, generous, ready to help poor writers and scholars, and a brilliant host. Only priests, the Church and religions were hated fanatically by him. His criticism of deism and theism challenged even Voltaire.

Holbach was a German nobleman who settled in Paris and adopted French nationality. He wrote many treatises on political, social and religious questions, generally hiding himself behind a pseudonym. His principal work *The System of Nature* (1770) has been called "the Bible of the atheists." It is something more. Holbach, while dealing with "the laws of the physical and moral world," represented nature not as a creation but as an immense workshop that provides man with tools by means of which he is enabled to give his life a better shape. He developed a philosophy of eternal change, and energetically rejected the assumption that all species have existed all the time or must exist in the future. He sneered at those philosophers or scientists who think nature incapable of giving rise to new organisms hitherto unknown. Man is not exempt from the law of change. Nature is indispensable to man, but man is not indispensable to nature which can continue her eternal course without man. Holbach must be credited for having, in 1770, pronounced evolutionism, declaring "Nature contains no constant forms."

THE ATHEIST

AN atheist is a man who knoweth nature and its laws, who knoweth his own nature, who knoweth what it imposes upon him: An atheist hath experience, and this experience, proveth to him, every moment, that vice can injure him, that his most concealed faults, that his most secret dispositions may be detected and display him in open day: this experience proveth to him that society is useful to his happiness; that his interest demands, that he should attach himself to the country which protects him, and which enables him to enjoy in security the benefits of nature; every thing shows him, that in order to be happy, he must make himself beloved; that his father is for him the most certain of friends; that ingratitude would remove from him his benefactor; that justice is necessary to the maintenance of every association; and that no man, whatever may be his power, can be content with himself, when he knoweth he is an object of public hatred.

He who hath maturely reflected upon himself, upon his own nature, and upon that of his associates, upon his own wants, and upon the means of procuring them, cannot prevent himself from knowing his duties, from discovering that which he oweth to himself, and that he hath morality, he hath real motives to conform himself to its dictates; he is obliged to feel, that these duties are necessary; and if his reason be not disturbed by blind passions, or by vicious habits, he will feel that virtue is for all men the surest road to felicity. The atheists, or the fatalists, found all their systems upon necessity; thus, their moral speculations, founded upon the necessity of things, are, at least, much more permanent and more invariable, than those which only rest upon a god who changes his aspect, according to the dispositions and the passions of all those who contemplate him. The nature of things, and its immutable laws, are not subject to vary; the atheist is always obliged to call that which injures him, vice and folly; to call that which injures others crime; to call that which is advantageous to society, or which contributes to its permanent happiness, virtue.

[169]

HOLMES, OLIVER WENDELL

HOLMES, OLIVER WENDELL (1809-1894). Oliver Wendell Holmes, professor of anatomy and physiology at Harvard Medical School and a popular figure in Boston, had become an American celebrity by 1860, due to the publication of his *Autocrat of the Breakfast Table*, a book of conversational charm, abundant in satirical glances at mankind and its good and bad customs, sharp and jovial judgments on life, the expression of common sense, love of nature, knowledge of nature, and a treasury of puns and anecdotes. The book became extremely popular in England too and was translated into French and German. Holmes' poems have sometimes been severely criticized, but among them there are many attractive creations of a sometimes robust, sometimes gracious humor, as well as witty and serious articulations of feelings which are shared by people of various levels of education. Some of them are representative of American sentiments of that time. Others surprise by their artful play with allusions and their skill in turning from joke to tender sensibility.

Holmes' mind was less profound than that of his son, Justice

Oliver Wendell Holmes. He was a successful teacher, admired and loved by his students, relying more on routine than on research. As a natural scientist, he was an independent yet not a creative thinker. As a physician, he was devoted to the welfare of his patients and eager to support medical progress. He introduced the term anaesthesia into medical practice by suggesting it to the dentist Morton, who was the first to use ether for making his patients insensible during operation.

WORKING OF THE UNCONSCIOUS

THERE are thoughts that never emerge into consciousness, which yet make their influence felt among the perceptible mental currents, just as the unseen planets sway the movements of those which are watched and mapped by the astronomer. Old prejudices, that are ashamed to confess themselves, nudge our talking thought to utter their magisterial veto. In hours of languor, as Mr. Lecky has remarked, the beliefs and fancies of obsolete conditions are apt to take advantage of us. We know very little of the contents of our minds until some sudden jar brings them to light, as an earthquake that shakes down a miser's house brings out the old stockings full of gold, and all the hoards that have hid away in holes and crannies.

We not rarely find our personality doubled in our dreams, and do battle with ourselves, unconscious that we are our own antagonists. Dr. Johnson dreamed that he had a contest of wit with an opponent, and got the worst of it: of course, he furnished the wit for both. Tartini heard the Devil play a wonderful sonata, and set it down on awaking. Who was the Devil but Tartini himself? I remember, in my youth, reading verses in a dream, written, as I thought, by a rival fledgling of the Muse. They were so far beyond my powers, that I despaired of equalling them; yet I must have made them unconsciously as I read them. Could I only have remembered them waking!

But I must here add another personal experience, of which I will say beforehand,—somewhat as honest Izaak Walton said of his pike, "This dish of meat is too good for any but anglers or very honest men,"—this story is good only for philosophers and very small children. I will merely hint to the former class of thinkers, that its moral bears on two points: first, the value of our self-estimate, sleeping,— possibly, also, waking; secondly, the significance of general formulae when looked at in certain exalted mental conditions.

I once inhaled a pretty full dose of ether, with the determination to put on record, at the earliest moment of regaining consciousness, the thought I should find uppermost in my mind. The mighty music of the triumphal march into nothingness reverberated through my brain, and filled me with a sense of infinite possibilities which made me an archangel for the moment. The veil of eternity was lifted. The one great truth which underlies all human experience, and is the key to all the mysteries that philosophy has sought in vain to solve, flashed upon me in a sudden revelation. Henceforth all was clear: a few words had lifted my intelligence to the level of the knowledge of the cherubim. As my natural condition returned, I remembered my resolution; and, staggering to my desk, I wrote in ill-shaped, straggling characters, the all-embracing truth still glimmering in my consciousness. The words were these (children may smile; the wise will ponder): "A strong smell of turpentine prevails throughout."

[170]

HOLMES, OLIVER WENDELL

HOLMES, OLIVER WENDELL (1841-1935). One day, when Justice Holmes was eighty-seven, a reporter, walking round Capitol Square in Washington, D. C., asked passers-by if they knew who Justice Holmes was. One of them answered "Holmes? Oh sure, that's the young judge on the Supreme Court that is always dissenting with the old guys."

Holmes has been called "the great dissenter." He often dissented from the majority of the United States Supreme Court because he thought that the law cannot be dealt with "as if it contains only the axioms and corollaries of a book of mathematics."

Holmes repeatedly emphasized that the life of the law is not logic, not logical cohesion of part with part, but experience, the history of the nation, the "felt necessities" of the present, and the endeavor of men, conscious of their national and human responsibilities, to shape the future development in harmony with the ideals of the common good. These views have been expounded by Holmes in his *Common Law* (1881), in numerous lectures, essays, addresses and, above all, in his written dissents. He regarded the Constitution of the United States not as the embodiment of any particular economic theory, but as "an experiment, as all life is an experiment." However, even though he admitted that the Constitution could be interpreted in various senses, he insisted that one of its principles "more imperatively calls for attachment than any other," namely, the principle of free thought. In accordance with Lord Acton, the British liberal historian, Holmes demanded "free thought not for those who agree with us but freedom for the thoughts that we hate."

When Holmes insisted that jurisdiction had to rest upon the "felt necessities" rather than upon logical conclusions he was not prepared to identify these "felt necessities" with the pressure of public opinion or vested interests. He was always remote from party politics. The philosophical foundation of his legal theory relied on John Stuart Mill, whose utilitarianism he found more acceptable than Kant's idealism, on Peirce and William James, his admired and admiring friend, and also upon a comprehensive study of history, of the causes of formation and dissolution of cultural patterns.

Holmes regarded his remoteness from political struggles as the essential condition of his judicial impartiality. But impartiality and scholarship were not to him the highest degree of human value. Scholars, men of letters, Holmes said, "give up half of their life" in order to be allowed to work in undisturbed detachment. But "the place for a man who is complete in all his powers is in the fight." Scholarship and freedom from prejudices did not prevent Holmes from making up his mind at his peril upon living questions, and to take his place in the fight, no matter how mighty his adversaries were.

THE OUGHT OF NATURAL LAW

THE jurists who believe in natural law seem to me to be in that naive state of mind that accepts what has been familiar and accepted by them and their neighbors as something that must be accepted by all men everywhere. No doubt it is true that, so far as we can see ahead, some arrangements and the rudiments of familiar institutions seem to be necessary elements in any society that may spring from our own and that would seem to us to be civilized—some form of permanent association between the sexes—some residue of property individually owned—some mode of binding oneself to specified future conduct—at the bottom of all, some protection for the person. But without speculating whether a group is imaginable in which all but the last of these might disappear and the last be subject to qualifications that most of us would abhor, the question remains as to the *Ought* of natural law.

It is true that beliefs and wishes have a transcendental basis in the sense that their foundation is arbitrary. You can not help entertaining and feeling them, and there is an end of it. As an arbitrary fact people wish to live, and we say with various degrees of certainty that they can do so only on certain conditions. To do it they must eat and drink. That necessity is absolute. It is a necessity of less degree but practically general that they should live in society. If they live in society, so far as we can see, there are further conditions. Reason working on experience does tell us, no doubt, that if our wish to live continues, we can do it only on those terms. But that seems to me the whole of the matter. I see no *a priori* duty to live with others and in that way, but simply a statement of what I must do if I wish to remain alive. If I do live with others they tell me that I must do and abstain from doing various things or they will put the screws on to me. I believe that they will, and being of the same mind as to their conduct I not only accept the rules but come in time to accept them with sympathy and emotional affirmation and begin to talk about duties and rights. But for legal purposes a right is only the hypostasis of a prophecy—the imagination of a substance supporting the fact that the public force will be brought to bear upon those who do things said to contravene it—just as we talk of the force of gravitation accounting for the conduct of bodies in space. One phrase adds no more than the other to what we know without it. No doubt behind these legal rights is the fighting will of the subject to maintain them, and the spread of his emotions to the general rules by which they are maintained; but that does not seem to me the same thing as the supposed *a priori* discernment of a duty or the assertion of a pre-existing right. A dog will fight for his bone.

The most fundamental of the supposed pre-existing rights—the right to life—is sacrificed without a scruple not only in war, but whenever the interest of society, that is, of the predominant power in the community, is thought to demand it. Whether that interest is the interest of mankind in the long run no one can tell, and as, in any event, to those who do not think with Kant and Hegel it is only an interest, the sanctity disappears. I remember a very tender-hearted judge being of opinion that closing a hatch to stop a fire and the destruction of a cargo was justified even if it was known that doing so would stifle a man below. It is idle to illustrate further, because to those who agree with me I am uttering commonplaces and to those who disagree I am ignoring the necessary foundations of thought. The *a priori* men generally call the dissentients superficial. But I do agree with them in believing that one's attitude on these matters is closely connected with one's general attitude toward the universe. Proximately, as has been suggested, it is determined largely by early associations and temperament, coupled with the desire to have an absolute guide. Men to a great extent believe what they want to—although I see in that no basis for a philosophy that tells us what we should want to want.

[171]

HSUN CHING

HSUN CHING (About 298-238 B.C.). The purely philosophical strain in Confucianism was developed to its highest point by Hsun Ching who, however, was also a great poet and a master of lyrical reflection, penetrating into the secrets of the human soul, inspired by the beauty of nature. Although he adopted views of Mo-Ti and some Taoists, he remained faithful to Confucianism, believing firmly in the necessity of moral order and individual self-perfection, and strongly opposing the belief in fate.

HEAVEN'S way of acting is unchanging. It did not act specially to make Yao [the Sage-Emperor] survive nor to bring Ch'ieh [the arch-criminal] to destruction. Respond to Heaven by governing well, then there will be good fortune: respond to it by governing badly, and then there will be bad fortune. If the basic industries [i.e. those in connection with agriculture] are in a flourishing state and economy is being practiced in public expenditure, Heaven cannot make the country poor; and if the supply of foodstuffs is complete and energy is exercised at the right times, Heaven cannot make the people sick; and if the Right Way is being cultivated, Heaven cannot send down calamities. The fact is that (by themselves) flood and drought cannot cause famine, extremes of cold and heat cannot cause distress, nor malicious spirits bring bad fortune. If, however, the basic industries are neglected, and expenditure is extravagant, then Heaven cannot make the country rich. . . . The fact is that famine is there before flood and drought, sickness arrives before the rigors of cold and heat. . . . Observance of the seasons and good government go together, whilst calamities and good government are incompatible; and it is wrong to inveigh against Heaven because its Way is so. Thus it is that only if a man be clear as to the relative spheres of Heaven and man may he be called a man of consummate understanding.

To carry to completion by actionless activity [*wu wei*], to accomplish without trying to, is to be described as Heaven's function. Deep though that function is, great though it is and of vital import, the man of consummate understanding nevertheless does not consider it to any extent, nor does he get additional ability through it, nor does he probe into it. This means that he does not try to complete Heaven. (For) Heaven has its times and seasons, Earth its wealth, and Man his work of making order: a blending into a trinity of powers, as it should be described.

Now the man who neglected the condition on which this

blending of powers depended, hoping to be the blender himself, would be on the wrong track altogether. The serried ranks of stars follow their courses: the sun and the moon take turns in shining: the four seasons successively take charge: the Yin and Yang make their great transformations: the wind and the rain exercise their all-pervading influence. Thus the myriad creatures come within the scope of this life-giving harmony (of forces) and in every case get the nourishment which brings them to completion. This we call a miraculous work, for we cannot see it going on, although we see the final accomplishment. We call it Heaven's accomplishment, for in every case we know that something has brought completion, although we have no knowledge of this something in its intangibility. The true sage does not try to know Heaven.

Heaven's function has been established once for all, its accomplishment brought to completion once for all. Thus man's body was prepared and the spirit of man came to life, and with loving and hating, delight and annoyance, sorrow and joy: that is, the 'Heaven-given emotions' were stored up within. Man has eyes, ears, nose, mouth, and limbs, 'the Heaven-given (natural) pipes,' each of them in contact with the others but not able to interchange its aptitude for the others. In the central emptiness dwells the mind [hsin], that is 'the Heaven-given (natural) sovereign,' controller of the five senses. The mind makes the arrangements by which the other species are used to nourish the human species: that is 'Heaven-given (natural) nourishing'; for to protect one's own species is what is called 'happiness,' to go against it is 'calamity.' This is 'the Heaven-given (natural) system of government.'

Now to darken man's Heaven-given sovereign, to throw his Heaven-given senses into confusion, to let go his Heaven-given nourishment, to disobey his Heaven-given system of governing, and to do violence to his Heaven-given emotions, this is the supreme evil fortune. The sage purifies his Heaven-given sovereign, rectifies his Heaven-given senses, prepares his Heaven-given nourishment [i.e. by attention to agricultural pursuits], protects his Heaven-given government, nourishes his Heaven-given emotions in order to bring to perfection his Heaven-given merit of accomplishment. If this be done, then he knows what he can do and what he cannot do, and with Heaven and Earth discharging their responsibilities the myriad creatures are at man's command. . . .

The high-minded man [*chun tzu*] is concerned about the matters in his own sphere and does not hanker after the matters in Heaven's sphere of action; whilst the low-minded man does the reverse. Because the former is so, his affairs daily go forward, and because the latter is so, his affairs daily go backward. There is a single reason for the one going forward and the other going backward. In this lies the difference between the two.

If a star falls or a tree groans, the people of the country are all in a panic. The question is, why (this state of panic)? The answer is, for no reason. There is some change in Heaven or in Earth, some Yin and Yang transformation, something which rarely happens in the material sphere. It is right to wonder at it; it is not right to fear it. In every generation there are these occurrences from time to time, eclipses of the sun or the moon, wind and rain at unseasonable times, strange stars appearing in groups. If those in authority are intelligent and their government is equable, then in spite of these occurrences in one generation after another there is no harm done. If they are unintelligent and their government leads in dangerous paths, in spite of there being no such occurrence they are not better off.

It follows that 'human omens' are the things to be feared, the scamped ploughing which affects the final crop, the sketchy hoeing which misses the weeds, the foolhardiness in government which saps the confidence of the people. When the fields are overgrown with weeds and the harvest is bad, the price of corn high and the people short of food and their dead bodies found on the roads, these are what I call human omens. When the official orders are stupid ones, when public undertakings are put in hand at the wrong times and the basic industries are not properly organized, these are what I call 'human omens.' If the (sense of) ritual-and-righteousness is not cultivated, if the women's and men's apartments are not kept separate and there is sex license, then father and son are suspicious of each other, rulers and ruled are at cross purposes, tyranny and distress go hand in hand. These I call human omens. They are born of disorder, and when these three kinds come together, peace is dead in that country. . . .

The question is put: What about the special sacrifices for rain and then the rain coming? The answer is that there is nothing to it. It would rain all the same if there were no sacrifices. When people 'save' the sun and moon from being devoured, or when they pray for rain at a time of drought, or when they divine the omens before taking an important decision, these prayers are not to be taken as being answered. They are superfluous embellishments, for that is how enlightened men regard them, although the people generally take them to be signs of the supernatural. (Rather) it is good fortune to see them as embellishments, bad fortune to see them as supernatural. . . . Which is better, to magnify Heaven and meditate on it or to have your goods properly cared for and systematically controlled; to submit to Heaven and sing its praises or to systematize its commissions and make good use of them; to rely on things multiplying of themselves or to exercise all one's ability in developing them? . . .

[172]

HUI SHIH

HUI SHIH (4th century B.C.). Documents of the teachings of Hui Shih are preserved only in the book of Chuang Chou, the brilliant precursor of Taoism, who considered him the worthiest of his adversaries, and evidently esteemed him higher than Confucius. Hui Shih probably was some years older than Chuang Chou and died before the latter had finished his book *Chuang Tzu.* In the aphorisms quoted by Chuang Chou, Hui Shih appears to be a disciple

of Confucius' grandson Tzu Ssu, deeply impressed by his awareness of eternal change and fond of pointing out the paradoxical.

THE APHORISMS

Hᴜɪ Shih explored the significance of things . . . and said:

1. That beyond which there is nothing greater should
be called the great unit. That beyond which there is nothing
smaller should be called the small unit.

2. That which has no thickness cannot be increased in
thickness, (but) its size can be a thousand miles (long).

3. The heavens are as low as the earth, mountains
on the same level as marshes.

4. The sun exactly at noon is exactly (beginning to)
go down. And a creature exactly when he is born is exactly
(beginning to) die.

5. A great similarity compared with a small similarity
is very different. This state of affairs should be described
as a small similarity-in-dissimilarity. The myriad things in
Nature are both completely similar and completely dissimilar. This state of affairs should be described as a great
similarity-in-dissimilarity.

6. The Southern region (beyond the borders of China
and not fully explored) has no limit and yet has a limit.

7. To-day I go to Yueh State and I arrive there in the
past.

8. Linked rings can be sundered.

9. I know that the hub of the world is north of Yen
State and south of Yueh State.

10. Love all things equally: the heavens and the earth
are one composite body.

[173]

HUIZINGA, JOHAN

HUIZINGA, JOHAN (1872-1945). After Huizinga had become internationally renowned as a historian of the civilization of the
later Middle Ages, the Renaissance and Humanism, he began to

develop his own philosophy of civilization. His books which deal with problems of contemporary culture, especially his *Shadow of Tomorrow* (1936), show clearly that the historical phenomenon of the *Waning of the Middle Ages*, as his most popular work is entitled, deeply influenced his thoughts about the present and future state of humanity. Although Huizinga regarded history as an irreversible process, he protested his belief in absolute principles of ethics and in eternal truth, which subsist "above the stream of change and evolution," and he regretted the loss of an universal authority, as was represented by the Medieval Church, bound to guide mankind in accordance with unchanging principles.

Culture was defined by Huizinga as cooperation of social life with spiritual productivity. He later abandoned this definition as too narrow, and, while retaining the emphasis on cooperation, tried to introduce the concept of human vocation into it. As the principal symptoms of the present cultural crisis, Huizinga recognized lack of mental concentration, weakening of judgment, renunciation of rationality, worship of life and lack of charity. The last-mentioned symptom became of increasing importance to Huizinga who was induced by the events of contemporary history to lean more and more upon Catholic moral theology. In a letter to Julien Benda he declared that the doctrine of the seven mortal sins is a better direction for human life than all modern psychology.

BARBARISM

JUST as barbarism can prevail in a society with a high degree of technical perfection, it may equally coincide with that other positive characteristic of modern society, universal education. To determine the level of culture from the degree of illiteracy is to deceive oneself with an outworn belief. A certain modicum of school knowledge in no way guarantees the possession of culture. It can hardly be called undue pessimism when, looking at the general state of mind of our time, one feels bound to speak in the following terms.

Delusion and misconception flourish everywhere. More than ever men seem to be slaves to a word, a motto, to kill one another with, to silence one another in the most literal sense. The world is filled with hate and misunderstanding. There is no way of measuring how great the percentage of the deluded is and whether it is greater than formerly, but delusion and folly have more power to harm and speak with greater authority. For the shallow, semi-educated person the beneficial restraints of respect for tradition, form and cult are gradually falling away. Worst of all is that widely prevalent indifference to truth which reaches its peak in the open advocacy of the political lie.

Barbarisation sets in when, in an old culture which once, in the course of many centuries, had raised itself to purity and clarity of thought and understanding, the vapours of the magic and fantastic rise up again from the seething brew of passions to cloud the understanding: when the *muthos* supplants the *logos*.

Again and again the new creed of the heroic will to power, with its exaltation of life over understanding, is seen to embody the very tendencies which to the believer in the Spirit spell the drift towards barbarism. For the "life-philosophy" does exactly this: it extols *muthos* over *logos*. To the prophets of the life-philosophy barbarism has no deprecatory implications. The term itself loses its meaning. The new rulers desire nothing else.

The gods of our time, mechanization and organization, have brought life and death. They have wired up the whole world, established contact throughout, created everywhere the possibility of co-operation, concentration of strength and mutual understanding. At the same time they have trapped the spirit, fettered it, stifled it. They have led man from individualism to collectivism. But with his unguided insight man has so far succeeded only in realizing the evil that is in every collectivism, the negation of the deepest personal values, the slavery of the spirit. Will the future be one of ever greater mechanization of society solely governed by the demands of utility and power?

[174]

HUMBOLDT, WILHELM VON

HUMBOLDT, WILHELM VON (1767-1835). As a contemporary observer remarked, Humboldt was not young at the age of sixteen and not old at the age of sixty. Although Humboldt did not dis-

552

agree with that statement, he claimed that his independence from change was the result of his self-education and striving and of the organization and economy of his living energies. Even if this assumption was incorrect, it is true that Humboldt endeavored, from his early years till his death, to construct his character in accordance with his ideals of human perfection and, although he persisted in wearing such a mask, his behavior was considered natural by men like Goethe and Schiller, his friends. This mask helped him, sensitive and sensual as he actually was, to appear serene and imperturbable. But he was by no means a hypocrite. He was deeply convinced that character was not a natural human quality but the result of will.

Humboldt was a man of highest culture and wide interests. He was a great linguist, a pioneer in studying the languages of American aborigines, of Sanskrit and Basque; in philosophy, an independent disciple of Kant and Schelling, not abandoning, however, the ideas of enlightenment; a historian; and a statesman who was an excellent minister of public education in Prussia, but was defeated when he struggled against routine and reaction and for a moderate liberalism.

In his early writings, Humboldt was an extreme individualist. Later he was interested in investigating the relations between the individual and the great movements of history, but he maintained, in opposition to Hegel, that the individual and the so-called spirit of the epoch or nation are incommensurable. He became convinced of the coherence of the spiritual life of all times and nations but his principal interest remained devoted to the individual. To him the diversity of men, times and nations constituted no objection to the establishment of a universal ideal of human education and perfection, and he constantly endeavored to give this ideal a telling, characteristic, concrete content.

SENSES AND REASON

THE impressions, inclinations, and passions which have their immediate source in the senses, are those which first and most violently manifest themselves in human nature. Wherever, before the refining influences of culture have imparted a new direction to the soul's energies, these impressions, etc., do not show themselves, all seeds of power have perished, and nothing either good or great can take root and flourish. They constitute the great original source of all spontaneous activity, and first inspire a glowing, genial warmth in human nature. They infuse life and elastic vigor into the soul: when unsatisfied, they render it active, buoyant, ingenious in the invention of schemes, and courageous in their execution; when satisfied, they promote an easy and unhindered play of ideas. In general, they animate and quicken all conceptions with a greater and more varied activity, suggest new views, point out hitherto unnoticed aspects, and, according to the manner in which they are satisfied, intimately react on the physical organization, which in its turn acts upon the soul, although we only notice how from the results.

The influence, however, of these impressions and inclinations differs, not only in its intensity, but in the manner of its operation. This is, to a certain extent, owing to their strength or weakness; but it is also partly to be attributed to their degree of affinity with the spiritual element in human nature, or from the difficulty or facility of raising them from mere animal gratifications to human pleasures. Thus, for instance, the eye imparts to the substance of its impressions that outline of form which is so full of enjoyment and fertile in ideas; while the ear lends to sound the proportionate succession of tones in the order of time. The nature of these impressions readily suggests many interesting reflections, if this were the proper place for such a topic, but I will only pause to notice their different importance as regards the culture of the soul.

The eye supplies the reason, so to speak, with a more prepared substance; and the inner part of our nature, with its own form and that of other things which stand in a relation to it, is thus presented to us in a single and distinct situation. If we conceive of the ear merely as an organ of sense, and in so far as it does not receive and communicate words, it conveys far less distinctness of impression. And it is for this reason that Kant assigns the preference to the plastic arts when compared with music. But he observes that the culture secured to the soul by the several arts, (and I would add, directly secured), is presupposed as a scale for determining this preference.

The question, however, presents itself whether this scale of previous culture is the just standard of appreciation. Energy appears to me to be the first and chiefest of human virtues. Whatever exalts our energy is of greater worth than anything that merely puts material into our hands for its exercise. . . .

But the sensual and spiritual are linked together by a mysterious bond, of which our hearts are distinctly conscious, though it remains hidden from our eyes. To this double nature of the visible and invisible world, and to the deep-implanted longing for the latter, coupled with the feeling of the sweet necessity of the former, we owe all sound and logical systems of philosophy, truly based on the immutable principles of our nature, just as to the same source we are able to trace the most visionary and incoherent reveries.

[175]

HUME, DAVID

HUME, DAVID (1711-1776). "If one reads Hume's books," Albert Einstein declared, "one is amazed that many sometimes highly esteemed philosophers after him have been able to write so much obscure stuff and even to find grateful readers for it. Hume has permanently influenced the development of the best of philosophers who came after him."

Sometimes, this influence had the very character of a revelation. Immanuel Kant "openly confessed" that Hume awakened him "from my dogmatic slumber and gave my investigation in the field of speculative philosophy quite a new direction." Jeremy Bentham described how, while reading Hume, "I felt as if scales had fallen from my eyes." In modern times, thinkers differing so widely from each other as William James, G. E. Moore, George Santayana and Bertrand Russell, agree in their devotion to Hume, although they have criticized and modified many of his statements.

Hume concentrated upon philosophy in his early years only. Later on he was a soldier, a diplomat, a politician, a member of the Tory party, Under-Secretary of State, and a librarian. He wrote on history, social sciences and religion. But he remained a philosopher, and part of his philosophy must be read out of his later

works. Hume called himself a sceptic. Modern philosophers characterize him more rightly as the precursor of positivism. His scepticism was mainly confined to his rejection of the principles of
induction. From this position, Hume proceeded to the statement
that the concept of causality cannot be gained from material given
by the senses. To connect one occurrence with some other by the
notions of cause and effect, is, according to Hume, not the result
of rational knowledge but of a habit of expecting the perception
of the second after having perceived the first, because that sequence
has previously taken place in innumerable cases. This habit is
founded upon a belief which can be explained psychologically
but cannot be derived by abstraction from either the ideas of
the two objects or the impressions of the senses. Hume did not
deny that causality works. He only denied that reason is capable
of understanding it. Neither did Hume deny the possibility of true
knowledge by comprehending resemblance, contrariety, proportions
in quantity or degrees in quality. Modern physicists, whose causal
laws are elaborated inferences from the observed course of nature,
have supported Hume's challenge to the traditional causal connection. Hume has often emphasized that the propensity to believe
in the existence of the world and in man's faculty to think and
judge is stronger than the awareness of the limits of human
reason. Occasionally Hume was depressed by doubts. But his enjoyment of life overcame his melancholy as soon as he recognized
that the inadequacy of his reason was natural and common to all
men. This insight was to him a cure. By critical examination of
facts Hume pioneered in the sciences of political and cultural history, economics, comparative history of religion and sociology.

ON THE ORIGIN OF OUR IDEAS

ALL the perceptions of the human mind resolve themselves
into two distinct kinds, which I shall call *impressions* and
ideas. The difference betwixt these consists in the degrees of
force and liveliness with which they strike upon the mind and
make their way into our thought or consciousness. Those
perceptions which enter with most force and violence we may
name *impressions;* and under this name I comprehend all our
sensations, passions, and emotions, as they make their first
appearance in the soul. By *ideas* I mean the faint images of
these in thinking and reasoning; such as, for instance, are all
the perceptions excited by the present discourse, excepting

only those which arise from the sight and touch, and excepting the immediate pleasure or uneasiness it may occasion.
I believe it will not be very necessary to employ many words
in explaining this distinction. Every one of himself will readily perceive the difference betwixt feeling and thinking. The
common degrees of these are easily distinguished, though
it is not impossible but in particular instances they may
very nearly approach to each other. Thus in sleep, in a
fever, in madness, or in any very violent emotions of soul,
our ideas may approach to our impressions; as on the other
hand it sometimes happens that our impressions are so faint
and low, that we cannot distinguish them from our ideas.
But notwithstanding this near resemblance in a few instances,
they are in general so very different that no one can make
a scruple to rank them under distinct heads, and assign to
each a peculiar name to mark the difference.

There is another division of our perceptions which it
will be convenient to observe, and which extends itself both
to our impressions and ideas. This division is into *simple* and
complex. Simple perceptions or impressions and ideas are
such as admit of no distinction nor separation. The complex
are the contrary to these, and may be distinguished into
parts. Though a particular color, taste, and smell are qualities all united together in this apple, 'tis easy to perceive
they are not the same but are at least distinguishable from
each other.

Having by these divisions given an order and arrangement to our objects, we may now apply ourselves to consider
with the more accuracy their qualities and relations. The
first circumstance that strikes my eye is the great resemblance betwixt our impressions and ideas in every other
particular except their degree of force and vivacity. The one
seem to be in a manner of the reflection of the other; so that
all the perceptions of the mind are double, and appear both
as impressions and ideas. When I shut my eyes and think
of my chamber, the ideas I form are exact representations
of the impressions I felt; nor is there any circumstance of

the one which is not to be found in the other. In running over my other perceptions I find still the same resemblance and representation. Ideas and impressions appear always to correspond to each other. This circumstance seems to me remarkable, and engages my attention for a moment.

Upon a more accurate survey I find I have been carried away too far by the first appearance, and that I must make use of the distinction of perceptions into simple and complex, to limit this general decision *that all our ideas and impressions are resembling.* I observe that many of our complex ideas never had impressions that corresponded to them, and that many of our complex impressions never are exactly copied in ideas. I can imagine to myself such a city as the New Jerusalem, whose pavement is gold and walls are rubies, though I never saw any such. I have seen Paris; but shall I affirm I can form such an idea of that city as will perfectly represent all its streets and houses in their real and just proportions?

I perceive, therefore, that though there is in general a great resemblance betwixt our *complex* impressions and ideas, yet the rule is not universally true that they are exact copies of each other. We may next consider how the case stands with our *simple* perceptions. After the most accurate examination of which I am capable, I venture to affirm that the rule here holds without any exception, and that every simple idea has a simple impression which resembles it, and every simple impression a correspondent idea. That idea of red which we form in the dark and that impression which strikes our eyes in sunshine differ only in degree, not in nature. That the case is the same with all our simple impressions and ideas 'tis impossible to prove by a particular enumeration of them. Everyone may satisfy himself in this point by running over as many as he pleases. But if anyone should deny this universal resemblance, I know no way of convincing him but by desiring him to show a simple impression that has not a correspondent idea, or a simple idea that has not a correspondent impression. If he does not answer this challenge, as 'tis certain he cannot, we may from his silence and our own observation establish our conclusion.

Thus we find that all simple ideas and impressions resemble each other; and as the complex are formed from them, we may affirm in general that these two species of perception are exactly correspondent. Having discovered this relation, which requires no farther examination, I am curious to find some other of their qualities. Let us consider how they stand with regard to their existence, and which of the impressions and ideas are causes and which effects.

The *full* examination of this question is the subject of the present treatise; and therefore we shall here content ourselves with establishing one general proposition, *that all our simple ideas in their first appearance are derived from simple impressions, which are correspondent to them, and which they exactly represent.*

In seeking for phenomena to prove this proposition I find only those of two kinds, but in each kind the phenomena are obvious, numerous, and conclusive. I first make myself certain, by a new review, of what I have already asserted, that every simple impression is attended with a correspondent idea and every simple idea with a correspondent impression. From this constant conjunction of resembling perceptions I immediately conclude that there is a great connection betwixt our correspondent impressions and ideas, and that the existence of the one has a considerable influence upon that of the other. Such a constant conjunction, in such an infinite number of instances, can never arise from chance; but clearly proves a dependence of the impressions on the ideas, or of the ideas on the impressions. That I may know on which side this dependence lies I consider the order of their *first appearance,* and find by constant experience that the simple impressions always take the precedence of their correspondent ideas, but never appear in the contrary order. To give a child an idea of scarlet or orange, of sweet or bitter, I present the objects, or in other words, convey to him these impressions; but proceed not so absurdly as to endeavor to produce the impressions by exciting the ideas. Our ideas upon their appearance produce not their correspondent impressions, nor do we perceive any color or feel any sensation merely upon thinking of them. On the other hand we find that any impression either of the mind or body is constantly followed by an idea which resembles it and is only different in the degrees of force and liveliness. The constant conjunction of our resembling perceptions is a convincing proof that the one are the causes of the other; and this priority of the impression is an equal proof that our impressions are the causes of our ideas, not our ideas of our impressions.

To confirm this I consider another plain and convincing phenomenon; which is, that wherever by any accident the faculties which give rise to any impressions are obstructed in their operations, as when one is born blind or deaf, not only the impressions are lost but also their correspondent ideas; so that there never appear in the mind the least traces of either of them. Nor is this only true where the organs of sensation are entirely destroyed, but likewise where they have never been put in action to produce a particular impression. We cannot form to ourselves a just idea of the taste of a pineapple without having actually tasted it.

There is however one contradictory phenomenon which may prove that 'tis not absolutely impossible for ideas to go before their correspondent impressions. I believe it will readily be allowed that the several distinct ideas of colors which enter by the eyes, or those of sounds which are conveyed by the hearing, are really different from each other, though at the same time resembling. Now if this be true of different colors, it must be no less so of the different shades of the same color, that each of them produces a distinct idea, independent of the rest. For if this should be denied, 'tis possible, by the continual gradation of shades, to run a color insensibly into what is most remote from it; and if you will not allow any of the means to be different, you cannot without absurdity deny the extremes to be the same. Suppose therefore a person to have enjoyed his sight for thirty years, and to have become perfectly well acquainted with colors of all kinds excepting one particular shade of blue, for instance, which it never has been his fortune to meet with. Let all the different shades of that color, except that single one, be placed before him, descending gradually from the deepest to the lightest, 'tis plain that he will perceive a blank where that shade is wanting, and will be sensible that there is a greater distance in that place betwixt the contiguous colors than in any other. Now I ask whether 'tis possible for him, from his own imagination, to supply this deficiency, and raise up to himself the idea of that particular shade, though it had never been conveyed to him by his senses? I believe there are few but will be of opinion that he can; and this may serve as a proof that the simple ideas are not always derived from the correspondent impressions; though the instance is so particular and singular that 'tis scarce worth our observing, and does not merit that for it alone we should alter our general maxim.

But besides this exception, it may be amiss to remark on this head that the principle of the priority of impressions to ideas must be understood with another limitation, *viz.*, that as our ideas are images of our impressions, so we can form secondary ideas which are images of the primary; as appears from this very reasoning concerning them. This is not, properly speaking, an exception to the rule so much as an explanation of it. Ideas produce the images of themselves in new ideas; but as the first ideas are supposed to be derived from impressions, it still remains true that all our simple ideas proceed either mediately or immediately from their correspondent impressions.

This then is the first principle I establish in the science of human nature; nor ought we to despise it because of the simplicity of its appearance. For 'tis remarkable that the present question concerning the precedency of our impressions or ideas is the same with what has made so much noise in other terms, when it has been disputed whether there be any *innate ideas*, or whether all ideas be derived from sen-

sation and reflection. We may observe that in order to prove
the ideas of extension and color not to be innate, philosophers
do nothing but show that they are conveyed by our senses.
To prove the ideas of passion and desire not to be innate,
they observe that we have a preceding experience of these
emotions in ourselves. Now if we carefully examine these
arguments. we shall find that they prove nothing but that
ideas are preceded by other more lively perceptions, from
which they are derived, and which they represent. I hope
this clear stating of the question will remove all disputes
concerning it, and will render this principle of more use
in our reasonings than it seems hitherto to have been.

[176]

HUNEIN IBN ISHAK

HUNEIN IBN ISHAK (809-873). The *Sayings of the Philosophers,*
written by Hunein Ibn Ishak, a Nestorian Christian who was born
in Syria and wrote in Syriac and Arabic, has been translated into
Hebrew, Spanish and other languages, and became a very popular
book among the intellectuals of the early Middle Ages in Europe
and the Middle East. This book, however, is highly significant of
the deformation of Greek philosophy in the sixth and seventh centuries. Hunein was a learned man. He wrote an *Introduction into
the Science of Medicine,* a Syriac-Arabic dictionary and grammar,
and many other books. He traveled a great deal and collected
Greek manuscripts, which he either translated into Syriac or Arabic,
or used as sources for his own books. Without any doubt, Hunein
was a careful writer and faithful translator, but the texts of the
manuscripts he had at hand were spoiled, because the copyists had
been incapable of understanding what they copied, and each succeeding scribe had added new errors to those of his predecessors.
Thus Hunein confounded Socrates with Diogenes, or Plato with
Bias. Even his own philosophy, whether it consisted of original
thoughts or of quotations, is more characteristic of the fate of
certain Greek thoughts in a time of spiritual decay.

A PHILOSOPHICAL COLLOQUY

AT a Greek holiday, four philosophers met in a temple which
was adorned with golden pictures. These philosophers were

the pillars of wisdom. They talked about the objects of wisdom, and discussed the philosophical principles of wisdom, while mentioning sayings of the old thinkers.

One of them said: This meeting shall not be forgotten. For the friends of wisdom will always like to learn wisdom. Now, we will utter wise sentences to be remembered by late generations so that posterity may learn from them. They shall be a moral school for those who come next, and established wisdom for those who come long after us.

The first said: Through noble souls and pure thoughts the spirits soar up to the air of spiritual understanding in the realm of light and power which are hidden to those who glance at the real world. There, they walk about celestial flower-beds, free from any misfortune. After the spirit has become pure, they will live an eternal life that cannot perish nor vanish into nothing. Then, ultimate ground will be united with ultimate ground, the pure will be united with the pure, and the obscure will be drowned into the obscure. Then the spirit will behold hidden mysteries, and will have sure possession of the knowledge that is obtained by the force of thought and by the union of ideas and concepts.

The second said: How can the spirit strive to grasp what is hidden, since the essence of truth is hidden to it? How can the pure be separated from the impure if the spirit is not imbued with the knowledge of pure thought? How can thought reach the depth of hiddenness since it is abiding in the darkness of foolishness, and since greed is spoiling the origin?

The third said: While grasping eternal truth, ideas get into the whirlpool of consideration, and thus are raised to the sphere of pure spirit, and strive with all their forces for grasping the hidden. Thus they arrive at the realm of high sublimity where the souls are resting in the shadow of Divine Majesty.

The fourth said: Contradictions can be reconciled, and the hidden can be recognized only if the spirit becomes allied with the other spirits; goes along the path of understanding;

becomes purified from obscure stupidity, and if it becomes separated from the abode of darkness in order to arrive at the free square of understanding. That is the highest happiness, the most magnificent and noble.

[177]

HUSSERL, EDMUND

HUSSERL, EDMUND (1859-1938). More than fifty years of strenuous work had to pass between the beginning and the accomplishment of Husserl's philosophy. At its completion he expressed his confidence in having established philosophy as a "rigorous science," as an "absolute discipline," and he classified all precedent philosophies as either superficial or poor, vague or sterile. In his early days, however, Husserl was tormented by doubts that his own talents were adequate to his aspirations, and that philosophy in itself could satisfy them. It was his teacher, Franz Brentano, who not only encouraged Husserl to devote his life to philosophy but gave him certainty that philosophy could clear up any doubt. Husserl did not find the way to Brentano spontaneously. He was brought into contact with him by his friend Thomas G. Masaryk, who was to become the founder and first president of the Czechoslovakian republic.

Brentano taught Husserl the importance of three points which remained characteristic of Husserl's own thinking, notwithstanding the modifications or even radical changes his philosophy underwent in the course of time. At first, he taught him to distinguish between logical laws and the laws of psychic facts which involved opposition to "psychologism," to any concept of logical notions as psychic formations apt to be explained by their genesis. Secondly, Husserl took from Brentano the Scholastic distinction between essence and existence, and, furthermore, the term of "intentionality" of thought, which means that thought is always directed toward things different from itself.

From this basis, Husserl proceeded to the foundation of phenomenology, which, before him, had been used as a theory of appearances, and, through him, became a full-fledged philosophy. It deals with insight into essences without regard to the empirical conditions of their perceptibility, even without regard to existence. Intuitive evidence is the criterion of truth. It is not to be confounded with certainty or proof of reality. Husserl would not deal with metaphysical considerations of any kind but he was convinced

564

that his phenomenology could provide answers to any "legitimate" metaphysical question, and he maintained that recognition and pursuit of phenomenological analysis, as developed by him, would produce true knowledge quite independently of the adherence of the analyzer to any philosopher in other regard. Husserl claimed to have established a doctrine of ideal conditions of the possibility of science, and to have served truth in a safer way than any philosophical system.

CONSCIOUSNESS AND NATURAL REALITY
THE VIEW OF THE "MAN IN THE STREET"

ALL THE ESSENTIAL characteristics of experience and consciousness which we have reached are for us necessary steps towards the attainment of the end which is unceasingly drawing us on, the discovery, namely, of the essence of that *"pure" consciousness* which is to fix the limits of the phenomenological field. Our inquiries were eidetic; but the individual instances of the essences we have referred to as experience, stream of experience, "consciousness" in all its senses, belonged as real events to the natural world. To that extent we have not abandoned the ground of the natural standpoint. Individual consciousness is interwoven with the *natural world* in a *twofold* way: it is some *man's* consciousness, or that of some *man* or *beast,* and in a large number at least of its particularizations it is a consciousness of this world. *In respect now of this intimate attachment with the real world, what is meant by saying that consciousness has an essence "of its own",* that with other consciousness it constitutes a self-contained *connexion determined purely through this, its own essence,* the connexion, namely, of the stream of consciousness? Moreover, since we can interpret consciousness in the widest sense to cover eventually whatever the concept of experience includes, the question concerns the experience-stream's own essential nature and that of all its components. To what extent, in the first place, must the *material world* be fundamentally different in kind, *excluded from the experience's own essential nature?* And if it is this, if over against all consciousness and the essential

565

being proper to it, it is that which is *"foreign"* and *"other"*, how can consciousness be *interwoven* with it, and consequently with the whole world that is alien to consciousness? For it is easy to convince oneself that the material world is not just any portion of the natural world, but its fundamental stratum to which all other real being is *essentially* related. It still fails to include the souls of men and animals; and the new factor which these introduce is first and foremost their "experiencing" together with their conscious relationship to the world surrounding them. *But here consciousness and thinghood form a connected whole,* connected within the particular psychological unities which we call *animalia,* and in the last resort within the *real unity of the world as a whole.* Can the unity of a whole be other than made one through the essential proper nature of its parts, which must therefore have some *community of essence* instead of a fundamental heterogeneity?

To be clear, let us seek out the ultimate sources whence the general thesis of the world which I adopt when taking up the natural standpoint draws its nourishment, thereby enabling me as a conscious being to discover over against me an existing world of things, to ascribe to myself in this world a body, and to find for myself within this world a proper place. This ultimate source is obviously *sensory experience.* For our purpose, however, it is sufficient to consider *sensory perception,* which in a certain proper sense plays among experiencing acts the part of an original experience, whence all other experiencing acts draw a chief part of their power to serve as a ground. Every perceiving consciousness has this peculiarity, that it is the consciousness of *the embodied* (*leibhaftigen*) *self-presence of an individual object,* which on its own side and in a pure logical sense of the term is an individual or some logico-categorical modification of the same. In our own instance, that of sensory perception, or, in distincter terms, perception of a world of things, the logical individual is the Thing; and it is sufficient for us to treat the perception of things as representing all other perception (of properties, processes, and the like).

The natural wakeful life of our Ego is a continuous perceiving, actual or potential. The world of things and our body within it are continuously present to our perception. How then does and can *Consciousness itself* separate out as a *concrete thing in itself,* from that within it, of which we are conscious, namely, the *perceived being, "standing over against"* consciousness *"in and for itself"*?

I meditate first as would the man "in the street." I see and grasp the thing itself in its bodily reality. It is true that I sometimes deceive myself, and not only in respect of the perceived constitution of the thing, but also in respect of its being there at all. I am subject to an illusion or hallucination. The perception is not the "genuine." But if it is, if, that is, we can "confirm" its presence in the actual context of experience, eventually with the help of correct empirical thinking, then the perceived thing *is real* and itself really given, and that bodily in perception. Here perceiving considered simply as consciousness, and apart from the body and the bodily organs, appears as something in itself essenceless, an empty looking of an empty "Ego" towards the object itself which comes into contact with it in some astonishing way.   [177A]

HUXLEY, THOMAS HENRY

HUXLEY, THOMAS HENRY (1825-1895). Huxley, the son of a poor schoolmaster, attended a regular school for only two years. He described that education as "a pandemonium." Thereafter, from his tenth year on, he had to pursue his studies by himself, which he did with such energy and clear-sightedness that he easily passed the examination for admission to the University. As a surgeon in the British Navy, Huxley was able to study tropical fauna and flora, and he became a pioneer in biology. His contributions to the anatomy of vertebrate and invertebrate animals are regarded as of lasting value. As a professor at London University, Lord Rector of the University of Aberdeen, president of the Royal So-

ciety and member of the Privy Council, Huxley used his authority
and influence for the promotion of all sciences and the defense of
science against detractors of any kind. Not the least of his accomplishments, Huxley was successful in popularizing science and
making the working classes acquainted with its principal results.
Full of energy and initiative, daring and circumspect in his way
of thinking, Huxley was a pugnacious but always courteous critic
who was fond of disputing with great authorities in science, in State
and Church.

Although Huxley, in his early years, was convinced of the
immutability of species, he became, immediately after the publication of Darwin's *Origin of Species*, a brilliant champion of evolutionism. He did not share Darwin's faith in the absolute rule of
small variations, and insisted on cases of sudden change observed
by himself. But this and other objections did not prevent him from
defending and continuously explaining Darwin's theory. As a philosophical thinker, Huxley, a great admirer of Hume, defined his
standpoint as *agnosticism*, a strict insistence on the impossibility of
knowing anything beyond observation of the senses, indifferent to
any theory of reality. Huxley's attitude was not a negative scepticism
but rather a plea for sceptical caution in the matter of belief. He
was as radically opposed to materialism as to the faith of the
Church.

THE RELATIONS OF MAN TO THE LOWER ANIMALS

THE question of questions to mankind—the problem which
underlies all others, and is more deeply interesting than
any other—is the ascertainment of the place which man occupies in nature, and of his relations to the universe of
things. Whence has our race come? what are the limits of
our power over nature, and of nature's power over us? To
what good are we tending?—these are the problems which
present themselves anew and with undiminished interest to
every man born into the world.

Most of us, shrinking from the difficulties and dangers
which beset the seeker after original answers to these riddles,
are contented to ignore them altogether, or to smother the
investigating spirit under the feather-bed of respected and
respectable tradition. But in every age one or two restless
spirits, blest with that constructive genius which can build

a secure foundation, or cursed with the mere spirit of scepticism, are unable to follow in the well-worn and comfortable
track of their forefathers and contemporaries; and, unmind-
ful of thorns and stumbling-blocks, strike out into paths of
their own. The sceptics end in the infidelity which asserts the
problem to be insoluble, or in the atheism which denies the
existence of any orderly progress and governance of things.
The men of genius propound solutions which grow into systems of theology or philosophy; or, veiled in musical language which suggests more than it asserts, take the shape
of the poetry of an epoch.

Each such answer to the great question—invariably
asserted by the followers of its propounder, if not by himself, to be complete and final—remains in high authority
and esteem, it may be for one century, or it may be for
twenty; but, as invariably, time proves each reply to have
been a mere approximation to the truth—tolerable chiefly
on account of the ignorance of those by whom it was accepted, and wholly intolerable when tested by the larger
knowledge of their successors.

In a well-worn metaphor a parallel is drawn between
the life of man and the metamorphosis of the caterpillar
into the butterfly; but the comparison may be more just, as
well as more novel, if for its former term we take the mental
progress of the race. History shows that the human mind, fed
by constant accessions of knowledge, periodically grows too
large for its theoretical coverings, and bursts them asunder
to appear in new habiliments, as the feeding and growing
grub at intervals casts its too narrow skin and assumes
another, itself but temporary. Truly the *imago* state of man
seems to be terribly distant; but every moult is a step gained,
and of such there have been many.

It will be admitted that some knowledge of man's position in the animated world is an indispensable preliminary
to the proper understanding of his position in the universe;
and this again resolves itself, in the long run, into an inquiry into the nature and the closeness of the ties which con-

nect him with those singular creatures which have been styled the man-like apes. The importance of such an inquiry is indeed intuitively manifest. Brought face to face with these blurred copies of himself, the least thoughtful of men is conscious of a certain shock, due, perhaps, not so much to disgust at the aspect of what looks like an insulting caricature, as to the awakening of a sudden and profound mistrust of time-honored theories and strongly rooted prejudices regarding his own position in nature, and his relations to the Under-world of life; while that which remains a dim suspicion for the unthinking becomes a vast argument, fraught with the deepest consequences, for all who are acquainted with the recent progress of anatomical and physiological sciences.

I now propose briefly to unfold that argument, and to set forth, in a form intelligible to those who possess no special acquaintance with anatomical science, the chief facts upon which all conclusions respecting the nature and the extent of the bonds which connect man with the brute world must be based. I shall then indicate the one immediate conclusion which, in my judgment, is justified by those facts; and I shall finally discuss the bearing of that conclusion upon the hypotheses which have been entertained respecting the origin of man.

*　　*　　*

Leaving Mr. Darwin's views aside, the whole analogy of natural operations furnishes so complete and crushing an argument against the intervention of any but what are termed secondary causes in the production of all the phenomena of the universe that, in view of the intimate relations between man and the rest of the living world, and between the forces exerted by the latter and all other forces, I can see no excuse for doubting that all are coordinated terms of nature's progression, from the formless to the formed—from the inorganic to the organic—from blind force to conscious intellect and will. Science has fulfilled her mission when she has ascertained and enunciated truth; and were these pages addressed to men of science only, I should now close this essay, knowing that my colleagues have learned to respect nothing but evidence, and to believe that their highest duty lies in submitting to it, however much it may jar against their inclinations.

But desiring, as I do, to reach the wider circle of the intelligent public, it would be unworthy cowardice were I to ignore the repugnance with which the majority of my readers are likely to meet the conclusions to which the most careful and conscientious study I have been able to give to this matter has led me. On all sides I shall hear the cry— "We are men and women, and not a mere better sort of ape—a little longer in the leg, more compact in the foot, and bigger in the brain, than your brutal chimpanzees and gorillas. The power of knowledge—the consciousness of good and evil—the pitiful tenderness of human affections—raise us out of all real fellowship with the brutes, however closely they may seem to approximate us."

To this I can only reply that the exclamation would be most just, and would have my own entire sympathy, if it were only relevant. But it is not I who seek to base man's dignity upon his great-toe, or insinuate that we are lost if an ape has a *hippocampus minor*. On the contrary, I have done my best to sweep away this vanity. I have endeavored to show that no absolute structural line of demarcation, wider than that between the animals which immediately succeed us in the scale, can be drawn between the animal world and ourselves. And I may add the expression of my belief that the attempt to draw a physical distinction is equally futile, and that even the highest faculties of feeling and intellect begin to germinate in the lower forms of life. At the same time, no one is more thoroughly convinced than I am of the vastness of the gulf between civilized man and the brutes; or is more certain that whether *from* them or not, he is assuredly not *of* them. No one is less disposed to think lightly of the present dignity, or despairingly of the future hopes, of the only consciously intelligent denizen of the world.

We are indeed told by those who assume authority in these matters that the two sets of opinions are incompatible, and that the belief of the unity of origin of man and brutes involves the brutalization and degradation of the former. But is this really so? Could not a sensible child confute, by obvious arguments, the shallow rhetoricians who would force this conclusion upon us? Is it indeed true that the poet, or the philosopher, or the artist, whose genius is the glory of his age, is degraded from his high estate by the undoubted historical probability—not to say certainty—that he is the direct lineal descendant of some naked and bestial savage, whose intelligence was just sufficient to make him a little more cunning than the fox, and by so much more dangerous than the tiger? Or is he bound to howl and grovel on all fours because of the wholly unquestionable fact that he was once an egg, which no ordinary power of discrimination could distinguish from that of the dog? Or is the philanthropist or the saint to give up his endeavors to lead a noble life because the simplest study of man's nature reveals, at its foundations, all the selfish passions and fierce appetites of the quadruped? Is the mother-love vile because the hen shows it; or fidelity base because dogs possess it?

The common-sense of the mass of mankind will answer these questions without a moment's hesitation. Healthy humanity, finding itself hard-pressed to escape from real sin and degradation, will leave the brooding over speculative pollution to the cynics and the "righteous overmuch," who, disagreeing in everything else, unite in blind insensibility to the nobleness of the visible world and inability to appreciate the grandeur of the place man occupies therein. Nay, more thoughtful men, once escaped from the blinding influences of traditional prejudice, will find in the lowly stock whence man has sprung the best evidence of the splendor of his capacities, and will discern in his long progress through the past a reasonable ground of faith in his attainment of a nobler future.

They will remember that in comparing civilized man with the animal world one is as the Alpine traveler who sees the mountains soaring into the sky, and can hardly discern where the deep-shadowed crags and roseate peaks end, and where the clouds of heaven begin. Surely the awe-struck voyager may be excused if he at first refuses to believe the geologist, who tells him that these glorious masses are, after all, the hardest mud of primeval seas, or the cooled slag of subterranean furnaces—of one substance with the dullest clay, but raised by inward forces to that place of proud and seemingly inaccessible glory. But the geologist is right; and the due reflection on his teachings, instead of diminishing our reverence and our wonder, adds all the force of intellectual sublimity to the more aesthetic intuition of the uninstructed beholder.

And after passion and prejudice have died away, the same result will attend the teachings of the naturalist respecting that great Alps and Andes of the living world—man. Our reverence for the nobility of manhood will not be lessened by the knowledge that man is, in substance and structure, one with the brutes; for he alone possesses the marvellous endowment of intelligible and rational speech, whereby, in the secular period of his existence, he has slowly accumulated and organized the experience which is almost wholly lost with the cessation of every individual life in other animals; so that he now stands on the mountain-top, far above the level of his humble fellows, and transfigured from the grosser nature by reflecting, here and there, a ray from the Infinite source of truth.

PROTOPLASM IN ANIMALS AND PLANTS

NOTWITHSTANDING all the fundamental resemblances which exist between the power of the protoplasm in plants and animals, they present one striking difference, in the fact that plants can manufacture fresh protoplasm out of mineral compounds, whereas animals are obliged to procure it ready-

573

made; and hence, in the long run, depend upon plants. Upon what condition this difference in the powers of the two great divisions of the world of life depends, nothing at present is known. With such qualification as arises out of this fact, it may be truly said that all the acts of all living things are fundamentally one. Is any such unity predicable of their forms? Let us seek in easily verified facts for a reply to this question.

If a drop of blood be drawn by pricking one's finger, and viewed with proper precautions, and under a sufficiently high microscopic power, there will be seen, among the innumerable multitude of little, circular, discloidal bodies, or corpuscles, which float in it and give it its color, a comparatively small number of colorless corpuscles, of somewhat large size and irregular shape. If the drop of blood be kept at the temperature of the body, these colorless corpuscles will seem to exhibit marvellous activity, changing their forms with great rapidity, drawing in and thrusting out prolongations of their substance, and creeping about as if they were independent organisms.

The substance which is thus active is a mass of protoplasm, and its activity differs in detail rather than in principle from that of the protoplasm of the nettle. Under sundry circumstances the corpuscle dies, and becomes distended into a round mass, in the midst of which is seen a smaller spherical body, which existed, but was more or less hidden, in the living corpuscle, and is called its *nucleus*. Corpuscles of essentially similar structure are to be found in the skin, in the lining of the mouth, and scattered through the whole framework of the body. Nay, more; in the earliest condition of the human organism—in that state in which it has just become distinguishable from the egg in which it arises —it is nothing but an aggregation of such corpuscles; and every organ of the body was once no more than an aggregation of such corpuscles. Thus a nucleated mass of protoplasm turns out to be what may be termed the structural unit of the human body. As a matter of fact, the body, in its

574

earliest state, is a mere multiple of such units, variously modified.

But does the formula which expresses the essential struc· tural character of the highest animal cover all the rest, as the statement of its powers and faculties covered that of all others? Very nearly. Beast and fowl, reptile and fish, mol· lusk, worm, and polype, are all composed of structural units of the same character—namely, masses of protoplasm with a nucleus. There are sundry very low animals each of which, structurally, is a mere colorless blood-corpuscle, leading an independent life. But at the very bottom of the animal scale even this simplicity becomes simplified, and all the phe· nomena of life are manifested by a particle of protoplasm without a nucleus. Nor are such organisms insignificant by reason of their want of complexity. It is a fair question whether the protoplasms of those simplest forms of life which people an immense extent of the bottom of the sea would not outweigh that of all the higher living beings which inhabit the land put together. And in ancient times, no less than at the present day, such living beings as these have been the greatest of rock-builders.

What has been said of the animal world is no less true of plants. Imbedded in the protoplasm at the broad or at· tached end of the nettle-hair there lies a spherical nucleus. Careful examination further proves that the whole substance of the nettle is made up of a repetition of such masses of nucleated protoplasm, each contained in a wooden case, which is modified in form, sometimes into a woody fibre, sometimes into a duct or spiral vessel, sometimes into a pollen-grain or an ovule. Traced back to its earliest state, the nettle arises, as a man does, in a particle of nucleated protoplasm. And in the lowest plants, as in the lowest ani· mals, a single mass of such protoplasm may constitute the whole plant, or the protoplasm may exist without a nucleus.

Under these circumstances, it may well be asked, How is one mass of non-nucleated protoplasm to be distinguished from another? Why call one plant and the other animal?

The only reply is that, so far as form is concerned, plants and animals are not separable; and that, in many cases, it is a mere matter of convention whether we call a given organism an animal or a plant.

There is a living body called *Aethalium septicum*, which appears upon decaying vegetable substances, and, in one of its forms, is common upon the surface of tanpits. In this condition, it is, to all intents and purposes, a fungus, and formerly was always regarded as such. But the remarkable investigations of De Bary have shown that in another condition, that *Aethalium* is an actively locomotive creature, and takes in solid matters upon which, apparently, it feeds, thus exhibiting the most characteristic features of animality. Is this a plant? or is it an animal? Is it both? or is it neither? Some decide in favor of the last supposition, and establish an intermediate kingdom— a sort of no man's land—for all these intermediate forms. But as it is admittedly impossible to draw any distinct boundary line between this no man's land and the vegetable world, on the one hand, or the animal, on the other, it appears to me that this proceeding merely doubles the difficulty, which before was single.

Protoplasm—simple or nucleated—is the formal basis of all life. It is the clay of the potter, which—bake it and paint it as he will—remains clay, separated by artifice, and not by nature, from the commonest brick or sun-dried clod. Thus it becomes clear that all living powers are cognate; and that all living forms are fundamentally of one character. The researches of the chemist have revealed a no less striking uniformity of material composition in living matter.

[178]

I

IBN BADJDJA. See AVENPACE.

IBN GABIROL, SOLOMON

IBN GABIROL, SOLOMON (About 1021-about 1058). From the middle of the 12th to the end of the 14th century, Dominicans and Franciscans struggled with great bitterness over the ideas expressed in the book *Fons Vitae*, which the monk Dominicus Gundisalvi, assisted by the baptized Jew John Hispalensis, had translated from the Arabic. Its author was called Avicebron. The Franciscans, among them famous philosophers like Alexander of Hales and Duns Scotus, accepted its ideas and used it as a source for their own work, while the majority of the Dominicans, including Thomas Aquinas, opposed them. The importance of *Fons Vitae* as a source of medieval Neo-Platonism can hardly be exaggerated. It was not until 1840 that the great orientalist Salomon Munk discovered the real author of the book—namely, Solomon Ibn Gabirol who, up to then, was known only as one of the greatest Spanish-Jewish poets. The Hebrew title of Ibn Gabirol's book is *Mekor Hayim* (Fountain of Life). It deals with the total subject matter from the point of view of the antagonism of form and matter, and establishes a hierarchy of all beings, a graduation which, on each higher level, shows a more perfect relation between form and matter. Gabirol, who continued to express his Jewish convictions in his poetry, dealt with the philosophical problems of his metaphysical work without any relation to Judaism.

SEEK WISDOM

A soul whose raging tempests wildly rise, whither shall she send her meditations? She rages, and is like a flame of fire, whose smoke constantly ascends. This time her meditations are like a wheel that turns around on the earth and the multitudes thereof, or like the seas wherein the earth's foun-

577

dations were fastened: "How canst thou be so strong and filled with courage, that thou disdainest a place upon the stars? From the path of wisdom turn thou away thy heart; the world shall then smooth thy path for thee."

Oh comfort ye my soul for that, my friends, and likewise for her sorrows comfort her; she thirsts for a man of prudence, but finds not a man to slake her thirst. Seek ye amongst the men of fame, perchance there may be one to grant her desires. If this world sins against me, my heart will regard it disdainfully. If it cannot see my light with its eye, let the world then be contented with its blindness. But afterwards, if it appeases me, I shall turn round, and forgive its sins. The earthly sphere would then be good; the hand of Time would place no yoke upon the wise.

Oh too much wrong didst thou commit; long have the gourds been as cedars of the earth. Despise the vile ones of the people, for stones are less burdensome to me than they. Cut off the tail of them that say to me: "Where is then wisdom and her votaries?" Oh that the world would judge them aright! oh that it would give food unto her sons! They would then rest, not toil, and would attain their goal, without knowing worldly joys. Some took the sun's daughters, and begot folly, but they were not its sons-in-law.

Why do ye chide me for my understanding, O ye thorns and briers of the earth? If wisdom is of light esteem to you, vile and despised are ye in her sight. Though she is closed, and reaches not your heart, lo, I shall open her chests. How shall I now abandon wisdom, since God's spirit made a covenant between us? or how shall she forsake me, since she is like a mother to me and I am the child of her old age? or like an ornament which adorns the soul, or like a necklace on her neck. How can ye say to me: "Take off thy ornaments, and remove the precious chain from her neck?" In her my heart rejoices, and is glad, because her rivers of delights are pure. Throughout my life I shall make my soul ascend until her abode is beyond the clouds. For she adjured me not to rest, until I find the knowledge of her Master.

[179]

578

IBN TUFAIL

IBN TUFAIL (About 1105-1185). The author of "Robinson Crusoe" certainly must have read the English version of Ibn Tufail's book *Hai Ebn Yokdhan* (Alive, Son of Awaken), the imaginary and allegorical story of a man who, living alone on an island, without any intercourse with human beings, discovered truth and conquered nature by reasonable thinking. This book became favorite reading in Europe. It was translated into French, Spanish, German and Dutch, and into English in 1674 and 1708. Its English title is *The Improvement of Human Reason*.

The full name of its author is Abu Bekr Mohammed ben Abd'el Malik ben Mohammed ben Mohemmed ben Tufail el-Quaici. His contemporaries also called him El Andaloci, which, at that time, meant Spaniard, or the man of Cordova, or the man of Seville. He was a physician in Granada who then became secretary to the governor and finally the vizier of Sultan Abu Yakub Yusuf, who ruled over Islamic Spain and Morocco. Ibn Tufail distinguished himself in medicine, poetry and astronomy. He criticized the Ptolemaic system as did other Arabic and Jewish thinkers of that period. He was highly respected as a scholar whose wisdom attracted men of all countries. The chronicles of his time also praise him as a Maecenas. Ibn Tufail especially protected Averroës and recommended him to his ruler as his successor when, in 1182, he retired from office. According to contemporary reports, Averroës was inspired to his commentaries on Aristotle by a conversation with Ibn Tufail and the Sultan, who complained that Aristotle was too obscure to him.

THE IMPROVEMENT OF HUMAN REASON

HE observed that if a star arose at any time in a great circle and another star at the same in a lesser circle, yet nevertheless, as they arose together, so they set together; and he observed it of all the stars, and at all times. From whence he concluded that the heaven was of a spherical figure; in which opinion he was confirmed by observing the return of the sun, moon and stars to the east after their setting; and also because they always appeared to him of the same bigness, both when they rose, and when they were in the midst of heaven, and at the time of their setting; whereas, if their motions had not been circular, they must have been nearer to sight, at some times than others; and consequently their dimensions would have appeared proportionably greater or lesser; but since there was no such appearance, he concluded that their motions were circular. Then he considered the motion of the moon and the planets from west to east, till at last he understood a great part of astronomy. Besides, he apprehended that their motions were in different spheres, all which were comprehended in another which was above them all, and which turned about all the rest in the space of a day and a night. But it would be too tedious to explain particularly how he advanced in this science; besides, 'tis taught in other books; and what we have already said is as much as is requisite for our present purpose.

When he had attained to this degree of knowledge, he found that the whole orb of the heavens, and whatsoever was contained in it was as one thing compacted and joined together; and that all those bodies which he used to consider before as earth, water, air, plants, animals and the like, were all of them so contained in it as never to go out of its bounds, and that the whole was like one animal, in which the luminaries represented the senses; the spheres so joined and compacted together answered to the limbs; and the sublunary world to the belly, in which the excrements and humors are contained, and which oftentimes breeds animals, as the greater world.

Now when it appeared to him that the whole world was only one substance, depending upon a voluntary agent, and he had united all the parts of it, by the same way of thinking which he had before made use of in considering the sublunary world; he proposed to his consideration the world in general, and debated with himself whether it did exist in *time*, after it had been; and came to *be* out of nothing; or whether it had been from eternity, without any privation preceding it. Concerning this matter, he had very many and great doubts; so that neither of these two opinions did prevail over the other. For when he proposed to himself the belief of its eternity, there arose a great many objections in his mind; because he thought that the notion of infinite existence was pressed with no less difficulties than that of infinite extension. And that such a being as was not free from accidents produced anew, must also itself be produced anew, because it cannot be said to be more ancient than those accidents. And that which cannot exist before accidents produced in time, must needs itself be produced in time. Then on the other hand, when he proposed to himself the belief of its being produced anew, other objections occurred to him; for he perceived that it was impossible to conceive any notion of its being produced anew, unless it was supposed that there was time before it; whereas time was one of those things which belonged to the world, and was inseparable from it; and therefore the world could not be supposed to be later than time. Then he considered that a thing created must needs have a Creator. And, if so, why did this Creator make the world now and not, as well before? Was it because of any new chance which happened to Him? That could not be, for there was nothing existent besides Himself? Was it then upon the account of any change in His own nature? But what should cause that change? Thus he continued for several years, arguing pro and con about this matter; and a great many arguments offered themselves on both sides so that neither of these two opinions in his judgment overbalanced the other.

This put him to a great deal of trouble, which made him begin to consider with himself what were the consequences which did follow from each of these opinions, and that perhaps they might be both alike. And he perceived that if he held the world was created in time and existed after a total privation, it would necessarily follow from thence that it could not exist of itself, without the help of some Agent to produce it. And that this Agent must needs be such an one as cannot be apprehended by our senses; for if He should be the object of sense, He must be *body*, and if *body*, then a part of the world, and consequently a created being; such an one as would have stood in need of some other cause to create Him. And if that second creator was *body*, He would depend upon a third, and that third upon a fourth, and so *ad infinitum*, which is absurd. Since therefore the world stands in need of an incorporeal Creator, and since the Creator thereof is really incorporeal, 'tis impossible for us to apprehend Him by any of our senses; for we perceive nothing by the help of them but *body*, or such accidents as adhere to bodies. And because He cannot be perceived by the senses, it is impossible He should be apprehended by the imagination; for the imagination does only represent to us the forms of things in their absence, which we have before learned by our senses. And since He is not *body*, we must not attribute to Him any of the properties of *body;* the first of which is extension, from which He is free, as also from all those properties of bodies which flow from it. And seeing that He is the maker of the world, doubtless He has the sovereign command over it. *Shall not he know it, that created it? He is wise, omniscient!*

On the other side, he saw that if he held the eternity of the world, and that it always was as it is, without any privation before it; then it would follow, that its motion must be eternal too; because there could be no rest before it, from whence it might commence its motion. Now all motion necessarily requires a mover; and this mover must be either a power diffused through the body, or else through some other body without it, or else a certain power, not diffused or dispersed through any body at all. Now every power which passeth or is diffused through any body is divided or doubled. For instance, the gravity in a stone, by which it tends downwards, if you divide the stone into two parts, is divided into two parts also; and if you add to it another like it, the gravity is doubled. And if it were possible to add stones *in infinitum*, the gravity would increase *in infinitum* too. And if it were possible, that stone should grow still bigger till it reached to an infinite extension, the weight would increase also in the same proportion; and if, on the other side, a stone should grow to a certain size, and stop there, the gravity would also increase to such a pitch, and no farther. Now it is demonstrated that all body must necessarily be finite; and consequently, that power which is in body is finite too. If therefore we can find any power, which produces an infinite effect, 'tis plain that it is not in body. Now we find that the heaven is moved about with a perpetual motion without any cessation. Therefore if we affirm the eternity of the world, it necessarily follows that the power which moves it is not in its own body, nor in the other exterior body; but proceeds from something altogether abstracted from body, and which cannot be described by corporeal adjuncts or properties. Now he had learned from his first contemplation of the sublunary world, that the true essence of body consisted in its *form,* which is its disposition to several sorts of motion; but that part of its essence which consisted in *matter* was very mean, and scarce possible to be conceived; therefore, the existence of the whole world consists in its disposition to be moved by this mover. Who is free from matter and the properties of body; abstracted from everything which we can perceive by our senses, or reach by our imagination. And since He is the efficient cause of the motion of the heavens, in which (notwithstanding their several kinds) there is no difference, no confusion, no cessation; without doubt He has power over it, and a perfect knowledge of it.

Thus his contemplation this way brought him to the same conclusion it did the other way. So that doubting concerning the eternity of the world and its existence *de novo,* did him no harm at all. For it was plain to him both ways, that there was a being, which was not body, nor joined to body, nor separated from it; nor within it, nor without it; because conjunction and separation, and being within any thing, or without it, are all properties of body, from which that being is altogether abstracted. And because all bodies stand in need of a form to be added to their matter, as not being able to subsist without it, nor exist really; and the form itself cannot exist, but by this Voluntary Agent, it appeared to him that all things owed their existence to this Agent; and that none of them could subsist but through Him, and, consequently, that He was the cause, and they the effects (whether they were newly created after a privation, or whether they had no beginning in respect of Him, 'twas all one), and creatures whose existence depended upon that Being; and that without His continuance they could not continue, nor exist without His existing, nor have been eternal without His being eternal; but that He was essentially independent of them and free from them. And how should it be othewise when it is demonstrated that His power and might are infinite, and that all bodies, and whatsoever belongs to them are finite? Consequently, that the whole world and whatsoever was in it, the heavens, the earth, the stars, and whatsoever was between them, above them, or beneath them, was all His work and creation and posterior to Him in nature, if not in time. As, if you take any body whatsoever in your hand, and then move your hand, the body will without doubt follow the motion of your hand with such a motion as shall be posterior to it in nature, though not in time, because they both began together. So all this world is caused and created by this Agent out of time, *Whose command is, when he would have anything done, BE, and it is.*

And when he perceived that all things which did exist were His workmanship, he looked them over again, considering attentively the power of the efficient, and admiring the wonderfulness of the workmanship, and such accurate wisdom and subtile knowledge. And there appeared to him in the most minute creatures (much more in the greater) such footsteps of wisdom and wonders of the work of creation that he was swallowed up with admiration, and fully assured that these things could not proceed from any other than a Voluntary Agent of infinite perfection, nay, that as above all perfection; such an one, to Whom the weight of the least atom was not unknown, whether in heaven or earth; no, nor any other thing, whether lesser or greater than it.

Then he considered all the kinds of animals and how this Agent had given such a fabric of body to every one of them, and then taught them how to use it. For if He had not directed them to apply those limbs which He had given them, to those respective uses for which they were designed, they would have been so far from being of any service that they would rather have been a burden. From whence he knew that the Creator of the world was supereminently bountiful and exceedingly gracious. And then when he perceived among the creatures any that had beauty, perfection, strength, or excellency of any kind whatever, he considered with himself, and knew that it all flowed from that Voluntary Agent (Whose name be praised) and from His essence and operation. And he knew that what the Agent had in His own nature was greater than that (which he saw in the creatures), more perfect and complete, more beautiful and glorious, and more lasting; and that there was no proportion between the one and the other. Neither did he cease to prosecute this search, till he had run through all the attributes of perfection, and found that they were all in this Agent, and all flowed from Him; and that He was most worthy to have them all ascribed to Him, above all the creatures which were described by them.

In like manner he enquired into all the attributes of imperfection and perceived that the Maker of the world was free from them all. And how was it possible for Him to be otherwise, since the notion of *imperfection* is nothing but *mere privation* or what depends upon it? And how can He any way partake of *privation* Who is *very essence,* and cannot but exist; Who gives being to everything that exists and besides Whom there is no existence? But HE is the Being, HE is the Absoluteness, HE is the Beauty, HE the Glory, HE the Power, HE the Knowledge. HE is HE, and besides Him all things are subject to perishing.

Thus far his knowledge had brought him towards the

end of the fifth septenary from his birth, viz., when he was 35 years old. And the consideration of this Supreme Agent was then so rooted in his heart that it diverted him from thinking upon anything else, and he so far forgot the consideration of the creatures and the enquiring into their natures, that as soon as e'er he cast his eyes upon anything of what kind soever, he immediately perceived in it the footsteps of this Agent; and in an instant his thoughts were taken off from the creature and transferred to the Creator. So that he was inflamed with the desire of Him, and his heart was altogether withdrawn from thinking upon this inferior world, which contains the objects of sense, and wholly taken up with the contemplation of the upper, intellectual world. [180]

IMITATION OF CHRIST. See AUTHOR OF THE IMITATION OF CHRIST.

INGE, WILLIAM RALPH

INGE, WILLIAM RALPH (1860-1954). Dean Inge is one of the most popular figures in Britain's public life, and his interpretation of English peculiarities has been heeded outside the kingdom. He has spoken about questions of the day quite as often as G. B. Shaw, and some people have grumbled that in England a playwright and a dean always fancy they know everything better than anybody else. In matters of public opinion, if not in those of religion, Inge is, in his own way, as heretic as was Shaw.

Inge has searched for a philosophy by which he could live. He found it in those Christian mystics who were steeped in the Platonic tradition, and it was Plotinus whose work he regarded as the summit of Platonism. Inge's *Philosophy of Plotinus* (1918) has been recognized as a work of penetrating scholarship, even by those who do not share Inge's appraisal of that thinker.

To Inge, Christianity is a religion of spiritual redemption, not one of social reform, and he has protested, "I am unable to distinguish between philosophy and religion." He holds that mythology, which rightly claims a large place in all religions, cannot be kept out of philosophy, provided that the thinker tries to "live by the rule of his thought." The real world is regarded by Inge neither as the material universe, assumed as existent independently of mind, nor as the thought of the universe in the mind of man, but rather as the unity of the thought and its object. Values are defined as the

586

attributes of the ultimate real. According to Inge, the founder of Christianity made the greatest contribution to the science or art of living by teaching that wisdom, knowledge and judgment of value are the result of love and sympathy. These ideas are explained in Inge's *Faith and Knowledge* (1904) and *Speculum Animae* (Mirror of the Soul, 1911).

MATTER AND MIND

MY own belief is that whatever is born in time must perish for time, and this must be true of world systems no less than of individual lives. Time and space are not part of the framework of the real or spiritual world; they are as real as the lives of those who live in them, while they live in them, but they are not—neither of them, nor the two rolled into one—the stuff of which reality is made. If the present world order had a beginning, "with time, not in time," as Augustine says, it will have an end, "not in time but with time," that is to say, with its own time framework. We are not obliged to believe that ours is the only world order. It is more natural to suppose that as God is eternal, so His creative activity is perpetual. The different world orders may be entirely independent of each other. But here we are guessing about what we neither know nor can ever hope to know.

It has been necessary to argue at length against the prevalent pantheistic theory that the world is as necessary to God as God is to the world. This error, as we regard it, comes from metaphysics, not from natural science. But though Christianity asserts the transcendence of God, it is equally emphatic in maintaining His immanence. On this subject a little more must be said.

However we regard matter and mind, and the relation between them, they are as a fact given to us in combination. We do not perceive matter by itself, but as it affects our minds through the senses. Colors and musical sounds come, as we know, from vibrations which have no sound and no color. To this extent we may claim that the immanence of mind in matter is given to us in experience. External nature has always had a religious influence upon mankind; we think we can find in the external world traces of divine working. Of course the interpretations differ widely. One man finds evidence for a good God; another for two warring principles; another for polytheism; another for pantheism. But the belief that there is a spiritual reality behind phenomena is itself, by its general prevalence, a very impressive phenomenon. I have emphasized . . . the great importance for philosophy of this apprehension of values, which though they are immanent in visible things plainly belong to a higher order. It is also worth saying that this spiritual vision is neither simply emotional nor moral nor intellectual; it is an affirmation of the undivided personality. If we may trust our own impressions, we are equally sure that we are in touch with the divine in our contact with these values, and that our knowledge of the divine mind is fitful and incomplete. From this we infer that though we live and move and have our being in God, He is immeasurably above us while we live here.

[181]

INGERSOLL, ROBERT GREEN

INGERSOLL, ROBERT GREEN (1833-1899). As soon as Thomas Henry Huxley coined the term "agnosticism" in 1869, Ingersoll enthusiastically adopted it because it gave adequate expression to what he had felt and tried to formulate himself for many years. Ingersoll, who tried untiringly to enlighten the American people by his speeches, lectures and books, was subsequently called "America's great agnostic." He was a gifted and powerful orator, a formidable debater who, in public discussions, was almost always victorious. Before he began his career as a lecturer on philosophical and religious questions, he had refined his oratorical techniques as a successful lawyer, and, for two years, he had been attorney general of Illinois. Of his publications, *Some Mistakes of Moses* (1879) and *Why I Am an Agnostic* (1896) became the most popular. But the effect of his lectures and speeches was incomparably greater. The enthusiasm of his audiences compensated him for the many setbacks in his professional and political career which were due to his provoking heresy.

Before the Civil War, Ingersoll adhered to the Democratic Party, but thereafter he was a Republican. His nomination speech in favor of James G. Blaine at the Republican Convention in Cincinnati, 1876, made him a national figure. Following that, he was recognized as one of America's greatest orators even by those who were strongly opposed to his utterances concerning religion.

THE DAMAGE RELIGION CAUSES

RELIGION makes enemies instead of friends. That one word, "religion," covers all the horizon of memory with visions of war, of outrage, of persecution, of tyranny, and death. That one word brings to the mind every instrument with which man has tortured man. In that one word are all the fagots and flames and dungeons of the past, and in that word is the infinite and eternal hell of the future.

In the name of universal benevolence Christians have hated their fellow-men. Although they have been preaching universal love, the Christian nations are the warlike nations of the world. The most destructive weapons of war have been invented by Christians. The musket, the revolver, the rifle, cannon, the bombshell, the torpedo, the explosive bullet, have been invented by Christian brains. Above all other arts, the Christian world has placed the art of war.

A Christian nation has never had the slightest respect for the rights of barbarians; neither has any Christian sect any respect for the rights of other sects. Anciently, the sects discussed with fire and sword, and even now, something happens almost every day to show that the old spirit that was in the Inquisition still slumbers in the Christian breast.

Whoever imagines himself a favorite with God, holds other people in contempt.

Whenever a man believes that he has the exact truth from God, there is in that man no spirit of compromise. He has not the modesty born of the imperfections of human nature; he has the arrogance of theological certainty and the tyranny born of ignorant assurance. Believing himself to be the slave of God, he imitates his master, and of all tyrants, the worst is a slave in power.

589

When a man really believes that it is necessary to do a certain thing to be happy forever, or that a certain belief is necessary to ensure eternal joy, there is in that man no spirit of concession. He divides the whole world into saints and sinners, into believers and unbelievers, into God's sheep and Devil's goats, into people who will be glorified and people who will be damned.

A Christian nation can make no compromise with one not Christian; it will either compel that nation to accept its doctrine, or it will wage war. If Christ, in fact, said "I came not to bring peace but a sword," it is the only prophecy in the New Testament that has been literally fulfilled.

[182]

ISOCRATES

ISOCRATES (436-338 B.C.). Isocrates, who, despite his delicate health and many misfortunes, lived to be nearly a hundred years old, was considered by the Greeks to be not the most powerful but the most skilled of all orators. After political events had ruined him financially, he established himself as a dealer in speeches and pamphlets which he wrote and sold or prepared on order. He was acquainted with Socrates, though not his disciple. Isocrates attacked the Sophists, as Socrates did, but not for the same reasons. Occasionally, he also attacked, or counter-attacked, Plato and Antisthenes.

Isocrates frequently dealt with political questions. His standpoint was very close to that of Aristotle. Both of them condemned the policy which was inaugurated by Themistocles and developed by Pericles, namely, Athens' claim to naval supremacy which, as Isocrates saw it, would provoke an overwhelming alliance of other powers against Athens' ambitions. Isocrates steadily advocated peace among all Greek states. He declared that all Greeks were united, less by blood than by common education and ideals.

PANEGYRIC OF ATHENS

THE inhabitants of Greece anciently led a wandering, unsettled life, uncultivated by laws, and unrestrained by any regular form of government. While one part fell a sacrifice to unbridled anarchy and sedition, another was oppressed

590

by the wanton insolence of tyrants. But Athens delivered them from these calamities, either by receiving them under her immediate protection, or by exhibiting herself as a model of a more equitable system of policy: for of all the states of Greece she was the first who established a government of laws, and rendered the voice of equity superior to the arm of violence. This is evident from the first criminal prosecutions, where the punishment was sought for in a legal manner and not by the decision of the sword. The parties, though strangers, came to Athens, and received the benefit of our laws.

Our ancestors bestowed their attention not merely on the useful arts, but likewise on those which are agreeable. Many of these they invented, others they carried to perfection, and all of them they communicated and diffused. Both their public institutions and the whole system of their private economics were founded on the most liberal and extensive principles. They were adapted to the enjoyments of the rich and the necessities of the poor. The prosperous and the unfortunate found themselves equally accommodated; to the one we offered an elegant retreat; to the other a comfortable asylum.

The commodities of the different states of Greece were different. No one sufficed for itself; but, while it could spare of its own productions, it stood in need of those of its neighbors. This occasioned everywhere a double inconveniency; for they could neither sell what was superfluous, nor purchase what they had occasion for. Athens erects the Piraeus: the evil immediately disappears. A trading town is established in the middle of Greece, where the merchandise of all the different countries is brought to market, and purchased at a cheaper rate than on the spot which produced them.

*   *   *

But I begin to think differently from what I did in the beginning of this discourse. I then imagined that it was possible to speak suitably to the grandeur of the subject; but

591

I am sensible how far I have fallen short of it. Several things
have escaped my memory. But do you yourselves consider the
advantages of carrying the war into the continent, and of
returning into Europe with all the wealth and happiness of
Asia. Think it not sufficient for you to hear and to approve of
what I have here advanced. Those who possess active talents
must vie with one another in effecting a reconciliation between Athens and Lacedaemon. Those who court literary
fame must abandon the study of deposits, and others equally
uninteresting; they must pursue the career which I have followed, and endeavor to outstrip me in the race. Let them consider that such as make great professions ought not to stoop
to mean objects; that they ought not to employ themselves on
inferior matters, which even to prove, would be attended
with small advantage; but that, making a proper distinction
between the subjects of eloquence, they should select and
cultivate those only which, if they succeed in, will establish
their own fame, and extend the glory of their country.

[183]

ISRAELI, ISAAC

ISRAELI, ISAAC (About 850-950). Israeli, who, during the one
hundred years of his life, was a famous physician and founder of
an influential medical school, did not escape the fate of many other
philosophers whose renown was founded upon their nonphilosoph-
ical activities. But it is just that objection made by some leaders of
philosophical schools that he has written his philosophical books
from the medical point of view, which should attract the interest of
modern scholars. For his description of the faculty of cogitation and
his distinction between the impressions received by "the five senses"
and the post-sensatory perceptions show him to have been an acute
psychologist whose hints at anthropology anticipated modern discoveries. His principal work *Kitab al Istiksat*, written in Arabic,
was translated into Hebrew under the title *Sefer Hayesodoth* and
into Latin under the title *De Elementis*. He also wrote a treatise on
definitions and commentaries on *Genesis* and the mystical *Sefer
Yetzirah*, the oldest Cabalistic work which is extant.

Israeli practiced medicine at Cairo, Egypt, and later at Kairwan, Tunisia. The Christian monk Constantine of Carthage translated several of Israeli's medical treatises into Latin in 1087, and used them as textbooks at the University of Salerno, the earliest university in Western Europe, but he omitted the real author's name, which was finally made known to the European public only in 1515 when *Opera Omnia Isaci* was printed at Lyons, France.

MAN AND GOD

MEN cannot obtain knowledge of the divine will except through God's envoys. For truth itself cannot have intercourse with everyone, since there are some people dominated by their animal soul, while others are dominated by their vegetative soul, and only a few have a cogitative soul.

Only a man who is exclusively dominated by his cogitative soul can be chosen by God as His envoy.

God cannot be known or grasped by human thought. He is exempt from change or alteration since He has no form which might turn from one state to another. We can only say that God is the Creator, but we must not think that we can conceive His attributes.

[184]

ISVARAKRSNA

ISVARAKRSNA (Fifth Century A.D.). The name of Isvarakrsna is connected with the *Samkya Karika,* composed about the middle of the fifth century, and probably the oldest of the six traditional systems of Indian philosophy. Its foundation is attributed to the sage Kapila. Samkya philosophy inspired Buddha who lived about a century later.

The Samkya school shares with other systems the belief in the Indian gods, demi-gods and demons, but it conceives them as mortal and subject to transmigration. Contrary to the Brahman concept, there is no place for a universal God in the Samkya system, which expressly denies the existence of such a god. The Samkya philosophy is pessimistic, regarding all existence as suffering, and dualistic, insisting on the fundamental difference between soul and matter. Salvation from suffering can be reached by cognitive grasping of the absolute difference between the soul and everything material. It is probable that the Samkya doctrine influenced Gnosticism and Neo-Platonism.

THE [present] inquiry is into the [problem] of how to obviate the three kinds of pain [arising within the individual, outside him, or from more remote causes, all presenting a person with the not too cheerful prospect of being reborn again and again]. Now, even though there are obvious means for getting rid of these difficulties, this enquiry is not superfluous, for conclusiveness and permanency is not theirs.

What rests on [sacred Vedic] tradition is like what is [ordinarily] experienced, for it is not pure, being at once deficient or too ornate. Something different from either is more worth-while, consisting in an analytical knowledge of the phenomenal (*vyakta*), the noumenal (*avyakta*), and the knower.

The root creative principle (*prakrti*) is not a modification [or development]. Seven, intelligence (*mahat*) and the rest [self-consciousness (*ahamkara*) and five principles (*tanmatras*)] are creative principles and modifications. Sixteen [or five powers of perception, five of action, mind and five elements] are modifications [merely]. The self (*purusa*) is neither a creative principle nor a modification.

Perception, inference and authority, in that they comprise all sources of knowledge, are respected as the threefold source of knowledge. By virtue of a source of knowledge, the object of knowledge is obtained.

Perception is ascertaining particular sense-objects. Inference is of three sorts, [antecedent, subsequent and by analogy, and] premises a predicate and [deduces] what it is predicated of. Authority is trustworthy tradition.

By inference, that is, reasoning by analogy, are things lying beyond the grasp of the senses ascertained; but what cannot be ascertained thus must be received by revelation.

Things may be imperceptible due to various reasons, such as distance, proximity, deficiency in the sense organ, inattention, minuteness, blocking out, ascendency and intermixture with identical things.

[The creative principle] is not apprehended in perception, not because it does not exist, but because of its subtlety; it is [properly] apprehended in its effects. Intelligence and the rest [of the principles named above] are effects which are [in one respect] identical with, [and in another] different from the creative principle.

The effect is existent [as a specific effect], for, [1.] a cause does not produce what is not; [2.] [one] appropriate cause may be assigned [to anything]; [3.] it is impossible that anything particular could connect up with anything and everything else; [4.] a cause operates only within its own competency; and [5.] there is a specificity of cause.

The phenomenal is causally conditioned, not eternal, specifically disperse, mutable, pluralistic, grounded in something, conjugial, tending to enter relationships, dependent on something else. The noumenal has just the opposite characteristics.

The phenomenal as well as matter (*pradhana*) have three moods (*gunas*), are undifferentiated, are an object of sense, public, unintelligible, full of urges. Soul (*pums*) has, like [the noumenal mentioned in the previous *sutra*], characteristics to these.

The moods consist of pleasure, pain and indifference, have as purpose manifestation, activity and restraint, and dominate, depend on and produce one another mutually, join up with one another and are interchangeable. . . .

In order to attain the intelligent comprehension of the self and the unity of matter, the two cooperate like the halt and the blind. This accomplished, there is creation.

From the creative principle comes forth intelligence, from thence self-consciousness, and from that the group of sixteen [mentioned above]. From five among the sixteen proceed five elements. . . .

The evolution of the creative principle from intelligence to the different elements is for the liberation of the individual selves, done for self as much as for the other.

Just as it is the function of milk, an unconscious [sub-

595

stance], to nourish the calf, so it is the function of matter to accomplish the liberation of the self.

Just as people engage in acts for the purpose of allaying anxiety, so the noumenal acts in order to liberate the self.

Just as a dancer, having exhibited herself to the spectator, desists from the dance, so the creative principle desists, having manifested itself to the self.

Without deriving benefits, the versatile servant serves unselfishly in multifarious ways the purposes of the selfish master (*pums*) who has no qualities whatever.

Nothing, in my opinion, is more delicate than the creative principle. Having once become aware of having been beheld, she does not again expose herself to the view of the self.

Indeed, nothing is bound, nor freed, nor is migrating. The creative principle alone is bound, freed and migrates in the various vehicles. . . .

[185]

J

JACOBI, FRIEDRICH HEINRICH

JACOBI, FRIEDRICH HEINRICH (1743-1819). As far as Jacobi's philosophy enjoyed any authority during his lifetime, it seemed to be definitely destroyed by the devastating criticism of Kant, Fichte, Schelling and Hegel. Jacobi died a defeated man. Today, however, he is regarded as a precursor of existentialism.

Jacobi called himself an aphoristic thinker. He was aware of his incapability to overcome all the contradictions which prevented him from being consistent. His principal propositions are presented in the form of novels. The first *Allwill* (1775) was intended as an encomium of Goethe, who was his friend, but it finally became a warning against the man of genius. Jacobi blamed contemporary civilization for its lack of original and immediate feelings, of natural behavior, for the decay of heart and intellect, and he exalted the morals of the man of genius who is independent of traditional ethical standards, whose life is dominated by passion which means confidence in life. Nevertheless, he recognized that surrendering to passion entails individual and social dangers. The second novel *Woldemar* (1777) is essentially the author's self-criticism.

It was Jacobi's principal intention to present "humanity as it is," no matter whether it be conceivable or inconceivable. He was inclined to attribute to life an absolute value but he was also aware of the ambiguity of life. He insisted that feeling, not knowledge, constitutes the contact between the ego and the external world, and that what cannot be proved by reason, can be comprehended by feeling; but he did not question traditional logic which secures experience by creating steadiness. Only when steadiness degenerates into rigidity does it become a danger. According to Jacobi, the only philosophical system that is logically irrefutable is that of Spinoza which, however, he rejected as metaphysically wrong. Jacobi's God, different from the pantheistic deity, is also

597

different from the Christian God. But, personally, Jacobi sympathized with Christian piety, and his conception of man is essentially Christian. Faith is, he said, intellectual evidence of logical principles as well as divination of Truth, imperfect knowledge as well as immediateness of feeling. The faithful disposition is the condition of any knowledge of truth and secures permanent certainty and peace of mind.

From this position, Jacobi proceeded to a severe criticism of the German idealists who replied with a roughness unheard of until then in the history of German controversies.

CHRISTIANITY AND PAGANISM

EVERY man has some kind of religion: that is, a supreme Truth by which he measures all his judgments— a supreme Will by which he measures all his endeavors. These everyone has who is at one with himself, who is everywhere decidedly the same. But the worth of such a religion and the honor due to it, and to him who has become one with it, cannot be determined by its *amount*. Its *quality* alone decides friendship, a higher value than to another. At bottom every religion is anti-Christian which makes the form the thing, the letter, the substance. Such a materialistic religion, in order to be consistent, ought to maintain a material infallibility.

There are but two religions—Christianity and Paganism—the worship of God and Idolatry. A third, between the two, is not possible. Where Idolatry ends, there Christianity begins; and where Idolatry begins, there Christianity ends. Thus the apparent contradiction is done away with between the two propositions— "Whoso is not against me is for me," and "Whoso is not for me is against me."

As all men are by nature liars, so all men are by nature idolators—drawn to the visible and averse to the invisible. Hamann called the body the first-born, because God first made a clod of earth, and then breathed into it a breath of life. The formation of the earth-clod and the spirit are both *of God*, but only the spirit is *from* God; and only on account of the spirit is man said to be made after the likeness of God. . . . Since man cannot do without the letter—

images and parables—no more than he can dispense with time, which is incidental to the finite, though both shall cease—I honor the letter, so long as there is a breath of life in it, for that breath's sake.

[186]

JAMBLICUS

JAMBLICUS (About 270-330 A.D.). So far as modern theosophy does not go back to Hindu mysticism, its adherents are using doctrines formulated mostly by Jamblicus, a Syrian and a disciple of Porphyry who tried to systematize the philosophy of Plotinus, wrote commentaries on Plato and about the Greek gods, the doctrines of the Egyptians, Chaldeans and Assyrians. Until the 19th century, Jamblicus was considered one of the great philosophers. In late antiquity his renown was enormous. He was glorified as "posterior to Plato only in time, not in genius," and his devoted disciples did not refrain from forging letters allegedly written by Emperor Julianus, in which Jamblicus was hailed as "Savior of Greece," "Treasury of the Hellenes" or "healer of the souls." For a long time these forgeries enjoyed full credit. For, in fact, Julianus did esteem Jamblicus highly and quoted him frequently in his genuine writings. Jamblicus was revered as a divine being, and many miracles were attributed to him. He attracted many adherents because he promised that the initiation into his philosophy would endow the adept with superhuman powers. Besides, he also promised success in practical life. His thoughts will not impress modern readers except by the eloquence with which they are displayed.

THE PROMISES OF PHILOSOPHY

THOSE things which are subject to us in our life, as the body, and those things about or connected with the body, were given to us as certain instruments. The use of these can be dangerous, causing much injury, to those who do not use them rightly. It is necessary, therefore, to seek and acquire scientific knowledge and to use it rightly so that we may use all these instruments properly and without detriment. We must philosophize, accordingly, if we wish to become good citizens and to pass through life usefully. . . .

If we pursue the heavenly way and live in our kindred

599

star, then we will philosophize, living truly, busied with the most profound and marvelous speculations, beholding the beauty in the soul immutably related to Truth, viewing the rules of the gods with joy, gaining perpetual delight and additional insight from contemplating and experiencing pure pleasure absolutely unmingled with any pain or sorrow. Turning this way, therefore, we will find that philosophy leads us to total felicity.

[187.]

JAMES, HENRY, SR.

JAMES, HENRY, SR. (1811-1882). What made Henry James, Sr., the father of the great philosopher William and the great novelist Henry James, critical of the existing order was not the accident which caused amputation of one of his legs and impaired him permanently, but the wealth of his family which seemed to grant him undue favor. His revolt against the existing social system led him to enthusiastic adherence to the views of the French socialist Fourier. His opposition to Presbyterian orthodoxy made him a radical religious individualist who combined ideas of enlightenment with Swedenborg's mysticism. James never ceased to fight for his ideals, but during the last thirty years of his life the care of the education and progress of his sons became his dominant interest. He published *The Church of Christ Not an Ecclesiasticism* (1854) and other works on religion and morality.

GOOD AND EVIL RELATIVE

ALL natural existence may be classified into forms of use; all spiritual existence into forms of power. Every real existence, whatsoever we rightly denominate a *thing* as addressing any of our senses, is a form of use to superior existence. Every spiritual existence, whatsoever we rightfully denominate a *person* as addressing our interior perception, is a form of power over inferior existence. Thus the vegetable on its material side is a form of use to the animal kingdom, as giving it sustenance; while on its spiritual side it is a form of power over the mineral kingdom, as compelling it into the service of its own distinctive individuality. The animal,

600

again, on its visible or corporeal side is a purely subjective implication of the human form, while on its spiritual or invisible side it furnishes the creative unity or objectivity of the vegetable world. So man, on his natural side, furnishes a helpful platform or basis to the manifestation of God's perfection, while to the power of his spiritual or individual aptitudes the animal and all the lower kingdoms of nature bear resistless testimony.

But in thus classifying all natural existence into forms of use, and all spiritual existence into forms of power, we must not forget to observe that the use promoted by the one class is never absolutely but only relatively good, nor the power exerted by the other class absolutely but only relatively benignant. That is to say, it is good and benignant not in itself, but in opposition to something else. Thus every natural form is a form of use, but some of these uses are relatively to others good, and some evil. And when we contemplate human nature we find some of its forms relatively accordant with the Divine perfection, others relatively to these prior ones again most discordant; the former exerting a decidedly benignant influence upon whatever is subject to them, the latter exerting a decidedly malignant influence.

This contrarious aspect both of nature and man has given rise, as the reader well knows, to a great amount of unsatisfactory speculation, because men have scarcely known how, apart from the light of Revelation, to shape their speculations into accordance with the demands of the Divine unity. The demand of unity in the Creator is so peremptory and inflexible that the mind utterly refuses in the long run to acquiesce in any scheme of creation which leaves creation divided, or puts the Creator in permanent hostility with any of His works. More than this: The mind not only rejects these puerile cosmologies which leave the Creator at war with His own creature, but it goes further, and insists, by an inevitable presentment of the great philosophic verity, that wherever we find a sphere of life antagonistic with itself, the antagonism is pure phenomenal; *i.e.*, is not final,

601

does not exist for its own sake but only in the interest of some higher unity.

The same rule holds in regard to moral existence, though the nonsensical pride we feel in ourselves habitually blinds us to the fact. I am not a bad man by virtue of any absolute or essential difference between us but altogether by virtue of the difference in our relation to that great unitary life of God in our nature which we call society, fraternity, fellowship, equality, and which from the beginning of human history has been struggling to work itself, by means of this strictly subjective antagonism, into final perfect and objective recognition; you as a morally good man being positively related to that life; I as a morally evil one being negatively related to it. The needs of this great life—which alone manifests God's spiritual presence in our nature—require the utmost conceivable intensity of human freedom; require, in other words, that man should be spontaneously good of himself, good without any antagonism of evil, infinitely good even as God is good. But clearly if we had had no preliminary acquaintance with imperfect or finite good, good as related to evil, we should be destitute of power to appreciate or even apprehend this higher and perfect good. If we had not first suffered, and suffered, too, most poignantly, from the experience of evil in ourselves as *morally, i.e.,* finitely, constituted, constituted in reciprocal independency each of every other, we should have been utterly unable even to discern that ineffable Divine and infinite good which is yet to be revealed in us as *socially, i.e.,* infinitely constituted, constituted in the closest reciprocal unity of all with each and each with all.

[188]

JAMES, WILLIAM

JAMES, WILLIAM (1842-1910). William James is generally considered not only the most influential of all American philosophers but the very representative of American thought. However, the results of his thinking are by no means confined to his native country, and his background is anything but exclusively American. Very few American families maintained such intimate contact with Europe as did Henry James, Senior, a theologian and philosophical writer, and a great amateur of wide culture, and his sons William and Henry, the great novelist, who, on his part, was more at home in France and England than in the land of his birth. William James often visited Europe where he became acquainted with Alexander Bain, Herbert Spencer, Wilhelm Wundt and Hermann von Helmholtz, whose works he appreciated as sources of information but whose principles he rejected. He became an intimate friend of James Ward and Carl Stumpf and felt himself much indebted to Charles Renouvier whose personality he revered.

In his youth, William James desired to become known as a painter. But, while living with art, he learned that he could live without art, and turned to medicine and the natural sciences. However, his early study of painting was no labor lost. On the contrary, James derived from it his pictorial manner of philosophizing, which does not involve picturesqueness of style but rather his talents for conveying the present aspect of a situation, for finding immediate joy in the variety of appearances from which he proceeded to enjoy the various psychic experiences, while being capable of describing them in scientific terms, coined afresh, without much regard to traditional terminology. Such blending of scientific sagacity with artistic sensibility, such psychological perspicacity, enriched and refined by his previous study of art, and disciplined by scientific training, are characteristic of James' brilliant lectures and writing, and the cause of his great success. His gifts became known to the public in 1890 when his *Principles of Psychology* appeared, marking a new period in this special branch of science and foreshadowing his turn to philosophy.

It was the latent artist in James that made his treatment of moral, epistemological, and metaphysical problems a revolt of the spirit of immediate concrete experience against the intellectualistic idealism. James' radical empiricism maintains the plurality of the real units of which, according to him, experience consists, against any harmonizing or simplifying monism. Pragmatism, as James defines his empiricism, has become of immense consequence in modern thinking. James surpasses Hume by denying consciousness. He acknowledges a stream of experiences but not a stream of conscious experiences. Therewith he denies that in knowledge the relation between the knowing subject and the object to be known is fundamental, which almost all modern philosophers had taken for granted. This denial has induced many contemporary philosophers, though opposed to James' views, to reconsider the bases and starting points of their own thoughts.

PRAGMATISM

TRUTH, as any dictionary will tell you, is a property of certain of our ideas. It means their "agreement," as falsity means their disagreement, with "reality." Pragmatists and intellectualists both accept this definition as a matter of course. They begin to quarrel only after the question is raised as to what may precisely be meant by the term "agreement," and what by the term "reality," when reality is taken as something for our ideas to agree with.

In answering these questions the pragmatists are more analytic and painstaking, the intellectualists more offhand and irreflective. The popular notion is that a true idea must copy its reality. Like other popular views, this one follows the analogy of the most usual experience. Our true ideas of sensible things do indeed copy them. Shut your eyes and think of yonder clock on the wall, and you get just such a true picture or copy of its dial. But your idea of its "works" (unless you are a clockmaker) is much less of a copy, yet it passes muster, for it in no way clashes with the reality. Even though it should shrink to the mere word "works," that word still serves you truly; and when you speak of the "time-keeping function" of the clock, or of its spring's "elasticity," it is hard to see exactly what your ideas can copy.

You perceive that there is a problem here. Where our ideas cannot copy definitely their object, what does agreement with that object mean? Some idealists seem to say that they are true whenever they are what God means that we ought to think about that object. Others hold the copy-view all through, and speak as if our ideas possessed truth just in proportion as they approach to being copies of the Absolute's eternal way of thinking.

These views, you see, invite pragmatistic discussion. But the great assumption of the intellectualists is that truth means essentially an inert static relation. When you've got your true idea of anything, there's an end of the matter. You're in possession; you *know*; you have fulfilled your thinking destiny. You are where you ought to be mentally; you have obeyed your categorical imperative; and nothing more need follow on that climax of your rational destiny. Epistemologically you are in stable equilibrium.

Pragmatism, on the other hand, asks its usual question. "Grant an idea or belief to be true," it says, "what concrete difference will its being true make in any one's actual life? How will the truth be realized? What experiences will be different from those which would obtain if the belief were false? What, in short, is the truth's cash-value in experiential terms?"

The moment pragmatism asks this question, it sees the answer: *True ideas are those that we can assimilate, validate, corroborate and verify. False ideas are those that we can not.* That is the practical difference it makes to us to have true ideas; that, therefore, is the meaning of truth, for it is all that truth is known as.

This thesis is what I have to defend. The truth of an idea is not a stagnant property inherent in it. Truth *happens* to an idea. It *becomes* true, is *made* true by events. Its verity *is* in fact an event, a process: the process namely of its verifying itself, its veri-*fication*. Its validity is the process of its valid-*ation*.

But what do the words verification and validation themselves pragmatically mean? They again signify certain practical consequences of the verified and validated idea. It is hard to find any one phrase that characterizes these consequences better than the ordinary agreement-formula—just such consequences being what we have in mind whenever we say that our ideas "agree" with reality. They lead us, namely, through the acts and other ideas which they instigate, into or up to, or towards, other parts of experience with which we feel all the while—such feeling being among our potentialities—that the original ideas remain in agreement. The connections and transitions come to us from point to point as being progressive, harmonious, satisfactory. This function of agreeable leading is what we mean by an idea's verification. Such an account is vague and it sounds at first quite trivial, but it has results which it will take the rest of my hour to explain.

Let me begin by reminding you of the fact that the possession of true thoughts means everywhere the possession of invaluable instruments of action; and that our duty to gain truth, so far from being a blank command from out of the blue, or a "stunt" self-imposed by our intellect, can account for itself by excellent practical reasons.

The importance to human life of having true beliefs about matters of fact is a thing too notorious. We live in a world of realities that can be infinitely useful or infinitely harmful. Ideas that tell us which of them to expect count as the true ideas in all this primary sphere of verification, and the pursuit of such ideas is a primary human duty. The possession of truth, so far from being here an end in itself, is only a preliminary means toward other vital satisfactions. If I am lost in the woods and starved, and find what looks like a cow path, it is of the utmost importance that I should think of a human habitation at the end of it, for if I do so and follow it, I save myself. The true thought is useful here because the house which is its object is useful. The practical value of true ideas is thus primarily derived from the practical importance of their objects to us. Their objects are, indeed, not important at all times. I may on another occasion have no use for the house; and then my idea of it, however verifiable, will be practically irrelevant, and had better remain latent. Yet since almost any object may some day become temporarily important, the advantage of having a general stock of *extra* truths, of ideas that shall be true of merely possible situations, is obvious. We store such extra truths away in our memories, and with the overflow we fill our books of reference. Whenever such an extra truth becomes practically relevant to one of our emergencies, it passes from cold storage to do work in the world and our belief in it grows active. You can say of it then either that "it is useful because it is true" or that "it is true because it is useful." Both these phrases mean exactly the same thing, namely that here is an idea that gets fulfilled and can be verified. True is the name for whatever idea starts the verification process, useful is the name for its completed function in experience. True ideas would never have been singled out as such, would never have acquired a class-name, least of all a name suggesting value, unless they had been useful from the outset in this way.

From this simple cue pragmatism gets her general notion of truth as something essentially bound up with the way in which one moment in our experience may lead us towards other moments which it will be worth while to have been led to. Primarily, and on the common sense level, the truth of a state of mind means this function of *a leading that is worth while*. When a moment in our experience, of any kind whatever, inspires us with a thought that is true, that means that sooner or later we dip by that thought's guidance into the particulars of experience again and make advantageous connection with them. This is a vague enough statement, but I beg you to retain it, for it is essential.

"The true," to put it briefly, is only the expedient in the way of our thinking, just as "the right" is only the expedient in the way of our behaving. Expedient in almost any fashion; and expedient in the long run and on the whole of course; for what meets expediently all the experience in sight won't necessarily meet all farther experiences equally satisfactorily. Experience, as we know, has ways of *boiling over*, and making us correct our present formulas.

The "absolutely" true, meaning what no farther experience will ever alter, is that ideal vanishing-point towards which we imagine that all our temporary truths will some day converge. It runs on all fours with the perfectly wise man, and with the absolutely complete experience; and, if these ideals are ever realized, they will all be realized together. Meanwhile we have to live to-day by what truth we can get to-day, and be ready to-morrow to call it falsehood. Ptolemaic astronomy, euclidean space, aristotelian logic, scholastic metaphysics, were expedient for centuries, but human experience has boiled over those limits, and we now call these things only relatively true, or true within those borders of experience. "Absolutely" they are false; for we know that those limits were casual, and might have been transcended by past theorists just as they are by present thinkers.

When new experiences lead to retrospective judgments, using the past tense, what these judgments utter *was* true, even though no past thinker had been led there. We live forwards, a Danish thinker has said, but we understand backwards. The present sheds a backward light on the world's previous processes. They may have been truth-processes for the actors in them. They are not so for one who knows the later revelations of the story.

This regulative notion of a potential better truth to be established later, possibly to be established some day absolutely, and having powers of retroactive legislation, turns its face, like all pragmatist notions, towards concreteness of fact, and towards the future. Like the half-truths, the absolute truth will have to be *made,* made as a relation incidental to the growth of a mass of verification-experience, to which the half true ideas are all along contributing their quota.

I have already insisted on the fact that truth is made largely out of previous truths. Men's beliefs at any time are so much experience *funded.* But the beliefs are themselves parts of the sum total of the world's experience, and become matter, therefore, for the next day's funding operations. So far as reality means experienceable reality, both it and the truths men gain about it are everlastingly in process of mutation towards a definite goal—it may be—but still mutation.

Mathematicians can solve problems with two variables. On the Newtonian theory, for instance, acceleration varies with distance, but distance also varies with acceleration. In the realm of truth-processes facts come independently and determine our beliefs provisionally. But these beliefs make us act, and as fast as they do so, they bring into sight or into existence new facts which re-determine the beliefs accordingly. So the whole coil and ball of truth, as it rolls up, is the product of a double influence. Truths emerge from facts; but they dip forward into facts again and add to them; which facts again create or reveal new truth (the word is indifferent) and so on indefinitely. The "facts" themselves meanwhile are not *true*. They simply *are*. Truth is the function of the beliefs that start and terminate among them.

The case is like a snowball's growth, due as it is to the distribution of the snow on the one hand, and to the successive pushes of the boys on the other, with these factors co-determining each other incessantly.

[189]

JASPERS, KARL

JASPERS, KARL (1883-   ). Since Germany's unconditional surrender, Jaspers has been the most respected, if not the most influential philosopher in that country. His prestige had already been great during the time of the Weimar Republic. He disliked Nazism and did not abandon his Jewish wife, but neither had he felt a predilection for the pre-Hitlerian republic and he cannot be considered a convert to parliamentarian democracy. Jaspers began his career as a psychiatrist. His *General Psychopathology* (1913), in which he offered a new classification of mental illnesses, has been of great consequence for the diagnosis of psychoses and neuroses. It was from the viewpoint of a psychiatrist that Jaspers first studied the philosophy of Friedrich Nietzsche and then the works of Kierkegaard, whose habits interested the student of abnormalities. As his *Psychology of Weltanschauungen* (1919) shows, Jaspers became more and more interested in inquiring into the relations between a philosopher's personality and his doctrine. The results of these studies remained valid to him when he exposed his own philosophy in *Principles of Philosophy* (1932), *Existenzphilosophie* (1938) and *The Perennial Scope of Philosophy* (1949). Despite all changes, Jaspers maintained the principle that philosophy is more than cogent intellectual knowledge and fundamentally different from, yet not opposite to science. The distinguishing feature of the philosophical mind, in contradistinction to the scientific mind, is characterized as personal faith. Though always allied with knowledge, philosophical faith transcends object cognition. Philosophical faith is neither grounded in any concept of anything objective or finite in the world nor subordinated to it. The truth of philosophical faith is not universal but both eternal and historical, a dynamism acting in time and longing for transcending time. The true value of man is seen by Jaspers not in the species or type but in the historical individual, and the situation of this individual—the conditions of his existence—is one of the principal problems of Jaspers' disquisitions.

Jaspers is one of the earliest contemporary existentialists. He belongs neither to the Christian nor to the atheistic group, and differs from most of them because he adopts Kant's idea of the phenomenality with its division into subject and object, and because he regards reason an indispensable element of philosophical faith, bluntly declining irrationalism.

The religious trend and the theistic conviction have become most conspicuous in Jaspers' latest works. He praises the values of the Old and New Testament but thinks that Judaism and Christianity are wrong in claiming absolute truth. According to Jaspers, the aim of philosophy is at all times to achieve the independence of man as an individual. To him independence is attachment to transcendence, and awareness of true being is identical with certainty of God. In his earlier works Jaspers stated that philosophy and religion will be in constant struggle with each other. Now he says that in all philosophical efforts lies a tendency to aid religious institutions whose practical values are affirmed by philosophy although philosophers cannot participate directly in them.

REASON

REASON is the comprehensive in us; it does not flow from the primal source of being, but is an instrument of existence. It is the existential absolute that serves to actualize the primal source and bring it to the widest manifestation.

There is something like a climate of reason. The passion for the open works in cool clarity. The rational man lives resolutely out of the root of his own historical soil, and at the same time he gives himself to every mode of historicity which he encounters, in order to penetrate to the depths of the world's historicity, through which alone a sympathetic under-standing of everything becomes possible. From this develops what was also the motive force from the outset—the love of being, of everything existent as existent in its transparency, thanks to which its relation to the primal source becomes visible. Reason enriches man by sharpening his hearing, in-creases his capacity for communication, makes him capable of change through new experience, but while doing all this it remains essentially one, unswerving in its faith, living in actually efficacious memory of everything that was once real to it.

He who engages in philosophy cannot sufficiently praise reason, to which he owes all his achievements. Reason is the bond that unites all the modes of the comprehensive. It al-lows no existent to separate itself absolutely, to sink into isolation, to be reduced to nothingness by fragmentation. Nothing must be lost. Where reason is effective, that which is strives for unification. A universal fellowship arises, in which men are open to all things and everything concerns them. Reason quickens dormant springs, frees what is hidden, makes possible authentic struggles. It presses toward the One that is all, it does away with the delusions that fixate the One prematurely, incompletely, in partisanship.

Reason demands boundless *communication*, it is itself the total will to communicate. Because, in time, we cannot have objective possession of a truth that is the eternal truth, and because being-here is possible only with other being-here, and existence can come into its own only with other existence, communication is the form in which truth is re-vealed in time.

The great seductions are: through belief in God to withdraw from men; through supposed knowledge of the absolute truth to justify one's isolation; through supposed possession of being itself to fall into a state of complacency that is in truth lovelessness. And to these may be added the assertion that every man is a self-contained monad, that no one can emerge from himself, that communication is a delusion.

In opposition to these stands philosophical faith, which may also be called faith in communication. For it upholds these two propositions: Truth is what joins us together; and, truth has its origin in communication. The only reality with which man can reliably and in self-understanding ally himself in the world, is his fellow man. At all the levels of communication among men, companions in fate lovingly find the road to the truth. This road is lost to the man who shuts himself off from others in stubborn self-will, who lives in a shell of solitude.

[190]

JEANS, JAMES HOPWOOD

JEANS, JAMES HOPWOOD (1877-1946). Jeans, one of the most eminent savants and an international authority in mathematics, theoretical physics and astronomy, has also been called "the Edgar Wallace of cosmology." Very few scientists of his rank have ever had his talents for combining profundity with a colorful, popular style. While his earlier books *The Dynamical Theory of Gases* (1904), *Theoretical Mechanics* (1906), *Mathematical Theory of Electricity and Magnetism* (1908) and numerous learned papers were written for experts, his later works *The Stars in Their Courses* (1931), *The New Background of Science* (1933) and *Through Space and Time* (1934) have been admired by tens of thousands of readers who were not prepared to read other scientific books. Jeans himself was fond of fiction and detective stories, and he knew how to charm the public, although he never made a confession to his readers which he could not justify before his scientific conscience.

Towards the end of his life, Jeans became more and more convinced that the scientific viewpoint was synonymous with that of the astronomer. Human life was to be seen as a chain of causes and effects. The problems of the day were to be set against a background of time into which the whole of human history shrinks to the twinkling of an eye. Abstract problems of philosophy did not trouble him. Nor did he feel a need for seeking a rational basis for morals. According to Jeans, neither science nor philosophy has a voice in the region of moral acting. This is left to the Christian religion only.

APPEARANCE AND REALITY

We may picture the world of reality as a deep-flowing stream, the world of appearance is its surface, below which we cannot see. Events deep down in the stream throw up bubbles and eddies on the surface of the stream. These are the transfers of energy and radiation of our common life which affect our senses and so activate our minds; below these lie deep waters which we can only know by inference. These bubbles and eddies show atomicity. . . .

Many philosophers have regarded the world of appearance as a kind of illusion, some sort of creation or selection of our minds which has in some way less existence in its own right than the underlying world of reality. Modern physics does not confirm this view; the phenomena are seen to be just a part of the real world which affects our senses, while the space and time in which they occur have the same sort of reality as the substratum which orders their motions. . . .

Because we have only complete photons at our disposal, and these form blunt probes, the world of phenomena can never be seen clearly and distinctly, either by us or by our instruments. Instead of seeing clearly defined particles clearly located in space and execution, clear-cut motions, we see only a collection of blurs, like a badly focused lantern side. . . . This is enough of itself to prevent our ever observing strict causality in the world of phenomena.

Each blur represents the unknown entity which the particle-picture depicts as a particle, or perhaps a group of such entities. The blurs may be pictured as wave-disturbances, the intensity of the waves at any point representing the probability that, with infinitely refined probes at our disposal, we should find a particle at that point. Or again, we may interpret the waves as representations of knowledge —they do not give us pictures of a particle, but of what we know as to the position and speed of motion of the particle. Now these waves of knowledge exhibit complete determinism; as they roll on, they show us knowledge growing out of knowledge and uncertainty following uncertainty according to a strict causal law. But this tells us nothing we do not already know. If we had found new knowledge appearing, not out of previous knowledge but spontaneously and of its own accord, we should have come upon something very startling and of profound philosophical significance; actually what we find is merely what was to be expected, and the problem of causality is left much where it was.

[191]

JEFFERSON, THOMAS

JEFFERSON, THOMAS (1743-1826). In accordance with Jefferson's own will, his tombstone reads:

Here was buried Thomas Jefferson
Author of the Declaration of American Independence
Of the Statute of Virginia for religious freedom
And Father of the University of Virginia.

Jefferson did not want to have mentioned that he had been Governor of Virginia, member of Congress, Minister to France, Secretary of State, Vice-President and third President of the United States. Jefferson often protested that he disliked politics and preferred the peaceful life on his farm and among his books. Undoubtedly these declarations were sincere. His was a meditative mind. He was not a man of action. But for decades he was involved in political struggles because they concerned not so much his material interests as his philosophy, and it was his philosophy, at least its broad outline, which caused a great political upheaval, resulting in Jefferson's victory over men of action, and his election to the Presidency.

Jefferson's political philosophy was founded upon his ideas on human nature. His motto was, "I cannot act as if all men were unfaithful because some are so. . . . I had rather be the victim of occasional infidelities than relinquish my general confidence in the honesty of man." His confidence disregarded differences of education, wealth, social position. The aim of his political activity was a life of freedom in which every individual would be able to develop his moral and intellectual nature and pursue his happiness. He was also confident that the common man would give authority to good and wise leaders. He firmly believed that Providence created man for society and endowed him with a sense of right and wrong so that an orderly society could subsist.

614

Jefferson, who in his youth had been engaged in "dancing, junketing and high jinks," was a man of solid studies in various fields. He was a profound jurist, versed in mathematics, botany and meteorology, interested in zoology, astronomy and ethnology, mechanics and architecture, well-read in classical and modern literature, a talented musician and a model farmer. He was opposed to Calvinist orthodoxy, advocated religious tolerance, emancipation of slaves and public education. Among modern political economists there are some who think it fashionable to deride Jefferson as "a petty bourgeois liberal." It is true, Jefferson, the leader of small farmers, shopkeepers and artisans, disliked big business and large-scale industrialization. But his philosophy was anything but the expression of his material interests or of his prejudices.

CHARACTER OF WASHINGTON

His mind was great and powerful, without being of the very first order; his penetration strong, though not so acute as that of a Newton, Bacon, or Locke; and, as far as he saw, no judgment was ever sounder. It was slow in operation, being little aided by invention or imagination, but sure in conclusion. Hence the common remark of his officers of the advantage he derived from councils of war, where, hearing all suggestions, he selected whatever was best; and certainly no general ever planned his battles more judiciously. But if deranged in the course of the action—if any member of his plan was dislocated by sudden circumstances, he was slow in a readjustment. The consequence was that he often failed in the field, and rarely against an enemy in station, as at Boston and York. He was incapable of fear, meeting personal dangers with the calmest unconcern. Perhaps the strongest feature in his character was prudence; never acting until every circumstance, every consideration, was maturely weighed; refraining if he saw doubt; but when once decided going through with his purpose, whatever obstacle interposed.

His integrity was most pure, his justice the most inflexible I have ever known; no motives of interest or consanguinity, of friendship or hatred, being able to bias his decision. He was, indeed, in every sense of the word a wise, a good, and a great man. His temper was naturally irritable and high-toned; but reflection and resolution had obtained a firm and habitual ascendancy over it. If, however, it broke its bonds, he was most tremendous in his wrath. In his expenses he was honorable, but exact; liberal in contributions to whatever promised utility, but frowning and unyielding on all visionary projects and all unworthy calls on his charity. His heart was not warm in its affections; but he exactly calculated every man's value, and gave him a solid esteem proportioned to it.

Although, in the circle of his friends, where he might be unreserved with safety, he took a free share in conversation, his colloquial talents were not above mediocrity, possessing neither copiousness of ideas nor fluency of words. In public, when called upon for a sudden effort, he was unready, short and embarrassed. Yet he wrote readily, rather diffusely, in an easy and correct style. This he had acquired by conversation with the world; for his education was merely reading, writing, and common arithmetic, to which he added surveying at a later day. His time was employed in action chiefly, reading little, and that only in agriculture and English history. His correspondence became necessarily extensive, and, with journalizing his agricultural proceedings, occupied most of his leisure time within doors.

On the whole, his character was, in its mass, perfect; in nothing bad; in few points indifferent; and it may be truly said that never did nature and fortune combine more perfectly to make a man great, and to place him in the same constellation with whatever worthies have merited from man an everlasting remembrance. For his was the singular destiny and merit of leading the armies of his country successfully through an arduous war for the establishment of its independence; of conducting its councils through the birth of a government, new in its forms and its principles, until it had settled down into an orderly train; and of scrupulously obeying the laws through the whole of his career, civil and military, of which the history of the world furnishes no other example.

Letter to Dr. Walter Jones, Thomas Jefferson.

THE PASSAGE OF THE POTOMAC
THROUGH THE BLUE RIDGE

THE passage of the Potomac through the Blue Ridge is perhaps one of the most stupendous scenes in Nature. You stand on a very high point of land. On your right comes up the Shenandoah, having ranged along the foot of the mountain a hundred miles to seek a vent. On your left approaches the Potomac, seeking a passage also. In the moment of their junction they rush together against the mountain, rend it asunder, and pass off to the sea. The first glance at this scene hurries our senses into the opinion that this earth has been created in time; that the mountains were formed first; that the rivers began to flow afterward; that in this place particularly, they have been dammed up by the Blue Ridge of mountains, and have formed an ocean which filled the whole valley; that, continuing to rise, they have at length broken over at this spot, and have torn the mountain down from its summit to its base. The piles of rock on each hand, but particularly on the banks of the Shenandoah; the evident marks of their disrupture and avulsion from their beds by the most powerful agents of Nature corroborate the impression.

But the distant finishing which Nature has given to the picture is of a very different character. It is a true contrast to the foreground. It is as placid and delightful as that is wild and tremendous. For, the mountains being cloven asunder, she presents to your eye, through the cleft, a small patch of smooth blue horizon, at an infinite distance in the plain country, inviting you, as it were, from the riot and tumult roaring around, to pass through the breach and participate of the calm below. Here the eye ultimately composes itself; and that way, too, the road happens actually to lead.

You cross the Potomac above its junction, pass along its side through the base of the mountain for three miles—its terrible precipices hanging in fragments over you—and within about twenty miles reach Fredericktown and the fine country round' that. This scene is worth a voyage across the Atlantic. Yet here—as in the neighborhood of the Natural Bridge—are people who have passed their lives within half a dozen miles, and have never been to survey these monuments of a war between rivers and mountains which must have shaken the earth itself to its centre.

THE INFLUENCE AND DOOM OF SLAVERY

THE whole commerce between master and slave is a perpetual exercise of the most boisterous passions; the most unremitting despotism on the one part and degrading submission on the other. Our children see this, and learn to imitate it—for man is an imitative animal. This quality is the germ of all education in him. From his cradle to his grave he is learning to do what he sees others do. If a parent could find no motives, either in his philanthropy or his self-love, for restraining the intemperance of passion toward his slave, it should always be a sufficient one that his child is present. But generally it is not sufficient. The parent storms, the child looks on, catches the lineaments of wrath, puts on the same airs in the circle of smaller slaves, gives loose to his worst passions, and thus, nursed, educated, and daily exercised in tyranny, cannot but be stamped by it with odious peculiarities. The man must be a prodigy who can retain his manners and his morals undepraved by such circumstances.

And with what execration should the statesman be loaded who, permitting one-half of the citizens thus to trample on the other, transforms those into despots and these into enemies; destroys the morals of the one part and the *amor patriae* of the other! For if the slave can have a country in this world, it must be any other in preference to that in which he is born to live and labor for another; in which he must lock up the faculties of his nature, contribute as far as depends on his individual endeavors to the banishment of the human race, or entail his own miserable condition on the endless generations proceeding from him. With the morals of a people their industry also is destroyed. For in a warm climate no man will labor for himself who can make another labor for him. This is so true, that of the proprietors of slaves a very small proportion indeed are ever seen to labor.

What an incomprehensible machine is man, who can endure toil, famine, stripes, imprisonment, and death itself, in vindication of his own liberty and the next moment be deaf to all those motives whose power supported him through his trial, and inflict upon his fellow-men a bondage, one hour of which is fraught with more misery than ages of that which he rose in rebellion to oppose! But we must wait with patience the workings of an over-ruling Providence, and hope that this is preparing the deliverance of these our suffering brethren. When the measure of their tears shall be full, doubtless a God of justice will awaken to their distress, and, by diffusing a light and liberality among their oppressors —or at length by His exterminating thunder—manifest His attention to things of this world, and that they are not left to the guidance of blind fatality.

[192]

JOAD, CYRIL E. M.

JOAD, CYRIL E. M. (1891-1953). As an Oxford student, Joad loathed the idealism in which he had been brought up. He felt himself to be a naive realist. Then, influenced by Bertrand Russell, he became an extreme realist and was satisfied that his views agreed completely with modern physics, although he found out that his realism was also quite compatible with metaphysics. Soon thereafter, Joad, the former grim adversary of idealism, came close to Plato's doctrine of Ideas, which must not necessarily be interpreted in accordance with the idealistic schools. Joad then became con-

619

spicuous as an ardent defender of religion against its materialistic and relativistic critics. He especially emphasized the fallacy of assuming that to lay bare the origins of a thing is tantamount to describing its present nature, and he continued, that to show how a belief arises does not constitute a description of it much less its refutation.

Joad's principal works are: *Matter, Life and Value* (1929), *The Present and Future of Religion* (1930) and *Return to Philosophy* (1935).

THE POWER OF THOUGHT

I BELIEVE in the practical efficacy of the intellect; I believe, that is to say, that what you think affects and may determine what you do. It follows that facts are not "hard," since they can be affected by thinking about them. If you change men's moral and political ideas, you can, I hold, thereby change society; if you can change their ideas about what is worth while, you can change their mode of living. It seems to me to be nonsense to suggest that the ideas which lay behind the French Revolution played no part in determining its outbreak or guiding its course, or that the ideas of Christ or Mahomet about how men should live have played no part in changing their modes of living. In no sphere, perhaps, does the student find more impressive verification of the power of the idea not only to persist but in the end to prevail than in victory which the claim to think freely gained over dogmatic religion. To trace the slow history of French free thought from the new springs of Renaissance discovery through Rabelais and Montaigne, thence to the Libertins and Bayle and from them to its full flowering in Holbach and Diderot and Voltaire, is to realize the power over men's minds of ideas that are rooted in objective fact. (Yet the phrase "rooted in objective fact" is, I think, merely a periphrasis for the word "true.") On the one side was all that authority could muster to suppress and destroy with the weapons of exile, imprisonment, torture and death; on the other, there was only the power of the idea. Yet in the last resort the idea prevailed, though only for a time, for the victories of the mind and spirit have to be won afresh in every age.

Nor are the changes which thought brings about negligible; on occasion they have profoundly affected man's way of living, and affected it for the better; indeed, it is the hope of bettering man's life and his societies that has inspired almost every system of philosophy which has concerned itself with human conduct and institutions. Most of us are at some time or other impelled, even if the impulse is brief, to take a hand in solving the problems of our society, and most of us know in our hearts that it is our business to try to leave the world a little better than we found it.

"There are no phenomena," says Herbert Spencer, "which a society presents but what have their origins in the phenomena of individual human life." This, I think, is true. To change men's lives is to change society, and to change their minds is to change their lives. Now, it is by ideas that men's minds are changed.

[193]

JOHN OF SALISBURY

JOHN OF SALISBURY (About 1115-1180). The first to personify the type of a cultivated Englishman who combines statesmanship with humanist learning and philosophical mind was John of Salisbury, who played a very important role in the English foreign and ecclesiastical policy of his days, and proved to be an independent thinker and a gifted writer. Numerous pages of his books strike one as most modern. His judgments on people and the state of culture were rather liberal. His descriptions were colorful, and his manner of expression shows a rare combination of humor and dignity, of restraint and acuteness. In 1148, John became secretary to Archbishop Theobald of Canterbury, and, in 1162, he began to serve in the same capacity to Thomas à Becket. He shared Becket's exile and witnessed his murder. He was a friend of Pope Hadrian IV, the only Englishman who ever was crowned with the tiara, and he directed the diplomatic negotiations between King Henry II of England and the Holy See on the occasion of the conquest of Ireland.

621

While secretary to Archbishop Theobald, John wrote the books *Polycraticus* and *Metalogicus*. The first is a theory of the state, defining the rights of the king who, according to him, is limited by religious laws only, but may be killed when he breaks these laws. The second is a defense and criticism of dialectics and a refutation of exaggerated realism. John also wrote biographies of St. Anselm and of Thomas à Becket, and, in *Metalogicus*, he inserted his charming autobiography. From 1176 until his death, he was Bishop of Chartres, France, and was associated with the famous school of the cathedral.

ON DREAM INTERPRETATION

In describing the methods of the interpreters of dreams I fear it may seem that I am not describing the art but am myself nodding, for it is no art or at best a meaningless one. For whoever involves himself in the deception of dreams is not sufficiently awake to the law of God, suffers a loss of faith, and drowses to his own ruin. Truth is indeed far removed from him, nor can he grasp it any more effectually than he who with blinded eyes gropes his way in broad daylight can lance a boil or treat a cancer.

Although this drowsiness of infidelity in the form of dream interpretation is to be aroused by the goad of faith, and this mockery of craftiness (shall we call it, rather than of a craft) is to be battled with, we do not propose to block the path of the disposition of divine grace nor prevent the Holy Spirit from breathing where it will and according to its will suffusing obedient souls with its truth. But all who are credulous enough to put faith in dreams have patently wandered not only from the orbit of pure belief but also from that of reason.

Surely if ambiguous language is used which lends itself to many interpretations would not one be justly regarded as quite ignorant who, as a result of it, stubbornly makes some particular decision without taking into consideration these meanings? All things involve varied and manifold meanings, as has been stated above. Careful discrimination is to be made amid this multiplicity of meanings, lest by following one line too enthusiastically there be a tendency to fall into error. Hence the dream interpreter which is inscribed with the name of Daniel is apparently lacking in the weight which truth carries, when it allows but one meaning to one thing. This matter really needs no further consideration since the whole tradition of this activity is foolish and the circulating manual of dream interpretation passes brazenly from hand to hand of the curious.

Daniel himself certainly had received from the Lord the gift of interpreting dreams and visions. God forbid that this prophet, who was aware that it had been prohibited by the law of Moses for any of the faithful to pay attention to dreams, should be the one to reduce this insane practice to an art, for he well knew that the accomplice of Satan is transformed into an angel of light for the ruin of man and that the Lord sent upon him wicked angels.

Joseph also, thanks to his gift of interpreting dreams, held the chief place in Egypt. His brothers, as if envying his dreams, sold him into slavery to the Ishmaelites, but the hand of the Lord, by a miracle as pleasant as it was favorable to him, revealed the face of the future which was presented to the king as he slept and, as it were by the medium of dreams, raised Joseph not only from servitude to freedom but to the chief place among the nobles and grandees; so that only in respect to the royal throne was the king above him. Now were this possible with regard to a profession based upon human wisdom, I would be inclined to believe that one of his predecessors had won distinction before him, or I would readily think that a holy man filled with the spirit of piety had bequeathed the knowledge of acquiring distinction, if not to man in general, which would have been but right, at least to his own sons and brothers.

Furthermore Moses, trained in all the wisdom of Egypt, either was not acquainted with this art or scorned it, since in his abhorrence of impiety he banished it from God's people. However Daniel, a holy man, acquired the learning and wisdom of the Chaldeans, which assuredly a pious man would not have done if he had believed that the educational system of the Gentiles were sinful. He had too as fellow students those whom he rejoiced to have as sharers in the law and justice of God. For Ananias, Azariah, and Michael received with him all that the Chaldeans had to teach. They too were inspired by God and refrained from partaking of the royal table. Their diet too was vegetarian; they were content with it and they attended the King on his military expeditions.

But behold! A unique gift which man was unable to confer had been conferred upon Daniel alone; he could solve the riddle of dreams and at the dictation of the Lord clarify the obscurity of allegory. To make his intimacy with divine favor more conspicuous, he knew what the king, when lying in bed, premeditated. Pondering upon his visions Daniel had the wisdom to expound the miracle of salvation, which then lay in shadow and took place or rather was to take place at the end of the ages.

Are interpreters of dreams thus wont to enter even into the thoughts of others, to banish darkness, to disclose the hidden, and to clarify the obscurity of allegory? If there be any who enjoys such special favor let him join Daniel and Joseph and like them attribute it to the Lord. But for him whom the spirit of truth has not illumined it is vain to place trust in the art, since every art has its source in nature and its development in experience and reason. But reason is so undependable in the case of interpreters of dreams that for the most part it knows not where to turn or what decision to make. That this is frequently the case may be gathered from a few instances.

A certain individual (his name escapes me though I remember that the great Augustine narrates the incident), much troubled by a matter which caused him to hesitate, demanded with great insistence the opinion of one to whom he was aware the matter at issue was well known. This person put off the request with promises, thwarting by his cunning the insistence of the other. It chanced that on the same night each had a dream, the one that he was giving the explanation as requested, the other that he was being instructed by his informant. The result was that when he awoke he marveled that he had obtained the knowledge without the help of the other and without effort on his own part. Afterward, when as usual pleading that the promised information be given him, "What you asked," replied the other, "was done the night I came to instruct you." Who can explain such an incident unless on the supposition that good or bad spirits, influenced by the good or bad deeds of men, instruct or lead them astray?

Our Holy Mother the Catholic Church knows on the authority of Jerome himself how he was hurried before the tribunal of God the Judge for the reason that he had been too devoted to pagan books, where he was forced to assert that he would not merely not read them further but would not even keep them. Before this declaration he had been questioned and had said that he was a Christian. His judge rebuked him sharply for being not His disciple but Cicero's.

I do not dare affirm that this should be classed as a dream since this same truthful and learned teacher most solemnly states that it was not a shadowy dream but an actual experience and that the Lord did indeed visit him. To prove his assertion beyond the shadow of a doubt, on arising he displayed the livid welts and scars of wounds upon his body.

When spirits act thus in the case of human beings the devout soul should reject every image except that which leaves its innocence unimpaired. For should the dream add fuel to vice, perchance by inducing lust and avarice or by inspiring greed for dominion or anything of the sort to destroy the soul, undoubtedly it is the flesh or the evil spirit that sends it. This spirit, with the permission of the Lord because of their sins, wreaks its unbridled wickedness upon some men so violently that what they suffer in the spirit they wretchedly but falsely believe comes to pass in the flesh.

For example it is said that some Moon or Herodias or

Mistress of the Night calls together councils and assemblies, that banquets are held, that different kinds of rites are performed, and that some are dragged to punishment for their deeds and others raised to glory. Moreover babes are exposed to witches and at one time their mangled limbs are eargly devoured, at another are flung back and restored to their cradles if the pity of her who presides is aroused.

Cannot even the blind see that this is but the wickedness of mocking demons? This is quite apparent from the fact that it is for the weaker sex and for men of little strength or sense that they disport themselves in such a cult. If in fact anyone who suffers from such illusion is firmly censured by someone or by some sign the malign influence is either overcome or yields, and, as the saying is, as soon as one is censured in the light the works of darkness cease. The most effective cure however for this bane is for one to embrace the true faith, refuse to listen to such lies, and never to give thought to follies and inanities of the sort.

[194]

JOHNSON, SAMUEL

JOHNSON, SAMUEL (1709-1784). Johnson was most popular among his British contemporaries, especially the citizens of London, as "the philosopher," but he disliked philosophers just as he disliked country life, music, learned women, Whigs, history for its own sake and a lot of other things. To him, Berkeley was a madman, Hume nothing but an infidel and Voltaire, whose literary skill he admired, a rascal. He was a critic of literature but he held that the fundamental aspects of life were not proper subjects for poetry.

Although Johnson was not a profound thinker, he was a man of deep convictions, acquired by hard experiences. His poem *The Vanity of Human Wishes* (1749) outlines his philosophy of life, which he formulated again and again in satirical and earnest, resigned and irate sayings. To him life is mostly bitter, and rarely sweet. It is endurable only because there are short intervals of satisfaction. The end of writing is to enable mankind "better to enjoy life or better to endure it." Poetry must stand the test of reason and common sense. Fabulous images, Johnson maintained, have worn thin.

In politics, Johnson was a staunch Tory, in religious questions uncompromisingly orthodox. He demanded that literature, in which he was mainly interested, does not have to explain the riddles of existence, but that it should support moral and religious doctrines and defend the king and the Church. Much of this philosophy was expressed by Johnson in casual remarks in his *Lives of the Poets* (1779-81). However, he is best known not by his own writings but rather by the book of his biographer James Boswell, who wrote down Johnson's remarks about daily life, literature, politics, and contemporary history. The biography presents a genial man, who— though difficult to deal with, a sarcastic conversationalist, sometimes sound, sometimes queer—was always sincere and original.

THE CRITIC

CRITICISM is a study by which men grow important and formidable at very small expense. The power of invention has been conferred by nature upon few, and the labor of learning those sciences which may, by mere labor, be obtained is too great to be willingly endured; but every man can exert such judgment as he has upon the works of others; and he whom nature has made weak, and idleness keeps ignorant, may yet support his vanity by the name of a critic.

I hope it will give comfort to great numbers who are passing through the world in obscurity, when I inform them how easily distinction may be obtained. All the other powers of literature are coy and haughty, they must be long courted, and at last are not always gained; but criticism is a goddess easy of access, and forward of advance, who will meet the slow, and encourage the timorous; the want of meaning she supplies with words, and the want of spirit she recompenses with malignity.

This profession has one recommendation peculiar to itself, that it gives vent to malignity without real mischief. No genius was ever blasted by the breath of critics. The poison which, if confined, would have burst the heart, fumes away in empty hisses, and malice is set at ease with very little danger to merit. The critic is the only man whose

627

triumph is without another's pain, and whose greatness does not rise upon another's ruin.

THE UNIVERSAL FALLACY

WE always make a secret comparison between a part and the whole; the termination of any period of life reminds us that life itself has likewise its termination; when we have done anything for the last time, we involuntarily reflect that a part of the days allotted us is past, and that as more is past there is less remaining.

It is very happily and kindly provided, that in every life there are certain pauses and interruptions, which force considerations upon the careless, and seriousness upon the light; points of time where one course of action ends and another begins; and by vicissitude of fortune, or alteration of employment, by change of place, or loss of friendship, we are forced to say of something, *this is the last.*

An even and unvaried tenor of life always hides from our apprehension the approach of its end. Succession is not perceived but by variation; he that lives today as he lived yesterday, and expects that, as the present day is, such will be the morrow, easily conceives time as running in a circle and returning to itself. This uncertainty of our duration is impressed commonly by dissimilitude of condition; it is only by finding life changeable that we are reminded of its shortness.

This conviction, however forcible at every new impression, is every moment fading from the mind; and partly by the inevitable incursion of new images, and partly by voluntary exclusion of unwelcome thoughts, we are again exposed to the universal fallacy; and we must do another thing for the last time, before we consider that the time is nigh when we shall do no more.

[195]

JONSON, BEN

JONSON, BEN (1573-1637). Starting as a bricklayer, Ben Jonson made his way to become a dramatic poet who held a dominant place in English literary life during the last years of Queen Elizabeth and the reign of James I. In his progress to this position, Jonson was a soldier who distinguished himself on the battlefield. He fought many duels, and attacked many of his fellow-writers with the weapon of sarcasm, though he respected the gentle Shakespeare. Because he killed an actor, Jonson narrowly escaped capital punishment. While in prison he became a convert to the Catholic Church, but twelve years thereafter, he returned to Protestantism.

Ben Jonson's best known works are his plays *Every Man in His Humour* (1598) and *Volpone* (1605). In his essays *Timber* or *Discoveries Made Upon Men and Matters,* he dealt mostly with the dignity and value of literature, while he also cast sidelights on the daily life of his time. Algernon Charles Swinburne praised these essays, and put them above those of Francis Bacon. Recent scholars have discovered that Jonson was much indebted to Latin authors, but they do not deny that he also relied on personal observation and expressed original views.

THE DIGNITY OF SPEECH

CUSTOM is the most certain mistress of language, as the public stamp makes the current money. But we must not be too frequent with the mint, every day coming. Nor fetch words from the extreme and utmost ages; since the chief virtue of a style is perspicuity, and nothing so vicious in it, as to need an interpreter. Words borrowed of antiquity do lend a kind of majesty to style, and are not without their delight sometimes. For they have the authority of years, and out of their intermission do win to themselves a kind of grace-like newness. But the eldest of the present, and newness of the past language, is the best. For what was the ancient language, which some men so dote upon, but the ancient custom? Yet when I name custom, I understand not the vulgar custom: For that were a precept no less dangerous to language, than life, if we should speak or live after the manners of the

629

vulgar: But that I call custom of speech, which is the consent of the learned; as custom of life, which is the consent of the good. Virgil was most loving of antiquity; yet how rarely doth he insert *aquai* and *pictai!* Lucretius is scabrous and rough in these; he seeks them: As some do Chaucerisms with us, which were better expunged and banished. Some words are to be culled out for ornament and color, as we gather flowers to strew houses, or make garlands; but they are better when they grow to our style; as in a meadow, where through the mere grass and greenness delights; yet the variety of flowers doth heighten and beautify. Marry, we must not play, or riot too much with them, as in *Paranomasies*: Nor use too swelling or ill-sounding words; *Quae per salebras, altaque saxa cadunt.* It is true, there is no sound but shall find some lovers, as the bitterest confections are grateful to some palates. Our composition must be more accurate in the beginning and end than in the midst; and in the end more than in the beginning; for through the midst the stream bears us. And this is attained by custom more than care or diligence. We must express readily, and fully, not profusely. There is difference between a liberal and a prodigal hand. As it is a great point of art, when our matter requires it, to enlarge, and veer out all sail; so to take it in and contract it is of no less praise when the argument doth ask it. Either of them hath their fitness in the place. A good man always profits by his endeavour, by his help; yea, when he is absent; nay, when he is dead by his example and memory. that, where you can take away nothing without loss, and that loss to be manifest.

[196]

JOUBERT, JOSEPH

JOUBERT, JOSEPH (1754-1824). With regard to psychological refinement and literary skill, Joubert belongs to that line of French moralists whose outstanding representatives are Montaigne and La Rochefoucauld. However, Joubert differs from them in that he is more interested in psychological curiosities than in truth and morals and he prefers aesthetical enjoyment to knowledge of the facts. In his youth, Joubert was a lay-brother but he left the cloister because he was fond of worldly life and could not renounce his associations with women. He was always sincere when he professed his predilection for the Catholic Church and his hatred of the philosophy, and even more so of the philosophers, of the Enlightenment. He did not conceal that his judgment relied on taste, not on faith. He disliked Diderot and D'Alembert because he considered them "vulgar," and for the same reason, he was horrified by the French Revolution. Under Napoleon, he was appointed inspector-general of the University. But the Emperor's favor entailed the disgrace of the restored Bourbons, and Joubert had always sympathized with royalism.

To Joubert, Plato did not Platonize enough. In fact, Joubert was more akin to Epicureanism, though he felt uneasy while enjoying life. Enjoyment of perfumes, flowers, refined cuisine, precious silk was a vital point to him. But enjoyment could not overcome his feelings of tediousness. Joubert was of very delicate health, but he enjoyed suffering because he believed that sickness made his soul more subtle. As a psychologist of morbidity, Joubert anticipated many psychological discoveries of recent times.

PLATO

PLATO shows us nothing; but he brings us brightness with him; he puts light into our eyes, and fills us with a clearness by which all objects afterward become illuminated. He teaches us nothing; but he prepares us, fashions us, and makes us ready to know all. Somehow or other, the habit of reading him augments in us the capacity for discerning and entertaining whatever fine truths may afterward present themselves. Like mountain air, it sharpens our organs, and gives us an appetite for wholesome food. . . . Plato loses himself in the void; but one sees the play of his wings, one hears their rustle. . . . It is good to breathe the air of Plato; but not to live upon him.

WHICH is best, if one wants to be useful and to be really understood, to get one's words in the world, or to get them in the schools? I maintain that the good plan is to employ words in their popular sense rather than in their philosophical sense; and the better plan still to employ them in their natural sense rather than in their popular sense. By their natural sense, I mean the popular and universal acceptation of them brought to that which in this is essential and invariable. To prove a thing by definition proves nothing if the definition is purely philosophical; for such definition only binds him who makes it. But to prove a thing by definition when the definition expresses the necessary, inevitable, and clear idea which the world at large attaches to the object, is, on the contrary, all in all; because then what one does is simply to show people what they do really think, in spite of themselves and without knowing it. The rule that one is free to give to words what sense one will, and that the only thing needful is to be agreed upon the sense one gives them, is very well for the mere purposes of argumentation; but in the true-born and noble science of metaphysics, and in the genuine world of literature, it is good for nothing.

[197]

JUNG, CARL GUSTAV

JUNG, CARL GUSTAV (1875-   ). From 1906 to 1913, Jung was one of the most enthusiastic adherents and disciples of Sigmund Freud. He was the editor of the *Annual for Psychoanalytic Research*, and, at Freud's suggestion, was appointed the first president of the International Psychoanalytical Association. His separation from Freud hurt the latter a great deal, and Freud subsequently criticized Jung's own theories with animosity, which was paid back in kind by Jung.

Jung started as a clinical psychiatrist but, at the same time he showed great sympathy for spiritism, and has retained in his late years a special interest in occult forces and mystical experiences. In addition to his temporary devotion to Freud's psychoanalysis, Jung has also been a student of the philosopher Heinrich Rickert, whose distinction between the methods of natural and social sciences he adopted.

Jung called his own doctrine "analytical psychology," at first and then "complex psychology." To him psychical is the true reality, and all conflicts between mind and nature are of no fundamental importance but are derived from the difference of origin of psychic contents. He conceives the psychic as of both individual and general character. The conscious personality is the focus of psychic processes. Without such a focus, no organized ego, no continuity of experience is possible. But the contents of psychic experience, Jung insists, reach beyond the range of individual consciousness. The individual is in a state of fusion with his environment, with the social group to which he belongs, with his nation and race. This fusion is taking place in the realm of the unconscious which completes and compensates the conscious in man. Any psychical structure of the human individual is shaped by the tension between the conscious and the unconscious, and the extension of the unconscious to the psychic life of the group, nation and race is of fundamental importance for the psychology of the individual. Its attitude toward the objects is determined by the tendency to either introversion or extraversion, one which is predominant and forms the humane type. This classification of men has aroused general interest and is the most frequently mentioned part of Jung's doctrine. However, according to Jung, the aim of mature man must be totality of the psychic, harmony between the cultivation of the self and the devotion to the outer world. He regards progress of culture as conditioned by the enlargement of the realm of consciousness. Both the progress of culture and the development of the individual are placed and kept in motion by what Jung calls energy, but which he tries to differentiate from physical energy.

Despite secession and mutual polemics, Jung has retained many of Freud's conceptions. However, Jung has substituted a general principle of energy for Freud's sexual drive as the moving cause of human life and destiny, and his interpretation of dreams and their symbols is different from the methods used by the founder of psychoanalysis. While Freud, notwithstanding his interest in instinctual drives, is essentially a rationalist, Jung, although proclaiming the increase of consciousness as the cultural goal, is, by nature, a romanticist.

THE HUMAN PSYCHE

IT is, to my mind, a fatal mistake to consider the human

psyche as a merely personal affair and to explain it exclusively from a personal point of view. Such a mode of explanation is only applicable to the individual in his ordinary everyday occupations and relationships, If, however, some slight trouble occurs, perhaps in the form of an unforeseen and somewhat extraordinary event, instantly instinctive forces are called up, forces which appear to be wholly unexpected, new, and even strange. They can no longer be explained by personal motives, being comparable rather to certain primitive occurrences like panics at solar eclipses and such things. To explain the murderous outburst of Bolshevistic ideas by a personal father complex appears to me as singularly inadequate.

The change of character that is brought about by the uprush of collective forces is amazing. A gentle and reasonable being can be transformed into a maniac or a savage beast. One is always inclined to lay the blame on external circumstances, but nothing could explode in us if it had not been there. As a matter of fact, we are always living upon a volcano and there is, as far as we know, no human means of protection against a possible outburst which will destroy everybody within its reach. It is certainly a good thing to preach reason and common sense, but what if your audience is a lunatic asylum or a crowd in a collective seizure? There is not much difference either, because the madman as well as the mob is moved by nonpersonal, overwhelming forces.

As a matter of fact, it needs as little as a neurosis to conjure up a force that cannot be dealt with by reasonable means. Our cancer case shows clearly how impotent human reason and intellect are against the most palpable nonsense. I always advise my patients to take such obvious but invincible nonsense as the manifestation of a power and a meaning not yet understood. Experience has taught me that it is a much more effective method of procedure to take such a fact seriously and to seek for a suitable explanation. But an explanation is suitable only when it produces a hypothesis equal to the morbid effect. Our case is confronted with a will power and a suggestion more than equal to anything his consciousness can put against it. In this precarious situation it would be bad strategy to convince the patient that he is somehow, though in a highly incomprehensible way, at the back of his own symptom, secretly inventing and supporting it. Such a suggestion would instantly paralyze his fighting spirit, and he would get demoralized. It is much better if he understands that his complex is an autonomous power directed against his conscious personality. Moreover, such an explanation fits the actual facts much better than a reduction to personal motives. An apparent personal motivation does exist, but it is not made by intention, it just happens to the patient.

[198]

JUSTIN MARTYR

JUSTIN MARTYR (About 110-165). The earliest defense of Christianity against paganism using philosophical arguments was written by Justin, who later suffered a martyr's death in Rome. Justin's *Apologies* is also of interest because it describes Christian worship as it was performed in early times, refutes accusations against members of the Christian community and tries to convince pagan philosophers by using their own terms. Justin, who was born in the Samaritan town of Flavia Neapolis, the old Shechem which had been destroyed by Vespasian in 67 A.D. and which is called Nablus today, probably was not of Samaritan but of pagan descent. Evidently he had studied pagan philosophy before his conversion, and acquired, if not profound knowledge, a fluency of style and ability in using philosophical terms. Justin also had a controversy with a Jewish scholar on which he reported in his *Dialogue with Tryphon*. Tryphon probably was a real person, known as Tarfon the Tanna, who was opposed to Christianity but who died before Justin was grown up.

THE EUCHARIST

AFTER the believer is baptized, and so incorporated or made one with us, we lead him to the congregation of the brethren, as we call them, and then with great fervency pour out our souls in common prayers both for ourselves, for the person baptized, and for all others all the world over; that having embraced the truth, our conversation might be as becometh the gospel, and that we may be found doers of the world, and so at length be favored with an everlasting salvation. Prayers being over we salute each other with a kiss; After this, bread and a cup of wine and water are brought to the president or bishop, which he takes, and offers up praise and glory to the Father of all things, through the name of His Son and the Holy Spirit; and this thanksgiving to God for vouchsafing us worthy of these His creatures, is a prayer of more than ordinary length. When the bishop has finished the prayers, and the thanksgiving service, all the people present conclude with an audible voice, saying, Amen; now Amen in the Hebrew tongue, is, so be it. The eucharistical office being thus performed by the bishop, and concluded with the acclamation of all the people, those we call deacons distribute to everyone present to partake of this eucharistical bread and wine, and water, and then they carry it to the absent.

This food we call the eucharist, of which none are allowed to be partakers, but such only as are true believers, and have been baptized in the Laver of Regeneration for the remission of sins, and live according to Christ's precepts; for we do not take this as common bread, and common wine. But as Jesus Christ our Saviour was made flesh by the *logos* of God, and had real flesh and blood for our salvation, so are we taught that this food, which the very same *logos* blessed by prayer and thanksgiving, is turned into the nourishment and substance of our flesh and blood; and is in some sense the flesh and blood of the incarnate Jesus. For the Apostles, in their commentaries called the Gospels, have left this command upon record, "That Jesus took bread, and when He had given thanks, He said, Do this in commemoration of Me, for this is My body; And in like manner He took the cup, and when He had given thanks, He said, This

636

is My blood," and delivered it to them only. And this very solemnity too the evil spirits have introduced in the mysteries of *Mithra;* for you do, or may know, that when any one is initiated into this religion, bread and a cup of water, with a certain form of words are made use of in the sacrifice. After this sacrament is over, we remind each other of the obligations to his duty, and the rich relieve the poor; and upon such charitable accounts we visit some or other every day.

[199]

637

K

KALLEN, HORACE MAYER

KALLEN, HORACE MAYER (1882-   ). A unique position in American philosophy is occupied by Kallen who resolved not to devote himself to philosophy exclusively, although he feels it as his very vocation, although he enjoys teaching it and has been a highly successful teacher, as he is a successful author of a large number of important books. Of all philosophical branches, it is aesthetics that attracts Kallen's highest and most enduring interest. But he has overcome this inclination because he held that active participation in political and economic movements is of greater importance and more urgent. Kallen has taken a leading part in the defense of civil rights, of freedom of thought and conscience, in advocating the demands of American labor, in the foundation of consumers' cooperatives, and in Jewish affairs, not least in Zionism. In doing so, he sometimes refrained from philosophizing although he did not abandon philosophy. For he always maintained that ideas are events in man's life; whatever else they may be, they certainly form human attitudes, determine the decisions of the individual and give experience its meaning. It is the belief in the power of ideas that supports Kallen's pluralistic views on life and culture. Philosophy should not rely on an exclusive system, but it must confront diverse passions, thoughts, experiences and find their point of junction. This pluralistic view is the basis for Kallen's conception of freedom, the "right to be different," and it has enabled him to clarify the extent and variety of experiencing freedom. In *The Liberal Spirit*, (1948) Kallen not only discussed the content and value of the idea of freedom but also the possibilities of its realization in a human community. In *The Education of Free Men* (1950) he developed his philosophy of education, refuting totalitarian despotism of any origin.

Pluralism has prevented Kallen from any over-simplification of philosophical and vital problems. According to Kallen, to deny difficulties and complications is to multiply them, just as to deny reality to evil is to aggravate evil. He holds that the world has not been created for the use and pleasure of mankind, but that Man is capable and, therefore, obliged to improve the world he lives in. Conscious of the fact that vital problems are and remain tough and complicated, and that ideals demand hard work and courageous fighting, Kallen need not be afraid that his seriousness may be questioned when he undertakes to harmonize modern science and religion, particularly Judaism, his own faith.

THE CHOICE OF FREEDOM

WHAT may be said of the impulsions of this freedom, which takes determinism for its instrument? What does it lead to? Where and how may it go?

Our time resounds with the warnings of Cassandras who prophesy that to these questions science can give no answer. All men, they chant, all values, are indifferent to science, for whose detached and impersonal view abundance signifies no more than scarcity, freedom than bondage, the tyrant than the slave. All are events in an indifferent sequence of cause and effect, and in the scientist's task of searching out measurable specific causes for measurable specific effects, a man is worth only as much as a thing. When psychologists, educators, college administrators equally with personnel managers and employment agents endeavor to define the qualities of men by means of machines that test and measure, do they not use the scientific understanding of nature in order to dissolve personal character into mechanical clockworks? Do they not dissolve the human being into the non-human event? Science can free men or enslave them, enrich men or impoverish them, but *which* is not itself a decision within the power of science to make.

The decision is not within the power of science because science, we are told, being the embodiment of modern man's insight into nature, takes determinism for its ground and postulates only uniformity, regularity, repetition in all things. The decision is not within the power of science because technics, being modern man's system of the applications of his embodied insight, postulates mechanism as the

639

ground of works, so that engineers and architects are but machinists *in excelsis*. And our modern psychologists and social scientists, are they, it is asked, anything different? Do they not start from these same postulates in their study of man? Do they not seek for their disciplines the same certainty of belief, the same precision of prediction and control which are the envied excellences of the sciences of nature? To merit the praise which the word *science* and its derivatives carry, the study of man must meet the determinist criteria of the study of the stars and the stuffs and articulations of earth. Until psychology and sociology and economics and politics become as physics and chemistry and biology and mechanics and astronomy, they will not merit the eulogium *science*.

But if they become like unto these, must they not also postulate that what the Declaration of Independence has written down about freedom as a self-evident truth is a self-evident error? Then what becomes of the problems of freedom which so vex our time? Are they not in truth abolished? If determinism is true, must not freedom be false, or else, with all the values men set their hearts upon, outside the realm of science altogether? And if they are outside, what good are the methods and results of science in solving the modern man's problem of freedom? Yet scientific determinist as he is, modern man's care for freedom is far more urgent than that of his unmodern forebears. He does believe with a fighting faith, that freedom *is* an inalienable right of every man, and he bled and died to vindicate this right throughout modern times. Only, uniquely, in modern times, have free men fought not alone for their own liberties but also to set slaves free as in the American Civil War. Daily modern man experiences freedom, seeks freedom, and uses freedom. So far as living his life goes, scientific determinism has been among his best means to freedom. Can science then make no deliverances about freedom's nature and intent?

So formulated, the question reinstates the dilemma of determinism with which William James challenged philosophers half a hundred years ago, and which he himself learned from the revolutionary French libertarian Charles Renouvier, a generation before. In a world all of whose events are automatic and predetermined—the argument runs —the urge and idea of freedom and its conflict with the idea of determinism must also be automatic and predetermined. The foreordained choice between them cannot fail to lead to momentous consequences for the chooser. Whichever he decides upon, he could not have decided otherwise. Yet the choice of one means necessity, repetition, everlastingly recurring cycles of old thoughts and old things moving in old directions upon old ways. It means there can be no contingencies and no disjunctions nor any true alternatives. It means that control must be error and the very choice which affirms it, illusion. It means that freedom is but the synonym for ignorance. Since events must be the necessary repetition of identicals, a passage from ignorance to knowledge is ruled out. Yet in fact such passages do occur, and in both directions. In fact, illusion is changed over into reality and error is confronted and overruled by truth, and vice versa. Such events strict determinism can neither explain nor explain away. It can only establish the believer as a resigned and submissive do-nothing or as a bullying fanatic. His world is inalterably either the best possible or the worst possible, and no thing in it can be otherwise than it is. Or, its compulsions—which he calls his Fate or Destiny and which he can neither confront nor escape—drive him against all men, and he cannot do otherwise than he does. World and man both, if they move at all, move inalterably to an inalterable end.

The choice of freedom, on the other hand, does not abolish determinism. The choice of freedom only limits and checks determinism. It simply adds to repetition and recurrence spontaneity and originality. It accepts our experiences of chance and contingency as experiences of the real. It takes at its face value the experience of new events confluent with old but not compelled by them; new events initiating new turns upon new ways in new directions toward new alternatives of thoughts or things. The choice of freedom grounds the fact that knowledge does replace ignorance, truth, error, and power helplessness. Choosing freedom, a man can stand up. A man can believe at his own risk and fight for his faith in his own power. Determinism, to this believer, is changed by his belief from a totalitarian metaphysics of existence into a method of understanding and managing an untotalizable existence. It becomes a consequence and vindication of freedom. In the daily life we experience existence now as free, now as determined, and again as both and neither. Carried down from the abstractions of the philosopher to the enterprises of the workaday world, in the daily life the sciences become transvalued from an effort to uncover an inert and immutable order into a succession of determinations, with which by trying out theories, experiments, and verifications and again and again revising them we slowly and assiduously shape new truths and transform old ones into new error. When freedom is the choice, science is realized as an open, imaginative, self-correcting adventure in perception, understanding and management —a free enterprise which works its way through a boundless world on hypotheses that aim at unguaranteed consequences, not at foregone conclusions.

[200]

KANT, IMMANUEL

KANT, IMMANUEL (1724-1804). The ancestors of Immanuel Kant on his father's side were Scotch. Had he kept the original spelling of Cant, the citizens of Königsberg would have pronounced his name "Zand." His entire well-ordered life, with the exception of a negligible period, was spent in that East Prussian city whose burghers used to set their watches when he passed under their windows on his daily walks. After mature reflection, Kant decided to stay single. From theological student he rose to Privatdozent and full professor of philosophy, and with his epoch-making answer to the problems posed by David Hume, he became not only Germany's greatest philosopher, but one of the greatest philosophers of all times.

In his famous *Critique of Pure Reason* he showed that knowledge *a priori* is possible, which means that by virtue of the forms and categories of the mind, like space, time and causality, man possesses the presuppositions for coherent and intelligible experience. To be sure, we know only appearances, colors, sounds and the like, never the thing-in-itself. Kant maintained that true knowledge cannot transcend or go beyond experience. Still, for the sake of religion and morality, we need such concepts as God, soul, freedom and immortality. To satisfy these demands of human nature, Kant wrote the *Critique of Practical Reason,* in which he acknowledged the necessity and validity of these values.

In the categorical imperative Kant laid a solid foundation for morality by enjoining man to act in such a way that the maxim of his will may at the same time be raised into a principle of universal law. Religionists called him the all-devourer, but they failed to recognize his deep piety expressed in these lines: "Two things fill the soul with ever new and increasing wonder and reverence the oftener and the more fervently reflection ponders on it: The starry heavens above and the moral law within." Scientists know him as the co-author of the Kant-Laplace theory of the heavens. And lovers of freedom are inspired by his treatise on eternal peace. All modern philosophy must orient itself to Kant.

JUDGMENTS

THIS may well be called the age of criticism, a criticism from which nothing need hope to escape. When religion seeks to shelter itself behind its sanctity, and law behind its majesty, they justly awaken suspicion against themselves, and lose all claim to the sincere respect which reason yields only to that which has been able to bear the test of its free and open scrutiny.

Metaphysics has been the battlefield of endless conflicts. Dogmatism at first held despotic sway; but . . . from time to time scepticism destroyed all settled order of society; . . . and now a widespread indifferentism prevails. Never has metaphysics been so fortunate as to strike into the sure path of science, but has kept groping about, and groping, too, among mere ideas. What can be the reason of this failure? Is a science of metaphysics impossible? Then, why should nature disquiet us with a restless longing after

643

it, as if it were one of our most important concerns? Nay more, how can we put any faith in human reason, if in one of the very things that we most desire to know, it not merely forsakes us, but lures us on by false hopes only to cheat us in the end? Or are there any indications that the true path has hitherto been missed, and that by starting afresh we may yet succeed where others have failed?

It seems to me that the intellectual revolution, by which at a bound mathematics and physics became what they now are, is so remarkable, that we are called upon to ask what was the essential feature of the change that proved so advantageous to them, and to try at least to apply to metaphysics as far as possible a method that has been successful in other sciences of reason. In mathematics I believe that, after a long period of groping, the true path was disclosed in the happy inspiration of a single man. If that man was Thales, things must suddenly have appeared to him in a new light, the moment he saw how the properties of the isosceles triangle could be demonstrated. The true method, as he found, was not to inspect the visible figure of the triangle, or to analyze the bare conception of it, and from this, as it were, to read off its properties, but to bring out what was necessarily implied in the conception that he had himself formed *a priori*, and put into the figure, in the construction by which he presented it to himself.

Physics took much longer time than mathematics to enter on the highway of science, but here, too, a sudden revolution in the way of looking at things took place. When Galileo caused balls which he had carefully weighed to roll down an inclined plane, or Torricelli made the air bear up a weight which he knew beforehand to be equal to a standard column of water, a new light broke on the mind of the scientific discoverer. It was seen that reason has insight only into that which it produces after a plan of its own, and that it must itself lead the way with principles of judgment based upon fixed laws, and force nature to answer its questions. Even experimental physics, therefore, owes the beneficial revolution in its point of view entirely to the idea, that, while reason can know nothing purely of itself, yet that which it has itself put into nature must be its guide to the discovery of all that it can learn from nature.

In metaphysical speculations it has always been assumed that all our knowledge must conform to objects; but every attempt from this point of view to extend our knowledge of objects *a priori* by means of conceptions has ended in failure. The time has now come to ask, whether better progress may not be made by supposing that objects must conform to our knowledge. Plainly this would better agree with the avowed aim of metaphysics, to determine the nature of objects *a priori*, or before they are actually presented. Our suggestion is similar to that of Copernicus in astronomy, who, finding it impossible to explain the movements of the heavenly bodies on the supposition that they turned round the spectator, tried whether he might succeed better by supposing the spectator to revolve and the stars to remain at rest. Let us make a similar experiment in metaphysics with *perception.* If it were really necessary for our perception to conform to the nature of objects, I do not see how we could know anything of it *a priori;* but if the sensible object must conform to the constitution of our faculty of perception, I see no difficulty in the matter. Perception, however, can become knowledge only if it is related in some way to the object which it determines. Now here again I may suppose, either that the *conceptions* through which I effect that determination conform to the objects, or that the objects, in other words the experience in which alone the objects are known, conform to conceptions. In the former case, I fall into the same perplexity as before, and fail to explain how such conceptions can be known *a priori.* In the latter case, the outlook is more hopeful. For, experience is itself a mode of knowledge which implies intelligence, and intelligence has a rule of its own, which must be an *a priori* condition of all knowledge of objects presented to it. To this rule, as expressed in *a priori* conceptions, all objects

645

of experience must necessarily conform, and with it they must agree.

Our experiment succeeds as well as we could wish, and gives promise that metaphysics may enter upon the sure course of a science, at least in its first part, where it is occupied with those *a priori* conceptions to which the corresponding objects can be given. The new point of view enables us to explain how there can be *a priori* knowledge, and what is more, to furnish satisfactory proofs of the laws that lie at the basis of nature as a totality of objects of experience. But the consequences that flow from this deduction of our faculty of *a priori* knowledge, which constitutes the first part of our inquiry, are unexpected, and at first sight seem to be fatal to the aims of metaphysics, with which we have to deal in the second part of it. For we are brought to the conclusion that we never can transcend the limits of possible experience, and therefore never can realize the object with which metaphysics is primarily concerned. In truth, however, no better indirect proof could be given that we were correct in holding, as the result of our first estimate of the *a priori* knowledge of reason, that such knowledge relates not at all to the thing as it exists in itself, but only to phenomena. For that which necessarily forces us to go beyond the limits of experience and of all phenomena is the *unconditioned,* which reason demands of things in themselves, and by right and necessity seeks in the complete series of conditions for everything conditioned. If, then, we find that we cannot think the unconditioned without contradiction, on the supposition of our experience conforming to objects as things in themselves; while, on the contrary, the contradiction disappears, on the supposition that our knowledge does not conform to things in themselves, but that objects as they are given to us as phenomena conform to our knowledge; we are entitled to conclude that what we at first assumed as an hypothesis is now established as a truth.

[200]

646

KIERKEGAARD, SÖREN

KIERKEGAARD, SÖREN AABY (1813-1855). A little boy of twelve, cold and hungry, tending the sheep on a lonely pasture, suddenly went in despair to the next hillock and there cursed God. This was not our philosopher, it was his father; but this deed hung heavily over the Kierkegaard family, denying the young Sören a happy youth and making him the prophet of anxiety. Only the comfortable income inherited from his father, who after that experience on the heath, had gone into the wool business and thrived, his native humor mixed with asceticism and an interest in the sorrows of his fellow men, preserved him from insanity. In excessive measure he shared the melancholy so typical of many a Dane; but, artist and poet that he was at heart and in language, he concealed much of it in his virile and colorful style which he devoted to showing that life ever leads to crossroads and demands decisions that need be made abruptly, by fits or jumps in attitude to tide us between the rational and the irrational. The title of one of his most important works *Either—Or* ironically became his nickname among the "common men" to whom he fled in his daily wanderings through Copenhagen. In a sense, he was the Danish counterpart of Schopenhauer with whom he shared his view of women.

Only recently influential, Kierkegaard, having admired Hegel and Schelling and discarded them, had the avowed intention of creating difficulties instead of solving them. The relation between the knowing mind and eternal truth he considered the great paradox. Truth is attainable only subjectively and subjectivity is truth.

Of Christianity he thought so much that he dissuaded people from joining the church. Having used up his inheritance, spent himself at last in argumentation and written all he wanted to write, he was picked up in the streets and died in a hospital, not yet 43 years of age.

NATURAL SCIENCES

IF the natural sciences had been developed in Socrates' day as they are now, all the sophists would have been scientists. One would have hung a microscope outside his shop in order to attract customers, and then would have had a sign painted saying: 'Learn and see through a giant microscope how a man thinks' (and on reading the advertisement Socrates would have said: 'that is how men who do not think behave'). An excellent subject for an Aristophanes, particularly if he let Socrates look through a microscope.

There is no use at all in going in for natural science. One stands there defenseless and without any control. The scientist begins at once to distract one with all his details, at one moment one is in Australia, at another in the moon, in the bowels of the earth, and the devil knows where—chasing a tape worm; at one moment one has to use a telescope and at the next a microscope, and who the devil can stand that kind of thing.

But joking apart; the confusion lies in the fact that it is never dialectically clear what is what, how philosophy is to make use of natural science. Is the whole thing a brilliant metaphor (so that one might just as well be ignorant of it)? is it an example and analogy? or is it of such importance that theory should be formed accordingly?

There is no more terrible torture for a thinker than to have to continue living under the strain of having details constantly uncovered, so that it always looks as though the thought is about to appear, the conclusion. If the natural scientist does not feel that torture he cannot be a thinker. Intellectually that is the most terrible tantalization! A thinker is, as it were, in hell until he has found spiritual certainty: *hic Rhodus, hic salta,* the sphere of faith where, even if the world broke to pieces and the elements melted, thou shalt nevertheless believe. There one cannot wait for the latest news, or till one's ship comes home. That spiritual certainty, the most humbling of all, the most painful to a vain spirit (for it is so superior to look through a microscope), is the only certainty.

The main objection, the whole objection to natural science may simply and formally be expressed thus, absolutely: it is incredible that a man who has thought infinitely about himself as a spirit could think of choosing natural science (with empirical material) as his life's work and aim. An observant scientist must *either* be a man of talent and instinct, for the characteristic of talent and instinct is not to be fundamentally dialectical, but only to dig up things and be brilliant—not to understand himself (and to be able to live on happily in that way, without feeling that anything is wrong because the deceptive variety of observations and discoveries continuously conceals the confusion of everything); *or* he must be a man who, from his earliest youth, half consciously, has become a scientist and continues out of habit to live in that way—the most frightful way of living: to fascinate and astonish the world by one's discoveries and brilliance, and not to understand oneself. It is self-evident that such a scientist is conscious, he is conscious within the limits of his talents, perhaps an astonishingly penetrating mind, the gift of combining things and an almost magical power of associating ideas, etc. But at the very most the relationship will be this: an eminent mind, unique in its gifts, explains the whole of nature—but does not understand itself. Spiritually he does not become transparent to himself in the moral appropriation of his gifts. But that relationship is scepticism, as may easily be seen (for scepticism means that an unknown, an X, explains everything. When everything is explained by an X which is not explained, then in the end nothing is explained at all). If that is not scepticism then it is superstition.

[202]

KLAGES, LUDWIG

KLAGES, LUDWIG (1872-   ). Between the two world wars, Klages was one of the most influential harbingers of German anti-intellectualism, and his latest utterances seem to indicate that, even after Germany's catastrophe, he is not prepared to recant. He has remained a rabid sympathizer with Nazism, although he preferred to live in democratic Switzerland and to admire the house Hitler built without moving in. But even after the end of World War II, Klages continued to express hostility toward democracy, Western civilization, reason and logic, while enjoying the indulgence of a democratic government.

649

In his youth, Klages was associated with the German poet Stefan George who, inspired by Baudelaire and Mallarmé, adhered to the theory of art for art's sake but declared that the cult of artistic form realized the highest ideals of human beings. Devoted to Roman Catholic traditionalism George and his circle detested the principal tendencies of 19th century civilization, especially positivism, naturalism, materialism and rationalism. From this position, Klages, after a period of graphological and character-ological studies, proceeded to extreme anti-intellectualism, denouncing thinking consciousness as a destroying force. In his principal work *Spirit, the Adversary of Soul*, Klages holds that body and soul form the natural unity of human existence in which spirit has invaded from outside in order to split this unity and in this way to kill the foundation of life. While the soul, directed by instincts, feelings and traditions, forms a sensually colorful world, spirit analyzes this world into abstract atoms, in order to subject nature to human will. This is condemned by Klages as sacrilege. While combating natural science as the main representative of the destructive spirit, Klages denies the value and right of any conscious and voluntary knowledge. Return to unconscious life is regarded by him as the way to salvation.

THE HYSTERICAL PERSON

THE typical hysterical person is incapable of not following his longing to represent; but that does not mean at all that he cannot control himself. If, for example, it is necessary to represent self-control, then he can endure with remarkable equanimity insults, mockery, degradations, and bodily torments of the severest kind. One thing only he can never repress—his desire to represent. For he has not a single substantial interest of real importance to oppose to this desire, and the rich store of energy at his disposal pours undivided and not to be dammed into this one craving. If one wanted to call him a mere actor, it would be necessary to add that he suffers from a passion to simulate passions, and that no genuine passion could be more irresistible, overpowering, and consistent (that is, like an impulse) than this. And if one wanted to call him thoroughly sophisticated, then it would have to be considered again that a permanent spice of intentionality does in fact flavor his every attitude, but in a different manner, and in one much harder to recognize than in a man who has ceased to be naive merely because he has inhibitions; for here the mask itself has become sovereign. He is not an actor so much as a man wearing a mask which has grown into his flesh; or rather, he carries behind the mask no living being but a clockwork, ready to follow the suggestions of the mask. In *Klein Zaches oder Zinnober,* Amadeus Hoffmann has prophetically dealt with the reflective nature which assimilates everything, and, by excelling makes it valueless; and, in the *Sandmann,* has given a fantastic treatment to the life-mimicking automaton.

The definite characteristic of the hysterical attitude is, that there is a relationship to the spectator. Those who must represent something, represent it for the benefit of a spectator; by choice a real stranger, if not an imaginary one, or as a last resource the spectator within himself. Accordingly no hysterical person is ever attentive to the matter in hand, and whatever he does or leaves undone is not done or left undone with a view to the effect, but is itself the effect by anticipation which itself suggests the idea of the goal from moment to moment; hence a change of surroundings may be accompanied by a change in behaviour of a kind which shows some points of similarity with that of a medium.

Here the type of hysterical exaltation is sharply distinguished from the vain man and from those who require to please or to win approval. The latter wish to appear superior in some respect, or to evoke affection or gain esteem; but the hysterical type wishes to excite attention either by creating amazement or admiration, or by challenging those other feelings, which are even more suitable for the purpose, of aversion, loathing, disgust, horror, indignation, contempt, and fury. It happens quite commonly that faults are invented, that a hysterical woman claims to have been raped, and a man to have raped, and even fictitious confessions of alleged murder have been known. The typically hysterical crime of Herostratus may here be recalled.

[203]

KOMENSKY, AMOS. See COMENIUS, JOHANN AMOS.

KREBS, NICHOLAS. See CUSA, NICHOLAS OF.

KROPOTKIN, PRINCE PETER

KROPOTKIN, PRINCE PETER (1842-1921). Administrative experience and Utopian vision became confused in the mind of Prince Kropotkin, the founder of communist, or, more precisely, communalist anarchism. For free communities are the political form which he thought social revolution should assume.

At the age of 19, Kropotkin, who had attended the Imperial Military School for Pages, became an officer of the Cossacks, and went with his regiment to Transbaikalia and Manchuria. In this capacity, he undertook numerous exploring expeditions and was also entrusted with administrative tasks. It was in this latter activity that he became imbued with animosity toward centralized government. Although he was decorated by the Tsar for his exploration and governmental services, Kropotkin became an ardent revolutionary. He professed socialist views, but was as opposed to the centralist systems of Saint-Simon and Marx as he was to centralist Tsarism. In 1874, Kropotkin was arrested by the Russian police because of his revolutionary activities. However, in 1876, he escaped to England. After a stay in Switzerland, he was expelled from that country at the request of the Tsarist police. In 1883 he was imprisoned in France, also at the instigation of the Russian police, but was released in 1886 at the personal order of President Jules Grévy. Thereafter he lived in England. Kropotkin made valuable contributions to geology, geography, chemistry, economics, sociology and history. Without systematic erudition, he proved to have vision in all fields of his scientific activities. He especially succeeded in elucidating important stages of the French Revolution in his book *The Great Revolution* (1909). His social system is explained in his book *Mutual Aid—A Factor in Evolution* (1902). The First World War isolated Kropotkin, who sided with the Western Allies against Germany and his anarchist followers. In 1917, he supported Kerensky against the Bolshevists.

ANARCHISM

ANARCHISM, the no-government system of socialism, has a double origin. It is an outgrowth of the two great movements of thought in the economic and the political fields which characterize the nineteenth century, and especially its second part. In common with all socialists, the anarchists hold that the private ownership of land, capital, and machinery has had its time; that it is condemned to disappear; and that all requisites for production must, and will, become the common property of society, and be managed in common by the producers of wealth. And in common with the most advanced representatives of political radicalism, they maintain that the ideal of the political organization of society is a condition of things where the functions of government are reduced to a minimum, and the individual recovers his full liberty of initiative and action for satisfying, by means of free groups and federations—freely constituted—all the infinitely varied needs of the human being.

As regards socialism, most of the anarchists arrive at its ultimate conclusion, that is, at a complete negation of the wage-system and at communism. And with reference to political organization, by giving a further development to the above-mentioned part of the radical program, they arrive at the conclusion that the ultimate aim of society is the reduction of the functions of government to *nil*—that is, to a society without government, to an-archy. The anarchists maintain, moreover, that such being the ideal of social and political organization, they must not remit it to future centuries, but that only those changes in our social organization which are in accordance with the above double ideal, and constitute an approach to it, will have a chance of life and be beneficial for the commonwealth.

As to the method followed by the anarchist thinker, it entirely differs from that followed by the utopists. The anarchist thinker does not resort to metaphysical conceptions (like "natural rights," the "duties of the State," and so on) to establish what are, in his opinion, the best conditions for realizing the greatest happiness of humanity. He follows, on the contrary, the course traced by the modern philosophy of evolution. He studies human society as it is now and was

653

in the past; and without either endowing humanity as a whole, or separate individuals, with superior qualities which they do not possess, he merely considers society as an aggregation of organisms trying to find out the best ways of combining the wants of the individual with those of cooperation for the welfare of the species. He studies society and tries to discover its *tendencies,* past and present, its growing needs, intellectual and economic, and in his ideal he merely points out in which direction evolution goes. He distinguishes between the real wants and tendencies of human aggregations and the accidents (want of knowledge, migrations, wars, conquests) which have prevented these tendencies from being satisfied. And he concludes that the two most prominent, although often unconscious, tendencies throughout our history have been: first, a tendency towards integrating labor for the production of all riches in common, so as finally to render it impossible to discriminate the part of the common production due to the separate individual; and second, a tendency towards the fullest freedom of the individual in the prosecution of all aims, beneficial both for himself and for society at large. The ideal of the anarchist is thus a mere summing-up of what he considers to be the next phase of evolution. It is no longer a matter of faith; it is a matter for scientific discussion.

[204]

KUNG FU TSE. See CONFUCIUS.

ℒ

LAIRD, JOHN

LAIRD, JOHN (1887-1946). Although in his early days, Laird was attached to the British movement of New Realism, he has since proceeded to metaphysical views. At first the problem of sensory perception was the center of his interests, and he rejected the subjective and phenomenalist theories of knowledge. In his books, *The Idea of Value* (1929) and *Knowledge, Belief, and Opinion* (1930), he dealt with the forms and motives of assent and valuation. Of special significance became his criticism of the subjectivist theory of value. Laird demonstrated that this theory is concerned with only one of several aspects of the value phenomenon, namely appreciation, which, however, has significance only through reference to objective values and even presupposes for its existence a class of valuing—namely, choosing within the cosmos. Laird holds, in agreement with Alfred Whitehead and Samuel Alexander, that value is to be read in the constituents of the universe. Turning to the philosophy of religion, Laird published, in 1942, *Theism and Cosmology*.

DEISM AND THEISM

CERTAINLY it may be argued that a creative God, in the more usual sense of creation, is volitional as well as intelligent, that mere intelligence may be as much of an abstraction and as little of a concrete reality in heaven as it is on earth, and that there would be a shocking lack of intelligence if an orderly world were created for any other purpose than the bringing of beauty or of moral excellence or of some other great value into existence. If so, it might very justly be inferred that the philosophy of a bolder and more opulent theism is more readily defensible than the precarious because over-cautious doctrines of a spare, unadventurous deism.

655

From this point of view the appearance of anthropomorphism may be simply another way of saying that man, in the finer part of him, is made in God's image and a little lower than the angels, or, more modestly, that God is less inadequately portrayed when he is represented as akin to man's nobler attributes than when all such resemblance is denied. Anthropomorphism itself, some would say, is defensible, and theism is the stronger for employing such conceptions.

However that may be, it is preposterous to assert either that mere deism is the sum of "natural" theology, or that there can be no philosophical grounds for a theism that exceeds mere deism. My plea for the recognition of deism in natural theology is not conceived in any such spirit, and I am anxious to say that it is not. On the other hand, the deist's caution, even if it is mistaken, should not be summarily condemned. His reluctance to wander blithely and almost carelessly on the resilient turf of familiar Christian apologetics is reasoned and may not be unreasonable. Deists may be illiberal and short-sighted in their views, and their opponents may be better cosmologists than they are; but even a narrow cosmology may be better than a perfunctory cosmology. If cosmology is an embarrassment to theism, such a theism is self-condemned.

Deism, to be brief, is a species of philosophical theism. It is a cosmological theory of the origin and stability of the universe, conceived upon principles that philosophical theism may rightly decide to incorporate. It is bad policy on the part of a theist to neglect what deists assert through distaste for what more deists deny. If deists draw their boundaries in the wrong places, their mistake, as regards the philosophy of it, has to be shown by philosophical argument to be a mistake. It has also to be shown that there are no similar boundaries in any other place for example, regarding God's "personality"; and the notion that there are such boundaries, to certain apologists, is an idea almost as distasteful as mere deism itself. Frontiers are obscured but not removed by raising a dust in their neighborhood.

[205]

LALANDE, ANDRÉ

LALANDE, ANDRÉ (1867-   ). One of the most comforting auguries of the spiritual recovery of France from the collapse of 1940
is the appearance of the fifth edition of Lalande's *Vocabulaire
Technique et Critique de la Philosophie* in 1947, a work of immense knowledge and acuteness, and universally hailed by historians of philosophy of all nations to whom it renders invaluable
services. Aided by an imposing array of French philosophers,
in this book, Lalande has given not the definitions of terms which
he himself considers adequate, but those which are used by various
philosophers from ancient times to the present day, and to these
semantics he has added a restrained critique of the philosophical
use of language.

Lalande's own philosophy, of course, is more disputable. He
revolts against favorite ideas, especially against monistic evolutionism. According to Lalande, two laws rule over the world.
The one, evolution, is dominant in biology, the other, involution,
a term nearly identical with entropy, in the physico-chemical world.
Life, as it can be observed, results from a compromise between two
antagonistic tendencies of which the one is directed toward increasing individual differences, and the other toward eliminating
them. Man's will must choose between these two tendencies. He is
bound to decide because Lalande denies that the vital impetus is
a reliable guide for the organization of human life. Opposed to
Spencer and critical of Bergson, Lalande adheres to a moral rationalism.

Lalande's principal work *Les Illusions Évolutionistes* was published, in its definitive form, in 1931.

INVOLUTION

SCIENCE is not "a development of the Homogeneous toward
the Heterogeneous," like the increase of species, but it is
a free assimilation of one mind to another, of one thing to
another, of the things to the minds. That is rather easily
recognized. But social progress, if observed without prejudice, becomes manifest not so much as an equilibrium organized by individual ambitions as rather as an *involution*.
That, above all, must penetrate to-day into common sense.
It must be inculcated as deeply as the contrary prejudice

has been inculcated. Practically, an improvement has taken place and continues to proceed through the lowering and even the extinction of the organic structures whereto social life at first had evolved spontaneously. The dissolution of the rule of caste and slavery, whose meticulous social differentiation was by heredity, has given room to aristocratic societies which were already less biomorphical but still neighboring, by virtue of their "states," to the organic structure of the living bodies and the societies of the animals; then these aristocratic societies have been dissolved almost everywhere into egalitarian states which appeal to an ideal of assimilation among their citizens. At the same time it has become evident that these egalitarian states are less warlike than the monarchies, dictatorships and oligarchies.

It might be objected that this great *involution* does not exclude inverse movements. Industrial, commercial, financial struggles are too clear examples of that fact. But when vast transformations of the entire status are at stake, there is no progress that is not accompanied by return-currents and reactionary turns. Who is the philosophical mind that would consider mercantilism a progress of civilization, or be happy that an oligarchy of money was established upon the ruins of an aristocracy of birth?

At the same time, the progress of civilization has universalized the principles and formulas of the law. There will be noticed also an assimilation of singular rapidity between the social functions of men and those of women, and a retrogression of the old forms of the family which had been organically differentiated. . . .

The essential task of science in our epoch is to make human masses understand that the *imago mundi* that led the first years of the 19th century back in the direction of barbary, has not been confirmed by an impartial and scientific reflection. . . . Without any doubt, the individual cannot live without conceding a minimum of satisfaction to its egoistical needs, and it is the same with the nations and social groups. But that is a concession and not an ideal.
[206]

LAMARCK, JEAN

LAMARCK, JEAN (1744-1829). The modern theory, called La-
marckism, according to which acquired properties of an organism
can become hereditary, has little connection with the thoughts of
Jean Lamarck who disregarded the phenomenon of heredity. But
he was one of the first scientists to transform the static conception
of the universe into an evolutionist one, and was a precursor of
modern theories of environment. In doing so, he experienced the
truth of Voltaire's saying that it is dangerous to be right while
all contemporary authorities are wrong. Cuvier's opposition to and
Comte's severe criticism of Lamarck's statements diverted the attention of the scientists from his work for more than one generation. Even Charles Darwin, generally reserved in the expression
of his opinion, found in Lamarck's works nothing but "nonsense,"
"rubbish" or, at best, "uselessness."

During his whole life, Lamarck, the descendant of an impov-
erished noble family, was a poor man, and in his last years he lost
the modest sum he had saved for his children. His temper revolted
against the ecclesiastical life to which he was dedicated in his
boyhood. At the age of seventeen he entered the French Army. Dis-
charged, after five years of service he became a clerk in a banking
house, in order to earn the money he needed to study medicine.
Having attained this end, he concentrated upon observing insects
and worms, and then proceeded to the investigation of the laws
which govern organic and inorganic bodies. In 1776, he wrote
Recherches sur les Causes des Principaux Faits Physiques, which
he could publish only in 1794, and then, as a sincere adherent
of the Jacobins, dedicated to the French people while the government of terror was at its height. In 1795, his *Système de la Nature*
appeared and, in 1809, his *Philosophie Zoologique.* Lamarck remained a republican under Napoleon and the restored Bourbons.

Lamarck took great care to distinguish between nature and
the Supreme Being, and between nature and the physical universe
which he regarded as an inactive and powerless mass of substances.
To him, the study of nature is the study of motion, and nature a
system of laws which rule over life. The motions which are peculiar
to beings endowed with life are clearly distinguished from the
physical motions. Life is marked by irritability and the faculty to
react to the challenge of influences from without. It is this faculty
which develops the nervous system. Changes of circumstances cause
changes of both needs and faculties. The lower forms of life are

moulded by environment. Higher forms, by virtue of their nervous system, tend to modify their environment by active urge or desire. The interaction of urge and environment produces new characters which either become permanent or perish, according to their respective capability of subsisting.

Lamarck combined sober observation with vivid imagination, which enabled him to behold ideal structures and the real characteristics of organic life.

UNDEVELOPED KNOWLEDGE

ONLY a vast and inconceivable man of genius could brace himself to the contemplation of the principal facts of the universe, and comprehend the extents, densities, distances and motions of the stars which seem to be its large and principal parts. Only a man of genius could embrace at one stretch the vast totality of all existing things. It seems to me, however, that man has to meet with no lesser difficulties when he tries to reduce the particular facts, witnessed daily by him, to their real causes. This is especially the case when he observes his immediate environment.

Our knowledge of the qualities of matter, of the nature of elements and their real properties, of their mutual relations, of the modifications of which several of them are susceptible, and of the real state of the compounds we observe in nature, is still, I think, mostly uncertain.

But of all the knowledge man tries to acquire, the possession of physical and chemical knowledge is most important because of the necessary connection of man's physical existence with all things that surround him or are needed by him. Now it seems that the great discoveries which are apparently outside the range of human mind, are just those by which human science distinguishes itself most, since we have made inconceivable progress in celestial physics, while there are still confused and poorly systematized ideas on the nature and properties of fire, air, etc., prevalent. Most of these ideas are incompatible with the facts which are to be explained. Just as man has surpassed himself by obtaining knowledge of sublime things, just so he seems to be inferior to himself in as far as mostly obscure and disparate hypotheses have been advanced to explain the particular phenomena which Man's environment constantly presents to his eyes.

[207]

LAMB, CHARLES

LAMB, CHARLES (1775-1834). The *Essays of Elia* (1823), one of the most popular books in English literature, is a kind of autobiography of its author, Charles Lamb, who was a clerk in the East India House, a very sociable man, loved by his friends, and a master of conversation. According to Hazlitt, Lamb "always made the best pun and the best remark in the course of the evening." He was capable of imparting the charm of his conversation to written words. But he never mentioned the misfortune of his life. Lamb never married because he had been insane for six weeks, and, until his death, he guarded with loving care his sister Mary who, in a fit of insanity, had killed her own mother.

MORALITY

NOT childhood alone, but the young man till thirty, never feels practically that he is mortal. He knows it indeed, and, if need were, he could preach a homily on the fragility of life; but he brings it not home to himself, any more than in a hot June we can appropriate to our imagination the freezing days of December. But now, shall I confess a truth?—I feel these audits but too powerfully. I begin to count the probabilities of my duration, and to grudge at the expenditure of moments and shortest periods, like misers' farthings. In proportion as the years both lessen and shorten, I set more count upon their periods, and would fain lay my ineffectual finger upon the spoke of the great wheel. I am not not content to pass away "like a weaver's shuttle." Those metaphors solace me not, nor sweeten the unpalatable draught of mortality. I care not to be carried with the tide, that smoothly bears human life to eternity; and reluct at the inevitable course of destiny. I am in love with this green earth; the face of town and country, the unspeakable rural solitudes, and the sweet security of streets.

[208]

LAMENNAIS, ROBERT FÉLICITÉ DE

LAMENNAIS, ROBERT FÉLICITÉ DE (1782-1854). Although Lamennais radically changed his religious and political standpoint at least three times and cursed what he had adored in the preceding period of his life, his mind preserved, despite all shifts, traits of imposing constancy. Lamennais was a keen metaphysician and, at the same time, a passionate sociologist, a thinker whom Schelling, after a long discussion with him, called "the greatest dialectician of the epoch," and an enthusiast whose imagination evidenced dramatic tension and power.

In his early youth, Lamennais, like his father who was a corsair and a descendant of corsairs, was an ardent supporter of the left wing of the French Revolution. In 1804 he abjured all revolutionary ideas and subsequently became a Catholic priest. His *Essai sur l'indifférence en matière de religion* (1817), translated into English, German, Italian and Spanish, maintains that religion is the fundamental principle of human action. Society, therefore, cannot be indifferent to religious doctrines, and must crush atheists, deists and heretics. In 1824, Lamennais reached the zenith of his ultramontanism, displaying more papal-mindedness than the Pope himself, as well as extreme royalism. But, in 1829, he advocated separation of Church and State, admonished the Church to sever its cause from that of the kings, and advocated the alliance between the Catholic Church and democracy, while maintaining the principle of the spiritual leadership of the Pope. Severely rebuked by the Pope, Lamennais, in 1834, published his *Paroles d'un Croyant* (Words of a Believer) of which more than 100,000 copies were sold within a few weeks. He returned to the deism of his youth, and became the herald of "spiritual democracy" and radical republicanism, yet always protesting that without faith in God, human rights and duties must collapse and no civil loyalty can persist.

Lamennais was one of the founders of the Second French Republic, the initiator of Catholic liberalism and Christian socialism.

JUSTICE AND LIBERTY

HE who asketh himself how much justice is worth profaneth

662

justice in his heart; and he who stops to calculate what liberty will cost hath renounced liberty in his heart. Liberty and justice will weigh you in the same balance in which you have weighed them. Learn, then, to know their value.

There have been nations who have not known that value, and never misery equalled theirs.

If there be upon earth anything truly great, it is the resolute firmness of a people who march on, under the eye of God, to the conquest of those rights which they hold from Him, without flagging for a moment; who think not of their wounds, their days of toil and sleepness nights, and say, "What are all these? Justice and liberty are well worthy of severer labors." Such a people may be tried by misfortunes, by reverses, by treachery; nay, may even be sold by some Judas: but let nothing discourage them. For in truth I say unto you that when, like the Saviour of the world, they shall go down into the tomb, like Him they shall come forth again, conquerors over death, and over the prince of this world and his servants.

The laborer beareth the burden of the day, exposed to the rain and sun and winds, that he may by his labor prepare that harvest which shall enrich his granaries in autumn.

Justice is the harvest of nations.

The workman rises before the dawn, he lights his little lamp, and endures ceaseless fatigue, that he may gain a little bread with which to feed himself and his children.

Justice is the bread of nations.

The merchant shrinks from no labor, complains of no trouble, exhausts his body, and forgets repose, that he may amass wealth.

Liberty is the wealth of nations.

The mariner traverses seas, trusts himself to wave and tempest, risks his body amid the rocks, and endures heat and cold, that he may secure repose in his old age.

Liberty is the repose of nations.

The soldier submits to many hard privations, he watches, fights, and sheds his blood, for what he calls glory.

Liberty is the glory of nations.

If there be on earth a people who think less of justice and liberty than the laborer does of his harvest, or the workman of his daily bread, or the merchant of his wealth, or the mariner of his repose, or the soldier of his glory:— build around that people a high wall, that their breath may not infect the rest of the world.

When the great day of judgment for nations shall come, it will be said to that people, "What hast thou done with thy soul? There is neither sign nor trace of it to be seen. The enjoyments of the brute have been everything to thee. Thou hast loved the mire—go, wallow in the mire."

And that people who, rising above mere material good, have placed their affections on the true good; who, to obtain that true good, have spared no labor, no fatigue, no sacrifice, shall hear this word: "For those who have a soul, there is the recompense of souls. Because thou hast loved justice and liberty before all things, come and possess forever liberty and justice."

[209]

LAMETTRIE, JULIEN OFFRAY DE

LAMETTRIE, JULIEN OFFRAY DE (1709-1751). This "scapegoat of 18th century materialism," as Friedrich Albert Lange rightly called him, has been blamed and despised by many who had not read a single page of his books. Lamettrie was a physician in the French army. In this capacity he entered into conflict first with medical routine, then with his superiors, and, finally, the government. He was dismissed, and emigrated to Holland. In his books *L' homme machine* and *L'homme plante* (1748), Lamettrie demonstrated by comparative methods the relationship between man and other living beings, and proceeded to a theory of the evolution of organisms. He stated that psychical life is observable already on the lowest level of the evolution. Investigating the functions of the brain, Lamettrie tried to discern various stages of its formation which are of primary importance in the development of mental life. Also, he protested against an evaluation of the moral character of men which depends on the acceptance of religious doctrines. Al-

hough Lamettrie was decried as a crude materialist, he also influenced idealist philosophers. To him Goethe owes the inspiration
for his botanical ideas.

FOOD AND TEMPER

THE human body is a machine that winds up its own springs:
it is a living image of the perpetual motion. Food nourishes
what a fever heats and excites. Without proper food the
soul languishes, raves, and dies with faintness. It is like a
taper, which revives in the moment it is going to be extinguished. Give but good nourishment to the body, pour into
its tubes vigorous juices and strong liquors; then the soul,
generous as these, arms itself with courage; and a soldier,
whom water would have made run away, becoming undaunted, meets death with alacrity amidst the rattle of
drums. Thus it is that hot water agitates the blood, which
cold had calmed.

What a vast power there is in a repast! Joy revives
in a disconsolate heart; it is transfused into the souls of all
the guests, who express it by amiable conversation, or music.
The hypochondriac mortal is overpowered with it; and the
lumpish pedant is unfit for the entertainment.

Raw meat gives a fierceness to animals; and man would
also become fierce by the same nourishment. This is so true
that the English, who eat not their meat so well roasted or
boiled as we, but red and bloody, seem to partake of this
fierceness more or less, which arises in part from such food,
and from other causes, which nothing but education can
render ineffectual. This fierceness produces in the soul pride,
hatred, contempt of other nations, indocility, and other bad
qualities that deprave man's character, just as gross phleg-
matic meat causes a heavy, cloudy spirit, whose favorite attributes are idleness and indolence.

* * *

There was, in Switzerland, a magistrate called Mon-
sieur Steiguer, of Wittighofen: this gentleman was, when

fasting, the most upright and merciful judge; but woe to the wretch who came before him when he had made a hearty dinner! He was then disposed to hang everybody, the innocent as well as the guilty.

We think not, nay, we are not honest men, but as we are cheerful, or brave; all depends on the manner of winding up our machine. A person would be tempted to think, at certain times that the soul is lodged in the stomach, and that Van Helmont in placing it in the pylorus is not deceived but by taking a part for the whole.

To what rage and extravagance cannot hunger drive us? No longer is there any respect shown to the bowels, to which we owe, or to which we have given, life. They are torn and devoured in a detestable feast; and in the madness that seizeth us, the weakest are always sure to fall a prey to the strongest.

[210]

LANGE, FRIEDRICH ALBERT

LANGE, FRIEDRICH ALBERT (1828-1875). Germany has produced very few philosophers who are as lucid, judicious and sincere as Lange, whose *History of Materialism* (1866) has maintained its value as a standard work and an example of philosophical historiography despite the change of time and the increase of knowledge. Lange, a leader of Neo-Kantianism, demonstrated materialism but, on the other hand, he taught us to appreciate the materialistic philosophers whose independence of idealistic traditions has often obtained sound results and has been directed by true critical insight. Above all, Lange destroyed the not uncommon prejudice that the adoption of idealistic views on metaphysics would guarantee higher moral standards than could be achieved by the conduct of life of those who professed materialism in metaphysics.

Before Lange published his history of materialism, his book *Die Arbeiterfrage* (The Workers' Question, 1865) created quite a stir in German social politics. Lange, a professor at the University of Marburg, energetically defended the interests of the workers and their political and economic demands, and he was eager to improve their educational and cultural conditions. He often debated with the earliest leaders of German socialism, and quite as often supported

hem, speaking at meetings arranged by them. Lange honestly tried
o ally German democrats and socialists. His premature death was
nourned by intellectuals and workers alike.

REALITY AND THE IDEAL WORLD

ONE thing is certain, that man needs to supplement reality
by an ideal world of his own creation, and that the highest
and noblest functions of his mind cooperate in such creations. But must this act of intellectual freedom always keep
on assuming the deceptive form of a demonstrative science?
In that case materialism, too, will always reappear, and will
destroy the bolder speculations with an attempt to satisfy
the instinct of the reason towards unity by a minimum of exaltation above the real and demonstrable.

We may not doubt of another solution of the problem,
especially in Germany, since we have in the philosophical
poems of Schiller a performance which unites with the
noblest vigor of thought the highest elevation above reality,
and which lends to the ideal an overpowering force by removing it openly and unhesitatingly into the realm of fan-
tasy. This must not be taken to mean that all speculation
must also assume the form of poetry. Schiller's philosophical
poems are more than mere products of the speculative instinct. They are emanations of a truly religious elevation of
the soul to the pure and troubled sources of all that man has
ever worshipped as divine and supermundane. May metaphysics ever continue its efforts towards the solution of its
insoluble problem! The more it continues theoretical, and
tries to compete in certainty with sciences of reality, all the
less will it succeed in obtaining general importance. The
more, on the other hand, it brings the world of existence
into connection with the world of values, and tries to raise
itself by its apprehension of phenomena to an ethical influence, the more will it make form predominate over matter,
and, without doing violence to the facts, will erect in the
architecture of its ideas a temple of worship to the eternal
and divine. Free poetry, however, may entirely leave the

ground of reality and make use of myth in order to lend words to the unutterable.

Here then we stand too before an entirely satisfactory solution of the question as to the immediate and more distant future of religion. There are only two ways which can permanently call for serious consideration, after it has been shown that mere rationalism loses itself in the sands of superficiality, without ever freeing itself from untenable dogmas. The one way is the complete suppression and abolition of all religions, and the transference of their functions to the state, science, and art; the other is to penetrate to the core of religion, and to overcome all fanaticism and superstition by conscious elevation above reality and definitive renunciation of the falsification of reality by myths, which, of course, can render no service to knowledge.

The first of these ways involves the danger of spiritual impoverishment; the second has to deal with the great question whether, at this very time, the core of religion is not undergoing a change which makes it difficult to apprehend it with certainty. But the second difficulty is the lesser one, because the very principle of the spiritualization of religion must facilitate and lend a more harmonious form to every transition rendered necessary by the intellectual requirements of a progressive age.   [211]

LAOTSE (Lao Tsu)

LAOTSE (LAO TSU) (About the 4th Century B.C.). The traditional assumption that Laotse was a contemporary of Confucius, and, as the author of the book *Tao Te Ching* (Teaching on the Power of the Way), the founder of Taoism, has been disproved by recent scholars. In all probability, the spiritual movement, later called Taoism, started long before the book *Tao* was written, and that book must be considered not so much the creation, as rather a condensation of already current Taoist ideas. It has been said that Lao was a custodian of documents and a priest-teacher. He has been worshipped since the third century A. D.

Tao, the Way, means the cosmic order of Nature that cannot be grasped by human intellects or expressed in words, according

668

to Taoism and contrary to the Confucian meaning of Tao that concerns guidance of moral conduct of life. Taoism is a doctrine of a reality which is different from the world perceptible by the senses. In many regards it is similar to the reality assumed by Plato, and even more so to the Hindu distinction between the world of appearances and true existence. In its later development, Taoism became mixed with ideas of various origin, but it has remained a mystical faith in the unity of Pure Being.

TAO TE CHING

IF the Tao could be comprised in words, it would not be the unchangeable Tao:
(For) if a name may be named, it is not an unchangeable name.
When the Tao had no name, that was the starting-point of heaven and earth:
Then when it had a name, this was 'mother of all creation.'
Because all this is so, to be constantly without desire is the way to have a vision of the mystery (of heaven and earth):
For constantly to have desire is the means by which their limitations are seen.
These two entities although they have different names emerged together;
And (emerging) together means 'in the very beginning.'
But the very beginning has also a beginning before it began—
This door into all mystery!

*   *   *

The whole world knows that beauty is beauty: and this is (to know) ugliness.
Every one knows that goodness is goodness; and this is (to know) what is not good.
Thus it is: existence and nonexistence give birth to each other:
The hard and the easy complete each other:
The long and the short are comparatively so:
The high and the less high are so by testing:
The orchestra and the choir make a harmony:
And the earlier and the later follow on each other.

And puts into practice wordless teaching.
Since all things have been made, he does not turn his back.
This is why the sage abides by actionless activity,
    on them:
Since they have life, he does not own them:
Since they act, he does not entrust himself to them.
When he has achieved any success, he does not stay by it.
In this not saying by his success he is unique;
And this is why he is not deprived of it.

*   *   *

Let there be no putting of the best people into office:
this will stop vicious rivalry among the people. Let there
be no prizing of rare merchandise; this will stop robbing
among the people. Let nothing desirable be visible; this
will save the people's minds from (moral) confusion.
This is why the sage's form of government
Empties the people's minds and fills their stomachs,
Weakens their ambitions and strengthens their bones,
Unfailingly makes the ordinary man ignorant and passion-
    less,
The wise man afraid to take action.
(For,) if action is actionless, there is nothing not under
    control.

*   *   *

The Tao is hollow: use it and there is no overflowing.
How fathomless it is! It makes one think of a common
    ancestor to all creatures,
One who blunts their cutting edges, unties their knots,
Makes a harmony of the lights (in the heavens) and lays the
    dust (of this grimy world).
How limpid it is, as if it would stay so for ever!
And yet we do not know whose son (this common ancestor
    could be),
This image of something before the High God!

*   *   *

Heaven and earth are not human-hearted: for them all
   creatures are but straw dogs.
A sage also is not human-hearted: for him also the hundred
   clans are but straw dogs.
Here is this space between heaven and earth, a bellows as
   it were,
Which is empty but does not buckle up, which the more it
   is worked the more it gives forth.
But, however many words are used, the number comes to an
   end.
It is better (to say nothing and) to hold fast to the mean
   (between too much and too little confidence in heaven and
   earth).

*   *   *

The spirit [divine significance?] of a valley is to be undying.
It is what is called 'the Original Female,'
And the Doorway of the Original Female is called 'the root
   from which heaven and earth sprang.'
On, on goes this spirit for ever, functioning without any
   special effort.

*   *   *

The heavens continue, and the earth endures;
And that in them which makes them so permanent
Is that they do not live for themselves.
Thus it is that they can live so long.
This is why a sage puts himself second and then (finds)
   himself in the forefront;
Puts himself outside (of things and events) and survives in
   them.
Surely it is because he has no personal desires that he is
   able to fulfil his desires.

*   *   *

The higher form of goodness is like water;
For water has the skill of profiting all creatures
Without striving with them.

It puts itself in the (lowly) place which everybody hates.
So near the Tao is it.
The goodness of houses consists in their being on the ground:
The goodness of men's minds consists in their being profound:
The goodness of companionship consists in human-heartedness:
The goodness of speech consists in its being reliable:
The goodness of government consists in bringing good order:
The goodness of any business consists in its being efficiently done:
The goodness of any movement consists in its being timely.
Only in all this there must be no striving,
For thus only can nothing go wrong.

*   *   *

To set out deliberately to be full to the brim [i.e. satisfy every desire] is not so good as (to know when) to stop.
If you are thorough in sharpening (a sword), you cannot preserve its edge for long.
If you fill your hall with gold and jade, there is no way by which you can guard it.
If you are rich and of exalted station, you become proud, and thus abandon yourself to unavoidable ruin.
When everything goes well, put yourself in the background:
That is the way Heaven acts.
Are you able, as you carry on with the restless physical soul, to embrace the oneness (of the universe) without ever losing hold?
Are you able as you control your breathing and make it more and more gentle, to become an (unself-conscious) babe?
Are you able, as you cleanse the Mysterious Mirror, to leave no traces of self-consciousness?
Are you able to love the people and rule a state, without being known to men?
Are you able, whether Heaven's Door is open or closed, to be the (passive, receptive) Female?

Are you able to have a right understanding of all creatures
   and never interfere?
Give life to them and nourish them;
(For) to give life but not to own, to make but not depend on,
To be chief amongst but not to order about,
This is what is meant by 'the Dark Power' (of unconscious
   influence).

*   *   *

Thirty spokes together make one wheel;
And they fit into 'nothing' (at the centre):
Herein lies the usefulness of a carriage.
The clay is moulded to make a pot;
And the clay fits round 'nothing':
Herein lies the usefulness of the pot.
Doors and windows are pierced in the walls of a house,
And they fit round 'nothing':
Herein lies the usefulness of the house.
Thus it is that, while it must be taken to be advantageous
   to have something there,
It must also be taken as useful to have 'nothing' there.

*   *   *

The men who set out to capture all under heaven and make
   it their own, according to my observation do not succeed.
What is under heaven is a sacred vessel,
Not to be treated in such fashion,
And those who do so bring it to ruin.
Those who hold on to it, lose it.
The truth is that some creatures go before and others follow
   behind,
Some breathe one way, and others breathe another,
Some feel strong, and others feel weak,
Some like constructing and others like destroying.
This is why the sage has nothing to do with the excessive,
   the extravagant, or with being exalted.

*   *   *

The man who uses the Tao in the service of an autocrat
Does not war down the states by force of arms.
His business is to long for the return (to peace and inaction);
For where soldiers are, there thorns and brambles grow:
After the passing of a great army,
The harvest is sure to be bad.
A really able commander stops when he has some success:
He dare not exploit his command of force.
Having some success he must not be elated:
Yes, having some success, he must not boast:
Yes, having some success, he must not become ungovernably
    proud.
That success may have been an unavoidable step,
But the (real) success must not be one of force;
For the weakness of old age accompanies the vigor of youth.
The explanation is this: force is not of the Tao;
And what is not of the Tao quickly perishes.

*   *   *

Tao is eternal, but has no fame (name);
The Uncarved Block, though seemingly of small account,
Is greater than anything that is under heaven.
If kings and barons would but possess themselves of it,
The ten thousand creatures would flock to do them homage.
Heaven-and-earth would conspire.
To send Sweet Dew,
Without law or compulsion, men would dwell in harmony.
Once the block is carved, there will be names,
And so soon as there are names
Know that it is time to stop.
Only by knowing when it is time to stop can danger be
    avoided.
To Tao all under heaven will come
As streams and torrents flow into a great river or sea.

*   *   *

To know men is to be wise:

674

To know one's self is to be illumined.
To conquer men is to have strength:
To conquer one's self is to be stronger still,
And to know when you have enough is to be rich:
For vigorous action may bring a man what he is determined
  to have,
But to keep one's place (in the order of the universe) is to
  endure;
And to die and not be lost, this is the real blessing of long
  life.

*   *   *

The Supreme Tao, how it floods in every direction!
This way and that, there is no place where it may not go.
All things look to it for life, and it refuses none of them:
(Yet) when it has done its work, it has no fame to be its
  distinctive clothing.
(For) while it nourishes all things, it does not lord it over
  them.
Since unfailingly it has no wants toward them,
It may be classed among things of low estate:
Since all things belong to it, but it does not lord it over
  them,
It may be named the Supreme:
But—to say the last word—it does not arrogate supremacy
to itself,
And thus it is that it fulfils its supremacy.

*   *   *

If you grasp the Supreme Symbol (of nothingness) and go
  all over the country,
There will be no harm (to any one) in your going.
Indeed, the peace and quiet will be beyond bounds:
Music and cake and ale,
And the passing stranger (made to) stop.
(Yet) the words from the mouth of the Tao, how insipid
  they are!

There is no taste to them at all.
Look for the Tao, and it is not enough to be seen,
Listen for the Tao, and it is not enough to be heard.
(Ah, but) use the Tao and it is not enough to come to a stop.

*   *   *

The high exponent of power in personality is without power
   [i.e. power personal to him]; and this is why he has
   (real) power in personality.
The inferior exponent is (set on) not losing his power; and
   this is why he has no (real) power in personality.
The high exponent taking no action has no ulterior ends,
Whilst the inferior exponent has ulterior ends to his activity.
(Thus) the high exponent of human-heartedness has no
   ulterior ends to his activity,
Whilst the high exponent of justice has.
(Thus) the high exponent of ritual [i.e. social and religious
   conventions], when he acts and fails to get the due
   response,
Bares his arm and uses force.
Thus it is that when the Tao is lost, there is personal power,
When that is lost, there is human-heartedness;
And when that is lost, there is justice;
And when that is lost, there are the conventions of ritual.
In relation to sincerity of heart and speech, ritual only goes
   skin-deep, and is thus the starting-point of moral anarchy;
And foreknowledge of events to come is but a pretentious
   display of the Tao, and is thus the door to benightedness.
This is why the really grown man concentrates on the core
   of things and not the husk,
And thus it is that he rejects 'the That' and lays hold of 'the
   This.'

*   *   *

The most yielding thing [the Tao?] in our world of experience can master the most immovable:
Since it is 'nothing' [i.e. immaterial], it can penetrate 'no
   space' [i.e. the material].

Hence we know that inaction is the profitable course.
(Yet) the truths which cannot be compassed in words,
And the profit which comes from inaction,
These men rarely grasp.

*   *   *

Not to go out of the house is to know the world of men,
Not to look out of the window is to know the ways of the
    heavens;
For the further a man travels,
The less he knows.
This is how the sage knows without going anywhere,
Can name things without seeing them,
Can bring them to completion without doing anything (to
    them).

[212]

LA ROCHEFOUCAULD, FRANÇOIS VI DUC DE

(Prince De Marsillac)

LA ROCHEFOUCAULD, FRANÇOIS VI DUC DE (PRINCE DE
MARSILLAC) (1613-1680). The almighty Cardinal Richelieu and
his successor, the no less powerful Cardinal Mazarin, were defied by
the Duke of La Rochefoucauld who, descending from a family as
noble and as old as the Plantagenets, treated the statesmen—virtually
absolute rulers over France—as snobs. Fearless on the military and
political battlefield, La Rochefoucauld lacked and detested brutal-
ity. He was a brilliant soldier, but no warrior. Twice exiled because
of his frankness, La Rochefoucauld was more inclined to observation and meditation, and thinking gave him solace for his experiences without mellowing his impressions. His sentiments were
benevolent but his eyes and ears were inexorable. He called himself
an Epicurean and a sceptic. In fact, La Rochefoucauld, a *grand-
seigneur* of the highest rank in the French kingdom, was melan-
cholic. What he had experienced and observed he condensed with
admirable artistic skill in his Maxims (1665). He had seen the
triumph of intrigues, the victory of meanness over generosity, and
he had penetrated into the secrets of statesmen and kings, of court-
cabals and political plotters. He had participated in foreign and

677

civil wars, and felt himself defeated and disappointed. From all these occurrences he drew the conclusion that egoism is the rule of human actions. His feelings were in constant revolt against this knowledge of his comprehensive mind. The *Maxims* scandalized the society of his time but were eagerly read and translated into many languages, and their resigned wisdom continues to attract philosophers and laymen in France and elsewhere, despite all cultural changes.

REFLECTIONS

WHAT we term virtue is often but a mass of various actions and divers interests, which fortune, or our own industry, manage to arrange; and it is not always from valor or from chastity that men are brave, and women chaste.

Self-love is the greatest of flatterers.

Passion often renders the most clever man a fool, and even sometimes renders the most foolish man clever.

Great and striking actions which dazzle the eyes are represented by politicians as the effect of great designs, instead of which they are commonly caused by the temper and the passions. Thus the war between Augustus and Antony, which is set down to the ambition they entertained of making themselves masters of the world, was probably but an effect of jealousy.

Passions often produce their contraries: avarice sometimes leads to prodigality, and prodigality to avarice; we are often obstinate through weakness and daring through timidity.

Whatever care we take to conceal our passions under the appearances of piety and honor, they are always to be seen through these veils.

The clemency of princes is often but policy to win the affections of the people.

This clemency, of which they make a merit, arises oftentimes from vanity, sometimes from idleness, oftentimes from fear, and almost always from all three combined.

We have all sufficient strength to support the misfortunes of others.

The constancy of the wise is only the talent of concealing the agitation of their hearts.

Those who are condemned to death affect sometimes a constancy and contempt for death which is only the fear of facing it; so that one may say that this constancy and contempt are to their mind what the bandage is to their eyes.

Few people know death, we only endure it, usually from determination, and even from stupidity and custom; and most men only die because they know not how to prevent dying.

We need greater virtues to sustain good than evil fortune.

Neither the sun nor death can be looked at without winking.

People are often vain of their passions, even of the worst, but envy is a passion so timid and shame-faced that no one ever dare avow her.

The evil that we do does not attract to us so much persecution and hatred as our good qualities.

Jealousy lives upon doubt; and comes to an end or becomes a fury as soon as it passes from doubt to certainty.

It would seem that nature, which has so wisely ordered the organs of our body for our happiness, has also given us pride to spare us the mortification of knowing our imperfections.

Those who apply themselves too closely to little things often become incapable of great things.

A man often believes himself leader when he is led; as his mind endeavors to reach one goal, his heart insensibly drags him towards another.

Whatever difference there appears in our fortunes, there is nevertheless a certain comprehension of good and evil which renders them equal.

The contempt of riches in philosophers was only a hidden desire to avenge their merit upon the injustice of fortune, by despising the very goods of which fortune had deprived them; it was a secret to guard themselves against the degradation of poverty, it was a back way by which to arrive at that distinction which they could not gain by riches.

To establish ourselves in the world we do everything to appear as if we were established.

Although men flatter themselves with their great actions, they are not so often the result of a great design as of chance.

Happiness is in the taste, and not in the things themselves; we are happy from possessing what we like, not from possessing what others like.

We are never so happy or so unhappy as we suppose.

[213]

LASSALLE, FERDINAND

LASSALLE, FERDINAND (1825-1864). It was one of the many paradoxes in Ferdinand Lassalle's life that he was mortally wounded in a duel, although he constantly struggled against obsolete institutions and conventions. He often perplexed both his admirers and his adversaries by the contradictory traits in his character. But it was just his inner contrasts that were the main constituents of the brilliancy and fascinating power of his personality.

August Boeckh, one of the most famous philologists and historians of that time, worded the epitaph of Lassalle's tombstone in the Breslau Jewish cemetery: "Here rests what was mortal of Ferdinand Lassalle, the thinker and fighter." Lassalle, when engaged in a conflict, fought recklessly and with relentless audacity. As a thinker he destroyed illusions but not ideals. While vindicating the rights of the working people, he appealed to the brutal facts of economic and political power as well as to humanitarian ideas. He was a profound scholar, whose work on Heraclitus is still consulted by students ninety years after its appearance, and whose *System der Erworbenen Rechte* (1861) contains remarks of great consequence for the philosophy of law. He was also a great organizer who created the first political party of workers in Germany, and a popular leader whose oratorical campaigns enraptured the masses. Adolf Hitler, despite his rabid anti-Semitism, studied Lassalle's public speeches, and tried to imitate some of their effects. But Hitler could grasp only the passionate, hypnotizing power of Lassalle's behavior. He was incapable of understanding Lassalle's clarity and mental culture, and his steady endeavor to raise the intellectual level of his audiences.

680

THE LAW OF WAGES

UNDER free competition the relation of an employer to the employed is the same as to any other merchandise. The worker is work, and work is the cost of its production. This is the leading feature of the present age. In former times the relations were those of man to man: after all, the relations of the slaveowner to the slave, and of the feudal lord to the serf, were human. The relations in former times were human, for they were those of rulers to the ruled; they were relations between one man and another man. Even the ill-treatment of the slaves and serfs proves this; for anger and love are human passions; and those ill-treated in anger were still treated as men. The cold, impersonal relation of the employer to the employed, as to a thing which is produced like any other ware on the market, is the specific and thoroughly inhuman feature of the Middle Class Age.

The Middle Class hate the idea of a State; they would replace the State by a Middle Class society permeated with free competition; for in a State, workers are still treated as men, while under the Middle Class regime the workers are like any other merchandise, and are only taken into consideration according to the cost of production.

Ancient civilization is shown by what Plutarch wrote of Marcus Crassus and his slaves: "He (Crassus) used to attend to their education and often gave them lessons himself; esteeming it the principal part of the business of a master to inspect and take care of his servants, whom he considered as the living instruments of economy. In this he was certainly right if he thought, as he frequently said, that other matters should be managed by servants, but the servants by the master." Contrast this with the words of a Liberal professor: "Swiss manufacturers boast that they can manufacture at less cost than the Germans because the Swiss have no compulsory education."

Wages, on the average, are reduced to the necessary

means of subsistence. But if this be the reward of labor, what becomes of the excess of the prices paid for the articles produced over the cost of subsistence of the workers whilst the articles are being made? This excess is divided between the employer and other capitalists, pure and simple, such as the holders of land, bankers, etc.

. . . There is not a single drop of the sweat of the workers that is not paid back to capital in the price of produce. Every pound in the hands of the employers produces another pound. With this increase the power of capital increases, so that every effort of the workers enables the capitalist to compel the workers to further toil. And when it is possible to reduce the prices of the products and thus cheapen the means of subsistence, then the increase of the workers does not increase with the increased produce of labor, but the power of capital does.

Take all those who have worked together in the production of some article—those who have worked with their brains as well as those who have worked with their hands; add together what they have received for their work, and they will not be able to recover the product of their labor! And when machinery is employed, thus causing a greater production with the same amount of labor, then it becomes more and more impossible for the workers to buy back with their wages the product of their work, and they become poorer and poorer.

[214]

LAVATER, JOHANN KASPAR

LAVATER, JOHANN KASPAR (1741-1801). Protestant orthodoxy and pietism, formerly opposed to each other, became allied in the mind of Lavater, whose complicated character made him sometimes obstinate, sometimes humble. He always tried to realize, by his thinking and conduct of life, the ideal of Christian humanity. He also tried to combine belief in miracles with the modern cult of poetic genius. Trained in psychological self-analysis, he was, nevertheless a helpless illusionist, whose extreme gullibility exposed him

682

to the suspicion of being insincere. A staunch adversary of rationalism, Lavater was often the victim of fanatics, charlatans and crooks who exploited his longing for miracles and the manifestation of supernatural forces. Notwithstanding his attempts to reach simple faith, an unsophisticated belief in the Word of the Bible, he was never satisfied with plain truth, and was always ready to take divination for knowledge and phantoms for reality because they stirred his imagination more than did reason. But when he was not occupied with the propaganda for his ideas, Lavater always proved to be a noble-minded and charitable man. However, it was not his theological writings that made him famous but his *Physiognomics* (1774-78), which was translated into several languages. This work contains a wealth of material and has inspired psychologists and poets, but it lacks scientific method. Lavater, who collected and interpreted a great number of historical or artistic portraits, was convinced that his physiognomical studies would promote not only a knowledge of man but also a mutual love of men.

MAXIMS

MAXIMS are as necessary for the weak as rules for a beginner: the master wants neither rule nor principle— he possesses both without thinking of them.

Who pursues means of enjoyment contradictory, irreconcilable, and self-destructive, is a fool, or what is called a sinner—sin and destruction of order are the same.

He knows not how to speak who cannot be silent; still less how to act with vigor and decision. Who hastens to the end is silent: loudness is impotence.

Wishes run over in loquacious impotence. *Will* presses on with laconic energy.

All affectation is the vain and ridiculous attempt of poverty to appear rich.

There are offenses against individuals, to all appearance trifling, which are capital offenses against the human race:—flay him who can commit them.

Who will sacrifice nothing, and enjoys all, is a fool.

Call him wise whose actions, words, and steps, are all a clear *because* to a clear *why*.

Say not you know another entirely till you have divided an inheritance with him.

Who without call or office, industriously recalls the remembrance of past errors to confound him who has repented of them is a villain.

Too much gravity argues a shallow mind.

Who makes too much or too little of himself has a false measure for everything.

The more honesty a man has, the less he affects the air of a saint—the affectation of sanctity is a blotch on the face of piety.

Kiss the hand of him who can renounce what he has publicly taught, when convicted of his error, and who with heartfelt joy embraces truth, though with the sacrifice of favorite opinions.

The friend of order has made half his way to virtue.

Whom mediocrity attracts, taste has abandoned.

The art to love your enemy consists in never losing sight of *man* in him. Humanity has power over all that is human: the most inhuman still remains man, and never can throw off all taste for what becomes a man—but you must learn to wait.

The merely just can generally bear great virtues as little as great vices.

He has not a little of the devil in him who prays and bites.

Be not the fourth friend of him who had three before, and lost them.

She neglects her heart who always studies her glass.

Who comes from the kitchen smells of its smoke; who adheres to a sect has something of its cant; the college air pursues the student, and dry inhumanity him who herds with literary pedants.

He knows little of the epicurism of reason and religion who examines the dinner in the kitchen.

Let none turn over books or scan the stars in quest of God who sees Him not in man.

He knows nothing of men who expects to convince a

determined party man; and he nothing of the world who despairs of the final impartiality of the public.

He who stands on a height sees farther than those beneath; but let him not fancy that he shall make them believe all he sees.

Pretend not to self-knowledge if you find nothing worse within you than what enmity or calumny dares loudly lay to your charge. Yet you are not very good if you are not better than your best friends imagine you to be.

He who wants witnesses in order to be good has neither virtue nor religion.

He submits to be seen through a microscope who suffers himself to be caught in a fit of passion.

Receive no satisfaction for premeditated impertinence. Forget it, forgive it—but keep him inexorably at a distance who offered it.

The public seldom forgives twice.

He surely is most in want of another's patience who has none of his own.

[215]

LEIBNIZ, GOTTFRIED WILHELM

LEIBNIZ, GOTTFRIED WILHELM (1646-1716). Born at the end of the Thirty Years' War, Leibniz constantly longed for peace and the reconciliation of warring parties. He was by nature one of the greatest mediators in the history of mankind. As a diplomat, he endeavored to unite the nations of Europe. As a theologian, he devoted much of his energy to a plan for the revision of the Christian Churches. As a philosopher, he tried, according to his own words, to connect Plato with Democritus, Aristotle with Descartes, the Scholastics with modern physicists, theology with reason. His philosophical conception of the Universe united aesthetical and mathematical, historical and logical, psychological and biological points of views with metaphysical feelings which were inspired by his confidence in God, the creator of the best of possible worlds. The elements of this world are called *monads* by Leibniz. They are characterized by him as the "true atoms," as metaphysical beings. They are not agglomerations of qualitatively undistinguishable

685

particles but individual centers of force, endowed with the faculty of perception and appetition. Insisting upon their immaterial, metaphysical essence, Leibniz denied the possibility of any physical interaction between them. Their coexistence and intercourse are regulated by the "pre-established harmony" which is the work of God.

Before Leibniz began to construct his philosophical system, he had, in 1684, discovered the differential calculus which, as he expected, would make the analytical method of mathematics applicable to all objects of science.

The belief in the intrinsic value of an infinite variety of individual beings, which he refused to regard as modifications of but one substance, made Leibniz the first modern pluralist. At the end of the 19th century, pluralism seemed to be definitely defeated. But it has been restored, particularly in America, by thinkers like William James, F. J. E. Woodbridge and John Dewey.

CONCERNING DIVINE PERFECTION

THE conception of God which is the most common and the most full of meaning is expressed well enough in the words: God is an absolutely perfect being. The implications, however, of these words fail to receive sufficient consideration. For instance, there are many different kinds of perfection, all of which God possesses, and each one of them pertains to him in the highest degree.

We must also know what perfection is. One thing which can surely be affirmed about it is that those forms or natures which are not susceptible of it to the highest degree, say the nature of numbers or of figures, do not permit of perfection. This is because the number which is the greatest of all (that is, the sum of all the numbers), and likewise the greatest of all figures, imply contradictions. The greatest knowledge, however, and omnipotence contain no impossibility. Consequently power and knowledge do admit of perfection, and in so far as they pertain to God they have no limits.

Whence it follows that God who possesses supreme and infinite wisdom acts in the most perfect manner not only metaphysically, but also from the moral standpoint. And with respect to our selves it can be said that the more we are enlightened and informed in regard to the works of God the more will we be disposed to find them excellent and conforming entirely to that which we might desire.

*   *   *

Therefore I am far removed from the opinion of those who maintain that there are no principles of goodness or perfection in the nature of things, or in the ideas which God has about them, and who say that the works of God are good only through the formal reason that God has made them. If this position were true, God, knowing that he is the author of things, would not have to regard them afterwards and find them good, as the Holy Scripture witnesses. Such anthropological expressions are used only to let us know that excellence is recognized in regarding the works themselves, even if we do not consider their evident dependence on their author. This is confirmed by the fact that it is in reflecting upon the works that we are able to discover the one who wrought. They must therefore bear in themselves his character. I confess that the contrary opinion seems to me extremely dangerous and closely approaches that of recent innovators who hold that the beauty of the universe and the goodness which we attribute to the works of God are chimeras of human beings who think of God in human terms. In saying, therefore, that things are not good according to any standard of goodness, but simply by the will of God, it seems to me that one destroys, without realizing it, all the love of God and all his glory; for why praise him for what he has done, if he would be equally praiseworthy in doing the contrary? Where will be his justice and his wisdom if he has only a certain despotic power, if arbitrary will takes the place of reasonableness, and if in accord with the definition of tyrants, justice consists in that which is pleasing to the most powerful? Besides it seems that every act of willing supposes some reason for the willing and this reason, of course, must precede the act. This is why, accordingly, I find so strange those expressions of certain philosophers who say that the eternal truths of metaphysics and Geometry, and consequently the principles of goodness, of justice, and of perfection, are effects only of the will of God. To me it seems that all these follow from his understanding, which does not depend upon his will any more than does his essence.

* * *

No more am I able to approve of the opinion of certain modern writers who boldly maintain that that which God has made is not perfect in the highest degree, and that he might have done better. It seems to me that the consequences of such an opinion are wholly inconsistent with the glory of God. *Uti minus malum habet rationem boni, ita minus bonum habet rationem mali.* I think that one acts imperfectly if he acts with less perfection than he is capable of. To show that an architect could have done better is to find fault with his work. Furthermore this opinion is contrary to the Holy Scriptures when they assure us of the goodness of God's work. For if comparative perfection were sufficient, then in whatever way God had accomplished his work, since there is an infinitude of possible imperfections, it would always have been good in comparison with the less perfect; but a thing is little praiseworthy when it can be praised only in this way.

I believe that a great many passages from the divine writings and from the holy fathers will be found favoring my position, while hardly any will be found in favor of that of these modern thinkers. Their opinion is, in my judgment, unknown to the writers of antiquity and is a deduction based upon the too slight acquaintance which we have with the general harmony of the universe and with the hidden reasons for God's conduct. In our ignorance, therefore, we are tempted to decide audaciously that many things might have been done better.

These modern thinkers insist upon certain hardly tenable subtleties, for they imagine that nothing is so perfect.

This is an error. They think, indeed, that they are thus safe-guarding the liberty of God. As if it were not the highest liberty to act in perfection according to the sovereign reason. For to think that God acts in anything without having any reason for his willing, even if we overlook the fact that such action seems impossible, is an opinion which conforms little to God's glory. For example, let us suppose that God chooses between A and B, and that he takes A without any reason for preferring it to B. I say that this action on the part of God is at least not praiseworthy, for all praise ought to be founded upon reason which *ex hypothesi* is not present here. My opinion is that God does nothing for which he does not deserve to be glorified.

The general knowledge of this great truth that God acts always in the most perfect and most desirable manner possible, is in my opinion the basis of the love which we owe to God in all things; for he who loves seeks his satis-faction in the felicity or perfection of the object loved and in the perfection of his actions. *Idem velle et idem nolle vera amicitia est.* I believe that it is difficult to love God truly when one, having the power to change his disposition, is not disposed to wish for that which God desires. In fact those who are not satisfied with what God does seem to me like dissatisfied subjects whose attitude is not very different from that of rebels. I hold therefore, that on these principles, to act conformably to the love of God it is not sufficient to force oneself to be patient, we must be really satisfied with all that comes to us according to his will. I mean this acquiescence in regard to the past; for as regards the future one should not be a quietist with the arms folded, open to ridicule, awaiting that which God will do; according to the sophism which the ancients called the lazy reason. It is necessary to act conformably to the presumptive will of God as far as we are able to judge of it, trying with all our might to contribute to the general welfare and particularly to the ornamentation and the perfection of that which touches us, or of that which is nigh and so to speak at our hand. For if the future shall perhaps show that God has not wished our good intention to have its way, it does not follow that he has not wished us to act as we have; on the contrary, since he is the best of all masters, he ever demands only the right intentions, and it is for him to know the hour and the proper place to let good designs succeed.

*　　*　　*

It is sufficient therefore to have this confidence in God, that he has done everything for the best and that nothing will be able to injure those who love him. To know in particular, however, the reasons which have moved him to choose this order of the universe, to permit sin, to dispense his salutary grace in a certain manner,—this passes the capacity of a finite mind, above all when such a mind has not come into the joy of the vision of God. Yet it is possible to make some general remarks touching the course of providence in the government of things. One is able to say, therefore, that he who acts perfectly is like an excellent Geometer who knows how to find the best construction for a problem; like a good architect who utilizes his location and the funds destined for the building in the most advantageous manner, leaving nothing which shocks or which does not display that beauty of which it is capable; like a good householder who employs his property in such a way that there shall be nothing uncultivated or sterile; like a clever machinist who makes his production in the least difficult way possible; and like an intelligent author who encloses the most of reality in the least possible compass.

Of all beings those which are the most perfect and occupy the least possible space, that is to say those which interfere with one another the least, are the spirits whose perfections are the virtues. That is why we may not doubt that the felicity of the spirits is the principal aim of God and that he puts this purpose into execution, as far as the general harmony will permit. We will recur to this subject again.

690

When the simplicity of God's way is spoken of, reference is specially made to the means which he employs, and on the other hand when the variety, richness and abundance are referred to, the ends or effects are had in mind. Thus one ought to be proportioned to the other, just as the cost of a building should balance the beauty and grandeur which is expected. It is true that nothing costs God anything, just as there is no cost for a philosopher who makes hypotheses in constructing his imaginary world, because God has only to make decrees in order that a real world come into being; but in matters of wisdom the decrees or hypotheses meet the expenditure in proportion as they are more independent of one another. The reason wishes to avoid multiplicity in hypotheses or principles very much as the simplest system is preferred in astronomy.

*   *   *

The activities or the acts of will of God are commonly divided into ordinary and extraordinary. But it is well to bear in mind that God does nothing out of order. Therefore, that which passes for extraordinary is so only with regard to a particular order established among the created things, for as regards the universal order, everything conforms to it. This is so true that not only does nothing occur in this world which is absolutely irregular, but it is even impossible to conceive of such an occurrence. Because, let us suppose for example that some one jots down a quantity of points upon a sheet of paper helter skelter, as do those who exercise the ridiculous art of Geomancy; now I say that it is possible to find a geometrical line whose concept shall be uniform and constant, that is, in accordance with a certain formula, and which line at the same time shall pass through all of those points, and in the same order in which the hand jotted them down; also if a continuous line be traced, which is now straight, now circular, and now of any other description, it is possible to find a mental equivalent, a formula or an equation common to all the points of this line by virtue of which formula the changes in the direction of the line must occur. There is no instance of a face whose contour does not form part of a geometric line and which can not be traced entire by a certain mathematical motion. But when the formula is very complex, that which conforms to it passes for irregular. Thus we may say that in whatever manner God might have created the world, it would always have been regular and in a certain order. God, however, has chosen the most perfect, that is to say the one which is at the same time the simplest in hypotheses and the richest in phenomena, as might be the case with a geometric line, whose construction was easy, but whose properties and effects were extremely remarkable and of great significance. I use these comparisons to picture a certain imperfect resemblance to the divine wisdom, and to point out that which may at least raise our minds to conceive in some sort what cannot otherwise be expressed. I do not pretend at all to explain thus the great mystery upon which depends the whole universe.

[216]

L E N I N ,   V.   I.

LENIN, V. I. (1870-1924). When, under the leadership of Lenin, the Bolshevik party seized political power in Russia on November 7, 1917, a new chapter was opened in the history not only of Russia but of the whole world. The character and effects of the Bolshevist revolution and of that party's regime are a matter of endless dispute. There is, furthermore, no agreement concerning Lenin's personality and the part played by him in the Russian revolution. But there is one fact that seems to be certain—that without Lenin, Marxian socialism in its rigid shape would not have been established and maintained as the exclusively ruling creed in Russia. Whether or not the governmental practice of the Bolshevist State has remained in accordance with the official creed is another question. However, it was Lenin, and he alone, who was responsible for the inauguration and continuance of a governmental course which, although in practice is sometimes ready to accept compromises or deviations, insists on the exclusive authority of socialism of the Marxian stamp and suppresses any attempt to express, let alone to practice, heterodox views. For this reason, Lenin is frequently considered, even by non-Bolshevists, as the greatest thinker of the Russian revolution. But his undisputed authority as leader of his party and as ruler over his country does not mean that he was equally superior in the realm of thought.

It is true that Lenin had spent about twenty years in preparing a theoretical and organizational basis for the Bolshevist revolution, and, undisturbed by delays and reverses, he had elaborated the main features of his governmental program when the moment came for seizing power. Lenin, whose original name was Vladimir Ilyich Ulianov, had studied the strategy of civil war, the tactics of sabotage, the weak points of dissenting groups, and the malleability of the mass of the Russian people. But, in his general ideas, he depended upon Marx. According to Lenin, Marx had sufficiently explained the world, and left to him the task of changing this world. He was not even interested in the philosophical foundation of Marxism. Lacking intellectual curiosity, Lenin was unwilling to indulge in thinking activity for its own sake. *Materialism and Empirio-Criticism*, (1909), Lenin's only work on philosophical principles, abounds in misunderstandings. Its aim is to deter socialists from reading Avenarius or Mach rather than to refute their arguments. Lenin's book on *Imperialism* (1916) is not an original analysis of political, economic or sociological facts, but it is, instead, a collection of comments on quotations from the German socialist Rudolph Hilferding's *Finanzkapital*. In his numerous disputes with dissenting socialists, Lenin contented himself with producing a text from Marx or Engels in order to crush his adversaries. This confidence in his masters was a source of strength for Lenin, the party leader and statesman. Apart from his Marxian orthodoxy, Lenin remained versatile and resourceful, not in the least because of his lack of philosophical interest. On the other hand, he was far from considering any of his collaborators as efficient if the latter was only an orthodox Marxian. Noncommunist foreigners were often impressed by Lenin's sarcastic remarks on incapable communist zealots, and took his frankness as a proof of his freedom from prejudice. But, although he judged men and their faculties with acuteness and almost without any bias, he remained fanatically devoted to his creed, and he was aware that he owed his leadership not to his theoretical thinking or his practical ability but to his fervor, his energy, his commanding glance, his educational talents and his skill in maintaining discipline.

THE THREE SOURCES OF MARXISM

THE teaching of Marx evokes throughout the civilized world

the greatest hostility and hatred on the part of all bourgeois science (both official and liberal) which regards Marxism as something in the nature of a "pernicious sect." No other attitude is to be expected, since there can be no "impartial" social science in a society which is built up on the class struggle. *All* official and liberal science *defends* wage slavery in one way or another, whereas Marxism has declared relentless war on that slavery. To expect science to be impartial in a society of wage slavery is as silly and naive as to expect impartiality from employers on the question as to whether the workers' wages should be increased by decreasing the profits of capital.

However, this is not all. The history of philosophy and that of social science shows with perfect clearness that there is nothing in Marxism resembling "sectarianism" in the sense of a secluded, fossilised doctrine originating somewhere away from the high road of development of world civilization. On the contrary, the genius of Marx manifested itself in that he provided the answers to questions which had already been put by the advanced brains of humanity. His teaching came as a direct and immediate *continuation* of the teaching of the greatest representatives of philosophy, political economy, and socialism.

The teaching of Marx is all-powerful because it is true. It is complete and harmonious, providing men with a consistent view of the universe, which cannot be reconciled with any superstition, any reaction, any defense of bourgeois oppression. It is the lawful successor of the best that has been created by humanity in the nineteenth century—German philosophy, English political economy and French socialism.

It is these three sources, which are also the three component parts of Marxism, that we will briefly dwell upon.

The philosophy of Marxism is *materialism*. Throughout the recent history of Europe, and particularly at the end of the eighteenth century in France, which was the scene of the decisive battle against every kind of medieval rubbish, against serfdom in institutions and ideas, materialism proved to be the only consistent philosophy, true to all the teachings of natural science, hostile to superstitions, cant, etc. The enemies of democracy tried, therefore, with all their energy, to "overthrow," undermine and defame materialism and defended various forms of philosophic idealism, which always leads, in one way or another, to the defense and support of religion.

Marx and Engels always defended philosophic materialism in the most determined manner, and repeatedly explained the profound error of every deviation from this basis. Their views are more clearly and fully expounded in the works of Engels, *Ludwig Feuerbach* and *Anti-Dühring*, which, like *The Communist Manifesto*, are household books for every conscious worker.

However, Marx did not stop at the materialism of the eighteenth century but moved philosophy forward. He enriched it by the achievements of German classical philosophy especially by Hegel's system, which in its turn had led to the materialism of Feuerbach. Of these the main achievement is *dialectics, i.e.,* the doctrine of development in its fuller, deeper form, free from one-sidedness—the doctrine, also, of the relativity of human knowledge that provides us with a reflection of eternally developing matter. The latest discoveries of natural science—radium, electrons, the transmutation of elements—are a remarkable confirmation of the dialectical materialism of Marx, despite the doctrines of bourgeois philosophers with their "new" returns to old and rotten idealism.

While deepening and developing philosophic materialism, Marx carried it to its conclusion; he extended its perception of nature to the perception of *human society*. The *historical materialism* of Marx represented the greatest conquest of scientific thought. Chaos and arbitrariness, which reigned until then in the views on history and politics, were replaced by a strikingly consistent and harmonious scientific theory, which shows how out of one order of social life another and higher order develops, in consequence of the growth of the productive forces—how capitalism, for instance, grows out of serfdom.

Just as the cognition of man reflects nature (*i.e.* developing matter) which exists independently of him, so also the *social cognition* of man (*i.e.* the various views and doctrines —philosophic, religious, political, etc.) reflects the *economic order* of society. Political institutions are a superstructure on the economic foundation. We see, for example, that the various political forms of modern European states serve the purpose of strengthening the domination of the bourgeoisie over the proletariat.

The philosophy of Marx is a perfected philosophic materialism which has provided humanity, and especially the working class, with a powerful instrument of knowledge.

Having recognized that the economic order is the foundation upon which the political superstructure is erected, Marx devoted all the greater attention to the study of that economic order. The principal work of Marx, *Capital,* is devoted to a study of the economic order of modern, *i.e.,* capitalist society.

Classical political economy, before Marx, was built up in England, the most developed capitalist country. Adam Smith and David Ricardo, in their investigations of the economic order, laid the foundations of the *labor theory of value.* Marx continued their work. He strictly proved and consistently developed this theory. He showed that the value of every commodity is determined by the quantity of socially-necessary labor time spent in its production.

Where the bourgeois economists saw a relation of things (the exchange of one commodity for another) Marx revealed a *relation between men.* The exchange of commodities expresses the connection between individual producers by means of the market. *Money* signifies that this connection is becoming closer and closer, inseparably combining the entire economic life of the individual producers into one whole. *Capital* signifies a further development of this connection: the labor power of man becomes a commodity. The wage laborer sells his labor power to the owner of land, of factories and instruments of labor. The worker uses one part of the labor day to cover the expenditure for the maintenance of himself and his family (wages), and the other part of the day he toils without remuneration and creates *surplus value* for the capitalist, which is the source of profit, the source of wealth of the capitalist class.

The doctrine of surplus value is the corner-stone of the economic theory of Marx.

Capital, created by the labor of the worker, presses upon the workers, ruins the petty owners and creates an army of unemployed. In industry the victory of large-scale production may be seen at once, but we also see the same phenomenon in agriculture: the superiority of big capitalist agriculture becomes greater, the application of machinery grows, peasant economy is caught in the noose of money-capital, it declines and becomes ruined under the burden of a backward technique. In agriculture, the forms of decline of petty production are different, but the decline itself is an indisputable fact.

By beating petty production, capital leads to the increase of the productivity of labor and to the establishment of a monopoly position for associations of the biggest capitalists. Production itself becomes more and more social; hundreds of thousands and millions of workers are linked up in a systematic economic organism, but the product of the collective labor is appropriated by a handful of capitalists. Anarchy of production, crises, a furious hunt after markets, and the insecurity of existence for the masses of the population, are on the increase.

While increasing the dependence of the workers upon capital the capitalist system creates the great power of combined labor.

Marx traced the development of capitalism from the first germs of commodity economy and simple exchange, to its highest forms, to large-scale production.

And the experience of all countries, whether old or new, clearly shows year after year, to an ever greater number of workers, the truth of Marx's teaching.

Capitalism has been victorious all over the world, but this victory is only the eve of the victory of labor over capital.

After the overthrow of serfdom, when a *"free"* capitalist society appeared, it was at once discovered that this freedom signified a new system of oppression and exploitation of the toilers. Various socialist doctrines immediately began to arise as a reflection of this oppression and protest against it. But socialism in its first origin was *utopian*. It criticised the capitalist society, it condemned it and damned it, it dreamed of its destruction, it drew phantastic pictures of a better order and endeavored to convince the rich of the wickedness of exploitation.

But utopian socialism was unable to show a real way out. It could not explain either the essence of wage slavery under capitalism, or discover the laws of its development, or find the *social force* which was capable of becoming the creator of a new society.

In the meantime, the stormy revolutions which accompanied the fall of feudalism and serfdom everywhere in Europe, and especially in France, revealed ever more clearly the *struggle of classes* as the basis of the whole development and its motive force.

Not a single victory of political freedom over the class of feudal lords was won without desperate resistance. Not a single capitalist country was established on a more or less free and democratic basis without a life and death struggle between the different classes of capitalist society.

Marx was a genius because he was able before anyone else to draw from these facts and consistently elaborate the conclusion which world history teaches. This conclusion is the doctrine of the *class struggle.*

People always were and always will be the stupid victims of deceit and self-deceit in politics, as long as they have not learned to discover the *interests* of one or another of the classes behind any moral, religious, political and social phrases, declarations and promises. The supporters of reforms and improvements will always be fooled by the defenders of the old, as long as they will not realize that every institution, however absurd and rotten it may appear, is kept in being by the forces of one or the other of the ruling classes. And there is *only one* way of breaking the resistance of these classes, and that is to find, in the very society which surrounds us, and to enlighten and organize for the struggle, the forces which can and, by their social position, *must* form the power capable of sweeping away the old and of establishing the new.

Only the philosophic materialism of Marx showed the proletariat the way out of the spiritual slavery in which all oppressed classes have languished up to the present. Only the economic theory of Marx explained the real position of the proletariat in the general system of capitalism.

The independent organizations of the proletariat are multiplying throughout the world from America to Japan and from Sweden to South Africa. The proletariat is being enlightened and educated in waging the class struggle, it is ridding itself of the prejudices of bourgeois society, consolidating itself ever more closely and learning to take the measure of its successes; it is hardening its forces and growing irresistibly.

[217]

LESSING, GOTTHOLD EPHRAIM

LESSING, GOTTHOLD EPHRAIM (1729-1781). The idea of religious tolerance has been given its noblest poetic symbolization in Lessing's drama *Nathan the Wise* (1779), which also became the model for Goethe's and Schiller's classical dramas. For admonishing the German people to love their fellow men without prejudice, Lessing was hated by German zealots of religious, political and racial orthodoxy, and considered to be not a genuine German but of Slavic origin.

Poet, dramatist, critic of art and literature, archeologist, historian and theologian, Lessing was the first man of letters in Germany who dared to earn his living as a free-lance writer. Living among people who recoiled from activities involving personal responsibility, Lessing valued independent thinking and feeling, criticism and knowledge as the highest energies of life and mind, and endeavored to awaken the spirit of responsibility among the German people. He rehabilitated wrongly depreciated or condemned thinkers of the past, he struggled against wrong authorities of his time, he tried to secure liberty of expression for a German literature that did not yet exist when he wrote his principal works. But he was not satisfied with his success in combating prejudices and narrowing rules. He also tried to establish standards of judgment and principles of poetic and artistic creation. This he did in his *Hamburgische Dramaturgie* and *Laokoon* (1766-67). Open revolt against the absolutist regime, in particular that of Frederick II of Prussia, was considered hopeless by Lessing, who limited his political criticism to some sporadic bitter remarks in his printed works but branded the political and social conditions of Germany with mordant sarcasm in his correspondence. At the end of his life, Lessing concentrated upon the theological disquisitions and defending himself against attacks on the part of orthodox clergymen. In this struggle that threatened his civil existence, Lessing proclaimed that he put striving for truth above possession of truth.

MAN'S FUTURE PERFECTION

WHAT education is for the individual, revelation is for the whole human race. Education is revelation that affects the individual; revelation is education which has affected and still affects the race. . . . In the early days of Christianity, the word "mystery" connoted something quite different from what we now understand by it. And the development of revealed truths into truths of reason is absolutely necessary if the human race is to be helped by them. When they were revealed, they were not, indeed, truths of reason; but they were revealed in order to become so.

Why should we not also be able to be conducted by a religion (notwithstanding that its historical truth, if you will, appears so doubtful), to more exact and better conceptions of the divine Being, of our nature, of our relation to God—conceptions to which the human reason would, of itself, never have strived.

Moreover, in this selfish state of the human heart, to incline to the exercise of the understanding only on those things which concern corporeal needs, would blunt it rather than whet it. It positively will be exercised on spiritual concerns if it is to attach to complete clarification and bring out this purity of heart which qualifies us to love virtue for its own sake.

Human education aims at that, and shall divine education not stretch so far? What art succeeds in doing for the individual, shall nature not succeed in doing for the whole? Blasphemy! Blasphemy!

No! it will come, it will surely come, the time of perfection when man—the more convinced his understanding feels of an ever better future—will not, however, have to borrow from this future motives for his actions, when he will do the good because it is the good, and not because there were imposed upon it arbitrary rewards which were earlier intended merely to steady his inconstant vision and strengthen it to recognize the inner, better rewards.

The time of a new, eternal gospel which is promised in the primers of the New Covenant will surely come to us.

[218]

LEONE, EBREO. See ABRAVANEL, JUDAH.

LEUCIPPUS

LEUCIPPUS (About 460 B.C.). All modern physicists may be regarded as followers of Leucippus of Miletus, the founder of atomism whose way of thinking has led to immense results in science and practical life. His theory that the Universe is composed of an infinite number of elements which are characterized by quantitative differences has undergone many and important modifications, but it has maintained its validity even after the "indivisible" atoms could be split.

All of Leucippus' works, among which the book *Megas Diakosmos* (The Great Order of the Universe) and *Peri Nou* (On Mind) were most famous, are lost. In the fourth century B.C. his writings were re-edited together with those of his disciple Democritus in one and the same collection. This led Epicurus to deny the historical existence of Leucippus, and some recent scholars have professed the same opinion. But, as Aristotle and Theophrastus remarked, there are differences between the doctrines of Leucippus and Democritus. Although Leucippus created the vocabulary of Greek atomism he remained in many respects more closely connected with the Ionian cosmologists of the older schools, while Democritus proceeded to a strictly scientific view on physical and mental phenomena.

ON ATOMISM

LEUCIPPUS thought he had a theory which was in harmony with sense-perception, and did not do away with coming into being and passing away, nor motion, nor the multiplicity of things. He made this concession to experience, while he conceded, on the other hand, to those who invented the One that motion was impossible without the void, that the void was not real, and that nothing of what was real was not real. "For," said he, "that which is, strictly speaking, real is an absolute plenum: but the plenum is not one. On the contrary, there are an infinite number of them, and they are invisible owing to the smallness of their bulk. They move in the void (for there is a void); and by their coming together they effect coming into being; by their separation, passing away."

He says that the worlds arise when many bodies are collected together into the mighty void from the surrounding space and rush together. They come into collision, and those which are of similar shape and like form become entangled, and from their entanglement the heavenly bodies arise.

[219]

702

LÉVY-BRUHL, LUCIEN

LÉVY-BRUHL, LUCIEN (1857-1939). When Lévy-Bruhl died, the Sorbonne, the University of Paris, deplored the loss of one of its most brilliant teachers; the French people mourned a staunch defender of human rights and a convinced and active republican and democrat; tens of thousands of political refugees, of human beings persecuted for religious or racial reasons, felt themselves deprived of the moral and material support of a true humanitarian; and experts in sociology, psychology, philosophy, epistemology and many branches of linguistics began to miss the inspiring influence of a scholar whose ideas had offered them new aspects.

Lévy-Bruhl had published solid and significant works on the history of German and French philosophy before he began his important investigations of primitive society. He penetrated into the soul of prelogical man who thought mystically. The philosophical problem that was raised by the results of his inquiries can be formulated as follows: Although all physio-psychological processes of perception of the primitive man are the same as those of modern, logical man—although both have the same structure of brain, the primitive man does not perceive as modern man does. The external world which the primitive man perceives is different from that of modern man, just as the social environments of both are different. Death forced Lévy-Bruhl to commit to his successors the responsibility of drawing further conclusions from his statements.

THE MIND OF THE PRIMITIVE MAN

THE primitive mind, like our own, is anxious to find the reasons for what happens, but it does not seek these in the same direction as we do. It moves in a world where innumerable occult powers are everywhere present, and always in action or ready to act. . . . Any circumstance, however slightly unusual it may be, is at once regarded as the manifestation of one or another of them. If the rain occurs at a time when the fields are badly needing water, it is because the ancestors and spirits of the neighborhood are content, and are thus manifesting their goodwill. If a persistent drought parches the corn and causes the cattle to perish, some *tabu* must have been violated, or possibly an ancestor considers himself injured, and his wrath must be appeased. In the same way, no enterprise will succeed unless the unseen powers give it their support. No one will start out hunting or fishing, nor begin a campaign; he will not attempt to cultivate a field or build a house, unless the auguries are favorable, and the mysterious guardians of the social group have explicitly promised their aid; it is necessary that the very animals needed should have given their consent, and the tools required have been consecrated and invested with magic qualities, and so forth. In short, the visible world and the unseen world are but one, and the events occurring in the visible world depend at all times upon forces which are not seen. Hence the place held in the life of primitives by dreams, omens, divination in its various forms, sacrifices, incantations, ritual ceremonies and magic. A man succumbs to some organic disease or to snake-bite; he is crushed to death by the fall of a tree, or devoured by a tiger or crocodile: to the primitive mind, his death is due neither to disease nor to snake-venom; it is not the tree or the wild beast or reptile that has killed him. If he has perished, it is undoubtedly because a wizard had "doomed" and "delivered him over." Both tree and animal are but instruments, and in default of the one, the other would have carried out the sentence. They were, as one might say, interchangeable, at the will of the unseen power employing them.

To minds thus orientated there is no circumstance which is purely physical. No question relating to natural phenomena presents itself to primitives as it does to us. When we want to explain any such we look for the conditions which would be necessary and sufficient to bring it about, in the series of similar phenomena. If we succeed in determining them, we ask no more; knowing the general law, we are satisfied. The primitive's attitude is entirely different. He may have remarked the unvarying antecedents of the phenomenon which interests him, and in acting he relies a good deal on what he has observed. But he will always seek the true cause in the world of unseen powers, above and beyond what we call Nature, in the "metaphysical" realm, using the word in its literal sense. In short, our problems are not his, and his are foreign to us. That is why we find ourselves in a blind alley, when we seek how he would treat one of ours, and imagine it and try to draw from it inferences which would explain such-and-such a primitive institution.

[220]

LEWES, GEORGE HENRY

LEWES, GEORGE HENRY (1817-1878). Victorian morality was challenged by Lewes who, from 1854 until his death, lived with Mary Ann Evans, the novelist known by the name of George Eliot. Lewes also broke through the moral framework of British life of his time on other occasions, but he knew how to maintain his social credit. He was a versatile, enterprising and often successful man of letters, the founder of the *Fortnightly Review*, which became of primary importance in British literary and political life and still exists, the author of a popular biography of Goethe, biographer of Robespierre, a novelist and playwright, an anatomist and physiologist, and a more gifted than trained thinker. His *Biographical History of Philosophy* (1845) met with great applause. His *Problems of Life and Mind* in four volumes (1874-79) became, despite its weak points, of major significance to the history of modern thought, although not all of those who were indebted to it have admitted the fact.

Lewes was inspired by Comte, whose philosophy he dealt with in *Comte's Philosophy of the Sciences* (1853). His first aim was to disentangle from philosophy all the metaphysical elements which he considered insoluble and meaningless, and to restate its problems in a form corresponding to terms of experience. Later Lewes admitted metaphysics as a science of highest generalities. His principal interest was directed to the question of what the conscious life means and how it is connected with the body. He criticized the mechanical interpretation of organic processes and introduced the concept of emergence which became important to C. L. Morgan, Broad and other thinkers. He also stressed the social factor in the development of the mind and tried to show its way of working. These efforts led him to form a new concept of the general mind and to connect biological, sociological and spiritual terms of evolution.

THE nature of philosophy condemns its followers to wander forever in the same labyrinth, and in this circumscribed space many will necessarily fall into the track of their predecessors. In other words, coincidences of doctrine at epochs widely distant from each other are inevitable.

Positive science is further distinguished from philosophy by the incontestable *progress* it everywhere makes. Its methods are stamped with certainty, because they are daily extending our certain knowledge; because the immense experience of years and of myriads of intelligences confirm their truth, without casting a shadow of suspicion on them. Science, then, progresses, and must continue to progress. Philosophy only moves in the same endless circle. Its first principles are as much a matter of dispute as they were two thousand years ago. It has made no progress, although in constant movement. Precisely the same questions are being agitated in Germany at this moment as were being discussed in ancient Greece, and with no better means of solving them, with no better hopes of success. The united force of thousands of intellects, some of them among the greatest that have made the past illustrious, has been steadily concentrated on problems, supposed to be of vital importance, and believed to be perfectly susceptible of solution, without the least result. All this meditation and discussion has not even established a few first principles. Centuries of labor have not produced any perceptible progress.

The history of science, on the other hand, is the history of progress. So far from the same questions being discussed in the same way as they were in ancient Greece, they do not remain the same for two generations. In some sciences —chemistry for example—ten years suffice to render a book so behind the state of knowledge as to be almost useless. Everywhere we see progress, more or less rapid, according to the greater or less facility of investigation.

In this constant movement of philosophy and constant linear progress of positive science, we see the condemnation of the former. It is in vain to argue that because no progress has yet been made, we are not therefore to conclude none will be made; it is in vain to argue that the difficulty of philosophy is much greater than that of any science, and therefore greater time is needed for its perfection. The difficulty is impossibility. No progress is made because no certainty is possible. To aspire to the knowledge of more than phenomena, their resemblances and successions, is to aspire to transcend the limitations of human faculties. To *know* more we must *be* more.

This is our conviction. It is also the conviction of the majority of thinking men. Consciously or unconsciously, they condemn philosophy. They discredit or disregard it. The proof of this is in the general neglect into which philosophy has fallen, and the greater assiduity bestowed on positive science. Loud complaints of this neglect are heard. Great contempt is expressed by the philosophers. They may rail, and they may sneer, but the world will go its way. The empire of positive science is established.

We trust that no one will suppose we think slightingly of philosophy. Assuredly we do not, or else why this work? . . . But we respect it as a great power that *has been,* and no longer *is.* It was the impulse to all early speculation: it was the parent of positive science. It nourished the infant mind of humanity; gave it aliment, and directed its faculties, rescued the nobler part of man from the dominion of brutish ignorance; stirred him with insatiable thirst for knowledge, to slake which he was content to undergo amazing toil. But its office has been fulfilled; it is no longer necessary to humanity, and should be set aside. The only interest it can have is a historical interest.

[221]

LEWIS, CLARENCE IRVING

LEWIS, CLARENCE IRVING (1883-1947). Lewis, professor of philosophy at Harvard and an outstanding representative of modern

707

philosophical naturalism, has given in *A Survey of Symbolic Logic* (1918) the most comprehensive and complete exposition of the various systems of symbolic logic, traced from Leibniz to the 20th century, and he has discussed therein the relation of a "system of strict implication" to systems of material implication and to the classical algebra of logic. In *Symbolic Logic* (1932), Lewis, in collaboration with Cooper Harold Langford, deals systematically with symbolic logic. The conception of consistency between propositions is brought into harmony with mathematical conception. The distinction between the logic of intension and the logic of extension is basic to the discussion of the whole book, in which the plurality of logical truth is maintained.

In *An Analysis of Knowledge and Valuation* (1947), Lewis exposes a naturalistic conception of values by dealing with the relations between the supreme good and justice. He holds that, for naturalistic ethics, determination of the good must precede the determination of what is right, since the justification of any action depends on the desirability of its contemplated effects. Contrary to many European theorists of values, Lewis characterizes valuation as a type of empirical cognition, not fundamentally different, in what determines their truth or falsity and what determines their validity or justification, from other kinds of empirical knowledge. According to Lewis, for contemporary empiricism, the theory of meaning has the same intimate connection with epistemology that rationalistic or idealistic conceptions previously assigned to metaphysics. Consequently, it has become useless to suppose that the *a priori* truth, known independently of sense particulars, describes something that is metaphysically relevant to reality. Ethics is the capstone of an edifice that rests upon the theory of meaning. Ethics, epistemology and the theory of meaning are essentially connected.

EVALUATION

WE cannot make even a good beginning in the consideration of evaluations in general until we untangle the question what basic good is and what goods are derivative, from the question of the subjectivity or objectivity of value-predications. And a first step here is to observe that there are three main types of value-predication, corresponding to the three main types of empirical statements in general.

First, there is expressive statement of a value-quality found in the directly experienced. One who says at the concert, "This is good," or who makes a similar remark at table, is presumably reporting a directly experienced character of the sensuously presented as such. He might, of course, have a quite different intention; he might be meaning to assert that the selection being played has a verifiably satisfactory character best attested by those endowed with musical discrimination and having long experience and training in music; or that the food verifiably meets all dietetic standards in high degree. In that case, the immediately experienced goodness would, presumably, provide the empirical cue to his judgment, but what is *judged* would be no more than partially verified in this directly apprehended quality of the given—which itself requires no judgment. Such judged and verifiable goodness of the musical selection or the viands, is an objective property, comparable to the objective roundness of a plate, or the objective frequency of vibrations in the surrounding atmosphere.

Directly experienced goodness or badness, like seen redness or felt hardness, may become, when attended, the matter of a formulation or report which intends nothing more than this apparent quality of what appears. There are any number of questions about value-quality as thus immediate, which will have to be discussed in the next chapter. But it will hardly be denied that there is what may be called 'apparent value' or 'felt goodness,' as there is seen redness or heard shrillness. And while the intent to formulate just this apparent value-quality of what is given, without implication of anything further, encounters linguistic difficulties, surely it will not be denied that there are such immediate experiences of good and bad to be formulated. We shall probably agree also that without such direct value-apprehensions, there could be no determination of values, or of what is valuable, in any *other* sense, or any significance for value-terms at all. Without the experience of felt value and disvalue, evaluations in general would have no meaning.

Any such formulation or report of apparent value, taken by itself and divested of all further implication, is an expressive statement; self-verifying (for him who makes it) in the only sense in which it could be called verifiable, and subject to no possible error, unless merely linguistic error in the words chosen to express it. Such a statement is true or false, since we could not tell lies about the quality of immediate experience; but the apprehension is not a judgment, and is not to be classed as knowledge, in the sense in which we have used that word.

Second, there are evaluations which are terminating judgments; the prediction, in the circumstances as apprehended, or in other and similarly apprehensible circumstances, of the possible accrual of value-quality in experience —for example, of enjoyment or of pain—conditional upon adoption of a particular mode of action. If I taste what is before me, I shall enjoy it: if I touch this red-glowing metal, I shall feel pain. Such judgments may be put to the test by acting on them, and are then decisively and completely verified or found false. Being predictive—verifiable but not verified—and subject to possible error, they represent a form of knowledge.

Third, there is that most important and most frequent type of evaluation which is the ascription of the objective property of being valuable to an existent or possible existent; to an object, a situation, a state of affairs, or to some *kind* of such thing. Such objective judgments of value are . . . considerably more complex than objective judgments of other characters than value. There is also much diversity amongst them: "*X* is valuable," in this objective sense, is a form of statement covering a great variety of meanings, and subject to troublesome ambiguities by reason of the difficulty of distinguishing these. But they all possess the common character of being what we have called non-terminating judgments.

[222]

710

LICHTENBERG, GEORG CHRISTOPH

LICHTENBERG, GEORG CHRISTOPH (1742-1799). Aphorism is a form of literary art that corresponds to the character of Lichtenberg, the ironic sceptic of German enlightenment. He liked to collect observations of daily life, curiosities, oddities, psychological experiences, and to shape them into short and easy sentences which mirrored his general philosophical outlook. Lichtenberg, professor of mathematics and natural sciences at the University of Göttingen, had a high idea of spiritual freedom, and he was not afraid to defend it. He particularly liked to ridicule orthodoxy and missionary zeal. Combining common sense and refinement of feeling, Lichtenberg remained lonely among German writers and thinkers.

ALL KINDS OF THOUGHTS

THE intercourse with reasonable people is advisable to everybody because, in this way, a blockhead can become wise by imitation, for the greatest blockheads can imitate, even apes and elephants can do it.

You must not allow your reading to dominate you but you should dominate your reading.

Before one blames, one should always find out whether one cannot excuse. To discover little faults has been always the particularity of such brains that are a little or not at all above the average. The superior ones keep quiet or say something against the whole and the great minds transform without blaming.

Do not have too artificial an idea of man but judge him naturally. Don't consider him too good or too bad. It is a golden rule that one should not judge people according to their opinions, but according to what these opinions make of them.

Popularizing should always be done in such a manner that one would elevate people by it. If one stoops down, one should always take care of elevating even those people to whom one descends.

The inclination of people to consider small things as important has produced many great things.

People don't think so differently about the events of life as they talk about them.

We live in a world in which one fool makes many fools but one wise man only a few wise men.

The highest point a poor brain can reach from experience is the ability to find out the weaknesses of superior people.

Concerning the body, there are at least as many, if not more, imaginary sick as really sick people. Concerning the mind, there are as many, if not more, imaginary sane people as really sane ones.

The late M. who had a Catholic maid, once told me entirely bona fide: This person is a Catholic, it is true, but she is an honest, good soul. Recently she committed a perjury on my behalf.

There are people that can believe everything they want. These are happy creatures.

People that never have time do the least of all.

How happy would many people live if they cared about other people's affairs as little as about their own.

One should never trust a person who, while assuring you of something, puts his hands on his heart.

[223]

LINCOLN, ABRAHAM

LINCOLN, ABRAHAM (1809-1865). Compared with Abraham Lincoln, many great figures in the history of the world, many really great leaders of nations, seem to be actors playing the roles of great men. There was nothing of the actor in Lincoln. His behavior was so simple that not only his adversaries but his political followers and many of his subordinates could not imagine that he was a hero. As Emerson said in his funeral discourse, Lincoln was a plain man of the people, a middle-class president, "yes, in manners and sympathies, but not in powers for his powers were superior." Lincoln never lost the characteristics of a small-town

712

lawyer, indulging often in the jocular talk in which he relished and in which he was a past master. But through the atmosphere of jocularity flashed the brilliance of his hard thinking and tragic earnestness, the flame of his devotion to the nation. To that which Lincoln considered identical with the spirit of the nation—the cause of popular government, his name remains inseparably connected. Little by little Lincoln's sagacity, his valor and patience, his sense of justice and his generosity were recognized, at first by the people of the Union, and thereafter by the whole world. He was recognized as a good and wise man whose wisdom was the result of strenuous life, self-education and appreciation of the apparently unimportant events and accidents in the lives of small people, of enjoyment and resignation. Even his famous Gettysburg Address, from which his expression of confidence in the "government of the people, by the people and for the people" has been and will be quoted again and again, did not immediately work up his audience. It took time before the public was moved by Lincoln's words, but then the deep impression lasted. Lincoln possessed the art of making simple words meaningful and of coining sentences which have become proverbial wisdom in almost all languages. He appealed to the intelligence not to the brute instincts of the public, and he knew how to make difficult decisions and questions understandable to the untrained mind.

THE PERPETUITY OF THE UNION

IT is seventy-two years since the first inauguration of a President under our National Constitution. During that period fifteen different and greatly distinguished citizens have in succession administered the Executive branch of the Government. They have conducted it through many perils, and generally with great success. Yet with all this scope for precedent, I now enter upon the same task for the brief constitutional term of four years under great and peculiar difficulty. A disruption of the Federal Union, heretofore only menaced, is now formidably attempted.

I hold that, in contemplation of universal law, and of the Constitution, the union of these States is perpetual. Perpetuity is implied, if not expressed in the fundamental law of all national governments. It is safe to assert that no government proper ever had a provision in its organic law for its own termination. Continue to execute all the express provisions of our national government, and the Union will endure forever—it being impossible to destroy it except by some action not provided for in the instrument itself. Again, if the United States be not a government proper, but an association of States in the nature of contract merely, can it, as a contract, be peaceably unmade by less than all the parties who made it? One party to a contract may violate it—break it, so to speak—but does it not require all to lawfully rescind it?

But if destruction of the Union by one or by a part only of the States be lawfully possible, the Union is less perfect than before—the Constitution having lost the vital element of perpetuity. It follows from these views that no State, upon its own motion, can lawfully get out of the Union; that resolves and ordinances to that effect are legally void; and that acts of violence within any State or States, against the authority of the United States, are insurrectionary or revolutionary, according to circumstances.

I therefore consider that, in view of the Constitution and the laws, the Union is unbroken; and to the extent of my ability I shall take care, as the Constitution expressly enjoins upon me, that the laws of the Union be faithfully executed in all the States. Doing this I deem to be only a simple duty on my part; and I shall perform it, so far as practicable, unless my rightful masters, the American people, shall withhold the requisite means, or in some authoritative manner direct the contrary. I trust that this will not be regarded as a menace, but only as the declared purpose of the Union that it will constantly defend and maintain itself.

In your hands, my dissatisfied fellow-countrymen, and not in mine, are the momentous issues of civil war. The Government will not assail you. You can have no conflict without being yourselves the aggressors. You have no oath registered in Heaven to destroy the Government, whilst I shall have the most solemn one to "Preserve, protect, and defend" it.

I am loath to close. We are not enemies but friends.

We must not be enemies. Though passion may have strained, it must not break our bonds of affection. The mystic cords of memory, stretching from every battlefield and patriot grave to every living heart and hearthstone all over this broad land, will yet swell the chorus of the Union, when again touched, as they surely will be, by the better angels of our nature.

THE EMANCIPATION PROCLAMATION

Now, therefore I, Abraham Lincoln, President of the United States, by virtue of the power in me vested as Commander-in-Chief of the Army and Navy of the United States in time of actual armed rebellion against the authority and government of the United States, and as a fit and necessary war measure for suppressing said rebellion, do on this first day of January, in the year of our Lord one thousand eight hundred and sixty-three, order and designate as States and parts of States wherein the people thereof respectively are this day in rebellion against the United States, the following, to wit: . . .

And by virtue of the power, and for the purpose aforesaid, I do order and declare that all persons held as slaves within such designated States and parts of States are, and henceforward shall be free; and the Executive Government of the United States, including the military and naval authorities thereof, will recognize and maintain the freedom of said persons. And upon this act, sincerely believed to be an act of justice, warranted by the Constitution upon military necessity, I invoke the considerate judgment of mankind, and the gracious favor of Almighty God.

THE GETTYSBURG ADDRESS

FOURSCORE and seven years ago our fathers brought forth upon this continent a new nation conceived in liberty, and

dedicated to the proposition that all men are created equal
Now we are engaged in a great civil war, testing whether
that nation or any nation so conceived and so dedicated
can long endure. We are met on a great battle-field of
that war. We have come to dedicate a portion of that field
as a final resting-place for those who here gave their lives
that that nation might live. It is altogether fitting and proper
that we should do this.

But in a larger sense *we* cannot dedicate, *we* cannot
consecrate, *we* cannot hallow this ground. The brave men,
living and dead, who struggled here, have consecrated it far
above our power to add or detract. The world will little
note nor long remember what we say here; but it can never
forget what *they* did here. It is for us—the living—rather,
to be dedicated here to the unfinished work which they who
fought here have thus far so nobly advanced. It is rather
for us to be here dedicated to the great task remaining
before us, that from these honored dead we take increased
devotion to that cause for which they gave the last full
measure of devotion; that we here highly resolve that these
dead shall not have died in vain, that this nation, under
God, shall have a new birth of freedom; and that government
of the people, by the people, and for the people, shall not
perish from the earth.

MALICE TOWARD NONE — CHARITY FOR ALL

FONDLY do we hope, fervently do we pray, that this mighty
scourge of war may speedily pass away. Yet if God wills
that it continue until all the wealth piled by the bondsman's
two hundred and fifty years of unrequited toil shall be sunk,
and until every drop of blood drawn with the lash shall be
paid by another drawn with the sword, as was said three
thousand years ago, so still it must be said, that the judgments of the Lord are true and righteous altogether.

With malice toward none, with charity for all, with

firmness in the right, as God gives us to see the right, let us finish the work we are in—to bind up the nation's wounds; to care for him who shall have borne the battle and for his widow and his orphans; to do all which may achieve and cherish a just and lasting peace among ourselves and with all nations.

[224]

LINNAEUS, CAROLUS

LINNAEUS, CAROLUS (1707-1778). On New Year's Day of 1730, the dean of the University of Upsala, Sweden, found on his desk a peculiar form of season's greetings. It was a manuscript, written by an unknown student and entitled *Preliminaries on the Marriage of Plants*. In his preface, the author of the manuscript confessed to his incapability of making verses, and excused himself for having, instead, written a juvenile treatise, in which he handled the analogy between plants and animals as he saw it.

This manuscript contained the germ of Linnaeus' great contribution to botany. Searching for a principle for the classification of plants, Linnaeus, dissatisfied with any division according to color, use or the season of flowering, found the key in the reproductive parts of the plants, and classified them according to their different ways of producing offshoots. In addition to this sexual system, Linnaeus also contributed to the natural sciences by originating the binominal system of naming plants and animals. The first name indicates the genus and the second, the particular species by Latin or Greek words. In this way, Linnaeus made his naming system internationally applicable. Linnaeus furthermore contributed to mineralogy and ethnology by his report on his scientific expedition to Lapland and his miscellaneous essays. He was a charming writer because he was a loving character and a unique observer. As a great scientist said, Linnaeus saw plants "just as an insect sees them." Born in a small farm cottage in a remote district of Sweden, Linnaeus as a little boy already astonished his relatives and teachers by his interest in, and knowledge of, plants. He liked to remember his native village and preserved his country-boy's outlook even after he had become internationally renowned. It is an almost general custom among botanists to make a botanical excursion on Linnaeus' birthday, although modern botany has ceased to concern itself with the flowers in the fields and has become a kind of department of physics and chemistry.

MANKIND, as well as all other creatures, being formed with such exquisite and wonderful skill that human wisdom is utterly insufficient to imitate the most simple fibre, vein, or nerve, much less a finger, it is perfectly evident, that all these things must originally have been made by an omnipotent and omniscient Being, for "He who formed the ear, shall He not hear; and He who made the eye, shall He not see?" If we consider the *generation* of animals, we find that each produces an offspring after its own kind; so that all living things, plants, animals, and even mankind themselves —form one "chain of universal being," from the beginning to the end of the world. While we turn our minds to the contemplation of the wonders and beauties which surround us, we are also permitted to employ them for our benefit. If the Maker of all things, who has done nothing without design, has furnished this earthly globe like a museum, with the most admirable proofs of His wisdom and power; if, moreover, this splendid theatre would be adorned in vain without a spectator, it follows that man is made for the purpose of studying the Creator's works, that he may be the publisher and interpreter of the wisdom of God. In order to lead us toward our duty, the Deity has so closely connected the study of His works with our general convenience and happiness that the more we examine them, the more we discover for our use and gratification. Can any work be imagined more forcibly to proclaim the majesty of its Author than a little inactive earth rendered capable of contemplating itself, as animated by the hand of God? of studying the dimensions and revolutions of the celestial bodies, rolling at an almost infinite distance, as well as the innumerable wonders dispersed by the Creator over this globe? The Author of Nature has frequently decorated even the minutest insects, and worms themselves, which inhabit the bottom of the sea, in so exquisite a manner that the most polished metal looks dull beside them. He who has given life to animals has given to them all different means of supporting it. The Silurus Callichthys, when the rivulet which it inhabits becomes dry, has a power of traveling over land till it finds more copious streams. The flying squirrel has a power of extending the skin on each side of its body in such a manner that, being enabled to descend by a precipitate flight from one branch to another, it easily avoids its enemies. Thus also has He lengthened out the fins on the breast of the flying-fish that it might seek for safety in the air, when pursued by its enemies in the water. He has likewise formed an appendage to the tail of the great cuttlefish (Sepia Loligo) by means of which it springs out of the sea, at the same time being furnished with a bladder, full of a sort of ink, with which it darkens the water and eludes the sight of its pursuers. The sucking-fish (Echeneis remora), which of itself could not, without great difficulty, swim fast enough to supply itself with food, has an instrument not unlike a saw, with which it affixes itself to ships and the larger kinds of fishes, and in this manner is transported gratis from one shore of the world to another. The same Divine Artificer has given the sluggish fishing-frog (Lophius piscatorius) a kind of rod, furnished with a bait, by which it beguiles little fishes into its jaws. The slow-paced Lemur tardigradus is supplied with double ears that he may betake himself to the trees in time to avoid danger. We cannot avoid thinking that those which we know of the Divine works are much fewer than those of which we are ignorant.

[225]

LIPPS, THEODOR

LIPPS, THEODOR (1851-1914). During the decade that preceded the outbreak of the First World War, Theodor Lipps was one of the most influential professors in the German universities. His name attracted many students from other countries. Because of his mordant sarcasm he was dreaded as a critic, but notwithstanding his fondness for irony, he was a rigorous though by no means a narrow-minded moralist. He professed political and cultural liberalism, and was not afraid of defending freedom of thought and art in public meetings. Sometimes he defied openly his government.

After experimental studies on optical illusions, Lipps adopted the notion of empathy (*Einfuehlung*), which had been formulated by Robert Vischer, a historian of art, and made it more and more the center of his thinking. At the same time, he enlarged its meaning and possibility of application. In particular, aesthetic experience was defined by Lipps as empathy, as a psychic process by means of which he who enjoys a work of art is enabled to penetrate into its form and essence, and into the soul of the creative artist. Consequently, Lipps was opposed to all theories of art according to which the artistic work produces the illusion of a reality, or the spectator becomes aware of an illusion. From the aesthetic empathy, Lipps proceeded to its conception as the basis of the feeling and recognition of other egos. Death prevented Lipps from further elaboration of these conceptions. In his last years he adopted some notions of Husserl. On the other hand, Lipps broached various questions which Max Scheler later tried to answer, though he did so a different way.

THE SCIENCE OF AESTHETICS

AESTHETICS is the science of the "beautiful"; implicitly also of the "ugly." An object is called beautiful because it arouses or is able to arouse within me a special feeling, that which we call the "sense of beauty." In any case, we call beauty the faculty of an object to provoke within me a certain effect. In whatever manner we might determine it more properly, this effect, as an effect within me, is a psychological fact. Aesthetics seeks to determine, to analyze, to describe, to delimit the nature of this effect. Moreover, aesthetics seeks to make it understandable. For the latter purpose, it must indicate the factors that combine within me to produce such an effect. Especially it has to demonstrate the conditions which have to be fulfilled in an object so that this object shall be capable of provoking such an effect within me. It must find out the laws according to which these conditions work. This is a psychological task. Aesthetics, therefore, is a psychological discipline.

720

At the same time the aesthetician looks necessarily at the beautiful objects existing in nature and art. Not just at any object but just at those objects he tries to make aesthetically understandable. He applies his psychological insight to them. In so far, aesthetics may be called a discipline of applied psychology.

In so far as aesthetics describes, clarifies or explains, it is a describing or explaining science. In sharp contrast to such sciences one has placed the normative sciences. This contrast seems to be entirely clear. It is something different whether I ask what a thing is and why it is the way it is, or whether I ask whether or how a thing shall be. There is a difference between the statement of a fact and the laws governing a fact and the prescription, the request, in one word—the norm.

Yet this contrast is no contrast at all. Supposing I know the conditions for the production of a feeling of beauty, I know that, and why, these particular factors are apt to produce it, while others are not likely to produce it. I know the laws according to which certain conditions in their action and combined action evoke the feeling of beauty while others interfere in a disturbing manner. Then I can also indicate without ado which conditions have to be fulfilled and which have to be avoided whenever feeling of beauty in question shall be produced. That means the insight into the real fact is at the same time a prescription. That matters not only here but in all possible fields—namely, wherever a theory is confronted with a technique. Physical insights are at the same time prescriptions for a physical technique, physiological insights prescriptions for a physiological technique (that is, the medical practice). And aesthetical insights are necessarily prescriptions for the aesthetical technique (that is, for art).

[226]

LOCKE, JOHN

LOCKE, JOHN (1632-1704). It is an incontestable fact that the germs of the American Declaration of Independence are contained in the second of John Locke's *Two Treatises on Government,* published in 1690 in order to justify the British Whig Revolution of two years before. It is also generally acknowledged that Locke by proving, in his *Letter on Toleration* (1689), the necessity of separating Church and State, deeply influenced constitutional and cultural life in the United States. For many decades during the 18th century, Americans could rightly claim to be the true inheritors of Locke's political will, which was neglected in England, the philosopher's home. British liberalism became powerful when it returned to Locke, whose ideas, with Montesquieu and Voltaire as intermediaries, had conquered France, and subsequently imbued the spirit of Holland and Scandinavia.

Locke's political theory was based upon his conception of human nature which was formed by extensive studies and, even more, by the experiences of his life. He had suffered in political persecution, had been active as a diplomat, and engaged in physical, chemical and medical observations before and while he was writing on philosophical subjects. Locke always stressed his conviction that philosophy must be of practical use. He disliked school-dust. He never consciously forced a fact to fit his theory. He rather risked being accused of inconsistency. Modern historians, however, have stated that Locke was very often more cautious in his wording than his numerous and most famous critics had been.

The great task of an inquiry into the faculties and limits of human mind was accomplished by Locke in his *Essay on Human Understanding* (1690), the result of seventeen years of work. This is an immense topography of the realm of mental activities and, since the problem of knowledge is placed upon a psychological basis, the first comprehensive study in analytical psychology. It inaugurated the age of empiricism, and directed the thoughts of many philosophers in various periods. Still in the 20th century, Alfred North Whitehead, though diverging widely from Locke's main positions, used to extol Locke's "admirable adequacy," and thought that Locke had anticipated the principal points of the philosophy of organism.

When King William III appointed Locke minister to the court of the Hohenzollerns at Berlin, the philosopher, who in his early years had been an attaché there, declined this honor, objecting that

ard drinking was indispensable for a minister at that court, and
1at he, "the soberest man in the kingdom," could not be of
ny use there. Locke was a sober man not only in the regard
entioned by him on that occasion.

IDEAS AND SENSES

T is an established opinion among some men that there are
n the understanding certain *innate principles;* some primary
otions, characters, as it were, stamped upon the mind of
1an; which the soul receives in its very first being, and
rings into the world with it. It would be sufficient to con-
ince unprejudiced readers of the falseness of this supposi-
ion, if I should only show . . . how men, barely by the
se of their natural faculties, may attain to all the knowl-
dge they have, without the help of any innate impressions;
nd may arrive at certainty, without any such original no-
ions or principles. For I imagine anyone will easily grant
hat it would be impertinent to suppose the ideas of colors
nnate in a creature to whom God hath given sight, and a
ower to receive them by the eyes from external objects: and
o less unreasonable would it be to attribute several truths
o the impressions of nature, and innate characters, when we
nay observe in ourselves faculties fit to attain as easy and
ertain knowledge of them as if they were originally im-
rinted on the mind.

But because a man is not permitted without censure to
ollow his own thoughts in the search of truth, when they
ead him ever so little out of the common road, I shall set
lown the reasons that made me doubt of the truth of that
opinion, as an excuse for my mistake, if I be in one; which
I leave to be considered by those who, with me, dispose themselves to embrace truth wherever they find it.

There is nothing more commonly taken for granted than
that there are certain *principles* both *speculative* and *practical,* (for they speak of both), universally agreed upon by
all mankind; which, therefore, they argue, must needs be
the constant impressions which the souls of men receive in

their first beings and which they bring into the world with them, as necessarily and really as they do any of their inherent faculties.

This argument, drawn from universal consent, has this misfortune in it, that if it were true in matter of fact, that there were certain truths wherein all mankind agreed, it would not prove them innate, if there can be any other way shown how men may come to that universal agreement, in the things they do consent in, which I presume may be done.

But, which is worse, this argument of universal consent, which is made use of to prove innate principles, seems to me a demonstration that there are none such: because there are none to which all mankind gives an universal assent. I shall begin with the speculative, and instance in those magnified principles of demonstration, "Whatever is, is," and "It is impossible for the same thing to be and not to be"; which, of all others, I think have the most allowed title to innate. These have so settled a reputation of maxims universally received, that it will no doubt be thought strange if anyone should seem to question it. But yet I take liberty to say, that these propositions are so far from having an universal assent, that there are a great part of mankind to whom they are not so much as known.

*   *   *

Every man being conscious to himself, that he thinks; and that which his mind is applied about while thinking being the ideas that are there, it is past doubt that men have in their minds several ideas,—such as are those expressed by the words *whiteness, hardness, sweetness, thinking, motion, man, elephant, army, drunkenness,* and others: it is in the first place, then, to be inquired, *How he comes by them?* I know it is a received doctrine, that men have native ideas, and original characters, stamped upon their minds in their very first being. This opinion I have at large examined already; and I suppose what I have said in the foregoing Book will be much more easily admitted, when I have shown whence the understanding may get all the ideas it has; and by what ways and degrees they may come into the mind;—for which I shall appeal to every one's own observation and experience.

Let us then suppose the mind to be, as we say, white paper, void of all characters, without any ideas;—how comes it to be furnished? Whence comes it by that vast store which the busy and boundless fancy of man has painted on it with an almost endless variety? Whence has it all the materials of reason and knowledge? To this I answer, in one word, from *experience*. In that all our knowledge is founded; and from that it ultimately derives itself. Our observation, employed either about external sensible objects, or about the internal operations of our minds, perceived and reflected on by ourselves, is that which supplies our understandings with all the *materials* of thinking. These two are the fountains of knowledge, from whence all the ideas we have, or can naturally have, do spring.

First our senses, conversant about particular sensible objects, do convey into the mind several distinct perceptions of things, according to those various ways wherein those objects do affect them. And thus we come by those ideas we have of *yellow, white, heat, cold, soft, hard, bitter, sweet,* and all those which we call sensible qualities; which when I say the senses convey into the mind, I mean, they from external objects convey into the mind what produces there those perceptions. This great source of most of the ideas we have, depending wholly upon our senses, and derived by them to the understanding, I call *Sensation.*

Secondly, the other fountain from which experience furnisheth the understanding with ideas is,—the perception of the operations of our own mind within us, as it is employed about the ideas it has got;—which operations, when the soul comes to reflect on and consider, do furnish the understanding with another set of ideas, which could not be had from things without. And such are *perception, thinking, doubting, believing, reasoning, knowing, willing,* and all the different actings of our own minds; which we being conscious of and observing in ourselves, do from these receive into our understandings as distinct ideas as we do from bodies affecting our senses. This source of ideas every man has wholly in himself; and though it be not sense, as having nothing to do with external objects be called *internal sense*. But as I call the other sensation, so I call this Reflection, the ideas it affords being such only as the mind gets by reflecting on its own operations within itself. By reflection then, in the following part of this discourse, I would be understood to mean that notice which the mind takes of its own operations, and the manner of them, by reason whereof there come to be ideas of these operations in the understanding. These two, I say, viz. external material things, as the objects of sensation, and the operations of our minds within, as the objects of reflection, are to me the only originals from whence all our ideas take their beginnings. The term *operations* here I use in a large sense, as comprehending not barely the actions of the mind about its ideas, but some sort of passions arising sometimes from them, such as is the satisfaction or uneasiness arising from any thought.

The understanding seems to me not to have the least glimmering of any ideas which it doth not receive from one of these two. *External objects* furnish the mind with the ideas of sensible qualities, which are all those different perceptions they produce in us; and the *mind* furnishes the understanding with ideas of its own operations.

These, when we have taken a full survey of them, and their several modes [combinations, and relations], we shall find to contain all our whole stock of ideas; and that we have nothing in our minds which did not come in one of these two ways. Let any one examine his own thoughts, and thoroughly search into his understanding; and then let him tell me, whether all the original ideas he has there, are any other than of the objects of his senses, or of the operations of his mind, considered as objects of his reflection. And how great a mass of knowledge soever he imagines to be lodged there, he will, upon taking a strict view, see that he has not any idea in his mind but what one of these two have imprinted,— though perhaps with infinite variety compounded and enlarged by the understanding, as we shall see hereafter.

*   *   *

To discover the nature of our ideas the better, and to discourse of them intelligibly, it will be convenient to distinguish them as they are *ideas or perceptions in our minds*; and as they are *modifications of matter in the bodies that cause such perceptions in us;* that so we may not think (as perhaps usually is done) that they are exactly the images and resemblances of something inherent in the subject; most of those of sensation being in the mind no more the likeness of something existing without us, than the names that stand for them are the likeness of our ideas, which yet upon hearing they are apt to excite in us.

Whatsoever the mind perceives in itself, or is the immediate object of perception, thought, or understanding, that I call *idea;* and the power to produce any idea in our mind, I call *quality* of the subject wherein that power is. Thus a snowball having the power to produce in us the ideas of white, cold, and round,— the power to produce those ideas in us, as they are in the snowball, I call qualities; and as they are sensations or perceptions in our understandings, I call them ideas; which ideas, if I speak of sometimes as in the things themselves, I would be understood to mean those qualities in the objects which produce them in us.

[Qualities thus considered in bodies are, *First,* such as are utterly inseparable from the body, in what estate soever it be]; and such as in all the alterations and changes it suffers, all the force can be used upon it, it constantly keeps; and such as sense constantly finds in every particle of matter which has bulk enough to be perceived; and the mind finds inseparable from every particle of matter, though less than to make itself singly be perceived by our senses: v.g. take a grain of wheat, divide it into two parts; each part has still

727

solidity, extension, figure, and mobility; divide it again, and it retains still the same qualities; and so divide it on, until the parts become insensible; they must retain still each of them all those qualities. For division (which is all that a mill, or pestle, or any other body, does upon another, in reducing it to insensible parts) can never take away either solidity, extension, figure, or mobility from any body, but only makes two or more distinct separate masses of matter, of that which was but one before; all which distinct masses, reckoned as so many distinct bodies, after division, make a certain number. [These I call *original* or *primary* qualities of body, which I think we may observe to produce simple ideas in us, viz. solidity, extension, figure, motion or rest, and number.]

Secondly, such qualities, which in truth are nothing in the objects themselves but powers to produce various sensations in us by their primary qualities, i.e., by the bulk, figure, texture, and motion of their insensible parts, as colors, sounds, tastes, etc. These I call *secondary qualities.* To these might be added a *third* sort, which are allowed to be barely powers; though they are as much real qualities in the subject as those which I, to comply with the common way of speaking, call qualities, but for distinction, *secondary* qualities. [For the power in fire to produce a new color, or consistency, in wax or clay,—by its primary qualities, is as much a quality in fire, as the power it has to produce in *me* a new idea or sensation of warmth or burning, which I felt not before,—by the same primary qualities, viz. the bulk, texture, and motion of its insensible parts].

[The next thing to be considered is, how bodies produce ideas in us; and that is manifestly by impulse, the only way which we can conceive bodies to operate in].

If, then, external objects be not united to our minds when they produce ideas therein; and yet we perceive these original qualities in such of them as singly fall under our senses, it is evident that some motion must be thence continued by our nerves, or animal spirits, by some parts of our

odies, to the brains or the seat of sensation, there to pro-
luce in our minds the particular ideas we have of them. And
ince the extension, figure, number, and motion of bodies of
an observable bigness, may be perceived at a distance by
the sight, it is evident some singly imperceptible bodies must
come from them to the eyes, and thereby convey to the brain
some motion; which produces these ideas which we have of
them in us.

After the same manner that the ideas of these original
qualities are produced in us, we may conceive that the ideas
of *secondary* qualities are also produced, viz. by the operation of insensible particles on our senses. For, it being
manifest that there are bodies and good store of bodies, each
whereof are so small, that we cannot by any of our senses
discover either their bulk, figure, or motion,—as is evident
in the particles of the air and water, and others extremely
smaller than those, perhaps as much smaller than the particles of air or water, as the particles of air or water are
smaller than peas or hail stones;—let us suppose at present
that the different motions and figures, bulk and number, of
such particles, affecting the several organs of our senses,
produce in us those different sensations which we have from
the colors and smells of bodies; v.g. that a violet, by the
impulse of such insensible particles of matter, of peculiar
figures and bulks, and in different degress and modifications
of their motions, causes the ideas of the blue color, and sweet
scent of that flower to be produced in our minds. It being
no more impossible to conceive that God should annex such
ideas to such motions, with which they have no similitude,
than that he should annex the idea of pain to the motion of
a piece of steel dividing our flesh, with which that idea hath
no resemblance.

What I have said concerning colors and smells, may be
understood also of tastes and sounds, and other the like
sensible qualities; which, whatever reality we by mistake
attribute to them, are in truth nothing in the objects themselves, but powers to produce various sensations in us; and

depend on those primary qualities, viz. bulk, figure, texture and motion of parts [as I have said].

From whence I think it is easy to draw this observation —that the ideas of primary qualities of bodies are resem blances of them, and their patterns do really exist in th bodies themselves, but the ideas produced in us by thes secondary qualities have no resemblance of them at all. Ther is nothing like our ideas, existing in the bodies themselves They are, in the bodies we denominate from them, only power to produce those sensations in us; and what is sweet blue, or warm in idea, is but the certain bulk, figure, an motion of the insensible parts, in the bodies themselves which we call so.

The qualities, then, that are in bodies, rightly consid ered, are of three sorts:—

First, The bulk, figure, number, situation, and motio or rest of their solid parts. Those are in them, whether w perceive them or not; and when they are of that size tha we can discover them, we have by these an idea of the thin as it is in itself; as is plain in artificial things. These I cal *primary qualities.*

Secondly, The power that is in any body, by reaso of its insensible primary qualities, to operate after a peculia manner on any of our senses, and thereby produce in *us* th different ideas of several colors, sounds, smells, tastes, etc These are usually called *sensible qualities.*

Thirdly, The power that is in any body, by reason o the particular constitution of its primary qualities, to mak such a change in the bulk, figure, texture, and motion o *another body,* as to make it operate on our senses differentl from what it did before. Thus the sun has a power to mak wax white, and fire to make lead fluid. [These are usuall called *powers*].

The first of these, as has been said, I think may be prop erly called real, original, or primary qualities; because the are in the things themselves, whether they are perceived o ot; and upon their different modifications it is that the secondary qualities depend.

The other two are only powers to act differently upon other things; which powers result from the different modifications of those primary qualities.

But, though the two latter sorts of qualities are powers barely, and nothing but powers, relating to several other bodies, and resulting from the different modifications of the original qualities, yet they are generally otherwise thought of. For the second sort, viz. the powers to produce several ideas in us, by our senses, are looked upon as real qualities in the things thus affecting us; but the *third* sort are called and esteemed barely powers. V.g. The idea of heat or light, which we receive by our eyes, or touch, from the sun are commonly thought real qualities existing in the sun, and something more than mere powers in it. But when we consider the sun in reference to wax, which it melts or blanches, we look on the whiteness and softness produced in the wax, not as qualities in the sun, but effects produced by powers in it. Whereas, if rightly considered, these qualities of light and warmth, which are perceptions in me when I am warmed or enlightened by the sun, are no otherwise in the sun, than the changes made in the wax, when it is blanched or melted, are in the sun. They are all of them equally *powers in the sun, depending on its primary qualities;* whereby it is able, in the one case, so to alter the bulk, figure, texture, or motion of some of the insensible parts of my eyes or hands, as thereby to produce in me the idea of light or heat; and in the other, it is able so to alter the bulk, figure, texture, or motion of the insensible parts of the wax, as to make them fit to produce in me the distinct ideas of white and fluid.

The reason why the one are ordinarily taken for real qualities and the other only for bare powers, seems to be, because the ideas we have of distinct colors, sounds, etc., containing nothing at all in them of bulk, figure, or motion, we are not apt to think them the effects of these primary qualities; which appear not, to our senses, to operate in their production, and with which they have not any apparent congruity or conceivable connection. Hence it is that we are so forward to imagine, that those ideas are the resemblances of something really existing in the objects themselves; since sensation discovers nothing of bulk, figure, or motion of parts in their production; nor can reason show how bodies *by their bulk, figure, and motion,* should produce in the mind the ideas of blue or yellow, etc. But, in the other case, in the operations of bodies changing the qualities one of another, we plainly discover that the quality produced hath commonly no resemblance with anything in the thing producing it; wherefore we look on it as a bare effect of power

For, through receiving the idea of heat or light from the sun, we are apt to think *it* is a perception and resemblance of such a quality in the sun; yet when we see wax, or a fair face, receive change of color from the sun, we cannot imagine *that* to be the reception or resemblance of anything in the sun, because we find not those different colors in the sun itself. For, our senses being able to observe a likeness or unlikeness of sensible qualities in two different external objects, we forwardly enough conclude the production of any sensible quality in any subject to be an effect of bare power, and not the communication of any quality which was really in the efficient, when we find no such sensible quality in the thing that produced it. But our senses, not being able to discover any likeness between the idea produced in us and the quality of the object producing it, we are apt to imagine that our ideas are resemblances of something in the objects, and not the effects of certain powers placed in the modification of their primary qualities, with which primary qualities the ideas produced in us have no resemblance.

[227

LOMBARD, PETER

LOMBARD, PETER (About 1100-1160). For more than two centuries, Peter Lombard's *Four Books of Sentences* has been used as the chief textbook by students of theology. Born in the town of Lumello in Lombardy, Peter became a professor of theology at the Cathedral School of Notre Dame, Paris, and in 1159, he was Bishop of Paris. He was associated with St. Bernard and the teacher of Abailard, his later adversary.

He thought little of logic and epistemology. According to him, human knowledge is bound to remain fragmentary, but true knowledge is higher than faith which, on its part is higher than opinion. The tenets of metaphysics are to be verified by the study of the Holy Scriptures and thereupon defended by "Catholic reason." In order to offer his pupils a reliable basis for disputations, he compiled his collection of *Sentences* from the Fathers and early teachers of the Church.

TRINITY

THE truth of God could be known in a great many ways. Although, then, God is a single, simple essence, which consists of no diversity of parts or of accidents, still the Apostle says in the plural: "the invisible things of God," because the truth of God is known in many ways through things which have been made. For the eternal author is understood from the perpetuity of creatures; the omnipotent author from the magnitude of creatures; the wise author from the order and disposition; the good author from their government. But all these relate to revealing the unity of Deity. . . .

The image of the Trinity is revealed in a certain manner of its creatures; to be sure, no sufficient knowledge of the Trinity can be had, nor could it be had by the contemplation of creatures without the revelation of doctrine or of inward inspiration, wherefore, those ancient philosophers saw truth as if through a shadow and from a distance, failing in the sight of the Trinity as did the magicians of Pharaoh in the third sign. We are aided, none the less, in the faith of invisible things by the things which have been made. . . .

Memory, understanding, will are one, one mind, one essence. . . . In those three a kind of Trinity appears. Consequently, the rational mind, considering these three and that one essence in which they are, extends itself to the contemplation of the Creator and sees unity in trinity, and

trinity in unity. For it understands that there is one God, one
essence, one principle. It understands also that, if there
were two, either both would be insufficient or one would be
superfluous; because if something were lacking to one, which
the other had, there would not be supreme perfection in it;
but if nothing were lacking to one which the other had, since
all things would be in one, the other would be superfluous.
The rational mind understood therefore, that there is one
God, one author of all things.

[228]

LONGINUS, CASSIUS

LONGINUS, CASSIUS (Third century A.D.). The author of the
treatise *On the Sublime* has been called "the most modern of all
the ancient Greek philosophers" and "next to Aristotle, the greatest
literary critic of ancient Greece." All that is known about his personality has been drawn from some passages of his essay, for no
other information about him exists. Only this fact is undisputed—
that Longinus, the minister of Queen Zenobia of Palmyra, is not
the author of the treatise. Longinus, to whom *On the Sublime* has
been attributed for centuries, lived from about 213 to 273 A.D.,
while the treatise must have been written about 50 A.D.

Many authorities agree with Theodor Mommsen that the author probably was a Jew, and those who do not adopt that supposition cannot refute it. For it would have been quite improbable
that any gentile author at that time or during the following century and a half could quote from the Old Testament, not even if
he were interested, for one reason or another, in the laws and
customs of the Jews.

The author surely revered Homer and Moses alike. He speaks
of himself as a Greek. But so does Philo whose loyalty to Judaism
is beyond doubt. The author, evidently a disciple of Plato and the
Stoics, attacks severely another Jew, named Cecilius, who had
mordantly criticized Plato in a work that is lost. Cecilius was probably the first to compare Greek, Latin and Hebrew poetry, and his
anonymous adversary follows this method.

From Boileau and Milton to Burke and Kant, European
aesthetics and literary criticism have been inspired by this anonymous writer. Some of his concepts have been only slightly modified by Hegel and his successors, and even in the twentieth cen-

734

tury more than one critic and poet continue to apply the principles of diction which were originally formulated by the unknown Jewish Platonist or perhaps by his fellow-Jew, Cecilius.

THE SUBLIME IN HOMER AND MOSES

I HAVE hinted in another place that the Sublime is an image reflected from the inward greatness of the soul. Hence it comes to pass that a naked thought, without words, challenges admiration, and strikes by its grandeur. Such is the silence of Ajax in the *Odyssey*, which is undoubtedly noble and far above expression. To arrive at excellence like this, we must needs suppose that which is the cause of it. I mean that an orator of true genius must have no mean and ungenerous ways of thinking. For it is impossible that those who have grovelling and servile ideas, or are engaged in the sordid pursuits of life should produce anything worthy of admiration and the perusal of all posterity. Grand and sublime expressions must flow from them—and them alone—whose conceptions are stored and big with greatness.

And hence it is that the greatest thoughts are always uttered by the greatest souls. When Parmenio cried, "I would accept these propositions if I were Alexander," Alexander made this reply, "And so would I, if I were Parmenio." His answer showed the greatness of his mind. So the space between heaven and earth marks out the vast reach and capacity of Homer's ideas when he says:

"Whilst scarce the skies her horrid head can bound, She stalks on earth."

This description may with more justice be applied to Homer's genius than to the extent of discord. But what disparity, what a fall there is in Hesiod's description of melancholy, if the poem of *The Shield* may be ascribed to him: "A filthy moisture from her nostrils flowed." He has not represented his image as terrible, but loathsome and nau-

seous. On the other hand, with what majesty and pomp does
Homer exalt his deities:

"Far as a shepherd, from some point on high
O'er the wide main extends his boundless eye;
Through such a space of air, with thundering sound
At one long leap the immortal coursers bound."

He measures the leap of the horses by the extent of the
world; and who is there that, considering the superlative
magnificence of this thought, would not with good reason
cry out that if the steeds of the Deity were to take another
leap, the world itself would want room for it? How grand
and pompous also are those descriptions of the combats of
the gods:

"Heaven in loud thunder bids the trumpets sound,
And wide beneath them groans the rending ground.
Deep in the dismal regions of the dead
The Infernal Monarch reared his horrid head;
Leapt from his throne lest Neptune's arm should lay
His dark dominions open to the day,
And pour in light on Pluto's drear abodes,
Abhorred by men, and dreadful e'en to gods."

What prospect is here! The earth is laid open to its
centre; Tartarus itself disclosed to view; the whole world
in commotion and tottering on its basis, and what is more,
Heaven and Hell—things mortal and immortal—all combating together, and, sharing in the danger of this immortal
battle. But yet these bold representations—if not allegori-
cally understood—are downright blasphemy, and extrava-
gantly shocking. For Homer, in my opinion, when he gives
us a detail of the wounds, the seditions, the punishments,
imprisonments, tears of the deities, with those evils of every
kind under which they languish, has to the utmost of his
power exalted his heroes who fought at Troy into gods, and

legraded his gods into men. Nay, he makes their condition
vorse than human, for when man is overwhelmed in mis-
'ortune death affords a comfortable port, and rescues him
rom misery. But he represents the infelicity of the gods
is everlasting as their nature. And how far does he excel
hose descriptions of the gods when he sets a deity in his
rue light, and paints him in all his majesty, grandeur, and
)erfection, as in that description of Neptune which has been
ilready applauded by several writers:

"Fierce, as he passed, the lofty, mountains nod,
The forests shake, earth trembled as he trod,
And felt the footsteps of the immortal god.
His whirling wheels the glassy surface sweep.
The enormous monsters rolling on the deep,
Gambol around him on the watery way,
And heavy whales in awkward measure play.
The sea subsiding spreads a level plain,
Exults, and owns the monarch of the main;
The parting waves before his coursers fly;
The wondering waters leave the axles dry."

So, likewise the Jewish legislator—not an ordinary person—having conceived a just idea of the power of God, has
nobly expressed it in the beginning of his law: "And God
said, Let there be light, and there was light; Let the earth
oe, and the earth was."

[229]

LOTZE, RUDOLPH HERMANN

LOTZE, RUDOLPH HERMANN (1817-1881). Lotze dealt with the
principal problems of his philosophy three times and each time
somewhat differently. At the age of 24, he published his first *Metaphysics*, and two years later, in 1843, his first *Logic*. He developed
his views on metaphysics, logic, ethics and other topics in his
Microcosmos (1856-1864), and wrote a third *Logic* (1874) and a
third *Metaphysics* (1879). Death prevented him from revising his

737

Ethics and other disquisitions. Although his *Microcosmos* was no
meant as his last word, his name remains connected with thi
work which is regarded as one of the most important document
of modern German philosophy, and has influenced many grea
thinkers in foreign countries, not least of all America. Before th
publication of *Microcosmos*, Lotze was regarded as a physiologi
rather than a philosopher. He had studied and taught medicine an
physiology, and had become known by his theory of "local signs,'
an attempt to establish relations between sensory affections an
areas of the brain, and even more by his rigorous criticism of th
concept of "vital force," by demonstrating that physiological pro
cesses can and must be explained by strictly mechanistic terms. I
his first *Logic*, he protested against any blending of logic with meta
physics. In his first *Metaphysics* he severely criticized German idea
ism. Lotze's *Microcosmos* is of anthropocentric character, and i
this work the effort to reconcile philosophy and religion, philosoph
and science, knowledge and the needs of human nature is conspic
uous. Maintaining his conviction of the mutual affection of min
and body, Lotze proceeds to a monism which he characterizes a
teleological idealism, sometimes as panpsychism. The mechanisti
interpretation of nature is considered unavoidable, but Lotze in
sists that there are ideal interests, values and duties which are no
to be rejected as phantoms because they cannot be proved mechan
istically, and that psychic life cannot be compared with external
natural occurrences. All concepts of the cosmic order are reduce
to a consciousness of truth, facts and values. Evidently inspired b
Malebranche, Lotze assumes God as the ultimate cause of all events
all becoming, and the condition of the possible.

In his third stage, Lotze tried to formulate his ideas more pre
cisely. He abandoned panpsychism. Always devoted to modern hu
manism, Lotze abhorred the idea of revolution, and did not lik
democracy.

SOUL-LIFE

IT is a strange and yet an intelligible pride that our scien
tific illuminati take in requiring for the explanatory recon
struction of reality in thought no other postulates than a
original store of matter and force, and the unshaken authorit
of a group of universal and immutable laws of Nature
Strange, because after all these are no trifling postulates
and because it might be expected to be more in accordanc
with the comprehensive spirit of the human reason t

cknowledge the unity of a creative cause than to have im-
osed on it as the starting-point of all explanation the prom-
scuous variety of merely actually existent things and no-
ons. And yet intelligible, for in return for this single sacri-
ce the finite understanding may now enjoy the satisfaction
f never again being overpowered by the transcendent sig-
ificance and beauty of any single phenomenon; however
ondrous and profound may appear to it any work of Na-
re, those universal laws, which are to it perfectly trans-
arent, give it the means of warding off a disagreeable im-
ression, and, while proving how perfectly it understands that
ven this phenomenon is but an incidental result of a well-
nown order of Nature, it succeeds in drawing within the
mits of its own finitude what to the unprejudiced mind is
nceivable only as a product of infinite wisdom.

These tendencies and habits of scientific culture it will
e hard to shake, especially by the arguments usually brought
 bear on them by the believers in a higher, intelligent guid-
nce of the course of Nature. For however distinctly un-
iased observation may suggest this belief, so that it may
em alike foolish and tedious to attempt to understand the
rder of Nature without it, the supporters of the mechan-
al conception can always with justice reply that neverthe-
ss in the explanation of details their road is always entered
y those who on the whole believe unquestioningly in the
overnment of an intelligent working power. They, too, are
t content till, for each result ordained by this power, they
ave one by one traced out the efficient means through whose
ecessary and blind causal connection the required effect
ust be brought about. Even they will never seriously be-
eve that within Nature as it lies patent to our senses, this
urposive power makes new beginnings of working, such as,
traced further back, would not always prove to be the
ecessary results of a prior state of things. While thus even
 those who hold the more religious view, the course of
ents is again converted into the unbroken chain of mechan-
al sequence, from the scientific point of view the latter

739

alone is conspicuous, and the idea of free action on the part of an intelligent force, to which no sphere of action can be assigned, is readily dropped. Science might be able to allow that the origin of the whole, whose internal relations alone form the subject of its investigations, may be attributed to a Divine Wisdom, but it would demand facts that, within the sphere of experience, made a continuous dependence of the creation on the preserving providence of its author a necessary condition of explanation. Too ingenuous and self-confident, the believers in this living interference of reason working towards an end bring forward only the fair aspect of life, and for the time forget its shadows; in their admiration of the wondrous harmony of organized bodies, and of their careful adaptation to the ends of mental life, they do not think of the bitter persistence with which this same organized life transmits ugliness and disease from generation to generation, or of the manifold hindrances that come in the way of the attainment even of modest human aims. How little, then, can this conception of the universe—to which the presence of evil is, if not an insoluble, at least an unsolved problem—hope by its assaults to overcome habit of mind that finds numberless special confirmation in observation, and is inaccessible to any feeling of the universal deficiency under which we suppose it to labor!

And is it compelled to make even the acknowledgment which it will perhaps make, that this world of blind necessity came forth at least primarily from the wisdom of supreme creator? Doubtless it can reply that even the positiveness of the present fabric, as it now is, could certainly have been evolved from the confusion of an original chaos under the sway of universal laws. For all that was brought together by a planless vortex, in unmeaning aggregation and without the internal equilibrium of constituents and force that might have secured to it a longer existence in the struggle with the onward-sweeping course of external Nature: all this has long since perished. Along with and after numberless unsuccessful attempts at formation, which per-

fill this hiatus, and weld
into the solid whole of
 Certainly it cannot;
selves, as a necessity pre
ticular cases? There car
inherent states; and a un
it is the order has come
tween beings as a self-ex
gether, an efficient, cont
our human life, we shall
lations do not exist besi
reality, are not powers to
because there they are;
of the individuals who
sanction and reality only
sons; they are nothing b
developed direction of n
later generalizing scrutin
externally-directing powe
over many it no longer
product of one. The law
ordinances of the human
said and disobeyed, the
limited and resistless; n
pass what is self-contrad
ence on that which can l
what is self-existent. We
speculations by a wide
speech that exercises no
of the incidents of daily
arisen. We speak of tie
which they enter, of an o
of laws under whose sw
hardly notice the contra
of relations lying ready l
them, of an order wait
finally, of ties stretched

haps filled primeval times in a rapid alternation of rise and decay, Nature gradually shrank into a narrower channel, and only those select creatures were preserved on which a happy combination of their constituent parts had bestowed the power of withstanding the pressure of surrounding stimuli, and of propagating their kind throughout an indefinite period. However little we may probably esteem this theory, we could yet hardly snatch it from those whom it satisfies, and we ourselves cannot wholly disallow the charm that scientific ingenuity will always find in the attempt to evolve from the formless chaos of whirling motions the necessity of a gradual sifting, and the spontaneous formation of permanent forms of succession of phenomena.

But all such attempts rest on the common assumption that the universal sway of unchanging laws prescribes the kind and amount of the reciprocal actions engaged in by the several substances of the original chaos, and thereby compels them to withdraw from combinations in which no equilibrium is possible, and to enter into others in which they are at rest, or can retain a constant mode of motion. This assumption it is whose trustworthiness we must now test; with it stands or falls the proud certainty of the mechanical conception of the universe. Is this veneration for an all-prevailing law of Nature, as the only bond that forces the scattered elements of the course of things into mutual active relations and determines the character of their results, itself a possible conception, and can it put the finishing touch to our view of Nature, whose perfecting in detail we ourselves have everywhere looked to it to accomplish?

Let us suppose two elements originally in existence, not produced by anything, not sprung from any common source, existing from eternity as things actual without any antecedents, but existing so that they have no other community than that of contemporaneous existence: how could the influence of the one be communicated to the other, seeing that each is as it were in a separate world, and that between them there is nothing? How is the efficacy of the one to make

its way to the
of transmissior
element consta
phere through
light where it
ing idly in vac
we have gaine
tion, either hc
that in which
interval of tin
be its object, i
in the end rea
forming powe
no obstacle to
arated by it, 1
in space woul
tion, or expla
of which in it
the other by
The transmiss
simple only to
ficial, commoi
in the externa
one examinin
inexplicable
force compell
states. As, be
outflow into
edge that all
and that the
prehensible p
suppose in ai
inadequate to
do not inher
course of Na
the idea of a

that we could not describe—across the abyss that divides one
being from another. We do not consider that all relations
and connections exist only in the unity of observing consciousness, which, passing from one element to another, knits
all together by its comprehensive activity, and that in like
manner all efficacious order, all laws, that we are fain to
conceive as existing between things independently of our
knowledge, can exist only in the unity of the One that binds
them all together. Not the empty shadow of an order of Nature, but only the full reality of an infinite living being of
whom all finite things are inwardly cherished parts, has
power so to knit together the multiplicity of the universe
that reciprocal actions shall make their way across the chasm
that would eternally divide the several distinct elements from
one another. For action, starting from one being, is not lost
in an abyss of nothing lying between it and another; but as
in all being the truly existent is one and the same, so in all
reciprocal action the infinite acts only on itself, and its activity never quits the sure foundation of being. The ener-
gizing of one of its parts is not confined to that and isolated
from the rest; the single state has not to travel along an
indescribable path in order to seek another element to which
it may impart itself, nor has it to exert an equally incomprehensible force in order to compel that indifferent other element to participate in it. Every excitation of the individual
is an excitation of the whole Infinite, that forms the living
basis even of the individual's existence, and every one can
therefore act upon every other which has the same living
basis; for it is this which from the unity of its own nature
causes the finite event here to be followed by its echo there.
It is not anything finite that out of itself as finite acts upon
something else; on the contrary, every stimulation of the
individual, seeing that it affects the eternal basis that in it,
as in all, forms the essence of its finite appearance, can
through this continuity of related being—but through this
alone—act upon the apparently remote.

We are not constrained to this recognition of an Infinite

Substance, that instead of an unsubstantial and unreal law unites all things by its actual reality, merely by admiration for single spheres of phenomena, by whose special significance we are impressed; nay, every example of reciprocal action however insignificant, every instance of causality, forces us, in order to understand the possibility of a transference of influence, to substitute for a merely natural connection a substantial Infinite, containing unseparated the manifold that in phenomenal existence is separated. We could not seek such a bond between the constituents of the living body alone, or between body and soul pre-eminently, as if we did not need it everywhere; on the contrary, seeing that we look on all that happens, however it may be designated, as but the manifested internal energy of a single Infinite Being, the later course of our speculations will carry us further from the resuscitated mythology that, like the ancient sagas, allots to certain distinguished phenomena their special genii, and leaves the remaining work-day reality to take care of itself.

For this Universal Being is not a mere bond, a mere indifferent bridge, having no other office than to form a way for the passage of action from one element to another: it is at the same time the sovereign power that for every antecedent fixes the form and degree of its consequent, for each individual the sphere of its possible activity, for every single manifestation of the latter its particular mode. We deceive ourselves when we imagine we can derive the modes in which things act on one another, as self-evident results, from the particular properties that now constitute their nature, and from the joint influence of the circumstances of each occasion. Honest consideration, on the contrary, leads us to make the acknowledgment that the effects actually presented to us by experience are not to be got as necessary conclusions from these premises alone, however we may analyze and recombine their content, but that an unknown power, as it were, having respect to something that we do not meet with among these prior conditions, has annexed to their form the particular form of the result. The Infinite is this secret power, and that to which it has respect in the determination of results is its own presence in all finite elements, by which the universe receives the unity of a being, and on account of which the course of its events must receive the unity of a connected manifestation of the content of that being. Every finite thing, therefore, possesses the capability of action only in such amount and such quality as it is permitted by the Infinite to contribute to the realization of the whole.

[230]

LOVEJOY, ARTHUR ONCKEN

LOVEJOY, ARTHUR ONCKEN (1873-). Shortly before the twentieth century began, two young, and then unknown, American philosophers made a horse-car trip during which one, named William P. Montague, asked the other whose name was Arthur O. Lovejoy, what he considered the chief end of man, and Lovejoy answered: self-consciousness, just what most philosophers regard as the starting point of their thinking. This viewpoint has remained characteristic of Lovejoy's philosophy. What other thinkers are apt to take for granted, he deals with as a problem.

Lovejoy calls his position "temporalized realism." To him, the most indubitable fact of all our experience is that experience itself is temporal. This cognition has been used by him as a touchstone to be applied to all theories about the nature of reality or of knowledge. He has used it for the rejection of all dominant forms of idealism and monism. He maintains that rationality, when conceived as complete and excluding all arbitrariness, becomes itself a kind of irrationality, excluding any limiting and selective principle. The world of concrete existence is a contingent world whose laws show some inexpugnable traits of arbitrariness. Otherwise it would be a world without power of choice, without character. Man is, by the most distinctive impulse of his nature, an interpretative animal who seeks to know the causes of things through trial and error in the course of time. The history of man's reflection, and the history of philosophy especially, is, to a large extent, a history of confusion of ideas, and Lovejoy has devoted much of his energy to analyze and unravel this confusion. An outstanding example of his method is in his book *The Great Chain of*

Being (1936). Thus Lovejoy's interest in critical philosophy is closely interwoven with his interest in historical thought and research.

THE COMPLEXITY OF ISMS

IDEALISM, romanticism, rationalism, transcendentalism, pragmatism—all these trouble-breeding and usually thought-obscuring terms . . . are names of complexes, not of simples. They stand, as a rule, not for one doctrine, but for several distinct and often conflicting doctrines held by different individuals or groups to whose way of thinking these appellations have been applied either by themselves or in the traditional terminology of historians; and each of these doctrines, in turn, is likely to be resolvable into simpler elements, often very strangely combined and derivative from a variety of dissimilar motives and historic influences. The term "Christianity," for example, is not the name for any single unit of the type for which the historian of specific ideas looks. I mean by this not merely the notorious fact that persons who have equally professed and called themselves Christians have, in the course of history, held all manner of distinct and conflicting beliefs under the one name, but also that any of these persons and sects has, as a rule, held under that name a very mixed collection of ideas, the combination of which into a conglomerate bearing a single name and supposed to constitute a real unity was usually the result of historic processes of a highly complicated and curious sort. It is, of course, proper and necessary that ecclesiastical historians should write books on the history of Christianity; but in doing so they are writing of a series of facts which, taken as a whole, have almost nothing in common except the name; the part of the world in which they occurred; the reverence for a certain person, whose nature and teaching, however, have been most variously conceived, so that the unity here too is largely a unity of name; and the identity of a part of their historic antecedents, of certain causes or influences which, diversely combined with other causes, have made each

747

of these systems what it is. In the whole series of creeds and movements going under the one name, and in each of them separately, it is needful to go behind the superficial appearance of singleness and identity, to crack the shell which holds the mass together, if we are to see the real units, the effective working ideas, which, in any given case, are present.

[231]

LUCRETIUS (Titus Lucretius Carus)

LUCRETIUS (TITUS LUCRETIUS CARUS) (98-55 B.C.). The system of Epicurus was converted into a striking picture of cosmic and human life by Lucretius in his poem *De Rerum Natura* (On the Nature of Things). A tense, electric atmosphere permeates this poem. Much more than a didactic work, it is the confession of a man of violent passions who is longing for equanimity, and, while cleansing his own mind of false ideas, proves to be ready to sacrifice even those illusions that apparently promise peace of mind.

The only extant report of Lucretius' life was written by Jerome, the Father of the Church, who certainly does not approve of the poet's opinions and quite possibly is not an impartial biographer. According to Jerome, Lucretius was afflicted by intermittent insanity, and committed suicide. Some sayings of Lucretius himself indicate that he was threatened by mental disease, and it is probable that he became resolved to die voluntarily when he felt that he had lost the tranquil mind which alone, in his belief, makes life tolerable.

It almost happened that Lucretius' poem was entirely lost. Emperor Augustus, who tried to restitute ancient religion, stigmatized Lucretius, whose memory vanished subsequently, and all but one manuscript of his poems was destroyed. The epoch of the Renaissance meant also the revival of Lucretius, who has since been considered one of the greatest poets of world literature. He was admired by Milton, Shelley and Walt Whitman, whose "Apostrophe to Death" may be traced to his reading of Lucretius. Alfred Tennyson, relying on Jerome, made Lucretius the object of a pathological study.

748

ATOMIC MATERIALISM

ALL nature, as it exists by itself, is founded on two things: there are bodies and there is void in which these bodies are placed and through which they move about. If room and space which we call void did not exist, bodies could not be placed anywhere nor move about at all to any side. Moreover, there is nothing which you can affirm to be at once separate from all body and quite distinct from void, which would, so to say, count as the discovery of a third nature. For whatever shall exist, this of itself must be something or other. Now if it shall admit of touch in however slight and small a measure, it will, be it with a large or be it with little addition, provided it does exist, increase the amount of body and join the sum. But if it shall be intangible and unable to hinder any thing from passing through it on any side, this you are to know will be that which we call empty void. Therefore, besides void and bodies no third nature taken by itself can be left in the number of things, either such as to fall at any time under the ken of our senses or such as any one can grasp by the reason of his mind.

Since there has been found to exist a twofold and widely dissimilar nature of two things, that is to say of body and of place in which things severally go on, each of the two must exist for and by itself and quite unmixed. For wherever there is empty space which we call void, there body is not; wherever again body maintains itself, there empty void nowise exists. First bodies, therefore, are solid and without void.

Again, since there is void in things begotten, solid matter must exist about this void, and no thing can be proved by true reason to conceal in its body and have within it void, unless you choose to allow that which holds it in is solid. Again that can be nothing but a union of matter which can keep in the void of things. Matter, therefore, which consists of a solid body, may be everlasting, though all things else are dissolved.

Moreover, if there were no empty void, the universe would be solid; unless, on the other hand, there were certain bodies to fill up whatever places they occupied, the existing universe would be empty and void space. Therefore, sure enough, body and void are marked off in alternate layers, since the universe is neither of a perfect fullness nor a perfect void.

Therefore, if first bodies (atoms) are, as I have shown, solid and without void, they must be everlasting. Again, unless matter had been eternal, all things before this would have utterly returned to nothing and whatever things we see would have been born anew from nothing. But since I have proved above that nothing can be produced from nothing, and that what is begotten cannot be recalled to nothing, first-beginnings must be of an imperishable body, into which all things can be dissolved at their last hour, that there may be a supply of matter for the reproduction of things. Therefore, first-beginnings (atoms) are of solid singleness, and in no other way can they have been preserved through ages during infinite time past in order to reproduce things.

The nature of the mind and soul is bodily; for when it is seen to push the limbs, rouse the body from sleep, and alter the countenance, and guide and turn about the whole man, and when we see that none of these effects can take place without touch nor touch without body, must we not admit that the mind and the soul are of a bodily matter? Therefore, the nature of the mind must be bodily, since it suffers from bodily weapons and blows.

I will now go on to explain of what kind of body the mind consists and out of what it is formed. First of all I say that it is extremely fine and formed by exceedingly minute bodies. That this is so you may perceive from what follows; nothing that is seen takes place with a velocity equal to that of the mind when it starts some suggestion and actually sets it agoing; the mind, therefore, is stirred with greater rapidity than any of the things whose nature stands out visible to sight. But that which is so passing nimble must consist of seeds exceedingly round and exceedingly minute, in order to be stirred and set in motion by a small moving power. Thus water is moved and heaves by ever so small a force, formed as it is of small particles apt to roll. But the nature of honey is more sticky, its liquid more sluggish, and its movement more dilatory; for the whole mass of matter coheres more closely, because it is made of bodies not so smooth, fine, and round. Since, then, the nature of the mind has been found to be eminently easy to move, it must consist of bodies exceedingly small, smooth, and round.

A tree cannot exist in the ether, nor clouds in the deep sea, nor fishes live in the fields, nor blood exist in woods, nor sap in stones. Where each thing can grow and abide is fixed and ordained. Thus the nature of the mind cannot come into being alone without the body nor exist far away from the sinews and blood. But since in our body even it is fixed and seen to be ordained where the soul and the mind can severally be and grow, it must still more strenuously be denied that it can abide and be born out of the body altogether. Therefore, when the body has died, we must admit that the soul has perished, wrenched away throughout the body.

Death, therefore, to us is nothing, concerns us not a jot, since the nature of the mind is proved to be mortal; and as in time long gone by we felt no distress when the Carthagian hosts came, and all things were shaken by war's troublous uproar, and mortal men were in doubt which of the two peoples it should be to whose empire all must fall by sea and land alike, thus when we shall no more, when there shall have been a separation of body and soul, out of both of which we are each formed into a single being, to us, you may be sure, who then shall be no more, nothing whatever can happen to excite sensation, not if earth shall mingle with sea and sea with heaven.

And even supposing the nature of the mind and power of the soul do feel, after they have been severed from our body, yet that is nothing to us who by the binding tie of marriage between body and soul are formed each into one single being. And if time should gather up our matter after our death and put it once more into position in which it now is, and the light of life be given to us again, this result even would concern us not at all, when the chain of our self-consciousness has once been snapped asunder.

[232]

LULLY, RAYMOND (Raymundus Lullus)

LULLY, RAYMOND (RAYMUNDUS LULLUS) (1235-1315). Because of his great learning, Lully was called "Doctor Illuminatus." He was born on the island of Majorca, where Christian civilization was in close contact with Jewish and Arabic lore. Lully was the first Christian scholar to study the Cabala, which he regarded as a divine science and a true revelation for the rational soul. He also studied Arabic philosophy but became a sworn adversary of Averröism. In 1275 he published his *Ars Generalis,* intended to serve as a basis for all sciences and as a key to invention and discovery. This work was much admired, even several hundred years later by Giordano Bruno and Leibniz. Lully was a great linguist and in 1311 he obtained the consent of the Council of Vienna for teachers of Hebrew and Arabic to be admitted to the papal schools and the great universities. His great ambition was to convert Moslems to Christianity. He agitated for crusades and travelled alone through Islamic North Africa. Probably he suffered a martyr's death. Lully was also a prolific poet, and is considered to have been a great master of the Catalan language.

ON LOVE

LONG and perilous are the paths by where the Lover seeks the Beloved. They are peopled by cares, sighs and tears. They are lit up by love.

Between Hope and Fear, Love made her home. She lives on thought, and when she is forgotten, dies. So unlike the pleasures of this world are their foundations.

There was a contention between the eyes and the memory of the Lover. For the eyes said that it was better to see the Beloved than to remember Him. But Memory said that re-

752

membering brings tears to the eyes, and makes the heart to burn with love.

The Lover asked the Understanding and the Will which of them was the nearer to his Beloved. And the two ran, and the Understanding came nearer to the Beloved than did the Will.

The keys of the gate of love are gilded with cares and desires, sighs and tears; the cord which binds them is woven of conscience, devotion, contrition and atonement; the door is kept by justice and mercy.

The path of love is both long and short. For love is clear, pure, and bright, subtle, yet simple, strong, diligent, brilliant, and abounding both in fresh thoughts and old memories.

"What meanest thou by love?" said the Beloved. And the Lover answered "It is to bear on one's heart the sacred marks and the sweet words of the Beloved. It is to long for Him with desire and with tears. It is boldness. It is fervor. It is fear. It is the desire for the Beloved above all things. It is that which causes the Lover to grow faint when he hears the Beloved's praises. It is that in which I die and in which is all my will."

[233]

LU WANG (Lu Hsiang-Shan)

LU WANG (LU HSIANG-SHAN) (1139-1192). Confucianism has become most scholastic in the philosophy of Lu Wang, whose thinking was imbued with the spirit of Buddhism although his terminology remained Confucian. He considered mind as the embodiment of reason, and taught training of the mind by "tranquil repose," in which state the essences of truth and goodness will be perceived by intuition, and the individual will be united with the universe. Neo-Confucianism revolted against Lu Wang's metaphysics which regards moral conduct as a mere consequence of intuitive insight into the essences of reality. In recent times, Lu Wang's philosophy was revived by Liang Sou-ming whose book *The Civilization and Philosophy of the East and the West* (1921) was a great sensation in China.

ON HUMAN NATURE

HUMAN Nature is originally good. Any evil in it results from the changes made upon it by [external] things. He who knows the injury caused by [those external] things and who can revert to himself [i.e. can return to his original condition], can then know that goodness is the innate possession of our Nature.

*   *   *

Mind should not be contaminated with anything; it should stand alone and independent. In its original state, the Mind of Man contains no disorder, [but gradually and] confusedly it is led astray by [external] things. If one has the proper spirit, he will immediately rise [above things], and will [attain the original] good. But if one continuously moves away [from the Original Mind], he will then become corrupted.

*   *   *

Where there is good there must be evil. [The transition from one to the other] is truly [like] the turning over of one's hand. Goodness, however, is so from the very beginning, whereas evil comes into existence only as a result of such a 'turning over.'

What is it that will injure your Mind? It is Desire. When Desires are many, what we can preserve of our [Original] Mind is inevitably little; and [conversely], when the Desires are few, what we can preserve of our [Original] Mind is inevitably much. Therefore, the Superior Man does not worry that his Mind is not preserved, but rather worries that his Desires are not made few. For if the Desires were eliminated, the Mind would automatically be preserved. Thus, then, does not the preserving of what is good in our Mind depend upon the elimination of what does it injury?

*   *   *

Common men and vulgarians are submerged [either] by poverty or wealth, or by high or low position, or by benefit or injury, or by profit or loss, or by sounds and colors, or by sensuality and Desire. They [thus] destroy their 'virtuous Mind,' and have no regard for Righteousness and Law. How very lamentable it is!

If scholars of today could only concentrate their attention on Truth and Law—in every affair being observant of the right, and refusing to follow the Passions and Desires—then, even though their understanding were not wholly complete and clear, and their conduct were not entirely according to the mean and moderate, yet they would not fail to be the successors of good men and correct scholars [i.e., of the sages and worthies of ancient times].

*　　*　　*

There is not one who does not love his parents and respect his elder brother. But when one is blinded by profit and Desire, then it is otherwise.

*　　*　　*

Those who follow Material Desires gallop [after them] without knowing [where] to stop. Those who follow [superficial] opinions also gallop [after them] without knowing [where] to stop. Therefore, 'although the Way is near, yet they seek for it afar; although a thing is easy [to deal with], yet they seek for it in its difficult [aspects].' But is the Truth [really] remote or the things [really] difficult? [It is because] their opinions are unsound, that they make difficulties for themselves. If one fully realizes one's error, then one's becloudings and doubts will be dissipated and one will reach the place in which to stop.

[234]

LUZZATTO, MOSES HAYIM

LUZZATTO, MOSES HAYIM (1707-1747). Some occurrences in Luzzatto's life show a parallel to that of Spinoza. Just as Spinoza earned his living by grinding optical lenses, Luzzatto did the same by lenses. Like Spinoza, he was ex-communicated from his coreligionists. But Luzzatto remained a faithful Jew, ardently devoted to the cause of Judaism. He even felt himself, like the Messiah, bound to rescue the Jewish people from danger and misery, and he believed that the study of the Cabala would enable him to perform that mission. Notwithstanding pressure on the part of orthodox rabbis, Luzzatto did not turn his thoughts from the mysticism that not only incited his loftiest aspirations but also inspired him to the conception of high ethical principles. Luzzatto was a versatile and gifted writer whose Hebrew style is much admired. He composed a drama, many liturgical poems and philosophical treatises in Hebrew, while his mystical works were written in Aramaic. His best-known book is *Mesillat Yesharim* (Path of the Upright, 1740) which has been compared with Bunyan's *Pilgrim's Progress* though it was not influenced by the latter. In 1746, Luzzatto emigrated to the Holy Land where he died shortly after his arrival.

UNDERSTANDING AND UPRIGHTNESS

UNDERSTANDING: O Uprightness, beloved of my soul, let thy heart take courage; like a girdle gird on strength! For when assistance seems very far away, relief comes suddenly to us. When in the blazing heat, in summer drought, the sky is covered with thick darkness of the clouds, whose thunder's roaring makes the earth beneath to quake; when lightning flashes like an arrow; when the wind rends the mounts, as though they were earthen pitchers; when at the sound of the abundance of rain, all ears grow deaf; then the beasts of the forest all together take refuge, and all the young doves flee unto the clefts of rocks. But in a moment, with the radiance of its light, the sun shines forth, and breaks through, and dispels all clouds and darkness, so that the storm is then as though it had not been. Thus likewise He, who rules the world with might, causes relief from trouble to spring forth within a moment unto the contrite.

Uprightness: O Understanding, O joy of my heart, thy comforting has surely enlarged my heart. For now it seems as though from the words of thy mouth I behold an opening for my hope. But be so kind, if thou hast good tidings, with-hold it not from me.

Understanding: Would that I had good tidings! I would not hide it. Howbeit, I hope to bring it to thee, though not now. For the worker of righteousness shall not forever fail, nor shall the hope of the perfect perish forever. Though Arrogance now rises high, reaches to the clouds, and rides prosperously on the high places of the earth; he is strong and firmly rooted, waxes mighty in his strength; he abstains not from all his lusts, and sees no trouble, neither does he know affliction's cords; but he will be brought down unto the nether-world, and there shall his pride of heart be humbled; instead of haughtiness he will clothe himself with disgrace like a garment; instead of glory, he shall take shame for ever. But thou, the fruit of thy faithfulness shalt thou find in due time; the end of all the troubles of thy soul shalt thou behold, and be for ever satisfied. And when relief comes, thou wilt be thankful for thy affliction; for sorrows which are past and gone are even as great joys esteemed on the day of bliss; for the recollection of them increases our gladness.

Uprightness: Fain would I (if I could muster strength) endure bravely by bitter lot, according to my wish, O Understanding; but it is hard for me, whenever mine eyes see the two stones of stumbling, Deceit and Folly, who take counsel together to be as pricks to me and cause me grief of soul. For noisily Folly shouts on the street; she treads on all the highest places of the town with impudent countenance; she knows no fear, and knows no shame; she breaks all covenants, annuls all laws; there is no faithfulness in her; falsehood is her right hand; her merchandise is violence, perjury, and treachery. She is a sister to all evil and a mother to all sin; but all the sons of prudence she oppresses unto death; she sits and speaks against them, and slanders them amidst bowls of wine; her inner thoughts are for evil against them; if she were able, she would devour them as a fish, or would bite them like an ass, and break their bones. And likewise is Deceit; for with the flattering of his mouth he hunts for souls as for a bird, and he feeds the dolt and fool with poison and death covered with honey; he bites when he kisses, and when his hands pretend to cure he bruises; he does according to all his desire, and yet succeeds.

Understanding: Indeed, it is but the illusion of our eyes, for they are eyes of flesh, and, therefore, they confound truth with falsehood. They change darkness into light, and light into darkness. Now, if in matters that they can perceive, they err at every occasion and chance, how greatly must they err in matters hidden and concealed from them! Look at the end of an oar put in the water: Lo, it appears to thee twisted and crooked, although thou knowest in thy heart that in reality it is straight. Sheshai and Talmai appear like ants, when reflected in a concave mirror; but in a convex mirror the effect is reversed. Consider now our spirit, which is like the sea ceaselessly agitated by the conflicts with the wind: its billows surge wildly, and are tossed about from place to place; even so our spirit is never free from grief. And as our sorrows change the moods of our spirit, so are our senses changed from time to time: We only see what we desire; our ears only hear what we long for, or that which our imagination conceives. If we would have seen this world with clear eyes but once, then could we have beheld these our enemies together so afflicted, stricken, and distressed, that we would have said: 'Enough! we have had our fill of vengeance!' Lo, as thine eyes see them all filled with bliss, and satisfied with ease, so truly are their feet entangled in the net, where they are held since long, and whence they will not escape; their steps take hold on the depth of the nether-world; as soon as their feet slip, they will have no power to rise there again. Now take thou courage, gird on strength! I shall go now and look about; if there is aught I hear, I shall return, and tell thee; for the present rest thou still, and direct the meditations of thy heart and all thy thoughts according to thy wisdom. Lo, there is no bravery like the bravery of a man who conquers his strong passions and rules over his spirit; only the heart that keeps vexation far away rests and reposes.

[235]

M

MACH, ERNST

MACH, ERNST (1838-1916). Mach made important discoveries and wrote a number of standard works in the fields of mechanics, theory of heat, optics and acoustics. He was also an academic teacher to whom his audience was enthusiastically devoted. While he refused to be called a philosopher, he did accept acknowledgment as a methodologist of science and a psychologist of knowledge. In fact, he formulated positivism anew, differing from Comte in attributing an equal importance to psychic as to physical facts. His aim was to attain a standpoint entirely free from metaphysics, and to eliminate all hypotheses which cannot be controlled by experience, to create an epistemology which preserves all advantages of empiricism without any ontological implication, be it idealistic or materialistic. Trying to avoid all anthropomorphical conceptions in science, he even regarded causality as a remainder of primitive religion, and would only admit functional dependence, as it is used in mathematical terminology. To him, laws of nature were only more and more improved propositions of experience. The ordinary conception of things was criticized by Mach's statement that language signifies them by the same proper names even when they change. Instead, things were characterized by Mach as symbols for a complex of sensations, such as sounds, colors, smells, pressures, temperature, spatial and temporal impressions. Consequently, the ego, as far as it is scientifically cognizable, is reduced to a bundle of changing sensations, and no fundamental difference between the psychic and physical world is admitted. However, Mach insisted that there are no isolated acts of sensing, feeling, willing and thinking, and that psychic life is not only receptive but also active, although his investigation concentrated upon its receptive side. Mach explained his theories in *Analysis of Sensations* (1886) and *Knowledge and Error* (1905).

To a person accustomed to looking at things from the point of view of the theory of evolution, the high development of modern music as well as the spontaneous and sudden appearance of great musical talent seem, at first glance, a most singular and problematic phenomenon. What could this remarkable development of the power of hearing have had to do with the preservation of the species? Does it not far exceed the measure of the necessary or the useful? What can possibly be the significance of a fine discriminative sense of pitch? Of what use to us is a perceptive sense of pitch? Of what use to us is a perceptive sense of intervals, or of the acoustic colorings of orchestral music?

As a matter of fact, the same question may be proposed with reference to every art, no matter from what province of sense its material is derived. The question is pertinent, also, with regard to the intelligence of a Newton, an Euler, or their like, which apparently far transcends the necessary measure. But the question is most obvious with reference to music, which satisfies no practical need and for the most part depicts nothing. Music, however, is closely allied to the decorative arts. In order to be able to see, a person must have the power of distinguishing the *directions* of lines. Having a *fine* power of distinction, such a person may acquire, as a sort of collateral product of his education, a feeling for *agreeable* combinations of lines. The case is the same with the sense of *color-harmony* following upon the development of the power of distinguishing colors, and so, too, it undoubtedly is with respect to music.

We must bear in mind that talent and genius, however gigantic their achievements may appear to us, constitute but a slight departure from normal endowment. Talent may be resolved into the possession of psychical power slightly above the average in a certain province. And as for genius, it is talent supplemented by a capacity of adaptation extending beyond the youthful period, and by the retention of freedom to overstep routine barriers. The naiveté of the child delights us, and produces almost always the impression of genius. But this impression as a rule quickly disappears, and we perceive that the very same utterances which, as adults, we are wont to ascribe to freedom, have their source, in the child, in a lack of fixed character.

[236]

MACHIAVELLI, NICCOLO

MACHIAVELLI, NICCOLO (1469-1527). In private life it is never a compliment to anyone of whom it is said that he thinks or acts as a Machiavellian. Statesmen, philosophers of history and historians, on the other hand, have often discussed whether or not Machiavelli's principles are sound and of basic importance for political success, or even for public welfare at all.

Machiavelli's disciples have rarely been frank. King Frederick II of Prussia wrote a book opposing Machiavelli, but he practically adopted his views and acted in accordance with them. Mussolini was a great admirer of Machiavelli, but he would not allow his subjects to read his idol's work, *The Prince*, which was written in 1514 and dedicated to Lorenzo de' Medici, whose daughter, Queen Catherine of France, and one of the earliest disciples of the author, was responsible for the notorious Massacre of St. Bartholomew (1572) where the leaders of French Protestantism were murdered.

The Prince contains advice to sovereigns about how to become successful, how to obtain and maintain power, and, especially, how to render political adversaries harmless and to check a dissatisfied people. This advice was founded upon the author's knowledge of, or ideas on, the possibilities and limitations of human nature. Any moral standard is consciously eliminated. Reality, as Machiavelli saw it, is put above ideals. Success, as the end, has to justify the means. Man, especially the man of genius, was regarded by Machiavelli as an aesthetic phenomenon, and his struggle for existence and power seemed to him like a drama on the stage.

Since Machiavelli professed republicanism in other writings, and since he served the republican government of Florence, his native city, for fourteen years it has often been doubted whether he meant what he said in *The Prince*. Probably he was a republican in principle, but, in the actual situation of Italy at that time, Machiavelli, an ardent Italian patriot, built all his hopes upon a tyrant.

As a statesman, Machiavelli was a failure. As a philosopher, he was to say the least, disputable. But he was a magnificent writer, and his work is, apart from its great influence, valuable as a document of the spirit, or, at least of a tendency, of the Renaissance.

PROMISES AND PRINCES

How honorable it is for a prince to keep his word, and act rather with integrity than collusion, I suppose everybody understands: nevertheless, experience has shown in our times that those princes who have not pinned themselves up to that punctuality and preciseness have done great things, and by their cunning and subtility have not only circumvented those with whom they had to deal, but have overcome and been too hard for those who have been so superstitiously exact. For further explanation you must understand there are two ways of contending—by law and by force: the first is proper to men; the second to beasts; but because many times the first is insufficient, recourse must be had to the second. It belongs, therefore, to a prince to understand both—when to make use of the rational and when of the brutal way; and this is recommended to princes, though abstrusely, by ancient writers, who tell them how Achilles and several other princes were committed for education to Chiron the Centaur, who was half man and half beast—thus showing how necessary it is for a prince to be acquainted with both natures, for one without the other will be of little duration. Seeing, therefore, it is of such importance to a prince to take upon him the nature and disposition of a beast, of all the whole flock he ought to imitate the lion and the fox; for the lion is in danger of toils and snares, and the fox of the wolf; so that he must be a fox to find out the snares, and a lion to fight away the wolves, but they who keep wholly to the lion have no true notion of themselves. A prince, therefore, who is wise and prudent, cannot or ought not to keep his word, when the keeping of it is to his prejudice, and the causes for which he promised removed. Were men all good this doctrine would not be taught, but because they are wicked and not likely to be punctual with you, you are not obliged to any such strictness with them; nor was there ever any prince that lacked lawful pretence to justify his breach of promise. I might give many modern examples, and show how many confederations, and peaces, and promises have been broken by the infidelity of princes, and how he that best personated the fox had the better success. Nevertheless, it is of great consequence to disguise your inclination, and to play the hypocrite well; and men are so simple in their temper and so submissive to their present necessities that he that is neat and cleanly in his collusions shall never want people to practice them upon. I cannot forbear one example which is still fresh in our memory. Alexander VI never did, nor thought of, anything but cheating, and never wanted matter to work upon; and though no man promised a thing with greater asseveration, nor confirmed it with more oaths and imprecations, and observed them less, yet understanding the world well he never miscarried.

A prince, therefore, is not obliged to have all the forementioned good qualities in reality, but it is necessary he have them in appearance; nay, I will be bold to affirm that, having them actually, and employing them upon all occasions, they are extremely prejudicial, whereas, having them only in appearance, they turn to better account; it is honorable to seem mild, and merciful, and courteous, and religious, and sincere and indeed to be so, provided your mind be so rectified and prepared that you can act quite contrary upon occasion. And this must be premised, that a prince, especially if come but lately to the throne, cannot observe all those things exactly which cause men to be esteemed virtuous, being oftentimes necessitated, for the preservation of his state, to do things inhuman, uncharitable, and irreligious; and, therefore, it is convenient for his mind to be at his command, and flexible to all the puffs and variations of fortune; not forbearing to be good while it is in his choice, but knowing how to be evil when there is a necessity. A prince, then, is to have particular care that nothing falls

from his mouth but what is full of the five qualities aforesaid, and that to see and hear him he appears all goodness,
integrity, humanity, and religion, which last he ought to pretend to more than ordinarily, because more men do judge by
the eye than by the touch; for everybody sees but few understand; everybody sees how you appear, but few know what
in reality you are, and those few dare not oppose the opinion of the multitude, who have the majesty of their prince
to defend them; and in the actions of all men, especially
princes, where no man has power to judge, everyone looks
to the end. Let a prince, therefore, do what he can to preserve his life, and continue his supremacy, the means which
he uses shall be thought honorable, and be commended by
everybody; because the people are always taken with the
appearance and event of things, and the greatest part of the
world consists of the people; those few who are wise taking
place when the multitude has nothing else to rely upon.
There is a prince at this time in being (but his name I shall
conceal) who has nothing in his mouth but fidelity and peace:
and yet had he exercised either the one or the other, they
had robbed him before this both of his power and reputation.
[237]

MAETERLINCK, MAURICE

MAETERLINCK, MAURICE (1862-1949). Motoring, canoeing,
skating, bicycling, and, in his earlier years, even boxing, were
Count Maeterlinck's recreations, even in his advanced age. Perhaps
he was the greatest sportsman among poets and thinkers, since the
end of the ancient Greek civilization. But, as a poet and thinker,
Maeterlinck has conceived of life mostly as a fragile, human existence troubled by indefinite fright or as the presentiment of an
inevitable catastrophe. His principal experience is the awareness
that the sentiments, instincts and ideas of humanity are incapable
of remaining consistent as soon as what he called the Unknown
appears in life. He was convinced that no human concept of reality
corresponds to the metaphysically Real, and that, when the Unknown and the metaphysically Real interfere with human life,
man's habitual connection between his ideas and senses is dis-

765

rupted. All this drove Maeterlinck to a mysticism, though it did not prevent him from remaining fond of science. He proved to be an excellent empirical scientist, observing the life of bees, ants and spiders with unsurpassed accuracy. Maeterlinck's mysticism was founded upon pantheism and a sympathy with whatever exists. He felt himself in intimate touch with whatever suffers and desires, and his moral teachings pronounced universal love.

Maeterlinck studied the mystical authors of the Christian Middle Ages, but it was two American authors who influenced him decisively in his formative years. Edgar Allan Poe impressed him by his poetry of horror, and Ralph Waldo Emerson revealed to him the sense of spiritual life, and gave his thinking the direction toward the contemplation of eternity. Maeterlinck also strongly sympathized with Walt Whitman with whom he shared the conviction that nothing can perish definitely. Maeterlinck was no traditionalist. He did not regret any abandonment of a creed, or even the collapse of a civilization that has lost its vitality. In his later years, Maeterlinck turned more and more from mysticism to modern science.

LOOK OVER YOUR SHOULDER

WE are all searching for happiness, yet can anyone define it? A friend of mine was recently trying to tell her small daughter what it is. After a long dissertation she asked the child: "Now do you understand?" Whereupon the little girl replied disarmingly: "Yes, Mother, except when you explain." Definitions abound, but I know perfectly as long as I am not asked!

How charming is the old Persian legend about the king who was very powerful but also very unhappy. He consulted his seers to find out what he must do to be happy. After diligent research they found a clue to the dilemma. "Your Majesty," they said, "you must wear the shirt of a happy man." There followed a long search and finally a poor peasant was found who was perfectly happy. He was a ragged fellow who wore no shirt.

The more we reflect on this phantom called happiness which we all seek so eagerly, the more we perceive its dependence upon the happiness of other people.

I once knew a man who died, leaving a vast fortune

which he himself said in an obituary letter was more than any one man should possess. He went on to say how he had spent futile years trying to find happiness. Doubtless he had everything that money could offer, yet the answer to his problem was actually unbuyable. It was probably over his shoulder, to be had free of charge.

Another man I knew was a helpless cripple, and utterly incurable. I could not help asking him whether his affliction colored his views. "Yes," he answered, "but I make the colors!"

Indeed, the strenuous soul would seem to be built up of disillusions. Every deception and disappointment, every hope that has crumbled to dust, is possessed of a hidden strength of its own that adds strength to all truths. The more disillusions that fall at our feet, the more surely and nobly will great reality shine on us.

Many a happiness in life, as many a disaster, can be due to chance, but the peace within us can never be governed by chance. Call it what you may, heart, will, soul or conscience, these words mean more or less the same thing: the spiritual riches of man. Without peace in our hearts how can we expect peace in the world?

I would not go so far as to say that it is given to all men to be happy in exterior things. External circumstances can do a lot; but it lies within the power of the least favored amongst us to find a happy inner life by being gentle and just and generous. He should learn to look on his fellows without envy or malice or futile regret, the things which most militate against true happiness.

Remember that happiness is as contagious as gloom. It should be the first duty of those who are happy to let others know of their gladness.

The French word for happiness is *bonheur*, meaning "good hour." Let us gather hours of gladness. So many are lost because we are not conscious of them at the time.

We are now living in a rare epoch of history when, in the space of a few raging years, the character and destiny of the world is being determined for an unknown length of time. The hope of earthly salvation should fill all of our hearts and should rest mainly on solidarity and her companion goodness.

With this anticipation for the benefit of collective mankind, let us start individually by making life less difficult for each other in every way possible.

Never forget that those who bring happiness to the lives of others cannot keep it from themselves. And more often than not the opportunity lies over your shoulder!

[238]

MAIMON, SALOMON

MAIMON, SALOMON (1753-1800). Immanuel Kant recognized Maimon as the most acute of all his critics. The famous author of the *Critique of Pure Reason* probably knew what hardships Maimon had endured before he could publish his *Versuch ueber die Transcendentalphilosophie*, in which he successfully dealt with problems not understandable to the great majority of German thinkers of that time. When Maimon, in 1778, left his native village of Nieszwicz, Lithuania, he had been trained in the Heder and Yeshiva, had studied the Talmud, the Cabala and Maimonides, but had had no opportunity to be taught a modern language. Without any teacher he had deciphered the German alphabet by means of adventurous combinations and immense labor; but he could not pronounce a German word correctly when he crossed the borders of Prussia. It took him a long time to learn German thoroughly. It took him even more time to adapt himself to the moderate mentality of his German contemporaries. For many years, his violent temper prevented him from concentrating upon the studies he had longed for. He provoked the indignation of his protector Moses Mendelssohn by his radical views and his licentiousness. He perplexed a Protestant minister who was to baptize him by his declaration that he regarded Judaism a religion superior to Christianity. After twelve years of wandering, Maimon anticipated many important views of post-Kantian philosophy, and influenced Fichte particularly. More than a century after Maimon's death, his thoughts became even more influential than during his lifetime. But great as his philosophical thinking has been, his most interesting work is his autobiography which, in 1792, the German psychologist Karl

Philipp Moritz edited under the title *Salomon Maimons Eigene Lebensgeschichte*. This book contains a charming description of Jewish life in Lithuania and a courageous vindication of rabbinic Judaism.

ON JEWISH RELIGION

POSITIVE religion is distinguished from *natural* in the very same way as the positive laws of a state from natural laws. The latter are those which rest on a self-acquired, indistinct knowledge, and are not duly defined in regard to their application, while the former rest on a distinct knowledge received from others, and are completely defined in regard to their application.

A *positive* religion however must be carefully distinguished from a *political* religion. The former has for its end merely the correction and accurate definition of knowledge, that is, *instruction* regarding the first cause: and the knowledge is communicated to another, according to the measure of his capacity, just as it has been received. But the latter has for its end mainly the welfare of the state. Knowledge is therefore communicated, not just as it has been received, but only in so far as it is found serviceable to this end. Politics, merely as politics, requires to concern itself about *true religion* as little as about *true morality*. The injury, that might arise from this, can be prevented by other means which influence men at the same time, and thus all can be kept in equilibrium. Every political religion is therefore at the same time positive, but every positive religion is not also political.

Natural religion has no *mysteries* any more than merely positive religion. For there is no mystery implied in one man being unable to communicate his knowledge to another of defective capacity with the same degree of completeness which he himself has attained; otherwise mysteries might be attributed to all the sciences, and there would then be *mysteries of mathematics* as well as *mysteries of religion*. Only *political religion* can have mysteries, in order to lead men in an indirect way to the attainment of the *political end*, inasmuch as they are made to believe that thereby they can best attain their *private ends,* though this is not always in reality the case. There are *lesser* and *greater* mysteries in the political religions. The former consist in the *material* knowledge of all particular operations and their connection with one another. The latter, on the contrary, consist in the knowledge of the *form,* that is, of the end by which the former are determined. The former constitute the totality of the *laws of religion,* but the latter contains the *spirit of the laws.*

The *Jewish religion,* even at its earliest origin among the nomadic patriarchs, is already distinguished from the *heathen* as *natural religion,* inasmuch as, instead of the *many incomprehensible* gods of heathenism, the *unity of an incomprehensible* God lies at its foundation. For as the particular causes of the effects, which in general give rise to a religion, are in themselves unknown, and we do not feel justified in transferring to the causes the attributes of the particular effects, in order thereby to characterize them, there remains nothing but the idea of cause in general, which must be related to all effects without distinction. This cause cannot even be *analogically* determined by the effects. For the effects are opposed to one another, and neutralize each other even in the same object. If therefore we ascribed them all to one and the same cause, the cause could not be analogically determined by any.

The *heathen* religion, on the other hand, refers every kind of effect to a special cause, which can of course be characterized by its effect. As a *positive* religion the Jewish is distinguished from the heathen by the fact, that it is not a merely political religion, that is, a religion which has for its end the social interest (in opposition to true knowledge and private interest); but in accordance with the spirit of its founder, it is adapted to the theocratic form of the national Government, which rests on the principle, that only the true religion, based on rational knowledge, can harmonize with the interest of the state as well as of the individual. Considered in its *purity*, therefore, it has no mysteries in the proper sense of the word; that is to say, it has no doctrines which, in order to reach their end, men *will* not disclose, but merely such as *can* not be disclosed to all.

[239]

MAIMONIDES (Moses Ben Maimon)

MAIMONIDES (MOSES BEN MAIMON) (1135-1204). Among the rabbis of the later Middle Ages and centuries thereafter, an adage was current, saying, "From Moses to Moses there is none like unto Moses." It means simply that Maimonides is to be regarded as the greatest figure in Jewish history since the man who delivered the Ten Commandments to the Jewish people. In fact, the spiritual development of Judaism up to the present age is incomprehensible without taking account of Maimonides' activities as a codifier, judge and commentator of the Bible and the Talmud. His *Mishneh Torah* (Copy of the Law) was the first systematic exposition of Jewish religion. His "articles of faith" are either quoted or poetically paraphrased in modern Jewish prayer books.

The philosophical thoughts of Maimonides strongly influenced not only Jewish but also Islamic and Christian philosophers. The intention of his main work *Moreh Nebuchim* (Guide of the Perplexed, in Arabic *Dalalat al Hairin*) was to prove that the teachings of Judaism are in harmony with the results of philosophical thinking, and that beyond that, they offer insight which reason alone cannot obtain. For this purpose, Maimonides prevalently used the works of Aristotle, and, to a lesser extent, those of Plato. Christian philosophers were eager to apply Maimonides' doctrine to the defense of their own religion or to the explanation of general principles. Thus did William of Auvergne, Alexander of Hales, Albertus Magnus, Meister Eckhart, Thomas Aquinas and, through him, all medieval and modern Thomists. The great jurist, Hugo Grotius, was inspired by Maimonides' views on the history of religion.

Born in Cordova, Spain, Maimonides was forced to emigrate, at first to Morocco, then to Egypt where he earned his living by practicing medicine. In his medical treatises he anticipated modern discoveries concerning the affliction of the body by psychic factors, allergies, epilepsy, the nervous system and individual constitution. Almost all of his books were written in Arabic and shortly thereafter translated into Hebrew and Latin.

771

A MAN MUST CHOOSE THE GOLDEN MEAN

MEN have various dispositions, which are different from, and diametrically opposed to, one another. There is one man who is irascible, and is continually angry; while there is another who is of a calm disposition and does not get angry at all; and even if he gets angry, his wrath is mild, and this only happens once in several years. There is one man who is exceedingly haughty, while there is another who is exceedingly meek. There is one man who is voluptuous, whose soul can never be satisfied with indulging in pleasures; while there is another whose heart is so pure, that he desires not even the bare necessities which the body requires. There is one man who is exceedingly avaricious, whose soul cannot be satisfied with all the riches of the world, as it is written: 'He that loveth silver shall not be satisfied with silver;' while there is another who is so unambitious, that he is content with a small thing which is hardly sufficient for him, and does not strive to obtain all that he needs. There is one man who emaciates himself by starvation, and saves all his money, and is very grieved when he has to spend a Perutah for his food; while there is another who wilfully squanders all his possessions. And in the same manner are all other dispositions, as for instance, one man is hilarious, while another is melancholy; one is niggardly, while another is generous; one is cruel, while another is merciful; one is faint-hearted, while another is courageous, and so forth.

Between two contrary dispositions which are at the two extremes there are intermediate dispositions which are likewise different from one another. There are some dispositions which are inherent in a man from his very birth, in accordance with the nature of his body; while there are others to which a man's nature is so predisposed, that they are readily adopted by him sooner than any other; and there are still others which are not inherent in a man from his very birth, but are acquired by him through imitating other men, or are

772

adopted by him of his own accord because of an idea that occurred to him, or because, having heard that this disposition was good for him and worthy of being cultivated, he regulated his conduct accordingly, until it has become fixed in his heart.

The two diametrically opposed extremes of all dispositions are not the good way, and it behooves no man to walk therein, nor to adopt them. If a man finds that his nature inclines toward one of them, or is predisposed to adopt it, or that he has already acquired it, and regulated his conduct accordingly, he should return to that which is good, and walk in the way of the good ones, which is the right way.

The right way is the intermediate quality of every disposition of man, and that is the disposition which is equidistant from both extremes, being neither nearer to the one nor to the other. The ancient sages have therefore commanded that a man should always put, arrange, and direct his dispositions in the middle course, so that he may be sound in his body. In what manner? He should not be irascible, easily provoked to anger, nor as a dead man that is insensible, but should take the middle course: he should only get angry on account of an important matter, when it behooves to show anger in order that a similar offense should not be again committed. Similarly, a man should only desire those things which are necessary and indispensable for his body, as it is written: 'The righteous eateth to the satisfying of his desire.' In like manner, he should not exert himself in his business more than to obtain the necessities of life, as it is written: 'A little is good for the righteous.' He should not be too niggardly, nor squander his money, but should give charity according to his means, and in a fitting manner lend to him who is in need. He should not be hilarious and mirthful, nor gloomy and melancholy, but always happy and contented and of cheerful countenance. In the same manner should all his dispositions be. This way is the way of the wise; every man whose dispositions are intermediate, that is to say, in the middle course, is called wise.

A man who is very strict with himself, and removes himself from the middle course slightly toward one side or another, is called pious. In what manner? He who removes himself from haughtiness toward the other extreme, and is very humble, is called pious; and this is the quality of piety. If, however, he moves only as far as the middle, and is modest, he is called wise; and this is the quality of wisdom. In the same manner are all other dispositions. The pious men of ancient times used to turn their dispositions from the middle course toward the extremes; some dispositions were made to incline toward the one extreme, while others toward the other extreme; this is beyond the line required by the law. We, however, are commanded to walk in middle courses, which are the good and upright ways, as it is written: 'And thou shalt walk in His ways.' In interpreting this commandment, the sages say: 'As He is called gracious, so shalt thou be gracious; as He is called merciful, so shalt thou be merciful; as He is called holy, so shalt thou be holy.' And for this reason did the prophets call God by all these attributes: slow to anger, abundant in lovingkindness, righteous, upright, perfect, mighty, strong, and so forth, in order to let us know that these are good and upright ways, according to which a man is obliged to regulate his conduct, so that he may be like unto Him, as far as lies in his power.

In what manner should a man accustom himself to these dispositions, so that they should become part of his nature? He should do once, and twice, and three times the deeds which he is to do according to the intermediate dispositions, and should always keep on repeating them until they have become so easy for him that he can do them without the slightest effort; the dispositions will then become fixed in his soul. Because the Creator is called by these names, they are according to the middle course wherein we are obliged to walk, and this way is called the way of God; it is the one which Abraham taught his children, as it is written: 'For I have known him, to the end that he may command. . . .' And he who walks in this way brings welfare and blessing to him-

self, as it is written: 'To the end that the Lord may bring
upon Abraham that which He hath spoken of Him.'

[240]

MAINE DE BIRAN
(Pierre Francois Gonthier De Biran)

MAINE DE BIRAN (PIERRE FRANÇOIS GONTHIER DE BI-
RAN) (1766-1824). Maine de Biran was a man of strong moral and
metaphysical feelings, but his psychological curiosity was always
stronger and sometimes diverted his thoughts from their initial aims.
For years his military and political activities prevented him from
concentrating upon philosophy. He was strictly opposed to Condillac and Cabanis whom he regarded as the representatives of the
spirit of the eighteenth century and whom he accused of evaporat-
ing human feelings by their analysis; but, in fact, as a psychologist,
Maine de Biran was closer to them than he supposed himself to
be. Nevertheless, many of his ideas seem to be anticipations of
those of Whitehead, Santayana, Hocking, Bergson, Scheler and
recent existentialism.

Serving in King Louis XVI's bodyguard, Maine de Biran was
wounded in the fight against the people of Paris during the early
revolutionary days of July 1789. After his regiment had been dis-
banded, he turned to mathematics and philosophy. Despite his ardent
royalism and hatred of the Revolution, he served under the Di-
rectory from 1795 on, and was elected a member of the Council
of the Five Hundred in 1797. The coup d'état of Fructidor induced
him to retire into private life until Napoleon, in 1805, appointed
him sub-prefect and member of the Corps Législatif. In 1811, Maine
de Biran abandoned the Emperor in favor of the Bourbons whose
return to power he openly demanded. King Louis XVIII awarded
him many honors but the ultra-reactionary faction accused him of
being too moderate.

From the time of his childhood, Maine de Biran was, as he
said, "astonished while feeling that I exist," and he was led by an
instinct to analyze his consciousness in order "to know how I can
live and be myself." Contrary to Descartes, he conceived man as a
willing creature. *Volo, ergo sum* is his device. Will signifies the
constant tension in man that urges him to act. Will is the primary
fact of consciousness that gives man the feeling of being united
with a body and brings him into contact with the outer world and
its resistance to his actions. The knowledge of substance is derived

775

from observation of the will. In his *New Essays on Anthropology* which were not finished when he died, Maine de Biran describes three stages of life. The first is that of animal life which is dominated by blind passions which are independent of the will. The second experience is will, intelligence, the meaning of ideas and words, and the conflict of wills. The third stage is that of spirit in which man identifies himself with the eternal source of power and insight. At its height, man is happy to lose his ego. At any stage, man needs the support of God.

Maine de Biran claimed to have overcome all difficulties which are the result of an erroneous tendency to comprehend in abstract or separate terms what is given in relatives or to divide into sections what really is a running stream.

THE IMPRESSIONS MOST WEAKENED BY REPETITION

OUR sensations certainly fade and vanish sooner and more completely in proportion to the *passivity* of their respective organs. This condition is bound up with the forced continuance of impressions, since then the will cannot directly react to distract or to stop them.

And first, inner impressions, however little they persist in the same degree, tend to be converted into habits of *temperament* and, although in this state they continue to influence the feeling of existence, which they make sad or painful, easy or agreeable, they cease nevertheless to be felt in themselves, but are lost and merged in this multitude of vague impressions, which cooperate to form the habitual inner feeling of our passive existence. Such an effect indeed seems to be connected with the equilibrium or the equal reaction of sensory forces which are coordinated with each other in course of time in such a way that one impression does not continue to dominate too much over the others. But we shall consider them soon in another connection.

Passive touch, spread over the whole surface of the body, is exposed at all points to the equal, continued or varied excitation of surrounding fluids or objects in motion, which stimulate it, titillate it, prick it, etc., without its being able to react in order to change or suspend their effects. But sensitivity is incessantly on the watch and puts itself on an equality with impressions by moderating and annulling them (always excepting cases of serious and sudden lesions).

The equilibrium of which we have spoken and the action of the sensory principle to re-establish it, are manifest in no other kind of impressions more clearly than in those which correspond to tactile sensations and particularly to those of heat or cold. It is well known how easily our bodies are adapted to changes of climate and temperature, provided that the transition is not too sudden; how a uniform temperature long continued becomes insensible to us; how the sensation is always proportional to the actual condition of the organ (so that such and such a degree alternately freezes or burns us); how from this organ it is extended from point to point and affects us the more intensely the more concentrated it is. In short, it is well known that the sensitive principle always tends to maintain in us an almost even heat, which it can do only by successively raising or lowering our temperature and restoring the inner equilibrium, which without this activity would be disturbed every instant.

Odors also gradually become fainter and end by becoming insensible. "My sachet scented with flowers," said Montaigne, "is first of service to my nose; but, after I have used it a week, it is no longer of any use except to the noses of bystanders." Odors are necessarily continuous since their organ is passive and breathing cannot be interrupted. First they stimulate the whole system, which attunes itself to them and soon ceases to experience any change from them. In relation to appetite they have other effects which we shall presently indicate.

Tastes become deadened more through repetition than through their continuance and always in proportion as the organ is more passive in experiencing them. Many an agreeable or disagreeable taste, which has affected us in the beginning, particularly in a drink, soon becomes through custom absolutely insensible—nauseous flavors excepted. Taste, like odor, becomes accustomed to the strongest artificial irritants and it is almost paralyzed by their repeated activity and, nevertheless, these same irritants become imperious needs.

Sounds, considered as passive impressions of an organ devoid of mobility, can undergo all the gradual fading which results from the repetition and continuance to which they are particularly susceptible. We experience daily how easy it is to become accustomed to every kind of noise to the point of becoming absolutely unconscious of it. This body, this *material* of sound, moreover, which in the beginning affects us so poignantly by itself and independently of any perceived relation, of any effect of melody, loses also through its frequency all power to stimulate. But though the impression in this case weakens like sensation, it is not obedient to the same law, to the same mode of diminishing, as perception. The motor activity, combined with the sensory, changes the simple results and gives rise to other habits. The auditory impression may lose its power of attraction, but the vocal impression will keep its distinctness.

Light stimulates the fibres of the retina with a certain force. Sensitivity—put into play—contracts or dilates the pupil through an activity quite independent of the will. It raises the tone of the organ, adjusts it, accommodates it to the degree of the external stimulus, in such a way that it is no longer affected, that it no longer feels the continued or repeated impression in the same degree.

[241]

MALEBRANCHE, NICOLAS

MALEBRANCHE, NICOLAS (1638-1715). Malebranche came to philosophy in a way that differs from that of many other philosophers. He began to study it, and, disappointed by its methods and results, turned to theology. He became a member of the Congregation of the Oratory, displayed religious ardor, accepted the doctrines of the Church as unchanging truth, though he was never quite satisfied with the arguments used by traditional theology. In

778

1664, by chance, he picked up in a bookstore Descartes' treatise *On Man*, and after perusing some pages fugitively, became fascinated by the author's ideas. For the following three years, Malebranche studied Descartes' works, doing nothing else. In 1674, ten years after his haphazard acquaintance with Descartes, he published the first volume of his *Recherche de la Vérité* (Investigation of Truth).

Following Descartes' example, Malebranche looked upon philosophical doubt as his indispensable starting point. But he deviated from his master by conceiving doubt as an act of will, of freedom.

Contrary to Descartes as well as to Bacon, Spinoza and many others, knowledge was not to him of causal determination or explanation. For, according to Malebranche there is no cause in the world but God. All creatures are united with God in an immediate manner. They depend essentially and directly on Him. There is no dependence of one creature or thing on another, since all things are powerless without God's will. All being, all knowing, all acting are produced by God. Man has only the faculties of desire and choice which are constituents of his liberty. As far as he has love of God, he has a will. As far he has a vision of God, he has reason. What he regards as causal connection of things is not conditional but only apparent, or as Malebranche says, occasional causes.

Since Malebranche reserved all causal acting to God alone, causality was completely abandoned by him as a principle of knowledge. Knowledge was to Malebranche evidence of intuition. He went so far as to declare evidence superior to faith. For faith may change but evidence shall subsist.

By emphasizing evidence, Malebranche influenced Leibniz, Locke, Berkeley and Hume. In modern times, Santayana, Husserl and Scheler adopted similar views.

ON GOD'S INTERVENTION

You cannot of yourself move your arm or alter your position, situation, posture, do to other men good or evil, or effect the least change in the world. You find yourself in the world, without any power, immovable as a rock, stupid, so to speak, as a log of wood. Let your soul be united to your body as closely as you please, let there come about a union between it and all the bodies of your environment. What advantage would you derive from this imaginary union? What

779

would you do in order merely to move the tip of your finger, or to utter even a monosyllable? Alas! unless God came to your aid, your efforts would be vain, the desires which you formed impotent; for just think, do you know what is necessary for the pronunciation of your best friend's name, or for bending or holding up that particular finger which you use most? But let us suppose that you know quite well what no one knows, about which even some scientists are not agreed, namely, that the arm can be moved only by means of the animal spirits, which flowing along the nerves to the muscles make them contract and draw towards themselves the bones to which they are attached. Let us suppose that you are acquainted with the anatomy and the action of your mechanism as well as a clockmaker is acquainted with his handiwork. But, at any rate, remember the principle that no one but the Creator of bodies can be their mover. This principle is sufficient to bind, indeed to annihilate, all your boasted faculties; for, after all, the animal spirits are bodies, however small they may be. They are, indeed, nothing but the subtlest parts of the blood and the humors. God alone, then, is able to move these small bodies. He alone knows how to make them flow from the brain along the nerves, from the nerves through the muscles, from one muscle to its antagonist—all of which is necessary for the movement of our limbs. It follows that, notwithstanding the conjunction of soul and body in whatever way it may please you to imagine it, you would be dead and inert if it were not for the fact that God wills to adapt his volitions to yours—His volitions, which are always effective, to your desires, which are always impotent. This then is the solution of the mystery. All creatures are united to God alone in an immediate union. They depend essentially and directly upon Him. Being all alike equally impotent, they cannot be in reciprocal dependence upon one another. One may, indeed, say that they are united to one another and that they depend upon one another. I grant this, provided it is not understood in the ordinary and vulgar sense of the term, provided that one agrees that

780

they are so only in consequence of the immutable and ever effective will of the Creator, only in consequence of the general laws which He has established, and by means of which He regulates the ordinary course of His providence. God has willed that my arm shall be set in motion at the instant that I will it myself (given the necessary conditions). His will is efficacious, His will is immutable, it alone is the source of my power and faculties. He has willed that I should experience certain feelings, certain emotions, whenever there are present in my brain certain traces, or whenever a certain disturbance takes place therein. In a word, He has willed—He wills incessantly—that the modifications of the mind and those of the body shall be reciprocal. This is the conjunction and the natural dependence of the two parts of which we are constituted. It is but the mutual and reciprocal dependence of our modifications based on the unshakable foundation of the divine decrees—decrees which through their efficacy endow me with the power which I have over my body, and through it over certain other bodies—decrees which through their immutability unite me with my body, and through it to my friends, my possessions, my whole environment. I derive nothing whatever from my own nature, nothing from the nature imagined by the philosophers—all comes from God and His decrees. God has linked together all His works, though He has not on that account produced in them entities charged with the function of union. He has subordinated them to one another without endowing them with active qualities. The latter are but the vain pretensions of human pride, the chimerical productions of the philosophers' ignorance. Men's senses being affected by the presence of objects, their minds being moved by the inner feeling which they have of their own movements, they have not recognized the invisible operations of the Creator, the uniformity of His mode of action, the fruitfulness of His laws, the ever-present efficacy of His volitions, the infinite wisdom of His providence. Do not say any more that your soul is united to your body more intimately than to anything else; since its immediate union is with God alone, since the divine decrees are the indissoluble bonds of union between the various parts of the universe and of the marvellous network of all the subordinate causes.

ON METAPHYSICS

THEOTIMUS. But let us return to metaphysics. Our soul is not united to our body in the ordinary sense of these terms. It is immediately and directly united to God alone. It is through the efficacy of His action alone that the three of us are here together; nay, more, that we all share the same opinion, are penetrated by the same truth, animated, it seems to me, by the same spirit, kindled with the same enthusiasm. God joins us together by means of the body, in consequence of the laws of the communication of movements. He affects us with the same feelings in consequence of the laws of the conjunction of body and soul. But, Aristes, how comes it about that we are so strongly united in mind? Theodore utters some words unto your ears. These are but the air struck by the organs of the voice. God transforms, so to speak, this air into words, into various sounds. He makes you understand these various sounds through the modifications by which you are affected. But where do you get the sense of the words from? Who is it that discloses to you and to myself the same truth as Theodore is contemplating? If the air which He forces back when speaking does not contain the sounds you hear, assuredly it will not contain the truths which you understand.

ARISTES. I follow you, Theotimus. We are united in mind because all of us are united to the universal Reason which illumines all intelligences. I am wiser than you think. Theodore has already led me to the point to which you wish to conduct me. He has convinced me that there is nothing visible, nothing which can act upon the mind and reveal itself thereto, but the substance of Reason, which is not only efficacious but also intelligent. Yes, nothing that is created can be the immediate object of our knowledge. We see things in this material world, wherein our bodies dwell, only because our mind through its attention lives in another world, only because it contemplates the beauties of the archetypal and intelligible world which Reason contains. As our bodies live upon the earth and find sustenance in the fruits which it produces, so our minds feed on the same truths as the intelligible and immutable substance of the divine Word contains. The words which Theodore utters into my ears urge me, in consequence of the law of the conjunction of soul and body, to be attentive to the truths which he is discovering in the supreme Reason. This turns my mind in the same direction as his. I see what he sees because I look where he looks, and by means of the words whereby I reply to his words, though both alike are, in themselves, devoid of sense, I discuss with him and enjoy with him a good which is common to all, for we are all essentially united to Reason, so united that without it we could enter into no social bond with anyone.

THEOTIMUS. Your reply, Aristes, surprises me extremely. How, knowing all that you are now telling me, could you reply to Theodore that we are united to our body more intimately than to anything else?

ARISTES. I did so because one is inclined to say only what is present to the memory, and because abstract truths do not present themselves to the mind so naturally as those that one has heard all one's life. When I have meditated as much as Theotimus I shall speak no more in mechanical fashion, but regulate my words in accordance with the deliverances of inner truth. I understand then now, and I shall not forget it all my life, that we are united immediately and directly to God. It is in the light of His wisdom that He makes us see the magnificence of His works, the model upon which He forms them, the immutable art which regulates their mechanism and movements, and it is through the efficacy of His will that He unites us to our body, and through our body to all those in our environment.

THEODORE. You might add that it is through the love

which He bears to Himself that He communicates to us that invincible enthusiasm which we have for the Good. But of this we shall speak on another occasion. It is sufficient for the present that you are quite convinced that the mind can be united immediately and directly to God alone, that we can have no intercourse with created beings except by the power of the Creator, which is communicated to us only in consequence of His laws, and that we can enter into no social union amongst ourselves and with Him except through the Reason with which He is consubstantial. This once granted, you will see that it is of the highest importance for us to try to acquire some knowledge of the attributes of this supreme Being, since we are so much dependent upon Him; for, after all, He acts upon us necessarily according to His nature. His mode of activity must bear the character of His attributes. Not only must our duties tend towards His perfections, but our whole course of action ought to be so regulated in accordance with His that we may take the proper measures for the realization of our purposes, and that we may find a combination of causes which is favorable to these designs. In this connection, faith and experience teach us many truths by means of the short-cut of authority and by the proofs of very pleasant and agreeable feelings. But all this intelligence does not give us forthwith; it ought to be the fruit and the recompense of our work and application. For the rest, being made to know and love God, it is clear that there is no occupation which is preferable to the meditation upon the divine perfections which should animate us with charity and regulate all the duties of a rational creature.

ARISTES. I understand quite well, Theodore, that the worship which God demands from minds is a spiritual worship. It consists in being full of the knowledge of Him, full of love of Him, in forming judgments of Him which are worthy of His attributes, and in regulating in accordance with His will all the movements of our heart. For God is spirit, and He wishes to be worshipped in spirit and in truth. But I must confess that I am extremely afraid lest I should form judgments on the divine perfections which would dishonor them. Is it not better to honor them by silence and admiration, and to devote ourselves solely to investigation of the less sublime truths and those which are more in proportion to the capacity of our minds?

THEODORE. How do you mean, Aristes? You are not thinking of what you are saying. We are made to know and love God. Do you mean, then, to say that you do not want us to think of Him, speak of Him, I might even add worship Him? We ought, you say, to worship Him by silence and admiration. Yes by a respectful silence which the contemplation of His greatness imposes upon us, by a religious silence to which the glory of His majesty reduces us, by a silence forced upon us, so to speak, due to our impotence, and not having as its source a criminal negligence or a misguided curiosity to know, instead of Him, objects less worthy of our application. What do you admire in the Divine if you know nothing of Him? How could you love Him if you did not contemplate Him? How can we instruct one another in charity if we banish from our discussion Him whom you have just recognized as the soul of all the intercourse which we have with one another, as the bond of our little society? Assuredly, Aristes, the more you know the supreme Being, the more you will admire His infinite perfections. Do not fear lest you should meditate too much upon Him and speak of Him in an unworthy way, providing you are led by faith. Do not fear lest you should entertain false opinions of Him so long as they are in conformity with the notion of the infinitely perfect Being. You will not dishonor the divine perfections by judgments unworthy of them, provided you never judge of Him by yourself, provided you do not ascribe to the Creator the imperfections and limitations of created beings. Think of this, therefore. I, too, shall think of it, and I hope Theotimus will do so likewise. That is necessary for the development of the principle which I think I ought to put before you. We shall meet to-morrow then, at the usual hour, for it is time for me to leave.

ARISTES. Adieu, Theodore. I beg of you, Theotimus, that the three of us should meet at the hour arranged.

THEOTIMUS. I am going with Theodore but I shall come back with him, as you desire it. Ah, Theodore, how changed Aristes is! He is attentive, he scoffs no more, he is no longer a stickler for forms—in a word, he listens to reason and submits to it in good faith.

THEODORE. That is true, but his prejudices still come in the way and somewhat confuse his ideas. Reason and prejudice both have their turn in what he says. Now truth makes him speak, now memory plays tricks upon him. But his imagination dares no longer to revolt. This indicates that he is sound at heart and encourages me a good deal.

THEOTIMUS. What do you expect, Theodore? Prejudices are not easily got rid of as an old coat which is no longer thought of. It seems to me that we have been like Aristes, for we were not born but became philosophers. It will be necessary to repeat to him the great principles ceaselessly, in order that he should think of them so often that his mind will obtain mastery over them, and that in the moment of need they may occur to him quite naturally.

THEODORE. That is what I have been trying to do hitherto. But this makes it difficult for him, for he loves detail and variety of thoughts. I beg of you always to dwell upon the necessity of a thorough understanding of principles, in order to stop the vivacity of his mind, and please do not forget to meditate upon the subject of our discussion.

[243]

MARITAIN, JACQUES

MARITAIN, JACQUES (1882-   ). Jacques Maritain, one of the most influential contemporary Neo-Thomists, is the descendant of a family of free-thinkers. His mother's father was Jules Favre, one of the founders of the Third French Republic and an ardent adversary of clericalism. Maritain kept himself outside the Catholic Church until he was converted by the mystic and eccentric poet, Léon Bloy, who lived in a world of supranatural symbols but was not at all interested in philosophy. After his conversion, which, in some respects, was prepared by his devotion to Henri Bergson, Maritain went to Heidelberg to study biology with Hans Driesch. Until 1926, Maritain was associated with the *Action Française*, the French royalist shock troop, and, in accordance with its program, he professed strong opposition to republicanism, democracy and liberal ideas. After the *Action Française* was condemned by Pope Pius XI in 1926, Maritain began to profess confidence in a democracy inspired by Christian faith. At the same time, he turned from speculative metaphysics to history and sociology.

Although Maritain has remained a staunch defender of the Catholic Church and Scholasticism, he does not regard the Christian Middle Ages as the obligatory model of human civilization. Rather, he is inclined to acknowledge the rights of a plurality of civilizations, all of which are guided by Divine providence, and proves his ability to expound historical and contemporary, human and social problems in Thomist terms, which, in his opinion, enable him to discover the relations between historical phenomena and the supratemporal order. Proceeding from these views, Maritain maintains that the value of the human person is rooted in an order which is created by God and strives toward God. The Catholic Church is acknowledged by Maritain as universal, supranational, supraracial and supratemporal, but he is eager to avoid any romanticizing of what he demands to be respected. He insists that the Church is not the home of the elect but the refuge of sinners. On the other hand, he is, on the ground of his conception of the Church, as strongly opposed to Nazism as he is to Bolshevism.

Any contradiction between the Christian faith and modern science is, according to Maritain, due to ontological ambitions on the part of Descartes and Newton, and will vanish after science will have elaborated a thoroughly nonmetaphysical approach. But he does not believe that, even in a distant future, science and faith will cooperate without friction.

THE DIVINE PLAN

THE divine plan is not a scenario prepared in advance, in which free subjects would play parts and act as performers. We must purge our thought of any idea of a play written in advance, at a time prior to time—a play in which time unfolds, and the characters of time read, the parts. On the contrary, everything is improvised, under the eternal and immutable direction of the almighty Stage Manager. The divine plan is the ordination of the infinite multiplicity of things, and of their becoming, by the absolutely simple gaze of the creative knowledge and the will of God. It is eternal and immutable, but it could have been otherwise (since it could not have been had there not been things). *Once fixed* from all eternity, once *assumed* as fixed in such and such a way from all eternity, it is immutable. And it is by virtue of the eternal presence of time in eternity (even before time was), by virtue of the embrace, by the eternal instant, of history in the making (perpetually fresh in its newness and indeed—as regards free acts—in its unforeseeability) that the divine plan is immutably fixed in heaven from all eternity, directing history towards the ends willed by God and disposing towards those ends all the actors in the drama and all the good God causes in them, while taking advantage, on behalf of those ends, of the evil itself of which they are the nihilating first cause and which God permits without having caused it.

By reason of this free nihilating, the creature has a portion of first initiative in the drama. Unless the free existent has received at one stroke an unshatterable impetus to good, it depends solely upon him whether he will or will not take the initiative of nihilating or of non-consideration of the rule, under the motions and activations which bear him towards good. Will he or will he not nihilate under the hand of the potter? As concerns his good or evil act, and the repercussions it may have upon what follows in the drama, it is at that instant in time, known from all eternity, that the immutable plan is simultaneously established from all eternity. Let us suppose that the free creature has not, in that instant, the initiative of the thing that is nothing. The initiative of nihilating not being seen (from all eternity) in the free existent by the 'science of vision,' from all eternity, the primordial will of God (which willed the good act of this creature in the direction of the particular end towards which it ordained him) is confirmed by the definitive or circumstanced will. Thus from all eternity the accomplishment of this good act by this creature is immutably fixed in the eternal plan.

[244]

MARX, KARL

MARX, KARL (1818-1883). To the impact of Marx's doctrine on political and social ideas and the subsequent changes of social structure there is no parallel in the whole history of philosophy. Only religious reformers have produced similar changes. What distinguishes Marx from other philosophers who more or less deeply influenced political and social ideas is the simple fact that his teachings directly affected the mind of the masses of working people in various nations, not only by appealing to their material interests but even more so by imbuing them with an apparently imperturbable confidence in the absolute truth of his statements and predictions. In his *Theses on Feuerbach* (1845), Marx, who had turned from the political radicalism of the Left Hegelians to what he then called communism and later scientific socialism, declared that the question of absolute truth is not one of theory but a practical one, and that the reality and power of thought must be demonstrated in practice by both interpreting and changing the world. But he always insisted that a vigorous theory is as indispensable to the destruction of a corrupted society and the construction of a new one as is drastically disciplined action. When, in his *Critique of Political Economics*, (1859), Marx called his method empirical, he did so in order to mark his opposition to abstract spiritualism. But he continued to sneer at pure empiricists. He turned Hegel's dialectic upside down because he thought that Hegel's way of proceeding from the abstract to the concrete, from the ideal to the real could reach reality, and that Hegel's conception of the dialectical motion as the development of consciousness was bound to miss human totality. But when Marx declared in opposition to Hegel that it is not consciousness that determines the existence of man but that the social existence of man determines his consciousness, he nevertheless, was regarding dialectic as the only infallible method of scientific thinking to which all empirical knowledge of facts is subordinated. He reproached Feuerbach for having abandoned not only idealism, of which he approved, but also dialectics of history which, to Marx, meant renouncing scientific exactness. In the same way, although he applied his theory mainly to economic and social life, and devoted much of his energy to the direction of political movements, Marx remained the philosopher of the dialectical movement who retained both Hegel's conviction that the real is rational and Hegel's dialectical concept of becoming. He continued to agree with Hegel that reality is a process, that life means itself and its contradiction, and that as soon as contradiction ceases to act, life will come to an end.

The fundamental characteristic of Marx's doctrine is not his theory of the concentration of wealth in the hands of a few powerful capitalists, or the condemnation of the "exploitation of man by his fellow-man." These views are borrowed from Saint-Simon, Sismondi and Constantin Pecqueur. Nor is it his theory of class struggle, borrowed from French historians of his time, or his theory of surplus value, owed to English economists. What really dominates the unity of his thinking is his conception of history, according to which the forms of economic production determine the formation of human society and the consciousness of its members so that ideas, moral values, aesthetic standards, political and social concepts, educational and religious systems are to be conceived as produced by the economic situation. As long as the "ideological superstructure" remains in accordance with the conditions of economic production, civilization is healthy. But, since these conditions are changing more rapidly than the superstructure, cultural crises are unavoidable, and, when people, incapable of understanding the laws of history, resist the changes dictated by it, revolution becomes necessary. In his principal work *Das Kapital* (1867 and later) Marx developed his philosophy by applying it to modern economic life, demonstrating by a historico-sociological analysis of economics that that which he calls the *bourgeoisie* has accomplished its historical task by great performances but that it is not capable any longer of adapting itself to the changed conditions of production and must give room to the proletariat.

Marx tried to regard phenomena as incessantly changing, life as continual movement of growth and destruction, so that nothing immutable remains except movement itself. For that reason, said his intimate friend and collaborator Friedrich Engels, Marx refrained from offering in his principal work any fixed and universally applicable definition. Marx even criticized the German Social Democratic Party which, in its program of 1875, mentioned the "present-day State." Marx maintained the "present-day State" to be a fiction since it differed from one country to another.

Although, in his later years, Marx became more and more reluctant to define concepts, because he was afraid lest he should admit in this way any fixed existence, he maintained his belief in the dynamics of economic change as the prime mover of historic life. He presented this conviction as an eternally valid law of nature, as the highest tribunal from which no appeal to another court is possible. He did it by an inexorable diction, fond of disillusioning and with dry irony, sneering at moralists, utopians, reformers who, as he said, tried in vain to escape the compulsion dictated by historical laws, such as are revealed by the right use of dialectics. He, on his part, claimed to teach how to cooperate with the due course of historical evolution. When each science will have become perfect, philosophy will be useless except formal logic and dialectic. Of these two disciplines, dialectic is declared superior, as a method of advancing from the known to the unknown. According to Marx, dialectic forces the way beyond the narrow horizon of formal logic, because it contains the germ of a more developed view of the world. He was fond of dialectic because he conceived of it as of constant fermentation. Marx's search for the causation and end of the historical process, which assumes that men, while producing the means of material existence, enter human relations independently of their will and change these human relations independently of their will when the way of production changes, has been much disputed. But many philosophers, historians and sociologists who contradict him, are ready to admit that he has created a working hypothesis.

THE HISTORICAL TENDENCY
OF CAPITALIST ACCUMULATION

WHAT does the *primitive accumulation of capital, i.e.,* its historical genesis, resolve itself into? In so far as it is not immediate transformation of slaves and serfs into wage laborers, and therefore a *mere change of form,* it only means the *expropriation of the immediate producers, i.e., the dissolution of private property based on the labor of its owner.* Private property, as the antithesis to social, collective property, exists only where the instruments of labor and the external conditions of labor belong to private individuals. But according as these private individuals are laborers or not laborers, private property has a different character. The numberless shades that it at first sight presents reflect only the intermediate stages lying between these two extremes. The private property of the laborer in his means of production is the foundation of petty industry whether agricultural, manufacturing, or both; petty industry, again, is an essential condition for the development of social production and of the free individuality of the laborer himself. Of course this petty mode of production exists also under slavery, serfdom, and other states of dependence. But it flourishes, it lets loose its whole energy, it attains its adequate classical form, only where the laborer is the free private owner of his own conditions of labor manipulated by himself: the peasant of the land which he cultivates, the artisan of the tool which he handles as a virtuoso. This model of production presupposes parcelling of the soil, and scattering of the other means of production. As it excludes the *concentration* of the means of production, so also its excludes cooperation, division of labor within each separate process of production, the social mastery and control over nature, and the free development of the *social* productive forces. It is compatible only with a system of production, and a society, moving within narrow and more or less primitive bounds. To perpetuate it would be, as Pecqueur rightly says, "to decree universal mediocrity." At a certain level of development it brings into being the material agencies for its own dissolution. From that moment new forces and new passions spring up in the bosom of society; but the old social organization fetters them and keeps them down. It must be annihilated; it is annihilated. Its annihilation, *the transformation of the individualized and scattered means of production into socially concentrated ones*, of the pigmy property of the many into the huge property of the few, *the expropriation of the great mass of the people from the soil, from the means of subsistence, and from the instruments of labor*, this fearful and painful *expropriation of the mass of the people*, forms the prelude to the history of capital. It comprises a series of forcible methods, of which we have passed in review only those that have been epoch-making as methods of the primitive accumulation of capital. The expropriation of the immediate producers was accomplished with merciless vandalism, and under the stimulus of

792

passions the most infamous, the most sordid, the pettiest, the most meanly odious. Self-earned private property that is based so to say, on the fusing together of the isolated, independent laboring individual with the conditions of his labor, is supplanted by capitalist private property, which rests on exploitation of the nominally free labor of others, *i.e.*, on wage labor.

As soon as this process of transformation has sufficiently decomposed the old society from top to bottom, as soon as the laborers are turned into proletarians, their means of labor into capital, as soon as the capitalist mode of production stands on its own feet, then the further socialization of labor and further transformation of the land and other means of production into socially exploited and, therefore, common means of production, as well as the further expropriation of private proprietors, takes a new form. That which is now to be expropriated is no longer the laborer working for himself, but the capitalist exploiting many laborers. This expropriation is accomplished by the action of the immanent laws of capitalist production itself, by the centralization of capital. One capitalist always kills many. Hand in hand with this centralization, or this expropriation of many capitalists by few, develop, on an ever extending scale, the co-operative form of the labor process, the conscious technical application of science, the methodical cultivation of the soil, the transformation of the instruments of labor into instruments of labor only usable in common, the economizing of all means of production by their use as the means of production of combined, socialized labor, the entanglement of all peoples in the net of the world market, and with this, the international character of the capitalist regime. Along with the constantly diminishing number of the magnates of capital who usurp and monopolize all advantages of this process of transformation, grows the mass of misery, oppression, slavery, degradation, exploitation; but with this, too, grows the revolt of the working class, a class always increasing in numbers, and disciplined, united, organized by the very mechanism of the process of capitalist production itself. The monopoly of capital becomes a fetter upon the mode of production, which has sprung up and flourished along with, and under it. Centralization of the means of production and socialization of labor reach a point where they become incompatible with their capitalist integument. This integument is burst asunder. The knell of capitalist private property sounds. The expropriators are expropriated.

The capitalist mode of appropriation, the result of the capitalist mode of production, produces capitalist private property. This is the first negation of individual private property, as founded on the labor of the proprietor. But capitalist production begets, with the inexorability of a law of nature, its own negation. It is the negation of negation. This does not reestablish property for the producer, but gives him individual property based on the acquisitions of the capitalist era: *i.e.*, on cooperation and the possession in common of the land and of the means of production produced by labor itself.

The transformation of scattered private property, arising from individual labor, into capitalist private property is, naturally, a process incomparably more protracted, violent, and difficult than the transformation of capitalist private property already in fact resting on socialized production, into socialized property. In the former case, we had the expropriation of the mass of the people by a few usurpers; in the latter, we have the expropriation of a few usurpers by the mass of the people.

[245]

MASARYK, THOMAS GARRIGUE

MASARYK, THOMAS GARRIGUE (1850-1937). The son of a blacksmith, Masaryk became the father of a democratic people. After achieving fame as a scholar, a political economist and a historian, he became a legendary figure, the founder of a modern state. In all situations of his life, as a teacher, a member of parliament,

794

an exile and a ruler, he proved to be a critical and constructive thinker.

"Truth conquers" was Masaryk's motto. He fought for truth when he discovered the forgery of an allegedly old document, without any regard to the fact that his discovery hurt Czech national pride. He fought for truth while denouncing the manner in which the "ritual murder" trial at Polna had been conducted in 1899, and he exposed the forgeries fabricated by members of the Austro-Hungarian Legation in Belgrade in 1910. He risked his popularity, his security and his life in order to prove the tenets of his philosophy, according to which Man is bound to collaborate with God, to follow the command of his conscience and to act as an individual responsible to humanity. Equally opposed to despotism and anarchy, Masaryk was a champion of democracy, convinced that the philosophy of history is identical with the philosophy of democracy. Dissatisfied with intellectualism and mysticism, Masaryk, as a thinker, endeavored to establish an equilibrium between emotional and intellectual tendencies. As a Czech, he professed solidarity with all Slavic nations, but he was a severe critic of Russian thought. His fundamental ideas were rooted in the philosophy of enlightenment and positivism, but he was very cautious concerning Locke and Comte, notwithstanding his personal sympathies with these thinkers. He regarded the leading trends of European history as the development of the ideas of the French Revolution of 1789 but, critical as he remained of religious, social and political traditions, he always tried to awake the sense of responsibility to the maintenance and promotion of the common good and to establish new norms of human conduct in accordance with the new forms of human life, to vivify religious feelings and to justify a sober criticism, to harmonize reason and living faith. Among Masaryk's philosophical works are *The Scientific and Philosophical Crisis of Contemporary Marxism* (1898), *The Ideals of Humanity* (1902) and *The Spirit of Russia* (1917).

MORALITY

I CLASS myself among those who base morality on emotion, but I do not think that emotion ought to be in opposition to reason. Among feelings there are: good and bad, noble and ignoble, exalted and brutal. Ethics based on sentiment should not lose itself in emotion. I think that the harmony of feeling with reason (and, to some extent, the supremacy of feeling over reason) is the foundation of morality. . . . The foremost principle of modern ethics . . . is not anything new but the old and universally acknowledged law: 'Love thy neighbor as thyself.' Who, however, is my neighbor? We speak of the ideal of humanity. I accept this ideal. It has for me a double meaning. It is, first of all, the ideal of proper manhood; to be a man. Secondly, it involves consideration for our fellow humans in the widest sense.

Love of humanity tends readily, however, to become abstract, to exist in fancy rather than in reality. Love needs to be concentrated on specific objects. One cannot love all men equally. We choose, and we ought to choose the objects of our love. We need to have some particular objective . . . Love, humanity, must be positive. People often take the hatred of another nation to be love of one's own. It is far higher to feel no hatred, but to love positively . . . Love is no sentimentality. We are too sentimental, and sentimentality is egoism. Morality is founded on emotion, but not every emotion is just and good. . . . Emotion is blind and needs illumination by reason.

True love rests on hope, the hope of eternal life. Such love alone is true, because the eternal cannot be indifferent to the eternal. Eternity does not just commence with death. Eternity is here now, at this moment, at every moment. . . . In fixing your gaze upon eternity do not despise matter, the body, because of the superiority of mind. There is no matter, there is no body which is worthless. It is not matter or the body which is the source of evil; it is mind. . . .

The hope in eternal life is, then, the basis of our faith in life. Our faith, I say, for life and work depend on faith.

[246]

MAZZINI, GIUSEPPE

MAZZINI, GIUSEPPE (1805-1872). When the Prince of Metternich was still considered the most powerful man in Europe, he said that "no one gave me more trouble than a devil of an Italian, emaciated, pale, poor, but eloquent as a tempest, inspired as an apostle, sly as a thief, and tireless as a lover—his name is Giuseppe Mazzini." In his private life, simple, kindly, affectionate, sometimes even playful, Mazzini, during the twenty years preceding 1850, was regarded by the revolutionaries of all the countries of Europe as their master, by the Italian people as the prophet of their future greatness, and, when he took refuge in England, Mazzini, a defeated man roused the enthusiasm of philosophers like Henry Sidgwick and John Morley, and of poets like Wordsworth, Swinburne and Meredith, and was, notwithstanding their dissension in fundamental political questions, a highly respected and dear friend of Thomas Carlyle.

It is characteristic of Mazzini that he embraced the cause of European revolution and the unification of Italy only when he saw proscripts who, after the collapse of their uprising of 1821, asked his mother for charity. His vision of the future was colored by pity for the poor and the suffering. He did not neglect the social aspect of the revolution, but he condemned the theory of class struggle and did not recognize chosen classes or chosen nations. He always put humanity above nations, his own included, and God above humanity. Equally opposed to Marx as to the Pope and the kings, Mazzini believed in the ultimate victory of disinterested motives over egoism, of idealism over materialism and utilitarianism, and in a religion of humanity freed from prejudices, aware of the cultural values of the Biblical tradition, and able to enhance the dignity of the human individual. He proclaimed the rights as well as the duties of Man. Although he did not conceive new ideas, he was a moral power of considerable influence.

INTERESTS AND PRINCIPLES

PRINCIPLES alone are constructive. Ideals are never translated into facts without the general recognition of some strong belief. Great things are never done except by the rejection of individualism and a constant sacrifice of self to the common progress. Now, self-sacrifice is the sense of Duty in action. And the sense of Duty cannot spring from individual interests, but postulates the knowledge of a superior, inviolable Law. Every law rests on a principle: otherwise it is arbitrary and its violation is *permissible*. This principle must be freely accepted by everybody: otherwise the law is despotic and its violation is a *duty*. The application of principle lies in a life in conformity with law. To discover, to study, to preach the *principle* which shall be the basis of the social law of the country and of the times in which he lives, should be the aim of every man who directs his thought to any political organization. *Faith* in that principle is the parent of effective and lasting work. The isolated and barren knowledge of *individual interests* can only lead to the isolated and barren knowledge of *individual right*. And the knowledge of individual right will, where that right is denied, lead in its turn to discontent, opposition, strife, sometimes insurrection, but insurrection which, like that of Lyons, results only in a bitterer hostility between the classes which compose society. Whenever, therefore, we desire to do one of those great deeds called Revolutions, we must always return to the knowledge and preaching of principles. The true instrument of the progress of the peoples is to be sought in the *moral* factor.

But do we, therefore, neglect the *economic* factors, material interests; the importance of industrial victories, and the labors that won them? Do we preach principles for principles' sake, faith for faith's sake, as the romantic school of literature to-day preaches *art for art's sake*.

God forbid! We do not suppress the *economic* factor: we believe, on the contrary, that it is destined in the society of the future to admit an ever-increasing extension of the principle of *equality*, and to incorporate the fruitful principle of *association*. But we subordinate the economic to the *moral* factor, because if withdrawn from its controlling influence, dissociated from principles, and abandoned to the theories of individualism which govern it to-day, it would result in brutish egotism; in perpetual strife between men who should be brothers; in the expression of the *appetites* of the human species, whilst it ought rather to represent on the ascending curve of progress the material translation of man's activity, the expression of man's industrial mission.

No, we do not neglect material interests: on the contrary, we reject as imperfect and irreconcilable with the needs of the age every doctrine which does not include them, or regards them as less important than they really are. We believe that to every stage of progress there should be a corresponding positive improvement in the material condition of the people; and this successive improvement, in a certain manner, verifies for us the progress made. But we maintain that material interests cannot be developed alone, that they are dependent on principles, that they are not the *end and aim* of society; because we know that such a theory is destructive of human dignity; because we remember that when the *material* factor began to hold the field in Rome, and duty to the people was reduced to giving them *bread* and *public shows*, Rome and its people were hastening to destruction; because we see to-day in France, in Spain, in every country, liberty trodden under foot or betrayed precisely in the name of commercial interests and that servile doctrine which parts material well-being from principles.

[247]

McDOUGALL, WILLIAM

McDOUGALL, WILLIAM (1871-1938). McDougall has called himself "arrogant," and the behaviorists, psychoanalysts, Gestalt psychologists, pragmatists and a host of men of other philosophical and psychological schools attacked by him are far from denying him that quality. Honored as McDougall was as a professor at Oxford and Harvard, he always felt himself living in an adverse intellectual atmosphere. Indeed, he had reason for becoming embittered, for he was aware that his theories were often misrepresented. His work has been discussed from the viewpoint of instinct theory. But, in fact, McDougall regarded the instinctive nature of man only as a foundation, and maintained that the theory of sentiments furnishes the key to his system according to which in the man of developed character very few actions proceed directly from his instinctive foundation.

In addition to extensive travels through India, Indonesia and China in order to "hear the East," McDougall prepared his approach to the problems of the human mind by neurological and psychological studies. However, after his *Physiological Psychology* (1905), he concentrated upon psychological introspection and retrospection. His *Introduction to Social Psychology* (1908) challenged all previous conceptions and provoked animated controversies. He held that neither instinct, regarded as a working hypothesis, nor the human individual, characterized as an abstraction, can provide the basic data for social psychology but rather molding influences of social environment. The basic fact of human behavior is *purposive striving*. Consequently, McDougall calls psychology *hormic*, from the Greek *horme*—vital impulse, urge to action, which is to him a property of the mind, while he regarded intellect not as a source of energy but as the integrated system of man's beliefs (later as the sum total of man's innate and acquired cognitive abilities). In *Body and Mind* (1911) McDougall stated that mind must be considered a potent cause of evolution. McDougall also wrote *The Group Mind* (1920), *The Frontiers of Psychology* (1936) and *The Riddle of Life* (1938).

INDIVIDUAL AND GROUPS

It is a notorious fact that, when a number of men think and feel and act together, the mental operations and the actions of each member of the group are apt to be very different from those he would achieve if he faced the situation as an isolated individual. Hence, though we may know each member of a group so intimately that we can, with some confidence, foretell his actions under given circumstances, we cannot foretell the behavior of the group from our knowledge of the individuals alone. If we would understand and be able to predict the behavior of the group, we must study the way in which the mental processes of its members are modified in virtue of their membership. That is to say, we must study the interactions between the members of the group and also those between the group as a whole and each member. We must examine also the forms of group organization and their influence upon the life of the group.

Groups differ greatly from one another in respect of the kind and degree of organization they possess. In the simplest case the group has no organization. In some cases the relations of the constituent individuals to one another and to the whole group are not in any way determined or fixed by previous events; such a group constitutes merely a mob. In other groups the individuals have certain determinate relations to one another which have arisen in one or more of three ways:

(1) Certain relations may have been established between the individuals, before they came together to form a group; for example, a parish council or a political meeting may be formed by persons belonging to various definitely recognized classes, and their previously recognized relations will continue to play a part in determining the collective deliberations and actions of the group; they will constitute an incipient organization.

(2) If any group enjoys continuity of existence, certain more or less constant relations, of subordination, deference, leadership and so forth, will inevitably become established between the individuals of which it is composed; and, of course, such relations will usually be deliberately established and maintained by any group that is united by a common purpose, in order that its efficiency may be promoted.

(3) The group may have a continued existence and a more or less elaborate and definite organization independent of the individuals of which it is composed; in such a case the individuals may change while the formal organization of the group persists; each person who enters it being received into some more or less well-defined and generally recognized position within the group, which formal position determines in great measure the nature of his relations to other members of the group and to the group as a whole.

We can hardly imagine any concourse of human beings, however fortuitous it may be, utterly devoid of the rudiments of organization of one or other of these three kinds; nevertheless, in many a fortuitous concourse the influence of such rudimentary organization is so slight as to be negligible. Such a group is an unorganized crowd or mob. The unorganized crowd presents many of the fundamental phenomena of collective psychology in relative simplicity; whereas the higher the degree of organization of a group, the more complicated is its psychology.

[248]

801

MEAD, GEORGE HERBERT

MEAD, GEORGE HERBERT (1863-1931). After Mead's death, one of his graduate students declared that for many years to come articles and even books would continue to be published of which the first author was George Mead. John Dewey, his intimate friend, has said that Mead had "a seminal mind of the first order," and Alfred Whitehead, after reading some of Mead's posthumously published books, publicly endorsed this view. Dewey also recognized that Mead, whose scholarship in the natural sciences was superior to his own, had influenced him by conversations which were continued over a period of years.

Mead published little during his lifetime, and wrote no systematic work, but he was a consistent thinker. He constantly expressed his antipathy for metaphysics and was equally opposed to idealism and materialism. His principal interests were devoted to the investigation of the consequence of biological theories to scientific psychology. He held that psychological phenomena, including those of thinking and knowing, must be described as actions or reactions of the organism that lives in an environment and regulates its relations to objective conditions of life by means of the nervous system of which the brain is a part. To Mead, the psychical is the state which occurs when previously formed relations of the organism to its environment break down and new ones are not yet built up. Acts are the unity of existence of the individual that is proclaimed as a concrete, inimitable, nonrationalizable unit, but modifiable through its relation to society. Mead tried to maintain a balance between the determination by the individual of the whole, be it society or the world, and the determination by the whole of the individual.

SOCIAL PSYCHOLOGY

SOCIAL Psychology studies the activity or behavior of the individual as it lies within the social process; the behavior of an individual can be understood only in terms of the behavior of the whole social group of which he is a member, since his individual acts are involved in larger, social acts which go beyond himself and which implicate the other members of that group.

We are not, in social psychology, building up the behavior of the social group in terms of the behavior of the separate individuals composing it; rather, we are starting out with a given social whole of complex group activity, into which we analyze (as elements) the behavior of each of the separate individuals composing it. We attempt, that is, to explain the conduct of the individual in terms of the organized conduct of the social group rather than to account for the organized conduct of the social group in terms of the conduct of the separate individuals belonging to it. For social psychology, the whole (society) is prior to the part (the individual), not the part to the whole; and the part is explained in terms of the whole, not the whole in terms of the part or parts. The social act is not explained by building it up out of stimulus plus response; it must be taken as a dynamic whole—as something going on—no part of which can be considered or understood by itself—a complex organic process implied by each individual stimulus and response involved in it.

In social psychology we get at the social process from the inside as well as from the outside. Social psychology is behavioristic in the sense of starting off with an observable activity—the dynamic, on-going social process, and the social acts which are its component elements—to be studied and analyzed scientifically. But it is not behavioristic in the sense of ignoring the inner experience of the individual—the inner phase of that process or activity. On the contrary, it is particularly concerned with the rise of such experience within the process as a whole. It simply works from the outside to the inside instead of from the inside to the outside, so to speak, in its endeavor to determine how such experience does arise within the process. The act, then, and not the tract, is the fundamental datum in both social and individual psychology when behavioristically conceived and it has both an inner and an outer phase, an internal and an external aspect.

These general remarks have had to do with our point of approach. It is behavioristic, but unlike Watsonian behavior-ism it recognizes the parts of the act which do not come to external observation, and it emphasizes the act of the human individual in its natural social situation.

[249]

MEINONG, ALEXIUS VON

MEINONG, ALEXIUS VON (1853-1920). When Meinong expressed opinions about political facts, he was convinced of being just and right. As a philosopher, however, he remained conscious that to err means to be a human being. He thought that scientists could not obtain definite results, save some fortunate exceptions that prove the rule, and that one might be satisfied with exploring more favorable starting points to broach old questions.

It is true that Meinong did not claim to have found definite truth. But he claimed to have established a new science, namely— the *Theory of Objects*, which, as he said, was bound to fill a gap which had been left by epistemology, metaphysics and psychology. His theory of objects differs from psychology because it does not envisage the psychic acts but the objects. It differs from metaphysics since it also comprises the non-real. It differs from ontology by stressing the experience of resistance to the experiencing subject on the part of the object. It was developed by its founder to a new doctrine of perception and of value and valuing. Ethics is regarded as a part of the theory of values, and ethical values comprise moral as well as nonmoral values.

Meinong, who first studied history and philology, came to philosophy, as he said, by chance and as an autodidact. He was encouraged by Franz Brentano, who later rejected many of Meinong's statements. Meinong was rather surprised when he was appointed a professor by the Austrian government. He had numerous disciples, some of whom modified Meinong's theory and brought it close to phenomenology.

THE PROBLEM OF CAUSALITY

HABENT *sua fata cogitationes*—and the idea of causality is without any doubt one of those whose fate has been eventful. Its fates have been recorded in the teachings of leading minds of both former and present days. But the manner in which public opinion of those who are more or less led has reacted to it should have been recorded, for history has to deal not only with kings but also with peoples. Especially at those times can you recognize it when its characteristic features lie above all in the specific manner of such reactions. A glance at the last few decades of our immediate past shows that the history of the idea of causality especially does not lack such times. When Hume, in spite of all sagacity, had played once with the sceptical fire not much more seriously than his predecessors—when Kant had hoped to forestall the threatening danger for good, one might consider these deeds as royal deeds. However, when the positivistic and empiriocritical wind blew the spark not into beaming but into singeing flames, then very little could be discovered of the characteristics of royal builders. In our days, wherever one deals with science in a philosophical manner, and even more so where one deals with it in an unphilosophical manner, there appears all the more clearly the tendency to defy the authority of the principle, if not examined afresh. In spite of some isolated attacks, this principle had been considered the pillar of science. Now it became fashionable to avoid, if possible, any reference to it if one was not downright resolved to deny the validity of the general law of causality. Needless to say how well that suits that agnosticism which otherwise promises satisfaction to many metaphysical and ethical needs. It goes without saying that there is no lack of those who, not because of their needs but because of their absence of needs, show great ease in considering everyone as backward who speaks of causal and not of functional relationships. One cannot therefore say that the destructive trend, proper to the more recent theories of causality, has begun to become a practice in our time. The general law of causality, claimed so often and with such emphasis as an indispensable requirement of scientific working, has lost its validity in the eyes of more than one who is resolved to think scientifically to the best of his capacity.

The question whether there is such a law has never been less academic than today.

[250]

MEISTER ECKHART. See ECKHART, JOHANNES.

MELISSOS

MELISSOS (Fifth Century, B.C.). We know practically nothing of the life of Melissos save the one great fact that he was the general of Samos that defeated the Athenian fleet in 440 B.C.

FRAGMENTS

IF nothing is, what can be said of it as of something real?

*　　　*　　　*

What was was ever, and ever shall be. For, if it had come into being, there must needs have been nothing before it came into being. Now, if nothing were to exist, in no wise could anything have arisen out of nothing.

*　　　*　　　*

Since, then, it has not come into being and since it is, it was ever and ever shall be, and has no beginning or end, but is infinite. For, if it had come into being, it would have had a beginning (or it would have begun to come into being at some time or other) and an end (for it would have ceased to come into being at some time or other); but, if it neither began nor ended, it ever was and ever shall be, and has no beginning or end; for it is not possible for anything to be ever without being all.

*　　　*　　　*

Further, just as it ever is, so it must ever be infinite in magnitude (for if it had bounds, it would be bounded by empty space).

But nothing which has a beginning or end is either eternal or infinite.

For if it is (infinite), it must be one; for if it were two, it could not be infinite; for then it would be bounded by another.

806

(And, since it is one, it is alike throughout; for if it were unlike, it would be many and not one).

So then it is eternal and infinite and one and all alike. And it cannot perish nor become greater, nor does it suffer pain or grief. For, if any of these happened to it, it would no longer be one. For, if it is altered, then the real must needs not be all alike, but what was before must pass away, and what was not must come into being. Now, if the all had changed by so much as a single hair, in thirty thousand years, it would all perish in the whole of time.

Further, it is not possible either that its order should be changed; for the order which it had before does not perish, nor does that which was not come into being. But, since nothing is either added to it or passes away or is altered, how can any real thing have had its order changed? For if anything became different, that would amount to a change in its order.

Nor does it suffer pain; for the All cannot be in pain. For a thing in pain could not be ever, nor could it have the same power as what is whole. It is only from the addition or subtraction of something that it could feel pain, and then it would no longer be like itself. Nor could what is whole possibly begin to feel pain; for then what was whole and what was real would pass away, and what was not would come into being. And the same argument applies to grief as to pain.

Nor is anything empty. For what is empty is nothing. . . . What is nothing, then, cannot be.

Nor does it move; for it has nowhere to betake itself to, but is full. For if there were empty space, it would betake itself to empty space. But, since there is no empty space, it has no place to betake itself to.

And it cannot be dense and rare; for it is not possible for what is rarefied to be as full as what is dense, but what is rare is ipso facto emptier than what is dense.

This is the way in which we must distinguish between what is full and what is not full. If a thing has room for anything else, and takes it in, it is not full; but if it has no room for anything and does not take it in, it is full.

Now, it must needs be full if there is no empty space, and if it is full, it does not move.

If what is real is divided, it moves; but if it moves, it cannot have body; for, if it had body it would have parts, and would no longer be one.

*   *   *

This argument, then, is the greatest proof that it is one alone; but the following are proofs of it also. If it were a many, these would have to be of the same kind as I say that the one is. For if there is earth and water, and air and iron, and gold and fire, and if one thing is living and another dead, and if things are black and white and all that men say they really are,—if that is so, and if we see and hear aright, each one of these must be such as we at first concluded that reality was, and they cannot be changed or altered. Whereas we say that we see and hear and understand aright, and yet we believe that what is warm becomes cold, and what is cold warm; that what is hard turns soft, and what is soft hard; that what is living dies, and that things are born from what lives not; and that all those things are changed. We think that iron, which is hard, is rubbed away with the finger, passing away in rust; and so with gold and stone and everything which we fancy to be strong, so that it turns out that we neither see nor know realities. Earth, too, and stone are formed out of water. Now these things do not agree with one another. We said that there were many things that were eternal and had forms and strength of their own, and yet we fancy that they all suffer alteration, and that they change with each perception. It is clear, then, that we did not see aright after all, nor are we right in believing that all these things are many. They would not change if they were real, but each thing would be just what we believed it to be; for nothing is stronger than true reality. But if it has changed, what was has passed away, and what was not is come into

being. So then, if there were many things they would have
to be just of the same nature as the one.

[251]

MENASSEH BEN ISRAEL

MENASSEH BEN ISRAEL (1604-1657). It was an apocalyptic mystic, expecting the fulfilment of the Messianic promises, who, in
1655, accomplished with extraordinary worldly ability the political
and diplomatic task of securing permission for the Jews to settle
again in England, from which they had been expelled in 1290.
Menasseh ben Israel, who was able to put Oliver Cromwell in a
mood favorable to his demands for readmission of the Jews to
England, was also highly respected by Queen Christina of Sweden,
had studied philosophy with Descartes, and his scholarship was
exalted by men like Hugo Grotius and the learned theologian Johannes Buxtorff. Until the end of the 18th century, Menasseh ben
Israel was considered a high authority in history, linguistics and
theology by great scholars in Holland, England, France and Germany. Even greater was his influence with Christian mystics. He
had studied the Cabala but was also well acquainted with orthodox
rabbinic literature. His own writings, devoted to the vindication of
Judaism, to its defense against accusations or to its reconciliation
with philosophical and mystical doctrines, show him to be a versatile rather than a profound thinker. Among them, *Hope of Israel*
(1650), dedicated to the Parliament of England, and *Vindication
of the Jews* (1656) were written for political purposes, while *The
Statue of Nebuchadnèzzar* (1656), a commentary on Daniel's interpretation of the Babylonian king's dream, outlines a mystical philosophy of history. This book, when first printed, was decorated
with four etchings by Rembrandt who, from 1645 on, was his intimate friend.

ON HUMAN LIFE

THE life of man has a determined and fixed period.

It may be considered in three modes; either according to the constitution and temperament of the body, the
strength communicated it to the natal hour or time of
conception by the planets, or the general period of existence
of the age.

809

This period considered in either way is not immutable but variable. Life may be shortened by providence, nature or accident.

The observance of the Divine precepts, both in theory and practice, and meditation in the Holy Law, lead to prolongation.

It is not only lawful but imperative that recourse should be had to physicians and medicines when requisite.

Although from eternity God knows the period of existence allotted to everyone yet it is in the power of man, by upright conduct, to ameliorate his condition.

The knowledge of how God's prescience and regulation of the future is consistent with existence of contingencies in nature, requires much longer detail and many arguments; but it may be briefly observed that . . . all contingencies are infallibly known to God, as they are subject to the Divine sight, from His omnipotence; and, withal, are only future contingencies when compared with their causes. Thus the First Cause not only sees the actions of man as future, but as present and already performed: in the same way as one person, seeing another do an act, would not say, because he was looking on, it was obliged to be done, so God, because he sees the action as present, does not oblige him who performs it, to do it, but leaves him to his liberty and the operating contingency.

God does not grant His grace to individuals, but He gives the same disposition to all mankind, by which every one may alike become meritorious, and by their own actions secure their felicity. Therefore, it being necessary that merit should precede grace, the Lord by His prophet said: "Turn unto Me, and I will turn unto you," for then grace and help infallibly follow.

The advantage a wise man has over a fool is the same as the humble has over the rich. For the humble knows how to walk to everlasting life, and the wealthy miser to death with eyes constantly fixed on the earth and its productions, gold and silver. But the wise man, with eyes raised to the heaven, satisfied with a moderate maintenance and clothing, walks to everlasting life.

[252]

MENCIUS (Meng Tzu)

MENCIUS (MENG TZU) (372-289 B.C.). In his efforts to educate kings, Meng Tzu (Master Meng) seems to have been no more successful than his Greek contemporary Aristotle. But to a greater extent than Aristotle, Meng used his personal experiences for the development of his philosophical teachings.

Meng was a disciple of Tzu, who was the grandson of Confucius and himself an influential philosopher, though of lesser importance to the history of Confucianism than his pupil Meng. It was Meng who restored the authority of Confucius by successfully combating deviating opinions such as were advanced by Mo-Ti and Yang Chou, both of whom had become extremely popular and had tried to discredit the cult and doctrine of Confucianism. At the end of his life, Meng composed the book that bears his name and, in the Sung era, was canonized. Extracts from the book became favorite reading in Europe early in the eighteenth century and have continued in their popularity. The book is the fruit of experiences collected during long, extensive travels, and of keen observations of people of all classes from kings down to beggars. Meng declared that man is good by nature but that he has to develop his own nature to the greatest possible perfection. The government, said Meng, must serve the people and promote their welfare. Revolt against bad rulers is permitted. War is branded as a crime. Meng has been quoted more than once by Voltaire and Rousseau. In this way he influenced, at least indirectly, many leaders of the French Revolution.

ON BENEVOLENCE

BENEVOLENCE brings glory to an individual and its opposite brings disgrace. For people of the present day to hate disgrace and yet live complacently doing what is not benevolent, is like hating moisture and yet living in low country.

If a man hates disgrace, the best course for him to pursue is to esteem virtue and honor virtuous scholars, giving the worthiest among them places of dignity, and the able offices of trust.

People take advantage of the time, when throughout the land there are leisure and rest, to abandon themselves to pleasure and indolent indifference; they, in fact, seek for calamities for themselves.

Calamity and happiness in all cases are men's own seeking. This is illustrated by what is said in The Book of Poetry:

> Be always studious to be in harmony with the ordinances of God,
> So you will certainly get for yourself much happiness;

and by the passages of the Tai Chia: "When Heaven sends down calamities, it is still possible to escape from them; when we occasion the calamities ourselves, it is not possible any longer to live."

*   *   *

If a ruler give honor to men of talents and virtue and employ the able, so that the offices shall all be filled by the individuals of distinction and mark—then all the scholars of the land will be pleased. . . .

All men have a mind which cannot bear to see the suffering of others. The ancient kings had this commiserating mind, and they, as a matter of course, had likewise a commiserating government. When with a commiserating mind was practiced a commiserating government, the government of the land was as easy a matter as the making anything go round in the palm.

When I say that all men have a mind which cannot bear to see the suffering of others, my meaning may be illustrated thus: even nowadays, if men suddenly see a child about to fall into a well, they will without exception experience a feeling of alarm and distress. They will feel so, not as a ground on which they may gain the favor of the child's parents, nor as a ground on which they may seek the praise of their neighbors and friends, nor from a dislike to the reputation of having been unmoved by such a thing.

From this case we may perceive that the feeling of commiseration is essential to man, that the feeling of shame and dislike is essential to man, that the feeling of modesty and complacence is essential to man.

*   *   *

The feeling of commiseration is the principle of benevolence. The feeling of shame and dislike is the principle of righteousness. The feeling of modesty and complacence is the principle of propriety. The feeling of approving and disapproving is the principle of knowledge.

Men have these four principles just as they have their four limbs. When men, having these four principles, yet say of themselves that they cannot develop them, they play the thief with themselves and he who says of his neighbor that he cannot develop them, plays the thief with his neighbor.

Since all men have these four principles in themselves, let them know to give them all their development and completion, and the issue will be like that of fire which has begun to burn, or that of a spring which has begun to find vent. Let them have their complete development and they will suffice to love and protect all within the four seas.

The choice of a profession, therefore, is a thing in which great caution is required. Confucius said, "It is virtuous manners which constitute the excellence of a neighborhood. If a man in selecting a residence, does not fix on one where such prevail, how can he be wise?"

Now, benevolence is the most honorable dignity conferred by heaven, and the quiet home in which man should dwell. Since no one can hinder us from being so, if yet we are not benevolent, we are unwise.

From the want of benevolence and the want of wisdom will ensue the entire absence of propriety and righteousness.

[253]

MENDELSSOHN, MOSES

MENDELSSOHN, MOSES (1729-1786). In the late seventeenth century, Father Pierre Bonhours, a Jesuit and a refined art critic, published a pamphlet in which he held that a German could never be a poet or an artist, nor could he understand aesthetical problems and phenomena. Of course, the booklet aroused indignation in Germany, and provoked violent counter-attacks. At that time, however, Frenchmen and Germans agreed that a Jew could never become integrated into modern culture, let alone contribute to its development. This opinion remained constant until, by 1755, the surprising news was spread in literary circles that there was in Berlin a Jew called Moses Mendelssohn who could not only speak and write German flawlessly but who could discuss philosophical and literary problems and was even esteemed by Lessing, the most feared German critic of his time, as an authority in aesthetics and psychology. Many otherwise independent thinkers would simply not believe that the news was true. Some of them went to Berlin in order to gaze in astonishment at such a curiosity. Then, for some years, even Mendelssohn's sincere admirers, such as Kant and Lessing, expressed doubts that he could continue to be devoted to German culture and at the same time remain loyal to Judaism. Later they recognized that he could do both.

Mendelssohn enriched descriptive psychology by his treatise on mixed sentiments. His essay on evidence in metaphysical sciences was awarded the prize by the Prussian Academy against his competitor, Immanuel Kant. His *Phaedon* (1767), defending the idea of the immortality of the soul, was a favorite book of German Jews and Christians alike for more than two generations. With his *Jerusalem* (1783), he deeply impressed Kant, who became convinced that Judaism was a true world religion. Mendelssohn also translated the Hebrew Bible into German and demanded civil rights for the Jews as well as the separation of Church and State. With him came the beginning of a new epoch in the history of the Jews, not only those of Germany. Still four decades after his death, hymns to his praise were sung by Christians and Jews united in their adherence to Mendelssohn's ideas. Lessing raised a poetic monument to his friend by using him as model for the hero of his drama *Nathan The Wise*.

ON PROGRESS

PROGRESS is for individual man, who is destined by Providence to pass a portion of his eternity here on earth. Every one goes his own way through life. One's route leads him over flowers and meadows; another's across desert plains, over steep mountains or by the side of dangerous precipices. Yet they all get on in the journey, pursuing the road to happiness, to which they are destined. But that the bulk, or the whole human race here on earth, should be constantly moving forth in progress of time, and perfecting itself, seems to me not to have been the design of Providence.

Do you want to divine the design of Providence with man? Then forge no hypotheses; look only around you at what actually does pass—and if you can take a general view of the history of all ages—at what has passed from the beginning. That is fact: that must have belonged to the design; that must have been approved of in the plan of Wisdom, or at least have been admitted in it. Providence never misses its aim. That which actually happens must have been its design from the beginning, or have belonged to it. Now, in respect to the human race at large, you do not perceive a constant progress of improvement that looks as if approaching nearer and nearer to perfection. On the contrary, we see the human race as a whole subject to slight swings; and it never yet made some steps forward but what it did, soon after, slide back again into its previous station, with double the celerity. Most nations of the earth pass many ages in the same degree of civilization in the same crepusculous light, which appears much too dim for our spoiled eyes. Now and then a particle of the grand mass will kindle, become a bright star, and run through an orbit, which, now after a longer, now after a shorter period, brings it back again, to its standstill, or sets it down at no great distance from it. Man goes on; but mankind is constantly swinging to and fro, within fixed boundaries; but, considered as a whole, retains, at all periods of time, about the same degree of morality, the same quality of religion and irreligion, of virtue and vice, of happiness and misery; the same result, when the same is taken into account against the same; of all the good

and evil as much as was required for the transit of individual
men, in order that they might be trained here on earth, and
approach as near to perfection as was allotted and appointed
to every one of them.

[254]

MILL, JOHN STUART

MILL, JOHN STUART (1806-1873). Modern progressive pedagog-
ists must be horrified by the methods which were employed for the
education of John Stuart Mill by his father, the stern utilitarian
James Mill. The latter was not only his son's sole teacher. He
was even his sole intercourse, instructing him on walks as well as
at home. At the age of three, John Stuart Mill learned Greek. At
seven he studied Plato's dialogues. At eight he had to teach his
sister Latin. When he was fifteen years old, he was initiated into
Bentham's doctrine of the greatest happiness of the greatest number, which struck him as a revelation and made him a convert to
utilitarianism for his lifetime.

But far from being an uncritical and orthodox adept of the
philosophy which was cherished by his father, John Stuart, recognizing its flaws, became interested in romantic poetry, and, though
opposed to Coleridge's political and religious standpoint, praised
him as "the awakener of the philosophical spirit in England." Of
greater importance, however, was the influence of Comte, Guizot and
Tocqueville, to whom Mill owed the enlargement of his historical
views and, above all, his awareness of the great social change and
its consequences. Mill remained a staunch defender of individual
liberty because he was convinced of its social usefulness. But he
was ready to sacrifice individual property rights when they endangered the common good. He remained the advocate of representative government, but he considered the social question of increasing importance and became more and more devoted to the cause
of the working class, without, however, any intention of idealizing
the workers. When he campaigned for a seat in Parliament, he
warned his constituents that he would do nothing for their special
interests but only what he thought to be right. He also fought for
women's suffrage and for the rights of colored people.

Mill's philosophy combined British utilitarianism and French
positivism, but, as his last essays prove, would have developed
farther if he had lived longer. The main task of his *System of Logic*
(1843) is the analysis of inductive proof. His canons of inductive

816

methods for comprehending the causal relations between phenomena are valid under the assumption of the validity of the law of causality; Mill, however, admitted that this law cannot be accepted except on the basis of induction, which, on its part, is fundamentally a matter of enumeration.

Mill was a courageous and considerate fighter for human rights, always trying to understand the fair side of his adversary. During the second half of the 19th century, his ascendancy over the spirit of European philosophy was immense. Since then it has withered. But many of those who used to belittle Mill are, in fact, obligated to him. What he has said of Bentham may be also true of Mill himself: "He was not a great philosopher but a great reformer in philosophy."

LIBERTY OF THE INDIVIDUAL

THERE is a sphere of action in which society, as distinguished from the individual, has, if any only an indirect interest; comprehending all that portion of a person's life and conduct which affects only himself or if it also affects others, only with their free, voluntary, and undeceived consent and participation. When I say only himself, I mean directly, and in the first instance: for whatever affects himself may affect others through himself; and the objection which may be grounded in this contingency, will receive consideration in the sequel. This, then, is the appropriate region of human liberty. It comprises, first, the inward domain of consciousness; demanding liberty of conscience, in the most comprehensive sense; liberty of thought and feeling; absolute freedom of opinion and sentiment on all subjects, practical or speculative, scientific, moral, or theological. The liberty of expressing and publishing opinions may seem to fall under a different principle, since it belongs to that part of the conduct of an individual which concerns other people; but, being almost of as much importance as the liberty of thought itself, and resting in great part on the same reasons, is practically inseparable from it. Secondly, the principle requires liberty of tastes and pursuits; of framing the plan of our life to suit our own character; of doing as we like, subject to such consequences as may follow: without impediment from our fellow creatures, so long as what we do does not harm them, even though they should think our conduct foolish, perverse, or wrong. Thirdly, from this liberty of each individual, follows the liberty, within the same limits, of combination among individuals; freedom to unite, for any purpose not involving harm to others: the persons combining being supposed to be of full age, and not forced or deceived.

No society in which these liberties are not, on the whole, respected, is free, whatever may be its form of government; and never is completely free in which they do not exist absolute and unqualified.

THE TRIUMPH OF TRUTH

THE dictum that truth always triumphs over persecution, is one of those pleasant falsehoods which men repeat after one another till they pass into commonplaces, but which all experience refutes. History teems with instances of truth put down by persecution. If not suppressed forever, it may be thrown back for centuries. To speak only of religious opinions: the Reformation broke out at least twenty times before Luther, and was put down. . . . Even after the era of Luther, wherever persecution was persisted in, it was successful. In Spain, Italy, Flanders, the Austrian Empire, Protestantism was rooted out; and most likely, would have been so in England, had Queen Mary lived, or Queen Elizabeth died. Persecution has always succeeded, save where the heretics were too strong a party to be effectually persecuted. No reasonable person can doubt that Christianity might have been extirpated in the Roman Empire. It spread, and became predominant, because the persecutions were only occasional, lasting but a short time, and separated by long intervals of almost undisturbed propagandism. It is a piece of idle sentimentality that truth, merely as truth, has any inherent power denied to error, of prevailing against the dungeon and the stake. Men are not more zealous for truth than they often are for error, and a sufficient application of legal or even of social penalties will generally succeed in stopping the propagation of either. The real advantage which truth has, consists in this, that when an opinion is true, it may be extinguished once, twice, or many times, but in the course of ages there will generally be found persons to rediscover it, until some one of its reappearances falls on a time when from favorable circumstances it escapes persecution until it has made such head as to withstand all subsequent attempts to suppress it.

INDIVIDUAL AND STATE

THE worth of a State, in the long run, is the worth of the individuals composing it; and a State which postpones the interests of *their* mental expansion and elevation, to a little more of administrative skill, or that semblance of it which practice gives, in the details of business; a State which dwarfs its men, in order that they may be more docile instruments in its hands even for beneficial purposes, will find that with small men no great thing can really be accomplished; and that the perfection of machinery to which it has sacrificed everything, will in the end avail it nothing, for want of the vital power which, in order that the machine might work more smoothly it has preferred to banish.

THE PUREST OF WISDOM

WHEN we consider either the history of opinion, or the ordinary conduct of human life, to what is to be ascribed that the one and the others are no worse than they are? Not certainly to the inherent force of the human understanding; for, on any matter not self-evident, there are ninety-nine persons totally incapable of judging it, for one who is capable; and the capacity of the hundredth person is only comparative; for the majority of the eminent men of every past generation held many opinions now known to be erroneous, and did or approved numerous things which no one will now justify. Why is it, then, that there is on the whole a preponderance among mankind of rational opinions and rational conduct? If there really is this preponderance—which there must be, unless human affairs are, and have always been, in an almost desperate state—it is owing to a quality of the human mind, the source of everything respectable in man either as an intellectual or as a moral being, namely, that his errors are corrigible. He is capable of rectifying his mistakes, by discussion and experience. Not by experience alone. There must be discussion, to show how experience is to be interpreted. Wrong opinions and practices gradually yield to fact and argument: but facts and arguments, to produce any effect on the mind, must be brought before it. Very few facts are able to tell their own story, without comments to bring out their meaning. The whole strength and value, then, of human judgment, depending on the one property, that it can be set right when it is wrong, reliance can be placed on it only when the means of setting it right are kept constantly at hand. In the case of any person whose judgment is really deserving of confidence how has it become so? Because he has kept his mind open to criticism of his opinions and conduct. Because it has been his practice to listen to all that could be said against him; to profit by as much of it as was just, and expound to himself, and upon occasion to others, the fallacy of what was fallacious. Because he has felt, that the only way in which a human being can make some approach to knowing the whole of a subject, is by hearing what can be said about it by persons of every variety of opinion, and studying all modes in which it can be looked at by every character of mind. No wise man ever acquired his wisdom in any other manner.

MAN THE INDIVIDUAL

HE who lets the world, or his own portion of it, choose his plan of life for him, has no need of any other faculty than the ape-like one of imitation. He who chooses his plan for himself employs all his faculties. He must use observation to see, reasoning and judgment to foresee, activity to gather materials for decision, discrimination to decide, and when he has decided, firmness and self-control to hold to his deliberate decision. And these qualities he requires and exercises exactly in proportion as the part of his conduct which he determines according to his own judgment and feelings is a large one. It is possible that he might be guided in some good path, and kept out of harm's way, without any of these things. But what will be his comparative worth as a human being? It really is of importance, not only what men do, but what manner of men they are that do it. Among the works of man, which human life is rightly employed in perfecting and beautifying, the first in importance is surely man himself. Supposing it were possible to get houses built, corn grown, battles fought, causes tried, and even churches erected and prayers said, by machinery—by automatons in human form—it would be a considerable loss to exchange for these automatons even the men and women who at present inhabit the more civilized parts of the world, and who assuredly are but starved specimens of what nature can and will produce. Human nature is not a machine to be built after a model, and set to do exactly the work prescribed for it, but a tree, which requires to grow and develop itself on all sides, according to the tendency of the inward forces which make it a living thing.

[255]

MOHAMMED

MOHAMMED (570-632). As with every founder of a religion, the life and personality of Mohammed, the founder of Islam, have been transformed by legends which picture him as the only perfect man, the greatest of all saints, the only one worthy of becoming the instrument of divine revelation. Mohammed himself, however, thought otherwise. He said that he was sent by God as a "witness, as a hopeful and warning messenger, as a torch," but he refused to be regarded as an example of virtue. He did not feel that he was a saint, and consciously refrained from performing miracles. He certainly was a fanatic but occasionally he showed a sense of humor, and several of his jokes have been transmitted to posterity.

The original name of Mohammed (The Praised One) was Ubu'l Kassim. He was a merchant in Mecca where plutocracy offended his social feelings, as the idolatry of the whole population offended his reason and piety. Broodings, dreams and visions led him to the belief that he was chosen by God to save the Arabian people from spiritual and moral corruption by announcing the coming judgment of humanity and teaching faith in Allah, the one and omnipotent God.

At the age of 40, Mohammed began his religious mission. The citizens of Mecca sneered at him and forced him to flee. In 622, he came to the city of Jathrib where he was well received and actively supported. Jathrib, therefore, was subsequently renamed Medina (City of the Prophet), and became the base of his power and his religious and military expeditions. The flight of 622 (Hejira) became an event of greatest importance to the history of the world. In Medina, Mohammed, once a lonesome missionary, became a spiritual and military ruler and conqueror, and his religious doctrine was shaped to the religion of Islam, an institution, and, at the same time, a warlike organization. Mohammed subdued Mecca, his native town that had expelled him. But when he died he could not foresee the future expansion of Islam.

The basis of Islamic religion is the *Koran* (Recitations), written by Mohammed who claimed to be inspired by Gabriel, the archangel. It consists of 114 sections (Suras), the first third of which was conceived in Mecca and deals with the creation and future fate of the world, the proofs of the omnipotence of Allah and the teachings of a moral conduct of life as a preparation for standing the test on the Day of Judgment. The remainder of the *Koran*, accomplished in Medina, contains polemics against other religious and civil legislation.

Mohammed claimed that he restored the religion of Abraham which, according to him, had been distorted by Judaism and Christianity. Mohammed adopted many of the Judaic and Christian, gnostic, and Babylonian traditions but, the older he grew, the more he stressed the importance of the sword as a means of propagating the right faith. Without Mohammed's *Koran*, the world religion of Islam cannot be understood. However, Islam cannot be understood only by the study of the *Koran*. The moral and dogmatic evolution of Mohammedanism did not stop by any means after Mohammed's death.

THE EXORDIUM

IN the name of God, the compassionate, Compassioner: Praise be to God, the Lord of the worlds, the compassionate Compassioner, the Sovereign of the day of judgment. Thee do we worship, and of Thee do we beg assistance. Direct us in the right way; in the way of those to whom Thou hast been gracious, on whom there is no wrath, and who go not astray.

CONCERNING ALMSGIVING

If ye make your alms to appear, it is well; but if ye conceal them, and give to the poor, this will be better for you, and will atone for your sins; and God is well informed of that which ye do. The direction of them belongeth not unto thee; but God directeth whom He pleaseth. The good that ye shall give in alms shall redound unto yourselves; and ye shall not give unless out of desire of seeing the face of God. And what good things ye shall give in alms, it shall be repaid you. They who distribute alms of their substance night and day, in private and in public, shall have their reward with their Lord; on them shall no fear come, neither shall they be grieved.

CONCERNING USURY

They who devour usury shall not arise from the dead, but as he ariseth whom Satan hath infected by a touch. This shall happen to them because they say, "Truly selling is but as usury;" and yet God hath permitted selling and forbidden usury. He therefore who, when there cometh unto him an admonition from his Lord, abstaineth from usury for the future, shall have what is past forgiven him; and his affair belongeth unto God. But whoever returneth to usury, they shall be the companions of hell-fire; they shall continue therein forever.

CONCERNING CONTRACTS

Deal not unjustly with others, and ye shall not be dealt

with unjustly. If there be any debtor under a difficulty of paying his debt, let his creditor wait till it be easy for him to do it; but if he remit it as alms, it will be better for you, if ye knew it. And fear the day when ye shall return unto God; then shall every soul be paid what it hath gained, and they shall not be treated unjustly.

O true believers, when ye bind yourselves one to the other in a debt for a certain time, write it down; and let a writer write between you according to justice; and let not a writer refuse writing according to what God hath taught him; but let him write, and let him who oweth the debt dictate, and let him fear God his Lord, and not diminish aught thereof. But if he who oweth the debt be foolish or weak, or be not able to dictate himself, let his agent dictate according to equity; and call to witness two witnesses of your neighboring men; but if there be not two men, let there be a man and two women of those whom ye shall choose for witnesses; if one of these women should mistake, the other of them shall cause her to recollect. And the witnesses shall not refuse, whensoever they shall be called. And disdain not to write it down, be it a large debt, or be it a small one, until its time of payment. This will be more just in the sight of God, and more right for bearing witness, and more easy, that ye may not doubt. And take witnesses when ye shall sell one to the other, and let no harm be done to the writer nor to the witness, which if ye do it will surely be injustice to you; and fear God, and God will instruct you, for God knoweth all things.

[256]

MONTAGUE, WILLIAM PEPPERELL

MONTAGUE, WILLIAM PEPPERELL (1873-1953). During his childhood, Montague used to bother his parents by questioning them about his soul, the relations between mind and body, and the soul of the universe. He was neither satisfied with his mother's evasive answers, nor terrified by his father's impatience. In his advanced age, Montague declared that he has continued ever since to ask

the same questions and that he has not been satisfied by the solutions
of the Church or of his teachers, among whom Royce, James, Santayana and Palmer were outstanding, or of his colleagues and
critics. However, reared in a New England congregation, he developed "a poignant sense of the beauty of the Christian doctrine."
He devoted his life to the reconciliation of his inquiring spirit
with his faith, seeking to establish God as the solid basis of
natural knowledge. He found out that the problem of God is
insoluble in terms of traditional theism and traditional atheism
but that Man craves infinity, and that higher religion has the
best chances of being proved to be true. To him it does not
matter whether his philosophy is called a cosmological spiritualism that, in a sense, can be expressed in physical terms, or as
spiritualistic, or even animistic, materialism.

Montague's metaphysics is founded upon an epistemological
realism which he had to defend on more than one front. Against
idealism Montague maintains the independence of reality from
consciousness. Against pragmatism he adheres to the idealist conception of truth as independent of its working in practice. In
1910 he was associated with the group of "New Realists," but
subsequently had to stress the difference of his views from those
of the other members of the group and from "objective" and
"critical" realism. None of these controversies could weaken his
conviction that theism is "an exciting and momentous hypothesis"
rather than either a dialectical truism or a dogma to be adopted
uncritically. But he declares that religion must claim a knowledge
of nature to go beyond what any reasonable person considers a
matter of course. To him, religion is concerned with the values
in the realm of existence, while philosophy is concerned with the
values in the life of the spirit. Philosophy is a vision as religion
is a faith.

PROMETHEAN CHALLENGE TO RELIGION

THE moral ideal of Christian love is like a pillar of flaming
light extending from earth to heaven, but the supernatural
religion of freedom, solace, and joy that should have evolved
from it was choked and poisoned. The successors of Christ,
from St. Paul down to the censors, obscurantists, and tyrants
of today have done their conscientious worst to hide the light
from men. The long series of authoritarians and ascetics have
changed the clear into the obscure, the beautiful into the

ugly, and with what was most gentle and generous they have associated what was most cruel and mean. They have debauched a religion of liberty, service, tolerance, and progress to their own base ends of persecution, reaction, and gloom.

Through all the world today there is an ominous muttering. Not only the small though growing army of scientists who view the efforts of religious fanatics to check the teachings of science with a contempt so deep and cold that they can hardly be brought to express it, and not only the men of letters and liberal authors who show a more voluble contempt for the spirit of censorious puritanism which is growing beyond the stage of an ugly American joke are significant; but far more meaningful than these is the sullen rage of the multitude of workers throughout the world who for the first time are really coming to hate the Christian scheme.

If religion is to be saved from destruction from without, it must be revolutionized from within. And it is a Promethean revolution that is needed: no new prophet as substitute for Christ, but a great purging and cleansing of Christianity and of all religion as it exists today.

What would a Prometheanized religion be like? Would there be left of Christianity, for example, anything more than a vague and worldly humanitarianism, a platitudinous philanthropy touched with inarticulate emotion? Many liberal and well-meaning people so believe, and, though aware of the anomalies of orthodoxy and of the growing dangers to the whole structure of religion, they fear that any breach in the ranks of authority would be more dangerous still. I think such fears are completely ungrounded, and by way of conclusion I will attempt to outline some of the principal characteristics of a religion transfigured by a Promethean revolution.

First of all, there would be the welcome and luminous absence of sacrosanct authority. Such dogmas as remained, and they would be many, would be transformed into hypothesis. The most fantastic theory of the supernatural, if held as a hypothesis, is honorable, and belief in it is honest and to be respected. There would be no lack of propaganda and missionary zeal. Those who had faith in a theory would be proud to have it vindicated by criticism. For the irreligious freethinking would be optional, but for religionists it would be compulsory. A church member who refused to allow his belief to be tested in the light of reason would be expelled as one of little faith. The various schools and sects would not persecute one another, for why should one seeker for truth hate another? Why should he not rather co-operate with him the better to realize their common end? If a theory is not true, no one would wish it to survive; if it is true, it will survive. How senseless and perverse not to test it!

Not only would theists cease to hate another—they would cease to hate atheists. They would love and respect them. For if you are walking comfortably in the light of a supernatural faith that the universe is on your side, why should you not love and respect the man who walks in darkness, crippled by the fear that the things we care for most are at the mercy of blind force—deprived of your hope of God and another world, yet fighting bravely by your side for the same ideals for which you fight? A strange inversion of Christian charity to hate such a one.

And in this Promethean religion, heaven would be no less free than earth of that hateful spirit of monarchical authority. We should not love goodness because it is commanded by God, but should love God because He is good. We should base our religion on our ethics; not as now, our ethics on a supernatural physics. And there would be no longer that curious double standard, according to which the same God who commands us to forgive our enemies no matter how many times they offend, reserves for Himself the right to wreak infinite vengeance on His enemies after one trial life on earth. That nightmare monster of authoritarian religion, veritable anti-Christ, would have been consigned to his own hell, the single one of all imagined beings who would really deserve it.

As in our religion, so in our ethics. The principle of authority would be gone, and with it the great clutter of prohibitions and taboos—rules taken as ends in themselves rather than as means to happiness. The one supreme and single purpose of morality would be the making of life more abundant, which means the developing to a maximum the potentialities of every creature. Love and work by all for the maximum well-being of all. All moral rules— the oldest and most revered, like those established for marriage and property, no less than the newest and queerest proposals— would be appraised without prejudice and in the cold light of intelligence, to be accepted or rejected only according to their efficiency in promoting the ideal of freer and more abundant living.

The banishment of asceticism and authoritarianism would for the first time in history bring human ethics into active partnership with human science. Once clear away the morality of taboos, and all the forces of intelligence could be mobilized in the service of progress, and the vast energies of thought and will that have been wasted in religious wars could be utilized for moral and religious work.

[257]

MONTAIGNE, MICHEL D'EYQUEM DE

MONTAIGNE, MICHEL D'EYQUEM DE (1533-1592). While noblemen used to adorn their coats-of-arms with grandiloquent devices, Montaigne wrote under his own: "Que sais-je?" (What do I know?). His lifetime was a period of constant quarreling between theologians, philosophers and scientists, and a time of bloody religious wars. Montaigne fought for peace and tolerance, using, for that purpose, the weapons of irony and scepticism. Against fanaticism he appealed to clear thinking and considerate reason, and, due to his literary skill, he succeeded in inspiring confidence in the value of reason at least in small circles of men everywhere in Europe, though most of the rulers, politicians and theologians continued to incite the fanaticism of the masses.

Montaigne, born in the castle of Montaigne near Bordeaux, France, was the son of a father who probably was of Jewish descent, and a mother, whose family was certainly Jewish. Some of Montaigne's relatives were Marranos, baptized Jews who secretly continued to profess Judaism, and Montaigne knew that. He admired the tenacity with which the Jews held to their faith in the face of persecution, and doubted that any one of them became a true convert to another religion.

Montaigne tried to undermine the position of any orthodoxy and fanaticism by showing the common weaknesses of men in order to make them aware of the possibility that other people might be right and they themselves could be wrong. He declared that arrogance is the natural and characteristic disease of man who, in fact, is the most fragile of all creatures. But his manner of exhorting to humility had nothing in common with that of ecclesiastical sermons. Montaigne completely changed the tone of religious and philosophical discussions. He did not express indignation. He emphasized the personal character of his views and experiences, and did not exclude other people's opinions on the same items. He understood men of genius as well as plain people. He studied Athens' civilization and was interested in the life of American Indians. At those who think that the entire universe is established and moving only for the commodity and the service of human beings he smiled. But while rejecting anthropocentric teleology and opposing any belief in absolute knowledge, Montaigne far from denied the values of human life and character, of nature, beauty, the arts and sciences. The relativity of values was to him no proof that there are no values or duties at all. Kindness toward fellow men was presented as an almost absolute value by Montaigne.

For his confessions, Montaigne created a new literary form— namely, the essay. It was used by Bacon, Descartes, Locke, Rousseau, and Voltaire, among others, and has remained popular to the present day. One of Montaigne's most interested readers was William Shakespeare and he was followed by Molière, Laurence Sterne, Anatole France and a host of others.

HAPPINESS CAN ONLY BE JUDGED AFTER DEATH

Scilicet ultima semper
Expectanda dies homini est, dicique beatus
Ante obitum nemo, supremaque funera debet.

Till man's last day is come we should not dare
Of happiness to say what was his share;

Since of no man can it be truly said
That he is happy till he first be dead.

CHILDREN know the story of King Croesus to this effect, that, having been taken prisoner by Cyrus and condemned to die, as he was on the point of execution he cried out, "O Solon, Solon!" This being reported to Cyrus, and he inquiring what it meant, Croesus gave him to understand that he now found the warning Solon had once given to him true to his cost, which was, that men, however fortune may smile upon them, cannot be called happy till they have been seen to pass through the last day of their lives, because of the uncertainty and mutability of human things, which at a very slight impulse change from one state to another, wholly different. And it was therefore that Agesilaus, to one who was saying that the King of Persia was happy to come so young to so mighty a kingdom, made answer: "'Tis true, but neither was Priam unhappy at his years." Sometime kings of Macedon, successors to that mighty Alexander, become joiners and scriveners at Rome; the tyrants of Sicily become schoolmasters at Corinth. A conqueror of one-half of the world and ruler of so many armies is turned into a miserable suppliant to the rascally officers of a king of Egypt: so much did the prolongation of five or six months of life cost the great Pompey. And, in our fathers' days, Ludovico Sforza, the tenth Duke of Milan, under whom all Italy had so long trembled, was seen to die a prisoner at Loches, but not till he had lived in that state ten years, which was the worst part of his fortune. *The fairest of queens, widow of the greatest king in Christendom, has she not just died by the hand of an executioner?* And a thousand such examples. For it seems that as storms and tempests are provoked against the pride and loftiness of our buildings, there are also spirits above that are envious of the grandeurs here below,

Usque adeo res humanas vis abdita quædam
Obterit, et pulchros fasces sævasque secures

830

Proculcare, ac ludibrio sibi habere videtur.

So greatly does some hidden power contemn
Our human fortunes, and is often seen
To trample down and make a laughing-stock
Of all the symbols of imperial power.

And it would seem that Fortune sometimes lies in wait
for precisely the last day of our lives, to show her power
to overthrow in a moment what she was so many years in
building, making us cry out with Laberius, "Nimirum hac
die una plus vixi, mihi quam vivendum fuit." "Truly I have
this day lived one day longer than I should."

In this sense may the good advice of Solon reasonably
be taken. But, inasmuch as he is a philosopher (with whom
the favors and disgraces of Fortune rank neither as happiness nor unhappiness, and grandeurs and power are accidents of a quality almost indifferent), I think it probable
that he had some further aim, and that his meaning was, that
this same felicity of our life, which depends upon the tranquillity and contentment of a well-born spirit, and the resolution and assurance of a well-ordered mind, ought never
to be attributed to any man till he has been seen to play the
last, and doubtless the hardest, act of his comedy. There
may be disguise in all the rest: either these fine philosophical
arguments are only by way of appearance, or circumstances,
not testing us to the quick, give us leisure still to preserve
the composure of our features. But in this last scene between
death and ourselves, there is no more counterfeiting: we must
speak out plain, and display what there is that is good and
clean at the bottom of the pot.

Nam veræ voces tum demum pectore ab imo
Ejiciuntur, et eripitur persona, manet res.

Truth then is forced
From his inmost heart: the mask is torn aside,
The real man remains.

That is why all the other actions of our life ought to be tried and tested by this final act. It is the master-day, it is the day that is judge of all the rest; "it is the day," says one of the ancients, "that must be judge of all my past years." To death do I refer the proof of the fruit of all my studies; we shall then see whether my reasonings come only from my mouth or from my heart.

I have seen many by their death give a reputation for good or ill to their whole life. Scipio, the father-in-law of Pompey, by a worthy death wiped away the ill opinion that till then everyone had conceived of him. Epaminondas, being asked which of the three he had in greatest esteem, Chabrias, Iphicrates, or himself, replied: "You must first see us die, before the question can be decided." In truth, Epaminondas himself would be deprived of much of his lustre if we should weigh him without regard to the honor and grandeur of his end.

God has ordered things as it has pleased Him; but in my time three of the most execrable persons that ever I knew in all manner of abominable living, and the most infamous, have had a death that was decorous and perfectly attuned in every circumstance.

There are brave and fortunate deaths. I have seen death cut the thread of the progress of a marvellous advancement, and that in the flower of its growth; and with an ending so magnificent that, in my opinion, the man's ambitious and courageous designs had nothing in them so high as their interruption. He reached, without moving, the place he was aiming at, more grandly and gloriously than he could either have hoped or desired. By his fall he carried his power and name beyond the point to which he aspired in his career. In the judgment I make of another man's life, I always observe how its last scene is passed; and among the principal concerns of my own life is that its last scene shall be passed well, that is to say, calmly and insensibly.

[258]

MONTESQUIEU, CHARLES DE SECONDAT

MONTESQUIEU, CHARLES DE SECONDAT (1689-1755). The principle of separation of powers, or of checks and balances, which is characteristic of the Constitution of the United States was formulated in such a striking manner by Montesquieu that Jefferson, Hamilton, Adams and Madison and other founders of the United States were deeply impressed by it, and held it more or less clearly in their minds when they gave the Constitution its shape.

Montesquieu was a high judge in France but he was very critical of the regime which he served. In his youth he had been a member of the "First Floor Club" in Paris, a secret society strongly opposed to absolutism and clerical orthodoxy. He remained faithful to the club's principles but became rather moderate in his judgment on the advantages of other political systems. His *Persian Letters* (1721) a thinly veiled satirical criticism of French life, made a great sensation. His *Reflections on the Causes of the Greatness and the Decadence of the Romans* (1734) is considered one of the most important monuments of modern historical literature. The very spirit of Roman civilization is grasped and brilliantly illustrated by Montesquieu, however much scholars of later times may object to his treatment of details. Montesquieu's principal work *The Spirit of the Laws* (1748) was the result of fourteen years of strenuous study into political history and comparative legislation, of reading sources and observing life by traveling through many countries of Europe, and above all, of a stay in England where he arrived on Lord Chesterfield's yacht. Montesquieu admired England, though not uncritically. Its institutions, in his opinion, guaranteed and realized the highest possible degree of freedom, and he derived this view from the application of the principle of checks and balances. This view is not shared by modern constitutional historians or jurists, least of all concerning the England of Montesquieu's days. But his work has been of lasting value to the development of methods of analyzing political, social and legal conditions and their connection. Next to Locke, Montesquieu was the most influential champion of liberalism in the 18th century.

LAWS, in their most general signification, are the necessary relations arising from the nature of things. In this sense all beings have their laws: the Deity His laws, the material world its laws, the intelligences superior to man their laws, the beasts their laws, man his laws.

They who assert that a blind fatality produced the various effects we behold in this world talk very absurdly; for can anything be more unreasonable than to pretend that a blind fatality could be productive of intelligent beings?

There is, then, a prime reason; and laws are the relations subsisting between it and different beings, and the relations of these to one another.

God is related to the universe, as Creator and Preserver; the laws by which He created all things are those by which He preserves them. He acts according to these rules, because He knows them; He knows them, because He made them; and He made them, because they are in relation to His wisdom and power.

Since we observe that the world, though formed by the motion of matter, and void of understanding, subsists through so long a succession of ages, its motions must certainly be directed by invariable laws, and could we imagine another world, it must also have constant rules, or it would inevitably perish.

Thus the creation, which seems an arbitrary act, supposes laws as invariable as those of the fatality of the Atheists. It would be absurd to say that the Creator might govern the world without those rules, since without them it could not subsist.

These rules are a fixed and invariable relation. In bodies moved, the motion is received, increased, diminished, or lost, according to the relations of the quantity of matter and velocity; each diversity is *uniformity*, each change is *constancy*.

Particular intelligent beings may have laws of their

own making, but they have some likewise which they never made. Before there were intelligent beings, they were possible; they had therefore possible relations, and consequently possible laws. Before laws were made, there were relations of possible justice. To say that there is nothing just or unjust but what is commanded or forbidden by positive laws, is the same as saying that before the describing of a circle all the radii were not equal.

We must therefore acknowledge relations of justice antecedent to the positive law by which they are established: as, for instance, if human societies existed, it would be right to conform to their laws; if there were intelligent beings that had received a benefit of another being, they ought to show their gratitude; if one intelligent being had created another intelligent being, the latter ought to continue in its original state of dependence; if one intelligent being injures another, it deserves a retaliation; and so on.

But the intelligent world is far from being so well governed as the physical. For though the former has also its laws, which of their own nature are invariable, it does not conform to them so exactly as the physical world. This is because, on the one hand, particular intelligent beings are of a finite nature, and consequently liable to error; and on the other, their nature requires them to be free agents. Hence they do not steadily conform to their primitive laws; and even those of their own instituting they frequently infringe.

Whether brutes be governed by the general laws of motion, or by particular movement, we cannot determine. Be that as it may, they have not a more intimate relation to God than the rest of the material world; and sensation is of no other use to them than in the relation they have either to other particular beings or to themselves.

By the allurement of pleasure they preserve the individual, and by the same allurement they preserve their species. They have natural laws, because they are united by sensation; positive laws they have none, because they are not connected by knowledge. And yet they do not invariably conform to their natural laws; these are better observed by vegetables, that have neither understanding nor sense.

Brutes are deprived of the high advantages which we have; but they have some which we have not. They have not our hopes, but they are without our fears; they are subject like us to death, but without knowing it; even most of them are more attentive than we to self-preservation, and do not make so bad a use of their passions.

Man, as a physical being, is like other bodies governed by invariable laws. As an intelligent being, he incessantly transgresses the laws established by God, and changes those of his own instituting. He is left to his private direction, though a limited being, and subject, like all finite intelligences, to ignorance and error: even his imperfect knowledge he loses; and as a sensible creature, he is hurried away by a thousand impetuous passions. Such a being might every instant forget his Creator; God has therefore reminded him of his duty by the laws of religion. Such a being is liable every moment to forget himself; philosophy has provided against this by the laws of morality. Formed to live in society, he might forget his fellow-creatures; legislators have therefore by political and civil laws confined him to his duty.

*　　*　　*

Antecedent to the above-mentioned laws are those of nature, so called, because they derive their force entirely from our frame and existence. In order to have a perfect knowledge of these laws, we must consider man before the establishment of society: the laws received in such a state would be those of nature.

The law which, impressing on our minds the idea of a Creator, inclines us towards Him, is the first in importance, though not in order, of natural laws. Man in a state of nature would have the faculty of knowing, before he had acquired any knowledge. Plain it is that his first ideas would not be of a speculative nature; he would think of the preservation of his being, before he would investigate its origin. Such a man would feel nothing in himself at first but impotency and weakness; his fears and apprehensions would be excessive; as appears from instances (were there any necessity of proving it) of savages found in forests, trembling at the motion of a leaf, and flying from every shadow.

In this state every man, instead of being sensible of his equality, would fancy himself inferior. There would therefore be no danger of their attacking one another; peace would be the first law of nature.

The natural impulse or desire which Hobbes attributes to mankind of subduing one another is far from being well founded. The idea of empire and dominion is so complex, and depends on so many other notions, that it could never be the first which occurred to the human understanding.

Hobbes inquires, *For what reason go men armed, and have locks and keys to fasten their doors, if they be not naturally in a state of war?* But is it not obvious that he attributes to mankind before the establishment of society what can happen but in consequence of this establishment, which furnishes them with motives for hostile attacks and self-defense?

Next to a sense of his weakness man would soon find that of his wants. Hence another law of nature would prompt him to seek for nourishment.

Fear, I have observed, would induce men to shun one another; but the marks of this fear being reciprocal, would soon engage them to associate. Besides, this association would quickly follow from the very pleasure one animal feels at the approach of another of the same species. Again, the attraction arising from the difference of sexes would enhance this pleasure, and the natural inclination they have for each other would form a third law.

Besides the sense or instinct which man possesses in common with brutes, he has the advantage of acquired knowledge; and thence arises a second tie, which brutes have not. Mankind have therefore a new motive of uniting; and a fourth law of nature results from the desire of living in society.

As soon as man enters into a state of society he loses the sense of his weakness; equality ceases, and then commences the state of war.

Each particular society begins to feel its strength, whence arises a state of war between different nations. The individuals likewise of each society become sensible of their force; hence the principal advantages of this society they endeavor to convert to their own emolument, which constitutes a state of war between individuals.

These two different kinds of states give rise to human laws. Considered as inhabitants of so great a planet, which necessarily contains a variety of nations, they have laws relating to their mutual intercourse, which is what we call the *law of nations.* As members of a society that must be properly supported, they have laws relating to the governors and the governed, and this we distinguish by the name of *political law.* They have also another sort of laws, as they stand in relation to each other; by which is understood the *civil law.*

The law of nations is naturally founded on this principle, that different nations ought in time of peace to do one another all the good they can, and in time of war as little injury as possible, without prejudicing their real interests.

The object of war is victory; that of victory is conquest; and that of conquest preservation. From this and the preceding principle all those rules are derived which constitute the *law of nations.*

All countries have a law of nations, not excepting the Iroquois themselves, though they devour their prisoners: for they send and receive ambassadors, and understand the rights of war and peace. The mischief is that their law of nations is not founded on true principles.

Besides the law of nations relating to all societies, there is a polity or civil constitution for each particularly considered. No society can subsist without a form of government. *The united strength of individuals,* as Gravina well observes, *constitutes what we call the body politic.*

The general strength may be found in the hands of a

single person, or of many. Some think that nature having established paternal authority, the most natural government was that of a single person. But the example of paternal authority proves nothing. For if the power of a father relates to a single government, that of brothers after the death of a father, and that of cousin-germans after the decease of brothers, refer to a government of many. The political power necessarily comprehends the union of several families.

Better is it to say, that the government most conformable to nature is that which best agrees with the humor and disposition of the people in whose favor it is established.

The strength of individuals cannot be united without a conjunction of all their wills. *The conjunction of those wills,* as Gravina again very justly observes, *is what we call the civil state.*

Law in general is human reason, inasmuch as it governs all the inhabitants of the earth: the political and civil laws of each nation ought to be only the particular cases in which human reason is applied.

They should be adapted in such a manner to the people for whom they are framed that it should be a great chance if those of one nation suit another.

They should be in relation to the nature and principle of each government; whether they form it, as may be said of political laws; or whether they support it, as in the case of civil institutions.

They should be in relation to the climate of each country, to the quality of its soil, to its situation and extent, to the principal occupation of the natives, whether husbandmen, huntsmen, or shepherds: they should have relation to the degree of liberty which the constitution will bear; to the religion of the inhabitants, to their inclinations, riches, numbers, commerce, manners, and customs.

[259]

839

MOORE, GEORGE EDWARD

MOORE, GEORGE EDWARD (1873-   ). There has been a debate between G. E. Moore and Bertrand Russell which is quite different from the usual disputes recorded in the history of philosophy. Russell declared in the preface to *Principia Mathematica*, "On fundamental questions of philosophy my position in all of its chief features is derived from G. E. Moore." But Moore, on his part, protested that if there were a question concerning who had learned from whom, then Russell was the teacher and himself the disciple. Literally, Moore was right but in reality Russell was right. It was Moore who started the movement of British New Realism by publishing his essay *Refutation of Idealism in Mind* in 1903. He holds that knowing means apprehension of the objectively real because in the mental act the object becomes transparent. A sense datum, therefore, is not the subjective image of the mind of something corresponding to it in the outer world but it is the object itself which immediately enters into the mind which looks through it. This view has been, with more or less modification, accepted by a great number of British philosophers of recent time. It has led to a partial rehabilitation of common sense.

Moore has also, especially in his *Principia Ethica* (1903) made a considerable contribution to axiology. Moore principally fought what he called the "naturalistic fallacy." He demonstrated the failure of any attempt to derive value from existent things or to define value in terms of relations between existing things. But together with evolutionary naturalism and utilitarianism he also refutes all metaphysical foundations of value, accusing all of them of trying in vain to derive the "ought" from the "is." He is also opposed to any subjectivist theory of value. According to Moore, value is not subjective but depends on intrinsic properties which, however, cannot be defined. "Good is good, and that is the end of the matter," says Moore. Good is not identical with being willed. Right and wrong are not names of the characteristic of values. They are emotive, not cognitive expressions, meaning only approval or disapproval, and do not mean any metaphysical or natural property.

Moore's method is called "microscopic." It concentrates on isolating and questioning, and most of its results lead to new questions.

WHAT IS GOOD?

WHAT . . . is good? How is good to be defined? Now, it
may be thought that this is a verbal question. A definition
does indeed often mean the expressing of one word's meaning
in other words. But this is not the sort of definition I am
asking for. Such a definition can never be of ultimate importance in any study except lexicography. If I wanted that kind
of definition I should have to consider in the first place how
people generally used the word 'good'; but my business is
not with its proper usage, as established by custom. I
should, indeed, be foolish, if I tried to use it for something
which it did not usually denote: if, for instance, I were to
announce that, whenever I used the word 'good,' I must be
understood to be thinking of that object which is usually
denoted by the word 'table.' I shall, therefore, use the word
in the sense in which I think it is ordinarily used; but at
the same time I am not anxious to discuss whether I am right
in thinking that it is so used. My business is solely with that
object or idea, which I hold, rightly or wrongly, that the
word is generally used to stand for. What I want to discover is the nature of that object or idea, and about this I
am extremely anxious to arrive at an agreement.

But, if we understand the question in this sense, my
answer to it may seem a very disappointing one. If I am
asked 'What is good?' my answer is that good is good, and
that is the end of the matter. Or if I am asked 'How is good
to be defined?' my answer is that it cannot be defined, and
that is all I have to say about it. But disappointing as these
answers may appear, they are of the very last importance.
To readers who are familiar with philosophic terminology,
I can express their importance by saying that they amount
to this: That propositions about the good are all of them
synthetic and never analytic; and that is plainly no trivial
matter. And the same thing may be expressed more popularly, by saying that, if I am right, then nobody can foist

upon us such an axiom as that 'Pleasure is the only good' or that 'The good is the desired' on the pretence that this is 'the very meaning of the word.'

Let us, then, consider this position. My point is that 'good' is a simple notion, just as 'yellow' is a simple notion; that, just as you cannot, by any manner of means, explain to any one who does not already know it, what yellow is, so you cannot explain what good is. Definitions of the kind that I was asking for, definitions which describe the real nature of the object or notion denoted by a word, and which do not merely tell us what the word is used to mean, are only possible when the object or notion in question is something complex. You can give a definition of a horse, because a horse has many different properties and qualities, all of which you can enumerate. But when you have enumerated them all, when you have reduced a horse to his simplest terms then you can no longer define those terms. They are simply something which you think of or perceive, and to any one who cannot think of or perceive them, you can never, by any definition, make their nature known. It may perhaps be objected to this that we are able to describe to others, objects which they have never seen or thought of. We can, for instance, make a man understand what a chimaera is, although he has never heard of one or seen one. You can tell him that it is an animal with a lioness's head and body, with a goat's head growing from the middle of its back, and with a snake in place of a tail. But here the object which you are describing is a complex object; it is entirely composed of parts, with which we are all perfectly familiar—a snake, a goat, a lioness; and we know, too, the manner in which those parts are to be put together, because we know what is meant by the middle of a lioness's back, and where her tail is wont to grow. And so it is with all objects, not previously known, which we are able to define: they are all complex; all composed of parts, which may themselves, in the first instance, be capable of similar definition, but which must in the end be reducible to simplest parts, which can no longer be defined. But yellow and good, we say, are not complex: they are notions of that simple kind, out of which definitions are composed and with which the power of further defining ceases.

When we say, as Webster says, 'The definition of horse is "A hoofed quadruped of the genus Equus," ' we may, in fact, mean three different things. (1) We may mean merely: 'When I say "horse," you are to understand that I am talking about a hoofed quadruped of the genus Equus.' This might be called the arbitrary verbal definition: and I do not mean that good is indefinable in that sense. (2) We may mean, as Webster ought to mean: 'When most English people say "horse," they mean a hoofed quadruped of the genus Equus.' This may be called the verbal definition proper, and I do not say that good is indefinable in this sense either; for it is certainly possible to discover how people use a word: otherwise, we could never have known that 'good' may be translated by 'gut' in German and by 'bon' in French. But (3) we may, when we define horse, mean something much more important. We may mean that a certain object, which we all of us know, is composed in a certain manner: that it has four legs, a head, a heart, a liver, etc., etc., all of them arranged in definite relations to one another. It is in this sense that I deny good to be definable. I say that it is not composed of any parts, which we can substitute for it in our minds when we are thinking of it. We might think just as clearly and correctly about a horse, if we thought of all its parts and their arrangement instead of thinking of the whole: we could, I say, think how a horse differed from a donkey just as well, just as truly, in this way, as now we do, only not so easily; but there is nothing whatsoever which we could so substitute for good; and that is what I mean, when I say that good is indefinable.

But I am afraid I have still not removed the chief difficulty which may prevent acceptance of the proposition that good is indefinable. I do not mean to say that *the* good, that which is good, is thus indefinable; if I did think so, I should not be writing on Ethics, for my main object is to

843

help towards discovering that definition. It is just because I think there will be less risk of error in our search for a definition of 'the good,' that I am now insisting that *good* is indefinable. I must try to explain the difference between these two. I suppose it may be granted that 'good' is an adjective. Well 'the good,' 'that which is good,' must therefore be the substantive to which the adjective 'good' will apply: it must be the whole of that to which the adjective will apply, and the adjective must *always* truly apply to it. But if it is that to which the adjective will apply, it must be something different from that adjective itself; and the whole of that something different, whatever it is, will be our definition of *the* good. Now it may be that this something will have other adjectives, beside 'good,' that will apply to it. It may be full of pleasure, for example; it may be intelligent: and if these two adjectives are really part of its definition, then it will certainly be true, that pleasure and intelligence are good. And many people appear to think that, if we say 'Pleasure and intelligence are good,' or if we say 'Only pleasure and intelligence are good,' we are defining 'good.' Well, I cannot deny that propositions of this nature may sometimes be called definitions; I do not know well enough how the word is generally used to decide upon this point. I only wish it to be understood that that is not what I mean when I say there is no possible definition of good, and that I shall not mean this if I use the word again. I do most fully believe that some true proposition of the form 'Intelligence is good and intelligence alone is good' can be found; if none could be found, our definition of *the* good would be impossible. As it is, I believe *the* good to be definable; and yet I still say that good itself is indefinable.

'Good,' then, if we mean by it that quality which we assert to belong to a thing, when we say that the thing is good, is incapable of any definition, in the most important sense of that word. The most important sense of 'definition' is that in which a definition states what are the parts which invariably compose a certain whole; and in this sense 'good' has no definition because it is simple and has no parts. It is one of those innumerable objects of thought which are themselves incapable of definition, because they are the ultimate terms by reference to which whatever *is* capable of definition must be defined. That there must be an indefinite number of such terms is obvious, on reflection; since we cannot define anything except by an analysis, which, when carried as far as it will go, refers us to something, which is simply different from anything else, and which by that ultimate difference explains the peculiarity of the whole which we are defining: for every whole contains some parts which are common to other wholes also. There is, therefore, no intrinsic difficulty in the contention that 'good' denotes a simple and indefinable quality.

[260]

MORE, THOMAS

MORE, THOMAS (1478-1535). Although Thomas More did not live in accordance with the ideas developed in his *Utopia* (1516), he was a man of principles and became a martyr to his convictions.

In the book *Utopia*, after which numerous utopias have been named, More described an imaginary island where a perfectly wise and happy people had established the best imaginable commonwealth by means of ideal institutions, living in peace and abhorring war and oppression of any kind.

More, however, had to live in Tudor England, and, although his spiritual horizon was larger and his moral consciousness was scrupulous, he had to adapt his thoughts and actions to the customs of his contemporary fellow Englishmen and, above all, to the desires of the king. For a time he seemed to be a conformist but when he had to choose between his loyalty to the king and the demands of his conscience, he decided against the royal arbitrary power and faced execution with equanimity.

Having intended to become a priest, More spent four years, from 1499 to 1503, in religious contemplation. Then he suddenly abandoned the idea of ecclesiastical life. Nevertheless, he remained a pious Catholic, although devoted to the "new learning" of humanism. He was an intimate friend of John Colet and Erasmus and participated in their efforts to reform the Catholic Church, to purify religious life and to reconcile religious traditions with the new science of humanism. He wrote poetry, books about English history, a biography of Pico della Mirandola, and protected the painter Hans Holbein and other artists.

After being elected member of Parliament in 1504, he had a brilliant career, was knighted in 1521, and succeeded Cardinal Wolsey as Lord Chancellor of England in 1529. But he was opposed to King Henry VIII's *Act of Supremacy* and *Act of Succession* because the former meant the secession from the Roman Catholic Church, and the latter the nullification of the king's first marriage. The whole of Catholic Europe was startled when it learned that More was executed for his decision to disobey the King. As a prisoner in the Tower, More wrote his *Dialogue of Comfort Against Tribulation* and died as an upright and courageous man.

MILITARY PRACTICE IN UTOPIA

WHEN they draw out troops of their own people, they take such out of every city as freely offer themselves, for none are forced to go against their wills, since they think that if any man is pressed that wants courage, he will not only act faintly, but by his cowardice dishearten others. But if an invasion is made on their country they make use of such men, if they have good bodies, though they are not brave; and either put them aboard their ships or place them on the walls of their towns, that being so posted they may find no opportunity of flying away; and thus either shame, the heat of action, or the impossibility of flying, bears down their cowardice; they often make a virtue of necessity and behave themselves well, because nothing else is left them. But as they force no man to go into any foreign war against his will, so they do not hinder those women who are willing to go along with their husbands; on the contrary, they encourage and praise them, and they stand often next their husbands in the front of the army. They also place together those who are related, parents and children, kindred, and those that are mutually allied, near one another; that those whom nature has inspired with the greatest zeal for assisting one another, may be the nearest and readiest to do it; and it is matter of great reproach if husband or wife survive one another, or if a child survives his parents, and therefore when they come to be engaged in action they continue to fight to the last man, if their enemies stand before them.

And as they use all prudent methods to avoid the endangering of their own men, and if it is possible let all the action and danger fall upon the troops that they hire, so if it becomes necessary for themselves to engage, they then charge with as much courage as they avoided it before with prudence; nor is it a fierce charge at first, but it increases by degrees; and as they continue in action, they grow more obstinate and press harder upon the enemy, insomuch that they will much sooner die than give ground; for the certainty that their children will be well looked after when they are dead, frees them from all that anxiety concerning them which often masters men of great courage; and thus they are animated by a noble and invincible resolution. Their skill in military affairs increases their courage; and the wise sentiments which, according to the laws of their country, are instilled into them in their education, give additional vigor to their minds: for as they do not undervalue life so as prodigally to throw it away, they are not so indecently fond of it as to preserve it by base and unbecoming methods. In the greatest heat of action, the bravest of their youth, who have devoted themselves to that service, single out the general of their enemies, set on him either openly or by ambuscade, pursue him everywhere, and when spent and wearied out, are relieved by others, who never give over the pursuit; either attacking him with close weapons when they can get near him, or with those which wound at a distance, when others get in between them; so that unless he secures himself by flight, they seldom fail at last to kill or to take him prisoner.

[261]

MORGAN, C. LLOYD

MORGAN, C. LLOYD (1852-1936). As a boy, Morgan had an almost exclusively literary education. He was devoted to Byron,

Keats, Shelley, Moore and Scott. Then, while in college, the philosophy of Spinoza, Berkeley and Hume had a strong appeal for him. He had intended to become an engineer but, as a student, was drawn by T. H. Huxley to the interpretation of nature by biological studies. His principal interest remained fixed on the borderline of life and mind, and he became more and more convinced that a synthesis of philosophy and science was possible and necessary.

Such a synthesis was, in Morgan's opinion, "bound to take a risk." The risk he took was to acknowledge things, to accept realism. Things were defined by him as "clusters of events," quite in accordance with modern physics. With his principal books *Animal Life and Intelligence* (1891), *Habit and Instinct* (1896) and *Emergent Evolution* (1923), Morgan has inspired biologists, psychologists and philosophers both in England, his homeland, and America. His ideas have also been accepted by outstanding French thinkers. Morgan defined evolution as a constructive scheme which shall provide for a physical realism but also for "something of at least in the same genre as Platonic realism." Emergent evolution was conceived as selective synthesis at certain critical turning points in the course of evolutionary advance. Darwin's conception of evolution as a steady, gradual process was abandoned by Morgan. On a broader basis, he developed T. H. Huxley's and G. H. Lewes's criticism of Darwin's theory and that which is called the theory of mutation. In this way he inspired Henri Bergson and Samuel Alexander, among others, at least by offering them rich material of concrete facts.

MAN'S THREE-FOLD NATURE

IF all art is constructive the comprehensive aim of philosophy as an art is to express in a representative 'vision' the whole nature of reality which shall include the whole nature of man.

Of any man I should say: He is body as a center which is recipient of physical influence from a material world of which he is part, and influences some of the physical events therein. He is mind as a center of experience from which there is reference to the physical world and to other minds. He is also a center of active causality.

Here I start with the frankly hypothetical assumption that such is man's three-fold nature. But what I reach is a considered assurance that this probably (I dare not say more) represents his real nature.

To this tripartite nature there are, as I think, three distinguishable avenues of approach which I label B inquiry (physical), C inquiry (psychological), and A inquiry (metaphysical). Philosophy includes all three.

Since on these terms the physical universe is not the subject-matter of C inquiry, the empirical psychologist, as such, has nothing to tell us about it. He leaves that to his colleague the physicist. Still in broader philosophical regard he may (or perhaps may not) acknowledge its continuant existence. So too since Activity is not the subject-matter of his empirical inquiry he has nothing to tell us about it, though, in his philosophical capacity, he may (or may not) acknowledge its abiding subsistence.

On these terms a physical world on the one hand and, on the other hand, activity as final cause, lie outside his specialized province of inquiry. None the less it *does* fall within that province to deal with the process and products of human thought. Since, then, an outcome of that thought is a distinction of body, mind, and active causality, the genetic origin of this distinction in thought falls within the subject-matter of psychological inquiry.

However it came about in the natural course of mental development, this distinction has taken definite form in some minds. I, for one, have been led to accept its representative validity. I may then be asked: How have these three—body, mind, and active causality—so come together in man as to constitute this tripartite nature? To this question I reply that I have no assurance that they have done so. I started long ago with this widespread animistic assumption. I cannot now endorse it with later assurance. My considered belief goes no further than the tenet that they *are* inseparably together in the three-fold nature of man.

Similarly when I pass to the whole nature of the cosmos of which man is a part. If in philosophical regard there be a directive Source of all processes current in things and in minds, such a Source there abidingly *is*, not apart from them, but always one with them.

[262]

MO-TI

MO-TI (About 470-396 B.C.). After Mencius had been successful in discrediting the doctrine of Mo-Ti, it was ignored by Chinese thinkers and the public for twelve centuries. Only Chinese Buddhism retained some of Mo-Ti's tenets. Recently Mohism, as the school of Mo-Ti is called, has been adopted anew by many young Chinese, who regard it as a way to China's salvation from the troubles of the present time. Mo-Ti was a victorious general and an efficient civil servant.

His philosophy combines religious spirituality and utilitarian rationalism. He was also a refined logician and experienced in dialectic. After having adhered to Confucianism he accused Confucius' successors of exaggerated ritualism and rejected his former Master's belief in fate. He set purity of the heart higher than formal correctness in fulfilling ceremonial laws. He pronounced universal love without regard to legal status, and therefore was called "an apostle of human brotherhood." While justifying his doctrine, he declared that universal love was demanded by Heaven, the Supreme Being, as well as by the innermost strivings of the human individual for happiness, and that it would always pay to love his fellow men. His aim was promotion of general welfare by both moral elevation and economic improvement. Devoted to the cause of peace, Mo-Ti allowed defensive war only, and he is credited with having averted several wars.

ON STANDARD PATTERNS

OUR Master Mo said: Any one in the Great Society who takes any business in hand, cannot dispense with a standard pattern. For there to be no standard and the business to succeed, this just does not happen. Even the best experts who act as generals and councillors-of-state, all have standards (of action); and so also even with the best craftsmen. They use a carpenter's square for making squares and compasses for making circles: a piece of string for making straight lines and a plumb line for getting the perpendicular. It makes no difference whether a craftsman is skilled or not: all alike use these five (devices) as standards, only the skilled are accurate. But, although the unskilled fail to be accurate, they nevertheless get much better results if they follow these standards in the work which they do. Thus it is that craftsmen in their work have the measurements which these standards give.

Now take the great ones who rule our Great Society, and the less great ones who rule the different states, but who have no standards of measurement (for their actions). In this they are less critically minded than the craftsman. That being so, what standard may be taken as suitable for ruling? Will it do if everybody imitates his father and mother? The number of fathers and mothers in the Great Society is large, but the number of human-hearted ones is small. If everybody were to imitate his father and mother, this standard would not be a human-hearted one. For a standard, however, to be not human-hearted makes it impossible for it to be a standard. Will it do then if everybody imitates his teacher? The number of teachers is large, but the number of human-hearted ones is small. If everybody were to imitate his teacher . . . this standard would not be a human-hearted one. Will it do then if everybody imitates his sovereign? The number of princes is large, but the number of human-hearted ones is small. If everybody imitated his sovereign, this standard would not be a human-hearted one. Hence, fathers and mothers, teachers and sovereigns cannot be taken as standards for ruling.

That being so, what standard may be taken as suitable for ruling? The answer is that nothing is equal to imitating Heaven. Heaven's actions are all-inclusive and not private-minded, its blessings substantial and unceasing, its revelations abiding and incorruptible. Thus it was that the Sage-kings imitated it. Having taken Heaven as their standard, their every movement and every action was bound to be measured in relation to Heaven. What Heaven wanted, that they did: what Heaven did not want, that they stopped doing.

The question now is, what does Heaven want and what does it hate? Heaven wants men to love and be profitable to each other, and does not want men to hate and maltreat each other. How do we know that Heaven wants men to love and be profitable to each other? Because it embraces all in its love of them, embraces all in its benefits to them. How do we know that Heaven embraces all . . .? Because it embraces all in its possession of them and in its gifts of food.

Take then the Great Society. There are no large or small states: all are Heaven's townships. Take men. There are no young men or old, no patricians or plebeians: all are Heaven's subjects. This is so, for there is no one who does not fatten oxen and sheep and dogs and pigs and make pure wine and sacrificial cakes with which to do reverence and service to Heaven. Can this be anything else than Heaven owning all and giving food to all? Assuming then that Heaven embraces all and gives food to all, how could it be said that it does not want men to love and benefit each other?

Hence I say that Heaven is sure to give happiness to those who love and benefit other men, and is sure to bring calamities on those who hate and maltreat other men. I maintain that the man who murders an innocent person will meet with misfortune. What other explanation is there of the fact that when men murder each other, Heaven brings calamity on them? This is the way in which we know that Heaven wants men to love and benefit each other and does not want them to hate and maltreat each other.

[263]

MUNK, KAJ

MUNK, KAJ (1898-1944). Kaj Munk, pastor of a village in Denmark, had inherited a bent posture from his father who had been a tanner, but he was one of the most upright men who ever defied Nazi tyranny. His moral power was rooted in the orthodox Lutheran faith that accepted the possibility of miracles as the basis of prayer. Munk regarded it as "God's way of telling me that my difficulty in keeping a straight back in a physical sense would help me keep a straight back in a spiritual sense."

When the Germans occupied Denmark in 1940, Munk was unrelenting in preaching resistance against the invaders. Standing by as a passive spectator would have meant to him to "feel myself a traitor to my Christian faith, my Danish outlook and my ordination vow."

In his sermons, Munk compared the people of Denmark to the people of Israel, exiled in Babylon and longing to become free from bondage. These sermons, delivered in the church of a small village, spread over the whole Danish country. The Gestapo took the preacher from his home on January 4, 1944, shot him through the head, and threw his body into a ditch by the roadside where it was found the following day.

MOSES AND CHRIST

MOSES and Jesus are two figures of the most tragic types, the one more tragic than the other.

It is almost laughable to think of them.

And yet they are the only two whose names today shine as stars over mankind. By them the name of man is, all things to the contrary, a noble name. It happens to the beasts of the jungle that one night a song sounds through the jungle forest. Some of them lift their heads and listen. This is the distant morning song of the stars.

And there are beasts among us whose hearts tremble in longing, a longing so great that the sneer dies on our lips, the sneer at the content of the song of the stars.

We know this is impossible. But the song is so powerful that we do not believe that it is impossible anyway.

Because there are some, and there always have been and always will be some in the jungle world in whom the song of the stars, the song of fight and hope, lives, we may believe that it will happen.

The great "thou shalt not" will change us into human beings, and the powerful "thou shalt" will perfect the work of the law.

[264]

MÜNSTERBERG, HUGO

MÜNSTERBERG, HUGO (1863-1916). The current of Münsterberg's life, which had seemed to take a slow course along German university lines, was suddenly turned to new tasks, experiences and ideas by a letter written to him by William James on February 21, 1892. James, who had met Münsterberg at an international congress three years before, had been impressed by his psychological methods and philosophical views, and now invited him to direct the Psychological Laboratory of Harvard University, claiming that in the whole world no better man could be found for that post than Münsterberg. The latter accepted and, apart from the years 1895 to 1897 and 1910 to 1911, taught at Harvard until his death.

Throughout his life in America, Münsterberg scientific interests were intertwined with cultural and political interests. Fascinated by American life, he tried to interpret it to Germany, his native country, and to acquaint Americans with German cultural performances and scientific methods. His position became precarious after the outbreak of the First World War, when Münsterberg did not conceal his sympathy with Germany, without, however, approving all the measures taken by the German government.

Münsterberg's scientific creed was that psychology must fit into a system of causally connected elements. The function of psychology is to analyze life into elements parallel to the elements of matter that physics reconstructs; but he emphatically warned against confusing that existence, postulated by psychological analysis, with the immediate reality of life, such as becomes manifest in moral and practical activities, in the arts and religion. Causal psychology must be completed by purposive psychology, and the latter must be founded upon a theory of values.

Münsterberg also took great care in applying psychology to education, psychotherapy, the courtroom, vocational training and increase of industrial efficiency. He was the first psychologist to recognize the artistic importance and possibilities of the motion picture.

RELATIVE AND ABSOLUTE VALUES

IN the realm of nature, the bodily and the mental nature, we could not find any values because nature as such has no relation to will. Now we enter the realm of immediate life-experience. Here we are subjects of will. Here our decision is no longer the effect of foregoing causes, but comes in question with reference to our purposes and to our aims. Have we now a firm anchorage for the values of the world? Can we understand the value in its pure validity from the will of individuals? But this question evidently has no meaning so long as we simply identify value with that which is the goal of our will. In that case we could not desire anything which would not by this mere fact of our desire be raised to the dignity of a value. For certain human interests we are accustomed to such terms. The political economist, for instance, is in the habit of calling the things which are desired, values. If the philosopher follows in this path, he needs of course, every time, qualifying additions, if his inquiry into values is to have any meaning. If he studies the character of values he does not intend to discuss the value of butter and eggs. The philosopher in his sphere of thought might even hesitate to call food valuable at all, in spite of the fact that the hungry man longs for it, that the consumer enjoys it, and that the grocer in buying and selling measures it by the standard of other desired things. If the philosopher is ready to use the word "value" in such a colorless way, and to concede to the economist that everything is valuable which is object of desire, he has simply to divide the values at once into two large groups. He must make from the start a sharp demarcation line between relative values and absolute values. Whether in reality two such kinds of values exist has to be examined. It would be thinkable that only the relative values have existence, that is, that everything would be valuable only for this or that individual, in this or that position, under this or that condition. But even if the reality of absolute values is denied, this separation remains necessary. In the spirit of critical philosophy, value always means an absolute value. But if we use the word in its wider sense, our question is now clear. That there exist relative values in the world of immediate life is then a matter of course to us. As it is a world in which the personalities are subjects of will, everything which is object of their will must have such conditional value. Our real question remains. It is the question whether, in this sphere of individual desires, there exist also unconditional absolute values, values which are valuable in themselves without reference to this or that individual and his wishes. So long as we were speaking of nature, the separation into relative and absolute values was superfluous, as a world in which there is no will can have no values whatever.

If all values in the world are based on the fact that individuals as individuals desire and prefer for themselves certain things, evidently we have only the one class of values, the relative ones. Every one who wants to acknowledge only the absolute values as true values would have to claim in this case that the world has merely pseudo-values. Indeed, it is impossible ever to deduce an absolute value from the world of individual personal desires. There exists no bridge from the individual pleasure and displeasure to the absolute value. So long as we start from the selfish desire of individuals,—and there may be unlimited millions of them,—we shall always come only to social and economic values which have relative validity. A value which without reference to individual pleasures and displeasures belongs to the world of reality itself, and which thus stands above all individual desires, remains out of the question there. Nature did not know any unconditional values, because nature had no relation at all to will; but the world of personal desires has no unconditional values, because in it every relation to will lacks the general necessary unconditional character. Whoever is convinced that all values in the world can be, and ultimately must be, based on the desire for pleasure in individuals, is certainly more consistent if he denies every absolute value than if, as frequently happens, he bolsters up the conditional values into eternal ones.

[265]

856

$\mathcal{N}$

NATORP, PAUL

NATORP, PAUL (1854-1924). Until his late years, Natorp was a faithful follower of Hermann Cohen. It was due to the excitement of the war years, 1914-1918, that he deviated slightly from his master's tenets and became more inclined to exalt the German national character and civilization in his book *Deutscher Weltberuf* (*Germany's Vocation in the World*, 1918). Natorp's interpretation of Plato's doctrine of ideas was much discussed. So was his *General Psychology* (1912). More successful was his *Socialpaedagogik* (1899) which was re-edited several times. According to Natorp, education must influence all social and economic activities as well as schools and universities in order to realize national solidarity and social peace.

ON COGNITION

THE objects are inexhaustible; cognition however which, tending toward the object, believes to draw closer and closer to it and still never reaches it, is following its inherent fundamental law always one and the same. The objects seem to stand outside of us at a certain distance. With the progress of cognition we believe we diminish this distance between them and us. To our amazement we discover that they remain always equally distant from us, nay that they draw farther and farther away from us. Only cognition remains ours, for it is consciousness and consciousness is, if anything, our own.

One well known example suffices to clarify this relationship. For the thinking of antiquity and the Middle Ages the outer universe ended with the ninth or eleventh etc. of these celestial spheres which, inserted one into the other like onion skins, one thought eternally revolving in changeless circular motions around their center the earth. Copernicus destroyed this artistically constructed edifice. The earth had to cede its central position to the sun and had to remain satisfied with a modest place among the planets. The sphere of the fixed stars withdrew to hitherto unexpected distances. This system too was superseded. The sun as little as the earth forms the center of the universe. The immovable sphere to which the fixed stars were attached has become a myth. Their name only (fixed stars) keeps, like a fossil remnant, the memory of their former importance. In reality they are only slowly moving planets of a superior order. The formerly assumed distances and periods of revolution have been surpassed by myriads. The aided eye finds only in its own imperfection and the imperfection of its instruments not in the object its barrier. Infinity has room for worlds and worlds of worlds without end. We call that progress of knowledge and count them among the greatest ones humanity has to record. Unfortunately, what we were looking forward to, the closed unity of the universe, the unity of the cosmos, has not been brought nearer to us, it has only been pushed farther and farther away from us. More than ever are we remote from a system of the universe. The Ancients had a system, Copernicus and still Kepler had theirs. We have none. But cognition has won immensely. And what is most amazing, the principle of cognition has remained the same. It is the same law of cognition to which Eudoxus and Ptolemy, Copernicus and Kepler, Newton, Kant and Laplace obeyed. Only its application to more remote fields of given phenomena, to the more thoroughly understood problems, had to lead to other results.

[266]

858

NICHOLAS OF CUSA. See CUSA, NICHOLAS OF.

NICOLAI, FRIEDRICH

NICOLAI, FRIEDRICH (1733-1811). The world record in being vilified by the greatest number of his most illustrious contemporaries can hardly be disputed to be held by Nicolai, who was a bookseller, publisher, editor of reviews, novelist, and theological and philosophical writer. For about a decade (1755-1765), Nicolai's good reputation was not attacked. He was the friend of Gotthold Ephraim Lessing and Moses Mendelssohn, and was considered a man of sound ideas, a fighter for the Enlightenment that flourished in Germany during that period. But then, for more than forty-five years, Nicolai was the object of satires, polemical pamphlets, literary assaults and expressions of indignation and contempt. Among Nicolai's most violent enemies were Immanuel Kant and Fichte, Goethe and Schiller, the poets of the movement of Storm and Stress and the leaders of German romanticism.

After Lessing's and Mendelssohn's deaths, Nicolai, almost alone, answered the attacks directed against him, sometimes with humor, sometimes with serious arguments, always with equanimity, though not always adequately. It cannot be denied that he was inferior to Kant, and that most of his debates with Kant resulted in his defeat. It cannot be denied that his devotion to the ideas of the Enlightenment was stiffened by a sort of orthodoxy. Nicolai was a fanatic adversary of sentimentalism, superstition, of obscurantism of any kind. He was a champion of common sense, and therefore became suspicious of Kant's criticism and Fichte's idealism. The poetry of Goethe, especially his *Werther*, was accused by him of favoring exaggeration of sentiments, and romanticism was, to him, identical with a return to the Middle Ages in politics, thought and religion. In all these struggles, the German public acclaimed Nicolai's adversaries. He was not discouraged nor afraid of replying to the romanticist Friedrich Schlegel, who exalted Fichte's doctrine of science, concerning which he, Nicolai, thought the introduction of planting potatoes was of greater importance to humanity. Nicolai's novels contain some interesting descriptions. His *Sebaldus Nothanker* (1773) gives a clear picture of Berlin under Frederick II.

German historians and philosophers still continue to sneer at Nicolai who defended common sense and felt that the German spirit took a dangerous route.

ON JEWISH PHILOSOPHY

WHICH philosophical writings I read and what influence they had on me during the 32 years which I spent and philosophized with Moses Mendelssohn—for I always found time for studies and the development of my spirit, though not for writing—all that would lead me into unnecessary and prolix details. Two very different philosophers, whose acquaintance I had made through Moses Mendelssohn, have given to my philosophical thinking an even more varified turn. Shaftesbury taught us both a more human manner of philosophizing which, with all the profoundness of this philosopher, gives an insight into the real world and unites again what the dry abstraction, for its commodity, has isolated although in nature it is coherent. And then I heard Moses Mendelssohn's excellent ideas on the cabalistic philosophy of the Hebrews. He explained in a very comprehensive manner that the strange aspect of the sentences of these oriental philosophers and their obscurity stems from the poverty of the Hebrew language in expressions of philosophical concepts, combined with the images customary in the Orient, so typical for uncultivated languages. In addition he showed that, given freedom from both cloaks, they have a very consistent sense, and that if one interprets the allegorical images literally and weaves them into new flowery commentaries the crudest nonsense and eccentricity is born, under which the religion of the Jews is still sighing and by which many Christian mystagogues have become complete fools. And then my friend showed very clearly how Spinoza, as a Jew, by combining the cabalistic philosophy, which he had inherited from his youth, with the sentences of Cartesius had to come quite naturally to the point where he imagined God as the only and general substance of which the world is only a modification. Through these lucid ideas I clarified my knowledge of ecclesiastical history commencing with Jewish and Christian gnostics, who played such an important

part in the formation of Christianity and whose opinions,
which originated in the cabalistic philosophy, modified the
Christian theology until the Middle Ages, as the study of the
Manicheans and Albigenses shows.

[267]

NIETZSCHE, FRIEDRICH

NIETZSCHE, FRIEDRICH (1844-1900). The fact that Nietzsche
was insane for the last twelve years of his life has often been
exploited by unfair adversaries who embarrassed serious critics
of his doctrines.

Before Nietzsche took his Ph.D. degree, he had already been
appointed a full professor of classical philology at the University
of Basel in 1869. But scholarship, which promised him a brilliant
career, did not satisfy him. The aim of his life was a philosophy
that would comprise both cool analysis and enthusiastic vision, a
synthesis of a new religious creed and merciless criticism. Apollo,
the god of lucid wisdom, and Dionysos, the god of orgiastic mysticism, were taken for its symbols.

Nietzsche is acknowledged, even by most of his opponents, as
a great psychologist who, particularly by using the concept of
"resentment," succeeded in unmasking hypocrisy, in exposing delusions, perversion of feeling and judgment or intellectual timidity,
and opened new ways by his much-disputed inquiry into the formation of morality.

But the view of the philosopher, as Nietzsche conceived it, is
not confined to things past and present. His task is not so much to
take care of the well-being of his contemporary fellow men as
rather to pave the way for the future development which will
change man into a higher type, the superman. For the sake of the
future, Nietzsche violently fought against Christianity, whose ethics
were depreciated by him as "slave morality," and he pronounced
the necessity of a general "trans-valuation of values." Nietzsche's
ideal of human personality meant the union of physical strength
and mental energy. It combined the virtues of the warrior and the
independent thinker. It was founded upon his conviction that the
"will to power" is the ruling principle of all life, and that life
on earth has an absolute value. Nietzsche's ethics, however, does not
preach self-indulgence or regard suffering as an evil. It demands
fearlessness, not love of pleasure. It prefers the dangerous life to
the comfortable one.

861

While endeavoring to grasp the essential features of cosmic life or to predict a far future, Nietzsche constantly kept his eye upon the cultural situation of his own time, foreboding a terrible catastrophe. Nihilism and decadence seemed to him the greatest dangers that threaten European civilization. He was equally opposed to democracy, socialism and nationalism, and most of all, to the national aspirations and pride of the Germans. He proclaimed the ideal of a "good European."

No philosopher has raged as vehemently against his own soul as Nietzsche did by glorifying physical strength and the will to power. In reality, he was gentle, always in poor health, hating noise and trying to avoid quarrels.

ZARATHUSTRA

WHEN Zarathustra arrived at the nearest town which adjoineth the forest, he found many people assembled in the market-place; for it had been announced that a rope-dancer would give a performance. And Zarathustra spake thus unto the people:

I teach you the Superman. Man is something that is to be surpassed. What have ye done to surpass man?

All beings hitherto have created something beyond themselves: and ye want to be the ebb of that great tide, and would rather go back to the beast than surpass man?

What is the ape to man? A laughing-stock, a thing of shame. And just the same shall man be to the Superman: a laughing-stock, a thing of shame.

Ye have made your way from the worm to man, and much within you is still worm. Once were ye apes, and even yet man is more of an ape than any of the apes.

Even the wisest among you is only a disharmony and hybrid of plant and phantom. But do I bid you become phantoms or plants?

Lo, I teach you the Superman!

The Superman is the meaning of the earth. Let your will say: The Superman *shall be* the meaning of the earth!

I conjure you, my brethren, *remain true to the earth,*

and believe not those who speak unto you of superearthly hopes! Poisoners are they, whether they know it or not.

Despisers of life are they, decaying ones and poisoned ones themselves, of whom the earth is weary: so away with them!

Once blasphemy against God was the greatest blasphemy; but God died, and therewith also those blasphemers. To blaspheme the earth is now the dreadfulest sin, and to rate the heart of the unknowable higher than the meaning of the earth!

Once the soul looked contemptuously on the body, and then that contempt was the supreme thing:—the soul wished the body meagre, ghastly, and famished. Thus it thought to escape from the body and the earth.

Oh, that soul was itself meagre, ghastly, and famished; and cruelty was the delight of that soul!

But ye, also, my brethren tell me: What doth your body say about your soul? Is your soul not poverty and pollution and wretched self-complacency?

Verily, a polluted stream is man. One must be a sea, to receive a polluted stream without becoming impure.

Lo, I teach you the Superman: he is that sea; in him can your great contempt be submerged.

What is the greatest thing ye can experience? It is the hour of great contempt. The hour in which even your happiness becometh loathsome unto you, and so also your reason and virtue.

The hour when ye say: "What good is my happiness! It is poverty and pollution and wretched self-complacency. But my happiness should justify existence itself!"

The hour when ye say: "What good is my reason! Doth it long for knowledge as the lion for his food? It is poverty and pollution and wretched self-complacency!"

The hour when ye say: "What good is my virtue! As yet it hath not made me passionate. How weary I am of my good and my bad! It is all poverty and pollution and wretched self-complacency!"

The hour when ye say: "What good is my justice! I do not see that I am fervour and fuel. The just, however, are fervour and fuel!"

The hour when we say: "What good is my pity! Is not pity the cross on which he is nailed who loveth man? But my pity is not a crucifixion."

Have ye ever spoken thus? Have ye ever cried thus? Ah! would that I have heard you crying thus!

It is not your sin—it is your self-satisfaction that crieth unto heaven; your very sparingness in sin crieth unto heaven!

Where is the lightning to lick you with its tongue? Where is the frenzy with which ye should be inoculated?

Lo, I teach you the Superman: he is that lightning, he is that frenzy!—

When Zarathustra had thus spoken, one of the people called out: "We have now heard enough of the rope-dancer; it is time now for us to see him!" And all the people laughed at Zarathustra. But the rope-dancer, who thought the words applied to him, began his performance.

*   *   *

Zarathustra, however, looked at the people and wondered. Then he spake thus:

Man is a rope stretched between the animal and the Superman—a rope over an abyss.

A dangerous crossing, a dangerous wayfaring, a dangerous looking-back, a dangerous trembling and halting.

What is great in man is that he is a bridge and not a goal: what is lovable in man is that he is an *over-going* and a *down-going*.

I love those that know not how to live except as downgoers, for they are the over-goers.

I love the great despisers, because they are the great adorers, and arrows of longing for the other shore.

I love those who do not first seek a reason beyond the stars for going down and being sacrifices, but sacrifice themselves to the earth, that the earth of the Superman may hereafter arrive.

I love him who liveth in order to know, and seeketh to know in order that the Superman may hereafter live. Thus seeketh he his own down-going.

I love him who laboreth and inventeth, that he may build the house for the Superman, and prepare for him earth, animal, and plant: for thus seeketh he his own down-going.

I love him who loveth his virtue: for virtue is the will to down-going, and an arrow of longing.

I love him who reserveth no share of spirit for himself, but wanteth to be wholly the spirit of his virtue: thus walketh he as spirit over the bridge.

I love him who maketh his virtue his inclination and destiny: thus, for the sake of his virtue, he is willing to live on, or live no more.

I love him who desireth not too many virtues. One virtue is more of a virtue than two, because it is more of a knot for one's destiny to cling to.

I love him whose soul is lavish, who wanteth no thanks and doth not give back: for he always bestoweth, and desireth not to keep for himself.

I love him who is ashamed when the dice fall in his favor, and who then asketh: "Am I a dishonest player?" —for he is willing to succumb.

I love him who scattereth golden words in advance of his deeds, and always doeth more than he promiseth: for he seeketh his own down-going.

I love him who justifieth the future ones, and redeemeth the past ones: for he is willing to succumb through the present ones.

I love him who chasteneth his God, because he loveth his God: for he must succumb through the wrath of his God.

I love him whose soul is deep even in the wounding, and may succumb through a small matter: thus goeth he willingly over the bridge.

I love him whose soul is so overfull that he forgetteth himself, and all things are in him: thus all things become his down-going.

I love him who is of a free spirit and a free heart:
thus is his head only the bowels of his heart; his heart, however, causeth his down-going.

I love all who are like heavy drops falling one by
one out of the dark cloud that lowereth over man: they
herald the coming of the lightning, and succumb as heralds.

Lo, I am a herald of the lightning, and a heavy drop
out of the cloud: the lightning, however, is the *Superman*.
[268]

NOÜY, PIERRE LECOMTE DU

NOÜY, PIERRE LECOMTE DU (1883-1947). A descendant of the
great French dramatist Pierre Corneille, and of many generations
of important artists, the son of an authoress of numerous novels,
one of which *Amitié Amoureuse* ran into six hundred editions in
France and was translated into sixteen languages, Pierre du Noüy
has been the first member of that family to turn to science. It was
in 1915, when he, then an officer in the French Army, met Dr.
Alexis Carrell, that he became interested in problems of science and
philosophy. Shortly thereafter du Noüy won international fame by
his pioneering efforts in applying mathematics to biology. Apart
from his sensational method of expressing mathematically the process
of healing of wounds by representing the process of cicatrization
through an equation, he introduced the concept of "physiological
age" as different from that measured by the calendar, and of "biological time" different from physical time, which led him to the
conclusion that time has different values for children and for
adults.

In *Human Destiny* (1947) du Noüy emphasizes that we must
have confidence in science but that we must be aware that we know
less about the material world than is usually believed. What we
know is subjective and conditioned by the structure of our brain.
He admits that the laws established by science express an order
of sequence and quantitative variations. But, he continues, that is
true only when life is inert. Du Noüy's principal tenet is that the
concept of evolution cannot be thought of without that of finality,
that finality dominates evolution. His doctrine of "telefinalism"
declares that the laws of inorganic evolution contradict those of the
evolution of life, and that the destiny of mankind is incomparable
to that of any other existent. In the evolution of mankind he finds
a striking parallel between biological, psychic and moral evolution,

but biological evolution is progressing far more slowly than the other two.

On this ground, Du Noüy confirms Christian religion and ethics, saying that man has to choose whether he will be a "co-worker with God" or a "dreg of evolution." Man has to use reason but he must also listen to heart. He must learn to think universally and to develop collective conscience for the sake of universal peace and solidarity.

ON EVOLUTION

IF we accept the idea of evolution, we must recognize the fact that, *on an average,* since the beginning of the world it has followed an ascending path, always oriented in the same direction. The objection has been made that many transformations of animals did not constitute a progress; the exaggerated development of the antlers of certain Cervidae, for instance. This is true, and that is the reason why we suggest the hypothesis of a finality comparable to gravitation in the above analogy, that is to say, a "telefinality" directing evolution as a whole. There is no doubt that there have been trials of all sorts, sometimes successful and sometimes unsuccessful. If we imagine a goal to be attained, acting like gravitation, once the start was given, all possible combinations had to be tried and their interest or their value proved by their reaction to the environment. If the new forms were badly adapted, incapable of serving as a starting point for a new stage of evolution, if they were surpassed by other strains, they disappeared progressively, or vegetated, cut off from the principal effort. The fate of the species itself thus becomes a secondary issue. What matters is the fate of the species *considered as a link in evolution as a whole.* Prodigies of adaptation were hardly more important than extraordinary performances in the circus. Adaptation and natural selection are no longer identified with evolution. The latter is differentiated from the former by its distant goal, which dominates all the species.

In this hypothesis, and in opposition to what Darwin thought, the survival of the fittest can no longer be considered as the *origin* of the evolving strain, and the fittest of a certain line can eventually give birth to a species destined to disappear or vegetate if the external conditions (climate, etc.), are modified or if other individuals, more apt from the final teleologic point of view, displace them.

Let us make this point quite clear: the properties or qualities of living organisms are *not* attributed to special principles as was done by the old vitalist doctrines, but it is simply assumed that a goal must be attained, by means of the most varied methods, *in conformity with the physico-chemical laws and the ordinary biological laws.* Nature often has recourse to chance, to probabilities, in living beings. Fish lay hundreds of thousands of eggs, as if they knew that, owing to the conditions under which these eggs will hatch, ninety per cent of them are destined to be destroyed.

We can no more consider evolutive transformations separately than we can consider physiological functions separately, if we aim to understand the evolution of living beings or the psychology of man.

In brief, evolution should be considered as a global phenomenon, irreversibly progressive, resulting from the combined activity of elementary mechanisms such as adaptation (Lamarck), natural selection (Darwin), and sudden mutations (Naudin—de Vries). Evolution begins with amorphous living matter or beings such as the Coenocytes, still without cell structure, and ends in thinking Man, endowed with a conscience. It is concerned *only* with the principal line thus defined. It represents *only* those living beings which constitute this unique line zigzagging intelligently through the colossal number of living forms.

Evolution, we repeat, is comprehensible only if we admit that it is dominated by a finality, a precise and distant goal. If we do not accept the reality of this orienting pole, not only are we forced to recognize that evolution is rigorously incompatible with our laws of matter, as we demonstrated above, but—and this is serious—that the appearance of moral and spiritual ideas remains an absolute mystery. Mystery for mystery, it seems wiser, more logical and more intelligent to choose the one which explains, thus satisfying our need to comprehend; the one which opens the doors to hope, rather than the one which closes those doors and explains nothing.

Adaptation, natural selection, mutations are, on the contrary, mechanisms which have contributed to the slow edification of evolution *without being themselves always progressive.* Strictly speaking these mechanisms are not determining factors in general evolution, any more than the mason is a determining factor in the cathedral on which he works. The mason represents, in himself, a very complex element obeying physico-chemical, biological, human, social laws. His sole contact with the cathedral is his trowel, and from the point of view of the architect, he is only a trowel. His private life, his intimate tragedies, his illnesses are immaterial. For the bishop, who willed the cathedral, the architect himself is but a means. The same is true of the processes lumped together under the generic name of "Mechanisms of Evolution." Each one contributes materially, statistically, to evolution, but the laws which they obey are not really identical with those of evolution which dominate and correlate them. In a similar way, the laws which govern the movements of particles in an atom are special and differ from those which govern the chemical properties of the atoms themselves. The latter are, as far as our actual science is concerned, without qualitative or quantitative relation to our psychological activity. To extrapolate and predict that such a relation will be discovered some day is not substantiated by facts, and entirely hypothetical.

Indeed, man must beware more of scientific extrapolations than of moral ones, because his scientific experience has been much shorter than his psychological experience. New facts are frequently found in science which compel him to revise completely his former concepts. The history of science is made up of such revolutions: the atomic theory, the kinetic theory, the granular theories of electricity, energy, and light, radioactivity, relativity have successively transformed our point of view from top to bottom. The future of science is always at the mercy of new discoveries and new theories. The science of matter is not two hundred years old, while the science of man is over five thousand years old. Empirical psychology was highly advanced at the time of the third Egyptian dynasty, and great philosophers twenty-six hundred years ago displayed a knowledge of man which has not been surpassed, but only confirmed today. Therefore, it can be reasonably assumed that moral extrapolations are much safer than scientific ones, even though they cannot be expressed mathematically.

[269]

O

OCKHAM, WILLIAM OF

OCKHAM, WILLIAM OF (1280-1348). No other Christian thinker of the Middle Ages rejected so many or such important assumptions which were prevalent in his times as did Ockham. His great aim was to teach men to think, and the result of his teachings was the elaboration of laic consciousness in the State, the reduction of the influence of the Church in human society, and the preparation for a new interpretation of the physical world. Although these results were counteracted by men and circumstances, Ockham must be considered as one of the principal agents of the dissolution of the Medieval synthesis of philosophy and theology. In the struggle between Pope John XXII and Emperor Louis of Bavaria, Ockham, collaborating with Marsilius of Padua, defended the rights of secular government against papal claims and contributed to the establishment of the modern political theory of the independence of the state from the church.

In his philosophical works, Ockham proclaimed the primacy of logical method in all disciplines. He rejected all attempts to evade reason but he restricted the range of reason. His epistemology destroyed any relation between knowledge of the universe and knowledge of God. He especially pronounced animosity against all those who claimed to know the psychology of God. He even maintained that monotheism can be derived only from the prime being and not from the prime efficient cause. He rejected Thomist ontology and Augustine's belief in eternal ideas which constitute the archetypes of the universe in the depth of divine essence, and he flatly denied the usefulness and truth of the speculations of all the great Doctors of the Church. He also held ethics to be independent of metaphysics.

In the struggle about universals, Ockham sided with those who held that universality can be attributed only to terms and propositions, not to things. But his interests did not center on this problem. To him, intuition of the singular is the basis of all concepts which

871

are signs of the real. Science has to verify the signs. All existing things depend on God's absolutely free will. All secondary causality is indemonstrable. It is only a fact which science has to interpret. While the will of God is absolutely free, Man has the freedom of alternative choice. Will is an essential attribute of any reasoning creature.

Ockham's diction is very precise but lacks charm. He influenced Wyclif and Erasmus. Luther borrowed some sentences from him, but would have repudiated his principal doctrines had he known them.

THE INDIVIDUAL AND THE UNIVERSAL

THE universals and second intentions are caused naturally by the knowledge of simple terms without any activity of the intellect and the will. They come about in this manner: first, I apprehend in particular some singular objects intuitively or abstractly. This is caused by the object or by a predisposition from a former act. This act consummated, presently, if there is no obstacle, another act follows naturally, distinct from the first and terminating in something of the same kind of logical reality as was seen before in the psychological reality. This second act produces the universals and second intentions. Something not there before is left behind in the imaginative faculty mediated by the intuitive cognition of particular sensation; yet this is not the object of the act, but some kind of a predisposition inclined to imagine the previously sensed object. I am certain that I perceive a stone in virtue of the sight of the stone and in virtue of primary vision. I am certain that I understand by experience because I see the image of the stone. The certainty of understanding the stone, however, comes by reasoning from effect to cause. I know fire by smoke when I see smoke alone, because I have on other occasions seen smoke caused by the presence of fire. In the same manner, I know the stone because on other occasions I have perceived intellectually the production of such an image in me.

Every universal is one singular thing and is universal only by the signification of many things. The universal is one and a single intention of the soul meant to be predicated of many things; in so far, however, as it is a single form subsisting really in the intellect, it is called singular.

The universal is twofold: natural and conventional. The first is a natural sign predicable of many things, as smoke naturally signifies fire, and a groan the pain of the sick man, and laughter a certain interior joy. Such a universal is nothing else than such an intention of the soul that no substance outside of the soul, nor any accident outside of the soul, is a counterpart of it. The conventional universal is one by voluntary institution. Such is the spoken word, which is an actual quality, numerically one, and universal because of its being a voluntarily instituted sign for the signification of many things. Therefore as the word is called common, the same also may be called universal, adding that this is not by the nature of the thing but only by the agreement of users. Of a universal that is such by discretion, I do not speak, but I do speak of that one which has whatever is universal in it by its very nature.

I am inquiring, now, whether this universal and univocally common entity is something real from the part of the thing which is outside of the soul. All of whom I meet agree by saying that the entity which is somehow universal is really in the individual, although some say that it is distinguished really, others that it is distinguished only formally, and some that it is not distinguished at all according to the nature of the thing, but only according to reason or by the consideration of the intellect. All these opinions coincide in that the universals are allowed to exist somehow from the side of the thing, so that their universality is held to be really present in the singular objects themselves.

This latter opinion is simply false and absurd. Against it this is my case. There is no unitary, unvaried or simple thing in a multiplicity of singular things nor in any kind of created individuals, together and at the same time. If such a thing were allowed, it would be numerically one; therefore, it would not be in many singular objects nor would ıt be of their essence. But the singular and the universal thing are by themselves two things, really distinct and equally simple; therefore, if the singular thing is numerically one, the universal thing will be numerically one also, and one does not include a greater plurality intrinsic to things than does the other.

[270]

ORIGEN

ORIGEN (185-253). While Clement of Alexandria is considered the father of Christian apologetics, his pupil Origen has been called the creator of Christian theology. But Origen was not only Clement's disciple; he was also taught by the pagan philosopher Ammonius Saccas, Plotinus' teacher. Origen tried to integrate the Christian faith into a comprehensive explanation of the universe, such as was adopted by Platonism and Stoicism, but he also leaned toward Neo-Platonism which was nascent during his lifetime. He was one of the greatest scholars who ever lived, whose *Hexapla,* the juxtaposition of versions of the Bible in six columns, was of great consequence to the criticism and exegesis of the Bible. He wrote a defense of Christianity *Against Celsus* which, however, was condemned by later orthodox Catholics as containing inadmissible concessions to paganism, and *On Principles,* a treatise on systematic theology which has been preserved in a Latin translation by Rufinus. In the fourth century, the number of Origen's works was estimated at about six thousand.

Origen lived a life of complete asceticism, having castrated himself. While orthodox Catholics continued to suspect him of heresy, the condemnation of his views by the Bishop of Alexandria was more than once confirmed. Protestant theologians and secular historians have always been sympathetically attracted to him whose soul lived in harmony with the course of nature and in confidence in the divine Logos, firm in his unselfish love of God and of his fellow men, longing for the return to the heavenly world of spirit which he conceived, in accordance with Plato, as behind and superior to the temporal world.

Many problems stemming from the doctrine of emanation or the eschatology of the Orphics and various Gnostics have been introduced into Christian thinking by Origen. Some of them became the cause of schism and heresy, while others contributed to the definite formation of the dogma of the Trinity.

874

THE FIRE OF HELL

THE FIRE OF HELL

WE find in the prophet Isaiah, that the fire with which each one is punished is described as his own; for he says, "Walk in the light of your own fire, and in the flame which ye have kindled." By these words it seems to be indicated that every sinner kindles for himself the flame of his own fire, and is not plunged into some fire which has been already kindled by another, or was in existence before himself. Of this fire the fuel and food are our sins, which are called by the Apostle Paul wood, and hay, and stubble. And I think that, as abundance of food, and provisions of a contrary kind and amount, breed fevers in the body, and fevers, too, of different sorts and duration according to the proportion in which the collected poison supplies material and fuel for disease (the quality of this material, gathered together from different poisons, proving the causes either of a more acute or more lingering disease); so, when the soul has gathered together a multitude of evil works, and an abundance of sins against itself, at a suitable time all that assembly of evils boils up to punishment, and is set on fire to chastisements; when the mind itself, or conscience, receiving by divine power into the memory all those things of which it had stamped on itself certain signs and forms at the moment of sinning, will see a kind of history, as it were, of all the foul, and shameful, and unholy deeds which it has done, exposed before its eyes: then is the conscience itself harassed, and, pierced by its own goads, becomes an accuser and a witness against itself. And this, I think, was the opinion of the Apostle Paul himself, when he said, "Their thoughts mutually accusing or excusing them in the day when God will judge the secrets of men by Jesus Christ, according to my Gospel." From which it is understood that around the substance of the soul certain tortures are produced by the hurtful affections of sins themselves.

And that the understanding of this matter may not appear very difficult, we may draw some considerations from the evil effects of those passions which are wont to befall some souls, as when a soul is consumed by the fire of love, or wasted away by zeal or envy, or when the passion of anger is kindled, or one is consumed by the greatness of his madness or his sorrow; on which occasions some, finding the excess of these evils unbearable, have deemed it more tolerable to submit to death than to endure perpetually torture of such a kind. You will ask indeed whether, in the case of those who have been entangled in the evils arising from those vices above enumerated, and who, while existing in this life, have been unable to procure any amelioration for themselves, and have in this condition departed from the world, it be sufficient in the way of punishment that they be tortured by the remaining in them of these hurtful affections, i.e., of the anger, or of the fury, or of the madness, or of the sorrow, whose fatal poison was in this life lessened by no healing medicine; or whether, these affections being changed, they will be subjected to the pains of a general punishment. Now I am of opinion that another species of punishment may be understood to exist; because, as we feel that when the limbs of the body are loosened and torn away from their mutual supports, there is produced pain of a most excruciating kind, so, when the soul shall be found to be beyond the order, and connection, and harmony in which it was created by God for the purposes of good and useful action and observation, and not to harmonize with itself in the connection of its rational movements, it must be deemed to bear the chastisement and torture of its own dissension, and to feel the punishments of its own disordered condition. And when this dissolution and rendering asunder of soul shall have been tested by the application of fire, a solidification undoubtedly into a firmer structure will take place, and a restoration be effected.

[271]

ORTEGA Y GASSET, JOSÉ

ORTEGA Y GASSET, JOSÉ (1883-). Although Ortega y Gasset disagrees with almost every important Spaniard of his time, he is generally acknowledged as the representative thinker of modern Spain. No wonder that he became an exile. He is strongly opposed to Franco's dictatorship; however, he had little sympathy with the government of the Spanish republic and its supporters. As the editor of the *Revista del Occidente,* he acquainted the Spanish public with the spiritual life of the Anglo-Saxon countries, of France and Germany, and he gave readers in foreign countries a striking presentation of the main features of Spanish thought and Spanish cultural tradition. But, above all, he has proved to be an original thinker who, rooted in Spanish civilization, universally cultivated, has developed personal ideas of great consequence.

Ortega y Gasset was educated by the Jesuits and studied at the Central University of Madrid, where he became a professor of metaphysics in 1910. Earlier, he had been a disciple of Hermann Cohen, but he became more interested in the philosophy of Husserl and Dilthey. The final result of his preoccupation with German thought was an opposition to idealism. He adopted Dilthey's concept of historical reason, but tried to avoid his shortcomings and went far beyond Dilthey's views.

He insists that human thinking is much less logical than it is generally supposed to be, that man is born at a definite date, formed by a definite tradition, and that his environment is equally determined by historical factors. Therefore, he concludes, whoever aspires to understand man, must throw overboard all immobile concepts and learn to think in ever-shifting terms. Because human life is radical reality that includes any other reality, history, and not physics, is the highest science.

Concerning the idealistic philosophy that starts from a concept of reality in which the subject, the ego, exists enclosed within itself, within its mental acts and states, he objects that such an existence is the opposite of living, whose meaning is to reach out of oneself, to be devoted to what is called the world. Consciousness is historical but the importance of history is not exhausted with the past. Historical knowledge is valued as a preparation for the future, and this conception involves a new appraisal of thinking. For, to Ortega, action without thought means chaos.

BOTH Bolshevism and Fascism are two false dawns; they do not bring the morning of a new day, but of some archaic day, spent over and over again: they are mere primitivism. And such will all movements be which fall into the stupidity of starting a boxing-match with some portion or other of the past, instead of proceeding to digest it. No doubt an advance must be made on the liberalism of the XIX century. But this is precisely what cannot be done by any movement such as Fascism, which declares itself anti-liberal. Because it was that fact—the being anti-liberal or non-liberal—which constituted man previous to liberalism. And as the latter triumphed over its opposite, it will either repeat its victory time and again, or else everything—liberalism and anti-liberalism—will be annihilated in the destruction of Europe. There is an inexorable chronology of life. In it liberalism is posterior to anti-liberalism, or what comes to the same, is more vital than it, just as the gun is more of a weapon than the lance.

At first sight, an attitude "anti-anything" seems posterior to this thing, inasmuch as it signifies a reaction against it and supposes its previous existence. But the innovation which the *anti* represents fades away into an empty negative attitude, leaving as its only positive content an "antique." When his attitude is translated into positive language, the man who declares himself anti-Peter does nothing more than declare himself the upholder of a world where Peter is non-existent. But that is exactly what happened to the world before Peter was born. The anti-Peterite, instead of placing himself after Peter, makes himself previous to him and reverses the whole film to the situation of the past, at the end of which the re-apparition of Peter is inevitable. The same thing happens to these *antis* as, according to the legend, happened to Confucius. He was born, naturally, after his father, but he was born at the age of eighty while his progenitor was only thirty! Every *anti* is nothing more than a simple, empty *No.*

This would be all very nice and fine if with a good, round *No* we could annihilate the past. But the past is of its essence a *revenant.* If put out, it comes back, inevitably. Hence, the only way to separate from it is not to put it out, but to accept its existence, and so to have in regard to it as to dodge it, to avoid it. In a word, to live "at the height of our time," with an exaggerated consciousness of the historical circumstances.

The past has reason on its side, its own reason. If that reason is not admitted, it will return to demand it. Liberalism had its reason, which will have to be admitted *per saecula saeculorum.* But it had not the whole of reason, and it is that part which was not reason that must be taken from it. Europe needs to preserve its essential liberalism. This is the condition for superseding it.

If I have spoken here of Fascism and Bolshevism it has been only indirectly, considering merely their aspect as anachronisms. This aspect is, to my mind, inseparable from all that is apparently triumphant to-day. For to-day it is the mass-man who triumphs, and consequently, only those designs inspired by him, saturated with his primitive style, can enjoy an apparent victory. But apart from this, I am not at present discussing the true inwardness of one or the other, just as I am not attempting to solve the eternal dilemma of revolution and evolution. The most that this essay dares to demand is that the revolution or the evolution be historical and not anachronistic.

The theme I am pursuing in these pages is politically neutral, because it breathes an air much ampler than that of politics and its dissensions. Conservative and Radical are none the less mass, and the difference between them—which at every period has been very superficial—does not in the least prevent them both being one and the same man—the common man in rebellion.

There is no hope for Europe unless its destiny is placed in the hands of men really "contemporaneous," men who feel palpitating beneath them the whole subsoil of history, who realize the present level of existence, and abhor every archaic and primitive attitude. We have need of history in its entirety, not to fall back into it, but to see if we can escape from it.

[272]

OWEN, ROBERT

OWEN, ROBERT (1771-1858). It is more by his activities than by his thoughts that Owen influenced the mind and practical life of later ages. He was a man of one idea which he called "socialism" but which rather means "cooperative settlements." He was obsessed by this idea, and not very capable of explaining and developing it in a scientific manner. But he devoted much of his time, energy and fortune to its realization, and influenced British social legislation by his restless insistence on the removal of the most flagrant abuses of the early industrial system.

After being a cotton-twist manufacturer in Manchester, Owen acquired, in 1797, a factory in New Lanfark which, under his direction, became a model factory and attracted the curiosity of many thousands of visitors from various countries. Employing 1,700 hands out of the 3,000 inhabitants of the village, Owen refused to employ children under the age of ten, or adults for more than ten and a half hours a day. He provided the families of his workers with schools, a cooperative store, the opportunity to hear music and to take physical exercises. Later he tried to organize cooperative settlements elsewhere in England and in the United States. But he was rather a despotic, though benevolent, ruler, and always a sworn foe of political democracy, educating his adherents to political indifference. In his book *New View of Society* (1813) and in numerous periodicals, he tried to propagate the idea that the existing evils were not due to lack of religion, against which Owen always proclaimed his animosity, but to a wrong distribution of wealth and to a deficient regulation of production which caused economic crises as a consequence of over-production. The rise of the factory system was defended by Owen, who, against Malthus, maintained that the increase of the productive capacity of the human race would be more rapid than the increase of the population. Owen's aim was revolutionary but not his method of realizing it.

880

It has been, and still is, a received opinion among theorists in political economy, that man can provide better for himself, and more advantageously for the public, when left to his own individual exertions, opposed to, and in competition with his fellows, than when aided by any social arrangements, which shall unite his interests individually and generally with society. This principle of individual interest, opposed, as it is perpetually, to the public good, is considered, by the most celebrated political economists, to be the cornerstone of the social system and without which, society could not subsist. Yet when they shall know themselves, and discover the wonderful effects, which combination and unity can produce, they will acknowledge that the present arrangement of society is the most antisocial, impolitic, and irrational, that can be devised; that under its influence, all the superior and valuable qualities of human nature are repressed from infancy, and that the most unnatural means are used to bring out the most injurious propensities; in short, that the utmost pains are taken to make that which by nature is the most delightful compound for producing excellence and happiness, absurd, imbecile, and wretched. Such is the conduct now pursued by those who are called the best and wisest of the present generation, although there is not one rational object to be gained by it. From this principle of individual interest have arisen all the divisions of mankind, the endless errors and mischiefs of class, sect, party, and of national antipathies, creating the angry and malevolent passions, and all the crimes and misery with which the human race has been hitherto afflicted. In short, if there be one closet doctrine more contrary to truth than another, it is the notion that individual interest, as the term is now understood, is a more advantageous principle on which to found the social system, for the benefit of all, or of any, than the principle of union and mutual cooperation. The former acts like an immense weight to repress the most valuable faculties and dispositions, and to give a wrong direction to all the human powers. It is one of those magnificent errors (if the expression may be allowed) that when enforced in practice, brings ten thousand evils in its train. The principle on which these economists proceed, instead of adding to the wealth of nations or of individuals, is itself the sole cause of poverty; and but for its operation, wealth would long ago have ceased to be a subject of contention in any part of the world. If, it may be asked, experience has proved that union, combination, and extensive arrangement among mankind, are a thousand times more powerful to *destroy*, than the efforts of an unconnected multitude, where each acts individually for himself,—would not a similar increased effect be produced by union, combination, and extensive arrangement, to *create and conserve?* Why should not the result be the same in the one case as in the other? But it is well known that a combination of men and of interests, can effect that which it would be futile to attempt, and impossible to accomplish, by individual exertions and separate interests. Then why, it may be inquired, have men so long acted individually, and in opposition to each other?

This is an important question, and merits the most serious attention.

Men have not yet been trained in principles that will permit them *to act in unison,* except to defend themselves or to destroy others. For self-preservation, they were early compelled to unite for these purposes in war. A necessity, however, equally powerful will now compel men to be trained to act together, to *create and conserve,* that in like manner they may preserve life in peace. Fortunately for mankind, the system of individual opposing interests, has now reached the extreme point of error and inconsistency;—in the midst of the most ample means to create wealth, all are in poverty, or in imminent danger, from the effects of poverty upon others.

The reflecting part of mankind, have admitted in theory, that the characters of men are formed chiefly by the circumstances in which they are placed; yet the science of the influence of circumstances, which is the most important of all the sciences, remains unknown for the great practical business of life. When it shall be fully developed, it will be discovered, that to unite the mental faculties of men, for the attainment of pacific and civil objects, will be a far more easy task than it has been to combine their physical powers to carry on extensive warlike operations.

The discovery of the distance and movements of the heavenly bodies; of the time-pieces; of a vessel to navigate the most distant parts of the ocean; of the steam engine, which performs, under the easy control of one man, the labor of many thousands; and of the press, by which knowledge and improvements may be speedily given to the most ignorant, in all parts of the earth;—these have, indeed, been discoveries of high import to mankind; but important as these and others have been in their effects, on the condition of human society, their combined benefits in practice, will fall far short of those which will be speedily attained by the new intellectual power, which men will acquire through the knowledge of "the science of the influence of circumstances over the whole conduct, character, and proceedings of the human race." By this latter discovery, more shall be accomplished in one year, for the well-being of human nature, including, without any exceptions, all ranks and descriptions of men, than has ever yet been effected in one or in many centuries. Strange as this language may seem to those whose minds have not yet had a glimpse of the real state in which society now is, it will prove to be not more strange than true.

Are not the mental energies of the world at this moment in a state of high effervescence. Is not society at a stand, incompetent to proceed in its present course, and do not all men cry out that "something must be done"? That "something," to produce the effect desired, must be a complete renovation of the whole social compact; one not forced on prematurely, by confusion and violence; not one to be brought about by the futile measures of the Radicals, Whigs, or Tories, of Britain,—the Liberals or Royalists of France, —the Illuminati of Germany, or the mere party proceedings of any little local portion of human beings, trained as they have hitherto been, in almost every kind of error, and without any true knowledge of themselves. No! The change sought for, must be preceded by the clear development of a great and universal principle which shall unite in one, all the petty jarring interests, by which, till now, nature has been made a most inveterate enemy to itself. No! extensive, nay, rather, universal as the rearrangement of society must be, to relieve it from the difficulties with which it is now overwhelmed, it will be effected in peace and quietness, with the good will and hearty concurrence of all parties, and of every people. It will necessarily commence by common consent, on account of its advantages, almost simultaneously among all civilized nations; and, once begun, will daily advance with an accelerating ratio, unopposed, and bearing down before it the existing systems of the world. The only astonishment then will be that such systems could so long have existed.

*   *   *

Under the present system, there is the most minute division of mental power and manual labor in the individuals of the working classes; private interests are placed perpetually at variance with the public good, and, in every nation, men are purposely trained from infancy to suppose that their well-being is incompatible with the progress and prosperity of other nations. Such are the means by which old society seeks to obtain the desired effects of life. The details now to be submitted, have been devised upon principles which will lead to an opposite practice; to the combination of extensive mental and manual powers in the individuals of the working classes; to a complete identity of private and public interest, and to the training of na-

884

tions to comprehend that their power and happiness cannot attain their full and natural development, but through an equal increase of the power and happiness of all other states. These, therefore, are the real points at variance between that which *is,* and that which *ought to be.*

[273]

𝒫

PAINE, THOMAS

PAINE, THOMAS (1737-1809). Contemporaries used to speak of Paine only in superlatives either of enthusiasm or contempt. Jefferson and Hamilton, though differing on so many points, agreed that Paine was a man to be avoided or distrusted. England, his native country, outlawed him. Jacobin France, where Paine at first had been made an honorary citizen and had been elected a member of the National Convention although he did not speak French, imprisoned him because he had agitated against the execution of the king. When Paine died, he had been poor, sick and ostracized for many years. A century after his death, Theodore Roosevelt sneered at him as a "filthy little atheist."

But independent historians have recognized that Paine, by his pamphlet *Common Sense* (1776) and by untiring agitation, convinced influential but hesitating Americans that independence should be declared because it was the only way to save the colonies. It was also Paine who insisted on the gathering of the Continental Congress, for the purpose of framing a Continental charter. Furthermore, it was Paine who earlier than any other proclaimed America's mission to be the defense of freedom and democracy by presenting to the whole world the example of a republic of free men.

Without any doubt, America and humanity in general owe him a grateful memory, although he was not free from vanity and his education was incomplete. But Paine was not a man to serve only one country. He defended the French Revolution against Edmund Burke in his book *The Rights of Man* (1791) with the same ardor as he had defended the American Revolution, and he tried to revolutionize England, though without success. In his *Age of Reason* (1794-96) he tried to emancipate humanity from Christian traditions and to establish a religion of deism. He did not recognize that the Age of Reason had ended when his book was printed.

After and throughout many failures in business while he lived in England, Paine had educated himself by confining his spiritual interests strictly to the science of his time. He was an artless writer although he displayed extraordinary talents for aphoristic formulas and for striking expressions.

THE RIGHTS OF MAN

EVERY history of the creation, and every traditional account, however they may vary in their opinion or belief of certain particulars, all agree in establishing one point, *the unity of man;* by which I mean that men are all of *one degree,* and consequently that all men are born equal, and with equal natural right, in the same manner as if posterity had been continued by *creation* instead of *generation,* the latter being the only mode by which the former is carried forward; and consequently every child born into the world must be considered as deriving its existence from God. The world is as new to him as it was to the first man that existed, and his natural right in it is of the same kind.

The duty of man is not a wilderness of turnpike gates through which he is to pass by tickets from one to the other. It is plain and simple, and consists but of two points: his duty to God, which every man must feel; and with respect to his neighbor, to do as he would be done by. If those to whom power is delegated do well, they will be respected; if not, they will be despised; and with regard to those to whom no power is delegated, but who assume it, the rational world can know nothing of them.

Natural rights are those which appertain to man in right of his existence. Of this kind are all the intellectual rights, or rights of the mind, and also all those rights of acting as an individual for his own comfort and happiness which are not injurious to the natural rights of others. Civil rights are those which appertain to man in right of his being a member of society. Every civil right has for its foundation some natural right pre-existing in the individual, but to the enjoyment of which his individual power is not, in all cases, sufficiently competent. Of this kind are all those which relate to security and protection.

From these premises two or three certain conclusions follow:

First, that every civil right grows out of a natural right; or, in other words, is a natural right exchanged.

Secondly, that civil power properly considered as such is made up of the aggregate of that class of the natural rights of man which becomes defective in the individual in point of power, and answers not his purpose, but when collected to a focus, becomes competent to the purpose of every one.

Thirdly, that the power produced from the aggregate of natural rights, imperfect in power in the individual, cannot be applied to invade the natural rights which are retained in the individual, and in which the power to execute is as perfect as the right itself.

We have now, in a few words, traced man from a natural individual to a member of society, and shown the quality of the natural rights retained, and of those which are exchanged for civil rights. Let us now apply these principles to governments.

It has been thought a considerable advance towards establishing the principle of freedom to say that government is a compact between those who govern and those who are governed; but this cannot be true, because it is putting the effect before the cause; for as man must have existed before governments existed, there necessarily was a time when governments did not exist.

Governments arising out of society do so by establishing a *constitution*. A constitution is not a thing in name only, but in fact. It has not an ideal, but a real existence; and wherever it cannot be produced in a visible form, there is none. A constitution is a thing *antecedent* to a government, and a government is only the creature of a constitution. The constitution of a country is not the act of its government, but of the people constituting its government. It is the body of elements to which you can refer and quote article by article; and which contains the principles on which the government shall be established, the manner in which it shall be organized, the powers it shall have, the mode of elections, the duration of parliaments, or by what other name such bodies may be called; the powers which the executive part of the government shall have; and, in fine, everything that relates to the complete organization of a civil government, and the principles on which it shall act, and by which it shall be bound.

A constitution, therefore, is to a government what the laws made afterward by that government are to a court of judicature. The court of judicature does not make the laws, neither can it alter them; it only acts in conformity to the laws made: and the government is in like manner governed by the constitution.

[274]

PARACELSUS

PARACELSUS (1493-1541). Theophrastus Bombastus of Hohenheim, called Paracelsus, has been decried as a charlatan, even as a scoundrel, and exalted as a precursor of modern knowledge and a martyr of modern science. In fact, he was an honest man who did wrong only when he was too exasperated by the obstinacy and evil tricks of his adversaries and competitors. He was a self-denying, and certainly also a very efficient physician, who fought routine and prejudices in his special field. But by no means did he attack routine and prejudice with the weapons of modern science, although he anticipated modern views in many ways. He demanded that a physician be an astrologist, an alchemist and a "philosopher," conceiving philosophy as knowledge of the arcana, founded upon a mystical grasp of the forces which work in the Universe. He warned his colleagues against observing the sick patient instead of contemplating the whole of nature, especially the qualities and the degeneration of metals from which he tried to draw conclusions about the sufferings of the human beings. Anatomy meant to him the astrological structure of the patient. Thus Paracelsus' criticism of medical traditions accepted alchemy, astrology, magic and the Church. "I write as a pagan," he declared, "but I am a Christian." His principal source was the Cabala which he thought proved the truth of Christianity.

889

But in the midst of his alchemist disquisitions, Paracelsus produced the elements of modern pharmacology. While trying to heal his patients by means of magic spells and sympathetic cures, he proceeded to treatments similar to those of modern psychotherapy, and his philosophy of the Universe led him to the idea of organic life. Although he declined to observe the patient and built his hopes for healing him upon speculation on the mystery of becoming and existence, he arrived at a sound view on the activities of medicine and pharmacology. Disease was considered by him to be a conflict between nature and demonic forces. In this conflict, the physician is "but the helper who furnishes nature with weapons," and the apothecary "the smith" who forges the needed weapons.

WHY NYMPHS, SYLPHS, ETC., EXIST

GOD has set guardians over nature, for all things, and he left nothing unguarded. Thus gnomes, pygmies and *mani* guard the treasures of the earth, the metals and similar treasures. Where they are, there are tremendous treasures, in tremendous quantities. They are guarded by such people, are kept hidden and secret so that they may not be found until the time for it has come. When they are found, people say: in times of old there used to be mountain manikins, earth people here, but now they are gone. This means that now the time has come for the treasures to be revealed. The treasures of the earth are distributed in such a way that the metals, silver, gold, iron, etc., have been found from the beginning of the world on, and are being discovered by and by. They are guarded and protected by these people so that they may not be found all at once, but one after another, by and by, now in this country, now in another. Thus the mines are shifted in the course of time from country to country and are distributed from the first day to the last. The same applies also to the fire people. They too are guardians, of the fireplaces, in which they live. In these places the treasures, that others guard, are forged, prepared, made ready. When the fire is extinguished, it is the earth manikins' turn to be on guard. And after the earth manikins' guard, the treasures are revealed. It is the same with the air people. They guard the rocks that lie on the surface, that have been made by the fire people, and put at the place where they belong, from where they get into man's hands. They guard them so long, until the time has come. Wherever there are treasures, such people are on hand. These are hidden treasures that must not be revealed yet. Since they are guardians of such matters, we can well understand that such guardians are not endowed with a soul, yet similar to and like men. The nymphs in the water are guardians of the great water treasures that lie in the sea and other waters, that have also been melted and forged by the fire people. It is, therefore, commonly understood that where nymphs are, there are considerable treasures and minerals and similar matters which they guard. This is apparent in many ways.

The cause of the sirens, giants, dwarfs, also of the will-o'-the-wisps, who are monsters of the fire people, is that they predict and indicate something new. They are not on guard, but signify that misfortune is threatening people. Thus when lights are seen it means the impending downfall of that country, that is, it commonly signifies the destruction of the monarchy and similar things. Thus the giants also signify great impending destruction of that country and land or some other such great disaster. The dwarfs signify great poverty among the people, in many parts. The sirens signify the downfall of princes and lords, the rise of sects or factions. For God wants us all to be of one essence. What is against it, He drops. And when this is going to happen, signs occur. These beings are such signs, as has been said, but not they alone; there are many more. You must know that the signs change each time. They do not appear in one way, but are hidden to our eyes.

And, finally, the last cause is unknown to us. But when the end of the world will come close, then all things will be revealed, from the smallest to the largest, from the first to the last, what everything has been and is, why it stood there and left, from what causes, and what its meaning was. And everything that is in the world will be disclosed and come to light. Then the fake scholars will be exposed, those who are highly learned in name only but know nothing by experience. Then, the thorough scholars and those who are mere talkers will be recognized for what they are, those who wrote truthfully and those who traded in lies, the thorough and the shallow ones. And to each will be measured according to his diligence, earnest endeavor and truth. At that place, not everyone will be or remain a master, or even a doctor, because there the tares will be separated from the wheat and the straw from the grain. He who now cries, will be quieted, and he who now counts the pages, will have his quills taken away. And all things will be revealed before the Day of Judgment breaks, in order that it be found of all scholars, from the past to that very day, who had knowledge and who not, whose writings were right and whose wrong. Now, in my time, this is still unknown. Blessed will be the people, in those days, whose intelligence will be revealed, for what they produced will be revealed to all the people as if it were written on their foreheads. For that time I also recommend my writings for judgment, asking that nothing be withheld. Thus it will be, for God makes the light manifest, that is, everyone will see how it has shone.

[275]

PARETO, VILFREDO

PARETO, VILFREDO (1848-1923). At the end of his life, Pareto, a professor of political economy at the University of Lausanne, Switzerland, was honored by Mussolini who had come to power. However, he remained indifferent to all Fascist eulogizers and even hinted that the Fascists misunderstood his thoughts. For a time, Pareto's ideas reached a position of power and prestige in democratic America too. Misunderstanding of Pareto's doctrines is not a little due to the fact, deplored by his most faithful admirers, that he had the habit of mentioning his most important points just casually, or even only in notes. Furthermore, he presented not a close and complete system but, rather a series of studies. What attracted Fascism to Pareto's ideas was not his doctrine itself, but some passages—namely his great admiration of

892

Machiavelli's *The Prince,* his small respect for ethics, and his contempt of metaphysics and religion.

Pareto was born in Paris. He was the son of an Italian nobleman who was a political refugee, and a French mother. When, in 1858, an amnesty allowed return to Italy, Pareto prepared himself for an engineering career and became manager of the railroad in the valley of the Arno River. In 1876, he began to write on economics and established "Pareto's law" which tries to express the relation between the amount of income and the number of its recipients. His *Manual of Political Economics* (1906) was much disputed. Even more controversies were provoked by his *Sociologia Generale* (1916) which was translated into English under the title *The Mind and Society* in 1935.

Pareto claimed to have raised sociology to a logico-experimental science. He stressed and explained the nonlogical factors in human actions by showing the components of social life which he divided into two principal groups—namely, the "residues" or fundamental factors and the derivations which often are erroneous and create myths. By "residues," of which he never gave a sufficient definition, Pareto meant the unexpressed postulates, the things one considers so obvious that they need no explanation, or beliefs which are not formed by logical processes. Social evolution is determined by economic interests, psychic and ideological factors and the "circulation of the elite." Pareto was opposed to "atomistic individualism," and he declared collectively to be "if not a person, at least a unity," and emphasized the importance of social classes.

ON CAUSE AND EFFECT

In nonmathematical language, the independent variable x in an algebraic equation corresponds to a *cause.* Sometimes that is an admissible translation, sometimes it is not. For *cause,* colloquially speaking, must necessarily come before its effect. Thus, you can consider the price of something as the *effect* and the cost of its production as the *cause,* or you can turn it about and consider the cost of production as *effect* and the selling price to be the *cause.* For in that case there are a series of actions and reactions which permit you to suppose either that the supply of the product precedes the demand or that the demand precedes the supply on the market. In fact, there is a mutual dependence between supply and demand, and this mutual dependence can theoretically be expressed by an equation. You could not, in collo-quial language, invert similarly the relation in which you call the freezing of water the cause and the breaking of a pipe its effect, and say that the break *caused* the water to freeze. But, leaving terminology aside, if you are concerned only with the experimental relation between these two facts, isolating them from all others, you could easily deduce the existence of a break in a pipe from the freezing of the water in it and *vice versa*. For, in fact, there is a mutual depend-ence between the change of temperature which turns the water into ice and the resistance of the pipe containing it. Thermodynamics, thanks to the language of mathematics, expresses this mutual dependence in a rigorous way; a collo-quial language expresses the same thing, but imperfectly.

Suppose we have two quantities, x and y, in a state of mutual dependence. In mathematical terms, we say that there is an equation between these two variables, and it is un-necessary to say more. But if we speak colloquially, we shall say that x is determined by y, which at once reacts on x, and so y finds itself depending on the new x. You can invert the terms and equally well say that y is determined by x, but that y reacts on x, and so x finds itself also dependent on y. Sometimes this method gives the same results as the mathema-tical equations; sometimes it does not. So we can substitute the colloquial method only with a good deal of circumspec-tion.

[276]

PARMENIDES

PARMENIDES (About 504-456 B.C.). Down to recent times, phil-osophy has accepted fundamental concepts from Parmenides, not-withstanding considerable criticisms, modifications and combinations with other ideas. It was Parmenides who initiated the distinction be-tween a sensible and an intelligible world. It was he who first as-sumed an indestructible *substance* and used it as the basis of his speculations, although he did not formulate its concept. It was he who began to distinguish between scientific truth and popular opinion. In this way, Parmenides influenced Empedocles, Leucippus and Democritus, the Sophists and Plato, while Hegel was not the last philosopher who followed Parmenides by founding metaphysics upon logic.

A principal characteristic of the Greek mind, which is significant not only of Greek philosophy but of Greek art and the Greek feeling of existence, was shaped by Parmenides, the founder of the Eleatic school. This is his preference for unity, composure, and the comprehension of limits and contours. This longing for unity made him suspicious of the senses; this want of composure made him deny change; this need of limits made him conceive the unchanging world as of spherical form and repudiate the idea of the infinite, or the empty space.

Little is known about Parmenides' life. He was born in Elea (Velia) in Southern Italy; probably he was a disciple of Xenophanes and Ameinias, a Pythagorean. In all probability, he resided for some years in Athens where, according to Plato, Socrates met him and learned much from the aged philosopher.

THE WAY OF TRUTH

COME now, I will tell thee—and do thou hearken to my saying and carry it away—the only two ways of search that can be thought of. The first, namely, that It is, and that it is impossible for anything not to be, is the way of conviction, for truth is its companion. The other, namely, that It is not, and that something must needs not be, that, I tell thee, is a wholly untrustworthy path. For you cannot know what is not—that is impossible—nor utter it; for it is the same thing that can be thought and that can be.

It needs must be that what can be thought and spoken of is; for it is possible for it to be, and it is not possible for what is nothing to be. This is what I bid thee ponder. I hold thee back from this first way of inquiry, and from this other also, upon which mortals knowing naught wander in two minds; for hesitation guides the wandering thought in their breasts, so that they are borne along stupefied like men deaf and blind. Undiscerning crowds, in whose eyes the same thing and not the same is and is not, and all things travel in opposite directions!

895

For this shall never be proved, that the things that are not are; and do thou restrain thy thought from this way of inquiry. Nor let habit force thee to cast a wandering eye upon this devious track, or to turn thither thy resounding ear or thy tongue; but do thou judge the subtle refutation of their discourse uttered by me. One path only is left for us to speak of, namely, that It is. In it are very many tokens that what is, is uncreated and indestructible, alone, complete, immovable and without end. Nor was it ever, nor will it be; for now it is, all at once, a continuous one. For what kind of origin for it will you look for? In what way and from what source could it have drawn its increase? I shall not let thee say nor think that it came from what is not; for it can neither be thought nor uttered that what is not is. And, if it came from nothing, what need could have made it arise later rather than sooner? Therefore must it either be altogether or be not at all. Nor will the force of truth suffer aught to arise besides itself from that which in any way is. Wherefore, Justice does not loose her fetters and let anything come into being or pass away, but holds it fast.

"Is it or is it not?" Surely it is adjudged, as it needs must be, that we are to set aside the one way as unthinkable and nameless (for it is no true way), and that the other path is real and true. How, then, can what is be going to be in the future? Or how could it come into being? If it came into being, it is not; nor is it if it is going to be in the future. Thus is becoming extinguished and passing away not to be heard of.

Nor is it divisible, since it is all alike, and there is no more of it in one place than in another, to hinder it from holding together, nor less of it, but everything is full of what is. Wherefore all holds together; for what is, is in contact with what is.

Moreover, it is immovable in the bonds of mighty chains, without beginning and without end; since coming into being and passing away have been driven afar, and true belief has cast them away. It is the same, and it rests in the self-same place; abiding in itself. And thus it remaineth constant in its place; for hard necessity keeps it in the bonds of the limit that holds it fast on every side. Wherefore it is not permitted to what is to be infinite; for it is in need of nothing; while, if it were infinite, it would stand in need of everything.

Look steadfastly with thy mind at things afar as if they were at hand. You cannot cut off what anywhere is from holding fast to what is anywhere; neither is it scattered abroad throughout the universe, nor does it come together.

It is the same thing that can be thought and for the sake of which the thought exists; for you cannot find thought without something that is, to which it is betrothed. And there is not, and never shall be, any time other than that which is present, since fate has chained it so as to be whole and immovable. Wherefore all these things are but the names which mortals have given, believing them to be true—coming into being and passing away, being and not being, change of place and alteration of bright color.

Where, then, it has its farthest boundary, it is complete on every side, equally poised from the centre in every direction, like the mass of a rounded sphere; for it cannot be greater or smaller in one place than in another. For there is nothing which is not that could keep it from reaching out equally, nor is it possible that there should be more of what is in this place and less in that, since it is all inviolable. For, since it is equal in all directions, it is equally confined within limits.

[277]

PASCAL, BLAISE

PASCAL, BLAISE (1623-1662). Scientists honor Pascal as one of the greatest mathematicians and physicists, as one of the founders of hydrodynamics and the mathematical theory of probability, and as a man who also made significant contributions by his investigations of vacuum, and gravity, and by his theory of conic sections. Men of all creeds revere Pascal's piety which was free from bigotry. Historians of literature admire Pascal's prose which contributed to the formation of modern French style. Philosophers highly esteem him as a profound psychologist and a thinker devoted to truth.

Success and fame meant nothing to Pascal. He sought peace of mind. Dissatisfied with abstract science, Pascal turned to the study of man and his spiritual problems. His conviction that self-complacency is the most dangerous obstacle in the way to true knowledge led him to a severe examination of his own inclinations and disinclinations. In his search of truth, Pascal was steadily tormented by his passions and inner conflicts, but he overcame all these obstacles by his honesty of thought. He was equally opposed to those who despise human reason and to those who are over-confident of it. According to him, God enabled man to know religious truth by means of reason, and to feel truth, due to His grace. He protested with energy and courage any attempt to convert men to any creed by force. But he fought religious and moral laxity with no less energy, as his *Lettres Provinciales*, masterworks of polemics, have shown. In his *Pensées* (Thoughts), Pascal dealt with the fundamental problems of human existence from the psychological and theological point of view. He regarded truth as the expression of God's will and as a means to know and to love Him.

THOUGHTS ON MIND AND ON STYLE

THE *difference between the mathematical and the intuitive mind.*—In the one the principles are palpable, but removed from ordinary use; so that for want of habit it is difficult to turn one's mind in that direction: but if one turns it thither ever so little, one sees the principles fully, and one must have a quite inaccurate mind who reasons wrongly from principles so plain that it is almost impossible they should escape notice.

But in the intuitive mind the principles are found in common use, and are before the eyes of everybody. One has only to look, and no effort is necessary; it is only a question of good eyesight, but it must be good, for the principles are so subtle and so numerous, that it is almost impossible but that some escape notice. Now the omission of one principle leads to error; thus one must have very clear sight to see all the principles, and in the next place an accurate mind not to draw false deductions from known principles.

All mathematicians would then be intuitive if they had clear sight, for they do not reason incorrectly from principles known to them; and intuitive minds would be mathematical if they could turn their eyes to the principles of mathematics to which they are unused.

The reason, therefore, that some intuitive minds are not mathematical is that they cannot at all turn their attention to the principles of mathematics. But the reason that mathematicians are not intuitive is that they do not see what is before them, and that, accustomed to the exact and plain principles of mathematics, and not reasoning till they have well inspected and arranged their principles, they are lost in matters of intuition where the principles do not allow of such arrangement. They are scarcely seen; they are felt rather than seen; there is the greatest difficulty in making them felt by those who do not of themselves perceive them. These principles are so fine and so numerous that a very delicate and very clear sense is needed to perceive them, and to judge rightly and justly when they are perceived, without for the most part being able to demonstrate them in order as in mathematics; because the principles are not known to us in the same way, and because it would be an endless matter to undertake it. We must see the matter at once, at one glance, and not by a process of reasoning, at least to a certain degree. And thus it is rare that mathematicians are intuitive, and that men of intuition are mathematicians, because mathematicians wish to treat matters of intuition mathematically, and make themselves ridiculous, wishing to begin with definitions and then with axioms, which is not the way to proceed in this kind of reasoning. Not that the mind does not do so, but it does it tacitly, naturally, and without technical rules; for the expression of it is beyond all men, and only a few can feel it.

Intuitive minds, on the contrary, being thus accustomed

to judge at a single glance, are so astonished when they are presented with propositions of which they understand nothing, and the way to which is through definitions and axioms so sterile, and which they are not accustomed to see thus in detail, that they are repelled and disheartened.

But dull minds are never either intuitive or mathematical.

Mathematicians who are only mathematicians have exact minds, provided all things are explained to them by means of definitions and axioms; otherwise they are inaccurate and insufferable, for they are only right when the principles are quite clear.

And men of intuition who are only intuitive cannot have the patience to reach to first principles of things speculative and conceptual, which they have never seen in the world, and which are altogether out of the common.

There are different kinds of right understanding; some have right understanding in a certain order of things, and not in others, where they go astray. Some draw conclusions well from a few premises, and this displays an acute judgment.

Others draw conclusions well where there are many premises.

For example, the former easily learn hydrostatics, where the premises are few, but the conclusions are so fine that only the greatest acuteness can reach them.

And in spite of that these persons would perhaps not be great mathematicians, because mathematics contains a great number of premises, and there is perhaps a kind of intellect that can search with ease a few premises to the bottom, and cannot in the least penetrate those matters in which there are many premises.

There are then two kinds of intellect: the one able to penetrate acutely and deeply into the conclusions of given premises, and this is the precise intellect; the other able to comprehend a great number of premises without confusing them, and this is the mathematical intellect. The one has force and exactness, the other comprehension. Now the one quality can exist without the other; the intellect can be strong and narrow, and can also be comprehensive and weak.

Those who are accustomed to judge by feeling do not understand the process of reasoning, for they would understand at first sight, and are not used to seek for principles. And others, on the contrary, who are accustomed to reason from principles, do not at all understand matters of feeling, seeking principles, and being unable to see at a glance.

Mathematics, intuition.— True eloquence makes light of eloquence, true morality makes light of morality; that is to say, the morality of the judgment, which has no rules, makes light of the morality of the intellect.

For it is to judgment that perception belongs, as science belongs to intellect. Intuition is the part of judgment, mathematics of intellect.

To make light of philosophy is to be a true philosopher.

Those who judge of a work by rule are in regard to others as those who have a watch are in regard to others. One says, "It is two hours ago"; the other says, "It is only three-quarters of an hour." I look at my watch, and say to the one, "You are weary," and to the other, "Time gallops with you"; for it is only an hour and a half ago, and I laugh at those who tell me that time goes slowly with me, and that I judge by imagination. They do not know that I judge by my watch.

Just as we harm the understanding, we harm the feelings also.

The understanding and the feelings are moulded by intercourse; the understanding and feelings are corrupted by intercourse. Thus good or bad society improves or corrupts them. It is, then, all-important to know how to choose in order to improve and not to corrupt them; and we cannot make this choice, if they be not already improved and not corrupted. Thus a circle is formed, and those are fortunate who escape it.

The greater intellect one has, the more originality one

finds in men. Ordinary persons find no difference between
men.

[278]

PATER, WALTER HORATIO

PATER, WALTER HORATIO (1839-1894). Most of Pater's disciples who pursued his doctrine of thrice-refined hedonism to its
extreme consequences finally took refuge in the Church of Rome,
and many of those who revolted against Pater's philosophy of life
or against his way of criticizing art, after becoming sure of their
victory, admitted their personal love of the man whose thoughts
and views they had attacked. Pater's belief that nothing which ever
has interested mankind can wholly lose its vitality, may be confirmed by the vicissitudes of his literary fame.

Oscar Wilde called Pater's *Renaissance* (1873) his "golden
book" and said in *De Profundis* that it had "such a strange influence over my life." George Moore took Pater's *Marius the Epicurean*
(1885), which he called his "Bible," as model for his own book
Confessions of a Young Man. William Butler Yeats and others who
later became noted poets and critics founded *The Rhymers' Club*
whose program was the cult of Pater's ideas.

Great scholars have praised Pater's principal work *Plato and
Platonism* (1893) because of its author's congeniality with the
great Greek thinker. But Pater was no Platonist. He called himself
an Epicurean, and was perhaps even more influenced by Heraclitus.
The essence of what he called his humanism is the conviction that
only the sharp apex of the present moment between two hypothetical eternities is secure, and that the art of living consists in the
ability of making such passing moments yield the utmost of enjoyment. He tried to show that devotion to enjoyment of beauty gives
the soul a strength and austerity which cannot be surpassed even
by moral ascetism, and that delicacy of feeling does not exclude
purity of thinking. Pater's way or regarding all things and principles as inconsistent did not allow him to acquiesce in any orthodoxy and maintained his curiosity in testing new opinions. But his
instincts, which were opposed to academic dullness, let him also
recoil from revolutionary excesses.

THREE WAYS OF CRITICISM

THERE are three different ways in which the criticism of
philosophic, of all speculative opinion whatever, may be

902

conducted. The doctrines of Plato's *Republic,* for instance, may be regarded as so much truth or falsehood, to be accepted or rejected as such by the student of today. That is the dogmatic method of criticism; judging every product of human thought, however alien or distant from one's self, by its congruity with the assumptions of Bacon or Spinoza, of Mill or Hegel, according to the mental preference of the particular critic. There is, secondly, the more generous, eclectic or syncretic method, which aims at a selection from contending schools of the various grains of truth dispersed among them. It is the method which has prevailed in periods of large reading but with little inceptive force of their own, like that of the Alexandrian Neo-Platonism in the third century, or the Neo-Platonism of Florence in the fifteenth. Its natural defect is in the tendency to misrepresent the true character of the doctrine it professes to explain, that it may harmonize thus the better with the other elements of a pre-conceived system.

Dogmatic and eclectic criticism alike have in our own century, under the influence of Hegel and his predominant theory of the ever-changing "Time-spirit" or *Zeit-geist,* given way to a third method of criticism, the historic method, which bids us replace the doctrine, or the system, we are busy with, or such an ancient monument of philosophic thought as *The Republic,* as far as possible in the group of conditions, intellectual, social, material, amid which it was actually produced if we would really understand it. That ages have their genius as well as the individual; that in every age there is a peculiar *ensemble* of conditions which determines a common character in every product of that age, in business and art, in fashion and speculation, in religion and manners, in men's very faces; that nothing man has projected from himself is really intelligible except at its own date, and from its proper point of view in the never-resting "secular process"; the solidarity of philosophy, of the intellectual life, with common or general history; that what it behooves the student of philosophic systems to cultivate is the "historic sense":

by force of these convictions many a normal, or at first sight abnormal, phase of speculation has found a reasonable meaning for us. As the strangely twisted pine tree, which would be a freak of nature on an English lawn, is seen, if we replace it, in thought, amid the contending forces of the Alpine torrent that actually shaped its growth, to have been the creature of necessity, of the logic of certain facts; so, beliefs the most fantastic, the "communism" of Plato, for instance, have their natural propriety when duly correlated with those facts, those conditions round about them, of which they are in truth a part.

[279]

PEANO, GIUSEPPE

PEANO, GIUSEPPE (1858-1932). Modest, simple, kind-hearted, benevolent, affable in his personal behavior, Peano impressed his audiences and readers with the strict precision of his thinking. He was principally a mathematical logician but was also devoted to the idea of the perfection of human relations, international communications, spiritual and technical advance and rapprochement. It was scientific and humanitarian interest that drove him to the problem of universal language or, as he called it "inter-language" and to the purpose of achieving what Leibniz had planned in his program of a universal characteristic.

After publishing, in 1884, *Differential Calculus and Principles of the Integral Calculus,* and, in 1888, *The Geometrical Calculus,* Peano introduced new concepts and methods into mathematics, whose vocabulary he reduced to three words. He became convinced that, in order to maintain the strict character of mathematics, it was necessary to renounce common language and to shape an instrument of language that renders to thought the same services as the microscope does in biology. The ideography created by Peano uses for logical operations symbols that are shaped differently from algebraic symbols. His system permits writing every proposition of logic in symbols exclusively, in order to emancipate the strictly logical part of reasoning from verbal language and its vagueness and ambiguity. In his *Formulary of Mathematics* (1894-1908) he reduced mathematics to symbolic notation. Besides his efforts to systematize logic as a mathematical science, Peano tried to make the idea of an international language popular and to develop its practical use. As the president of the *Academia pro Inter-lingua* he was a devoted apostle of this idea.

ON UNIVERSAL LANGUAGE

Since most people are in mutual contact for reasons of politics, science and commerce, a need for an international language has always been manifest.

Under the Roman Empire various peoples adopted popular Latin with simplifications. Saxon people, in contact with Angles, have formed the modern English language which has simplified cases, genders, and, in part, person and mood. The English language has a tendency to get rid of all inflection and to become monosyllabic.

Likewise in historical time, *Lingua Franca* was formed in Mediterranean ports, pidgin-English in China, Urdu in India.

Today, every man in Europe and America who has relations with foreign countries, wants an international language. For a national language is sufficient only for those who have relations only within their own country. Knowledge of three or four principal languages may be sufficient for reading books which either in their original version or in translations have already become famous. But today Russians, Poles, Roumanians, Japanese and others are publishing important works in their own language.

The adoption of a living language as international language is, for political reasons, not possible.

Many scholars recommend classical Latin.

Dr. Zamenhof published, in 1887, Esperanto which simplifies gender and person but does not continue simplification in case and number. Esperanto reduces the whole grammar to sixteen rules, none of which is necessary.

Artificial language is analytic. It decomposes the idea of a common language. If, in the future, analysis and synthesis meet one another, just as two sources of mining workers meet each another after driving a tunnel, rational language and Leibniz' universal characteristics will do the same.

[280]

PEIRCE, CHARLES SAUNDERS

PEIRCE, CHARLES SAUNDERS (1839-1914). Until William James turned to philosophy and made pragmatism popular, his life-long friend, Peirce, the initiator of this movement, had been almost unknown. Peirce had lectured at Harvard during the periods 1864-65 and 1869-70 and at Johns Hopkins during 1879-84. He had contributed to scientific and general reviews, but no University was induced by his publications to appoint him a professor. For thirty years he had been associated with the United States Coast and Geodetic Survey. He had had no time to complete a book, except his *Grand Logic* which, however, was published after his death, together with other works he had left.

Before men like James and Dewey made Peirce's name famous, he could state: "I am a man of whom critics never found anything good to say." But once he was rather happy to be blamed by a malicious critic who reproached him for not being sure of his own conclusions. Peirce regarded this reproof as a praise. For to him any truth is provisional. In any proposition there must be taken account of coefficient of probability. This theory, called by Peirce "fallibilism," is a substitute for scepticism, and a constituent of his philosophical system, of no lesser importance than pragmatism, which he substitutes for positivism.

Peirce was the son of the great mathematician, Benjamin Peirce, and himself a mathematician who pioneered in various fields. Before he concentrated upon philosophical studies, he had worked for ten years in chemical laboratories, and had been devoted to exact sciences. He was, by nature, a logician, and it was his interest in logic that made him a philosopher. His conception of pragmatism was not a metaphysical but a logical theory. After studying German and English philosophies, Peirce declared that the Germans acquainted him with "a rich mine of suggestions," which were "of little argumentative weight," while the results of the British were "meager but more accurate."

Peirce's pragmatism, though a logical theory, interprets thought in terms of operation and control. Its striking feature is the inseparable connection between rational cognition and rational purpose. The whole function of thinking, says Peirce, is but one step in the production of habits of action. His statement of the close relation between thought and human conduct has often been misunderstood as though Peirce had proclaimed subordination of reason to action, or even to profit and particular interests. In fact, Peirce defined the meaning of a concept or proposition as that form which is most directly applicable to self-control in any situation and to any purpose. To him, the rational meaning of every proposition lies in the future which is regarded as the ultimate test of what truth means.

DIVISIONS OF SCIENCE

I RECOGNIZE two branches of science: theoretical, whose purpose is simply and solely knowledge of God's truth; and practical, for the uses of life. In branch 1, I recognize two subbranches, of which, at present, I consider only the first, [the sciences of discovery]. Among the theoretical sciences [of discovery], I distinguish three classes, all resting upon observation, but being observational in very different senses.

The first is mathematics, which does not undertake to ascertain any matter of fact whatever, but merely posits hypotheses, and traces out their consequences. It is observational, in so far as it makes constructions in the imagination according to abstract precepts, and then observes these imaginary objects, finding in them relations of parts not specified in the precept of construction. This is truly observation, yet certainly in a very peculiar sense; and no other kind of observation would at all answer the purpose of mathematics.

Class II is philosophy, which deals with positive truth, indeed, yet contents itself with observations such as come within the range of every man's normal experience, and for the most part in every waking hour of his life. Hence Bentham calls this class, *coenoscopic*. These observations escape the untrained eye precisely because they permeate our whole lives, just as a man who never takes off his blue spectacles soon ceases to see the blue tinge. Evidently, therefore, no microscope or sensitive film would be of the least use in this class. The observation is observation in a peculiar, yet perfectly legitimate, sense. If philosophy glances now and then at the results of special sciences, it is only as a sort of condiment to excite its own proper observation.

907

Class III is Bentham's *idioscopic;* that is, the special sciences, depending upon special observation, which travel or other exploration, or some assistance to the senses, either instrumental or given by training, together with unusual diligence, has put within the power of its students. This class manifestly divides itself into two subclasses, the physical and the psychical sciences; or, as I will call them, physiognosy and psychognosy. Under the former is to be included physics, chemistry, biology, astronomy, geognosy, and whatever may be like these sciences; under the latter, psychology, linguistics, ethnology, sociology, history, etc. Physiognosy sets forth the workings of efficient causation, psychognosy of final causation. But the two things call for different eyes. A man will be no whit the worse physiognosist for being utterly blind to facts of mind; and if we sometimes find observation in a psychognosist, it will, unless by exception, be found not to be of a purely physical fact. Thus, a philologist may have a fine ear for language-sounds; but it is by no means pure physical resemblance which determines whether a given sound is or is not "the" Italian close *o,* for example, as it is naively called: it is psychical habit. In any simple physical sense the sounds not distinguished from that differ much more from one another than almost any of them do from sounds which would not be tolerated for "the" close *o.* So, this fine phonetic observation of the linguist is a knack of understanding a virtual convention. The two kinds of observation are different; but they do not seem to be quite so different as both alike are from the observation of the philosopher and the mathematician; and this is why, though I, at first, was inclined to give each of them equal rank with those classes, it has at length appeared certain that they should be placed a little lower.

I still persist in leaving unnoticed a certain sub-branch of theoretical science [the sciences of review]; and as for the practical sciences, I shall merely mention a few of them, just to give an idea of what I refer to under that name. I mean, then, all such well-recognized sciences now *in actu,* as pedagogics, gold-beating, etiquette, pigeon-fancying, vulgar arithmetic, horology, surveying, navigation, telegraphy, printing, bookbinding, paper-making, deciphering, ink-making, librarian's work, engraving, etc. In short, this is by far the more various of the two branches of science. I must confess to being utterly bewildered by its motley crowd, but fortunately the natural classification of this branch will not concern us in logic—at least, will not do so as far as I can perceive.

Now let us consider the relations of the classes of science to one another. We have already remarked that relations of generation must always be of the highest concern to natural classification, which is, in fact, no more nor less than an account of the existential, or *natural*, birth concerning relations of things; meaning by birth the relations of a thing to its originating final causes.

Beginning with Class I, mathematics meddles with every other science without exception. There is no science whatever to which is not attached an application of mathematics. This is not true of any other science, since pure mathematics has not, as a part of it, any application of any other science, inasmuch as every other science is limited to finding out what is positively true, either as an individual fact, as a class, or as a law; while pure mathematics has no interest in whether a proposition is existentially true or not. In particular, mathematics has such a close intimacy with one of the classes of philosophy, that is, with logic, that no small acumen is required to find the joint between them.

Next, passing to Class II, philosophy, whose business it is to find out all that can be found out from those universal experiences which confront every man in every waking hour of his life, must necessarily have its application in every other science. For be this science of philosophy that is founded on those universal phenomena as small as you please, as long as it amounts to anything at all, it is evident that every special science ought to take that little into account before it begins work with its microscope, or telescope, or whatever special means of ascertaining truth it may be provided with.

It might, indeed, very easily be supposed that even pure mathematics itself would have need of one department of philosophy; that is to say, of logic. Yet a little reflection would show, what the history of science confirms, that that is not true. Logic will, indeed, like every other science, have its mathematical parts. There will be a mathematical logic just as there is a mathematical physics and a mathematical economics. If there is any part of logic of which mathematics stands in need—logic being a science of fact and mathematics only a science of the consequences of hypotheses—it can only be that very part of logic which consists merely in an application of mathematics so that the appeal will be, not of mathematics to a prior science of logic, but of mathematics to mathematics. Let us look at the rationale of this a little more closely. Mathematics is engaged solely in tracing out the consequences of hypotheses. As such, she never at all considers whether or not anything be existentially true, or not. But now suppose that mathematics strikes upon a snag; and that one mathematician says that it is evident that a consequence follows from a hypothesis, while another mathematician says it evidently does not. Here, then, the mathematicians find themselves suddenly abutting against brute fact; for certainly a dispute is not a rational consequence of anything. True, this fact, this dispute, is no part of mathematics. Yet it would seem to give occasion for an appeal to logic, which is generally a science of fact, being a science of truth; and whether or not there be any such thing as truth is a question of fact. However, because this dispute relates merely to the consequence of a hypothesis, the mere careful study of the hypothesis, which is pure mathematics, resolves it; and after all, it turns out that there was no occasion for the intervention of a science of reasoning.

It is often said that the truths of mathematics are infallible. So they are, if you mean practical infallibility,

infallibility such as that of conscience. They appear even as theoretically infallible, if they are viewed through spectacles that cut off the rays of blunder. I never yet met with boy or man whose addition of a long column, of fifty to a hundred lines, was absolutely infallible, so that adding it a second time could in no degree increase one's confidence in the result, nor ought to do so. The addition of that column is, however, merely a repetition of $1+1=2$; so that, however improbable it may be, there is a certain finite probability that everybody who has ever performed this addition of 1 and 1 has blundered, except on those very occasions on which we are accustomed to suppose (on grounds of probability merely) that they *did* blunder. Looked at in this light, every mathematical inference is merely a matter of probability. At any rate, in the sense in which anything in mathematics is certain, it is most certain that the whole mathematical world has often fallen into error, and that, in some cases, such errors have stood undetected for a couple of millennia. But no case is adducible in which the science of logic has availed to set mathematicians right or to save them from tripping. On the contrary, attention once having been called to a supposed inferential blunder in mathematics, short time has ever elapsed before the whole mathematical world has been in accord, either that the step was correct, or else that it was fallacious; and this without appeal to logic, but merely by the careful review of the mathematics as such. Thus, historically mathematics does not, as *a priori* it cannot, stand in need of any separate science of reasoning.

But mathematics is the only science which can be said to stand in no need of philosophy, excepting, of course, some branches of philosophy itself. It so happens that at this very moment the dependence of physics upon philosophy is illustrated by several questions now on the *tapis*. The question of non-Euclidean geometry may be said to be closed. It is apparent now that geometry, while in its main outlines, it must ever remain within the borders of philosophy, since it depends and must depend upon the scrutinizing of every-day experience, yet at certain special points it stretches over into the domain of physics. Thus, space, as far as we can see, has three dimensions; but are we quite sure that the corpuscles into which atoms are now minced have not room enough to wiggle a little in a fourth? Is physical space hyperbolic, that is, infinite and limited, or is it elliptic, that is, finite and unlimited? Only the exactest measurements upon the stars can decide. Yet even with them the question cannot be answered without recourse to philosophy. But a question at this moment under consideration by physicists is whether matter consists ultimately of minute solids, or whether it consists merely of vortices of an ultimate fluid. The third possibility, which there seems to be reason to suspect is the true one, that it may consist of vortices in a fluid which itself consists of far minuter solids, these, however, being themselves vortices of a fluid, itself consisting of ultimate solids, and so on in endless alternation, has hardly been broached. The question as it stands must evidently depend upon what we ought to conclude from everyday, unspecialized observations, and particularly upon a question of logic. Another still warmer controversy is whether or not it is proper to endeavor to find a mechanical explanation of electricity, or whether it is proper, on the contrary, to leave the differential equations of electrodynamics as the last word of science. This is manifestly only to be decided by a scientific philosophy very different from the amateurish, superficial stuff in which the contestants are now entangling themselves. A third pretty well defended opinion, by the way, is that instead of explaining electricity by molar dynamics, molar dynamics ought to be explained as a special consequence of the laws of electricity. Another appeal to philosophy was not long ago virtually made by the eminent electrician, the lamented Hertz, who wished to explain force, in general, as a consequence of unseen constraints. Philosophy alone can pronounce for or against such a theory. I will not undertake to anticipate questions which have not yet emerged; otherwise, I might suggest that chemists must ere long be making appeal to philosophy to decide whether compounds are held together by force or by some other agency. In biology, besides the old logico-metaphysical dispute about the reality of classifications, the momentous question of evolution has unmistakable dependence on philosophy. Then again, caryocinesis has emboldened some naturalists, having certain philosophical leanings, to rebel against the empire of experimental physiology. The origin of life is another topic where philosophy asserts itself; and with this I close my list, not at all because I have mentioned all the points at which just now the physical sciences are influenced by a philosophy, such as it is, but simply because I have mentioned enough of them for my present purpose.

The dependence of the psychical sciences upon philosophy is no less manifest. A few years ago, indeed, regenerate psychology, in the flush of her first success, not very wisely proposed to do without metaphysics; but I think that today psychologists generally perceive the impossibility of such a thing. It is true that the psychical sciences are not quite so dependent upon metaphysics as are the physical sciences; but, by way of compensation, they must lean more upon logic. The mind works by final causation, and final causation is logical causation. Note, for example, the intimate bearing of logic upon grammatical syntax. Moreover, everything in the psychical sciences is inferential. Not the smallest fact about the mind can be directly perceived as psychical. An emotion is directly felt as a bodily state, or else it is only known inferentially. That a thing is agreeable appears to direct observation as a character of an object, and it is only by inference that it is referred to the mind. If this statement be disputed (and some will dispute it), all the more need is there for the intervention of logic. Very difficult problems of inference are continually emerging in the psychical sciences. In psychology, there are such questions as free-will and innate ideas; in linguistics, there is the question of the origin of language, which must be settled before linquistics takes its final form. The whole business of deriving ancient history from documents that are always insufficient and, even when not conflicting, frequently pretty obviously false, must be carried on under the supervision of logic, or else be badly done.

The influence of philosophy upon the practical sciences is less direct. It is only here and there that it can be detected; and ethics is the division of philosophy which most concerns these sciences. Ethics is courteously invited to make a suggestion now and then in law, jurisprudence, and sociology. Its sedulous exclusion from diplomacy and economics is immense folly. We are unhappily debarred from calling this folly stupendous or egregious, because it is merely the ordinary blindness of those who profoundly believe that lies are the most wholesome of diet, who, as Edgar Poe sagaciously said, when they get home, have once locked themselves in their several chambers, have undressed, knelt down by the bedside and said their prayers, got into bed, and blown out the candle, then, at length, and not till then, indulge in one veracious wink—the only veracious act of the day—and lull themselves to sleep with an inward ditty that Right is a silly thing without wealth or vigor in this work-a-day world. One day man shall start up out of his slumber to see by broad daylight that that despised idea has all along been the one irresistible power. Then may begin an era when it is counted within the practical sciences, one and all—when, in a word, a man will not design a stove nor order a coat without stopping first and sifting out his real desire—and it is prophecy as simple as *Barbara*, that, when that comes to pass, those sciences will answer even their lower and nearest purposes far more perfectly than at present they do. So, at any rate, the student of minute logic will be forced to think.

[281]

PENN, WILLIAM

PENN, WILLIAM (1644-1718). The part that William Penn played in making freedom of conscience prevail in America is of primary importance, even granted that many other men and groups of people have struggled for the same cause. As soon as he had been converted to Quakerism, he gave powerful expression to his longing for freedom of worship and his opposition to religious intolerance. He was ready to sacrifice his own liberty for his faith, and while in prison, he told his jailer that he "scorned that religion which is not worth suffering for, and able to sustain those that are afflicted for it." But when he himself became the ruler over a territory that now is a state of the Union, second in its population, he provided that no one should be obliged "to frequent or maintain any religious worship, place or ministry contrary" to his conscience. Many of his provisions became basic to corresponding articles in the Constitution of the United States.

A curious combination of circumstances enabled Penn to undertake what he called "a holy experiment" and to establish a "theocratic democracy," different from all the other great British colonies in America. The inheritance of a claim for money advanced to the Crown by his father, Admiral Sir William Penn, gave him the opportunity of acquiring the territory of Pennsylvania and of founding there a state in accordance with his religious and political ideas. Without this opportunity, Penn would have been no more than an agitator, however influential and self-denying, confined to an environment which did not promise great success, or else merely the author of a Utopian scheme. He could not secure permanent realization of his ideal, but he established and maintained his government "without ever drawing a sword." His treaties with the Indians aroused even the admiration of Voltaire, who praised them because they were "not ratified by an oath and were never infringed."

Penn was a religious perfectionist and a man of the world. He wrote with great clarity of his religious experiences, but his interests were not limited to religion and theology. Many of his works reveal great erudition. Religious tolerance was the cornerstone of his political system, in which fundamental and circumstantial laws are distinguished. He repeatedly emphasized that "the political union of loyal citizens does not depend upon unity of belief."

THE world is the stage in which all men do act for eternity, and every venture of this brings its true weight of eternal life or death.

By revelation we understand the discovery and illumination of the light and spirit of God relating to those things that properly and immediately concern the daily information and satisfaction of our souls in the way of our duty to Him and our neighbors.

As there is this natural and intelligent spirit by which man is daily informed of the concerns of mortal life, so is a divine principle communicated to him, which we call the Light and that does illuminate and discover to his understanding the condition of his soul, and gives him a true knowledge of what is good, what he himself is, and what is regarded at his hands, either in obeying or suffering.

I know no religion that destroys courtesy, civility and kindness.

All men have reason, but all men are not reasonable. Is it the fault of the grain in the granary that it yields no increase, or of the talent in the napkin that it is not improved?

Conscience, truly speaking, is no other than the sense a man has, or judgment he makes of his duty to God, according to the understanding God gives him of his will.

Justice is the means of peace betwixt the government and the people and one man and company and another.

Liberty without obedience is confusion, and obedience without liberty is slavery.

Liberty of conscience is every man's natural right, and he who is deprived of it is a slave in the midst of the greatest liberty.

[282]

PERICLES

PERICLES (495-429 B.C.). Pericles' name is inseparably connected with a period that is generally considered the height of ancient Greek civilization. During the time he ruled Athens, the Parthenon was built, sculptors like Phidias, Myron, Polycletus, painters like Zeuxis, Parrhasius and Polygnotus, dramatists like Aeschylus, Sophocles and Euripides, created their immortal works, and Socrates began to meditate about the value of life. Pericles himself was taught philosophy by Anaxagoras. He entrusted to Protagoras an important mission. He developed what in Athens' democracy became of lasting political and humanitarian value, though he could not remove its shortcomings. As a statesman, Pericles has been judged differently. While Thucydides exalts him, Aristoteles and Isocrates think that Pericles' policy was not in Athens' best interest. Modern historians hold that his foreign policy was a failure but that he later learned to calculate the forces of Athens' adversaries more rightly. Even his enemies have recognized that Pericles never resorted to the tricks of a demagogue. As a speaker he was regarded by his contemporaries as the most powerful they knew or could even imagine. He was not a frequent orator but when he delivered a speech, his political success was almost certain. Despite all rivalries, he was elected commander-in-chief for fifteen terms. Until his last years his authority in matters of state was supreme.

In 430, at the close of the first year of the Peloponnesian War, which ended with Sparta's victory over Athens, Pericles, in an address celebrating the memory of the citizen-soldiers who were killed in action, defended Athens' democratic way of life.

THE DEMOCRATIC WAY OF LIFE

I WILL speak first of our ancestors, for it is right and becoming that now, when we are lamenting the dead, a tribute should be paid to their memory. There has never been a time when they did not inhabit this land, which by their valor they have handed down from generation to generation, and we have received from them a free state. But if they were worthy of praise, still more were our fathers, who added to their inheritance, and after many a struggle transmitted to us, their sons, this great empire. And we ourselves, as-

917

sembled here today, who are still most of us in the vigor of life, have chiefly done the work of improvement, and have richly endowed our city with all things, so that she is sufficient for herself both in peace and war. Of the military exploits by which our various possessions were acquired, or of the energy with which we or our fathers drove back the tide of war, Hellenic or Barbarian, I will not speak, for the tale would be long and is familiar to you. But before I praise the dead, I should like to point out by what principles of action we rose to power, and under what institutions and through what manner of life our empire became great. For I conceive that such thoughts are not unsuited to the occasion, and that this numerous assembly of citizens and strangers may profitably listen to them.

Our form of government does not enter into rivalry with the institutions of others. We do not copy our neighbors, but are an example to them. It is true that we are called a democracy, for the administration is in the hands of the many and not of the few. But while the law secures equal justice to all alike in their private disputes, the claim of excellence is also recognized; and when a citizen is in any way distinguished, he is preferred to the public service, not as a matter of privilege but as the reward of merit. Neither is poverty a bar, but a man may benefit his country whatever be the obscurity of his condition. There is no exclusiveness in our public life, and in our private intercourse we are not suspicious of one another, nor angry with our neighbor if he does what he likes; we do not put on sour looks at him which, though harmless, are not pleasant. While we are thus unconstrained in our private intercourse, a spirit of reverence pervades our public acts; we are prevented from doing wrong by respect for authority and for the laws, having an especial regard to those which are ordained for the protection of the injured as well as to those unwritten laws which bring upon the transgressor of them the reprobation of the general sentiment.

And we have not forgotten to provide for our weary

spirits many relaxations from toil; we have regular games and sacrifices throughout the year; at home the style of our life is refined; and the delight which we daily feel in all these things helps to banish melancholy. Because of the greatness of our city the fruits of the whole earth flow in upon us; so that we enjoy the goods of other countries as freely as of our own.

We are lovers of the beautiful, yet simple in our tastes, and we cultivate the mind without loss of manliness. Wealth we employ, not for talk and ostentation, but when there is a real use for it. To avow poverty with us is no disgrace; the true disgrace is in doing nothing to avoid it. An Athenian citizen does not neglect the state because he takes care of his own household; and even those of us who are engaged in business have a very fair idea of politics. We alone regard a man who takes no interest in public affairs, not as a harmless, but as a useless character; and if few of us are originators, we are all sound judges of a policy. The great impediment to action is, in our opinion, not discussion, but the want of that knowledge which is gained by discussion preparatory to action. For we have a peculiar power of thinking before we act and of acting too, whereas other men are courageous from ignorance, but hesitate upon reflection. And they are surely to be esteemed the bravest spirits who, having the clearest sense both of the pains and pleasures of life, do not on that account shrink from danger. In doing good, again, we are unlike others—we make our friends by conferring, not by receiving, favors.

To sum up: I say that Athens is the school of Hellas, and that the individual Athenian in his own person seems to have the power of adapting himself to the most varied forms of action with the utmost versatility and grace. This is no passing and idle word, but truth and fact; and the assertion is verified by the position to which these qualities have raised the state. For in the hour of trial, Athens alone among her contemporaries is superior to the report of her. No enemy who comes against her is indignant at the reverses which he sustains at the hands of such a city; no subject complains that his masters are unworthy of him. And we shall assuredly not be without witnesses; there are mighty monuments of our power which will make us the wonder of all ages.

We have compelled every land and every sea to open a path for our valor, and have everywhere planted eternal memorials of our friendship and of our enmity. Such is the city for whose sake these men fought and died; they could not bear to think that she might be taken from them; and every one of us who survive should gladly toil on her behalf.

[283]

PERRY, RALPH BARTON

PERRY, RALPH BARTON (1876-   ). From his study of Kant, Perry, the author of the classic biography of William James, proceeded to a revision of the critical approach to natural knowledge. He was one of the most active members of the group of American philosophers who, about 1910, elaborated the program of the "New Realism." However, soon thereafter he dissented from its majority and, banishing "moral and spiritual ontology" of any kind, arrived at a point which, based upon a philosophy of disillusionment, allowed him to take a stand on the "hazard of faith."

In his booklet *The Hope for Immortality* (1935), Perry confesses to be empty-handed as far as theoretical evidence or even arguments for the probability of immortality are concerned. But he holds that, even in default of knowledge, belief is sometimes justified by the insistence or depth of the need which it satisfies. Assuming a less extremist attitude, Perry later explained his belief in freedom, which he defines as the exercise of enlightened choice. Freedom constitutes the dignity of Man but is also his generic attribute. Cultivation of freedom therefore does not set a man apart from his fellows but implies a sense of universal kinship. Consequently freedom and humanitarian consciousness, far from excluding one another, are inseparable. Philosophy, the social sciences and history are justified only as far as they contribute to the growth of freedom and humanitarian solidarity. The natural sciences can be regarded as part of humanitarian culture in so far as

920

they reveal the real world as a condition or source of human life. Neither does utility as such constitute the humanitarian character of a science, nor is science as such inescapably human. The philosopher of disillusionment maintains that humanity is always escapable. But, for that reason, Perry is an ardent advocate of a militant democracy which must be "total but not totalitarian."

LOVE

LOVE means . . . a favorable interest in the satisfaction of a second interest. In the present context it is assumed that the second interest is the interest of a second person. Love begins and ends abroad. That "charity begins at home" is one of those many proverbs which have been coined by the devil to flatter human weakness. Love is, in the next place, essentially *indulgent;* it coincides with, and supports, the interest which is its object. The success or defeat of the loving interest will be a function of what is judged to be the success or defeat of the loved interest. Other-love, in this sense, may be directed to any one, or to the whole system, of the second person's interest. Where love is directed to the whole person it may oppose one of that person's particular interests, in so far as the person is imperfectly integrated. Where a person suffers from internal conflict, another's love may side with the integral self against the insubordinate element; but if love is to be indulgent, there must already be such an integral self in some form or stage of development. Love, in other words, is an interested support of another's preexisting and independently existing interest.

There are several common meanings of love which this definition excludes. In the first place, love is neither approving nor censorious. It does not prescribe the object of the loved interest, but desires that that interest shall have its object *whatever* that object. Suppose a son to desire fame; then the father's desire for the son's fame, if founded on the father's admiration of fame, is not love; nor is it love if the father desires that the son shall substitute for fame some other object, such as knowledge, which he, the father, prefers. Action towards another dictated by the agent's belief that he knows better what is good for the other than does the other himself, may be praiseworthy, but it is not love. The true quality of love is to be found in that sensitive imagination which can find its way into the secret sources of a man's joy and sorrow. Similarly, censoriousness, though it may be just, is not love. Love does not rebuke the sinner, or rejoice in his merited punishment; but grieves for him, and seeks to *bring him in,* as the shepherd seeks his lost sheep. Love, like Thomson's "Hound of Heaven," follows its object relentlessly into every corner of the universe and refuses to be offended or repelled.

The support of another's interest that springs from a sense of plenitude and power, or that looks to bind the other in gratitude, is not love. Nor is it love when an appetite feeds upon another individual, even though the other be of the same species. So-called sex-love may be as unloving as cannibalism. Finally, love must have an object other than itself. To love another's love of oneself, supposing oneself to consist only in love of the other, would be meaningless, even though it occurs in poetry and fiction. The circle must be broken at some point by an interest directed to an object, in order that there may be something for love to indulge. What seems to be circular love is the gratification afforded to each of two individuals by the presence of the other. Other-love finds itself most purely embodied in parental love, for the very reason that it is commonly one-sided or unreciprocated. Reciprocity adds to the intensity of love, but tends to impair its purity through introducing an element of sensuous gratification or of self-reference.

Love in the present sense consists essentially, then, in an activity which supports the interested activity of another person; seeking to promote that other person's achievement of what he desires, or enjoyment of what he likes. Universal love would be such a disposition on the part of one person towards all persons. If it is psychologically possible (in the sense of the general capacity of human nature) towards one,

it is psychologically possible towards two or more; or towards all members of a class, such as the family, the nation,
mankind, or sentient creatures. This attitude of general
kindly interest, or of amiability, has its negative form, as
in Lincoln's maxim, "with malice toward none, with charity for all"; and its positive form, as in good Samaritanism
and humanity. A personal integration dominated by such a
purpose is known in the tradition of moral philosophy as
'good will.'   [284]

PESTALOZZI, JOHANN HEINRICH

PESTALOZZI, JOHANN HEINRICH (1746-1827). Pestalozzi is
generally regarded as the father of modern European pedagogics.
Born in Switzerland, an ardent Swiss patriot, he not only influenced the educational system of his own country and of Germany,
but also inspired French and Scandinavian educators, and men like
Horace Mann and Henry Barnard in the United States.

It is true, Pestalozzi could never heed to order in his own
house or in his enterprises, and neglected his appearance to a
degree no progressive educator could approve if one of his pupils
did so. But he was an extraordinarily gifted leader of young people. He thoroughly knew and loved children, and also knew and
loved humanity. His educational ideas are embedded in a totality
of ideas on the perfection of Man. Indignant of individual wickedness and terrified by events of contemporary history, Pestalozzi
never lost confidence in what he considered true human nature.
His pedagogical skill was founded upon a large experience. He
had been not only a teacher of children and a teacher of teachers,
but also a trustee of orphans, and it was from the observation of
abandoned children that he learned the most.

Educational ardor made Pestalozzi write philosophical treatises, as it also caused him to write novels, the best known of
which is *Lienhard and Gertrude*, which was widely read. By no
means did he claim to be a philosopher. He was neither a rationalist nor an intellectual, and he declared that his whole work was
a work of the heart, not of understanding. He even felt uneasy
while writing on philosophical problems. But he thought it necessary in order to explain his aims and methods which are conditional
on broad views on the destiny of humanity. He considered man
as an animal, a member of society and an ethical power. After

trying to outline the course of nature in the development of humanity, he proceeded to the establishment of an ethical humanism which has to dominate the education of children and the conduct of adults—their economic, political and spiritual life. Development of the mind, the heart and manual work were the principal points of Pestalozzi's education. He did not ignore the fact that any political community is threatened by inner contradictions; but he hoped to overcome many difficulties by pedagogical care.

WHAT I AM AS THE WORK OF MYSELF

Is it true that state of nature is to civilization, and civilization is to morality as childhood is to years of apprenticeship and these to mature age?

Is it true that I could never obtain a disposition to morality without the error of my sensual enjoyment and without the wrong of my social claims?

Is it true that truth and Justice are the exclusive property of that disposition?

Is it true that this disposition is exclusively the matter of the individual? That morality in relation to two people, as a matter of these two, cannot subsist? That the natural state does not know that disposition, and society does not rely on it?

Is it true that animal proximity or distance of moral objects is the definite natural turn to true morality?

Is it true that my civil duty as such does not make me moral?

Is it true that everything I owe to my community or as a member of the masses incites me to immorality?

All that is true!

In the individual, morality is closely connected with its animal nature and its social relations. But essentially it is entirely founded upon the freedom of my will—that means upon that quality of myself through which I feel myself independent of my animal greeds.

As a moral being I walk in the way to perfection of myself, and thus I become capable of overcoming the contradictions that seem to lie in my nature.

[285]

PHILO JUDAEUS

PHILO JUDAEUS (About 25 B.C.—Before 50 A.D.). The importance of Philo to the history of philosophy is incomparably greater than the power of his personality or the relevance of his personal thinking. For about seventeen centuries his example was, consciously and unconsciously, followed by all European thinkers, notwithstanding their differences, no matter whether they were nominalists or realists, idealists or naturalists, orthodox or heretics, and today Catholic Neo-Scholasticism is still following him, not to mention his influence on Islamic and Jewish philosophy.

Philo was the first thinker to introduce into epistemology, metaphysics, physics and ethics the problem of reconciling speculative thought with the data of Biblical revelation; or, rather, he established these data, especially their characteristics of God, Man and Nature as the perfect truth with which the philosopher had to harmonize the results of his thinking. In this way, Philo created a spiritual situation, completely unknown in pagan Greek philosophy which had not to regard Sacred Scripture as the standard and source of truth. The impact of the belief in the pagan gods on philosophical thoughts had only occasionally caused conflicts and had become negligible. As a positive support of thinking, as a source of knowledge, the belief in the pagan gods was of no account even when some philosophers used the gods as symbols of forces which were comprehended by speculative methods. Philo initiated a new era in the history of philosophy, the earliest documents of which can be noted in the Gospel of St. John. Its great development begins with the Fathers of the Church, comprises the whole Middle Ages and part of modern times, Descartes included. It was Spinoza, a Jew like Philo, who removed Biblical revelation from the realm of philosophy.

But, unlike Spinoza, Philo, a contemporary of Jesus Christ and St. Paul, remained a faithful, professing Jew. He devoted the main part of his life to the interpretation of the Pentateuch and to the defense of the Jewish faith against attacks on the part of gentile critics by explaining the essence of Judaism from the historical, philosophical, ethical and juridical points of view. When he was elected leader of a Jewish embassy to Rome in 40 A.D., he tried also to defend his co-religionists against the arbitrary power of Emperor Caligula.

Although Philo borrowed much from Greek philosophers, his

system deviates widely from purely Greek lines. It is the doctrine of monotheistic mysticism, teaching that human mind is capable, by intuition, not by reasoning, to apprehend God's existence but not His nature. In this way, Philo was the first to outline a psychology of faith.

ALLEGORICAL MEANING
OF THE DOWNFALL OF MANKIND

Its juggleries and deceits pleasure does not venture to bring directly to the man, but first offers them to the woman, and by her means to the man; acting in a very natural and sagacious manner. For in human beings the mind occupies the rank of the man, and the sensations that of the woman. And pleasure joins itself to and associates itself with the sensations first of all, and then by their means cajoles also the mind, which is the dominant part. For, after each of the senses has been subjected to the charms of pleasure, and has learnt to delight in what is offered to it, the sight being fascinated by varieties of colors and shapes, the hearing by harmonious sounds, the taste by the sweetness of flowers, and the smell by the delicious fragrance of the odors which are brought before it, these all having received these offerings, like handmaids, bring them to the mind as their master, leading with them persuasion as an advocate, to warn it against rejecting any of them whatever. And the mind being immediately caught by the bait, becomes a subject instead of a ruler, and a slave instead of a master, and an exile instead of a citizen, and a mortal instead of an immortal. For we must altogether not be ignorant that pleasure, being like a courtesan or mistress, is eager to meet with a lover, and seeks for panders in order by their means to catch a lover. And the sensations are her panders, and conciliate love to her, and she employing them as baits, easily brings the mind into subjection to her. And the sensations conveying within the mind the things which have been seen externally, explain and display the forms of each of them setting their seal upon a similar affection. For the mind is like wax, and receives the impressions of appearances through the sensations, by means of which it makes itself master of the body, which of itself it would not be able to do, as I have already said.

And those who have previously become the slaves of pleasure immediately receive the wages of this miserable and incurable passion. For the woman having received vehement pains, partly in her travail, and partly such as are a rapid succession of agonies during the other portions of her life, and especially with reference to the bringing forth and bringing up of her children, to their diseases and their health, to their good or evil fortune, to an extent that utterly deprives her of her freedom and subjects her to the dominion of the man who is her companion, finds it unavoidable to obey all his commands. And the man in his turn endures toils and labors, and continual sweats, in order to the providing of himself with necessaries, and he also bears the deprivation of all those spontaneous good things which the earth was originally taught to produce without requiring the skill of the farmer, and he is subjected to a state in which he lives in incessant labor, for the purpose of seeking for food and means of subsistence, in order to avoid perishing by hunger.

[286]

PICO DELLA MIRANDOLA, GIOVANNI

PICO DELLA MIRANDOLA, GIOVANNI (1463-1494). Popular legends and scholarly tradition used to represent Pico as a resuscitated Greek god who had taught, by means of Platonic ideas, a new religion of worldly individualism. But, in fact, Pico, who charmed his greatest contemporaries and was admired by Reuchlin and Erasmus, by Lorenzo of Medici and Savonarola, was no pagan thinker, no heretic, no pantheist. His great aim was to reconcile all philosophies which, according to him, conflicted with one another only in appearance. He especially tried to synthesize Plato and Aristotle, and constantly refused to depreciate Aquinas or Scholasticism in general, although his aesthetic sense was captivated by Platonism.

But it was the Jewish Cabala that inspired him most. He held that Christian faith was not fundamentally different from the Cabala and expressed his strong conviction that every great phil-

927

osophical or religious doctrine uses esoteric wisdom to veil secret teachings, which only the cabalist scholar is able to unveil.

At the age of 24, Pico planned to challenge all scholars of the known world by defending 900 conclusions or theses in a public disputation at Rome, but papal authorities prevented him from doing so and condemned thirteen of his conclusions.

Pico's metaphysics, despite its Platonic wrappings, depended largely on Aquinas as well as on the Cabala. His *Heptaplas* is a commentary on the Cabalist doctrine of Sefiroth, the ten creative powers. His last work *De Ente et Uno* (On Being and One) was inspired by his Hebrew teacher Eliah Del Medigo who had written a book *De Esse, Essentia et Uno*.

Pico was one of the most elegant stylists. He had an extraordinary talent for striking formulas. Thus he expressed his standpoint in the short sentence: "No philosophy turns us away from the trend to mysticism; philosophy seeks, theology finds, religion possesses truth." Of princely descent, related to almost all ruling dynasties in Italy, handsome, learned, an untiring worker, a reliable friend, Pico enchanted everyone he met, except the officers of papal jurisdiction.

THE ATTRIBUTES OF GOD
AND HUMAN CONDUCT OF LIFE

WE conceive God first of all as the perfect totality of act, the plenitude of being itself. It follows from this concept that He is one, that a term opposite to Him cannot be imagined. See then how much they err who fashion many first principles, many gods! At once it is clear that God is truth itself. For, what can He have which appears to be and is not, He who is being itself? It follows with certainty that He is truth itself. But He is likewise goodness itself. Three conditions are required for the good as Plato writes in his *Philebus*: perfection, sufficiency, and desirability. Now the good which we conceive will be perfect, since nothing can be lacking to that which is everything; it will be sufficient, since nothing can be lacking to those who possess that in which they will find all; it will be desirable, since from Him and in Him are all things which can possibly be desired. God is therefore the fullest plenitude of being, undivided unity, the most solid truth, the most perfect good. This, if I am not mistaken, is that quaternity, by which Pythagoras swore and which he called the principle of ever-flowing nature. Indeed, in this quarternity, which is One God, we have demonstrated the principle of all things. But we also swear by that which is holy, true, divine; now, what more true, more holy, more divine than these four characters? If we attribute them to God as the cause of things, the entire order is inverted. First He will be one, because He is conceived in Himself before He is conceived as cause. Then He will be good, true, and finally being (*ens*). For since the final cause has priority over the exemplary cause, and that over the efficient (we first desire to have something to protect us from the weather, then we conceive the idea of a house, and finally we construct one by making it materially), if the good pertains to the final cause, the true to the exemplary, being to the efficient, God as cause will have first of all the attribute of good, then of true, and finally of being. We shall here terminate these brief remarks on a subject teeming with many important problems.

Let us, lest we speak more of other things than of ourselves, take care that, while we scrutinize the heights, we do not live too basely, in a manner unworthy of beings to whom has been given the divine power of inquiring into things divine. We ought, then, to consider assiduously that our mind, with its divine privileges, cannot have a mortal origin nor can find happiness otherwise than in the possession of things divine, and that the more it elevates and inflames itself with the contemplation of the Divine by renouncing earthly preoccupations while yet a traveller on this pilgrimage here below, the more it will approach felicity. The best precept, then, which this discussion can give us, seems to be that, if we wish to be happy we ought to imitate the most happy and blessed of all beings, God, by establishing in ourselves unity, truth, and goodness.

What disturbs the peace of unity is ambition, the vice that steals away from itself the soul which abandons itself to it, tearing it, as it were, in pieces, and dispersing it. The resplendent light of truth, who will not lose it in the mud, in the darkness of lust? Avarice and cupidity steal from us goodness, for it is the peculiar property of goodness to communicate to others the goods which it possesses. Thus, when Plato asked himself why God had created the world, he answered: 'Because He was good.' These are the three vices: pride of life, concupiscence of the flesh, concupiscence of the eyes, which, as St. John says, are of the world and not of the Father who is unity, goodness, and truth indeed.

[287]

PLANCK, MAX

PLANCK, MAX (1858-1947). The first revolutionary novelty since Newton was introduced into the science of physics by Planck, the founder of the quantum theory. Before Planck, physical thinking rested on the assumption that all causal interactions are continuous. Planck, after studying entropy and radiation, showed that in a light or heat wave of frequency, the energy of the wave does not vary continuously, and established an "elementary quantum of action" of a definite numerical value as the unit of these variations. Quantum theory has made an inroad upon the concept of mass but it is most important in the regular occurrences of all atomic processes.

Planck's elementary quantum of action could not be welded in the framework of classical physics. All theoretical difficulties were removed by Einstein's special theory of relativity which was published in 1905, five years after Planck had established his quantum theory. Through the cooperation of Planck and Einstein a new picture of the world emerged. Its elements are no longer chemical atoms but electrons and protons whose mutual interactions are governed by the velocity of light and the elementary quantum of action.

Planck regarded the quanta as the building blocks of the universe and as proof of the existence in nature of something real and independent of every human measurement. He rejected positivism and believed in the possibility of reconciling natural science and religion.

SCIENCE AND FAITH

A VAST volume of experiences reaches each one of us in the course of a year; such is the progress made in the various means of communication that new impressions from far and near rush upon us in a never-ending stream. It is true that many of them are forgotten as quickly as they arrive and that every trace of them is often effaced within a day; and it is as well that it should be so: if it were otherwise modern man would be fairly suffocated under the weight of different impressions. Yet every person who wishes to lead more than an ephemeral intellectual existence must be impelled by the very variety of these kaleidoscopic changes to seek for some element of permanence, for some lasting intellectual possession to afford him a *point d'appui* in the confusing claims of everyday life. In the younger generation this impulse manifests itself in a passionate desire for a comprehensive philosophy of the world; a desire which looks for satisfaction in groping attempts turning in every direction where peace and refreshment for a weary spirit is believed to reside.

It is the Church whose function it would be to meet such aspirations; but in these days its demands for an unquestioning belief serve rather to repel the doubters. The latter have recourse to more or less dubious substitutes, and hasten to throw themselves into the arms of one or other of the many prophets who appear preaching new gospels. It is surprising to find how many people even of the educated classes allow themselves to be fascinated by these new religions—beliefs which vary from the obscurest mysticism to the crudest superstition.

It would be easy to suggest that a philosophy of the world might be reached from a scientific basis; but such a suggestion is usually rejected by these seekers on the ground that the scientific view is bankrupt. There is an element of truth in this suggestion, and, indeed, it is entirely correct if the term science is taken in the traditional and still surviving sense where it implies a reliance on the understanding. Such a method, however, proves that those who adopt it have no sense of real science. The truth is very different. Anyone who has taken part in the building up of a branch of science is well aware from personal experience that every endeavor in this direction is guided by an unpretentious but essential principle. This principle is faith—a faith which looks ahead. It is said that science has no preconceived ideas: there is no saying that has been more thoroughly or more disastrously misunderstood. It is true that every branch of science must have an empirical foundation: but it is equally true that the essence of science does not consist in this raw material but in the manner in which it is used. The material always is incomplete: it consists of a number of parts which however numerous are discrete, and this is equally true of the tabulated figures of the natural sciences, and of the various documents of the intellectual sciences.

The material must therefore be completed, and this must be done by filling the gaps; and this in turn is done by means of associations of ideas. And associations of ideas are not the work of the understanding but the offspring of the investigator's imagination—an activity which may be described as faith, or, more cautiously, as a working hypothesis. The essential point is that its content in one way or another goes beyond the data of experience. The chaos of individual masses cannot be wrought into a cosmos without some harmonizing force and, similarly, the disjointed data of experience can never furnish a veritable science without the intelligent interference of a spirit actuated by faith. . . .

[288]

PLATO

PLATO (427-347 B.C.). For two thousand and three hundred years Plato's work has been a living force that has given to some the firmest certainty while causing creative unrest in the minds of others. Plato's ascendancy over the philosophers of ancient Greco-

Roman civilization was immense. It remained great in the Middle Ages, increased in the Renaissance as well as in the eras of Descartes, Berkeley and Hegel, and still today there are outstanding thinkers in America and Europe who adhere to his doctrine. The discussion about its real meaning has not come to an end, and entails re-examinations of the principal methods of modern science and philosophy.

The man whose influence was so deep and lasting is known to posterity by his nickname which means "the Broad." His real name was Aristocles. Belonging to one of the oldest and noblest families of Athens' aristocracy whose members used to take part in governing the state, Plato also felt a leaning toward statesmanship. However, his attempts to play a political role resulted in frustration and disappointment. To these painful experiences Plato reacted by founding and directing his "Academy" which was a University and a center of research as well as a training school for future political leaders. For Plato was convinced that any state must perish if its rulers were not philosophers, and philosophy meant to him the ability to perceive the world of Ideas, immaterial essences, Forms which contain the true and ultimate realities while the world of sensible things is only a vague, transitory and untrustworthy copy. Only the cognition of the Ideas enables man to act with wisdom. The rules of rightful conduct of human life were derived by Plato from the laws that rule the universe. Plato's criteria of human behavior were rooted in his metaphysical conceptions.

Although Plato constantly emphasized his conviction that true knowledge can be obtained only by cognition of the eternal and immutable Ideas or Forms, he by no means neglected the phenomena of change or the imperfect phases of knowledge which are given by sensations or expressed by mere opinions. He was a keen observer of daily life, acquainted with arts and crafts, versed in empirical sciences and literature. He was a tough warrior and sportsman. He even proved to be a clever traveling salesman who dealt in oil when he visited Egypt, and he succeeded well although he found the Egyptians to be extremely shrewd businessmen.

Every work published by Plato is written in the form of a dialogue. Most of them are full of dramatic life. Some are gay comedies. Speech has been given to both historical and fictitious persons but hardly ever to the author himself who attributed most of his own thoughts to his teacher Socrates. The discussions allow representation of various, even opposed, points of view. Their principal means of explanation is the dialectic whose function is to illustrate the logical consequences of a hypothesis. In order to explain ideas difficult to understand, or to elucidate a hypothesis impossible to be proved true, Plato often resorts to the use of a myth which elucidates a thought or truth by means of images.

Plato's doctrine contains the elements of a religion, of positive sciences, of a political system and of legislation. He recognized the complexity of the problems with which he dealt and was aware of the precariousness of the results of his thinking. Until his death he continued to develop his ideas.

GOVERNMENT BY PHILOSOPHERS

WE were inquiring into the nature of absolute justice and into the character of the perfectly just, and into injustice and the perfectly unjust, that we might have an ideal. We were to look at these in order that we might judge of our own happiness and unhappiness according to the standard which they exhibited and the degree in which we resembled them, but not with any view of showing that they could exist in fact.

True, he said.

Would a painter be any the worse because, after having delineated with consummate art an ideal of a perfectly beautiful man, he was unable to show that any such man could ever have existed?

He would be none the worse.

Well, and were we not creating an ideal of a perfect state?

To be sure.

And is our theory a worse theory because we are unable to prove the possibility of a city being ordered in the manner described?

Surely not, he replied.

That is the truth, I said. But if, at your request, I am to try and show how and under what conditions the possibility is highest, I must ask you, having this in view, to repeat your former admissions.

What admissions?

I want to know whether ideals are ever fully realized in

language? Does not the word express more than the fact, and must not the actual, whatever a man may think, always, in the nature of things, fall short of the truth? What do you say?

I agree.

Then you must not insist on my proving the actual state will in every respect coincide with the ideal: if we are only able to discover how a city may be governed nearly as we proposed, you will admit that we have discovered the possibility which you demand; and will be contented. I am sure that I should be contented—will not you?

Yes, I will.

Let me next endeavor to show what is that fault in states which is the cause of their present maladministration, and what is the least change which will enable a state to pass into the truer form; and let the change, if possible, be of one thing only, or, if not, of two; at any rate, let the changes be as few and slight as possible.

Certainly, he replied.

I think, I said, that there might be a reform of the state if only one change were made, which is not a slight or easy though still a possible one.

What is it? he said.

Now then, I said, I go to meet that which I liken to the greatest of the waves; yet shall the word be spoken, even though the wave break and drown me in laughter and dishonor; and do you mark my words.

Proceed.

I said: *Until philosophers are kings, or the kings and princes of this world have the spirit and power of philosophy, and political greatness and wisdom meet in one, and those commoner natures who pursue either to the exclusion of the other are compelled to stand aside, cities will never have rest from their evils,—no, nor the human race, as I believe, —and then only will this our state have a possibility of life and behold the light of day.* Such was the thought, my dear Glaucon, which I would fain have uttered if it had not seemed too extravagant; for to be convinced that in no other state can there be happiness private or public is indeed a hard thing.

*   *   *

And thus, Glaucon, after the argument has gone a weary way, the true and the false philosophers have at length appeared in view.

I do not think, he said, that the way could have been shortened.

I suppose not, I said; and yet I believe that we might have had a better view of both of them if the discussion could have been confined to this one subject and if there were not many other questions awaiting us, which he who desires to see in what respect the life of the just differs from that of the unjust must consider.

And what is the next question? he asked.

Surely, I said, the one which follows next in order. Inasmuch as philosophers only are able to grasp the eternal and unchangeable, and those who wander in the region of the many and variable are not philosophers, I must ask you which of the two classes should be the rulers of our state?

And how can we rightly answer that question?

Whichever of the two are best able to guard the laws and institutions of our state—let them be our guardians.

Very good.

Neither, I said, can there be any question that the guardian who is to keep anything should have eyes rather than no eyes?

There can be no question of that.

And are not those who are verily and indeed wanting in the knowledge of the true being of each thing, and who have in their souls no clear pattern, and are unable as with a painter's eye to look at the absolute truth and to that original to repair, and having perfect vision of the other world to order the laws about beauty, goodness, justice in this, if not already ordered, and to guard and preserve the order of them—are not such persons, I ask, simply blind?

Truly, he replied, they are much in that condition.

And shall they be our guardians when there are others who, besides being their equals in experience and falling short of them in no particular of virtue, also know the very truth of each thing?

There can be no reason, he said, for rejecting those who have this greatest of all great qualities; they must always have the first place unless they fail in some other respect.

Suppose then, I said, that we determine how far they can unite this and the other excellences.

By all means.

In the first place, as we began by observing, the nature of the philosopher has to be ascertained. We must come to an understanding about him, and, when we have done so, then, if I am not mistaken, we shall also acknowledge that such a union of qualities is possible and that those in whom they are united, and those only, should be rulers in the state.

What do you mean?

Let us suppose that philosophical minds always love knowledge of a sort which shows them the eternal nature not varying from generation and corruption.

Agreed.

And further, I said, let us agree that they are lovers of all true being; there is no part whether greater or less, or more or less honorable, which they are willing to renounce; as we said before of the lover and the man of ambition.

True.

And if they are to be what we were describing, is there not another quality which they should also possess?

What quality?

Truthfulness: they will never intentionally receive into their mind falsehood, which is their detestation, and they will love the truth.

Yes, that may be safely affirmed of them.

"May be," my friend, I replied, is not the word; say rather, "must be affirmed": for he whose nature is amorous of anything cannot help loving all that belongs or is akin to the object of his affections.

Right, he said.

And is there anything more akin to wisdom than truth?

How can there be?

Can the same nature be a lover of wisdom and a lover of falsehood?

Never.

The true lover of learning then must from his earliest youth, as far as in him lies, desire all truth?

Assuredly.

But then again, as we know by experience, he whose desires are strong in one direction will have them weaker in others; they will be like a stream which has been drawn off into another channel.

True.

He whose desires are drawn towards knowledge in every form will be absorbed in the pleasures of the soul, and will hardly feel bodily pleasure—I mean, if he be a true philosopher and not a sham one.

That is most certain.

Such a one is sure to be temperate and the reverse of covetous; for the motives which make another man desirous of having and spending, have no place in his character.

Very true.

Another criterion of the philosophical nature has also to be considered.

What is that?

There should be no secret corner of illiberality; nothing can be more antagonistic than meanness to a soul which is ever longing after the whole of things both divine and human.

Most true, he replied.

Then how can he who has magnificence of mind and is the spectator of all time and all existence, think much of human life?

He cannot.

Or can such a one account death fearful?

No indeed.

Then the cowardly and mean nature has no part in true philosophy?

Certainly not.

Or again: can he who is harmoniously constituted, who is not covetous or mean, or a boaster, or a coward—can he, I say, ever be unjust or hard in his dealings?

Impossible.

Then you will soon observe whether a man is just and gentle, or rude and unsociable; these are the signs which distinguish even in youth the philosophical nature from the unphilosophical.

True.

There is another point which should be remarked.

What point?

Whether he has or has not a pleasure in learning; for no one will love that which gives him pain, and in which after much toil he makes little progress.

Certainly not.

And again, if he is forgetful and retains nothing of what he learns, will he not be an empty vessel?

That is certain.

Laboring in vain, he must end in hating himself and his fruitless occupation?

Yes.

Then a soul which forgets cannot be ranked among genuine philosophic natures; we must insist that the philosopher should have a good memory?

Certainly.

And one more, the inharmonious and unseemly nature can only tend to disproportion?

Undoubtedly.

And do you consider truth to be akin to proportion or to disproportion?

To proportion.

Then, besides other qualities, we must try to find a

naturally well-proportioned and gracious mind, which will move spontaneously towards the true being of everything.

Certainly.

Well, and do not all these qualities, which we have been enumerating, go together, and are they not, in a manner, necessary to a soul, which is to have a full and perfect participation of being?

They are absolutely necessary, he replied.

And must not that be a blameless study which he only can pursue who has the gift of a good memory, and is quick to learn,—noble, gracious, the friend of truth, justice, courage, temperance, who are his kindred?

The god of jealousy himself, he said, could find no fault with such a study.

And to men like him, I said, when perfected by years and education, and to these only you will intrust the state.

Here Adeimantus interposed and said: To these statements, Socrates, no one can offer a reply; but when you talk in this way, a strange feeling passes over the minds of your hearers: They fancy that they are led astray a little at each step in the argument, owing to their own want of skill in asking and answering questions; these littles accumulate, and at the end of the discussion they are found to have sustained a mighty overthrow and all their former notions appear to be turned upside down. And as unskilful players of draughts are at last shut up by their more skilful adversaries and have no piece to move, so they too find themselves shut up at last; for they have nothing to say in this new game of which words are the counters; and yet all the time they are in the right. The observation is suggested to me by what is now occurring. For any one of us might say, that although in words he is not able to meet you at at each step of the argument, he sees as a fact that the votaries of philosophy, when they carry on the study, not only in youth as a part of education, but as the pursuit of their maturer years, most of them become strange monsters, not to say utter rogues, and that those who may be considered the best of them are made useless to the world by the very study which you extol.

Well, and do you think that those who say so are wrong?

I cannot tell, he replied; but I should like to know what is your opinion.

Hear my answer; I am of opinion that they are quite right.

Then how can you be justified in saying that cities will not cease from evil until philosophers rule in them, when philosophers are acknowledged by us to be of no use to them?

You ask a question, I said, to which a reply can only be given in a parable.

Yes, Socrates; and that is a way of speaking to which you are not at all accustomed, I suppose.

I perceive, I said, that you are vastly amused at having plunged me into such a hopeless discussion; but now hear the parable, and then you will be still more amused at the meagerness of my imagination: for the manner in which the best men are treated in their own states is so grievous that no single thing on earth is comparable to it; and therefore, if I am to plead their cause, I must have recourse to fiction, and put together a figure made up of many things, like the fabulous unions of goats and stags which are found in pictures. Imagine then a fleet or a ship in which there is a captain who is taller and stronger than any of the crew, but he is a little deaf and has a similar infirmity in sight, and his knowledge of navigation is not much better. The sailors are quarreling with one another about the steering—every one is of opinion that he has a right to steer, though he has never learned the art of navigation and cannot tell who taught him or when he learned, and will further assert that it cannot be taught, and they are ready to cut in pieces any one who says the contrary. They throng about the captain, begging and praying him to commit the helm to them; and if at any time they do not prevail, but others are preferred to them, they kill the others or throw them overboard, and having first chained up the noble captain's senses with drink or some narcotic drug, they mutiny and take possession of the ship and make free with the stores; thus, eating and drinking, they proceed on their voyage in such manner as might be expected of them. Him who is their partisan and cleverly aids them in their plot for getting the ship out of the captain's hands into their own whether by force or persuasion, they compliment with the name of sailor, pilot, able seaman, and abuse the other sort of man, whom they call a good-for-nothing; but that the true pilot must pay attention to the year and seasons and sky and stars and winds, and whatever else belongs to his art, if he intends to be really qualified for the command of a ship, and that he must and will be the steerer, whether other people like or not—the possibility of this union of authority with the steerer's art has never seriously entered into their thoughts or been made part of their calling. Now in vessels which are in a state of mutiny and by sailors who are mutineers, how will the true pilot be regarded? Will he not be called by them a prater, a star-gazer, a good-for-nothing?

Of course, said Adeimantus.

Then you will hardly need, I said, to hear the interpretation of the figure, which describes the true philosopher in his relation to the state; for you understand already.

Certainly.

Then suppose you now take this parable to the gentleman who is surprised at finding that philosophers have no honor in their cities; explain it to him and try to convince him that their having honor would be far more extraordinary.

I will.

Say to him, that, in deeming the best votaries of philosophy to be useless to the rest of the world, he is right; but also tell him to attribute their uselessness to the fault of those who will not use them, and not to themselves. The pilot should not humbly beg the sailors to be commanded by him—that is not the order of nature; neither are "the wise to go to the doors of the rich"—the ingenious author of this saying told a lie—but the truth is, that, when a man is ill, whether he be rich or poor, to the physician he must go, and he who wants to be governed, to him who is able to govern. The ruler who is good for anything ought not to beg his subjects to be ruled by him; although the present governors of mankind are of a different stamp; they may be justly compared to the mutinous sailors, and the true helmsmen to those who are called by them good-for-nothings and star-gazers.

Precisely so, he said.

For these reasons, and among men like these, philosophy, the noblest pursuit of all, is not likely to be much esteemed by those of the opposite faction; not that the greatest and most lasting injury is done to her by her opponents, but by her own professing followers, the same of whom you suppose the accuser to say, that the greater number of them are arrant rogues, and the best are useless; in which opinion I agreed.

Yes.

And the reason why the good are useless has now been explained?

True.

Then shall we proceed to show that the corruption of the majority is also unavoidable, and that this is not to be laid to the charge of philosophy any more than the other?

By all means.

And let us ask and answer in turn, first going back to the description of the gentle and noble nature. Truth, as you will remember, was his leader, whom he followed always and in all things; failing in this, he was an imposter, and had no part or lot in true philosophy.

Yes, that was said.

Well, and is not this one quality, to mention no others, greatly at variance with present notions of him?

Certainly, he said.

And have we not a right to say in his defense, that the true lover of knowledge is always striving after being—that is his nature; he will not rest in the multiplicity of individuals which is an appearance only, but will go on—the keen edge will not be blunted, nor the force of his desire abate until we have attained the knowledge of the true nature of every essence by a sympathetic and kindred power in the soul, and by that power drawing near and mingling and becoming incorporate with very being, having begotten mind and truth, he will have knowledge and will live and grow truly, and then, and not till then, will he cease from his travail.

Nothing, he said, can be more just than such a description of him.

And will the love of a lie be any part of a philosopher's nature? Will he not utterly hate a lie?

He will.

And when truth is the captain, we cannot suspect any evil of the band which he leads?

Impossible.

Justice and health of mind will be of the company, and temperance will follow after?

True, he replied.

*　　*　　*

I omitted the troublesome business of the possession of women, and the procreation of children, and the appointment of the rulers, because I knew that the perfect state would be eyed with jealousy and was difficult of attainment; but that piece of cleverness was not of much service to me, for I had to discuss them all the same. The women and children are now disposed of, but the other question of the rulers must be investigated from the very beginning. We were saying, as you will remember, that they were to be lovers of their country, tried by the test of pleasures and pains, and neither in hardships, nor in dangers, nor at any other critical moment were to lose their patriotism—he was to be rejected who failed, but he who always come forth pure, like gold tried in the refiner's fire, was to be made a ruler, and to receive honors and rewards in life and after death. This was the sort of thing which was being said, and then the argument turned aside and veiled her face; not liking to stir the question which has now arisen.

I perfectly remember, he said.

Yes, my friend, I said, and I then shrank from hazarding the bold word; but now let me dare to say—that the perfect guardian must be a philosopher.

Yes, he said, let that be affirmed.

And do not suppose that there will be many of them; for the gifts which were deemed by us to be essential rarely grow together; they are mostly found in shreds and patches.

What do you mean? he said.

You are aware, I replied, that quick intelligence, memory, sagacity, cleverness, and similar qualities, do not often grow together, and that persons who possess them and are at the same time high-spirited and magnanimous are not so constituted by nature as to live orderly and in a peaceful and settled manner; they are driven any way by their impulses, and all solid principle goes out of them.

Very true, he said.

On the other hand, those steadfast natures which can better be depended upon, which in a battle are impregnable to fear and immovable, are equally immovable when there is anything to be learned; they are always in a torpid state, and are apt to yawn and go to sleep over any intellectual toil.

Quite true.

And yet we were saying that both qualities were necessary in those to whom the higher education is to be imparted, and who are to share in any office or command.

Certainly, he said.

And will they be a class which is rarely found?

Yes, indeed.

Then the aspirant must not only be tested in those labors and dangers and pleasures which we mentioned before, but there is another kind of probation which we did not mention—he must be exercised also in many kinds of knowledge, to see whether the soul will be able to endure the highest of all, or will faint under them as in any other studies and exercises.

* * *

Observe, Glaucon, that there will be no injustice in compelling our philosophers to have a care and providence of others; we shall explain to them that in other states, men of their class are not obliged to share in the toils of politics: and this is reasonable, for they grow up at their own sweet will, and the government would rather not have them. Being self-taught, they cannot be expected to show any gratitude for a culture which they have never received. But we have brought you into the world to be rulers of the hive, kings of yourselves and of the other citizens, and have educated you far better and more perfectly than they have been educated, and you are better able to share in the double duty. Wherefore each of you, when his turn comes, must go down to the general underground abode, and get the habit of seeing in the dark. When you have acquired the habit, you will see ten thousand times better than the inhabitants of the den, and you will know what the several images are, and what they represent, because you have seen the beautiful and just and good in their truth. And thus our state, which is also yours, will be a reality, and not a dream only, and will be administered in a spirit unlike that of other states, in which men fight with one another about shadows only and are distracted in the struggle for power, which in their eyes is a great good. Whereas the truth is that the state in which the rulers are most reluctant to govern is always the best and most quietly governed, and the state in which they are most eager, the worst.

Quite true, he replied.

And will our pupils, when they hear this, refuse to take their turn at the toils of state, when they are allowed to spend the greater part of their time with one another in the heavenly light?

Impossible, he answered; for they are just men, and the commands which we impose upon them are just; there can be no doubt that every one of them will take office as a stern necessity, and not after the fashion of our present rulers of state.

Yes, my friend, I said; and there lies the point. You must contrive for your future rulers another and a better life than that of a ruler, and then you may have a well-ordered state; for only in the state which offers this, will they rule who are truly rich, not in silver and gold, but in virtue and wisdom, which are the true blessings of life. Whereas if they go to the administration of public affairs, poor and hungering after their own private advantage, thinking that hence they are to snatch the chief good, order there can never be; for they will be fighting about office, and the civil and domestic broils which thus arise will be the ruin of the rulers themselves and of the whole state.

Most true, he replied.

And the only life which looks down upon the life of political ambition is that of true philosophy. Do you know of any other?

Indeed, I do not, he said.

And those who govern ought not to be lovers of the task? For, if they are, there will be rival lovers, and they will fight.

No question.

Who then are those whom we shall compel to be guardians? Surely they will be the men who are wisest about affairs of state, and by whom the state is administered, and who at the same time have other honors and another and better life than that of politics?

They are the men, and I will choose them, he replied.

*   *   *

And now let me remind you that, although in our former selection we chose old men, we must not do so in this. Solon was under a delusion when he said that a man when

947

he grows old may learn many things—for he can no more learn much than he can run much; youth is the time for any extraordinary toil.

Of course.

And, therefore, calculation and geometry and all the other elements of instruction, which are a preparation for dialectic, should be presented to the mind in childhood; not, however, under any notion of forcing our system of education.

Why not?

Because a freeman ought not to be a slave in the acquisition of knowledge of any kind. Bodily exercise, when compulsory, does no harm to the body; but knowledge which is acquired under compulsion obtains no hold on the mind.

Very true.

Then, my good friend, I said, do not use compulsion, but let early education be a sort of amusement; you will then be better able to find out the natural bent.

That is a very rational notion, he said.

Do you remember that the children, too, were to be taken to see the battle on horseback; and that if there were no danger they were to be brought close up and, like young hounds, have a taste of blood given them?

Yes, I remember.

The same practice may be followed, I said, in all these things—labors, lessons, dangers—and he who is most at home in all of them ought to be enrolled in a select number.

At what age?

At the age when the necessary gymnastics are over: the period whether of two or three years which passes in this sort of training is useless for any purpose; for sleep and exercise are unpropitious to learning; and the trial of who is first in gymnastic exercises is one of the most important tests to which our youth are subjected.

Certainly, he replied.

After that time those who are selected from the class of twenty years old will be promoted to higher honor, and the sciences which they learned without any order in their early education will now be brought together, and they will be able to see the natural relationship of them to one another and to true being.

Yes, he said, that is the only kind of knowledge which takes lasting root.

Yes, I said; and the capacity for such knowledge is the great criterion of dialectical talent: the comprehensive mind is always the dialectical.

I agree with you, he said.

These, I said, are the points which you must consider; and those who have most of this comprehension, and who are most steadfast in their learning, and in their military and other appointed duties, when they have arrived at the age of thirty will have to be chosen by you out of the select class, and elevated to higher honor; and you will have to prove them by the help of dialectic, in order to learn which of them is able to give up the use of sight and the other senses, and in company with truth to attain absolute being.

* * *

Suppose, I said, the study of philosophy to take the place of gymnastics and to be continued diligently and earnestly and exclusively for twice the number of years which were passed in bodily exercise—will that be enough?

Would you say six or four years? he asked.

Say five years, I replied; at the end of the time they must be sent down again into the den and compelled to hold any military or other office which young men are qualified to hold: in this way they will get their experience of life, and there will be an opportunity of trying whether, when they are drawn all manner of ways of temptation, they will stand firm or flinch.

And how long is this stage of their lives to last?

Fifteen years, I answered; and when they have reached fifty years of age, then let those who still survive and have distinguished themselves in every action of their lives and in every branch of knowledge come at last to their consummation: the time has now arrived at which they must raise the eye of the soul to the universal light which lightens all things, and behold the absolute good; for that is the pattern according to which they are to order the state and the lives of individuals, and the remainder of their own lives also; making philosophy their chief pursuit, but, when their turn comes, toiling also at politics and ruling for the public good, not as though they were performing some heroic action, but simply as a matter of duty; and when they have brought up in each generation others like themselves and left them in their place to be governors of the state, then they will depart to the Islands of the Blest and dwell there; and the city will give them public memorials and sacrifices and honor them, if the Pythian oracle consent, as demigods, but if not, as in any case blessed and divine.

You are a sculptor, Socrates, and have made statues of our governors faultless in beauty.

Yes, I said, Glaucon, and of our governesses too; for you must not suppose that what I have been saying applies to men only and not to women as far as their natures go.

There you are right, he said, since we have made them to share in all things like the men.

Well, I said, and you would agree (would you not?) that what has been said about the state and the government is not a mere dream, and although difficult not impossible, but only possible in the way which has been supposed; that is to say, when the true philosopher kings are born in a state, one or more of them, despising the honors of this present world which they deem mean and worthless, esteeming above all things right and the honor that springs from right, and regarding justice as the greatest and most necessary of all things, whose ministers they are, and whose principles will be exalted by them when they set in order their own city?

How will they proceed?

They will begin by sending out into the country all the

inhabitants of the city who are more than ten years old, and will take possession of their children, who will be unaffected by the habits of their parents; these they will train in their own habits and laws, I mean in the laws which we have given them: and in this way the state and constitution of which we were speaking will soonest and most easily attain happiness, and the nation which has such a constitution will gain most.

Yes, that will be the best way. And I think, Socrates, that you have very well described how, if ever, such a constitution might come into being.

Enough then of the perfect state and of the man who bears its image—there is no difficulty in seeing how we shall describe him.

There is no difficulty, he replied; and I agree with you in thinking that nothing more need be said.

[289]

PLEKHANOV, GEORGE

PLEKHANOV, GEORGE (1857-1918). Although for many years, from 1904 until his death, Plekhanov strongly opposed Lenin and the Bolshevists, and was arrested by them after their victory in 1917, Lenin did not deny his spiritual indebtedness to his adversary and the rulers of Soviet Russia acknowledged the value of Plekhanov's works and permitted them to be re-edited by the Marx-Engels-Institute.

Plekhanov was the founder of the Russian Social-Democratic party which was subsequently divided into the Menshevik and Bolshevik parties.

He was the son of a noble, but not wealthy, landowner who treated his serfs ruthlessly. When, after his father's death, his mother tried to cheat her peasants, the son prevented her from doing so by threatening to set fire to the paternal home.

As a student, Plekhanov joined the Narodniki (Friends of the People) who advocated immediate socialization of Russia. But in 1880 he was converted to Marxism, and, on the ground of his interpretation of this doctrine, he opposed the Narodniki by arguing that Russian economic conditions had to ripen before socialism could be introduced into that country. Because of his revolutionary

951

activities, Plekhanov was exiled in 1882. In the following year he founded the "Union for Emancipation of Labor," the germ-cell of the Social-Democratic Party of Russia, whose program was elaborated by him. At the request of the German Social Democrats, he wrote *Anarchism and Socialism* (1894); in the following year he wrote against the Narodniki in *On the Question of the Development of the Monist View in History;* and in 1896 his *Essay on the History of Materialism* was published, which, like his *Fundamental Problems of Marxism* (1908), was generally acknowledged to be an authoritative interpretation of Marxism. Plekhanov fought the socialist revisionists in Germany and France but sided, in 1904, with the Russian Mensheviks against Lenin. When Plekhanov returned to Russia after the overthrow of Tsarism, he was hopelessly suffering from tuberculosis but struggled against Bolshevism to his last gasp.

BOURGEOIS AND SOCIALISTIC ART

UNDER socialism, the theory of art for art's sake will be logically impossible, in so far as social morality will lose its vulgarity, a vulgarity that is at present the inevitable consequence of the desire of the ruling class to retain its privileges.

Flaubert said: "Art is the quest for the useless," and in this sentence the principal theme of Pushkin's *The Mob* is observable. The fondness for this theme is simply an indication of the artist's protest against the narrow utilitarianism of a given ruling class or caste. With the disappearance of social classes, this narrow utilitarianism, so closely linked with selfishness, will also disappear. Selfishness has nothing to do with aesthetics. Artistic judgment invariably presupposes an absence of desire for personal gain on the part of him who exercises that judgment. Desire for collective gain, however, is quite another matter. The desire to be useful to society, which was the basis of ancient morality, inspired a spirit of self-sacrifice; and self-sacrifice, as the history of art so eloquently proves, inspires artistic creation. It is sufficient to note the songs of primitive peoples; or, less remotely, the monument to Harmodius and Aristogiton at Athens.

The thinkers of antiquity, including Plato and Aristotle, already realized how man is degraded by having to expend all his energy in the struggle for existence. Contemporary bourgeois philosophers also realize this, and feel the necessity of relieving man of the staggering burden of constant economic anxiety. But the man they have in mind is the man of the upper classes, who lives by exploiting the workers. Their solution of the problem is the same as that of the philosophers of antiquity: enslavement of the producers by a select few individuals, who approach more or less the ideal of the "superman." This solution, conservative in the time of Plato and Aristotle, in our time is ultra-reactionary. While the conservative slave-owners of ancient Greece believed that they could maintain their dominant position by relying upon their own "valor," contemporary advocates of the enslavement of the masses of the people are sceptical of the "valor" of bourgeois exploiters. For this reason they like to dream of the coming of a great genius, an omniscient superman who, if placed at the head of the state, by sheer force of his iron will would bolster up the now tottering structure of class rule. That is why decadents who are not averse to politics are often found to be ardent admirers of Napoleon.

Like Renan, who desired a powerful government, one that would compel the "good peasant" to work for him while he spent his time in meditation, our contemporary aesthetes want a social order that will compel the proletariat to labor while they indulge in loftier pursuits—such as the painting and tinting of little cubes and other stereometric figures. Organically incapable of any constructive effort, they become genuinely indignant at the thought of a society without idlers.

"He who lives with wolves usually learns to howl." While combatting philistinism verbally, our contemporary bourgeois aesthetes worship the golden calf as much as any bourgeois philistine. "They imagine there is a movement in the sphere of art," says Mauclair, "while in reality the movement is only in the picture market, where speculation goes on also in undiscovered genius." I might add in passing that one reason for this speculation in "undiscovered genius" is the feverish quest for "something new" which occupies so many artists today. When people look for "something new" it is because the old fails to satisfy them. The question is why it fails to satisfy them. A great many contemporary artists are dissatisfied with the old for the sole reason that so long as the public continues to hold it in esteem their own genius remains undiscovered. Their rebellion against the old is motivated not by love of new ideas, but rather by love for that "sole reality," their precious ego. Such a love does not inspire an artist except in so far as it tends to make him judge everything, even the Apollo Belvedere, by the standard of utility.

"The subject of money is so closely bound up with that of art," Mauclair continues, "that art criticism feels as if it were crushed in a vise. The best critics are unable to say what they think; the others say only that which is expedient in any given instance, since as they aver, they make their living by writing. I do not say that we should become indignant over this, but it would not be amiss to bear in mind the complexity of the problem." Thus we see that *art for art's sake has become art for money's sake*. Mauclair wished to determine the cause of this phenomenon; and this we can easily trace.

There was a time, as in the Middle Ages, when only the superfluity, the excess of production over consumption, was exchanged.

There was again a time, when not only the superfluity, but all products, all industrial existence, had passed into commerce, when the whole of production depended on exchange. . . .

Finally, there came a time when everything that men had considered as inalienable became an object of exchange, of traffic and could be alienated. This is the time when the very things which till then had been communicated, but never exchanged; given, but never sold;

acquired, but never bought—virtue, love, conviction, knowledge, conscience, etc.—when everything in short, passed into commerce. It is the time of general corruption, of universal venality, or, to speak in terms of political economy, the time when everything, moral or physical, having become a marketable value, is brought to the market to be assessed at its truest value.

Is it any wonder that in this period of universal venality, art, too, has become a commodity?

Mauclair says that we should not become indignant about this phenomena, and neither do I wish to judge it from the standpoint of morality. As the saying goes, I wish neither to cry nor to laugh, but simply to understand. I do not say that contemporary artists *must* seek inspiration in the emancipatory movement of the proletariat. Not at all. Just as apple-trees must give forth apples and pear-trees pears, so must artists who share the bourgeois point of view struggle against this movement. The art of a decadent epoch *must* be decadent. This is inevitable and it would be futile to become indignant about it. *The Communist Manifesto* correctly states:

In times when the class struggle nears the decisive hour, the process of dissolution going on within the ruling class, in fact within the whole range of old society, assumes such a violent, glaring character, that a small section of the ruling class cuts itself adrift, and joins the revolutionary class, the class that holds the future in its hands. Just as, therefore, at an earlier period, a section of the nobility went over to the bourgeoisie, so now a portion of the bourgeoisie goes over to the proletariat, and in particular, a portion of the bourgeois ideologists, who have raised themselves to the level of comprehending theoretically the historical movement as a whole.

Among bourgeois ideologists going over to the side of the proletariat, we find very few artists. This is probably due to the fact that to comprehend theoretically the historical process as a whole it is necessary to think; and contemporary artists, unlike the great masters of the Renaissance, for instance, think very little. *At any rate, there is no doubt that any artist of proven talent will increase considerably the forcefulness of his work by steeping himself in the great emancipatory ideas of our time. For this, it is necessary that these ideas permeate his spirit and that he express them through his artist's temperament.* He must also know how to assess correctly the "modernist" art of contemporary bourgeois ideologists. The ruling class is now in such a position that to go forward can only mean to go downward, and this sad fate is shared by all their ideologists as well. The foremost among them are those who have sunk lower than all their predecessors.

[290]

PLINY THE YOUNGER

PLINY THE YOUNGER (62-113). Among the most famous reports ever written are two letters of Pliny the Younger, who, at the age of seventeen, eye-witnessed the eruption of Mount Vesuvius in 79 A.D. and described the destruction of the city of Herculaneum to Tacitus, the historian. He was the nephew and adopted son of Pliny the Elder, admiral of the Roman fleet and noted naturalist, who was a victim of that disaster.

Pliny the Younger had a brilliant career under Emperor Trajan. He was appointed consul and later governor of Bithynia. In his reports to the Emperor, Pliny also mentioned the Christians whose customs he had to investigate. He described their conduct of life as impeccable, but censured their disobedience to the Roman authorities in matters of religion. His letters, most of which are real essays, give valuable information about the political, social and literary life in the Roman Empire during his lifetime. Pliny studied philosophy with Musonius Rufus, who was also the teacher of Epictetus. But Pliny's ideal was Cicero, the orator, the philosopher and letter-writer, and his ambition was to imitate his model. He followed Cicero's example too by branding corruption, and accusing officials who abused their power.

ON GOVERNMENT

CONSIDER that you are sent to that noble province to regulate the condition of free cities; sent, that is, to a society of men who breathe the spirit of true manhood and liberty; who have maintained the rights they received from Nature, by courage, by virtue, by alliances; in a word, by civil and religious faith.

Revere the gods their founders; their ancient glory, and even that very antiquity itself, venerable in men, is sacred in states.

Honor them therefore for their deeds of old renown, nay, their very legendary traditions.

Grant to every one his full dignity, privileges, yes, and the indulgence of his very vanity.

Remember it was from this nation we derived our laws; that she did not receive ours by conquest, but gave us hers by favor.

Reflect what these cities once were; but so reflect as not to despise them for what they are now.

Far be pride and asperity from you my friend; nor fear, by a proper condescension, to lay yourself open to contempt.

Can he who is vested with the power and bears the ensigns of authority, can he fail of meeting with respect, unless by pursuing base and sordid measures, and first breaking through that reverence he owes to himself?

*   *   *

Ill, believe me, is power proved by insult; ill can terror command veneration, and far more effectual is affection in obtaining one's purpose than fear. For terror operates no longer than its object is present, but love produces its effects with its object at a distance: and as absence changes the former into hatred, it raises the latter into respect.

Therefore you ought (and I cannot but repeat it too often) you ought to well consider the nature of your office, and to represent to yourself how great and important the task is of governing a free state. For what can be better for society than such government, what can be more precious than freedom? How ignominious then must his conduct be who turns good government into anarchy, and liberty into slavery?

To these considerations let me add, that you have an established reputation to maintain; the fame you have acquired by good administration elsewhere, the good opinion of the Emperor, the credit you obtained in other offices, in a word, this very government, which may be looked upon as the reward of your former services, are all so many glorious weights which are incumbent upon you to support with suitable dignity.

The more strenuously therefore you ought to endeavor that it may not be said you showed greater urbanity, integrity and ability in a province remote from the capital, than in one which lies so much nearer the capital; in the midst of a nation of slaves, than among a free people; that it may not be remarked, that it was chance, and not judgment, appointed you to this office; that your character was unknown and inexperienced, not tried and approved.

*　　*　　*

It should be an invariable rule to refer to the Emperor in all matters where there is doubt, for the highest authority is alone capable of removing scruples or informing one's ignorance.

If you are unacquainted with the nature of a particular crime or the measure of punishment, it is not wholly proper for you to enter into an examination concerning these things.

Force of character, or whatever else you may call a fixed determination in obtaining what one has a mind for, rightly applied, can effect infinite good. The misfortune is that there is less of this quality about good people than about bad people, and as ignorance begets rashness, and thoughtfulness produces deliberation, so modesty is apt to cripple the action of virtue, while confidence will become the aid of vice.

For (and it is a maxim which your reading and conversation must have often suggested to you) it is a far greater disgrace losing the name one has once acquired than never to have attained it.

I again beg you to be persuaded that I did not write this with a design of instruction, but of reminder.

Indeed, however, if I had, it would have only been in consequence of the great affection I bear you. It is a sentiment I am in no fear of carrying beyond its just bounds, for there can be no danger of excess where one cannot love too well.

[291]

PLOTINUS

PLOTINUS (205-270). Despite careful inquiries and heated controversies, no satisfying answer has been given to the question as to whether or not Plotinus possessed a real knowledge of the religion and philosophy of India to which his own teachings bear surprising analogies. It is, however, certain that Plotinus was eager to study the wisdom of India. For that purpose he participated in Emperor Gordianus' campaign against Perisia.

At any rate, Plotinus seems to be nearer to the spirit of India than any other thinker of the Mediterranean civilization. His doctrine that the reality perceived by the senses is a dispersion and degradation of the true Reality, conceived by Plotinus as the Trinity of the One, the *Nous* (Spirit) and the Soul, seems as much of Hindu origin as his advice that asceticism and ecstasy lead to wisdom. But, on the other hand, Saint Augustine was not entirely wrong in saying that Plotinus, in order to become a Christian, would have to change "only a few words." In fact, Christian theology and philosophy of the Middle Ages adopted many of Plotinus' thoughts. So did European mysticism and romanticism up to the present day.

Plotinus, notwithstanding the resemblance to, or affinity with, India and Christianity, persisted in honoring the gods of pagan Greece. Born in Egypt, he was the disciple of Ammonius Saccas who had been converted from Christianity to paganism, and, in all probability, also studied the works of the Jewish philosopher Philo. From 245 until his death, Plotinus taught philosophy in Rome. He was consulted more than once by Emperor Gallienus. His disciples followed him with a religious devotion. Plotinus is also highly esteemed as a keen psychologist and a refined aesthete.

THE ONE

ALL things that exist do so by virtue of "unity"—in so far as they exist in any ultimate sense and in so far as they may be said to be real. For what would anything be if it were not "one"? Without the unity of which we speak things do not exist. There can be no army which is not a unit, nor a chorus, nor herd, unless each is "one." Neither is there a household or ship without unity; for the house is a unit and the ship is a unit, and if one took away the unity the household would no longer be a household nor the ship a ship. Continuous magnitudes would not exist if there were no unity to them. When divided, in so far as they lose unity they lose existence. So also with the bodies of plants and animals, each of which is a unit, if unity is lost—being broken up into multiplicity—they lose the being which they had, and no longer continue as they were. And they become other things even then only in so far as these have unity. Similarly there is health when the body is harmonized into unity, and beauty when the essence of unity controls the parts, and virtue in the soul when it is unified and brought into a single harmonious whole.

There must be something prior to all, simple, and different from the things which are posterior to it, self-existent, unmingled with the things which come from it, and yet able in another way to be present with the others, being really one, not something else first then secondarily one, of which it is false even that it is one; but of this One no description nor scientific knowledge is possible. Indeed it must be said to be beyond "being"; for if it were not simple, without any composition and synthesis, and really one, it would not be a first principle. And it is wholly self-sufficient by virtue of its being simple and prior to all things. What is not first needs that which is prior to itself, and that which is not simple demands those simple elements which are within it, that it may be composed of them. Such a One must be unique, for if there were another such both together would constitute a larger unit. For we hold that they are not two bodies nor is the Primary One a body. For no body is simple, and a body is subject to generation; it is not an ultimate principle. The ultimate principle is unoriginated, and being incorporeal and really one it is able to stand first.

Since substances which have an origin are of some form (for no one could say anything else of what is generated from the One), and since it is not any particular form but all, without exception, the first principle must be formless. And being formless it is not substance; for substance must be particular; and a particular is determinate. But this can not be regarded as particular, for it would not be a principle, but merely that particular thing which you may have called it. If then all things are included among what are generated, which of them will you say is the first principle? Only what is none of them could be said to stand above the rest. But these constitute existing things and Being in general. The First Principle then is beyond Being. To say that it is beyond Being does not assert it to be any definite thing. It does not define it. Nor does it give it a name. It applies to it only the appellation "not-this." In doing so it nowhere sets limits to it. It would be absurd to seek to delimit such a boundless nature. He who wishes to do this prevents himself from getting upon its track in any wise, even little by little. But just as he who wishes to see the Intelligible must abandon all imagery of the perceptible in order to contemplate what is beyond the perceptible, so he who wishes to contemplate what is beyond the Intelligible will attain the contemplation of it by letting go everything intelligible, through this means learning *that* it is, abandoning the search for *what* it is. To tell what it is would involve a reference to what it is not, for there is no quality in what has no particular character. But we are in painful doubt as to what we should say of it; so we speak of the ineffable and give it a name, meaning to endow it with some significance to ourselves so far as we can. Perhaps this name "The One" implies merely opposition to plurality. . . . But if The One were given positive content, a name and signification, it would be less appropriately designated than when one does not give any name. It may be said that description of it is carried thus far in order that he who seeks it beginning with that which indicates the simplicity of all things may end by negating even this, on the ground that it was taken simply as the most adequate and the nearest description possible for him who used it, but not even this is adequate to the revelation of that nature, because it is inaudible, not to be understood through hearing, and if by any sense at all by vision alone. But if the eye that sees seeks to behold a form it will not descry even this.

[292]

PLUTARCH OF CHAERONEA

PLUTARCH OF CHAERONEA (50-120). In the ancient world, Plutarch was considered "the true philanthropist"; in America, Emerson called him the embodiment of the highest ideal of humanity. As a biographer of heroes, as a moralist, as an unorthodox Platonist, Plutarch has been the world's most popular author for many centuries.

His spiritual life was centered in Athens and Delphi, in the Academy, founded by Plato, and in the temple whose priest he was. Plutarch was a pious man, an advocate of general peace and reconciliation. He was a cautious adviser of his troubled fellow men, and an experienced observer of human characters and customs. Notwithstanding his devotion to the old gods, the Fathers of the Church sympathized with him. Among the reformers of the sixteenth century Zwingli and Melanchthon loved him, while Calvin remained cool, and Luther ignored him. Montaigne was called

Plutarch's best disciple, and Shakespeare could have been called so. It was only in the nineteenth century, when the historical importance of collective factors was stressed, that Plutarch's influence weakened. But as long as people are interested in individual life, he will be read and re-read, and those who think that history must be conceived as the development of group life, will find in Plutarch's writings highly important information. For he was also one of the greatest folklorists. He wrote on almost everything that could interest, educate or edify his contemporaries, and, in doing so, he amassed a treasury of knowledge, from which modern psychologists, sociologists, educators and students of comparative science of religion may profit as much as historians and philosophers.

WISDOM AND PRUDENCE

THERE are those who thought that all human actions depended upon mere casualty, and were not guided by wisdom. If this be so, justice and equity have no place at all in the world, and temperance and modesty can do nothing in the direction and managing of our affairs.

We may grant that many occurrences came by fortune, but it is true that the world has in it temperance, justice and fortitude. What reason is there to say that there is no prudence and wisdom therein? Now if it be yielded that the world is not void of prudence, how can it be maintained that there should not be in it sage counsel? For temperance is a kind of prudence, and most certain it is that justice should be assisted by prudence, or to say more truly, ought to have it present with her continually.

*   *   *

Certainly, sage counsel and wisdom in the good use of pleasures and delights, whereby we continue honest, we ordinarily do call continence and temperance; the same in dangers and travails, we term tolerance, patience and fortitude; in contracts and management of state affairs, we give the name of loyalty, equity and justice; whereby it comes to pass, that if we will attribute the effects of counsel and wisdom unto fortune, we must likewise ascribe unto her the works of justice and temperance.

963

Take away sage and discreet counsel; farewell then all consultation as touching affairs, away with deliberation, consideration and inquisition into that which is useful and expedient, for surely then Sophocles talked idly when he said:

> *"Seek, and be sure to find with diligence,*
> *But lose what you forfeit by negligence."*

Now would I gladly know, what is it that men may find and what can they learn, in case all things in the world be directed by fortune? What senate house would not be dissolved and abolished? What council chamber would not be overthrown and put down, if all were at the disposition of fortune? We do her wrong in reproaching her for blindness, when we run upon her as we do, blind, and debasing ourselves unto her; for how can we choose but stumble upon her indeed, if we pluck out our own eyes, to wit, our wisdom and dexterity of counsel, and take a blind guide to lead us by the hand in the course of this our life?

Nature has bestowed upon us sight, hearing, taste and smell, with all of the parts of the body endowed with the rest of their faculties and powers, as ministers of counsel and wisdom. For it is the soul that sees, it is the soul and understanding that hears, all the rest are deaf and blind: and like as if there were no sun at all we should live in perpetual blindness. Even so, if man had not reason and intelligence, notwithstanding all his other senses, he should not differ in the whole race of his life from brute and wild beasts; but now in that we excel and rule them all, it is not by chance and fortune, but the use and discourse of reason is the very cause that has given us this in recompense. By experience, memory, wisdom and artifice we go beyond all animals, and thereby we have the mastery and use of them. We take from them whatsoever they have.

*   *   *

Artificers use altogether in every piece of work their squares, their rules, their lines and levels; they go by measures and numbers, to the end that in all their works there should not be anything found done rashly or at adventure. These arts are petty kinds of prudence, sprinkled and dispersed among the necessities of this life. It is a wonderful thing how these arts and sciences should have no dealing with fortune nor need her help, to attain their proper ends.

Shall we say then that the greatest and most principal things that are, even those that be most material and necessary for man's felicity, use not wisdom, nor participate one whit with providence and the judgment of reason? There is no man so void of understanding, that after he has tempered clay and water together, lets it alone and goes his way, when he has done, expecting that by fortune there will be bricks and tiles made; nor is anyone such a fool as when he has bought wool and leather, sits him down and prays fortune that he may have garments and shoes; or, being possessed of divers fair and stately houses, with their rich and costly furniture, will he deem that these can make him live happily, without pain, without grief, secure of change and alteration, if he does not possess wisdom.

[293]

POINCARÉ, HENRI

POINCARÉ, HENRI (1854-1912). The name of Poincaré is mostly associated with the person of Raymond Poincaré who was President of the Third French Republic during the First World War. Henri was his first cousin, and outside France he was known in the scientific world only. Eight foreign Universities conferred honorary doctors' degrees upon him; twenty-one foreign academies made him their honorary member, not to mention the honors he enjoyed in his native country. Poincaré himself, however, was more satisfied with the great influence he exercised on succeeding generations through his writings and lectures.

Poincaré made great strides in the history of mathematics, especially by his disquisitions on differential equations and analytical functions. The development of mechanics and astronomy owes to him admirable results concerning the capillarity, the equilibrium of fluid masses and rotating liquids, and, above all, the form of the planets. He made also very important contributions to geography and geodesy. In the field of physics, Poincaré dealt with the problems of vibration and elasticity, electricity and radioactivity, electro-dynamics and gravitation, and published his views on relativity some months before Albert Einstein made known his famous theory.

Poincaré's philosophical inquiries concerned especially the process of hypothesis making, the relations between the logical and empirical elements of knowledge. From the statement that for any consistent and verifiable hypothesis there is a host of other likewise consistent and verifiable hypotheses, he proceeded to the conclusion that the choice between them is not dictated by logic or observation but by what he called convention. According to Poincaré, the value of science lies not so much in its usefulness as in its intrinsic worth, in the elevation of the soul which the true scientist feels while working. Poincaré was a fighter for human ideals. He courageously and successfully participated in the struggle for Dreyfus by destroying the arguments of the experts who were hired by the French general staff.

THE CHOICE OF FACTS IN SCIENCE

Tolstoy somewhere explains why 'science for its own sake' is in his eyes an absurd conception. We can not know *all* facts, since their number is practically infinite. It is necessary to choose; then we may let this choice depend on the pure caprice of our curiosity; would it not be better to let ourselves be guided by utility, by our practical and above all by our moral needs; have we nothing better to do than to count the number of ladybugs on our planet?

It is clear the word utility has not for him the sense men of affairs give it, and following them most of our contemporaries. Little cares he for industrial applications, for the marvels of electricity or of automobilism, which he regards rather as obstacles to moral progress; utility for him is solely what can make man better.

For my part, it need scarce be said, I could never be content with either the one or the other ideal; I want neither that plutocracy grasping and mean, nor that democracy goody and mediocre, occupied solely in turning the other cheek, where would dwell sages without curiosity, who, shunning excess, would not die of disease, but would surely die of ennui. But that is a matter of taste and is not what I wish to discuss.

The question nevertheless remains and should fix our attention; if our choice can only be determined by caprice or by immediate utility, there can be no science for its own sake, and consequently no science. But is that true? That a choice must be made is incontestable; whatever be our activity, facts go quicker than we, and we can not catch them; while the scientists discover one fact, there happen milliards of milliards in a cubic millimeter of his body. To wish to comprise nature in science would be to want to put the whole into the part.

But scientists believe there is a hierarchy of facts and that among them may be made a judicious choice. They are right, since otherwise there would be no science, yet science exists. *One need only open the eyes to see that the conquests of industry which have enriched so many practical men would never have seen the light, if these practical men alone had existed and if they had not been preceded by unselfish devotees who died poor, who never thought of utility, and yet had a guide far other than caprice.*

As Mach says, *these devotees have spared their successors the trouble of thinking.* Those who might have worked solely in view of an immediate application would have left nothing behind them, and, in face of a new need, all must have been begun over again. Now most men do not love to think, and this is perhaps fortunate when instinct guides them, for most often, when they pursue an aim which is immediate and ever the same, instinct guides them better than reason would guide a pure intelligence. But instinct is routine, and if thought did not fecundate it, it would no more progress in man than in the bee or ant. It is needful then to think for those who love not thinking, and, as they are numerous, it is needful that each of our thoughts be as often useful as possible, and this is why a law will be the more precious the more general it is.

967

This shows us how we should choose: the most interesting facts are those which may serve many times, these are the facts which have a chance of coming up again. We have been so fortunate as to be born in a world where there are such. Suppose that instead of 60 chemical elements there were 60 milliards of them, that they were not some common, the others rare, but that they were uniformly distributed. Then, every time we picked up a new pebble there would be great probability of its being formed of some unknown substance; all that we knew of other pebbles would be worthless for it; before each new object we should be as the new-born babe; like it we could only obey our caprices or our needs. Biologists would be just as much at a loss if there were only individuals and no species and if heredity did not make sons like their fathers.

In such a world there would be no science; perhaps thought and even life would be impossible, since evolution could not there develop the preservational instincts. Happily it is not so; like all good fortune to which we are accustomed, this is not appreciated at its true worth.

[294]

POMPONAZZI, PIETRO

POMPONAZZI, PIETRO (1462-1524). While the philosophy of the Renaissance is characterized by the overthrow of the authority of Aristotle and the revival of Platonism, Pomponazzi, one of the most acute thinkers who lived in that period, remained a staunch Aristotelian, for he was not affected by the religious and artistic currents of his time, and possessed neither a reactionary nor traditional but rather a progressive and independent mind. He was the philosophical teacher of Copernicus, and in the middle of the 19th century his example encouraged Roberto Ardigo, the leader of Italian positivism to abandon the Church and to devote himself to secular science.

Pomponazzi was by no means uncritical when he adopted Aristotle's views, and he was opposed to both Aquinas' and Averroës' interpretation of his master, although he had also learned much from Averroës. His principal work *On the Immortality of the Soul*

968

(1516), in which he denied immortality, aroused a storm of indignation, and Pope Leo X charged Agostino Nifo with refuting it. Pomponazzi was insistent that the conviction of mortality of the soul allows man to be good and virtuous.

Pomponazzi's general design was to defend and secure experience, which he conceived so broadly that it included magic and miracles which he explained as natural and not performed by angels or demons. What he considered outside the wide range of natural causes assumed by him, he combated as superstition. From his investigation of the relation between prayer and fulfilment of the wishes expressed by prayer, he proceeded to views on the history of religions. He stated that religions are subject to the law of change and necessary decline, and he did not except Christianity from these laws. But he distinguished simple faith from the spirit of inquiry, and declared that philosophical thoughts must not influence man's behavior as a faithful Christian and member of the Catholic Church. This version of the Averroist assumption of "double truth" allowed him to remain unmolested as a professor at the Universities of Padua, Ferrara and Bologna.

TRUTH

TRUTH is a certain adequacy or mensurableness of the thing to the intellect, or of the intellect to the thing. . . . If a thing corresponds to a practical intellect it is true as far as it corresponds to such an intellect. All things in their totality are true as far as they are corresponding to the Divine intellect. For as far as every thing is an effect of God, either on the ground of efficient cause or of finality, everything has its idea within the Divine mind. Furthermore, since things have a similitude to their ideas, they are true, and the more they become similar to their ideas, the more they will become true. . . .

But if the question is broached whether God himself is true, I declare that all modes of truth are in God. He is true in all His modes, because in God there is total adequacy of all things to the intellect, and of the intellect to all things. For His essence is equal to His intellect, and His intellect is equal to His essence, and in no way can He practice any deception upon Himself.

[295]

PORPHYRY

PORPHYRY (232-304). Porphyry, a Syrian whose original name was Malchos, was one of the last defenders of classical paganism against the Sceptics and Christians. He was a disciple and friend of Plotinus, whose writings he edited. He was also an excellent interpreter of Aristotle.

In his objections to Christianity, Porphyry tried to do justice to the views he fought by informing himself as fully as possible about the history and doctrines of his adversaries, and he took a great many pains to refrain from open hostility. His book *Against the Christians* was considered very dangerous by Christian apologists. Porphyry was convinced that truly religious men do not desire formulas, cults, sacrifices or incantations. But, he said, men of pure heart and wise conduct of life being very rare, people need the images of the gods for their moral discipline and spiritual satisfaction.

VEGETARIANISM

HE who says that the man who extends the just as far as to brutes, corrupts the just, is ignorant that he does not himself preserve justice, but increases pleasure, which is hostile to justice. By admitting, therefore, that pleasure is the end [of our actions], justice is evidently destroyed. For to whom is it not manifest that justice is increased through abstinence? For he who abstains from every thing animated, though he may abstain from such animals as do not contribute to the benefit of society, will be much more careful not to injure those of his own species. For he who loves the genus, will not hate any species of animals; and by how much the greater his love of the genus is, by so much the more will he preserve justice towards a part of the genus, and that to which he is allied. He, therefore, who admits that he is allied to all animals, will not injure any animal. But he who confines justice to man alone, is prepared, like one enclosed in a narrow space, to hurl from him the prohibition of injustice. So that the Pythagorean is more pleasing than the Socratic banquet. For Socrates said that hunger is the sauce of food; but Pythagoras said that to injure no one, and to be exhilarated with justice, is the sweetest sauce; as the avoidance of animal food, will also be the avoidance of unjust conduct with respect to food. For God has not so constituted things that we cannot preserve ourselves without injuring others; since, if this were the case, he would have connected us with a nature which is the principle of injustice. Do not they, however, appear to be ignorant of the peculiarity of justice, who think that it was introduced from the alliance of men to each other? For this will be nothing more than a certain philanthropy; but justice consists in abstaining from injuring any thing which is not noxious. And our conception of the just man must be formed according to the latter, and not according to the former mode. Hence, therefore, since justice consists in not injuring any thing, it must be extended as far as to every animated nature. On this account, also, the essence of justice consists in the rational ruling over the irrational, and in the irrational being obedient to the rational part. For when reason governs, and the irrational part is obedient to its mandates, it follows, by the greatest necessity, that man will be innoxious towards every thing. For the passions being restrained, and desire and anger wasting away, but reason possessing its proper empire, a similitude to a more excellent nature [and to deity] immediately follows. But the more excellent nature in the universe is entirely innoxious, and, through possessing a power which preserves and benefits all things, is itself not in want of any thing. We, however, through justice [when we exercise it], are innoxious towards all things, but, through being connected with mortality, are indigent of things of a necessary nature. But the assumption of what is necessary does not injure even plants, when we take what they cast off; nor fruits, when we use such of them as are dead; nor sheep, when through shearing we rather benefit than injure them, and by partaking of their milk, we in return afford them every proper attention. Hence, the just man appears to be one who deprives himself of things pertaining to the body; yet he does not [in reality] injure himself. For, by this management of his body, and continence, he increases his inward good, *i.e.* his similitude to God.

[296]

POSIDONIUS

POSIDONIUS (About 135-51 B.C.). The remnants of the works of Posidonius consist of sentences which have been quoted by later authors. In his time and by many succeeding generations, he was esteemed as the most learned scholar who was able to present dry matter in a popular, even picturesque style. Posidonius was born in Syria but taught mostly on the island of Rhodes and at Rome. He traveled through North Africa, Spain, France and Italy and wrote on philosophy, history, geography, physics, and astronomy. Religion played an important part in his thinking. He revered the Greek, Roman, and Oriental gods and rites, and combined the beliefs in the gods and demons with the traditional Stoic pantheism. His picture of the Universe, though preserved in fragments only, influenced many thinkers of the Middle Ages and the Renaissance, and his sayings, which blend reason with mysticism, sober experience with daring conjectures, inspired Leibniz and the romanticists.

MAN AND THE GODS

EVERY creature is attracted by what is identical with its intrinsic property. Man is a reasonable being. He therefore is not attracted to himself as an animal but to himself as a reasonable being. Man loves himself in so far as he is really human.

Everything that is visible, including the divine and the human, is one. We are members of a great body. Nature has made us related because it has created all of us out of one and the same. This origin makes us love one another and be sociable.

The whole world is a state, comprising gods and men. We cannot deny our duties to revere the gods. Utility is not the father of the law but rather equality, which is taught by Nature.

A holy demon abides within us. He is watching our good and evil actions. Just as we treat him, he will treat us. He is not born together with our body, and will not perish together with it. Under no circumstance can the state be interested in committing a crime. No state is allowed to command a citizen to do ugly things, because the state is founded upon law.

[297]

PROCLUS

PROCLUS (411-485). Pagan Neo-Platonism reached its last peak in the philosophy of Proclus who was revered as the embodiment of the ideal of the Sage. In accordance with the ideas of late antiquity, Proclus was, at the same time, a refined rationalist, an irresistible logician and dialectician, and a mystic to whom no secret was hidden. His mind is pictured by his contemporaries as the triumph of human reason and the source of superhuman powers. He was the priest of the gods of Greece, Asia Minor and Arabia, and conducted their worship with scientific knowledge and artistic skill. Only Christianity and Judaism were despised and defied by him.

But so great was his fame and the charm of his writings that the Fathers of the Church relied on the commentaries on Plato written by the enemy of Christianity, and Proclus' *Elementa Theologica*, the defense and glorification of paganism, became of basic importance to Christian theology of the Middle Ages. His influence extended even to the thinkers of the Renaissance and Hegelianism.

HYMN TO THE CULTURAL MUSES

I

With hymns let us celebrate the educative light that shows us the path to Heaven,
The sonorous Nine Daughters of the Supreme, who redeem
The souls that have lost their way along the depths of life,
With the blameless, inspiring mysteries of books,

973

FROM unseen sorrows preserving the terrestrials,
Teaching them to hasten to follow the path that leads above
the depths of oblivion,
Aiding them to arrive still pure at their native star,
Whence they had come; when they rushed into the childbirth
bed,
While intoxicated with the fumes of material pleasure.

II

I PRAY you, Goddesses, calm my tumultuous impulses,
And sober me with the liberal intelligible words of the wise;
Nor let the race of superstitious men stray from the path
divine;
The Path of ample splendor, and luxurious fruits!
Ever from the tumult of the straying generations
Allure my wandering soul to your chaste light,
Weighted by, and sanctified from your prolific books,
And may my soul ever enjoy the alluring glory of fine
diction!

III

LISTEN, Divinities, you hold the reins of sacred wisdom.
Who set men's souls on fire with flames indomitable,
Drawing them, through the cloudy depths, far up to the
Immortals,
Purging us with mystic rites of indescribable hymns;
LISTEN great saviors! from divine books
Grant me the innocent, blameless light that dissipates the
clouds,
So I may discover the truth about Man, and the immortal
Divinity!
Neither let the Evil-working Spirit restrain me under the
Lethean waters of Oblivion,
Ever far from the Blessed; for my soul
Would no longer continue to stray,
Nor suffer the cruel pains of imprisonment in the bands of
life!

IV

NAY, Gods of high and illustrious wisdom,
Masters and leaders, hear me, the hastener
Along the Upward Way!—Initiate me into the orgiac
    mysteries
And reveal them by the ceremonies of sacred words!

[298]

PROTAGORAS

PROTAGORAS (About 480-410 B.C.). Professor F. C. Schiller, the
founder of the English branch of modern pragmatism, used to call
himself a disciple of Protagoras. Possibly he did so because Plato
reports a saying of Protagoras, that expressed his disbelief in absolute truth, and maintains that one opinion can be better than
another one though it is not true.

For around 2300 years, the Sophists of whom Protagoras is
the oldest known in history, have been despised as unscrupulous
distorters of facts. It was Friedrich Nietzsche who rehabilitated them,
and since then their contribution to philosophy can no longer be
disregarded. Plato, who initiated the unfavorable opinion about the
Sophists and induced posterity to condemn them without hearing,
however, exempted Protagoras from that sentence.

Protagoras was born in Abdera and studied philosophy, if
not as a personal disciple of Democritus, yet as a pupil of atomistic
materialism. He came to Athens where his conditions seem to have
changed more than once. Pericles highly esteemed him and entrusted
him with drawing up a constitution for the Attic colony of Thurii.
But his books were publicly burned in Athens, and he was persecuted because of blasphemy. In 416, Protagoras was sentenced to
death but escaped to his native town.

Several disciples of Socrates had been previously taught by
Protagoras. None of them seems to have regarded the change of
teachers as a conversion to a very different philosophy. Protagoras,
however, insisted on sensation as the only source of knowledge and
claimed that the art of the Sophist could modify the sensations of
his audience. Any sensation is true as long as it is perceived, and
only that is true which is actually sensed. Protagoras was one of
the creators of Greek rhetoric, the science of language, and scientific
prose. He wrote numerous books, of which only four small fragments are extant.

I DO not know whether or not there are gods, or what they are like. There are many circumstances that prevent us from knowing. The subject is obscure, and the span of time that is given to mortals is short. Man is the measure of all things, of being things that they exist, and of nonentities that they do not exist.

What seems to be just to a man is just only for him. What seems to be just to a city is just for that city.

[299]

PROUDHON, PIERRE JOSEPH

PROUDHON, PIERRE JOSEPH (1809-1865). Of all socialist theorists of the 19th century, Proudhon was the most abounding in ideas but the least capable of mastering them. He was a vigorous but poorly trained thinker, often very original and independent, but sometimes haunted by prejudices and whims. To him philosophy was only a means of changing the thoughts of men. Karl Marx, who met Proudhon in Paris, and admired him greatly though he shortly thereafter vilified him, adopted Proudhon's view that the philosopher has not only to interpret the world but to alter it. Marx learned much more from Proudhon, and gave him information about Hegel that confused Proudhon rather than inspired him. Proudhon, as Marx did after him, criticized his socialist predecessors with no lesser severity than the classical economists. He rejected any Utopian system and also communism as forms of government. He was fundamentally not a revolutionary but a reformer who intended to improve the existing methods of production and distribution instead of overthrowing them. His often quoted saying *La propriété c'est le vol* ("Property is theft") is not meant as a definition of property but as a condemnation of what he considers an abuse of it—namely, the power to provide unearned income. Apart from the right of escheat and lending on interest, private property, the disposal of the results of labor and savings, was declared by Proudhon as the essence of liberty and a necessary stimulant to labor and energy.

Proudhon's philosophy maintains that solidarity is a natural and original characteristic of human beings, and egoism the result of a deviation from natural conditions. Man must be guided back from his present isolation to a community in which the equilibrium between the rights of the individual and "public" or "collective" reason must be established anew, and too great inequality of wealth must be prohibited. He was opposed to the assumption that ideas of justice and morality are dependent on economic or social conditions. In this regard he professed to be a Platonist.

Proudhon was the son of a poor cooper who had not the means to give his children a higher education, and who died in misery because he refused to earn more than the medieval theory of the "just price" allowed. Proudhon therefore had to earn his living as a printer, compositor and proofreader before he became a freelance writer. The first studies he made as an economist concerned his father's fate. From it he drew the conclusion that the world must be altered although he maintained his father's belief that no one should be permitted to earn beyond the "just price."

THE COMPLEXITY OF HUMAN NATURE

HUMAN society is *complex* in its nature. Though this expression is inaccurate, the fact to which it refers is none the less true; namely, the classification of talents and capacities. But who does not see that these talents and capacities, owing to their infinite variety, give rise to an infinite variety of wills, and that the character, the inclinations, and—if I may venture to use the expression—the form of the *ego*, are necessarily changed; so that in the order of liberty, as in the order of intelligence, there are as many types of individuals, as many characters as heads, whose tastes, fancies, and propensities, being modified by dissimilar ideas, must necessarily conflict? Man, by his nature and his instinct, is predestined to society; but his personality, ever varying, is adverse to it.

In societies of animals, all the members do exactly the same things. The same genius directs them; the same will animates them. A society of beasts is a collection of atoms, round, hooked, cubical, or triangular, but always perfectly identical. These personalities do not vary, and we might say that a single *ego* governs them all. The labors which animals perform whether alone or in society, are exact reproductions of their character. Just as the swarm of bees is composed of individual bees, alike in nature and equal in value, so the honeycomb is formed of individual cells, constantly and invariably repeated.

But man's intelligence, fitted for his social destiny and his personal needs, is of a very different composition, and therefore gives rise to a wonderful variety of human wills. In the bee, the will is constant and uniform, because the instinct which guides it is invariable, and constitutes the animal's whole life and nature. In man, talent varies, and the mind wavers; consequently, his will is multiform and vague. He seeks society, but dislikes constraint and monotony; he is an imitator, but fond of his own ideas, and passionately in love with his works.

If, like the bees, every man were born possessed of talent, perfect knowledge of certain kinds, and, in a word, an innate acquaintance with the functions he has to perform, but destitute of reflective and reasoning faculties, society would organize itself. We should see one man plowing a field, another building houses; this one forging metals, that one cutting clothes; and still others storing the products and superintending their distribution. Each one, without inquiring as to the object of his labor, and without troubling himself about the extent of his task, would obey orders, bring his product, receive his salary, and would then rest for a time; keeping meanwhile no accounts, envious of nobody, and satisfied with the distributor, who never would be unjust to any one. Kings would govern, but would not reign; for to reign is to be a *proprietor à l'engrais*, as Bonaparte said: and having no commands to give, since all would be at their posts, they would serve rather as rallying centers than as authorities or counsellors. It would be a state of ordered communism, but not a society entered into deliberately and freely.

But man acquires skill only by observation and experiment. He reflects, then, since to observe and experiment is to reflect; he reasons, since he cannot help reasoning. In reflecting, he becomes deluded; in reasoning, he makes mistakes, and, thinking himself right, persists in them. He is wedded to his opinions; he esteems himself, and despises others. Consequently, he isolates himself; for he could not submit to the majority without renouncing his will and his reason,—that is, without disowning himself, which is impossible. And this isolation, this intellectual egotism, this individuality of opinion, lasts until the truth is demonstrated to him by observation and experience.

[300]

PYTHAGORAS

PYTHAGORAS (578?-510? B.C.). Already in the days of Xenophanes and Heraclitus of Ephesus, about 500 B.C., Pythagoras had become a legendary figure, and all the efforts of ancient and modern scholars, to distinguish between fiction and truth or between Pythagoras' own performances and those of his disciples, the Pythagoreans, have resulted only in more or less probable conjectures. But his historical existence cannot be doubted. Some ancient authorities assert that he was born in Syria, but most of them think that he was born on the island of Samos, and that he emigrated to Southern Italy after Polycrates had seized power over his native country in 538 B.C. In Italy, Pythagoras seems to have founded a school which was like a religious and political order, and to have tried to interfere with politics.

There is general agreement that Pythagoras is regarded as the initiator of mathematical demonstration and deduction. Whether he himself or one of his disciples discovered the proposition about right-angled triangles which is named after him, cannot be ascertained. Pythagoras also is credited with having discovered the importance of numbers in music and having laid the fundaments of the theory of that art.

There is also general agreement that Pythagoras combined rational science and religious mysticism, and endeavored to use mathematical concepts and axioms for otherworldly speculations. He influenced Plato and Plotinus, and, through them, many mystics and metaphysicians up to the present day.

PAY honor first to the Immortal Gods,
As Order hath established Their Choirs:
Reverence the Oath. The heroes great and good
Revere thou next, and earth's good geniuses,
Paying to them such honors as are due.
Honor thy parents and thy nearest kin;
Of others make the virtuous thy friend:
Yield to his gentle words, his timely acts;
Nor for a petty fault take back thy love.
Bear what thou canst: pow'r cometh at man's need.
Know this for truth, and learn to conquer these:
Thy belly first; sloth, luxury, and rage.
Do nothing base with others or alone,
And, above all things, thine own self respect.
Next practice justice in thy word and deed
And learn to act unreasonably in naught;
But know that all must die. Wealth comes and goes.
Of ills the Goddess Fortune gives to man
Bear meekly thou thy lot, nor grieve at it;
But cure it as thou canst. Remember this:
Fate gives the least of evil to the good.
Many the reasonings that on men's ears
Fall; good and bad. Admire not all of such
Nor shun them neither. If one speaketh false,
Be calm. And practice ever this that now
I say. Let no man's word or deed seduce thee
To do or say aught not to thy best good.
First think, then act; lest foolish be thy deed.
Unhappy he who thoughtless acts and speaks:
But that which after vexes not do thou.
Do naught thou dost not understand; but learn
That which is right, and sweet will be thy life.
Nor shouldest thou thy body's health neglect,
But give it food and drink and exercise
In measure; that is, to cause it no distress.

Decent, without vain show, thy way of life:
Look well to this, that none thou envious make
By unmeet expense, like one who lacks good taste.
Nor niggard be: in all the mean is best.
Do that which cannot harm thee. Think, then act.
When first thou dost from soothing sleep uprise,
Hasten about thy day's intended work;
Nor suffer sleep to fall on thy soft lids
Till thrice thou hast each act of the day recalled:
How have I sinned? What done? What duty missed?
Go through them first to last; and, if they seem
Evil, reproach thyself; if good, rejoice.
Toil at and practice this; this must thou love;
This to the Path of Heavenly Virtue leads.
By Him Who gave the Tetractys to our soul,
Fount of Eternal Nature, this I swear.
Begin thy work, first having prayed the Gods
To accomplish it. Thou, having mastered this,
That essence of Gods and mortal men shalt know,
Which all things permeate, which all obey.
And thou shalt know that Law hath stablishéd
The inner nature of all things alike;
So shalt thou hope not for what may not be,
Nor aught, that may, escape thee. Thou shalt know
Self-chosen are the woes that fall on men—
How wretched, for they see not good so near,
Nor hearken to its voice—few only know
The Pathway of Deliverance from ill.
Such fate doth blind mankind, who, up and down,
With countless woes are carried by its wheel.
For bitter inborn strife companions them
And does them secret harm. Provoke it not,
O men, but yield, and yielding, find escape.
O Father Zeus, 'twould free from countless ills
Didst Thou but show what Genius works in each!
But courage! Men are children of the Gods,
And Sacred Nature all things hid reveals.

And if the Mysteries have part in thee,
Thou shalt prevail in all I bade thee do,
And, thoroughly cured, shalt save thy soul from toil.
Eat not the foods proscribed, but use discretion
In lustral rites and the freeing of thy soul:
Ponder all things, and stablish high thy mind,
That best of charioteers. And if at length,
Leaving behind thy body, thou dost come
To the free Upper Air, then shalt thou be
Deathless, divine, a mortal man no more.

[301]

$\mathcal{R}$

RAMSEY, FRANK PLUMPTON

RAMSEY, FRANK PLUMPTON (1903-1930). The premature death of Ramsey at the age of twenty-six has been felt as a heavy loss by leading thinkers in the field of philosophy, mathematical logic, and theory of economics.

Ramsey tried to tackle problems at the point where Bertrand Russell and Ludwig Wittgenstein had left them. He makes a fundamental distinction between *human logic,* which deals with useful mental habits and is applicable to the logic of probability, and *formal logic,* which is concerned with the rules of consistent thought. Against John Maynard Keynes he holds that probability is concerned not with objective relations between propositions but with degrees of belief. Keynes partly yielded to Ramsey without abandoning his efforts to make induction an application of mathematical probability.

MY OUTLOOK ON THE WORLD

IF I was to write a *Weltanschauung* I should call it not "What I believe" but "What I feel." This is connected with Wittgenstein's view that philosophy does not give us beliefs, but merely relieves feelings of intellectual discomfort. Also, if I were to quarrel with Russell, it would not be with what he believed but with the indications given as to what he felt. Not that one can really quarrel with a man's feelings; one can only have different feelings oneself, and perhaps also regard one's own as more admirable or more conducive to a happy life. From this point of view, that it is a matter not of fact but of feeling, I shall conclude by some remarks on things in general, or, as I would rather say, not things but *life* in general.

Where I seem to differ from some of my friends is in attaching little importance to physical size. I don't feel the least humble before the vastness of the heavens. The stars may be large, but they cannot think or love; and these are qualities which impress me far more than size does. I take no credit for weighing nearly seventeen stone.

My picture of the world is drawn in perspective, and not like a model to scale. The foreground is occupied by human beings and the stars are all as small as threepenny bits. I don't really believe in astronomy, except as a complicated description of part of the course of human and possibly animal sensation. I apply my perspective not merely to space but also to time. In time the world will cool and everything will die; but that is a long time off still, and its present value at compound discount is almost nothing. Nor is the present less valuable because the future will be blank. Humanity, which fills the foreground of my picture, I find interesting and on the whole admirable. I find, just now at least, the world a pleasant and exciting place. You may find it depressing; I am sorry for you, and you despise me. But I have reason and you have none; you would only have a reason for despising me if your feeling corresponded to the fact in a way mine didn't. But neither can correspond to the fact. The fact is not in itself good or bad; it is just that it thrills me but depresses you. On the other hand, I pity you with reason, because it is pleasanter to be thrilled than to be depressed, and not merely pleasanter but better for all one's activities.

[302]

REICHENBACH, HANS

REICHENBACH, HANS (1891-1953). Reichenbach belongs to a generation of scientists who began to study after most of their teachers had already abandoned the concepts of classical physics; thus they were able to start with ideas and modes of thought found by their predecessors after much hardship, trial and error. Reichenbach, however, has actively participated in the further advance

984

of science and philosophy. His contributions have been discussed by the greatest contemporary scientists and philosophers with respect if not with general consent, and are recognized either as real contributions or at least as working hypotheses or useful suggestions.

At first, Reichenbach was preoccupied with the clarification of the concepts of space and time, their relations, and the way of assimilating one to another. As a theorist of knowledge, Reichenbach comes in his own way closer to the methods of the Vienna Circle, but he even more vigorously insists that all our knowledge is only probable. The doctrine of probability, advanced by R. von Mises and Reichenbach, is based on the concept of "frequency," a statistical concept. Every definition of induction is involved in this doctrine. Induction is described as a process of predicting future events with the aid of propositions of probability which serve as instruments of indication. Reichenbach objects to classical logic that it classifies propositions according to their truth or falsity instead of lower or higher degrees of probability. He holds that true logic is probability logic, and has presented his views in *Wahrscheinlichkeitslehre* (Doctrine of Probability, 1935) and *Experience and Prediction* (1938).

In his *Elements of Symbolic Logic* (1947), Reichenbach acknowledges classical logic as the "mother of all logics" and admits that it can be carried through in the sense of approximation, even if refined analysis demands probability logic.

LOGIC AND LANGUAGE

IF it is true that to a certain extent we can improve our thinking by studying logic, the fact is to be explained as a conditioning of our thought operations in such a way that the relative number of right results is increased.

When we call logic *analysis of thought* the expression should be interpreted so as to leave no doubt that it is not actual thought which we pretend to analyze. It is rather a substitute for thinking processes, their *rational reconstruction,* which constitutes the basis of logical analysis. Once a result of thinking is obtained, we can reorder our thoughts in a cogent way, constructing a chain of thoughts between point of departure and point of arrival; it is this rational reconstruction of thinking that is controlled by logic, and whose analysis reveals those rules which we call logical laws.

The two realms of analysis to be distinguished may be called *context of discovery* and *context of justification*. The context of discovery is left to psychological analysis, whereas logic is concerned with the context of justification, i.e., with the analysis of ordered series of thought operations so constructed that they make the results of thought justifiable. We speak of a justification when we possess a proof which shows that we have good grounds to rely upon those results.

It has been questioned whether all thinking processes are accompanied by linguistic utterances, and behavioristic theories stating that thinking *consists* in linguistic utterances have been attacked by other psychologists. We need not enter into this controversy here for the very reason that we connect logical analysis, not with actual thinking, but with thinking in the form of its rational reconstruction. There can be no doubt that this reconstruction is bound to linguistic form; this is the reason that logic is so closely connected with language. Only after thinking processes have been cast into linguistic form do they attain the precision that makes them accessible to logical tests; logical validity is therefore a predicate of linguistic forms. Considerations of this kind have led to the contention that logic is *analysis of language*, and that the term "logical laws" should be replaced by the term "rules of language." Thus in the theory of deduction we study the rules leading from true linguistic utterances to other true linguistic utterances. This terminology appears admissible when it is made clear that the term "rules of language" is not synonymous with "arbitrary rules." Not all rules of language are arbitrary; for instance, the rules of deduction are not, but are determined by the postulate that they must lead from true sentences to true sentences.

It is the value of such an analysis of language˙that it makes thought processes clear, that it distinguishes meanings and the relations between meanings from the blurred background of psychological motives and intentions. The student of logic will find that an essential instrument for such clarification is supplied by the method of symbolization, which has given its name to the modern form of logic. It is true that simple logical operations can be performed without the help of symbolic representation; but the structure of complicated relations cannot be seen without the aid of symbolism. The reason is that the symbolism eliminates the specific meanings of words and expresses the general structure which controls these words, allotting to them their places within comprehensive relations. The great advantage of modern logic over the older forms of the science results from the fact that this logic is able to analyze structures that traditional logic never has understood, and that it is able to solve problems of whose existence the older logic has never been aware.

We said that logic cannot claim to replace creative thought. This limitation includes symbolic logic; we do not wish to say that the methods of symbolic logic will make unnecessary the imaginative forms of thought used in all domains of life, and it certainly would be a misunderstanding to believe that symbolic logic represents a sort of slide-rule technique by which all problems can be solved. The practical value of a new scientific technique is always a secondary question. Logic is primarily a theoretical science; and it proceeds by giving a determinate form to notions that until then had been employed without a clear understanding of their nature. Whoever has had such an insight into the structure of thought, whoever has experienced in his own mind the great clarification process which logical analysis accomplishes, will know what logic can achieve.

[303]

RICARDO, DAVID

RICARDO, DAVID (1772-1823). One of Ricardo's basic convictions, namely, the belief that businessmen are always acting with a full knowledge of all possible consequences of their actions, has been proved to be wrong. Also, some of his other propositions have been definitely refuted. Nevertheless, Ricardo's authority as an acute and informed thinker remains unshattered, and many of his discoveries have become commonplace. Important concepts, formulated by him, have been adopted by economists who defend either private enterprise or socialism.

Ricardo, the son of a Jewish stockbroker who had come to England from Holland, was a financier and member of the London Stock Exchange. He lacked classical education, having attended only an elementary school, but he had learned, as an autodidact, natural sciences and political economics. From 1819 until his death, he was a member of Parliament, and was, despite his radical opinions, revered by both sides of the House as the highest authority in matters of finance and currency. Although Ricardo was a clever businessman, his political and economic demands took no regard of vested interests, not even his own private interests. In his *Principles of Political Economy and Taxation* (1817), Ricardo states an "iron law" in virtue of which rent is always rising while real wages remain stationary, and the profits of the manufacturer and the farmer, kept at the same level by the competition of capital, are constantly declining. In order to change this state of things, Ricardo attempted in vain to ally the rest of the nations against the great landowners. His statements are founded upon exact observations of the economic situation of his own time and the preceding fifty years of British history, but from this reliable knowledge, Ricardo proceeded to rash generalizations. A powerful advocate of free trade, Ricardo was by no means an optimist. He expressed grave apprehensions concerning class struggle. Marx borrowed this and some other formulas from Ricardo but drew different conclusions from them. Bulwer-Lytton's novel *Pelham* and many other literary documents of the second and third decades of the 19th century testify to Ricardo's popularity, although his own style was rather dry. His premature death was mourned by the entire British nation.

ON WAGES

LABOR, like all other things which are purchased and sold, and which may be increased or diminished in quantity, has its natural and its market price. The natural price of labor is that price which is necessary to enable the laborers, one with another, to subsist and to perpetuate their race, without either increase or diminution.

The power of the laborer to support himself, and the

family which may be necessary to keep up the number of laborers, does not depend on the quantity of money which he may receive for wages, but on the quantity of food, necessaries, and conveniences become essential to him from habit which that money will purchase. The natural price of labor, therefore, depends on the price of the food, necessaries, and conveniences required for the support of the laborer and his family. With a rise in the price of food and necessaries, the natural price of labor will rise; with the fall in their price, the natural price of labor will fall.

With the progress of society the natural price of labor has always a tendency to rise, because one of the principal commodities by which its natural price is regulated has a tendency to become dearer from the greater difficulty of producing it. As, however, the improvements in agriculture, the discovery of new markets, whence provisions may be imported, may for a time counteract the tendency to a rise in the price of necessaries, and may even occasion their natural price to fall, so will the same causes produce the correspondent effects on the natural price of labor.

The natural price of all commodities, excepting raw produce and labor, has a tendency to fall in the progress of wealth and population; for though, on one hand, they are enhanced in real value, from the rise in the natural price of the raw material of which they are made, this is more than counter-balanced by the improvements in machinery, by the better division and distribution of labor, and by the increasing skill, both in science and art, of the producers.

The market price of labor is the price which is really paid for it, from the natural operation of the proportion of the supply to the demand; labor is dear when it is scarce and cheap when it is plentiful. However much the market price of labor may deviate from its natural price, it has, like commodities, a tendency to conform to it.

It is when the market price of labor exceeds its natural price that the condition of the laborers is flourishing and happy, that he has it in his power to command a greater proportion of the necessaries and enjoyments of life, and therefore to rear a healthy and numerous family. When, however, by the encouragement which high wages give to the increase of population, the number of laborers is increased, wages again fall to their natural price, and indeed from a reaction sometimes fall below it.

When the market price of labor is below its natural price, the condition of the laborers is most wretched: then poverty deprives them of those comforts which custom renders absolute necessaries. It is only after their privations have reduced their number, or the demand for labor has increased, that the market price of labor will rise to its natural price, and that the laborer will have the moderate comforts which the natural rate of wages will afford.

Notwithstanding the tendency of wages to conform to their natural rate, their market rate may, in an improving society, for an indefinite period, be constantly above it; for no sooner may the impulse which an increased capital gives to a new demand for labor be obeyed, than another increase of capital may produce the same effect; and thus, if the increase of capital be gradual and constant, the demand for labor may give a continued stimulus to an increase of people.

Capital is that part of the wealth of a country which is employed in production, and consists of food, clothing, tools, raw materials, machinery, etc., necessary to give effect to labor.

Capital may increase in quantity at the same time that its value rises. An addition may be made to the food and clothing of a country at the same time that more labor may be required to produce the additional quantity than before; in that case not only the quantity but the value of capital will rise.

Or capital may increase without its value increasing, and even while its value is actually diminishing; not only may an addition be made to the food and clothing of a country, but the addition may be made by the aid of machinery, without any increase, and even with an absolute diminution in the proportional quantity of labor required to produce them. The quantity of capital may increase, while neither the whole together, nor any part of it singly, will have a greater value than before, but may actually have a less.

In the first case, the natural price of labor, which always depends on the price of food, clothing, and other necessaries, will rise; in the second, it will remain stationary or fall; but in both cases the market rate of wages will rise, for in proportion to the increase of capital will be the increase in the demand for labor; in proportion to the work to be done will be the demand for those who are to do it.

In both cases, too, the market price of labor will rise above its natural price; and in both cases it will have a tendency to conform to its natural price, but in the first case this agreement will be most speedily effected. The situation of the laborer will be improved, but not much more improved; for the increased price of food and necessaries will absorb a large portion of his increased wages; consequently a small supply of labor, or a trifling increase in the population, will soon reduce the market price to the then increased natural price of labor.

In the second case, the condition of the laborer will be very greatly improved; he will receive increased money wages without having to pay any increased price, and perhaps even a diminished price for the commodities which he and his family consume; and it will not be till after a great addition has been made to the population that the market price of labor will again sink to its then low and reduced natural price.

Thus, then, with every improvement of society, with every increase in its capital, the market wages of labor will rise; but the permanence of their rise will depend on the question whether the natural price of labor has also risen; and this again will depend on the rise in the natural price of those necessaries on which the wages of labor are expended.

[304]

991

RICKERT, HEINRICH

RICKERT, HEINRICH (1863-1936). Closely associated with Wilhelm Windelband and his successor as professor of philosophy at the University of Heidelberg, Rickert was also a leader of the "South-West-German school of philosophy" and fought, as Windelband did, against a concept of science that comprises natural sciences only. His early works were concerned with the demonstration of the limits of the formation of concepts which natural sciences cannot extend, or with the thesis that natural sciences envisage only part of nature, leaving it to other sciences, namely historical sciences, to deal with the neglected aspects of reality.

In his later years, Rickert, without abandoning the views he shared with Windelband, concentrated more and more upon the problem of values. While declaring that the values of civilization are the real object of philosophy, Rickert refuted the doctrines according to which life in itself is the supreme value. Contrary to philosophers like Nietzsche and Bergson, Rickert emphasized that values demand a distance from life, and that what Bergson, Dilthey or Simmel called "vital values" were not true values. For Rickert, the connection between value and life was secured by the realm of meaning. While reality is to be explained and values are to be understood, meanings are to be interpreted. According to Rickert, the meaning of life can be interpreted only by understanding the value of civilization, even if civilization might be recognized as of no value.

NATURAL AND CULTURAL SCIENCE

IF we conceive the notion of natural science broadly enough so that it coincides with the conception of a generalizing science, is then knowledge of the material world by any procedure other than that of the natural sciences possible at all? . . . There are sciences that do not tend toward the establishment of natural laws, not even toward the formulation of general conceptions, and these are the historical sciences in the widest sense of the word. They don't seek to make only "ready-made suits" which fit Paul as well as Peter—that means, they want to present reality being never general but always individual in its complete individuality and, as soon as this individuality is to be considered, the concept of the natural science must fail because it is the characteristic of this concept that it eliminates the individual as negligible.

With Goethe, the historians will think concerning the general: "We use it but we don't like it; we like only the individual," and they certainly want to present this individual scientifically just as far as the object that shall be investigated is concerned as a whole. Let us, for a moment, leave it undecided in what way historical science presents the peculiarity and individuality of reality. Since reality as such, on account of its immense diversity, cannot be comprised in one concept, and since the elements of all concepts are general, the idea of an individualizing formation of concepts must appear problematical. One cannot, however, dispute the fact that history sees its task in the presentation of the peculiar and individual, and from the viewpoint of this task one has to explain its formal essence. For all concepts of sciences are concepts of tasks, and to understand them logically is only possible if one proceeds from comprehending their purposes to penetrating into the logical structure of their method. This is the road that leads to the goal. History, as "History," does not want to generalize in the manner as natural sciences do. That is as the decisive point of logic.

Recently the contradistinction between the procedure of the natural sciences, that is, the generalizing procedure, and the historical procedure has been clarified, at least in this one, if only negative, regard. . . . Without dwelling upon other contributions to the clarification of this point, I refer only to the studies of Windelband. He places at the side of the "nomothetical" procedure of the natural sciences the "idiographical" procedure of history, namely, the procedure that tends toward the presentation of what happens only once and in a particular way.

In order to obtain two exclusively logical and therefore exclusively formal concepts of nature and history, signifying not two different realities but the same reality under different aspects, I have formulated the logical fundamental problem of a division of the sciences according to their methods, as follows: Reality becomes nature if we consider it with regard to the general. It becomes history if we consider it with regard to the special and individual and, accordingly, I want to oppose the individualizing procedure of history to the generalizing procedure of natural sciences.

[305]

RIDPATH, JOHN CLARK

RIDPATH, JOHN CLARK (1840-1900). Ridpath, the editor of some of America's most popular encyclopedias, was by nature an encyclopedist, surveying the whole range of knowledge of his time, always working hard, aided by an extraordinarily reliable memory, reading untiringly, learning constantly, and able to teach what he had read and learned. In fact, his great talents for teaching are also the conspicuous quality of his writings.

Ridpath was born and grew up on a farm in the frontier community of Putnam County, Indiana, remote from high schools. He owed it to his highly cultivated parents that he could attend Indiana Asbury University, where he later had a brilliant career as teacher, professor, and vice-president. He taught English literature, history and normal instruction. In 1885, he renounced his professorship in order to devote his full time to writing. His principal works are *Encyclopedia of Universal History* (1880-85), *The Great Races of Mankind* (1884-94), and *The Ridpath Library of Universal Literature*, comprising 25 volumes (1898).

LITERATURE

LITERATURE is the highest blossom of the human spirit. It is higher than art; for if art survives for ages, literature survives forever; it is immortal.

Such is the nature of literature that it is susceptible of being translated from language to language, from race to race, from century to century, and, it may be, from world to world. For thought, we doubt not, is in some measure common to the inhabitants of all the spheres. Is not thought indeed a part and essence of the eternities?

While the conditions of purely aesthetic production suffer change, and while the canons of artistic criticism are frequently amended and reversed, literature remains coeval with mankind; it cannot suffer save in the decadence of the race and in the collapse of civilization.

Literature is recorded in the book; the book is its receptacle. Literature is the soul of the book, and the book is the body of the soul. The book is multifarious in form and presence. It may be of papyrus, and its pictured symbols may be the hieratic images and fictions of old Egypt. The book may be the sacred scroll of Brahma. It may be the inaccessible wedges on the sculptured face of the rocks of Behistun. It may be the parchment roll of Herodotus, from which he reads to the assembled Greeks. It may be the bark of the *beech* (from which, indeed, is the name of the *book*) written in runes on its inner, sappy surface, as by the old Goths beyond the Danube. The book may be the parchment rolls of Roman poet or orator. It may be the crude sheets marked from the black-letter blocks of Gutenberg and Faust. It may be the primitive book of Wyclif or of the old printers of Venice. It may be the printed paper book (albeit "paper" is *papyrus*) of our modern age, born of revolving cylinders and clattering binderies going always, pouring forth their infinity of volumes into the lap of civilization. And in these books is embodied the literature of the world.

Literature is not of one race, but of all enlightened races. Even the barbarians, though they have it not, possess its rudiments. No sooner do they become self-conscious than they begin to essay the expression of that consciousness in some record of themselves and their deeds.

To gather and preserve in an acceptable form the literature of the world, or the best of that literature, is a work not to be overlooked in estimating the means by which the civilized life is preserved and promoted. Certainly not all literature can be brought within the reach of all intelligences. Only *some* can be preserved and offered as a treasure *to* some; and perhaps a portion to all.

[306]

ROMAINS, JULES

ROMAINS, JULES (1885-). At the height of his literary successes as one of the greatest French novelists of our time, Jules Romains has been faithful to the ideal of "unanimism" which has dominated the poetry of his youth, but he has modified it and changed the means of expression.

"Unanimism" originally meant an opposition to individualism, or at least to the exaltation of individual particularities, universal sympathy with life, existence, humanity. In later years, the end of literature has been defined by Romains as "representation of the world without judgment," and his social ideal seems to comprise as well the highest conception of solidarity as the defense of individual rights. In his immense series of novels, *Men of Good Will*, Romains has not limited his task to the invention of characters and events but has also tried to live the lives of his figures with extreme concreteness, to let them think about questions of the day and the universe, about the principal problems of civilization, to let them criticize one another, develop their judgment, and he has indeed succeeded in uniting intellectual force, artistic vision, colorful description, and narrative dynamics. The result is a picture of French cultural life in its stratification, with its fundamental conflicts and common tendencies, on a scale which can be compared only with Balzac and Zola, but surpassing its rivals in spirituality and psychological refinement.

Romains is no sceptic. He does not believe that human mind is capable of discovering absolute and definite truth. He holds that there will always be an aspect of reality which challenges the dominant one. Reality means change. When man becomes tired of broaching new questions and when he acquiesces in a creed or system, he will lose contact with reality. But he believes that in the course of history man will come closer and closer to truth, although new aspects will be opened which let him see new problems. His "men of good will" respect reason and give experience the last word, though they do not exclude the possibility that intuition, in exceptional cases, may also discover reality.

996

THE ADVENTURE OF HUMANITY

It is in the human sphere that the problem takes on breadth and vital interest. The reader may know that I have devoted a great deal of attention to human groups. When *unanimism* is discussed it ordinarily designates a specialized study, largely a literary one, of the life of human groups, and the relationship between the individual and these groups.

I believe, in fact, that the adventure of humanity is essentially an adventure of groups. It is also an adventure of individuals in conflict with groups or with each other. This conflict is maintained under conditions which bring into constant play the aptitude for forming multiple ties, truly biological associations, as well as the aptitude for warding off the forces of "dispossession," both spiritual and physical, which groups or collectivities of various kinds may exercise over the individual.

Reduced to its simplest form, this statement contains very little originality. The life of society, at whatever level, has always been considered important as a key to the explanation of human action.

Experience, however, has proved that this bare statement takes on a special power of illumination when one endows the idea of the group with its full richness of content, its efficacy, one might almost say its virulence. Especially when one need not be afraid to look for the organic bond elsewhere than in mere metaphors and abstractions.

This patient and painstaking quest for the organic bond down to its weakest manifestation is in brief the essence of unanimism: a quest rather than a doctrine.

It will be noted that this quest profits by one very remarkable circumstance. Man forms part of the groups, the organizations which he seeks to understand. The situation is analogous to that in which he finds himself when he attempts to probe human consciousness. As he himself is "human consciousness," the facts he investigates occur within him, form a part of himself. He manages to grasp many of them, and to grasp them (without detriment to other methods) in a firm and essential way by the direct means of introspection, that is to say by consciousness carried to a high degree of acuteness and subtlety. There is a direct connection of the same kind between man and the groups or communities of which he is part. This connection cannot be questioned even by the most positivist, the most critical minds. They, for instance, admit that as part of society we can more readily than if we were not part of it, take account of the internal mechanisms of that society and understand the *raison d'être* of the varied behavior of social man, his customs and manners, the influence exerted on him by group emotions, public institutions, etc.—even if this internal awareness does not reveal everything. But I for one go further. I hold, on the basis of an experience of a special nature, that we are able, with the aid of certain refinements of attention, to grasp the interhuman organic bond, even in its most essential and invisible form, its most fugitive nascent stages. This is, if you will, the counterpart of introspection when it functions most profoundly and permits us to grasp the psychic reality within us.

Now it becomes a question of reaching a psychic reality which is not external to us but which envelops us. I am far from believing—even if I have appeared to say so at certain times—that this enveloping psychic reality does not exceed the bounds of human groups. But human groups elaborate and condense it in a fashion, raise it one degree higher, just as the human consciousness condenses and raises to a higher plane some psychic reality which exceeds the limitations of personal identity.

It is not astonishing—and I emphasize this—that I have attributed a prominent part in this investigation to literature in all its forms. Literature has, for the same reasons, played an important part in the investigation of the spirit.

I have been reproached for having "deified" the group. And it is true I have pronounced words on the subject dangerous to the extent that they might provoke a confusion between the order of fact and the order of right, between the real and desirable. That groups, having achieved a certain degree of organic reality, should be termed by the poet "gods" or, better, "divine animals"—this is merely to express on the lyric or mystic plane a real fact. That fact arises from the disproportion in dimension and power (physical and psychic) between groups and individuals. It implies the change of magnitude occurring when one rises from one plane to the other. But it would obviously be hazardous to draw from this the unqualified conclusion that the group as opposed to the individual is always right, and that the individual's only attitude should be submission and worship.

In any case, formerly no less than now, I have always insisted that the power of the group over the individual is justified only to the extent to which it finds expression in and by the spontaneity of the individual. I condemned the restrictions imposed upon the individual from without by society and its institutions. As forcibly as I could, I emphasized the contrast between "society," conceived as a system of restraints and conventions, and "the unanimous life," conceived as the "free respiration" of human groups and implying the voluntary surrender of the individual to their influence and attractions. I indicated the danger lying in the very idea of the state, with all its germs of juridical formalism and of oppression. I even declared that a certain infusion of "anarchy" is indispensable to avert the demoniacal mechanization of society and salvage "the unanimous life." On the other hand, I have always maintained the extreme importance—for good or evil—of the leader.

The political and social events of the last twenty years have but confirmed these opinions. It has been said, ironically —and hardly to make me feel happy—that the founders of totalitarian governments are to some extent my disciples. My reply was that these governments are merely a burlesque of unanimism, and that they err and err gravely in two important respects. First, they proceed by coercion and are as far as possible from fostering the "free respiration" of the masses. Second, they have a shockingly over-simplified idea of unanimity. They interpret it as an inexorable uniformity of thought, an inflexible and sterile "union." Unanimism postulates the richest possible variety of individual states of consciousness, in a "harmony" made valuable by its richness and density. This harmony is necessary before any glimpse can be given of the birth of those states of consciousness that transcend the individual spirit.

[307]

ROMERO, FRANCISCO

ROMERO, FRANCISCO (1891-). As far as opposition to positivism prevails in Latin America, Romero is to be considered the present leader of the philosophic movement in these countries, especially in Argentina. Romero has become influential as a critic, as a translator from the German, and, even more so, as a stimulating teacher. He has not yet published systematic works but his treatises, *Old and New Concepts of Reality* (1932), *The Problems of Philosophy of Culture* (1938) and *Program of a Philosophy* (1940), attracted general attention and were much discussed. Inspired by Gestalt theory, Romero defends a structural conception of reality against Hume and rationalism, biological evolutionism and any atomistic conception. True being is identified by Romero with transcendence, and personality is its function.

THE MARCH OF PHILOSOPHY FOR CENTURIES

PHILOSOPHY has investigated with growing exactness and profoundness the problem of nature, the order and constitution of the physical world. The problem of cognition, namely, the question of how we obtain knowledge of this world, has been raised afterwards. And only much later has philosophy dealt with questions concerning the world of culture, meaning the world of the products of man and his manners of living. At first glance, it seems surprising that the object of research has been at first that which is farthest and most remote from us, the external world, and that only afterwards philosophical curiosity has spread to cognition itself and to culture, which is our most immediate environment, nearest to us not only as environment but also as our creation.

But this fact is strange only in appearance. That which concerns us most immediately is not generally the first to be noticed by us. In order to see things, a certain distance that permits perspective is indicated. If the distance does not exist, an effort must be made to adapt the sight in such a manner as to concentrate upon the object which, just by its immediacy and intimacy, is invisible for a spontaneous act of cognition. Of the whole field forming our natural scenery at any moment only a fraction is totally invisible: precisely what concerns us most closely, the square stones which support our feet. The piece of ground which sustains us is at any moment the one we cannot see.

This strange rule, according to which the cognition of that which is closest to us is the most difficult and the last, is fulfilled with relative, if not absolute, regularity. The movement of the stars was studied before the evolution of the insects. The child discovers above all the surrounding world and must wait until adolescence in order to realize with anxiety and astonishment the discovery of its intimate feelings. Philosophical thinking seems to follow the same path. The first philosophers of the Occident are called pre-Socratics, a designation which comprises the thinkers from Thales to the atomists, Leucippus and Democritus. Their problem is essentially the problem of being, of the things, the structure and the law of the world. The human spirit that thinks and knows the world, this center of all thought to be reality, this reality incomparable to any other, which is man, remains invisible to them. The pre-Socratics are the ancestors of western philosophy, but, at the same time, they are like children, absorbed by the magnificent spectacle of the exterior world, and ignoring that world which is their own personality. The adolescence of Greek thought, the discovery of the subject, of the problems man is confronted with occurs in the Attic stage with the much abused Sophists and with Socrates. When they formulated first questions concerning the essence of man, the problems of the things had already been examined from all sides.

[308]

ROSCELLIN

ROSCELLIN (About 1050-1120). The war waged by Roscellin against Platonism and every kind of realism is interesting because it induced him to adumbrate a criticism of language which impresses one as most modern. Proceeding from the statement that in nature only individuals exist and species are not things, Roscellin has inquired into the generalizing character of words and language. In 1092 he was accused of adhering to Tritheism, i.e., that he conceived of the Trinity as of three distinct deities. He denied such a doctrine but later returned to it. Roscellin taught at the schools of several French towns. Among his pupils was Abailard who later criticized him. Roscellin's thoughts are known to us only by quotations which his adversaries made. Of all his writings only a letter to Abailard is extant.

A TEACHER'S DEFENSE AGAINST HIS DISCIPLE

You assert, I be excluded from Christianity. I have been educated in the schools of the churches of Soissons and Rheims, as can be testified. Rome, the capital of the world, has friendlily received me, and listened to my words with great joy. In Tours where I was canon, you have been sitting at my feet as my humblest disciple as long as you have stayed in that town. . . .

I am very sad that you have called me the persecutor of good men. Maybe, I am not good: but I have always revered good men. . . . I will not justify myself, because, if I were seeking for my own glory, my glory would be nothing. . . .

If I have somewhat lapsed in my words and deviated from truth, I would not obstinately defend either words or

1002

assertion, but I am always more prepared to learn than to teach. . . . Words are only breaths of the voice.

ROSENZWEIG, FRANZ

ROSENZWEIG, FRANZ (1886-1929). Shortly before the outbreak of the First World War, a young German scholar of Jewish origin, who had become renowned because of his epoch-making discovery of the earliest outline of German idealism and his acute investigation of the relations between Schelling and Hegel, intended to embrace Christianity. But before making the decisive step he thought it would be appropriate to know what he intended to abandon. He therefore began to study Judaism, and subsequently became resolved not only to remain a Jew, but also to devote his life to the elaboration of a new conception of Judaism, based upon historical, linguistic, and philosophical research, and aimed at a moral and spiritual rejuvenation of his fellow Jews. The first fruit of these efforts was the book *Der Stern der Erloesung* (Star of Salvation), written during the war in the trenches and edited posthumously in 1930.

Rosenzweig's vindication of Judaism is anything but polemical toward Christianity. He is opposed to atheism and irreligion, but his historical consciousness prevents him from attacking, even from disputing, any religious tradition or any living faith. On the contrary, he has encouraged his closest friend and first cousin to embrace Christianity rather than to live apart from any religious community. Although opposed to Jewish nationalism, Rosenzweig thinks that Jewish religion concerns only born Jews, and, without any concession to racialism, founds his philosophy of history upon the fact that the Jews form a cultural unit with a common history and certain relatively constant characteristics. He even maintains that only the Jews, by virtue of being such a unit, can have a genuine philosophy of history in which their fate, regarded as a unit, is the decisive factor. The historical aspect is also of primary importance to Rosenzweig's philosophy of religion which, notwithstanding the tensions between religion and civilization, is at the same time a philosophy of culture.

THE NEW WAY OF THINKING

PEOPLE are still accustomed to thinking that philosophy must begin with epistemological considerations. In fact, however, philosophy might rather end with them. Kant's criticism, initiating the epistemological prejudice of our days, is nothing but the finishing accomplishment of a historical epoch that began with the natural sciences of the era of the Baroque. Kant's criticism proves to be correct only as far as the philosophy of that epoch is concerned. To the "Copernican revolution" of Copernicus that made man a particle of dust in the universe corresponds the "Copernican revolution" of Kant that, in order to compensate man, elevated him on the throne of the world. The two revolutions correspond one to another more precisely than Kant ever imagined. A dreadful humiliation of man at the expense of his humanity has been compensated, equally at the expense of his humanity, by a reckless correction. . . .

In truth, even in ultimate truth, there must be contained an "and." It must be, different from the philosopher's truth that knows only itself, truth for somebody. If it shall be the one truth, then it can be only truth for one. Our truth, therefore, necessarily becomes multifarious, and "the truth" will be transformed into "our truth." Truth ceases to be "what is true," and becomes what will stand the test of truth. The concept of standing the test becomes the fundamental concept of the new epistemology which replaces the old theory of consistency and objectivity by a dynamic one.

[310]

ROSHD, IBN. See AVERROÉS.

ROSMINI-SERBATI, ANTONIO

ROSMINI-SERBATI, ANTONIO (1797-1855). Even to organize charity and enjoin poverty is not without grave consequences and above suspicion. That is what Rosmini-Serbati had to learn. This thinker who is classed as an ontologist in philosophy, is better known for the world-wide Institutes of Charity, the first of which he established in 1828 on Monte Calvario near Domodossola, Italy. Rosminians have to take vows of absolute poverty, which have been criticized at times as more affective than effective, and they must subscribe in their charitable work to two principles, that of passivity or not seeking out their cases and that of personal indifference or disinterestedness in the performance of their duty.

Rosmini was born at Rovereto in the Austrian Tyrol, studied at Trient and Padua, and in 1823 went to Rome with the avowed intention to resuscitate Catholic philosophy and fortify it against disbelief and doubt, in which purpose Pope Pius VII encouraged him. Deeply influenced by Cartesian thinking, he poured over the philosophy of St. Thomas, modifying it in the direction of an ideological psychologism.

Followers of the Society of Jesus opened a feud lasting for many years until silence was imposed by order of the Pope. Rosmini was devoted to Pius IX, even following him into exile. Still, even these circumstances did not prevent his books from being put on the *Index* at a later date, but, nothing detrimental to the Church being found in them, they were dismissed and thus given a semblance of papal approval. Rosmini lived just long enough to see himself thus partially justified.

THE FUNCTIONS OF THE HUMAN MIND
AND ITS METHODS

1. METHOD is a part of logic, and if taken in all its bearings, may be said to be itself logic, since the aim of the latter is throughout to establish the method of conducting our reasoning processes. . . .

2. The human mind has truth for its object, and, in relation to this most noble object, it exercises various functions. Some of these functions relate to truth already known; others, to truth which is still unknown, and the knowledge of which is sought for.

3. The functions of the mind, in relation to truths already known, may be reduced to three, namely, 1. The communication of it to others; 2. The defense of it; and, 3. The disentanglement of it from error.

4. The functions of the mind, in relation to truth as yet unknown, and which it seeks to know, may also be reduced to three, namely, 1. To find the demonstration of the truths known; 2. To find the consequences to be derived from them through their development and application; and, 3. and

lastly, to attain through the senses, by observation and experience, new data on which to base entirely new arguments.

5. Each of these functions of the human mind has its own method, which consists of an assemblage of rules for the guidance of the mind itself in the performance of its work: hence we may distinguish six kinds of method, as we have distinguished six functions of the mind in relation to truth.

6. These are, *the method of exposition,* which teaches how best to impart our knowledge to others; the *polemical method,* which teaches us how to defend truth and repel its assailants; the *critical method,* which teaches how to separate the true from the false. These are the three methods which must govern our mental processes in relation to truths already known. The remaining three are, the *demonstrative method,* which gives the rules for arriving at exact demonstrations; the *inductive,* which teaches how to reach the truths yet unknown, through inductions and conclusions from the known, developing from the knowledge we have ascertained in germ, as it were, the far larger body of that which we do not know; and, finally, the method we shall call the *perceptive-inductive,* which is not satisfied with arriving at new cognitions by inductions and conclusions from previously known data, but which leads us to the discovery of wholly new data through the perception of new phenomena, skilfully produced and made apparent to our senses. These are the three methods which govern the functions of the mind in relation to truths yet unknown. The last alone is the experimental method proper, the Baconian, to which is due the immense progress of physical science in modern times.

[311]

ROUSSEAU, JEAN JACQUES

ROUSSEAU, JEAN JACQUES (1712-1778). Rousseau was the first to diagnose, from secular aspects, the symptoms of the crisis of modern civilization. Both his approach and many of his conclusions have been exposed to criticism. Nevertheless, he gave us an early and powerful expression of a current of thoughts and sentiments that transformed cultural life and that has not yet come to an end in the age of two world wars.

Both modern civilization and the entire history that shaped its features were condemned by Rousseau as deviation from nature. Rousseau asserted that every man has a unique personality, and that all men are equal. But, in his eyes, state and society are the triumph of oppression, men have become unequal because of artificial conventions, and cultural life is degenerating more and more because vital needs of the human heart are neglected. He demanded a radical reform that does not mean return to primitive barbarism, but rather, a restitution of the natural order in which reason and sentiments become harmonized, and in which man meets his fellow man with neither artificial subordination nor any intention of subordinating him, both respecting the general will which is expressed by the majority of citizens.

Rousseau's criticism was determined to a large degree by his sense of justice and his aesthetic sentiments. In this way, he became the precursor of the French Revolution, and caused a literary revolution that started soon after the publication of his principal works. His call "back to nature" was echoed by the masses of oppressed peoples and by individuals who longed for a free development of their faculties. Since Rousseau, sincerity and intensity of feelings and expression, rather than formal perfection, have become the principal criteria of literary and artistic criticism. Rousseau enhanced the effects of his teachings by the charm and vigor of his style and, even more, by the unrestrained exhibition of his inner life, for he was by no means afraid of showing his flaws and vices to the public. His political doctrine emphasizes that the sovereignty belongs to the people. His religious creed is a deism that relies more on feelings than on reason, without excluding rational principles. Rousseau's literary influence remained strong from the times of Goethe and Byron to the days of R. L. Stevenson and D. H. Lawrence. Among the philosophers, his most important disciples, were Kant, Fichte and Hegel and, not the least among them, Karl Marx. In politics, Maximilian Robespierre was Rousseau's most devoted follower. Notwithstanding the excesses of the French Revolution, Rousseau continued to be regarded the apostle of democracy, although it was discovered that some of the aspects of his philosophy favor totalitarian dictatorship.

THE GENERAL WILL AND THE LAW

THE general will is always right and always tends to the public advantage; but it does not follow that the resolutions of the people have always the same rectitude. Men always desire their own good, but do not always discern it; the people are never corrupted, though often deceived, and it is only then that they seem to will what is evil.

There is often a great deal of difference between the will of all and the general will; the latter regards only the common interest, while the former has regard to private interests, and is merely a sum of particular wills; but take away from these same wills the pluses and minuses which cancel one another, and the general will remains as the sum of the differences.

If the people came to a resolution when adequately informed and without any communication among the citizens, the general will would always result from the great number of slight differences, and the resolution would always be good. But when factions, partial associations, are formed to the detriment of the whole society, the will of each of these associations becomes general with reference to its members, and particular with reference to the state; it may then be said that there are no longer as many voters as there are men, but only as many voters as there are associations. The differences become less numerous and yield a less general result. Lastly, when one of these associations becomes so great that it predominates over all the rest, you no longer have as the result a sum of small differences, but a single difference; there is then no longer a general will, and the opinion which prevails is only a particular opinion.

It is important, then, in order to have a clear declaration of the general will, that there should be no partial association in the state, and that every citizen should express his own opinion. Such was the unique and sublime institution of the great Lycurgus. But if there are partial associations, it is necessary to multiply their number and prevent inequality, as Solon, Numa, and Servius did. These are the only proper precautions for insuring that the general will may always be enlightened, and that the people may not be deceived.

*   *   *

If the state or city is nothing but a moral person, the life of which consists in the union of its members, and if the most important of its cares is that of self-preservation, it needs a universal and compulsive force to move and dispose of every part in the manner most expedient for the whole. As nature gives every man an absolute power over all his limbs, the social pact gives the body politic an absolute power over all its members; and it is this same power which when directed by the general will, bears the name of sovereignty.

But besides the public person, we have to consider the private persons who compose it, and whose life and liberty are naturally independent of it. The question, then, is to distinguish clearly between the respective rights of the citizens and of the sovereign, as well as between the duties which the former have to fulfill in their capacity as subjects and the natural rights which they ought to enjoy in their character as men.

It is admitted that whatever part of his power, property, and liberty each one alienates by the social compact is only that part of the whole of which the use is important to the community; but we must also admit that the sovereign alone is judge of what is important.

All the services that a citizen can render to the state he owes to it as soon as the sovereign demands them; but the sovereign, on its part, cannot impose on its subjects any burden which is useless to the community; it cannot even wish to do so, for, by the law of reason, just as by the law of nature, nothing is done without a cause.

The engagements which bind us to the social body are

obligatory only because they are mutual; and their nature is such that in fulfilling them we cannot work for others without also working for ourselves. Why is the general will always right, and why do all invariably desire the prosperity of each, unless it is because there is no one but appropriates to himself this word *each* and thinks of himself in voting on behalf of all? This proves that equality of rights and the notion of justice that it produces are derived from the preference which each gives to himself, and consequently from man's nature; that the general will, to be truly such, should be so in its object as well as in its essence; that it ought to proceed from all in order to be applicable to all; and that it loses its natural rectitude when it tends to some individual and determinate object, because in that case, judging of what is unknown to us, we have no true principle of equity to guide us.

Indeed so soon as a particular fact or right is in question with regard to a point which has not been regulated by an anterior general convention, the matter becomes contentious; it is a process in which the private persons interested are one of the parties and the public the other, but in which I perceive neither the law which must be followed, nor the judge who should decide. It would be ridiculous in such a case to wish to refer the matter for an express decision of the general will, which can be nothing but the decision of one of the parties, and which, consequently, is for the other party only a will that is foreign, partial, and inclined on such an occasion to injustice as well as liable to error. Therefore, just as a particular will cannot represent the general will, the general will in turn changes its nature when it has a particular end, and cannot, as general, decide about either a person or a fact. When the people of Athens, for instance, elected or deposed their chiefs, decreed honors to one, imposed penalties on another, and by multitudes of particular decrees exercised indiscriminately all the functions of government, the people no longer had any general will properly so called; they no longer acted as a sovereign power, but as magistrates. This will appear contrary to common ideas, but I must be allowed time to expound my own.

From this we must understand that what generalizes the will is not so much the number of voices as the common interest which unites them; for, under this system, each necessarily submits to the conditions which he imposes on others —an admirable union of interest and justice, which gives to the deliberations of the community a spirit of equity that seems to disappear in the discussion of any private affair, for want of a common interest to unite and identify the ruling principle of the judge with that of the party.

By whatever path we return to our principle we always arrive at the same conclusion, viz., that the social compact establishes among the citizens such an equality that they all pledge themselves under the same conditions and ought all to enjoy the same rights. Thus, by the nature of the compact, every act of sovereignty, that is, every authentic act of the general will, binds or favors equally all the citizens; so that the sovereign knows only the body of the nation, and distinguishes none of those that compose it.

What, then, is an act of sovereignty properly so called? It is not an agreement between a superior and an inferior, but an agreement of the body with each of its members; a lawful agreement, because it has the social contract as its foundation; equitable, because it is common to all; useful, because it can have no other object than the general welfare; and stable, because it has the public force and the supreme power as a guarantee. So long as the subjects submit only to such conventions, they obey no one, but simply their own will; and to ask how far the respective rights of the sovereign and citizens extend is to ask up to what point the latter can make engagements among themselves, each with all and all with each.

Thus we see that the sovereign power, wholly absolute, wholly sacred, and wholly inviolable as it is, does not, and cannot, pass the limits of general conventions, and that every man can fully dispose of what is left to him of his property and liberty by these conventions; so that the sovereign never has a right to burden one subject more than another, because then the matter becomes particular and his power is no longer competent.

These distinctions once admitted, so untrue is it that in the social contract there is on the part of individuals any real renunciation, that their situation, as a result of this contract, is in reality preferable to what it was before, and that, instead of an alienation, they have only made an advantageous exchange of an uncertain and precarious mode of existence for a better and more assured one, of natural independence for liberty, of the power to injure others for their own safety, and of their strength, which others might overcome, for a right which the social union renders inviolable. Their lives, also, which they have devoted to the state, are continually protected by it; and in exposing their lives for its defense, what do they do but restore what they have received from it? What do they do but what they would do more frequently and with more risk in the state of nature, when, engaging in inevitable struggles, they would defend at the peril of their lives their means of preservation? All have to fight for their country in case of need, it is true; but then no one ever has to fight for himself. Do we not gain, moreover, by incurring, for what insures our safety, a part of the risks that we should have to incur for ourselves individually, as soon as we were deprived of it?

*   *   *

By the social compact we have given existence and life to the body politic; the question now is to endow it with movement and will by legislation. For the original act by which this body is formed and consolidated determines nothing in addition as to what it must do for its own preservation.

What is right and conformable to order is such by the nature of things, and independently of human conventions. All justice comes from God, he alone is the source of it;

but could we receive it direct from so lofty a source, we should need neither government nor laws. Without doubt there is a universal justice emanating from reason alone; but this justice, in order to be admitted among us, should be reciprocal. Regarding things from a human standpoint, the laws of justice are inoperative among men for want of a natural sanction; they only bring good to the wicked and evil to the just when the latter observe them with every one, and no one observes them in return. Conventions and laws, then, are necessary to couple rights with duties and apply justice to its object. In the state of nature, where everything is in common, I owe nothing to those to whom I have promised nothing; I recognize as belonging to others only what is useless to me. This is not the case in the civil state, in which all rights are determined by law.

But then, finally, what is law? So long as men are content to attach to this word only metaphysical ideas, they will continue to argue without being understood; and when they have stated what a law of nature is, they will know no better what a law of the state is.

I have already said that there is no general will with reference to a particular object. In fact, this particular object is either in the state or outside of it. If it is outside the state, a will which is foreign to it is not general in relation to it; and if it is within the state, it forms part of it; then there is formed between the whole and its part a relation which makes of it two separate beings, of which the part is one, and the whole, less this same part, is the other. But the whole less one part is not the whole, and so long as the relation subsists, there is no longer any whole, but two unequal parts; whence it follows that the will of the one is no longer general in relation to the other.

But when the whole people decree concerning the whole people, they consider themselves alone; and if a relation is then constituted, it is between the whole object under one point of view and the whole object under another point of view, without any division at all. Then the matter respecting which they decree is general like the will that decrees. It is this act that I call law.

When I say that the object of the laws is always general, I mean that the law considers collectively, and actions as abstract, never a man as an individual nor a particular action. Thus the law may indeed decree that there shall be privileges, but cannot confer them on any person by name; the law can create several classes of citizens, and even assign the qualifications which shall entitle them to rank in these classes, but it cannot nominate such and such persons to be admitted to them; it can establish a royal government and a hereditary succession, but cannot elect a king or appoint a royal family; in a word, no function which has reference to an individual object appertains to the legislative power.

From this standpoint we see immediately that it is no longer necessary to ask whose office it is to make laws, since they are acts of the general will; nor whether the prince is above the laws, since he is a member of the state; nor whether the law can be unjust, since no one is unjust to himself; nor how we are free and yet subject to the laws, since the laws are only registers of our wills.

We see, further, that since the law combines the universality of the will with the universality of the object, whatever any man prescribes on his own authority is not a law; and whatever the sovereign itself prescribes respecting a particular object is not a law, but a decree, not an act of sovereignty, but of magistracy.

I therefore call any state a republic which is governed by laws, under whatever form of administration it may be; for then only does the public interest predominate and the commonwealth count for something. Every legitimate government is republican; I will explain hereafter what government is.

Laws are properly only the conditions of civil association. The people, being subjected to the laws, should be the authors of them; it concerns only the associates to determine the conditions of association. But how will they be determined? Will it be by a common agreement, by a sudden inspiration? Has a body politic an organ for expressing its will? Who will give it the foresight necessary to frame its acts and publish them at the outset? Or shall it declare them in the hour of need? How would a blind multitude, which often knows not what it wishes because it rarely knows what is good for it, execute of itself an enterprise so great, so difficult, as a system of legislation? Of themselves, the people always desire what is good, but do not always discern it. The general will is always right, but the judgment which guides it is not always enlightened. It must be made to see objects as they are, sometimes as they ought to appear; it must be shown the good path that it is seeking, and guarded from the seduction of private interests; it must be made to observe closely times and places, and to balance the attraction of immediate and palpable advantages against the danger of remote and concealed evils. Individuals see the good which they reject; the public desire the good which they do not see. All alike have need of guides. The former must be compelled to conform their wills to their reason; the people must be taught to know what they require. Then from the public enlightenment results the union of the understanding and the will in the social body; and from that the close cooperation of the parts, and, lastly, the maximum power of the whole. Hence arises the need of a legislator.

[312]

ROYCE, JOSIAH

ROYCE, JOSIAH (1855-1916). Royce was born in Grass Valley, Nevada County, California, a mining town which was about five years older than himself. Living among rough-handed pioneer people, the sensitive, timid boy who lacked physical strength and skill very early became aware of the value of an established social order because his environment was devoid of it. When his sixtieth birthday was celebrated, Royce, reviewing his mental development, expressed his strong feeling that his deepest motives and problems had centered about the idea of a community, although this idea had come only gradually to his clear consciousness. A Platonist vein in his mind caused him to base the idea of human community upon a theory of life and upon a conception of the nature of truth and reality. Idealistic metaphysics was to him the guarantee not only for absolute certainty, but also for a rule over the whole life by right judgment, directed by the sense of absolute truth. Royce's theoretical thinking, however, was always connected with and supported by his experience of religious life. His mother had been his first teacher in philosophy and the Bible his first textbook. Although he could claim to be born nonconformist and to be without connection with "any visible religious body," it was religious problems that drove him to philosophy, and it was religious faith that was regarded by him as the foundation of human solidarity and social loyalty, as the binding element of a community.

While in Royce's *Religious Aspect of Philosophy* (1885) the influence of Hegel is prevalent, Royce later, in *The World and the Individual* (1900-01) came closer to Fichte and Schopenhauer, and shifted his emphasis from thought, which in the earlier work designates the processus of the Absolute, to will, calling himself "a voluntarist and empiricist who yet believes in the Absolute." To Royce, will, as the manifestation of the Absolute, seems fit to reconcile idealist metaphysics and human experience; to corroborate in man the cardinal virtues of courage, industry, loyalty, and solidarity; and above all to unite the religious conception of God with the philosophical idea of the Absolute. While the Absolute had been conceived at first as the universal knower, as the unity of infinite thought, in Royce's later development the God of the idealist is presented as "no merely indifferent onlooker upon this our temporal world of warfare and dust and blood and sin and glory." Absolute reason is not abandoned by Royce but, according to him, does not exclude but rather implies absolute choice, and the divine unity of reason and will implies freedom of the individual which, in accordance with Kant, belongs not to the phenomenal and temporal world but to a higher order of which man is a part.

In his last years, Royce studied the works of Charles Peirce and, in *The Problem of Christianity* (1913), exposed a triple logic of perception, conception, and interpretation. Voluntarism became an integral factor in Royce's theory of knowledge. Knowing is characterized as an act. An idea, to become cognitive, must be part of a judgment or itself a judgment. This change, however, confirms Royce's early conviction that all reality is reality because true judgments can be made about it. The decision as to which judgments are true and which are false is up to the infinite thought of the Absolute, Supreme Being.

For about thirty years, Royce and William James were intimate friends and staunch adversaries. James secured Royce's appointment as professor at Harvard. While criticizing one another, they inevitably also influenced one another, be it by provoking contrasting ideas or by agreeing on certain views. Royce sometimes expressed his sadness about being forced to attack the philosophy of James to whom he felt himself obliged for practically everything he had written. James, whose criticism of Royce's books sometimes could be devastating, once exclaimed, "Two hundred and fifty years from now, Harvard will be known as the place where Josiah Royce once taught."

IMMORTALITY

So far as we live and strive at all, our lives are various, are needed for the whole, and are unique. No one of these lives can be substituted for another. No one of us finite beings can take another's place. And all this is true just because the Universe is one significant whole.

That follows from our general doctrine concerning our unique relation, as various finite expressions taking place within the single whole of the divine life. But now, with this result in mind, let us return again to the finite realms, and descend from our glimpse of the divine life to the dim shadows and to the wilderness of this world, and ask afresh: But *what* is the unique meaning of my life just now? What place do I fill in God's world that nobody else either fills or can fill?

How disheartening in one sense is still the inevitable answer. I state that answer again in all its negative harshness. I reply simply: For myself, I do not now know in any concrete human terms wherein my individuality consists. In my present human form of consciousness I simply cannot tell. If I look to see what I ever did that, for all I now know, some other man might not have done, I am utterly unable to discover the certainly unique deed. When I was a child I learned by imitation as the rest did. I have gone on copying models in my poor way ever since. I never felt a feeling that I knew or could know to be unlike the feelings of other people. I never consciously thought, except after patterns that the world or my fellows set for me. Of myself, I seem in this life to be nothing but a mere meeting-place in this stream of time where a mass of the driftwood from the ages has collected. I only know that I have always tried to be myself and nobody else. This mere aim I indeed have observed, but that is all. As for you, my beloved friend, I loyally believe in your uniqueness; but whenever I try to tell to you wherein it consists, I helplessly describe only a type. That type may be uncommon. But it is not you. For as soon as described, it might have other examples. But you are alone. Yet I never tell what you are. And if your face lights up my world as no other can—well, this feeling too, when viewed as the mere psychologist has to view it, appears to be simply what all the other friends report about their friends. It is an old story, this life of ours. There is nothing new under our sun. Nothing new, that is, for us, as we now feel and think. When we imagine that we have seen or defined uniqueness and novelty, we soon feel a little later the illusion. We live thus, in one sense, so lonesomely here. For we love individuals; we trust in them; we honor and pursue them; we glorify them and hope to know them. But after we have once become keenly critical and worldly wise, we know, if we are sufficiently thoughtful, that we men can never either find them with our eyes, or define them in our minds; and that hopelessness of finding what we most love makes some of us cynical, and turns others of us into lovers of barren abstractions, and renders still others of us slaves to monotonous affairs that have lost for us the true individual meaning and novelty that we had hoped to find in them. Ah, one of the deepest tragedies of this human existence of ours lies in this very loneliness of the awakened critics of life. We seek true individuality and the true individuals. But we find them not. For lo, we mortals see what our poor eyes can see; and they, the true individuals,—they belong not to this world of our merely human sense and thought.

They belong not to this world, in so far as our sense and our thought now show us this world! Ah, therein,—just therein lies the very proof that they even now belong to a higher and to a richer realm than ours. Herein lies the very sign of their true immortality. For they are indeed real, these individuals. We know this, first, because we mean them and seek them. We know this, secondly, because, in this very longing of ours, God too longs; and because the Absolute Life itself, which dwells in our life, and inspires these very longings, possesses the true world, and *is* that world. For the Absolute, as we now know, all life is individual, but is individual as expressing a meaning. Precisely what is unexpressed here, then, in our world of mortal glimpses of truth, precisely what is sought and longed for, but never won in this our human form of consciousness, just that is interpreted, is developed into its true wholeness, is won in its fitting form, and is expressed, in all the rich variety of individual meaning that love here seeks, but cannot find, and is expressed too as a portion, unique, conscious, and individual, of an Absolute Life that even now pulsates in every one of our desires for the ideal and for the individual. We all even now really dwell in this realm of a reality that is not visible to human eyes. We dwell there as individuals. The oneness of the Absolute Will lives in and through all this variety of life and love and longing that now is ours, but cannot live in and through all without working out to the full precisely that individuality of purpose, that will to choose and to love the unique, which is in all of us the deepest expression of the ideal. Just because, then, God is One, all our lives have various and unique places in the harmony of the divine life. And just because God attains and wins and finds this uniqueness, all our lives win in our union with him the individuality which is essential to their true meaning. And just because individuals whose lives have uniqueness of meaning are here only objects of pursuit, the attainment of this very individuality, since it is indeed real, occurs not in our present form of consciousness, but in a life that now we see not, yet in a life whose genuine meaning is continuous with our own human life, however far from our present flickering form of disappointed human consciousness that life of the final individuality may be. Of this our true individual life, our present life is a glimpse, a fragment, a hint, and in its best moments a visible beginning. That this individual life of all of us is not something limited in its temporal expression to the life that now we experience, follows from the very fact that here nothing final or individual is found expressed.

[313]

RUSH, BENJAMIN

RUSH, BENJAMIN (1745-1813). Rush Medical College, now affiliated with the University of Chicago, was so named in honor of Benjamin Rush, one of the most successful physicians of 18th century America, surgeon general in the Revolutionary Army, a signer of the Declaration of Independence, author of the first textbook on chemistry in America, treasurer of the United States Mint, social reformer, and a prolific writer on medicine, social problems, natural sciences and philosophy.

His approach to philosophy was determined by his medical profession, especially his experiences in psychiatry. He was mainly interested in investigating the effects of physical causes on the mind and the effects of psychic changes on the body. His *Inquiry Upon Physical Causes Upon the Moral Faculty* (1786) and *Medical Inquiries and Observations Upon the Diseases of the Mind* (1812) were for a long time considered standard works on psychiatry. Rush energetically advocated human understanding of mentally ill people, and he also advocated human treatment of criminals. He demanded abolition of capital punishment and slavery. However, his philanthropy did not imply any laxity in moral principles. Rush was firmly convinced that science and religion are in harmony, that ethics is founded upon the Christian faith, and he untiringly protested against any materialistic interpretation of the results of his psychological research. It was on religious grounds that Rush became an ardent American patriot, a revolutionary fighter, and a defender of popular government. He was an intimate friend of Thomas Paine who owed the title of his pamphlet *Common Sense* to Rush's suggestion. Rush was no deist but a Christian who was politically closely allied with Paine, together with whom he even challenged the authority of George Washington. His religious and political ideas made Rush a supporter of the advancement of learning and the improvement of public education. He actively participated in the foundation of colleges and elementary schools, always confident that the increase of knowledge would strengthen democracy and religious belief.

ATTRACTION, COMPOSITION AND DECOMPOSITION

ATTRACTION, composition, and decomposition belong to the passions as well as to the matter. Vices of the same species attract each other with the most force—hence the bad consequences of crowding young men (whose propensities are generally the same) under one roof, in our modern plans of education. The effects of composition and decomposition upon vices appear in the meanness of the school boy, being often cured by the prodigality of a military life, and by the precipitation of avarice, which is often produced by ambition and love.

If physical causes influence morals, may they not also influence religious principles and opinions?—I answer in the affirmative; and I have authority, from the records of physic, as well as from my own observations, to declare, that religious melancholy and madness, in all their variety of species, yield with more facility to medicine, than simply to polemical discourses, or to casuistical advice. But this subject is foreign to the business of the present inquiry.

We are led to contemplate with admiration, the curious structure of the human mind. How distinct are the number, and yet how united! How subordinate and yet how coequal are all its faculties! How wonderful is the action of the mind upon the body! Of the body upon the mind!—And of the divine spirit upon both! What a mystery is the mind of man to itself!—O! nature!—Or to speak more properly, —O! thou God of Nature!—In vain do we attempt to scan thy immensity, or to comprehend thy various modes of existence, when a single particle of light issued from thyself, and kindled into intelligence in the bosom of man, thus dazzles and confounds our understandings!

[314]

RUSKIN, JOHN

RUSKIN, JOHN (1819-1900). No understatement can be found in Ruskin's writing which is, as he himself said, as vacillating as his temper, changing from delight into horror, from indignation into enthusiasm. Ruskin was a critic and historian of art, bitterly opposed to the conception of art for art's sake, always considering the artist's work as the test of his moral disposition, acknowledging only those as artists who are recognized as men of a pure heart, and using "sincerity" as the standard of his aesthetic judgment. He limited sincerity to the Gothic style only and upheld it as much on moral as on aesthetical grounds, while he branded the Renaissance, and even the "flamboyant style" of the end of the Gothic period, as moral and artistic decay.

Ruskin was by nature a zealot, even an eccentric. His dislike of modern technics, railroads included, induced him to expensive efforts to become independent of modern means of transportation. Criticism of art was for him a solemn duty, but his moralist aesthetics did not allow him to confine his views to the realm of the arts. He was sensitive to injustice and misery. When, in Venice, he read in the newspaper that a seamstress in London had died of starvation, he became incapable of enjoying his beloved pictures. Ruskin, therefore, by 1860, turned to political economy, and proceeded to regard economic justice, moral and artistic sincerity as one and inseparable. He complained of the substitution of factory work for handicraft, and protested violently against reckless competition. Above all, Ruskin indignantly fought any evaluation of the human individual which identified wealth with worth. Ruskin was one of the first to deny the "economic man."

"In the height of black anger," as Ruskin said, he wrote the first volume of his *Modern Painters* (1842-60) in which he excepted modern landscape painting from his general condemnation of his

own time. Another deviation from his general attitude was his defense of British colonial expansion. As a professor at Oxford, he
used his lectures on art for converting his audience to imperialism.
Among the undergraduates who listened to Ruskin were Cecil
Rhodes and Alfred Milner, bound to enlarge the British empire.

TRUE BOOKS

THE good book of the hour, then,—I do not speak of the
bad ones,—is simply the useful or pleasant talk of some person whom you cannot otherwise converse with, printed for
you. Very useful often, telling you what you need to know;
very pleasant often, as a sensible friend's present talk would
be. These bright accounts of travels; good-humoured and
witty discussions of question; lively or pathetic story-telling
in the form of novel; firm fact-telling, by the real agents
concerned in the events of passing history;—all these books
of the hour, multiplying among us as education becomes
more general, are a peculiar possession of the present age;
we ought to be entirely thankful for them, and entirely
ashamed of ourselves if we make no good use of them. But
we make the worst possible use if we allow them to usurp
the place of true books; for, strictly speaking, they are not
books at all, but merely letters or newspapers in good print.
Our friend's letter may be delightful, or necessary, to-day;
whether worth keeping or not, is to be considered. The newspaper may be entirely proper at breakfast time, but assuredly it is not reading for all day. So, though bound up in
a volume, the long letter which gives you so pleasant an
account of the inns, and roads, and weather, last year at
such a place, or which tells you that amusing story, or gives
you the real circumstances of such and such events, however valuable for occasional reference, may not be, in the
real sense of the word, a 'book' at all, nor, in the real sense,
to be read. A book is essentially not a talking thing, but a
written thing; and written, not with a view of mere communication, but of permanence. The book of talk is printed only
because its author cannot speak to thousands of people at

once; if he could, he would—the volume is mere multiplication of his voice. You cannot talk to your friend in India; if you could, you would; you write instead; that is mere conveyance of voice. But a book is written, not to multiply the voice merely, not to carry it merely, but to perpetuate it. The author has something to say which he perceives to be true and useful, or helpfully beautiful. So far as he knows, no one has yet said it; so far as he knows, no one else can say it. He is bound to say it, clearly and melodiously if he may; clearly at all events. In the sum of his life he finds this to be the thing, or group of things, manifest to him;— this, the piece of true knowledge, or sight which his share of sunshine and earth has permitted him to seize. He would fain set it down forever; engrave it on rock, if he could; saying, "This is the best of me; for the rest, I ate, and drank, and slept, loved, and hated, like another; my life was as the vapor, and is not; but this I saw and knew; this, if anything of mine, is worth your memory." That is his "writing"; it is, in his small human way, and with whatever degree of true inspiration is in him, his inscription, or scripture. That is a "Book."

MAN'S BEST WISDOM

VERY ready we are to say of a book, "How good this is— that's exactly what I think!" But the right feeling is, "How strange that is! I never thought of that before, and yet I see it is true; or if I do not now, I hope I shall some day." But whether thus submissively or not, at least be sure that you go to the author to get at his meaning, not to find yours. Judge it afterwards if you think yourself qualified to do so; but ascertain it first. And be sure, also, if the author is worth anything, that you will not get at his meaning all at once;—nay, that at his whole meaning you will not for a long time arrive in any wise. Not that he does not say what he means, and in strong words too; but he cannot say it all;

1024

and what is more strange, will not, but in a hidden way and in parables, in order that he may be sure you want it. I cannot quite see the reason of this, nor analyze that cruel reticence in the breasts of wise men which makes them always hide their deeper thought. They do not give it you by way of help, but of reward; and will make themselves sure that you deserve it before they allow you to reach it. But it is the same with the physical type of wisdom, gold. There seems, to you and me, no reason why the electric forces of the earth should not carry whatever there is of gold within it at once to the mountain tops, so that kings and people might know that all the gold they could get was there; and without any trouble of digging, or anxiety, or chance, or waste of time, cut it away, and coin as much as they needed. But Nature does not manage it so. She puts it in little fissures in the earth, nobody knows where; you may dig long and find none; you must dig painfully to find any.

And it is just the same with men's best wisdom. When you come to a good book, you must ask yourself, "Am I inclined to work as an Australian miner would? Are my pickaxes and shovels in good order, and am I in good trim myself, my sleeves well up to the elbow, and my breath good, and my temper?" And, keeping the figure a little longer, even at cost of tiresomeness, for it is a thoroughly useful one, the metal you are in search of being the author's mind or meaning, his words are as the rock which you have to crush and smelt in order to get at it. And your pickaxes are your own care, wit, and learning; your smelting furnace is your own thoughtful soul. Do not hope to get at any good author's meaning without those tools and that fire; often you will need sharpest, finest chiselling, and patientest fusing, before you can gather one grain of the metal.

[315]

RUSSELL, BERTRAND

RUSSELL, BERTRAND (1872-   ). As late as in 1940, the appointment of Bertrand Russell as professor of philosophy at the College
of the City of New York has roused the fury of bigots of all denominations. It was denounced as "the establishment of a chair of
indecency" and withdrawn by the Board of Education after a trial
had ended with Russell's condemnation as "immoral" and a danger
for the youth of the city.

The victim of this persecution has been accustomed to making
sacrifices for his convictions. During World War I he had been
imprisoned because of his radical pacifism. He had also been accustomed to having his opinions explained by radical leftists as
being determined by his connection with the British aristocracy.
His grandfather, Lord John Russell, who had been Prime Minister
and Foreign Secretary, had tried to defend European solidarity
against Bismarck's national egoism, and had brought about the
repeal of the Test and Corporation Act which barred from public
office anyone not belonging to the established Church of England.

Russell is regarded as the most controversial figure of modern
Anglo-Saxon philosophy, even by those who recognize him as one
of the greatest thinkers of the twentieth century and who agree
with Albert Einstein who has confessed that he owes "innumerable
happiness to the reading of Russell's works." Russell's mind is
uncompromising, not afraid of running risks, yet always ready to
change and to admit errors. He always has maintained the independence of his thought and judgment although he underwent many
influences. Russell is a prolific writer who attributes the clarity and
fluency of his style to his absence from the influence of public
school education. Conspicuous qualities of his books are the firm
direction of the course of ideas, his ability to continue or check
a discussion according to his principal intention, and particularly
his easy humor and his devastating irony.

Russell has taken an outstanding part in the foundation of
modern mathematical logic. Together with Alfred North Whitehead he has written *Principia Mathematica* (1910-13), one of the
most comprehensive systems of mathematics. At first, Russell regarded mathematics as the ideal of philosophy. Then, abandoning
Platonism, he thought of mathematics as an instrument of science,
and finally declared that logic is not a part of philosophy but of
a general theory of science.

To Russell, philosophy is a conception of life and the world which is the product of two factors. The one consists of inherited religious and ethical concepts, the other of investigations which may be called scientific. Philosophy is regarded as something intermediate between theology and science. Like theology it is concerned with speculations on matters concerning which knowledge has been unascertainable. Like science it appeals to human reason rather than to authority. Russell holds that all human knowledge remains uncertain, inexact and partial, and that scepticism, while logically faultless, is psychologically impossible. To obtain some results which may be useful for humanity, philosophy should take its problems from natural sciences, not from theology or ethics.

At least in its broad outline, scientific knowledge is to be accepted. But, against traditional concepts, Russell maintains that knowledge is an intimate, almost mystical contact between subject and object by perception. Although perception is far more complicated than is generally supposed, common-sense realism comes closer to truth than idealism. Subjectivism is justified to ask how knowledge of the world is obtained but not to say what sort of world exists in which we live. Kant's claim to have effected a "Copernican revolution" is refuted by Russell who declares that Kant rather achieved a "Ptolemaic counter-revolution." Knowledge is characterized as a subclass of true belief, but not every true belief is to be recognized as knowledge. In *Human Knowledge* (1948) Russell deals with the problem of the relation between individual experience and the general body of scientific knowledge, and arrives at the result that science cannot be wholly interpreted in terms of experience. He demands that the description of the world be kept free from influences derived from the nature of human knowledge, and declares that "cosmically and causally, knowledge is an unimportant feature of the universe." Like Whitehead, he holds that the distinction between mind and body is a dubious one. It will be better to speak of organism, leaving the division of its activities between the mind and the body undetermined. What is true or false is a state of organism. But it is true or false in general, in virtue of occurrences outside the organism.

THE LIMITS OF PHILOSOPHICAL KNOWLEDGE

MOST philosophers—or, at any rate, very many—profess to be able to prove, by *a priori* metaphysical reasoning, such things as the fundamental dogmas of religion, the essential rationality of the universe, the illusoriness of matter, the unreality of all evil, and so on. There can be no doubt that the hope of finding reason to believe such theses as these has been the chief inspiration of many life-long students of philosophy. This hope, I believe, is vain. It would seem that knowledge concerning the universe as a whole is not to be obtained by metaphysics, and that the proposed proofs that, in virtue of the laws of logic, such and such things *must* exist and such and such others cannot, are not capable of surviving a critical scrutiny. . . . We shall briefly consider the kind of way in which such reasoning is attempted, with a view to discovering whether we can hope that it may be valid.

The great representative, in modern times, of the kind of view which we wish to examine, was Hegel (1770-1831). Hegel's philosophy is very difficult, and commentators differ as to the true interpretation of it. According to the interpretation I shall adopt, which is that of many, if not most, of the commentators, and has the merit of giving an interesting and important type of philosophy, his main thesis is that everything short of the Whole is obviously fragmentary, and obviously incapable of existing without the complement supplied by the rest of the world. Just as a comparative anatomist, from a single bone, sees what kind of animal the whole must have been, so the metaphysician, according to Hegel, sees from any one piece of reality, what the whole of reality must be—at least in its large outlines. Every apparently separate piece of reality has, as it were, hooks which grapple it to the next piece; the next piece, in turn, has fresh hooks, and so on, until the whole universe is reconstructed. This essential incompleteness appears, according to Hegel, equally in the world of thought and in the world of things. In the world of thought, if we take any idea which is abstract or incomplete, we find, on examination, that if we forget its incompleteness, we become involved in contradictions; these contradictions turn the idea in question into its opposite, or antithesis; and in order to escape, we have to find a new, less incomplete idea, which is the synthesis of our original idea and its antithesis. This new idea we started with, will be found, nevertheless, to be still not wholly complete, but to pass into its antithesis, with which it must be combined in a new synthesis. In this way Hegel advances until he reaches the "Absolute Idea," which, according to him, has no incompleteness, no opposite, and no need of further development. The Absolute Idea, therefore, is adequate to describe Absolute Reality; but all lower ideas only describe reality as it appears to a partial view, not as it is to one who simultaneously surveys the Whole. Thus Hegel reaches the conclusion that Absolute Reality forms one single harmonious system, not in space or time, not in any degree evil, wholly rational, and wholly spiritual. Any appearance to the contrary, in the world we know, can be proved logically—so he believes—to be entirely due to our fragmentary piecemeal view of the universe. If we saw the universe whole, as we may suppose God sees it, space and time and matter and evil and all striving and struggling would disappear, and we should see instead an eternal perfect unchanging spiritual unity.

In this conception, there is undeniably something sublime, something to which we could wish to yield assent. Nevertheless, when the arguments in support of it are carefully examined, they appear to involve much confusion and many unwarrantable assumptions. The fundamental tenet upon which the system is built up is that what is incomplete must be not self-subsistent, but must need the support of other things before it can exist. It is held that whatever has relations to things outside itself must contain some reference to those outside things in its own *nature*, and could not, therefore, be what it is if those outside things did not exist. A man's nature, for example, is constituted by his memories and the rest of his knowledge, by his loves and hatreds, and so on; thus, but for the objects which he knows or loves or hates, he could not be what he is. He is essentially and obviously a fragment: taken as the sum-total of reality he would be self-contradictory.

This whole point of view, however, turns upon the notion of the "nature" of a thing, which seems to mean "all the truths about the thing." It is of course the case that a truth which connects one thing with another thing could not subsist if the other thing did not subsist. But a truth about a thing is not part of the thing itself, although it must, according to the above usage, be part of the "nature" of the thing. If we mean by a thing's "nature" all the truths about the thing, then plainly we cannot know a thing's "nature" unless we know all the thing's relations to all the other things in the universe. But if the word "nature" is used in this sense, we shall have to hold that the thing may be known when its "nature" is not known, or at any rate is not known completely. There is a confusion, when this use of the word "nature" is employed, between knowledge of things and knowledge of truths. We may have knowledge of a thing by acquaintance even if we know very few propositions about it—theoretically we need not know any propositions about it. Thus, acquaintance with a thing does not involve knowledge of its "nature" in the above sense. And although acquaintance with a thing is involved in our knowing any one proposition about a thing, knowledge of its "nature," in the above sense, is not involved. Hence, (1) acquaintance with a thing does not logically involve a knowledge of its relations, and (2) a knowledge of some of its relations does not involve a knowledge of all of its relations nor a knowledge of its "nature" in the above sense. I may be acquainted, for example, with my toothache, and this knowledge may be as complete as knowledge by acquaintance ever can be, without knowing all that the dentist (who is not acquainted with it) can tell me about its cause, and without therefore knowing its "nature" in the above sense. Thus the fact that a thing has relations does not prove that its relations are logically necessary. That is to say, from the mere fact that it is the thing it is we cannot deduce that it must have the various relations which in fact it has. This only *seems* to follow because we know it already.

It follows that we cannot prove that the universe as a

whole forms a single harmonious system such as Hegel believes that it forms. And if we cannot prove this, we also cannot prove the unreality of space and time and matter and evil, for this is deduced by Hegel from the fragmentary and relational character of these things. Thus we are left to the piecemeal investigation of the world, and are unable to know the characters of those parts of the universe that are remote from our experience. This result, disappointing as it is to those whose hopes have been raised by the systems of philosophers, is in harmony with the inductive and scientific temper of our age, and is borne out by the whole examination of human knowledge which has occupied our previous chapters.

Most of the great ambitious attempts of metaphysicians have proceeded by the attempt to prove that such and such apparent features of the actual world were self-contradictory, and therefore could not be real. The whole tendency of modern thought, however, is more and more in the direction of showing that the supposed contradictions were illusory, and that very little can be proved *a priori* from considerations of what *must* be. A good illustration of this is afforded by space and time. Space and time appear to be infinite in extent, and infinitely divisible. If we travel along a straight line in either direction, it is difficult to believe that we shall finally reach a last point, beyond which there is nothing, not even empty space. Similarly, if in imagination we travel backwards or forwards in time, it is difficult to believe that we shall reach a first or last time, with not even empty time beyond it. Thus space and time appear to be infinite in extent.

Again, if we take any two points on a line, it seems evident that there must be other points between them, however small the distance between them may be: every distance can be halved, and the halves can be halved again, and so on *ad infinitum*. In time, similarly, however little time may elapse between two moments, it seems evident that there will be other moments between them. Thus space and time appear to be infinitely divisible. But as against these apparent facts—infinite extent and infinite divisibility—philosophers have advanced arguments tending to show that there could be no infinite collections of things, and that therefore the number of points in space, or of instants in time, must be finite. Thus a contradiction emerged between the apparent nature of space and time and the supposed impossibility of infinite collections.

Kant, who first emphasized this contradiction, deduced the impossibility of space and time, which he declared to be merely subjective; and since his time very many philosophers have believed that space and time are mere appearance, not characteristic of the world as it really is. Now, however, owing to the labors of the mathematicians, notably Georg Cantor, it has appeared that the impossibility of infinite collections was a mistake. They are not in fact self-contradictory, but only contradictory of certain rather obstinate mental prejudices. Hence the reasons for regarding space and time as unreal have become inoperative, and one of the great sources of metaphysical constructions is dried up.

The mathematicians, however, have not been content with showing that space as it is commonly supposed to be is possible; they have shown also that many other forms of space are equally possible, so far as logic can show. Some of Euclid's axioms, which appear to common sense to be necessary, and were formerly supposed to be necessary by philosophers, are now known to derive their appearance of necessity from our mere familiarity with actual space, and not from any *a priori* logical foundation. By imagining worlds in which these axioms are false, the mathematicians have used logic to loosen the prejudices of common sense, and to show the possibility of spaces differing—some more, some less— from that in which we live. And some of these spaces differ so little from Euclidean space, where distances such as we can measure are concerned, that it is impossible to discover by observation whether our actual space is strictly

Euclidean or of one of these other kinds. Thus the position is completely reversed. Formerly it appeared that experience left only one kind of space to logic, and logic showed this one kind to be impossible. Now, logic presents many kinds of space as possible apart from experience, and experience only partially decides between them. Thus, while our knowledge of what is has become less than it was formerly supposed to be, our knowledge of what may be is enormously increased. Instead of being shut in within narrow walls, of which every nook and cranny could be explored, we find ourselves in an open world of free possibilities, where much remains unknown because there is so much to know.

What has happened in the case of space and time has happened, to some extent, in other directions as well. The attempt to prescribe to the universe by means of *a priori* principles has broken down; logic, instead of being, as formerly, the bar to possibilities, has become the great liberator of the imagination, presenting innumerable alternatives which are closed to unreflective common sense, and leaving to experience the task of deciding, where decision is possible, between the many worlds which logic offers for our choice. Thus knowledge as to what exists becomes limited to what we can learn from experience—not to what we can actually experience, for, as we have seen, there is much knowledge by description concerning things of which we have no direct experience. But in all cases of knowledge by description, we need some connection of universals, enabling us, from such and such a datum, to infer an object of a certain sort as implied by our datum. Thus in regard to physical objects, for example, the principle that sense data are signs of physical objects is itself a connection of universals; and it is only in virtue of this principle that experience enables us to acquire knowledge concerning physical objects. The same applies to the law of causality, or, to descend to what is less general, to such principles as the law of gravitation.

Principles such as the law of gravitation are proved, or rather are rendered highly probable, by a combination of experience with some wholly *a priori* principle, such as the principle of induction. Thus our intuitive knowledge, which is the source of all our other knowledge of truths, is of two sorts: pure empirical knowledge, which tells us of the existence and some of the properties of particular things with which we are acquainted, and pure *a priori* knowledge, which gives us connections between universals, and enables us to draw inferences from the particular facts given in empirical knowledge. Our derivative knowledge always depends upon some pure *a priori* knowledge and usually also depends upon some pure empirical knowledge.

Philosophical knowledge, if what has been said above is true, does not differ essentially from scientific knowledge; there is no special source of wisdom which is open to philosophy but not to science, and the results obtained by philosophy are not radically different from those obtained from science. The essential characteristic of philosophy, which makes it a study distinct from science, is *criticism*. It examines critically the principles employed in science and in daily life; it searches out any inconsistencies there may be in these principles, and it only accepts them when, as the result of a critical inquiry, no reason for rejecting them has appeared. If, as many philosophers have believed, the principles underlying the sciences were capable, when disengaged from irrelevant detail, of giving us knowledge concerning the universe as a whole, such knowledge would have the same claim on our belief as scientific knowledge has; but our inquiry has not revealed any such knowledge, and therefore, as regards the special doctrines of the bolder metaphysicians, has had a mainly negative result. But as regards what would be commonly accepted as knowledge, our result is in the main positive: we have seldom found reason to reject such knowledge as the result of our criticism, and we have seen no reason to suppose man incapable of the kind of knowledge which he is generally believed to possess.

When, however, we speak of philosophy as a *criticism* of knowledge, it is necessary to impose a certain limitation.

If we adopt the attitude of the complete sceptic, placing ourselves wholly outside all knowledge, and asking, from this outside position, to be compelled to return within the circle of knowledge, we are demanding what is impossible, and our scepticism can never be refuted. For all refutation must begin with some piece of knowledge which the disputants share; from blank doubt, no argument can begin. Hence the criticism of knowledge which philosophy employs must not be of this destructive kind, if any result is to be achieved. Against this absolute scepticism, no *logical* argument can be advanced. But it is not difficult to see that scepticism of this kind is unreasonable. Descartes' "methodical doubt," with which modern philosophy began, is not of this kind, but is rather the kind of criticism which we are asserting to be the essence of philosophy. His "methodical doubt" consisted in doubting whatever seemed doubtful; in pausing, with each apparent piece of knowledge, to ask himself whether, on reflection, he could feel certain that he really knew it. This is the kind of criticism which constitutes philosophy. Some knowledge, such as knowledge of the existence of our sense data, appears quite indubitable, however calmly and thoroughly we reflect upon it. In regard to such knowledge, philosophical criticism does not require that we should abstain from belief. But there are beliefs—such, for example, as the belief that physical objects exactly resemble our sense data—which are entertained until we begin to reflect, but are found to melt away when subjected to a close inquiry. Such beliefs philosophy will bid us reject, unless some new line of argument is found to support them. But to reject the beliefs which do not appear open to any objections, however closely we examine them, is not reasonable, and is not what philosophy advocates.

The criticism aimed at, in a word, is not that which, without reason, determines to reject, but that which considers each piece of apparent knowledge on its merits, and retains whatever still appears to be knowledge when this consideration is completed. That some risk of error remains must be admitted, since human beings are fallible. Philosophy may claim justly that it diminishes the risk of error, and that in some cases it renders the risk so small as to be practically negligible. To do more than this is not possible in a world where mistakes must occur; and more than this no prudent advocate of philosophy would claim to have performed.

[316]

S

S A A D I A

SAADIA (892-942). Until Saadia began to formulate his ideas, the spiritual atmosphere of his times had been, as one of his contemporaries complained, as follows:

> Muslims, Jews, Christians and Magicians, they all are walking in error and darkness. There are two kinds of people left in the world: the one group is intelligent but lacking in faith, the other has faith but is lacking in intelligence.

And so it became Saadia's purpose to teach not only his Jewish co-religionists but also Islamic and Christian thinkers that faith is not opposed to reason but only to pseudo-reason.

Born in Egypt, and educated as well in all branches of Arabian culture as in Biblical and Talmudic scholarship, Saadia went to Palestine, and then to Babylonia. There he accomplished his great work which became the foundation of Jewish philosophy and science. Acquainted with Greek philosophy, the various formulations of the Christian dogma, the doctrines of the Manicheans, of Zoroaster and even with the philosophy of India, Saadia developed the idea that Judaism is compatible with all truth, whatever its source. In his explanation of the nature of religion, the character of man and the way of conceiving God, Saadia criticized Plato's cosmology and refuted gnostic doctrines. He tried to reconcile the idea of freedom of man with that of the all-embracing foreknowledge of God.

Saadia was also a learned mathematician and a trained philologist, and he composed the first Hebrew dictionary as well as the first Jewish prayer-book.

ON ABEL'S DEATH AND ON THE PUNISHMENT OF THE WICKED ONES

WHEN his sons brought offerings God favored the younger, because he brought of the best of his fatlings to the ruling

King: what was vile and refuse, that the elder brought to the sanctuary. So He let him know that he was despised; but he did not repent, he hated.

He struck his brother, and God inquired of him so that he might confess, but in his reply he feigned [innocence] with cunning and craft. Therefore hath God wreaked His vengeance on him with a ruling anger; for He avengeth the blood of His servants and redeemeth their soul.

I shall reply to thy question with a strong reply. Thou sayest: "Why hath He not guarded him [Abel] so that his posterity should not have been destroyed?" Thus shouldst thou have said if there were but one world and one habitation, but since there is a second world, He chose everything with a view for reproof.

Let them not rejoice who exercise oppression here [in this world], for at the time when their foot shall slide there [in the next world] He will choose to pay with vengeance; and let him not mourn who is oppressed and crushed and circumvented, for God can change it into good, and he shall not return empty.

Because the oppressor will not cease from putting forth his hand, and the one who suffereth violence will not always rescue his possessions, therefore there is a day when everyone will be measured by His law, both he that serveth God and he that serveth Him not.

Thou hast asked further concerning the kinds of suffering; hunger and sickness, fear and desolation and destruction, and heat and cold, why they are not kept from men. All these are but one question and thou hast multiplied words.

Know thou and understand, that God chastiseth His creatures for their good, that they may know the pain of chastisement and the bitterness thereof; He delivereth them to it that they may forbear to do wrong. For they would not know [what punishment was] if He had withheld [suffering] from them.

Thou hast expressed wonder and amazement and hast

asked a difficult question, "Why doth man not live forever so that he shall not go down to Sheol?" Would that from the beginning he were created to be in the world that is to come for redemption, but thou desirest him to remain in siege and under a curse.

Though He doth all these things, there are many who yet rebel, and though He frighteneth them with calamities, there are [many] who are yet faithless to His decree. How much more if they had no cause to fear. They would then all with one accord not serve Him.

It is wise to make thy image live forever, or to save it from distress and anguish and trembling? What knowledge, dost thou judge, will save thee from falling [into ruin] that thou hast spoken rebellion against Him who dwelleth forever?

For the scorners judgments and stripes are prepared, Topheth is of old prepared for them in wrath. He preserved it against the time of trouble, against the day of battle and war. Thou also like one of them wilt share the anger of the God of vengeance.

[317]

SAINT-SIMON, CLAUDE HENRI, COMTE DE

SAINT-SIMON, CLAUDE HENRI, COMTE DE (1760-1825). In Saint-Simon's personality, the mind of a true philosopher was coupled with that of a smart businessman, that of a sincere philanthropist with that of an adventurous schemer. He fought at Yorktown for American independence. He was the first to advocate the building of the canals of Suez and Panama. More than a hundred years before the Young Plan, he demanded the foundation of an international bank, and his most faithful disciples became founders of joint-stock societies and constructors of canals and railroads, which, as Saint-Simon taught them, are necessary for the organization of human welfare and the realization of the ideals of human solidarity. Saint-Simon was the first to denounce "exploitation of men by their fellow men," and to prognosticate the increasing concentration of capital and industry. But he was also one of those "wicked speculators" who were branded by Robes-

1039

pierre, and he narrowly escaped execution. During the French Revolution he amassed a large fortune, but he died in poverty.

Saint-Simon's dominant idea was that the social system must be an application of the philosophical system, and that the function of philosophy is a prevalently social one. After ten years of studies devoted to physics, astronomy and chemistry, he turned to the study of human society and pronounced as its result that philosophical changes cause social changes, and that philosophy, as he conceived of it, must found a new society, a new religion, and a new evaluation of men. He especially emphasized that in modern times the industrial worker had become of far greater importance than the nobleman, the soldier and the priest, and, consequently, that he must occupy a higher social position than the former dignitaries. To industrial workers, scholars, and bankers he entrusted the organization of his new social system, which may be characterized as a kind of technocratic socialism. But the form of government was, in Saint-Simon's opinion, of lesser importance than the problem of administration. Therefore, he was not radically opposed to monarchism. After the publication of his works on the *Reorganization of Europe* (1814), *The Industrial System* and *Catechism of Industrials* (1821-1824), he wrote *The New Christianity* in the year of his death, 1825, by which he intended to substitute a secular religion of pantheistic and sensualistic color for the Christian faith. A small circle of enthusiastic disciples revered Saint-Simon who lived in obscurity and poverty as the founder of the religion of the future. After his death he became famous the world over, due to the propagandistic ardor of his pupils. He particularly influenced Goethe, Carlyle, Auguste Comte and Karl Marx.

APPEAL TO THE PRINCES TO BRING ABOUT
SOCIAL JUSTICE

PRINCES, What is, in the eyes of God and Christians, the nature and character of the power which you exercise? What is the basis of the system of social organization which you seek to establish? What measures have you taken to ameliorate the moral and physical existence of the poor classes? You call yourselves Christians and still you found your power upon physical force. You are still only the successors of Caesar, and you forget that the true Christians set as the ultimate end of their work the complete annihilation of the power of the sword, the power of Caesar, which by its nature is essentially provisional. And this is the power which you have undertaken to form as the basis of social organization! According to you, the initiative to perform all the general reforms which the progress of enlightenment has been calling for is left to this power exclusively. In order to support this monstrous system you keep two million people under arms. All the tribunals had to adopt your principle and you have made the Catholic, Protestant and Greek clergy profess loudly the heresy that Caesar's power is the regulating power of the Christian society.

While reminding the nations of the Christian religion by the symbol of your union, while making them enjoy a peace which, for them, is the first of all goods, you have nevertheless not aroused their gratitude toward yourselves. Your personal interest dominates too much in the combinations which you present as being of a general interest. The supreme European power which lies in your hands is far from being a Christian power, as it should have become. Ever since you have acted, you have displayed the character and the insignia of physical force, of anti-Christian force.

All the measures of whatever importance which you have taken since you united one with another in the Holy Alliance, all these measures tend toward worsening the lot of the poor classes, not only for this actual generation, but even for the generations to come. You have raised the taxes, you raise them every year in order to cover the increase of expenses brought about by your armies of soldiers and by the luxury of your courts. The class of your subjects to which you grant a special protection is the aristocracy, a class which, like you, founds its rights upon the sword. However, your blamable conduct seems excusable from several angles: that which has led you into error is the approval received by your efforts to smash the power of the modern Caesar. While fighting him, you have acted in a very Christian manner, but so it was only because in his hands the authority of Caesar, which Napoleon has conquered, had much more force than in yours where it has come only by heritage. Your conduct has also another excuse: It should have been the task of the clergymen to stop you at the edge of the abyss; instead they precipitated themselves into it, together with you.

[318]

SANTAYANA, GEORGE

SANTAYANA, GEORGE (1863-1952). Santayana was the son of a Spanish father and an American mother. He hints at his own Spanish strain when he describes the southern mind as long-indoctrinated, disillusioned, distinct, sceptical, malicious, yet in its reflective phase detached and contemplative, able to despise all entanglements, to dominate will and to look truth in the eye without blinking. He thinks of the American mind as being more ingenuous than wise. American is the texture, Spanish is the structure of Santayana's mind. America impressed his spiritual outlook. But, successful as he was as an influential professor at Harvard, he never felt himself at ease there. The Spanish tradition corresponded more by far to his inclinations, and, although he did not care about authorities, he highly esteemed the soil of history, tradition or human institutions without which thought and imagination became trivial.

When Santayana resolved to spend the rest of his life in an Italian convent as guest, he did not give up his philosophical conviction, one of whose striking features was unrelenting materialism. He was "attached to Catholicism" but "entirely divorced from faith," and protested that his scepticism had rather confirmed than dispelled this attachment. He continued to hold that "most conventional ideals, the religious ones included, are not adequate to the actual nature and capacities of men who accept them." He did not acknowledge any Christian dogma but liked the Christian religion for aesthetic and historical reasons. Nevertheless he was far from holding romanticist predilections, and even farther from having any adoration of the tragic sense of living.

What was true for Santayana's attachment to Catholicism was also true for his relation to Platonism. Santayana thought in terms of two realms of being, that of existence and that of essences.

1042

Concerning existence, he professed materialism. His realm of essences was of Platonist origin. But Santayana declined to regard essences as truer realities than existent things, or to found the realm of essences upon divine activity or to oppose essence to accident and modification.

According to Santayana, essences neither necessitate nor explain thoughts, nor do they determine the ground of concrete existence. The seat and principle of genesis is matter, not essence, which, for its part, is explanatory of intuition, assures the form of apperception, elucidates existence, and helps the mind to grasp and to retain the character and identity of the changing existences. However, while the evolution of existing things changes their character at every moment, the essences, representing every moment of this change, remain in their logical identity. An essence is anything definite capable of appearing and being thought of: it is senseless to believe in it because belief involves the assumption of real existence. Intuition of essence is no knowledge at all because illusion and error are also intuitions. Knowledge is a compound of instinctive conviction and expectation, animal faith and intuition of essence. It is essence by means of which the pursuit, attention and feelings which contribute to knowledge are transcribed in aesthetic, moral or verbal terms into consciousness. Matter is in flux; mind, conceived by Santayana as "simply sensibility in bodies," is existentially carried along the movement of that flux but is capable of arresting some datum, different from what the stimulated sensibility can articulate. This datum is essence in whose language alone mind can express its experiences.

Disillusioned, Santayana, although convinced of the truth of his work, did not except his philosophy from his general judgment of philosophical systems. To him they were all personal, temperamental, even premature. They were human heresies. The orthodoxy around which these heresies play, is no private or closed body of doctrine. It is "the current imagination and good sense of .mankind," a body of beliefs and evaluations far too chaotic, subject to errors and too conventional to satisfy a reflective mind, but capable of correcting its errors. Hence the need for personal philosophical thought, hence the impossibility to attain the goal to shape a philosophy satisfying mankind. As for Santayana he acquiesced in this insight, and was fond of stating divergencies between his mind and that of his critics.

1043

ART IN INSTINCT AND EXPERIENCE

Man Affects His Environment, Sometimes to Good Purpose.

MAN exists amid a universal ferment of being, and not only needs plasticity in his habits and pursuits but finds plasticity also in the surrounding world. Life is an equilibrium which is maintained now by accepting modification and now by imposing it. Since the organ for all activity is a body in mechanical relation to other material objects, objects which the creature's instincts often compel him to appropriate or transform, changes in his habits and pursuits leave their mark on whatever he touches. His habitat must needs bear many a trace of his presence, from which intelligent observers might infer something about his life and action. These vestiges of action are for the most part imprinted unconsciously and aimlessly on the world. They are in themselves generally useless, like footprints; and yet almost any sign of man's passage might, under certain conditions, interest a man. A footprint could fill Robinson Crusoe with emotion, the devastation wrought by an army's march might prove many things to a historian, and even the disorder in which a room is casually left may express very vividly the owner's ways and character.

Sometimes, however, man's traces are traces of useful action which has so changed natural objects as to make them congenial to his mind. Instead of a footprint we might find an arrow; instead of a disordered room, a well-planted orchard—things which would not only have betrayed the agent's habits, but would have served and expressed his intent. Such propitious forms given by man to matter are no less instrumental in the life of reason than are propitious forms assumed by man's own habit or fancy. Any operation which thus humanizes and rationalizes objects is called art.

Art Is Plastic Instinct Conscious of Its Aim.

All art has an instinctive source and a material embodiment. If the birds in building nests felt the utility of what

1044

they do, they would be practicing an art; and for the instinct to be called rational it would even suffice that their traditional purpose and method should became conscious occasionally. Thus weaving is an art, although the weaver may not be at every moment conscious of its purpose, but may be carried along, like any other workman, by the routine of his art; and language is a rational product, not because it always has a use or meaning, but because it is sometimes felt to have one. Arts are no less automatic than instincts, and usually, as Aristotle observed, less thoroughly purposive; for instincts, being transmitted by inheritance and imbedded in congenital structure, have to be economically and deeply organized. If they go far wrong they constitute a burden impossible to throw off and impossible to bear. The man harassed by inordinate instincts perishes through want, vice, disease, or madness. Arts, on the contrary, being transmitted only by imitation and teaching, hover more lightly over life. If ill-adjusted they make less havoc and cause less drain. The more superficial they are and the more detached from practical habits, the more extravagant and meaningless they can dare to become so that the higher products of life are the most often gratuitous. No instinct or institution was ever so absurd as is a large part of human poetry and philosophy, while the margin of ineptitude is much broader in religious myth than in religious ethics.

It Is Automatic.

Arts are instincts bred and reared in the open, creative habits acquired in the light of reason. Consciousness accompanies their formation; a certain uneasiness or desire and a more or less definite conception of what is wanted often precedes their full organization. That the need should be felt before the means for satisfying it have been found has led the unreflecting to imagine that in art the need produces the discovery and the idea the work. Causes at best are lightly assigned by mortals, and this particular superstition is no worse than any other. The data—the plan and its execution—as conjoined empirically in the few interesting cases which show successful achievement, are made into a law, in oblivion of the fact that in more numerous cases such conjunction fails wholly or in part, and that even in the successful cases other natural conditions are present, and must be present, to secure the result. In a matter where custom is so ingrained and supported by a constant apperceptive illusion, there is little hope of making thought suddenly exact, or exact language not paradoxical. We must observe, however, that only by virtue of a false perspective do ideas seem to govern action, or is a felt necessity the mother of invention. In truth invention is the child of abundance, and the genius or vital premonition and groping which achieve art simultaneously achieve the ideas which that art embodies; or, rather, ideas are themselves products of an inner movement which has an automatic extension outwards; and this extension manifests the ideas. Mere craving has no lights of its own to prophesy by, no prescience of what the world may contain that would satisfy, no power of imagining what would allay its unrest. Images and satisfactions have to come of themselves; then the blind craving, as it turns into an incipient pleasure, first recognizes its object. The pure will's impotence is absolute, and it would writhe for ever and consume itself in darkness if perception gave it no light and experience no premonition.

So Are the Ideas It Expresses.

Now, a man cannot draw bodily from external perception the ideas he is supposed to create or invent; and as his will or uneasiness, before he creates the satisfying ideas, is by hypothesis without them, it follows that creation or invention is automatic. The ideas come of themselves, being new and unthought-of figments, similar, no doubt, to old perceptions and compacted of familiar materials, but reproduced in a novel fashion and dropping in their sudden form from the blue. However instantly they may be welcomed, they were not already known and never could have been summoned. In the stock example, for instance, of groping for a forgotten name, we know the context in which that name should lie; we feel the environment of our local void; but what finally pops into that place, reinstated there by the surrounding tensions, is itself unforeseen, for it was just this that was forgotten. Could we have invoked the name we should not have needed to do so, having it already at our disposal. It is in fact a palpable impossibility that any idea should call itself into being, or that any act or any preference should be its own ground. The responsibility assumed for these things is not a determination to conceive them before they are conceived (which is a contradiction in terms) but an embrace and appropriation of them once they have appeared. It is thus that ebullitions in parts of our nature become touchstones for the whole; and the incidents within us seem hardly our own work till they are accepted and incorporated into the main current of our being. All invention is tentative, all art experimental, and to be sought, like salvation, with fear and trembling. There is a painful pregnancy in genius, a long incubation and waiting for the spirit, a thousand rejections and futile birthpangs, before the wonderful child appears, a gift of the gods, utterly undeserved and inexplicably perfect. Even this unaccountable success comes only in rare and fortunate instances. What is ordinarily produced is so base a hybrid, so lame and ridiculous a changeling, that we reconcile ourselves with difficulty to our offspring and blush to be represented by our fated works.

We Are Said to Control Whatever Obeys Us.

The propensity to attribute happy events to our own agency, little as we understand what we mean by it, and to attribute only untoward results to external forces, has its ground in the primitive nexus of experience. What we call ourselves is a certain cycle of vegetative processes, bringing a round of familiar impulses and ideas; this stream has a general direction, a conscious vital inertia, in harmony with which it moves. Many of the developments within it are dialectical; that is, they go forward by inner necessity, like an egg hatching within its shell, warmed but undisturbed by an environment of which they are wholly oblivious; and this sort of growth, when there is adequate consciousness of it, is felt to be both absolutely obvious and absolutely free. The emotion that accompanies it is pleasurable, but is too active and proud to call itself a pleasure; it has rather the quality of assurance and right. This part of life, however, is only its courageous core; about it play all sorts of incidental processes, allying themselves to it in more or less congruous movement. Whatever peripheral events fall in with the central impulse are accordingly lost in its energy and felt to be not so much peripheral and accidental as inwardly grounded, being, like the stages of a prosperous dialectic, spontaneously demanded and instantly justified when they come.

The sphere of the self's power is accordingly, for primitive consciousness, simply the sphere of what happens well; it is the entire unoffending and obedient part of the world. A man who has good luck at dice prides himself upon it, and believes that to have it is his destiny and desert. If his luck were absolutely constant, he would say he had the *power* to throw high; and as the event would, by hypothesis, sustain his boast, there would be no practical error in that assumption. A will that never found anything to thwart it would think itself omnipotent; and as the psychological essence of omniscience is not to suspect there is anything which you do not know, so the psychological essence of omnipotence is not to suspect that anything can happen which you do not desire. Such claims would undoubtedly be made if experience lent them the least color; but would even the most comfortable and innocent assurances of this sort cease to be precarious? Might not any moment of eternity bring the unimagined contradiction, and shake the dreaming god?

Utility Is a Result.

Utility like significance, is an eventual harmony in the arts and by no means their ground. All useful things have been discovered as ancient China discovered roast pig; and the casual feat has furthermore to be supported by a situation favorable to maintaining the art. The most useful act will never be repeated unless its secret remains embodied in structure. Practice and endeavor will not help an artist to remain long at his best; and many a performance is applauded which cannot be imitated. To create the requisite structure two preformed structures are needed: one in the agent, to give him skill and perseverance, and another in the material, to give it the right plasticity. Human progress would long ago have reached its goal if every man who recognized a good could at once appropriate it, and possess wisdom for ever by virtue of one moment's insight. Insight, unfortunately, is in itself perfectly useless and inconsequential; it can neither have produced its own occasion nor now insure its own recurrence. Nevertheless, being proof positive that whatever basis it needs is actual, insight is also an indication that the extant structure, if circumstances maintain it, may continue to operate with the same moral results, maintaining the vision which it has once supported.

The Useful Naturally Stable.

When men find that by chance they have started a useful change in the world, they congratulate themselves upon it and call their persistence in that practice a free activity. And the activity is indeed rational, since it subserves an end. The happy organization which enables us to continue in that rational course is the very organization which enabled us to initiate it. If this new process was formed under external influences, the same influences, when they operate again, will reconstitute the process each time more easily; while if it was formed quite spontaneously, its own inertia will maintain it quietly in the brain and bring it to the surface whenever circumstances permit. This is what is called learning by experiences. Such lessons are far from indelible and are not always at command. Yet what has once been done may be repeated; repetition reinforces itself and becomes habit; and a clear memory of the benefit once attained by fortunate action representing as it does the trace left by that action in the system, and its harmony with the man's usual impulses (for the action is felt to be *beneficial*), constitutes a strong presumption that the act will be repeated automatically on occasion; i.e., that it has really been learned. Consciousness, which willingly attends to results only, will judge either the memory or the benefit, or both confusedly, to be the ground of this readiness to act; and only if some hitch occurs in the machinery, so that rational behavior fails to take place, will a surprised appeal be made to material accidents, or to a guilty forgetfulness or indocility in the soul.

Intelligence Is Docility.

The idiot cannot learn from experience at all, because a new process, in his liquid brain, does not modify structure; while the fool uses what he has learned only inaptly and in frivolous fragments, because his stretches of linked experience are short and their connections insecure. But when the cerebral plasm is fresh and well disposed and when the paths are clear, attention is consecutive and learning easy; a multitude of details can be gathered into a single cycle of memory or of potential regard. Under such circumstances action is the unimpeded expression of healthy instinct in an environment squarely faced. Conduct from the first then issues in progress, and, by reinforcing its own organization at each rehearsal, makes progress continual. For there will subsist not only a readiness to act and a great precision in action, but if any significant circumstance has varied in the conditions or in the interests at stake, this change will make itself felt; it will check the process and prevent precipitate action. Deliberation or well-founded scruple has the same source as facility—a plastic and quick organization. To be sensitive to difficulties and dangers goes with being sensitive to opportunities.

Art Is Reason Propagating Itself.

Of all reason's embodiments art is therefore the most splendid and complete. Merely to attain categories by which inner experience may be articulated, or to feign analogies by which a universe may be conceived, would be but a visionary triumph if it remained ineffectual and went with no actual remodelling of the outer world, to render man's dwelling more appropriate and his mind better fed and more largely transmissible. Mind grows self-perpetuating only by its expression in matter. What makes progress possible is that rational action may leave traces in nature, such that nature in consequence furnishes a better basis for the life of reason; in other words progress is art bettering the conditions of existence. Until art arises, all achievement is internal to the brain, dies with the individual, and even in him spends itself without recovery, like music heard in a dream. Art, in establishing instruments for human life beyond the human body, and moulding outer things into sympathy with inner values, establishes a ground whence values may continually spring up; the thatch that protects from to-day's rain will last and keep out tomorrow's rain also; the sign that once expresses an idea will serve to recall it in future.

Not only does the work of art thus perpetuate its own function and produce a better experience, but the process of art also perpetuates itself, because it is teachable. Every animal learns something by living; but if his offspring inherit only what he possessed at birth, they have to learn life's lessons over again from the beginning, with at best some vague help given by their parent's example. But when the fruits of experience exist in the common environment, when new instruments, unknown to nature, are offered to each individual for his better equipment, although he must still learn for himself how to live, he may learn in a humaner school, where artificial occasions are constantly open to him for expanding his powers. It is no longer merely hidden inner processes that he must reproduce to attain his predecessors' wisdom; he may acquire much of it more expeditiously by imitating their outward habit—an imitation which, furthermore, they have some means of exacting from him. Wherever there is art there is a possibility of training. A father who calls his idle sons from the jungle to help him hold the plough not only inures them to labor but compels them to observe the earth upturned and refreshed, and to watch the germination there; their wandering thought, their incipient rebellions, will be met by the hope of harvest; and it will not be impossible for them, when their father is dead, to follow the plough of their own initiative and for their own children's sake. So great is the sustained advance in rationality made possible by art which, being embodied in matter, is teachable and transmissible by training; for in art the values secured are recognized the more easily for having been first enjoyed when other people furnished the means to them; while the maintenance of these values is facilitated by an external tradition imposing itself contagiously or by force on each new generation.

Beauty an Incident in Rational Art.

Art is action which transcending the body makes the world a more congenial stimulus to the soul. All art is therefore useful and practical, and the notable æsthetic value which some works of art possess, for reasons flowing for the most part out of their moral significance, is itself one of the satisfactions which art offers to human nature as a whole. Between sensation and abstract discourse lies a region of deployed sensibility or synthetic representation, a region where more is seen at arm's length than in any one moment could be felt at close quarters, and yet where the remote parts of experience, which discourse reaches only through symbols, are recovered and recomposed in something like their native colors and experienced relations. This region, called imagination, has pleasures more airy and luminous than those of sense. more massive and rapturous than those of intelligence. The values inherent in imagination, in instant intuition, in sense endowed with form, are called æsthetic values; they are found mainly in nature and living beings, but often also in man's artificial works, in images evoked by language, and in the realm of sound.

Inseparable from the Others.

Productions in which an æsthetic value is or is supposed to be prominent take the name of fine art; but the work of fine art so defined is almost always an abstraction from the actual object, which has many non-æsthetic functions and values. To separate the æsthetic element, abstract and de-dependent as it often is, is an artifice which is more mislead-ing than helpful; for neither in the history of art nor in a rational estimate of its value can the æsthetic function of things be divorced from the practical and moral. What had to be done was, by imaginative races, done imaginatively; what had to be spoken or made, was spoken or made fitly, lovingly, beautifully. Or to take the matter up on its psy-chological side, the ceaseless experimentation and ferment of ideas, in breeding what it had a propensity to breed, came sometimes on figments that gave it delightful pause; these beauties were the first knowledges and these arrests the first hints of real and useful things. The rose's grace could more easily be plucked from its petals than the beauty of art from its subject, occasion, and use. An æsthetic fragrance, indeed, all things may have, if in soliciting man's senses or reason they can awaken his imagination as well; but this middle zone is so mixed and nebulous and its limits are so vague, that it cannot well be treated in theory otherwise than as it exists in fact—as a phase of man's sympathy with the world he moves in. If art is that element in the life of reason which consists in modifying its environment the better to attain its end, art may be expected to subserve all parts of the human ideal, to increase man's comfort, knowledge, and de-light. And as nature, in her measure, is wont to satisfy these interests together, so art, in seeking to increase that satis-faction, will work simultaneously in every ideal direction. Nor will any of these directions be on the whole good, or tempt a well-trained will, if it leads to estrangement from all other interests. The æsthetic good will be accordingly hatched in the same nest with the others, and incapable of flying far in a different air.

[319]

SARTRE, JEAN PAUL

SARTRE, JEAN PAUL (1905-   ). Evidently and avowedly, Sartre, of all younger French authors the one whose works are most eagerly read in America, has not yet come to a final formulation of his philosophical thoughts. In his *Baudelaire* (1947) and in his critical essays *Situations* (1947), he expresses ideas and sentiments which indicate some changes of viewpoint and standard of evaluation when compared with his principal philosophical works *Being and Nothingness* (1943) and *Existentialism is a Humanism* (1946). Also his drama *The Flies* (1943) leads to conclusions concerning human destiny which are not yet theoretically expressed by Sartre.

Sartre, always a man of delicate health, and an orphan at an early age, was a professor of philosophy at one of Paris' greatest colleges, after having studied at the Sorbonne and at the German University of Göttingen where he was a student of Husserl. In World War II he was made a prisoner but was released from the German prisoners' camp because of his sickness. When he returned to Paris, he became a leader of the resistance.

Sartre's philosophy as far as it has so far developed is deeply influenced by Heidegger. But Sartre's existentialism departs from that of Heidegger's by establishing an anti-theological morale, a phenomenology of the body, and principles of existential psychoanalysis. While anguish is Heidegger's fundamental experience, Sartre's is that which he calls nausea, disgust, revulsion against being, duration, repetition and continuance of life, as well as against the unending mobility of human existence. Sartre tried to banish all vagueness while confronting personal existence with general life but he also tried to find a way to vindicate freedom and the value of the individual.

REASONS AND WRITING

EACH one has his reasons: for one, art is a flight; for another, a means of conquering. But one can flee into a hermitage, into madness, into death. One can conquer by arms. Why does

1054

it have to be *writing*, why does one have to manage his escapes and conquests by *writing?* Because, behind the various aims of authors, there is a deeper and more immediate choice which is common to all of us. We shall try to elucidate this choice, and we shall see whether it is not in the name of this very choice of writing that the engagement of writers must be required.

Each of our perceptions is accompanied by the consciousness that human reality is a "revealer," that is, it is through human reality that "there is" being, or, to put it differently, that man is the means by which things are manifested. It is our presence in the world which multiplies relations. It is we who set up a relationship between this tree and that bit of sky. Thanks to us, that star which has been dead for millennia, that quarter moon, and that dark river are disclosed in the unity of landscape. It is the speed of our auto and our airplane which organizes the great masses of the earth. With each of our acts, the world reveals to us a new face. But, if we know that we are directors of being, we also know that we are not its producers. If we turn away from this landscape, it will sink back into its dark permanence. At least, it will sink back; there is no one mad enough to think that it is going to be annihilated. It is we who shall be annihilated, and the earth will remain in its lethargy until another consciousness comes along to awaken it. Thus, to our inner certainty of being "revealers" is added that of being inessential in relation to the thing revealed.

One of the chief motives of artistic creation is certainly the need of feeling that we are essential in relationship to the world. If I fix on canvas or in writing a certain aspect of the fields or the sea or a look on someone's face which I have disclosed, I am conscious of having produced them by condensing relationship, by introducing order where there was none, by imposing the unity of mind on the diversity of things. That is, I feel myself essential in relation to my creation. But this time it is the created object which escapes me;

1055

I can not reveal and produce at the same time. The creation becomes inessential in relation to the creative activity. First of all, even if it appears to others as definitive, the created object always seems to us in a state of suspension; we can always change this line, that shade, that word. Thus, it never *forces itself*. A novice painter asked his teacher, "When should I consider my painting finished?" And the teacher answered, "When you can look at it in amazement and say to yourself '*I'm* the one who did *that!*'"

[320]

SCHELLING, FRIEDRICH WILHELM JOSEPH VON

SCHELLING, FRIEDRICH WILHELM JOSEPH VON (1775-1854). Schelling has been called the Proteus among philosophers. His mind was as changeable as it was impressible. In his early years, Schelling fascinated everyone he met. He was overflowing with ideas, versatile, and apt in understanding men and problems. Goethe considered him the most congenial philosopher he knew, and it was Schelling who inspired Hegel, although the latter would not admit it.

Schelling created the philosophy of identity by asserting that nature is not essentially different from mind; his way of representing the various forms of existence as the work of an unconsciously creating activity which is the same in shaping nature and mind, influenced not only his German contemporaries but English and French thinkers as well, and not the least among them—Bergson.

The aged Schelling was rigid in his attitude toward man and the universe. He recanted his earlier pantheistic belief in the identity of nature and mind and repudiated transcendental idealism, even idealism and judgments *a priori* at all. The "positive philosophy" of Schelling's last years considered empiricism the lesser evil compared with any kind of rational deduction. Originally an admirer of Epicurus and Spinoza, he had become the defender of Protestant and Catholic orthodoxy and the champion of political reaction. But he could not prevent liberals from referring to his words, spoken in earlier days, which extolled eternal change.

1056

ALL knowledge is based upon the agreement of an objective with a subjective. For we *know* only the true, and the truth is universally held to be the agreement of representations with their objects.

The sum of all that is purely objective in our knowledge we may call Nature; whereas the sum of everything subjective may be termed the *Ego*, or Intelligence. These two concepts are mutually opposed. Intelligence is originally conceived as that which solely represents, and nature as that which is merely capable of representation; the former as the conscious—the latter as the unconscious. But in all knowledge there is necessary a mutual agreement of the two—the conscious and the unconscious *per se*. The problem is to explain this agreement.

In knowledge itself, in that I know, the objective and subjective are so united that one cannot say which of the two has priority. There is here no first and no second—the two are contemporaneous and one. In any attempt to explain this identity, I must already have resolved it. In order to explain it, inasmuch as there is nothing else given me as a principle of explanation except these two factors of knowledge, I must of necessity place the one before the other, that is to say, must set out from the one in order to arrive at the other. From which of the two I shall set out is not determined by the problem.

There are, consequently, only two cases possible:

I. *Either the objective is made first, and the question arises how a subjective agreeing with it is superinduced.*

The idea of the subjective is not contained in the idea of the objective; on the contrary they mutually exclude each other. The subjective must therefore be *superinduced* upon the objective. It forms no part of the conception of nature that there must be likewise an intelligence to represent it.

Nature, to all appearance, would exist even if there were nothing to represent it. The problem may therefore likewise be expressed thus: How is the intelligent superinduced upon nature? or, How does nature come to be represented?

The problem assumes nature, or the objective, as the first. It is, therefore, undoubtedly the task of natural science, which does the same. That natural science actually, and without knowing it, approximates, at least, to the solution of this problem can here be only briefly shown.

If all knowledge has, as it were, two poles, which mutually presuppose and demand each other, then they must seek each other in all sciences. There must, therefore, of necessity, exist two fundamental sciences; and it must be impossible to set out from one pole without being driven to the other. The necessary tendency of all natural science, therefore, is to proceed from nature to the intelligent. This, and this alone, lies at the foundation of the effort to bring theory into natural phenomena. The final perfection of natural science would be the complete intellectualization of all the laws of nature into laws of intuition and of thought. The phenomena, that is, the material, must completely vanish, and leave only the laws,—that is, the formal. Hence it happens that the more the conformity to law is manifested in nature so much the more the wrapping disappears—the phenomena themselves become more intellectualized, and at length entirely cease. Optical phenomena are nothing more than a geometry whose lines are drawn by aid of the light; and even this light itself is already of doubtful materiality. In the phenomena of magnetism every trace of matter has already vanished; and of the phenomena of gravitation, which even the natural philosopher believed could be attributed only to direct spiritual influence, there remains nothing but their law, whose performance on a large scale is the mechanism of the heavenly motions. The complete theory of nature would be that by virtue of which the whole of nature should be resolved into an intelligence. The dead and unconscious products of nature are only unsuccessful attempts of nature to reflect itself, but the so-called dead nature is merely an unripe intelligence; hence in its phenomena the intelligent character appears, though still unconscious. Its highest aim, that is of becoming wholly self-objective, nature does not attain, except in its highest and last reflection, which is none other than man, or more generally what we call reason. By its means nature first turns completely back upon itself, and thereby it is manifest that nature is originally identical with what in us is known as intelligent and conscious.

This may suffice to prove that natural science has a necessary tendency to render nature intelligent. By this very tendency it becomes natural philosophy, which is one of the two necessary fundamental sciences of philosophy.

II. Or the subjective is made first, and the problem is, how an objective is superinduced agreeing with it.

If all knowledge is based upon the agreement of these two, then the problem to explain this agreement is undoubtedly the highest for all knowledge; and if, as is generally admitted, philosophy is the highest and loftiest of all sciences, it becomes certainly the chief task of philosophy.

But the problem demands only the explanation of that agreement generally, and leaves it entirely undetermined where the explanation shall begin, what it shall make its first, and what its second. Since also the two opposites are mutually necessary, the result of the operation is the same, from whichever point one sets out. To make the objective the first, and to derive the subjective from it, is, as has just been shown, the task of natural philosophy.

If, therefore, there is a transcendental philosophy, the only direction remaining for it is the opposite, that is: to proceed from the subjective as the first and the absolute, and to deduce the origin of the objective from it. Natural and transcendental philosophy have divided between themselves these two possible directions of philosophy. And if all philosophy must have for an aim to make either an intelligence out of nature or a nature out of intelligence, then transcendental philosophy, to which this latter problem belongs, is the other necessary fundamental science of philosophy.

[321]

SCHILLER, FERDINAND CANNING SCOTT

SCHILLER, FERDINAND CANNING SCOTT (1864-1917). In strong opposition to the Hegelianism prevailing at Oxford University since T. H. Green and strengthened by F. H. Bradley, another professor of that same University, though a namesake of the German idealistic poet Schiller, combated any idealism of German provenience. F. C. S. Schiller called his philosophy *Humanism*, while calling himself a disciple of the sophist Protagoras, who said that man is the measure of all things. Schiller proceeds from the statement that all mental life is purposive to the establishment of a concept of truth whose criteria are given by the consequences of a proposition. This does not mean that truth corresponds to the organic or sentimental needs of the knower. As Schiller says, his humanism is merely the perception that the philosophic problem concerns human beings striving to comprehend a world of human experience by the resources of the human mind. He distinguishes humanism from pragmatism, to which it is in fact akin, by the claim that humanism is of larger range and is able to be applied not only to logic but to ethics, aesthetics, metaphysic and theology, and furthermore by his readiness to acknowledge as many metaphysics as there are tempers, while rejecting any absolute metaphysic. Schiller's principal works about humanism are *Humanism* (1903) and *Studies in Humanism* (1907). He wrote also about the problems of the day. In one of his pamphlets he declared that a government of the world administered by international bankers would by no means be the worst possible.

HOW IS "EXACTNESS" POSSIBLE?

IT is amazing what a spell the ideal of exactness has cast upon the philosophic mind. For hundreds, nay thousands, of years philosophers seem to have been yearning for exactness, and hoping that, if only they could attain it, all their troubles would be over. All the pitfalls in the way of phil-

osophic progress would be circumvented, and every philosophic science, from psychology and logic to the remotest
heights of metaphysics, would become accessible to the
meanest understanding.

Yet what a gap there is between these professions and
the practice of philosophers! Despite of their zeal for exactness, what body of learned men is more careless in their
terminology and more contemptuous of all the devices which
seem conducive to exactness?

Experience shows that it is quite impossible to pin any
philosophic term down to any single meaning, even for a
little while, or even to keep its meaning stable enough to
avoid gross misunderstanding. Even the most express and
solemn definitions are set at naught by the very writers who
propounded them. The most famed philosophers are the
very ones who have been the worst offenders. For example,
Kant's fame rests in no small measure on the tricks he played
with words like "*a priori*," "category," "object," and his
systematic confusion of "transcendental" and "transcendent." There is hardly a philosophy which does not juggle
thus with ambiguous terms. If the theories of philosophers
may be interpreted in the light of their practice, they should
be the last persons in the world to laud "exactness."

On the other hand, they might fairly be expected to
inform us what "exactness" means, or at least what they
wish it to mean. I do not find, however, that they are at all
eager to do this. Apparently they are content to refer to
mathematics as an "exact" science, and to admonish philosophy to respect and aspire to the mathematical ideal.

To understand exactness, therefore, we must go to
mathematics and inquire whether and in what senses mathematics are "exact." Now it is clear that mathematics are not
exact in the sense that mathematical objects exactly reproduce physical realities; nor do physical realities exactly
exemplify mathematical ideals. There are no straight lines
nor circles to be found in nature, while all the physical con-

stants, like the year, month, and day, are inexact. Plato knew this, but yet thought of God as a mathematician; he should have added that if God geometrizes, He does so very inexactly.

Hence, if the relation between realities and mathematical ideals is conceived as a *copying* or *reproduction*, it cannot possibly be "exact." Which is the archetype, and which the copy, does not matter: alike whether the real copies the mathematical ideal, or the latter is moulded upon the former, no exactness can be found.

There is, however, a sense in which exactness depends on definition; and mathematicians take great pride in the exactness of their definitions. A definition can be exact, because it is a *command* addressed to nature, and it sounds quite uncompromising. If the real will not come up to the definition, so much the worse for the real! In so far therefore as exactness depends on definitions, mathematics can be exact. It can be as exact as anything defined exactly.

But there appear to be limits to the exactness thus attainable. The exactness of a definition is limited by two difficulties. (a) In the first place things must be found to which the definition, when made, does actually apply. And secondly, (b) the definition has to be maintained against the growth of knowledge. Both these difficulties may easily prove fatal to exactness.

As to (a), it is clear that we cannot arbitrarily "define" the creatures of our fancy, without limits. Definitions which apply to nothing have no real meaning. The only sure way, therefore, of securing that a definition will be operative and will have application to the real, is to allow the real, idealized if necessary, to suggest the definition to the mathematician. The mathematician was sensible enough to adopt this procedure. He allowed a ray of sunlight to suggest the definition of a straight line, and this assured to Euclidean geometry a profitable field of application.

But it did *not* render the definition immutable, and immune to the growth of knowledge. The mathematical definition remains dependent on the behavior of the real. If, therefore, rays of light are found to curve in a gravitational field, a far-reaching doubt is cast on the use of Euclidean geometry for cosmic calculations.

As to (b), the definer retains the right to revise his definitions. So the very framing of his definition may suggest to the mathematician the idea of developing it in some promising and interesting direction. But this procedure may entail a further definition, or redefinition, which destroys the exactness of the first formula. Thus when he has accomplished the "exact" definition of a circle and an ellipse, it may occur to a mathematician that after all a circle may be taken as a special case of an ellipse, and that it would be interesting to see what happens if he followed out this line of thought. He does so, and arrives at "the points at infinity," with their paradoxical properties. Again the development of non-Euclidean geometries has rendered ambiguous and inexact the Euclidean conceptions, e.g. of "triangle." Even so elementary and apparently stable a conception as that of the unit of common arithmetic undergoes subtle transformations of meaning as others beyond the original operation of addition are admitted.

In mathematics then, as in the other sciences, it is inevitable that the conceptions used should *grow*. It is impossible to prohibit their growth, and to restrict them to the definitions as they were conceived at first. Indeed the process of stretching old definitions so as to permit of new operations is even particularly evident in mathematics.

The method by which it is justified is that of *analogy*. If an analogy can be found which promises to bridge a gap between one notion and another, their identity is experimentally assumed. And if the experiment works for the purposes of those who made it, the differences between them are slurred over and ignored. If it were not possible to take the infinitesimal, now as something, now as nothing, what would be left of the logic of the calculus? But the logician at least should remind himself that analogy is not an exact and valid form of argument.

Can exactness be said to inhere in the symbols used by mathematicians? Hardly. $+$ and $-$, and even $=$, have many uses, and therefore senses, even in the exactest mathematics.

The truth is that mathematical definitions cannot be more exact than our knowledge of the realities to which, sooner or later, directly or indirectly, they refer. Nor can mathematical symbols be more exact than *words*. It is sheer delusion to think otherwise.

And what about words? Whence do they get their meanings, and how are they stabilized and modified?

Words get their meaning by being used successfully by those who have meanings to convey. *Verbal* meaning, therefore, is derivative from *personal* meaning. Once a verbal meaning is established and can be presumed to be familiar, personal meaning can employ a word for the purpose of transmitting a new meaning judged appropriate to a situation in which a transfer of meaning to others is judged necessary or desirable. Thus a transfer of meaning is always experimental, and generally problematic and inexact.

Moreover the situation which calls for it is always more or less *new*. Hence a successful transfer, that is the understanding of a meaning, always involves an *extension* of an old meaning; and in the course of time this may result in a complete reversal of the initial definition. For example, when the "atom" was first imported into physics, it was defined as the ultimate and indivisible particle of matter. Now, notoriously, it has been subdivided so often that there seems to be room in it for an unending multitude of parts; and its exploration is the most progressive part of physics. The word remains, but its definition has been radically changed. For the scientist always has an option when he finds that his old words are no longer adequate: he can either change his terms, or else his definitions. But there is, and can be, no fixity and no exactness about either.

There is a further difficulty about definitions. All words cannot be defined. Wherever the definer begins, or ends, he makes use of terms not yet defined, or has recourse to definitions revolving in a circle. So, if he hankers after exactness, he declares that some terms are indefinable and need no definition. This subterfuge is utterly unworthy of an exact logician. For if he holds that these indefinables are yet intuitively understood or apprehended, he enslaves his "logic" to psychology. If he admits that he cannot guarantee that any two reasoners will understand the indefinables alike, he explodes the basis of all exactness. Thus even the exactest definitions are left to float in a sea of inexactitude.

The situation grows still more desperate if the logician realizes that, to achieve exactness, he must eradicate and overcome the potential ambiguity of words. He must devise words which exactly fit the particular situation in which the words are used. For otherwise the same word will be permitted to mean one thing in one context, another in another. It will be what logicians have been wont to call "ambiguous." In this, however, they may have been mistaking for a flaw the most convenient property of words, namely their plasticity and capacity for repeated use as vehicles of *many* meanings.

For the alternative of demanding a one-one correspondence between words and meanings, seems incomparably worse. I remember this was tried once by Earl Bertrand Russell, in a sportive mood. It was not long after the war, and he had just emerged from the dungeon to which he had been consigned for an ill-timed jest, that he came to Oxford to read a paper to a society of undergraduate philosophers, on what he called "vagueness." I was requested to "open the discussion" on this paper, and so obtained what in Hollywood is called a "preview" of it. What was my amazement when I found that Russell's cure for "vagueness," that is, the applicability of the same word to different situations, was

1065

that there should be distinctive words enough for every situation! Certainly that would be a radical cure; but in what a state would it leave language! A language freed from "vagueness" would be composed entirely of *nonce words,* "hapax legomena," and almost wholly unintelligible. When I pointed out this consequence, Russell cheerfully accepted it, and I retired from the fray.

Russell had rightly diagnosed what was the condition of exactness. But he had ignored the fact that his cure was impracticable, and far worse than the alleged disease. Nor had he considered the alternative, the inference that *therefore* the capacity of words to convey a multitude of meanings must not be regarded as a flaw, but that a distinction must be made between plurality of meanings and actual ambiguity.

It is vital to logic that the part words play in transmitting meaning from one person to another should be rightly understood; but does not such understanding reduce the demand for "exactness" to a false ideal?

What finally is the bearing of these results on the pretensions of logistics?

It seems to reduce itself to a game with fictions and verbal meanings. (1) It is clear that it is a fiction that meanings can be fixed, and embodied in unvarying symbols. (2) It is clear that the verbal meanings to be fixed are never the personal meanings to be conveyed in actual knowing. The assumption that they can be identified is just a fiction too. (3) There appears to be no point of contact between the conventions of this game and the real problems of scientific knowing. This is the essential difference between logistics and mathematics. Pure mathematics is a game too, but it has application to reality. But logistics seems to be a game more remote from science than chess is from strategy. For in a science the meanings concerned are those of the investigators, that is, are *personal.* They are also experimental. They respond to every advance in knowledge, and are modified accordingly. Their fixity would mean stagnation, and the death of science. Words need have only enough stability of meaning, when they are used, for the old senses (which determine their selection) to yield a sufficient clue to the new senses to be conveyed, to render the latter intelligible. In their context, not in the abstract. In the abstract they may remain infinitely "ambiguous," that is, *potentially useful.* This does no harm, so long as it does not mislead in actual use. And when an experimenter ventures on too audacious innovations upon the conventional meanings of his words, the right rebuke to him is not "You contradict the meaning of the words you use," but "I do not understand; what do you mean?"

I am driven then to the conclusion that logistics is an intellectual game. It is a game of make-believe, which mathematically trained pedants love to play, but which does not on this account become incumbent on every one. It may have the advantage that it keeps logisticians out of other mischief. But I fail to see that it has either any serious significance for understanding scientific knowing or any educational importance for sharpening wits!

[322]

SCHLEGEL, FRIEDRICH VON

SCHLEGEL, FRIEDRICH VON (1772-1829). Friedrich Schlegel is one of the most characteristic representatives of German romanticism whose principal trait is the longing for a reality different from that which is determined by natural laws and historical circumstances. Dissatisfied with the civilization of his own time, Schlegel at first exalted the French Revolution, then the Middle Ages, and finally, considering the Roman Catholic Church as the keeper of the medieval mind, he was converted to it, and became a champion of political and cultural reaction. He began as an admirer and pupil of Kant, Fichte and Goethe, and later turned to Metternich and Joseph de Maistre who asserted the superiority of tradition over reason, and proclaimed papacy as the one legitimate ruler over humanity.

Schlegel was a poor poet. His novel *Lucinde*, although it scandalized middle-class morals, proved to be unreadable. His tragedy *Alarcos*, produced by Goethe in Weimar, fell flat. But in his early aphorisms and essays, Schlegel refined the understanding of poetry and evoked the sense of personality in every kind of spiritual activity, be it poetic, scientific, philosophical or religious. In his later works, Schlegel stiffened his opposition to Enlightenment, natural law, democracy and liberalism, but, despite his turn to traditionalism, he preserved a revolutionary strain of which he was conscious. He defined it as his faculty to perceive historical changes without sympathizing with them, and to combat the revolution with what he called "revolutionary spirit in a valid sense but different from the common conception." He therefore was as distrusted by Catholics as he was blamed by Protestants.

For many years, Schlegel led a destitute life for he was rather indolent. He would have perished without the help of his wife Dorothea, Moses Mendelssohn's daughter with whom he had eloped from the house of her husband Simon Veit. Dorothea, the "child of enlightenment," nine years older than Schlegel, followed him from folly to folly and, at the same time, provided him with money by writing novels and articles with untiring energy.

PHILOSOPHY OF LIFE

"THERE are," says a poet as ingenious as profound, "more things in heaven and earth, than are dreamt of in our philosophy." This sentiment, which Genius accidentally let drop, is in the main applicable also to the philosophy of our own day; and, with a slight modification, I shall be ready to adopt it as my own. The only change that is requisite to make it available for my purpose would be the addition— "and also between heaven and earth are there many things which are not dreamt of in our philosophy." And exactly because philosophy, for the most part, does nothing but dream —scientifically dream, it may be—therefore is it ignorant, ay, has no inkling even of much which nevertheless, in all propriety it ought to know. It loses sight of its true object, it quits the firm ground where, standing secure, it might pursue its own avocations without let or hindrance, whenever, abandoning its own proper region, it either soars up to heaven to weave there its fine-spun webs of dialectics, and to build its metaphysical castles in the air, or else, losing itself on the earth, it violently interferes with external reality, and determines to shape the world according to its own fancy, and to reform it at will. Half-way between these two devious courses lies the true road; and the proper region of philosophy is even that spiritual inner life between heaven and earth.

On both sides, many and manifold errors were committed, even in the earlier and better days of enlightened antiquity. Plato himself, the greatest of the great thinkers of Greece, set up in his Republic the model of an ideal polity, which, in this respect, cannot bear the test of examination. His design indeed finds, in some measure, its apology in the disorders and corruption which even in his day, had infected all the free states of Greece, whether great or small. His work too, by the highly finished style of the whole, the vivid perspicuity of its narrative, its rich profusion of pregnant ideas and noble sentiments, stands out in dignified contrast to the crude and ill-designed schemes of legislation so hastily propounded in our own day. Still, it will ever remain the weak point of this great man. One needs not to be a Plato to see how absolutely unfeasible, not to say practically absurd, are many of the propositions of this Platonic ideal. Accordingly it has ever been the fruitful occasion, not only among contemporaries, but also with posterity, of ridicule to the ignorant and of censure to the wise. In this respect it cannot but excite our regret that such great and noble powers of mind should have been wasted in following a false direction, and in pursuit of an unattainable end. The oldest philosophers of Greece, on the other hand—those first bold adventurers on the wide ocean of thought, combined together the elements of things, water, or air, or fire, or atoms, or lastly the all-ruling Intellect itself, into as many different systems of the universe. If, however, each in his own way thus set forth a peculiar creed of nature, we must ever bear in mind that the popular religion, with its poetical imagery, and the fabulous mythology of antiquity, as affording not only no sufficient, but absolutely

1069

no answer to the inquiring mind, as to the essence of things, and the first cause of all, could not possibly satisfy these earlier thinkers. Consequently they might well feel tempted to find, each for himself, a way to honor nature, and to contemplate the supreme Being. Since then, however, the world has grown older by nearly twenty-five centuries, and much in the meanwhile has been accomplished by, or fallen to the share of, the human race. But when philosophy would pretend to regard this long succession of ages, and all its fruits, as suddenly erased from the records of existence, and for the sake of change would start afresh, so perilous an experiment can scarcely lead to any good result, but in all probability, and to judge from past experience, will only give rise to numberless and interminable disputes. Such an open space in thought—cleared from all the traces of an earlier existence (a smoothly polished marble tablet, as it were, like the *tabula rasa* of a recent ephemeral philosophy)—would only serve as an arena for the useless though daring ventures of unprofitable speculation, and could never form a safe basis for solid thought, or for any permanent manifestation of intellectual life.

In itself it is nothing surprising if young and inexperienced minds, occupying themselves prematurely, or in a perverted sense, with the grand ideas of God and nature, liberty and the march of thought, should be wholly overmastered and carried away with them. It has often happened before now, and it is no new thing if youthful and ardent temperaments should either yield to the seductive temptation to make, not to say create, a new religion of their own; or else feel a deceitful impulse to censure and to change all that is already in existence, and, if possible, to reform the whole world by their newly acquired ideas.

That this twofold aberration and misuse of philosophical thought must prove universally injurious, and prejudicial both to education and the whole world, is so evident that it can scarcely be necessary to dwell upon it. Its effect has been to cause men, especially those whose minds have been formed in the great and comprehensive duties of practical life, to view the thing altogether in an evil light, although it must be confessed there is much injustice in this sweeping condemnation. In several of the great statesmen of Rome we may observe a similar contempt for Grecian philosophy as useless and unprofitable. And yet, as is happily indicated by its Greek name, this whole effort was assuredly based upon a noble conception, and, when duly regulated, a salutary principle. For in this beautiful word, according to its original acceptation, science is not regarded as already finished and mature, but is rather set forth as an object of search—of a noble curiosity and of a pure enthusiasm for great and sublime truths, while at the same time it implies the wise use of such knowledge. Merely, however, to check and to hinder the aberrations of a false philosophy, is not by itself sufficient. It is only by laying down and levelling the right road of a philosophy of life, that a thorough remedy for the evil is to be found. True philosophy, therefore, honoring that which has been given from above and that which is existent from without, must neither raise itself in hostility to the one, nor attempt to interfere violently with the other. For it is exactly when, keeping modestly within its proper limits of the inner spiritual life, it makes itself the handmaid neither of theology nor of politics, that it best asserts its true dignity and maintains its independence in its own peculiar domain. And thus, even while it abstains most scrupulously from intermeddling with the positive and actual, will it operate most powerfully on alien and remote branches of inquiry, and by teaching them to consider objects in a freer and more general light, indirectly it will exercise on them a salutary influence. Thus while it proceeds along its appointed path, it will, as it were, without effort disperse many a mist which spreads its dangerous delusion over the whole of human existence, or remove perhaps many a stone of stumbling, which offends the age and divides the minds of men in strife and discord. In this manner consequently will it most beautifully

1071

attest its healing virtue, and at the same time best fulfil its proper destination.

The object therefore of philosophy is the inner mental life (*geistige Leben*), not merely this or that individual faculty in any partial direction, but man's spiritual life with all its rich and manifold energies. With respect to form and method: the philosophy of life sets out from a single assumption—that of life, or in other words, of a consciousness to a certain degree awakened and manifoldly developed by experience—since it has for its object, and purposes to make known the entire consciousness and not merely a single phase of it. Now, such an end would be hindered rather than promoted by a highly elaborate or minutely exhaustive form and a painfully artificial method; and it is herein that the difference lies between a philosophy of life and the philosophy of the school. If philosophy be regarded merely as one part of a general scientific education, then is the instruction in method (whether under the old traditionary name of logic or any other) the chief point to be regarded. For such a mere elementary course, passing over, or at least postponing for a while the consideration of the matter, as possessing as yet but a very remote interest for the student, and, in the default of an adequate internal experience of his own, incapable of being understood by him, concerns itself rather with the practice of methodical thought, both as necessary for the future, and as applicable to all matters. But the preliminary exercise in philosophical thinking is only the introduction to philosophy, and not philosophy itself. This school-teaching of philosophy might perhaps be rendered productive of the most excellent consequences, if only it were directed to the history of the human intellect. What could be more interesting than a history which should enter into the spirit, and distinctly embody the various systems which the inventive subtlety of the Greeks gave birth to, or which, taking a still wider range, should embrace the science of the Egyptians, and some Asiatic nations, and illustrate the no less wonderful nor less manifold systems of the

Hindoos—those Greeks of the primeval world! But this, perhaps, would be to encroach upon the peculiar domain of erudition, and might, moreover, fail to furnish equal interest for all; and at any rate the history of philosophy is not philosophy itself.

Now, the distinction between the philosophy of life and the philosophy of the school will appear in very different lights according to the peculiarity of view which predominates in the several philosophical systems. That species of philosophy which revolves in the dialectical orbit of abstract ideas, according to its peculiar character presupposes and requires a well-practiced talent of abstraction, perpetually ascending through higher grades to the very highest, and even then boldly venturing a step beyond. In short, as may be easily shown in the instance of modern German science, the being unintelligible is set up as a kind of essential characteristic of a true and truly scientific philosophy. I, for my part, must confess, that I feel a great distrust of that philosophy which dwells in inaccessible light, where the inventor indeed asserts of himself, that he finds himself in an unattainable certainty and clearness of insight, giving us all the while to understand thereby, that he does see well enough how of all other mortals scarcely any, or perhaps, strictly speaking, no one, understands or is capable of understanding him. In all such cases it is only the false light of some internal *ignis fatuus* that produces this illusion of the unintelligible, or rather of nonsense. In this pursuit of wholly abstract and unintelligible thought, the philosophy of the school is naturally enough esteemed above every other, and regarded as pre-eminently the true science—i.e., the unintelligible.

In such a system a philosophy of life means nothing more than a kind of translation of its abstruser mysteries into a more popular form, and an adaptation of them to the capacity of ordinary minds. But even such popular adaptations, though evincing no common powers of language and illustration, in spite of their apparent clearness, when closer examined, are found as unintelligible as the recondite originals. For inasmuch as the subject matter of these abstract speculations was, from the very first, confused and unintelligible, it was consequently incapable of being made clear even by the most perspicuous of styles. But the true living philosophy has no relation or sympathy with this continuous advance up to the unintelligible heights of empty abstraction. Since the objects it treats of are none other than those which every man of a cultivated mind and in any degree accustomed to observe his own consciousness, both has and recognizes within himself, there is nothing to prevent its exposition being throughout clear, easy, and forcible. Here the relation is reversed. In such a system the philosophy of life is the chief and paramount object of interest; while the philosophy of the school, or the scientific teaching of it in the schools, however necessary and valuable in its place, is still, as compared with the whole thing itself, only secondary and subordinate. In the philosophy of life, moreover, the method adopted must also be a living one. Consequently it is not, by any means, a thing to be neglected. But still it need not to be applied with equal rigor throughout, or to appear prominently in every part, but on all occasions must be governed in these respects by what the particular end in view may demand.

A few illustrations, drawn from daily experience, will perhaps serve to explain my meaning. Generally speaking, the most important arts and pursuits of life are ultimately based on mathematics. This science furnishes them, as it were, with the method they observe; but it is not practicable, nor indeed has man the leisure, to revert on every occasion, with methodical exactness, to these elements, but, assuming the principles to be well known and admitted, he attends rather to the results essential to the end he has in view. The economical management of the smallest as well as of the largest household, rests in the end on the elementary principles of arithmetic; but what would come of it, if, on every occasion, we were to go back to the simple "one-times-one" of the multiplication table, and reflected upon and sought for the proofs that the principle is really valid and can confidently be relied on in practice? In the same way the art of war is founded on geometry, but when the general arranges his troops for battle does he consult his Euclid to satisfy himself of the correctness and advantages of his position? Lastly, even the astronomer, whose vocation is preeminently dependent on accurate calculation, when he would make us acquainted with the phenomena of the sidereal heavens, confines himself almost entirely to them, without wearying those whom he wishes to interest, with the complicated reckonings which, however, in all probability, he was obliged himself to go through. With all these arts and pursuits of practical life, the intellectual business of thinking—of such thinking at least as is common to most men—and of communicating thought, has a sort of affinity and resemblance. For, unquestionably, it is one among the many problems of philosophy to establish a wise economy and prudent stewardship of that ever-shifting mass of incoming and outgoing thoughts which make up our intellectual estate and property. And this is the more necessary, the greater are the treasures of thought possessed by our age. For, in the highly rapid interchange of, and traffic in ideas, which is carrying on, the receipts and disbursements are not always duly balanced. There is much cause, therefore, to fear lest a thoughtless and lavish dissipation of the noblest mental endowments should become prevalent, or a false and baseless credit system in thought spring up amidst an absolute deficiency of a solid and permanent capital safely invested in fundamental ideas and lasting truths. As for the second simile: I should, by all means, wish to gain a victory, not indeed for you, but with you, over some of the many errors and many semblances of thought, which are, however, but cheats and counterfeits which distract the minds of the present generation, disturb the harmony of life, and banish peace even from the intellectual world. And as respects the third illustration: I should indeed rejoice as having, in a great

1075

measure, attained my object, if only I shall succeed in directing your attention to some star in the higher region of intellect, which hitherto was either totally unknown, or, at least, never before fully observed.

But above all, I think it necessary to observe further, that in the same way as philosophy loses sight of its true object and appropriate matter, when either it passes into and merges in theology, or meddles with external politics, so also does it mar its proper form when it attempts to mimic the rigorous method of mathematics. In the middle of the last century scarcely was there to be found a German manual for any of the sciences that did not ape the mathematical style, and where every single position in the long array of interminable paragraphs did not conclude with the solemn act of demonstrative phraseology. But it is also well known that the philosophy which was propounded in this inappropriate form and method was crammed full of, nay, rather, was hardly anything more than a tissue of arbitrary, now forgotten, hypotheses, which have not brought the world at all nearer to the truth,—not at least to that truth which philosophy is in search of, and which is something higher than a mere example of accurate computation.

[323]

SCHLEIERMACHER, FRIEDRICH DANIEL

SCHLEIERMACHER, FRIEDRICH DANIEL (1768-1834). The life, theology and philosophy of Schleiermacher may be characterized as a steady concordance of contraries. He was a minister of the Reformed Church, devoted to the spiritual welfare of his community and an influential professor of theology, but he shocked faithful Christians by his close association with Friedrich Schlegel when this romanticist author was an avowed libertine and defied Christian morality with his lascivious novel *Lucinde*, which Schleiermacher defended against general indignation. He offended not only the members of his congregation by his intimate friendship with the Jewess, Henriette Herz, but, even more so, by his love of a married woman, which was the talk of the town. Wilhelm Dilthey,

1076

his biographer, destroyed much of Schleiermacher's correspondence in order to remove, as he said, "ugly spots" from his memory. Yet all this could not, and cannot, cause us to question the sincerity of Schleiermacher's religious feelings, his spiritual dignity and the originality of his thinking.

Schleiermacher became known by his book *On Religion* (1799), in which he defended religion "against its educated scorners." He intended to found an eternal covenant between the Christian faith and independent science. He professed firm confidence that no rational criticism could destroy Christian religion, which he conceived as the "feeling of absolute dependence," indispensable to human life but not closely connected with thought, knowledge and will. Personally convinced of the truth of Christianity, Schleiermacher nevertheless denied its claim "to be universal and to rule alone over mankind as the sole religion." He was strongly opposed to uniformity, and, above all, to uniformity in religion. He was an ardent defender of the rights of each person to have a religion of his own that corresponds to the uniqueness of his individuality. But Schleiermacher, who, in theology and philosophy, vindicated the cause of the individual, regarded him always as a link in the chain of history. As a historically minded thinker and as a philosopher of religion he refused to identify the infinite value of the individual, whom he acknowledged, with his independence from historical tradition and present society, and regarded this standpoint as justification of his activities as a churchman. Theology was to him no rational science but a compound of knowledge and rules which are needed for the maintenance and direction of the Christian community, and individual faith, valuable as it remains, requires emotional response and moral support on the part of a community of voluntary and devoted members. In the history of the Church, Schleiermacher achieved a notable success by effecting the union between Lutheranism and Calvinism in Prussia.

In his philosophical writings, Schleiermacher also insisted on the value of the individual, whom he regarded in his connection with nature and history. Fichte sneered at him and Hegel hated him, but Schleiermacher retaliated shrewdly. In his frequent quarrels with his fellow professors he did not rely on the teachings of the Sermon on the Mount.

ON THE GORGIAS

THE intuition of the true and perfectly existent, in other words, of the eternal and unalterable, with which, as we have

1077

seen, every exposition of Plato's philosophy commenced, has its opposite pole in the equally general, and, to common thought and being, no less original and underived, intuition of the imperfectly existent, ever flowing and mutable, which yet holds bound under its form all action and thought as they can be apprehended in actual, tangible reality. Therefore the highest and most general problem of philosophy is exclusively this—to apprehend and fix the *essential* in that fleeting chaos, to display it as the essential and good therein, and so, drawing forth to the full light of consciousness the apparent contradiction between those two intuitions, to reconcile it at the same time. This harmonizing process necessarily resolves itself into two factors, upon whose different relation to each other rests the difference of the methods. Setting out from the intuition of the perfectly existent to advance in the exposition up to the semblance, and thus, simultaneously with its solution, for the first time to awaken and explain the consciousness of this contradiction; this is, in relation to philosophy, the immediate way of proceeding. On the other hand, starting from the consciousness of the contradiction as a thing given to advance to the primary intuition as the means of its solution, and to lead up by force of the very necessity of such a mean toward it, this is the method which we have named the indirect or mediate, and which, being for many reasons especially suited to one who commences on ethical ground, is here placed by Plato in the center, as the true mean of connection and progressive formation from the original intuition, his elementary starting post, to the constructive exposition, the goal of his systematic conclusion.

Now the relation which, in the sphere of nature, being and semblance or sensation bear to one another in this antithesis, is the same as that which in ethics exists between good and pleasure or feeling. Therefore the principal object for the second part of Plato's works, and their common problem, will be to show, that science and art cannot be discovered, but only a deceitful semblance of both must be ever predominant, so long as these two are exchanged with each other—being with appearance, and good with pleasure. And advances are made to the solution of this problem naturally in a two-fold way, yet without holding each course entirely apart in different writings: on the one hand, namely, that which hitherto had passed for science and art is laid bare in its utter worthlessness; on the other, attempts are made, from the very position of knowing and acknowledging that antithesis to develop rightly the essence of science and art and their fundamental outlines. The Gorgias stands at the head of this class, because it rather limits itself as preparatory to the former task, then ventures upon the latter; and starting entirely from the ethical side, attacks at both ends the confusion existing herein, fixing on its inmost spirit, as the root, and it is openly displayed, as the fruits. The remaining dialogues observe this general distinction: they partly go farther back in the observation of the scientific in mere seeming, partly farther forward in the idea of true science, and partly contain other later consequences of what is here first advanced in preparation.

From this point, then, we observe a natural connection between the two main positions demonstrated to the interlocutors with Socrates in this dialogue. The first, that their pretensions to this possession of an art properly so called in their art of speaking are entirely unfounded; and the second, that they are involved in a profound mistake in their confusion of the good with the pleasant. And, from the same point likewise, the particular manner in which each is proved, and the arrangement of the whole, may be explained. For when it is the good that is under consideration, and the ethical object is predominant, truth must be considered more in reference to art than science, if, that is, unity is to be preserved in the work generally. And, moreover, it is art in its most general and comprehensive form that is here discussed, for the dialogue embraces everything connected with it, from its greatest object, the state, to its least, the embellishment of sensuous existence. Only, as his custom is, Plato is most fond of using the greater form as the scheme and representation of the general, and the less, on the other hand, as an example and illustration of the greater; that no one may lose himself, contrary to Plato's purpose, in the object of the latter, which can never be anything but a particular.

[324]

SCHLICK, MORITZ

SCHLICK, MORITZ (1882-1936). When, in 1936 a lunatic murdered Professor Schlick, many of the numerous admirers of the assassinated scholar considered it a particularly tragic irony that this nonsensical misdeed put an end to a life that was devoted to the inquiry into the meaning of life.

Schlick's aim was not the construction of a system of ideas or thoughts but the investigation of the way of philosophizing that satisfies the demands of the most scrupulous scientific conscience. This task involved skill in seeing through wrongly set problems and in surveying the consequences of wrong approaches to them, and Schlick himself was never afraid of abandoning previously elaborated views when, in the course of his development, he recognized **their** falsehood.

The principal results of Schlick's thinking are: a distinct demarcation between experience which is immediate and knowledge which is no vision but rather calculation and organization by means of concepts and symbols, and, furthermore, a new foundation of empiricism, which leans upon Berkeley and Hume but profits from modern logic. Reality is defined as happening in time. Every Real has a definite place in time. The task of science is to obtain knowledge of reality, and the true achievements of science can neither be destroyed nor altered by philosophy. But the aim of philosophy is to interpret these achievements correctly and to expound their deepest meaning.

Schlick was fundamentally a man who preferred aesthetic contemplation to exact science. But as a thinker he was convinced of the unique philosophical significance of natural science, and he branded it as a grave mistake to believe that the arts and cultural sciences are in any way equivalent to natural science.

THE CONSTRUCTION OF THEORIES

THEORETICAL science, as is obvious from its name, consists of theories—that is, of systems of propositions. Propositions constitute a system when they are related to one another through being concerned with the same objects; or even when they can be deduced from one another. The process of formulating a law of nature is, fundamentally, always the same. It consists, in the first place, of recording the observations of a natural process in a table which always contains the relevant measured values of those variable magnitudes which characterize the process. The next step is to discover a function which will represent in a single formula the distribution of values in this table. This formula is then considered to be the law describing the process as long as all new observations are in agreement with it. Inasmuch as the formula always contains more than what is actually observed, and also because it must hold for all processes of a similar kind, the formulation of any law involves a generalization, or a so-called induction. There is no such thing as a logically valid deduction going from the particular to the general: the latter can only be conjectured, but never logically inferred. Thus, the universal validity, or truth, of laws must always remain hypothetical. All laws of nature have the character of hypotheses: their truth is never absolutely certain. Hence, natural science consists of a combination of brilliant guesses and exact measurements. . . .

In the same way as a special law is the result of a series of single observations, a general law is the consequence of the inductive combination of several individual laws, until finally a relatively small number of general propositions which include the totality of natural laws is obtained. Thus today, for instance, all chemical laws can, in principle, be reduced to physical laws; and the dividing line between the different domains of physics which used to be externally related to one another (mechanics, acoustics, optics, theory of heat, etc.) has long since completely disappeared. At the present time, only mechanics and electrodynamics are left; and these are nowise independent of each other, but interpenetrate everywhere. Whether biology will continue to remain a special province, or whether it also will become incorporated in the domain of physics, is a question that will be discussed in due course.

In order to obtain a concrete description of nature (i.e., of nature as it really is), it is not sufficient to formulate laws: the abstract laws must, as it were, be given content. And in addition to these abstract laws, the constellation of reality (at the time of consideration), to which the formulas can be applied, must be stated. Such constellations are called by physicists boundary or initial conditions; and mathematically, they are expressed by the introduction of constants.

Here, we are considering the system of laws in itself, independently of all applications—that is to say, we are only studying general, and not particular, propositions. We can thus select out of this system, a group of the most general propositions from which all the others are derivable. This derivation is a purely logical deduction which can be undertaken without knowledge of the meaning of the symbols which occur in the laws. Hence, we will disregard, not only all application to individual cases, but also the meaning of all words and symbols—until the system is reduced to a purely formal structure, or empty framework which does not consist of actual propositions, but only of their forms (in logic, these are known as propositional functions). A system of this kind, which does not represent nature in actuality, but *all the possibilities in nature,* or in other words, its most general form—is known as a hypothetico-deductive system (Pieri). The propositions forming a group at the apex of this system, are called axioms; and the choice as to which propositions shall be taken as axioms is, to a certain extent, arbitrary. We may regard any proposition as an axiom, so long as we fulfil one condition, which is that all the other propositions in the system be derivable from the chosen group of axioms. Thus, the quality of being an axiom is not only in any sense a natural, intrinsic attribute or characteristic of a law; the only reason for choosing certain propositions as axioms, are those of their expediency or convenience. In the propositions derived from these axioms, further symbols, other than those used in the axioms, are introduced *by definition*. A definition consists of the introduction of new symbols, or signs, for the purpose of abbreviation. The choice as to which of these signs shall be regarded as fundamental symbols and which as derived from the latter by definition, is likewise arbitrary.

Examples:

$$E = \tfrac{1}{2}mv^2 \qquad\qquad M = mv$$

Definition of Energy   *Definition of Momentum*

But instead of mass and velocity, we can also write:

$$\frac{\text{Energy}}{\text{Momentum}} \quad : \quad v = \frac{2E}{M}$$

Thus, it is immaterial which magnitudes or quantities occur in the axioms.

Hence, the structure of a theory consists of: 1) axioms; 2) derived propositions and 3) definitions. In the symbolic representation of natural science, whether by means of words or of mathematical symbols, the three structural elements cannot be outwardly distinguished from one another.

The symbolic representation of a theory consists of sentences which in their turn are constituted of certain series of spoken or written signs: the theory itself consists primarily of "propositions." The question as to whether a sentence represents a true proposition or only a definition for example depends on the interpretations which explain it and give it its meaning. These do not form part of the symbolic representation itself, but are added to it—that is, they are added to a hypothetico-deductive system—from outside as it were, for example, in the form of ostensive definitions. They constitute the rules of the application of the sentences and are conclusive for the philosophical interpretation of the latter. It is, after all, necessary to refer to a reality which is described by the system of signs or symbols since, at some time or another, we must break out from their system. Only those sentences which, by virtue of their interpretation, represent genuine propositions, can communicate something about nature; the others are merely internal rules for signs and consequently are definitions.

[325]

SCHOPENHAUER, ARTHUR

SCHOPENHAUER, ARTHUR (1788-1860). Schopenhauer almost became an Englishman when his father, a citizen of Danzig, then in Poland, fearing the annexation of his native town by Prussia (which in fact was imminent), intended to take his wife, who was expecting a baby, to England, so that his son would not be a subject of the hated Prussian monarchy. However, the son was born before the parents could reach the land of their hope.

Arthur Schopenhauer did not share his father's predilection for England or his opposition to Prussian despotism. But he nevertheless adopted some English habits, read the *London Times* regularly, and remained aloof from any political movement in Germany, indifferent to nationalism, yet hating democracy, Judaism and Christianity. He preferred animals to his fellow men, and particularly he disliked women. British empiricism did not satisfy him, and his German contemporaries, Fichte, Schelling and Hegel, were branded by him as humbugs. He respected Kant from whose criticism he proceeded to his own philosophy. The wisdom and religion of India, the Vedas, Upanishads and Buddhism, aroused his enthusiasm, and he untiringly proclaimed the superiority of Indian thought to the European mind.

Although to his father's satisfaction, Schopenhauer had forgotten the German language during his stay in Paris and London, and had had to learn it again, when, at the age of seventeen, he returned to Germany, he became one of the greatest masters of German prose style. His clear and well-organized sentences proved able to captivate readers who recoil from the language of most of the German philosophers. Goethe, whom Schopenhauer knew personally and highly esteemed both as a poet and thinker, wrote in

Schopenhauer's album an epigram, saying: "If you will enjoy the value of your own personality you must enjoy the value of the world." Nothing could be more contrary to Schopenhauer's doctrine, for, according to it, the world is fundamentally evil. Its reality cannot be grasped by reason which is only capable of perceiving delusive appearances of the real things. The only real, metaphysical, cosmic being is the will which comprises both mental acts of the human individual and the drive, urge or instinctive force of the entire organic world. Even the crystallization of the diamond, or the turning of the magnet to the pole, or chemical affinities are regarded by Schopenhauer as utterances of the will which is essentially one. The fact that man takes cognizance of his body as much by way of reason as by immediate feeling, enables him to become aware of the will that works within his organism, and thus of the cosmic will which is identical with the former. To Schopenhauer this procedure offers the key to the understanding of the real world.

But, while the world of appearances or ideas is delusive, the world of the will is fundamentally evil. Will is the source of crime and suffering. The only salvation available to mankind is mortification of the will, complete resignation, extinction of the self.

Schopenhauer's pessimism had many followers. Of even greater influence was his doctrine of the superiority of instinct, the will, the unconscious drive to reason and knowledge, after Nietzsche had dissolved its connection with pessimism.

WILL AND IDEA

"THE world is my idea:"—this is a truth which holds good for everything that lives and knows, though man alone can bring it into reflective and abstract consciousness: If he really does this, he has attained to philosophical wisdom. It then becomes clear and certain to him that what he knows is not a sun and an earth, but only an eye that sees a sun, a hand that feels the earth; that the world which surrounds him is there only as idea, i.e., only in relation to something else, the consciousness, which is himself. If any truth can be asserted *a priori*, it is this: for it is the expression of the most general form of all possible and thinkable experience: a form which is more general than time, or space, or causality, for they all presuppose it; and each of these, which we have seen to be just so many modes of the principle of sufficient reason, is valid only for a particular class of ideas; whereas the antithesis of object and subject is the common form of all these classes, is that form under which alone any idea of whatever kind it may be, abstract or intuitive, pure or empirical, is possible and thinkable. No truth therefore is more certain, more independent of all others, and less in need of proof than this, that all that exists for knowledge and therefore this whole world, is only object in relation to subject, perception of a perceiver, in a word, idea. This is obviously true of the past and the future, as well as of the present, of what is furthest off, as of what is near; for it is true of time and space themselves, in which alone these distinctions arise. All that in any way belongs or can belong to the world is inevitably thus conditioned through the subject, and exists only for the subject. The world is idea.

*　　　*　　　*

This world in which we live and have our being is in its whole nature through and through *will*, and at the same time through and through *idea;* that this idea, as such, already presupposes a form, object and subject, is therefore relative; and if we ask what remains if we take away this form and all those forms which are subordinate to it, and which express the principle of sufficient reason, the answer must be that as something *toto genere* different from idea, this can be nothing but *will*, which is thus properly the *thing-in-itself.* Every one finds that he himself is this will, in which the real nature of the world consists, and he also finds that he is the knowing subject, whose idea the whole world is, the world which exists only in relation to his consciousness, as its necessary supporter. Every one is thus himself in a double aspect the whole world, the microcosm; finds both sides whole and complete in himself. And what he thus recognizes as his own real being also exhausts the being of the whole world—the macrocosm; thus the world, like man, is through and through *will*, and through and through *idea*, and nothing more than this. So we see the philosophy of Thales, which concerned the macrocosm, unite at this point with the philosophy of Socrates, which dealt with the microcosm, for the object of both is found to be the same.

One question may be more particularly considered, for it can only properly arise so long as one has not fully penetrated the meaning of the foregoing exposition, and may so far serve as an illustration of it. It is this: Every will is a will towards something, has an object, and end of its willing; what then is the final end, or towards what is that will striving that is exhibited to us as the being-in-itself of the world? This question rests, like so many others, upon the confusion of the thing-in-itself with the manifestation. The principle of sufficient reason, of which the law of motivation is also a form, extends only to the latter, not to the former. It is only of phenomena, of individual things, that a ground can be given, never of the will itself, nor of the idea in which it adequately objectifies itself. So then of every particular movement or change of any kind in nature, a cause is to be sought, that is, a condition that of necessity produced it, but never of the natural force itself which is revealed in this and innumerable similar phenomena; and it is therefore simple misunderstanding, arising from want of consideration, to ask for a cause of gravity, electricity, and so on. Only if one had somehow shown that gravity and electricity were not original special forces of nature, but only the manifestations of a more general force already known, would it be allowable to ask for the cause which made this force produce the phenomena of gravity or of electricity here. All this has been explained at length above. In the same way every particular act of will of a knowing individual (which is itself only a manifestation of will as the thing-in-itself) has necessarily a motive without which that act would never have occurred; but just as material causes contain merely the determination that at this time, in this place, and in this manner, a manifestation of this or that natural force must take place, so the motive determines only the act of will of a knowing being, at this time, in this place, and under these circumstances, as a particular act, but by no means determines that that being wills in general or wills in this manner; this is the expression of his intelligible character, which, as will itself, the thing-in-itself, is without ground, for it lies outside the province of the principle of sufficient reason. Therefore every man has permanent aims and motives by which he guides his conduct, and he can always give an account of his particular actions; but if he were asked why he wills at all, or why in general he wills to exist, he would have no answer, and the question would indeed seem to him meaningless; and this would be just the expression of his consciousness that he himself is nothing but will, whose willing stands by itself and requires more particular determination by motives only in its individual acts at each point of time.

In fact, freedom from all aim, from all limits, belongs to the nature of the will, which is an endless striving. This was already touched on above in the reference to centrifugal force. It also discloses itself in its simplest form in the lowest grade of the objectification of will, in gravitation, which we see constantly exerting itself, though a final goal is obviously impossible for it. For if, according to its will, all existing matter were collected in one mass, yet within this mass gravity, ever striving towards the center, would still wage war with impenetrability as rigidity or elasticity. The tendency of matter can therefore only be confined, never completed or appeased. But this is precisely the case with all tendencies of all phenomena of will. Every attained end is also the beginning of a new course, and so on *ad infinitum*. The plant raises its manifestation from the seed through the stem and the leaf to the blossom and the fruit, which again is the beginning of a new seed, a new individual, that runs through the old course, and so on through endless time. Such also is the life of the animal; procreation is its highest point, and after attaining to it, the life of the first individual

1088

quickly or slowly sinks, while a new life insures to nature the endurance of the species, and repeats the same phenomena. Indeed, the constant renewal of the matter of every organism is also to be regarded as merely the manifestation of this continual pressure and change, and physiologists are now ceasing to hold that it is the necessary reparation of the matter wasted in motion for the possible wearing out of the machine can by no means be equivalent to the support it is constantly receiving through nourishment. Eternal becoming, endless flux, characterizes the revelation of the inner nature of will. Finally, the same thing shows itself in human endeavors and desires, which always delude us by presenting their satisfaction as the final end of will. As soon as we attain to them they no longer appear the same, and therefore they soon grow stale, are forgotten, and though not openly disowned, are yet always thrown aside as vanished illusions. We are fortunate enough if there still remains something to wish for and to strive after, that the game may be kept up of constant transition from desire to satisfaction, and from satisfaction to a new desire, the rapid course of which is called happiness, and the slow course sorrow, and does not sink into that stagnation that shows itself in fearful *ennui* that paralyzes life, vain yearning without a definite object, deadening languor. According to all this, when the will is enlightened by knowledge, it always knows what it wills now and here, never what it wills in general; every particular act of will has its end, the whole will has none; just as every particular phenomenon of nature is determined by a sufficient cause so far as concerns its appearance in this place at this time, but the force which manifests itself in it has no general cause, for it belongs to the thing-in-itself, to the groundless will. The single example of self-knowledge of the will as a whole is the idea as a whole, the whole world of perception. It is the objectification, the revelation, the mirror of the will.

[326]

1089

SCHWEITZER, ALBERT

SCHWEITZER, ALBERT (1875-). The greatest and most famous Universities of the world have offered to Albert Schweitzer a professorship endowed with all possible advantages. As the historian of *The Quest of the Historical Jesus* (Geschichte der Leben Jesu Forschung, 1906; English edition, 1910), of *Paul and his Interpreters* (1912), and *The Mysticism of Paul the Apostle* (1931); as the authoritative biographer of *Johann Sebastian Bach* (1904); as the author of *Civilization and Ethics* (1929) and *The Philosophy of Civilization* (1932), Schweitzer could have made his own choice whether to become a professor of theology or of philosophy, of musicology or of history, in America, England, France or Germany. But he declined the most promising offers. Sacrificing a brilliant academic career in order to study medicine, he became a missionary-physician in Lambarene, French West Africa. Since 1913, Schweitzer has lived in that plague-stricken area, devoting himself to the medical treatment and spiritual education of the Negroes. He travelled to Europe and, in 1949, to America to deliver lectures, to do research for his books, and to gather funds for the maintenance of his activities in Africa.

In the wilderness, Schweitzer remained a man of widest interests and original views on life, science, philosophy and religion. He interprets the teachings of Jesus as determined by the expectation of the imminent end of the world. Although far from Europe, he warned against Hitler's savageness, but was not heeded. The fundamental idea of Schweitzer's ethics and philosophy is "reverence for life," which involves sympathy with and respect for all creatures, as well as human solidarity and devotion to spiritual progress. While most other philosophers of life are somewhat inclined to exalt egoism, will to power or sensualism, to Schweitzer the cult of life means altruism, love of mankind without regard to origin, creed or color. Further, altruism does not mean resignation but rather enhanced activity on behalf of humanity.

INDIVIDUAL AND SOCIETY

ETHICAL conflicts between society and the individual continue to exist because the individual has not only a personal but also a supra-personal sense of responsibility. Where my own person only is in question I can always be patient, always forgive, always be sympathetic, always be compassionate. But we all have the experience of being placed in positions where we are responsible not only for ourselves but also for some affair or business, and are then forced to make decisions which run counter to personal morality. The manufacturer who directs a business, be it ever such a small one; the musician who conducts performances; these can no longer remain human beings merely, however much they would prefer to do so. The one must dismiss an inefficient or drunken workman, in spite of all the sympathy which he may feel with him and his family; the other must prevent a singer whose voice has given way from taking any further part, however much pain this may cause to her.

The more comprehensive is a man's activity the more he comes into the position of being obliged to surrender some portion of his humanity to his supra-personal responsibility. Current thought usually tries to escape from this dilemma by laying down as a dogma that personal responsibility is covered and superseded by that of society in general. In this way the community tries to console the individual. For the comfort of those to whom this dogma seems too categorical it may perhaps add certain other principles which undertake to determine in a universally valid manner to what extent personal morality has ever a right to interfere.

Current ethics cannot possibly avoid subscription to this surrender. It has not the means for defending the stronghold of personal morality, since it has no absolute notions of good and evil at its disposal. Not so the ethic of reverence for life. It is in actual possession of what the other lacks. Therefore it never surrenders the fortress, even when this is in a state of constant siege. It feels itself capable of holding it permanently, and of keeping the besiegers in a breathless condition by making repeated sallies.

Only that entirely universal and absolute purposiveness with regard to the maintenance and enhancement of life, which is the aim of reverence for life, is really ethical. All other necessity or purposiveness is not ethical, but more or less urgent necessity or more or less purposive purposiveness. In the conflict which goes on between the maintenance of my own existence and the destruction and injury of other existence, I can never unite the ethical and the necessary in a relatively ethical, but must always make my own decision between what is ethical and what is necessary, and, if I choose the latter, must shoulder the guilt of having injured life. Similarly, I may never imagine that in the struggle between personal and supra-personal responsibility it is possible to make a compromise between the ethical and the purposive in the shape of a relative ethic, or to let the ethical be superseded by the purposive. On the contrary, it is my duty to make my own decision as between the two. If, under the pressure of supra-personal responsibility, I surrender to the purposive, I am guilty to some extent through my failure to uphold the principle of reverence for life.

The attempt to combine in a relative ethic the purposive, dictated by supra-personal responsibility, and the really ethical, is particularly blatant, because it logically follows that the man who obeys the commands of supra-personal responsibility is acting unegoistically.

[327]

SENECA, LUCIUS ANNAEUS

SENECA, LUCIUS ANNAEUS (4 B.C.-65 A.D.). Before Seneca fell into disgrace with Emperor Nero and was forced to commit suicide, he was generally considered, as Elder Pliny said, "the leader in letters and in government;" he was Nero's prime minister. The tragedies he wrote inspired dramatic authors until the days of Queen Elizabeth of England, Louis XIV of France and Napoleon I. Calling himself a Stoic, Seneca wrote treatises on the natural sciences, psychology and moral questions. He was a prominent jurist, and was acknowledged by his contemporaries to be an authority on geology, meteorology and marine zoology. The rise of Christianity

1092

was by no means detrimental to Seneca's fame and influence. He was said to have exchanged letters with Paul the Apostle; but these letters, often quoted, were evidently forged. Although the fathers of the Church knew that Seneca was no Christian, they highly appreciated his moral doctrines. So did later Christian philosophers and theologians until Thomas à Kempis. However, it was the age of the Renaissance that enhanced Seneca's importance to Western civilization. His Stoicism penetrated into the minds of Montaigne, Rabelais, Bacon, Shakespeare, Ben Jonson, Corneille and Racine, Milton and Dryden. Even in the 19th century it attracted poets like Wordsworth and thinkers like Emerson.

ON THE HAPPY LIFE

ALL men wish to live happily, but are dull at perceiving exactly what it is that makes life happy: and so far is it from being easy to attain to happiness that the more eagerly a man struggles to reach it the further he departs from it, if he takes the wrong road.

Let us not therefore decide whither we must tend, and by what path, without the advice of some experienced person who has explored the region which we are about to enter, because this journey is not subject to the same conditions as others.

True happiness consists in not departing from nature and in molding our conduct according to her laws and model. A happy life is one which is in accordance with its own nature, and cannot be brought about unless in the first place the mind be sound and vigorous, enduring all things with most admirable courage suited to the times in which it lives, and must be able to enjoy the bounty of Fortune without becoming her slave.

*   *   *

A happy life consists in a mind which is free, upright, undaunted and steadfast beyond the influence of fear or desire. A man must be accompanied by a continual cheerfulness, a high happiness, which comes indeed from on high because he delights in what he has. If we attain to this, then there will dawn upon us those invaluable blessings, the repose of a mind that is at rest in a safe haven, its lofty imaginings, its great and steady delight at casting out errors and learning to know the truth, its courtesy and its cheerfulness, in all of which we shall take delight.

Virtue is a lofty quality, sublime, royal, unconquerable, untiring. You will meet virtue in the temple, the market-place, the senate-house, manning the walls, covered with dust, sunburnt, horny-handed; you will find pleasure sulking out of sight, seeking for shady nooks.

The highest good is immortal. It knows no ending, and does not admit of either satiety or regret; for a right-thinking mind never alters or becomes hateful to itself, nor do the best things ever undergo any change. But pleasure dies at the very moment when it charms us most. It has no great scope, and therefore it soon cloys and wearies us, and fades away as soon as its first impulse is over. Indeed, we cannot depend upon anything whose nature is to change.

A man should be unbiased and ought not to be conquered by external things. He ought to feel confidence in his own spirit, and so order his life as to be ready alike for good or bad fortune. But let not his confidence be without knowledge, nor his knowledge without steadfastness. Let him abide by what he has determined, and let there be no erasure in his doctrine.

*   *   *

Let reason be encouraged by the senses to seek for the truth, and draw its first principles from thence. Indeed, it has no other base of operations or place from which to start in pursuit of truth: it must fall back upon itself. Even the all-embracing universe and God who is its guide extends Himself forth into outward things, and yet altogether returns from all sides back to Himself. Let our mind do the same thing.

By this means we shall obtain a strength and an ability which are united; we shall derive from it that reason which never halts between two opinions, nor is dull in forming its perceptions, beliefs or convictions. Such a mind, when it has ranged itself in order, made its various parts agree together, and, if I may so express myself, harmonized them, has attained to the highest good. For it has nothing evil or hazardous remaining, nothing to shake it or make it stumble. It will do everything under the guidance of its own will, and nothing unexpected will befall it, but whatever may be done by it will turn out well, and that, too, readily and easily, without the doer having recourse to any underhand devices.

You may, then, boldly declare that the highest good is singleness of mind, for where agreement and unity are, there must the virtues be. It is the vices that are at war with one another.

[328]

SEXTUS EMPIRICUS

SEXTUS EMPIRICUS (About 200 A.D.). The writings of Sextus Empiricus are an arsenal of scepticism which has furnished pagan thinkers with weapons to combat Christianity, Christian apologists with arguments to refute paganism, and, in later centuries, philosophers like Montaigne with reasons in defense of the independence of their minds on dogmatism of any kind.

Sextus, a physician by profession, was not so much an original thinker as an informed popularizer, a skilful and vigorous writer, who was able to summarize his thoughts by striking formulas. He attacked not only dogmatic philosophers and theologians but any expert, whether of mathematics or grammar, who claimed infallibility. In this way he has also given highly valuable information about the history of various sciences such as they had developed in his time.

TEN MODES OF THOUGHT

THEY are these: The first is based upon the differences in animals; the second upon the differences in men; the third upon the difference in the constitution of the organs of sense; the fourth upon circumstances; the fifth upon position, distance, and place; the sixth upon mixtures; the seventh upon the quantity and constitution of objects; the eighth upon rela-

1095

tion; the ninth upon frequency or rarity of occurrences; the tenth upon systems, customs, laws, mythical beliefs, and dogmatic opinions. We make this order ourselves. These tropes come under three general heads: the standpoint of the judge, the standpoint of the thing judged, and the standpoint of both together. . . .

It is probable therefore, that the inequalities and differences in origin cause great antipathies, in the animals, and the result is incompatibility, discord, and conflict between the sensations of the different animals. Again, the differences in the principal parts of the body, especially in those fitted by nature to judge and to perceive, may cause the greatest differences in their ideas of objects, according to the differences in the animals themselves. As for example, those who have the jaundice call that yellow which appears to us white, and those who have bloodshot eyes call it blood-red. Accordingly, as some animals have yellow eyes, and others blood-shot ones, and still others whitish ones, and others eyes of other colors, it is probable, I think, that they have a different perception of colors. Furthermore, when we look steadily at the sun for a long time, and then look down at a book, the letters seem to us gold colored, and dance around. Now some animals have by nature a luster in their eyes, and these emit a fine and sparkling light so that they see at night, and we may reasonably suppose that external things do not appear the same to them as to us. Jugglers by lightly rubbing the wick of the lamp with metal rust, or with the dark yellow fluid of the sepia, make those who are present appear now copper colored and now black, according to the amount of the mixture used; if this be so, it is much more reasonable to suppose that because of the mixture of different fluids in the eyes of animals, their ideas of objects would be different. Furthermore, when we press the eye on the side, the figures, forms and sizes of things seen appear elongated and narrow. It is, therefore, probable that such animals as have the pupil oblique and long, as goats, cats, and similar

1096

animals, have ideas different from those of the animals which have a round pupil. Mirrors according to their different construction, sometimes show the external object smaller than reality, as concave ones, and sometimes long and narrow, as the convex ones do; others show the head of the one looking into it down, and the feet up. As some of the vessels around the eye fall entirely outside the eye, on account of their protuberance, while others are more sunken, and still others are placed in an even surface, it is probable that for this reason also the ideas vary, and dogs, fishes, lions, men and grasshoppers do not see the same things, either of the same size, or of similar form, but according to the impression on the organ of sight of each animal respectively. The same thing is true in regard to the other senses; for how can it be said that shellfish, birds of prey, animals covered with spines, those with feathers and those with scales would be affected in the same way by the sense of touch? And how can the sense of hearing perceive alike in animals which have the narrowest auditory passages, and in those that are furnished with the widest, or in those with hairy ears and those with smooth ones? For we, even, hear differently when we partially stop up the ears, from what we do when we use them naturally. The sense of smell also varies according to differences in animals, since even our sense of smell is affected when we have taken cold and the phlegm is too abundant, and also parts around our head are flooded with too much blood, for we then avoid odors that seem agreeable to others, and feel as if we were injured by them. Since also some of the animals are moist by nature and full of secretions, and still others have either yellow or black bile prevalent and abundant, it is reasonable because of this to think that odorous things appear different to each one of them. And it is the same in regard to things of taste, as some animals have the tongue rough and dry and others very moist. We too, when we have a dry tongue in fever, think that whatever we take is gritty, bad tasting, or bitter; and this we experience because of the varying degrees of the humors that are said to be in us. Since, then, different animals have different organs for taste, and a greater or less amount of the various humors, it can well be that they form different ideas of the same objects as regards their taste. For just as the same food on being absorbed becomes in some places veins, in other places arteries, and in other places bones, nerves, or other tissues, showing different power according to the difference of the parts receiving it; just as the same water absorbed by the trees becomes in some places bark, in other places branches, and in other places fruit, perhaps a fig or a pomegranate, or something else; just as the breath of the musician, one and the same when blown into the flute, becomes sometimes a high tone and sometimes a low one, and the same pressure of the hand upon the lyre sometimes causes a deep tone and sometimes a high tone, so it is natural to suppose that external objects are regarded differently according to the different constitution of the animals which perceive them. We may see this more clearly in the things that are sought for and avoided by animals. For example, myrrh appears very agreeable to men and intolerable to beetles and bees. Oil also, which is useful to men, destroys wasps and bees if sprinkled on them; and sea-water, while it is unpleasant and poisonous to men if they drink it, is most agreeable and sweet to fishes. Swine also prefer to wash in vile filth rather than in pure clean water. Furthermore, some animals eat grass and some eat herbs; some live in the woods, others eat seeds; some are carnivorous, and others lactivorous; some enjoy putrefied food, and others fresh food; some raw food, and others that which is prepared by cooking; and in general that which is agreeable to some is disagreeable and fatal to others, and should be avoided by them. Thus hemlock makes the quail fat, and henbane the hogs, and these, as it is known, enjoy eating lizards; deer also eat poisonous animals, and swallows, the cantharidae. Moreover, ants and flying ants, when swallowed by men, cause discomfort and colic; but the bear, on the contrary, whatever sickness he may have, becomes stronger by devouring them. The viper is benumbed if one twig of the oak touches it, as is also the bat by a leaf of the plane tree. The elephant flees before the ram, and the lion before the cock, and seals from the rattling of beans that are being pounded, and the tiger from the sound of the drum. Many other examples could be given, but that we may not seem to dwell longer than is necessary on this subject, we conclude by saying that since the same things are pleasant to some and unpleasant to others, and the pleasure and displeasure depend on the ideas, it must be that different animals have different ideas of objects. And since the same things appear different according to the difference in the animals, it will be possible for us to say how the external object appears to us, but as to how it is in reality we shall suspend our judgment. For we cannot ourselves judge between our own ideas and those of other animals, being ourselves involved in the difference, and therefore much more in need of being judged than being ourselves able to judge. And furthermore, we cannot give the preference to our own mental representations over those of other animals, either without evidence or with evidence, for besides the fact that perhaps there is no evidence, as we shall show, the evidence so called will be either manifest to us or not. If it is not manifest to us, then we cannot accept it with conviction; if it is manifest to us, since the question is in regard to what is manifest to animals, and we use as evidence that which is manifest to us who are animals, then it is to be questioned if it is true as it is manifest to us. It is absurd, however, to try to base the questionable on the questionable, because the same thing is to be believed and not to be believed, which is certainly impossible. The evidence is to be believed in so far as it will furnish a proof, and disbelieved in so far as it is itself to be proved. We shall therefore have no evidence according to which we can give preference to our own ideas over those so-called irrational animals. Since, therefore, ideas differ according to the difference in animals, and it is impossible to judge them, it is necessary to suspend the judgment in regard to external objects.

[329]

SHANKARA

SHANKARA (9th century A.D.). The reports on the life of Shankara, who is considered by some authorities the greatest commentator, even the greatest philosopher of the Hindus, are adorned with myths and legends that ascribe to him superhuman powers and the performance of many miracles. He was revered as a saint and as a scholar whose theoretical and practical teachings became of great consequence. He systematized the philosophy of the Upanishads, and, in his commentaries, elucidated many passages of the Vedanta. He is characterized as a gentle and tolerant reformer and also as an everready controversialist who was eager to refute any doctrine that differed from his own. He denied the relevance of caste and lineage, and denounced the desire for personal separateness as the cause of bondage to conditional existence, birth and death. Devotion is an instrument of emancipation from ignorance and enslavement. Devotion is not to be distinguished from contemplation. Truth is to be understood intellectually, but the highest spiritual intuition leads to the union of the knower, the known and knowledge. Shankara often described the way to that goal as the denial of selfness in thought, feeling and action.

THE KNOWLEDGE OF SOUL

KNOWLEDGE alone effects emancipation.
As fire is indispensable to cooking,
So knowledge is essential to deliverance.
Knowledge alone disperses ignorance,
As sunlight scatters darkness—not so acts;
For ignorance originates in works.
The world and all the course of mundane things
Are like the vain creation of a dream,
In which Ambition, Hatred, Pride and Passion
Appear like phantoms mixing in confusion.
While the dream lasts the universe seems real,
But when 'tis past the world exists no longer.

1100

Like the deceptive silver of a shell,
So at first sight the world deludes the man
Who takes mere semblance for reality.
As golden bracelets are in substance one
With gold, so are all visible appearances
And each distinct existence one with Brahma.
By action of the fivefold elements
Through acts performed in former states of being,
Are formed corporeal bodies, which become
The dwelling-place of pleasure and of pain.
The soul inwrapped in five investing sheaths
Seems formed of these, and all its purity
Darkened, like crystal laid on colored cloth.
As winnowed rice is purified from husk
So is the soul disburdened of its sheaths
By force of meditation, as by threshing.
The soul is like a king whose ministers
Are body, senses, mind and understanding.
The soul is wholly separate from these,
Yet witnesses and overlooks their actions.
The foolish think the spirit acts, whereas
The senses are the actors; so the moon
Is thought to move when clouds are passing o'er it.
When intellect and mind are present, then
Afflictions, inclinations, pleasures, pains
Are active; in profound and dreamless sleep
When intellect is non-existent, these
Exist not; therefore they belong to mind.
As brightness is inherent in the sun,
Coolness in water, warmness in the fire,
E'en so existence, knowledge, perfect bliss,
And perfect purity inhere in soul.
The understanding cannot recognize
The soul, nor does the soul need other knowledge
To know itself, e'en as a shining light
Requires no light to make itself perceived.
The soul declares its own condition thus:

"I am distinct from body, I am free
From birth, old age, infirmity and death.
I have no senses; I have no connection
With sound or sight or objects of sensation.
I am distinct from mind, and so exempt
From passion, pride, aversion, fear and pain.
I have no qualities, I am without
Activity and destitute of option,
Changeless, eternal, formless, without taint,
Forever free, forever without stain.
I, like the boundless ether, permeate
The universe within, without, abiding
Always, forever similar in all,
Perfect, immovable, without affection,
Existence, knowledge, undivided bliss,
Without a second, One, Supreme am I."

*   *   *

That which is through, above, below, complete,
Existence, wisdom, bliss, without a second,
Endless, eternal, one—know that as Brahma.
That which is neither coarse nor yet minute,
That which is neither short nor long, unborn,
Imperishable, without form, unbound
By qualities, without distinctive marks,
Without a name—know that indeed as Brahma.
Nothing exists but Brahma, when aught else
Appears to be, 'tis, like the mirage, false.

[330]

SIDGWICK, HENRY

SIDGWICK, HENRY (1838-1900). Sidgwick, one of the founders of the Society for Psychical Research and the Ethical Society in Cambridge, England, where he was a professor, gave a number of suggestions which have been of consequence for the latest development of philosophical thinking in England and America. A follower of John Stuart Mill in ethics, politics and economics, Sidgwick endeavored, especially in his *Methods of Ethics* (1874) to found utilitarianism anew by resorting to Thomas Reid's "natural realism" and sweeping away all hedonistic theories. His efforts to combine utilitarian ethics with intuitionist theory of knowledge did not entirely satisfy Sidgwick, who was aware of the difficulty of his task and constantly tried to improve or correct his arguments without abandoning his fundamental position. He recognized that philosophical empiricism was based upon conceptions that cannot be traced back to experience but declined Kant's theory of experience. Sidgwick has studied "with reverent care and patience" what is called the morality of common sense. For he was convinced that, despite all historical changes and diversities of thoughts and actions, there is a large region of broad agreement in the details of morality, without any attempt to penetrate into the ultimate grounds upon which principles of moral action may be constructed. Sidgwick did not only regard this common-sense morality as the proper starting point for philosophical inquiries into ethical problems, but he thought that the work of the philosopher has to be aided, and, in a way, controlled by the moral judgment of "persons with less philosophy but more special experience."

MORALITY OF COMMON SENSE

THE philosopher's practical judgment on particular problems of duty is liable to be untrustworthy, unless it is aided and controlled by the practical judgment of others who are not philosophers. This may seem to some a paradox. It may be thought that so far as a philosopher has a sound general theory of right, he must be able to apply it to determine the duties of any particular station in life, if he has taken due pains to inform himself as to that station and its circumstances. And this would doubtless be true if his information could be made complete; but this it cannot be. He can only learn from others the facts which they have consciously observed and remembered; but there is an important element in the experience of themselves and their predecessors—the continuous experience of social generations—which finds no place in any statement of facts or reasoned forecast of consequences that they could furnish; it is only represented in their judgments as to what ought to be done and aimed at. Hence it is a common observation that the judgments of practical men as to what ought to be done in particular circumstances are often far sounder than the reasons they give for them; the judgments represent the result of experience unconsciously as well as consciously imbibed; the reasons have to be drawn from that more limited part of experience which has been the subject of conscious observation, information, and memory. This is why a moral philosopher, in my opinion, should always study with reverent care and patience what I am accustomed to call the morality of common sense. By this I do not mean the morality of "the world"—*i.e.*, the moral notions and judgments of persons who are not seriously concerned about their moral duty—who are always perhaps in a majority. Such persons, indeed, have a morality, and it is better than their actions; they approve rules which they do not carry out, and admire virtues which they do not imitate. Still, taking the morality of the worldly at its best, it would be wasted labor to try to construct it into a consistent system of thought; what there is in it of wisdom and truth is too much intermixed with a baser element, resulting from want of singleness of heart and aim in those whose thoughts it represents. What the worldly really want—if I may speak plainly—is not simply to realize the good life in virtue of its supreme worth to humanity, but to realize it as much as they can while keeping terms with all their appetites and passions, their sordid interests and vulgar ambitions. The morality that the world works out in different ages and countries and different sections of society, under the influence of the spirit of compromise, is not without interest for the historian and the sociologist; but it was not to this mixed stuff that I just now referred when I said that the moral philosopher should study with reverent and patient care the morality of common sense. I referred to the moral judgments—and especially the spontaneous unreflected judgments on particular cases, which are sometimes called moral intuitions—of those persons, to be found in all walks and stations of life, whose earnest and predominant aim is to do their duty; of whom it may be said that

"though they slip and fall,
They do not blind their souls with clay,"

but after each lapse and failure recover and renew their rectitude of purpose and their sense of the supreme value of goodness. Such persons are to be found, not alone or chiefly in hermitages and retreats—if there are still any hermitages and retreats—but in the thick and heat of the struggle of active life, in all stations and ranks, in the Churches and outside the Churches. It is to their judgments on the duties of their station, in whatever station they may be found, that the moral philosopher should, as I have said, give reverent attention, in order that he may be aided and controlled by them in his theoretical construction of the science of right.

[331]

SIMMEL, GEORG

SIMMEL, GEORG (1858-1918). From about 1900 to the outbreak of the First World War, Simmel was considered one of the greatest contemporary philosophers. Not favored by the Prussian government, Simmel was a lecturer, then an associate professor at the University of Berlin, and only a few years before his death he was appointed full professor at the University of Strasbourg. As long as he lectured in Berlin, his audience was composed mostly of students from Russia and Central and Southern Europe where his fame was even greater than in Germany. Nevertheless, he did not form a school. Many of his former pupils died on the battlefield, others, uprooted by the events of war and revolution, were forced to renounce philosophy altogether, or turned to radical Marxism or nationalism, both of which were contrary to Simmel's mind which, despite all changes, maintained a relativist attitude.

Simmel's talents for psychological analysis are unsurpassed, and he always succeeded in elucidating psychological insight by philosophical aspects, no matter whether he dealt with Platonic ideas or fashions, Schopenhauer's pessimism or the flirt, the effects of money lending or the question of theistic faith. He interpreted Kant's *a priori*, which he himself adopted, psychologically and as

1105

supporting relativism. Later he developed, independently of American thinkers, a kind of pragmatism. Likewise, he was independent of Bergson when he tried to overcome his relativism by a belief in the self-transcendence of life. From a purely descriptive ethics he proceeded to one of valid values. He always remained an unorthodox Kantian, stressing the antagonism between immediate experience and the elaboration of this experience by the creative human spirit, insisting that the natural sciences as well as history offer only an image of reality that is transformed by the theoretical or historical *a priori*. According to Simmel, sociology does not belong to philosophy. Sociology and philosophy offer two different aspects of the situation of man in the world. They are two autonomous interpretations of mental life. Simmel started with studies *On Social Differentiation* (1890), then published his *Philosophy of Money* (1900) and *Sociology* (1908). A thorough student of Marx, he admitted the influence of economic facts on intellectual attitudes but insisted that the effects of intellectual patterns on economics act likewise. He maintained that the decisive factor of human attitudes is antecedent to changes of social or economic institutions. Sociology is conceived by Simmel as the doctrine of the forms of the relations between individuals, independent of spiritual contents which are subject to historical change. It is the "geometry of social life."

Religion and the arts represent to Simmel autonomous worlds which are independent of science but accessible to the philosopher, provided he does not disregard their autonomous foundations. In his monographies on *Goethe* (1913) and *Rembrandt* (1916), Simmel tried to show that the poet and artist while forming his own image of life, although determined by the historical situation of his lifetime, transcends historical conditions and testifies that life always hints beyond itself. The principal problem of culture is formulated by Simmel as the difficulty to seize life without violating it.

SOCIETY

SOCIETY, in its broadest sense, is found wherever several individuals enter into reciprocal relations. From a purely ephemeral association for the purpose of a casual promenade to the complete unity of a family, or a guild of the Middle Ages, one must recognize socialization of the most varying kind and degree. The particular causes and aims, without which socialization never takes place, comprise, to a certain extent, the body, the *material* of the social process. That the result of these causes, and the pursuance of these aims call forth, among the persons concerned, a reciprocal relationship, or a socialization, this is the *form* in which the content of social organization clothes itself. The entire existence of a special science of society rests upon the isolation of this form by means of scientific abstraction. For it is evident that the same form and the same kind of socialization can arise in connection with the most varied elements and take place for the most diverse ends. Socialization in general takes place as well in a religious congregation as in a band of conspirators, in a trust as well as in a school of art, in a public gathering as well as in a family; and we find also certain formal similarities in the special characteristics and development of all such unions. We find, for example, the same forms of authority and subordination, of competition, imitation, opposition, division of labor in social groups which are the most different possible in their aims and in their moral character. We find the formation of a hierarchy the embodiment of the group-forming principles in symbols, the division in parties, all stages of freedom or restriction of the individual in relation to the group, interaction and stratification of groups themselves, and definite forms of reaction against external influence. This similarity of form and its development, in the case of groups with the most complete heterogeneity of material conditions, reveals forces lying back of these immediate conditions, and suggests the possibility of constituting, by abstraction, a legitimate realm of investigation, namely that of socialization as such and the study of its forms. These forms are evolved through contact of the individuals, but relatively independent of the basis of such contact, and their sum makes up that concrete thing which we designate by the abstraction—society. [332]

SIRACH, JESUS

SIRACH, JESUS, son of (About 200 B.C.). Ever since the book written by Jesus, son of Sirach, has become known it has edified readers of all succeeding generations up to the present day. It has confirmed pious people in their faith. It has impressed sceptical-minded readers by its vigorous conviction. It has inspired poets, philosophers, statesmen and plain people. Above all, it has been valued as a rich fountain of proverbial wisdom and the personal confession of a man of large experience. Although it has not been accepted into the Protestant canon and was placed among the books of Apocrypha, it has generally been as highly appreciated as the books of the Bible itself.

The author was a contemporary of the high priest Simon II who died in 199 B.C., and he certainly was no longer alive when the Jewish people were afflicted by the persecutions which preceded the rise of the Maccabees. In his youth, Jesus ben Sirach had studied the Bible and books of popular wisdom. Then a calumniator endangered his life and forced him to flee from his native town, but after a while he was vindicated and lived for the rest of his life in Jerusalem. During his exile, he meditated on his misfortune, and observed the vicissitudes of life which others had to endure. These experiences, and not so much his previous readings, are the substance of his book. He was neither a priest nor a *Sofer* (skilled interpreter of the law), but a layman who used to deliver popular speeches. His book was translated into Greek by his grandson under the title *Wisdom of Jesus the Son of Sirach*. Its Latin title is *Ecclesiasticus*. It also was translated into many other languages. The Hebrew original was lost. In 1896, some parts of it were found in a cellar of the Ezra Synagogue in Cain. Later these were augmented so that now about three fifths of the original are extant.

WISE MEN AND FOOLS

THERE is a reproof that is not comely: again, some man holdeth his tongue, and he is wise.

It is much better to reprove, than to be angry secretly: and he that confesseth his fault shall be preserved from hurt.

How good is it, when thou art reproved, to shew repentance! for so shalt thou escape wilful sin.

As is the lust of a eunuch to deflower a virgin; so is he that executeth judgment with violence.

There is one that keepeth silence, and is found wise: and another by much babbling becometh hateful.

1108

Some man holdeth his tongue, because he hath not to answer: and some keepeth silence, knowing his time.

A wise man will hold his tongue till he see opportunity: but a babbler and a fool will regard no time.

He that useth many words shall be abhorred; and he that taketh to himself authority therein shall be hated.

There is a sinner that hath good success in evil things; and there is a gain that turneth to loss.

There is a gift that shall not profit thee; and there is a gift whose recompense is double.

There is an abasement because of glory; and there is that lifteth up his head from a low estate.

There is that buyeth much for a little, and repayeth it sevenfold.

A wise man by his words maketh himself beloved: but the graces of fools shall be poured out.

The gift of a fool shall do thee no good when thou hast it; neither yet of the envious for his necessity: for he looketh to receive many things for one.

He giveth little, and upbraideth much; he openeth his mouth like a crier; to-day he lendeth, and to-morrow will he ask it again: such a one is to be hated of God and man.

The fool saith, I have no friends, I have no thanks for all my good deeds, and they that eat my bread speak evil of me.

How oft, and of how many shall he be laughed to scorn! for he knoweth not aright what it is to have; and it is all one unto him as if he had it not.

To slip upon a pavement is better than to slip with the tongue: so the fall of the wicked shall come speedily.

An unseasonable tale will always be in the mouth of the unwise.

A wise sentence shall be rejected when it cometh out of a fool's mouth; for he will not speak it in due season.

There is that is hindered from sinning through want: and when he taketh rest, he shall not be troubled.

There is that destroyeth his own soul through bashfulness, and by accepting of persons overthroweth himself.

There is that for bashfulness promiseth to his friend, and maketh him his enemy for nothing.

A lie is a foul blot in a man, yet it is continually in the mouth of the untaught.

A thief is better than a man that is accustomed to lie: but they both shall have destruction to heritage.

The disposition of a liar is dishonorable, and his shame is ever with him.

A wise man shall promote himself to *honor* with his words: and he that hath understanding will please great men.

He that tilleth his land shall increase his heap: and he that pleaseth great men shall get pardon for iniquity.

Presents and gifts blind the eyes of the wise, and stop up his mouth that he cannot reprove.

Wisdom that is hid, and treasure that is hoarded up, what profit is in them both?

Better is he that hideth his folly than a man that hideth his wisdom.

Necessary patience in seeking the Lord is better than he that leadeth his life without a guide.

[333]

SOCRATES

SOCRATES (470-399 B.C.). The Delphic Oracle, regarded as omniscient by great and small and old and young in ancient Greece, used to communicate its knowledge in obscure and equivocal phrases. However, when asked whether there was any man wiser than Socrates, it replied simply and clearly: No one is wiser.

Hearing of this pronouncement, Socrates himself was rather disturbed. For he had steadily disclaimed that he was wise or that he possessed any knowledge. Rather, it was his manner to proceed from the statement that he was an ignorant person, and the only merit he claimed was to be aware of his ignorance. So he went among pretentious people of various professions, particularly rhetoricians and sophists, questioning their knowledge, until he became convinced that they were quite as ignorant as he, but that they did not admit, nor were they even aware of, their ignorance.

Socrates was the son of a stone-cutter and a midwife, and he liked to draw a parallel between his method of making people think and his mother's calling. Before he began to teach, Socrates had served in the army of Athens, his native city, had distinguished himself on the battlefield, and had held offices in the Athenian administration. He owned a house in the city and a modest capital sum, which he was wise enough to entrust for investment to his friend and pupil Crito, an experienced businessman. Socrates, therefore, could afford to teach without demanding fees. While doing so, he embittered other teachers, and aroused suspicion in the minds of influential fellow citizens. His rather eccentric manners, his fondness of jesting, and, above all, his repeated refusal to subordinate his judgment to political party purposes aggravated his situation. Accused of corrupting the youth of Athens by his teaching, Socrates was sentenced to death. On several occasions he could have escaped from jail, but he insisted on his obligation to respect the sentence even though it be wrong. His preparedness to die and his serene fortitude during the last hours of his life gained the admiration of both his contemporaries and posterity.

Socrates did not put his doctrines into writing; he taught orally. His pupils adored him despite his ugliness and slovenliness. Many of them belonged to Athens' aristocracy, while others were humble people. Some of them became outstanding philosophers, like Euclid, Phaedo, Antisthenes, Aristippus, and Plato, the greatest of all of them. All these pupils agree that Socrates insisted on the belief on moral values, on an austere conduct of life, and on the unity of wisdom, knowledge and virtue. While Plato made him the mouthpiece of the doctrine of ideas, all other philosophers who were close to Socrates were opposed to that doctrine. It is therefore quite probable that Plato went far beyond the philosophical position of his master.

I AM A PHILOSOPHICAL MIDWIFE

Theaetetus. I can assure you, Socrates, that I have tried very often, when the report of questions asked by you was brought to me; but I can neither persuade myself that I have a satisfactory answer to give, nor hear of any one who answers as you would have him; and I cannot shake off a feeling of anxiety.

1111

Socrates. These are the pangs of labor, my dear Theae-tetus; you have something within you which you are bring-ing to the birth.

Theaetetus. I do not know, Socrates; I only say what I feel.

Socrates. And have you never heard, simpleton, that I am the son of a midwife, brave and burly, whose name was Phaenarete?

Theaetetus. Yes, I have.

Socrates. And that I myself practice midwifery?

Theaetetus. No, never.

Socrates. Well, my art of midwifery is in most respects like theirs; but differs, in that I attend men and not women, and I look after their souls when they are in labor, and not after their bodies: and the triumph of my art is in thor-oughly examining whether the thought which the mind of the young man brings forth is a false idol or a noble and true birth. And like the midwives, I am barren, and the reproach which is often made against me, that I ask ques-tions of others and have not the wit to answer them myself, is very just—the reason is, that the god compels me to be a midwife, but does not allow me to bring forth. And there-fore I am not myself at all wise, nor have I anything to show which is the invention or birth of my own soul, but those who converse with me profit. Some of them appear dull enough at first, but afterwards, as our acquaintance ripens, if the god is gracious to them, they all make astonish-ing progress; and this is in the opinion of others as well as in their own. It is quite clear that they never learned any-thing from me; the many fine discoveries to which they cling are of their own making. But to me and the god they owe their delivery. And the proof of my words, is that many of them in their ignorance, either in their self-conceit de-spising me, or falling under the influence of others, have gone away too soon; and have not only lost the children of whom I had previously delivered them by an ill bringing up, but have stifled whatever else they had in them by evil communications, being fonder of lies and shams than of the truth; and they have at last ended by seeing themselves, as others see them, to be great fools. Aristides, the son of Lysimachus, is one of them, and there are many others. The truants often return to me, and beg that I would consort with them again—they are ready to go to me on their knees—and then, if my familiar allows, which is not always the case, I receive them. My art is able to arouse and to allay in those who consort with me, just like the pangs of women in childbirth; night and day they are full of perplexity and travail which is even worse than that of the women. So much for them. And there are others, Theaetetus, who come to me apparently having nothing in them; and as I know that they have no need of my art, I coax them into marrying some one, and by the grace of God I can generally tell who is likely to do them good. Many of them I have given away to Prodicus, and many to other inspired sages. I tell you this long story, friend Theaetetus, because I suspect, as indeed you seem to think yourself, that you are in labor—great with some conception. Come then to me,—who am a midwife's son and myself a midwife, and do your best to answer the questions which I will ask you. And if I abstract and expose your first-born, because I discover upon inspection that the conception which you have formed is a vain shadow, do not quarrel with me on that account, as the manner of women is when their first children are taken from them. For I have actually known some who were ready to bite me when I deprived them of a darling folly; they did not perceive that I acted from goodwill, not knowing that no god is the enemy of man—that was not within the range of their ideas; neither am I their enemy in all this, but it would be wrong for me to admit falsehood, or to stifle the truth. Once more, then, Theaetetus, I repeat my old question, "What is knowledge?"—and do not say that you cannot tell; but quit yourself like a man, and by the help of God you will be able to tell.

Theaetetus. At any rate, Socrates, after such an exhortation I should be ashamed of not trying to do my best.

[334]

SOLOVIEV, VLADIMIR

SOLOVIEV, VLADIMIR (1853-1900). Soloviev has been called "the Russian Newman" or "the Russian Carlyle," and he could easily be called "the Russian Kierkegaard" with equal, or even more justice. For the struggle against the established Church, against the alliance between Church and State, which, in his opinion, meant domination of the Church by the State, and the effort to take the doctrine of Christ seriously was Soloviev's great purpose just as it was Kierkegaard's. Soloviev protested against the division of mankind into a Church which claimed to possess divine truth and to represent the will of God, and all the rest. This division, as it has been developed in the history of Christianity, was deplored by Soloviev and regarded by him as seducing the Church to abuse its lust of power. Deeply convinced of the truth of Christianity, Soloviev asserted the idea of "Godmanhood," bequeathed to humanity, and the ideal of universal theocracy, which he conceived as absolutely incompatible with the claims of the Orthodox Church.

Soloviev was the son of the noted Russian historian Sergius Soloviev, who was devoted to Tsarism, the Orthodox Church and Slavophile ideas. His career promised to become brilliant, but he renounced it, in 1881, after the assassination of Tsar Alexander II, when he publicly asked for mercy for the assassins. He always was a strong adversary of capital punishment. Then retired to private life, Soloviev became one of the greatest Russian philosophers of religion.

It is not so much the originality of Soloviev's ideas that makes his works important as rather their connection with fundamental trends of Russian thought, and his view of the crisis of European civilization. Soloviev's hostility against nationalism, especially Russian nationalism, is no less ardent than his opposition to the claims of the Orthodox Church. At the end of his life, he recognized Rome as the center of Christianity, without, however, converting to the Roman Church. His positive doctrine culminated in the "justification of the good," founded upon a psychology of human conscience and upon his strong belief that man cannot be entirely wicked. He was a man who lived in accordance with his

1114

ideas, and was revered as a saint by people of all classes. His tombstone became a place of pilgrimage.

HUMANITY BEFORE NATIONALITY

THE good embraces all the details of life, but in itself it is *indivisible*. Patriotism as a virtue is part of the right attitude to everything, and in the moral order this part cannot be separated from the whole and opposed to it. In the moral organization not a single nation can prosper *at the expense of* others; it cannot positively affirm itself to the detriment or the disadvantage of others. Just as the positive moral dignity of a private person is known from the fact that his prosperity is truly useful to all others, so the prosperity of a nation true to the moral principle is necessarily connected with the universal good. This logical and moral axiom is crudely distorted in the popular sophism that we must think of our own nation only, because it is good, and therefore its prosperity is a benefit to every one. It either thoughtlessly overlooks or impudently rejects the obvious truth that this very alienation of one's own nation from others, this *exclusive* recognition of it as pre-eminently good, is in itself evil, and that nothing but evil can spring from this evil root. It must be one or the other. Either we must renounce Christianity and monotheism in general, according to which "there is none but one, that is, God," and recognize our nation *as such* to be the highest good—that is, put it in the place of God—or we must admit that a people becomes good not in virtue of the simple fact of its particular nationality, but only in so far as it conforms to and participates in the absolute good. And it can only do so if it has a right attitude to everything, and, in the first place, to other nations. A nation cannot be really good so long as it feels malice or hostility against other nations, and fails to recognize them as its neighbors and to love them as itself.

The moral duty of a true patriot is then to serve the nation in the good, or to serve the true good of a nation, inseparable from the good of all, or, what is the same thing,

1115

to serve the nation in humanity, and humanity in the nation.
Such a patriot will discover a positive aspect in every foreign race and people, and by means of it will seek to relate
this race or people with his own for the benefit of both.

When we hear of a *rapprochement* between nations, of
inter-national agreements, friendships, and alliances, we
must, before rejoicing or being grieved about it, know *in
what* it is that the nations are being united, in good or
in evil. The fact of union as such decides nothing. If two
private people or two nations are united by the hatred of
a third, their union is an evil and a source of fresh evil.
If they are united by mutual interest or by common gain,
the question still remains open. The interest may be unworthy, the gain may be fictitious, and in that case the
union of nations, as well as of individuals, even if it is
not a direct evil, can certainly not be a good desirable
for its own sake. The union of men and nations can be
positively approved only in so far as it furthers the moral
organization of humanity, or the organization of the absolute good in it. We have seen that the ultimate *subject* of
this organization, the real bearer of the *moral order*, is the
collective man or humanity, successively differentiated into
its organs and elements—nations, families, persons.

[335]

SOREL, GEORGES

SOREL, GEORGES (1847-1922). The name of Georges Sorel has
been connected with the history of both bolshevism and fascism.
Jean Jaurès called him "the metaphysician of syndicalism." But, in
fact, Sorel was a metaphysician of industrial production, and tried
to utilize the working class and its ideologies as the instrument for
attaining his aims.

By vocation an engineer and always very bourgeois in his
conduct of life, Sorel turned to social and economic studies only
after his fortieth year. From 1893 to 1897, he adopted Marx's
ideas; thereafter, he professed animosity not only toward Marx but
also toward democracy, rationalism and intellectualism, expressing

his views in his principal books, *The Decomposition of Marxism,*
Reflections on Violence (both 1908) and *Illusions of Progress*
(1911). Inspired by Henri Bergson, whom he respected despite his
constant animosity toward the Jews, Sorel heralded the "Myth of
the General Strike," and took great care to distinguish between
the Utopia and the myth. The latter term was used by Sorel as
the image of a fictitious, even unrealizable future that expresses
the sentiments of the revolutionary masses and incites them to
revolutionary action. "Violence" was proclaimed by Sorel as the
way to power. But this "Violence," Sorel protested, is not meant
as "Jacobinic" action but as "psychic warfare" whose means are
sabotage, strike and the boycott of workers who decline to participate in that warfare.

For a time, Sorel succeeded in winning over the French syndi-
calists. But very soon, the militant workers turned against him
who, with his pupil Georges Valois as intermediary, negotiated
with the royalist Charles Maurras, the leader of the "Action Française." The outbreak of the war, in 1914, prevented their alliance.
After the war, Sorel built his hopes upon bolshevism, but Lenin
rebuked him in his polemics against empiriocriticism. Only Mussolini acknowledged Sorel and frequently proclaimed his indebtedness to him.

Sorel was not interested in socialism, communism or any
other politico-economic system but in the increase of industrial
production to the highest possible degree. His experiences as an
engineer had convinced him that capitalists or industrial entrepre-
neurs would be incapable of attaining this goal. He therefore entrusted the employees and workers with the fulfillment of the task.
This idea of Sorel's might have impressed Thorstein Veblen, who
expressed similar views on the incompetency of capitalists.

OPTIMISM AND PESSIMISM
IN SOCIAL DEVELOPMENT

THE immense successes obtained by industrial civilization
have created the belief that, in the near future, happiness will
be produced automatically for everybody. "The present century," writes Hartmann, "has for the last forty years only
entered the third period of illusion. In the enthusiasm and
enchantment of its hopes, it rushes towards the realization
of the promise of a new age of gold. Providence takes care
that the anticipations of the isolated thinker do not disar-

range the course of history by prematurely gaining too many adherents." He thinks that for this reason his readers will have some difficulty in accepting his criticism of the illusion of future happiness. The leaders of the contemporary world are pushed towards optimism by economic forces.

So little are we prepared to understand pessimism, that we generally employ the word quite incorrectly: we call pessimists people who are in reality only disillusioned optimists. When we meet a man who, having been unfortunate in his enterprises, deceived in his most legitimate ambitions, humiliated in his affections, expresses his grief in the form of a violent revolt against the duplicity of his associates, the stupidity of society, or the blindness of destiny, we are disposed to look upon him as a pessimist; whereas we ought nearly always to regard him as a disheartened optimist who has not had the courage to start afresh, and who is unable to understand why so many misfortunes have befallen him, contrary to what he supposes to be the general law governing the production of happiness.

The optimist in politics is an inconstant and even dangerous man, because he takes no account of the great difficulties presented by his projects; these projects seem to him to possess a force of their own, which tends to bring about their realization all the more easily as they are, in his opinion, destined to produce the happiest results. He frequently thinks that small reforms in the political constitution, and, above all, in the personnel of the government, will be sufficient to direct social development in such a way as to mitigate those evils of the contemporary world which seem so harsh to the sensitive mind. As soon as his friends come into power, he declares that it is necessary to let things alone for a little, not to hurry too much, and to learn how to be content with whatever their own benevolent intentions prompt them to do. It is not always self-interest that suggests these expressions of satisfaction, as people have often believed; self-interest is strongly aided by vanity and by the illusions of philosophy. The optimist passes with remarkable facility from revolutionary anger to the most ridiculous social pacifism.

If he possesses an exalted temperament, and if unhappily he finds himself armed with great power, permitting him to realize the ideal he has fashioned, the optimist may lead his country into the worst disasters. He is not long in finding out that social transformations are not brought about with the ease that he had counted on; he then supposes that this is the fault of his contemporaries, instead of explaining what actually happens by historical necessities; he is tempted to get rid of people whose obstinacy seems to him to be so dangerous to the happiness of all. During the Terror, the men who spilt most blood were precisely those who had the greatest desire to let their equals enjoy the golden age they had dreamt of, and who had the most sympathy with human wretchedness: optimists, idealists, and sensitive men, the greater desire they had for universal happiness the more inexorable they showed themselves.

Pessimism is quite a different thing from the caricatures of it which are usually presented to us; it is a philosophy of conduct rather than a theory of the world; it considers the *march towards deliverance* as narrowly conditioned, on the one hand, by the experimental knowledge that we have acquired from the obstacles which oppose themselves to the satisfaction of our imaginations (or, if we like, by the feeling of social determinism), and, on the other, by a profound conviction of our natural weakness. These two aspects of pessimism should never be separated although, as a rule, scarcely any attention is paid to their close connection.

The conception of pessimism springs from the fact that literary historians have been very much struck with the complaints made by the great poets of antiquity on the subject of the griefs which constantly threaten mankind. There are few people who have not, at one time or another, experienced a piece of good fortune; but we are surrounded by malevolent forces always ready to spring out on us from some ambuscade and overwhelm us. Hence the very real sufferings which arouse the sympathy of nearly all men, even of those who have been more favorably treated by fortune; so that the literature of grief has always had a certain success throughout the whole course of history. But a study of this kind of literature would give us a very imperfect idea of pessimism. It may be laid down as a general rule, that in order to understand a doctrine it is not sufficient to study it in an abstract manner, nor even as it occurs in isolated people: it is necessary to find out how it has been manifested in historical groups.

The pessimist regards social conditions as forming a system bound together by an iron law which cannot be evaded, so that the system is given, as it were, in one block, and cannot disappear except in a catastrophe which involves the whole. If this theory is admitted, it then becomes absurd to make certain wicked men responsible for the evils from which society suffers; the pessimist is not subject to the sanguinary follies of the optimist, infatuated by the unexpected obstacles that his projects meet with; he does not dream of bringing about the happiness of future generations by slaughtering existing egoists.

[336]

SPENCER, HERBERT

SPENCER, HERBERT (1820-1903). An engineer by training, Spencer tried to survey the whole range of human thought with the intention of interpreting "the phenomena of life, mind and society in terms of matter, motion and force." Defining philosophy as "knowledge of the highest degree of generality," he established the formula of evolution as the general law which enabled him to explain all phenomena in the above mentioned terms. Under its simplest and most general aspect, evolution is characterized by Spencer as "the integration of matter and concomitant dissipation of movement: while dissolution is the absorption of motion and concomitant disintegration of matter." To Spencer, evolution was universal and one, dominating the realms of biology, psychology, ethics and sociology. He was the first philosopher to maintain the genetic principle, according to which the more developed thing must be interpreted by the less developed one. He was also the first to use a biological standard for human ethics. He complained that "men do not even know that their sensations are their natural guides and (when not rendered morbid by long-continued disobedience) their most trustworthy guides," because he thought that the senses of man were molded in accordance with the all-embracing law of evolution from a less perfect to a more perfect state. In this way, Spencer identified evolution with progress.

Spencer's notion of evolution has a curious history. At first he borrowed it from Coleridge, and adopted at the same time the latter's idea of social organism, both of which have been conceived of as in opposition to utilitarianism. Later, he came closer to the utilitarian point of view, espoused the cause of rugged individualism, strictly opposed any encroachment upon private enterprise by the state, and became a grim adversary of socialism. He was deeply disappointed when Beatrice Potter, his favorite pupil, married Sidney Webb, the theorist of British labor, and he then cancelled her appointment as his literary executor. At the end of his life, Spencer expressed very pessimistic views about the future of humanity.

PHILOSOPHY DEFINED

AFTER concluding that we cannot know the ultimate nature of that which is manifested to us, there arise the questions —What is it that we know? In what sense do we know it? And in what consists our highest knowledge of it? Having repudiated as impossible the philosophy which professes to formulate being as distinguished from appearance, it becomes needful to say what philosophy truly is—not simply to specify its limits, but to specify its character within those limits. Given a certain sphere as the sphere to which human intelligence is restricted, there remains to define the peculiar product of human intelligence which may still be called philosophy.

In doing this, we may advantageously avail ourselves of the method followed at the outset, of separating from conceptions that are partially or mainly erroneous, the element of truth they contain. It was previously inferred that religious beliefs, wrong as they might individually be in their particular forms, nevertheless probably each contained an essential verity, and that this was most likely common to them all; so in this place it is to be inferred that past and present beliefs respecting the nature of philosophy, are none of them wholly false, and that that in which they are true is that in which they agree. We have here, then, to do what was done there—"to compare all opinions of the same genus; to set aside as more or less discrediting one another those various special and concrete elements in which such opinions disagree; to observe what remains after the discordant constituents have been eliminated; and to find for this remaining constituent that abstract expression which holds true throughout its divergent modifications."

Earlier speculations being passed over, we see that among the Greeks, before there had arisen any notion of philosophy in general, apart from particular forms of philosophy, the particular forms of it from which the general notion was to arise, were hypotheses respecting some universal principle that constituted the essence of all concrete kinds of being. To the question—"What is that *invariable existence* of which these are *variable states?*" there were sundry answers—water, air, fire. A class of hypotheses of this all-embracing character having been propounded, it became possible for Pythagoras to conceive of philosophy in the abstract, as knowledge the most remote from practical ends; and to define it as "knowledge of immaterial and eternal things:" "the cause of the material existence of things," being, in his view, number. Thereafter, we find continued a pursuit of philosophy as some ultimate interpretation of the universe, assumed to be possible, whether actually reached in any case or not. And in the course of this pursuit, various such ultimate interpretations were given us as that "One is the beginning of all things;" that "the One is God;" that "the One is Finite;" that "the One is Infinite;" that "Intelligence is the governing principle of things;" and so on. From all which it is plain that the knowledge supposed to constitute philosophy, differed from other knowledge in its transcendent, exhaustive character. In the subsequent course of speculation, after the sceptics had shaken men's faith in their powers of reaching such transcendent knowledge, there grew up a much-restricted conception of philosophy. Under Socrates, and still more under the Stoics, philosophy became little else than the doctrine of right living. Its subject matter was practically cut down to the proper ruling of conduct, public and private. Not indeed that the proper ruling of conduct, as conceived by sundry of the later Greek thinkers to constitute subject matter of philosophy, answered to what was popularly understood by the proper ruling of conduct. The injunctions of Zeno were not of the same class as those which guided men from early times downwards, in their daily observances, sacrifices, customs, all having more or less of religious sanction; but they were principles of action enunciated without reference to times, or persons, or special cases. What, then, was the constant element in these unlike ideas of philosophy held by the ancient? Clearly the character in which this last idea agrees with the first is that within its sphere of inquiry, philosophy seeks for wide and deep truths, as distinguished from the multitudinous detailed truths which the surfaces of things and actions present.

By comparing the conceptions of philosophy that have been current in modern times, we get a like result. The disciples of Schelling, Fichte, and their kindred, join the Hegelian in ridiculing the so-called philosophy which has usurped the title in England. Not without reason, they laugh on reading of "philosophical instruments;" and would deny that any one of the papers in the *Philosophical Transactions* has the least claim to come under such a title. Retaliating on their critics, the English may, and most of them do, reject as absurd the imagined philosophy of the German schools. As consciousness cannot be transcended, they hold that whether consciousness does or does not vouch for the existence of something beyond itself, it at any rate cannot comprehend that something; and that hence, in so far as any philosophy professes to be an ontology, it is false. These two views cancel one another over large parts of their areas. The English criticism of the German cuts off from philosophy all that is regarded as absolute knowledge. The German criticism of the English tacitly implies that if philosophy is limited to the relative, it is at any rate not concerned with those aspects of the relative which are embodied in mathematical formulas, in accounts of physical researches, in chemical analyses, or in descriptions of species and reports of physiological experiments. Now what has the too-wide German conception in common with the conception general among the English men of science; which, narrow and crude as it is, is not so narrow and crude as their misuse of the word philosophical indicates? The two have this in common, that neither Germans nor English apply the word to unsystematized knowledge—to knowledge quite uncoordinated with other knowledge. Even the most limited specialist would not describe as philosophical, an essay which, dealing wholly with details, manifested no perception of the bearings of those details on wider truths.

The vague idea thus raised of that in which the various conceptions of philosophy agree, may be rendered more definite by comparing what has been known in England as natural philosophy with that development of it called positive philosophy. Though, as M. Comte admits, the two consist of knowledge essentially the same in kind; yet, by having put this kind of knowledge into a more coherent form, he has given it more of that character to which the term philosophical is applied. Without expressing any opinion respecting the truth of his co-ordination, it must be conceded that by the fact of its co-ordination, the body of knowledge organized by him has a better claim to the title philosophy, than has the comparatively unorganized body of knowledge named natural philosophy.

If subdivisions of philosophy, or more special forms of it, be contrasted with one another, or with the whole, the same implication comes out. Moral philosophy and political philosophy agree with philosophy at large in the comprehensiveness of their reasonings and conclusions. Though under the head of moral philosophy, we treat of human actions as right or wrong, we do not include special directions for behavior in the nursery, at table, or on the exchange; and though political philosophy has for its topic the conduct of men in their public relations, it does not concern itself with modes of voting or details of administration. Both of these sections of philosophy contemplate particular instances, only as illustrating truths of wide application.

Thus every one of these conceptions implies the belief in a possible way of knowing things more completely than they are known through simple experiences, mechanically accumulated in memory or heaped up in cyclopedias. Though in the extent of the sphere which they have supposed philosophy to fill, men have differed and still differ very widely; yet there is a real if unavowed agreement among them in signifying by this title a knowledge which transcends ordinary knowledge. That which remains as the common element in these conceptions of philosophy, after the elimination of their discordant elements, is—*knowledge of the highest degree of generality.* We see this tacitly asserted by the simultaneous inclusion of God, nature, and man, within its scope; or still more distinctly by the division of philosophy as a whole into theological, physical, ethical, etc. For that which characterizes the genus of which these are species, must be something more general than that which distinguishes any one species.

What must be the specific shape here given to this conception? The range of intelligence we find to be limited to the relative. Though persistently conscious of a power manifested to us, we have abandoned as futile the attempt to learn anything respecting the nature of that power; and so have shut out philosophy from much of the domain supposed to belong to it. The domain left is that occupied by science. Science concerns itself with the coexistences and sequences among phenomena; grouping these at first into generalizations of a simple or low order, and rising gradually to higher and more extended generalizations. But if so, where remains any subject matter for philosophy?

The reply is—philosophy may still properly be the title retained for knowledge of the highest generality. Science means merely the family of the sciences—stands for nothing more than the sum of knowledge formed of their contributions; and ignores the knowledge constituted by the *fusion* of all these contributions into a whole. As usage has defined it, science consists of truths existing more or less separated; and does not recognize these truths as entirely integrated. An illustration will make the difference clear.

If we ascribe the flow of a river to the same force which causes the fall of a stone, we make a statement, true as far as it goes, that belongs to a certain division of science. If, in further explanation of a movement produced by gravitation in a direction almost horizontal, we cite the law that fluids subject to mechanical forces exert reactive forces which are equal in all directions, we formulate a wider fact, containing the scientific interpretation of many other phenomena; as those presented by the fountain, the hydraulic press, the steamengine, the airpump. And when this proposition, extending only to the dynamics of fluids, is merged in a proposition of general dynamics, comprehending the laws of movement of solids as well as of fluids, there is reached a yet higher truth; but still a truth that comes wholly within the realm of science. Again, looking around at birds and mammals, suppose we say that airbreathing animals are hot-blooded; and that then, remembering how reptiles, which also breathe air, are not much warmer than their media, we say, more truly, that animals (bulks being equal) have temperatures proportionate to the quantities of air they breathe; and that then, calling to mind certain large fish which maintain a heat considerably above that of the water they swim in, we further correct the generalization by saying that the temperature varies as the rate of oxygenation of the blood; and that then, modifying the statement to meet other criticisms, we finally assert the relation to be between the amount of heat and the amount of molecular change— supposing we do all this, we state scientific truths that are successively wider and more complete, but truths which, to the last, remain purely scientific. Once more if, guided by mercantile experiences, we reach the conclusion that prices rise when the demand exceeds the supply; and that commodities flow from places where they are abundant to places where they are scarce; and that the industries of different localities are determined in their kinds mainly by the facilities which the localities afford them; and if, studying these generalizations of political economy, we trace them all to the truth that each man seeks satisfaction for his desires in ways costing the smallest efforts—such social phenomena being *resultants* of individual actions so guided; we are still dealing with the propositions of science only.

And now how is philosophy constituted? It is constituted by carrying a stage further the process indicated. So long as these truths are known only apart and regarded as independent, even the most general of them cannot without laxity of speech be called philosophical. But when, having been severally reduced to a simple mechanical axiom, a principle of molecular physics, and a law of social action, they are contemplated together as corollaries of some ultimate truth, then we rise to the kind of knowledge that constitutes philosophy proper.

The truths of philosophy thus bear the same relation to the highest scientific truths, that each of these bears to lower scientific truths. As each widest generalization of science comprehends and consolidates the narrower generalizations of its own division; so the generalizations of philosophy comprehend and consolidate the widest generalizations of science. It is therefore a knowledge the extreme opposite in kind to that which experience first accumulates. It is the final product of that process which begins with a mere colligation of crude observations, goes on establishing propositions that are broader and more separated from particular cases, and ends in universal propositions. Or to bring the definition to its simplest and clearest form:—knowledge of the lowest kind is *un-unified* knowledge; science is *partially unified* knowledge; philosophy is *completely unified* knowledge.

Such, at least, is the meaning we must here give to the word philosophy, if we employ it at all. In so defining it, we accept that which is common to the various conceptions of it current among both ancients and moderns—rejecting those elements in which these conceptions disagree, or exceed the possible range of intelligence. In short, we are simply giving precision to that application of the word which is gradually establishing itself.

Two forms of philosophy, as thus understood, may be distinguished. On the one hand, the things contemplated may be the universal truths: all particular truths referred to being used simply for proof or elucidation of these universal truths. On the other hand, setting out with the universal truths as granted, the things contemplated may be the particular truths as interpreted by them. In both cases we deal with the universal truths; but in the one case they are passive and in the other case active—in the one case they form the products of exploration and in the other case the instruments of exploration. These divisions we may appropriately call general philosophy and special philosophy respectively.

[337]

SPINOZA, BENEDICTUS DE
(Baruch de Spinoza)

SPINOZA, BENEDICTUS DE (BARUCH DE SPINOZA) (1632-1677). For more than a century after Spinoza's works were published, their author was objurgated with embitterment by Catholics, Protestants, Jews and freethinkers alike. Even David Hume, in general a man of kindly disposition, branded him as "infame," and Moses Mendelssohn, the affable advocate of tolerance, was horrified and disbelieving when he heard that his friend Lessing had adopted Spinoza's doctrine. A great change was inaugurated by Herder and Goethe who became Spinozists, and revered Spinoza as a saint. So did Heinrich Heine. Post-Kantian philosophers and Romantic poets in Germany were deeply influenced by Spinoza's conception of nature. In modern times, Spinoza is universally recognized as a philosopher of unsurpassed sublimity and profundity. Even his critics agree that Spinoza had a most lovable personality, one of the purest characters in the history of mankind. Despite his delicate feelings and the subtlety of his definitions, Spinoza's mind was unsophisticated, and regardless of the boldness of his thoughts and the sternness of his will to draw his conclusions logically and without any regard to personal inclinations, Spinoza was calm, benevolent, fond of plain people. He earned his living by grinding optical lenses and declined an appointment as professor at the University of Heidelberg because he preferred independence to honor.

Spinoza belonged to a Jewish family which had been exiled from Spain and Portugal, and had finally settled in Holland. Before studying Latin, the natural sciences, and the philosophy of Hobbes and Descartes, he had studied the Hebrew Bible, the Talmud, medieval Jewish literature, and probably cabala. In 1656, he was put under the ban by the Jewish community of Amsterdam because of his opposition to traditional doctrines of Judaism, including those that were also sacred tenets of Christianity. Detached from the Jewish community, Spinoza manifested indifference to Jews and Judaism. With his investigation of the sacred Scriptures he gave an impetus to modern Biblical criticism. But the elements of his Jewish education, especially his acquaintance with medieval Jewish philosophy, remain visible in his conception of the oneness of God and in his personal piety.

Spinoza's chief work is entitled *Ethics*. It could have been named "Metaphysics" with equal justice, for Spinoza was thoroughly convinced that the knowledge of the ultimate reality involves the norm of human action and implies the measure of personal perfection. Philosophical thinking was, to Spinoza, self-education and improvement of the mind of the thinker. His aim was to obtain, by means of reason and science, the same trust in rules of human behavior that religious traditions claimed to grant their believers. Contrary to Descartes, he denied the possibility of harmonizing reason with Biblical revelation, and, in that way, Spinoza, not Descartes, became the symbol of the end of medieval philosophy. The scientific method offered to Spinoza not only the measure of moral evaluation but a means of gaining eternal bliss. To win supreme happiness or "unceasing joy," Spinoza said, man has to attain knowledge of his union with the whole of nature.

All individual beings, whatever is popularly supposed to be a real thing, are regarded by Spinoza as mere modifications of but one infinite substance which has an infinite number of attributes, of which, however, only two, namely thought and extension, are perceptible by man. This one substance which is in itself and conceived through itself alone, is the only object of true knowledge, and is identical with God whose will is identical with the laws of nature. He who knows nature knows God. Increasing knowledge of nature means increasing love of God. From this proposition of the oneness and universality of God, Spinoza has deduced *more geometrico*, in a manner following the example of geometrical demonstrations, his definitions of all particular objects in the realms of extension and thought. He finally arrived at his much admired description of the intellectual love of God which is characterized as an absolutely disinterested feeling, the humble cognizance of all-governing necessity and at the same time the complete liberation of the soul from disturbing passions. Neither to laud nor to blame but to understand is the principle of Spinoza's attitude toward life.

ON THE IMPROVEMENT OF THE MIND

AFTER experience had taught me that all things which are ordinarily encountered in common life are vain and futile, and when I saw that all things which occasioned me any anxiety or fear had in themselves nothing of good or evil, except in so far as the mind was moved by them; I at length determined to inquire if there were anything which was a true good capable of imparting itself, by which the mind could be solely affected to the exclusion of all else; whether, indeed, anything existed by whose discovery and acquisition I might be put in possession of a joy continuous and supreme to all eternity. I say that *I at length deter-*

mined; for at the first glance it appeared to me to be foolish to be willing to part with something certain for something then uncertain. I saw, forsooth, the advantages which accrue from honor and riches, and that I should be forced to abstain from seeking these if I wished to apply myself seriously to another and new undertaking; and if, by chance, perfect happiness should lie in those things, I perceived that I must go without it; but if, on the other hand, it did not lie in them, and I applied myself only to them, I must then also go without the highest happiness. I turned it over, therefore, in my mind whether it might not perchance be possible to carry out my new purpose or, at least, to arrive at some certainty with regard to it, without changing the order and ordinary plan of my life, a thing I had often attempted in vain. Now, the things which generally present themselves in life, and are considered by men as the highest good, so far as can be gathered from their actions, are included in these three, riches, honor, and sensual indulgence. By these three the mind is so distracted, that it is scarcely possible for it to think of any other good thing. For example, as regards sensual indulgence, the mind is engrossed by it to such a degree as to rest in it as in some good, and is thereby entirely prevented from thinking of anything else, but, after it has been satisfied, there follows a very great melancholy, which, if it does not check the action of the mind, nevertheless disturbs and blunts it. Through the pursuit of honor and riches also the mind is not a little distracted, especially if the latter are sought for their own sake, because in that case they are supposed to be the highest good. By honor the mind is even more distracted; for it is always regarded as a good in itself, and, as it were, the ultimate end to which everything is directed. Again, in the case of honor and riches there is no repentance, as in the case of sensual indulgence, but the more we have of them, the more our joy is increased; and consequently we are more and more incited to increase them; nevertheless, if by any chance our expectations are deceived, then very great sorrow arises.

Finally, honor is a great hindrance to us, because it is necessary, if we would attain it, to direct our lives according to the notions of men—that is to say, by avoiding what they commonly avoid, and seeking what they commonly seek.

Since, therefore, I saw that all these things stood in the way of my devoting myself to any new purpose; that, in fact, they were so opposed to it, that either they or it must be relinquished, I was compelled to inquire what was most useful to me, for as I have said, it seemed as if I were willing to lose a certain good for that which was uncertain. But after I had reflected a little on the subject, I discovered, in the first place, that if forsaking riches and honor and sensual indulgence, I should address myself to my new purpose, I should be giving up a good uncertain in its very nature, as may clearly be seen from what has already been said, for one uncertain not in its very nature (for I sought a good which was stable), but only so far as its attainment was concerned, and after careful reflection, I came to see that, if only I could apply myself wholly to thought, I should then be giving up certain evils for a certain good. For I saw that I was situated in the greatest danger, and I forced myself to seek with all my strength a remedy, even although it might be uncertain, just as a sick man suffering from a mortal disease, who foresees certain death unless a remedy be applied, is forced to seek it with all his strength, even though it be uncertain, for therein lies the whole of his hope. All those things, however, which the majority of persons pursue, not only contribute no means whereby to preserve our being, but even are a hindrance to its preservation. They frequently cause the destruction of those who possess them, and always cause the destruction of those who are possessed by them.

For there are very many examples of men who have suffered persecution even to death for the sake of their riches, and also of men, who, in order that they might obtain wealth, have exposed themselves to so many dangers that at length they have paid with their lives the penalty of their folly. Nor are there fewer examples of men, who, in order that they might obtain honor, or guard it, have endured most miserable calamities; and, lastly, innumerable are the examples of those who, through excess of sensual indulgence, have hastened their death. The cause of these evils appeared to be that all happiness or unhappiness solely depends upon the quality of the object to which we are attached by love. For on account of that which is not loved no strife will arise, there will be no sorrow if it perishes, no jealousy if it is appropriated by another, no fear, no hatred, and, in a word, no agitations of the mind. All these, however, arise from the love of that which is perishable, as all those things are of which we have just spoken. But love for an object eternal and infinite feeds the mind with joy alone, and a joy which is free from all sorrow. This is something greatly to be desired and to be sought with all our strength.

But not without reason did I use the words *if I could but apply myself wholly to thought.* For although I saw all this so clearly in my mind, I could not therefore put aside all avarice, sensual desire, and love of honor. This one thing I saw, that so long as my mind was occupied with these thoughts, so long it was turned away from the things mentioned above, and seriously reflected on the new purpose. This confronted me greatly. For I saw that those evils were not of such a kind that they would not yield to remedies. And although in the beginning these intervals were rare and lasted but for a very short time, nevertheless, when the true good was by degrees better known to me, they became more frequent and longer, especially when I came to see that the acquisition of wealth, or sensual desire and love of honor, are injurious so long as they are sought for their own sake and not as means for other things; but if they are sought as means they will be enjoyed in moderation and will not be injurious: on the contrary, they will be very conducive to the end for which they are sought, as we shall show in the proper place.

Here I will explain, but only briefly, what I understand by a true good, and at the same time what is the highest good. In order that this may be rightly understood, it is to be observed that the words "good" and "evil" are only used relatively, so that one and the same thing may be called good and evil according to its different relations, just as from different points of view it may be called perfect or imperfect. For nothing considered in its own nature can be called perfect or imperfect, especially after we have discerned that everything comes to pass according to an eternal order and according to fixed laws of nature. But since human weakness cannot reach that order by its own thought, and meanwhile man can imagine a human nature much stronger than his own, and sees no obstacle to prevent his acquiring such a nature, he is urged to seek the means which may lead him to such perfection. Everything, therefore, which may be a means by which to arrive thereat, he calls a true good, but the highest good is to obtain, with as many other individuals as possible, the enjoyment of that nature. But what that nature is we shall show in the proper place— that it is a knowledge of the union between the mind and the whole of nature. This, therefore, is the end towards which I strive—to acquire this nature and to endeavor that others may acquire it with me—that is to say, it is essential to my happiness to try to make many others understand what I understand, so that their intellect and desire may entirely agree with my intellect and desire. In order to achieve this end, it is necessary to understand so much of nature as may be sufficient for acquiring the desired nature; then to form a society such as is desirable for enabling as many people as possible with the greatest ease and security to acquire it. Furthermore, we must pay attention to moral philosophy as well as to the science of the education of children, and because health is by no means an insignificant means to the attainment of this end, the whole of medicine is to be studied. Because also many things which are difficult are rendered easier by art and we can thereby gain much time and comfort in life, mechanics are by no means to be despised. But above everything a means of healing the mind must be sought out, and of purifying it as much as possible at the outset so that it may happily understand things without error and as completely as possible. Hence everybody can now see that I wish to direct all the sciences to a single end and purpose, namely, that we may reach the highest human perfection of which we have spoken. Therefore everything in the sciences which in no way advances us towards our end will be rejected as useless, that is to say, in one word, all our actions as well as our thoughts are to be directed to this end. Since, however, while we are seeking to attain it and are endeavoring to constrain our intellect into the right way, it is necessary to live, we must first of all assume certain rules of life to be good. They are these:—

I. To speak and act in accordance with the notions of the majority, provided no hindrance thereby arises to the attainment of our purpose. For we can obtain not a little profit from them, if we conform as much as possible to their notions, and, besides, in this way they will lend friendly ears to listen to the truth.

II. To indulge in pleasures only so far as is consistent with the preservation of health.

III. To seek only so much of wealth or of anything else as is sufficient to preserve life and health, and to conform to such customs of the state as are not opposed to our purpose.

Having laid down these rules, I will attempt that which stands first, and is to be achieved before anything, that is to say, to improve the intellect and make it fit to understand things in the way which is necessary in order to obtain our end. To do this, natural order requires that I should here review all the kinds of knowledge which I have hitherto possessed whereby to affirm or deny positively, in order that I may choose the best of them all, and at the same time may begin to know my powers and that nature which I wish to perfect.

If I consider accurately, they may all be reduced generally to four.

I. There is the knowledge which we derive from hearing or from some arbitrary sign.

II. There is the knowledge which we derive from vague experience, that is to say, from experience which is independent of the intellect and which is so called only because it presents itself casually and we have no experimental proof to the contrary. Therefore it abides with us undisturbed.

III. There is the knowledge which arises when the essence of a thing is deduced from another thing, but not adequately. This happens when we either infer the cause from some effect, or when we make an inference from some universal which is always accompanied by some property.

IV. Finally there is the knowledge which arises when a thing is perceived through its essence alone, or through the knowledge of its proximate cause.

All this I will illustrate by examples. From mere *hearing* I know my birthday, and that I had certain parents, and other things of the same kind which I have never doubted. Through *vague experience* I know that I shall die, for I affirm it because I have seen other people die of the same nature as myself, although they have not all lived equally long, nor have they died of the same disease. Again through vague experience I also know that oil is the proper food for feeding flame, and that water is fit for extinguishing it; I know also that a dog is a barking animal and man is a rational animal, and in this way I have learned nearly everything which appertains to the service of life. We deduce *from some other thing* in this way: when we clearly perceive that we are sensible of a particular body and no other, then we clearly deduce, I say, from that perception that our mind is united to that body, and that this union is the cause of that sensation but we cannot understand directly from it the nature of that union and of sensation. Again, after I have come to know the nature of sight, and at the same time that it has this property, that at a great distance we see one and the same thing to be less than when we see it near at hand, I deduce that the sun is greater than he appears to be, and other conclusions of the same kind.

Finally, a thing is perceived through *its essence alone*, when from the fact that I have known something, I understand what it is to have known something; as, for instance, from the fact that I have known the essence of the soul I understand it to be united to the body. By this kind of knowledge we know that two and three are five, and that if there be two lines parallel to a third, they are parallel to one another. But the things which I can as yet understand by this kind of knowledge are very few.

In order that all these things may be better understood I will give only one example as follows. Three numbers are given: a fourth is required which shall be to the third as the second is to the first. In such a case merchants generally say that they know what is to be done in order to find the fourth, because they have not as yet forgotten the rule which they heard nakedly, without any demonstration, from their teachers. Others from their experience of particular cases construct a universal axiom. When, for example, the fourth number is self-evident, as in the series 2, 4, 3, 6, they see that if the second be multiplied by the third and the product divided by the first the quotient is 6. Since they observe that the quotient is the same number which, without this rule, they knew to be the proportional, they conclude that the rule is always valid for the discovery of a fourth proportional number. Mathematicians, however, by the help of the demonstration of Euclid, Prop. 19, bk. vii, know what numbers are proportional to one another—that is to say, that from the nature and property of proportion a number which is the product of the first and fourth is equal to a number which is the product of the second and third, but they do not see the adequate proportionality of the given numbers, or if they do see it, it is not by the help of this proposition, but intuitively and without any calculation.

In order to select the best of these kinds of knowledge it is necessary that we should briefly enumerate what are the necessary means to the attainment of our end. They are these:—

1. To know exactly our own nature which we desire to perfect, and at the same time so much of the nature of things as is necessary.

2. To form correct inductions with regard to the differences, agreements, and oppositions of things.

3. To understand properly how far they can and how far they cannot be acted upon.

4. To compare the result with the nature and power of man. It will then clearly appear what is the highest perfection to which man can attain. Having thus considered these matters, let us see what kind of knowledge we ought to choose.

As to the first, without taking into account that it is something altogether uncertain, it is self-evident that from hearing, as appears from our example, no essence of a thing can be perceived, and since, as will afterwards be seen, the particular existence of a thing is not known unless its essence be known, we clearly infer that all the certainty which we derive from hearing must be distinguished from science. For no one can be affected by simple hearing unless his own intellect has first acted.

As to the second, no one can say that he obtains thereby the idea of that proportion which he seeks. Not only is it something altogether uncertain, not only is no definite object in view, but by means of it nothing of natural objects is ever perceived save accidents, which are never clearly understood unless the essences of the things be previously known. Therefore also this method is to be set aside.

By the third it may in some measure be said that we have an idea of the thing, and that thence we can conclude without danger of error, but, nevertheless, this by itself will not be the means whereby we may obtain our perfection.

The fourth mode alone grasps the adequate essence of the thing without danger of error, and therefore is the one of which we are to avail ourselves above all others. We will take care to explain in what manner it is to be applied, so that by this kind of knowledge unknown things may be understood by us, and how this may be achieved as succinctly as possible.

[338]

SPIR, AFRICAN

SPIR, AFRICAN (1837-1890). During the siege of Sevastopol in the Crimean War, two young Russian officers distinguished themselves while defending the same bastion. Both of them were decorated with the high order of St. George's Cross. But, although they fought next to each other, they never became acquainted one with another. The one was Count Leo Tolstoy, then an artillery officer, who soon thereafter became world-famous as a great novelist and religious thinker. The other was African Spir, a lieutenant in the Russian navy who, in 1856, renounced his military career and emigrated from Russia in 1867, and whose philosophical writings remained relatively unknown. One of the few who were vitally interested in Spir's philosophy was Friedrich Nietzsche. With his friend, the theologian Franz Overbeck, he discussed Spir's ideas and adopted some of Spir's views.

Only six years after Spir's death, Tolstoy read the books written by his former companion in arms, whose existence he had ignored until then. He was deeply and sympathetically impressed, and succeeded in gaining permission from the Russian censorship for the publication of a Russian version of Spir's works, which had been written in German.

Spir's intention, especially in his principal work *Thought and Reality* (1873), was to establish philosophy as the science of first principles, and he held that its task was to investigate immediate knowledge, to demonstrate the delusion of the empirical world and the true nature of things by strict statements of facts and logically controlled inference. This method led him to proclaim the principle of identity as the fundamental law of knowledge which is opposed to the changing appearance of the empirical world, and the superiority of the moral over the physical elements. Spir was a profoundly religious thinker, but he regarded God as not responsible for the crimes committed by mankind because God has nothing to do with external causality. Spir therefore felt that the old religions are of merely historical importance. He demanded just distribution of material goods but disapproved collectivism.

ON INDIVIDUAL IMMORTALITY

WHAT I intend to consider here is not so much the question of whether individual immortality is probable, but rather the question of whether it is desirable or whether the desire for it is justified. These two questions, however, cannot be entirely separated one from another. For the same reasons which prove that individual immortality is not desirable also prove that it is not probable, and, inversely, men are inclined to regard their very desires as a guarantee for the fulfilment of that which they desire.

There are principally four reasons for desiring, and believing in, individual immortality. One of them is theoretical; the second is, so to speak, animal; the others are moral or ethical. . . . The theoretical reason lies in the fact that everyone recognizes, and must recognize, himself in his consciousness as an absolute entity, a substance. A substance, however, is by virtue of its concept imperishable. It is, therefore, inconceivable and incredible to us that our ego or self could be destroyed. As it is generally known, the spiritualists have asserted that this reason that our ego or self is a substance and therefore imperishable, is a scientifically valid proof of immortality. But Kant and others have shown that this argument is untenable. . . .

A substance is nothing but an object which has an essence proper to itself, not borrowed from outside and not determined by external conditions. A substance therefore is something in itself, independent of other things.

If we inspect ourselves closely, it undoubtedly becomes

evident that we are no substance, and that we do not possess a truly proper essence that is independent of other things. What we find in ourselves are only feelings, desires, ideas and the like, which are only various ways and manners of our reacting to effects from without, but which show nothing in themselves, nothing that exists independently of these effects. A closer inquiry demonstrates that we are a compound and a mere product of conditions, and that all our essence is constantly floating and changing. Even the apparently persistent ego or self is in fact created anew at every moment. For that reason, this ego or self can be destroyed or suspended at any moment. A mere pressure on the brain is sufficient to suppress all our psychic life.

Just because we are not real substances, and do not possess a real self or a content really proper to us, our individuality could not subsist without the natural delusion by virtue of which we appear as substances in our self-consciousness and by which we apparently have a proper, persistent and independent essence, without this delusion we would not be ourselves, and there would be no question of our ego. Our existence is therefore inseparable from our self-consciousness, or rather our existence consists of it. We only exist because we are understanding ourselves.

[339]

STEINER, RUDOLF

STEINER, RUDOLF (1861-1925). By 1900, Rudolf Steiner, then at the age of forty, surprised his friends by a complete change of personality. He had been a faithful disciple of Ernst Haeckel and a devoted adherent of evolutionist materialism, when he suddenly became a mystic. He had been a Bohemian, and suddenly became a saint. He had been nonchalant, and suddenly proved to be a fanatic. Only his admiration of Goethe did not change; but now Steiner interpreted his works in a new way, claiming that his understanding of Goethe was the only correct and congenial one, and that it was, at the same time, a justification of his new creed. Dissatisfied with natural sciences, Steiner became devoted to the-

1141

osophy which he regarded as the legitimate and consequent continuance of biology and psychology. For a time he adopted the
doctrine of Annie Besant, and was its enthusiastic propagator in
Germany, winning influential adherents among the industrialists,
army officers, even clergymen and poets. But when he tried to
graft European ideas upon the "ancient wisdom," he and his followers were excluded from the Theosophical Society. Thereupon
Steiner founded the "Anthroposophical Society" whose center was
in Dornach, Switzerland. Steiner, who regarded himself an occult
scientist rather than a mystic, taught that moral purification, emancipation from egoistic drives, and training in meditation developed
spiritual qualities which enabled him and his followers to know
realms of human and cosmic existence which otherwise remain
hidden to the profane mind. Steiner was also interested in rhythm-
ics, dancing, social questions and medicine. In 1917 he advanced
a program for general peace. He exposed his doctrine in *Vom
Menschenraetsel* (On the Riddle of Man, 1916) and *Von Seelen-
raetseln* (On the Riddles of the Soul, 1917).

INTUITION

INTUITION. In the language of occult science this word expresses, in many respects, the exact opposite of that to which
it is often applied in ordinary life. People talk of intuition
as if they mean some notion, dimly felt to be true, but lacking any clear and exact knowledge. They imagine it to be a
preliminary step towards cognition rather than as cognition
itself. Such a fancy as this may illuminate a great truth as
by a flash of lightning, but it can only be counted as cognition when confirmed by accurate judgment. Further, by intuition is generally denoted something which is "felt" as
truth, and of which a person is quite convinced, but which
he will not burden with intellectual judgment. People who
are approaching a knowledge of occult science often say
that this or that was always clear to them "intuitively." But
we must put all this entirely aside and fix our attention on
the true meaning which the term intuition here implies. It
is, from this point of view, a method of cognition in no way
inferior in clearness to intellectual knowledge, and far surpassing it.

Through inspiration the experiences of the higher worlds speak out what they mean. The observer lives in the qualities and deeds of beings of those higher worlds. When he follows with his ego, as described above, the direction of a line or the shape of a form, he knows that he is not within the being itself but within its qualities and deeds. In imaginative cognition he has already experienced the feeling of being no longer outside but inside the color-pictures, and now he understands just as clearly that these color-pictures are not in themselves independent beings but only the *qualities* of those beings. In inspiration he is conscious of becoming one with the *deeds* of such beings and with the manifestations of their will. In intuition he first melts his own personality with beings which are in themselves complete. This can only happen in the right way when the melting together takes place, not through the obliteration of his own being but with its perfect maintenance. To "lose oneself" in another being is wrong. Therefore it is only an ego fortified within itself to a very high degree that can be submerged in the being of another with impunity.

[340]

STERN, WILLIAM

STERN, WILLIAM (1871-1938). When William Stern, in 1927, wrote his autobiography, he summarized his external life in two lines by naming three cities: Berlin where he was born and had studied philosophy, and Breslau and Hamburg where he had been, and was then, a professor. He had no idea that six years later Hitler would oust him, notwithstanding all his merits, and that he would thus come to teach at Duke University and Harvard.

Stern became famous as a pioneer in applied psychology. His contributions to the psychology of deposition created a sensation among jurists, and his investigations of the psychology of childhood attracted the attention of educators. Of equal importance were Stern's concept of the intelligence quotient and other studies on intelligence testing.

This successful psychologist also became a highly respected and influential philosopher. According to Stern, psychology and philosophy must follow the strategic principle of "marching separately and battling commonly."

Stern was strongly opposed to what he called "scientification of psychology" because its result was "mechanization of spiritual life." His philosophy of critical personalism tries to overcome the antagonism between common sense, which believes in separate persons, gods, or vital forces, and impersonal science, which regards the whole world as a system of elementary units and all individuals as physico-chemical aggregates. Stern declared that the person is the primordial and most pervasive unity in the range of the experimental world. Any attempt to dissect it, to typify or to reduce it to notions or principles he rejected as distortion of facts. Stern's concept of person is larger that that of the human individual. It comprises also groups. The person is to be distinguished from the thing. The person is a whole, individuality, quality, while the thing is an aggregate, quantity, comparable with other things. Personal development is no mechanical interchange between the person and his environment. It involves a constant, though not necessarily conscious, readiness to realize values which are suggested by environment. Stern's concept of history denies both biological evolution and the dialectical process, and also Rickert's reference to general values. Stern's personalism begins as ontology and proceeds to "axiosophy."

PLAY

IF we compare the play of children and adults a common principle is revealed; *make-believe* is produced in the midst of the world of reality. Like the playing of soldiers by youngsters, the billiard playing of grownups is a sham battle between people who in reality bear no enmity toward each other; an actor's role is as fictitious as the role of mother assumed by a girl playing with dolls. In both instances all the meaning of the play lies in the *present;* unlike work or artistic creation, play does not incline toward some systematic objective; it has no sequels, and it is not serious, however seriously the player may take it during its course.

The differences between the play of young and old become clear when certain *lines of development* are disclosed. In early childhood, play is definitely central to the child's behavior (wherefore this period is also called the "playing age"). Here there is no sharp separation of the world of play and the world of real earnest; all environmental objects and all the child's actions, including the realistic ones like eating, dressing, etc., become entangled in play and charged with playfulness; even when things are frankly "taken seriously" there is no clear-cut distinction between make-believe and reality. In terms of inner experience there is scarcely any difference between a girl's helping her mother dress the baby by handing her the garments, and dressing her own doll. The school age brings about fundamental changes, inasmuch as the child experiences *side by side* the two spheres of work and play, which are now clearly separate; at this point serious activity begins to develop with increasing strength, along with restraint of playfulness. In adolescence the intermediate and mixed forms appear; intermediate forms are athletics, which, by the principle of constant increase of prowess, no longer yields gratification purely in the present but imposes future goals, collecting, and other hobbies directed upon the promotion of lasting concerns. A mixed form is "serious play" (*Ernstspiel*), a behavior which, while subjectively of serious import, retains objectively the freedom and lack of consequence of play.

In adulthood play, sports, and hobbies become more and more definitely a mere adjunct to life, supplementing and completing it while affording a contrast to the severity of occupational routine and to the momentous responsibilities of domestic and public concerns.

The changing place of *imagination* also correlates with development. In early childhood imagination is very free and spontaneous, wanton, unorganized and bubbling. In play everything is grist for the mill; both player and objects played with can assume any sort of "part" without rules or restrictions; the child is sole ruler of his world of play.

When socialized play becomes more prominent, the individual's imagination must be curbed in certain respects; the game, its setting, and its rules impose limitations and directions which, without eliminating imagination, discipline and organize it. In athletics the principle of organization attains great strictness; each action is prescribed and established, and there is little room for free imagination, which receives new impulsion in the "serious play" of adolescence where instincts, desires, and anxieties are elaborated in an highly imaginative manner.

The play of adults, however, is well-nigh devoid of imagination; forms of solitary amusement like collecting have their course laid out for them in greater or less strictness by the objective and the material. Social games (cards, table games, sporting games) are hedged by such a mass of fixed rules that very limited freedom of action remains to creative imagination.

[341]

STIRNER, MAX

STIRNER, MAX (1806-1856). In the daytime, Herr Kaspar Schmidt was a teacher at a young ladies' school, a respectable citizen of Berlin and a loyal subject of his king, Frederick William IV of Prussia. In the evening, he drank wine in a restaurant where he met some writers of left-wing Hegelianism and discussed with them philosophical problems. More often than not, these debates and the wine fired the imagination of the speakers who competed one with another in exalting, both earnestly and parodistically, their personal mission as radical revolutionaries. Some members of that company later became notorious as political adventurers, others became more or less prominent socialists. Kaspar Schmidt, after coming home, worked, late in the night, at a manuscript which he published under the title *Der Einzige und sein Eigentum* (The Ego and his Own, 1845). The author of this book, calling himself Max Stirner is generally considered as the founder of theoretical anarchism and the most radical individualist in the history of philosophy. While most of his contemporaries conceived the individual as determined by collective factors of various kinds, Stirner proclaimed the uniqueness and absolute independence of his ego. For even the notion of the individual is in Stirner's opinion a useless concession to collectivism. He leaves it to other egos to claim the same uniqueness for themselves. While establishing the ego as the

1146

sole reality and the sole value, Stirner emphasizes his opposition against society, against the state, against reactionary and revolutionary parties, against liberalism and socialism, against any legislation and social conventions. For Stirner, the negation of all values except the ego means the only guarantee of personal freedom and the sole way of constructing a philosophical system by independent thinking. His motto is, "I am dependent on nothing," and his cardinal principle is, "For me there is nothing like myself." Whatever other people regard as value, ideas, notions, tenets or laws, are dealt with by Stirner as spectres which haunt unenlightened men. While trying to exorcise these spectres by exposing their unreality, Stirner becomes a mythologist on his own. He was severely attacked by Marx and Engels; however, his book remained practically ignored during his lifetime. Stirner gave his adventurous spirit a free course only in his inward life. What later became known as political anarchism would have terrified him, and he would have opposed it as contrary to his cult of the ego.

THE POSSESSED

MAN, your head is haunted; you have wheels in your head! You imagine great things, and depict to yourself a whole world of gods that has an existence for you, a spirit-realm to which you suppose yourself to be called, an ideal that beckons to you. You have a fixed idea!

Do not think that I am jesting or speaking figuratively when I regard those persons who cling to the Higher, and (because the vast majority belongs under this head) almost the whole world of men, as veritable fools, fools in a madhouse. What is it, then, that is called a "fixed idea"? An idea that has subjected the man to itself. When you recognize, with regard to such a fixed idea, that it is a folly, you shut its slave up in an asylum. And is the truth of the faith, say, which we are not to doubt; the majesty of (e.g.) the people, which we are not to strike at (he who does is guilty of lesemajesty); virtue, against which the censor is not to let a word pass, that morality may be kept pure; etc.,—are these not "fixed ideas"? Is not all the stupid chatter of (e.g.) most of our newspapers the babble of fools who suffer from the fixed idea of morality, legality, Christianity, etc., and only seem to go about free because the madhouse in which they walk takes in so broad a space? Touch the fixed idea of such a fool, and you will at once have to guard your back against the lunatic's stealthy malice. For these great lunatics are like the little so-called lunatics in this point too, that they assail by stealth him who touches their fixed idea. They first steal his weapon, steal free speech from him, and then they fall upon him with their nails. Every day now lays bare the cowardice and vindictiveness of these maniacs, and the stupid populace hurrahs for their crazy measures. One must read the journals of this period, and must hear the Philistines talk, to get the horrible conviction that one is shut up in a house with fools. "Thou shalt not call thy brother a fool; if thou dost—etc." But I do not fear the curse, and I say, my brothers are arch-fools. Whether a poor fool of the insane asylum is possessed by the fancy that he is God the Father, Emperor of Japan, the Holy Spirit, etc., or whether a citizen in comfortable circumstances conceives that it is his mission to be a good Christian, a faithful Protestant, a loyal citizen, a virtuous man, etc.,—both these are one and the same "fixed idea." He who has never tried and dared not to be a good Christian, a faithful Protestant, a virtuous man, etc., is *possessed* and prepossessed by faith, virtuousness, etc. Just as the schoolmen philosophized only *inside* the belief of the church; as Pope Benedict XIV wrote fat books *inside* the papist superstition, without ever throwing a doubt upon this belief; as authors fill whole folios on the State without calling in question the fixed idea of the State itself; as our newspapers are crammed with politics because they are conjured into the fancy that man was created to be a *zoon politicon,*—so also subjects vegetate in subjection, virtuous people in virtue, liberals in humanity, etc., without ever putting to these fixed ideas of theirs the searching knife of criticism. Undislodgeable, like a madman's delusion, those thoughts stand on a firm footing, and he who doubts them lays hands on the *sacred!* Yes, the "fixed idea," that is the truly sacred!

1148

Is it perchance only people possessed by the devil that meet us, or do we as often come upon people *possessed* in the contrary way,—possessed by "the good," by virtue, morality, the law, or some "principle" or other? Possessions of the devil are not the only ones. God works on us, and the devil does; the former "workings of grace," the latter "workings of the devil." Possessed people are *set* in their opinions.

If the word "possession" displeases you, then call it prepossession; yes, since the spirit possesses you, and all "inspirations" come from it, call it inspiration and enthusiasm. I add that complete enthusiasm—for we cannot stop with the sluggish, half-way kind—is called fanaticism.

It is precisely among cultured people that *fanaticism* is at home; for man is cultured so far as he takes an interest in spiritual things, and interest in spiritual things, when it is alive, is and must be *fanaticism;* it is a fanatical interest in the sacred (*fanum*). Observe our liberals, look into the *Saechsischen Vaterlandsblaetter,* hear what Schlosser says: "Holbach's company constituted a regular plot against the traditional doctrine and the existing system, and its members were as fanatical on behalf of their unbelief as monks and priests, Jesuits and Pietists, Methodists, missionary and Bible societies, commonly are for mechanical worship and orthodoxy."

Take notice how a "moral man" behaves, who today often thinks he is through with God and throws off Christianity as a bygone thing. If you ask him whether he has ever doubted that the copulation of brother and sister is incest, that monogamy is the truth of marriage, that filial piety is a sacred duty, etc., then a moral shudder will come over him at the conception of one's being allowed to touch his sister as wife also, etc. And whence this shudder? Because he *believes* in those moral commandments. This moral *faith* is deeply rooted in his breast. Much as he rages against the *pious* Christians, he himself has nevertheless as thoroughly remained a Christian,—to wit, a *moral* Christian. In the form of morality Christianity holds him a prisoner, and a pris-

1149

oner under *faith*. Monogamy is to be something sacred, and he who may live in bigamy is punished as a *criminal*; he who commits incest suffers as a *criminal*. Those who are always crying that religion is not to be regarded in the state, and the Jew is to be a citizen equally with the Christian, show themselves in accord with this. Is not this of incest and monogamy a *dogma of faith*? Touch it, and you will learn by experience how this moral man is a *hero of faith* too, not less than Krummacher, not less than Philip II. These fight for the faith of the Church, he for the faith of the State, or the moral laws of the State; for articles of faith, both condemn him who acts otherwise than *their faith* will allow. The brand of "crime" is stamped upon him, and he may languish in reformatories, in jails. Moral faith is as fanatical as religious faith! They call that "liberty of faith" then, when brother and sister, on account of a relation that they should have settled with their "conscience," are thrown into prison. "But they set a pernicious example." Yes, indeed: others might have taken the notion that the State had no business to meddle with their relation, and thereupon "purity of morals" would go to ruin. So then the religious heroes of faith are zealous for the "sacred God," the moral ones for the "sacred good."

Those who are zealous for something sacred often look very little like each other. How the strictly orthodox or old-style believers differ from the fighters for "truth, light, and justice," from the Philalethes, the Friends of Light, the Rationalists, etc. And yet, how utterly unessential is this difference! If one buffets single traditional truths (*e.g.* miracles, unlimited power of princes, etc.), then the rationalists buffet them too, and only the old-style believers wail. But, if one buffets truth itself, he immediately has both, as *believers*, for opponents. So with moralities; the strict believers are relentless, the clearer heads are more tolerant. But he who attacks morality itself gets both to deal with. "Truth, morality, justice, light, etc.," are to be and remain "sacred." What any one finds to censure in Christianity is simply supposed to be "unchristian" according to the view of these rationalists; but Christianity must remain a "fixture," to buffet it is outrageous, "an outrage." To be sure, the heretic against pure faith no longer exposes himself to the earlier fury of persecution, but so much more does it now fall upon the heretic against pure morals.

[342]

STRAUSS, DAVID FRIEDRICH

STRAUSS, DAVID FRIEDRICH (1808-1874). Before Strauss published his *Life of Jesus* (1835), it seemed that the authority of the Christian faith was defended in Germany far more efficiently than it had been during the preceding century. Hegel and Schleiermacher, bitterly opposed one to another, had produced a synthesis of Christian religion and modern thought that was supposed to satisfy all spiritual needs of German intellectuals, not to mention that pressure was exercised by more orthodox theologians who used to denounce really or allegedly un-Christian opinions, and by the governments which were always ready to punish the expression of such opinions. The appearance of Strauss' book had the effect of a bombshell and changed the situation completely. It made Germany the arena of a religious struggle whose violence was unheard of since the end of the Thirty Years War.

Strauss, without denying the historical existence of Jesus, inexorably criticized the sources of the New Testament, proved their inner contradictions in principal and minor points, and demonstrated that many reports on the life of Jesus, narrated in the Gospels, were entirely unreliable, products of, as he said, "mythical" literature which, to a large extent, was patterned on tales and sayings of the Old Testament. The synthesis of theology and science was destroyed, and could not be saved either by orthodox theologians who called for the police or by rightist Hegelians who protested that Strauss had misunderstood their master.

The book that made Strauss famous, destroyed his happiness. He was not a fighter, and the permanent hostilities which culminated in an open revolt of the people of Zurich, where he had been appointed professor, undermined his health. But his sense of truth remained unshattered. In his *Doctrine of the Christian Faith* (1840), Strauss definitely broke with Christian theology and Christianity completely. His frankness surpassed that of the most daring thinkers

1151

in Germany previous to him. He maintained his standpoint in his
later works, especially in his *The Old Faith and the New* (1872),
while flatly answering "No" to the question "Can we still be
Christians?," and trying to harmonize the doctrine of Ludwig Feuerbach with Darwinism. Certainly, this last work of a tired, constantly persecuted and physically suffering man has many weak
points. But it did not deserve the violent attack made by Friedrich Nietzsche who ignored that Strauss, at least in his early writings, had accomplished that which Nietzsche himself demanded from
a valiant thinker.

POLYTHEISM AND MONOTHEISM

POLYTHEISM was the original, and in some respects the natural form of religion. A multiplicity of phenomena presented themselves to man, a multiplicity of forces pressed
in upon him, from which he either wished himself protected,
or of whose favor he desired to be assured; then also a variety of relations which he craved to have sanctified and se-
curely established; thus naturally arose, also, a multiplicity
of divinities. This conclusion is confirmed by the observation, that all those tribes of the earth which are still to a
certain extent in a state of nature, continue now, as formerly,
to be polytheists. Monotheism appears everywhere in history,
the Jewish not excepted, as something secondary, as something educed in the lapse of time out of a more primitive
polytheism. How was this transition effected?

It is said, certainly, that a more exact observation of
Nature must have led man to perceive the connection of all
her phenomena, the unity of design in which all her laws
converge. And in like manner the development of man's
powers of reflection must have rendered it evident that a
plurality of deities must mutually limit each other, and in
consequence deprive each other of the very attributes of
divinity, so that the deity, in the true and complete sense
of that word, could only be a unit. Insight of this kind, it
is argued, came to a few highly gifted individuals of antiquity, and these became in consequence the founders of monotheism.

1152

We know full well the highly gifted individuals who acquired insight in this manner: they were the Greek philosophers; but they became founders, not of religion, but of philosophical systems and schools. Of a like nature is the oscillating monotheism of the Indian religion: it is an esoteric, mystical doctrine, the presentiment of a few, developed from the popular polytheism.

Monotheism first occurs among the Jews in the firm serried form of a popular religion. And here also we can clearly apprehend its origin. Hebrew monotheism was certainly not produced by a deeper observation of nature; the Hebrews for a long while caring only for nature in its relation to their own wants. Neither did it arise from philosophical speculation; for before the impulse communicated to them by the Greeks, the Jews did not speculate, at least not in the philosophical sense. Monotheism (the fact becomes evident in that of the Jews, and is further confirmed by Islamism) is originally and essentially the religion of a wandering clan. The requirements of such a nomadic band are very simple, as are also its social arrangements; and although at first (as may also here be assumed to have been the primitive idea) these may have been presided over by distinct fetishes, dæmons, or deities, nevertheless this distinction disappeared in proportion as the horde concentrated itself (as did, for example, the Israelites in their invasion of Canaan) and receded more and more, as in course of warfare with hordes like themselves, or with tribes and nations of different institutions, the contrast to these latter gained prominence. As it was but a single enthusiasm which inspired the clan, which strengthened it in its conflict with others, gave it hope in victory, and even in defeat the trust in future triumph; even thus it was only one god whom it served, from whom it expected all things; or, rather even this god was, in fact, only its deified popular spirit. True, at first the gods of other tribes and nations were conceived as antagonistic to the one god of the clan—the gods of the Canaanites

1153

to the god of Israel; but as the weaker, the inferior, destined
to be overcome by the god of the clan—vain gods, who at
last must actually vanish into nothing, leaving the one true
God alone.

[343]

SWEDENBORG, EMANUEL

SWEDENBORG, EMANUEL (1688-1772). Emerson once remarked
that it would require "a colony of men" to do justice to Swedenborg's work. Goethe adopted several of Swedenborg's ideas. Balzac
founded essential views on human and cosmic nature on Swedenborg's doctrine. So have many modern authors. And today there are
thousands of faithful Swedenborgians in Europe and America.

Until his fifty-third year, Swedenborg had been known as a
great engineer, a scholar and a scientist. He had written important
books on mathematics, mechanics, physiology and astronomy. Then
he experienced a grave crisis. As a lad, he had already yearned to
know God and had eagerly discussed theological questions with
clergymen. In his advanced age he became more and more anxious
about his spiritual conditions. He was deeply impressed by dreams
in which he had visions. In 1757 he became convinced of having
witnessed in one of his visions the Last Judgment. In his *Arcana
Coelestia* (in 12 volumes, 1749-56) he offered a mystical interpretation of the first books of the Old Testament which, according
to him, was purposely written to prevent profanation, and by exposing their true meaning, he developed his own religious and
philosophical system.

Of fundamental importance to Swedenborg's system is his
doctrine of correspondence, which, as he asserts, was known to the
ancient peoples in Canaan, Chaldea, Syria and Egypt and since
had been forgotten. Greek travelers who visited these countries
misunderstood the doctrine and changed it into fabulous stories
which, however, allow a reconstruction of the true sense. According to this doctrine, everything in our visible, natural or material
world corresponds to something in the invisible, spiritual astral
world. The total natural world corresponds to the spiritual world
not only in general but in particular. Thus, everything in the natural world represents an idea.

Swedenborg distinguishes four styles in the world. The first,
the style of the most ancient mankind which extends until Noah and
the Flood, has been transcribed by Moses but has an offspring in

1154

the third style, the prophetic, while the second, the historic, extends from Abraham to the time of the kings of Judah and Israel. The fourth style, that of David's psalms, is mixed with the prophetic style and common speech. The restitution of the most ancient religion is Swedenborg's purpose. He claims to be sent by God to announce the end of the Christian and the beginning of the New Jerusalem dispensation. He recognizes Jesus Christ as Saviour but rejects the Christian doctrine of Trinity and excludes the Epistles of Paul from the Biblical Canon. God is one, both in essence and person. He is uncreated, eternal, infinite, omnipotent, the union of love and wisdom.

Related with the doctrine of correspondence is Swedenborg's doctrine of degrees. Man is a recipient of three degrees, and capable of thinking analytically and rationally of things within the sphere of nature, and of spiritual and celestial things above the natural sphere. At the highest degree, man may see God.

Swedenborg's behavior showed nothing eccentric. Apart from his visions, he was very practical and free from emotion. He was a strict vegetarian and admonished his disciples to refrain from eating meat. His modesty and simplicity won him many friends and admirers even among those who did not share his opinions.

ON HUMAN MIND

EVERY created thing is finite; and the Infinite is in finite things as in its receptacles, and is in men as in its images. Every created thing is finite because all things are from Jehovah God through the sun of the spiritual world, which most nearly encompasses Him; and that sun is composed of the substance that has gone forth from Him, the essence of which is love. From the sun, by means of its heat and light, the universe has been created from its firsts to its lasts. But this is not the proper place to set forth in order the process of creation. . . . All that is important now is to know that one thing was formed from another, and thus degrees were constituted, three in the spiritual world and three corresponding to them in the natural world, and the same number in the passive materials of which the terraqueous globe is composed. The origin and nature of these degrees has been fully explained in the *Angelic Wisdom concerning the Divine Love and the Divine Wisdom* (published at Amsterdam in 1763), and a small work on *The Intercourse of the Soul and the Body* (published at London in 1769). Through these degrees all things posterior are made receptacles of things prior, and these again of things still prior, and so on in succession receptacles of the primitive elements which constitute the sun of the angelic heaven; and thus have things finite been made receptacles of the infinite. This is in agreement with the wisdom of the ancients, according to which each thing and all things are divisible to infinity. It is a common idea that, because the finite cannot grasp the infinite, things finite cannot be receptacles of the infinite; but in what has been set forth in my works respecting creation it has been shown that God first rendered His infinity finite by means of substances emitted from Himself, from which His nearest surrounding sphere, which constitutes the sun of the spiritual world, came into existence; and that then through that sun He perfected the other surrounding spheres, even to the outmost, which consists of passive materials; and in this manner, by means of degrees, He rendered the world more and more finite. This much has been said to satisfy human reason, which never rests until it perceives a cause.

That the infinite Divine is in men as in its images is evident from the Word, where we read:—

And God said, Let us make man in Our image, after Our likeness. So God created man to His own image, into the image of God created He him (*Gen.* i. 26, 27).

From this it follows that man is an organic form recipient of God, and is an organic form that is in accordance with the kind of reception. The human mind, which makes man to be man, and in accordance with which man is man, is formed into three regions in accordance with the three degrees; in the first degree, in which also are the angels of the highest heaven, the mind is celestial; in the second degree, in which are the angels of the middle heaven, it is spiritual; and in the third degree, in which are the angels of the lowest heaven, it is natural. The human mind, organized in accordance with these three degrees, is a receptacle of Divine influx; nevertheless, the Divine flows into it no further than man prepares the way or opens the door. If man does this as far as to the highest or celestial degree he becomes truly an image of God, and after death an angel of the highest heaven; but if he prepares the way or opens the door only to the middle or spiritual degree, he becomes an image of God, but not in the same perfection; and after death he becomes an angel of the middle heaven. But if man prepares the way or opens the door only to the lowest or natural degree, in case he acknowledges God and worships Him with actual piety he becomes an image of God in the lowest degree, and after death an angel of the lowest heaven. But if man does not acknowledge God and does not worship Him with actual piety he puts off the image of God and becomes like some animal, except that he enjoys the faculty of understanding, and consequently of speech; and if he then closes up the highest natural degree, which corresponds to the highest celestial, he becomes as to his loves like a beast of the earth; and if he closes up the middle natural degree, which corresponds to the middle spiritual degree, he becomes in his love like a fox, and in his intellectual vision like a bird of night; while if he also closes up the lowest natural degree in its relation to his spiritual he becomes in his love like a wild beast, and in his understanding of truth like a fish.

[344]

T

TAGORE, RABINDRANATH

TAGORE, RABINDRANATH (1861-1941). Rabindranath Tagore, the greatest lyrical poet of modern India, also a successful dramatist and novelist, and a highly respected author of philosophical treatises, was the descendant of an old Brahman family. The great aim of his life was to revive the ideals of ancient India and at the same time to obtain a better understanding between East and West. His attitude was opposed to that of Gandhi, whose methods he held in contempt.

After studying law in England, Tagore managed his family's estate for seventeen years. In 1901 he founded his school, *Abode of Peace,* where pupils were educated in accordance with his principles. When he came to England in 1911, where his poems *Gitanjali* (Song of Offerings) were published in an English version prepared by the author, he was enthusiastically received, and his fame spread over Europe and America. He was the first Asian to receive, in 1913, the Nobel Prize. In 1915, he was knighted. After the massacre of Amritsar he intended to renounce his knightship in order to protest against the British administration of India but instead consented to a compromise.

Tagore's poems have been translated into many languages, and the music of his diction remained charming and strong in most of the versions. The harmonious balance of his personality, which found expression in his writings, never failed to impress everyone he met. His ethics did not tolerate morals of expediency or sanction of means according to their ends. Always ready to protest against injustice and persecution, he was a staunch adversary of German nationalism and Hitler's regime. His philosophy is based on the belief in the progressive realization of the divine in man, and it shows little interest in celestial destiny. He insists that man's perfection shall come in the world in which he is living.

LOVE AS THE FULFILLMENT OF LIFE

ONE DAY I was out in a boat on the Ganges. It was a beautiful evening in autumn. The sun had just set; the silence of the sky was full to the brim with ineffable peace and beauty. The vast expanse of water was without a ripple, mirroring all the changing shades of the sunset glow. Miles and miles of a desolate sandbank lay like a huge amphibious reptile of some antediluvian age, with its scales glistening in shining colours. As our boat was silently gliding by the precipitous river-bank, riddled with the nest-holes of a colony of birds, suddenly a big fish leapt up to the surface of the water and then disappeared, displaying on its vanishing figure all the colours of the evening sky. It drew aside for a moment the many-coloured screen behind which there was a silent world full of the joy of life. It came up from the depths of its mysterious dwelling with a beautiful dancing motion and added its own music to the silent symphony of the dying day. I felt as if I had a friendly greeting from an alien world in its own language, and it touched my heart with a flash of gladness. Then suddenly the man at the helm exclaimed with a distinct note of regret, "Ah, what a big fish!" It at once brought before his vision the picture of the fish caught and made ready for his supper. He could only look at the fish through his desire, and thus missed the whole truth of its existence. But man is not entirely an animal. He aspires to a spiritual vision, which is the vision of the whole truth. This gives him the highest delight, because it reveals to him the deepest harmony that exists between him and his surroundings. It is our desires that limit the scope of our self-realisation, hinder our extension of consciousness, and give rise to sin, which is the innermost barrier that keeps us apart from our God, setting up disunion and the arrogance of exclusiveness. For sin is not one mere action, but it is an attitude of life which takes for granted that our goal is finite, that our self is the ultimate truth,

1159

and that we are not all essentially one but exist each for his own separate individual existence.

So I repeat we never can have a true view of man unless we have a love for him. Civilisation must be judged and prized, not by the amount of power it has developed, but by how much it has evolved and given expression to, by its laws and institutions, the love of humanity. The first question and the last which it has to answer is, Whether and how far it recognises man more as a spirit than as a machine? Whenever some ancient civilisation fell into decay and died, it was owing to causes which produced callousness of heart and led to the cheapening of man's worth; when either the state or some powerful group of men began to look upon the people as a mere instrument of their power; when, by compelling weaker races to slavery and trying to keep them down by every means, man struck at the foundation of his greatness, his own love of freedom and fairplay. Civilisation can never sustain itself upon cannibalism of any form. For that by which alone man is true can only be nourished by love and justice.

As with man, so with this universe. When we look at the world through the veil of our desires we make it small and narrow, and fail to perceive its full truth. Of course it is obvious that the world serves us and fulfills our needs, but our relation to it does not end there. We are bound to it with a deeper and truer bond than that of necessity. Our soul is drawn to it. [345]

TELESIO, BERNARDINO

TELESIO, BERNARDINO (1508-1588). By his refusal to be nominated Archbishop by Pope Paul IV, Telesio renounced a brilliant ecclesiastical career in order to devote his life to independent thought and the study of the sciences. He did not break with the Church, but became one of the initiators of the scientific movement which, though not identical with it, resulted from the spirit of the Renaissance.

Telesio accepted the traditional division of psychic life into vegetative, sensitive and intellectual spheres, and he followed the tradition by insisting upon the fundamental difference between the human soul, created by and endowed with the divine spirit, and the animal soul, which is considered a natural formation. But these traditional views allowed him to state numerous physiological and psychical qualities which are common to both man and animals, and to observe that man's psychic life is not sufficiently characterized by the divine origin of his soul but that its description must be completed by a purely empirical study which shows the part played by the animal character in him.

Knowledge is founded, according to Telesio, upon sensation and memory. Essential as sensual perception is considered, an at least equal importance is attributed to the memory of perceiving. Without memory, Telesio said, no formation of thought is possible. While adumbrating a doctrine of psychic atomism, Telesio anticipated both the sensualism and the associationism of later centuries. He also tried to establish the compatibility of psychic and physical motions, as well as relations between time and motion. Physical facts were reduced to contraction and expansion, which are caused by heat and cold.

In his later years, Telesio founded and directed his own academy, the *Academia Telesiana* at Naples, which became instrumental to the propagation and growth of the scientific spirit in Galileo's epoch.

MAN HAS A DIVINE SOUL

BE it permitted to mention that even though the spirit in animals drawn from the sperms shall be considered the substance of the soul, it does not follow that one shall also take this spirit as the substance of the soul of man, because not only the Holy Script but even human reasons convince us that in man dwells another entirely divine substance placed here by God himself. We recognize in man, namely, actions, sufferings and strivings quite distinct from animals, which must be ascribed to a higher substance than the spirit drawn from the sperms; for man is not satisfied, as the rest of the animals are, with sensation, cognitions and enjoyments of the things that feed, conserve and please him, but he also investigates with greatest zeal the substance and effects of such things as are of no use to him and cannot even be conceived by any sense, especially those concerning the di-

1161

vine essence and divinity. Nay, he even forgets, disdains
and neglects, while persistently and blissfully contemplating them, even that which pertains to the well-being and
enjoyment of his body. Entirely in opposition to the other
animals, which are satisfied with the goods that maintain
them and make them sufficiently happy and neither desire
nor ask for anything beyond that man alone finds no satisfaction in the present goods, whatever they might be, but
shows by his outlook on the future, his longing for the remote and the prediction of a still happier life that there is
a substance, a spirit in him that tends anxiously toward his
Creator and Father (God) as toward his highest and proper
good, and, being deprived of the intuition of it, he cannot
be enticed by anything to such a degree that he could forget
it or would not crave it. Finally, the intellect of man considers evil men, even if he sees them in highest abundance
and happiness, as contemptible and pitiful, but he likes,
honors and considers happy the good ones. This proves too
that here is in man a divine sense that is a divine substance
and nature.

[346]

TEMPLE, WILLIAM

TEMPLE, WILLIAM (1881-1944). When William Temple, who had
been Archbishop of York since 1929, became in 1942, Archbishop
of Canterbury and in this way succeeded his father, Frederick
Temple, the event was considered unheard of in the history of
the English Church. But even greater astonishment was caused by
the fact that the new Archbishop, the highest ecclesiastical dignitary of the British kingdom, was an avowed student of Karl Marx.
Temple had had a thorough classical education, combined with
training in logic, ethics, metaphysics and the history of philosophy.
His tutor, Edward Caird, had initiated him in the philosophy of
Plato and Hegel, but he also read with admiration Aristotle and
Aquinas, and finally two such different thinkers as Bergson and
Marx induced him to break with traditional idealism and to adopt
a kind of dialectical realism. He adopted Marxian dialectics and
subscribed to many points of the socialist program, especially those

1162

concerning public ownership; but the most radical realization of socialist ideas seemed to him insufficient for the thorough reform of human conditions. He remained convinced that only Christian faith can fulfil this task and that Christianity is necessary for the completion of human thought and life, as well as for the cultural progress in which he firmly believed.

While in philosophy Temple turned from idealism to realism, in theology he turned from liberalism to orthodoxy. But just as he could say that, while being a liberal, he never for a moment had doubted the divinity of Christ, Temple, while an orthodox theologian, retained a liberal and tolerant attitude in questions of religious convictions. He defended discussion and believed in democracy, vital need for which is discussion. Temple never faced doubt as a personal problem. He was as happy as he was pious, and as simple and good-humored as he was dignified. The energetic manner in which he insisted on the close connection between faith and life revealed his judgment on mystical religion. Temple would not deny that the mystical experience might be the purest and intensest of all religious experiences. But just for the reason that it claims to be the most detached from nonreligious interests, he held that it is the least representative and least important of all religious forms. He declared that any philosophy that arrives at theism arrives at the study of the real world which is created and explained by God.

THE PROBLEM OF EVIL

THE problem of evil is always a problem in terms of purpose. No one is much interested in finding out how it came here, as a matter of historical fact; that does not much matter. The problem is, what is it doing here? What is it for? Why does God permit it? Or, if God is omnipotent, in which case permission and creation are the same, why did God create it? While we are sitting at our ease it generally seems to us that the world would be very much better if all evil were abolished, and indeed had never existed. But would it? Which are our own best days,—the days when we have nothing to perplex us, or trouble us? or the days when, at considerable cost to ourselves, we have made some real effort against the evil which afflicted either ourselves or other people? Surely the latter. Surely we know that one of the

best of the good things in life is victory and particularly
moral victory. But to demand victory without an antagonist
is to demand something with no meaning. If, then, goodness
is to exist up to the limit of what even we can understand,
there must at least be an antagonist to be overcome. If you
take all the evil out of the world you will remove the possibility of the best thing in life. That does not mean that evil
is good. What one means by calling a thing good is that the
spirit rests permanently content with it for its own sake. Evil
is precisely that with which no spirit can rest content; and
yet it is the condition, not the accidental but the essential
condition, of what is in and for itself the best thing in life,
namely moral victory.

[347]

TERTULLIAN

TERTULLIAN (About 165-220). At the age of forty, Tertullian,
the son of a Roman army officer, was converted to Christianity and
became its most ardent apologist. Living during the reigns of emperors Septimius Severus and Caracalla, he courageously protested
against the cruelties committed by the magistrates and against the
excesses of the mob against Christians, but he was equally prepared to recommend violence against any adversary of his new co-
religionists in case persuasion did not help. His works, of which,
besides the *Apology*, thirty-three are extant, exhibit fervor, zeal-
otism, knowledge of his times and of past history, and an extremely
aggressive spirit. Tertullian was untiring in expressing his contempt
of pagan philosophers. To him faith was above reason, and logical
contradiction a means to refutation of creed. His saying *Credo
quia absurdum est,* however, is often quoted in a sense which its
author did not mean. For twenty years, Tertullian intervened in
every controversy concerning Christian doctrine. He introduced, in
his book *Adversus Praxean,* the term *Trinitas* into the Latin language in order to signify the one God in three persons, although
he did not live to see the dogma of the Trinity firmly established.
With uncompromising rigor he fought aggressively against Jews,
pagans, heretics and secular authorities. He eagerly objected to
second marriages and branded Christians who held offices in the
imperial administration or did military service. Further, he could

not tolerate Christian artists. However in his last years, Tertullian. with ascetic leanings adhering to the sect of Montanists, became himself a heretic.

THE PARTS OF THE SOUL

THAT position of Plato's is quite in keeping with the faith, in which he divides the soul into two parts—the rational and the irrational. To this definition we take no exception, except that we would not ascribe this twofold distinction to the nature (of the soul). It is the rational element which we must believe to be its natural condition, impressed upon it from its very first creation by its Author, who is Himself essentially rational. For how should that be other than rational, which God produced on His own prompting; nay more, which He expressly sent forth by His own *afflatus* or breath? The irrational element, however, we must understand to have accrued later, as having proceeded from the instigation of the serpent—the very achievement of (the first) transgression—which thenceforward became inherent in the soul, and grew with its growth, assuming the manner by this time of a natural development, happening as it did immediately at the beginning of nature. But, inasmuch as the same Plato speaks of the rational element only as existing in the soul of God Himself, if we were to ascribe the irrational element likewise to the nature which our soul has received from God, then the irrational element will be equally derived from God, as being a natural production, because God is the author of nature. Now from the devil proceeds the incentive to sin. All sin, however, is irrational: therefore the irrational proceeds from the devil, from whom sin proceeds; and it is extraneous to God, to whom also the irrational is an alien principle. The diversity, then, between these two elements arises from the difference of their authors. When, therefore, Plato reserves the rational element (of the soul) to God alone, and subdivides it into two departments the *irascible*, which they call *tymikon*, and the *concupiscible*, which they designate by the term *epitymetikon* (in such a way as to make the first common to us and lions, and the second shared between ourselves and flies, whilst the rational element is confined to us and God)—I see that this point will have to be treated by us, owing to the facts which we find operating also in Christ. For you may behold this triad of qualities in the Lord. There was the *rational* element, by which He taught, by which He discoursed, by which He prepared the way of salvation; there was moreover *indignation* in Him, by which He inveighed against the scribes and the Pharisees; and there was the principle of *desire*, by which He so earnestly desired to eat the passover with His disciples. In our own cases, accordingly, the irascible and the concupiscible elements of our soul must not invariably be put to the account of the irrational (nature), since we are sure that in our Lord these elements operated in entire accordance with reason. God will be angry, with perfect reason, with all who deserve His wrath; and with reason, too, will God desire whatever objects and claims are worthy of Himself. For He will show indignation against the evil man, and for the good man will He desire salvation. To ourselves even does the apostle allow the concupiscible quality. "If any man," says he, "desireth the office of a bishop, he desireth a good work." Now, by saying "a good work," he shows us that the desire is a reasonable one. He permits us likewise to feel indignation. How should he not, when he himself experiences the same? "I would," says he, "that they were even cut off which trouble you." In perfect agreement with reason was that indignation which resulted from his desire to maintain discipline and order. When, however, he says, "We were formerly the children of wrath," he censures an irrational irascibility, such as proceeds not from that nature which is the production of God, but from that which the devil brought in, who is himself styled the lord or "master" of his own class, "Ye cannot serve *two masters*," and has the actual designation of "father:" "Ye are of your *father* the devil." So that you need not be afraid to ascribe to him the mastery and dominion over that second, later, and deteriorated nature (of which we have been speaking), when you read of him as "the sower of tares," and the nocturnal spoiler of the crop of corn.

[348]

THALES

THALES (About 625-545 B.C.). The earliest philosophical school in the history of Western civilization was founded by Thales, a citizen of Miletus in Asia Minor. Although he is unanimously recognized as the initiator of Greek philosophy, he was not of Greek origin but descended from a Semitic (Carian) family, and he owed much of his scientific and technical knowledge to Babylonian and Egyptian influences.

Thales took the initiative in Greek philosophical thinking with his conception of the existing world as the transformation of a single cosmic matter, declaring that water was the fundamental substance and source of all living beings. Although this special hypothesis did not satisfy his successors, his way of distinguishing between the apparent nature and a reality which becomes comprehensible through the unifying and relating functions of reason was of lasting consequence and continued to inspire Greek thinkers.

The whole Græco-Roman antiquity revered Thales as one of the "Seven Sages." He became famous because of his many important inventions and discoveries in the fields of astronomy, geometry, meteorology and navigation, and above all because he predicted the solar eclipse which took place on May 28, 585 B.C., while a great battle was raging between the Lydian and Median armies. He was also a clever businessman who made a fortune by monopolizing the olive trade in years of shortage, which he had foreseen. Thales taught in the Greek language but wrote no books.

FRAGMENTS

THALES was the first person who affirmed that the souls of men were immortal; and he was the first person, too, who discovered the path of the sun from one end of the ecliptic to the other; and who, as one account tells us, defined the magnitude of the sun as being seven hundred and twenty times as great as that of the moon. He was also the first person who called the last day of the month the thirtieth.

And likewise the first to converse about natural philosophy, as some say. But Aristotle and Hippias say that he attributed souls also to lifeless things, forming his conjecture from the nature of the magnet, and of amber.

He asserted water to be the principle of all things, and that the world had life, and was full of demons; they say, too, that he was the original definer of the seasons of the year, and that it was he who divided the year into three hundred and sixty-five days. And he never had any teacher except during the time that he went to Egypt, and associated with the priests. Hieronymus also says that he measured the Pyramids: watching their shadow, and calculating when they were of the same size as that was. He lived with Thrasybulus the tyrant of Miletus, as we are informed by Minyas.

These are quoted as some of his lines:

It is not many words that real wisdom proves;
    Breathe rather one wise thought,
    Select one worthy object,
So shall you best the endless prate of silly men reprove.
And the following are quoted as sayings of his:—"God is the most ancient of all things, for he had no birth: the world is the most beautiful of things, for it is the work of God; place is the greatest of things, for it contains all things: intellect is the swiftest of things, for it runs through everything, necessity is the strongest of things, for it rules everything: time is the wisest of things, for it finds out everything."

He said also that there was no difference between life and death. "Why, then," said some one to him, "do not you die?" "Because," said he, "it does make no difference." A man asked him which was made first, night or day, and he replied, "Night was made first by one day." Another man asked him whether a man who did wrong, could escape the notice of the gods. "No, not even if he thinks wrong," said he. An adulterer inquired of him whether he should swear that he had not committed adultery. "Perjury," said he, "is no worse than adultery." When he was asked what was very difficult, he said, "To know one's self." And what was easy,

"To advise another." What was most pleasant? "To be successful." To the question, "What is the divinity?" he replied, "That which has neither beginning nor end." When asked what hard thing he had seen, he said, "An old man a tyrant." When the question was put to him how a man might most easily endure misfortune, he said, "If he saw his enemies more unfortunate still." When asked how men might live most virtuously and most justly, he said, "If we never do ourselves what we blame in others." To the question, "Who was happy?" he made answer, "He who is healthy in his body, easy in his circumstances, and well-instructed as to his mind." He said that men ought to remember those friends who were absent as well as those who were present, and not to care about adorning their faces, but to be beautified by their studies. "Do not," said he, "get rich by evil actions, and let not any one ever be able to reproach you with speaking against those who partake of your friendship. All the assistance you give to your parents, the same you have a right to expect from your children." He said that the reason of the Nile overflowing was that its streams were beaten back by the Etesian winds blowing in a contrary direction.

[349]

THOREAU, HENRY DAVID

THOREAU, HENRY DAVID (1817-1862). Thoreau was not satisfied merely to entertain an opinion and to enjoy it; he was resolved to live it. For himself and for any individual he claimed the right of revolution against bad government, and he regarded the authority of good government still an impure one, defended civil disobedience, and refused to pay taxes after facing and suffering imprisonment. "Under a government," Thoreau wrote, "which imprisons any unjustly, the true place for a just man is also a prison." The spirit of revolt, the impulse to isolation, the ideal to live alone with thought, nature and God, as well as practical considerations, caused him to retreat to Walden Pond (1845-46) where he contemplated nature and meditated upon it.

Thoreau was a scholar and poet, an eccentric and a shrewd

realist. His *Walden* (1854), the work of a great naturalist and an even greater poet of nature, has been translated into many languages.

"To be a philosopher," says Thoreau, "is not merely to have subtle thought, or even to found a school but so to love wisdom as to live, according to its dictates, a life of simplicity, independence, magnanimity and trust." No serene sage, Thoreau's ferocity often disturbed his most faithful friends, and estranged from him Emerson with whom he had been, for a time, closely associated. His temperament committed him to action, his faith to contemplation. Until 1850, Thoreau was an enthusiast of community life. Thereafter he became a staunch opponent of popular movements.

The essential life meant to him life in nature. To him, the burden of the civilization of his age was not caused by mere defects in industrial organization and distribution, but rather by the domination of industry itself over human interests. Against a cultural evolution which he condemned as resulting in the neglect of human values, Thoreau was resolved to live his own time by his own terms.

HIGHER LAWS

OUR whole life is startlingly moral. There is never an instant's truce between virtue and vice. Goodness is the only investment that never fails. In the music of the harp which trembles round the world it is the insisting on this which thrills us. The harp is the traveling patterer for the Universe's Insurance Company, recommending its laws, and our little goodness is all the assessment that we can pay. Though the youth at last grows indifferent, the laws of the universe are not indifferent, but are forever on the side of the most sensitive. Listen to every zephyr for some reproof, for it is surely there, and he is unfortunate who does not hear it. We cannot touch a string or move a stop but the charming moral transfixes us. Many an irksome noise, go a long way off, is heard as music, a proud sweet satire on the meanness of our lives.

We are conscious of an animal in us, which awakens in proportion as our higher nature slumbers. It is reptile and sensual, and perhaps cannot be wholly expelled; like the worms which, even in life and health, occupy our bodies. Possibly we may withdraw from it, but never change its nature. I fear that it may enjoy a certain health of its own; that we may be well, yet not pure. The other day I picked up the lower jaw of a hog, with white and sound teeth and tusks, which suggested that there was an animal health and vigor distinct from the spiritual. This creature succeeded by other means than temperance and purity. "That in which men differ from brute beasts," says Mencius, "is a thing very inconsiderable; the common herd lose it very soon; superior men preserve it carefully." Who knows what sort of life would result if we had attained to purity? If I knew so wise a man as could teach me purity I would go to seek him forthwith. "A command over our passions, and over the external senses of the body, and good acts, are declared by the Veda to be indispensable in the mind's approximation to God." Yet the spirit can for a time pervade and control every member and function of the body, and transmute what in form is the grossest sensuality into purity and devotion. The generative energy, which, when we are loose, dissipates and makes us unclean, when we are continent invigorates and inspires us. Chastity is the flowering of man; and what are called genius, heroism, holiness, and the like, are but various fruits which succeed it. Man flows at once to God when the channel of purity is open. By turns our purity inspires and our impurity casts us down. He is blessed who is assured that the animal is dying out in him day by day, and the divine being established. Perhaps there is none but has cause for shame on account of the inferior and brutish nature to which he is allied. I fear that we are such gods or demigods only as fauns and satyrs, the divine allied to beasts, the creatures of appetite, and that, to some extent, our very life is our disgrace—

"How happy's he who hath due place assigned
To his beasts and disafforested his mind! . . .
Can use his horse, goat, wolf, and ev'ry beast,
And is not ass himself to all the rest!

1171

Else man not only is the herd of swine,
But he's those devils too which did incline
Them to headlong rage and made them worse."

All sensuality is one, though it takes many forms; all purity is one. It is the same whether a man eat, or drink, or cohabit, or sleep sensually. They are but one appetite, and we only need to see a person do any one of these things to know how great a sensualist he is. The impure can neither stand nor sit with purity. When the reptile is attacked at one mouth of his burrow, he shows himself at another. If you would be chaste, you must be temperate. What is chastity? How shall a man know if he is chaste? He shall not know it. We have heard of this virtue, but we know not what it is. We speak conformably to the rumor which we have heard. From exertion come wisdom and purity; from sloth ignorance and sensuality. In the student sensuality is a sluggish habit of mind. An unclean person is universally a slothful one, one who sits by a stove, whom the sun shines on prostrate, who reposes without being fatigued. If you would avoid uncleanness, and all the sins, work earnestly, though it be at cleaning a stable. Nature is hard to be overcome, but she must be overcome. What avails that you are Christian, if you are not purer than the heathen, if you deny yourself no more, if you are not more religious? I know of many systems of religion esteemed heathenish whose precepts fill the reader with shame, and provoke him to new endeavors, though it be to the performance of rites merely.

I hesitate to say these things, but it is not because of the subject,—I care not how obscene my *words* are,—but because I cannot speak of them without betraying my impurity. We discourse freely without shame of one form of sensuality, and are silent about another. We are so degraded that we cannot speak simply of the necessary functions of human nature. In earlier ages, in some countries, every function was reverently spoken of and regulated by law. Nothing was too trivial for the Hindoo lawgiver, however offensive it may be to modern taste. He teaches how to eat, drink, cohabit, void excrement and urine, and the like, elevating what is mean and does not falsely excuse himself by calling these things trifles.

Every man is the builder of a temple, called his body, to the god he worships, after a style purely his own, nor can he get off by hammering marble instead. We are all sculptors and painters, and our material is our own flesh and blood and bones. Any nobleness begins at once to refine a man's features, any meanness or sensuality to imbrute them.

[350]

TOLSTOY, LEO

TOLSTOY, LEO (1828-1910). In *Resurrection* (1899), the third of Tolstoy's great novels, the author summarized the experiences of his life by asserting his conviction that in every human being a spiritual and altruistic principle is working against an animal and egoistic one "which is ready to sacrifice the well-being of the whole world to one's own comfort." The defeat of the animal in man by the spirit, which was identified by Tolstoy with conscience, is the underlying principle in all Tolstoy's works, as well as the aim of his life. The antagonism between spirit and animal is the standard of valuing which Tolstoy applied to modern humanity and civilization, and he has not concealed that he himself could not stand its test. Tolstoy was a rigorous moralist but he far from simplified the things his moral judgment condemned. His art penetrated into the inner secrets of a society and of persons despised by him. He knew what was important to an officer of the imperial bodyguard, what troubled the nerves of a lady of fashion, what lured the ambition of an official, and he showed the vanity of their hopes and apprehensions with such a power that the outstanding critics of all civilized nations agree with William Dean Howells who said that "Tolstoy's imagination leaves all tricks of fancy, all effects of art immeasurably behind."

Yet it was Tolstoy's moralism that turned against his own art. Though in his youth he had been very fond of the power of literary imagination, in his later years he rejected every kind of power, not the least of which being the power of art. He had conquered the world with his novel *War and Peace* (1869), and he seemed to have secured this conquest by his novel *Anna Karenina* (1877). But in

1173

My Confession (1882) he declared: "When I had ended *Anna Karenina* my despair reached such a height that I could do nothing but think of the horrible condition in which I found myself. I saw only one thing, Death. Everything else was a lie."

Tolstoy saw only one way out of his crisis, namely the strict obeyance to the Sermon on the Mount which, according to him, involves social repentance, religious purification, radical opposition to the interests and institutions of the world, rejection of property, power, war, oath and political statutes. He fought the Church because, while ruling the world, it was dominated by the world. He revered Christ but did not look back to the events narrated in the New Testament. He was looking forward, expecting the coming kingdom of God and the end of the rule of earthly power.

Every philosophy was to Tolstoy an evil in so far as it tried to form a system, an artificial order of thoughts. But he was interested in the efforts of some philosophers—especially Descartes, Leibniz, Rousseau, Kant, Schopenhauer and African Spir—to deal with the power of evil or to know God, although he protested that no philosopher had given more than a vague idea of God. Tolstoy himself conceived of God not as a person in the proper sense of the word but rather through man's relations to God as comparable with personal loyalty, and the feeling of God as the source of love and moral law. He regarded the uneducated, poor, enslaved Russian peasant as the most reliable guide to the way to God and as the true representative of humanity.

CHURCH AND HERESY

In the Gospels the word "Church" is used twice. Once in the sense of an assembly of men to settle a dispute, and again in connection with the obscure utterance about the rock, Peter and the gates of hell. From these two mentions of the word "Church" (means merely an assembly) what is now meant by the word "Church," has been deduced.

But Christ could certainly not have established the Church, that is, the institution we now call by that name, for nothing resembling our present conception of the Church—with its sacraments, its hierarchy, and especially its claim to infallibility—is to be found either in Christ's words or in the conception of the men of his time.

The fact that people called an institution established

later by a name Christ has used to designate something quite different, in no way gives them the right to assert that Jesus founded "the one true Church." Besides, had Christ really founded such an institution as the Church for the basis of our entire faith and doctrine, he would probably have announced this institution clearly and definitely . . . and would have given this one true Church unmistakable tokens of genuineness. . . . The conception of one holy Church only arose from the quarrels and strife of two parties, each of which, denouncing the other as a heresy, claimed to be the one infallible Church. . . .

Heresy is the obverse side of the Church. Wherever the Church exists, there must be the conception of heresy. A Church is a body of men who assert that they are the possessors of infallible truth. Heresy is the opinion of people who do not admit the indubitability of the Church's truth. . . .

Whatever stage of comprehension and perfection a follower of Christ may reach, he always feels the inadequacy of his conception and of his fulfilment of Christ's teaching, and always strives towards an increase of both. Therefore a claim by any individual or society to be in possession of a perfect understanding and a complete fulfilment of Christ's teaching is to renounce the spirit of Christ's teaching.

[351]

TUFTS, JAMES HAYDEN

TUFTS, JAMES HAYDEN (1862-1942). After having hesitated between mathematics and philosophy, Tufts concentrated upon studies in the history of philosophy but turned to ethics because he considered changes in moral values and concepts to be of even more significance than changes in science and knowledge. However, his ethical research was not limited to the reading of books. As a professor at the then newly founded Chicago University, Tufts was also a member of the Board of Arbitration, and the chairman of a committee of the social agencies of Chicago; through these affiliations he acquired insight into economic and social struggles which inspired his thinking about the questions of justice, responsibility, rights of the underdog, conflicts of relatively justified claims and other moral problems quite as much as through his studies in the history of ethical principles. In *Ethics* (in collaboration with John Dewey, 1917), Tufts grouped the various factors of moral changes under the captions of "psychological" and "sociological" agencies. According to him, moral ideas are shaped under the influence of religious, social and economic forces but that they do not remain objects of pure contemplation; they themselves become patterns of action, and thereby modify the state of mind of men involved in social, political and economic struggles. This conception of mutual influences is opposed to both Marxism and idealism. The most urgent task of ethical analysis in the present time was defined by Tufts as the endeavor not to conceive an image of a perfect state of society but to watch the forces which are at work and challenge the habitual concepts of political democracy, capitalism, religious and social institutions. From this point of view Tufts dealt with *America's Social Morality* (1933).

DEMOCRACY AT TRIAL

WHETHER democracies in Europe and the Americas are to be permitted to retain any of the progress gained in freedom, welfare, equality, and peace seems likely to be decided, not by reason but by arms. But in the faith that right makes might we may at least consider what internal policies and course of action will tend to safeguard from destruction not only our way of life but also what we have come to hold as right and good.

As regards our institutions and organizations, how can we be safe from the rise of despotic power? The outstanding lessons from Communism and National Socialism would seem to be the danger of concentration of all power in a single organization as contrasted with such pluralism, or division of power, as is found, for instance, in Scandinavian countries and the United States. Power is a necessary instrument of civilization. The preservation and advancement of moral ideals need the support of collective agencies as do trade, industry, and the administration of justice. But power, either over natural forces or over actions and minds of men is now seen to be, if possible, more dangerous than ever, to freedom and to life itself. History has seen various attempts to resist oppressive power, but effective restraint of power wielded by collective organization has usually been secured only by the collective strength of some other organization. Both Communism and National Socialism are totalitarian states. They are systems of absolute power. They permit no counter-balancing or restraining agency. No opposition may organize. Secret police are vigilant to prevent even the beginnings of questioning. Neither organized wealth nor organized labor is allowed to influence. No opposition party appears at the polls.

In the free democracies, on the contrary, are numerous collective agencies, not only for manifold educational, philanthropic, recreational, and social purposes, but for representing interests or groups of those who wish to influence or even to oppose government. In the United States there are a chamber of commerce, a manufacturers' association, two labor unions, a farm group, various religious groups, scientific and educational associations. All these inform or shape public opinion, secure or oppose legislation, influence national policies. At times, indeed, it has been charged that organized wealth was writing tariffs or controlling the press, or that organized labor was carrying elections. And at times government has seemed to be unable to act promptly in emergencies because of the numerous checks and balances provided by the cautious founders. Yet, on the whole, we have both kept our freedom and advanced justice. In the light of what totalitarian governments are doing we may well think that we have built better than we knew in encouraging such a variety of organized groups. Pluralism seems safer than totalitarianism.

Yet pluralism is no sure reliance for maintenance of rights or for ensuring advance in moral ideals or moral standards. It affords agencies through which the spirit may act, but if the spirit is dead or lacking, the agencies are dead likewise. The spirit which must preserve moral gains is the same spirit which has won them; it lives only as it grows. Life for institutional as for individual morality must combine stability with change. Reverence for what we hold right, just, and good, must be matched with open-minded sensitiveness to new claims by or for those who hitherto have had small share in the vast increase in goods provided by science, invention, and mass production. Moral dilemmas are experienced when older morals and institutions fail as yet to meet new situations. Hard resistance to just changes provokes either violence or despair or apathy. Certain forces of the day, notably the power of mass—in industry, in business, in social and political pressure groups, in subtler forms of propaganda—make for disintegration of older moral structures. Family and religious influence has suffered. On the other hand, in the present century we have made fairly steady progress in protection against disease, ignorance, hunger, industrial accidents, excessive hours of labor in factories, waste of natural resources. We have made provision for old age, have given legal standing to collective bargaining, and have recognized the plight of the farmer caught between low prices for his products and high prices for what he must buy. We have not yet learned how to prevent business depressions, but we have at least come to see that the moral injury of prolonged unemployment for workmen and of closed opportunity for youth is a more serious and difficult problem than that of bodily hunger. It is hard to believe that the enormous advances in means of communication through transport, electricity, and radio will not ultimately lower older barriers between peoples and make for better international understanding.

But there is no prospect of Utopia, either for individuals or for peoples. Moral life will continue to need alertness, courage, faith in the good cause, and at times sacrifice. A new invention like the airplane may place at the disposal of ruthless force a terrible weapon; a new idea like that of *Lebensraum* may touch off with explosive violence a new train; an economics of force may change the problem of just distribution. What we may hope for, if the present threat to all our rights and values can be met, is the opportunity to work out further the promise of free American life.

[352]

TYNDALL, JOHN

TYNDALL, JOHN (1820-1893). There are scientists who occupy themselves with the facts of their research without ever asking what implications they may be effecting. There are other scientists who keep science and religion separate and remain untroubled by any incongruity between them. Tyndall did not belong to either of these groups. Always he was conscious that every scientific inquiry, pursued to the end, must leave him face to face with metaphysics or religion. Always he felt himself obliged to become aware of the consequences of his scientific work, and to express them publicly, all the more so since he liked to combine daring research work in unknown fields and pioneering in many branches of science with the dissemination of knowledge by popular writings and lectures. As a result, he was brilliantly successful in popularizing science. Tyndall made highly important contributions to molecular physics, to the knowledge of magnetism, electricity, theory of heat, optics and acoustics, and he promoted bacteriology by his method of sterilizing liquids. His achievements were greatly respected by Pasteur, Maxwell, Lister, Kelvin and his intimate friend Thomas Henry Huxley; and Herbert Spencer especially praised him because of his "scientific use of imagination." It is the combination of enthusiasm and reason, rightly characterized by Spencer, that is significant of Tyndall's mind. To him, man is not mere intellect; he cannot be satisfied with the products of understanding alone. Tyndall held that the scientist, too, is a man. He protested: "Believing in continuity of nature, I cannot stop abruptly where our miscroscope ceases to be of use." But he spoke of himself when he defined the calling of a scientist as a continued exercise of realization and self-correction. His endeavor was to draw a sharp line to mark the boundary where, in his view, science ends and speculation begins. Although he refuted the claims of theologians, Tyndall was not at war with religion. But he was devoted to humanitarian ideals, and strongly opposed to any kind of injustice and oppression.

1179

THE POSITION OF SCIENCE

THE doctrine of evolution derives man, in his totality, from the interaction of organism and environment through count-less ages past. The human understanding, for example—that faculty which Mr. Spencer has turned so skilfully round upon its own antecedents—is itself a result of the play between organism and environment through cosmic ranges of time. Never, surely, did prescription plead so irresistible a claim. But then it comes to pass that, over and above his understanding, there are many other things appertaining to man whose prescriptive rights are quite as strong as those of the understanding itself. It is a result, for example, of the play of organism and environment that sugar is sweet, and that aloes are bitter; that the smell of henbane differs from the perfume of a rose. Such facts of consciousness (for which, by the way, no adequate reason has ever been rendered) are quite as old as the understanding; and many other things can boast an equally ancient origin. Mr. Spencer at one place refers to that most powerful of passions—the amatory passion—as one which, when it first occurs, is antecedent to all relative experience whatever; and we may press its claim as being at least as ancient, and as valid, as that of the understanding itself. Then there are such things woven into the texture of man as the feeling of awe, reverence, wonder—and not alone the sexual love just referred to, but the love of the beautiful, physical, and moral, in nature, poetry, and art. There is also that deep-set feeling, which, since the earliest dawn of history, and probably for ages prior to all history, incorporated itself in the religions of the world. You, who have escaped from these religions into the high-and-dry light of the intellect, may deride them; but in so doing you deride accidents of form merely, and fail to touch the immovable basis of the religious sentiment in the nature of man. To yield this sentiment reasonable satisfaction is the problem of problems at the present hour.

And grotesque in relation to scientific culture as many of the religions of the world have been and are—dangerous, nay, destructive, to the dearest privileges of freemen as some of them undoubtedly have been, and would, if they could, be again—it will be wise to recognize them as the forms of a force, mischievous if permitted to intrude on the region of objective *knowledge*, over which it holds no command, but capable of adding, in the region of *poetry* and *emotion*, inward completeness and dignity to man.

Feeling, I say again, dates from as old an origin and as high a source as intelligence, and it equally demands its range of play. The wise teacher of humanity will recognize the necessity of meeting this demand, rather than of resisting it on account of errors and absurdities of form. What we should resist, at all hazards, is the attempt made in the past, and now repeated, to found upon this elemental bias of man's nature a system which should exercise despotic sway over his intellect. I have no fear of such a consummation. Science has already to some extent leavened the world; it will leaven it more and more. I should look upon the mild light of science breaking in upon the minds of the youth of Ireland, and strengthening gradually to the perfect day, as a surer check to any intellectual or spiritual tyranny which may threaten this island than the laws of princes or the swords of emperors. We fought and won our battle even in the Middle Ages: should we doubt the issue of another conflict with our broken foe?

The impregnable position of science may be described in a few words. We claim, and we shall wrest from theology, the entire domain of cosmological theory. All schemes and systems which thus infringe upon the domain of science must, in so far as they do this, submit to its control, and relinquish all thought of controlling it. Acting otherwise proved always disastrous in the past, and it is simply fatuous to-day. Every system which would escape the fate of an organism too rigid to adjust itself to its environment must be plastic to the extent that the growth of knowledge demands. When this truth has been thoroughly taken in, rigidity will be relaxed, exclusiveness diminished, things now deemed essential will be dropped, and elements now rejected will be assimilated. The lifting of the life is the essential point, and as long as dogmatism, fanaticism, and intolerance are kept out, various modes of leverage may be employed to raise life to a higher level.

[353]

TZU SSU

TZU SSU (About 335-288 B.C.). Tzu Ssu was a grandson of Confucius. Often he evoked his ancestor's authority; but he also expressed thoughts of his own. Confucius had begun to distinguish between true and supposed knowledge, while Tzu Ssu proceeded to meditations on the relativity of human knowledge of the Universe. He tried to analyze as many types of action as possible, and believed that the reality of the universe can be copied in the character of any wise man who is conscious of his moral and intellectual duties.

THE WAY OF THE MEAN

CHUNG-NI [Confucius] said, "The man of true breeding is the mean in action. The man of no breeding is the reverse. The relation of the man of true breeding to the mean in action is that, being a man of true breeding, he consistently holds to the Mean. The reverse relationship of the man of no breeding is that, being what he is, he has no sense of moral caution."

The Master said, "Perfect is the mean in action, and for a long time now very few people have had the capacity for it."

The Master said, "I know why the Way is not pursued. (It is because) the learned run to excess and the ignorant fall short. I know why the Way is not understood. The good run to excess and the bad fall short. . . ."

The Master said, "Alas, this failure to pursue the Way!"

The Master said, "Consider Shun, the man of great wisdom. He loved to ask advice and to examine plain speech. He never referred to what was evil, and publicly praised what was good. By grasping these two extremes he put into effect the Mean among his people. In this way he was Shun [i.e. a sage-emperor], was he not?"

The Master said. "All men say 'I know,' but they are driven into nets, caught in traps, fall into pitfalls, and not one knows how to avoid this. All men say 'I know,' but, should they choose the mean in action, they could not persist in it for a round month."

The Master said, "Hui, a real man! He chose the mean in action, and, if he succeeded in one element of good, he grasped it firmly cherished it in his bosom, and never let it go."

The Master said, "The states and families of the Great Society might have equal divisions of land: men might refuse noble station and the wealth that goes with it: they might trample the naked sword under foot; but the mean in action, it is impossible for them to achieve that."

Tzu Lu inquired about strong men, and the Master said, "It is strong men of the southern kind, or strong men of the northern kind, or, maybe, making yourself strong (that you have in mind)? The (typical) strong man of the south is magnanimous and gentle in instructing people, and he takes no revenge for being treated vilely: it is the habit of a man of true breeding to be like this. The (typical) strong man of the north lives under arms and dies without a murmur: it is the habit of a man of true force to be like this. Hence the man of true breeding, how steadfast he is in his strength, having a spirit of concord and not giving way to pressure. He takes up a central position, and does not waver one way or another. How steadfast his strength, for, when there is good government, he does not change his original principles, and, when there is vile government, he does not change, even though his life be at stake."

The Way of the enlightened man is widely apparent and yet hidden. Thus the ordinary man and woman, ignorant though they are, can yet have some knowledge of it; and yet in its perfection even a sage finds that there is something there which he does not know. Take the vast size of heaven and earth; men can still find room for criticism of it. Hence, when the enlightened man speaks of supreme bigness, it cannot be contained within the world of our experience; nor, when he speaks of supreme smallness, can it be split up in the world of our experience into nothing. As is said in the *Odes*: "The hawk beats its way up to the height of heaven, the fish dives down into the abyss." That refers to things being examined from above and from below. Thus the Way of the enlightened man, its early shoots coming into existence in the ordinary man and woman, but in its ultimate extent to be examined in the light of heaven and earth.

The master said, "The Way is not far removed from men. If a man pursues a way which removes him from men, he cannot be in the Way. In the *Odes* there is the word, 'When hewing an axe handle, hew an axe handle. The pattern of it is close at hand.' You grasp an axe handle to hew an axe handle, although, when you look from the one to the other [i.e. from the axe in your hand to the block of wood], they are very different." Therefore the right kind of ruler uses men to control men and attempts nothing beyond their correction; and fidelity and mutual service (these two human qualities) cannot be outside the scope of the Way. The treatment which you do not like for yourself you must not hand out to others. . . .

The acts of the enlightened man agree with the station in life in which he finds himself, and he is not concerned with matters outside that station. If he is a man of wealth and high position, he acts as such. If he is a poor man and low in the social scale, he acts accordingly. So also if he is among barbarians, or if he meets trouble. In fact, there is no situation into which he comes in which he is not himself.

In a high station he does not disdain those beneath him. In a low station he does not cling round those above him. He puts himself in the right and seeks no favors. Thus he is free from ill will, having no resentment against either Heaven or men. He preserves an easy mind, as he awaits the will of Heaven: (in contrast to) the man who is not true, who walks in perilous paths and hopes for good luck.

The Way of the enlightened man is like a long journey, since it must begin with the near at hand. It is like the ascent of a high mountain, since it must begin with the low ground. As is said in the *Odes*:

> The happy union with wife and child
> Is like the music of lutes and harps.
> When concord grows between brother and brother,
> The harmony is sweet and intimate.
> The ordering of your household!
> Your joy in wife and child!

The Master said, "How greatly parents are served in this!" He also said, "How irrepressible is the spiritual power in the spirits of the great dead! Look for them, and they are not to be seen. Listen for them, and they are not to be heard. They are in things, and there is nothing without them. They stir all the people in the Great Society to fast and purify themselves and wear their ritual robes, in order that they may sacrifice to them. They fill the air, as if above, as if on the left, as if on the right. The *Odes* has it, 'The coming of the Spirits! Incalculable! And yet they cannot be disregarded.'" Even so is the manifestation of the imperceptible and the impossibility of hiding the real.

[354]

1185

U

UNAMUNO Y JUGO, MIGUEL DE

UNAMUNO Y JUGO, MIGUEL DE (1864-1936). Any appraisal of Unamuno's philosophy is incomplete without taking into account his poetry. Unamuno the thinker and Unamuno the poet are one and inseparable. He accepted the word of a French critic, according to which Unamuno, the poet, had written only commentaries, perpetual analyses of his ego, the Spanish people, their dreams and ideals, but he maintained that Homer and Dante equally had written only commentaries. His greatest commentary was devoted to the figure of Don Quixote whom he presents as a fighter for glory, life and survival. The mortal Quixote is a comic character. The immortal, realizing his own comicalness, superimposes himself upon it and triumphs over it without renouncing it. The longing for immortality is the ever-recurring theme of Unamuno's philosophy and poetry. It finds no consolation in reason, which is regarded as a dissolving force, or in the intellect, which means identity and which, on its part, means death. Rather, it relies on faith. But faith is a matter of will, and will needs reason and intellect. Thus faith and reason, or philosophy and religion, are enemies which nevertheless need one another. Neither a purely religious nor a purely rationalistic tradition is possible. This insight leads not to compromise but creates instead the tragic sentiment. The tragic history of human thought is the history of the struggle between veracity and sincerity, between the truth that is thought and the truth that is felt, and no harmony between the two adversaries is possible, although they never cease to need each other.

Unamuno called himself "an incorrigible Spaniard." But his erudition was universal. In a conversation he was able to explain the particular Scotticism in a verse of Robert Burns, or the difference between two German mystics of whom only German specialists had ever heard. He combined a utilitarian mind with the search for God. But he confessed that his idea of God was different each time that he conceived it. Proud of his Basque origin, Unamuno, like Loyola, another Basque, was imbued with stern earnestness and a tragic sense of life. He felt himself as the descendant of saints and mystics. But he loved fools and regarded even Jesus as a divine fool. To him, dreaming meant the essence of life, and systematic thinking the destruction of that essence. He declined any philosophic system, but contemplation of the way of philosophizing was to him a source of profound wisdom. He was indeed the knight errant of the searching spirit.

LANGUAGE AND PHILOSOPHERS

OUR language itself, like every cultured language, contains within itself an implicit philosophy.

A language, in effect, is a potential philosophy. Platonism is the Greek language which discourses in Plato, unfolding its secular metaphors; scholasticism is the philosophy of the dead Latin of the Middle Ages wrestling with the popular tongues; the French language discourses in Descartes, the German in Kant and in Hegel, and the English in Hume and in Stuart Mill. For the truth is that the logical starting point of all philosophical speculation is not the I, neither is it representation (*Vorstellung*), nor the world as it presents itself immediately to the senses; but it is mediate or historical representation, humanly elaborated and such as it is given to us principally in the language by means of which we know the world; it is not psychical but spiritual representation. When we think, we are obliged to set out, whether we know it not and whether we will or not, from what has been thought by others who came before us and who environ us. Thought is an inheritance. Kant thought in German, and into German he translated Hume and Rousseau, who thought in English and French respectively. And did not Spinoza think in Judeo-Portuguese, obstructed by and contending with Dutch?

Thought rests upon prejudgments, and prejudgments pass into language. To language Bacon rightly ascribed not a few of the errors of the *idola fori*. But is it possible to philosophize in pure algebra or even in Esperanto? In order to see the result of such an attempt one has only to read the work of Avenarius on the criticism of pure experience (*reine Erfahrung*), of this prehuman or inhuman experience. And even Avenarius, who was obliged to invent a language, invented one that was based upon the Latin tradition, with roots which carry in their metaphorical implications a content of impure experience, of human social experience.

All philosophy is, therefore, at bottom philology. And philology, with its great and fruitful law of analogical formations, opens wide the door to chance, to the irrational, to the absolutely incommensurable. History is not mathematics, neither is philosophy. And how many philosophical ideas are not strictly owing to something akin to rhyme, to the necessity of rightly placing a consonant! In Kant himself there is a great deal of this, of esthetic symmetry, rhyme.

Representation is, therefore, like language, like reason itself—which is simply internal language—a social and racial product, and race, the blood of the spirit, is language, as Oliver Wendell Holmes has said, and as I have often repeated.

It was in Athens and with Socrates that our Western philosophy first became mature, conscious of itself, and it arrived at this consciousness by means of the dialogue, of social conversation. And it is profoundly significant that the doctrine of innate ideas, of the objective and normative value of ideas, of what scholasticism afterwards knew as realism, should have formulated itself in dialogues. And these ideas, which constitute reality, are names, as nominalism showed. Not that they may not be more than names (*flatus vocis*), but that they are nothing less than names. Language is that which gives us reality, and not as a mere vehicle of reality, but as its true flesh, of which all the rest, dumb or inarticulate representation, is merely the skeleton. And thus logic operates upon aesthetics, the concept upon the expression, upon the word, and not upon the brute perception.

[355]

V

VEBLEN, THORSTEIN

VEBLEN, THORSTEIN (1857-1929). Before Veblen turned to the study of social and economic facts and theories, he had concentrated upon philosophy, especially the works of Kant, Comte and Spencer, and, in his later years, the problems of economics remained closely connected in Veblen's mind with fundamental problems of life, civilization and the general theory of science. Intending to integrate political economy into the general movement of science, Veblen discussed the evolution of the scientific point of view, the place of science within the framework of civilization, and the function of evolution within political economy. Although Veblen was strongly impressed by the doctrine of evolution, he was opposed to the simple application of the evolutionary principles to the study of social phenomena. He was also strongly opposed to positivism, and relied more upon German idealism and romanticism. He sometimes flirted with theorists of racialism like Gobineau and H. S. Chamberlain, and, if not influenced by Georges Sorel, he came in his own way very close to the latter's standpoint. Both Sorel and Veblen were inspired by Marx and criticized him by similar arguments. Both were enthusiasts of the idea of promoting industrial production by social and political changes. Also, both considered the capitalist unfit to achieve technical progress and they advocated recruitment of industrial leaders from the classes of salaried technicians and workers.

Veblen's violent attacks on the business class and its ideology have caused violent controversies in America. In Europe Veblen remained nearly unknown. Brought up in a clannish community of immigrants from Norway, Veblen never became completely at ease with the American way of living. He had no talent for teaching, and his academic career was hampered by the troubles of his private life. But his writing, especially his first and principal book *Theory of the Leisure Class* (1899), had a fermenting effect on economic and social thinking in America.

1189

THE PLACE OF WOMEN AND PETS
IN THE ECONOMIC SYSTEM

Barnyard fowl, hogs, cattle, sheep, goats, draught horses are of the productive nature of goods, and serve a useful, often a lucrative end; therefore beauty is not readily imputed to them. The case is different with those domestic animals which ordinarily serve no industrial end; such as pigeons, parrots and other cage birds, cats, dogs, and fast horses. These commonly are items of conspicuous consumption, and are therefore honorific in their nature and may be accounted beautiful. This class of animals is conventionally admired by the body of the upper classes, while the pecuniarily lower classes—and that select minority of the leisure class among which the rigorous canon that abjures thrift is in a measure obsolescent—find beauty in one class of animals as in another, without drawing a hard and fast line of pecuniary demarcation between the beautiful and the ugly.

In the case of those domestic animals which are honorific and are reputed beautiful, there is a subsidiary basis of merit that should be spoken of. Apart from the birds which belong in the honorific class of domestic animals, and which owe their place in this class to their nonlucrative character alone, the animals which merit particular attention are cats, dogs, and fast horses. The cat is less reputable than the other two just named, because she is less wasteful; she may even serve a useful end. At the same time the cat's temperament does not fit her for the honorific purpose. She lives with man on terms of equality, knows nothing of what is the ancient basis of all distinctions of worth, honor, and repute, and she does not lend herself with facility to an invidious comparison between her owner and his neighbors. The exception to this last rule occurs in the case of such scarce and fanciful products as the Angora cat, which have some slight honorific value on the ground of expensiveness, and have, therefore, some special claim to beauty on pecuniary grounds.

1190

The dog has advantages in the way of usefulness as well as in special gifts of temperament. He is often spoken of, in an eminent sense, as the friend of man, and his intelligence and fidelity are praised. The meaning of this is that the dog is man's servant and that he has the gift of an unquestioning subservience and a slave's quickness in guessing his master's mood. Coupled with these traits, which fit him well for the relation of status—and which must for the present purpose be set down as serviceable traits—the dog has some characteristics which are of a more equivocal aesthetic value. He is the filthiest of the domestic animals in his person and the nastiest in his habits. For this he makes up in a servile, fawning attitude towards his master, and a readiness to inflict damage and discomfort on all else. The dog, then, commends himself to our favor by affording play to our propensity for mastery, and as he is also an item of expense, and commonly serves no industrial purpose, he holds a well-assured place in men's regards as a thing of good repute. The dog is at the same time associated in our imagination with the chase—a meritorious employment.

Even those varieties of the dog which have been bred into grotesque deformity by the dog-fancier are in good faith accounted beautiful by many. These varieties of dogs—and the like is true of other fancy-bred animals—are rated and graded in aesthetic value somewhat in proportion to the degree of grotesqueness and instability of the particular fashion which the deformity takes in the given case. For the purpose in hand, this differential utility on the ground of grotesqueness and instability of structure is reducible to terms of a greater scarcity and consequent expense. The commercial value of canine monstrosities, such as the prevailing styles of pet dogs both for men's and women's use, rests on their high costs of production, and their value to their owners lies chiefly in their utility as items of conspicuous consumption. Indirectly, through reflection upon their honorific expensiveness, a social worth is imputed to them; and so, by an easy substitution of words and ideas, they come to be admired and reputed beautiful.

The case of the fast horse is much like that of the dog. He is on the whole expensive, or wasteful and useless—for the industrial purpose. What productive use he may possess, in the way of enhancing the well-being of the community or making the way of life easier for men, takes the form of exhibitions of force and facility of motion that gratify the popular aesthetic sense. This is of course a substantial serviceability. The horse is not endowed with the same spiritual aptitude for servile dependence in the same measure as the dog; but he ministers effectually to his master's impulse to convert the "animate" forces of environment to his own use and discretion and so express his own dominating individuality through them. The fast horse is at least potentially a race horse, of high or low degree; and it is as such that he is peculiarly serviceable to his owner. The utility of the fast horse lies largely in his efficiency as a means of emulation; it gratifies the owner's sense of aggression and dominance to have his own horse outstrip his neighbor's. This use not being lucrative, but on the whole pretty consistently wasteful, and quite conspicuously so, it is honorific, and therefore gives the fast horse a strong presumptive position of reputability. Beyond this, the race horse proper has also a similarly nonindustrial but honorific use as a gambling instrument.

It is only with respect to consumable goods—including domestic animals—that the canons of taste have been colored by the canons of pecuniary reputation. Something to the like effect is to be said for beauty in persons. In order to avoid whatever may be matter of controversy, no weight will be given in this connection to such popular predilection as there may be for the dignified (leisurely) bearing and portly presence that are by vulgar tradition associated with opulence in mature men. These traits are in some measure accepted as elements of personal beauty. But there are certain elements of feminine beauty, on the other hand, which come under this head, and which are of so concrete and

1192

specific a character as to admit of itemized appreciation. It is more or less a rule that in communities at which women are valued by the upper class for their service, the ideal of female beauty is a robust, large-limbed woman. The ground of appreciation is the physique, while the conformation of the face is of secondary weight only. A well-known instance of this ideal of the early predatory culture is that of the maidens of the Homeric poems.

This ideal suffers a change in the succeeding development, when, in the conventional scheme, the office of the high-class wife comes to be a vicarious leisure simply. This ideal then includes the characteristics which are supposed to result from or go with a life of leisure consistently enforced. The ideal accepted under these circumstances may be gathered from descriptions of beautiful women by poets and writers of the chivalric times. In the conventional scheme of those days ladies of high degree were conceived to be in perpetual tutelage, and to be scrupulously exempt from all useful work. The resulting chivalric or romantic ideal of beauty takes cognizance chiefly of the face, and dwells on its delicacy, and on the delicacy of the hands and feet, the slender figure, and especially the slender waist. In the pictured representations of the women of that time, and in modern romantic imitators of the chivalric thought and feeling, the waist is attenuated to a degree that implies extreme debility. The same ideal is still extant among a considerable portion of the population of modern industrial communities; but it is said that it has retained its hold most tenaciously in those modern communities which are least advanced in point of economic and civil development, and which show the most considerable survivals of status and predatory institutions. That is to say, the chivalric ideal is best preserved in those existing communities which are substantially least modern. Survivals of this lackadaisical or romantic ideal occur freely in the tastes of the well-to-do classes of Continental countries.

In modern communities which have reached the higher

levels of industrial development, the upper leisure class has accumulated so great a mass of wealth as to place its women above all imputation of vulgarly productive labor. Here the status of women as vicarious consumers is beginning to lose its place in the affections of the body of the people, and as a consequence the ideal of feminine beauty is beginning to change back again from the infirmly delicate, translucent, and hazardously slender, to a woman of the archaic type that does not disown her hands and feet, nor, indeed, the other gross material facts of her person. In the course of economic development the ideal of beauty among the peoples of Western culture has shifted from the woman of physical presence to the lady, and it is beginning to shift back again to the woman; and all in obedience to the changing conditions of pecuniary emulation. The exigencies of emulation at one time required lusty slaves; at another time they required a conspicuous performance of vicarious leisure and consequently an obvious disability; but the situation is now beginning to outgrow this last requirement, since, under the higher efficiency of modern industry, leisure in women is possible so far down the scale of reputability that it will no longer serve as a definitive mark of the highest pecuniary grade.

It has already been noticed that at the stages of economic evolution at which conspicuous leisure is much regarded as a means of good repute, the ideal requires delicate and diminutive hands and feet and a slender waist. These features, together with the other, related faults of structure that commonly go with them, go to show that the person so affected is incapable of useful effort and must therefore be supported in idleness by her owner. She is useless and expensive, and she is consequently valuable as evidence of pecuniary strength. It results that at this cultural stage women take thought to alter their persons, so as to conform more nearly to the requirements of the instructed taste of the time; and under the guidance of the canon of pecuniary decency, the men find the resulting artificially induced pathological features attractive. So, for instance, the constricted waist which has had so wide and persistent a vogue in the communities of the Western culture, and so also the deformed foot of the Chinese. Both of these are mutilations of unquestioned repulsiveness to the untrained sense. Yet there is no room to question their attractiveness to men into whose scheme of life they fit as honorific items sanctioned by the requirements of pecuniary reputability. They are items of pecuniary and cultural beauty which have come to do duty as elements of the ideal of womanliness.

In the so-called "New Woman" movement there are at least two elements discernible, both of which are of an economic character. These two elements or motives are expressed by the double watchword, "emancipation" and "work." Each of these words is recognized to stand for something in the way of a widespread sense of grievance. The prevalence of the sentiment is recognized even by people who do not see that there is any real ground for a grievance in the situation as it stands today. It is among the women of the well-to-do classes, in the communities which are farthest advanced in industrial development, that this sense of grievance to be redressed is most alive and finds most frequent expression. The demand comes from that portion of womankind which is excluded by the canons of good repute from all effectual work, and which is closely reserved for a life of leisure and conspicuous consumption.

More than one critic of this new-woman movement has misapprehended its motive. The case of the average American "new woman" has lately been summed up with some warmth by a popular observer of social phenomena: "She is petted by her husband, the most devoted and hard-working of husbands in the world. . . . She is the superior of her husband in education, and in almost every respect. She is surrounded by the most numerous and delicate attentions. Yet she is not satisfied. . . . The Anglo-Saxon 'new woman' is the most ridiculous production of modern times, and destined to be the most ghastly failure of the century." Apart from the deprecation—perhaps well placed—which is contained in this presentment, it adds nothing but obscurity to the woman question. The grievance of the new woman is made up of those things which this typical characterization of the movement urges as reasons why she should be content. She is petted, and she is permitted, or even required, to consume largely and conspicuously—vicariously for her husband or other natural guardian. She is exempted, or debarred, from vulgarly useful employment—in order to perform leisure vicariously for the good repute of her natural (pecuniary) guardian. These offices are the conventional marks of the un-free, at the same time that they are incompatible with the human impulse to purposeful activity. But the woman is endowed with her share—which there is reason to believe is more than an even share—of the instinct of workmanship, to which futility of life or of expenditure is obnoxious. She must unfold her life activity in response to the direct, unmediated stimuli of the economic environment with which she is in contact. The impulse is perhaps stronger upon the woman than upon the man to live her own life in her own way and to enter the industrial process of the community at something nearer than the second remove.

So long as woman's place is consistently that of a drudge, she is, in the average of cases, fairly contented with her lot. She not only has something tangible and purposeful to do, but she has also no time or thought to spare for a rebellious assertion of such human propensity to self-direction as she has inherited.

[356]

VINCI, LEONARDO DA

VINCI, LEONARDO DA (1452-1519). For nearly four centuries after Leonardo's death, humanity remained uninformed about the scientific and philosophical performances of one of the greatest painters of the Italian Renaissance. Leonardo himself published only his *Treatise on Painting* in which the author combined the display of his artistic skill and experiences with epistemological and mathematical disquisitions. But the immense range of Leonardo's studies, researches and knowledge remained hidden in his diaries, notebooks and sketchbooks, which were printed late in the nineteenth century. They make manifest that Leonardo anticipated many important discoveries. He knew that the earth is a star which turns around the sun, and that moonlight is a result of reflection. He invented a submarine and an airplane, a parachute, poison gas and shrapnel. But, as one of his notes clearly indicates, he kept his inventions secret because he did not wish these instruments of destruction to be used.

To Leonardo, sensual experience is the interpreter between man and nature. But the visible form is regarded by him as the symbol of a spiritual reality. The artist's eye is a perfect instrument of experience but mathematical thought has to control it, and every practice must be founded upon sound theory. Leonardo was of a religious mind though independent of traditional faith. No other artist of the Renaissance but Leonardo could have dared to portray St. John the Baptist and Bacchus, the pagan god, as resembling one another like brothers. And none of that age could combine the character of an altar piece with that of a psychological study, as Leonardo did in his "Last Supper."

ON PAINTING

How painting surpasses all human works by reason of the subtle possibilities which it contains:

The eye, which is called the window of the soul, is the chief means whereby the understanding may most fully and abundantly appreciate the infinite works of Nature; and the ear is the second, inasmuch as it acquires its importance from the fact that it hears the things which the eye has seen. If you historians, or poets, or mathematicians had never seen things with your eyes, you would be ill able to describe them in your writings. And if you, O poet, represent a story by depicting it with your pen, the painter with his brush will so render it as to be more easily satisfying and less tedious to understand. If you call painting "dumb poetry," then the painter may say of the poet that his art is "blind painting." Consider then which is the more grievous affliction, to be blind or to be dumb! Although the poet has as wide a choice of subjects as the painter, his creations fail to afford as much satisfaction to mankind as do paintings, for while poetry attempts to represent forms, actions, and scenes with words, the painter employs the exact images of these forms in order to reproduce them. Consider, then, which is more fundamental to man, the name of man or his image? The name changes with change of country; the form is unchanged except by death.

And if the poet serves the understanding by way of the ear, the painter does so by the eye, which is the nobler sense.

I will only cite as an instance of this how, if a good painter represents the fury of a battle and a poet also describes one, and the two descriptions are shown together to the public, you will soon see which will draw most of the spectators, and where there will be most discussion, to which most praise will be given and which will satisfy the more. There is no doubt that the painting, which is by far the more useful and beautiful, will give the greater pleasure. Inscribe in any place the name of God and set opposite to it His image, you will see which will be held in greater reverence!

Since painting embraces within itself all the forms of Nature, you have omitted nothing except the names, and these are not universal like the forms. If you have the results of her processes we have the processes of her results.

Take the case of a poet describing the beauties of a lady to her lover and that of a painter who makes a portrait of her; you will see whither nature will the more incline the enamoured judge. Surely the proof of the matter ought to rest upon the verdict of experience!

In art we may be said to be grandsons unto God. If poetry treats of moral philosophy, painting has to do with natural philosophy; if the one describes the workings of the mind, the other considers what the mind effects by movements of the body; if the one dismays folk by hellish fictions, the other does the like by showing the same things in action. Suppose the poet sets himself to represent some image of beauty or terror, something vile and foul, or some monstrous thing, in contest with the painter, and suppose in his own way he makes a change of forms at his pleasure, will not the painter still satisfy the more? Have we not seen pictures which bear so close a resemblance to the actual thing that they have deceived both men and beasts?

If you know how to describe and write down the appearance of the forms, the painter can make them so that they appear enlivened with lights and shadows which create the very expression of the faces; herein you cannot attain with the pen where he attains with the brush.

That sculpture is less intellectual than painting, and lacks many of its natural parts:

As practicing myself the art of sculpture no less than that of painting, and doing both the one and the other in the same degree, it seems to me that without suspicion of unfairness I may venture to give an opinion as to which of the two is the more intellectual, and of the greater difficulty and perfection.

In the first place, sculpture is dependent on certain lights, namely, those from above, while a picture carries everywhere with its own light and shade; light and shade, therefore, are essential to sculpture. In this respect, the sculptor is aided by the nature of the relief, which produces these of its own accord, but the painter artificially creates them by his art in places where Nature would normally do the like. The sculptor cannot render the difference in the varying natures of the colors of objects; painting does not fail to do so in any particular. The lines of perspective of sculptors do not seem in any way true; those of painters may appear to extend a hundred miles beyond the work itself. The effects of aerial perspective are outside the scope of sculptors' work: they can neither represent transparent bodies nor luminous bodies nor angles of reflection nor shining bodies, such as mirrors and like things of glittering surface, nor mists, nor dull weather, nor an infinite number of things which I forbear to mention lest they should prove wearisome.

The one advantage which sculpture has is that of offering greater resistance to time; yet painting offers a like resistance if it is done upon thick copper covered with white enamel and then painted upon with enamel colors and placed in a fire and fused. In degree of permanence it then surpasses even sculpture.

* * *

Show first the smoke of the artillery mingled in the air with the dust stirred up by the movement of the horses and of the combatants. This process you should express as follows: the dust, since it is made up of earth and has weight, although by reason of its fineness it may easily rise and mingle with the air, will nevertheless readily fall down again, and the greatest height will be attained by such part of it as is the finest, and this will in consequence be the least visible and will seem almost the color of the air itself.

The smoke which is mingled with the dust-laden air will as it rises to a certain height have more and more the appearance of a dark cloud, at the summit of which the smoke will be more distinctly visible than the dust. The smoke will assume a bluish tinge, and the dust will keep its natural color. From the side whence the light comes this mixture of air and smoke and dust will seem far brighter than on the opposite side.

As for the combatants, the more they are in the midst of this turmoil, the less they will be visible, and the less will be the contrast between their lights and shadows.

You should give a ruddy glow to the faces and the figures and the air around them, and to the gunners and those near to them, and this glow should grow fainter as it is farther away from its cause. The figures which are between you and the light, if far away, will appear dark against a light background, and the nearer their limbs are to the ground, the less will they be visible, for there the dust is greater and thicker. And if you make horses galloping away from the throng, make little clouds of dust as far distant one from another as is the space between the strides made by the horse, and that cloud which is farthest away from the horse should be the least visible, for it should be high and spread out and thin, while that which is nearest should be most conspicuous and smallest and most compact.

Let the air be full of arrows going in various directions, some mounting upwards, others falling, others flying horizontally; and let the balls shot from the guns have a train of smoke following their course. Show the figures in the foreground covered with dust on their hair and eyebrows and such other level parts as afford the dust a space to lodge.

Make the conquerors running, with their hair and other light things streaming in the wind, and with brows bent down; and they should be thrusting forward opposite limbs; that is, if a man advances the right foot, the left arm should also come forward. If you represent anyone fallen, you should also show the mark where he has been dragged through the dust which has become changed to blood-stained mire, and roundabout in the half-liquid earth you should show the marks of the trampling of men and horses who have passed over it.

Make a horse dragging the dead body of his master, and leaving behind him in the dust and mud the track of where the body was dragged along.

Make the beaten and conquered pallid, with brows raised and knit together, and let the skin above the brows be all full of lines of pain; at the sides of the nose show the furrows going in an arch from the nostrils and ending where the eye begins, and show the dilatation of the nostrils which is the cause of these lines; and let the lips be arched displaying the upper row of teeth, and let the teeth be parted after the manner of such as cry in lamentation. Show someone using his hand as a shield for his terrified eyes, turning the palm of it towards the enemy, and having the other resting on the ground to support the weight of his body; let others be crying out with their mouths wide open, and fleeing away. Put all sorts of armour lying between the feet of the combatants, such as broken shields, lances, swords, and other things like these. Make the dead, some half-buried in dust, others with the dust all mingled with the oozing blood and changing into crimson mud; and let the line of the blood be discerned by its color, flowing in a sinuous stream from the corpse to the dust. Show others in the death agony grinding their teeth and rolling their eyes, with clenched fists grinding against their bodies and with legs distorted. Then you might show one, disarmed and struck down by the enemy, turning on him with teeth and nails to take fierce and inhuman vengeance; and let a riderless horse be seen galloping with mane streaming in the wind, charging among the enemy and doing them great mischief with his hoofs.

You may see there one of the combatants, maimed and fallen on the ground, protecting himself with his shield, and the enemy bending down over him and striving to give him the fatal stroke; there might also be seen many men fallen in a heap on top of a dead horse; and you should show some of the victors leaving the combat and retiring apart from the crowd, and with both hands wiping away from eyes and cheeks the thick layer of mud caused by the smarting of their eyes from the dust.

And the squadrons of the reserves should be seen standing full of hope but cautious, with eyebrows raised, and shading their eyes with their hands, peering into the thick, heavy mist in readiness for the commands of their captain; and so, too, the captain with his staff raised, hurrying to the reserves and pointing out to them the quarter of the field where they are needed; and you should show a river, within which horses are galloping, stirring the water all around with a heaving mass of waves and foam and broken water, leaping high into the air and over the legs and bodies of the horses; but see that you make no level spot of ground that is not trampled over with blood.

[357]

VIVEKANANDA, SWAMI

VIVEKANANDA, SWAMI (1862-1902). Educated abroad, Swami Vivekananda was an agnostic, whose rationalistic doubts were dispersed by the teachings of Ramakrishna Paramahamsa. His simple belief in the philosophy of the monistic Vedanta of Sankara and the attempt to re-emphasize the unity of all religions made Vivekananda a disciple, who devoted the remainder of his life to the dissemination of his teacher's ideas. He founded the Ramakrishna Mission for humanitarian service, brought to Hinduism an enthusiastic missionary approach, and emphasized the positive aspect of Vedanta: "that all is Brahma, and, therefore, that service of man as God is better than quiescent meditation." His influence has been seen in the works of such philosophers as Radhakrishnan and Aurobindo, in the social service and spread of Hindu ideas throughout the world, and it is even apparent in the political attitude of Mahatma Gandhi.

SWAMI VIVEKANANDA'S WORKS

SIDE BY SIDE with the modern theory of evolution, there is another thing: atavism. There is a tendency in us to revert to old ideas, in religion. Let us think something new, even if it be wrong. It is better to do that. Why should you not try to hit the mark? We become wiser through failures. Time is infinite. Look at the wall. Did the wall ever tell a lie? It is always the wall. Man tells a lie,—and becomes a god, too. It is better to do something; never mind even if it proves to be wrong; it is better than doing nothing. The cow never tells a lie, but she remains a cow, all the time. Do something! Think some thought; it doesn't matter whether you are right or wrong. But think something! Because my forefathers did not think this way, shall I sit down quietly and gradually lose my sense of feeling, and my own think-

1203

ing faculties? 1 may as well be dead! And what is life worth if we have no living ideas, no convictions of our own about religion? There is some hope for the Atheists because though they differ from others, they think for themselves. The people who never think anything for themselves, are not yet born into the world of religion; they have a mere jelly-fish existence. They will not think; they do not care for religion. But the disbeliever, the atheist, cares, and he is struggling. So think something! Struggle Godward! Never mind if you fail, never mind if you get hold of a queer theory. If you are afraid to be called queer, keep it in your own mind;— you need not go and preach it to others. But do something! Struggle Godward! Light must come. If a man feeds me every day of my life, in the long run I shall lose the use of my hands. Spiritual death is the result of following each other like a flock of sheep. Death is the result of inaction. Be active; and wherever there is activity, there must be difference. Difference is the sauce of life; it is the beauty, it is the art of everything: difference makes all beautiful here. It is variety that is the source of life, the sign of life. Why should we be afraid of it?   [357A]

VOLTAIRE, FRANÇOIS MARIE AROUET DE

VOLTAIRE, FRANÇOIS MARIE AROUET DE (1694-1778). W. Somerset Maugham, the well-known novelist and playwright, has declared: "Before I start writing a novel, I read *Candide* over again so that I may have in the back of my mind the touchstone of that lucidity, grace and wit."

Voltaire's *Candide* is, however, not only a literary masterwork that defies the change of time and taste; it is also an attack on Leibniz' *Theodicy*. With mordant irony it castigates the belief that the existing world is the best of all possible ones. Life and studies confirmed Voltaire in his bitter criticism of man and human institutions. Three times imprisoned in the *Bastille* in Paris, Voltaire was then banished from France. As an exile in England, he studied Locke and Newton, and adopted Bolingbroke's deism. The result of these studies, Voltaire's *Lettres philosophiques* (1734), was publicly burned by the hangman in Paris. Dissatisfied with his own time, Voltaire, one of the initiators of modern history of civilization, saw that in the past the triumph of error and injustice had been even more outrageous. But he persisted in teaching that man is capable of shaping the future of humanity in accordance with true morality by making prevail the results of secular science and by resisting arbitrary power and intolerance. Until the last day of his life, Voltaire struggled for liberty of thought and conscience. He, a single man, defeated the organized power of fanaticism by rehabilitating Jean Calas, the victim of a judicial murder, and by saving his relatives from imprisonment. Voltaire passed the watchword of resistance to fanaticism. It became a battle cry that is heard and echoed in the present time.

ON TOLERANCE

ONE does not need great art and skilful eloquence to prove that Christians ought to tolerate each other—nay, even to regard all men as brothers. Why, you say, is the Turk, the Chinese, or the Jew my brother? Assuredly; are we not all children of the same father, creatures of the same God?

But these people despise us and treat us as idolaters. Very well; I will tell them that they are quite wrong. It seems to me that I might astonish, at least, the stubborn pride of a Mohammedan or a Buddhist priest if I spoke to them somewhat as follows:

This little globe, which is but a point, travels in space like many other globes; we are lost in the immensity. Man, about five feet high, is certainly a small thing in the universe. One of these imperceptible beings says to some of his neighbors, in Arabia or South Africa: "Listen to me, for the God of all these worlds has enlightened me. There are nine hundred million little ants like us on the earth, but my ant-hole alone is dear to God. All the others are eternally reprobated by him. Mine alone will be happy."

They would then interrupt me, and ask who was the fool that talked all this nonsense. I should be obliged to tell them that it was themselves. I would then try to appease them, which would be difficult.

I would next address myself to the Christians, and would venture to say to, for instance, a Dominican friar—an inquisitor of the faith: "Brother, you are aware that each province in Italy has its own dialect, and that people do not speak at Venice and Bergamo as they do at Florence. The Academy of La Crusca has fixed the language. Its dictionary is a rule that has to be followed, and the grammar of Matei is an infallible guide. But do you think that the consul of the Academy; or Matei in his absence, could in conscience cut out the tongues of all the Venetians and the Bergamese who persisted in speaking their own dialect?"

The inquisitor replies: "The two cases are very different. In our case it is a question of your eternal salvation. It is for your good that the heads of the inquisition direct that you shall be seized on the information of any one person, however infamous or criminal; that you shall have no advocate to defend you; that the name of your accuser shall not be made known to you; that the inquisitor shall promise you pardon and then condemn you; and that you shall then be subjected to five kinds of torture, and afterwards either flogged or sent to the galleys or ceremoniously burned. On this Father Ivonet, Doctor Chucalon, Zanchinus, Campegius, Royas, Telinus, Gomarus, Diabarus, and Gemelinus are explicit, and this pious practice admits of no exception."

I would take the liberty of replying: "Brother, possibly you are right. I am convinced that you wish to do me good. But could I not be saved without all that?"

It is true that these absurd horrors do not stain the face of the earth every day; but they have often done so, and the record of them would make up a volume much larger than the gospels which condemn them. Not only is it cruel to persecute, in this brief life, those who differ from us, but I am not sure if it is not too bold to declare that they are damned eternally. It seems to me that it is not the place of the atoms of a moment, such as we are, thus to anticipate the decrees of the Creator. Far be it from me to question the principle, "Out of the Church there is no salvation." I respect it, and all that it teaches; but do we really know all the ways of God, and the full range of his mercies? May we not hope in him as much as fear him? Is it not enough to be loyal to the Church? Must each individual usurp the rights of the Deity, and decide, before he does, the eternal lot of all men?

When we wear mourning for a king of Sweden, Denmark, England, or Prussia, do we say that we wear mourning for one who burns eternally in hell? There are in Europe forty million people who are not of the Church of Rome. Shall we say to each of them: "Sir, seeing that you are infallibly damned, I will neither eat, nor deal, nor speak with you"?

What ambassador of France, presented in audience to the Sultan, would say in the depths of his heart: "His Highness will undoubtedly burn for all eternity because he has been circumcised"? If he really believed that the Sultan is the mortal enemy of God, the object of his vengeance, could he speak to him? Ought he to be sent to him? With whom could we have intercourse? What duty of civil life could we ever fulfil if we were really convinced that we were dealing with damned souls?

Followers of a merciful God, if you were cruel of heart; if, in worshipping him whose whole law consisted in loving one's neighbor as oneself, you had burdened this pure and holy law with sophistry and unintelligible disputes; if you had lit the fires of discord for the sake of a new word or a single letter of the alphabet; if you had attached eternal torment to the omission of a few words or ceremonies that other peoples could not know, I should say to you:

"Transport yourselves with me to the day on which all men will be judged, when God will deal with each according to his works. I see all the dead of former ages and of our own stand in his presence. Are you sure that our Creator and Father will say to the wise and virtuous Confucius, to the lawgiver Solon, to Pythagoras, to Zaleucus, to Socrates, to

Plato, to the divine Antonines, to the good Trajan, to Titus, the delight of the human race, to Epictetus, and to so many other model men: 'Go, monsters, go and submit to a chastisement infinite in its intensity and duration; your torment shall be eternal as I. And you, my beloved, Jean Chatel, Ravaillac, Damiens, Cartouche, etc. [assassins in the cause of the Church], who have died with the prescribed formulæ, come and share my empire and felicity for ever.' "

You shrink with horror from such sentiments; and, now that they have escaped me, I have no more to say to you.

[358]

VON BAADER, FRANCIS XAVIER. See BAADER, FRANCIS XAVIER VON.

W

WAHLE, RICHARD

WAHLE, RICHARD (1857-1935). Proceeding from extreme positivism, Wahle, once a professor of philosophy at the Universities of Czernovitz and Vienna, pronounced in his *Tragicomedy of Wisdom* (2nd edition, 1925) his death sentence on philosophy. He acknowledged only "definite, agnostic, absolute critique of knowledge" and psychology as surviving, or rather he maintained that critiques of knowledge, logic and psychology have nothing to do with philosophy. As a consequence of his fundamental attitude, Wahle did not recognize the ego as a nucleus of forces but only as a changing whirl or as some stitches in the texture of the universe. But in his *Formation of Character* (2nd edition, 1928) he made important contributions to modern characterology. Wahle's devastating criticism of philosophers has spared only very few such as Spinoza, Hume and Herbart, whose works he praised as useful.

TIME

TIME—it is embarrassing for philosophy still to have to talk about such things—is not as Kant wanted it an *a priori* conception; it has no real being, no special content of consciousness, no quality, but it is an afterwards reflected abstraction concerning changes altogether. To consider time, a continuously flowing, developing thing or an ever-existing, everlasting thing, as a substance, is as absurd as if somebody wanted to believe that the stupidity which becomes manifest in some person is a stupidity substance that is permeating the whole world. Time can only be thought of and measured by increases, decreases and changes. Duration and rest can only be thought about through the possibility of changes which, however, do not occur. Time is not the stuff out of which everything is made, nor is it the place in which everything would become. As little as the concept of youth or age designates an undivided objective real thing an entity, but rather, as we understand it, only an abstract comprehension of all processes occurring in young or old individuals—so time too does not refer to an entity existing for itself but it, instead, is nothing but a completely dependent reflected abstraction of a possibility on the basis of real increases or decreases, of growth or reduction. Each being noticing an increment—for instance, a beginning increase—in a thing could build the abstraction "time" immediately, the content of which would be just the idea of such changes together with the thought that if there are changes there are also possibilities for mutations, developments and innovations. The possibility of the continuous accumulation of changes is "time."

Since time is an abstraction of the possibilities of changes, it could be conceived as an abstraction of the possibility of increases; it could also be an abstraction from numbers, but only by counting them through the successive intentional increase of the series of numbers. The ideal series of numbers, therefore, does not need to have any relation to time, for the series of numbers can be imagined as stationary. Also in another sense it is rather unfortunate to symbolize time by means of the number, for the series of numbers is not absolutely continuous but rather the unities and even their smallest differences are separated from each other.

[359]

WEBER, MAX

WEBER, MAX (1864-1920). Very few scholars have been so severely tormented by the conflict between their scientific convictions and their vital instincts as was Max Weber, and hardly any other one has, in his writings and teachings, so sternly disciplined himself as did he. His penetrating analysis of social formations, of the economic factor in history, of the relations between religion and economics and the general trends of human civilization, proceeds from and results in the statement that the victory of rational impersonality over irrational impulses is inevitable and historically justified. But Weber himself, a man of impulsive vehemence, afflicted by psychic tensions and disturbances, bitterly resented any loss of irrational privacy which was imposed on him by the development of depersonalizing tendencies, although his insight forced him to accept it. His constant endeavor was not to betray personal feelings in his teachings and to keep his statements and characteristics of the objects of his science free from intrinsic value judgments. According to him, science has to give only technical knowledge which may be useful for the domination of things and human beings. Social science is defined by him as a method of interpreting social action and of explaining its course and its effects by the quest for its intention and the means of its accomplishment, without any regard to its desirability.

Only on the occasion of literary feuds and political debates did Weber allow eruptions of his feelings. He was a formidable controversialist, capable of knocking down his adversaries with ice-cold irony or with truculent impetuosity. He was an ardent German nationalist but, for the greater part of his life, believed that democracy was more efficient than any authoritarian regime, and therefore he advocated Germany's democratization. Still opposed to the Treaty of Versailles, Weber, at the end of his life, came closer to nationalist extremists whom he had energetically combated during the war.

THE FATE OF SCIENCE

IN science, each of us knows that what he has accomplished will be antiquated in ten, twenty, fifty years. That is the fate to which science is subjected; it is the very *meaning* of scientific work, to which it is devoted in a quite specific sense, as compared with other spheres of culture for which in general the same holds. Every scientific "fulfilment" raises new "questions"; it *asks* to be "surpassed" and outdated. Whoever wishes to serve science has to resign himself to this fact. Scientific works certainly can last as "gratifications" because of their artistic quality, or they may remain important as a means of training. Yet they will be surpassed scientifically—let that be repeated—for it is our common fate and, more, our common goal. We cannot work without hoping that others will advance further than we have. In principle, this progress goes on *ad infinitum*. And with this we come to inquire into the *meaning* of science. For, after all, it is not self-evident that something subordinate to such a law is sensible and meaningful in itself. Why does one engage in doing something that in reality never comes, and never can come, to an end?

One does it, first, for purely practical, in the broader sense of the word, for technical, purposes: in order to be able to orient our practical activities to the expectations that scientific experience places at our disposal. Good. Yet this has meaning only to practitioners. What is the attitude of the academic man towards his vocation—that is, if he is at all in quest of such a personal attitude? He maintains that he engages in "science for science's sake" and not merely because others, by exploiting science, bring about commercial or technical success and can better feed, dress, illuminate, and govern. But what does he who allows himself to be integrated into this specialized organization, running on *ad infinitum*, hope to accomplish that is significant in these productions that are always destined to be outdated? This question requires a few general considerations.

Scientific progress is a fraction, the most important fraction, of the process of intellectualization which we have been undergoing for thousands of years and which nowadays is usually judged in such an extremely negative way. Let us first clarify what this intellectualist rationalization, created by science and by scientifically oriented technology, means practically.

Does it mean that we, today, for instance, have a greater knowledge of the conditions of life under which we exist than has an American Indian or a Hottentot? Hardly. Unless he is a physicist, one who rides on the streetcar has no idea how the car happened to get into motion. And he does not need to know. He is satisfied that he may "count" on the behavior of the streetcar, and he orients his conduct according to this expectation; but he knows nothing about what it takes to produce such a car so that it can move. The savage knows incomparably more about his tools. When we spend money today I bet that almost every one will hold a different answer in readiness to the question: How does it happen that one can buy something for money—sometimes more and sometimes less? The savage knows what he does in order to get his daily food and which institutions serve him in this pursuit. The increasing intellectualization and rationalization do *not*, therefore, indicate an increased and general knowledge of the conditions under which one lives.

It means something else, namely, the knowledge or belief that if one but wished one *could* learn it at any time. Hence, it means that principally there are no mysterious incalculable forces that come into play, but rather that one can, in principle, master all things by calculation. This means that the world is disenchanted. One need no longer have recourse to magical means in order to master or implore the spirits, as did the savage, for whom such mysterious powers existed. Technical means and calculations perform the service. This above all is what intellectualization means.

[360]

WERTHEIMER, MAX

WERTHEIMER, MAX (1880-1943). Wertheimer's article *Experimental Studies on the Vision of Movement*, published in *Zeitschrift für Psychologie* (1912), led to the development of *Gestalt* theory which has been formulated at first psychologically, and then enlarged into a philosophical conception of physical, biological and social facts. Wertheimer broke away from the purely summative theory of sensory experience. Instead he held that the phenomena must be considered autonomous unities, coherent wholes, that the existence of each element of such an unity is dependent on the latter's structure, and that the knowledge of the whole cannot be derived from that of its elements. Neither psychologically nor physiologically is the element anterior to the whole.

In his *Productive Thinking*, published posthumously in 1945, Wertheimer defined thinking as "envisaging, realizing structural

1213

features, structural requirements, proceeding in accordance with, and determined by, these requirements; thereby changing the situation in the direction of structural improvement." He claimed that *Gestalt* theory had started scientific study of the problems of thinking, clarified them theoretically, and that it tried to form appropriate tools for dealing with the facts and laws involved in them in a scientific manner.

GESTALT THEORY

GESTALT theory does *not* attempt to patch up or evade, nor does it endeavor to settle the problem by decreeing: this is science, life is different; other factors are at work in the spiritual realm than in the material. Gestalt theory does not seek a solution in a separation of the subject matter of knowledge. It endeavors at a crucial point to probe the innermost core of the problem, by asking: at this precise point is there not something in the approach, the basic thesis, the fundamental preconceptions, that used to be considered indispensable to the realm of science but in actuality is not so at all?

For a long time it seemed self-evident, and very characteristic of European epistemology and science, that the scientist could only proceed in the following way: if I have before me a phenomenon to be investigated and understood, I must view it first as an aggregate, as something to be dissected into piecemeal elements; then I must study the laws governing such elements. Only by compounding the elementary data and by establishing the relations between the separate pieces can the problem be solved. All this is not new; during recent decades it has raised problems in the minds of most scientists. Briefly characterized, one might say that the paramount presupposition was to go back to particles, to revert to piecemeal single relations existing between such individual particles or elements, to analyze and synthesize by combining the elements and particles into larger complexes.

Gestalt theory believes it has discovered a decisive aspect in recognizing the existence of phenomena and contexts of a different—of a formally different—nature. And this not merely in the humanities. The basic thesis of gestalt theory might be formulated thus: there are contexts in which what is happening in the world cannot be deduced from the characteristics of the separate pieces, but conversely; what happens to a part of the whole is, in clear-cut cases, determined by the laws of the inner structure of its whole. . . .

If I view the situation from the standpoint of set theory, and ask, how would a world look in which there was no science, no understanding, no penetration or grasp of inner relationships, the answer is very simple. Such a world would consist of a mere agglomeration of disparate elements. The next question would be: what would a world be like, how must a plurality be conceived, if science should be able to proceed in a piecemeal way? This can also be quite simply characterized. The only requirements would be the recurrence of couplings of a senseless, piecemeal nature; then everything needed to operate traditional logic, piecemeal mathematics and science would be at hand. There is a third kind of formation of set theory which, up to now, has not been sufficiently studied—that is, those sets where a manifold is not built up of separate elements but the whole conditions of a set determine the character and place of any particular part of this set.

Figuratively speaking, then, what is the situation we are in? Everyone sees one particular sector of this world and this sector in itself is small indeed. Imagine the world consisting of a large plateau on which musicians are seated, each playing. As I walk around I hear and see. Here there are various possibilities, which are different in principle. Firstly, the world could be a senseless plurality. Everyone acts arbitrarily—everyone for himself. The combination I would gain if I could hear ten of them or all of them at the same time, would be an accidental effect of what each of them does individually. This would correspond to a radically piecemeal theory such as the kinetic theory of gases. A second possibility would be that whenever one musician played C, another would play F so and so many seconds later; I would establish some blind piecemeal relationship linking the acts of the individual musicians which would again result in something totally meaningless. That is the conception most people have of physics. However, correctly regarded, physics interprets the world differently. Our third possibility would for instance be a Beethoven symphony where from a part of the whole we could grasp something of the inner structure of the whole itself. The fundamental laws, then, would not be piecemeal laws but structural characteristics of the whole. And with this I will conclude.

[361]

WHITEHEAD, ALFRED NORTH

WHITEHEAD, ALFRED NORTH (1861-1947). Whitehead had become famous as a scientist, as one of the founders of modern mathematical logic, before he concentrated upon philosophy. He was sixty-three years old when he renounced his professorship of mathematics at the Imperial College of Science and Technology, London, in order to become professor of philosophy at Harvard. However, his mathematical investigations remained relevant to his metaphysics, and even Whitehead, the metaphysician who protested that "the final outlook of philosophical thought cannot be based upon the exact statements which form the basis of special sciences," retained his grand vision of the possibilities of abstract theory.

Whitehead never hesitated to confess his indebtedness to William James, Samuel Alexander and Henri Bergson for the development of his own philosophical thoughts, or that Minkowski's assimilation of space and time and Einstein's theory of relativity had stimulated his thought. But this indebtedness meant not so much an actual influence as rather the creation of a new situation which allowed Whitehead to proceed in his own way.

The decisive feature of this new situation was shaped by James' denial that the subject-object relation is fundamental to knowledge. By denying that in the occurrence of knowing one entity, regarded as the knower, as a mind or soul, standing in front of an object, be it externally existent or the self-consciousness of the knower himself, James also removed the habitual distinction

1216

of mind and matter. Whitehead, while constantly contending that the "bifurcation of nature," the sharp division between nature and mind, established by Descartes, had "poisoned all subsequent philosophy" and jeopardized the very meaning of life, restored the subject-object relation as a fundamental structural pattern of experience, "but not in the sense in which subject-object is identified with knower-known." To Whitehead, "the living organ or experience is the living body as a whole." Human experience has its origin in the physical activities of the whole organism which tends to readjustment when any part of it becomes unstable. Although such experience seems to be more particularly related to the brain, Whitehead held that "we cannot determine with what molecules the brain begins and the rest of the body ends." Human experience therefore is defined as "an act of self-origination, including the whole of nature, limited to the perspective of a focal region, located within the body, but not necessarily persisting in any fixed coordination within a definite part of the brain."

Upon this concept of human experience, Whitehead founded his new philosophy of the organism, his cosmology, his defense of speculative reason, his ideas on the process of nature, his rational approach to God. The aim of his speculative philosophy was "to frame a coherent, logical, necessary system of general ideas in terms of which every item of our experience can be interpreted." Whitehead thought that philosophy, speculative metaphysics included, was not, or should not be, a ferocious debate between irritable professors but "a survey of possibilities and their comparison with actualities," balancing the fact, the theory, the alternatives and the ideal. In this way the fundamental beliefs which determine human character, will be clarified.

The first period of Whitehead's activities was devoted to mathematics and logic. It began with *Universal Algebra* published in 1898 after seven years of work, continued with *Mathematical Concepts of the Material World* (1905) and culminated in the monumental *Principia Mathematica* (1910-1913) written in collaboration with Bertrand Russell. Characteristic of Whitehead's second period, in which he was preoccupied with a philosophy of natural science without metaphysical exposition, are *An Enquiry Concerning the Principles of Natural Knowledge* (1919), *The Concept of Nature* (1920), *The Principle of Relativity* (1922) and *Science and the Modern World* (1925), which already mentions but not yet attempts a metaphysical synthesis of existence.

Most significant of Whitehead's metaphysical views are *Process and Reality* (1929), *Adventures of Ideas* (1933) and *Modes of Thought* (1938).

1217

THE proper satisfaction to be derived from speculative thought is elucidation. It is for this reason that fact is supreme over thought. This supremacy is the basis of authority. We scan the world to find evidence for this elucidatory power.

Thus the supreme verification of the speculative flight is that it issues in the establishment of a practical technique for well-attested ends, and that the speculative system maintains itself as the elucidation of that technique. In this way there is the progress from thought to practice, and regress from practice to the same thought. This interplay of thought and practice is the supreme authority. It is the test by which the charlatanism of speculation is restrained.

In human history, a practical technique embodies itself in established institutions—professional associations, scientific associations, business associations, universities, churches, governments. Thus the study of the ideas which underlie the sociological structure is an appeal to the supreme authority. It is the Stoic appeal to the "voice of nature."

But even this supreme authority fails to be final, and this for two reasons. In the first place the evidence is confused, ambiguous, and contradictory. In the second place, if at any period of human history it had been accepted as final, all progress would have been stopped. The horrid practices of the past, brutish and nasty, would have been fastened upon us for all ages. Nor can we accept the present age as our final standard. We can live, and we can live well. But we feel the urge of the trend upwards: we still look toward the better life.

We have to seek for a discipline of the speculative reason. It is of the essence of such speculation that it transcends immediate fact. Its business is to make thought creative of the future. It effects this by its vision of systems of ideas, including observation but generalized beyond it. The need of discipline arises because the history of speculation is analogous to the history of practice. If we survey mankind, their speculations have been foolish, brutish, and nasty. The true use of history is that we extract from it general principles as to the discipline of practice and the discipline of speculation.

The object of this discipline is not stability but progress. There is no true stability. What looks like stability is a relatively slow process of atrophied decay. The stable universe is slipping away from under us. Our aim is upwards.

The men who made speculation effective were the Greek thinkers. We owe to them the progressive European civilization. It is therefore common sense to observe the methods which they introduced into the conduct of thought.

In the first place, they were unboundedly curious. They probed into everything, questioned everything, and sought to understand everything. This is merely to say that they were speculative to a superlative degree. In the second place, they were rigidly systematic both in their aim at clear definition and at logical consistency. In fact, they invented logic in order to be consistent. Thirdly, they were omnivorous in their interests—natural science, ethics, mathematics, political philosophy, metaphysics, theology, esthetics, and all alike attracted their curiosity. Nor did they keep these subjects rigidly apart. They very deliberately strove to combine them into one coherent system of ideas. Fourthly, they sought truths of the highest generality. Also in seeking these truths, they paid attention to the whole body of their varied interests. Fifthly, they were men with active practical interests. Plato went to Sicily in order to assist in a political experiment, and throughout his life studied mathematics. In those days mathematics and its applications were not so separated as they can be today. No doubt, the sort of facts that he observed were the applications of mathematical theory. But no one had a keener appreciation than Plato of the divergence between the exactness of abstract thought and the vague margin of ambiguity which haunts all observation. Indeed in this respect Plato, the abstract thinker, far surpasses John Stuart Mill, the inductive philosopher. Mill in his account of the inductive methods of science never faces the difficulty that no observation ever does exactly verify the law which it is presumed to support. Plato's feeling for the inexactness of physical experience in contrast to the exactness of thought certainly suggests that he could look for himself. Mill's determinism is, according to his own theory, an induction respecting the exactness of conformation to the conditions set by antecedent circumstances. But no one has ever had any such experience of exact conformation. No observational basis whatsoever can be obtained for the support of Mill's doctrine. Plato knew this primary fact about experience, Mill did not. Determinism may be the true doctrine, but it can never be proved by the methods prescribed by English empiricism.

When we come to Aristotle the enumeration of his practical activities makes us wonder that he had any time for thought at all. He analyzed the constitutions of the leading Greek states, he dissected the great dramatic literature of his age, he dissected fishes, he dissected sentences and arguments, he taught the youthful Alexander. A man, who had done these things and others, might well have been excused if he had pleaded lack of time for mere abstract thought.

In considering the culmination of Greek speculation in Plato and Aristotle the characteristics which finally stand out are the universality of their interests, the systematic exactness at which they aimed, and the generality of their thoughts. It is no rash induction to conclude that these combined characteristics constitute one main preservative of speculation from folly.

The speculative reason works in two ways so as to submit itself to the authority of facts without loss of its mission to transcend the existing analysis of facts. In one way it accepts the limitations of a special topic, such as a science or a practical methodology. It then seeks speculatively to enlarge and recast the categorical ideas within the limits of that topic. This is speculative reason in its closest alliance with the methodological reason.

In the other way, it seeks to build a cosmology expressing the general nature of the world as disclosed in human interests. In order to keep such a cosmology in contact with reality, account must be taken of the welter of established institutions constituting the structures of human society throughout the ages. It is only in this way that we can appeal to the widespread effective elements in the experience of mankind. What those institutions stood for in the experience of their contemporaries represents the massive facts of ultimate authority.

The discordance at once disclosed among the beliefs and purposes of men is commonplace. But in a way, the task is simplified. The superficial details at once disclose themselves by the discordance which they disclose. The concordance in general notions stands out. The very fact of institutions to effect purposes witnesses to unquestioned belief that foresight and purpose can shape the attainment of ends. The discordance over moral codes witnesses to the fact of moral experience. You cannot quarrel about unknown elements. The basis of every discord is some common experience, discordantly realized.

A cosmology should above all things be adequate. It should not confine itself to the categorical notions of one science, and explain away everything which will not fit in. Its business is not to refuse experience but to find the most general interpretive system. Also it is not a mere juxtaposition of the various categorical notions of the various sciences. It generalizes beyond any special science, and thus provides the interpretive system which expresses their interconnection. Cosmology, since it is the outcome of the highest generality of speculation, is the critic of all speculation inferior to itself in generality.

But cosmology shares the imperfections of all the efforts of finite intelligence. The special sciences fall short of their aim, and cosmology equally fails. Thus when the novel speculation is produced a threefold problem is set. Some special science, the cosmological scheme, and the novel concept will have points of agreement and points of variance. Reason intervenes in the capacity of arbiter and yet with a further exercise of speculation. The science is modified, the cosmological outlook is modified, and the novel concept is modified. The joint discipline has eliminated elements of folly, or of mere omission, from all three. The purposes of mankind receive the consequential modification, and the shock is transmitted through the whole sociological structure of technical methods and of institutions.

Every construction of human intelligence is more special, more limited than was its original aim. Cosmology sets out to be the general system of general ideas applicable to this epoch of the universe. Abstraction is to be made from all subordinate details. Thus there should be one cosmology presiding over many sciences. Unfortunately this ideal has not been realized. The cosmological outlooks of different schools of philosophy differ. They do more than differ, they are largely inconsistent with each other. The discredit of philosophy has largely arisen from this warring of the schools.

So long as the dogmatic fallacy infests the world, this discordance will continue to be misinterpreted. If philosophy be erected upon clear and distinct ideas, then the discord of philosophers, competent and sincere men, implies that they are pursuing a will-o'-the-wisp. But as soon as the true function of rationalism is understood, that it is a gradual approach to ideas of clarity and generality, the discord is what may be expected.

The various cosmologies have in various degrees failed to achieve the generality and the clarity at which they aim. They are inadequate, vague, and push special notions beyond the proper limits of their application. For example, Descartes is obviously right, in some sense or other, when he says that we have bodies and that we have minds, and that they can be studied in some disconnection. It is what we do daily in practical life. This philosophy makes a large generalization which obviously has some important validity. But if you turn it into a final cosmology, errors will creep in. The same is true of other schools of philosophy. They all say something which is importantly true. Some types of philosophy have produced more penetrating cosmologies than other schools. At certain epochs a cosmology may be produced which includes its predecessors and assigns to them their scope of validity. But at length, that cosmology will be found out. Rivals will appear correcting it, and perhaps failing to include some of its general truths.

In this way mankind stumbles on in its task of understanding the world.

[362]

WHITMAN, WALT

WHITMAN, WALT (1819-1892). Not only in America but also in England, France, Germany and other countries, Whitman has been celebrated as the prophet of the age of democracy, a title which the poet himself relished. The new technique of lyrical expression and description which he initiated has been adopted by outstanding French poets and by many minor poets in several languages.

The function of poetry was conceived by Whitman as not only enjoying but leading and teaching mankind, and in many of his poems he attempted to answer philosophical questions. Whitman also dealt with philosophical problems in his notebooks. In 1847 he did not believe himself to have become a great philosopher, and in 1860 he wrote, in a similar mood, that he had not founded a philosophical school. In a way, he even repudiated philosophy as a bond of thinking, and exclaimed: "I leave all free, I charge you to leave all free." But he also claimed that the poet of the cosmos "advances through all interpositions, coverings and turmoils and stratagems to first principles." In *Passage to India* he declared that the poet fuses nature and man who were diffused before. In fact, Whitman was devoted to a philosophy which combined pantheism with a strong belief in human action, which unites the human soul with cosmic life but stresses the uniqueness of human personality and human relations. His civil, democratic, human consciousness was rooted in an all-embracing feeling of cosmic solidarity, and he was anxious to avoid any attenuation, and not to be deterred by psychic transmigration to the remotest objects. There is a tension between Whitman's firmness of conviction and his universal receptivity for impressions, sensations, ideas and phenomena, between his feelings of being a missionary of democracy and his mythical imagination. But this same tension strengthened his poetical power and did not endanger the unity of his character. From cosmic vagaries he always found the way back to simple truth and common sense.

LITERATURE'S SERVICE

THE chief trait of any given poet is always the spirit he brings to the observation of humanity and nature—the mood out of which he contemplates his subjects. What kind of temper and what amount of faith report these things? Up to how recent a date is the song carried? What the equipment, and special raciness of the singer—what his tinge of coloring? The last value of artistic expressers, past and present —Greek aesthetes, Shakespeare—or in our own day Tennyson, Victor Hugo, Carlyle, Emerson—is certainly involv'd in such questions. I say the profoundest service that poems or any other writings can do for their reader is not merely to satisfy the intellect, or supply something polish'd or interesting, nor even to depict great passions, or persons or events, but to fill him with vigorous and clean manliness, religiousness, and give him *good heart* as a radical possession and habit. The educated world seems to have been growing more and more ennuied for ages, leaving to our time the inheritance of it all. Fortunately there is the original inexhaustible fund of buoyancy, normally resident in the race, forever eligible to be appeal'd to and relied on.

Democracy's Need

I SAY that democracy can never prove itself beyond cavil, until it founds and luxuriantly grows its own forms of art, poems, schools, theology, displacing all that exists, or that

1224

has been produced anywhere in the past, under opposite influences. It is curious to me that while so many voices, pens, minds, in the press, lecture rooms, in our Congress, etc., are discussing intellectual topics, pecuniary dangers, legislative problems, the suffrage, tariff and labor questions, and the various business and benevolent needs of America, with propositions, remedies, often worth deep attention, there is one need, a hiatus the profoundest, that no eye seems to perceive, no voice to state. Our fundamental want today in the United States, with closest, amplest reference to present conditions, and to the future, is of a class, and the clear idea of a class, of native authors, literatures, far different, far higher in grade, than any yet known, sacerdotal, modern, fit to cope with our occasions, lands, permeating the whole mass of American mentality, taste, belief, breathing into it a new breath of life, giving it decision, affecting politics far more than the popular superficial suffrage, with results inside and underneath the elections of Presidents or Congresses—radiating, begetting appropriate teachers, schools, manners, and as its grandest result, accomplishing (what neither the schools nor the churches and their clergy have hitherto accomplished, and without which this nation will no more stand, permanently, soundly, than a house will stand without a substratum), a religious and moral character beneath the political and productive and intellectual bases of the States. For know you not, dear, earnest reader, that the people of our land may all read and write, and may all possess the right to vote—and yet the main things may be entirely lacking?— (and this to suggest them).

Viewed, today, from a point of view sufficiently overarching, the problem of humanity all over the civilized world is social and religious, and is to be finally met and treated by literature. The priest departs, the divine literatus comes. . . .

Few are aware how the great literature penetrates all, gives hue to all, shapes aggregates and individuals, and, after subtle ways, with irresistible power, constructs, sustains, demolishes at will. Why tower, in reminiscence, above all the nations of the earth, two special lands, petty in themselves, yet inexpressibly gigantic, beautiful, columnar? Immortal Judah lives, and Greece immortal lives, in a couple of poems.

[363]

WILSON, WOODROW

WILSON, WOODROW (1856-1924). Most of Wilson's admirers hold that his idealism enhanced his statesmanship while most of his adversaries assert that it was his idealism that led him astray. But neither his sound nor his erroneous judgments and measures can be explained by his philosophical or religious attitude alone. At times, Wilson, the idealist, was rightly considered "America's most practical president," and sometimes Wilson became the victim of his illusions when he tried to act as a shrewd politician. His power to exercise sound judgment increased and deteriorated independently of his idealism that always was a constant element of his personality. The mystical faith in his mission must be distinguished from his religious belief and his philosophical conviction, both of which nourished his missionary zeal but were not identical with it. He was not the man to create original ideas but rather to make the adopted ideas into living forces which had to serve his mission, and the efforts to accomplish this mission made evident the conflicting tendencies of his personality which finally caused his personal failure without refuting the principal ideas supported by him.

Wilson was moved by strong emotional impulses though always on guard against his own emotions. He was a deeply convinced Christian but humility was not the significant trait of his nature. He struggled for the rights of the individual but confessed that he was "not fond of thinking of Christianity as the means of saving individual souls." Service and sacrifice of selfish interests was preached by him, and he earnestly endeavored to live and act in accordance with his teaching, but he was intolerant of any dissent. No President of the United States had studied so intensely the lives, achievements and failures of his predecessors in office as Wilson had done. The result of these studies was his firm belief that he, the President, by virtue of his election, "can speak what no man else knows, the common meaning of the common voice." But in

1226

case of disagreement with the majority of the people, Wilson believed in his higher judgment. It was this mystical belief in his faculty to express the innermost thoughts of the nations that led him on a dangerous way when he tried to impose on the world a peace treaty which should be, as ex-President Taft remarked, "his and nobody's else's peace" because he claimed to know better than anyone else the meaning of justice. It was not vanity that let him make such assumptions. If Wilson did not distrust his convictions he at least steadily distrusted his emotions. His motives have been best expressed in Rudyard Kipling's poem *If*, which Wilson regarded as his personal credo, and which he carried in his pocket and later had framed to hang beside him when he died, a hero in defeat. It was Wilson's motto "to keep your head when all about you are losing theirs and blaming it on you," to "trust yourself when all men doubt you," to "dream and not make dream your master" and to "talk with crowds and keep your virtue."

CONDITIONS OF SOCIAL LIFE

Co-operation is the vital principle of social life, not organization merely. I think I know something about organization. I can make an organization, but it is one thing to have an organization and another thing to fill it with life. And then it is a very important matter what sort of life you fill it with. If the object of the organization is what the object of some business organizations is, to absorb the life of the community for its own benefit, then there is nothing beneficial in it. But if the object of the organization is to afford a mechanism by which the whole community can cooperatively use its life, then there is a great deal in it. An organization without the spirit of cooperation is dead and may be dangerous. . . .

Legislation cannot save society. Legislation cannot even rectify society. The law that will work is merely the summing up in legislative form of the moral judgment that the community has already reached. Law records how far society has got; there have got to be instrumentalities preceding the law that get society up to that point where it will be ready to record. . . . Law is a record of achievement. It is not a process of regeneration. Our wills have to be regenerated, and our purposes rectified before we are in a position to enact laws that record those moral achievements. And that is the business, primarily, it seems to me, of the Christian. . . .

All the transforming influences in the world are unselfish. There is not a single selfish force in the world that is not touched with sinister power, and the church is the only embodiment of the things that are entirely unselfish, the principles of self-sacrifice and devotion. . . . America is great in the world, not as she is a successful government merely, but as she is the successful embodiment of a great ideal of unselfish citizenship.

[364]

WINDELBAND, WILHELM

WINDELBAND, WILHELM (1848-1915). As a historian of philosophy and as the founder of the "South-West-German school of philosophy," Windelband exercised considerable influence. In both activities, he emphasized that philosophy must reflect on civilization and its historical evolution. Windelband belongs to those German philosophers who proceed from Kant's criticism, but he protested against other neo-Kantians who mainly confined their thinking to a renewal of Kant's epistemology, and he stressed the importance of his inquiries into ethics, aesthetics, and philosophy of law and religion. Windelband's program, however, maintained that "to understand Kant rightly means to go beyond him." While Kant considered only mathematics and natural sciences, founded upon mathematics, as real sciences, Windelband held that history in the broadest sense of the word, comprising views on all kinds of human activities, must be acknowledged as a true science. He distinguished between the natural sciences, which are concerned with the establishment of laws, and the historical sciences, which try to grasp, to describe and explain individual facts. The methods of the natural sciences are characterized as being of a generalizing, nomothetic character, those of the historical sciences as "idiographic." From this distinction, Windelband proceeded to a sharp opposition to epistemological naturalism, and broached the question, of whether the nomothetic or the idiographic sciences are of more essential importance to philosophy. He decided in favor of the historical sciences, because, according to him philosophy must interpret spiritual life and explain values, and the sense of values is rooted in the sense of the individual.

In his efforts to "go beyond Kant," Windelband relied on Hegel, Herbart and Lotze. Closely associated with Windelband was Heinrich Rickert. Among Windelband's disciples were not only noted philosophers but sociologists like Max Weber and theologians like Ernst Troeltsch.

PHILOSOPHY

THE man who wishes to make a serious study of philosophy must be prepared to find that in its light the world and life will present a different aspect from that which he saw previously; to sacrifice, if it prove necessary, the preconceived ideas with which he approached it.

It is quite possible, perhaps inevitable, that the results of philosophy will diverge considerably from the conclusions that one had in advance, but the things which philosophy discusses are not remote and obscure objects that need some skill to discover them. On the contrary, they are precisely the things which life itself and the work of the various sciences force upon a man's attention. It is the very essence of philosophy to examine thoroughly what lies at hand and all round us. In the whole of our intellectual life there are uncritized assumptions and ideas lightly borrowed from life and science. The practical life of man is pervaded and dominated by the pre-scientific ideas, naively developed, which usage has incorporated in our speech. These ideas, it is true, are modified and clarified in the special sciences as far as it is necessary for their particular purpose of arranging and controlling their material; but they still demand consideration in connection with the problems and inquiries of philosophy. Just as life affords material to the scientific worker in its pre-scientific ideas, so life and the sciences together provide, in their pre-scientific and *pre-philosophic* ideas, material for the operations of the philosopher. Hence it is that the frontier between the special sciences and philosophy is not a definite line, but depends in each age on the state of knowledge. In common life we conceive a body as a thing that occupies space and is endowed with all sorts of properties. Out of this pre-scientific notion physics and chemistry form their ideas of atoms, molecules, and elements. They were first formed in the general impulse to acquire knowledge which the Greeks called "philosophy." To-day these scientific ideas are pre-philosophic concepts, and they suggest to us so many problems of philosophy.

These assumptions which have not been thoroughly examined have a legitimate use in the field for which they are intended. Practical life manages very well with its pre-scientific ideas of bodies; and the pre-philosophical ideas of atoms, etc., are just as satisfactory for the special needs of physics and chemistry. While, however, they are thus suited to the demands of empirical theory it may be that they will present serious problems in the more general aspects in which philosophy has to consider them. The idea of natural law is an indispensable requirement both for practical life and for scientific research, which has to discover the several laws of nature. But what a natural law is, and what is the nature of the dependence of our various concrete experiences upon this general idea, are difficult problems which must be approached, not by empirical investigation, but by philosophical reflection.

In the special sciences and in common life, therefore, these fundamental assumptions are justified by success; but the moment they are considered more deeply, the moment a man asks himself whether these things which are naively taken for granted are really sound, philosophy is born. It is, as Aristotle says, the *taumagein*, the hour in which the mind is puzzled and turns upon itself. It is the *esetagein*, the demand of proof, with which Socrates disturbed the illusory self-complacency of himself and his fellow-citizens. It is complete honesty of the intellect with itself. We can never reflect on things without assumptions which must be taken for granted; but we must not leave them indefinitely without investigation, and we must be prepared to abandon them if

1230

they are found to be wrong. This testing of one's assumptions is philosophy.

Every great philosopher has passed through this phase of examining what had been taken for granted, and it is the same impulse which directs a man to the study of philosophy. In the life of every thoughtful man there comes a time when everything that had been assumed, and on which we had confidently built, collapses like a house of cards, and, as during an earthquake, even the most solid-looking structure totters. Descartes has very vividly described this, with the most exquisite simplicity and fineness, in his first *Meditation*. He experiences, as Socrates did, the real mission of scepticism; which is, both in history and in the very nature of human thought, to lead us onward to a final security through the dissolution of our unreflecting assumptions.

[365]

WITTGENSTEIN, LUDWIG

WITTGENSTEIN, LUDWIG (1889-1951). For a time, Wittgenstein was preoccupied with architecture and only intermittently interested in philosophy. But his *Tractatus Logico-Philosophicus* (1922) became of great consequence to the development of logical positivism or scientific empiricism, while its author, then about thirty years old, inspired older thinkers like Moritz Schlick, Bertrand Russell and Alfred Whitehead.

In this treatise, Wittgenstein offers a general way of removing philosophical difficulties by investigating the logical structure of language. Incapability of seeing through the logic of language, or at least neglect of its importance, is the cause of apparently or really insoluble philosophical problems. Wittgenstein insists that whatever can be said, can be said clearly. Philosophy is not a doctrine but, rather, an activity. Its result is not new propositions but clarification of propositions. Philosophy will mean the inexpressible by presenting the expressible as clearly as possible.

Some years after the publication of his treatise, Wittgenstein concentrated upon his philosophical studies, and was called to Cambridge, England, where later he was appointed successor to G. E. Moore.

BEGINNING OF THE TRACTATUS
LOGICO-PHILOSOPHICUS

1	The world is everything that is the case.*
1.1	The world is the totality of facts, not of things.
1.11	The world is determined by the facts, and by these being *all* the facts.
1.12	For the totality of facts determines both what is the case, and also all that is not the case.
1.13	The facts in logical space are the world.
1.2	The world divides into facts.
1.21	Any one can either be the case or not be the case, and everything else remain the same.
2	What is the case, the fact, is the existence of atomic facts.
2.01	An atomic fact is a combination of objects (entities, things).
2.011	It is essential to a thing that it can be a constituent part of an atomic fact.
2.012	In logic nothing is accidental: if a thing *can* occur in an atomic fact the possibility of that atomic fact must already be prejudged in the thing.
2.0121	It would, so to speak, appear as an accident, when to a thing that could exist alone on its own account, subsequently a state of affairs could be made to fit.

If things can occur in atomic facts, this possibility must already lie in them.

(A logical entity cannot be merely possible. Logic treats of every possibility, and all possibilities are its facts.)

Just as we cannot think of spatial objects at all apart from space, or temporal objects apart from

* The decimal figures as numbers of the separate propositions indicate the logical importance of the propositions, the emphasis laid upon them in my exposition. The propositions *n*.1, *n*.2, *n*.3, etc., are comments on proposition No. *n*; the propositions *n.m*1, *n.m*2, etc., are comments on the proposition No. *n.m*; and so on.

time, so we cannot think of *any* object apart from the possibility of its connection with other things.

If I can think of an object in the context of an atomic fact, I cannot think of it apart from the *possibility* of this context.

2.0122 The thing is independent, in so far as it can occur in all *possible* circumstances, but this form of independence is a form of connection with the atomic fact, a form of dependence. (It is impossible for words to occur in two different ways, alone and in the proposition.)

2.0123 If I know an object, then I also know all the possibilities of its occurrence in atomic facts.

(Every such possibility must lie in the nature of the object.)

A new possibility cannot subsequently be found.

2.01231 In order to know an object, I must know not its external but all its internal qualities.

2.0124 If all objects are given, then thereby are all *possible* atomic facts also given.

2.013 Every thing is, as it were, in a space of possible atomic facts. I can think of this space as empty, but not of the thing without the space.

2.0131 A spatial object must lie in infinite space. (A point in space is a place for an argument.)

[366]

WOLFF, CHRISTIAN

WOLFF, CHRISTIAN (1679-1754). Frederick William I, the "soldier king" of Prussia, dismissed Wolff, in 1723, from his post as professor at the University of Halle, forced him to leave the kingdom within forty-eight hours, and, some years later, decreed that everyone who used a book of Wolff's should be sentenced to wheelbarrow labor. What incited the fury of the king was an address given by Wolff in which he had praised the ethical teachings of Confucius, and had added that a man could be happy and good without the Divine grace or revelation. Furthermore, the king was impressed by the apprehension, expressed by some of his generals, that Wolff, as an adherent of determinism, might endanger the discipline of the Prussian army.

Wolff's international fame was enhanced by the King's measures. Other governments offered him a professorship. Learned societies in France and England awarded him degrees and honors. However, the University of Halle suffered from the consequences of Wolff's expulsion, so that the King, reluctantly, invited Wolff to come back. Before the negotiations were completed, Frederick William I died, and his successor Frederick II used Wolff's final reappointment to exhibit himself as a tolerant ruler.

Wolff was a disciple of Leibniz, but he completed the latter's system, or, as Leibniz saw it, deformed it, by concessions to Aquinas, Descartes, and even to Locke. Despite different opinions, Leibniz remained friendly to Wolff, and continued to recommend and advise him. For Leibniz was aware that Wolff had a faculty of clear expression and systematization which he himself lacked. Wolff's authority and influence with the German Enlightenment were immense until Kant shook the fundamentals of Wolff's system. But even Kant revered him as "the most powerful representative of dogmatic rationalism, of the standpoint of pure, unshaken confidence in the strength of reason."

DUTIES TOWARD OTHERS

SINCE Man shall not only perfect himself and his status and make himself safe from imperfection, but since he shall contribute, as far as possible and without failing in his duties toward himself, to the perfection of others and their status whenever they need his help, and since he shall also refrain from everything which would make them and their status more imperfect, it follows that each man owes to his fellow men the same things he owes to himself in the same measure as far as the other person has these things not in his powers and he himself can do them for this other person without neglecting his duty toward himself. Consequently, the duties of a person toward others are the same as his duties toward himself. Therefore these duties be incumbent on others.

Every man, therefore, shall, as far as it is in his power, help any other person who needs his help; he shall improve the goods of the soul, of the body and of fortune and consequently take precautions lest the others would be overtaken by the diseases of the soul or of the body and ill fortune. Since natural law does not restrict help to certain goods we shall not refuse our help to others so that they may enjoy better welfare than we enjoy ourselves. That could not be so if we envied another person for his happiness. One shall never envy anyone for a joy he lacks. Envy is opposed to the very nature of Man.

Natural obligation is absolutely unchangeable. If another person does not fulfil this obligation, this fact does not allow you not to fulfil it either. Consequently it is not permissible to transgress natural law by referring to the examples of others, and our duties toward others do not cease because they fail in their duties toward us. This being understood also concerning the things the natural law prohibits, it follows too that we owe the duties of humanity to those who harm us.

The duties of Man toward others being the same as those toward himself, everybody shall have a constant and perpetual will to advance the perfection and happiness of any other person. Consequently, because love or our fellow man is the essence of this will, and love the essence of the disposition of the soul to feel pleasure through the happiness of another person, everybody should have sympathy and love for his fellow man as well as for himself, and should not hate him

Since men shall be friends to each other, each shall strive not to make others his enemies but to obtain and to keep their friendship. However, one cannot be exempted from natural obligation. One shall, therefore, not do anything out of friendship which would be contrary to natural law

Perfection of the soul consists in the intellectual and moral virtues. We have therefore to be careful to extend them and, by our example, we have to teach them to others and make them love those virtues. Consequently we shall give

1235

them good examples—that means examples that teach those virtues—and inspire them to like them and not to give them bad ones—that means examples by which one teaches them vices and which inspire them to vices. One shall not mislead anybody to vices. Since we shall omit actions by which another or his status is made more imperfect, and since we shall contribute to the perfection of other people as much as we can, it follows that nobody shall prevent another from obtaining any perfection nor shall he prevent a third person from helping him in it. This concerns any good of the soul, the body of the fortune. It seems also that nobody shall prevent anyone from eliminating another person's sickness of the soul or of the body or ill fortune, or from delivering him from these evils. Even less shall one deprive him from any good, either by acting himself or through others.

[367]

WOODBRIDGE, FREDERICK JAMES EUGENE

WOODBRIDGE, FREDERICK JAMES EUGENE (1867-1940). Woodbridge, one of the most attractive and stimulating teachers in the history of American universities, called himself a naive realist. In his later years he was deeply impressed by Santayana's writings which he highly praised and acknowledged as illuminating and enhancing his own understanding of philosophical and cultural problems. But the basis of his philosophy, such as it is presented in his books *The Purpose of History* (1916) and *The Realm of Mind* (1926), was laid before he became acquainted with Santayana's thoughts.

The originality of Woodbridge's realism is veiled by his own characterization of his philosophy as "a synthesis of Aristotle and Spinoza, tempered by Locke's empiricism." Woodbridge avowed his indebtedness to Aristotle's naturalism and the conception of productivity, and to Spinoza's "rigid insistence on structure," while it was Locke who he said had taught him "fundamentally sound thinking." "Far less acute than Descartes, and far less subtle than Kant, he was far more solid than any of them."

But it is taken for granted that Woodbridge, by historically deriving his own thoughts from Aristotle, Spinoza and Locke, had wronged himself. The three philosophers were more influential to him as examples of philosophizing than as transmitters of ideas, and Spinoza and Locke particularly impressed him more as human personalities than as shapers of doctrines. Woodbridge's inquiry into the nature of structure and activity and their relations is the work of an independent thinker. To him, structure determines what is possible, and activity determines what exists. These concepts were elaborated by cautious and flexible analysis of reality as Woodbridge himself saw it.

WHAT IS PERSONALITY

WHAT is personality? If by the question we mean to ask, What is the nature of personality as a given conscious fact to be analyzed?, we get the answer from psychology. As such a fact personality is found to be, not a cause of consciousness, not something back of it and distinct from it, but is itself a content, an arrangement of element. But if we mean by the question what an individual with such a conduct of life, what is he a factor in society, what is he revealed in the fullness of human experience, we get the answer from history—to be a person is to use the material and machinery of life in the service of ideals. Let us think of ourselves as masses of sensations if we must; but let us never be so absurd as to forget that such masses of sensations have made human history what it is, and can, if they will, make the history of the future immeasurably more glorious. Let us not quarrel with psychology or the results of science, but let the wonder of it all possess us; that there should appear in the natural history of the world creatures whose lot in life should be constantly to reach beyond themselves in order to live at all, whose whole existence should be a world-transformation and a self-tranformation in the interest of what they would have prevail, who, while they must draw the materials of their work from what they could discover of nature's constitution and their own, must none the less draw life's inspiration and motives, must get the mainspring of the activity and progress, not from what they are, but from what they might be; creatures who, under this necessity and this compulsion, should find no permanent peace until they would commit themselves, freely and wholly, in complete self-surrender, to what their ideals reveal them to be—let us wonder at it. And we should be wondering, not at some theory of things, but at one of the plainest facts we know. No psychology can destroy that fact, and no metaphysics enhance the wonder of it. It is the truth of experience, and in that truth our personality is disclosed.

[368]

WUNDT, WILHELM

WUNDT, WILHELM (1832-1920). The first psychological laboratory was founded in 1879 at Leipzig by Wundt who was a professor at that University from 1875 until his death, and who attracted to his lectures and demonstrations not only young students but scholars who had distinguished themselves, from almost all countries. Wundt developed physiological psychology by experimental methods, measuring reactions to physical and physiological changes, effects, stimulations. But, to him, physiological psychology covers only part of psychology. It is to be completed by introspective analysis of "internal experience," founded upon a philosophical system and integrated into the general doctrine of science. Wundt's introspective psychology is characterized by his conviction that will, together with the emotional states closely connected with it, is the constituent of psychological experience, and is far more important than sensations and ideas; all the other psychical processes must be conceived of by analogy to the experience of will. To him, the soul is a subject but no substance. It is event, activity, evolution.

Wundt's philosophical system is described by himself as a synthesis of Hegelianism and positivism, though he intended to avoid the one-sidedness of each. The fundamental principle of his metaphysics maintained that all material and mechanical things are but the outer shell behind which spiritual activities and strivings are hidden. According to Wundt, the world is the purposive evolution of the spirit. To this extent, Wundt agreed with Hegel. However, he tried to found his philosophy upon a thorough study of the empirical sciences.

GENERAL LAWS OF PSYCHICAL DEVELOPMENTS

THE *law of mental growth* is as little applicable to all con-

1238

tents of psychical experience as is any other law of psychical development. It holds only under the limiting condition which applies to the principle of resultants, the application of which is, namely, the condition of the *continuity of the processes*. But since the circumstances that tend to prevent the realization of this condition, are, of course, much more frequent when the mental developments concerned include a greater number of psychical syntheses, than in the case of the simple syntheses themselves, it follows that the law of mental growth can be demonstrated only for certain developments taking place under normal conditions, and even here only within certain limits. Within these limits, however, the more comprehensive developments, as for example the mental development of the normal individual and the development of mental communities, are obviously the best exemplifications of the fundamental principle of resultants, which principle lies at the basis of this development.

The *law of heterogony of ends* is most closely connected with the principle of relations, but it is also based on the principle of resultants, which latter is always to be taken into consideration when dealing with the larger interconnections of psychical development. In fact, we may regard this law of heterogony of ends as a principle of development which controls the changes arising as results of successive creative syntheses, in the relations between the single partial contents of psychical compounds. The resultants arising from united psychical processes include contents which were not present in the components, and these new contents may in turn enter into relation with the old components, thus changing again the relations between these old components and consequently changing the new resultants which arise. This principle of continually changing relations is most strikingly illustrated when an *idea of ends* is formed on the basis of the given relations. In such cases the relation of the single factors to one another is regarded as an interconnection of means, which interconnection has for its end the product arising from the interconnection. The relation in such a case between the actual *effects* and the ideated ends, is such that secondary effects always arise which were not thought of in the first ideas of end. These new effects enter into new series of motives, and thus modify the earlier ends or add new ends to those which existed at first.

The law of heterogony of ends in its broadest sense dominates all psychical processes. In the special teleological coloring which has given it its name, however, it is to be found primarily in the sphere of *volitional processes,* for here the ideas of end together with their affective motives are of the chief importance. Of the various spheres of applied psychology, it is especially *ethics* for which this law is of great importance.

The *law of development towards opposites* is an application of the principle of intensification through contrast, to more comprehensive interconnections which form in themselves series of developments. In such series of developments there is a constant play of contrasting feelings in accordance with the fundamental principle of contrasts. First, certain feelings and impulses of small intensity begin to arise. Through contrast with the predominating feelings this rising group increases in intensity until finally it gains the complete ascendency. This ascendency is retained for a time and then from this point on the same alteration may be, once, or even several times, repeated. But generally the laws of mental growth and heterogony of ends operate in the case of such an oscillation, so that succeeding phases, though they are like corresponding antecedent phases in their general affective direction, yet differ essentially in their special components.

The law of development towards opposites shows itself in the mental development of the individual, partly in a purely individual way within shorter periods of time, and partly in certain universal regularities in the relation of various periods of life. It has long been recognized that the predominating temperaments of different periods of life present certain contrasts. Thus, the light, sanguine excitability of childhood, which is seldom more than superficial, is followed by the slower but more retentive temperament of youth with its frequent touch of melancholy. Then comes manhood with the mature character, generally quick and active in decision and execution, and last of all, old age with its leaning towards contemplative quiet. Even more than in the individual does the principle of development toward opposites find expression in the alternation of mental tendencies which appear in social and historical life, and in the reaction of those mental tendencies on civilization and customs and on social and political development.

As the law of heterogony of ends applies chiefly to the domain of *moral* life, so the law of development towards opposites finds its chief significance in the more general sphere of *historical* life.

[369]

X

XENOPHANES

XENOPHANES (About 580-485 B.C.). Xenophanes was born in Colophon in Asia Minor. He was the first thinker of Greek culture to present the idea of the one, true, eternal, supreme God in opposition to the ideas of the gods of the poets and the popular cults which, as Xenophanes vigorously declared, were shaped after human images. God, as conceived by Xenophanes, defies all human ways of comprehending. In his ideas on physics, Xenophanes, a contemporary of Pythagoras, relied principally on the Milesian school. Possibly it was because of his religious rigorism that Xenophanes led a migratory life, wandering restlessly after he had left his native country for Italy.

FRAGMENTS

THERE is one god, supreme among gods and men; resembling mortals neither in form nor in mind.

The whole of him sees, the whole of him thinks, the whole of him hears.

Without toil he rules all things by the power of his mind.

And he stays always in the same place, nor moves at all, for it is not seemly that he wander about now here, now there.

But mortals fancy gods are born, and wear clothes, and have voice and form like themselves.

Yet if oxen and lions had hands, and could paint with their hands, and fashion images, as men do, they would make the pictures and images of their gods in their own likeness; horses would make them like horses, oxen like oxen.

Ethiopians make their gods black and snub-nosed;
Thracians give theirs blue eyes and red hair.

Homer and Hesiod have ascribed to the gods all deeds
that are a shame and a disgrace among men: thieving, adultery, fraud.

The gods did not reveal all things to men at the start;
but, as time goes on, by searching, they discover more and
more.

There never was, nor ever will be, any man who knows
with certainty the things about the gods and about all things
which I tell of. For even if he does happen to get most things
right, still he himself does not know it. But mere opinions all
may have.

[370]

XIRAU PALAU, JOAQUIN

XIRAU PALAU, JOAQUIN (1895-   ). After a brilliant academic
career in Spain, his native country, Xirau became a refugee from
the Franco dictatorship, and went to Mexico. Next to Ortega y Gasset, with whom he studied philosophy, Xirau is considered the most
profound thinker of modern Spain. Firmly rooted in the spiritual
tradition of his country and well-acquainted with French, German
and Anglo-Saxon philosophy, Xirau was particularly inspired by
Bergson, Husserl and Heidegger, though he by no means adopted
their views uncritically. His main objection to modern existentialism
is that in it all ideas of transcendence disappear. He holds that
fundamental existence is a preconscious experience of pure tempor-
ality, and that reality is revealed by prerational intuition. Reality
is conceived by Xirau as destiny which remains unfulfilled, and the
task of philosophy is to explore the ways to advance fulfilment, although it cannot be reached. After historical and critical studies on
Descartes, Leibniz and Rousseau, Xirau affirmed his principal
views in *Amor y Mundo* (Love and World, 1940).

THE METAPHYSICAL BACKGROUND
OF THE CRISIS OF CIVILIZATION

THE social and political crisis through which the world is
passing has a metaphysical background that has been little

noticed or is wholly unknown to the great majority of men. It persists in the very air that we breathe, its presence is so familiar as to be imperceptible. Only by withdrawing can we contemplate it "en masse." Hence our surprise in the face of unprecedented events which in reality were foresee-able and natural. The lightning flames from the heights and fire from the depth of the volcano, and since both spring from invisible sources they seem instantaneous. For a long time man lived heedless, caring not for the disasters that the gods were forging in his midst. Men continued to speak of progress, of liberty, of civilization, failing to see that even the strains of their voices were dying in the echo. Every alarming symptom was summarily dispatched with a solemn declaration that in "these days" certain things were no longer possible. Whence dismay and terror when it was realized that in these times "Things" were possible such as no century has ever suspected. . . .

Modern life is chaos, not Cosmos. As such it lacks a center, is meaningless, aimless. The ancient world was an organism. And, as in every organism, each part served the whole, and the whole gave service to the parts. Life was lived centered between the material which constituted the telluric root and the luminous crown of the ideal. The living body of reality had its foundation in the contents of the material and its culmination in the splendor of the spirit. Both were functions of a central organism that gave them meaning and form. Descartes stripped away the living flesh of the world. The organism splits and disappears. We are left only the base and the apex, matter and spirit, the real and the ideal. The pomp and glory of the world is reduced to one or the other. Thus transformed into a thin thread of ideas or an endless flux of causes and effects, the world becomes an illusion, and through idealism and materialization, mathe-matical calculus or atomic movement, tends to dissolve into nothingness.

[371]

Y

YAJNAVALKYA

YAJNAVALKYA (About 600 B.C.). There is no agreement among scholars whether Yajnavalkya was a historical person or the fictitious name for a group of thinkers and teachers. At any rate, this name is connected with the *Brhadaranyaka Upanishad* which does not only belong to the thirteen oldest Upanishads but is considered the most coherent and illuminating of all of them. It is representative of the earliest philosophical development of the Vedic religion, previous to the earliest beginnings of Greek philosophy.

The Upanishads teach the belief in Brahma, the one great reality, as the ground of existence, the belief in transmigration and *karma*, which originally meant sacrificial acts, but later the influence of human action, as the explanation of apparently unjust or incomprehensible distribution of good and evil and the home of liberation of the soul through union of the individual with Brahma. The *Brhadaranyaka Upanishad* presents these tenets in a relatively concentrated form.

THE SELF

In sooth, a husband is dear,—not because you love the husband; but a husband is dear because you love the Self. In sooth, a wife is dear,—not because you love the wife; but a wife is dear because you love the Self. . . . In sooth, the gods are dear,—not because you love the gods; but gods are dear because you love the Self. In sooth, beings are dear,—not because you love beings; but beings are dear because you love the Self. In sooth, the whole world is dear, —not because you love the whole world; but the whole world is dear because you love the Self.

In very truth, it is the Self that should be seen, heard, thought and meditated. . . . Indeed, when the Self is seen, heard, thought and understood, everything is comprehended. . . .

It is as when a drum is beaten: You cannot lay hold of the sound at large, but by laying hold of the drum or the beater of the drum, the sound is seized. . . .

It is as with a lump of salt: Thrown into water, it dissolves [making] it impossible to retrieve it; but wherever you may dip, it is salty throughout. In the same manner it is, truly, with this great, infinite, boundless Being which consists of intelligence: Emerging from the elements, it becomes immersed in them again. After death there is no consciousness. . . . For, where there is, as it were, a duality, there you see one another, smell one another, hear one another, talk to one another, understand one another, recognize one another. But where everything has become one's self,—how could you smell anything, see anything, hear anything, talk to anyone, think anything, discern anything? How could you discern that by which all is discerned? How could you discern the discerner? . . .

. . . It is your self which is in all things. . . . You could not see the seer in seeing, you could not hear the hearer in hearing, you could not think the thinker in thinking, you could not discern the discerner in discerning. It is your self that is in everything. Anything else [means] woe. . . .

. . . That which [though] dwelling in all being, beings do not know, whose body all beings are, governs all beings from within,—that is your Self, the inner controller, the immortal one. . . . It is the seer that is not seen, the hearer that is not heard, the thinker that is not thought, the discerner that is not discerned. There is nothing apart from it that sees, nothing apart from it that hears, nothing apart from it that thinks, nothing apart from it that discerns. It is your Self, the inner controller, the immortal. . . .

. . . That which is above the heavens, that which is below the earth, that which is between both heaven and earth, is what is called the past, present and future. It is woven, warp and woof, in space. . That [which space is woven in] Brahmans call the Imperishable: It is not coarse, not fine, not short, not long, not glowing, not clinging, not shadowy, not dark; it is windless, etherless, unattached, tasteless, odorless, eyeless, earless, speechless, nonenergetic, breathless, mouthless, descentless, endless, without inside or outside; it does not consume anything, nor is it consumed by anything. .

Verily, . . he who does not know this Imperishable and [yet] sacrifices, worships and practices penance in this world for thousands of years on end,—to him it is of limited [avail]. Indeed, . . . who departs from this world and does not know this Imperishable, he is to be pitied. But he . . . who departs from this world and knows that Imperishable, he is a Brahman.

. The Self is not this, it is not that. It is inconceivable, for it cannot be conceived. It is indestructible, for it cannot be destroyed. It is unattached, for it does not attach itself. It is unbound. It does not come to naught. It does not fail. . . .

[372]

YU-LAN FUNG

YU-LAN FUNG (1895-   ). Professor Yu-Lan Fung, the author of the standard *History of Chinese Philosophy* (1930-33) and *The New Rational Philosophy* (1939), is not only a historian of philosophy but a systematic philosopher whose way of thinking and conceiving reality shows striking analogies to George Santayana's views, though he is firmly rooted in the traditions of Confucianism. He has revived the rational philosophy of the brothers Ch'eng Ming-tao and Ch'eng I Ch'uan (1032-1086 and 1033-1107, respectively) in order to "continue" but not to "follow" them. He distinguishes two realms, that of truth and that of actuality. Reason, according to him, belongs to the realm of truth. It is not in or above the world but rather it is a regulating principle of everything that appears in the actual world. The realm of actuality is not created by reason; it is self-existent. Since reason cannot create, it

1247

is a principle which is neither in reason nor in the actual world that brings things into real existence. This principle is called "the Vital Principle of the True Prime Unit." The essences of the realm of truth which are not the causes but the models of the real things can be known only by the objective and systematic studies, by means of inductive method and experimental logic. In this way, Fung has purified Neo-Confucianism from the Buddhist elements which had pervaded it in previous times.

PHILOSOPHY OF CONTEMPORARY CHINA

CHINA is now at a present that is not the natural growth of her past, but something forced upon her against her will. In the completely new situation that she has to face, she has been much bewildered. In order to make the situation more intelligible and to adapt to it more intelligently, she has to interpret sometimes the present in terms of the past and sometimes the past in terms of the present. In other words, she has to connect the new civilization that she has to face with the old that she already has and to make them not alien but intelligible to each other. Besides interpretation, there is also criticism. In interpreting the new civilization in terms of the old, or the old in terms of the new, she cannot help but to criticize sometimes the new in the light of the old, and sometimes the old in the light of the new. Thus the interpretation and criticism of civilizations is the natural product in China of the meeting of the West and the East and is what has interested the Chinese mind and has constituted the main current of Chinese thought during the last fifty years.

It may be noticed that the interpretation and criticism of the civilizations new and old, within the last fifty years, differ in different periods according to the degree of the knowledge or of the ignorance of the time regarding the new civilization that comes from outside. Generally speaking there have been three periods. The first period is marked with the ill-fated political reformation with the leadership of Kan Yu-wei under the Emperor Kuang-su in 1898. Kan Yu-wei was a scholar of one of the Confucianist schools, known as the Kung Yang school. According to this school,

Confucius was a teacher with divine personality. He devised a scheme that would cover all stages of human progress. There are mainly three stages. The first is the stage of disorder; the second, the stage of progressive peace; and the third, the stage of great peace. In the stage of disorder, every one is for one's own country. In the stage of progressive peace, all the civilized countries are united in one. In the stage of great peace, all men are civilized and humanity is united in one harmonious whole. Confucius knew beforehand all these that are to come. He devised accordingly three systems of social organization. According to Kan Yu-wei, the communication between the East and the West and the political and social reformations in Europe and America show that men are progressing from the stage of disorder to the higher stage, the stage of progressive peace. Most, if not all, of the political and social institutions of the West are already implied in the teaching of Confucius. Kan Yu-wei was the leader of the New Movement at his time. But in his opinion, what he was doing was not the adoption of the new civilization of the West, but rather the realization of the old teaching of Confucius. He wrote many Commentaries to the Confucian classics, reading into them his new ideas. Besides these he also wrote a book entitled *The Book on The Great Unity*, in which he gave a concrete picture of the utopia that will become a fact in the third stage of human progress according to the Confucianist scheme. Although the nature of this book is so bold and revolutionary that it will startle even most of the utopian writers, Kan Yu-wei himself was not an utopian. He insisted that the programme he set forth in his book cannot be put into practice except in the highest stage of human civilization, the last stage of human progress. In his practical political programme he insisted to have a constitutional monarchy.

One of the colleagues of Kan Yu-wei in the New Movement of that time was Tan Tse-tung, who was a more philosophical thinker. He wrote a book entitled *On Benevolence* in which he also taught the Confucianist teaching of the three stages of human progress. According to him although Confucius set forth the general scheme of the three stages, most of the teaching of Confucius was for the stage of disorder. It is the reason why Confucius was often misunderstood as the champion of traditional institutions and conventional morality. The Christian teaching of universal love and the equality of men before God is quite near the Confucian teaching for the stage of progressive peace. The teaching that is near the Confucian teaching for the last stage of human progress is Buddhism which goes beyond all human distinctions and conventional morality.

The main spirit of this time is that the leaders were not antagonistic to the new civilization that came from the West, nor did they lack appreciation of its value. But they appreciated its value only in so far as it fits in the imaginary Confucian scheme. They interpreted the new in terms of, and criticized it in the light of, the old. It is to be noticed that the philosophical justification of the Revolution of 1911 with the result of the establishment of the Republic was mainly taken from Chinese philosophy. The saying of Mencius that "the people is first important, the country the second, the sovereign unimportant" was much quoted and interpreted. The teaching of the European revolutionary writers such as Rousseau also played its role, but people often thought that they are right because they agree with Mencius.

The second period is marked with the New Culture Movement which reached its climax in 1919. In this period the spirit of the time is the criticism of the old in the light of the new. Chen Tu-siu and Hui Shih were the leaders of the criticism. The latter philosopher wrote *An Outline of the History of Chinese Philosophy*, of which only the first part was published. It is in fact a criticism of Chinese philosophy rather than a history of it. The two most influential schools of Chinese philosophy, Confucianism and Taoism, were much criticized and questioned from a utilitarian and pragmatic point of view. He is for individual liberty and development and therefore he found that Confucianism is wrong in the teaching of the subordination of the individual to his sovereign and his father, to his state and his family. He is for the spirit of struggle and conquering nature and therefore he found that Taoism is wrong in the teaching of enjoying nature. In reading his book one cannot but feel that in his opinion the whole Chinese civilization is entirely on the wrong track.

In reaction there was a defender of the old civilization. Soon after the publication of Hui Shih's *History*, another philosopher, Lu Wang, published another book entitled *The Civilizations of the East and the West and their Philosophies*. In this book Liang Shu-ming maintained that every civilization represents a way of living. There are mainly three ways of living: the way of aiming at the satisfaction of desires, that at the limitation of desires and that at the negation of desires. If we choose the first way of living, we have the European civilization; if the second, the Chinese civilization; if the third, the Indian civilization. These three civilizations should represent three stages of human progress. Men should at first try their best to know and to conquer nature. After having secured sufficient ground for their place in nature, they should limit their desires and know how to be content. But there are certain inner contradictions in life that can not be settled within life. Therefore the last resort of humanity is the way of negating desires, negating life. The Chinese and the Indians are wrong not in the fact that they produced civilizations that seem to be useless. Their civilizations are of the first order and in them there are some things that humanity is bound to adopt. The Chinese and the Indians are wrong in the fact that they adopted the second and the third ways of living without living through the first. They are on the right track but at the wrong time. Thus the defender of the East also thought there must be something wrong in it. His book therefore is also an expression of the spirit of his time.

The third period is marked with the Nationalist Movement of 1926 with the result of the establishment of the National Government. This movement was originally undertaken with the combined force of the Nationalists and the Communists. Sun Yat-sen, the leader of the Revolution of 1911 and of this movement, held the communistic society as the highest social ideal. But he was not a communist in that he was against the theory of class struggle and the dictatorship of the proletariat. He thought that the ideal society should be the product of love, not that of hatred. The Nationalists and the Communists soon split. With this movement the attitude of the Chinese towards the new civilization of the West takes a new turn. The new civilization of the West as represented in its political and economical organizations, once considered as the very perfection of human institutions, is now to be considered as but one stage of human progress. History is not closed; it is in the making. And what is now considered as the final goal that history is achieving, the peace of the world and the unity of man, looks more congenial to the old East than to the modern West. In fact, if we take the Marxian theory of human progress without its economical explanation of it, we see that between it and the teaching of the Kung Yang school as represented by Kan Yu-wei there is some similarity. Indeed Tan Tse-tung, in his book *On Benevolence*, knowing nothing about either Hegel or Marx, also pointed out what the Marxists may call the dialectical nature of human progress. He pointed out that there is some similarity between the future ideal society and the original primitive ones. But when we attain to the ideal, we are not returning to the primitive, we advance.

Is the spirit of this third period the same as that of the first? No, while the intellectual leaders of the first period were interested primarily in interpreting the new in terms of the old, we are now also interested in interpreting the old in terms of the new. While the intellectual leaders of the second period were interested in pointing out the difference between the East and the West, we are now interested in seeing what is common to them. We hold that if there is any difference between the East and the West, it is the product of different circumstances. In different circumstances men have different responses. If we see the response with the circumstances that produce it, we may probably say with Hegel that what is actual is also reasonable. Thus we are not interested now in criticizing one civilization in the light of the other, as the intellectual leaders of the first and the second periods did, but in illustrating the one with the other so that they may both be better understood. We are now interested in the mutual interpretation of the East and the West rather than their mutual criticism. They are seen to be the illustrations of the same tendency of human progress and the expressions of the same principle of human nature. Thus the East and the West are not only connected, they are united.

The same spirit is also seen in the work in technical philosophy. The Chinese and European philosophical ideas are compared and studied not with any intention of judging which is necessarily right and which is necessarily wrong, but simply with the interest of finding what the one is in terms of the other. It is expected that before long we will see that the European philosophical ideas will be supplemented with the Chinese intuition and experience, and the Chinese philosophical ideas will be clarified by the European logic and clear thinking.

These are what I consider to be the characteristics of the spirit of time in the three periods within the last fifty years in Chinese history. If we are to apply the Hegelian dialectic, we may say that the first period is the thesis, the second the antithesis, and the third the synthesis.

[373]

1253

Z

ZENO of ELEA

ZENO of ELEA (About 490-430 B.C.). The subtleties of Zeno of Elea have been endlessly discussed by philosophers and mathematicians, including those of the twentieth century.

Zeno was a scholar and a politician. According to tradition, he combated tyranny and, when a Sicilian tyrant tortured him in order to make him betray his political associates, Zeno cut his own tongue with his teeth, and threw it in the face of the torturer.

Zeno shared his teacher Parmenides' ideas on unity and the impossibility of change. He denied the Pythagorean identification of arithmetical units with geometrical points. His paradoxical arguments against the concept of motion, of which those of Achilles and the tortoise and the flying arrow became famous, were advanced in order to defend the doctrine of Parmenides; they are the crude precursors of the mathematical concepts of continuity and infinity.

Like Parmenides, Zeno resided for some years in Athens. He is said to have invented the art of dialectics which Socrates learned from him.

FRAGMENTS

IF things are a many, they must be just as many as they are, and neither more nor less. Now, if they are as many as they are, they will be finite in number.

But again, if things are a many, they will be infinite in number; for there will always be other things between them, and others again between them.

*   *   *

If things are a many, they are both great and small; so great as to be of an infinite magnitude, and so small as to have no magnitude at all.

That which has neither magnitude nor thickness nor bulk, will not even be. For, moreover, if it be added to any other thing it will not make it any larger; for nothing can gain in magnitude by the addition of what has no magnitude, and thus it follows at once that what was added was nothing. . . . But if, when this is taken away from another thing, that thing is no less; and again, if, when it is added to another thing, that does not increase, it is plain that what was added was nothing, and what was taken away was nothing.

But, if we assume that the unit is something, each one must have a certain magnitude and a certain thickness. One part of it must be at a certain distance from another, and the same may be said of what surpasses it in smallness; for it, too, will have magnitude, and something will surpass it in smallness. It is all the same to say this once and to say it always; for no such part of it will be the last, nor will one thing be nonexistent compared with another. So, if things are a many, they must be both small and great, so small as not to have any magnitude at all, and so great as to be infinite.

If there is space, it will be in something; for all that is is in something, and to be in something is to be in space. This goes on ad infinitum, therefore there is no space.

You cannot traverse an infinite number of points in a finite time. You must traverse the half of any given distance before you traverse the whole, and the half of that again before you can traverse it. This goes on ad infinitum, so that (if space is made up of points) there are an infinite number in any given space, and it cannot be traversed in a finite time.

And then is the famous puzzle of Achilles and the tortoise. Achilles must first reach the place from which the tortoise started. By that time the tortoise will have got on a little way. Achilles must then traverse that, and still the tortoise will be ahead. He is always coming nearer, but he never makes up to it.

The third argument against the possibility of motion through a space made up of points is that, on this hypothesis, an arrow in any given moment of its flight must be at rest in some particular point. Aristotle observes quite rightly that this argument depends upon the assumption that time is made up of "nows," that is, of indivisible instants. This, no doubt, was the Pythagorean view.

[374]

ZENO the STOIC

ZENO the STOIC (About 340-265 B.C.). Stoicism has a long history. It was initiated by Zeno of Citium who was of Phoenician descent, and almost all of its early representatives were not Greeks but Asians. For a time Stoicism was regarded as the last bulwark of Greek paganism. Then it was harmonized with the spirit of Christianity by some Fathers of the Church. Although Stoicism was by no means dormant in the thought of the Middle Ages, the great period of its revival began with the Renaissance and lasted until the beginning of the nineteenth century. Stoic morality inspired Shakespeare, Corneille and Schiller, Spinoza, Immanuel Kant and many leaders of the French Revolution.

Stoicism takes its name from a portico (*stoa*) in Athens, where Zeno, the founder of the school, taught his disciples. He had come to that city from his native town, situated on the island of Cyprus, after having made a fortune as a clever businessman. Fragments of twenty-six books written by him are extant. But more of his works have been lost. His successors often changed the Stoic doctrine and deviated from many original views, or enlarged them, or assumed a considerably more austere attitude toward life. But all of them adhered to the ideal of the sage who endeavors to act in accordance with his self and with nature, indifferent to the vicissitudes of life, and most of them proclaimed the equality of all men, as Zeno did.

FRAGMENTS

NOTHING incorporeal feels with body, nor does body feel

1256

with the incorporeal, but body with body. Now the soul feels with the body in sickness or under the knife, and the body feels with the soul turning red when the soul is ashamed, and pale when the soul is afraid. Therefore the soul is body.

Death is separation of soul from the body. But nothing incorporeal is separated from the body, as, on the other hand, there is no contact between the incorporeal and the body. But the soul is in contact with body, and is separated from body. Therefore the soul is body.

No evil is glorious. But there are cases of a glorious death Death therefore is no evil.

*   *   ‘

Time is the extension of motion

*   *   *

The parts of the world are sensing. The world does not lack feeling.

*   *   *

To live in accordance with nature is to live in accordance with virtue. In doing so, the wise man secures a happy and peaceful course to his own life

[375]

References

REFERENCES

1. *The Ethics*, Abailard, tr. J. Ramsay McCallum; Basil Blackwell & Mott, Ltd., Oxford.
2. *In Time and Eternity*, ed. Nahum Glatzer; Schocken Books, Inc., New York, 1946.
2A. *Dialoghi di Amore*.
3. *Die Schriften des Uriel Da Costa*.
4. *The Works of John Adams*, John Adams, 1851.
5. *The Science of Living*, Alfred Adler; Greenberg, Publisher, New York, 1929.
6. *Creed and Deed*, Felix Adler, 1878.
7. *Analogy Between God and Man*, Albertus Magnus.
8. *Sefer Ha-Ikkarim*, Joseph Albo, tr. Isaac Husik; Jewish P blication Society of America, Philadelphia, 1929.
9. *Orphic Sayings* and *Table Talk*, Amos Bronson Alcott.
10. *Dialogue on the Virtues*, Flaccus Albinus Alcuin, tr. Slee.
11. *Elements of Intellectual Philosophy*, Joseph Alden, 1866.
12. *Philosophical & Literary Pieces*, Samuel Alexander; St. Martin's Press, Inc., New York, 1939.
13. *The Main Problems of Abu Nasr Al-Farabi*.
14. *The Renovation of the Science of Religion*, Abu Hamid Mohammed Ibn Ghazzali Alghazzali, tr. Syed Nawab Ali.
15. *The Book of Alkindi on the Subject of Intellect*, Albino Nagy edition.
16. *Reason the Only Oracle of Man*, Ethan Allen, 1784.
17 *Classifications of Science in Medieval Jewish Philosophy*, David Ibn Merwan Al-Mukammas, ed. H. A. Wolfson, 1925.
18. *Early Greek Philosophy*, ed. and tr. John Burnet, A & C. Black Ltd., London, 1930
19. *Early Greek Philosophy*, ed. and tr. John Burnet; A. & C. Black Ltd., London, 1930.
20 *Early Greek Philosophy*, ed and tr. John Burnet; A. & C. Black Ltd., London, 1930.
21 *Prologium*, Anselm, tr Sidney N. Deane, Open Court Publ. Co., LaSalle, Illinois.
22. *Diogenes Laertius*.
23 *Summa Theologica*, Thomas Aquinas, tr. Dominican Fathers, Burns, Oates & Washbourne Ltd., London, 1912
24. *Source Book*, Bakewell.
25. *La Revue Internationale de Sociologie*, 1898
26. *Diogenes Laertius*.
27. *Metaphysics*, Aristotle.
28 *Enchiridon*, Augustine, tr J E. Shaw, Charles Scribner's Sons, New York; 1917
28A. *Meditations*, tr. George Long, Cassell.
28B. The Indian Philosophical Congress *Silver Jubilee Commemoration Volume* –1950.
29 Attributed to Thomas à Kempis.
30. *Critique of Pure Experience*.
31 *Regime of the Solitary Man*, Avenpace, tr. Moses Narboni

1261

32. *The Metaphysics of Averroes,* Fourth Treatise.
33. *A Compendium on the Soul,* tr. Edward A. van Dyck.
34. *Die Russische Revolution.*
35. *Die Weltalter,* ed. Franz Hoffmann, 1868.
36. *In Time and Eternity,* ed. Nahum Glatzer; Schocken Books, Inc., New York, 1946.
37. *Novum Organum,* tr. James Spedding from *The Philosophical Works of Francis Bacon.*
38. *Opus Majus,* tr. Robert B. Burke; Univ. of Pennsylvania Press, Philadelphia, 1928.
39. *Hobot ha-Lebabot,* tr. Benzion Halper in *Post-Biblical Hebrew Literature;* Jewish Publication Society of America, Philadelphia.
40. *God and the State,* tr. Benjamin R. Tucker, 1885.
41. *Dogmatics in Outline;* Philosophical Library, New York, 1949.
42. *Talks About Farming,* 1842; *Star Papers,* 1851; *The Overture of Angels,* 1870; *Yale Lectures on Preaching,* 1873; *A Summer Parish,* 1875; *Sermons on Evolution and Religion,* 1885.
43. *The Treason of the Intellectuals,* Julien Benda, tr. Richard Aldington; William Morrow & Co., Inc., New York, 1928.
44. *Adam Smith to Karl Marx,* edited by A. Castell & M. Shaw; Webb Publishing Company, St. Paul, 1946.
45. *Wisdom of the Hebrews,* ed. Brian Brown, tr. H. Gollanez; Brentano Publ. Co., New York, 1925.
46. *The End of Our Time,* Nicolas Berdyaev, tr. Donald Atwater; Geoffrey Bles, Ltd., London, 1933.
47. *Creative Evolution,* Henri Bergson, tr. Arthur Mitchell; Henry Holt & Co., Inc., New York, 1911.
48. *A Treatise Concerning the Principles of Human Knowledge;* Dublin, 1710.
49. *Meditations of Saint Bernard;* tr. Stanhope.
50. *The Three Principles of Divine Essence,* Jacob Boehme.
51. *De Consolatione Philosophiae,* Boethius.
52. *Wissenschaftslehre.*
53. *The Life of St. Francis of Assisi,* tr. Lockhart; New York, 1898.
54. *Laws of Thought,* Boole.
55. *The Philosophical Theory of the State,* London, 1899.
56. *The Contingency of the Laws of Nature,* tr. Fred Rothwell; Chicago, 1916.
57. *The Principles of Ethics,* 1892.
58. *Appearance and Reality,* Francis H. Bradley, 1893.
59. *The Brandeis Guide to the Modern World,* ed. Alfred Lief; Little Brown & Co., Boston, 1941.
60. *Von der Klassifikation der Psychischen Phänomene.*
61. *Reflections of a Physicist,* Bridgman; Philosophical Library, New York.
62. *A Philosophy of the Infinite Universe,* Bruno, tr. John Toland.
63. *Religion et Philosophie,* Brunschwicg.
64. *Hasidism,* Buber; Philosophical Library, New York, 1948.
65. *Nyayasutras.*
66. *Reflections on History,* Jakob Burckhardt; George Allen & Unwin Ltd., London, 1943.
67. *Thoughts on the Cause of the Present Discontents; Letters on a Regicide Peace;* Burke.
68. *Under the Apple-Trees;* Houghton Mifflin Co., Boston, 1916.
69. *The Note-Book of Samuel Butler,* ed. Henry F. Jones; New York, 1913.
70. *The Good Man and the Good;* New York, 1918.
71. *The City of the Sun in Total Commonwealths,* tr. Thomas Halliday, London, 1901.

72. *Paradoxes of Legal Science*, Benjamin N. Cardozo; Columbia University Press, 1928.
73. *On Heroes, Hero Worship and the Heroic in History*, New York, 1893.
74. *The Fallacy of the Criterion of Truth.*
75. *The Point of View*, ed. Catherine Cook; Chicago, 1927.
76. *An Essay on Man*, Ernst Cassirer; Yale University Press, New Haven, 1944.
77. *La Possession du Sol.*
78. *The Common Nature and Its Reason.*
79. From the book *Chinese Philosophy in Classical Times*, edited by E. H. R. Hughes, Everyman's Library, published by E. P. Dutton & Co., Inc., New York.
80. *On Friendship.*
80A. *On Justice*, from the *De Officiis.*
81. *Hymn to Zeus*, tr. Edward Beecher.
82. *In the Evening of My Thought*, Georges Clemenceau, tr. C. M. Thompson & John Heard, Jr.; Houghton Mifflin Co., Boston, 1929.
83. *Clement of Alexandria*, tr. G. W. Butterworth.
84. *Kant as the Founder of the Philosophy of Science*, Hermann Cohen.
85. *Conception of Philosophy in Recent Discussion*, 1910.
86. a. *Lectures on Shakespeare.*
    b. *Notebooks.*
    c. *Anima Poetae.*
    d. *The Friend, Essay VII.*
    e. *Preface to Aids to Reflection.*
87 *The Confession*, Comenius.
88. *Cours de Philosophie Positive*, tr. Paul Descours and H. G. Jones.
89. *Treatise on Sensations*, tr. Geraldine Carr; Univ. Southern California, Los Angeles, 1930.
90. *The Doctrine of the Mean.*
90A. *The Great Learning.*
91. *Biology*, Cook, 1877.
92. *Researches into the Mathematical Principles of the Theory of Wealth*, A. A. Cournot; trans. by Nathaniel Bacon; Macmillan Company, New York, 1927.
93. *Philosophical Essays*, tr. George Ripley, Edinburgh, 1839.
93A. *Cours de l'Histoire de la Philosophie.*
94. *Studies in Speculative Philosophy*; New York, 1925.
95. *Or Adonai, Crescas' Critique of Aristotle*, tr. Harry A. Wolfson; Harvard Univ. Press, Cambridge, 1929.
96. *History, Its Theory and Practice*, tr. Douglas Ainstre; New York, 1921.
97. *A Treatise Concerning Eternal and Immutable Morality*, London, 1731.
98. *The Vision of God*, Nicolaus de Cusa, tr. Emma Gurney Salter; E. P Dutton & Co., Inc., New York, 1928.
99. *Anecdotes of Bossuet*, tr. John Aikin.
100. *Charles Darwin*, Francis Darwin, New York, 1893.
101. *L'Essor de la Physique en France.*
102. *Essays on the Theory of Numbers*, tr. Wooster W Beman; Chicago, 1909
103. *Elim* (Psalms).
104. *Die Fragments der Vorsokratiker* (Diels) and *Source Book in Ancient Philosophy*, Bakewell.
105. *Formal Logic*, London, 1847.
106. *History of Italian Literature*, Francesco De Sanctis, tr. Joan Redfern, Harcourt Brace & Co., Inc., New York, 1931.
107. *Meditationes de prima philosophia*, tr. John Veitch; Paris, 1641.
108. *Problems of Men*. Dewey; Philosophical Library, New York.

109. *Thoughts on Religion*, London, 1819.
110. *Studies on the Foundations of the Sciences of the Mind.*
111. *Naturwissenschaft und Philosophie* (Records of the Eighth International Congress of Philosophy.)
112. *The Value of Life.*
113. *Selections from Medieval Philosophers*, from *Oxford Commentary on the Four Books of the Master of the Sentences*, Richard McKeon; Charles Scribner's Sons, New York, 1929.
114. *The Rules of Sociological Method.* Emile Durkheim, tr. S. A. Solovay and J. Mueller, ed. G. E. G. Catlin; copyright University of Chicago, 1938.
115. *Master Eckhart's Writings and Sermons.*
116. *Freedom of Will;* New York, 1840.
117. *The World as I See It;* Philosophical Library, New York.
118. *Essays,* George Eliot.
119. *Self-Reliance,* R. W. Emerson.
120. *Early Greek Thinkers,* edited and translated by John Burnet; A. & C. Black, Ltd., London, 1930.
121. *Revolution in Science,* tr. Emile Burns; New York, 1931.
122. *Meditations,* tr. George Long, Cassell & Co., Ltd., London.
123. *Epicurus, the Extant Remains,* tr. Sir Cyril Bailey; Clarendon Press, Oxford, 1926.
124. *The Whole Familiar Colloquies of Erasmus;* London, 1877.
125. Reprinted from *Selections from Medieval Philosophers* ed. and tr. by Richard McKeon; Charles Scribner's Sons, New York, 1929. Used by permission of the publisher.
126. *The Life of the Spirit,* tr. F. L. Pogson; New York, 1909.
127. *The Twelve Books of Euclid's Elements,* tr. Sir Thomas L. Heath; Cambridge University Press, New York, 1926.
128. *Life After Death,* tr. Mary C. Wadsworth; Pantheon Books, New York, 1944.
129. *Das Wesen des Christentums,* tr. Marian Evans, 1840.
130. *Grundlage der Gesammten Wissenschaftslehre,* tr. A. F. Kroeger, 1794.
131. "Poor Richard's" Editorials. Courtesy Think Magazine.
132. *Teachings of Mahatma Gandhi.* Indian Printing Works. Lahore, 1949.
134. *Summary of Gassendi's Philosophy,* ed. F. Bernier, vol. 7; Lyon, 1864.
135. *The Theory of Mind as Pure Act,* Giovanni Gentile, tr. H. Wildon Carr; Macmillan & Co., Ltd., London, & St. Martin's Press, New York, 1922.
136. *Progress and Poverty,* Henry George.
137. *Milhamot ha-Shem,* tr. by Benzion Halper, in *Post-Biblical Hebrew Literature;* Jewish Publication Society of America, Philadelphia.
138. *Ethica.*
139. *The Unity of Philosophical Experience,* Etienne Gilson; Charles Scribner's Sons, New York, 1937.
140. *Selected Essays by Ahad Ha-'Am,* tr. Leon Simon; Jewish Publication Society of America, Philadelphia, 1944.
141. *Introduction to the Study of Philosophy;* Brussels, 1844.
142. *The Inequality of Human Races,* tr. Adrian Collins; New York, 1915.
142A. *The Consistence of the Continuum Hypothesis,* Kurt Goedel.
143. *Wilhelm Meister's Apprenticeship.*
144. *Aristotle.*
145. *Prolegomena to Ethics.*
146. *De Jure Belli ac Pacis,* tr. Whewell; 1853.
147. *The Object of Psychology,* Berlin, 1921.
148. *The Book of the Chazars,* tr. H. Hirschfeld.
149. *Main Writings,* ed. Otto Mann; Leipzig, 1937
150. *The Federalist,* ed. G. Smith.

151 From the book *Chinese Philosophy in Classical Times* edited by E. H. Hughes, Everyman's Library, published by E. P. Dutton & Co., Inc., New York.
152. *The Last Judgment*, W. T. Harris.
153. *Philosophie des Unbewussten*, tr. W. C. Coupland.
154. *Das Wertproblem in der Philosophie der Gegenwart* (Actes du Huitième Congres Internationale de Philosophie, 1934.)
155. *Lectures on the Philosophy of History*, tr. J. Sibree, 1902.
156 *Sefer Hasidim*, tr. by Benzion Halper, in *Post-Biblical Hebrew Literature*; Jewish Publication Society of America, Philadelphia.
157 *Was ist Metaphysik?*; Bonn, 1930.
158. *Popular Lectures on Scientific Subjects*, tr. E. Atkinson
159. *De l'Esprit, or, Essays on the Mind*; London, 1809.
160 *Early Greek Philosophy*, edited and translated by John Burnet; A. & C. Black Ltd., London, 1930.
161 *Letters and Lectures on Education*, tr. Henry M. and E. Felkin; London, 1898.
162. *Outlines of a Philosophy of Humanity*, tr. T. Churchill.
163. *Moses Hess et la Gauche Hegelienne*; in *Vorwaerts*, Dec. 12, 1844.
164. *Hegyon he-Nefesh*, from *Studies in Pre-Tibbonian Terminology*. Jewish Quarterly Review, New Series, vol. 17
165. *Leviathan.*
166 *Human Nature and Its Remaking*, William E. Hocking; Yale University Press, New Haven, 1929.
167. *The Metaphysic of Experience.*
168. *A Philosophical Confession*, in *Journal of Philosophy, Psychology and Scientific Methods*; February 16, 1905
169 *The System of Nature*, London, 1797
170 *Pages from An Old Volume of Life.*
171. *The Mind and Faith of Justice Holmes*, Max Lerner; Little Brown & Co., 1943.
172 From the book *Chinese Philosophy in Classical Times*, edited by E. H. Hughes. Everyman's Library, published by E. P. Dutton & Co., Inc., New York.
173 From the book *Chinese Philosophy in Classical Times*, edited by E. H. Hughes. Everyman's Library, published by E. P Dutton & Co., Inc., New York.
174. Reprinted from *In the Shadow of Tomorrow* by Jacob Huizinga, tr. J. F. Huizinga, copyright 1936 by W W Norton & Co., Inc. By permission of the publisher.
175. *The Sphere and Duties of Government*, tr Joseph Coulthard
176. *A Treatise of Human Nature*, 1739
177. *The Sayings of the Philosophers.*
177A. *Ideas*, Edmund Husserl, tr. by W R. B. Gibson; Macmillan Co., New York.
178. *The Evolution of Theology.*
179 *Seek Wisdom*, tr. by Benzion Halper, in *Post-Biblical Hebrew Literature*, Jewish Publication Society of America, Philadelphia.
180 *The Improvement of Human Reason, (Hai Ebn Yokdhan)* tr. Simon Ockley.
181. *God and the Astronomers*, Dean Inge; Longmans Green & Co., London
182. *The Works of Robert G. Ingersoll*, New York, 1900
183. *Panegyric of Athens*, tr. Gillies.
184 *Das Buch ueber die Elemente*. Salomon Fried, Leipzig, 1885
185 *Samkya Karika.*
186 *Christianity and Paganism*, tr F H. Hedge

187. *Jamblicus' Exhortations*, tr. Thomas H. Johnson; Osceola, Mo., 1917.
188. *Substance and Shadow*, 1863.
189. *Pragmatism;* Longmans Green & Co., New York, 1907.
190. *The Perennial Scope of Philosophy*, Karl Jaspers; Philosophical Library, New York.
191. *Physics and Philosophy*, James H. Jeans; Cambridge University Press, New York, 1942.
192. *Letter to Dr. Walter Jones;* and *Notes on Virginia.*
193. *Decadence*, C. E. M. Joad; Philosophical Library, New York.
194. *Frivolities of Courtiers and Footprints of Philosophers*, Joseph P. Pike; University of Minnesota Press, Minneapolis, 1938.
195. *The Idler.*
196. *Relaxation of Studies;* and *Discoveries.*
197. *The Use of Words*, tr. Matthew Arnold.
198. *Psychology and Religion*, C. G. Jung; Yale University Press, New Haven.
199. *The Apologies of Martyr Justin*, tr. William Reeves.
200. *The Liberal Spirit*, H. M. Kallen; Cornell University Press, Ithaca, 1948.
201. *Kritik der reinen Vernunft*, tr. John Watson; Riga, 1787.
202. *Sören Kierkegaard's Papirer*, tr. Alexander Dru.
203. *The Science of Character*, Ludwig Klages, tr. Johnston; George Allen & Unwin Ltd., London, 1929
204. *Revolutionary Pamphlets*, edited by Roger Baldwin; Vanguard Press, Inc., New York, 1927.
205. *Theism and Cosmology*, John Laird; Philosophical Library, New York.
206. *On the Mission of Philosophy in Our time* (Actes du Huitième Congres Internationale de Philosophie, 1943.)
207. *Recherches sur les Causes des Principaux Faits Physiques*, Paris, 1794.
208. *Essays of Elia.*
209. *Words of a Believer.*
210. *Man a Machine*, tr. Marquis d'Argens.
211. *History of Materialism*, tr. Ernest C. Thomas; London, 1881.
212. From the book *Chinese Philosophy in Classical Times*, edited by E. H. Hughes. Everyman's Library, published by E. P. Dutton & Co., Inc., New York.
213. *Reflections.*
214. *What is Capital?*, tr. F. Keddez; New York, 1900.
215. *Aphorisms on Man.*
216. *Discours de la metaphysique*, tr. George R. Montgomery; 1686.
217. *Karl Marx, Selected Works*, ed. V. Adoratsky and C. P. Dutt.
218. *The Education of the Human Race*, tr. John Dearling Haney; New York, 1913.
219. *Early Greek Philosophy*, edited and translated by John Burnet; A. &. C. Black Ltd., London, 1930.
220. *Primitive Mentality*, tr. Lilian A. Clare; New York, 1923.
221. *A Biographical History of Philosophy.*
222. *An Analysis of Knowledge and Valuation*, Clarence Irving Lewis; Open Court Publishing Company, La Salle, 1947.
223. *Selected Writings of George C. Lichtenberg*, ed. Adolf Wilbrandt; Stuttgart, 1893.
224. *The First Inaugural; The Emancipation Proclamation; The Gettysburg Address.*
225. *The Study of Nature*, tr. Sir James Edward Smith.
226. *Aesthetics;* Hamburg and Leipzig, 1903.
227. *An Essay Concerning Human Understanding.*
228. Reprinted from *Selections from Medieval Philosophers* by Richard McKeon; used by permission of the publishers, Charles Scribner's Sons.
229. *On the Sublime.*

230 *Microcosmus*, tr Elizabeth Hamilton and E. E. Constance Jones, Edinburgh, 1888.

231 *The Great Chain of Being*. Arthur O. Lovejoy; Harvard University Press, Cambridge, 1942.

232. *On the Nature of Things*, tr. H. A. J Munro; G. Bell & Sons Ltd., London, 1914.

233 *The Book of the Lover and the Beloved*, tr. E. A. Peers; New York, 1923.

234. *Lu Shian-Shan—A Dissertation in Philosophy* by Siu-Chi Huang, taken from *Lu Hsiang-Shan—A Twelfth Century Chinese Idealist Philosopher*, American Oriental Series, Volume 27, publ. by American Oriental Society, New Haven, Conn., 1944.

235 *Mesillat Yesharim*, tr. by Benzion Halper, in *Post-Biblical Hebrew Literature*; Jewish Publication Society of America, Philadelphia.

236. *Analysis of the Sensations*; Open Court Publishing Co., 1897

237. *Il Principe*, tr. Henry Morley

238. *Think Magazine*.

239. *Salomon Maimon, An Autobiography*, tr. S. Clark Murray; London, 1888.

240. *Code, Hilkot De'ot*, tr. by Benzion Halper, in *Post-Biblical Hebrew Literature*; Jewish Publication Society of America, Philadelphia.

241. *The Influence of Habit on the Faculty of Thinking*, Psychology Classics, Vol. III, tr. Margaret Donaldson Boehm; Williams & Wilkins Co., Baltimore, 1929

243. *Dialogues on Metaphysics and on Religion*, tr. Morris Ginsberg. The Macmillan Company, New York, 1923.

244. *Existence and the Existent*, Jacques Maritain, tr. Galantiere and Phelan; Pantheon Books, Inc., New York.

245. *Capital*.

246. *The Ideals of Humanity*, Thomas G Masaryk; tr. W P Warren; George Allen & Unwin Ltd., London, 1938.

247 *The Duties of Man and Other Essays*; London, 1907

248. *The Group Mind*; New York, 1920.

249. *Mind, Self, and Society*, H. Mead; University of Chicago Press, 1924.

250. *Proof of the General Law of Causality*.

251. *Early Greek Philosophy*, edited and translated by John Burnet; A. & C. Black Ltd., London, 1930.

252. *The Conciliator*, tr. E. H. Lindo; London, 1842

253. *Four Books*; from *Think Magazine*.

254. *Jerusalem: A Treatise on Ecclesiastical Authority and Judaism*, tr. M. Samuels, in *Wisdom of the Hebrews*, ed Brian Brown, Brentano Publ. Co., New York, 1925

255. *On Liberty*.

256. *The Koran*.

257 Reprinted by permission from *The Ways of Things*, by William P. Montague (copyright, 1940, by Prentice-Hall, Inc., New York), pp. 526-529.

258. *Essays*, Montaigne; tr. Jacob Zeitlin; Alfred A. Knopf, Inc., New York, 1934.

259. *L'Esprit des Lois*, tr. Thomas Nugent; London, 1878.

260. *Principia Ethica*, Moore; Cambridge University Press, New York, 1929.

261. *Hellenistic Philosophies*, P. E. More; Princeton University Press.

262. *Emergent Evolution*, C. Lloyd Morgan, Williams & Norgate Ltd., London, 1933.

263 From the book *Chinese Philosophy in Classical Times*, edited by E. H. Hughes. Everyman's Library, published by E. P. Dutton & Co., Inc., New York.

264 *By The River of Babylon*, Kaj Munk; Lutheran Publishing House, Blair, Nebraska, 1945.

265. *The External Values;* Boston, 1909.
266. *Philosophy, its Problem and its Problems.* Gottingen, 1911.
267. *About My Scholarly Upbringing,* Leipzig, 1934.
268. *Also Spake Zarathustra,* tr. Thomas Common.
269. *Human Destiny,* Lecomte de Noüy; Longmans Green & Co., Inc., New York.
270. *Ockham: Studies and Selections,* ed. Stephen Tornay; Open Court Publishing Co., La Salle, 1938
271. *De Principiis,* Origen, tr. Frederick Crombie; Charles Scribner's Sons, New York, 1925.
272. *The Revolt of the Masses,* José Ortega y Gasset; W. W. Norton & Co., Inc., New York, 1932.
273. *Adam Smith to Karl Marx,* edited by A. Castell & Mary Shaw; Webb Publishing Company, St. Paul, 1946.
274. *The Rights of Man.*
275. *Four Treatises on Theophrastus from Hohenheim,* ed. and tr. Henry E. Sigerist, Johns Hopkins Press, Baltimore, 1941.
276. *The Mind and Society,* Harcourt, Brale & Co., Inc., New York.
277. *Early Greek Philosophy,* edited and translated by John Burnet; A. & C. Black, Ltd., London, 1930.
278. *Pensées,* tr. by William F. Trotter, appearing in *Harvard Classics,* Volume 48; P. F. Collier & Son, Publisher, New York.
279. *Plato and Platonism;* London, 1893.
280. *Revista Matematica.* Vol. 8; 1902.
281. *Collected Papers,* ed. Charles Hartshorne and Paul Weiss.
282. *Fruits of An Active Life,* ed. William Wistar Comfort; Friends Central Bureau, Philadelphia, Pa., 1943.
283. *Funeral Oration,* delivered in Athens in 430 B.C., Courtesy Think Magazine.
284. *General Theory of Value,* Ralph B. Perry; Longmans Green & Co., New York, 1926.
285. *Meine Nachforschungen ueber den Gang der Natur in der Entwicklung des Menschengeschlechts,* 1797.
286. *The Works of Philo;* tr. C. D. Jonge; London, 1854.
287. *On Being and One.*
288. *The Philosophy of Physics.*
289. *The Republic,* tr. Benjamin Jowett.
290. *Art and Society,* tr. Paul S. Leitner, Alfred Goldstein, L. H. Crout; Critics Group, New York, 1936.
291. *Letters.* Courtesy Think Magazine.
292. *Enneads,* tr. Albert Edwin Avey.
293. *Morals,* Courtesy Think Magazine.
294. *The Foundations of Science,* Henri Poincaré, tr. Halsted; The Science Press, Lancaster, 1913.
295. *Commentarii in Libros Aristotelis De Anima,* ed. L. Ferri; Rome, 1871.
296. *Selected Works,* tr. N. Taylor; London, 1823.
297. *Poseidonios' Metaphysische Schriften,* I. Heinemann; Breslau, 1921.
298. *Life, Hymns & Works,* ed. K. S. Guthrie, tr. Johnson; Platonist Press, New York, 1925.
299. *Fragments.*
300. *What is Property?* tr. Benj. R. Tucker; Princeton, Mass., 1876.
301. *The Golden Verses,* in *Shrines of Wisdom.*
302. *The Foundations of Mathematics and Other Logical Essays,* Ramsay, ed. Braithwaite; Routledge & Kegan Paul, Ltd., London, 1931; distributed in U. S. by Humanities Press, New York.

303 *Symbolic Logic*, Hans Reichenbach; Macmillan Co., New York, 1947 **By** permission of the publishers.
304 *Adam Smith to Karl Marx*, edited by A. Castell & Mary Shaw, Webb Publishing Company, St. Paul, 1946
305. *Cultural and Natural Sciences.*
306. *The Ridpath Library of Universal Literature.*
307 *I Believe: The Personal Philosophies of 23 Eminent Men and Women*, copyright Simon & Schuster, Inc., 1939.
308. *The Problems of the Philosophy of Culture.*
309 *Roscellin's Letter to Abailard;* ed. Johan Andreas Schmeller; Munich, 1849.
310. *Kleinere Schriften;* Berlin, 1937.
311 *The Ruling Principle of Method Applied to Education*, tr. Mrs. William Grey; Boston, 1893.
312 *Social Contract*, tr. Henry J. Tozer.
313. *The Conception of Immortality*, Houghton Mifflin Co., Boston, 1900
314. *The Influence of Physical Causes Upon the Moral Faculty*
315. *Sesame and Lilies.*
316 *The Problems of Philosophy*, Oxford Univ. Press, London.
317 *Polemic Against Hiwi al-Balkhi*, ed. and tr Israel Davidson, New York. 1915.
318. *The Work of St. Simon*
319 Reprinted from *Reason in Art* by George Santayana, copyright 1905, 1933, by the author; used by permission of the publisher, Charles Scrib ner's Sons, New York.
320. *What is Literature?*, Jean-Paul Sartre, Philosophical Library, New York.
321 *System des transcendentalen Idealismus*, tr Benjamin Rand; Tubingen 1800.
322. *Actes du Huitième Congres Internationale de Philosophie*, 1934
323 *Philosophie des Lebens*, tr. A. J. W. Morrison.
324. *Introduction to the Dialogues of Plato*, tr. William Dobson.
325 *Philosophy of Nature*, Moritz Schlick, Philosophical Library, New York.
326. *Die Welt als Wille und Vorstellung*. tr. R. B. Haldane and J. Kemp.
327 *The Philosophy of Civilization* by Albert Schweitzer, tr C. T Campion Macmillan Company, New York, 1949
328 *Essays.*
329 *Pyrrhonic Sketches*, tr Mary M Patrick, Courtesy Think Magazine
330 *Atma-Bodha.*
331. *Ethics and Religion*, ed. Society of Ethical Propa., London, 1900
332. *The Problem of Sociology;* Philadelphia, 1895.
333 *A Bible for the Liberal;* ed. D D. Runes, Philosophical Library, New York.
334. *Theatetus*, tr. Benjamin Jowett.
335. *The Justification of the Good*, tr Nathalie A Duddington, New York, 1918.
336. *Reflections on Violence*, tr. T. E. Holme, New York, 1912
337 *First Principles.*
338. *De Intellectus Emendatione*, tr. Amelia Hutchison Stirling.
339. *Collected Works;* Leipzig, 1885.
340. *Stages of Higher Knowledge*, G. P Putnam's Sons, New York. 19··`
341. *Play.*
342. *The Ego and His Own*, tr. Steven T. Byington.
343. *The Old Faith and the New*. tr. Mathilde Blind; New York, 1873.
344. *The True Christian Religion·* The Swedenborg Foundation, New York, 1925.
345 *Sadhana*, Rabindranath Tagore; Macmillan Company, New York **1914**

346. *Life and Scientific Opinions of Famous Physicists.*
347. *The Faith and Modern Thought;* London, 1910.
348. *The Ante-Nicene Fathers,* ed. Rev. Alex Robert and James Donaldson, tr. Peter Holmes.
349. *Early Greek Philosophy,* edited and translated by John Burnet; A. & C. Black Ltd., London, 1930.
350. *Walden.*
351. *The Kingdom of God is Within You,* Tolstoy, tr. Louise and Aylmer Maude; Oxford University Press, London, 1941.
352. *Twentieth Century Philosophy,* ed. D. D. Runes; Philosophical Library, New York.
353. The Belfast Address, Lectures and Essays.
354. From the book *Chinese Philosophy in Classical Times,* edited by E. H. Hughes. Everyman's Library, published by E. P. Dutton & Co., Inc., New York.
355. *The Tragic Sense of Life,* tr. E. Crawford Flitch; St. Martin's Press, London and New York, 1921.
356. *The Theory of the Leisure Class.*
357. *On Cause and Effect.*
357A. *The Complete Works of the Swami Vivekananada.*
358. *Selected Works,* tr. Joseph McCabe; Watts & Co., London, 1921.
359. *The Tragicomedy of Wisdom.*
360. From Max Weber: *Essays in Sociology,* translated, edited and with introduction by H. H. Gerth and C. Wright Mills, copyright 1946 by Oxford University Press, Inc., New York.
361. *Gestalt Theory,* Max Wertheimer, tr. N. Nairn-Allison; Social Research for February, 1944. New School for Social Research, New York.
362. *The Function of Reason,* Alfred North Whitehead; Princeton University Press, 1929.
363. *A Backward Glance; Democratic Vistas.*
364. *Memorial Day Address,* Arlington, Virginia, May 31, 1915.
365. *An Introduction to Philosophy,* tr. Joseph McCabe; Heidelberg, 1914.
366. *Tractatus Logico-Philosophicus,* Ludwig Wittgenstein, tr. C. K. Ogden; Routledge & Kegan Paul, Ltd., London, 1922, distributed in U. S. by Humanities Press, New York.
367. *Institutions of the Natural Right and the Right of Men.*
368. *Nature and Mind. Selected Essays,* F. J. E. Woodbridge; Columbia University Press, 1937.
369. *Outlines of Psychology.*
370. *Die Fragmente der Vorsokratiker* (Diels) and *Source Book in Ancient Philosophy,* Bakewell.
371. *"Crisis", The Personalist,* Summer, 1946; by Joaquin Xirau.
372. *Brhadaranyaka Upanishad.*
373. Actes du Huitième Congres Internationale de Philosophie, 1934.
374. *Early Greek Philosophy,* tr. by John Burnet; A. & C. Black, Ltd., London, 1930.
375. *Hellenistic Philosophies,* tr. Paul Elmer More; *Fragments from Cicero and Seneca.*

Index

INDEX